A SELECT LIBRARY

OF THE

NICENE AND POST-NICENE FATHERS

OF

THE CHRISTIAN CHURCH

EDITED BY

PHILIP SCHAFF, D.D., LL.D.,

PROFESSOR OF CHURCH HISTORY IN THE UNION THEOLOGICAL SEMINARY, NEW YORK

IN CONNECTION WITH A NUMBER OF PATRISTIC SCHOLARS OF EUROPE
AND AMERICA

VOLUME VII

ST. AUGUSTIN:

HOMILIES ON THE GOSPEL OF JOHN
HOMILIES ON THE FIRST EPISTLE OF JOHN
SOLILOQUIES

T&T CLARK
EDINBURGH

WM. B. EERDMANS PUBLISHING COMPANY
GRAND RAPIDS, MICHIGAN

British Library Cataloguing in Publication Data

Nicene & Post-Nicene Fathers. — 1st series
1. Fathers of the church
I. Title   II. Schaff, Philip
230′.11   BR60.A62

T&T Clark ISBN 0 567 09396 4

Eerdmans ISBN 0-8028-8104-1

Reprinted, June 1991

PREFACE.

AUGUSTIN was an indefatigable preacher. He considered regular preaching an indispensable part of the duty of a bishop. To his homilies we owe most of his exegetical labors. The homilies were delivered *extempore*, taken down by scribes and slightly revised by Augustin. They retain their colloquial form, devotional tone, frequent repetitions, and want of literary finish. He would rather be deficient in rhetoric than not be understood by the people. He was cheered by the eager attention and acclamations of his hearers, but never fully satisfied with his performance. "My preaching," he says, "almost always displeases me. I eagerly long for something better, of which I often have an inward enjoyment in my thoughts before I can put them into audible words. Then when I find that my power of expression is not equal to my inner apprehension, I am grieved at the inability of my tongue to answer to my heart" (*De Catech. Rudibus*, ch. II. 3, in this Series, Vol. III. 284). His chief merit as an interpreter is his profound theological insight, which makes his exegetical works permanently useful. Comp. the introductory essay in the sixth volume.

This volume contains:

I. The Homilies or Tractates on the GOSPEL OF JOHN (*In Joannis Evangelium Tractatus CXXIV*).[1] Augustin delivered them to his flock at Hippo about A.D. 416 or later. The Latin text is in the third Tome of the Benedictine edition (in Migne's reprint, Tom. III. Part II. fol. 1379–1976). The first English translation appeared in the Oxford "Library of Fathers of the Holy Catholic Church," Oxford, 1848, In 2 Vols., and was prepared by Rev. H. Browne, M. A., of Corpus Christi College, Cambridge. The present translation was made jointly by Rev. John Gibb, D.D., Professor in the Presbyterian Theological College at London (Vol. I., Tractates 1–37), and Rev. James Innes, of Panbride, near Dundee, Scotland (Vol. II., Tractates 38 to 124), for Dr. Dods' Series of Augustin's Works, published by T. & T. Clark, Edinburgh, 1873. Dr. Gibb was requested to revise it, but did not deem it necessary. The Indices of topics and texts are added to the American edition.

II. The Homilies on the FIRST EPISTLE OF JOHN (*In Epistolam Joannis ad Parthos [2] Tractatus decem*) were preached about the same time as those on the Gospel, or shortly after-

---

[1] The manuscripts vary in their headings between *Tractatus, Sermones,* and *Homiliæ.* In three copies used by the Benedictine editors the title is thus given: "*Aurelii Augustini Doctoris Hippon. Episc. Homiliæ in Evangelium Dom. Jesu secundum Joannem incipiunt, quas ipse colloquendo prius ad populum habuit, et inter loquendum a notariis exceptas, eo quo habitæ sunt ordine, verbum ex verbo postea dictavit.*"—Migne III. II. 1378.

[2] *Ad Parthos* is a mistake which is found also in some MSS. of the Vulgate and has led to different conjectures. See note to the Prologue, p. 4' 1, and Critical Introductions to the N. T., *e. g.* that of Weiss (1886), p. 468. He favors the conjecture πρὸς παρθένους, *ad virgines*, which Clement of Alex. gives as the superscription to the second Epistle of John. Others conjecture τοῦ παρθένου, (*virginis*), or *Ad sparsos*, etc.

wards. They are also included in the third volume of the Benedictine edition (Migne, T. III. P. II. 1977–2062). The translation by Rev. H. Browne is taken from the Oxford Library of the Fathers (Clark's edition has none), and was slightly revised and edited with additional notes and an introduction by the Rev. Dr. Myers, of Washington.

III. The SOLILOQUIES (in Vol. I., 869–905, Migne's ed.) were translated for this Library by the Rev. C. C. Starbuck, of Andover, Mass. They were written by Augustin shortly after his conversion (387), and are here added as a specimen of his earliest philosophical writings. Neither the Oxford nor the Clark Series give them a place. King Alfred translated parts of the SOLILOQUIES into the Anglo-Saxon of his day, and a partial translation appeared in 1631, but I have not seen it.

This volume completes Augustin's exegetical writings on the New Testament. The eighth and last volume will contain his Homilies on the Psalms, as translated for the Oxford Library, and edited by Bishop Coxe. It will be ready for publication in July of this year.

PHILIP SCHAFF.

NEW YORK, March 23, 1888.

CONTENTS.

ST. AUGUSTIN:

LECTURES OR TRACTATES

ON THE

GOSPEL ACCORDING TO ST. JOHN.

TRANSLATED BY

REV. JOHN GIBB, D.D.,

PROFESSOR IN THE THEOLOGICAL COLLEGE, GUILFORD STREET, LONDON.

AND

REV. JAMES INNES,

MINISTER AT PANBRIDE, NEAR DUNDEE, SCOTLAND.

CONTENTS OF TRACTATES.

LECTURES OR TRACTATES

ON THE

GOSPEL ACCORDING TO ST. JOHN.

TRACTATE I.

CHAPTER I. 1–5.

1. WHEN I give heed to what we have just read from the apostolic lesson, that "the natural man perceiveth not the things which are of the Spirit of God,"[1] and consider that in the present assembly, my beloved, there must of neccessity be among you many natural men, who know only according to the flesh, and cannot yet raise themselves to spiritual understanding, I am in great difficulty how, as the Lord shall grant, I may be able to express, or in my small measure to explain, what has been read from the Gospel, "In the beginning was the Word, and the Word was with God, and the Word was God;" for this the natural man does not perceive. What then, brethren? Shall we be silent for this cause? Why then is it read, if we are to be silent regarding it? Or why is it heard, if it be not explained? And why is it explained, if it be not understood? And so, on the other hand, since I do not doubt that there are among your number some who can not only receive it when explained, but even understand it before it is explained, I shall not defraud those who are able to receive it, from fear of my words being wasted on the ears of those who are not able to receive it. Finally, there will be present with us the compassion of God, so that perchance there may be enough for all, and each receive what he is able, while he who speaks says what he is able.

For to speak of the matter as it is, who is able? I venture to say, my brethren, perhaps not John himself spoke of the matter as it is, but even he only as he was able; for it was man that spoke of God, inspired indeed by God, but still man. Because he was inspired he said something; if he had not been inspired, he would have said 'nothing; but because a man inspired, he spoke not the whole, but what a man could he spoke.

2. For this John, dearly beloved brethren, was one of those mountains concerning which it is written: "Let the mountains receive peace for thy people, and the hills righteousness."[2] The mountains are lofty souls, the hills little souls. But for this reason do the mountains receive peace, that the hills may be able to receive righteousness. What is the righteousness which the hills receive? Faith, for "the just doth live by faith."[3] The smaller souls, however, would not receive faith unless the greater souls, which are called mountains, were illuminated by Wisdom herself, that they may be able to transmit to the little ones what the little ones can receive; and the hills live by faith, because the mountains receive peace. By the mountains themselves it was said to the Church, "Peace be with you;" and the mountains themselves in proclaiming peace to the Church did not divide themselves against Him from whom

---

[1] 1 Cor. ii. 14.

[2] Ps. lxxii. 3.

[3] Hab. ii. 4; Rom. i. 17.

they received peace,[1] that truly, not feignedly, they might proclaim peace.

3. For there are other mountains which cause shipwreck, on which, if any one drive his ship, she is dashed to pieces. For it is easy, when land is seen by men in peril, to make a venture as it were to reach it; but sometimes land is seen on a mountain, and rocks lie hid under the mountain; and when any one makes for the mountain, he falls on the rocks, and finds there not rest, but wrecking. So there have been certain mountains, and great have they appeared among men, and they have created heresies and schisms, and have divided the Church of God; but those who divided the Church of God were not those mountains concerning which it is said, " Let the mountains receive peace." For in what manner have they received peace who have severed unity ?

4. But those who received peace to proclaim it to the people have made Wisdom herself an object of contemplation, so far as human hearts could lay hold on that which " eye hath not seen, nor ear heard, neither has ascended into the heart of man."[2] If it has not ascended into the heart of man, how has it ascended into the heart of John ? Was not John a man ? Or perhaps neither into John's heart did it ascend, but John's heart ascended into it ? For that which ascends into the heart of man is from beneath, to man; but that to which the heart of man ascends is above, from man. Even so brethren, can it be said that, if it ascended into the heart of John (if in any way it can be said), it ascended into his heart in so far as he was not man. What means " was not man"? In so far as he had begun to be an angel. For all saints are angels, since they are messengers of God. Therefore to carnal and natural men, who are not able to perceive the things that are of God, what says the apostle ? " For whereas ye say, I am of Paul, I of Apollos, are ye not men ?"[3] What did he wish to make them whom he upbraided because they were men ? Do you wish to know what he wished to make them ? Hear in the Psalms: " I have said, ye are gods; and all of you are children of the Most High."[4] To this, then, God calls us, that we be not men. But then will it be for the better that we be not men, if first we recognize the fact that we are men, that is, to the end that we may rise to that height from humility; lest, when we think that we are something when we are nothing, we not only do not receive what we are not, but even lose what we are.

5. Accordingly, brethren, of these mountains was John also, who said, " In the beginning was the Word, and the Word was with God, and the Word was God." This mountain had received peace; he was contemplating the divinity of the Word. Of what sort was this mountain ? How lofty ? He had risen above all peaks of the earth, he had risen above all plains of the sky, he had risen above all heights of the stars, he had risen above all choirs and legions of the angels. For unless he rose above all those things which were created, he would not arrive at Him by whom all things were made. You cannot imagine what he rose above, unless you see at what he arrived. Dost thou inquire concerning heaven and earth ? They were made. Dost thou inquire concerning the things that are in heaven and earth ? Surely much more were they made. Dost thou inquire concerning spiritual beings, concerning angels, archangels, thrones, dominions, powers, principalities ? These also were made. For when the Psalm enumerated all these things, it finished thus: " He spoke, and they were made; He commanded, and they were created."[5] If " He spoke and they were made," it was by the Word that they were made; but if it was by the Word they were made, the heart of John could not reach to that which he says, " In the beginning was the Word, and the Word was with God, and the Word was God," unless he had risen above all things that were made by the Word. What a mountain this ! How holy ! How high among those mountains that received peace for the people of God, that the hills might receive righteousness !

6. Consider, then, brethren, if perchance John is not one of those mountains concerning whom we sang a little while ago, " I have lifted up mine eyes to the mountains, from whence shall come my help." Therefore, my brethren, if you would understand, lift up your eyes to this mountain, that is, raise yourselves up to the evangelist, rise to his meaning. But, because though these mountains receive peace he cannot be in peace who places his hope in man, do not so raise your eyes to the mountain as to think that your hope should be placed in man; and so say, " I have lifted up mine eyes to the mountains, from whence shall come my help," that you immediately add, " My help is from the Lord, who made heaven and earth."[6] Therefore let us lift our eyes to the mountains,

---

[1] John xx. 19.   [2] 1 Cor. ii. 9.
[3] 1 Cor iii. 4.   [4] Ps. lxxxii. 6

[5] Ps. cxlviii. 5   [6] Ps. cxxi. 1, 2.

from whence shall come our help; and yet it is not in the mountains themselves that our hope should be placed, for the mountains receive what they may minister to us; therefore, from whence the mountains also receive, there should our hope be placed. When we lift our eyes to the Scriptures, since it was through men the Scriptures were ministered, we are lifting our eyes to the mountains, from whence shall come our help; but still, since they were men who wrote the Scriptures, they did not shine of themselves, but "He was the true light,[1] who lighteth every man that cometh into the world." A mountain also was that John the Baptist, who said, "I am not the Christ,"[2] lest any one, placing his hope in the mountain, should fall from Him who illuminates the mountain. He also confessed, saying, "Since of His fullness have all we received."[3] So thou oughtest to say, "I have lifted up mine eyes to the mountains, from whence shall come my help," so as not to ascribe to the mountains the help that comes to thee; but continue and say, "My help is from the Lord, who made heaven and earth."

7. Therefore, brethren, may this be the result of my admonition, that you understand that in raising your hearts to the Scriptures (when the gospel was sounding forth, "In the beginning was the Word, and the Word was with God, and the Word was God," and the rest that was read), you were lifting your eyes to the mountains. For unless the mountains said these things, you would not find out how to think of them at all. Therefore from the mountains came your help, that you even heard of these things; but you cannot yet understand what you have heard. Call for help from the Lord, who made heaven and earth; for the mountains were enabled only so to speak as not of themselves to illuminate, because they themselves are also illuminated by hearing. Thence John, who said these things, received them—he who lay on the Lord's breast, and from the Lord's breast drank in what he might give us to drink. But he gave us words to drink. Thou oughtest then to receive understanding from the source from which he drank who gave thee to drink; so that thou mayest lift up thine eyes to the mountains from whence shall come thine aid, so that from thence thou mayest receive, as it were, the cup, that is, the word, given the eto drink; and yet, since thy help is from the Lord, who made heaven and earth, thou mayest fill thy breast from the source from which he filled his; whence thou saidst, "My help is from

the Lord, who made heaven and earth:" let him, then, fill who can. Brethren, this is what I have said: Let each one lift up his heart in the manner that seems fitting, and receive what is spoken. But perhaps you will say that I am more present to you than God. Far be such a thought from you! He is much more present to you; for I appear to your eyes, He presides over your consciences. Give me then your ears, Him your hearts, that you may fill both. Behold, your eyes, and those your bodily senses, you lift up to us; and yet not to us, for we are not of those mountains, but to the gospel itself, to the evangelist himself: your hearts, however, to the Lord to be filled. Moreover, let each one so lift up as to see what he lifts up, and whither. What do I mean by saying, "what he lifts up, and whither?" Let him see to it what sort of a heart he lifts up, because it is to the Lord he lifts it up, lest, encumbered by a load of fleshly pleasure, it fall ere ever it is raised. But does each one see that he bears a burden of flesh? Let him strive by continence to purify that which he may lift up to God. For "Blessed are the pure in heart, because they shall see God."[4]

8. But let us see what advantage it is that these words have sounded, "In the beginning was the Word, and the Word was with God, and the Word was God." We also uttered words when we spoke. Was it such a word that was with God? Did not those words which we uttered sound and pass away? Did God's Word, then, sound and come to an end? If so, how were all things made by it, and without it was nothing made? how is that which it created ruled by it, if it sounded and passed away? What sort of a word, then, is that which is both uttered and passes not away? Give ear, my beloved, it is a great matter. By everyday talk, words here become despicable to us, because through their sounding and passing away they are despised, and seem nothing but words. But there is a word in the man himself which remains within; for the sound proceeds from the mouth. There is a word which is spoken in a truly spiritual manner, that which you understand from the sound, not the sound itself. Mark, I speak a word when I say "God." How short the word which I have spoken—four letters and two syllables![5] Is this all that God is, four letters and two syllables? Or is that which is signified as costly as the word is paltry? What took place in thy heart when thou heardest "God"? What took place in my heart when I said "God"?

---

[1] John i. 9.   [2] John i. 30.   [3] John i. 16.   [4] Matt. v. 8.   [5] Deus.

A certain great and perfect substance was in our thoughts, transcending every changeable creature of flesh or of soul. And if I say to thee, " Is God changeable or unchangeable?" thou wilt answer immediately, " Far be it from me either to believe or imagine that God is changeable: God is unchangeable." Thy soul, though small, though perhaps still carnal, could not answer me otherwise than that God is unchangeable: but every creature is changeable; how then wert thou able to enter, by a glance of thy spirit, into that which is above the creature, so as confidently to answer me, " God is unchangeable"? What, then, is that in thy heart, when thou thinkest of a certain substance, living, eternal, all-powerful, infinite, everywhere present, everywhere whole, nowhere shut in? When thou thinkest of these qualities, this is the word concerning God in thy heart. But is this that sound which consists of four letters and two syllables? Therefore, whatever things are spoken and pass away are sounds, are letters, are syllables. His word which sounds passes away; but that which the sound signified, and was in the speaker as he thought of it, and in the hearer as he understood it, that remains while the sounds pass away.

9. Turn thy attention to that word. Thou canst have a word in thy heart, as it were a design born in thy mind, so that thy mind brings forth the design; and the design is, so to speak, the offspring of thy mind, the child of thy heart. For first thy heart brings forth a design to construct some fabric, to set up something great on the earth; already the design is conceived, and the work is not yet finished: thou seest what thou wilt make; but another does not admire, until thou hast made and constructed the pile, and brought that fabric into shape and to completion; then men regard the admirable fabric, and admire the design of the architect; they are astonished at what they see, and are pleased with what they do not see: who is there who can see a design? If, then, on account of some great building a human design receives praise, do you wish to see what a design of God is the Lord Jesus Christ, that is, the Word of God? Mark this fabric of the world. View what was made by the Word, and then thou wilt understand what is the nature of the world. Mark these two bodies of the world, the heavens and the earth. Who will unfold in words the beauty of the heavens? Who will unfold in words the fruitfulness of the earth? Who will worthily extol the changes of the seasons? Who will worthily extol the power of seeds? You see what things I do not mention, lest in giving a long list I should

perhaps tell of less than you can call up to your own minds. From this fabric, then, judge the nature of the Word by which it was made: and not it alone; for all these things are seen, because they have to do with the bodily sense. By that Word angels also were made; by that Word archangels were made, powers, thrones, dominions, principalities; by that Word were made all things. Hence, judge what a Word this is.

10. Perhaps some one now answers me, "Who so conceives this Word?" Do not then imagine, as it were, some paltry thing when thou hearest "the Word," nor suppose it to be words such as thou hearest them every day—" he spoke such words," "such words he uttered," " such words you tell me;" for by constant repetition the term *word* has become, so to speak, worthless. And when thou hearest, "In the beginning was the Word," lest thou shouldest imagine something worthless, such as thou hast been accustomed to think of when thou wert wont to listen to human words, hearken to what thou must think of: " The Word was God."

11. Now some unbelieving Arian may come forth and say that " the Word of God was made." How can it be that the Word of God was made, when God by the Word made all things? If the Word of God was itself also made, by what other Word was it made? But if thou sayest that there is a Word of the Word, I say, that by which it was made is itself the only Son of God. But if thou dost not say there is a Word of the Word, allow that that was not made by which all things were made. For that by which all things were made could not be made by itself. Believe the evangelist then. For he might have said, " In the beginning God made the Word:" even as Moses said, " In the beginning God made the heavens and the earth;" and enumerates all things thus: "God said, Let it be made, and it was made." [1] If " said," who said? God. And what was made? Some creature. Between the speaking of God and the making of the creature, what was there by which it was made but the Word? For God said, " Let it be made, and it was made." This Word is unchangeable; although changeable things are made by it, the Word itself is unchangeable.

12. Do not then believe that that was made by which were made all things, lest thou be not new-made by the Word, which makes all things new. For already hast thou been made by the Word, but it behoves thee to be new-made by the Word. If, however, thy

[1] Gen. i.

belief about the Word be wrong, thou wilt not be able to be new-made by the Word. And although creation by the Word has happened to thee, so that thou hast been made by Him, thou art unmade by thyself: if by thyself thou art unmade, let Him who made thee make thee new: if by thyself thou hast been made worse, let Him who created thee re-create thee. But how can He re-create thee by the Word, if thou holdest a wrong opinion about the Word? The evangelist says, "In the beginning was the Word;" and thou sayest, "In the beginning the Word was made." He says, "All things were made by Him;" and thou sayest that the Word Himself was made. The evangelist might have said, "In the beginning the Word was made:" but what does he say? "In the beginning was the Word." If He was, He was not made; that all things might be made by it, and without Him nothing be made. If, then, "in the beginning the Word was, and the Word was with God, and the Word was God;" if thou canst not imagine what it is, wait till thou art grown. That is strong meat: receive thou milk that thou mayest be nourished, and be able to receive strong meat.

13. Give good heed to what follows, brethren, "All things were made by Him, and without Him was nothing made," so as not to imagine that "nothing" is something. For many, wrongly understanding "without Him was nothing made," are wont to fancy that "nothing" is something. Sin, indeed, was not made by Him; and it is plain that sin is nothing, and men become nothing when they sin. An idol also was not made by the Word;—it has indeed a sort of human form, but man himself was made by the Word;— for the form of man in an idol was not made by the Word, and it is written, "We know that an idol is nothing."[1] Therefore these things were not made by the Word; but whatever was made in the natural manner, whatever belongs to the creature, everything that is fixed in the sky, that shines from above, that flies under the heavens, and that moves in universal nature, every creature whatsoever: I will speak more plainly, brethren, that you may understand me; I will say, from an angel even to a worm. What more excellent than an angel among created things? what lower than a worm? He who made the angel made the worm also; but the angel is fit for heaven, the worm for earth. He who created also arranged. If He had placed the worm in heaven, thou mightest have found fault; if He had willed that angels should spring from

decaying flesh, thou mightest have found fault: and yet God almost does this, and He is not to be found fault with. For all men born of flesh, what are they but worms? and of these worms God makes angels. For if the Lord Himself says, "But I am a worm and no man,"[2] who will hesitate to say what is written also in Job, "How much more is man rottenness, and the son of man a worm?"[3] First he said, "Man is rottenness;" and afterwards, "The son of man a worm:" because a worm springs from rottenness, therefore "man is rottenness," and "the son of man a worm." Behold what for thy sake He was willing to become, who "in the beginning was the Word, and the Word was with God, and the Word was God!" Why did He for thy sake become this? That thou mightest suck, who wert not able to chew. Wholly in this sense, then, brethren, understand "All things were made by Him, and without Him was nothing made." For every creature, great and small, was made by Him: by Him were made things above and things beneath; spiritual and corporeal, by Him were they made. For no form, no structure, no agreement of parts, no substance whatever that can have weight, number, measure, exists but by that Word, and by that Creator Word, to whom it is said, "Thou hast ordered all things in measure, and in number, and in weight."[4]

14. Therefore, let no one deceive you, when perchance you suffer annoyance from flies. For some have been mocked by the devil, and taken with flies. As fowlers are accustomed to put flies in their traps to deceive hungry birds, so these have been deceived with flies by the devil. Some one or other was suffering annoyance from flies; a Manichæan found him in his trouble, and when he said that he could not bear flies, and hated them exceedingly, immediately the Manichæan said, "Who made them?" And since he was suffering from annoyance, and hated them, he dared not say, "God made them," though he was a Catholic. The other immediately added, "If God did not make them, who made them?" "Truly," replied the Catholic, "I believe the devil made them." And the other immediately said, "If the devil made the fly, as I see you allow, because you understand the matter well, who made the bee, which is a little larger than the fly?" The Catholic dared not say that God made the bee and not the fly, for the case was much the same. From the bee he led him to the locust; from the locust to the

lizard; from the lizard to the bird; from the bird to the sheep; from the sheep to the cow; from that to the elephant, and at last to man; and persuaded a man that man was not made by God. Thus the miserable man, being troubled with the flies, became himself a fly, and the property of the devil. In fact, Beelzebub, they say, means "Prince of flies;" and of these it is written, "Dying flies deprive the ointment of its sweetness."[1]

15. What then, brethren? why have I said these things? Shut the ears of your hearts against the wiles of the enemy. Understand that God made all things, and arranged them in their orders. Why, then, do we suffer many evils from a creature that God made? Because we have offended God? Do angels suffer these things? Perhaps we, too, in that life of theirs, would have no such thing to fear. For thy punishment, accuse thy sin, not the Judge. For, on account of our pride, God appointed that tiny and contemptible creature to torment us; so that, since man has become proud and has boasted himself against God, and, though mortal, has oppressed mortals, and, though man, has not acknowledged his fellowman,—since he has lifted himself up, he may be brought low by gnats. Why art thou inflated with human pride? Some one has censured thee, and thou art swollen with rage. Drive off the gnats, that thou mayest sleep: understand who thou art. For, that you may know, brethren, it was for the taming of our pride these things were created to be troublesome to us, God could have humbled Pharaoh's proud people by bears, by lions, by serpents; He sent flies and frogs upon them,[2] that their pride might be subdued by the meanest creatures.

16. "All things," then, brethren, "all things were made by Him, and without Him was nothing made." But how were all things made by Him? "That, which was made, in Him is life." It can also be read thus: "That, which was made in Him, is life;" and if we so read it, everything is life. For what is there that was not made in Him? For He is the Wisdom of God, and it is said in the Psalm,[3] "In Wisdom hast Thou made all things." If, then, Christ is the Wisdom of God, and the Psalm says, "In Wisdom hast Thou made all things:" as all things were made by Him, so all things were made in Him. If, then, all things were made in Him, dearly beloved brethren, and that, which was made in Him, is life, both the earth is life and wood is life. We do indeed say wood is life, but in the sense of the wood of

the cross, whence we have received life. A stone, then, is life. It is not seemly so to understand the passage, as the same most vile sect of the Manichæans creep stealthily on us again, and say that a stone has life, that a wall has a soul, and a cord has a soul, and wool, and clothing. For so they are accustomed to talk in their raving; and when they have been driven back and refuted, they in some sort bring forward Scripture, saying, "Why is it said, 'That, which was made in Him, is life'?" For if all things were made in Him, all things are life. Be not carried away by them; read thus "That which was made;" here make a short pause, and then go on, "in Him is life." What is the meaning of this? The earth was made, but the very earth that was made is not life; but there exists spiritually in the Wisdom itself a certain reason by which the earth was made: this is life.

17. As far as I can, I shall explain my meaning to you, beloved. A carpenter makes a box. First he has the box in design; for if he had it not in design, how could he produce it by workmanship? But the box in theory is not the very box as it appears to the eyes. It exists invisibly in design, it will be visible in the work. Behold, it is made in the work; has it ceased to exist in design? The one is made in the work, and the other remains which exists in design; for that box may rot, and another be fashioned according to that which exists in design. Give heed, then, to the box as it is in design, and the box as it is in fact. The actual box is not life, the box in design is life; because the soul of the artificer, where all these things are before they are brought forth, is living. So, dearly beloved brethren, because the Wisdom of God, by which all things have been made, contains everything according to design before it is made, therefore those things which are made through this design itself are not forthwith life, but whatever has been made is life in Him. You see the earth, there is an earth in design; you see the sky, there is a sky in design; you see the sun and the moon, these also exist in design: but externally they are bodies, in design they are life. Understand, if in any way you are able, for a great matter has been spoken. If I am not great by whom it is spoken, or through whom it is spoken, still it is from a great authority. For these things are not spoken by me who am small; He is not small to whom I refer in saying these things. Let each one take in what he can, and to what extent he can; and he who is not able to take in any of it, let him nourish his heart, that he may become able.

How is he to nourish it? Let him nourish it with milk, that he may come to strong meat. Let him not leave Christ born through the flesh till he arrive at Christ born of the Father alone, the God-Word with God, through whom all things were made; for that is life, which in Him is the light of men.

18. For this follows: "and the life was the light of men;" and from this very life are men illuminated. Cattle are not illuminated, because cattle have not rational minds capable of seeing wisdom. But man was made in the image of God, and has a rational mind, by which he can perceive wisdom. That life, then, by which all things were made, is itself the light; yet not the light of every animal, but of men. Wherefore a little after he says, "That was the true light, which lighteth every man that cometh into the world." By that light John the Baptist was illuminated; by the same light also was John the Evangelist himself illuminated. He was filled with that light who said, "I am not the Christ; but He that cometh after me, whose shoe's latchet I am not worthy to unloose."[1] By that light he had been illuminated who said, "In the beginning was the Word, and the Word was with God, and the Word was God." Therefore that life is the light of men.

19. But perhaps the slow hearts of some of you cannot yet receive that light, because they are burdened by their sins, so that they cannot see. Let them not on that account think that the light is in any way absent, because they are not able to see it; for they themselves are darkness on account of their sins. "And the light shineth in darkness, and the darkness comprehended it not." Accordingly, brethren, as in the case of a blind man placed in the sun, the sun is present to him, but he is absent from the sun. So every foolish man, every unjust man, every irreligious man, is blind in heart. Wisdom is present; but it is present to a blind man, and is absent from his eyes; not because it is absent from him, but because he is absent from it. What then is he to do? Let him become pure, that he may be able to see God. Just as if a man could not see because his eyes were dirty and sore with dust, rheum, or smoke, the physician would say to him: "Cleanse from your eye whatever bad thing is in it, so that you may be able to see the light of your eyes." Dust, rheum, and smoke are sins and iniquities: remove then all these things, and you will see the wisdom that is present; for God is that wisdom, and it has been said, "Blessed are the pure in heart; for they shall see God."[2]

[1] John i. 26, 27.

[2] Matt. v. 8.

TRACTATE II.

CHAPTER I. 6–14.

It is fitting, brethren, that as far as possible we should treat of the text of Holy Scripture, and especially of the Holy Gospel, without omitting any portion, that both we ourselves may derive nourishment according to our capacity, and may minister to you from that source from which we have been nourished. Last Lord's day, we remember, we treated of the first section; that is, "In the beginning was the Word, and the Word was with God, and the Word was God. The same was in the beginning with God. All things were made by Him; and without Him was nothing made. That which was made, in Him is life; and the life was the light of men. And the light shineth in darkness; and the darkness comprehended it not." So far, I believe, had I advanced in the treatment of the passage: let all who were present recall

what was then said; and those of you who were not present, believe me and those who chose to be present. Now therefore,—because we cannot always be repeating everything, out of justice to those who desire to hear what follows, and because repetition of the former thought is a burden to them and deprives them of what succeeds,—let those who were absent on the former occasion refrain from demanding repetition, but, together with those who were here, listen to the present exposition.

2. It goes on, "There was a man sent from God whose name was John." Truly, brethren beloved, those things which were said before, were said regarding the ineffable divinity of Christ, and almost ineffably. For who shall comprehend "In the beginning was the Word, and the Word was with God"?

And do not allow the name word to appear mean to you, through the habit of daily words, for it is added, "and the Word was God." This Word is He of whom yesterday we spoke much; and I trust that God was present, and that even from only thus much speaking something reached your hearts. "In the beginning was the Word." He is the same, and is in the same manner; as He is, so He is always; He cannot be changed; that is, He *is*. This His name He spoke to His servant Moses: "I am that I am; and He that *is* hath sent me."[1] Who then shall comprehend this when you see that all mortal things are variable; when you see that not only do bodies vary as to their qualities, by being born, by increasing, by becoming less, by dying, but that even souls themselves through the effect of divers volitions are distended and divided; when you see that men can obtain wisdom if they apply themselves to its light and heat, and also lose wisdom if they remove themselves from it through some evil influence? When, therefore, you see that all those things are variable, what is that which is, unless that which transcends all things which are so that they are not? Who then can receive this? Or who, in what manner soever he may have applied the strength of his mind to touch that which is, can reach to that which he may in any way have touched with his mind? It is as if one were to see his native land at a distance, and the sea intervening; he sees whither he would go, but he has not the means of going. So we desire to arrive at that our stability where that which is, is, because this alone always is as it is: the sea of this world interrupts our course, even although already we see whither we go; for many do not even see whither they go. That there might be a way by which we could go, He has come from Him to whom we wished to go. And what has He done? He has appointed a tree by which we may cross the sea. For no one is able to cross the sea of this world, unless borne by the cross of Christ. Even he who is of weak eyesight sometimes embraces this cross; and he who does not see from afar whither he goes, let him not depart from it, and it will carry him over.

3. Therefore, my brethren, I would desire to have impressed this upon your hearts: if you wish to live in a pious and Christian manner, cling to Christ according to that which He became for us, that you may arrive at Him according to that which is, and according to that which was. He approached, that

for us He might become this; because He became that for us, on which the weak may be borne, and cross the sea of this world and reach their native country; where there will be no need of a ship, for no sea is crossed. It is better then not to see with the mind that which is, and yet not to depart from the cross of Christ, than to see it with the mind, and despise the cross of Christ. It is good beyond this, and best of all, if it be possible, that we both see whither we ought to go, and hold fast that which carries us as we go. This they were able to do, the great minds of the mountains, who have been called mountains, whom the light of divine justice pre-eminently illuminates; they were able to do this, and saw that which is. For John seeing said, "In the beginning was the Word, and the Word was with God, and the Word was God." They saw this, and in order that they might arrive at that which they saw from afar, they did not depart from the cross of Christ, and did not despise Christ's lowliness. But little ones who cannot understand this, who do not depart from the cross and passion and resurrection of Christ, are conducted in that same ship to that which they do not see, in which they also arrive who do see.

4. But truly there have been some philosophers of this world who have sought for the Creator by means of the creature; for He can be found by means of the creature, as the apostle plainly says, "For the invisible things of Him from the creation of the world are clearly seen, being understood by the things that are made, even His eternal power and glory; so they are without excuse." And it follows, "Because that, when they knew God;" he did not say, Because they did not know, but "Because that, when they knew God, they glorified Him not as God, neither were thankful; but became vain in their imaginations, and their foolish heart was darkened." How darkened? It follows, when he says more plainly: "Professing themselves to be wise, they became fools."[2] They saw whither they must come; but ungrateful to Him who afforded them what they saw, they wished to ascribe to themselves what they saw; and having become proud, they lost what they saw, and were turned from it to idols and images, and to the worship of demons, to adore the creature and to despise the Creator. But these having been blinded did those things, and became proud, that they might be blinded: when they were proud they said that they were wise. Those, therefore, concerning whom he said, "Who,

when they had known God," saw this which John says, that by the Word of God all things were made. For these things are also found in the books of the philosophers: and that God has an only-begotten Son, by whom are all things. They were able to see that which is, but they saw it from afar: they were unwilling to hold the lowliness of Christ, in which ship they might have arrived in safety at that which they were able to see from afar; and the cross of Christ appeared vile to them. The sea has to be crossed, and dost thou despise the wood? Oh, proud wisdom! thou laughest to scorn the crucified Christ; it is He whom thou dost see from afar: "In the beginning was the Word, and the Word was with God." But wherefore was He crucified? Because the wood of His humiliation was needful to thee. For thou hadst become swollen with pride, and hadst been cast out far from that fatherland; and by the waves of this world has the way been intercepted, and there is no means of passing to the fatherland unless borne by the wood. Ungrateful one! thou laughest Him to scorn who has come to thee that thou mayest return: He has become the way, and that through the sea:[1] thence He walked in the sea to show that there is a way in the sea. But thou who art not able in any way thyself to walk in the sea, be carried in a ship, be carried by the wood: believe in the crucified One, and thou shalt arrive thither. On account of thee He was crucified, to teach thee humility; and because if He should come as God, He would not be recognized. For if He should come as God, He would not come to those who were not able to see God. For not according to His Godhead does He either come or depart; since He is everywhere present, and is contained in no place. But, according to what did He come? He appeared as a man.

5. Therefore, because He was so man, that the God lay hid in Him, there was sent before Him a great man, by whose testimony He might be found to be more than man. And who is this? "He was a man." And how could that man speak the truth concerning God? "He was sent by God." What was he called? "Whose name was John." Wherefore did he come? "He came for a witness, that he might bear witness concerning the light, that all might believe through him." What sort of man was he who was to bear witness concerning the light? Something great was that John, vast merit, great grace, great loftiness! Admire, by all means,

admire; but as it were a mountain. But a mountain is in darkness unless it be clothed with light. Therefore only admire John that you may hear what follows, "He was not that light;" lest if, when thou thinkest the mountain to be the light, thou make shipwreck on the mountain, and find not consolation. But what oughtest thou to admire? The mountain as a mountain. But lift thyself up to Him who illuminates the mountain, which for this end was elevated that it might be the first to receive the rays, and make them known to your eyes. Therefore, "he was not that light."

6. Wherefore then did he come? "But that he might bear witness concerning the light." Why so? "That all might believe through him." And concerning what light was he to bear witness? "That was the true light." Wherefore is it added true? Because an enlightened man is also called a light; but the true light is that which enlightens. For even our eyes are called lights; and nevertheless, unless either during the night a lamp is lighted, or during the day the sun goes forth, these lights are open in vain. Thus, therefore, John was a light, but not the true light; because, if not enlightened, he would have been darkness; but, by enlightenment, he became a light. For unless he had been enlightened he would have been darkness, as all those once impious men, to whom, as believers, the apostle said, "Ye were sometimes darkness." But now, because they had believed, what?—"but now are ye light," he says, "in the Lord."[2] Unless he had added "in the Lord," we should not have understood. "Light," he says, "in the Lord:" darkness you were not in the Lord. "For ye were sometimes darkness," where he did not add in the Lord. Therefore, darkness in you, light in the Lord. And thus "he was not that light, but was sent to bear witness of the light."

7. But where is that light? "He was the true light, which lighteth every man that cometh into the world." If every man that cometh, then also John. The true light, therefore, enlightened him by whom He desired Himself to be pointed out. Understand, beloved, for He came to infirm minds, to wounded hearts, to the gaze of dim-eyed souls. For this purpose had He come. And whence was the soul able to see that which perfectly is? Even as it commonly happens, that by means of some illuminated body, the sun, which we cannot see with the eyes, is known to have arisen. Because even those

---

[1] Matt. xiv. 25.   [2] Eph. v. 8.

who have wounded eyes are able to see a wall illuminated and enlightened by the sun, or a mountain, or a tree, or anything of that sort; and, by means of another body illuminated, that arising is shown to those who are not as yet able to gaze on it. Thus, therefore, all those to whom Christ came were not fit to see Him: upon John He shed the beams of His light; and by means of him confessing himself to have been irradiated and enlightened, not claiming to be one who irradiates and enlightens, He is known who enlightens, He is known who illuminates, He is known who fills. And who is it? "He who lighteth every man," he says, "who cometh into the world." For if man had not receded from that light, he would not have required to be illuminated; but for this reason has he to be illuminated here, because he departed from that light by which man might always have been illuminated.

8. What then? If He came hither, where was He? "He was in this world." He was both here and came hither; He was here according to His divinity, and He came hither according to the flesh; because when He was here according to His divinity, He could not be seen by the foolish, by the blind, and the wicked. These wicked men are the darkness, concerning which it was said, "The light shineth in darkness, and the darkness comprehended it not."[1] Behold, both here He is now, and here He was, and here He is always; and He never departs, departs nowhither. There is need that thou have some means whereby thou mayest see that which never departs from thee; there is need that thou depart not from Him who departs nowhither; there is need that thou desert not, and thou shalt not be deserted. Do not fall, and His sun will not set to thee. If thou fallest, His sun setteth upon thee; but if thou standest, He is present with thee. But thou hast not stood: remember how thou hast fallen, how he who fell before thee cast thee down. For he cast thee down, not by violence, not by assault, but by thine own will. For hadst thou not consented unto evil, thou wouldest have stood, thou wouldest have remained enlightened. But now, because thou hast already fallen, and hast become wounded in heart,—the organ by which that light can be seen,—He came to thee such as thou mightest see; and He in such fashion manifested Himself as man, that He sought testimony from man. From man God seeks testimony, and God has man as a witness;— God has man as a witness, but on account of

man: so infirm are we. By a lamp we seek the day; because John himself was called a lamp, the Lord saying," He was a burning and a shining light; and ye were willing for a season to rejoice in his light: but I have greater witness than John."[2]

9. Therefore He showed that for the sake of men He desired to have Himself revealed by a lamp to the faith of those who believed, that by means of the same lamp His enemies might be confounded. There were enemies who tempted Him, and said, "Tell us by what authority doest thou these things?" "I also," saith He, "will ask you one question; answer me. The baptism of John, whence was it? from heaven, or of men? And they were troubled, and said among themselves, If we shall say, From heaven, he will say unto us, Why did ye not believe him?" (Because he had borne testimony to Christ, and had said, I am not the Christ, but He.[3] "But if we shall say, Of men, we fear the people, lest they should stone us: for they held John as a prophet." Afraid of stoning, but fearing more to confess the truth, they answered a lie to the Truth; and "wickedness imposed a lie upon itself."[4] For they said, "We know not." And the Lord, because they shut the door against themselves, by professing ignorance of what they knew, did not open to them, because they did not knock. For it is said, Knock, and it shall be opened unto you."[5] Not only did these not knock that it might be opened to them; but, by denying that they knew, they barred that door against themselves. And the Lord says to them, Neither tell I you by what authority I do these things."[6] And they were confounded by means of John; and in them were the words fulfilled,"I have ordained a lamp for mine anointed. His enemies will I clothe with shame."[7]

10. "He was in the world, and the world was made by Him." Think not that He was in the world as the earth is in the world, as the sky is in the world, as the sun is in the world, the moon and the stars, trees, cattle, and men. He was not thus in the world. But in what manner then? As the Artificer governing what He had made. For He did not make it as a carpenter makes a chest. The chest which he makes is outside the carpenter, and so it is put in another place, while being made; and although the workman is nigh, he sits in another place, and is external to that which he fashions. But God, infused into

---

[1] John i. 5.

[2] John v. 35. [3] John i. 20, 27.
[4] Ps. xxvii. 12. [5] Matt. vii. 7.
[6] Matt. xxi. 23–27; Mark xii. 28–33; Luke xx. 2–8.
[7] Ps. cxxxii. 17.

the world, fashions it; being everywhere present He fashions, and withdraweth not Himself elsewhere, nor doth He, as it were, handle from without, the matter which He fashions. By the presence of His majesty He maketh what He maketh; His presence governs what He made. Therefore was He in the world as the Maker of the world; for, " The world was made by Him, and the world knew Him not."

11. What meaneth " the world was made by Him " ? The heaven, the earth, the sea, and all things which are therein, are called the world. Again, in another signification, those who love the world are called the world. " The world was made by Him, and the world knew Him not." Did not the heavens know their Creator, or did the angels not know their Creator, or did the stars not know their Creator, whom the demons confess ? All things from all sides gave testimony. But who did not know ? Those who, for their love of the world, are called the world. By loving we dwell with the heart; but because of their loving the world they deserved to be called after the name of that in which they dwelt. In the same manner as we say, This house is bad, or this house is good, we do not in calling the one bad or the other good accuse or praise the walls; but by a bad house we mean a house with bad inhabitants, and by a good house, a house with good inhabitants. In like manner we call those the world who by loving it, inhabit the world. Who are they ? Those who love the world; for they dwell with their hearts in the world. For those who do not love the world in the flesh, indeed, sojourn in the world, but in their hearts they dwell in heaven, as the apostle says, " Our conversation is in heaven." [1] Therefore " the world was made by Him, and the world knew Him not."

12. " He came unto His own,"—because all these things were made by Him,—" and His own received Him not." Who are they ? The men whom He made. The Jews whom He at the first made to be above all nations. Because other nations worshipped idols and served demons; but that people was born of the seed of Abraham, and in an eminent sense His own, because kindred through that flesh which He deigned to assume. " He came unto His own, and His own received Him not." Did they not receive Him at all ? did no one receive Him ? Was there no one saved ? For no one shall be saved unless he who shall have received the coming Christ.

13. But John adds: " As many as received Him." What did He afford to them ? Great benevolence ! Great mercy ! He was born the only Son of God, and was unwilling to remain alone. Many men, when they have not sons, in advanced age adopt a son, and thus obtain by an exercise of will what nature has denied to them: this men do. But if any one have an only son, he rejoices the more in him; because he alone will possess everything, and he will not have any one to divide with him the inheritance, so that he should be poorer. Not so God: that same only Son whom He had begotten, and by whom He created all things, He sent into this world that He might not be alone, but might have adopted brethren. For we were not born of God in the manner in which the Only-begotten was born of Him, but were adopted by His grace. For He, the Only-begotten, came to loose the sins in which we were entangled, and whose burden hindered our adoption: those whom He wished to make brethren to Himself, He Himself loosed, and made joint-heirs. For so saith the apostle, " But if a son, then an heir through God." And again, " Heirs of God, and joint-heirs with Christ." He did not fear to have joint-heirs, because His heritage does not become narrow if many are possessors. Those very persons, He being possessor, become His inheritance, and He in turn becomes their inheritance. Hear in what manner they become His inheritance: " The Lord hath said unto me, Thou art my Son, this day have I begotten Thee. Ask of me, and I will give Thee the nations for Thine inheritance." [2] Hear in what manner He becomes their inheritance. He says in the Psalms: " The Lord is the portion of mine inheritance, and of my cup." [3] Let us possess Him, and let Him possess us: let Him possess us as Lord; let us possess Him as salvation, let us possess Him as light. What then did He give to them who received Him ? " To them He gave power to become sons of God, even to them that believe on His name;" that they may cling to the wood and cross the sea.

14. And how are they born ? Because they become sons of God and brethren of Christ, they are certainly born. For if they are not born, how can they be sons ? But the sons of men are born of flesh and blood, and of the will of man, and of the embrace of wedlock. But in what manner are they born ? " Who not of bloods," as if of male and female. Bloods is not Latin; but because it is plural in Greek, the interpreter preferred so to express it, and to speak bad Latin according to

the grammarian that he might make the matter plain to the understanding of the weak among his hearers. For if he had said blood in the singular number, he would not have explained what he desired; for men are born of the bloods of male and female. Let us say so, then, and not fear the ferule of grammarians, so long as we reach the solid and certain truth. He who understands it and blames it, is thankless for his having understood. "Not of bloods, nor of the will of the flesh, nor of the will of man." The apostle puts flesh for woman; because, when she was made of his rib, Adam said, "This is now bone of my bone, and flesh of my flesh." [1] And the apostle saith, "He that loveth his wife loveth himself; for no one ever hated his own flesh." [2] Flesh, then, is put for woman, in the same manner that spirit is sometimes put for husband. Wherefore? Because the one rules, the other is ruled; the one ought to command, the other to serve. For where the flesh commands and the spirit serves, the house is turned the wrong way. What can be worse than a house where the woman has the mastery over the man? But that house is rightly ordered where the man commands and the woman obeys. In like manner that man is rightly ordered where the spirit commands and the flesh serves.

15. These, then, "were born not of the will of the flesh, nor of the will of man, but of God." But that men might be born of God, God was first born of them. For Christ is God, and Christ was born of men. It was only a mother, indeed, that He sought upon earth; because He had already a Father in heaven: He by whom we were to be created was born of God, and He by whom we were to be re-created was born of a woman. Marvel not, then, O man, that thou art made a son by grace, that thou art born of God according to His Word. The Word Himself first chose to be born of man, that thou mightest be born of God unto salvation, and say to thyself, Not without reason did God wish to be born of man, but because He counted me of some importance, that He might make me immortal, and for me be born as a mortal man. When, therefore, he had

said, "born of God," lest we should, as it were, be filled with amazement and trembling at such grace, at grace so great as to exceed belief that men are born of God, as if assuring thee, he says, "And the Word was made flesh, and dwelt among us." Why, then, dost thou marvel that men are born of God? Consider God Himself born of men: "And the Word was made flesh, and dwelt among us."

16. But because "the Word was made flesh, and dwelt among us," by His very nativity he made an eye-salve to cleanse the eyes of our heart, and to enable us to see His majesty by means of His humility. Therefore "the Word was made flesh, and dwelt among us:" He healed our eyes; and what follows? "And we beheld His glory." His glory can no one see unless healed by the humility of His flesh. Wherefore were we not able to see? Consider, then, dearly beloved, and see what I say. There had dashed into man's eye, as it were, dust, earth; it had wounded the eye, and it could not see the light: that wounded eye is anointed; by earth it was wounded, and earth is applied to it for healing. For all eye-salves and medicines are derived from the earth alone. By dust thou wert blinded, and by dust thou art healed: flesh, then, had wounded thee, flesh heals thee. The soul had become carnal by consenting to the affections of the flesh; thus had the eye of the heart been blinded. "The Word was made flesh:" that Physician made for thee an eye-salve. And as He thus came by flesh to extinguish the vices of the flesh, and by death to slay death; therefore did this take place in thee, that, as "the Word became flesh," thou mayest be able to say, "And we beheld His glory." What sort of glory? Such as He became as Son of man? That was His humility, not His glory. But to what is the sight of man brought when cured by means of flesh? "We beheld His glory, the glory as of the Only-begotten from the Father, full of grace and truth." Of grace and truth we shall speak more fully in another place in this same Gospel, if the Lord vouchsafe us opportunity. Let these things suffice for the present, and be ye edified in Christ: be ye comforted in faith, and watch in good works, and see that ye do not depart from the wood by which ye may cross the sea.

---

[1] Gen. ii. 23.　　　[2] Eph. v. 28, 29.

TRACTATE III.

CHAPTER I. 15-18.

WE undertook, in the name of the Lord, and promised to you, beloved, to treat of that grace and truth of God, full of which the only-begotten Son, our Lord and Saviour Jesus Christ, appeared to the saints, and to show how, as a matter belonging to the New Testament, it is to be distinguished from the Old Testament. Give, then, your attention, that what I receive in my measure from God, you in your measure may receive and hear the same. For it will only remain if, when the seed is scattered in your hearts, the birds take it not away, nor thorns choke it, nor heat scorch it, and there descend upon it the rain of daily exhortations and your own good thoughts, by which that is done in the heart which in the field is done by means of harrows, so that the clod is broken, and the seed covered and enabled to germinate: that you bear fruit at which the husbandman may be glad and rejoice. But if, in return for good seed and good rain, you bring forth not fruit but thorns, the seed will not be blamed, nor will the rain be in fault; but for thorns due fire is prepared.[1]

2. I do not think that I need spend much time in endeavoring to persuade you that we are Christian men; and if Christians, by virtue of the name, belonging to Christ. Upon the forehead we bear His sign; and we do not blush because of it, if we also bear it in the heart. His sign is His humility. By a star the Magi knew Him;[2] and this sign was given by the Lord, and it was heavenly and beautiful. He did not desire that a star should be His sign on the forehead of the faithful, but His cross. By it humbled, by it also glorified; by it He raised the humble, even by that to which He, when humbled, descended. We belong, then, to the gospel, we belong to the New Testament. "The law was given by Moses, but grace and truth came by Jesus Christ." We ask the apostle, and he says to us, since we are not under the law but under grace.[3] "He sent therefore His Son, made of a woman, made under the law, that He might redeem those who were under the law, that we might receive the adoption of sons."[4] Behold, for this end Christ came, that He might redeem those who were under the law; that now we may not be under the law, but under grace. Who, then, gave the law? He gave the law who gave likewise grace; but the law He sent by a servant, with grace He Himself came down. And in what manner were men made under the law? By not fulfilling the law. For he who fulfills the law is not under the law, but with the law; but he who is under the law is not raised up, but pressed down by the law. All men, therefore, being placed under the law, are by the law made guilty; and for this purpose it is over their head, that it may show sins, not take them away. The law then commands, the Giver of the law showeth pity in that which the law commands. Men, endeavoring by their own strength to fulfill that which the law commands, fell by their own rash and headstrong presumption; and not with the law, but under the law, became guilty: and since by their own strength they were unable to fulfill the law, and were become guilty under the law, they implored the aid of the Deliverer; and the guilt which the law brought caused sickness to the proud. The sickness of the proud became the confession of the humble. Now the sick confess that they are sick; let the physician come to heal the sick.

3. Who is the Physician? Our Lord Jesus Christ. Who is our Lord Jesus Christ? He who was seen even by those by whom He was crucified. He who was seized, buffeted, scourged, spit upon, crowned with thorns, suspended upon the cross, died, pierced by the spear, taken down from the cross, laid in the sepulchre. That same Jesus Christ our Lord, that same Jesus exactly, He is the complete Physician of our wounds. That crucified One at whom insults were cast, and while He hung on the cross His persecutors wagging the head, and saying, "If he be the Son of God, let him come down from the cross,"[5]—He, and no other, is our complete Physician. Wherefore, then, did He not show to his deriders that He was the Son of God; so that if He allowed Himself to be lifted up upon the cross, at least when they said, "If he be the Son of God, let him come down from the cross," He should then come down, and show to them that He was the very Son of God whom they had dared to deride? He would not. Wherefore would He not? Was it because He could not? Manifestly

---

[1] Matt. xiii. 3-25.   [2] Matt. ii. 2.
[3] Rom. vi. 14.   [4] Gal. iv. 4, 5.   [5] Matt. xxvii. 39, 40.

He could. For which is greater, to descend from the cross or to rise from the sepulchre? But He bore with His insulters; for the cross was taken not as a proof of power, but as an example of patience. There He cured thy wounds, where He long bore His own; there He healed thee of death eternal, where He vouchsafed to die the temporal death. And did He die, or in Him did death die? What a death was that, which slew death!

4. Is it, however, our Lord Jesus Christ Himself—His whole self—who was seen, and held, and crucified? Is the whole very self that? It is the same, but not the whole, that which the Jews saw; this is not the whole Christ. And what is? "In the beginning was the Word." In what beginning? "And the Word was with God." And what word? "And the Word was God." Was then perhaps this Word made by God? No. For "the same was in the beginning with God." What then? Are the other things which God made not like unto the Word? No: because "all things were made by Him, and without Him was not anything made." In what manner were all things made by Him? Because "that which was made in Him was life;" and before it was made there was life. That which was made is not life; but in the art, that is, in the wisdom of God, before it was made, it was life. That which was made passes away; that which is in wisdom cannot pass away. There was life, therefore, in that which was made. And what sort of life, since the soul also is the life of the body? Our body has its own life; and when it has lost it, the death of the body ensues. Was then the life such as this? No; but "the life was the light of men." Was it the light of cattle? For this light is the light of men and of cattle. There is a certain light of men: let us see how far men differ from the cattle, and then we shall understand what is the light of men. Thou dost not differ from the cattle except in intellect; do not glory in anything besides. Dost thou presume upon thy strength? By the wild beasts thou art surpassed. Upon thy swiftness dost thou presume? By the flies thou art surpassed. Upon thy beauty dost thou presume? How great beauty is there in the feathers of a peacock! Wherein then art thou better? In the image of God. Where is the image of God? In the mind, in the intellect. If then thou art in this respect better than the cattle, that thou hast a mind by which thou mayest understand what the cattle cannot understand; and therein a man, because better than the cattle; the light of men is the light of minds. The light of minds is above minds and surpasses all minds.

This was that life by which all things were made.

5. Where was it? Was it here? was it with the Father, and was it not here? or, what is more true, was it both with the Father and here also? If then it was here, wherefore was it not seen? Because "the light shineth in darkness, and the darkness comprehended it not." Oh men, be not darkness, be not unbelieving, unjust, unrighteous, rapacious, avaricious lovers of this world: for these are the darkness. The light is not absent, but you are absent from the light. A blind man in the sunshine has the sun present to him, but is himself absent from the sun. Be ye not then darkness. For this is perhaps the grace regarding which we are about to speak, that now we be no more darkness, and that the apostle may say to us, "We were sometime darkness, but now light in the Lord."[1] Because then the light of men was not seen, that is, the light of minds, there was a necessity that a man should give testimony regarding the light, who was not in darkness, but who was already enlightened; and nevertheless, because enlightened, not the light itself, "but that He might bear witness of the light." For "he was not that light." And what was the light? "That was the true light which enlightened every man that cometh into this world." And where was that light? "In this world it was." And how was it "in this world?" As the light of the sun, of the moon, and of lamps, was that light thus in the world? No. Because "the world was made by Him, and the world knew Him not;" that is to say, "the light shineth in darkness, and the darkness comprehended it not." For the world is darkness; because the lovers of the world are the world. For did not the creature acknowledge its Creator? The heavens gave testimony by a star;[2] the sea gave testimony, and bore its Lord when He walked upon it;[3] the winds gave testimony, and were quiet at His bidding;[4] the earth gave testimony, and trembled when He was crucified.[5] If all these gave testimony, in what sense did the world not know Him, unless that the world signifies the lovers of the world, those who with their hearts dwell in the world? And the world is evil, because the inhabitants of the world are evil; just as a house is evil, not because of its walls, but because of its inhabitants.

6. "He came unto His own;" that is to say, He came to that which belonged to Himself; "and His own received Him not." What, then, is the hope, unless that "as many

[1] Eph. v. 8.　　[2] Matt. ii. 2.　　[3] Matt. xiv. 26.
[4] Matt. xxiii. 27.　　[5] Matt. xxvii. 51.

as received Him, to them gave He power to become the sons of God"? If they become sons, they are born; if born, how are they born? Not of flesh, "nor of blood, nor of the will of the flesh, nor of the will of man; but of God are they born." Let them rejoice, therefore, that they are born of God; let them believe that they are born of God; let them receive the proof that they are born of God: "And the Word became flesh, and dwelt among us." If the Word was not ashamed to be born of man, are men ashamed to be born of God? And because He did this, He cured us; and because He cured us, we see. For this, "that the Word was made flesh, and dwelt among us," became a medicine unto us, so that as by earth we were made blind, by earth we might be healed; and having been healed, might behold what? "And we beheld," he says, "His glory, the glory as of the Only-begotten of the Father, full of grace and truth."

7. "John beareth witness of Him, and crieth, saying, This was He of whom I spake, He that cometh after me is made before me." He came after me, and He preceded me. What is it, "He is made before me"? He preceded me. Not was made before I was made, but was preferred before me, this is "He was made before me." Wherefore was He made before thee, when He came after thee? "Because He was before me." Before thee, O John! what great thing to be before thee! It is well that thou dost bear witness to Him; let us, however, hear Himself saying, "Even before Abraham, I am." [1] But Abraham also was born in the midst of the human race: there were many before him, many after him. Listen to the voice of the Father to the Son: "Before Lucifer I have begotten Thee." [2] He who was begotten before Lucifer Himself illuminates all. A certain one was named Lucifer, who fell; for he was an angel and became a devil; and concerning him the Scripture said, "Lucifer, who did arise in the morning, fell." [3] And why was he *Lucifer?* Because, being enlightened, he gave forth light. But for what reason did he become dark! Because he abode not in the truth. [4] Therefore He was before Lucifer, before every one that is enlightened; since before every one that is enlightened, of necessity He must be by whom all are enlightened who can be enlightened.

8. Therefore this follows: "And of His fullness have all we received." What have ye received? "And grace for grace." For so run the words of the Gospel, as we find by a comparison of the Greek copies. He does not say, And of His fullness have all we received grace for grace; but thus He says: "And of His fullness have all we received, and grace for grace,"—that is, have we received; so that He would wish us to understand that we have received from His fullness something unexpressed, and something besides, grace for grace. For we received of His fullness grace in the first instance; and again we received grace, grace for grace. What grace did we, in the first instance, receive? Faith: walking in faith, we walk in grace. How have we merited this? by what previous merits of ours? Let not each one flatter himself, but let him return into his own conscience, seek out the secret places of his own thoughts, recall the series of his deeds; let him not consider what he is if now he is something, but what he was that he might be something: he will find that he was not worthy of anything save punishment. If, then, thou wast worthy of punishment, and He came not to punish sins, but to forgive sins, grace was given to thee, and not reward rendered. Wherefore is it called grace? Because it is bestowed gratuitously. For thou didst not, by previous merits, purchase that which thou didst receive. This first grace, then, the sinner received, that his sins were forgiven. What did he deserve? Let him interrogate justice, he finds punishment; let him interrogate mercy, he finds grace. But God promised this also through the prophets; therefore, when He came to give what He had promised, He not only gave grace, but also truth. How was truth exhibited? Because that was done which had been promised.

9. What, then, is "grace for grace"? By faith we render God favorable to us; and inasmuch as we were not worthy to have our sins forgiven, and because we, who were unworthy, received so great a benefit, it is called grace. What is grace? That which is freely given. What is "freely given"? Given, not paid. If it was due, wages were given, not grace bestowed; but if it was really due, thou wast good; but if, as is true, thou wast evil, but didst believe on Him who justifieth the ungodly [5] (What is, Who justifieth the ungodly? Of the ungodly maketh pious), consider what did by right hang over thee by the law, and what thou hast obtained by grace. But having obtained that grace of faith, thou shalt be just by faith (for the just lives by faith); [6] and thou shalt obtain favor of God by living by faith. And having obtained favor from God by living by faith,

[1] John viii. 58. [2] Ps. cx. 3.—Vulgate.
[3] Isa. xiv. 27. [4] John viii. 44.
[5] Rom. iv. 5. [6] Hab. ii. 4; Rom. i. 17.

thou shalt receive immortality as a reward, and life eternal. And that is grace. For because of what merit dost thou receive life eternal? Because of grace. For if faith is grace, life eternal is, as it were, the wages of faith: God, indeed, appears to bestow eternal life as if it were due (To whom due? To the faithful, because he had merited it by faith); but because faith itself is grace, life eternal also is grace for grace.

10. Listen to the Apostle Paul acknowledging grace, and afterwards desiring the payment of a debt. What acknowledgment of grace is there in Paul? "Who was before a blasphemer, and a persecutor, and injurious; but I obtained," saith he, "mercy."[1] He said that he who obtained it was unworthy; that he had, however, obtained it, not through his own merits, but through the mercy of God. Listen to him now demanding the payment of a debt, who had first received unmerited grace: "For," saith he, "I am now ready to be offered up, and the time of my departure is at hand. I have fought a good fight, I have finished my course, I have kept the faith: henceforth there is laid up for me a crown of righteousness."[2] Now he demands a debt, he exacts what is due. For consider the following words: "Which the Lord, the righteous Judge, shall render unto me in that day." That he might in the former instance receive grace, he stood in need of a merciful Father; for the reward of grace, of a just judge. Will He who did not condemn the ungodly man condemn the faithful man? And yet, if thou dost rightly consider, it was He who first gave thee faith, whereby thou didst obtain favor; for not of thine own didst thou so obtain favor that anything should be due to thee. Wherefore, then, in afterwards bestowing the reward of immortality, He crowns His own gifts, not thy merits. Therefore, brethren, "we all of His fullness have received;" of the fullness of His mercy, of the abundance of His goodness have we received. What? The remission of sins that we might be justified by faith. And what besides? "And grace for grace;" that is, for this grace by which we live by faith we shall receive another grace. What, then, is it except grace? For if I shall say that this also is due, I attribute something to myself as if to me it were due. But God crowns in us the gifts of His own mercy; but on condition that we walk with perseverance in that grace which in the first instance we received.

11. "For the law was given by Moses;" which law held the guilty. For what saith the apostle? "The law entered that the offense might abound." It was a benefit to the proud that the offense abounded, for they gave much to themselves, and, as it were, attributed much to their own strength; and they were unable to fulfill righteousness without the aid of Him who had commanded it. God, desirous to subdue their pride, gave the law, as if saying: Behold, fulfill, and do not think that there is One wanting to command. One to command is not wanting, but one to fulfill.

12. If, then, there is one wanting to fulfill, whence does he not fulfill? Because born with the heritage of sin and death. Born of Adam, he drew with him that which was there conceived. The first man fell, and all who were born of him from him derived the concupiscence of the flesh. It was needful that another man should be born who derived no concupiscence. A man and a man: a man to death and a man to life. Thus saith the apostle: "Since, indeed, by man death, by man also the resurrection of the dead." By which man death, and by which man the resurrection of the dead? Do not make haste: he goes on to say, "For as in Adam all die, so also in Christ shall all be made alive."[3] Who belong to Adam? All who are born of Adam. Who to Christ? All who were born through Christ. Wherefore all in sin? Because no one was born except through Adam. But that they were born of Adam was of necessity, arising from damnation; to be born through Christ is of will and grace. Men are not compelled to be born through Christ: not because they wished were they born of Adam. All, however, who are of Adam are sinners with sin: all who are through Christ are justified, and just not in themselves, but in Him. For in themselves, if thou shouldest ask, they belong to Adam: in Him, if thou shouldest ask, they belong to Christ. Wherefore? Because He, the Head, our Lord Jesus Christ, did not come with the heritage of sin; but He came nevertheless with mortal flesh.

13. Death was the punishment of sins; in the Lord was the gift of mercy, not the punishment of sin. For the Lord had nothing on account of which He should justly die. He Himself says, "Behold, the prince of this world cometh, and findeth nothing in me." Wherefore then dost Thou die? "But that all may know that I do the will of my Father, arise, let us go hence."[4] He had not in Himself any reason why He should die, and He died: thou hast such a reason, and

---

dost thou refuse to die? Do not refuse to bear with an equal mind thy desert, when He did not refuse to suffer, to deliver thee from eternal death. A man and a man; but the one nothing but man, the other God-man. The one a man of sin, the other of righteousness. Thou didst die in Adam, rise in Christ; for both are due to thee. Now thou hast believed in Christ, render nevertheless that which thou owest through Adam. But the chain of sin shall not hold thee eternally; because the temporal death of thy Lord slew thine eternal death. The same is grace, my brethren, the same is truth, because promised and manifested.

14. This grace was not in the Old Testament, because the law threatened, did not bring aid; commanded, did not heal; made manifest, but did not take away our feebleness: but it prepared the way for that Physician who was to come with grace and truth; as a physician who, about to come to any one to cure him, might first send his servant that he might find the sick man bound. He was not sound; he did not wish to be made sound; and lest he should be made sound, he boasted that he was so. The law was sent, it bound him; he finds himself accused, now he exclaims against the bandage. The Lord comes, cures with somewhat bitter and sharp medicines: for He says to the sick, Bear; He says, Endure; He says, Love not the world, have patience, let the fire of continence cure thee, let thy wounds endure the sword of persecutions. Wert thou greatly terrified although bound? He, free and unbound, drank what He gave to thee; He first suffered that He might console thee, saying, as it were, that which thou fearest to suffer for thyself, I first suffer for thee. This is grace, and great grace. Who can praise it in a worthy manner?

15. I speak, my brethren, regarding the humility of Christ. Who can speak regarding the majesty of Christ, and the divinity of Christ? In explaining and speaking of the humility of Christ, to do so in any fashion we find ourselves not sufficient, indeed wholly insufficient: we commend Him entire to your thoughts, we do not endeavor to fill Him up to your hearing. Consider the humility of Christ. But who, thou sayest, may explain it to us, unless thou declare it? Let Him declare it within. Better does He declare it who dwelleth within, than he who crieth without. Let Himself show to you the grace of His humility, who has begun to dwell in your hearts. But now, if in explaining and setting forth His humility we are deficient, who can speak of His majesty? If "the Word made flesh" disturbs us, who shall explain "In the beginning was the Word"? Keep hold then, brethren, upon the entireness of Christ.

16. "The law was given by Moses: grace and truth came by Jesus Christ." By a servant was the law given, and made men guilty: by an Emperor was pardon given, and delivered the guilty. "The law was given by Moses." Let not the servant attribute to himself more than was done through him. Chosen to a great ministry as one faithful in his house, but yet a servant, he is able to act according to the law, but cannot release from the guilt of the law. "The law," then, "was given by Moses: grace and truth came by Jesus Christ."

17. And lest, perhaps, any one should say, And did not grace and truth come through Moses, who saw God? immediately he adds, "No one hath seen God at any time." And how did God become known to Moses? Because the Lord revealed Himself to His servant. What Lord? The same Christ, who sent the law beforehand by His servant, that He might Himself come with grace and truth. "For no one hath seen God at any time." And whence did He appear to that servant as far as he was able to receive Him? But "the Only-begotten," he says, "who is in the bosom of the Father, He has declared Him." What signifieth "in the bosom of the Father?" In the secret of the Father. For God has not a bosom, as we have, in our garments, nor is He to be thought of sitting, as we do, nor is He girt with a girdle so as to have a bosom; but because our bosom is within, the secret of the Father is called the bosom of the Father. And He who knew the Father, being in the secret of the Father, He declared Him. "For no man hath seen God at any time." He then came and narrated whatever He saw. What did Moses see? Moses saw a cloud, he saw an angel, he saw a fire. All that is the creature: it bore the type of its Lord, but did not manifest the presence of the Lord Himself. For thou hast it plainly stated in the law: "And Moses spake with the Lord face to face, as a friend with his friend."[1] Following the same scripture, thou findest Moses saying: "If I have found grace in Thy sight, show me Thyself plainly, that I may see Thee." And it is little that he said this: he received the reply, "Thou canst not see my face." An angel then spake with Moses, my brethren, bearing the type of the Lord; and all those things which were done by the angel promised that future grace and truth. Those who

---

[1] Ex. xxxiii. 11, 13, 20.

examine the law well know this; and when we have opportunity to speak somewhat of this matter also, we shall not fail to speak to you, beloved brethren, as far as the Lord may reveal to us.

18. But know this, that all those things which were seen in bodily form were not that substance of God. For we saw those things with the eyes of the flesh: how is the substance of God seen? Interrogate the Gospel: "Blessed are the pure in heart; for they shall see God."[1] There have been men who, deceived by the vanity of their hearts, have said, The Father is invisible, but the Son is visible. How visible? If on account of His flesh, because He took flesh, the matter is manifest. For of those who saw the flesh of Christ, some believed, some crucified; and those who believed doubted when He was crucified; and unless they had touched the flesh after the resurrection, their faith would not have been recalled. If, then, on account of His flesh the Son was visible, that we also grant, and it is the Catholic faith; but if before He took flesh, as they say, that is, before He became incarnate, they are greatly deluded, and grievously err. For those visible and bodily appearances took place though the creature, in which a type might be exhibited: not in any fashion was the substance itself shown and made manifest. Give heed, beloved brethren, to this easy proof. The wisdom of God cannot be beheld by the eyes. Brethren, if Christ is the Wisdom of God and the Power of God;[2] if Christ is the Word of God, and if the word of man is not seen with the eyes, can the Word of God be so seen?

19. Expel, therefore, from your hearts carnal thoughts, that you may be really under grace, that you may belong to the New Testament. Therefore is life eternal promised in the New Testament. Read the Old Testament, and see that the same things were enjoined upon a people yet carnal as upon us. For to worship one God is also enjoined upon us. "Thou shalt not take the name of the Lord thy God in vain" is also enjoined upon us, which is the second commandment. "Observe the Sabbath-day" is enjoined on us more than on them, because it is commanded to be spiritually observed. For the Jews observe the Sabbath in a servile manner, using it for luxuriousness and drunkenness. How much better would their women be employed in spinning wool than in dancing on that day in the balconies? God forbid, brethren, that we should call that an observance of the Sabbath. The Christian observes the Sabbath spiritually, abstaining from servile work. For what is it to abstain from servile work? From sin. And how do we prove it? Ask the Lord· "Whosoever committeth sin is the servant of sin."[3] Therefore is the spiritual observance of the Sabbath enjoined upon us. Now all those commandments are more enjoined on us, and are to be observed: "Thou shalt not kill. Thou shalt not commit adultery. Thou shalt not steal. Thou shalt not bear false witness. Honor thy father and thy mother. Thou shalt not covet thy neighbor's goods. Thou shalt not covet thy neighbor's wife."[4] Are not all these things enjoined upon us also? But ask what is the reward, and thou wilt find it there said: "That thine enemies may be driven forth before thy face, and that you may receive the land which God promised to your fathers."[5] Because they were not able to comprehend invisible things, they were held by the visible. Wherefore held? Lest they should perish altogether, and slip into idol-worship. For they did this, my brethren, as we read, forgetful of the great miracles which God performed before their eyes. The sea was divided; a way was made in the midst of the waves; their enemies following, were covered by the same waves through which they passed:[6] and yet when Moses, the man of God, had departed from their sight, they asked for an idol, and said, "Make us gods to go before us; for this man has deserted us." Their whole hope was placed in man, not in God. Behold, the man is dead: was God dead who had rescued them from the land of Egypt? And when they had made to themselves the image of a calf, they offered it adoration, and said, "These be thy gods, O Israel, which delivered thee out of the land of Egypt."[7] How soon forgetful of such manifest grace! By what means could such a people be held except by carnal promises?

20. The same things are commanded in the Decalogue as we are commanded to observe; but the same promises are not made as to us. What is promised to us? Life eternal. "And this is life eternal, that they know Thee, the only true God, and Jesus Christ whom Thou hast sent."[8] The knowledge of God is promised: that is, grace for grace. Brethren, we now believe, we do not see; for faith the reward will be to see what we believe The prophets knew this, but it was concealed before He came. For a certain lover sighing, says in the Psalms: "One thing have I desired of the Lord, that will

---

[1] Matt. v. 8.   [2] 1 Cor. i. 24.

[3] John viii. 34.   [4] Ex. xx. 3.-17.   [5] Lev. xxvi. 1-13.
[6] Ex. xiv. 21-31.   [7] Ex. xxxii. 1-4.   [8] John xvii. 3.

I seek after." And dost thou ask what he seeks? For perhaps he seeks a land flowing with milk and honey carnally, although this is to be spiritually sought and desired; or perhaps the subjection of his enemies, or the death of foes, or the power and riches of this world. For he glows with love, and sighs greatly, and burns and pants. Let us see what he desires: "One thing have I desired of the Lord, that will I seek after." What is it that he doth seek after? "That I may well," saith he, "in the house of the Lord all the days of my life." And suppose that thou dwellest in the house of the Lord, from what source will thy joy there be derived? "That I may behold," saith he, "the beauty of the Lord." [1]

21. My brethren, wherefore do you cry out, wherefore do you exult, wherefore do you love, unless that a spark of this love is there? What do you desire? I ask you. Can it be seen with the eyes? Can it be touched? Is it some fairness which delights the eyes? Are not the martyrs vehemently beloved; and when we commemorate them do we not burn with love? What is it that we love in them, brethren? Limbs torn by wild beasts? What is more revolting if thou askest the eyes of the flesh? what more fair if thou askest the eyes of the heart? How appears in your eyes a very fair young man who is a thief? How shocked are your eyes! Are the eyes of the flesh shocked? If you interrogate them, nothing is more shapely and better formed than that body; the symmetry of the limbs and the beauty of the color attract the eyes; and yet, when thou hearest that he is a thief, your mind recoils from the man. Thou beholdest on the other hand a bent old man,

leaning upon a staff, scarcely moving himself, ploughed all over with wrinkles. Thou hearest that he is just: thou lovest and embracest him. Such are the rewards promised to us, my brethren: love such, sigh after such a kingdom, desire such a country, if you wish to arrive at that with which our Lord came, that is, at grace and truth. But if you covet bodily rewards from God, thou art still under the law, and therefore thou shalt not fulfill the law. For when thou seest those temporal things granted to those who offend God, thy steps falter, and thou sayest to thyself: Behold, I worship God, daily I run to church, my knees are worn with prayers, and yet I am constantly sick: there are men who commit murders, who are guilty of robberies, and yet they exult and have abundance; it is well with them. Was it such things that thou soughtest from God? Surely thou didst belong to grace. If, therefore, God gave to thee grace, because He gave freely, love freely. Do not for the sake of reward love God; let Him be the reward. Let thy soul say, "One thing have I desired of the Lord, that will I seek after; that I may dwell in the house of the Lord all the days of my life, that I may behold the beauty of the Lord." Do not fear that thine enjoyment will fail through satiety: such will be that enjoyment of beauty that it will ever be present to thee, and thou shalt never be satisfied; indeed thou shalt be always satisfied, and yet never satisfied. For if I shall say that thou shalt not be satisfied, it will mean famine; and if I shall say thou shalt be satisfied, I fear satiety: where neither satiety nor famine are, I know not what to say; but God has that which He can manifest to those who know not how to express it, yet believe that they shall receive.

---

[1] Ps. xxvi. 4.

TRACTATE IV.

JOHN I. 19–33.

You have very often heard, holy brethren, and you know well, that John the Baptist, in proportion as he was greater than those born of women, and was more humble in his acknowledgment of the Lord, obtained the grace of being the friend of the Bridegroom; zealous for the Bridegroom, not for himself; not seeking his own honor, but that of his Judge, whom as a herald he preceded. Therefore, to the prophets who went before, it was granted to predict concerning Christ; but to

this man, to point Him out with the finger. For as Christ was unknown by those who did not believe the prophets before He came, He remained unknown to them even when present. For He had come humbly and concealed from the first; the more concealed in proportion as He was more humble: but the people, despising in their pride the humility of God, crucified their Saviour, and made Him their condemner.

2. But will not He who at first came con-

cealed, because humble, come again manifested, because exalted? You have just listened to the Psalm: "God shall come manifestly, and our God shall not keep silence."[1] He was silent that He might be judged, He will not be silent when He begins to judge. It would not have been said, "He will come manifestly," unless at first He had come concealed; nor would it have been said, "He shall not keep silence," unless He had first kept silence. How was He silent? Interrogate Isaiah: "He was brought as a sheep to the slaughter, and as a lamb before his shearer was dumb, so He opened not His mouth.'[2] "But He shall come manifestly, and shall not keep silence." In what manner "manifestly"? "A fire shall go before Him, and round about Him a strong tempest."[3] That tempest has to carry away all the chaff from the floor, which is now being threshed; and the fire has to burn what the tempest carries away. But now He is silent; silent in judgment, but not silent in precept. For if Christ is silent, what is the purpose of these Gospels? what the purpose of the voices of the apostles, what of the canticles of the Psalms, what of the declarations of the prophets? In all these Christ is not silent. But now He is silent in not taking vengeance: He is not silent in not giving warning. But He will come in glory to take vengeance, and will manifest Himself even to all who do not believe on Him. But now, because when present He was concealed, it behoved that He should be despised. For unless He had been despised, He would not have been crucified; if He had not been crucified, He would not have shed His blood—the price by which He redeemed us. But that He might give a price for us, He was crucified; that He might be crucified, He was despised; that He might be despised, He appeared in humility.

3. Yet because He appeared as it were in the night, in a mortal body, He lighted for Himself a lamp by which He might be seen. That lamp was John,[4] concerning whom you lately heard many things: and the present passage of the evangelist contains the words of John; in the first place, and it is the chief point, his confession that he was not the Christ. But so great was the excellence of John, that men might have believed him to be the Christ: and in this he gave a proof of his humility, that he said he was not when he might have been believed to have been the Christ; therefore, "This is the testimony of John, when the Jews sent priests and Levites to him from Jerusalem to ask him, Who art thou?" But they would not have sent unless they had been moved by the excellence of his authority who ventured to baptize. "And he confessed, and denied not." What did he confess? "And he confessed, I am not the Christ."

4. 'And they asked him, What then? Art thou Elias?" For they knew that Elias was to precede Christ. For to no Jew was the name of Christ unknown. They did not think that he was the Christ; but they did not think that Christ would not come at all. When they were hoping that He would come, they were offended at Him when He was present. and stumbled at Him as on a low stone. For He was as yet a small stone, already indeed cut out of the mountain without hands; as saith Daniel the prophet, that he saw a stone cut out of the mountain without hands. But what follows? "And that stone," saith he, "grew, and became a great mountain, and filled the whole face of the earth."[5] Mark then, my beloved brethren, what I say: Christ, before the Jews, was already cut out from the mountain. The prophet wishes that by the mountain should be understood the Jewish kingdom. But the kingdom of the Jews had not filled the whole face of the earth. The stone was cut out from thence, because from thence was the Lord born on His advent among men. And wherefore without hands? Because without the co-operation of man did the Virgin bear Christ. Now then was that stone cut out without hands before the eyes of the Jews; but it was humble. Not without reason; because not yet had that stone increased and filled the whole earth: that He showed in His kingdom, which is the Church, with which He has filled the whole face of the earth. Because then it had not yet increased, they stumbled at Him as at a stone: and that happened in them which is written, "Whosoever shall fall upon that stone shall be broken; but on whomsoever that stone shall fall, it will grind them to powder."[6] At first they fell upon Him lowly: as the lofty One He shall come upon them; but that He may grind them to powder when He comes in His exaltation, He first broke them in His lowliness. They stumbled at Him, and were broken; they were not ground, but broken: He will come exalted and will grind them. But the Jews were to be pardoned because they stumbled at a stone which had not yet increased. What sort of persons are those who stumble at the mountain itself? Already you know who they are of whom I speak. Those who deny the Church diffused

through the whole world, do not stumble at the lowly stone, but at the mountain itself: because this the stone became as it grew. The blind Jews did not see the lowly stone: but how great blindness not to see the mountain!

5. They saw Him then lowly, and did not know Him. He was pointed out to them by a lamp. For in the first place he, than whom no greater had arisen of those born of women, said, "I am not the Christ." It was said to him, "Art thou Elias? He answered, I am not." For Christ sends Elias before Him: and he said, "I am not," and occasioned a question for us. For it is to be feared lest men, insufficiently understanding, think that John contradicted what Christ said. For in a certain place, when the Lord Jesus Christ said certain things in the Gospel regarding Himself, His disciples answered Him: "How then say the scribes," that is, those skilled in the law, "that Elias must first come?" And the Lord said, "Elias is already come, and they have done unto him what they listed;" and, if you wish to know, John the Baptist is he.[1] The Lord Jesus Christ said, "Elias is already come, and John the Baptist" is he; but John, being interrogated, confessed that he was not Elias, in the same manner that he confessed that he was not Christ. And as his confession that he was not Christ was true, so was his confession that he was not Elias. How then shall we compare the words of the herald with the words of the Judge? Away with the thought that the herald speaks falsehood; for that which he speaks he hears from the Judge. Wherefore then did he say, "I am not Elias;" and the Lord, "He is Elias"? Because the Lord Jesus Christ wished in him to prefigure His own advent, and to say that John was in the spirit of Elias. And what John was to the first advent, that will Elias be to the second advent. As there are two advents of the Judge, so are there two heralds. The Judge indeed was the same, but the heralds two, but not two judges. It was needful that in the first instance the Judge should come to be judged. He sent before Him His first herald; He called him Elias, because Elias will be in the second advent what John was in the first.

6. For mark, beloved brethren, how true it is what I say. When John was conceived, or rather when he was born, the Holy Spirit prophesied that this would be fulfilled in him: "And he shall be," he said, "the forerunner of the Highest, in the spirit and power of Elias."[2] What signifieth "in the spirit and power of Elias"? In the same Holy Spirit in the room of Elias. Wherefore in room of Elias? Because what Elias will be to the second, that John was to the first advent. Rightly therefore, speaking literally, did John reply. For the Lord spoke figuratively, "Elias, the same is John;" but he, as I have said, spoke literally when he said, "I am not Elias." Neither did John speak falsely, nor did the Lord speak falsely; neither was the word of the herald nor of the Judge false, if only thou understand. But who shall understand? He who shall have imitated the lowliness of the herald, and shall have acknowledged the loftiness of the Judge. For nothing was more lowly than the herald. My brethren, in nothing had John greater merit than in this humility, inasmuch as when he was able to deceive men, and to be thought Christ, and to have been received in the place of Christ (for so great were his grace and his excellency), nevertheless he openly confessed and said, "I am not the Christ." "Art thou Elias?" If he had said I am Elias, it would have been as if Christ were already coming in His second advent to judge, not in His first to be judged. As if saying, Elias is yet to come, "I am not," said he, "Elias." But give heed to the lowly One before whom John came, that you may not feel the lofty One before whom Elias came. For thus also did the Lord complete the saying: "John the Baptist is he which is to come." He came as a figure of that in which Elias is to come in his own person. Then Elias will in his own proper person be Elias, now in similitude he was John. Now John in his own proper person is John, in similitude Elias. The two heralds gave to each other their similitudes, and kept their own proper persons; but the Judge is one Lord, whether preceded by this herald or by that.

7. "And they asked him, What then? Art thou Elias? And he said, No. And they said unto him, Art thou a prophet? and he answered, No! They said therefore unto him, Who art thou? that we may give an answer to them that sent us. What sayest thou of thyself? He saith, I am the voice of one crying in the wilderness."[3] That said Isaiah. This prophecy was fulfilled in John, "I am the voice of one crying in the wilderness." Crying what? "Prepare ye the way of the Lord, make straight the paths of our God." Would it not have seemed to you that a herald would have cried, "Go away, make room." Instead of the herald's cry

---

1 Matt. xvii. 10-13; Matt. xi. 14, Vulg.　　2 Luke i. 17.　　3 Isa. xl. 3.

"Go away," John says "Come." The herald makes men stand back from the judge; to the Judge John calls. Yes, indeed, John calls men to the lowly One, that they may not experience what He will be as the exalted Judge. "I am the voice of one crying in the wilderness, Prepare ye the way of the Lord, as said the prophet Isaiah." He did not say, I am John, I am Elias, I am a prophet. But what did he say? This I am called, "The voice of one crying in the wilderness, Prepare the way for the Lord: I am the prophecy itself."

8. "And they which were sent were of the Pharisees," that is, of the chief men among the Jews; "and they asked him and said unto him, Why baptizest thou then, if thou be not the Christ, nor Elias, nor a prophet?" As if it seemed to them audacity to baptize, as if they meant to inquire, in what character baptizest thou? We ask whether thou art the Christ; thou sayest that thou art not. We ask whether thou perchance art His precursor, for we know that before the advent of Christ, Elias will come; thou answerest that thou art not. We ask, if perchance thou art some herald come long before, that is, a prophet, and hast received that power, and thou sayest that thou art not a prophet. And John was not a prophet; he was greater than a prophet. The Lord gave such testimony concerning him: "What went ye out into the wilderness to see? A reed shaken with the wind?" Of course implying that he was not shaken by the wind; because John was not such an one as is moved by the wind; for he who is moved by the wind is blown upon by every seductive blast. "But what went ye out for to see? A man clothed in soft raiment?" For John was clothed in rough garments; that is, his tunic was of camel's hair. "Behold, they who are clothed in soft raiment are in kings' houses." You did not then go out to see a man clothed in soft raiment. "But what went ye out for to see? A prophet? Yea, I say unto you, one greater than a prophet is here;"[1] for the prophets prophesied of Christ a long time before, John pointed Him out as present.

9. "Why baptizest thou then, if thou be not the Christ, nor Elias, nor a prophet? John answered them, saying, I baptize with water; but there standeth One among you whom ye know not." For, very truly, He was not seen, being humble, and therefore was the lamp lighted. Observe how John gives place, who might have been accounted other than he was. "He it is who cometh after me, who is made before me" (that is, as we have already said, is "preferred before me"), whose shoe's latchet I am not worthy to unloose." How greatly did he humble himself! And therefore he was greatly lifted up; for he that humbleth himself shall be exalted.[2] Hence, holy brethren, you ought to note that if John so humbled himself as to say, "I am not worthy to unloose His shoe-latchet," what need they have to be humbled who say, "We baptize; what we give is ours, and what is ours is holy." He said, Not I, but He; they say, We. John is not worthy to unloose His shoe's latchet; and if he had said he was worthy, how humble would he still have been! And if he had said he was worthy, and had spoken thus, "He came after me who is made before me, the latchet of whose shoe I am only worthy to unloose," he would have greatly humbled himself. But when he says that he is not worthy even to do this, truly was he full of the Holy Spirit, who in such fashion as a servant acknowledged his Lord, and merited to be made a friend instead of a servant.

10. "These things were done in Bethany, beyond Jordan, where John was baptizing. The next day John saw Jesus coming unto him, and saith, Behold the Lamb of God; behold Him who taketh away the sin of the world!" Let no one so arrogate to himself as to say that he taketh away the sin of the world. Give heed now to the proud men at whom John pointed the finger. The heretics were not yet born, but already were they pointed out; against them he then cried from the river, against whom he now cries from the Gospel. Jesus comes, and what says he? "Behold the Lamb of God!" If to be innocent is to be a lamb, then John was a lamb, for was not he innocent? But who is innocent? To what extent innocent? All come from that branch and shoot, concerning which David sings, even with groanings, "Behold, I was shapen in iniquity; and in sin did my mother conceive me."[3] Alone, then, was He, the Lamb who came, not so. For He was not conceived in iniquity, because not conceived of mortality; nor did His mother conceive Him in sin, whom the Virgin conceived, whom the Virgin brought forth; because by faith she conceived, and by faith received Him. Therefore, "Behold the Lamb of God." He is not a branch derived from Adam: flesh only did he derive from Adam, Adam's sin He did not assume. He who took not upon Him sin from our lump, He it is who taketh away our sin. "Behold

the Lamb of God, who taketh away the sin of the world ! ''

You know that certain men say sometimes, We take away sin from men, we who are holy; for if he be not holy who baptizeth, how taketh he away the sin of another, when he is a man himself full of sin ? In opposition to these disputations, let us not speak our own words, let us read what John says: " Behold the Lamb of God; behold Him who taketh away the sin of the world ! '' Let there not be presumptuous confidence of men upon men; let not the sparrow flee to the mountains, but let it trust in the Lord;[1] and if it lift its eyes to the mountains, from whence cometh aid to it, let it understand that its aid is from the Lord who made heaven and earth. [2] So great is the excellence of John, that to him it is said, " Art thou the Christ ? '' He says, No. Art thou Elias ? He says, No. Art thou a prophet ? He says, No. Wherefore then dost thou baptize ? " Behold the Lamb of God; behold Him who taketh away the sin of the world ! This is He of whom I spake, After me cometh a Man who was made before me; for He was before me.'' " Cometh after me,'' because He was born later; " was made before me,'' because preferred before me; " He was before me,'' because, " In the beginning was the Word, and the Word was with God, and the Word was God.''

12. " And I knew Him not,'' he said; " but that He might be made manifest to Israel, therefore came I baptizing with water. And John bare record, saying, I saw the Spirit descending from heaven like a dove, and it abode upon Him. And I knew Him not: but He that sent me to baptize with water, the same said unto me, Upon whom thou shalt see the Spirit descending, and abiding upon Him, the same is He who baptizeth with the Holy Ghost. And I saw, and bare record that this is the Son of God.'' Give heed for a little, beloved. When did John learn Christ ? For he was sent to baptize with water. They asked, Wherefore ? That He might be made manifest to Israel, he said. Of what profit was the baptism of John ? My brethren, if it had profited in any respect, it would have remained now, and men would have been baptized with the baptism of John, and thus have come to the baptism of Christ. But what saith he ? " That He might be made manifest to Israel,''—that is, to Israel itself, to the people Israel, so that Christ might be made manifest to it,—therefore he came baptizing with water. John received the ministry

of baptism, that by the water of repentance he might prepare the way for the Lord, not being himself the Lord; but where the Lord was known, it was superfluous to prepare for Him the way, for to those who knew Him He became Himself the way; therefore the baptism of John did not last long. But how was the Lord pointed out? Lowly, that John might so receive a baptism in which the Lord Himself should be baptized.

13. And was it needful for the Lord to be baptized ? I instantly reply to any one who asks this question: Was it needful for the Lord to be born? Was it needful for the Lord to be crucified ? Was it needful for the Lord to die ? Was it needful for the Lord to be buried ? If He undertook for us so great humiliation, might He not also receive baptism ? And what profit was there that he received the baptism of a servant ? That thou mightest not disdain to receive the baptism of the Lord. Give heed, beloved brethren. Certain catechumens were to arise in the Church of higher grace. It sometimes comes to pass that you see a catechumen who practises continence, bids farewell to the world, renounces all his possessions, distributing them to the poor; and although but a catechumen, instructed in the saving doctrine better, perhaps, than many of the faithful. It is to be feared regarding such an one that he may say to himself about holy baptism, whereby sins are remitted, What more shall I receive ? Behold, I am better than this faithful man, and this,—having in his mind those among the faithful who are either married, or who are perhaps ignorant, or who keep possession of their property, while he has given his to the poor,—and considering himself better than those who have been already baptized, he deigns not to come to baptism, saying, Am I to receive what this man has, and this ? thinking of persons whom he despises, and, as it were, considers it an indignity to receive that which inferiors have received, because he appears to himself to be already better than they; and, nevertheless, all his sins are upon him, and without coming to saving baptism, wherein all sins are remitted, he cannot, with all his excellence, enter into the kingdom of heaven. But the Lord, in order to invite such excellence to his baptism, that sins might be remitted, Himself came to the baptism of His servant; and although He had no sin to be remitted, nor was there anything in Him that needed to be washed, He received baptism from a servant; and by so doing, addressed Himself to the son carrying himself proudly, and exalting himself, and disdaining, perhaps, to receive along with the ignorant

[1] Ps. x. 2.   [2] Ps. cxii. 1, 2.

that from which salvation comes to him, and said to him: How dost thou extend thyself? How dost thou exalt thyself? How great is thy excellence? How great is thy grace? Can it be greater than mine? If I come to the servant, dost thou disdain to come to the Lord? If I have received the baptism of the servant, dost thou disdain to be baptized by the Lord?

14. But that you may know, my brethren, that not from a necessity of any chain of sin did the Lord come to this John, as the other evangelists say when the Lord came to him to be baptized, John himself said, "Comest Thou to me? I have need to be baptized of Thee."[1] What did He reply to him? "Suffer it to be so now: let all righteousness be fulfilled?" What meaneth this, "let all righteousness be fulfilled"? I came to die for men, have I not to be baptized for men? What meaneth "let all righteousness be fulfilled"? Let all humility be fulfilled. What then? Was not He to accept baptism from a good servant who accepted suffering at the hands of evil servants? Give heed then. The Lord being baptized, if John for this end baptized, that by means of his baptism the Lord might manifest His humility, should no one else have been baptized with the baptism of John? But many were baptized with the baptism of John. When the Lord was baptized with the baptism of John, the baptism of John ceased. John was forthwith cast into prison. Afterwards we do not find that any one is baptized with that baptism. If, then, John came baptizing for this end, that the humility of the Lord might be made manifest to us, in order that we might not disdain to receive from the Lord that which the Lord had received from a servant, should John have baptized the Lord alone? But if John had baptized the Lord alone, some would have thought that the baptism of John was more holy than that of Christ: as if Christ alone had been found worthy to be baptized with the baptism of John, but the human race with that of Christ. Give heed, beloved brethren. With the baptism of Christ we have been baptized, and not only we, but the whole world, and this will continue to the end. Which of us can in any respect be compared with Christ, whose shoe's latchet John declared himself unworthy to unloose? If, then, the Christ, a man of such excellence, a man who is God, had been alone baptized with the baptism of John, what were men likely to say? What a baptism was that of John! His was a great baptism, an ineffable sacrament; behold, Christ alone de-

served to be baptized with the baptism of John. And thus the baptism of the servant would appear greater than the baptism of the Lord. Others were also baptized with the baptism of John, that the baptism of John might not appear better than the baptism of Christ; but baptized also was the Lord, that through the Lord receiving the baptism of the servant, other servants might not disdain to receive the baptism of the Lord: for this end, then, was John sent.

15. But did he know Christ, or did he not know Him? If he did not know Him, wherefore did He say, when Christ came to the river, " I have need to be baptized of Thee"? that is to say, I know who Thou art. If, then, he already knew Him, assuredly he knew Him when he saw the dove descending. It is evident that the dove did not descend upon the Lord until after He went up out of the water of baptism. "The Lord having been baptized, went up out of the water, and the heavens were opened, and he saw a dove descending on Him." If, then, the dove descended after the baptism, and if, before the Lord was baptized, John said to Him, "Comest Thou to me? I have need to be baptized of Thee;" that is to say, before he knew Him to whom he said, "Comest Thou to me? I have need to be baptized of Thee;" —how then said he, "And I knew Him not: but He who sent me to baptize with water, the same said to me, Upon whom thou seest the Spirit descending as a dove, and abiding upon Him, the same is He which baptizeth with the Holy Ghost?" It is not an insignificant question, my brethren. If you have seen the question, you have seen not a little; it remains that the Lord give the solution of it. This, however, I say, if you have seen the question, it is no small matter. Behold, John is placed before your eyes, standing beside the river. Behold John the Baptist. Behold, the Lord comes, as yet to be baptized, not yet baptized. Hear the voice of John, "Comest Thou to me? I have need to be baptized of Thee." Behold, already he knew the Lord, by whom He wishes to be baptized. The Lord, having been baptized, goes up out of the water; the heavens are opened, the Spirit descends; then John knows Him. If then for the first time he knew Him, why did he say before, "I have need to be baptized of Thee"? But if he did not then recognize Him for the first time, because he knew Him already, what is the meaning of what he said, "I knew Him not: but He that sent me to baptize with water, the same said unto me, Upon whom thou shalt see the Spirit descending, and abiding upon Him, as a dove, the

---

[1] Matt. iii. 14, 15.

same is He which baptizeth with the Holy Ghost"?

16. My brethren, this question if solved to-day would oppress you, I do not doubt, for already have I spoken many words. But know that the question is of such a character that alone it is able to extinguish the party of Donatus. I have said thus much, my beloved, in order to gain your attention, as is my wont; and also in order that you may pray for us, that the Lord may grant to us to speak what is suitable, and that you may be found worthy to receive what is suitable. In the meantime, be pleased to defer the question for to-day. But in the meantime, I say this briefly, until I give a fuller solution: Inquire peacefully, without quarreling, without contention, without altercations, without enmities; both seek by yourselves, and inquire of others, and say, "This question our bishop proposed to us to-day, and he will resolve it at a future time, if the Lord will." But whether it be resolved or not, reckon that I have propounded what appears to me of importance; for it does seem of considerable importance. John says, "I have need to be baptized of Thee," as if he knew Christ. For if he did not know Him by whom he wished to be baptized, he spoke rashly when he said, "I have need to be baptized of Thee." Therefore he knew Him. If he knew Him,

what is the meaning of the saying, "I knew Him not: but He that sent me to baptize with water, the same said unto me, Upon whom thou shalt see the Spirit descending, and abiding upon Him, as a dove, the same is He which baptizeth with the Holy Ghost"? What shall we say? That we do not know when the dove came? Lest perchance they [1] take refuge in this, let the other evangelists be read, who have spoken of this matter more plainly, and we find most evidently that the dove then descended when the Lord came up out of the water. Upon Him baptized the heavens opened, and He saw the Spirit descending. [2] If it was when He was already baptized that John knew Him, how saith he to Him, coming to baptism, "I have need to be baptized of Thee"? Ponder this in the meantime with yourselves, confer upon it, treat of it, one with another. The Lord our God grant that before you hear it from me, the explanation may be revealed to some of you first. Nevertheless, brethren, know this, that by means of the solution of this question, the allegation of the party of Donatus, if they have any sense of shame, will be silenced, and their mouths will be shut regarding the grace of baptism, a matter about which they raise mists to confuse the uninstructed, and spread nets for flying birds.

[1] The Donatists.　　[2] Matt. iii. 16; Mark i. 10; Luke iii. 21, 22.

TRACTATE V.

CHAPTER I. 33.

WE have arrived, as the Lord hath willed it, to the day of our promise. He will grant this also, that we may arrive at the fulfillment of the promise. For then those things which we say, if they are useful to us and to you, are from Him; but those things which proceed from man are false, as our Lord Jesus Christ Himself has said, "He that speaketh a lie speaketh of his own." [1] No one has anything of his own except falsehood and sin. But if man has any truth and justice, it is from that fountain after which we ought to thirst in this desert, so that being, as it were, bedewed by some drops from it, and comforted in the meantime in this pilgrimage, we may not fail by the way, but reach His rest and satisfying fullness. If then "he that

speaketh a lie speaketh of his own," he who speaketh the truth speaketh of God. John is true, Christ is the Truth; John is true, but every true man is true from the Truth. If, then, John is true, and a man cannot be true except from the Truth, from whom was he true, unless from Him who said, "I am the truth"? [2] The Truth, then, could not speak contrary to the true man, or the true man contrary to the Truth. The Truth sent the true man, and he was true because sent by the Truth. If it was the Truth that sent John, then it was Christ that sent him. But that which Christ does with the Father, the Father does; and what the Father does with Christ, Christ does. The Father does nothing apart from the Son, nor the Son anything apart from the

[1] John viii. 44.　　[2] John xiv. 6.

Father: inseparable love, inseparable unity, inseparable majesty, inseparable power, according to these words which He Himself propounded," I and my Father are one." [1] Who then sent John? If we say the Father, we speak truly; if we say the Son, we speak truly; but to speak more plainly, we say the Father and the Son. But whom the Father and the Son sent, one God sent; because the Son said, "I and the Father are one." How, then, did he not know Him by whom he was sent? For he said, "I knew Him not: but He that sent me to baptize with water, the same said unto me." I interrogate John: "Who sent thee to baptize with water? what did He say to thee?' "Upon whom thou shalt see the Spirit descending as a dove, and abiding upon Him, the same is He which baptizeth with the Holy Ghost." Is it this, O John, that He said to thee who sent thee? It is manifest that it was this; who, then, sent thee? Perhaps the Father. True God is the Father, and the Truth is God the Son: if the Father without the Son sent thee, God without the Truth sent thee; but if thou art true, because thou dost speak the truth, and dost speak of the Truth, the Father did not send thee without the Son, but the Father and the Son together sent thee. If, then, the Son sent thee with the Father, how didst thou not know Him by whom thou wast sent? He whom thou hadst seen in the Truth, Himself sent thee that He might be recognized in the flesh, and said, "Upon whom thou shalt see the Spirit descending as a dove, and abiding upon Him, the same is He which baptizeth with the Holy Ghost.'

2. Did John hear this that he might know Him whom he had not known, or that he might more fully know Him whom he had already known? For if he had been entirely ignorant of Him, he would not have said to Him when He came to the river to be baptized, "I have need to be baptized of Thee, and comest Thou to me?" [2] He knew Him therefore. But when did the dove descend? When the Lord had been baptized, and was ascending from the water. But if He who sent Him said, "Upon whom thou shalt see the Spirit descending as a dove, and abiding upon Him, the same is He which baptizeth with the Holy Ghost," and he knew Him not, but when the dove descended he learned to know Him, and the time at which the dove descended was when the Lord was going up from the water; but John had known the Lord, when the Lord came to him to the water: it is made plain to us that John after a manner knew, and after a manner did not at first know the Lord. And unless we understand it so, he was a liar. How was he true acknowledging the Lord and saying, "Comest Thou to me to be baptized," and, "I have need to be baptized of Thee"? Is he true when he said this? And how is he again true when he saith, "I knew Him not: but He that sent me to baptize with water, the same said unto me, Upon whom thou shalt see the Spirit descending as a dove, and abiding upon Him, the same is He who baptizeth with the Holy Ghost"? The Lord was made known by a dove, not to him who knew Him not, but to him who in a manner knew Him, and in a manner knew Him not. It is for us to discover what, in Him, John did not know, and learned by the dove.

3. Why was John sent baptizing? Already, I recollect, I have explained that to you, beloved, according to my ability. For if the baptism of John was necessary for our salvation, it ought even now to be used. For we cannot think that men are not saved now, or that more are not saved now, or that there was one salvation then, another now. If Christ has been changed, the salvation has also been changed; if salvation is in Christ, and Christ Himself is the same, there is the same salvation to us. But why was John sent baptizing? Because it behoved Christ to be baptized. Wherefore did it behove Christ to be baptized? Wherefore did it behove Christ to be born? Wherefore did it behove Christ to be crucified? For if He had come to point out the way of humility, and to make Himself the way of humility; in all things had humility to be fulfilled by Him. He deigned from this to give authority to His own baptism, that His servants might know with what alacrity they ought to run to the baptism of the Lord, when He Himself did not refuse to receive the baptism of a servant. This favor was bestowed upon John that it should be called his baptism.

4. Give heed to this, exercise your discrimination, and know it, beloved. The baptism which John received is called the baptism of John: alone he received such a gift. No one of the just before him and no one after him so received a baptism that it should be called his baptism. He received it indeed, for of himself he could do nothing: for if any one speaketh of his own, he speaketh of his own a lie. And whence did he receive it except from the Lord Jesus Christ? From Him he received power to baptize whom he afterwards baptized. Do not marvel; for Christ acted in the same manner in respect to John as in respect to His mother. For concerning

---

[1] John x. 30.　　[2] Matt. iii. 14.

Christ it was said, "All things were made by Him."[1] If all things were made by him, Mary also was made by Him, of whom Christ was afterwards born. Give heed, beloved; in the same manner that He did create Mary, and was created by Mary, so did He give the baptism of John, and was baptized by John.

5. For this purpose therefore did He receive baptism from John, in order that, receiving what was inferior from an inferior, He might exhort inferiors to receive that which was superior. But wherefore was not He alone baptized by John, if John, by whom Christ was baptized, was sent for this end, to prepare a way for the Lord, that is, for Christ Himself? This we have already explained, but we recur to it, because it is necessary for the present question. If our Lord Jesus Christ had been alone baptized with the baptism of John;—hold fast what we say; let not the world have such power as to efface from your hearts what the Spirit of God has written there; let not the thorns of care have such power as to choke the seed which is being sown in you: for why are we compelled to repeat the same things, but because we are not sure of the memory of your hearts?—and if then the Lord alone had been baptized with the baptism of John, there would be persons who would so reckon it, that the baptism of John was greater than is the baptism of Christ. For they would say, that baptism is so much the greater, that Christ alone deserved to be baptized with it. Therefore, that an example of humility might be given us by the Lord, that the salvation of baptism might be obtained by us, Christ accepted what for Him was not necessary, but on our account was necessary. And again, lest that which Christ received from John should be preferred to the baptism of Christ, others also were permitted to be baptized by John. But for those who were baptized by John that baptism did not suffice: for they were baptized with the baptism of Christ; because the baptism of John was not the baptism of Christ. Those who receive the baptism of Christ do not seek the baptism of John; those who received the baptism of John sought the baptism of Christ. Therefore was the baptism of John sufficient for Christ. How should it not be sufficient, when not even it was necessary? For to Him was no baptism necessary; but in order to exhort us to receive His baptism, He received the baptism of His servant. And lest the baptism of the servant should be preferred to the baptism of the Lord, other fellow-servants were baptized with the baptism of the ser-

vant. But it behoved those fellow-servants who were baptized with that baptism to be likewise baptized with the baptism of the Lord: but those who were baptized with the baptism of the Lord do not require the baptism of the fellow-servant.

6. Since, then, John had accepted a baptism which may be properly called the baptism of John, but the Lord Jesus Christ would not give His baptism to any, not that no one should be baptized with the baptism of the Lord, but that the Lord Himself should always baptize: that was done, that the Lord should baptize by means of servants; that is to say, those whom the servants of the Lord were to baptize, the Lord baptized, not they. For it is one thing to baptize in the capacity of a servant, another thing to baptize with power. For baptism derives its character from Him through whose power it is given; not from him through whose ministry it is given. As was John, so was his baptism: the righteous baptism of a righteous man; but of a man who had received from the Lord that grace, and so great grace, that he was worthy to be the forerunner of the Judge, and to point Him out with the finger, and to fulfill the saying of that prophecy: "The voice of one crying in the wilderness, Prepare ye the way for the Lord."[2] As was the Lord, such was His baptism: the baptism of the Lord, then, was divine, because the Lord was God.

7. But the Lord Jesus Christ could, if He wished, have given power to one of His servants to give a baptism of his own, as it were, in His stead, and have transferred from Himself the power of baptizing, and assigned it to one of His servants, and have given the same power to the baptism transferred to the servant as it had when bestowed by the Lord. This He would not do, in order that the hope of the baptized might be in him by whom they acknowledged themselves to have been baptized. He would not, therefore, that the servant should place his hope in the servant. And therefore the apostle exclaimed, when he saw men wishing to place their hope in himself, "Was Paul crucified for you? or were ye baptized in the name of Paul?"[3] Paul then baptized as a servant, not as the power itself; but the Lord baptized as the power. Give heed. He was both able to give this power to His servants, and unwilling. For if He had given this power to His servants— that is to say, that what belonged to the Lord should be theirs—there would have been as many baptisms as servants; so that, as we speak of the baptism of John, we should also

---

[1] John i. 3.   [2] Isa. xl. 3.   [3] 1 Cor. i. 13.

have spoken of the baptism of Peter, the baptism of Paul, the baptism of James, the baptism of Thomas, of Matthew, of Bartholomew: for we spoke of that baptism as that of John. But perhaps some one objects, and says, Prove to us that that baptism was called the baptism of John. I will prove it from the very words of the Truth Himself, when He asked the Jews, "The baptism of John, whence was it? from heaven, or of men?"[1] Therefore, lest as many baptisms should be spoken of as there are servants who received power from the Lord to baptize, the Lord kept to Himself the power of baptizing, and gave to His servants the ministry. The servant says that he baptizes; he says so rightly, as the apostle says, "And I baptized also the household of Stephanas;"[2] but as a servant. Therefore, if even he be bad, and he happen to have the ministration of baptism, and if men do not know him, but God knows him, God, who has kept the power to Himself, permits baptism to be administered through him.

8. But this John did not know in the Lord. That He was the Lord he knew, and that he ought to be baptized by Him he knew; and he confessed that He was the Truth, and that he, the true man, was sent by the Truth: this he knew. But what was in Him which he knew not? That he was about to retain to Himself the power of His baptism, and was not to transmit or transfer it to any servant; but that, whether a good servant baptized in a ministerial manner, or whether an evil servant baptized, the person baptized should not know that he was baptized, unless by Him who kept to Himself the power of baptizing. And that you may know, brethren, what John did not know in Him, he learned it by means of the dove: for he knew the Lord; but that He was to retain to Himself the power of baptizing, and not to give it to any servant, he did not yet know. Regarding this he said, "I knew Him not." And that you may know that he there learnt this, give heed to what follows: "But He that sent me to baptize with water, the same said unto me, Upon whom thou shalt see the Spirit descending as a dove, and abiding upon Him, the same is He." What same is He? The Lord? But he already knew the Lord. Suppose, then, that John had said thus far, "I knew Him not: but He that sent me to baptize with water, the same said unto me—" We ask, what He said? It follows: "Upon whom thou shalt see the Spirit descending as a dove, and abiding upon Him." I do not say what follows. In the meantime give heed: "Upon

whom thou shalt see the Spirit descending as a dove, and abiding upon Him, the same is He." But what same is He? What did He who sent me mean to teach me by means of a dove? That He was Himself the Lord. Already I knew by whom I was sent; already I knew Him to whom I said, "Comest Thou to me to be baptized? I have need to be baptized of Thee." So far, then, did I know the Lord, that I wished to be baptized by Him, not that He should be baptized by me; and then He said to me, "Suffer it to be so now; for thus it becometh us to fulfill all righteousness." I came to suffer; do I not come to be baptized? "Let all righteousness be fulfilled," says my God to me. Let all righteousness be fulfilled; let me teach entire humility. I know that there will be proud ones in my future people; I know that some men then will be eminent in some grace, so that when they see ordinary persons baptized, they, because they consider themselves better, whether in continence, or in alms-giving, or in doctrine, will perhaps not deign to receive what has been received by their inferiors. It was needful that I should heal them, so that they should not disdain to come to the baptism of the Lord, because I came to the baptism of the servant.

9. Already, then, John knew this, and he knew the Lord. What then did the dove teach? What did He desire to teach by means of the dove—that is, by means of the Holy Spirit thus coming to teach who had sent him to whom He said, "Upon whom thou shalt see the Spirit descending as a dove, and abiding upon Him, the same is He"? Who is this He? The Lord? I know. But didst thou already know this, that the same Lord having the power to baptize, was not to give that power to any servant, but to retain it to Himself, so that all who were baptized by the ministration of the servant, should not impute their baptism to the servant, but to the Lord? Didst thou already know this? I did not know this: so what did He say to me? "Upon whom thou shalt see the Spirit descending as a dove, and abiding upon Him, the same is He who baptizeth with the Holy Ghost." He does not say, "He is the Lord;" He does not say, "He is the Christ;" He does not say, "He is God;" He does not say, "He is Jesus;" He does not say, "He is the One who was born of the Virgin Mary, after thee, before thee." This He does not say, for this John did already know. But what did he not know? That this great authority of baptism the Lord Himself was to have, and to

retain to Himself, whether present in the earth or absent in body in the heaven, and present in majesty; lest Paul should say, my baptism; lest Peter should say, my baptism. Therefore see, give heed to the words of the apostles. None of the apostles said, my baptism. Although there was one gospel of all, yet thou findest that they said, my gospel: thou dost not find that they say, my baptism.

10. This, then, my brethren, John learned. What John learned by means of the dove let us also learn. For the dove did not teach John without teaching the Church, the Church to which it was said, "My dove is one."[1] Let the dove teach the dove; let the dove know what John learned by the dove. The Holy Spirit descended in the form of a dove. But this which John learned in the dove, wherefore did he learn it in the dove? For it behoved him to learn, and perhaps it did not so much behove him to learn as to learn by the dove. What shall I say, my brethren, concerning the dove? or when will faculty of tongue or heart suffice to speak as I wish? And, perchance, my wish falls short of my duty in speaking; even if I were able to speak as I wish, how much less am I able to speak as I ought? I could wish to hear one better than myself speak this, rather than speak of it to you.

11. John learns to know Him whom he knew; but he learns in Him with regard to what he did not know; with regard to what he did know, he does not learn. And what did he know? The Lord. What did he not know? That the power of the Lord's baptism was not to pass from the Lord to any man, but that the ministration of it plainly would do so; the power from the Lord to no one, the ministration both to good and bad. Let not the dove shrink from the ministration of the bad, but have regard to the power of the Lord. What injury does a bad servant do to you where the Lord is good? What impediment can the malicious herald put in your way if the judge is well-disposed? John learned by means of the dove this. What is it that he learned? Let him repeat it himself. "The same said unto me," saith he, "Upon whom thou shalt see the Spirit descending as a dove, and abiding on Him, this is He which baptizeth with the Holy Ghost." Let not those seducers deceive thee, O dove, who say, We baptize. Acknowledge, dove, what the dove has taught: "This is He which baptizeth with the Holy Ghost." By means of the dove we are taught that this is He; and dost thou think that thou art baptized by his au-

thority by whose ministration thou art baptized? If thou thinkest this, thou art not as yet in the body of the dove; and if thou art not in the body of the dove, it is not to be wondered at that thou hast not simplicity; for by means of the dove, simplicity is chiefly designated.

12. Wherefore, my brethren, by the simplicity of the dove did John learn that "This is He which baptizeth with the Holy Ghost," unless to show that these are not doves who have scattered the Church? Hawks they were, and kites. The dove does not tear. And thou seest that they hold us up to hatred, for the persecutions, as they call them, which they have suffered. Bodily persecutions, indeed, if they are to be so called, they have suffered, since these were the scourges of the Lord, plainly administering temporal correction, lest He should have to condemn them eternally, if they did not acknowledge it and amend themselves. They truly persecute the Church who persecute by means of deceit; they strike the heart more heavily who strike with the sword of the tongue; they shed blood more bitterly who, as far as they can, slay Christ in man. They seem to be in fear, as it were, of the judgment of the authorities. What does the authority do to thee if thou art good? but if thou art evil, fear the authority; "For he beareth not the sword in vain,"[2] saith the apostle. Draw not the sword wherewith thou dost strike Christ. Christian, what dost thou persecute in a Christian? What did the Emperor persecute in thee? He persecuted the flesh; thou in a Christian persecutest the Spirit. Thou dost not slay the flesh. And, nevertheless, they do not spare the flesh; as many as they were able, they slew with the sword; they spared neither their own nor strangers. This is known to all. The authority is hated because it is legitimate; he acts in a hated manner who acts according to the law; he acts without incurring hatred who acts contrary to the laws. Give heed, each one of you, my brethren, to what the Christian possesses. His humanity he has in common with many, his Christianity distinguishes him from many, and his Christianity belongs to him more strictly than his humanity. For, as a Christian, he is renewed after the image of God, by whom man was made after the image of God;[3] but as a man he might be bad, he might be a pagan, he might be an idolater. This thou dost persecute in the Christian, which is his better part; for this by which he lives thou wishest to take away from him. For he lives tempo-

---

[1] Cant. vi. 8.   [2] Rom xiii. 4.   [2] Col. iii. 10.

rally according to the spirit of life, by which his body is animated, but he lives for eternity according to the baptism which he received from the Lord; thou wishest to take this away from him which he received from the Lord, this thou wishest to take away from him by which he lives. Robbers, with regard to those whom they wish to despoil, have the purpose to enrich themselves and to deprive their victims of all that they have; but thou takest from him, and with thee there will not be anything more, for there does not accrue more to thee because thou takest from him. But, truly, they do the same as those who take away the natural life: they take it away from another, and yet they themselves have not two lives.

13. What, then, dost thou wish to take away? What displeases thee in the man whom thou wishest to rebaptize? Thou art not able to give what he already has, but thou makest him deny what he has. What greater cruelty did the pagan persecutor of the Church commit? Swords were stretched out against the martyrs, wild beasts were let loose, fires were applied: for what purpose these things? In order that the sufferer might be induced to say, I am not a Christian. What dost thou teach him whom thou wishest to rebaptize, unless that he first say, I am not a Christian? For the same purpose for which the persecutor put forth the flame, thou puttest forth the tongue; thou dost by seducing what he did not do by slaying. And what is it thou dost give, and to whom art thou to give it? If he tells thee the truth, and does not lie, seduced by thee, he will say, I have. Thou askest, Hast thou baptism? I have, he says. As long as he says, I have, thou sayest, I will not give. And do not give, for that which thou wishest to give cannot cleave to me; because what I received cannot be taken away from me. But wait, nevertheless; let me see what thou wouldest teach me. Say, he said, in the first place, I have not. But this I have; if I shall say, I have not, I lie; for what I have I have. Thou hast not, he says. Teach me that I have it not. An evil man gave it to thee. If Christ is evil, an evil man did give it to me. Christ, he says, is not evil; but Christ did not give it to thee. Who then gave it to me? Reply, I know that I received it from Christ. He who gave it to thee, he says, was not Christ, but some *traditor*. I shall see to it who was the minister; I shall see who was the herald. Concerning the official, I do not dispute; I give heed to the Judge: and, perchance, in thy objection to the official, thou speakest falsely. But I decline to discuss it; let the

Lord of both decide the cause of His own official. If, perhaps, I were to ask for proof, thou couldst give none; indeed, thou liest; it has been proved that thou wert not able to give proof. But I do not place my case on this, lest from my zealous defense of innocent men thou infer that I have placed my hope even on innocent men. Let the men be what they may, I received from Christ, I was baptized by Christ. No, he says; not Christ, but that bishop baptized thee, and that bishop communicates to them. By Christ I have been baptized, I know. How dost thou know? The dove taught me, which John saw. O evil kite, thou mayest not tear me from the bowels of the dove. I am numbered among the members of the dove, because what the dove taught, this I know. Thou sayest to me, This man or that baptized thee: by means of the dove it is said to me and to thee, "This is He which baptizeth." Which shall I believe, the kite or the dove?

14. Tell me certainly, that thou mayest be confounded by that lamp by which also were the former enemies confounded, who were like to thee, the Pharisees, who, when they questioned the Lord by what authority He did those things: "I also," said He, "will ask you this question, Tell me, the baptism of John, whence is it? from heaven, or of men?" And they, who were preparing to spread their wiles, were entangled by the question, and began to debate with themselves, and say, "If we shall answer, It is from heaven, He will say unto us, Wherefore did ye not believe him?" For John had said of the Lord, "Behold the Lamb of God, who taketh away the sin of the world!"[1] Why then do you inquire by what authority I act? O wolves, what I do, I do by the authority of the Lamb. But that you may know the Lamb, why do you not believe John, who said, "Behold the Lamb of God, who taketh away the sin of the world"? They, then, knowing what John had said regarding the Lord, said among themselves, "If we shall say that John's baptism is from heaven, He will say unto us, Wherefore then did ye not believe him? If we shall say, It is of men, the people will stone us; for they hold John as a prophet." Hence, they feared men; hence, they were confounded to confess the truth. Darkness replied with darkness; but they were overcome by the light. For what did they reply? "We know not;" regarding that which they knew, they said, "We know not." And the Lord said, "Neither tell I you by what authority I do these things."[2]

---

[1] John i. 29.   [2] Matt. xxi. 23-27.

And the first enemies were confounded. How? By the lamp. Who was the lamp? John. Can we prove that he was the lamp? We can prove it; for the Lord says: "He was a burning and a shining lamp."[1] Can we prove also that the enemies were confounded by him? Listen to the psalm: "I have prepared," he says, "a lamp for my Christ. His enemies I will clothe with shame."[2]

15. As yet, in the darkness of this life, we walk by the lamp of faith: let us hold also to the lamp John, and let us confound by him the enemies of Christ; indeed, let Christ Himself confound His own enemies by His own lamp. Let us put the question which the Lord put to the Jews, let us ask and say, "The baptism of John, whence is it? from heaven, or of men?" What will they say? Mark, if they are not as enemies confounded by the lamp. What will they say? If they shall say, Of men, even their own will stone them; but if they shall say, From heaven, let us say to them, Wherefore, then, did ye not believe him? They perhaps say, We believe him. Wherefore, then, do you say that you baptize, when John says, "This is He which baptizeth"? But it behoveth, they say, the ministers of so great a Judge who baptize, to be righteous. And I also say, and all say, that it behoveth the ministers of so great a Judge to be righteous; let the ministers, by all means, be righteous if they will; but if they will not be righteous who sit in the seat of Moses, my Master made me safe, of whom His Spirit said, "This is He which baptizeth." How did He make me safe? "The scribes and the Pharisees," He says, "sit in Moses' seat: what they say, do; but what they do, that do not ye: for they say, and do not."[3] If the minister is righteous, I reckon him with Paul, I reckon him with Peter; with those I reckon righteous ministers: because, in truth, righteous ministers seek not their own glory; for they are ministers, they do not wish to be thought judges, they abhor that one should place his hope on them; therefore, I reckon the righteous minister with Paul. For what does Paul say? "I have planted, Apollos watered; but God gave the increase. Neither is he that planteth anything, nor he that watereth; but God who giveth the increase."[4] But he who is a proud minister is reckoned with the devil; but the gift of Christ is not contaminated, which flows through him pure, which passes through him liquid, and comes to the fertile earth. Suppose that he is stony, that he cannot from water rear fruit; even through the stony channel the water passes, the water passes to the garden beds; in the stony channel it causes nothing to grow, but nevertheless it brings much fruit to the gardens. For the spiritual virtue of the sacrament is like the light: both by those who are to be enlightened is it received pure, and if it passes through the impure it is not stained. Let the ministers be by all means righteous, and seek not their own glory, but His glory whose ministers they are; let them not say, The baptism is mine; for it is not theirs. Let them give heed unto John. Behold, John was full of the Holy Spirit; and he had his baptism from heaven, not from men; but how long had he it? He said himself, "Prepare ye the way for the Lord."[5] But when the Lord was known, Himself became the way; there was no longer need for the baptism of John to prepare the way for the Lord.

16. What, however, are they accustomed to say against us? "Behold, after John, baptism was given." For before that question was properly treated in the Catholic Church, many erred in it, both great and good men; but because they were members of the dove, they did not cut themselves off, and in their case that happened which the apostle said, "If in any thing ye are otherwise minded, God shall reveal even this unto you."[6] Whence those who separated themselves became unteachable. What then are they wont to say? Behold, after John baptism was given; after heretical baptism is it not to be given? because certain who had the baptism of John were commanded by Paul to be baptized,[7] for they had not the baptism of Christ. Why then, say they, dost thou exaggerate the merit of John, and, as it were, underrate the misery of heretics? I also grant to you that the heretics are wicked; but the heretics gave the baptism of Christ, which baptism John did not give.

17. I go back to John, and say, "This is he which baptizeth." For John is better than a heretic, just as John is better than a drunkard, as John is better than a murderer. If we ought to baptize after the worse because the apostles baptized after the better, whosoever among them were baptized by a drunkard,—I do not say by a murderer, I do not say by the satellite of some wicked man, I do not say by the robber of other men's goods, I do not say by the oppressor of orphans, or a separater of married persons; I speak of none of these; I speak of what happens every year, of what happens every day; I speak of what all are called to, even in

---

[1] John v. 35. [2] Ps. cxxxi. 17, 18.
[3] Matt. xxiii. 2, 3. [4] 1 Cor. iii. 6, 7. [5] John i. 23. [6] Phil. iii. 15. [7] Acts xix. 3-5.

this city, when it is said to them, Let us play the part of the irrational, let us have pleasure, and on such a day as this of the calends of January we ought not to fast: these are the things I speak of, these trifling everyday proceedings;—when one is baptized by a drunkard, who is better? John or the drunkard? Reply, if thou canst, that the drunkard is better than John! This thou wilt never venture to do. Do you then, as a sober man, baptize after thy drunkard. For if the apostles baptized after John, how much more ought the sober to baptize after the drunkard? Or dost thou say, the drunkard is in unity with me? Was not John then, the friend of the Bridegroom, in unity with the Bridegroom?

18. But I say to thee thyself, whoever thou art, Art thou better than John? Thou wilt not venture to say: I am better than John. Then let thine own baptize after thee if they are better. For if baptism was administered after John, blush that baptism is not administered after thee. Thou wilt say, But I have and teach the baptism of Christ. Acknowledge, then, now the Judge, and do not be a proud herald. Thou givest the baptism of Christ, therefore baptism is not administered after thee: after John it was administered, because he gave not the baptism of Christ, but his own; for he had in such manner received it that it was his own. Thou art then not better than John: but the baptism given through thee is better than that of John; for the one is Christ's, but the other is that of John. And that which was given by Paul, and that which was given by Peter, is Christ's; and if baptism was given by Judas it was Christ's. Judas gave baptism and after Judas baptism was not repeated; John gave baptism, and baptism was repeated after John: because if baptism was given by Judas, it was the baptism of Christ; but that which was given by John, was John's baptism. We prefer not Judas to John; but the baptism of Christ, even when given by the hand of Judas, we prefer to the baptism of John, rightly given even by the hand of John. For it was said of the Lord before He suffered, that He baptized more than John; then it was added: "Howbeit, Jesus Himself baptized not, but His disciples." [1] He, and not He: He by power, they by ministry; they performed the service of baptizing, the power of baptizing remained in Christ. His disciples, then, baptized, and Judas was still among his disciples: and were those, then, whom Judas baptized not again baptized; and those whom John baptized were they again baptized?

Plainly there was a repetition, but not a repetition of the same baptism. For those whom John baptized, John baptized; those whom Judas baptized, Christ baptized. In like manner, then, they whom a drunkard baptized, those whom a murderer baptized, those whom an adulterer baptized, if it was the baptism of Christ, were baptized by Christ. I do not fear the adulterer, the drunkard, or the murderer, because I give heed unto the dove, through whom it is said to me, "This is He which baptizeth."

19. But, my brethren, it is madness to say that—I will not say Judas—but that any man was better than he of whom it was said, that "Among those that are born of women, there hath not arisen a greater than John the Baptist." [2] No servant then is preferred to him; but the baptism of the Lord, even when given through an evil servant, is preferred to the baptism even of a servant who was a friend. Listen to the sort of persons whom the Apostle Paul mentions, false brethren, preaching the word of God through envy, and what he says of them: "And I therein do rejoice, yea, and will rejoice." [3] They proclaimed Christ, through envy indeed, but still they proclaimed Christ. Consider not the why, but the whom: through envy is Christ preached to thee. Behold Christ, avoid envy. Do not imitate the evil preacher, but imitate the Good One who is preached to thee. Christ then was preached by some out of envy. And what is envy? A shocking evil. By this evil was the devil cast down; this malignant pest it was which cast him down; and certain preachers of Christ were possessed by it, whom, nevertheless, the apostle permitted to preach. Wherefore? Because they preached Christ But he who envies, hates; and he who hates, what is said concerning him? Listen to the Apostle John: "He who hateth his brother is a murderer." [4] Behold, after John baptism was given, after a murderer baptism was not given; because John gave his own baptism, the murderer gave the baptism of Christ. That sacrament is so sacred that not even the ministration of a murderer pollutes it.

20. I do not reject John, but rather I believe John. In what do I believe John? In that which he learned through the dove? What did he learn through the dove? "This is He which baptizeth with the Holy Ghost." Now therefore, brethren, hold this fast and impress it upon your hearts; for if I would more fully explain to-day, Wherefore through the dove? time fails. For I have, I think, to

some extent made plain to you, holy brethren, that a matter which had to be learned was instilled into John by means of the dove, a matter with regard to Christ which John did not know, although he already knew Christ; but why it behoved this matter to be pointed out by means of the dove, I would say, were it possible to say it briefly: but because it would take long to say, and I am unwilling to burden you, since I have been helped by your prayers to perform my promise; with the renewed help of your pious attention and good wishes, it will likewise become clear to you, wherefore John with regard to that matter which he learned regarding the Lord, namely, that it is " He which baptizeth with the Holy Ghost," and that to none of His servants had he transferred the power of baptizing—why this it became him not to learn except through the dove.

TRACTATE VI.

CHAPTER I. 32, 33.

1. I NFESS to you, holy brethren, I was afraid the cold would have made you cold in assembling yourselves together; but since you prove by this, your crowded assembly, that you are fervent in spirit, I doubt not that you have also prayed for me, that I may pay you what I owe. For I promised you in the name of Christ that, as the shortness of the time prevented us from expounding it before, I would to-day discuss why God was pleased to manifest the Holy Ghost in the form of a dove. That this may be explained, this day has dawned on us; and I perceive that from eagerness to hear, and pious devotion, you have come together in greater number than usual. May God, by our mouth, fulfill your expectation. For your coming together is of your love; but love of what? If of us, even that is well; for we desire to be loved by you, but not in ourselves. Because we love you in Christ, do you love us in Christ in return, and let our love mutually sigh towards God; for the note of the dove is a sighing or moaning.

2. Now if the dove's note is a moaning, as we all know it to be, and doves moan in love, hear what the apostle says, and wonder not that the Holy Ghost willed to be manifested in the form of a dove: " For what we should pray for as we ought," says he, " we know not; but the Spirit Himself intercedes for us with groanings which cannot be uttered."[1] What then, my brethren? shall we say this, that the Spirit groans where He has perfect and eternal blessedness with the Father and the Son? For the Holy Spirit is God, even as the Son of God is God, and the Father God. I have said " God " thrice, but not three Gods; for indeed it is God *thrice* rather than three Gods; because the Father, and the Son, and the Holy Ghost are one God: this you know full well. It is not then in Himself with Himself in that Trinity, in that blessedness, in that His eternal substance, that the Holy Spirit groans; but in us He groans because He makes us to groan. Nor is it a little matter that the Holy Spirit teaches us to groan, for He gives us to know that we are sojourners in a foreign land, and He teaches us to sigh after our native country; and through that very longing do we groan. He with whom it is well in this world, or rather he who thinks it is well with him, who exults in the joy of carnal things, in the abundance of things temporal, in an empty felicity, has the cry of the raven; for the raven's cry is full of clamor, not of groaning. But he who knows that he is in the pressure of this mortal life, a pilgrim " absent from the Lord,"[2] that he does not yet possess that perpetual blessedness which is promised to us, but that he has it in hope, and will have it in reality when the Lord shall come openly in glory who came before in humility concealed; he, I say, who knows this doth groan. And so long as it is for this he groans, he does well to groan; it was the Spirit that taught him to groan, he learnt it from the dove. Many indeed groan by reason of earthly misery. They are shattered, it may be, by losses, or weighed down by bodily ailment, or shut up in prisons, or bound with chains, or tossed about on the waves of the sea, or hedged in by the ensnaring devices of their enemies. Therefore do they groan, but not with the moaning of the dove, not with love of God, not in the Spirit. Accordingly, when such are delivered from

---

these same afflictions, they exult with loud voices, whereby it is made manifest that they are ravens, not doves. It was with good reason that a raven was sent forth from the ark, and returned not again; a dove was sent forth, and it returned. These two birds Noah sent forth.[1] He had there-the raven, and also the dove. That ark contained both kinds; and if the ark was a figure of the Church, you see indeed that in the present deluge of the world, the Church must of necessity contain both kinds, as well the raven as the dove. Who are the ravens? They who seek their own. Who are the doves? They who seek the things that are Christ's.[2]

3. Therefore, when He sent the Holy Spirit He manifested Him visibly in two ways—by a dove and by fire: by a dove upon the Lord when He was baptized, by fire upon the disciples when they were gathered together. For when the Lord had ascended into heaven after His resurrection, having spent forty days with His disciples, and the day of Pentecost being fully come, He sent unto them the Holy Spirit as He had promised. Accordingly the Spirit coming at that time filled the place, and there was first a sound from heaven as of a rushing mighty wind, as we read in the Acts of the Apostles, and "there appeared unto them," it says, "cloven tongues as of fire, and it sat upon each of them; and they began to speak with tongues, as the Spirit gave them utterance."[3] Here we have seen a dove descending upon the Lord; there, cloven tongues upon the assembled disciples: in the former, simplicity is shown; in the latter, fervency. Now there are who are said to be simple, who are only indolent; they are called simple, but they are only slow. Not such was Stephen, full of the Holy Ghost: he was simple, because he injured no one; he was fervent, because he reproved the ungodly. For he held not his peace before the Jews. His are those burning words: "Ye stiff-necked and uncircumcised of heart and ears, ye do always resist the Holy Spirit." Mighty impetuosity; but it is the dove without gall raging. For that you know that he was fierce without gall, see how, upon hearing these words, they who were the ravens immediately took up stones and rushed together upon this dove. They begin to stone Stephen; and he who a little before stormed and glowed with ardor of spirit,—who had, as it were, made an onset on his enemies, and like one full of violence had attacked them in such fiery and burning words as you have heard, "Ye stiff-necked and uncircumcised in heart and ears," that any one who heard those

words might fancy that Stephen, if he were allowed, would have them consumed at once, —but when the stones thrown from their hands reached him, with fixed knee he saith, "Lord, lay not this sin to their charge."[4] He held fast to the unity of the dove. For his Master, upon whom the dove descended, had done the same thing before him; who, while hanging on the cross, said, "Father, forgive them, for they know not what they do."[5] Wherefore by the dove it is shown that they who are sanctified by the Spirit should be without guile; and that their simplicity should not continue cold is shown us by the fire. Nor let it trouble you that the tongues were divided; for tongues are diverse, therefore the appearance was that of cloven tongues. "Cloven tongues," it saith, "as of fire, and it sat upon each of them." There is a diversity of tongues, but the diversity of tongues does not imply schisms. Be not afraid of separation in the cloven tongues; in the dove recognize unity.

4. Hence in this manner it behoved the Holy Spirit to be manifested when coming upon the Lord, that every one might understand that if he has the Holy Spirit he ought to be simple as the dove, to have true peace with his brethren, that peace which the kisses of doves signify. Ravens have their kisses too; but in the case of the ravens it is a false peace, in that of the dove a true peace. Not every one, therefore, who says, "Peace be with you," is to be listened to as if he were a dove. How then are the kisses of ravens distinguished from those of doves? Ravens kiss, but they tear; the nature of doves is innocent of tearing. Where consequently there is tearing, there is not true peace in the kisses. They have true peace who have not torn the Church. Ravens feed upon carrion, it is not so with the dove; it lives on the fruits of the earth, its food is innocent. This, brethren, is really worthy of admiration in the dove. Sparrows are very small birds, but yet they kill flies at least. The dove does nothing of this sort, for it does not feed on what is dead. They who have torn the Church feed on the dead. God is mighty; let us pray that they who are devoured by them, and perceive it not, may come to life again. Many acknowledge that they do come to life again, for at their coming we daily express joy with them in the name of Christ. Be ye simple, but only in such wise that ye be fervent, and let your fervor be in your tongues. Hold not your peace, speak with glowing tongues, set those that are cold on fire.

5. For why, my brethren? Who does not

see what they do not? And no wonder; for they who are unwilling to return from that are just like the raven that was sent forth from the ark. For who does not see what they see not? They are unthankful even to the Holy Spirit Himself. See, the dove descended upon the Lord, upon the Lord when baptized: and thereupon was manifested that holy and real Trinity, which to us is one God. For the Lord went up out of the water, as we read in the Gospel: "And, lo, the heavens were opened unto Him, and He saw the Spirit descending like a dove, and it abode upon Him: and immediately a voice followed, Thou art my beloved Son, in whom I am well pleased."[1] The Trinity most manifestly appears: the Father in the voice, the Son in the man, the Spirit in the dove. In this Trinity let us see, as we do see, whereunto the apostles were sent forth, and what it is wonderful those men do not see. Not indeed that they really do not see, but that they really shut their eyes to that which strikes them in the very face: that whereunto the disciples were sent forth in the name of the Father, and of the Son, and of the Holy Ghost, by Him of whom it is said, "This is He that baptizeth:" it was said, in fact, to His ministers, by Him who has retained this authority to Himself.

6. Now this it was in Him that John saw, and came to know which he did not know. Not that he did not know Him to be the Son of God, or that he did not know Him to be the Lord, or not know Him to be the Christ; or that he did not know this too, that it was He who should baptize with water and with the Holy Ghost. This he did know; but that he should do this so as to retain the authority to Himself and transfer it to none of His ministers, this is what he learnt in the dove. For by this authority, which Christ has retained to Himself alone, and conferred upon none of His ministers, though He has deigned to baptize by His ministers; by this authority, I say, stands the unity of the Church, which is figured in the dove, concerning which it is said, "My dove is one, the only one of her mother."[2] For if, as I have already said, my brethren, the authority were transferred by the Lord to His minister, there would be as many baptisms as ministers, and the unity of baptism would no longer exist.

7. Mark, brethren; before our Lord Jesus Christ came to His baptism (for it was after the baptism that the dove descended, whereby John recognized something that was peculiar to Him, since he was told, "Upon whom thou

shalt see the Spirit descending like a dove, and remaining on Him, the same is He that baptizeth with the Holy Ghost"), John knew that He it was that baptizeth with the Holy Ghost; but that it should be with this peculiarity, that the authority should not pass from Him to another, notwithstanding He confers it, this is what he learnt there. And whence do we prove that John did already know that the Lord was to baptize with the Holy Ghost; so that what he must be understood to have learned by the dove is, that the Lord was to baptize with the Holy Ghost in such wise that the authority should not pass from Him to any other man? Whence do we prove this? The dove descended after the Lord was baptized; but before the Lord came to be baptized by John in the Jordan, we have said that John knew Him, on the evidence of those words, in which he says, "Comest Thou to me to be baptized? I have need to be baptized of Thee." Well, he did know Him to be the Lord, knew Him to be the Son of God; how do we prove that he knew already that the same was He who should baptize with the Holy Ghost? Before He came to the river, whilst many people were running together to John to be baptized, he says to them, "I indeed baptize you with water; but He that cometh after me is greater than I, the latchet of whose shoes I am not worthy to loose; the same shall baptize you with the Holy Ghost, and with fire."[3] Already he knew this also. What then did he learn from the dove, that he may not afterwards be found a liar (which God forbid we should think), if it be not this, that there was to be a certain peculiarity in Christ, such that, although many ministers, be they righteous or unrighteous, should baptize, the virtue of baptism would be attributed to Him alone on whom the dove descended, and of whom it was said, "This is He that baptizeth with the Holy Ghost"? Peter may baptize, but this is He that baptizeth; Paul may baptize, yet this is He that baptizeth; Judas may baptize, still this is He that baptizeth.

8. For if the sanctity of baptism be according to the diversity of merits in them that administer it, then as merits are diverse there will be diverse baptisms; and the recipient will imagine that what he receives is so much the better, the better he appears to be from whom he received it. The saints themselves —understand brethren, they that belong to the dove, that have their part in that city of Jerusalem, the good themselves in the Church, of whom the apostle says, "The Lord know-

---

[1] Matt. iii. 16.   [2] Cant. vi. 8.   [3] Matt. iii. 14.

eth them that are His " [1]—are endued with different graces, and do not all possess like merits. Some are more holy than others, some are better than others. Therefore if one receive baptism from him, for example, who is a righteous saint, another from another who is of inferior merit with God, of inferior degree, of inferior continence, of inferior life, how notwithstanding is that which they receive one, equal and like, if it be not because, "This is He that baptizeth"? Just, then, as when the good and the better administer baptism, one man does not receive a good thing, another a better; but, notwithstanding that the ministers were one good the other better, they receive what is one and equal, not a better in the one case and a worse in the other; so, too, when a bad man administers baptism, through the ignorance or forbearance of the Church (for bad men either are not known as such, or are borne with; the chaff is tolerated until the floor be fully purged at the last), that which is given is one, not unlike because the ministers are unlike, but like and equal because "This is He that baptizeth."

9. Therefore, beloved, let us see what those men desire not to see; not what they may not see, but what they grieve to see, as though it were shut against them. Whither were the disciples sent to baptize as ministers, in the name of the Father, and of the Son, and of the Holy Ghost? Whither were they sent? "Go," said He, "baptize the nations." You have heard, brethren, how that inheritance comes, "Ask of me, and I will give Thee the nations for Thine inheritance, and the utmost bounds of the earth for Thy possessions." [2] You have heard how that "from Sion went forth the law, and the word of the Lord from Jerusalem." [3] For it was there the disciples were told, "Go, baptize the nations in the name of the Father, and of the Son, and of the Holy Ghost." [4] We became attentive when we heard, "Go, baptize the nations." In whose name? "In the name of the Father, and of the Son, and of the Holy Ghost." This is one God; for it says not in the "names" of the Father, and of the Son, and of the Holy Ghost, but "in the name of the Father, and of the Son, and of the Holy Ghost." Where thou hearest one name, there is one God; just as it was said of Abraham's seed, and the Apostle Paul expounds it, "In thy seed shall all nations be blessed; he said not, In seeds, as in many, but as in one, and in thy seed which is Christ." [5] Wherefore, just as the apostle wished to show thee that,

because in that place it is not said "in seeds," Christ is one; so here too, when it is said, "in the name," not in the names, even as these, "in seed," not in seeds, is it proved that the Father, and the Son, and the Holy Ghost are one God.

10. But lo, say the disciples to the Lord, we are told in what name we are to baptize; Thou hast made us ministers, and hast said to us, "Go, baptize in the name of the Father, and of the Son, and of the Holy Ghost." Whither shall we go? Whither? Have you not heard? To Mine inheritance. You ask, Whither shall we go? To that which I bought with my blood. Whither then? To the nations, saith He. I fancied that He said, Go, baptize the Africans in the name of the Father, and of the Son, and of the Holy Ghost. Thanks be to God, the Lord has solved the question the dove has taught us. Thanks be to God, it was to the nations the apostles were sent; if to the nations, then to all tongues. The Holy Spirit signified this, being divided in the tongues, united in the dove. Here the tongues are divided, there the dove unites them. The tongues of the nations agreed, perhaps that of Africa alone disagreed. What can be more evident, my brethren? In the dove the unity, in the tongues the community of the nations. For once the tongues became discordant through pride, and then of one became many tongues. For after the flood certain proud men, as if endeavoring to fortify themselves against God, as if aught were high for God, or aught could give security to pride, raised a tower, apparently that they might not be destroyed by a flood, should there come one thereafter. For they had heard and considered that all iniquity was swept away by a flood; to abstain from iniquity they would not; they sought the height of a tower as a defense against a flood; they built a lofty tower. "God saw their pride, and frustrated their purpose by causing that they should not understand one another's speech, and thus tongues became diverse through pride." If pride caused diversities of tongues, Christ's humility has united these diversities in one. The Church is now bringing together what that tower had sundered. Of one tongue there were made many; marvel not: this was the doing of pride. Of many tongues there is made one; marvel not: this was the doing of charity. For although the sounds of tongues are various, in the heart one God is invoked, one peace preserved. How then should the Holy Spirit have been manifested when signifying a unity, if

---

[1] 2 Tim. ii. 19.   [2] Ps. ii. 8.   [3] Isa. ii. 3.
[4] Matt. xxviii. 19.   [5] Gen. xxii. 18; Gal. iii. 16.   [6] Gen. xi. 1-9.

not by the dove, so that it might be said to the Church brought into a state of peace, " My dove is one " ? How ought humility to have been represented but by an innocent, sorrowing bird; not by a proud, exulting bird like the raven ?

11. But perhaps they will say: Well, as it is a dove, and the dove is one, baptism there cannot be apart from the one dove. Therefore if the dove is with thee, or if thou be thyself a dove, do thou give me, when I come to thee, that which I have not. You know that this is what they say; but you will presently see that it is not of the voice of the dove, but of the clamor of the raven. For attend a little, beloved, and fear their devices; nay, beware of them, and listen to the words of gainsayers only to reject them, not to swallow them and take them into your bowels. Do therein what the Lord did when they offered Him the bitter draught, " He tasted, and spat it out;"[1] so also you hear and cast away. What indeed say they ? Let us see. Lo, says he, " Thou art the dove." O Catholic Church, it is to thee it is said, " My dove is one, the only one of her mother," to thee certainly is it said. Stop, do not question me; prove first whether to me it was said; if it was said to me, I would hear it at once. " To thee," saith he, " it was said." I answer, in the voice of the Catholic Church, " To me." And this answer, brethren, sounding forth from my mouth alone, has sounded, as I believe, also from your hearts, and we all affirmed together, yea, to the Catholic Church was it said, " One is my dove, the only one of her mother." Apart from this dove, says he further, there is no baptism: I was baptized apart from this dove, consequently have not baptism; if I have not baptism, why dost thou not give it me when I come to thee ?

12. I also will put questions; let us meanwhile lay aside the inquiry as to whom this was said, " My dove is one, the only one of her mother;"—as yet we are inquiring;—it was said either to me or to thee; let us postpone the question as to whom it was said. This is what I ask, if the dove is simple, innocent, without gall, peaceful in its kisses, not fierce with its talons, I ask whether the covetous, the rapacious, the crafty, the sottish, the infamous, belong to the members of this dove? are they members of this dove? Far be the thought, says he. And who would really say this, brethren? To speak of nothing else, if I mention the rapacious alone, members of the hawk they may be, not members of the dove. Kites seize and plunder, so do hawks,

so do ravens; doves do not plunder nor tear, consequently they who snatch and rob are not members of the dove. Was there not even one rapacious person among you? Why abides the baptism, which in this case the hawk, not the dove, has given? Why do you not among yourselves baptize after robbers, after adulterers, after drunkards? why not baptize after the avaricious among yourselves? Are these all members of the dove? You so dishonor your dove that you make those that have the nature of the vulture her members. What, then, brethren, what say we? There are the bad and the good in the Catholic Church, but with them the bad only. But perhaps I say this with a hostile feeling: let this too be afterwards examined. They do say, certainly, that among them are the good and the bad; for, should they assert that they have only the good, let their own credit it, and I subscribe. With us, let them say, there are none but holy, righteous, chaste, sober men; no adulterers, no usurers, no deceivers, no false swearers, no wine-bibbers;—let them say this, for I heed not their tongues, I touch their hearts. But since they are well known to us, and to you, and to their own, just as you are known both to yourselves in the Catholic Church and to them, neither let us find fault with them, nor let them flatter themselves. We confess that in the Church there are good and bad, yet as the grain and the chaff. Sometimes he who is baptized by the grain is chaff, and he who is baptized by the chaff is grain. Otherwise, if his baptism who is baptized by the grain stands good, and his who is baptized by the chaff not, then it is not true, " This is He that baptizeth." But if it is true " This is He that baptizeth," then what is given by the chaff stands good, and he baptizeth in like manner as the dove. For the bad man (who administers baptism) is not the dove, nor belongs to the members of the dove, nor can he possibly be affirmed to be so, either with us in the Catholic Church or with them, if they assert that their Church is the dove. What then are we to understand, brethren? Since it is evident, and known to all, and they must admit, though it be against their will, that when with them bad men give baptism, it is not given after those bad men; and with us, too, when the bad give baptism, it is not given after them. The dove does not baptize after the raven; why then would the raven baptize after the dove?

13. Consider, beloved, why also was there a something pointed out by means of the dove, as that the dove—namely, the Holy Spirit in the shape of a dove—came to the Lord on being baptized, and rested upon Him, whilst

---

[1] Matt. xxvii. 34.

by the coming of the dove John learned this, that there dwelt in the Lord a power peculiarly His own to baptize? Because it was by this power peculiar to Himself, as I have said, the peace of the Church was made secure. And yet it may be that one may have baptism apart from the dove; but that baptism apart from the dove should do him good, is impossible. Consider, beloved, and understand what I say, for by this deception they mislead such of our brethren as are dull and cold. Let us be more simple and more fervent. See, say they, have I received, or have I not? I answer, Thou hast received. Well, if I have received, there is nothing which thou canst give me; I am safe, even on thine own evidence. For I affirm that I have received, and thou, too, dost confess that I have received: I am safe by the confession of both: what then dost thou promise me? Why wouldst thou make me a Catholic, when thou wouldst not give me anything further, seeing thou confessest that I have already received that which thou affirmest thyself to possess? But when I say, Come to me, I say that thou dost not possess, who yet confessest that I do. Why dost thou say, Come to me?

14. The dove teaches us. From the head of the Lord she answers, and says, Thou hast baptism, but the charity with which I groan thou hast not. How is this, says he, I have baptism, and have not charity? Have I the sacraments, and not charity? Do not shout: show me how can he who divides unity have charity? I, saith he, have baptism. Thou hast; but that baptism, without charity, profits thee nothing; because without charity thou art nothing. The baptism itself, even in him who is nothing, is not nothing. Baptism, indeed, is something, aye, something great, for His sake, of whom it is said, "This is He that baptizeth." But lest thou shouldst fancy that that which is great can profit thee aught, if thou be not in unity, it was after He was baptized that the dove descended, as if intimating, If thou hast baptism, be in the dove, lest what thou hast profit thee not. Come, then, to the dove, we say; not that thou mayest begin to have what thou hadst not before, but that what thou didst have may begin to profit thee. For thou didst have baptism to destruction without; if thou shalt have it within, it begins to profit thee to salvation.

15. For not only was baptism not profitable to thee, and not also hurtful. Even holy things may be hurtful. In the good, indeed, holy things are to salvation; in the evil, to judgment. For we certainly know, brethren, what we receive, and what we receive is at any rate holy, and no one says that it is not:

and what says the apostle? "But he that eateth and drinketh unworthily, eateth and drinketh judgment to himself."[1] He does not say that the thing itself is bad, but that the evil man, by receiving it amis, receives the good thing which he does receive to judgment. Was that morsel which the Lord delivered to Judas evil? God forbid. The physician would not give poison; it was health the physician gave; but by unworthily receiving it, he who received it not being at peace, received it unto destruction. So likewise also he who is baptized. I have (baptism), says he, for myself. Thou hast it, I admit. Give good heed to what thou hast; by that very thing which thou hast thou wilt be condemned. Wherefore? Because thou hast what belongs to the dove apart from the dove. If thou hast what is the dove's in the dove, thou art safe. Suppose thyself a soldier: if thou hast thy general's mark within the lines, thou servest in safety; but if thou hast it out of bounds, not only that mark will not be of advantage to thee for service, but thou wilt even be punished as a deserter. Come, then, come, and do not say, I have already, I have enough. Come; the dove is calling thee, calling thee by her sighing. My brethren, to you I say, call by groaning, not by quarreling; call by praying, by invitation, by fasting; let them by your charity understand that you pity them. I doubt not, my brethren, that if they see your sorrow they will be astonished, and will come to life again. Come, then, come; be not afraid; be afraid if thou do not come; nay, be not afraid, rather bewail thyself. Come, thou wilt rejoice if thou wilt come; thou wilt indeed groan in the tribulations of thy pilgrimage, but thou wilt rejoice in hope. Come where the dove is, to whom it was said, "My dove is one, the only one of her mother." Seest thou not the one dove upon the head of Christ? seest thou not the tongues throughout the whole world? It is the same Spirit by the dove and by the tongues: if by the dove the same Spirit, and by the tongues the same Spirit, then was the Holy Spirit given to the whole world, from which Spirit thou hast cut thyself off, that thou mightest clamor with the raven, not that thou mightest sigh with the dove. Come, then.

16. But thou art anxious, it may be, and sayest, I was baptized without; I fear lest therefore I am guilty, in that I was baptized without. Already thou beginnest to know what thou hast to bewail. Thou sayest truly that thou art guilty, not because of thy re-

---

[1] 1 Cor. xi. 29.

ceiving, but because of thy receiving without. Keep then what thou hast received; amend thy receiving it without. Thou hast received what is the dove's apart from the dove. Here are two things said to thee: Thou hast received, and, Apart from the dove thou hast received. In that thou hast received, I approve; that thou hast received without, I disappprove. Keep then what thou hast received, it is not changed, but recognized: it is the mark of my king, I will not profane it. I will correct the deserter, not change the mark.

17. Boast not of thy baptism because I call it a real baptism. Behold, I say that it is so; the whole Catholic Church says that it is so; the dove regards it, and acknowledges it, and groans because thou hast it without; she sees therein what she may acknowledge, sees also what she may correct. It is a real baptism, come. Thou boastest that it is real, and yet wilt thou not come? What then of the wicked, who do not belong to the dove? Saith the dove to thee, Even the wicked, among whom I groan, who belong not to my members, and it must needs be that I groan among them, have not they that which thou boastest of having? Have not many drunkards baptism? Have not many covetous? Have not many idolaters, and, what is worse, who are such by stealth? Do not the pagans resort, or at least did resort, publicly to idols? And now Christians secretly seek out diviners and consult astrologers. And yet these have baptism; but the dove groans among ravens. Why then dost thou boast in the having it? This that thou hast, the wicked man also has. Have thou humility, charity, peace; have thou the good thing which as yet thou hast not, so that the good thing which thou hast may profit thee.

18. For what thou hast, even Simon Magus had: the Acts of the Apostles are witness, that canonical book which has to be read in the Church every year. You know that every year, in the season following the Lord's Passion, that book is read, wherein it is written, how the apostle was converted, and from a persecutor became a preacher;[1] also, how on the day of Pentecost the Holy Spirit was sent in cloven tongues as of fire.[2] There we read that in Samaria many believed through the preaching of Philip: and he is understood to have been either one of the apostles or one of the deacons; for we read there that seven deacons were ordained, among whom is the name of Philip. Well, then, through the preaching of Philip the Samaritans believed; Samaria began to abound in believers. This

Simon Magus was there. By his magical arts he had so befooled the people, that they fancied him to be the power of God. Impressed, however, by the signs which were done by Philip, he also believed; but in what manner he believed, the events that followed afterwards proved. And Simon also was baptized. The apostles, who were at Jerusalem, heard this. Peter and John were sent to those in Samaria; they found many baptized; and as none of them had as yet received the Holy Ghost,—in like manner as He at that time descended, so as that they on whom the Holy Spirit came should speak with tongues, for a manifest token that the nations would believe,—they laid their hands on them, praying for them, and they received the Holy Ghost. This Simon,—who was not a dove but a raven in the Church, because he sought his own things, not the things which are Jesus Christ's; whence he loved the power which was in the Christians more than the righteousness,—Simon, I say, saw that the Holy Spirit was given by the laying on of the hands of the apostles (not that it was given by them, but given in answer to their prayers), and he said to them, " How much money will ye that I give you, so that by the laying on of my hands also, the Holy Ghost may be given? And Peter said unto him, Thy money perish with thee, because thou thoughtest that the gift of God was to be bought with money." To whom said he, " Thy money perish with thee "? Undoubtedly to one that was baptized. Baptism he had already; but he did not cleave to the bowels of the dove. Understand that he did not; attend to the very words of the Apostle Peter, for he goes on, " Thou hast no part nor lot in this faith: for I see that thou art in the gall of bitterness."[3] The dove has no gall; Simon had, and for that reason he was separated from the bowels of the dove. What did baptism profit him? Do not therefore boast of thy baptism, as if that were of itself enough for thy salvation. Be not angry, put away thy gall, come to the dove. Here that will profit thee, which without not only did not profit thee, but even was prejudicial to thee.

19. Neither say, I will not come, because I was baptized without. So, begin to have charity, begin to have fruit, let there be fruit found in thee, and the dove will send thee within. We find this in Scripture. The ark was made of incorruptible wood. The incorruptible timbers are the saints, the faithful that belong to Christ. For as in the temple the living stones of which it is built are said

to be faithful men, so likewise the incorruptible timbers are they who persevere in the faith. In that same ark, then, the timbers were incorruptible. Now the ark is the Church, it is there the dove baptizeth; for the ark was borne on the water, the incorruptible timbers were baptized within. We find that certain timbers were baptized without, such as all the trees that were in the world. Nevertheless the water was the same, not another sort; all had come from heaven, or from abysses of the fountains. It was the same water in which the incorruptible timbers which were in the ark were baptized, and in which the timbers that were without were baptized. The dove was sent forth, and at first found no rest for its feet; it returned to the ark, for all was full of water, and it preferred to return rather than be rebaptized. But the raven was sent out before the water was dried up. Rebaptized, it desired not to return, and died in those waters. May God avert from us that raven's death. For why did not the raven return, unless because it was taken off by the waters? But on the other hand, the dove not finding rest for its feet, whilst the water was crying to it on every side, "Come, come, dip thyself here;" just as these heretics cry, "Come, come, here thou hast it;" the dove, finding no rest for its feet, returned to the ark. And Noah sent it out a second time, just as the ark sends you out to speak to them; and what did the dove afterwards? Because there were timbers without that were baptized, it brought back to the ark an olive branch. That branch had both leaves and fruit. Let there not be in thee words only, nor leaves only; let there be fruit, and thou returnest to the ark, not of thyself, the dove calls thee back. Groan ye without, that ye may call them back within.

20. Moreover, as to this fruit of the olive, if the matter be examined, you will find what it was. The fruit of the olive signifies charity. How do we prove this? Just as oil is kept down by no liquid, but bursting through all, bounds up and overtops them; so likewise charity cannot be pressed to the bottom, but must of necessity show itself at the top. Therefore the apostle says of it, "Yet show I unto you a more excellent[1] way." Since we have said of oil that it overtops other liquids, in case it should not be of charity, the apostle said, "I show you a more excellent way," let us hear what follows. "Though I speak with the tongues of men and of angels, and have not charity, I am become as sounding brass, or a tinkling cymbal." Go now, Donatus, and cry, "I am eloquent;" go now, and cry, "I am learned." How far eloquent? How far learned? Hast thou spoken with the tongues of angels? Yet though thou wert to speak with the tongues of angels, not having charity, I should hear only sounding brass and tinkling cymbals. I want solidity; let me find fruit among the leaves; let there be not words merely, let them have the olive, let them return to the ark.

21. But I have the sacrament, thou wilt say. Thou sayest the truth; the sacrament is divine; thou hast baptism, and that I confess. But what says the apostle? "If I should know all mysteries,[2] and have prophecy and all faith, so that I could remove mountains;" in case thou shouldest say this, "I believe; enough for me." But what says James? "The devils believe and tremble."[3] Faith is mighty, but without charity it profits nothing. The devils confessed Christ. Accordingly it was from believing, but not from loving, they said, "What have we to do with Thee?"[4] They had faith, but not charity; hence they were devils. Boast not of faith; so far thou art on a level with the devils. Say not to Christ, What have I to do with Thee? For Christ's unity speaks to thee. Come, learn peace, return to the bowels of the dove. Thou hast been baptized without; have fruit, and thou returnest to the ark.

22. But sayest thou, "Why do you seek us if we are bad men?" That you may be good. The reason why we seek you is, because you are bad; for if you were not bad, we should have found you, and would not be seeking you. He who is good is already found; he who is bad is still sought after. Consequently, we are seeking you; return ye to the ark. "But I have baptism already." "Though I should know all mysteries,[5] and have prophecy and all faith, so as to remove mountains, but have not charity, I am nothing." Let me see fruit there; let me see the olive there, and thou art called back to the ark.

23. But what sayest thou? "Behold, we suffer many evils." Would that ye suffered these for Christ, not for your own honor! Hear what follows: They, indeed, boast sometimes, because they do many alms, give to the poor; because they suffer afflictions: but it is for Donatus, not for Christ. Consider how thou sufferest; for if thou sufferest for Donatus, it is for a proud man: thou art not in the dove if thou art suffering for Donatus. Donatus was not the friend of the Bridegroom; for had he been, he would have sought the glory of the Bridegroom, not his own. See the

---

[1] Supereminentiorem.
[2] Sacramenta.
[4] Mark i. 24.
[3] Jas. ii. 19.
[5] Sacramenta.

friend of the Bridegroom saying, "This is He that baptizeth." He, for whom thou art suffering, was not the friend of the Bridegroom. Thou hast not the wedding garment; and if thou art come to the feast, thou wilt be put out of doors; nay, thou hast been cast out of doors already, and for that reason thou art wretched: return at length, and do not boast. Hear what the apostle says: "Though I should distribute all my goods to the poor, and give my body to be burnt, but have not charity." See what thou dost not have. "Though," he saith, "I should give my body to be burnt;" and that, too, for the name of Christ; but since there are many who do this boastfully, not with charity, therefore, "Though I should give my body to be burnt, and have not charity, it profiteth me nothing."[1] It was by charity those martyrs, who suffered in time of persecution, did this; but these men do it of their vanity and pride; for in the absence of a persecutor, they throw themselves headlong into destruction. Come, then, that thou mayest have charity. "But we have our martyrs." What martyrs? They are not doves; hence they attempted to fly, and fell over the rock.

24. You see then, my brethren, that all things cry against them, all the divine pages, all prophecy, the whole gospel, all the apostolic letters, every sigh of the dove, and yet they awake not, they do not yet rouse from their sleep. But if we are the dove, let us groan, let us persevere, let us hope; God's compassion will be with you, that the fire of the Holy Spirit may glow in your simplicity; and they will come. There must be no despairing; pray, preach, love; the Lord is able to the utmost. Already they begin to be sensible of their shame; many have become sensible of it, and blushed; Christ will aid, that the rest also may become sensible of it. However, my brethren, at least let the chaff alone remain there; let all the grain be gathered together; let whatever has borne fruit among them return to the ark by the dove.

25. Failing everywhere else, what do they now allege against us, not finding what to say? They have taken away our houses, they have taken away our estates. They bring forward wills. "See, Gaius Seius made a grant of an estate to the church over which Faustinus presided." Of what church was Faustinus bishop? What is the church? To the church over which Faustinus presided, said he. But Faustinus presided not over a church, but over a sect. The dove, however, is the Church. Why cry out? We have not

devoured houses; let the dove have them. Let inquiry be made who the dove is, and let her have them. For you know, my brethren, that those houses of theirs are not Augustin's; and if you know it not, and imagine that I delight in the possession of them, God knows, yea, knows my judgment respecting those estates, and even what I suffer in that matter; He knows my groaning, since He has deigned to impart to me somewhat of the dove. Behold, there are those estates; by what right dost thou assert thy claim to them? By divine right, or by human? Let them answer: Divine right we have in the Scriptures, human right in the laws of kings. By what right does every man possess what he possesses? Is it not by human right? For by divine right, "The earth is the Lord's, and the fullness thereof."[2] The poor and the rich God made of one clay; the same earth supports alike the poor and the rich. By human right, however, one says, This estate is mine, this house is mine, this servant is mine. By human right, therefore, is by right of the emperors. Why so? Because God has distributed to mankind these very human rights through the emperors and kings of this world. Do you wish us to read the laws of the emperors, and to act by the estates according to these laws? If you will have your possession by human right, let us recite the laws of the emperors; let us see whether they would have the heretics possess anything. But what is the emperor to me? thou sayest. It is by right from him that thou possessest the land. Or take away rights created by emperors, and then who will dare say, That estate is mine, or that slave is mine, or this house is mine? If, however, in order to their possessing these things, men have received rights derived from kings, will ye that we read the laws, that you may be glad in having even a single garden, and impute it to nothing but the clemency of the dove that you are permitted to remain in possession even there? For there are to be read well known laws, in which the emperors have directed that those who, being outside the communion of the Catholic Church, usurp to themselves the name of Christians, and are not willing in peace to worship the Author of peace, may not dare to possess anything in the name of the Church.

26. But what have we to do with the emperor? But I have already said that we are treating of human right. And yet the apostle would have us obey kings, would have us honor kings, and said, "Honor the king."[3] Do not say, What have I to do with the king?

[1] 1 Cor. xiii. 2, 3.   [2] Ps. xxiv. 1.   [3] 1 Pet. ii. 17.

as in that case, what have you to do with the possession? It is by the rights derived from kings that possessions are enjoyed. Thou hast said, What have I to do with the king? Say not then that the possessions are thine; because it is to those same human rights, by which men enjoy their possessions, thou hast referred them. But it is with divine right I have to do, saith he. Well, let us read the Gospel; let us see how far extends the Catholic Church of Christ, upon whom the dove came, which taught, "This is He that baptizeth." In what way, then, can he possess by divine right, who says, "I baptize;" whilst the dove says, "This is He that baptizeth;" whilst the Scripture says, "My dove is one, the only one of her mother"? Why have you torn the dove?—nay, rather, have torn your own bowels? for while you are yourselves torn to pieces, the dove continues entire. Therefore, my brethren, if, driven from every point, they have nothing to say, I will tell them what to do; let them come to the Catholic Church, and together with us, they will have not only the earth, but Him also who made heaven and earth.

TRACTATE VII.

Chapter I. 34–51.

1. WE rejoice at your numbers, for you have come together with readiness and in greater numbers than we could have hoped. This it is that delights and consoles us in all the labors and dangers of this life, your love towards God, and pious zeal, and assured hope, and fervor of spirit. You heard when the psalm was read, "that the needy and poor man cries to God in this world."[1] For it is the voice, as you have often heard, and ought to remember, not of one man, and yet of one man; not of one, because the faithful are many—many grains groaning amid the chaff diffused throughout the whole world—but of one, because all are members of Christ, and thus one body. This people, then, poor and needy, does not know to rejoice with the world: its grief is within, and its joy is within, where no one sees but He who listens to him who groans, and crowns him who hopes. The rejoicing of the world is vanity. With great expectation is it hoped for, and it cannot, when it comes, be held fast. For this day which is a day of rejoicing in this city to the lost, to-morrow will, of course, cease to be; nor will they themselves be the same to-morrow that they are to-day. And all things pass away, fly away, and vanish like smoke; and woe to those who love such things! For every soul follows what it loves. "All flesh is grass, and all the goodliness thereof as the flower of the field: the grass withereth, the flower fadeth; but the word of the Lord abideth forever."[2] Behold what thou must love if thou dost desire to abide for ever.

But thou hadst this to reply: How can I apprehend the word of God? "The Word was made flesh, and dwelt among us."[3]

2. Wherefore, beloved, let it belong to our neediness and poverty to grieve for those who seem to themselves to abound. For their joy is as that of madmen. But as a madman rejoices for the most part in his madness, and laughs, and grieves over him who is in his senses, so let us, beloved, if we have received the medicine coming from heaven, because we all were madmen, as if made whole, because those things which we did love we do not love,—let us, I say, groan unto God for those who are yet in madness, for He is able to save them also. And there is need that they should look upon themselves and be displeased with themselves: to behold they desire, and to behold themselves they have not known. For if they for a little turn their eyes upon themselves, they see their own confusion. But until this take place, let our pursuits be different, let the recreations of our souls be different; our grief avails more than their joy. As far as regards the number of the brethren, it is difficult to conceive that any one of the men should have been carried away by that celebration; but as regards the number of the sisters, it grieves us, and this is a greater cause for grief, that they do not rather repair to the Church, whom if not fear, modesty at all events ought to deter from the public scene. May He see to this who sees it; and may His mercy be present to heal all. Let us who have come together feed upon the

feast of God, and let our joy be His word. For He has invited us to His gospel, and He is our food, than whom nothing is sweeter, if only a man have a healthy palate in his heart.

3. But I imagine, beloved brethren, that you remember that this Gospel is read in order in suitable portions; and I think that it has not escaped you what has lately been treated of, specially the recent matters concerning John and the dove. Concerning John, namely, what new thing he learned concerning the Lord by means of the dove, although he had already known the Lord. And this was discovered by the inspiration of the Spirit of God, that John indeed already knew the Lord, but that the Lord Himself was to baptize, that the power of baptizing He would not transfer from Himself to any one, this he learned by means of the dove, because it was said to him, " On whom thou shalt see the Spirit descending as a dove, and abiding upon Him, this is He which baptizeth with the Holy Ghost." [1] What is " This is He " ? Not another, although by means of another. But why by means of a dove ? Many things were said, and I am not able, nor is there need that I should go over all;—principally, however, to denote peace, because also the trees which were baptized outside, because the dove found in them fruit, it brought to the ark, as you remember the dove sent out by Noah from the ark, which floated on the flood and was washed by baptism, was not submerged. When, then, it was sent forth, it brought an olive branch; but it had not leaves alone, it had also fruit. [2] This, then, we ought to wish for our brethren who are baptized outside, that they may have fruit; the dove will not permit them to remain outside, but bring them back to the ark. For the whole of fruit is charity, without which a man is nothing, whatever else he have. And this, which is most fully said by the apostle, we have mentioned and recounted. For he says, " Though I speak with the tongues of men and of angels, and have not charity, I am become as sounding brass or a tinkling cymbal; and though I should have all knowledge, and know all mysteries, and have all prophecy, and should have all faith " (but in what sense did he say all faith ?), " so that I could remove mountains, and have not charity, I am nothing. And though I should distribute all my goods to the poor, and though I should give my body to be burned, and have not charity, it profiteth me nothing." [3] But in no manner are they able to say that they have charity who divide

unity. These things were said: let us see what follows.

4. John bare record because he saw. What record did he bear ? " That this is the Son of God." It behoved, then, that He should baptize who is God's only Son, not His adopted son. Adopted sons are the ministers of the only Son: the only Son has power; the adopted, the ministry. In the case that a minister baptizes who does not belong to the number of sons, because he lives evilly and acts evilly, what is our consolation ? " This is He which baptizeth."

5. " The next day, John stood, and two of his disciples; and looking upon Jesus as He walked, he saith, Behold the Lamb of God ! " Assuredly, in a special sense, the Lamb; for the disciples were also called lambs: " Behold, I send you as lambs in the midst of wolves." [4] They were also called light: " Ye are the light of the world; " [5] but in another sense is He called so, concerning whom it was said, " That was the true light, which lighteth every man that cometh into the world." [6] In like manner was He called the dove in a special sense, alone without stain, without sin; not one whose sins have been washed away, but One who never had stain. For what ? Because John said concerning the Lord, " Behold the Lamb of God," was not John himself a lamb? Was he not a holy man ? Was he not the friend of the Bridegroom ? Wherefore, with a special meaning, said John of Him, " This is the Lamb of God;" because solely by the blood of this Lamb alone could men be redeemed.

6. My brethren, if we acknowledge our price, that it is the blood of the Lamb, who are they who this day celebrate the festival of the blood of I know not what woman ? and how ungrateful are they ! The gold was snatched, they say, from the ear of a woman, and the blood ran, and the gold was placed on a pair of scales or on a balance, and the advantage was much on the side of the blood. If the blood of a woman was sufficiently weighty to outweigh the gold, what power to outweigh the world has the blood of the Lamb by whom the world was made ? And, indeed, that spirit, I know not who, was pacified by the blood that he should depress the weight. Impure spirits knew that Jesus Christ would come, they had heard of His coming from the angels, they had heard of it from the prophets, and they expected it. For if they were not expecting it, why did they exclaim, " What have we to do with Thee ? art Thou come before the time to destroy us ?

---

[1] John i. 33.   [2] Gen. viii. 8-11.   [3] 1 Cor. xiii. 1-3.   [4] Matt. x. 16.   [5] Matt. v. 14.   [6] John i. 9.

We know who Thou art; the Holy One of God."[1] They expected that He would come, but they were ignorant of the time. But what have you heard in the psalm regarding Jerusalem? "For Thy servants have taken pleasure in her stones, and will pity the dust thereof. Thou shalt arise," says he, "and have mercy upon Zion: for the time is come that Thou wilt have mercy upon her."[2] When the time came for God to have mercy, the Lamb came. What sort of a Lamb whom wolves fear? What sort of a Lamb is it who, when slain, slew a lion? For the devil is called a lion, going about and roaring, seeking whom he may devour.[3] By the blood of the Lamb the lion was vanquished. Behold the spectacles of Christians. And what is more: they with the eyes of the flesh behold vanity, we with the eyes of the heart behold truth. Do not think, brethren, that our Lord God has dismissed us without spectacles; for if there are no spectacles, why have ye come together to-day? Behold, what we have said you saw, and you exclaimed; you would not have exclaimed if you had not seen. And this is a great thing to see in the whole world, the lion vanquished by the blood of the Lamb; members of Christ delivered from the teeth of the lions, and joined to the body of Christ. Therefore some spirit or other contrived the counterfeit that His image should be bought for blood, because he knew that the human race was at some time to be redeemed by the precious blood. For evil spirits counterfeit certain shadows of honor to themselves, that they may deceive those who follow Christ. So much so, my brethren, that those who seduce by means of amulets, by incantations, by the devices of the enemy, mingle the name of Christ with their incantations: because they are not now able to seduce Christians, so as to give them poison they add some honey, that by means of the sweet the bitter may be concealed, and be drunk to ruin. So much so, that I know that the priest of that Pilleatus was sometimes in the habit of saying, Pilleatus himself also is a Christian. Why so, brethren, unless that they were not able otherwise to seduce Christians?

7. Do not, then, seek Christ elsewhere than where Christ wished Himself to be preached to you; and as He wished Himself to be preached to you, in that fashion hold Him fast, in that manner write Him on your heart. It is a wall against all the assaults, and against all the snares of the enemy. Do not fear, he does not tempt unless he has been permitted; it is certain that he does nothing unless permitted or sent. He is sent as an evil angel by a power holding him in control: he is permitted when he asks anything; and this, brethren, does not take place unless that the just may be tried, the unjust punished. Why, then, dost thou fear? Walk in the Lord thy God; be thou assured, what He does not wish thee to suffer thou dost not suffer; what He permits thee to suffer is the scourge of one correcting, not the punishment of one condemning. We are being educated for an eternal inheritance, and do we spurn to be scourged? My brethren, if a boy were to refuse the punishment of cuffs or stripes from his father, would he not be called proud, incorrigible, ungrateful towards paternal discipline? And for what does an earthly father educate his son? That he may not lose the temporal things which he has acquired for him, which he has collected for him, which he does not wish him to lose, which he who leaves them cannot retain eternally. He does not teach a son with whom he is to possess, but one who is to possess after him   My brethren, if a father teaches a son who is to succeed him, and teaches him also that he will have to pass through all these things, in same way as he who is admonishing him is destined to pass through them, how do you wish that He educate us, our Father to whom we are not to succeed, but to whom we are to approach, and with whom we are to abide eternally in an inheritance which does not decay nor die, and which no storms can desolate? He is Himself both the inheritance and the Father. Shall we possess Him, and ought we not to undergo training? Let us hear the instruction of the Father. When our head aches, let us not have recourse to the superstitious intercessor, to the diviners and remedies of vanity. My brethren, shall I not mourn over you? Daily do I find these things; and what shall I do? Not yet have I persuaded Christians that their hope ought to be placed in God. Behold, if one dies to whom one of these remedies has been given (and how many have died with remedies, and how many have lived without them!), with what confidence does the spirit go forth to God? He has lost the sign of Christ, and has received the sign of the devil. Perhaps he may say that he has not lost the sign of Christ. Thou canst have, then, the sign of Christ along with the sign of the devil. Christ does not desire community of ownership, but He desires to possess alone what He has purchased. He has bought at so great a price that He may possess alone: thou makest Him the partner of that devil to whom thou didst sell thyself by thy sin. "Woe to the double-hearted,"[4] to those who in

---

[1] Mark i. 24.   [2] Ps. cii. 13, 14.   [3] 1 Pet. v. 8.   [4] Ecclus. ii. 12.

their hearts give part to God and part to the devil. God, being angry that the devil has part there, departs, and the devil will possess the whole. Not in vain, therefore, says the apostle, "Neither give place to the devil."[1] Let us know the Lamb, then, brethren; let us know our price.

8. "John stood, and two of his disciples." Behold two of John's disciples: since John, the friend of the Bridegroom, was such as he was, he sought not his own glory, but bore witness to the truth. Did he wish that his disciples should remain with him and not follow the Lord? Rather he himself showed his disciples whom they should follow. For they accounted of him as though he were the lamb; and he said, "Why do you give heed to me? I am not the lamb; behold the Lamb of God," of whom also he had already said, Behold the Lamb of God. And what benefit does the Lamb of God confer upon us? "Behold," he says, "who taketh away the sin of the world." The two who were with John followed Him when they heard this.

9. Let us see what follows: "Behold the Lamb of God." This John said, and the two disciples heard him speak, and followed Jesus. Then Jesus turned and saw them following, and saith unto them, "What seek ye?" And they said, "Rabbi (that is to say, being interpreted, Master), where dwellest Thou?" They did not follow Him in such manner as that they should cleave to Him; for it is plain when they clave unto Him, for He called them from the ship. For one of the two was Andrew, as you have just heard, and Andrew was the brother of Peter; and we know from the Gospel that the Lord called Peter and Andrew from the ship, saying, "Come ye after me, and I will make you fishers of men."[2] And from that time they clave unto Him, so as not to go away. On the present occasion these two followed Him, not as those who were not again to leave Him, but to see where He dwelt, and to fulfill the Scripture: "Let thy foot wear out the threshold of His doors; arise to come to Him continually, and be instructed in His precepts."[3] He showed them where He dwelt: they came and remained with Him. What a blessed day they spent, what a blessed night! Who can make known to us those things which they heard from the Lord? Let us also build in our heart, and make a house into which He may come and teach us, and have converse with us.

10. "What seek ye?" They said unto Him, "Rabbi (which is to say, being inter-preted, Master), where dwellest Thou? He says to them, Come and see. And they came and saw where He dwelt, and abode with Him that day: and it was about the tenth hour." Do we think that it did in no wise pertain to the evangelist to tell us what hour it was? Is it possible that he wished us to give heed to nothing in that, to inquire after nothing? It was the tenth hour. That number signifies the law, because the law was given in ten commandments. But the time had come for the law to be fulfilled by love, because it could not be fulfilled by the Jews by fear. Hence the Lord says, "I am not come to destroy the law, but to fulfill."[4] Suitably, then, at the tenth hour did these two follow Him, at the testimony of the friend of the Bridegroom, and that He at the tenth hour heard "Rabbi (which is interpreted, Master)." If at the tenth hour the Lord heard Rabbi, and the tenth number pertains to the law, the master of the law is no other than the giver of the law. Let no one say that one gave the law, and that another teaches the law: for the same teaches it who gave it; He is the Master of His own law, and teaches it. And mercy is in His tongue, therefore mercifully teacheth He the law, as it is said regarding wisdom, "The law and mercy doth she carry in her tongue."[5] Do not fear that thou art not able to fulfill the law, flee to mercy. If thou canst not fulfill the law, make use of that covenant, make use of the bond, make use of the prayers which the heavenly One, skilled in the law, has ordained and composed for you.

11. For those who have a cause, and wish to supplicate the emperor, seek for some one skilled in the law, and trained in the schools, to compose their petition for them; lest perchance, if they ask in an unbecoming manner, they not only do not obtain what they seek, but get punishment instead of a benefit. When, therefore, the apostles sought to petition, and could not find how to approach the Emperor God, they said unto Christ, "Lord, teach us to pray;" that is to say, "O thou who art our skilled One in the law, our Assessor, yea, the Concessor of God, compose for us prayers." And the Lord taught them from the book of the celestial law, taught them how to pray; and in that which He taught, He laid down a certain condition: "Forgive us our debts, as we also forgive our debtors."[6] If thou seekest not according to the law, thou becomest guilty. Dost thou not tremble before the Emperor, having become guilty? Offer the sacrifice of humility, offer the sacrifice of mercy; pray, saying,

[1] Eph. iv. 27.　　[2] Matt. iv. 19.　　[3] Ecclus. vi. 36, 37.　　[4] Matt. v. 17.　　[5] Prov. xxxi. 26.　　[6] Luke xi. 1-4.

Forgive me, for I also forgive. But if thou sayest, do. For what wilt thou do? whither wilt thou go if thou hast lied in thy prayers? Not as it is said in the forum, thou shalt lose the benefit of the rescript; but thou shalt not obtain a rescript. For it is the law of the forum that he who shall have lied in his petition shall derive no benefit from that which he has obtained. But this among men, because a man can be deceived: the emperor might have been deceived, when thou didst address to him thy petition; for thou saidest what thou wouldest, and he to whom thou didst speak knew not whether it was true or false; he sent thee away to thy adversary to be confuted if possible, so that if before the judge thou shouldest be convicted of falsehood (because he was not able not to grant the rescript, not knowing whether thou hadst lied), thou shouldest lose the benefit of the rescript, in the place to which thou hadst taken it. But God, who knows whether thou liest or speakest the truth, does not cause thee to lose in the judgment the benefit, but does not permit thee to obtain it, because thou hast dared to lie to the Truth.

12. What, then, wilt thou do? Tell me. To fulfill the law in every part, so as to offend in nothing, is difficult: the condition of guilt is therefore certain; wilt thou refuse to use the remedy? Behold, my brethren, what a remedy the Lord hath provided for the sicknesses of the soul! What then? When thy head aches, we praise thee if thou placest the gospel at thy head, instead of having recourse to an amulet. For so far has human weakness proceeded, and so lamentable is the estate of those who have recourse to amulets, that we rejoice when we see a man who is upon his bed, and tossed about with fevers and pains, placing his hope on nothing else than that the gospel lies at his head; not because it is done for this purpose, but because the gospel is preferred to amulets. If, then, it is placed at the head to allay the pain of the head, is it not placed at the heart to heal it from sin? Let it be done then. Let what be done? Let it be placed at the heart, let the heart be healed. It is well,—well that thou shouldest have no further care regarding the safety of the body, than to ask it from God. If He knows that it will do thee good, He will give it thee; if He give it not to thee, it would not have profited thee to have it. How many are sick in bed, and for that reason are innocent! for if they were to recover, they would go forth to commit acts of wickedness. To how many is health an injury! The robber who goes forth to the narrow path to slay a man, how much better for him would it have been to have been sick! And he who rises by night to dig through his neighbor's wall, how much better for him to be tossed by fever! If he were ill, he would have been comparatively innocent; being well, he is guilty of wickedness. It is known, then, to God what is expedient for us: let us make this only our endeavor, that our hearts be whole from sins; and when it happens that we are scourged in the body, let us pray to Him for relief. The Apostle Paul besought Him that He would take away the thorn in his flesh, and He would not. Was he disturbed? Was he filled with sadness, and did he speak of himself as deserted? Rather did he say that he was not deserted, because that was not taken away which he desired to be taken away, to the end that infirmity might be cured. For this he found in the voice of the Physician, "My grace is sufficient for thee; for my strength is made perfect in weakness."[1] Whence knowest thou, then, that God does not wish to heal thee? As yet it is expedient for thee to be scourged. Whence knowest thou how diseased that is which the physician cuts, using his knife on the diseased parts? Does he not know the measure, what he is to do, and how far he is to do it? Does the shrieking of him he cuts restrain the hands of the physician cutting according to his art? The one cries, the other cuts. Is he cruel who does not listen to the man crying out, or is he not rather merciful in following the wound, that he may heal the sick man? These things have I said, my brethren, in order that no one seek any other aid than that of God, when we happen to be under the reproof of God. See that ye perish not; see that ye do not depart from the Lamb, and be devoured by the lion.

13. We have declared, then, why it was at the tenth hour. Let us see what follows: "One of the two which heard John speak, and followed Him, was Andrew. Simon Peter's brother. He findeth his own brother Simon, and saith unto him, We have found the Messias, which is, being interpreted, the Christ." Messias, in Hebrew; Christ, in Greek; in Latin, Anointed. Χρίσμα is anointing in Greek; Christ, therefore, is the Anointed. He is peculiarly anointed, pre-eminently anointed; wherewith all Christians are anointed, He is pre-eminently anointed. Hear how He speaks in the psalm: "Wherefore God, Thy God, hath anointed Thee with the oil of gladness above Thy fellows." For all the holy ones are His fellows, but He in a peculiar sense is the Holy of Holies, peculiarly anointed, peculiarly Christ.

---

[1] 2 Cor. xii. 8, 9.

14. "And he brought him to Jesus; and when Jesus beheld him, He said, Thou art Simon the son of Joannes: thou shalt be called Cephas, which is, by interpretation, Peter." It is not a great thing that the Lord said whose son Peter was. What is great to the Lord? He knew all the names of His own saints, whom He predestinated before the foundation of the world; and dost thou wonder that He said to one man, Thou art the son of this man, and thou shalt be called this or that? Is it a great matter that He changed his name, and converted it from Simon to Peter? Peter is from *petra*, a rock, but the *petra* [rock]; is the Church; in the name of Peter, then, was the Church figured. And who is safe, unless he who builds upon the rock? And what saith the Lord Himself? "He that heareth these my words, and doeth them, I will liken him unto a wise man building his house upon a rock" (he doth not yield to temptation). "The rain descended, the floods came, the winds blew, and beat upon that house; and it fell not: for it was founded upon a rock. But he that heareth my words, and doeth them not" (now let each one of us fear and beware), "I will liken him to a foolish man, who built his house upon the sand: the rain descended, the floods came, the winds blew, and beat upon that house; and it fell: and great was the fall of it."[1] What profit is it to enter the Church for him who builds upon the sand? For, by hearing and not doing, he builds indeed, but on the sand. For if he hears nothing, he builds nothing; but if he hears, he builds. But we ask, Where? For if he hears and does, he builds upon the rock; if he hears and does not, he builds upon the sand. There are two kinds of builders, those building upon the rock, and those building upon the sand. What, then, are those who do not hear? Are they safe? Does He say that they are safe because they do not build? They are naked beneath the rains, before the winds, before the floods; when these come, they carry away those persons before they overthrow the houses. It is then the only security, both to build, and to build upon the rock. If thou wilt hear and do not, thou buildest; but thou buildest a ruin: and when temptation comes it overthrows the house, and carries away thee with the ruin. But if thou dost not hear, thou art naked; thou thyself art dragged away by those temptations. Hear, then, and do; it is the only remedy. How many, perchance, on this day, by hearing and not doing, are hurried away on the stream of this festi-

val! For, through hearing and not doing, the flood cometh, this annual festival; the torrent is filled, it will pass away and become dry, but woe to him whom it shall carry away! Know this, then, beloved, that unless a man hears and does, he builds not upon the rock, and he does not belong to that great name which the Lord so commended. For He has called thy attention. For if Simon had been called Peter before, thou wouldest not have so clearly seen the mystery of the rock, and thou wouldest have thought that he was called so by chance, not by the providence of God; therefore God willed that he should be called first something else, that by the very change of name the reality of the sacrament might be commended to our notice.

15. "And the day following He would go forth into Galilee, and finding Philip, He saith unto him, Follow me. Now he was of the city of Andrew and Peter. And Philip findeth Nathanael" (Philip who had been already called by the Lord); "and he said unto him, We have found Him, of whom Moses in the law, and the prophets, did write, Jesus, the son of Joseph." He was called the son of that man to whom His mother had been espoused. For that He was conceived and born while she was still a virgin, all Christians know well from the Gospel. This Philip said to Nathanael, and he added the place, "from Nazareth." And Nathanael said unto him, "From Nazareth something good can come." What is the meaning, brethren? Not as some read, for it is likewise wont to be read, "Can any good thing come out of Nazareth?" For the words of Philip follow, who says, "Come and see." But the words of Philip can suitably follow both readings, whether you read it thus, as confirming, "From Nazareth something good can come," to which Philip replies, "Come and see;" or whether as doubting, and making the whole a question, "Can any good thing come out of Nazareth? Come and see." Since then, whether read in this manner or in that, the words following are not incompatible, it is for us to inquire which of the two interpretations we shall adopt.

16. What sort of a man this Nathanael was, we prove by the words which follow. Hear what sort of a man he was; the Lord Himself bears testimony. Great is the Lord, known by the testimony of John; blessed Nathanael, known by the testimony of the truth. Because the Lord, although He had not been commended by the testimony of John, Himself to Himself bore testimony, because the truth is sufficient for its own testimony. But because men were not able to receive the truth,

---

[1] Matt. vii. 24-27.

they sought the truth by means of a lamp, and therefore John was sent to show them the Lord. Hear the Lord bearing testimony to Nathanael: "Nathanael said unto him, Can any good thing come out of Nazareth? Philip says to him, Come and see. And Jesus sees Nathanael coming to Him, and says concerning him, Behold an Israelite indeed, in whom is no guile." Great testimony! Not of Andrew, nor of Peter, nor of Philip was that said which was said of Nathanael, "Behold an Israelite indeed, in whom is no guile."

17. What do we then, brethren? Ought this man to be the first among the apostles? Not only is Nathanael not found as first among the apostles, but he is neither the middle nor the last among the twelve, although the Son of God bore such testimony to him, saying, "Behold an Israelite indeed, in whom is no guile." Is the reason asked for? In so far as the Lord intimates, we find a probable reason. For we ought to understand that Nathanael was learned and skilled in the law; and for that reason was the Lord unwilling to place him among His disciples, because He chose unlearned persons, that He might by them confound the world. Listen to the apostle speaking these things: "For ye see," saith he, "your calling, brethren, how that not many wise men after the flesh, not many mighty, not many noble, are called: but God hath chosen the weak things of the world to confound the things which are mighty; and base things of the world, and things that are despised, hath God chosen, yea, and things which are not, as though they were things that are, to bring to nought things that are."[1] If a learned man had been chosen, perhaps he would have said that he was chosen for the reason that his learning made him worthy of choice. Our Lord Jesus Christ, wishing to break the necks of the proud, did not seek the orator by means of the fisherman, but by the fisherman He gained the emperor. Great was Cyprian as an orator, but before him was Peter the fisherman, by means of whom not only the orator, but also the emperor, should believe. No noble was chosen in the first place, no learned man, because God chose the weak things of the world that He might confound the strong. This man, then, was great and without guile, and for this reason only was not chosen, lest the Lord should seem to any to have chosen the learned. And from this same learning in the law, it came that when he heard "from Nazareth,"—for he had searched the Scripture, and knew that the Saviour was to be expected thence, what

the other scribes and Pharisees had difficulty in knowing,—this man, then, very learned in the law, when he heard Philip saying, "We have found Him, of whom Moses in the law, and the prophets, did write, Jesus of Nazareth, the son of Joseph;"—this man, who knew the Scriptures excellently well, when he heard the name "Nazareth," was filled with hope, and said, "From Nazareth something good can come."

18. Let us now see the rest concerning this man. "Behold an Israelite indeed, in whom is no guile." What is "in whom is no guile?" Perhaps he had no sin? Perhaps he was not sick? Perhaps he did not need a physician? God forbid. No one is born here in such fashion as not to need that Physician. What, then, is the meaning of the words, "in whom is no guile"? Let us search a little more intently—it will appear presently—in the name of the Lord. The Lord says *dolus* [guile]; and every one who understands Latin knows that *dolus* is when one thing is done and another feigned. Give heed, beloved. *Dolus* (guile) is not *dolor* (pain). I say this because many brethren, not well skilled in Latin, so speak as to say, *Dolus* torments him, using it for *dolor*. *Dolus* is fraud, it is deceit. When a man conceals one thing in his heart, and speaks another, it is guile, and he has, as it were, two hearts; he has, as it were, one recess of his heart where he sees the truth, and another recess where he conceives falsehood. And that you may know that this is guile, it is said in the Psalms, "Lips of guile." What are "lips of guile"? It follows, "In a heart and in a heart have they spoken evil."[2] What is "in a heart and in a heart," unless in a double heart? If, then, guile was not in Nathanael, the Physician judged him to be curable, not whole. A whole man is one thing, a curable another, an incurable a third: he who is sick, but not hopelessly sick, is called curable; he who is sick hopelessly, incurable; but he who is already whole does not need a physician. The Physician, then, who had come to cure, saw that he was curable, because there was no guile in him. How was guile not in him, if he is a sinner? He confesses that he is a sinner. For if he is a sinner, and says that he is a just man, there is guile in his mouth. Therefore in Nathanael He praised the confession of sin, He did not judge that he was not a sinner.

19. Wherefore, when the Pharisees, who seemed righteous to themselves, blamed the Lord, because, as physician, he mixed with

---

[1] 1 Cor. i. 20-28.

[2] Ps. xi. 3.

the sick, and when they said, "Behold with whom he eats, with publicans and sinners," the Physician replied to the madmen, "They that are whole need not a physician, but they that are sick: I came not to call the righteous, but sinners."[1] That is to say, because you call yourselves righteous when you are sinners, because you judge yourselves to be whole when you are languishing, you put away from you the medicine, and do not hold fast health. Hence that Pharisee who had asked the Lord to dinner, was whole in his own eyes; but that sick woman rushed into the house to which she had not been invited, and, made impudent by the desire of health, approached not the head of the Lord, nor the hands, but the feet; washed them with tears, wiped them with her hair, kissed them, anointed them with ointment,—made peace, sinner as she was, with the footprints of the Lord. The Pharisee who sat at meat there, as though whole himself, blamed the Physician, and said within himself, "This man, if he were a prophet, would have known what woman touched his feet." He suspected that He knew not, because He did not repulse her to prevent His being touched with unclean hands; but He did know, He permitted Himself to be touched, that the touch itself might heal. The Lord, seeing the heart of the Pharisee, put forth a parable: "There was a certain creditor, which had two debtors; the one owed five hundred denars, and the other fifty; and when they had nothing to pay, he frankly forgave them both. Which of them loved him most?" He answered, "I suppose, Lord, he to whom he forgave most." And turning to the woman, He said unto Simon, "Seest thou this woman? I entered into thine house, thou gavest me no water for my feet; but she hath washed my feet with tears, and wiped them with the hairs of her head: thou gavest me no kiss; she hath not ceased to kiss my feet: thou gavest me no oil; she hath anointed my feet with ointment. Wherefore, I say unto thee, to her are forgiven many sins, for she loved much; but to whom little is forgiven, the same loveth little."[2] That is to say, thou art more sick, but thou thinkest thyself whole; thou thinkest that little is forgiven thee when thou owest more. Well did she, because guile was not in her, deserve medicine. What means, guile was not in her? She confessed her sins. This He also praises in Nathanael, that guile was not in him; for many Pharisees who abounded in sins said that they were righteous, and brought guile with

them, which made it impossible for them to be healed.

20. Jesus then saw this man in whom was no guile, and said, "Behold an Israelite indeed, in whom is no guile." Nathanael saith unto Him, "Whence knowest Thou me?" Jesus answered and said, "Before that Philip called thee, when thou wast under the fig (that is, under the fig-tree), I saw thee." Nathanael answered and said unto Him, "Rabbi, Thou art the Son of God; Thou art the King of Israel." Some great thing Nathanael may have understood in the saying, "When thou wast under the fig-tree, I saw thee, before that Philip called thee;" for his words, "Thou art the Son of God, Thou art the King of Israel," were not dissimilar to those of Peter so long afterwards, when the Lord said unto him, "Blessed art thou, Simon Barjona, for flesh and blood hath not revealed it unto thee, but my Father which is in heaven." And there He named the rock, and praised the strength of the Church's support in this faith. Here already Nathanael says, "Thou art the Son of God; Thou art the King of Israel." Wherefore? Because it was said to him, "Before that Philip called thee, when thou wast under the fig-tree, I saw thee."

21. We must inquire whether this fig-tree signifies anything. Listen, my brethren. We find the fig-tree cursed because it had leaves only, and not fruit.[3] In the beginning of the human race, when Adam and Eve had sinned, they made themselves girdles of fig leaves.[4] Fig leaves then signify sins. Nathanael then was under the fig-tree, as it were under the shadow of death. The Lord saw him, he concerning whom it was said, "They that sat under the shadow of death, unto them hath light arisen."[5] What then was said to Nathanael? Thou sayest to me, O Nathanael, "Whence knowest thou me?" Even now thou speakest to me, because Philip called thee. He whom an apostle had already called, He perceived to belong to His Church. O thou Church, O thou Israel, in whom is no guile! if thou art the people, Israel, in whom is no guile, thou hast even now known Christ by His apostles, as Nathanael knew Christ by Philip. But His compassion beheld thee before thou knewest Him, when thou wert lying under sin. For did we first seek Christ, and not He seek us? Did we come sick to the Physician, and not the Physician to the sick? Was not that sheep lost, and did not the shepherd, leaving the ninety and nine in the wilderness, seek and find it, and joyfully

---

[1] Matt. xi. 11-13.   [2] Luke vii. 36-47.   [3] Matt. xx. 19.   [4] Gen. iii. 7.   [5] Isa. ix. 2.

carry it back on his shoulders? Was not that piece of money lost, and the woman lighted the lamp, and searched in the whole house until she found it? And when she had found it, "Rejoice with me," she said to her neighbors, "for I have found the piece of money which I lost."[1] In like manner were we lost as the sheep, lost as the piece of money; and our Shepherd found the sheep, but sought the sheep; the woman found the piece of money, but sought the piece of money. What is the woman? The flesh of Christ. What is the lamp? "I have prepared a lamp for my Christ."[2] Therefore were we sought that we might be found; having been found, we speak. Let us not be proud, for before we were found we were lost, if we had not been sought. Let them then not say to us whom we love, and whom we desire to gain to the peace of the Catholic Church, "What do you wish with us? Why seek you us if we are sinners?" We seek you for this reason that you perish not: we seek you because we were sought; we wish to find you because we have been found.

22. When, then, Nathanael had said, "Whence knowest Thou me?" the Lord said to him, "Before that Philip called thee, when thou wast under the fig-tree, I saw thee." O thou Israel without guile, whosoever thou art; O people living by faith, before I called thee by my apostles, when thou wast under the shadow of death, and thou sawest not me, I saw thee. The Lord then says to him, "Because I said unto thee, I saw thee under the fig-tree, thou believest: thou shalt see a greater thing than these." What is this, thou shalt see a greater thing than these? And He saith unto him, "Verily, verily, I say unto you, ye shall see heaven open, and angels ascending and descending upon the Son of man." Brethren, this is something greater than "under the fig-tree I saw thee." For it is more that the Lord justified us when called than that He saw us lying under the shadow of death. For what profit would it have been to us if we had remained where He saw us? Should we not be lying there? What is this greater thing? When have we seen angels ascending and descending upon the Son of man?

23. Already on a former occasion I have spoken of these ascending and descending angels; but lest you should have forgotten, I shall speak of the latter briefly by way of recalling it to your recollection. I should use more words if I were introducing, not recalling the subject. Jacob saw a ladder in a dream; and on a ladder he saw angels ascending and descending: and he anointed the stone which he had placed at his head.[3] You have heard that the Messias is Christ; you have heard that Christ is the Anointed. For Jacob did not place the stone, the anointed stone, that he might come and adore it: otherwise that would have been idolatry, not a pointing out of Christ. What was done was a pointing out of Christ, so far as it behoved such a pointing out to be made, and it was Christ that was pointed out. A stone was anointed, but not for an idol. A stone anointed; why a stone? "Behold, I lay in Zion a stone, elect, precious: and he that believeth on Him shall not be confounded."[4] Why anointed? Because Christus comes from chrisma. But what saw he then on the ladder? Ascending and descending angels. So it is the Church, brethren: the angels of God are good preachers, preaching Christ; this is the meaning of, "they ascend and descend upon the Son of man." How do they ascend, and how do they descend? In one case we have an example; listen to the Apostle Paul. What we find in him, let us believe regarding the other preachers of the truth. Behold Paul ascending: "I know a man in Christ fourteen years ago was caught up into the third heaven (whether in the body, or whether out of the body, I cannot tell: God knoweth), and that he heard unspeakable words, which it is not lawful for a man to utter."[5] You have heard him ascending, hear him descending: "I could not speak unto you as unto spiritual, but as unto carnal; as babes in Christ I have fed you with milk, not with meat."[6] Behold he descended who had ascended. Ask whether he ascended to the third heaven. Ask whether he descended to give milk to babes. Hear that he descended: "I became a babe in the midst of you, even as a nurse cherisheth her children."[7] For we see both nurses and mothers descend to babes, and although they be able to speak Latin, they shorten the words, shake their tongues in a certain manner, in order to frame childish endearments from a methodical language; because if they speak according to rule, the infant does not understand nor profit. And if there be a father well skilled in speaking, and such an orator that the forum resounds with his eloquence, and the judgment-seats shake, if he have a little son, on his return home he puts aside the forensic eloquence to which he had ascended, and in child's language descends to his little one. Hear in one place the

---

[1] Luke xv. 4-10. [2] Ps. cxxxii. 17. [3] Gen. xxviii. 12-18. [4] Isa. xxviii. 16; 1 Pet. ii. 6. [5] 2 Cor. xii. 2-4. [6] 1 Cor. iii. 1, 2. [7] 1 Thess. ii. 7.

apostle himself ascending and descending in the same sentence: " For whether," says he, " we be beside ourselves, it is to God; or whether we be sober, it is for your cause."[1] What is " we are beside ourselves"? That we see those things which it is not lawful for a man to speak. What is " we are sober for your cause? Have I judged myself to know anything among you, save Jesus Christ and Him crucified?" If the Lord Himself ascended and descended, it is evident that His preachers ascend by imitation. descend by preaching.

24. And if we have detained you somewhat longer than is our wont, the design was that the dangerous hours might pass: we imagine that those people have now brought their vanity to a close. But let us, brethren, having fed upon the feasts of salvation, do what remains, that we may in a religious manner fill up the Lord's day with spiritual joys, and compare the joys of verity with the joys of vanity;[2] and if we are horrified, let us grieve; if we grieve, let us pray; if we pray, may we be heard; if we are heard, we gain them also.

[1] 2 Cor. v. 13.

[2] [The heathen spectacles.]

TRACTATE VIII.

CHAPTER II. 1–4.

1. THE miracle indeed of our Lord Jesus Christ, whereby He made the water into wine, is not marvellous to those who know that it was God's doing. For He who made wine on that day at the marriage feast, in those six water-pots, which He commanded to be filled with water, the self-same does this every year in vines. For even as that which the servants put into the water-pots was turned into wine by the doing of the Lord, so in like manner also is what the clouds pour forth changed into wine by the doing of the same Lord. But we do not wonder at the latter, because it happens every year: it has lost its marvellousness by its constant recurrence. And yet it suggests a greater consideration than that which was done in the water-pots. For who is there that considers the works of God, whereby this whole world is governed and regulated, who is not amazed and overwhelmed with miracles? If he considers the vigorous power of a single grain of any seed whatever, it is a mighty thing, it inspires him with awe. But since men, intent on a different matter, have lost the consideration of the works of God, by which they should daily praise Him as the Creator, God has, as it were, reserved to Himself the doing of certain extraordinary actions, that, by striking them with wonder, He might rouse men as from sleep to worship Him. A dead man has risen again; men marvel: so many are born daily, and none marvels. If we reflect more considerately, it is a matter of greater wonder for one to be who was not before, than for one who was to come to life again. Yet the same God, the Father of our Lord Jesus Christ, doeth by His word all these things; and it is He who created that governs also. The former miracles He did by His Word, God with Himself; the latter miracles He did by the same Word incarnate, and for us made man. As we wonder at the things which were done by the man Jesus, so let us wonder at the things which where done by Jesus God. By Jesus God were made heaven, and earth, and the sea, all the garniture of heaven, the abounding riches of the earth, and the fruitfulness of the sea;—all these things which lie within the reach of our eyes were made by Jesus God. And we look at these things, and if His own spirit is in us they in such manner please us, that we praise Him that contrived them; not in such manner that turning ourselves to the works we turn away from the Maker, and, in a manner, turning our face to the things made and our backs to Him that made them.

2. And these things indeed we see; they lie before our eyes. But what of those we do not see, as angels, virtues, powers, dominions, and every inhabitant of this fabric which is above the heavens, and beyond the reach of our eyes? Yet angels, too, when necessary, often showed themselves to men. Has not God made all these too by His Word, that is, by His only Son, our Lord Jesus Christ? What of the human soul itself, which is not seen, and yet by its works shown in the flesh excites great admiration in those that duly reflect on them,—by whom was it made, unless by God? And through whom

was it made, unless through the Son of God? Not to speak as yet of the soul of man: the soul of any brute whatever, see how it regulates the huge body, puts forth the senses, the eyes to see, the ears to hear, the nostrils to smell, the taste to discern flavors,—the members, in short, to execute their respective functions! Is it the body, not the soul, namely the inhabitant of the body, that doeth these things? The soul is not apparent to the eyes, nevertheless it excites admiration by these its actions. Direct now thy consideration to the soul of man, on which God has bestowed understanding to know its Creator, to discern and distinguish between good and evil, that is, between right and wrong: see how many things it does through the body! Observe this whole world arranged in the same human commonwealth, with what administrations, with what orderly degrees of authority, with what conditions of citizenship, with what laws, manners, arts! The whole of this is brought about by the soul, and yet this power of the soul is not visible. When withdrawn from the body, the latter is a mere carcase: first, it in a manner preserves it from rottenness. For all flesh is corruptible, and falls off into putridity unless preserved by the soul as by a kind of seasoning. But the human soul has this quality in common with the soul of the brute; those qualities rather are to be admired which I have stated, such as belong to the mind and intellect, wherein also it is renewed after the image of its Creator, after whose image man was formed.[1] What will this power of the soul be when this body shall have put on incorruption, and this mortal shall have put on immortality?[2] If such is its power, acting through corruptible flesh, what shall be its power through a spiritual body, after the resurrection of the dead? Yet this soul, as I have said, of admirable nature and substance, is a thing invisible, intellectual; this soul also was made by God Jesus, for He is the Word of God. "All things were made by Him, and without Him was nothing made."

3. When we see, therefore, such deeds wrought by Jesus God, why should we wonder at water being turned into wine by the man Jesus? For He was not made man in such manner that He lost His being God. Man was added to Him, God not lost to Him. This miracle was wrought by the same who made all those things Let us not therefore wonder that God did it, but love Him because He did it in our midst, and for the purpose of our restoration. For He gives us certain intimations by the very circumstances of the case. I suppose that it was not without cause He came to the marriage. The miracle apart, there lies something mysterious and sacramental in the very fact. Let us knock, that He may open to us, and fill us with the invisible wine: for we were water, and He made us wine, made us wise; for He gave us the wisdom of His faith, whilst before we were foolish. And it appertains, it may be, to this wisdom, together with the honor of God, and with the praise of His majesty, and with the charity of His most powerful mercy, to understand what was done in this miracle.

4. The Lord, on being invited, came to the marriage. What wonder if He came to that house to a marriage, having come into this world to a marriage? For, indeed, if He came not to a marriage, He has not here a bride. But what says the apostle? "I have espoused you to one husband, to present you a chaste virgin to Christ." Why does he fear lest the virginity of Christ's bride should be corrupted by the subtilty of the devil? "I fear," saith he, "lest as the serpent beguiled Eve by his subtilty, so also your minds should be corrupted from the simplicity and chastity which is in Christ."[3] Thus has He here a bride whom He has redeemed by His blood, and to whom He has given the Holy Spirit as a pledge. He has freed her from the bondage of the devil: He died for her sins, and is risen again for her justification.[4] Who will make such offerings to his bride? Men may offer to a bride every sort of earthly ornament, —gold, silver, precious stones, houses, slaves, estates, farms,—but will any give his own blood? For if one should give his own blood to his bride, he would not live to take her for his wife. But the Lord, dying without fear, gave His own blood for her, whom rising again He was to have, whom He had already united to Himself in the Virgin's womb. For the Word was the Bridegroom, and human flesh the bride; and both one, the Son of God, the same also being Son of man. The womb of the Virgin Mary, in which He became head of the Church, was His bridal chamber: thence He came forth, as a bridegroom from his chamber, as the Scripture foretold, "And rejoiced as a giant to run his way." From His chamber He came forth as a bridegroom; and being invited, came to the marriage.

5. It is because of an indubitable mystery that He appears not to acknowledge His mother, from whom as the Bridegroom He came forth, when He says to her, "Woman, what have I to do with thee? mine hour is

[1] Col. iii. 10.   [2] 1 Cor. xv. 54.   [3] 2 Cor. xi. 3.   [4] Rom. iv. 25.   [5] Ps. xix. 5.

not yet come." What is this? Did He come to the marriage for the purpose of teaching men to treat their mothers with contempt? Surely he to whose marriage He had come was taking a wife with the view of having children, and surely he wished to be honored by those children he would beget: had Jesus then come to the marriage in order to dishonor His mother, when marriages are celebrated and wives married with the view of having children, whom God commands to honor their parents? Beyond all doubt, brethren, there is some mystery lurking here. It is really a matter of such importance that some,—of whom the apostle, as we have mentioned before, has forewarned us to be on our guard, saying, "I fear, lest, as the serpent beguiled Eve by his subtilty, so also your minds should be corrupted from the simplicity and chastity which is in Christ,"—taking away from the credibility of the gospel, and asserting that Jesus was not born of the Virgin Mary, used to endeavor to draw from this place an argument in support of their error, so far as to say, How could she be His mother, to whom He said, "Woman, what have I to do with thee?" Wherefore we must answer them, and show them why the Lord said this, lest in their insanity they appear to themselves to have discovered something contrary to wholesome belief, whereby the chastity of the virgin bride may be corrupted, that is, whereby the faith of the Church may be injured. For in very deed, brethren, their faith is corrupted who prefer a lie to the truth. For these men, who appear to honor Christ in such wise as to deny that He had flesh, do nothing short of proclaiming Him a liar. Now they who build up a lie in men, what do they but drive the truth out of them? They let in the devil, they drive Christ out; they let in an adulterer, shut out the bridegroom, being evidently paranymphs, or rather, the panderers of the serpent. For it is for this object they speak, that the serpent may possess, and Christ be shut out. How doth the serpent possess? When a lie possesses. When falsehood possesses, then the serpent possesses; when truth possesses, then Christ possesses. For Himself has said, "I am the truth;"[1] but of that other He said, "He stood not in the truth, because the truth is not in him."[2] And Christ is the truth in such wise that thou shouldst receive the whole to be true in Him. The true Word, God equal with the Father, true soul, true flesh, true man, true God, true nativity, true passion, true death, true resurrection. If thou say that any of

these is false, rottenness enters, the worms of falsehood are bred of the poison of the serpent, and nothing sound will remain.

6. What, then, is this, saith one, which the Lord saith, "Woman, what have I to do with thee?" Perhaps the Lord shows us in the sequel why He said this: "Mine hour," saith He, "is not yet come." For thus is how He saith, "Woman, what have I to do with thee? mine hour is not yet come." And we must seek to know why this was said. But first let us therefrom withstand the heretics. What says the old serpent, of old the hissing instiller of poison? What saith he? That Jesus had not a woman for His mother. Whence provest thou that? From this, saith he, because Jesus said, "Woman, what have I to do with thee?" Who has related this, that we should believe that Jesus said it? Who has related it? None other than John the evangelist. But the same John the evangelist said, "And the mother of Jesus was there." For this is how he has told us: "The next day there was a marriage in Cana of Galilee, and the mother of Jesus was there. And having been invited to the marriage, Jesus had come thither with His disciples." We have here two sayings uttered by the evangelist. "The mother of Jesus was there," said the evangelist; and it is the same evangelist that has told us what Jesus said to His mother. And see, brethren, how he has told us that Jesus answered His *mother*, having said first, "His mother said unto Him," in order that you may keep the virginity of your heart secure against the tongue of the serpent. Here we are told in the same Gospel, the record of the same evangelist, "The mother of Jesus was there," and "His mother said unto Him." Who related this? John the evangelist. And what said Jesus in answer to His mother? "Woman, what have I to do with thee? Who relates this? The very same Evangelist John. O most faithful and truth-speaking evangelist, thou tellest me that Jesus said, "Woman, what have I to do with thee?" why hast thou added His mother, whom He does not acknowledge? For thou hast said that "the mother of Jesus was there," and that "His mother said unto Him;" why didst thou not rather say, Mary was there, and Mary said unto Him. Thou tellest us these two facts, "His mother said unto Him," and, "Jesus answered her, Woman, why have I to do with thee?" Why doest thou this, if it be not because both are true? Now, those men are willing to believe the evangelist in the one case, when he tells us that Jesus said to His mother, "Woman, what have I to do with thee?" and yet they

[1] John xiv. 6.   [2] John viii. 44.

will not believe him in the other, when he says, "The mother of Jesus was there," and "His mother said unto Him." But who is he that resisteth the serpent and holds fast the truth, whose virginity of heart is not corrupted by the subtilty of the devil? He who believes both to be true, namely, that the mother of Jesus was there, and that Jesus made that answer to His mother. But if he does not as yet understand in what manner Jesus said, "Woman, what have I to do with thee?" let him meanwhile believe that He said it, and said it, moreover, to His mother. Let him first have the piety to believe, and he will then have fruit in understanding.

7. I ask you, O faithful Christians, Was the mother of Jesus there? Answer ye, She was. Whence know you? Answer, The Gospel says it. What answer made Jesus to His mother? Answer ye, "Woman, what have I to do with thee? mine hour is not yet come." And whence know you this? Answer, The Gospel says it. Let no man corrupt this your faith, if you desire to preserve a chaste virginity for the Bridegroom. But if it be asked of you, why He made this answer to His mother, let him declare who understands; but he who does not as yet understand, let him most firmly believe that Jesus made this answer, and made it moreover to His mother. By this piety he will learn to understand also why Jesus answered thus, if by praying he knock at the door of truth, and do not approach it with wrangling. Only this much, while he fancies himself to know, or is ashamed because he does not know, why Jesus answered thus, let him beware lest he be constrained to believe either that the evangelist lied when he said, "The mother of Jesus was there," or that Jesus Himself suffered for our sins by a counterfeit death, and for our justification showed counterfeit scars; and that He spoke falsely in saying, "If ye continue in my word, ye are my disciples indeed; and ye shall know the truth, and the truth shall make you free."[1] For if He had a false mother, false flesh, false death, false wounds in His death, false scars in His resurrection, then it will not be the truth, but rather falsehood, that shall make free those that believe on Him. Nay, on the contrary, let falsehood yield to truth, and let all be confounded who would have themselves be accounted truthspeaking, because they endeavor to prove Christ a deceiver, and will not have it said to them, We do not believe you because you lie, when they affirm that truth itself has lied. Nevertheless, if we ask them,

Whence know you that Christ said, "Woman, what have I to do with thee?" they answer that they believe the Gospel. Then why do they not believe the Gospel when it says, "The mother of Jesus was there," and, "His mother said unto Him"? Or if the Gospel lies here, how are we to believe it there, that Jesus said this, "Woman, what have I to do with thee?" Why do not those miserable men rather faithfully believe that the Lord did so answer, not to a stranger, but to His mother; and also piously seek to know why He did so answer? There is a great difference between him who says, I would know why Christ made this answer to His mother, and him who says, I know that it was not to His mother that Christ made this answer. It is one thing to be willing to understand what is shut up, another thing to be unwilling to believe what is open. He who says, I would know why Christ thus made answer to His mother, wishes the Gospel, in which he believes, opened up to him; but he who says, I know that it was not to His mother that Christ made this answer, accuses of falsehood the very Gospel, wherein he believed that Christ did so answer.

8. Now then, if it seem good, brethren, those men being repulsed, and ever wandering in their own blindness, unless in humility they be healed, let us inquire why our Lord answered His mother in such a manner. He was in an extraordinary manner begotten of the Father without a mother, born of a mother without a father; without a mother He was God, without a father He was man; without a mother before all time, without a father in the end of times. What He said was said in answer to His mother, for "the mother of Jesus was there," and "His mother said unto Him." All this the Gospel says. It is there we learn that "the mother of Jesus was there," just where we learn that He said unto her, "Woman, what have I to do with thee? mine hour is not yet come." Let us believe the whole; and what we do not yet understand, let us search out. And first take care, lest perhaps, as the Manichæans found occasion for their falsehood, because the Lord said, "Woman, what have I to do with thee?" the astrologers in like manner may find occasion for their deception, in that He said, "Mine hour is not yet come." If it was in the sense of the astrologers He said this, we have committed a sacrilege in burning their books. But if we have acted rightly, as was done in the times of the apostles,[2] it was not according to their notion that the Lord said, "Mine

hour is not yet come." For, say those vain-talkers and deceived seducers, thou seest that Christ was under fate, as He says, "Mine hour is not yet come." To whom then must we make answer first—to the heretics or to the astrologers? For both come of the serpent, and desire to corrupt the Church's virginity of heart, which she holds in undefiled faith. Let us first reply to those whom we proposed, to whom, indeed, we have already replied in great measure. But lest they should think that we have not what to say of the words which the Lord uttered in answer to His mother, we prepare you further against them; for I suppose what has already been said is sufficient for their refutation.

9. Why, then, said the Son to the mother, "Woman, what have I to do with thee? mine hour is not yet come?" Our Lord Jesus Christ was both God and man. According as He was God, He had not a mother; according as He was man, He had. She was the mother, then, of His flesh, of His humanity, of the weakness which for our sakes He took upon Him. But the miracle which He was about to do, He was about to do according to His divine nature, not according to His weakness; according to that wherein He was God, not according to that wherein He was born weak. But the weakness of God is stronger than men.[1] His mother then demanded a miracle of Him; but He, about to perform divine works, so far did not recognize a human womb; saying in effect, "That in me which works a miracle was not born of thee, thou gavest not birth to my divine nature; but because my weakness was born of thee, I will recognize thee at the time when that same weakness shall hang upon the cross." This, indeed, is the meaning of "Mine hour is not yet come." For then it was that He recognized, who, in truth, always did know. He knew His mother in predestination, even before He was born of her; even before, as God, He created her of whom, as man, He was to be created, He knew her as His mother: but at a certain hour in a mystery He did not recognize her; and at a certain hour which had not yet come, again in a mystery, He does recognize her. For then did He recognize her, when that to which she gave birth was a-dying. That by which Mary was made did not die, but that which was made of Mary; not the eternity of the divine nature, but the weakness of the flesh, was dying. He made that answer therefore, making a distinction in the faith of believers, between the *who*, and the *how*, He came.

For while He was God and the Lord of heaven and earth, He came by a mother who was a woman. In that He was Lord of the world, Lord of heaven and earth, He was, of course, the Lord of Mary also; but in that wherein it is said, "Made of a woman, made under the law," He was Mary's son. The same both the Lord of Mary and the son of Mary; the same both the Creator of Mary and created from Mary. Marvel not that He was both son and Lord. For just as He is called the son of Mary, so likewise is He called the son of David; and son of David because son of Mary. Hear the apostle openly declaring, "Who was made of the seed of David according to the flesh." [2] Hear Him also declared the Lord of David; let David himself declare this: "The Lord said to my Lord, Sit Thou on my right hand." [3] And this passage Jesus Himself brought forward to the Jews, and refuted them from it.[4] How then was He both David's son and David's Lord? David's son according to the flesh, David's Lord according to His divinity; so also Mary's son after the flesh, and Mary's Lord after His majesty. Now as she was not the mother of His divine nature, whilst it was by His divinity the miracle she asked for would be wrought, therefore He answered her, "Woman, what have I to do with thee?" But think not that I deny thee to be my mother: "Mine hour is not yet come;" for in that hour I will acknowledge thee, when the weakness of which thou art the mother comes to hang on the cross. Let us prove the truth of this. When the Lord suffered, the same evangelist tells us, who knew the mother of the Lord, and who has given us to know about her in this marriage feast,—the same, I say, tells us, "There was there near the cross the mother of Jesus; and Jesus saith to His mother, Woman, behold thy son! and to the disciple, Behold thy mother!" [5] He commends His mother to the care of the disciple; commends His mother, as about to die before her, and to rise again before her death. The man commends her a human being to man's care. This humanity had Mary given birth to. That hour had now come, the hour of which He had then said, "Mine hour is not yet come."

10. In my opinion, brethren, we have answered the heretics. Let us now answer the astrologers. And how do they attempt to prove that Jesus was under fate? Because, say they, Himself said, "Mine hour is not yet come." Therefore we believe Him; and if He had said, "I have no hour," He would

[1] 1 Cor. i. 25.

[2] Rom. i. 3.
[3] Ps. cx. 1.
[4] Matt. xxii. 45.
[5] John xix. 25, 27.

have excluded the astrologers: but behold, say they, He said, "Mine hour is not yet come." If then He had said, "I have no hour," the astrologers would have been shut out, and would have no ground for their slander; but now that He said, "Mine hour is not yet come," how can we contradict His own words? 'Tis wonderful that the astrologers, by believing Christ's words, endeavor to convince Christians that Christ lived under an hour of fate. Well, let them believe Christ when He saith, "I have power to lay down my life and to take it up again: no man taketh it from me, but I lay it down of myself, and I take it again."[1] Is this power then under fate? Let them show us a man who has it in his power when to die, how long to live: this they can never do. Let them, therefore, believe God when He says, "I have power to lay down my life, and to take it up again;" and let them inquire why it was said, "Mine hour is not yet come;" and let them not, because of these words, be imposing fate on the Maker of heaven, the Creator and Ruler of the stars. For even if fate were from the stars, the Maker of the stars could not be subject to their destiny. Moreover, not only Christ had not what thou callest fate, but not even hast thou, or I, or he there, or any human being whatsoever.

11. Nevertheless, being deceived, they deceive others, and propound fallacies to men. They lay snares to catch men, and that, too, in the open streets. They who spread nets to catch wild beasts even do it in woods and desert places: how miserably vain are men, for catching whom the net is spread in the forum! When men sell themselves to men, they receive money; but these give money in order to sell themselves to vanities. For they go in to an astrologer to buy themselves masters, such as the astrologer is pleased to give them: be it Saturn, Jupiter, Mercury, or any other named profanity. The man went in free, that having given his money he might come out a slave. Nay, rather, had he been free he would not have gone in; but he entered whither his master Error and his mistress Avarice dragged him. Whence also the truth says, "Every one that doeth sin is the slave of sin."[2]

12. Why then did He say, "Mine hour is not yet come?" Rather because, having it in His power when to die, He did not yet see it fit to use that power. Just as we, brethren, say, for example, "Now is the appointed hour for us to go out to celebrate the sacraments." If we go out before it is necessary,

do we not act perversely and absurdly? And because we act only at the proper time, do we therefore in this action regard fate when we so express ourselves? What means then, "Mine hour is not yet come?" When I know that it is the fitting time for me to suffer, when my suffering will be profitable, then I will willingly suffer. That hour is not yet: that thou mayest preserve both, this, "Mine hour is not yet come;" and that, "I have power to lay down my life, and power to take it again." He had come, then, having it in His power when to die. And surely it would not have been right were He to die before He had chosen disciples. Had he been a man who had not his hour in his own power, he might have died before he had chosen disciples; and if haply he had died when his disciples were now chosen and instructed, it would be something conferred on him, not his own doing. But, on the contrary, He who had come having in His power when to go, when to return, how far to advance, and for whom the regions of the grave were open, not only when dying but when rising again; He, I say, in order to show us His Church's hope of immortality, showed in the head what it behoved the members to expect. For He who has risen again in the head will also rise again in all His members. The hour then had not yet come, the fit time was not yet. Disciples had to be called, the kingdom of heaven to be proclaimed, the Lord's divinity to be shown forth in miracles, and His humanity in His very sympathy with mortal men. For He who hungered because He was man, fed so many thousands with five loaves because He was God; He who slept because He was man, commanded the winds and the waves because He was God. All these things had first to be set forth, that the evangelists might have whereof to write, that there might be what should be preached to the Church. But when He had done as much as He judged to be sufficient, then His hour came, not of necessity, but of will,—not of condition, but of power.

13. What then, brethren? Because we have replied to these and those, shall we say nothing as to what the water-pots signify? what the water turned into wine? what the master of the feast? what the bridegroom? what in mystery the mother of Jesus? what the marriage itself? We must speak of all these, but we must not burden you. I would have preached to you in Christ's name yesterday also, when the usual sermon was due to you, my beloved, but I was hindered by certain necessities. If you please then, holy brethren, let us defer until to-morrow what

---

1 John x. 18   2 John viii. 34.

pertains to the hidden meaning of this translation, and not burden both your and our own weakness. There are many of you, perhaps, who have to-day come together on account of the solemnity of the day, not to hear the sermon. Let those who come to-morrow come to hear, so that we may not defraud those who are eager to learn, nor burden those who are fastidious.

TRACTATE IX.

CHAPTER II. 1–11.

1. MAY the Lord our God be present, that He may grant us to render you what we promised. For yesterday, if you remember, holy brethren, when the shortness of the time prevented us from completing the sermon we had begun, we put off until to-day the unfolding, by God's assistance, of those things which are mystically put in hidden meanings in this fact of the Gospel lesson. We need not, therefore, now stay any longer to commend the miracle of God. For He is the same God who, throughout the whole creation, worketh miracles every day, which become lightly esteemed by men, not because of the ease with which they are wrought, but by reason of their constant recurrence. Those uncommon works, however, which were done by the same Lord—that is, by the Word for us made flesh—occasioned greater astonishment to men, not because they are greater than those which He daily performs in the creation, but because these which happen every day are accomplished as it were in the course of nature; but the others appear exhibited to the eyes of men, wrought by the efficacy of a power, as it were, immediately present. We said, as you remember, one dead man rose again, people were amazed, whilst no man wonders at the birth every day of those who were not in being. In like manner, who does not wonder at water turned into wine, although God is doing this every year in vines? But since all the works which the Lord Jesus did, serve not only to rouse our hearts by their miraculous character, but also to edify our hearts in the doctrine of faith, it behoves us thoroughly to examine into the meaning and significance of those works. For the consideration of the meaning of all these things we deferred, as you remember, till to-day.

2. The Lord, in that He came to the marriage to which He was invited, wished, apart from the mystical signification, to assure us that marriage was His own institution. For there were to be those of whom the apostle spoke, " forbidding to marry," [1] and asserting that marriage was an evil, and of the devil's institution: notwithstanding the same Lord declares in the Gospel, on being asked whether it be lawful for a man to put away his wife for any cause, that it is not lawful save for the cause of fornication. In His answer, if you remember, He said, " What God hath joined together let not man put asunder." [2] And they that are well instructed in the catholic faith know that God instituted marriage; and as the union of man and wife is from God, so divorce is from the devil. But in the case of fornication it is lawful for a man to put away his wife, because she first chose to be no longer wife in not preserving conjugal fidelity to her husband. Nor are those women who vow virginity to God, although they hold a higher place of honor and sanctity in the Church, without marriage. For they too, together with the whole Church, attain to a marriage, a marriage in which Christ is the Bridegroom. And for this cause, therefore, did the Lord, on being invited, come to the marriage, to confirm conjugal chastity, and to show forth the sacrament of marriage. For the bridegroom in that marriage, to whom it was said, " Thou hast kept the good wine until now," represented the person of the Lord. For the good wine—namely, the gospel—Christ has kept until now.

3. For now let us begin to uncover the hidden meanings of the mysteries, so far as He in whose name we made you the promise may enable us. In the ancient times there was prophecy, and no times were left without the dispensation of prophecy. But the prophecy, since Christ was not understood therein, was water. For in water wine is in some manner latent. The apostle tells us what we are to understand by this water: " Even unto this day," saith he, " whilst

---

[1] 1 Tim. iv. 3.   [2] Matt. xix. 6.

Moses is read, that same veil is upon their heart; that it is not unveiled because it is done away in Christ. And when thou shalt have passed over," saith he, "to the Lord, the veil shall be taken away."[1] By the veil he means the covering over of prophecy, so that it was not understood. When thou hast passed over to the Lord, the veil is taken away; so likewise is tastelessness taken away when thou hast passed over to the Lord; and what was water now becomes wine to thee. Read all the prophetic books; and if Christ be not understood therein, what canst thou find so insipid and silly? Understand Christ in them, and what thou readest not only has a taste, but even inebriates thee; transporting the mind from the body, so that forgetting the things that are past, thou reachest forth to the things that are before.[2]

4. Wherefore, prophecy from ancient times, even from the time when the series of human births began to run onwards, was not silent concerning Christ; but the import of the prophecy was concealed therein, for as yet it was water. Whence do we prove that in all former times, until the age in which the Lord came, prophecy did not fail concerning Him? From the Lord's own saying. For when He had risen from the dead, He found His disciples doubting concerning Himself whom they had followed. For they saw that He was dead, and they had no hope that He would rise again; all their hope was gone. On what ground was the thief, after receiving praise, deemed worthy to be that same day in Paradise? Because when bound on the cross he confessed Christ, while the disciples doubted concerning Him. Well, He found them wavering, and in a manner reproving themselves because they had looked for redemption in Him. Yet they sorrowed for Him as cut off without fault, for they knew Him to be innocent. And this is what the disciples themselves said, after His resurrection, when He had found certain of them in the way, sorrowful, "Art thou only a stranger in Jerusalem, and hast not known the things which are come to pass there in these days? And He said unto them, What things? And they said, Concerning Jesus of Nazareth, who was a prophet mighty in deeds and words before God and all the people: how our priests and rulers delivered Him to be condemned to death, and bound Him to the cross. But we trusted that it was He who should have redeemed Israel; and to-day is now the third day since these things were done." After one of the two whom He found in the way

going to a neighboring village had spoken these and other words, Jesus answered and said, "O irrational, and slow of heart to believe all that the prophets have spoken. Ought not Christ to have suffered all these things, and to enter into His glory? And beginning from Moses and all the prophets, He expounded unto them in all the Scriptures the things concerning Himself." And likewise, in another place, when He would even have His disciples touch Him with their hands, that they might believe that He had risen in the body, He saith, "These are the words which I have spoken unto you, while I was yet with you, that all things must be fulfilled which were written in the law of Moses, and in the prophets, and in the Psalms, concerning me. Then opened He their understanding, that they might understand the Scriptures, and said unto them, Thus it is written, that Christ should suffer, and rise again from the dead the third day: and that repentance and remission of sins should be preached in His name among all nations, beginning at Jerusalem."

5. When these words of the Gospel are understood, and they are certainly clear, all the mysteries which are latent in this miracle of the Lord will be laid open. Observe what He says, that it behoved the things to be fulfilled in Christ that were written of Him. Where were they written? "In the law," saith He, "and in the prophets, and in the Psalms." He omitted no part of the Old Scriptures. These were water; and hence the disciples were called *irrational* by the Lord, because as yet they tasted to them as water, not as wine. And how did He make of the water wine? When He opened their understanding, and expounded to them the Scriptures, beginning from Moses, through all the prophets; with which being now inebriated, they said, "Did not our hearts burn within us in the way, when He opened to us the Scriptures?" For they understood Christ in those books in which they knew Him not before. Thus our Lord Jesus Christ changed the water into wine, and that has now taste which before had not, that now inebriates which before did not. For if He had commanded the water to be poured out of the water-pots, and so Himself had put in the wine from the secret repositories of the creature, whence He made bread when He satisfied so many thousands; for five loaves were not in themselves sufficient to satisfy five thousand men, nor even to fill twelve baskets, but the omnipotence of the Lord was, as it were, a fountain of bread; so likewise He might, on the water being poured

---

[1] 2 Cor. iii. 14-16   [2] Phil. iii. 13.

out, have poured in wine: but had He done this, He would appear to have rejected the Old Scriptures. When, however, He turns the water itself into wine, He shows us that the Old Scripture also is from Himself, for at His own command were the water-pots filled. It is from the Lord, indeed, that the Old Scripture also is; but it has no taste unless Christ is understood therein.

6. But observe what Himself saith, "The things which were written in the law, and in the prophets, and in the Psalms concerning me." And we know that the law extends from the time of which we have record, that is, from the beginning of the world: "In the beginning God made the heaven and the earth."[1] Thence down to the time in which we are now living are six ages, this being the sixth, as you have often heard and know. The first age is reckoned from Adam to Noah; the second, from Noah to Abraham; and, as Matthew the evangelist duly follows and distinguishes, the third, from Abraham to David; the fourth, from David to the carrying away into Babylon; the fifth, from the carrying away into Babylon to John the Baptist;[2] the sixth, from John the Baptist to the end of the world. Moreover, God made man after His own image on the *sixth day*, because in this sixth age is manifested the renewing of our mind through the gospel, after the image of Him who created us;[3] and the water is turned into wine, that we may taste of Christ, now manifested in the law and the prophets. Hence "there were there six water-pots," which He bade be filled with water. Now the six water-pots signify the six ages, which were not without prophecy. And those six periods, divided and separated as it were by joints, would be as empty vessels unless they were filled by Christ. Why did I say, the periods which would run fruitlessly on, unless the Lord Jesus were preached in them? Prophecies are fulfilled, the water-pots are full; but that the water may be turned into wine, Christ must be understood in that whole prophecy.

7. But what means this: "They contained two or three metretæ apiece"? This phrase certainly conveys to us a mysterious meaning. For by "metretæ" he means certain measures, as if he should say jars, flasks, or something of that sort. *Metreta* is the name of a measure, and takes its name from the word "measure." For μέτρον is the Greek word for measure, whence the word "metretæ" is derived. "They contained," then, "two or three metretæ apiece." What are we to say, brethren? If He had simply said "three apiece," our mind would at once have run to the mystery of the Trinity. And, perhaps, we ought not at once to reject this application of the meaning, because He said, "two or three apiece;" for when the Father and Son are named, the Holy Spirit must necessarily be understood. For the Holy Spirit is not that of the Father only, nor of the Son only, but the Spirit of the Father and of the Son. For it is written, "If any man love the world, the Spirit of the Father is not in him."[4] And again, "Whoso hath not the Spirit of Christ is none of His."[5] The same, then, is the Spirit of the Father and of the Son. Therefore, the Father and the Son being named, the Holy Spirit also is understood, because He is the Spirit of the Father and of the Son. And when there is mention of the Father and Son, "two metretæ," as it were, are mentioned; but since the Holy Spirit is understood in them, "three metretæ." That is the reason why it is not said, "Some containing two metretæ apiece, others three apiece;" but the same six water-pots contained "two or three metretæ apiece." It is as if he had said, When I say two apiece, I would have the Spirit of the Father and of the Son to be understood together with them; and when I say three apiece, I declare the same Trinity more plainly.

8. Wherefore, whoso names the Father and the Son ought thereby to understand the mutual love of the Father and Son, which is the Holy Spirit. And perhaps the Scriptures on being examined (I do not say that I am able to show you this to-day, or as if another proof cannot be found),—nevertheless, the Scriptures, perhaps, on being searched, do show us that the Holy Spirit is charity. And do not count charity a thing cheap. How, indeed, can it be cheap, when all things that are said to be not cheap are called dear (*chara*)? Therefore, if what is not cheap is dear, what is dearer than dearness itself (*charitas*)? The apostle so commends charity to us that he says, "I show unto you a more excellent way. Though I speak with the tongues of men and of angels, and have not charity, I am become as sounding brass, or a tinkling cymbal. And though I know all mysteries and all knowledge, and have prophecy and all faith, so that I could remove mountains, and have not charity, I am nothing. And though I distribute all my goods to the poor, and give my body to be burned, and have not charity, it profiteth me nothing."[6] How great, then, is charity, which, if

---

[1] Gen. i. 1.　　[2] Matt. i. 17.　　[3] Col. iii. 10.　　[4] 1 John ii. 15.　　[5] Rom. viii. 9.　　[6] 1 Cor. xiii. 1-3.

wanting, in vain have we all things else; if present, rightly have we all things! Yet the Apostle Paul, setting forth the praise of charity with copiousness and fullness, has said less of it than did the Apostle John in brief, whose Gospel this is. For he has not hesitated to say, "God is love." It is also written, "Because the love of God is shed abroad in our hearts by the Holy Spirit which is given us."[1] Who, then, can name the Father and the Son without thereby understanding the love of the Father and Son? Which when one begins to have, he will have the Holy Spirit; which if one has not, he will not have the Holy Spirit. And just as thy body, if it be without spirit, namely thy soul, is dead; so likewise thy soul, if it be without the Holy Spirit, that is, without charity, will be reckoned dead. Therefore "The water-pots contained two metretæ apiece," because the Father and the Son are proclaimed in the prophecy of all the periods; but the Holy Spirit is there also, and therefore it is added, "or three apiece." "I and the Father," saith He, "are one."[2] But far be it from us to suppose that where we are told, "I and the Father are one," the Holy Spirit is not there. Yet since he named the Father and the Son, let the water-pots contain "two metretæ apiece;" but attend to this, "or three apiece." "Go, baptize the nations in the name of the Father, and of the Son, and of the Holy Ghost." So, therefore, when it says "two apiece," the Trinity is not expressed but understood; but when it says, "or three," the Trinity is expressed also.

9. But there is also another meaning that must not be passed over, and which I will declare: let every man choose which he likes best. We keep not back what is suggested to us. For it is the Lord's table, and the minister ought not to defraud the guests, especially when they hunger as you now do, so that your longing is manifest. Prophecy, which is dispensed from the ancient times, has for its object the salvation of all nations. True, Moses was sent to the people of Israel alone, and to that people alone was the law given by him; and the prophets, too, were of that people, and the very distribution of times was marked out according to the same people; whence also the water-pots are said to be "according to the purification of the Jews:" nevertheless, that the prophecy was proclaimed to all other nations also is manifest, forasmuch as Christ was concealed in him in whom all nations are blessed, as it was promised to Abraham by the Lord, saying, "In thy seed shall all nations be blessed."[3] But

this was not as yet understood, for as yet the water was not turned into wine. The prophecy therefore was dispensed to all nations. But that this may appear more agreeably, let us, so far as our time permits, mention certain facts respecting the several ages, as represented respectively by the water-pots.

10. In the very beginning, Adam and Eve were the parents of all nations, not of the Jews only; and whatever was represented in Adam concerning Christ, undoubtedly concerned all nations, whose salvation is in Christ. What better can I say of the water of the first water-pot than what the apostle says of Adam and Eve? For no man will say that I misunderstand the meaning when I produce, not my own, but the apostle's. How great a mystery, then, concerning Christ does that of which the apostle makes mention contain, when he says, "And the two shall be in one flesh: this is a great mystery!"[4] And lest any man should understand that greatness of mystery to exist in the case of the individual men that have wives, he says, "But I speak concerning Christ and the Church." What great mystery is this, "the two shall be one flesh?" While Scripture, in the Book of Genesis, was speaking of Adam and Eve, it came to these words, "Therefore shall a man leave his father and mother, and shall cleave to his wife; and they two shall be one flesh."[5] Now, if Christ cleave to the Church, so that the two should be one flesh, in what manner did He leave His Father and His mother? He left His Father in this sense, that when He was in the form of God, He thought it not robbery to be equal with God, but emptied Himself, taking to Him the form of a servant.[6] In this sense He left His Father, not that He forsook or departed from His Father, but that He did not appear unto men in that form in which He was equal with the Father. But how did He leave His mother? By leaving the synagogue of the Jews, of which, after the flesh, He was born, and by cleaving to the Church which He has gathered out of all nations. Thus the first water-pot then held a prophecy of Christ; but so long as these things of which I speak were not preached among the peoples, the prophecy was water, it was not yet changed into wine. And since the Lord has enlightened us through the apostle, to show us what we were in search of, by this one sentence, "The two shall be one flesh; a great mystery concerning Christ and the Church;" we are now permitted to seek Christ everywhere, and to drink wine from all the water-pots. Adam sleeps, that Eve may be formed; Christ dies, that the Church may

---

[1] Rom. v. 5.   [2] John x. 30.   [3] Gen. xxii. 18.   [4] Eph. iii. 31.   [5] Gen. ii. 24.   [6] Phil. ii. 6.

be formed. When Adam sleeps, Eve is formed from his side; when Christ is dead, the spear pierces His side, that the mysteries may flow forth whereby the Church is formed. Is it not evident to every man that in those things then done, things to come were foreshadowed, since the apostle says that Adam himself was the figure of Him that was to come? "Who is," saith he, "the figure of Him that was to come."[1] All was mystically prefigured. For, in reality, God could have taken the rib from Adam when he was awake, and formed the woman. Or was it, haply, necessary for him to sleep lest he should feel pain in his side when the rib was taken away? Who is there that sleeps so soundly that his bones may be torn from him without his awaking? Or was it because it was God that tore it out, that the man did not feel it? Well, He who could take it from him without pain when he was asleep, could do it also when he was awake. But, without doubt, the first water-pot was being filled, there was a dispensation of the prophecy of that time concerning this which was to be.

11. Christ was represented also in Noah, and in that ark of the whole world. For why were all kinds of animals shut in, in the ark, but to signify all nations? For God could again create every kind of animals. When as yet they were not, did He not say, "Let the earth bring forth," and the earth brought forth? From the same source He could make anew, whence He then made; by a word He made, by a word He could make again: were it not that He was setting before us a mystery, and filling up the second water-pot of prophetical dispensation, that the world might by the wood be delivered in a figure; because the life of the world was to be nailed on wood.

12. Now, in the third water-pot, to Abraham, as I have mentioned before, it was said, "In thy seed shall all nations be blessed." And who does not see whose figure Abraham's only son was, he who bore the wood for the sacrifice of himself, to that place whither he was being led to be offered up? For the Lord bore his own cross, as the Gospel tells us. This will be enough to say concerning the third water-pot.

13. But as to David, why do I say that his prophecy extends to all nations, when we have just heard the psalm (and it is difficult to mention a psalm in which the same is not sounded forth)? But certainly, as I have said, we have been just singing, "Arise, O God, judge the earth; for Thou shalt inherit among all nations."[2] And this is why the

Donatists are as men cast forth from the marriage: just as the man who had not a wedding garment was invited, and came, but was cast forth from the number of the guests because he had not the garment to the glory of the bridegroom; for he who seeks his own glory, not Christ's, has not the wedding garment: for they refuse to agree with him who was the friend of the Bridegroom, and says, "This is He that baptizeth." And deservedly was that which he was not made, by way of rebuke, an objection to him who had not the wedding garment, "Friend, how art thou come hither?"[3] And just as he was speechless, so also are these. For what can tongue-clatter avail when the heart is mute? For they know that inwardly, and with their own selves, they have not anything to say. Within, they are mute; without, they make a din. But whether they will or no, they hear this sung even among themselves, "Arise, O God, judge the earth; for Thou shalt inherit among the nations:" and by not communicating with all nations, what do they but acknowledge themselves to be disinherited?

14. Now what I said, brethren, that prophecy extends to all nations (for I wish to show you another meaning in the expression, "Containing two or three metretæ apiece"), —that prophecy, I say, extends to all nations, is pointed out, as we have just now reminded you, in Adam, "who is the figure of Him that was to come." Who does not know that from him all nations are sprung; and that in the four letters of his name the four quarters of the globe, by their Greek appellations, are indicated? For if the east, west, north, and south are expressed in Greek even as Holy Scripture mentions them in various places, the initial letters of the words, thou wilt find, make the word Adam: for in Greek the four quarters of the world are called Anatole, Dysis, Arktos, Mesembria. If thou write these four words, one under the other, like four verses, the capital letters form the word Adam. The same is represented in Noah, by reason of the ark, in which were all animals, significant of all nations: the same in Abraham, to whom it was said more clearly, "In thy seed shall all nations be blessed:" the same in David, from whose psalms, to omit other expressions, we have just been singing, "Arise, O God, judge the earth; for Thou shalt inherit among all nations." Now to what God is it said "Arise," but to Him who slept? "Arise, O God, judge the earth." As if it were said, Thou hast been asleep, having been judged by the earth; arise, to

---

[1] Rom. v. 14.   [2] Ps. lxxxii. 8.   [3] Matt. xxii. 13.

judge the earth. And whither does that prophecy extend, "For Thou shalt inherit among all nations"?

15. Moreover, in the fifth age, in the fifth water-pot as it were, Daniel saw a stone that had been cut from a mountain without hands, and had broken all the kingdoms of the earth; and he saw the stone grow and become a great mountain, so as to fill the whole face of the earth.[1] What can be plainer, my brethren? The stone is cut from a mountain: the same is the stone which the builders rejected, and is become the head of the corner.[2] From what mountain is it cut, if not from the kingdom of the Jews, of which our Lord Jesus Christ was born according to the flesh? And it is cut without hands, without human exertion; because Christ sprung from a virgin, without a husband's embrace. The mountain from which it was cut had not filled the whole face of the earth; for the kingdom of the Jews did not possess all nations. But, on the other hand, the kingdom of Christ we see occupying the whole world.

16. To the sixth age belongs John the Baptist, than whom none greater has arisen among those born of women; of whom it was said, that he was "greater than a prophet."[3] And how did John show that Christ was sent to all nations? When the Jews came to him to be baptized, that they might not pride themselves on the name of Abraham, he said to them, "O generation of vipers, who has proclaimed to you to flee from the wrath to come? Bring forth therefore fruit worthy of repentance;" that is, be humble; for he was speaking to proud people. But whereof were they proud? Of their descent according to the flesh, not of the fruit of imitating their father Abraham. What said he to them? "Say not, We have Abraham for our father: for God is able of these stones to raise up children to Abraham."[4] Meaning by stones all nations, not on account of their durable strength, as in the case of that stone which the builders rejected, but on account of their stupidity and their foolish insensibility, because they had become like the things which they were accustomed to worship: for they worshipped senseless images, themselves equally senseless. "They that make them are like them, and so are all they that trust in them."[5] Accordingly, when men begin to worship God, what do they hear said to them? "That ye may be the children of your Father who is in heaven; who maketh His sun to rise on the good and on the evil, and sendeth rain on the just and on the unjust."[6] Wherefore, if

a man becomes like that which he worships, what is meant by "God is able of these stones to raise up children unto Abraham"? Let us ask ourselves and we shall see that it is a fact. For of those nations are we come, but we should not have come of them had not God of the stones raised up children unto Abraham. We are made children of Abraham by imitating his faith, not by being born of his flesh. For just as they by their degeneracy have been disinherited, so have we by imitating been adopted. Therefore, brethren, this prophecy also of the sixth water-pot extended to all nations; and hence it was said concerning all, "containing two or three metretæ apiece."

17. But how do we show that all nations belong to the "two or three metretæ apiece"? It was a matter of reckoning, in some measure, that he should say the same water-pots contained "two apiece," which he had said contained "three apiece;" evidently in order to intimate to us a mystery therein. How are there "two metretæ apiece"? Circumcision and uncircumcision. Scripture mentions these two classes of people, and leaves out no kind of men, when it says, "Circumcision and uncircumcision;"[7] in these two appellations thou hast all nations: they are the two metretæ apiece. In these two walls, meeting from different quarters, "Christ became the corner-stone, in order to make peace in Himself."[8] Let us show also the "three metretæ apiece" in the case of these same all nations. Noah had three sons, through whom the human race was restored. Hence the Lord says, "The kingdom of heaven is like leaven, which a woman took and hid in three measures of meal, till the whole was leavened."[9] What is this woman, but the flesh of the Lord? What is the leaven, but the gospel? What the three measures, but all nations, on account of the three sons of Noah? Therefore the "six water-pots containing two or three metretæ apiece" are six periods of time, containing the prophecy relating to all nations, whether as represented in two sorts of men, namely, Jews and Greeks, as the apostle often mentions them;[10] or in three sorts, on account of the three sons of Noah. For the prophecy was represented as reaching unto all nations. And because of that reaching it is called a measure,[11] even as the apostle says, "We have received a measure for reaching unto you."[12] For in preaching the gospel to the Gentiles, he says, "A measure for reaching unto you."

1 Dan. ii. 34. 2 Ps. cxviii. 22. 3 Matt. xi. 11.
4 Matt. iii. 9. 5 Ps. cxv. 8. 6 Matt. v. 45.

7 Col iii. 11. 8 Eph. ii. 14.
9 Luke xiii. 21. 10 Rom. ii. 9; 1 Cor. i. 24, etc.
11 Metreta. 12 2 Cor. x. 13.

TRACTATE X.

CHAPTER II. 12–21.

1. IN the psalm you have heard the groaning of the poor, whose members endure tribulations over the whole earth, even unto the end of the world. Make it your chief business, my brethren, to be among and of these members: for all tribulation is to pass away. "Woe to them that rejoice!"[1] "Blessed," says the Truth, "are they that mourn, for they shall be comforted." God has become man: what shall man be, for whom God is become man? Let this hope comfort us in every tribulation and temptation of this life. For the enemy does not cease to persecute; and when he does not openly rage, he plots in secret. How does he plot? "And for wrath, they worked deceitfully."[2] Thence is he called a lion and a dragon. But what is said to Christ? "Thou shalt tread on the lion and the dragon." Lion, for open rage; dragon, for hidden treachery. The dragon cast Adam out of Paradise; as a lion, the same persecuted the Church, as Peter says: "For your adversary, the devil, goeth about as a roaring lion, seeking whom he may devour."[3] Let it not seem to you as if the devil had lost his ferocity. When he blandly flatters, then is he the more vigilantly to be guarded against. But amid all these treacherous devices and temptations of his, what shall we do but that which we have heard in the psalm: "And I, when they were troublesome to me, clothed me in sackcloth, and humbled my soul in fasting."[4] There is one that heareth prayer, hesitate not to pray; but He that heareth abideth within. You need not direct your eyes towards some mountain; you need not raise your face to the stars, or to the sun, or to the moon; nor must you suppose that you are heard when you pray beside the sea: rather detest such prayers. Only cleanse the chamber of thy heart; wheresoever thou art, wherever thou prayest, He that hears is within, within in the secret place, which the psalmist calls his bosom, when he says, "And my prayer shall be turned in my own bosom."[5] He that heareth thee is not beyond thee; thou hast not to travel far, nor to lift thyself up, so as to reach Him as it were with thy hands. Rather, if thou lift thyself up, thou shalt fall; if thou humble thyself, He will draw near thee. Our Lord God is here, the Word of God, the Word made flesh, the Son of the Father, the Son of God, the Son of man; the lofty One to make us, the humble to make us anew, walking among men, bearing the human, concealing the divine.

2. "He went down," as the evangelist says, "to Capernaum, He, and His mother, and His brethren, and His disciples; and they continued there not many days." Behold He has a mother, and brethren, and disciples: whence He has a mother, thence brethren. For our Scripture is wont to call them brethren, not only that are sprung from the same man and woman, or from the same mother, or from the same father, though by different mothers; or, in truth, that are of the same degree as cousins by the father's or mother's side: not these alone is our Scripture wont to call brethren. The Scripture must be understood as it speaks. It has its own language; one who does not know this language is perplexed and says, Whence had the Lord brethren? For surely Mary did not give birth a second time? Far from it! With her begins the dignity of virgins. She could be a mother, but a woman known of man she could not be. She is spoken of as *mulier* [which usually signifies a *wife*], but only in reference to her sex, not as implying loss of virgin purity: and this follows from the language of Scripture itself. For Eve, too, immediately she was formed from the side of her husband, and as yet not known of her husband, is, as you know, called mulier: "And he made her a woman [mulier]." Then, whence the brethren? The kinsmen of Mary, of whatever degree, are the brethren of the Lord. How do we prove this? From Scripture itself. Lot is called "Abraham's brother;"[6] he was his brother's son. Read, and thou wilt find that Abraham was Lot's uncle on the father's side, and yet they are called brethren. Why, but because they were kinsmen? Laban the Syrian was Jacob's uncle by the mother's side, for he was the brother of Rebecca, Isaac's wife and Jacob's mother.[7] Read the Scripture, and thou wilt find that uncle and sister's son are called brothers.[8] When thou hast known this rule, thou wilt find that all the blood relations of Mary are the brethren of Christ.

3. But rather were those disciples brethren;

---

[1] Luke vi. 25. [2] Ps. xxxv. 20. [3] 1 Pet. v. 8.
[4] Ps. xxxv. 13. [5] Ps. xxxv. 13.

[6] Gen. xiii. 8; xiv. 14. [7] Gen. xxviii. 5.
[8] Gen. xxix. 12–15.

for even those kinsmen would not be brethren were they not disciples: and to no advantage brethren, if they did not recognize their brother as their master. For in a certain place, when He was informed that His mother and His brethren were standing without, at the time He was speaking to His disciples, He said: "Who is my mother? or who are my brethren? And stretching out His hand over His disciples, He said, These are my brethren;" and, "Whosoever shall do the will of my Father, the same is my mother, and brother, and sister." [1] Therefore also Mary, because she did the will of the Father. What the Lord magnified in her was, that she did the will of the Father, not that flesh gave birth to flesh. Give good heed, beloved. Moreover, when the Lord was regarded with admiration by the multitude, while doing signs and wonders, and showing forth what lay concealed under the flesh, certain admiring souls said: "Happy is the womb that bare Thee: and He said, Yea, rather, happy are they that hear the word of God, and keep it." [2] That is to say, even my mother, whom ye have called happy, is happy in that she keeps the word of God: not because in her the Word was made flesh and dwelt in us; but because she keeps that same word of God by which she was made, and which in her was made flesh. Let not men rejoice in temporal offspring, but let them exult if in spirit they are joined to God. We have spoken these things on account of that which the evangelist says, that He dwelt in Capernaum a few days, with His mother, and His brethren, and His disciples.

4. What follows upon this? "And the Jews' passover was at hand; and He went up to Jerusalem." The narrator relates another matter, as it came to his recollection. "And He found in the temple those that sold oxen, and sheep, and doves, and the changers of money sitting: and when He had made, as it were, a scourge of small cords, He drove them all out of the temple; the oxen likewise, and the sheep; and poured out the changers' money, and overthrew the tables; and said unto them that sold doves, Take these things hence; and make not my Father's house a house of merchandise." What have we heard, brethren? See, that temple was still a figure, and yet the Lord cast out of it all that sought their own, all who had come to market. And what did they sell there? Things which people needed in the sacrifices of that time. For you know, beloved, that sacrifices were given to that people, in consideration of the

carnal mind and stony heart yet in them, to keep them from falling away to idols: and they offered there for sacrifices oxen, sheep, and doves: you know this, for you have read it. It was not a great sin, then, if they sold in the temple that which was bought for the purpose of offering in the temple: and yet He cast them out thence. If, while they were selling what was lawful and not against justice (for it is not unlawful to sell what it is honorable to buy), He nevertheless drove those men out, and suffered not the house of prayer to be made a house of merchandise; how, if He found drunkards there, what would the Lord do? If the house of God ought not to be made a house of trading, ought it to be made a house of drinking? But when we say this, they gnash upon us with their teeth; but the psalm which you have heard comforts us: "They gnashed upon me with their teeth." Yet we know how we may be cured, although the strokes of the lash are multiplied on Christ, for His word is made to bear the scourge: "The scourges," saith He, "were gathered together against me, and they knew not." He was scourged by the scourges of the Jews; He is now scourged by the blasphemies of false Christians: they multiply scourges for their Lord, and know it not. Let us, so far as He aids us, do as the psalmist did: "But as for me, when they were troublesome to me, I put on sackcloth, and humbled my soul with fasting." [3]

5. Yet we say, brethren (for He did not spare those men: He who was to be scourged by them first scourged them), that He gave us a certain sign, in that He made a scourge of small cords, and with it lashed the unruly, who were making merchandise of God's temple. For indeed every man twists for himself a rope by his sins: "Woe to them who draw sins as a long rope?" [4] Who makes a long rope? He who adds sin to sin. How are sins added to sins? When the sins which have been committed are covered over by other sins. One has committed a theft: that he may not be found out to have committed it, he seeks the astrologer. It were enough to have committed theft: why wilt thou add sin to sin? Behold two sins committed. When thou art forbidden to go to the astrologer, thou revilest the bishop: behold three sins. When thou hearest it said of thee, Cast him forth from the Church; thou sayest, I will betake me to the party of Donatus: behold thou addest a fourth sin. The rope is growing; be thou afraid of the rope. It is good for thee to be corrected

---

[1] Matt. xii. 46-50. [2] Luke xi. 27. [3] Ps. xxxv. 13. [4] Isa. v. 18; LXX.

here, when thou art scourged with it; that it may not be said of thee at the last, "Bind ye his hands and feet, and cast him forth into outer darkness."[1] For, "With the cords of his own sins is every one bound."[2] The former of these is the saying of the Lord, the latter that of another Scripture; but yet both are the sayings of the Lord. With their own sins are men bound and cast into outer darkness.

6. However, to seek the mystery of the deed in the figure, who are they that sell oxen? Who are they that sell sheep and doves? They are they who seek their own in the Church, not the things which are Christ's. They account all a matter of sale, while they will not be redeemed: they have no wish to be bought, and yet they wish to sell. Yes; good indeed is it for them that they may be redeemed by the blood of Christ, that they may come to the peace of Christ. Now, what does it profit to acquire in this world any temporal and transitory thing whatsoever, be it money, or pleasure of the palate, or honor that consists in the praise of men? Are they not all wind and smoke? Do they not all pass by and flee away? Are they not all as a river rushing headlong into the sea? And woe to him who shall fall into it, for he shall be swept into the sea. Therefore ought we to curb all our affections from such desires. My brethren, they that seek such things are they that sell. For that Simon, too, wished to buy the Holy Ghost, just because he meant to sell the Holy Ghost; and he thought the apostles to be just such traders as they whom the Lord cast out of the temple with a scourge. For such an one he was himself, and desired to buy what he might sell: he was of those who sell doves. Now it was in a dove that the Holy Ghost appeared.[3] Who, then, are they, brethren, that sell doves, but they who say, "We give the Holy Ghost"? But why do they say this? and at what price do they sell? At the price of honor to themselves. They receive as the price, temporal seats of honor, that they may be seen to be sellers of doves. Let them beware of the scourge of small cords. The dove is not for sale: it is given freely; for grace, or favor, it is called. Therefore, my brethren, just as you see them that sell, common chapmen, each cries up what he sells: how many stalls they have set up! Primianus has a stall at Carthage, Maximianus has another, Rogatus has another in Mauritania, they have another in Numidia, this party and that, which it is not in our power now to name. Accordingly,

one goes round to buy the dove, and every one at his own stall cries up what he sells. Let the heart of such an one turn away from every seller; let him come where he receives freely. Aye, brethren, and they do not blush, that, by these bitter and malicious dissensions of theirs, they have made of themselves so many parties, while they assume to be what they are not, while they are lifted up, thinking themselves to be something when they are nothing.[4] But what is fulfilled in them, since that they will not be corrected, but that which you have heard in the psalm: "They were rent asunder, and felt no remorse"?

7. Well, who sell oxen? They who have dispensed to us the Holy Scriptures are understood to mean the oxen. The apostles were oxen, the prophets were oxen. Whence the apostle says: "Thou shalt not muzzle the mouth of the ox that treadeth out the corn. Doth God take care for oxen? Or saith He it for our sakes? Yea, for our sakes He saith it: that he who ploweth should plow in hope; and he that thresheth, in hope of partaking."[5] Those oxen, then, have left to us the narration of the Scriptures. For it was not of their own that they dispensed, because they sought the glory of the Lord. Now, what have ye heard in that psalm? "And let them say continually, The Lord be magnified, they that wish the peace of His servant."[6] God's servant, God's people, God's Church. Let them who wish the peace of that Church magnify the Lord, not the servant: "and let them say continually, The Lord be magnified." Who, let say? "Them who wish the peace of His servant." The voice of that people, of that servant, is clearly that voice which you have heard in lamentations in the psalm, and were moved at hearing, because you are of that people. What was sung by one, re-echoed from the hearts of all. Happy they who recognized themselves in those voices as in a mirror. Who, then, are they that wish the peace of His servant, the peace of His people, the peace of the one whom He calls His "only one," and whom He wishes to be delivered from the lion: "Deliver mine only one from the power of the dog?"[7] They who say always, "The Lord be magnified." Those oxen, then, magnified the Lord, not themselves. See this ox magnifying his Lord, because "the ox knoweth his owner;"[8] observe that ox in fear lest men desert the ox's owner and rely on the ox: how he dreads them that are willing to put their confidence in him: "Was Paul crucified for you? or

[1] Matt. xxii. 3.   [2] Prov. v. 22.   [3] Matt. iii. 16.

[4] Gal. vi. 3.   [5] 1 Cor. ix. 9, 10.   [6] Ps. xxxv. 27.
[7] Ps. xxii. 20.   [8] Isa. i. 3.

were ye baptized in the name of Paul?"[1] Of what I gave, I was not the giver: freely ye have received; the dove came down from heaven. "I have planted," saith he, "Apollos watered; but God gave the increase: neither he that planteth is anything, neither he that watereth; but God that giveth the increase."[2] "And let them say always, The Lord be magnified, they that wish the peace of His servant."

8. These men, however, deceive the people by the very Scriptures, that they may receive honors and praises at their hand, and that men may not turn to the truth. But in that they deceive, by the very Scriptures, the people of whom they seek honors, they do in fact sell oxen: they sell sheep too; that is, the common people themselves. And to whom do they sell them, but to the devil? For if the Church be Christ's sole and only one, who is it that carries off whatever is cut away from it, but that lion that roars and goes about, "seeking whom he may devour?"[3] Woe to them that are cut off from the Church! As for her, she will remain entire. "For the Lord knoweth them that are His."[4] These, however, so far as they can, sell oxen and sheep, they sell doves too: let them guard against the scourge of their own sins. But when they suffer some such things for these their iniquities, let them acknowledge that the Lord has made a scourge of small cords, and is admonishing them to change themselves and be no longer traffickers: for if they will not change, they shall at the end hear it said, "Bind ye these men's hands and feet, and cast them forth into outer darkness."

9. "Then the disciples remembered that it was written, The zeal of Thine house hath eaten me up:" because by this zeal of God's house, the Lord cast these men out of the temple. Brethren, let every Christian among the members of Christ be eaten up with zeal of God's house. Who is eaten up with zeal of God's house? He who exerts himself to have all that he may happen to see wrong there corrected, desires it to be mended, does not rest idle: who if he cannot mend it, endures it, laments it. The grain is not shaken out on the threshing-floor that it may enter the barn when the chaff shall have been separated. If thou art a grain, be not shaken out from the floor before the putting into the granary; lest thou be picked up by the birds before thou be gathered into the granary. For the birds of heaven, the powers of the air, are waiting to snatch up something off the threshing-floor, and they can snatch up only

what has been shaken out of it. Therefore, let the zeal of God's house eat thee up: let the zeal of God's house eat up every Christian, zeal of that house of God of which he is a member. For thy own house is not more important than that wherein thou hast everlasting rest. Thou goest into thine own house for temporal rest, thou enterest God's house for everlasting rest. If, then, thou busiest thyself to see that nothing wrong be done in thine own house, is it fit that thou suffer, so far as thou canst help, if thou shouldst chance to see aught wrong in the house of God, where salvation is set before thee, and rest without end? For example, seest thou a brother rushing to the theatre? Stop him, warn him, make him sorry, if the zeal of God's house doth eat thee up. Seest thou others running and desiring to get drunk, and that, too, in holy places, which is not decent to be done in any place? Stop those whom thou canst, restrain whom thou canst, frighten whom thou canst, allure gently whom thou canst: do not, however, rest silent. Is it a friend? Let him be admonished gently. Is it a wife? Let her be bridled with the utmost rigor. Is it a maid-servant? Let her be curbed even with blows. Do whatever thou canst for the part thou bearest; and so thou fulfillest, "The zeal of Thy house hath eaten me up." But if thou wilt be cold, languid, having regard only to thyself, and as if thyself were enough to thee, and saying in thy heart, What have I to do with looking after other men's sins? enough for me is the care of my own soul: this let me keep undefiled for God;—come, does there not recur to thy mind the case of that servant who hid his talent and would not lay it out? Was he accused because he lost it, and not because he kept it without profit?[5] So hear ye then, my brethren, that ye may not rest idle. I am about to give you counsel: may He who is within give it; for though it be through me, it is He that gives it. You know what to do, each one of you, in his own house, with his friend, his tenant, his client, with greater, with less: as God grants an entrance, as He opens a door for His word, do not cease to win for Christ; because you were won by Christ.

10. "The Jews said unto Him, What sign showest thou unto us, seeing that thou doest these things?" And the Lord answered, "Destroy this temple, and in three days I will raise it up. Then said the Jews, Forty and six years was this temple in building, and dost thou say, In three days I will rear it up?"

Flesh they were, fleshly things they minded; but He was speaking spiritually. But who could understand of what temple He spoke? But yet we have not far to seek; He has discovered it to us through the evangelist, he has told us of what temple He said it. "But He spake," saith the evangelist, "of the temple of His body." And it is manifest that, being slain, the Lord did rise again after three days. This is known to us all now: and if from the Jews it is concealed, it is because they stand without; yet to us it is open, because we know in whom we believe. The destroying and rearing again of that temple, we are about to celebrate in its yearly solemnity: for which we exhort you to prepare yourselves, such of you as are catechumens, that you may receive grace; even now is the time, even now let that be purposed which may then come to the birth. Now, that thing we know.

11. But perhaps this is demanded of us, whether the fact that the temple was forty and six years in building may not have in it some mystery. There are, indeed, many things that may be said of this matter; but what may briefly be said, and easily understood, that we say meanwhile. Brethren, we have said yesterday, if I mistake not, that Adam was one man, and is yet the whole human race. For thus we said, if you remember. He was broken, as it were, in pieces; and, being scattered, is now being gathered together, and, as it were, conjoined into one by a spiritual fellowship and concord. And "the poor that groan," as one man, is that same Adam, but in Christ he is being renewed: because an Adam is come without sin, to destroy the sin of Adam in His own flesh, and that Adam might renew to himself the image of God. Of Adam then is Christ's flesh: of Adam the temple which the Jews destroyed, and the Lord raised up in three days. For He raised His own flesh: see, that He was thus God equal with the Father. My brethren, the apostle says, "Who raised Him from the dead." Of whom says he this? Of the Father. "He became," saith he, "obedient unto death, even the death of the cross; wherefore also God raised Him from the dead, and gave Him a name which is above every name."[1] He who was raised and exalted is the Lord. Who raised Him? The Father, to whom He said in the psalms, "Raise me up and I will requite them."[2] Hence, the Father raised Him up. Did He not raise Himself? And doeth the Father anything without the Word? What doeth the Father

without His only One? For, hear that He also was God. "Destroy this temple, and in three days I will raise it up." Did He say, Destroy the temple, which in three days the Father will raise up? But as when the Father raiseth, the Son also raiseth; so when the Son raiseth, the Father also raiseth: because the Son has said, "I and the Father are one."[3]

12. Now, what does the number Forty-six mean? Meanwhile, how Adam extends over the whole globe, you have already heard explained yesterday, by the four Greek letters of four Greek words. For if thou write the four words, one under the other, that is, the names of the four quarters of the world, of east, west, north, and south, which is the whole globe,—whence the Lord says that He will gather His elect from the four winds when He shall come to judgment;[4]—if, I say, you take these four Greek words,—ἀνατολή, which is east; δύσις, which is west; ἄρκτος, which is north; μεσημβρία, which is south; Anatole, Dysis, Arctos, Mesembria,—the first letters of the words make Adam. How, then, do we find there, too, the number forty-six? Because Christ's flesh was of Adam. The Greeks compute numbers by letters. What we make the letter A, they in their tongue put Alpha, α, and Alpha, α, is called one. And where in numbers they write Beta, β, which is their b, it is called in numbers two. Where they write Gamma, γ, it is called in their numbers three. Where they write Delta, δ, it is called in their numbers four; and so by means of all the letters they have numbers. The letter we call M, and they call My, μ, signifies forty; for they say My, μ, τεσσαράκοντα. Now look at the number which these letters make, and you will find in it that the temple was built in forty-six years. For the word Adam has Alpha, α, which is one: it has Delta, δ, which is four; there are five for thee: it has Alpha, α, again, which is one; there are six for thee: it has also My, μ, which is forty; there hast thou forty-six. These things, my brethren, were said by our elders before us, and that number forty-six was found by them in letters. And because our Lord Jesus Christ took of Adam a body, not of Adam derived sin; took of him a corporeal temple, not iniquity which must be driven from the temple: and that the Jews crucified that very flesh which He derived from Adam (for Mary was of Adam, and the Lord's flesh was of Mary); and that, further, He was in three days to raise that same flesh which they were about to slay on the cross: they destroyed

---

the temple which was forty-six years in building, and that temple He raised up in three days.

13. We bless the Lord our God, who gathered us together to spiritual joy. Let us be ever in humility of heart, and let our joy be with Him. Let us not be elated with any prosperity of this world, but know that our happiness is not until these things shall have passed way. Now, my brethren, let our joy be in hope: let none rejoice as in a present thing, lest he stick fast in the way. Let joy be wholly of hope to come, desire be wholly of eternal life. Let all sighings breathe after Christ. Let that fairest one alone, who loved the foul to make them fair, be all our desire; after Him alone let us run, for Him alone pant and sigh; "and let them say always, The Lord be magnified, that wish the peace of His servant."

TRACTATE XI.

CHAPTER II. 23–25; III. 1–5.

1. OPPORTUNELY has the Lord procured for us that this passage should occur in its order to-day: for I suppose you have observed, beloved, that we have undertaken to consider and explain the Gospel according to John in due course. Opportunely then it occurs, that to-day you should hear from the Gospel, that, "Except a man be born again of water and of the Spirit, he shall not see the kingdom of God." For it is time that we exhort you, who are still catechumens, who have believed in Christ in such wise, that you are still bearing your sins. And none shall see the kingdom of heaven while burdened with sins; for none shall reign with Christ, but he to whom they have been forgiven: but forgiven they cannot be, but to him who is born again of water and of the Holy Spirit. But let us observe all the words what they imply, that here the sluggish may find with what earnestness they must haste to put off their burden. For were they bearing some heavy load, either of stone, or of wood, or even of some gain; if they were carrying corn, or wine, or money, they would run to put off their loads: they are carrying a burden of sins, and yet are sluggish to run. You must run to put off this burden; it weighs you down, it drowns you.

2. Behold, you have heard that when our Lord Jesus Christ "was in Jerusalem at the Passover, on the feast day, many believed in His name, seeing the signs which He did." "Many believed in His name;" and what follows? "But Jesus did not trust Himself to them." Now what does this mean, "They believed," or trusted, "in His name;" and yet "Jesus did not trust Himself to them;"? Was it, perhaps, that they had not believed on Him, but were feigning to have believed, and that therefore Jesus did not trust Himself to them? But the evangelist would not have said, "Many believed in His name," if he were not giving a true testimony to them. A great thing, then, it is, and a wonderful thing: men believe on Christ, and Christ trusts not Himself to men. Especially is it wonderful, since, being the Son of God, He of course suffered willingly. If He were not willing, He would never have suffered, since, had He not willed it, He had not been born; and if He had willed this only, merely to be born and not to die, He might have done even whatever He willed, because He is the almighty Son of the almighty Father. Let us prove it by facts. For when they wished to hold Him, He departed from them. The Gospel says, "And when they would have cast Him headlong from the top of the mountain, He departed from them unhurt."[1] And when they came to lay hold of Him, after He was sold by Judas the traitor, who imagined that he had it in his power to deliver up his Master and Lord, there also the Lord showed that He suffered of His own will, not of necessity. For when the Jews desired to lay hold of Him, He said to them, "Whom seek ye? But they said, Jesus of Nazareth. And said He, I am He. On hearing this saying, they went backward, and fell to the ground."[2] In this, that in answering them He threw them to the ground, He showed His power; that in His being taken by them He might show His will. It was of compassion, then, that He suffered. For "He was delivered up for our sins, and rose again for our justification."[3] Hear His own words: "I have power to lay down my life, and I have power to take it

---

1 Luke iv. 30.   2 John xviii. 4–6.   3 Rom. iv. 25.

again: no man taketh it from me, but I lay it down of myself, that I may take it again."[1] Since, therefore, He had such power, since He declared it by words, showed it by deeds, what then does it mean that Jesus did not trust Himself to them, as if they would do Him some harm against His will, or would do something to Him against His will, especially seeing that they had already believed in His name? Moreover, of the same persons the evangelist says, "They believed in His name," of whom he says, "But Jesus did not trust Himself to them." Why? "Because He knew all men, and needed not that any should bear witness of man: for Himself knew what was in man." The artificer knew what was in His own work better than the work knew what was in itself. The Creator of man knew what was in man, which the created man himself knew not. Do we not prove this of Peter, that he knew not what was in himself, when he said, "With Thee, even to death"? Hear that the Lord knew what was in man: "Thou with me even to death? Verily, verily, I say unto thee, Before the cock crow, thou shalt deny me thrice."[2] The man, then, knew not what was in himself; but the Creator of the man knew what was in the man. Nevertheless, many believed in His name, and yet Jesus did not trust Himself to them. What can we say, brethren? Perhaps the circumstances that follow will indicate to us what the mystery of these words is. That men had believed in Him is manifest, is true; none doubts it, the Gospel says it, the truth-speaking evangelist testifies to it. Again, that Jesus trusted not Himself to them is also manifest, and no Christian doubts it; for the Gospel says this also, and the same truth-speaking evangelist testifies to it. Why, then, is it that they believed in His name, and yet Jesus did not trust Himself to them? Let us see what follows.

3. "And there was a man of the Pharisees, Nicodemus by name, a ruler of the Jews: the same came to Him by night, and said unto Him, Rabbi (you already know that Master is called Rabbi), we know that Thou art a teacher come from God; for no man can do these signs which Thou doest, except God be with him." This Nicodemus, then, was of those who had believed in His name, as they saw the signs and prodigies which He did. For this is what he said above: "Now, when He was in Jerusalem at the passover on the feast-day, many believed in His name." Why did they believe? He goes on to say, "Seeing His signs which He did." And what

says he of Nicodemus? "There was a ruler of the Jews, Nicodemus by name· the same came to Him by night, and says to Him, Rabbi, we know that Thou art a teacher come from God." Therefore this man also had believed in His name. And why had he believed? He goes on, "For no man can do these signs which Thou doest, except God be with him." If, therefore, Nicodemus was of those who had believed in His name, let us now consider, in the case of this Nicodemus, why Jesus did not trust Himself to them. "Jesus answered and said unto him, Verily, verily, I say unto thee, Except a man be born again, he cannot see the kingdom of God." Therefore to them who have been born again doth Jesus trust Himself. Behold, those men had believed on Him, and yet Jesus trusted not Himself to them. Such are all catechumens: already they believe in the name of Christ, but Jesus does not trust Himself to them. Give good heed, my beloved, and understand. If we say to a catechumen, Dost thou believe on Christ? he answers, I believe, and signs himself; already he bears the cross of Christ on his forehead, and is not ashamed of the cross of his Lord. Behold, he has believed in His name. Let us ask him, Dost thou eat the flesh of the Son of man, and drink the blood of the Son of man? he knows not what we say, because Jesus has not trusted Himself to him.

4. Therefore, since Nicodemus was of that number, he came to the Lord, but came by night; and this perhaps pertains to the matter. Came to the Lord, and came by night; came to the Light, and came in the darkness. But what do they that are born again of water and of the Spirit hear from the apostle? "Ye were once darkness, but now light in the Lord; walk as children of light;"[3] and again, "But we who are of the day, let us be sober."[4] Therefore they who are born again were of the night, and are of the day; were darkness, and are light. Now Jesus trusts Himself to them, and they come to Jesus, not by night, like Nicodemus; not in darkness do they seek the day. For such now also profess: Jesus has come near to them, has made salvation in them; for He said, "Except a man eat my flesh, and drink my blood, he shall not have life in him."[5] And as the catechumens have the sign of the cross on their forehead, they are already of the great house; but from servants let them become sons. For they are something who already belong to the great house. But when did the people Israel eat the manna?

---

[1] John x. 18.   [2] Matt. xxvi. 33, 34; Luke xxii. 33, 34.   [3] Eph. v. 8.   [4] 1 Thess. v. 8.   [5] John vi. 54.

After they had passed the Red Sea. And as to what the Red Sea signifies, hear the apostle: "Moreover, brethren, I would not have you ignorant, that all our fathers were under the cloud, and all passed through the sea." To what purpose passed they through the sea? As if thou wert asking of him, he goes on to say, "And all were baptized by Moses in the cloud and in the sea."[1] Now, if the figure of the sea had such efficacy, how great will be the efficacy of the true form of baptism! If what was done in a figure brought the people, after they had crossed over, to the manna, what will Christ impart, in the verity of His baptism, to His own people, brought over through Himself? By His baptism He brings over them that believe; all their sins, the enemies as it were that pursue them, being slain, as all the Egyptians perished in that sea. Whither does He bring over, my brethren? Whither does Jesus bring over by baptism, of which Moses then showed the figure, when he brought them through the sea? Whither? To the manna. What is the manna? "I am," saith He, "the living bread, which came down from heaven."[2] The faithful receive the manna, having now been brought through the Red Sea? Why Red Sea? Besides sea, why also "red"? That "Red Sea" signified the baptism of Christ. How is the baptism of Christ red, but as consecrated by Christ's blood? Whither, then, does He lead those that believe and are baptized? To the manna. Behold, "manna," I say: what the Jews, that people Israel, received, is well known, well known what God had rained on them from heaven; and yet catechumens know not what Christians receive. Let them blush, then, for their ignorance; let them pass through the Red Sea, let them eat the manna, that as they have believed in the name of Jesus, so likewise Jesus may trust Himself to them.

5. Therefore mark, my brethren, what answer this man who came to Jesus by night makes. Although he came to Jesus, yet because he came by night, he still speaks from the darkness of his own flesh. He understands not what he hears from the Lord, understands not what he hears from the Light, "which lighteth every man that cometh into this world."[3] Already hath the Lord said to him, "Except a man be born again, he shall not see the kingdom of God. Nicodemus saith unto Him, How can a man be born again when he is old?" The Spirit speaks to him, and he thinks of the flesh. He thinks of his own flesh, because as yet he thinks not of

Christ's flesh. For when the Lord Jesus had said, "Except a man eat my flesh, and drink my blood, he shall not have life in him," some who followed Him were offended, and said among themselves, "This is a hard saying; who can hear it?" For they fancied that, in saying this, Jesus meant that they would be able to cook Him, after being cut up like a lamb, and eat Him: horrified at His words, they went back, and no more followed Him. Thus speaks the evangelist: "And the Lord Himself remained with the twelve; and they said to Him, Lo, those have left Thee. And He said, Will ye also go away?" —wishing to show them that He was necessary to them, not they necessary to Christ. Let no man fancy that he frightens Christ, when he tells Him that he is a Christian; as if Christ will be more blessed if thou be a Christian. It is a good thing for thee to be a Christian; but if thou be not, it will not be ill for Christ. Hear the voice of the psalm, "I said to the Lord, Thou art my God, since Thou hast no need of my goods."[4] For that reason, "Thou art my God, since of my goods Thou hast no need." If thou be without God, thou wilt be less; if thou be with God, God will not be greater. Not from thee will He be greater, but thou without Him wilt be less. Grow, therefore, in Him; do not withdraw thyself, that He may, as it were, diminish. Thou wilt be renewed if thou come to Him, wilt suffer loss if thou depart from Him. He remains entire when thou comest to Him, remains entire even when thou fallest away. When, therefore, He had said to His disciples, "Will ye also go away?" Peter, that Rock, answered with the voice of all, "Lord, to whom shall we go? Thou hast the words of eternal life." Pleasantly savored the Lord's flesh in his mouth. The Lord, however, expounded to them, and said, "It is the Spirit that quickeneth." After He had said, "Except a man eat my flesh, and drink my blood, he shall not have life in him," lest they should understand it carnally, He said, "It is the Spirit that quickeneth, but the flesh profiteth nothing: the words which I have spoken unto you are spirit and life."[5]

6. This Nicodemus, who had come to Jesus by night, did not savor of this spirit and this life. Saith Jesus to him, "Except a man be born again, he shall not see the kingdom of God." And he, savoring of his own flesh, while as yet he savored not of the flesh of Christ in his mouth, saith, "How can a man be born a second time, when he is old? Can he enter a second time into his mother's

---

[1] 1 Cor. x. 1. [2] John vi. 51. [3] John i. 9. [4] Ps. xvi. 2. [5] John vi. 54-59.

womb, and be born?" This man knew but one birth, that from Adam and Eve; that which is from God and the Church he knew not yet: he knew only those parents that bring forth to death, knew not yet the parents that bring forth to life; he knew but the parents that bring forth successors, knew not yet the ever-living parents that bring forth those that shall abide.

Whilst there are two births, then, he understood only one. One is of the earth, the other of heaven; one of the flesh, the other of the Spirit; one of mortality, the other of eternity; one of male and female, the other of God and the Church. But these two are each single; there can be no repeating the one or the other. Rightly did Nicodemus understand the birth of the flesh; so understand thou also the birth of the Spirit, as Nicodemus understood the birth of the flesh. What did Nicodemus understand? "Can a man enter a second time into his mother's womb, and be born?" Thus, whosoever shall tell thee to be spiritually born a second time, answer in the words of Nicodemus, "Can a man enter a second time into his mother's womb, and be born?" I am already born of Adam, Adam cannot beget me a second time. I am already born of Christ, Christ cannot beget me again. As there is no repeating from the womb, so neither from baptism.

7. He that is born of the Catholic Church, is born, as it were, of Sarah, of the free woman; he that is born of heresy is, as it were, born of the bond woman, but of Abraham's seed. Consider, beloved, how great a mystery. God testifies, saying, "I am the God of Abraham, and the God of Isaac, and the God of Jacob." Were there not other patriarchs? Before these, was there not holy Noah, who alone of the whole human race, with all his house, was worthy to be delivered from the flood,—he in whom, and in his sons, the Church was prefigured? Borne by wood, they escaped the flood. Then afterwards great men whom we know, whom Holy Scriptures commends, Moses faithful in all his house.[1] And yet those three are named, just as if they alone deserved well of him: "I am the God of Abraham, and the God of Isaac, and the God of Jacob: this is my name for ever."[2] Sublime mystery! It is the Lord that is able to open both our mouth and your hearts, that we may speak as He has deigned to reveal, and that you may receive even as it is expedient for you.

8. The patriarchs, then, are these three, Abraham, Isaac, and Jacob. You know that the sons of Jacob were twelve, and thence the people Israel; for Jacob himself is Israel, and the people Israel in twelve tribes pertaining to the twelve sons of Israel. Abraham, Isaac, and Jacob three fathers, and one people. The fathers three, as it were in the beginning of the people; three fathers in whom the people was figured: and the former people itself the present people. For in the Jewish people was figured the Christian people. There a figure, here the truth; there a shadow, here the body: as the apostle says, "Now these things happened to them in a figure." It is the apostle's voice: "They were written," saith he, "for our sakes, upon whom the end of the ages is come."[3] Let your mind now recur to Abraham, Isaac, and Jacob. In the case of these three, we find that free women bear children, and that bond women bear children: we find there offspring of free women, we find there also offspring of bond women. The bond woman signifies nothing good: "Cast out the bond woman," saith he, "and her son; for the son of the bond woman shall not be heir with the son of the free." The apostle recounts this; and he says that in those two sons of Abraham was a figure of the two Testaments, the Old and the New. To the Old Testament belong the lovers of temporal things, the lovers of the world: to the New Testament belong the lovers of eternal life. Hence, that Jerusalem on earth was the shadow of the heavenly Jerusalem, the mother of us all, which is in heaven; and these are the apostle's words.[4] And of that city from which we are absent on our sojourn, you know much, you have now heard much. But we find a wonderful thing in these births, in these fruits of the womb, in these generations of free and bond women: namely, four sorts of men; in which four sorts is completed the figure of the future Christian people, so that what was said in the case of those three patriarchs is not surprising, "I am the God of Abraham, and the God of Isaac, and the God of Jacob." For in the case of all Christians, observe, brethren, either good men are born of evil men, or evil men of good; or good men of good, or evil men of evil: more than these four sorts you cannot find. These things I will again repeat: Give heed, keep them, excite your hearts, be not dull; take in, lest ye be taken, how of all Christians there are four sorts. Either of the good are born good, or of the evil, are born evil; or of the good are born evil, or of the evil good. I think it is plain. Of the good, good; if they

who baptize are good, and also they who are baptized rightly believe, and are rightly numbered among the members of Christ. Of the evil, evil; if they who baptize are evil, and they who are baptized approach God with a double heart, and do not observe the morals which they hear urged in the Church, so as not to be chaff, but grain, there. How many such there are, you know, beloved. Of the evil, good; sometimes an adulterer baptizes, and he that is baptized is justified. Of the good, evil; sometimes they who baptize are holy, they who are baptized do not desire to keep the way of God.

9. I suppose, brethren, that this is known in the Church, and that what we are saying is manifest by daily examples; but let us consider these things in the case of our fathers before us, how they also had these four kinds. Of the good, good; Ananias baptized Paul. How of the evil, evil? The apostle declares that there were certain preachers of the gospel, who, he says, did not use to preach the gospel with a pure motive, whom, however, he tolerates in the Christian society, saying, "What then? notwithstanding every way, whether by occasion or in truth, Christ is preached, and in this I rejoice."[1] Was he therefore malevolent, and did he rejoice in another's evil? No, but rejoiced because through evil men the truth was preached, and by the mouths of evil men Christ was preached. If these men baptized any persons like themselves, evil men baptized evil men: if they baptized such as the Lord admonishes, when He says, "Whatsoever they bid you, do; but do not ye after their works,"[2] they were evil men that were baptizing good. Good men baptized evil men, as Simon the sorcerer was baptized by Philip, a holy man.[3] Therefore these four sorts, my brethren, are known. See, I repeat them again, hold them, count them, think upon them; guard against what is evil; keep what is good. Good men are born of good, when holy men are baptized by holy; evil men are born of evil, when both they that baptize and they that are baptized live unrighteously and ungodly; good men are born of evil, when they are evil that baptize, and they good that are baptized; evil men are born of good, when they are good that baptize, and they evil that are baptized.

10. How do we find this in these three names, "I am the God of Abraham, and the God of Isaac, and the God of Jacob"? We hold the bond women among the evil, and the free women among the good. Free women bear the good; Sarah bare Isaac: bond women

bear the evil; Hagar bare Ishmael. We have in the case of Abraham alone the two sorts, both when the good are of the good, and also when the evil are of the evil. But where have we evil of good figured? Rebecca, Isaac's wife, was a free woman: read, She bare twins; one was good, the other evil. Thou hast the Scripture openly declaring by the voice of God, "Jacob have I loved, but Esau have I hated."[4] Rebecca bare two, Jacob and Esau: one of them is chosen, the other is reprobated; one succeeds to the inheritance, the other is disinherited. God does not make His people of Esau, but makes it of Jacob. The seed is one, those conceived are dissimilar: the womb is one, those born of it are diverse. Was not the free woman that bare Jacob, the same free woman that bare Esau? They strove in the mother's womb; and when they strove there, it was said to Rebecca, "Two peoples are in thy womb." Two men, two peoples; a good people, and a bad people: but yet they strive in one womb. How many evil men there are in the Church! And one womb carries them until they are separated in the end: and the good cry out against the evil, and the evil in turn cry out against the good, and both strive together in the bowels of one mother. Will they be always together? There is a going forth to the light in the end; the birth which is here figured in a mystery is declared; and it will then appear that "Jacob have I loved, but Esau have I hated."

11. Accordingly we have now found, brethren, of the good, good—of the free woman, Isaac; and of the evil, evil—of the bond woman, Ishmael; and of the good, evil—of Rebecca, Esau: where shall we find of the evil, good? There remains Jacob, that the completion of these four sorts may be concluded in the three patriarchs. Jacob had for wives free women, he had also bond women: the free bear children, as do also the bond, and thus come the twelve sons of Israel. If you count them all, of whom they were born, they were not all of the free women, nor all of the bond women; but yet they were all of one seed. What, then, my brethren? Did not they who were born of the bond women possess the land of promise together with their brethren? We have there found good sons of Jacob born of bond women, and good sons of Jacob born of free women. Their birth of the wombs of bond women was nothing against them, when they knew their seed in the father, and consequently they held the kingdom with their brethren. Therefore,

---

[1] Phil. i. 18. [2] Matt. xxiii. 3. [3] Acts viii. 13. [4] Mal. i. 3; Rom. ix. 13.

as in the case of Jacob's sons, that they were born of bond women did not hinder their holding the kingdom, and receiving the land of promise on an equality with their brothers; their birth of bond women did not hinder them, but the father's seed prevailed: so, whoever are baptized by evil men, appear as if born of bond women; nevertheless, because they are of the seed of the Word of God, which is figured in Jacob, let them not be cast down, they shall possess the inheritance with their brethren. Therefore, let him who is born of the good seed be without fear; only let him not imitate the bond woman, if he is born of a bond woman. Do not thou imitate the evil, proud, bond woman. For how came the sons of Jacob, that were born of bond women, to possess the land of promise with their brethren, whilst Ishmael, born of a bond woman, was cast out from the inheritance? How, but because he was proud, they were humble? He proudly reared his neck, and wished to seduce his brother while he was playing with him.

12. A great mystery is there. They were playing together, Ishmael and Isaac: Sarah sees them playing, and says to Abraham, "Cast out the bond woman and her son; for the son of the bond woman shall not be heir with my son Isaac." And when Abraham was sorrowful, the Lord confirmed to him the saying of his wife. Now here is evidently a mystery, that the event was somehow pregnant with something future. She sees them playing, and says, "Cast out the bond woman and her son." What is this, brethren? For what evil had Ishmael done to the boy Isaac, in playing with him? That playing was a mocking; that playing signified deception. Now attend, beloved, to this great mystery. The apostle calls it persecution; that playing, that play, he calls persecution: for he says, "But as then he that was born after the flesh, persecuted him that was born after the Spirit, so also now;" that is, they that are born after the flesh persecute them that are born after the Spirit. Who are born after the flesh? Lovers of the world, lovers of this life. Who are born after the Spirit? Lovers of the kingdom of heaven, lovers of Christ, men that long for eternal life, that worship God freely. They play, and the apostle calls it persecution. For after he said these words, "And as then he that was born after the flesh persecuted him that was born after the Spirit, so also now;" the apostle went on, and showed of what persecution, he was speaking: "But what says the Scripture? Cast out the bond woman and her son: for the son of the bond woman shall not

be heir with my son Isaac."[1] We search where the Scripture says this, to see whether any persecution on Ishmael's part against Isaac preceded this; and we find that this was said by Sarah when she saw the boys playing together. The playing which Scripture says that Sarah saw, the apostle calls persecution. Hence, they who seduce you by playing, persecute you the more. "Come," say they, "Come, be baptized here, here is true baptism for thee." Do not play, there is one true baptism; that other is play: thou wilt be seduced, and that will be a grievous persecution to thee. It were better for thee to make Ishmael a present of the kingdom; but Ishmael will not have it, for he means to play. Keep thou thy father's inheritance, and hear this: "Cast out the bond woman and her son; for the son of the bond woman shall not be heir with my son Isaac."

13. These men, too, dare to say that they are wont to suffer persecution from catholic kings, or from catholic princes. What persecution do they bear? Affliction of body: yet if at times they have suffered, and how they suffered, let themselves know, and settle it with their consciences; still they suffered only affliction of body: the persecution which they cause is more grievous. Beware when Ishmael wishes to play with Isaac, when he fawns on thee, when he offers another baptism: answer him, I have baptism already. For if this baptism is true, he who would give thee another would be mocking thee. Beware of the persecution of the soul. For though the party of Donatus has at times suffered somewhat at the hands of catholic princes, it was a bodily suffering, not the suffering of spiritual deception. Hear and see in the very facts of Old Testament history all the signs and indications of things to come. Sarah is found to have afflicted her maid Hagar: Sarah is free. After her maid began to be proud, Sarah complained to Abraham, and said, "Cast out the bond woman;" she has lifted her neck against me. His wife complains of Abraham, as if it were his doing. But Abraham, who was not bound to the maid by lust, but by the duty of begetting children, inasmuch as Sarah had given her to him to have offspring by her, says to her: "Behold, she is thy handmaid; do unto her as thou wilt." And Sarah grievously afflicted her, and she fled from her face. See, the free woman afflicted the bond woman, and the apostle does not call that a persecution; the slave plays with his master, and he calls it persecution: this afflicting is not called persecution; that playing is. How does it appear to

---

[1] Gen. xxi. 9-12 ; Gal. iv. 30.

you, brethren? Do you not understand what is signified? Thus, then, when God wills to stir up powers against heretics, against schismatics, against those that scatter the Church, that blow on Christ as if they abhorred Him, that blaspheme baptism, let them not wonder; because God stirs them up, that Hagar may be beaten by Sarah. Let Hagar know herself, and yield her neck: for when, after being humiliated, she departed from her mistress, an angel met her, and said to her, "What is the matter with thee, Hagar, Sarah's handmaid?" When she complained of her mistress, what did she hear from the angel? "Return to thy mistress."[1] It is for this that she is afflicted, that she may return; and would that she may return, for her offspring, just like the sons of Jacob, will obtain the inheritance with their brethren.

14. But they wonder that Christian powers are roused against detestable scatterers of the Church. Should they not be moved, then? How otherwise should they give an account of their rule to God? Observe, beloved, what I say, that it concerns Christian kings of this world to wish their mother the Church, of which they have been spiritually born, to have peace in their times. We read Daniel's visions and prophetical histories. The three children praised the Lord in the fire: King Nebuchadnezzar wondered at the children praising God, and at the fire around them doing them no harm: and whilst he wondered, what did King Nebuchadnezzar say, he who was neither a Jew nor circumcised, who had set up his own image and compelled all men to adore it; but, impressed by the praises of the three children when he saw the majesty of God present in the fire, what said he? "And I will publish a decree to all tribes and tongues in the whole earth." What sort of decree? "Whosoever shall speak blasphemy against the God of Shadrach, Meshach, and Abednego, shall be cut off, and their houses shall be made a ruin."[2] See how an alien king acts with raging indignation that the God of Israel might not be blasphemed, because He was able to deliver the three children from the fire: and yet they would not have Christian kings to act with severity when Christ is contemptuously rejected, by whom not three children, but the whole world, with these very kings, is delivered from the fire of hell! For those three children, my brethren, were delivered from temporal fire. Is He not the same God who was the God of the Maccabees and the God of the three children? The latter He deliv-

ered from the fire; the former did in body perish in the torments of fire, but in mind they remained steadfast in the ordinances of the law. The latter were openly delivered, the former were crowned in secret.[3] It is a greater thing to be delivered from the flame of hell than from the furnace of a human power. If, then, Nebuchadnezzar praised and extolled and gave glory to God because He delivered three children from the fire, and gave such glory as to send forth a decree throughout his kingdom, "Whosoever shall speak blasphemy against the God of Shadrach, Meshach, and Abednego, shall be cut off, and their houses shall be brought to ruin," how should not these kings be moved, who observe, not three children delivered from the flame, but their very selves delivered from hell, when they see Christ, by whom they have been delivered, contemptuously spurned in Christians, when they hear it said to a Christian, "Say that thou art not a Christian"? Men are willing to do such deeds, but they do not wish to suffer, at all events, such punishments.

15. For see what they do and what they suffer. They slay souls, they suffer in body: they cause everlasting deaths, and yet they complain that they themselves suffer temporal deaths. And yet what deaths do they suffer? They allege to us some martyrs of theirs in persecution. See, Marculus was hurled headlong from a rock; see, Donatus of Bagaia was thrown into a well. When have the Roman authorities decreed such punishments as casting men down rocks? But what do those of our party reply? What was done I know not; what, however, do ours tell? That they flung themselves headlong and cast the infamy of it upon the authorities. Let us call to mind the custom of the Roman authorities, and see to whom we are to give credit. Our men declare that those men cast themselves down headlong. If they are not the very disciples of those men, who now cast themselves down precipices, while no man persecutes them, let us not credit the allegation of our men: what wonder if those men did what these are wont to do? The Roman authorities never did employ such punishments: for had they not the power to put them to death openly? But those men, while they wished to be honored when dead, found not a death to make them more famous. In short, whatever the fact was, I do not know. And even if thou hast suffered corporal affliction, O party of Donatus, at the hand of the Catholic Church, as an Hagar thou hast suf-

fered it at the hand of Sarah; "return to thy mistress."' A point which it was indeed necessary to discuss has detained us somewhat too long to be at all able to expound the whole text of the Gospel Lesson. Let this suffice you in the meantime, beloved brethren, lest, by speaking of other matters, what has been spoken might be shut out from your hearts. Hold fast these things, declare such things; and while yourselves are inflamed, go your way thither, and set on fire them that are cold.

TRACTATE XII.

CHAPTER III. 6-21.

1. WE observe, beloved, that the intimation with which we yesterday excited your attention has brought you together with more alacrity, and in greater number than usual; but meanwhile let us, if you please, pay our debt of a discourse on the Gospel Lesson, which comes in due course. You shall then hear, beloved, as well what we have already effected concerning the peace of the Church, and what we hope yet further to accomplish. For the present, then, let the whole attention of your hearts be given to the gospel; let none be thinking of anything else. For if he who attends to it wholly apprehends with difficulty, must not he who divides himself by diverse thoughts let go what he has received? Moreover, you remember, beloved, that on the last Lord's day, as the Lord deigned to help us, we discoursed of spiritual regeneration. That lesson we have caused to be read. to you again, so that what was then left unspoken, we may now, by the aid of your prayers in the name of Christ, fulfill.

2. Spiritual regeneration is one, just as the generation of the flesh is one. And Nicodemus said the truth when he said to the Lord that a man cannot, when he is old, return again into his mother's womb and be born. He indeed said that a man cannot do this when he is old, as if he could do it even were he an infant. But be he fresh from the womb, or now in years, he cannot possibly return again into the mother's bowels and be born. But just as for the birth of the flesh, the bowels of woman avail to bring forth the child only once, so for the spiritual birth the bowels of the Church avail that a man be baptized only once. Therefore, in case one should say, "Well, but this man was born in heresy, and this in schism:" all that was cut away, if you remember what was debated to you about our three fathers, of whom God willed to be called the God, not that they were thus alone. but because in them alone the figure of the future people was made up in its completeness. For we find one born of a bond woman disinherited, one born of a free woman made heir: again, we find one born of a free woman disinherited, one born of a bond woman made heir. Ishmael, born of a bond woman, disinherited; Isaac, born of a free woman, made heir: Esau, born of a free woman, disinherited; the sons of Jacob, born of bond women, made heirs. Thus, in these three fathers the figure of the whole future people is seen: and not without reason God saith, "I am the God of Abraham, and the God of Isaac, and the God of Jacob: this," saith He, "is my name for ever."[1] Rather let us remember what was promised to Abraham himself: for this was promised to Isaac, and also to Jacob. What do we find? "In thy seed shall all nations be blessed."[2] At that time the one man believed what as yet he saw not: men now see, and are blinded. What was promised to the one man is fulfilled in the nations; and they who will not see what is already fulfilled, are separating themselves from the communion of the nations. But what avails it them that they will not see? See they do, whether they will or no; the open truth strikes against their closed eyes.

3. It was in answer to Nicodemus, who was of them that had believed on Jesus, that it was said, And Jesus did not trust Himself to them. To certain men, indeed, He did not trust Himself, though they had already believed on Him. Thus it is written, "Many believed in His name, seeing the signs which He did. But Jesus did not trust Himself to them. For He needed not that any should testify of man; for Himself knew what was in man." Behold, they already believed on Jesus, and yet Jesus did not trust Himself to them. Why? because they were not yet born again of water and of the Spirit. From this have we ex-

---

[1] Ex. iii. 6, 15.　　　[2] Gen. xxii. 18.

horted and do exhort our brethren the catechumens. For if you ask them, they have
already believed in Jesus; but because they
have not yet received His flesh and blood,
Jesus has not yet trusted Himself to them.
What must they do that Jesus may trust Himself to them? They must be born again of
water and of the Spirit; the Church that is in
travail with them must bring them forth.
They have been conceived; they must be
brought forth to the light: they have breasts
to be nourished at; let them not fear lest,
being born, they may be smothered; let them
not depart from the mother's breasts.

4. No man can return into his mother's
bowels and be born again. But some one is
born of a bond woman? Well, did they who
were born of bond women at the former time,
return into the wombs of the free to be born
anew? The seed of Abraham was in Ishmael
also; but that Abraham might have a son of
the bond maid, it was at the advice of his wife.
The child was of the husband's seed, not of
the womb, but at the sole pleasure of the
wife. Was his birth of a bond woman the
reason why he was disinherited? Then, if
he was disinherited because he was the son
of a bond woman, no sons of bond women
would be admitted to the inheritance. The
sons of Jacob were admitted to the inheritance;
but Ishmael was put out of it, not because
born of a bond woman, but because he was
proud to his mother, proud to his mother's
son; for his mother was Sarah rather than
Hagar. The one gave her womb, the other's
will was added: Abraham would not have
done what Sarah willed not: therefore was he
Sarah's son rather. But because he was proud
to his brother, proud in playing, that is, in
mocking him; what said Sarah? "Cast out
the bond woman and her son; for the son of
the bond woman shall not be heir with my
son Isaac."[1] It was not, therefore, the bowels of the bond woman that caused his rejec-
tion, but the slave's neck. For the free-born
is a slave if he is proud, and, what is worse,
the slave of a bad mistress, of pride itself.
Thus, my brethren, answer the man, that a
man cannot be born a second time; answer
fearlessly, that a man cannot be born a second
time. Whatever is done a second time is
mockery, whatever is done a second time is
play. It is Ishmael playing, let him be cast
out. For Sarah observed them playing, saith
the Scripture, and said to Abraham, "Cast
out the bond woman and her son." The
playing of the boys displeased Sarah. She
saw something strange in their play. Do

not they who have sons like to see them playing? She saw and disapproved it. Something or other she saw in their play; she saw
mockery in it, observed the pride of the slave;
she was displeased with it, and she cast him
out. The children of bond women, when
wicked, are cast out; and the child of the free
woman, when an Esau, is cast out. Let none,
therefore, presume on his birth of good
parents; let none presume on his being baptized by holy men. Let him that is baptized
by holy men still beware lest he be not a
Jacob, but an Esau. This would I say then,
brethren, it is better to be baptized by men
that seek their own and love the world, which
is what the name of bond woman imports,
and to be spiritually seeking the inheritance of
Christ, so as to be as it were a son of Jacob
by a bond woman, than to be baptized by
holy men and to become proud, so as to be
an Esau to be cast out, though born of a free
woman. Hold ye this fast, brethren. We are
not coaxing you, let none of your hope be in
us; we flatter neither ourselves nor you;
every man bears his own burden. It is our
duty to speak, that we be not judged unhappily: yours to hear, and that with the
heart, lest what we give be required of you;
nay, that when it is required, it may be
found a gain, not a loss.

5. The Lord says to Nicodemus, and explains to him: "Verily, verily, I say unto
thee, Except a man be born again of water
and of the Spirit, he cannot enter into the
kingdom of God." Thou, says He, understandest a carnal generation, when thou sayest, Can a man return into his mother's bowels? The birth for the kingdom of God must
be of water and of the Spirit. If one is born
to the temporal inheritance of a human
father, be he born of the bowels of a carnal
mother; if one is born to the everlasting inheritance of God as his Father, be he born of
the bowels of the Church. A father, as one
that will die, begets a son by his wife to succeed him; but God begets of the Church
sons, not to succeed Him, but to abide with
Himself. And He goes on: "That which is
born of the flesh is flesh; and that which is
born of the Spirit is spirit." We are born
spiritually then, and in spirit we are born
by the word and sacrament. The Spirit is
present that we may be born; the Spirit is
invisibly present whereof thou art born, for
thou too must be invisibly born. For He
goes on to say: "Marvel not that I said unto
thee, Ye must be born again. The Spirit
bloweth where it listeth, and thou hearest its
voice, but knowest not whence it cometh, or
whither it goeth." None sees the Spirit; and

---

[1] Gen. xxi. 9, 10.

how do we hear the Spirit's voice? There sounds a psalm, it is the Spirit's voice; the gospel sounds, it is the Spirit's voice; the divine word sounds, it is the Spirit's voice. "Thou hearest its voice, and knowest not whence it cometh, and whither it goeth." But if thou art born of the Spirit, thou too shalt be so, that one who is not born of the Spirit knows not, as for thee, whence thou comest, or whither thou goest. For He said, as He went on, "So is also every one that is born of the Spirit."

6. "Nicodemus answered and said unto Him, How can these things be?" And, in fact, in the carnal sense, he knew not how. In him occurred what the Lord had said; the Spirit's voice he heard, but knew not whence it came, and whither it was going. "Jesus answered and said unto him, Art thou a master in Israel, and knowest not these things?" Oh, brethren! what? do we think that the Lord meant to taunt scornfully this master of the Jews? The Lord knew what He was doing; He wished the man to be born of the Spirit. No man is born of the Spirit if he be not humble, for humility itself makes us to be born of the Spirit; "for the Lord is nigh to them that are of broken heart."[1] The man was puffed up with his mastership, and it appeared of some importance to himself that he was a teacher of the Jews. Jesus pulled down his pride, that he might be born of the Spirit: He taunted him as an unlearned man; not that the Lord wished to appear his superior. What comparison can there be, God compared to man, truth to falsehood? Christ greater than Nicodemus! Ought this to be said, can it be said, is it to be thought? If it were said, "Christ is greater than angels," it were ridiculous: for incomparably greater than every creature is He by whom every creature was made. But yet He rallies the man on his pride: "Art thou a master in Israel, and knowest not these things?" As if He said, Behold, thou knowest nothing, thou art a proud chief; be thou born of the Spirit: for if thou be born of the Spirit, thou wilt keep the ways of God, so as to follow Christ's humility. So, indeed, is He high above all angels, that, "being in the form of God, He thought it not robbery to be equal with God, but emptied Himself, taking upon Him the form of a servant, being made into the likeness of men, and found in fashion as a man: He humbled Himself, being made obedient unto death" (and lest any kind of death should please thee), "even the death of the cross."[2] He hung on the cross, and they scoffed at Him. He could have come down from the cross; but He deferred, that He might rise again from the tomb. He, the Lord, bore with proud slaves;[3] the physician with the sick. If He did this, how ought they to act whom it behoves to be born of the Spirit!—if He did this, He who is the true Master in heaven, not of men only, but also of angels. For if the angels are learned, they are so by the Word of God. If they are learned by the Word of God, ask of what they are learned; and you shall find, "In the beginning was the Word, and the Word was with God, and the Word was God." The neck of man is done away with, only the hard and stiff neck, that it may be gentle to bear the yoke of Christ, of which it is said, "My yoke is easy, and my burden is light."[3]

7. And He goes on, "If I have told you earthly things, and ye believe not; how shall ye believe, if I tell you heavenly things?" What earthly things did He tell, brethren? "Except a man be born again;" is that an earthly thing? "The Spirit bloweth where it listeth, and thou hearest its voice, and knowest not whence it cometh, or whither it goeth;" is that earthly? For if He spoke it of the wind, as some have understood it, when they were asked what earthly thing the Lord meant, when He said, "If I told you earthly things, and ye believe not; how shall ye believe, if I tell you heavenly things?"— when, I say, it was asked of certain men what "earthly thing" the Lord meant, being in difficulty, they said, What He said, "The Spirit bloweth where it listeth," and "its voice thou hearest, and knowest not whence it cometh, or whither it goeth," He said concerning the wind. Now what did He name earthly? He was speaking of the spiritual birth; and going on, saith, "So is every one that is born of the Spirit." Then, brethren, which of us does not see, for example, the south wind going from south to north, or another wind coming from east to west? How, then, know we not whence it cometh and whither it goeth? What earthly thing, then, did He tell, which men did not believe? Was it that which He had said about raising the temple again? Surely, for He had received His body of the earth, and that earth taken of the earthly body He was preparing to raise up. They did not believe Him as about to raise up earth. "If I told you earthly things," saith He, "and ye believe not; how shall ye believe if I tell you heavenly things?" That is, if ye believe not that I can raise up the temple cast down by you, how shall ye believe that men can be regenerated by the Spirit?

---

[1] Ps. xxxiv. 18.   [2] Phil. ii. 6-8.   [3] Matt. xi. 30.

8. And He goes on: "And no man hath ascended into heaven, but He that came down from heaven, the Son of man who is in heaven." Behold, He was here, and was also in heaven; was here in His flesh, in heaven by His divinity; yea, everywhere by His divinity. Born of a mother, not quitting the Father. Two nativities of Christ are understood: one divine, the other human: one, that by which we were to be made; the other, that by which we were to be made anew: both marvellous; that without mother, this without father. But because He had taken a body of Adam,—for Mary was of Adam,—and was about to raise that same body again, it was an earthly thing He had said in saying, "Destroy this temple, and in three days I will raise it up." But this was a heavenly thing, when He said, "Except a man be born again of water and of the Spirit, he shall not see the kingdom of God." Come then, brethren! God has willed to be the Son of man; and willed men to be sons of God. He came down for our sakes; let us ascend for His sake. For He alone descended and ascended, He who saith, "No man hath ascended into heaven, but He who came down from heaven." Are they not therefore to ascend into heaven whom He makes sons of God? Certainly they are: this is the promise to us, "They shall be equal to the angels of God."[1] Then how is it that no man ascends, but He that descended? Because one only descended, only one ascends. What of the rest? What are we to understand, but that they shall be His members, that one may ascend? Therefore it follows that "no man hath ascended into heaven, but He who came down from heaven, the Son of man who is in heaven." Dost thou marvel that He was both here and in heaven? Such He made His disciples. Hear the Apostle Paul saying, "But our conversation is in heaven."[2] If the Apostle Paul, a man, walked in the flesh on earth, and yet had his conversation in heaven, was the God of heaven and earth not able to be both in heaven and on earth?

9. Therefore, if none but He descended and ascended, what hope is there for the rest? The hope for the rest is this, that He came down in order that in Him and with Him they might be one, who should ascend through Him. "He saith not, And to seeds," saith the apostle, "as in many; but as in one, And to thy seed, which is Christ." And to believers he saith, "And ye are Christ's; and if Christ's, then are Abraham's seed."[3] What he said to be one, that he said that we all are.

Hence, in the Psalms, many sometimes sing, to show that one is made of many; sometimes one sings, to show what is made of many. Therefore was it only one that was healed in the pool; and whoever else went down into it was not healed. Now this one shows forth the oneness of the Church. Woe to them who hate unity, and make to themselves parties among men! Let them hear him who wished to make them one, in one, for one: let them hear him who says, Be not ye making many: "I have planted, Apollos watered; but God gave the increase. But neither he that planteth is anything, neither he that watereth; but God that giveth the increase."[4] They were saying, "I am of Paul, I of Apollos, I of Cephas." And he says, "Is Christ divided?" Be ye in one, be one thing, be one person: "No man hath ascended into heaven, but He who came down from heaven." Lo! we wish to be thine, they said to Paul. And he said to them, I will not that ye be Paul's, but be ye His whose is Paul together with you.

10. For He came down and died, and by that death delivered us from death: being slain by death, He slew death. And you know, brethren, that this death entered into the world through the devil's envy. "God made not death," saith the Scripture, "nor delights He in the destruction of the living; but He created all things to be." But what saith it here? "But by the devil's envy, death entered into the whole world."[5] To the death offered for our entertainment by the devil, man would not come by constraint; for the devil had not the power of forcing, but only cunning to persuade. Hadst thou not consented, the devil had brought in nothing: thy own consenting, O man, led thee to death. Of the mortal are mortals born; from immortals we are become mortals. From Adam all men are mortal; but Jesus the Son of God, the Word of God, by which all things were made, the only Son equal with the Father, was made mortal: "for the Word was made flesh, and dwelt among us."

11. He endured death, then; but death He hanged on the cross, and mortal men are delivered from death. The Lord calls to mind a great matter, which was done in a figure with them of old: "And as Moses," saith He, "lifted up the serpent in the wilderness, so must the Son of man be lifted up; that every one who believeth on Him may not perish, but have everlasting life." A great mystery is here, as they who read know. Again, let them hear, as well they who have

---

[1] Matt. xxii. 30.   [2] Phil. iii. 20.   [3] Gal. iii. 16, 29.   [4] 1 Cor. iii. 6, 7.   [5] Wisd. i. 2.

not read as they who have forgotten what perhaps they had heard or read. The people Israel were fallen helplessly in the wilderness by the bite of serpents; they suffered a great calamity by many deaths: for it was the stroke of God correcting and scourging them that He might instruct them. In this was shown a great mystery, the figure of a thing to come: the Lord Himself testifies in this passage, so that no man can give another interpretation than that which the truth indicates concerning itself. Now Moses was ordered by the Lord to make a brazen serpent, and to raise it on a pole in the wilderness, and to admonish the people Israel, that, when any had been bitten by a serpent, he should look to that serpent raised up on the pole. This was done: men were bitten; they looked and were healed.[1] What are the biting serpents? Sins, from the mortality of the flesh. What is the serpent lifted up? The Lord's death on the cross. For as death came by the serpent, it was figured by the image of a serpent. The serpent's bite was deadly, the Lord's death is life-giving. A serpent is gazed on that the serpent may have no power. What is this? A death is gazed on, that death may have no power. But whose death? The death of life: if it may be said, the death of life; ay, for it may be said, but said wonderfully. But should it not be spoken, seeing it was a thing to be done? Shall I hesitate to utter that which the Lord has deigned to do for me? Is not Christ the life? And yet Christ hung on the cross. Is not Christ life? And yet Christ was dead. But in Christ's death, death died. Life dead slew death; the fullness of life swallowed up death; death was absorbed in the body of Christ. So also shall we say in the resurrection, when now triumphant we shall sing, "Where, O death, is thy contest? Where, O death, is thy sting?"[2] Meanwhile, brethren, that we may be healed from sin, let us now gaze on Christ crucified; for "as Moses," saith He, "lifted up the serpent in the wilderness, so must the Son of man be lifted up; that whosoever believeth on Him may not perish, but have everlasting life." Just as they who looked on that serpent perished not by the serpent's bites, so they who look in faith on Christ's death are healed from the bites of sins. But those were healed from death to temporal life; whilst here He saith, "that they may have everlasting life." Now there is this difference between the figurative image and the real thing: the figure procured temporal life; the reality, of which that was the figure, procures eternal life.

12. "For God sent not His Son into the world to judge the world, but that the world through Him may be saved." So far, then, as it lies in the physician, He is come to heal the sick. He that will not observe the orders of the physician destroys himself. He is come a Saviour to the world: why is he called the Saviour of the world, but that He is come to save the world, not to judge the world? Thou wilt not be saved by Him; thou shalt be judged of thyself. And why do I say, "shalt be judged"? See what He says: "He that believeth on Him is not judged, but he that believeth not." What dost thou expect He is going to say, but "is judged"? "Already," saith He, "has been judged." The judgment has not yet appeared, but already it has taken place. For the Lord knoweth them that are His: He knows who are persevering for the crown, and who for the flame; knows the wheat on His threshing-floor, and knows the chaff; knows the good corn, and knows the tares. He that believeth not is already judged. Why judged? "Because he has not believed in the name of the only-begotten Son of God."

13. "And this is the judgment, that light is come into the world, and men loved darkness rather than light, because their deeds were evil." My brethren, whose works does the Lord find to be good? The works of none: He finds the works of all evil. How is it, then, that some have done the truth, and are come to the light? For this is what follows: "But he that doeth truth cometh to the light, that his deeds may be made manifest, that they are wrought in God." In what way have some done a good work to come to the light, namely, to Christ? And how have some loved darkness? For if He finds all men sinners, and healeth all of sin, and that serpent in which the Lord's death was figured healed them that were bitten, and on account of the serpent's bite the serpent was set up, namely, the Lord's death on account of mortal men, whom He finds unrighteous; how are we to understand that "this is the judgment, that light is come into the world, and men loved darkness rather than light, because their deeds were evil"? How is this? Whose works, in fact, are good? Hast Thou not come to justify the ungodly? "But they loved," saith He, "darkness rather than light." There He laid the emphasis: for many loved their sins; many confessed their sins; and he who confesses his sins, and accuses them, doth now work with God. God accuses thy sins: and if thou also accusest, thou art united to God. There are, as it were, two things, man and sinner. That thou

---

[1] Num. xxi. 6-9.   [2] 1 Cor. xv. 54.

art called man, is God's doing; that thou art called sinner, is man's own doing. Blot out what thou hast done, that God may save what He has done. It behoves thee to hate thine own work in thee, and to love the work of God in thee. And when thy own deeds will begin to displease thee, from that time thy good works begin, as thou findest fault with thy evil works. The confession of evil works is the beginning of good works. Thou doest the truth, and comest to the light. How is it thou doest the truth? Thou dost not caress, nor soothe, nor flatter thyself; nor say, " I am righteous," whilst thou art unrighteous: thus, thou beginnest to do the truth. Thou comest to the light, that thy works may be made manifest that they are wrought in God; for thy sin, the very thing that has given thee displeasure, would not have displeased thee, if God did not shine into thee, and His truth show it thee. But he that loves his sins, even after being admonished, hates the light admonishing him, and flees from it, that his works which he loves may not be proved to be evil. But he that doeth truth accuses his evil works in himself, spares not himself, forgives not himself, that God may forgive him: for that which he desires God to forgive, he himself acknowledges, and he comes to the light; to which he is thankful for showing him what he should hate in himself. He says to God, " Turn away Thy face from my sins:" yet with what countenance says it, unless he adds, "For I acknowledge mine iniquity, and my sin is ever before me?"[1] Be that before thyself which thou desirest not to be before God. But if thou wilt put thy sin behind thee, God will thrust it back before thine eyes; and this He will do at a time when there will be no more fruit of repentance.

14. Run, my brethren, lest the darkness

[1] Ps. li. 11.

lay hold of you. Awake to your salvation, awake while there is time; let none be kept back from the temple of God, none kept back from the work of the Lord, none called away from continual prayer, none be defrauded of wonted devotion. Awake, then, while it is day: the day shines, Christ is the day. He is ready to forgive sins, but to them that acknowledge them; ready to punish the self-defenders, who boast that they are righteous, and think themselves to be something when they are nothing. But he that walks in His love and mercy, even being free from those great and deadly sins, such crimes as murder, theft, adultery; still, because of those which seem to be minute sins, of tongue, or of thought, or of intemperance in things permitted, he doeth the truth in confession, and cometh to the light in good works: since many minute sins, if they be neglected, kill. Minute are the drops that swell the rivers; minute are the grains of sand; but if much sand is put together, the heap presses and crushes. Bilge-water neglected in the hold does the same thing as a rushing wave. Gradually it leaks in through the hold; and by long leaking in and no pumping out, it sinks the ship. Now what is this pumping out, but by good works, by sighing, fasting, giving, forgiving, so to effect that sins may not overwhelm us? The path of this life, however, is troublesome, full of temptations: in prosperity, let it not lift us up; in adversity, let it not crush us. He who gave the happiness of this world gave it for thy comfort, not for thy ruin. Again, He who scourgeth thee in this life, doeth it for thy improvement, not for thy condemnation. Bear the Father that corrects thee for thy training, lest thou feel the judge in punishing thee. These things we tell you every day, and they must be often said, because they are good and wholesome.

TRACTATE XIII.

Chapter III. 22–29.

1. The course of reading from the Gospel of John, as those of you who are concerned for your own progress may remember, so proceeds in regular order, that the passage which has now been read comes before us for exposition to-day. You remember that we have expounded it, in the preceding dis-

courses, from the very beginning of the Gospel, as far as the lesson of to-day. And though perhaps you have forgotten much of it, at least it remains in your memory that we have done our part in it. What you have heard from it about the baptism of John, even though you retain not all, yet I believe you have heard that which you may retain. Also, what was said as to why the Holy Spirit appeared in the shape of a dove; and how that most knotty question was solved, namely, what was that something in the Lord which John did not know, and which he learned by means of the dove, whilst already John knew Him, since, as Jesus came to be baptized, he said to Him, "I ought to be baptized by Thee, and comest Thou to me?" when the Lord answered him, "Suffer it now, that all righteousness may be fulfilled." [1]

2. Now, therefore, the order of our reading obliges us to return to that same John. The same is he who was prophesied of by Isaiah, "The voice of one crying in the wilderness, Prepare ye a way for the Lord, make His paths straight." [2] Such testimony gave he to his Lord and (for the Lord deemed him worthy) his friend. And the Lord, even his friend, did also Himself bear witness to John. For concerning John He said, "Among them that are born of women, there hath not arisen a greater than John the Baptist." But as He put Himself before John, in that wherein He was greater, He was God. "But he that is less," saith He, "in the kingdom of heaven is greater than he." [3] Less in age; greater in power, in deity, in majesty, in brightness: even as "in the beginning was the Word, and the Word was with God, and the Word was God." In the preceding passages, however, John had given testimony to the Lord, in such wise that he did indeed call Him Son of God, but said not that He was God, nor yet denied it: he was silent as to His being God, not denied that He was God; but yet he was not altogether silent as to His being God, for perhaps we find this in the lesson of to-day. He had called Him Son of God; but men, too, have been called sons of God. He had declared Him to be of such excellence, that he was not himself worthy to loose the latchet of His shoe. Now this greatness gives us much to understand: whose shoe-latchet he was not worthy to loose, he than whom none greater had arisen among them that are born of women. He was more, indeed, than all men and angels. For we find an angel forbidding a man to fall at his feet. For example, when in the Apocalypse an angel was showing certain things to John, the writer of this Gospel, John, terrified at the greatness of the vision, fell down at the angel's feet. But said the angel, "Rise; see thou do it not: worship God, for I am thy fellow-servant, and the brethren's." [4] An angel, then, forbade a man to fall down at his feet. Is it

not manifest that He must be above all angels, for whom a man, such that a greater than he has not risen among them that are born of women, declares himself to be not worthy to loose the latchet of His shoe?

3. John, however, may say something more evidently, that our Lord Jesus Christ is God. We may find this in the present passage, that it is perhaps of Him we have been singing, "The Lord reigned over all the earth;" against which they are deaf who imagine that He reigns only in Africa. But let them not suppose that it is not of Christ it is spoken when it is said, "God reigned over all the earth." For who else is our King, but our Lord Jesus Christ? It is He that is our King. And what have you heard in the same psalm, in the verse just sung? "Sing praises to our God, sing praises: sing praises to our King, sing praises." Whom he called God, the same he called our King: "Sing praises to our God, sing praises: sing praises to our King, sing ye praises with understanding." And that thou shouldest not understand Him to whom thou singest praises to reign in one part, he says, "For God is King of all the earth." [5] And how is He King of all the earth, who appeared in one part of the earth, in Jerusalem, in Judea, walking among men, born, sucking the breast, growing, eating, drinking, waking, sleeping, sitting at a well, wearied; laid hold of, scourged, spat upon, crowned with thorns, hanged on a tree, wounded with a spear, dead, buried? How then King of all the earth? What was seen locally was flesh, to carnal eyes only flesh was visible; the immortal majesty was concealed in mortal flesh. And with what eyes shall we be able to behold the immortal majesty, after penetrating through the structure of the flesh? There is another eye, there is an inner eye. Tobias, for example, was not without eyes, when, blind in his bodily eyes, he was giving precepts of life to his son. [6] The son was holding the father's hand, that the father might walk with his feet, whilst the father was giving the son counsel to walk in the way of righteousness. Here I see eyes, and there I understand eyes. And better are the eyes of him that gives counsel of life, than his who holds the hand. Such eyes Jesus also required when He said to Philip, "Am I so long time with you, and ye have not known me?" Such eyes He required when He said, "Philip, he that seeth me, seeth the Father." These are the eyes of the understanding, these are the eyes of the mind. It is for that reason that the psalm, when it

---

[1] Matt. iii. 14.　　[2] Isa. xl. 3.
[3] Matt. xi. 11.　　[4] Rev. xxii. 8, 9.　　[5] Ps. xlvii. 3-8.　　[6] Tobit iv.

had said, "For God is King of all the earth," immediately added, "Sing ye praises with understanding." For in that I say, "Sing ye praises to our God," I say that God is our King. But yet our King you have seen among men, as man; you have seen Him suffering, crucified, dead: there was in that flesh something concealed, which you might have seen with eyes of flesh. What was there concealed? "Sing ye praises with understanding." Do not seek to see with the eyes what is beheld by the mind. "Sing praises" with the tongue, for He is among you as flesh; but because "the Word was made flesh, and dwelt among us," render the sound to the flesh, render to God the gaze of the mind. "Sing ye praises with understanding," and you see that the "Word was made flesh, and dwelt among us."

4. Now let John also declare his witness: "After these things came Jesus and His disciples into the land of Judea; and there He tarried with them, and baptized." Being baptized, He baptized. Not with that baptism with which He was baptized did He baptize. The Lord, being baptized by a servant, gives baptism, showing the path of humility and leading to the baptism of the Lord, that is, His own baptism, by giving an example of humility, in not Himself refusing baptism from a servant. And in the baptism by a servant, a way was prepared for the Lord; the Lord also being baptized, made Himself a way for them that come to Him. Let us hear Himself: "I am the way, the truth, and the life." If thou seekest truth, keep the way, for the way and the truth are the same. The way that thou art going is the same as the *whither* thou art going: thou art not going by a way as one thing, to an object as another thing; not coming to Christ by something else as a way, thou comest to Christ by Christ. How by Christ to Christ? By Christ the man, to Christ God; by the Word made flesh, to the Word which in the beginning was God with God; from that which man ate, to that which angels daily eat. For so it is written, "He gave them bread of heaven: man ate the bread of angels."[1] What is the bread of angels? "In the beginning was the Word, and the Word was with God, and the Word was God." How has man eaten the bread of angels? "And the Word was made flesh, and dwelt among us."

5. But though we have said that angels eat, do not fancy, brethren, that this is done with teeth. For if you think so, God, of whom the angels eat, is as it were torn in pieces.

Who tears righteousness in pieces? But still, some one asks me, And who is it that can eat righteousness? Well, how is it said, "Blessed are they that hunger and thirst after righteousness, for they shall be filled"? The food which thou eatest carnally perishes, in order to refresh thee; to repair thy waste it is consumed: eat righteousness; and while thou art refreshed, it continues entire. Just as by seeing this corporeal light, these eyes of ours are refreshed, and yet it is a corporeal thing that is seen by corporeal eyes. Many there have been, when too long in darkness, whose eyesight is weakened by fasting, as it were, from light. The eyes, deprived of their food (for they feed on light), become wearied by fasting, and weakened, so that they cannot bear to see the light by which they are refreshed; and if the light is too long absent, they are quenched, and the very sense of sight dies as it were in them. What then? Does the light become less, because so many eyes are daily fed by it? Thy eyes are refreshed, and the light remains entire. As God was able to show this in the case of corporeal light to corporeal eyes, does He not show that other light to clean hearts as unwearied, continuing entire, and in no respect failing? What light? "In the beginning was the Word, and the Word was with God." Let us see if this is light. "For with Thee is the fountain of light, and in Thy light shall we see light." On earth, fountain is one thing, light another. When thirsting, thou seekest a fountain, and to get to the fountain thou seekest light; and if it is not day, thou lightest a lamp to get to the fountain. That fountain is the very light: to the thirsting a fountain, to the blind a light. Let the eyes be opened to see the light, let the lips of the heart be opened to drink of the fountain; that which thou drinkest, thou seest, thou hearest. God becomes all to thee; for He is to thee the whole of these things which thou lovest. If thou regardest things visible, neither is God bread, nor is God water, nor is God this light, nor is He garment nor house. For all these are things visible, and single separate things. What bread is, water is not; and what a garment is, a house is not; and what these things are, God is not, for they are visible things. God is all this to thee: if thou hungerest, He is bread to thee; if thou thirstest, He is water to thee; if thou art in darkness, He is light to thee: for He remains incorruptible. If thou art naked, He is a garment of immortality to thee, when this corruptible shall put on incorruption, and this mortal shall put on immortality. All things can be said of God,

---

[1] Ps. lxxviii. 24.

and nothing is worthily said of God. Nothing is wider than this poverty of expression. Thou seekest a fitting name for Him, thou canst not find it; thou seekest to speak of Him in any way soever, thou findest that He is all. What likeness have the lamb and the lion? Both is said of Christ. "Behold the Lamb of God!" How a lion? "The Lion of the tribe of Judah hath prevailed." [1]

6. Let us hear John: "Jesus baptized." We said that Jesus baptized. How Jesus? How the Lord? How the Son of God? How the Word? Well, but the Word was made flesh. "And John also was baptizing in Ænon, near to Salim." A certain lake, "Ænon." [2] How do we know it was a lake? "Because there was much water there, and they came and were baptized. For John was not yet cast into prison." If you remember (see, I say it again), I told you why John baptized: because the Lord must needs be baptized. And why must the Lord be baptized? Because many there would be to despise baptism, that they might appear to be endowed with greater grace than they saw other believers endowed with. For example, a catechumen, now living continently, might despise a married person, and say of himself that he was better than the other believer. That catechumen might possibly say in his heart, "What need have I to receive baptism, to have just what that other man has, than whom I am already better?" Therefore, lest that neck of pride should hurl to destruction certain men much elated with the merits of their own righteousness, the Lord was willing to be baptized by a servant, as if addressing His chief sons: "Why do you extol yourselves? Why lift yourselves up because you have, one prudence, another learning, another chastity, another the courage of patience? Can you possibly have as much as I who gave you these? And yet I was baptized by a servant, you disdain to be baptized by the Lord." This is the sense of "to fulfill all righteousness."

7. But some one will say, "It were enough, then, that John baptized only the Lord; what need was there for others to be baptized by John?" Now we have said this too, that if John had baptized only the Lord, men would not be without this thought, that John had a better baptism than the Lord had. They would say, in fact, "So great was the baptism of John, that Christ alone was worthy to be baptized therewith." Therefore, to show that the baptism which the Lord was to give was better than that of John,—that the

one might be understood as that of a servant, the other as that of the Lord,—the Lord was baptized to give an example of humility; but He was not the only one baptized by John, lest John's baptism should appear to be better than the baptism of the Lord. To this end, however, our Lord Jesus Christ showed the way, as you have heard, brethren, lest any man, arrogating to himself that he has abundance of some particular grace, should disdain to be baptized with the baptism of the Lord. For whatever the catechumen's proficiency, he still carries the load of his iniquity: it is not forgiven him until he shall have come to baptism. Just as the people Israel were not rid of the Egyptians until they had come to the Red Sea, so no man is rid of the pressure of sins until he has come to the font of baptism.

8. "Then there arose a question on the part of John's disciples with the Jews about purifying." John baptized, Christ baptized. John's disciples were moved; there was a running after Christ, people were coming to John. Those who came to John, he sent to Jesus to be baptized; but they who were baptized by Christ were not sent to John. John's disciples were alarmed, and began to dispute with the Jews, as usually happens. Understand the Jews to have declared that Christ was greater, and that to His baptism people ought to have recourse. John's disciples, not yet understanding this, defended John's baptism. They came to John himself, that he might solve the question. Understand, beloved. And here we are given to see the use of humility, and, when people were erring in the subject of dispute, are shown whether John desired to glory in himself. Now probably he said, "You say the truth, you contend rightly; mine is the better baptism, I baptized Christ Himself." John could say this after Christ was baptized. If he wished to exalt himself, what an opportunity he had to do so! But he knew better before whom to humble himself: to Him whom he knew to have come after himself by birth, he willingly yielded precedence by confessing Him. He understood his own salvation to be in Christ. He had already said above, "We all have received out of His fullness;" and this is to confess Him to be God. For how can all men receive of His fullness, if He be not God? For if He is man in such wise that He is not God, then Himself also receives of the fullness of God, and so is not God. But if all men receive of His fullness, He is the fountain, they are drinkers. They that drink of a fountain, both thirst and drink. The fountain never thirsts; it has never need of itself.

---

[1] Rev. v. 5.　　　　[2] [An error.]

Men need a fountain. With thirsty stomachs and parched lips they run to the fountain to be refreshed. The fountain flows to refresh, so does the Lord Jesus.

9. Let us see, then, what answer John gives: "They came unto John, and said unto him, Rabbi, he that was with thee beyond Jordan, to whom thou barest witness, behold the same baptizeth, and all men come to him:" that is, What sayest thou? Ought they not to be hindered, that they may rather come to thee? "He answered and said, A man cannot receive anything, except it be given him from heaven." Of whom, think you, had John said this? Of himself. "As a man, I received," saith he, "from heaven." Note, my beloved: "A man cannot receive anything, except it be given him from heaven. Ye yourselves bear me witness that I said, I am not the Christ." As much as to say, "Why do ye deceive yourselves? See how you have put this question before me. What have you said to me? 'Rabbi, he that was with thee beyond Jordan, to whom thou barest witness.' Then you know what sort of witness I bare to Him. Am I now to say that He is not the same whom I declared Him to be? And because I received somewhat from heaven, in order to be something, do you wish me to be empty of it, so as to speak against the truth? 'A man cannot receive anything, except it be given him from heaven. Ye yourselves bear me witness that I said, I am not the Christ.'" Thou art not the Christ; but what if thou art greater than He, since thou didst baptize Him? "I am sent:" I am the herald, He is the Judge.

10. But hear a far stronger, a far more expressive testimony. See ye what it is we are treating of; see ye that to love any person in place of Christ is adultery. Why do I say this? Let us attend to the voice of John. People could be mistaken in him, could think him to be the person he was not. He rejects the false honor, in order to hold the truth complete. See what he declares Christ to be; what does he say himself is? "He that hath the bride is the bridegroom." Be chaste, love the bridegroom. But what art thou, who sayest to us, "He that hath the bride is the bridegroom? But the friend of the bridegroom, who standeth and heareth him, rejoiceth greatly because of the bridegroom's voice." The Lord our God will help me in proportion to the tumult of my heart, for it is full of sadness, to utter the grief I feel; but I beseech you by Christ Himself to imagine in thought what it will not be possible for me to utter; for I know that my grief cannot be expressed with befitting impressiveness.

Now I see many adulterers who desire to get possession of the bride, purchased at so great a price, loved while deformed that she might be made fair, having been purchased and delivered and adorned by such an one; and those adulterers strive with their words to be loved instead of the bridegroom. Of that One it is said, "This is He that baptizeth." [1] Who is he that goes forth from us and says, "I am he that baptizeth"? Who is he that goes forth from us and says, "That is holy which I give"? Who is he that goes hence and says, "It is good for thee to be born of me"? Let us hear the friend of the bridegroom, not the adulterers against the bridegroom; let us hear one jealous, but not for himself.

11. Brethen, return in thought to your own homes. I speak of carnal, I speak of earthly things; I speak after the manner of men, for the infirmity of your flesh. Many of you have, many of you wish to have, many, though you wish not to have, still have had wives; many who do not at all wish to have wives, are born of the wives of your fathers. This is a feeling that touches every heart. There is no man so alien from mankind in human affairs as not to feel what I say. Suppose that a man, having set out on a journey, had commended his bride to the care of his friend: "See, I pray thee, thou art my dear friend; see to it, lest in my absence some other may perchance be loved in my stead." Then what sort of a person must he be, who, while the guardian of the bride or wife of his friend, does indeed endeavor that none other be loved, but if he wishes himself to be loved instead of his friend, and desires to enjoy her who was committed to his care, how detestable must he appear to all mankind! Let him see her gazing out of the window, or joking with some one somewhat too heedlessly, he forbids her as one who is jealous. I see him jealous, but let me see for whom he is jealous; whether for his absent friend or for his present self. Think that our Lord Jesus Christ has done this. He has committed His bride to the care of His friend; He has set out on a journey to a far country to receive a kingdom, as He says Himself in the Gospel, [2] but yet is present in His majesty. Let the friend who has gone beyond the sea be deceived; and if he is deceived, woe to him who deceives! Why do men attempt to deceive God,—God who looks at the hearts of all, and searches the secrets of all? But some heretic shows himself, and says, "'Tis I that give, 'tis I that sanctify, 'tis I that justify; go not

1 John i. 33.   2 Luke xix. 12.

thou to that other sect." He does well indeed to be jealous, but see for whom. "Go
not thou to idols," saith he,—he is rightly jealous; "nor to diviners,"—still rightly jealous.
Let us see for whom he is jealous: "What I
give is holy, because it is *I* that give it; he
is baptized whom I baptize; he whom I baptize not is not baptized." Hear thou the
friend of the bridegroom, learn to be jealous
for thy friend; hear His voice who is " He
that baptizeth." Why desire to arrogate to
thyself what is not thine? Is he so very absent who has left here his bride? Knowest
thou not, that He who rose from the dead is
sitting at the right hand of the Father? If
the Jews despised Him hanging on the tree,
dost thou despise Him sitting in heaven? Be
assured, beloved, that I suffer great grief of
this matter; but, as I have said, I leave the rest
to your thoughts. I cannot utter it if I speak
the whole day. If I bewail it the whole day,
I do not enough. I cannot utter it, if I
should have, as the prophet says, "a fountain
of tears;" and were I changed into tears,
and to become all tears, were I turned into
tongues, and to become all tongues, it were
not enough.

12. Let us return and see what this John
saith: " He that hath the bride is the bridegroom; " she is not my bride. And dost
thou not rejoice in the marriage? Yea, saith
he, I do rejoice: "But the friend of the
bridegroom, who standeth and heareth him,
rejoiceth greatly because of the voice of the
bridegroom." Not because of mine own
voice, saith he, do I rejoice, but because of
the Bridegroom's voice. I am in the place
of hearer; He, of speaker: I am as one that
must be enlightened, He is the light; I am as
the ear, He is the word. Therefore the friend
of the Bridegroom standeth and heareth Him.
Why standeth? Because he falls not. How falls
not? Because he is humble. See him standing on solid ground; "I am not worthy to
loose the latchet of His shoe." Thou doest
well to be humble; deservedly thou dost not
fall; deservedly thou standest, and hearest
Him, and rejoicest greatly for the Bridegroom's voice. So also the apostle is the
Bridegroom's friend; he too is jealous, not
for himself, but for the Bridegroom. Hear
his voice when he is jealous: " I am jealous
over you," said he, "with the jealousy of
God:" not with my own, nor for myself, but
with the jealousy of God. Why? How?
Over whom art thou jealous, and for whom?
" For I have espoused you to one husband,
to present a chaste virgin to Christ." Why
dost thou fear, then? Why art thou jealous?
" I fear," saith he, " lest, as the serpent be-

guiled Eve by his subtilty, so your minds
should be corrupted from the chastity which
is in Christ." [1] The whole Church is called a
virgin. You see that the members of the
Church are divers, that they are endowed
with and do rejoice in divers gifts: some men
wedded, some women wedded; some are wid-
owers who seek no more to have wives, some
are widows who seek no more to have husbands; some men preserve continence from
their youth, some women have vowed their
virginity to God: divers are the gifts, but all
these are one virgin. Where is this virginity?
for it is not in the body. It belongs to few
women; and if virginity can be said of men,
to few men in the Church belongs a holy
integrity even of body; yet one such is a
more honorable member. Other members,
however, preserve virginity, not in body, but
all in mind. What is the virginity of the
mind? Entire faith, firm hope, sincere charity. This is the virginity which he, who,
was jealous for the Bridegroom, feared might
be corrupted by the serpent. For, just as
the bodily member is marred in a certain part,
so the seduction of the tongue defiles the
virginity of the heart. Let her who does not
desire without cause to keep virginity of body,
see to it that she be not corrupted in mind.

13. What shall I say, then, brethren?
Even the heretics have virgins, and there are
many virgins among heretics. Let us see
whether they love the Bridegroom, so that
this virginity may be guarded. For whom
is it guarded? "For Christ." Let us see if
it be for Christ, and not for Donatus: let us
see for whom this virginity is preserved: you
can easily prove. Behold, I show you the
Bridegroom, for He shows Himself. John
bears witness to Him: " This is He that baptizeth." O thou virgin, if for this Bridegroom thou preservest thy virginity, why runnest thou to him who says, "I am he that
baptizeth," while the friend of the Bridegroom tells thee, " This is He that baptizeth"? Again, thy Bridegroom possesseth
the whole world; why, then, shouldst thou be
defiled with a part of it? Who is the Bridegroom? " For God is King of all the earth."
This thy Bridegroom possesses the whole,
because He purchased the whole. See at
what price He purchased it, that thou mayest
understand what He has purchased. What
price has He given? He gave His blood.
Where gave He, where shed He, His blood?
In His passion. Is it not to thy Bridegroom
thou singest, or feignest to sing, when the
whole world was purchased: " They pierced

---

[1] 2 Cor. xi. 2, 3.

my hands and my feet, they counted all my bones: but they themselves considered me, they looked upon me, they divided my garments among them, and upon my vesture they cast lots"? Thou art the bride, acknowledge thy Bridegroom's vesture. Upon what vesture was the lot cast? Ask the Gospel; see to whom thou art espoused, see from whom thou receivest pledges. Ask the Gospel; see what it tells thee in the suffering of the Lord. "There was a coat" there: let us see what kind; "woven from the top throughout." What does the coat woven from the top signify, but charity? What does this coat signify, but unity? Consider this coat, which not even the persecutors of Christ divided. For it saith, "They said among themselves, Let us not divide it, but let us cast lots upon it." Behold that of which the psalm spoke! Christ's persecutors did not rend His garment; Christians divide the Church.

14. But what shall I say, brethren? Let us see plainly what He purchased. For there He bought, where He paid the price. Paid it for how much? If He paid it only for Africa, let us be Donatists, and not be called Donatists, but Christians; since Christ bought only Africa: although even here are other than Donatists. But He has not been silent of what He bought in this transaction. He has made up the account: thanks be to God, He has not tricked us. Need there is for that bride to hear, and then to understand to whom she has vowed her virginity. There, in that psalm where it says, "They pierced my hands and my feet, they counted all my bones;" wherein the Lord's passion is most openly declared;—the psalm which is read every year on the last week, in the hearing of the whole people, at the approach of Christ's passion; and this psalm is read both among them and us;—there, I say, note, brethren, what He has bought: let the bill of merchandise be read: hear ye what He bought: "All the ends of the earth shall remember, and turn unto the Lord; and all the kindreds of the nations shall worship in His sight: for the kingdom is His, and He shall rule the nations." Behold what it is He has bought! Behold! "For God, the King of all the earth," is thy Bridegroom. Why, then, wouldst thou have one so rich reduced to rags? Acknowledge Him: He bought the whole; yet thou sayest, "Thou hast a part of it here." Oh, would that thou wert well-pleasing to thy Spouse; would that thou who speakest wert not defiled, and, what is worse, defiled in heart, not in body! Thou lovest a man instead of Christ; lovest one that says, "'Tis I that baptize;" not hearing the friend of the Bridegroom when he says, "This is He that baptizeth;" not hearing him when he says, "He that hath the bride is the Bridegroom." I have not the bride, said he; but what am I? "But the friend of the Bridegroom, who standeth and heareth Him, rejoiceth greatly, because of the Bridegroom's voice."

15. Evidently, then, my brethren, it profits those men nothing to keep virginity, to have continence, to give alms. All those doings which are praised in the Church profit them nothing; because they rend unity, namely, that "coat" of charity. What do they? Many among them are eloquent; great tongues, streams of tongues. Do they speak like angels? Let them hear the friend of the Bridegroom, jealous for the Bridegroom, not for himself: "Though I speak with the tongues of men and of angels, and have not charity, I am become as sounding brass, or a tinkling cymbal." [1]

16. But what say they? "We have baptism." Thou hast, but not thine. It is one thing to have, another to own. Baptism thou hast, for thou hast received to be baptized, received as one enlightened, provided thou be not darkened of thyself; and when thou givest, thou givest as a minister, not as owner; as a herald proclaiming, not as judge. The judge speaks through the herald, and nevertheless it is not written in the registers, "The herald said," but, "The judge said." Therefore see if what thou givest is thine by authority. But if thou hast received, confess with the friend of the Bridegroom, "A man cannot receive anything, except it be given him from heaven." Confess with the friend of the Bridegroom, "He that hath the bride is the Bridegroom; but the friend of the Bridegroom standeth and heareth Him." But O, would thou didst stand and hear Him, and not fall, to hear thyself! For by hearing Him, thou wouldst stand and hear; for thou wilt speak, and thy head is puffed with pride. I, saith the Church, if I am the bride, if I have received pledges, if I have been redeemed at the price of that blood, do hear the voice of the Bridegroom; and I do hear the voice of the Bridegroom's friend too, if he give glory to my Bridegroom, not to himself. Let the friend speak: "He that hath the bride is the Bridegroom; but the friend of the Bridegroom standeth and heareth Him, and rejoices greatly because of the voice of the Bridegroom." Behold, thou hast sacraments; and I grant that thou hast. Thou hast the form, but thou art a branch

---

[1] 1 Cor. xiii. 1.

cut off from the vine; thou hast a form, I want the root. There is no fruit of the form, except where there is a root; but where is the root but in charity? Hear the form of the cut-off branches; let Paul speak: "Though I know all mysteries," saith he, "and have all prophecy, and all faith" (and how great a faith!), "so as to remove mountains, and have not charity, I am nothing."

17. Let no man tell you fables, then. "Pontius wrought a miracle; and Donatus prayed, and God answered him from heaven." In the first place, either they are deceived, or they deceive. In the last place, grant that he removes mountains: "And have not charity," saith the apostle, "I am nothing." Let us see whether he has charity. I would believe that he had, if he had not divided unity. For against those whom I may call marvel-workers, my God has put me on my guard, saying, "In the last times there shall arise false prophets, doing signs and wonders, to lead into error, if it were possible, even the elect: Lo, I have foretold it to you."[1] Therefore the Bridegroom has cautioned us, that we ought not to be deceived even by miracles. Sometimes, indeed, a deserter frightens a plain countryman; but whether he is of the camp, and whether he is the better of that character with which he is marked, is what he who would not be frightened or seduced attends to. Let us then, my brethren, hold unity: without unity, even he who works miracles is nothing. The people Israel was in unity, and yet wrought no miracles: Pharaoh's magicians were out of unity, and yet they wrought the like works as Moses.[2] The people Israel, as I have said, wrought no miracles. Who were saved with God—they who did, or they who did not, work miracles? The Apostle Peter raised a dead person: Simon Magus did many things: there were there certain Christians who were not able to do either what Peter did or what Simon did;

and wherein did they rejoice? In this, that their names were written in heaven. For this is what our Lord Jesus Christ said to the disciples on their return, because of the faith of the Gentiles. The disciples, in truth, themselves said, boasting, "Behold, Lord, in Thy name even the devils are subject to us." Rightly indeed they confessed, they brought the honor to the name of Christ; and yet what does He say to them? "Do not ye glory in this, that the devils are subject to you; but rejoice that your names are written in heaven."[3] Peter cast out devils. Some old widow, some lay person or other, having charity, and holding the integrity of faith, forsooth does not do this. Peter is the eye in the body, that man is the finger, yet is he in the same body in which Peter is; and if the finger has less power than the eye, yet it is not cut off from the body. Better is it to be a finger and to be in the body, than to be an eye and to be plucked out of the body.

18. Therefore, my brethren, let no man deceive you, let no man seduce you: love the peace of Christ, who was crucified for you, whilst He was God. Paul says, "Neither he that planteth is anything, neither he that watereth, but God who giveth the increase."[4] And does any of us say that he is something? If we say that we are something, and give not the glory to Him, we are adulterers; we desire ourselves to be loved, not the Bridegroom. Love ye Christ, and us in Him, in whom also you are beloved by us. Let the members love one another, but live all under the Head. With grief indeed, my brethren, I have been obliged to speak much, and yet I have said little: I have not been able to finish the passage; God will help us to finish it in due season. I did not wish to burden your hearts further; I wish them to be free for sighs and prayers in behalf of those who are still deaf and do not understand.

---

[1] Mark xiii. 22, 23.   [2] Ex. vii. 12.   [3] Luke x. 17.   [4] 1 Cor. iii. 7.

TRACTATE XIV.

Chapter III. 29–36.

1. This lesson from the holy Gospel shows us the excellency of our Lord Jesus Christ's divinity, and the humility of the man who earned the title of the Bridegroom's friend; that we may distinguish between the man who is man, and the Man who is God. For the Man who is God is our Lord Jesus Christ, God before all ages, Man in the age of our world: God of the Father, man of the Virgin, yet one and the same Lord and Saviour Jesus Christ, Son of God, God and man. But John, a man of distinguished grace, was sent

before Him, a man enlightened by Him who is the Light. For of John it is said, "He was not the Light, but that he should bear witness of the Light." He may himself be called a light indeed, and rightly so; but an enlightened, not an enlightening light. The light that enlightens, and that which is enlightened, are different things: for even our eyes are called lights (*lumina*), and yet when we open them in the dark, they do not see. But the light that enlightens is a light both from itself and for itself, and does not need another light for its shining; but all the rest need it, that they may shine.

2. Accordingly John confessed Him: as you have heard that when Jesus was making many disciples, and they reported to John as if to excite him to jealousy,—for they told the matter as if moved by envy, " Lo, he is making more disciples than thou,"—John confessed what he was, and thereby merited to belong to Him, because he dared not affirm himself to be that which Jesus is. Now this is what John said: " A man cannot receive anything, except it be given him from heaven." Therefore Christ gives, man receives. " Ye yourselves bear me witness that I said, I am not the Christ, but that I am sent before Him. He that hath the bride is the Bridegroom; but the friend of the Bridegroom, who standeth and heareth Him, rejoiceth greatly because of the Bridegroom's voice." Not of himself did he give himself joy. He that will have joy of himself shall be sad; but he that will have his joy of God will ever rejoice, because God is everlasting. Dost thou desire to have everlasting joy? Cleave to Him who is everlasting. Such an one John declared himself to be. " Because of the Bridegroom's voice, the friend of the Bridegroom rejoiceth," not because of his own voice, and " standeth and heareth." Therefore, if he falls, he heareth Him not: for of a certain one who fell it is said, " And he stood not in the truth;" [1] this is said of the devil. It behoves the Bridegroom's friend, then, " to stand and to hear." What is it to stand? It is to abide in His grace, which he received. And he hears a voice at which he rejoices. Such was John: he knew whereof he rejoiced; he did not arrogate to himself to be what he was not; he knew himself as one enlightened, not the enlightener. " But that was the true Light," saith the evangelist, " that lighteneth every man coming into this world." If " every man," then also John himself; for he too is of men. Moreover, although none hath arisen among them that are born of women greater than John, yet he was himself one of those that are born of women. Is he to be compared with Him who, because He willed it, was born by a singular and extraordinary birth? For both generations of the Lord are unexampled, both the divine and the human: by the divine He has no mother; by the human, no father. Therefore John was but one of the rest: of greater grace, however, so that of those born of women none arose greater than he; so great a testimony he gave to our Lord Jesus Christ as to call Him the Bridegroom, and himself the Bridegroom's friend, not worthy however to loose the latchet of the Bridegroom's shoe. You have already heard much on this point, beloved: let us look to what follows; for it is somewhat hard to understand. But as John himself says, that " no man can receive anything, except it be given him from heaven," whatever we shall not have understood, let us ask Him who gives from heaven: for we are men, and cannot receive anything, except He, who is not man, give it us.

3. Now this is what follows: and John says, " This my joy therefore is fulfilled." What is his joy? To rejoice at the Bridegroom's voice. It is fulfilled in me, I have my grace; more I do not assume to myself, lest also I lose what I have received. What is this joy? " With joy rejoiceth for the Bridegroom's voice." A man may understand, then, that he ought not to rejoice of his own wisdom, but of the wisdom which he has received from God. Let him ask nothing more, and he loses not what he found. For many, in that they affirmed themselves to be wise, became fools. The apostle convicts them, and says of them, " Because that which is known of God is manifest to them; for God has showed it unto them." Hear ye what he says of certain unthankful, ungodly men: " For the invisible things of Him from the creation of the world are seen, being understood by the things that are made, His eternal power likewise, and Godhead; so that they are without excuse." Why without excuse? " Because, knowing God " (he said not, " because they knew Him not "), " they glorified Him not as God, nor were thankful; but became vain in their imaginations, and their foolish heart was darkened: professing themselves to be wise, they became fools." [2] If they had known God, they had known at the same time that God, and none other, had made them wise; and they would not then attribute to themselves that which they did not have from themselves, but to Him from whom they

---

[1] John viii. 44.　　　　[2] Rom. i. 19-22.

had received it. But by their unthankfulness they became fools. Therefore, what God gave freely, He took from the unthankful. John would not be this; he would be thankful: he confessed to have received, and declared that he rejoiced for the Bridegroom's voice, saying, "Therefore this my joy is fulfilled."

4. "He must increase, but I must decrease." What is this? He must be exalted, but I must be humbled. How is Jesus to increase? How is God to increase? The perfect does not increase. God neither increases nor decreases. For if He increases, He is not perfect; if He decreases, he is not God. And how can Jesus increase, being God? If to man's estate, since He deigned to be man and was a child; and, though the Word of God, lay an infant in a manger; and, though His mother's Creator, yet sucked the milk of infancy of her: then Jesus having grown in age of the flesh, that perhaps is the reason why it is said, "He must increase, but I must decrease." But why in this? As regards the flesh, John and Jesus were of the same age, there being six months between them: they had grown up together; and if our Lord Jesus Christ had willed to be here longer before His death, and that John should be here with Him, then, as they had grown up together, so would they have grown old together: in what way, then, "He must increase, but I must decrease"? Above all, our Lord Jesus Christ being now thirty years old, does a man who is already thirty years old still grow? From that same age, men begin to go downward, and to decline to graver age, thence to old age. Again, even had they both been lads, he would not have said, "He must increase," but, We must increase together. But now each is thirty years of age. The interval of six months makes no difference in age; the difference is discovered by reading rather than by the look of the persons.

5. What means, then, "He must increase, but I must decrease"? This is a great mystery! Before the Lord Jesus came, men were glorying of themselves; He came a man, to lessen man's glory, and to increase the glory of God. Now He came without sin, and found all men in sin. If thus He came to put away sin, God may freely give, man may confess. For man's confession is man's lowliness: God's pity is God's loftiness. Therefore, since He came to forgive man his sins, let man acknowledge his own lowliness and let God show His pity. "He must increase, but I must decrease:" that is, He must give, but I must receive; He must be glorified, but I must confess. Let man know

his own condition, and confess to God; and hear the apostle as he says to a proud, elated man, bent on extolling himself: "What hast thou that thou didst not receive? And if thou didst receive it, why dost thou glory as if thou didst not receive it?"[1] Then let man understand that he has received; and when he would call that his own which is not his, let him decrease: for it is good for him that God be glorified in him. Let him decrease in himself, that he may be increased in God. These testimonies and this truth, Christ and John signified by their deaths. For John was lessened by the Head: Christ was exalted on the cross; so that even there it appeared what this is, "He must increase, but I must decrease." Again, Christ was born when the days were just beginning to lengthen; John was born when they began to shorten. Thus their very creation and deaths testify to the words of John, when he says, "He must increase, but I must decrease." May the glory of God then increase in us, and our own glory decrease, that even ours may increase in God! For this is what the apostle says, this is what Holy Scripture says: "He that glorieth, let him glory in the Lord."[2] Wilt thou glory in thyself? Thou wilt grow; but grow worse in thy evil. For whoso grows worse is justly decreased. Let God, then, who is ever perfect, grow, and grow in thee. For the more thou understandest God, and apprehendest Him, He seems to be growing in thee; but in Himself He grows not, being ever perfect. Thou didst understand a little yesterday; thou understandest more to-day, wilt understand much more to-morrow: the very light of God increases in thee; as if thus God increases, who remains ever perfect. It is as if one's eyes were being cured of former blindness, and he began to see a little glimmer of light, and the next day he saw more, and the third day still more: to him the light would seem to grow; yet the light is perfect, whether he see it or not. Thus it is also with the inner man: he makes progress indeed in God, and God seems to be increasing in him; yet man himself is decreasing, that he may fall from his own glory, and rise into the glory of God.

6. What we have just heard, appears now distinctly and clearly. "He that cometh from above, is above all." See what he says of Christ. What of himself? "He that is of the earth, is of earth, and speaketh of the earth. He that cometh from above is above all"— this is Christ; and "he that is of the earth, is of earth, and speaketh of the earth"—this is John. And is this the whole: John is of the

---

[1] 1 Cor. iv. 7.   [2] 1 Cor. i. 31.

earth, and speaks of the earth? Is the whole testimony that he bears of Christ a speaking of the earth? Are they not voices of God that are heard from John, when he bears witness of Christ? Then how does he speak of the earth? He said this of man. So far as relates to man in himself, he is of earth, and speaks of the earth; and when he speaks some divine things, he is enlightened by God. For, were he not enlightened, he would be earth speaking of earth. God's grace is apart by itself, the nature of man apart by itself. Do but examine the nature of man: man is born and grows, he learns the customs of men. What does he know but earth, of earth? He speaks the things of men, knows the things of men, minds the things of men; carnal, he judges carnally, conjectures carnally: lo! it is man all over. Let the grace of God come, and enlighten his darkness, as it saith, "Thou wilt lighten my candle, O Lord; my God, enlighten my darkness;"[1] let it take the mind of man, and turn it to its own light; immediately he begins to say, as the apostle says, "Yet not I, but the grace of God that is with me;"[2] and, "Now I live; yet not I, but Christ liveth in me."[3] That is to say, "He must increase, but I must decrease." Thus John: as regards John, he is of the earth, and speaks of the earth; whatever that is divine thou hast heard from John, is of Him that enlightens, not of him that receives.

7. "He that cometh from heaven is above all; and what He hath seen and heard, that He testifieth: and no man receiveth His testimony." Cometh from heaven, is above all, our Lord Jesus Christ; of whom it was said above, "No man hath ascended into heaven, but He that came down from heaven, the Son of man who is in heaven." And He is above all; "and what He hath seen and heard, that He speaks." Moreover, He hath a Father, being Himself the Son of God; He hath a Father, and He also hears of the Father. And what is that which He hears of the Father? Who can unfold this? When can my tongue, when can my heart be sufficient, either the heart to understand, or the tongue to utter, what that is which the Son hath heard from the Father? May it be the Son has heard the Word of the Father? Nay, the Son is the Word of the Father. You see how all human effort is here wearied out; you see how all guessing of our heart, all straining of our darkened mind, here fails. I hear the Scripture saying that the Son speaks that which He heareth from the Father; and again,

I hear the Scripture saying that the Son is Himself the Word of the Father: "In the beginning was the Word, and the Word was with God, and the Word was God." The words that we speak are fleeting and transient: as soon as thy word has sounded from thy mouth, it passeth away; it makes its noise, and passes away into silence. Canst thou follow thy sound, and hold it to make it stand? Thy thought, however, remains, and of that thought that remains thou utterest many words that pass away. What say we, brethren? When God spake, did He give out a voice, or sounds, or syllables? If He did, in what tongue spake He? In Hebrew, or in Greek, or in Latin? Tongues are necessary where there is a distinction of nations. But there none can say that God spake in this tongue, or in that. Observe thy own heart. When thou conceivest a word which thou mayest utter,—For I will say, if I can, what we may note in ourselves, not whereby we may comprehend that,—well, when thou conceivest a word to utter, thou meanest to utter a thing, and the very conception of the thing is already a word in thy heart: it has not yet come forth, but it is already born in the heart, and is waiting to come forth. But thou considerest the person to whom it is to come forth, with whom thou art to speak: if he is a Latin, thou seekest a Latin expression; if a Greek, thou thinkest of Greek words; if a Punic, thou considerest whether thou knowest the Punic language: for the diversity of hearers thou hast recourse to divers tongues to utter the word conceived; but the conception itself was bound by no tongue in particular. Whilst therefore God, when speaking, required not a language, nor took up any kind of speech, how was He heard by the Son, seeing that God's speaking is the Son Himself? As, in fact, thou hast in thy heart the word that thou speakest, and as it is with thee, and is none other than the spiritual conception itself (for just as thy soul is spirit, so also the word which thou hast conceived is spirit; for it has not yet received sound to be divided by syllables, but remains in the conception of thy heart, and in the mirror of the mind); so God gave out His Word, that is, begat the Son. And thou, indeed, begettest the word even in thy heart according to time; God without time begat the Son by whom He created all times. Whilst, therefore, the Son is the Word of God, and the Son spoke to us not His own word, but the word of the Father, He willed to speak Himself to us when He was speaking the word of the Father. This it is that John said, as was fit and necessary; and we have expounded according to our ability.

---

[1] Ps. xviii. 28.   [2] 1 Cor. xv. 10.   [3] Gal. ii. 20.

He whose heart has not yet attained to a proper perception of so great a matter, has whither to turn himself, has where to knock, has from whom to ask, from whom to seek, of whom to receive.

8. "He that cometh from heaven is above all; and what He hath seen and heard, that testifieth He; and His testimony no man receiveth." If no man, to what purpose came He? He means, no man of a certain class. There are some people prepared for the wrath of God, to be damned with the devil; of these, none receiveth the testimony of Christ. For if none at all, not any man, received, what could these words mean, "But he that received His testimony hath set to his seal that God is true"? Not certainly, then, *no man*, if thou sayest thyself, "He that received His testimony has set to his seal that God is true." Perhaps John, on being questioned, would answer and say, I know what I have said, in saying *no man*. There are, in fact, people born to God's wrath, and thereunto foreknown. For God knows who they are that will and that will not believe; He knows who they are that shall persevere in that in which they have believed, and who that shall fall away; and all that shall be for eternal life are numbered by God; and He knows already the people set apart. And if He knows this, and has given to the prophets by His Spirit to know it, He gave this also to John. Now John was observing, not with his eye,—for as regards himself he is earth, and speaketh of earth,—but with that grace of the Spirit which he received of God, he saw a certain people, ungodly, unbelieving. Contemplating that people in its unbelief, he says, "His testimony, who came from heaven, no man receiveth." No man of whom? Of them who shall be on the left hand, of them to whom it shall be said, "Go into the everlasting fire, which is prepared for the devil and his angels." Who are they that do receive it? They who shall be at the right hand, they to whom it shall be said, "Come, ye blessed of my Father, receive the kingdom which is prepared for you from the beginning of the world." He observes, then, in the Spirit a dividing, but in the human race a mingling together; and that which is not yet separated locally, he separated in the understanding, in the view of the heart; and he saw two peoples, one of believers, one of unbelievers. Fixing his thought on the unbelievers, he says, "He that cometh from heaven is above all; and what He hath seen and heard, that He testifieth, and no man receiveth His testimony." He then turned his thought from the left hand, and looked at the right, and proceeded to

say, "He that received His testimony has set to his seal that God is true." What means "has set to his seal that God is true," if it be not that man is a liar, and God is true? For no human being can speak any truth, unless he be enlightened by Him who cannot lie. God, then, is true; but Christ is God. Wouldest thou prove this? Receive His testimony and thou findest it. For "he that hath received His testimony has set to his seal that God is true." Who is true? The same who came from heaven, and is above all, is God, and true. But if thou dost not yet understand Him to be God, thou hast not yet received His testimony: receive it, and thou puttest thy seal to it; confidently thou understandest, definitely thou acknowledgest, that God is true.

9. "For He whom God hath sent speaketh the words of God." Himself is the true God, and God sent Him: God sent God. Join both, one God, true God sent by God. Ask concerning them singly, He is God; ask concerning them both, they are God. Not individually God, and both Gods; but each individual God, and both God. For so great is the charity of the Holy Spirit there, so great the peace of unity, that when thou questionest about them individually, the answer to thee is, God; when thou askest concerning the Trinity, thou gettest for answer, God. For if the spirit of man, when it cleaves to God, is one spirit, as the apostle openly declares, "He that is joined to the Lord is one spirit;"[1] how much more is the equal Son, joined to the Father, together with Him one God! Hear another testimony. You know how many believed, when they sold all they had and laid it at the apostles' feet, that it might be distributed to each according to his need; and what saith the Scripture of that gathering of the saints? "They had one soul and one heart in the Lord."[2] If charity made one soul of so many souls, and one heart of so many hearts, how great must be the charity between the Father and the Son! Surely it must be greater than that between those men who had one heart. If, then, the heart of many brethren was one by charity, if the soul of many brethren was one by charity, wouldst thou say that God the Father and God the Son are two? If they are two Gods, there is not the highest charity between them. For if charity is here so great as to make thy soul and thy friend's soul one soul, how can it be then that the Father and the Son is not one God? Far be unfeigned faith from this thought. In short, how excellent that charity is, understand

7

---

[1] 1 Cor. vi. 17.   [2] Acts iv. 32.

hence: the souls of many men are many, and if they love one another, it is one soul; still, in the case of men, they may be called many souls, because the union is not so strong. But there it is right for thee to say one God; two or three Gods it is not right for thee to say. From this, the supreme and surpassing excellency of charity is shown thee to be such, that a greater cannot be.

10. "For He whom God hath sent speaketh the words of God." This, of course, he said of Christ, to distinguish himself from Christ. What then? Did not God send John himself? Did he not say himself, "I am sent before Him"? and, "He that sent me to baptize with water"? And is it not of John that it is said, "Behold, I send my messenger before Thee, and he shall prepare Thy way"?[1] Does he not himself speak the words of God, he of whom it is said that he is more than a prophet? Then, if God sent him too, and he speaks the words of God, how do we understand him to have distinctly said of Christ, "He whom God hath sent speaketh the words of God"? But see what he adds: "For God giveth not the Spirit by measure." What is this, "For God giveth not the Spirit by measure"? We find that God does give the Spirit by measure. Hear the apostle when he says, "According to the measure of the gift of Christ."[2] To men He gives by measure, to the only Son He gives not by measure. How does He give to men by measure? "To one is given by the Spirit the word of wisdom; to another the word of wisdom according to the same Spirit; to another faith by the same Spirit; to another prophecy; to another discerning of spirits; to another kinds of tongues; to another the gift of healing. Are all apostles? Are all prophets? Are all teachers? Are all workers of miracles? Have all the gift of healing? Do all speak with tongues? Do all interpret?"[3] This man has one gift, that man another; and what that man has, this has not: there is a measure, a certain division of gifts. To men, therefore, it is given by measure, and concord among them makes one body. As the hand receives one kind of gift to work, the eye another to see, the ear another to hear, the foot another to walk; nevertheless the soul that does all is one, in the hand to work, in the foot to walk, in the ear to hear, in the eye to see; so are also the gifts of believers diverse, distributed to them as to members, to each according to his proper measure. But Christ, who gives, receives not by measure.

11. Now hear further what follows: because

He had said of the Son, "For God giveth not the Spirit by measure: the Father loveth the Son, and hath given all things into His hand," He added, "hath given all things into His hands," that thou mightest know also here with what distinction it is said, "The Father loveth the Son." And why? Does the Father not love John? And yet He has not given all things into his hand. Does the Father not love Paul? And yet He has not given all things into his hand. "The Father loveth the Son:" but as father loveth, not as master loveth a servant; as the Only Son, not as an adopted son. And so "hath given all things into His hand." What means "all things"? That the Son should be such as the Father is. To equality with Himself He begat Him in whom it was no robbery to be in the form of God, equal to God. "The Father loveth the Son, and hath given all things into His hand." Therefore, having deigned to send us the Son, let us not imagine that it is something less than the Father that is sent to us. The Father, in sending the Son, sent His other self.

12. But the disciples, still thinking that the Father is something greater than the Son, seeing only the flesh, and not understanding His divinity, said to Him, "Lord, show us the Father and it sufficeth us." As much as to say, "We know Thee already, and bless Thee that we know Thee: for we thank that Thou hast shown Thyself to us. But as yet we know not the Father: therefore our heart is inflamed, and occupied with a certain holy longing of seeing Thy Father who sent Thee. Show us Him, and we shall desire nothing more of Thee: for it sufficeth us when He has been shown, than whom none can be greater." A good longing, a good desire; but small intelligence. Now the Lord Jesus Himself, regarding them as small men seeking great things, and Himself great among the small, and yet small among the small, says to Philip, one of the disciples, who had said this: "Am I so long time with you, and ye have not known me, Philip?" Here Philip might have answered, Thee we have known, but did we say to Thee, Show us Thyself? We have known Thee, but it is the Father we seek to know. He immediately adds, "He that hath seen me, hath seen the Father also."[4] If, then, One equal with the Father has been sent, let us not estimate Him from the weakness of the flesh, but think of the majesty clothed in flesh, but not weighed down by the flesh. For, remaining God with the Father, He was made man among men,

---

[1] Mal. iii. 1.   [2] Eph. iv. 7.   [3] 1 Cor. xii. 8–30.   [4] John xiv. 8, 9.

that, through Him who was made man, thou mightest become such as to receive God. For man could not receive God. Man could see man; God he could not apprehend. Why could he not apprehend God? Because he had not the eye of the heart, by which to apprehend Him. There was something within disordered, something without sound: man had the eyes of the body sound, but the eyes of the heart sick. He was made man to the eye of the body; so that, believing on Him who could be seen in bodily form, thou mightst be healed for seeing Him whom thou wast not able to see spiritually. "Am I so long time with you, and ye know me not, Philip? He that hath seen me, hath seen the Father also." Why did they not see Him? Lo, they did see Him, and yet saw not the Father: they saw the flesh, but the majesty was concealed. What the disciples who loved Him saw, saw also the Jews who crucified Him. Inwardly, then, was He all; and in such manner inwardly in the flesh, that He remained with the Father when He came to the flesh.

13. Carnal thought does not apprehend what I say: let it defer understanding, and begin by faith; let it hear what follows: "He that believeth on the Son hath everlasting life: and he that believeth not the Son shall not see life; but the wrath of God abideth on him." He has not said, The wrath of God cometh to him; but, "The wrath of God abideth on him." All that are born mortals have the wrath of God with them. What wrath of God? That wrath which Adam first received. For if the first man sinned, and heard the sentence, "Thou shalt die the death," he became mortal, and we began to be born mortal; and we have been born with the wrath of God. From this stock came the Son, not having sin, and He was clothed with flesh and mortality. If He partook with us of the wrath of God, are we slow to partake with Him the grace of God? He, then, that will not believe the Son, on the same "the wrath of God abideth." What wrath of God? That of which the apostle says, "We also were by nature the children of wrath, even as the rest."[1] All are therefore children of wrath, because coming of the curse of death. Believe on Christ, for thee made mortal, that thou mayest receive Him, the immortal; and when thou shalt have received His immortality, thou shalt no longer be mortal. He lived, thou wast dead; He died that thou shouldst live. He has brought us the grace of God, and has taken away the wrath of God. God has conquered death, lest death should conquer man.

[1] Eph. ii. 3.

TRACTATE XV.

Chapter IV. 1–42.

1. It is nothing new to your ears, beloved, that the Evangelist John, like an eagle, takes a loftier flight, and soars above the dark mist of earth, to gaze with steadier eyes upon the light of truth. From his Gospel much has already been treated of and discussed through our ministry, with the Lord's help; and the passage which has been read to-day follows in due order. What I am about to say, with the Lord's permission, many of you will hear in such wise that you will be reviewing what you know, rather than learning what you know not. Yet, for all that, your attention ought not to be slack, because it is not an acquiring, but a reviewing, of knowledge. This has been read, and we have in our hands to discourse upon this passage—that which the Lord Jesus spoke with the Samaritan woman at Jacob's well. The things spoken there are great mysteries, and the similitudes of great things; feeding the hungry, and refreshing the weary soul.

2. Now when the Lord knew this, "when He had heard that the Pharisees had learned that He was making more disciples than John, and baptized more (though Jesus baptized not, but His disciples), He left Judea, and departed again into Galilee." We must not discourse of this too long, lest, by dwelling on what is manifest, we shall lack the time to investigate and lay open what is obscure. Certainly, if the Lord saw that the fact of their coming to know that He made more disciples, and baptized more, would so avail to salvation to the Pharisees in following Him, as to become themselves His disciples, and to desire to be baptized by Him; rather would He not have left Judea, but would have remained there for their sakes. But because He knew their knowledge of the

fact, and at the same time knew their envy, and that they learned this, not to follow, but to persecute him, He departed thence. He could, indeed, even when present, cause that He should not be taken of them, if He would not; He had it in His power not to be put to death, if He would not, since He had the power not to be born, if He would not. But because, in everything that He did as man, He was showing an example to them who were to believe on Him (that any one servant of God sinneth not if he retire into another place, when he sees, it may be, the rage of his persecutors, or of them that seek to bring his soul into evil; but if a servant of God did this he might appear to commit sin, had not the Lord led the way in doing it), that good Master did this to teach us, not because He feared it.

3. It may perhaps surprise you why it is said, that "Jesus baptized more than John;" and after this was said, it is subjoined, "although Jesus baptized not, but His disciples." What then? Was the statement made false, and then corrected by this addition? Or are both true, viz. that Jesus both did and also did not baptize? He did in fact baptize, because it was He that cleansed; and He did not baptize, because it was not He that touched. The disciples supplied the ministry of the body; He afforded the aid of His majesty. Now, when could He cease from baptizing, so long as He ceased not from cleansing? Of Him it is said by the same John, in the person of the Baptist, who saith, "This is He that baptizeth." Jesus, therefore, is still baptizing; and so long as we continue to be baptized, Jesus baptizeth. Let a man come without fear to the minister below; for he has a Master above.

4. But it may be one saith, Christ does indeed baptize, but in spirit, not in body. As if, indeed, it were by the gift of another than He that any is imbued even with the sacrament of corporal and visible baptism. Wouldest thou know that it is He that baptizeth, not only with the Spirit, but also with water? Hear the apostle: "Even as Christ," saith he, "loved the Church, and gave Himself for it, purifying it with the washing of water by the Word, that He might present to Himself a glorious Church, not having spot, or wrinkle, or any such thing."[1] Purifying it. How? "With the washing of water by the Word." What is the baptism of Christ? The washing of water by the Word. Take away the water, it is no baptism; take away the Word, it is no baptism.

[1] Eph. v. 25-27.

5. This much, then, on the preliminary circumstances, by occasion of which He came to a conversation with that woman, let us look at the matters that remain; matters full of mysteries and pregnant with sacraments. "And He must needs pass through Samaria. He cometh then to a city of Samaria which is called Sychar, near to the parcel of ground which Jacob gave to his son Joseph. Now Jacob's fountain was there." It was a well; but every well is a fountain, yet not every fountain a well. For where the water flows from the earth, and offers itself for use to them that draw it, it is called a fountain; but if accessible, and on the surface, it is called only a fountain: if, however, it be deep and far down, it is called a well, but in such wise as not to lose the name of fountain.

6. "Jesus therefore, being wearied with His journey, sat thus on the well. It was about the sixth hour." Now begin the mysteries. For it is not without a purpose that Jesus is weary; not indeed without a purpose that the strength of God is weary; not without a purpose that He is weary, by whom the wearied are refreshed; not without a purpose is He weary, by whose absence we are wearied, by whose presence we are strengthened. Nevertheless Jesus is weary, and weary with His journey; and He sits down, and that, too, near a well; and it is at the sixth hour that, being wearied, He sits down. All these things hint something, are intended to intimate something, they make us eager, and encourage us to knock. May Himself open to us and to you; He who has deigned to exhort us, so as to say, "Knock, and it shall be opened to you." It was for thee that Jesus was wearied with His journey. We find Jesus to be strength, and we find Jesus to be weak: we find a strong and a weak Jesus: strong, because "in the beginning was the Word, and the Word was with God, and the Word was God: the same was in the beginning with God." Wouldest thou see how this Son of God is strong? "All things were made by Him, and without Him was nothing made:" and without labor, too, were they made. Then what can be stronger than He, by whom all things were made without labor? Wouldest thou know Him weak? "The Word was made flesh, and dwelt among us." The strength of Christ created thee, the weakness of Christ created thee anew. The strength of Christ caused that to be which was not: the weakness of Christ caused that what was should not perish. He fashioned us by His strength, He sought us by His weakness.

7. As weak, then, He nourishes the weak, as a hen her chickens; for He likened Him-

self to a hen: "How often," He saith to Jerusalem, "would I have gathered thy children under my wings, as a hen her chickens; but thou wouldest not!"[1] And you see, brethren, how a hen becomes weak with her chickens. No other bird, when it is a mother, is recognized at once to be so. We see all kinds of sparrows building their nests before our eyes; we see swallows, storks, doves, every day building their nests; but we do not know them to be parents, except when we see them on their nests. But the hen is so enfeebled over her brood, that even if the chickens are not following her, if thou see not the young ones, yet thou knowest her at once to be a mother. With her wings drooping, her feathers ruffled, her note hoarse, in all her limbs she becomes so sunken and abject, that, as I have said, even though thou seest not her young, yet thou perceivest her to be a mother. In such manner was Jesus weak, wearied with His journey. His journey is the flesh assumed for us. For how can He, who is present everywhere, have a journey, He who is nowhere absent? Whither does He go, or whence, but that He could not come to us, except He had assumed the form of visible flesh? Therefore, as He deigned to come to us in such manner, that He appeared in the form of a servant by the flesh assumed, that same assumption of flesh is His journey. Thus, "wearied with His journey," what else is it but wearied in the flesh? Jesus was weak in the flesh: but do not thou become weak; but in His weakness be strong, because what is "the weakness of God is stronger than men."

8. Under this image of things, Adam, who was the figure of Him that was to be, afforded us a great indication of this mystery; rather, God afforded it in him. For he was deemed worthy to receive a wife while he slept, and that wife was made for him of his own rib: since from Christ, sleeping on the cross, was the Church to come,—from His side, namely, as He slept; for it was from His side, pierced with the spear, as He hung on the cross, that the sacraments of the Church flowed forth. But why have I chosen to say this, brethren? Because it is the weakness of Christ that makes us strong. A remarkable figure of this went before in the case of Adam. God could have taken flesh from the man to make of it a woman, and it seems that this might have been the more suitable. For it was the weaker sex that was being made, and weakness ought to have been made of flesh rather than of bone; for the bones are the stronger parts in the flesh. He took not flesh to make of it a woman; but took a bone, and of the bone was the woman shaped, and flesh was filled in into the place of the bone. He could have restored bone for bone; He could have taken, not a rib, but flesh, for the making of the woman. What, then, did this signify? Woman was made, as it were, strong, from the rib; Adam was made, as it were, weak, from the flesh. It is Christ and the Church; His weakness is our strength.

9. But why at the sixth hour? Because at the sixth age of the world. In the Gospel, count up as an hour each, the first age from Adam to Noah; the second, from Noah to Abraham; the third, from Abraham to David; the fourth, from David to the removing to Babylon; the fifth, from the removing to Babylon to the baptism of John: thence is the sixth being enacted. Why dost thou marvel? Jesus came, and, by humbling Himself, came to a well. He came wearied, because He carried weak flesh. At the sixth hour, because in the sixth age of the world. To a well, because to the depth of this our habitation. For which reason it is said in the psalm: "From the depth have I cried unto Thee, O Lord."[2] He sat, as I said, because He was humbled.

10. "And there came a woman." Figure of the Church not yet justified, but now about to be justified: for this is the subject of the discourse. She comes ignorant, she finds Him, and there is a dealing with her. Let us see what, and wherefore. "There cometh a woman of Samaria to draw water." The Samaritans did not belong to the nation of the Jews: they were foreigners, though they inhabited neighboring lands. It would take a long time to relate the origin of the Samaritans; that we may not be detained by long discourse of this, and leave necessary matters unsaid, suffice to say, then, that we regard the Samaritans as aliens. And, lest you should think that I have said this with more boldness than truth, hear the Lord Jesus Himself, what He said of that Samaritan, one of the ten lepers whom He had cleansed, who alone returned to give thanks: "Were there not ten cleansed? And where are the nine? There was not another to give glory to God, save this stranger."[3] It is pertinent to the image of the reality, that this woman, who bore the type of the Church, comes of strangers: for the Church was to come of the Gentiles, an alien from the race of the Jews. In that woman, then, let us hear ourselves, and in her acknowledge ourselves, and in her give

---

[1] Matt. xxiii. 37.　　　[2] Ps. cxxx. 1.　　　[3] Luke xvii. 17.

thanks to God for ourselves. For she was the figure, not the reality; for she both first showed forth the figure and became the reality. For she believed on Him who, of her, set the figure before us. "She cometh, then, to draw water." Had simply come to draw water, as people are wont to do, be they men or women.

11. "Jesus saith unto her, Give me to drink. For His disciples were gone away into the city to buy meat. Then saith the Samaritan woman unto Him, How is it that thou, being a Jew, askest drink of me, who am a Samaritan woman? For the Jews have no dealings with the Samaritans." You see that they were aliens: indeed, the Jews would not use their vessels. And as the woman brought with her a vessel with which to draw the water, it made her wonder that a Jew sought drink of her,—a thing which the Jews were not accustomed to do. But He who was asking drink was thirsting for the faith of the woman herself.

12. At length, hear who it is that asketh drink: "Jesus answered and said unto her, If thou knewest the gift of God, and who it is that saith to thee, Give me to drink, thou wouldest, it may be, have asked of Him, and He would have given thee living water." He asks to drink, and promises to give drink. He longs as one about to receive; He abounds as one about to satisfy. "If thou knewest," saith He, "the gift of God." The gift of God is the Holy Spirit. But as yet He speaks to the woman guardedly, and enters into her heart by degrees. It may be He is now teaching her. For what can be sweeter and kinder than that exhortation? "If thou knewest the gift of God," etc.: thus far He keeps her in suspense. That is commonly called living water which issues from a spring: that which is collected from rain in pools and cisterns is not called living water. And it may have flowed from a spring; yet if it should stand collected in some place, not admitting to it that from which it flowed, but, with the course interrupted, separated, as it were, from the channel of the fountain, it is not called "living water:" but that is called living water which is taken as it flows. Such water there was in that fountain. Why, then, did He promise to give that which He was asking?

13. The woman, however, being in suspense, saith to Him, "Lord, thou hast nothing to draw with, and the well is deep." See how she understood the living water, simply the water which was in that fountain. "Thou wouldst give me living water, and I carry that with which to draw, and thou dost not. The

living water is here; how art thou to give it me?" Understanding another thing, and taking it carnally, sne does in a manner knock, that the Master may open up that which is closed. She was knocking in ignorance, not with earnest purpose; she is still an object of pity, not yet of instruction.

14. The Lord speaks somewhat more clearly of that living water. Now the woman had said, "Art thou greater than our father Jacob, who gave us the well, and drank of it himself, his children, and his cattle?" Thou canst not give me of the living water of this well, because thou hast nothing to draw with: perhaps thou promisest another fountain? Canst thou be better than our father, who dug this well, and used it himself, and his? Let the Lord, then, declare what He called living water. "Jesus answered and said unto her, Every one that drinketh of this water shall thirst again: but he that drinketh of the water that I shall give him, shall not thirst forever; but the water which I shall give him will become in him a fountain of water, springing up into everlasting life." The Lord has spoken more openly: "It shall become in him a fountain of water, springing up into everlasting life. He that drinketh of this water shall not thirst forever." What more evident than that it was not visible, but invisible water, that He was promising? What more evident than that He was speaking, not in a carnal, but in a spiritual sense?

15. Still, however, the woman has her mind on the flesh: she is delighted with the thought of thirsting no more, and fancies that this was promised to her by the Lord after a carnal sense; which it will be indeed, but in the resurrection of the dead. She desired this now. God had indeed granted once to His servant Elias, that during forty days he neither hungered nor thirsted. Could not He give this always, seeing He had power to give it during forty days? She, however, sighed for it, desiring to have no want, no toil. To be always coming to that fountain, to be burdened with a weight with which to supply her want, and, when that which she had drawn is spent, to be obliged to return again: this was a daily toil to her; because that want of hers was to be relieved, not extinguished. Such a gift as Jesus promised delighted her; she asks Him to give her living water.

16. Nevertheless, let us not overlook the fact that it is something spiritual that the Lord was promising. What means, "Whoso shall drink of this water shall thirst again?" It is true as to this water; it is true as to what the water signified. Since the water in the

well is the pleasure of the world in its dark depth: from this men draw it with the vessel of lusts. Stooping forward, they let down the lust to reach the pleasure fetched from the depth of the well, and enjoy the pleasure and the preceding lust let down to fetch it. For he who has not despatched his lust in advance cannot get to the pleasure. Consider lust, then, as the vessel; and pleasure as the water from the depth of the well: when one has got at the pleasure of this world, it is meat to him, it is drink, it is a bath, a show, an amour; can it be that he will not thirst again? Therefore, " Whoso shall drink of this water," saith He, " will thirst again;" but if he shall receive water of me, " he shall never thirst." " We shall be satisfied," it saith, " with the good things of Thy house." [1] Of what water, then, is He to give, but of that of which it is said, " With Thee is the fountain of life"? For how shall they thirst, who " shall be drunk with the fatness of Thy house"? [2]

17. What He was promising them was a certain feeding and abundant fullness of the Holy Spirit: but the woman did not yet understand; and not understanding, how did she answer? " The woman saith unto Him, Sir, give me this water, that I thirst not, neither come hither to draw." Want forced her to labor, and her weakness was pleading against the toil. Would that she heard the invitation, " Come unto me, all ye that labor and are heavy laden, and I will refresh you ! " [3] This is, in fact, what Jesus was saying to her, that she might no longer labor: but she did not yet understand.

18. At length, wishing her to understand, " Jesus saith unto her, Go, call thy husband, and come hither." What means this, " Call thy husband"? Was it through her husband that He wished to give her that water? Or, because she did not understand, did He wish to teach her through her husband? Perhaps it was as the apostle says concerning women, "If they wish to learn anything, let them ask their husbands at home." But this the apostle says of that where there is no Jesus present to teach. It is said, in short, to women whom the apostle was forbidding to speak in the Church. [4] But when the Lord Himself was at hand, and in person speaking to her, what need was there that He should speak to her by her husband? Was it through her husband that he spoke to Mary, while sitting at His feet and receiving His word; while Martha, wholly occupied with much serving, murmured at the happiness of her sister? [5] Wherefore, my brethren, let us hear and understand what it is that the Lord says to the woman, " Call thy husband." For it may be that He is saying also to our soul, " Call thy husband." Let us inquire also concerning the soul's husband. Why, is not Jesus Himself already the soul's real husband? Let the understanding be present, since what we are about to say can hardly be apprehended but by attentive hearers: therefore let the understanding be present to apprehend, and perhaps that same understanding will be found to be the husband of the soul.

19. Now Jesus, seeing that the woman did not understand, and willing her to understand, says to her, " Call thy husband." " For the reason why thou knowest not what I say is, because thy understanding is not present: I am speaking after the Spirit, and thou art hearing after the flesh. The things which I speak relate neither to the pleasure of the ears, nor to the eyes, nor to the smell, nor to the taste, nor to the touch; by the mind alone are they received, by the understanding alone are they drawn up: that understanding is not with thee, how canst thou apprehend what I am saying? ' Call thy husband,' bring thy understanding forward. What is it for thee to have a soul? It is not much, for a beast has a soul. Wherein art thou better than the beast? In having understanding, which the beast has not." Then what is " Call thy husband"? " Thou dost not apprehend me, thou dost not understand me: I am speaking to thee of the gift of God, and thy thought is of the flesh; thou wishest not to thirst in a carnal sense, I am addressing myself to the spirit: thy understanding is absent. ' Call thy husband.' Be not as the horse and mule, which have no understanding.'" Therefore, my brethren, to have a soul, and not to have understanding, that is, not to use it, not to live according to it, is a beast's life. For we have somewhat in common with the beasts, that by which we live in the flesh, but it must be ruled by the understanding. For the motions of the soul, which moves after the flesh, and longs to run unrestrainedly loose after carnal delights, are ruled over by the understanding. Which is to be called the husband?—that which rules, or that which is ruled? Without doubt, when the life is well ordered the understanding rules the soul, for itself belongs to the soul. For the understanding is not something other than the soul, but a thing of the soul: as the eye is not something other than the flesh, but a thing of the flesh. But whilst the eye is a thing of the flesh, yet it alone enjoys the light; and the other fleshy members may be steeped in light, but they cannot feel the light: the eye

---

[1] Ps. lxv. 4.　　　[2] Ps. xxxvi. 9, 10.　　　[3] Matt. xi. 28.
[4] 1 Cor. xiv. 34.　　[5] Luke x. 40.

alone is both bathed in it, and enjoys it. Thus in our soul there is a something called the understanding. This something of the soul, which is called understanding and mind, is enlightened by the higher light. Now that higher light, by which the human mind is enlightened, is God; for "that was the true light which enlighteneth every man coming into this world." Such a light was Christ, such a light was speaking with the woman: yet she was not present with the understanding, to have it enlightened with that light; not merely to have it shed upon it, but to enjoy it. Therefore the Lord said, "Call thy husband," as if He were to say, I wish to enlighten, and yet there is not here whom I may enlighten: bring hither the understanding through which thou mayest be taught, by which thou mayest be ruled. Thus, put the soul without the understanding for the woman; and having the understanding as having the husband. But this husband does not rule the wife well, except when he is ruled by a higher. "For the head of the woman is the man, but the head of the man is Christ."[1] The head of the man was talking with the woman, and the man was not present. And so the Lord, as if He said, Bring hither thy head, that he may receive his head, says, "Call thy husband, and come hither;" that is, Be here, be present: for thou art as absent, while thou understandest not the voice of the Truth here present; be thou present here, but not alone; be thou here with thy husband.

20. And, the husband being not yet called, still she does not understand, still she minds the flesh; for the man is absent: "I have not," saith she, "a husband." And the Lord proceeds and utters mysteries. Thou mayest understand that woman really to have had at that time no husband; she was living with some man, not a lawful husband, rather a paramour than a husband. And the Lord said to her, "Thou hast well said, I have not a husband." How then didst Thou say, "Call thy husband"? Now hear how the Lord knew well that she had not a husband. "He says to her," etc. In case the woman might suppose that the Lord had said, "Thou hast well said, I have not a husband," just because He had learned this fact of her, and not because he knew it by His own divinity, hear something which thou hast not said: "For thou hast had five husbands, and he whom thou now hast is not thy husband; this thou hast said truly."

21. Once more He urges us to investigate the matter somewhat more exactly concerning these five husbands. Many have in fact understood, not indeed absurdly, nor so far improbably, the five husbands of this woman to mean the five books of Moses. For the Samaritans made use of these books, and were under the same law: for it was from it they had circumcision. But since we are hemmed in by what follows, "And he whom thou now hast is not thy husband," it appears to me that we can more easily take the five senses of the body to be the five former husbands of the soul. For when one is born, before he can make use of the mind and reason, he is ruled only by the senses of the flesh. In a little child, the soul seeks for or shuns what is heard, and seen, and smells, and tastes, and is perceived by the touch. It seeks for whatever soothes, and shuns whatever offends, those five senses. At first, the soul lives according to these five senses, as five husbands; because it is ruled by them. But why are they called husbands? Because they are lawful and right: made indeed by God, and are the gifts of God to the soul. The soul is still weak while ruled by these five husbands, and living under these five husbands; but when she comes to years of exercising reason, if she is taken in hand by the noble discipline and teaching of wisdom, these five men are succeeded in their rule by no other than the true and lawful husband, and one better than they, who both rules better and rules for eternity, who cultivates and instructs her for eternity. For the five senses rule us, not for eternity, but for those temporal things that are to be sought or shunned. But when the understanding, imbued by wisdom, begins to rule the soul, it knows now not only how to avoid a pit, and to walk on even ground—a thing which the eyes show to the soul even in its weakness; nor merely to be charmed with musical voices, and to repel harsh sounds; nor to delight in agreeable scents, and to refuse offensive smells; nor to be captivated by sweetness, and displeased with bitterness; nor to be soothed with what is soft, and hurt with what is rough. For all these things are necessary to the soul in its weakness. Then what rule is made use of by that understanding? Not one to discern between black and white, but between just and unjust, between good and evil, between the profitable and the unprofitable, between chastity and impurity, that it may love the one and avoid the other; between charity and hatred, to be in the one, not to be in the other.

22. This husband had not yet succeeded to those five husbands in that woman. And

---

[1] 1 Cor. xi. 3.

where he does not succeed, error sways. For when the soul has begun to be capable of reason, it is ruled either by the wise mind or by error: but yet error does not *rule* but destroys. Wherefore, after these five senses was that woman still wandering, and error was tossing her to and fro. And this error was not a lawful husband, but a paramour: for that reason the Lord saith to her, "Thou hast well said, I have not a husband. For thou hast had five husbands." The five senses of the flesh ruled thee at first; thou art come to the age of using reason, and yet thou art not come to wisdom, but art fallen into error. Therefore, after those five husbands, "this whom thou now hast is not thy husband." And if not a husband, what was he but a paramour? And so, "Call," not the paramour, but "thy husband," that thou mayest receive me with the understanding, and not by error have some false notion of me. For the woman was still in error, as she was thinking of that water; whilst the Lord was now speaking of the Holy Ghost. Why was she erring, but because she had a paramour, not a husband? Put away, therefore, that paramour who corrupts thee, and "go, call thy husband." Call, and come that thou mayest understand me.

23. "The woman saith unto Him, Sir, I see that thou art a prophet." The husband begins to come, he is not yet fully come. She accounted the Lord a prophet, and a prophet indeed He was; for it was of Himself He said, that "a prophet is not without honor, save in his own country."[1] Again, of Him it was said to Moses, "A Prophet will I raise up to them of their brethren, like unto thee."[2] Like, namely, as to the form of the flesh, but not in the eminence of His majesty. Accordingly we find the Lord Jesus called a Prophet. Hence this woman is now not far wrong. "I see," she saith, "that thou art a prophet." She begins to call the husband, and to shut out the paramour; she begins to ask about a matter that is wont to disquiet her. For there was a contention between the Samaritans and the Jews, because the Jews worshipped God in the temple built by Solomon; but the Samaritans, being situated at a distance from it, did not worship there. For this reason the Jews, because they worshipped God in the temple, boasted themselves to be better than the Samaritans. "For the Jews have no dealings with the Samaritans:" because the latter said to them, How is it you boast and account yourselves to be better than we, just because you have a temple which

we have not? Did our fathers, who were pleasing to God, worship in that temple? Was it not in this mountain where we are they worshipped? We then do better, say they, who pray to God in this mountain, where our fathers prayed. Both peoples contended in ignorance, because they had not the husband: they were inflated against each other, on the one side in behalf of the temple, on the other in behalf of the mountain.

24. What, however, does the Lord teach the woman now, as one whose husband has begun to be present? "The woman saith unto Him, Sir, I perceive that thou art a prophet. Our fathers worshipped in this mountain; and ye say that in Jerusalem is the place where men ought to worship. Jesus saith unto her, Woman, believe me." For the Church will come, as it is said in the Song of Songs, "will come, and will pass over from the beginning of faith."[3] She will come in order to pass through; and pass through she cannot, except from the beginning of faith. Rightly she now hears, the husband being present: "Woman, believe me." For there is that in thee now which can believe, since thy husband is present. Thou hast begun to be present with the understanding when thou calledst me a prophet. Woman, believe me; for if ye believe not, ye will not understand.[4] Therefore, "Woman, believe me, for the hour will come when ye shall neither in this mountain nor in Jerusalem worship the Father. Ye worship ye know not what: we worship what we know; for salvation is of the Jews. But the hour will come." When? "And now is." Well, what hour? "When the true worshippers shall worship the Father in spirit and in truth," not in this mountain, not in the temple, but in spirit and in truth. "For the Father seeketh such to worship Him." Why does the Father seek such to worship Him, not on a mountain, not in the temple, but in spirit and in truth? "God is Spirit." If God were body, it were right that He should be worshipped on a mountain, for a mountain is corporeal; it were right He should be worshipped in the temple, for a temple is corporeal. "God is Spirit; and they that worship Him, must worship in spirit and in truth."

25. We have heard, and it is manifest; we had gone out of doors, and we are sent inward. Would I could find, thou didst say, some high and lonely mountain! For I think that, because God is on high, He hears me the rather from a high place. Because thou art on a mountain, dost thou imagine thyself near to

---

[1] Luke iv. 24. [2] Deut. xviii. 18. [3] Cant. iv. 8, LXX. [4] Isa. vii. 9, LXX.

God, and that He will quickly hear thee, as if calling to Him from the nearest place? He dwells on high, but regards the lowly. "The Lord is near." To whom? To the high, perhaps? "To them who are contrite of heart."[1] 'Tis a wonderful thing: He dwelleth on high, and yet is near to the lowly; "He hath regard to lowly things, but lofty things He knoweth from afar;"[2] He seeth the proud afar off, and He is the less near to them the higher they appear to themselves to be. Didst thou seek a mountain, then? Come down, that thou mayest come near Him. But wouldest thou ascend? Ascend, but do not seek a mountain. "The ascents," it saith, "are in his heart, in the valley of weeping."[3] The valley is humility. Therefore do all within. Even if perhaps thou seekest some lofty place, some holy place, make thyself a temple for God within thee. "For the temple of God is holy, which temple are ye."[4] Wouldest thou pray in a temple? Pray in thyself. But be thou first a temple of God, for He in His temple heareth him that prays.

26. "The hour cometh, and now is, when the true worshippers shall worship the Father in spirit and in truth. We worship that which we know: ye worship ye know not what; for salvation is of the Jews." A great thing has He attributed to the Jews; but do not understand Him to mean those spurious Jews. Understand that wall to which another is joined, that they may be joined together, resting on the corner-stone, which is Christ. For there is one wall from the Jews, another from the Gentiles; these walls are far apart, only until they are united in the Corner. Now the aliens were strangers and foreigners from the covenants of God.[5] According to this, it is said, "We worship what we know." It is said, indeed, in the person of the Jews, but not of all Jews, not of reprobate Jews, but of such as were the apostles, as were the prophets, as were all those saints who sold all their goods, and laid the price of their goods at the apostles' feet. "For God hath not rejected His people which He foreknew."[6]

27. The woman heard this, and proceeded. She had already called Him a prophet; she observes that He with whom she was speaking uttered such things as still more pertained to the prophet; and what answer did she make? See: "The woman saith unto Him, I know that Messias will come, who is called Christ: when He then is come, He will show us all things." What is this? Just now she saith, The Jews are contending for the temple, and we for this mountain: when He has come, He will despise the mountain, and overthrow the temple; He will teach us all things, that we may know how to worship in spirit and in truth. She knew who could teach her, but she did not yet know Him that was now teaching her. But now she was worthy to receive the manifestation of Him. Now Messias is Anointed: Anointed, in Greek, is Christ; in Hebrew, Messias; whence also, in Punic, Messe means Anoint. For the Hebrew, Punic and Syriac are cognate and neighboring languages.

28. Then, "The woman saith unto Him, I know that Messias will come, who is called Christ: when He then is come, He will tell us all things. Jesus saith unto her, I that speak with thee am He." She called her husband; he is made the head of the woman, and Christ is made the head of the man. Now is the woman constituted in faith, and ruled, as about to live rightly. After she heard this, "I that speak with thee am He," what further could she say, when the Lord Jesus willed to manifest Himself to the woman, to whom He had said, "Believe me?"

29. "And immediately came His disciples, and marvelled that He talked with the woman." That He was seeking her that was lost, He who came to seek that which was lost: they marvelled at this. They marvelled at a good thing, they were not suspecting an evil thing. "Yet no man said, What seekest Thou, or why talkest Thou with her?"

30. "The woman then left her water-pot." Having heard, "I that speak with thee am He," and having received Christ the Lord into her heart, what could she do but now leave her water-pot, and run to preach the gospel? She cast out lust, and hastened to proclaim the truth. Let them who would preach the gospel learn; let them throw away their water-pot at the well. You remember what I said before of the water-pot: it was a vessel with which the water was drawn, called *hydria*, from its Greek name, because water is *hydor* in Greek; just as if it were called *aquarium*, from the Latin. She threw away her water-pot then, which was no longer of use, but a burden to her, such was her avidity to be satisfied with that water. Throwing her burden away, to make known Christ, "she ran to the city, and says to those men, Come, and see a man that told me all things that ever I did." Step by step, lest those men should get angry and indignant, and should persecute her. "Is this Christ? Then they went out of the city, and came to Him."

31. "And in the meanwhile His disciples besought Him, saying, Master, eat." For

1 Ps. xxxiv. 18.   2 Ps. cxxxviii. 6.   3 Ps. lxxxiv. 6.
4 1 Cor. iii. 17.   5 Eph. ii. 11-22.   6 Rom. xi. 2.

they had gone to buy meat, and had returned. "But He said, I have meat to eat which ye know not of. Therefore said the disciples one to another, Hath any man brought Him aught to eat?" What wonder if that woman did not understand about the water? See; the disciples do not yet understand the meat. But He heard their thoughts, and now as a master instructs them, not in a round-about way, as He did the woman while He still sought her husband, but openly at once: "My meat," saith He, "is to do the will of Him that sent me." Therefore, in the case of that woman, it was even His drink to do the will of Him that sent Him. That was the reason why He said, "I thirst, give me to drink;" namely, to work faith in her, and to drink of her faith, and to transplant her into His own body, for His body is the Church. Therefore He saith, "My meat is to do the will of Him that sent me."

32. "Say ye not, that there are yet four months, and then cometh harvest?" He was aglow for the work, and was arranging to send forth laborers. You count four months to the harvest; I show you another harvest, white and ready. Behold, I say unto you, "Lift up your eyes, and see that the fields are already white for the harvest." Therefore He is going to send forth the reapers. "For in this is the saying true, that one reapeth, another soweth: that both he that soweth and he that reapeth may rejoice together. I have sent you to reap that on which ye have not labored: others have labored, and ye are entered into their labor." What then? He sent reapers; sent He not the sowers? Whither the reapers? Where others labored already. For where labor had already been bestowed, surely there had been sowing; and what had been sown had now become ripe, and required the sickle and the threshing. Whither, then, were the reapers to be sent? Where the prophets had already preached before; for they were the sowers. For had they not been the sowers, whence had this come to the woman, "I know that Messias will come"? That woman was now ripened fruit, and the harvest fields were white, and sought the sickle. "I sent you," then. Whither? "To reap what ye have not sown: others sowed, and ye are entered into their labors." Who labored? Abraham, Isaac, and Jacob. Read their labors; in all their labors there is a prophecy of Christ, and for that reason they were sowers. Moses, and all the other patriarchs, and all the prophets, how much they suffered in that cold season when they sowed! Therefore was the harvest

now ready in Judea. Justly was the corn there said to be as it were ripe, when so many thousands of men brought the price of their goods, and, laying them at the apostles' feet, having eased their shoulders of this worldly baggage, began to follow the Lord Christ. Verily the harvest was ripe. What was made of it? Of that harvest a few grains were thrown out, and sowed the whole world; and another harvest is rising which is to be reaped in the end of the world. Of that harvest it is said, "They that sow in tears shall reap with joy."[1] But to that harvest not apostles, but angels, shall be sent forth. "The reapers," saith He, "are the angels."[2] That harvest, then, is growing among tares, and is awaiting to be purged in the end of the world. But that harvest to which the disciples were sent first, where the prophets labored, was already ripe. But yet, brethren, observe what was said: "may rejoice together, both he that soweth and he that reapeth." They had dissimilar labors in time, but the rejoicing they shall enjoy alike equally; they shall receive for their wages together eternal life.

33. "And many Samaritans of that city believed on Him, because of the saying of the woman, who testified, He told me all that ever I did. And when the Samaritans came to Him, they besought Him that He would tarry with them; and He tarried there two days. And many more believed because of His word; and said to the woman, Now we believe, not because of thy words; for we have heard Him ourselves, and we know that this is indeed the Saviour of the world." This also must be slightly noticed, for the lesson is come to an end. The woman first announced Him, and the Samaritans believed her testimony; and they besought Him to stay with them, and He stayed there two days, and many more believed. And when they had believed, they said to the woman, "Now we believe, not because of thy word; but we are come to know Him ourselves, and we know that this is indeed the Saviour of the world:" first by report, then by His presence. So it is to-day with them that are without, and are not yet Christians. Christ is made known to them by Christian friends; and just upon the report of that woman, that is, the Church, they come to Christ, they believe through this report. He stays with them two days, that is, gives them two precepts of charity; and many more believe, and more firmly believe, on Him, because He is in truth the Saviour of the world.

---

[1] Ps. cxxvi. 5.   [2] Matt. xiii. 39.

TRACTATE XVI.

CHAPTER IV. 43-54.

1. THE Gospel Lesson of to-day follows that of yesterday, and this is the subject of our discourse. In this passage the meaning, indeed, is not difficult of investigation, but worthy of preaching, worthy of admiration and praise. Accordingly, in reciting this passage of the Gospel, we must commend it to your attention, rather than laboriously expound it.

Now Jesus, after His stay of two days in Samaria, "departed into Galilee," where He was brought up. And the evangelist, as he goes on, says, "For Jesus Himself testified that a prophet hath no honor in his own country." It was not because He had no honor in Samaria that Jesus departed thence after two days; for Samaria was not His own country, but Galilee. Whilst, therefore, He left Samaria so quickly, and came to Galilee, where He had been brought up, how does He testify that "a prophet hath no honor in his own country"? Rather does it seem that He might have testified that a prophet has no honor in his own country, had He disdained to go into Galilee, and had stayed in Samaria.

2. Now mark well, beloved, while the Lord suggests and bestows what I may speak, that here is intimated to us no slight mystery. You know the question before us; seek ye out the solution of it. But, to make the solution desirable, let us repeat the theme. The point that troubles us is, why the evangelist said, "For Jesus Himself testified that a prophet hath no honor in his own country." Urged by this, we go back to the preceding words, to discover the evangelist's intention in saying this; and we find him relating, in the preceding words of the narrative, that after two days Jesus departed from Samaria into Galilee. Was it for this, then, thou saidst, O evangelist, that Jesus testified that a prophet hath no honor in his own country, just because He left Samaria after two days, and made haste to come to Galilee? On the contrary, I should have thought it more likely, that if Jesus had no honor in His own country, He should not have hastened to it, and left Samaria. But if I am not mistaken, or rather, because it is true, and I am not mistaken; for the evangelist saw what he was saying better than I can see it, saw the truth better than I do, he who drank it in from the Lord's bosom: for the evangelist is the same John

who, among all the disciples, reclined on the Lord's breast, and whom the Lord, owing love to all, yet loved above the rest. Is it he, then, that should be mistaken, and I right in my opinion? Rather, if I am piously-minded, let me obediently hear what he said, that I may be worthy of thinking as he thought.

3. Hear then, dearly beloved, what I think in this matter, without prejudice to your own judgment, if you have formed a better. For we have all one Master, and we are fellow-disciples in one school. This, then, is my opinion, and see whether my opinion is not true, or near the truth. In Samaria He spent two days, and the Samaritans believed on Him; many were the days He spent in Galilee, and yet the Galileans did not believe on Him. Look back to the passage, or recall in memory the lesson and the discourse of yesterday. He came into Samaria, where at first He had been preached by that woman with whom He had spoken great mysteries at Jacob's well. After they had seen and heard Him, the Samaritans believed on Him because of the woman's word, and believed more firmly because of His own word, even many more believed: thus it is written. After passing two days there (in which number of days is mystically indicated the number of the two precepts on which hang the whole law and the prophets, as you remember we intimated to you yesterday), He goes into Galilee, and comes to the city Cana of Galilee, where He made the water wine. And there, when He turned the water into wine, as John himself writes, His disciples believed on Him; but, of course, the house was full with a crowd of guests. So great a miracle was wrought, and yet only His disciples believed on Him. He has now returned to this city of Galilee. "And, behold, a certain ruler, whose son was sick, came to Him, and began to beseech Him to go down" to that city or house, "and heal his son; for he was at the point of death." Did he who besought not believe? What dost thou expect to hear from me? Ask the Lord what He thought of him. Having been besought, this is what He answered: "Except ye see signs and wonders, ye believe not." He shows us a man luke-warm, or cold in faith, or of no faith at all; but eager to try by the healing of his son what manner of person Christ was, who He

was, what He could do. The words of the suppliant, indeed, we have heard: we have not seen the heart of the doubter; but He who both heard the words and saw the heart has told us this. In short, the evangelist himself, by the testimony of his narrative, shows us that the man who desired the Lord to come to his house to heal his son, had not yet believed. For after he had been informed that his son was whole, and found that he had been made whole at that hour in which the Lord had said, "Go thy way, thy son liveth;" then he saith, "And himself believed, and all his house." Now, if the reason why he believed, and all his house, was that he was told that his son was whole, and found the hour they told him agreed with the hour of Christ's foretelling it, it follows that when he was making the request he did not yet believe. The Samaritans had waited for no sign, they believed simply His word; but His own fellow-citizens deserved to hear this said to them, "Except ye see signs and wonders, ye believe not;" and even there, notwithstanding so great a miracle was wrought, there did not believe but "himself and his house." At His discourse alone many of the Samaritans believed; at that miracle, in the place where it was wrought, only that house believed. What is it, then, brethren, that the Lord doth show us here? Galilee of Judea was then the Lord's own country, because He was brought up in it. But now that the circumstance portends something,—for it is not without cause that "prodigies" are so called, but because they portend or presage something: for the word "prodigy" is so termed as if it were *porrodicium, quod porro dicat,* what betokens something to come, and portends something future,—now all those circumstances portended something, predicted something; let us just now assume the country of our Lord Jesus Christ after the flesh (for He had no country on earth, except after the flesh which He took on earth); let us, I say, assume the Lord's own country to mean the people of the Jews. Lo, in His own country He hath no honor. Observe at this moment the multitudes of the Jews; observe that nation now scattered over the whole world, and plucked up by the roots; observe the broken branches, cut off, scattered, withered, which being broken off, the wild olive has deserved to be grafted in; look at the multitude of the Jews: what do they say to us even now? "He whom you worship and adore was our brother." And we reply, "A prophet hath no honor in his own country." In short, those Jews saw the Lord as He walked on the earth and worked miracles; they saw Him

giving sight to the blind, opening the ears of the deaf, loosing the tongues of the dumb, bracing up the limbs of the paralytics, walking on the sea, commanding the winds and waves, raising the dead: they saw Him working such great signs, and after all that scarcely a few believed. I am speaking to God's people; so many of us have believed, what signs have we seen? It is thus, therefore, that what occurred at that time betokened what is now going on. The Jews were, or rather are, like the Galileans; we, like those Samaritans. We have heard the gospel, have given it our consent, have believed on Christ through the gospel; we have seen no signs, none do we demand.

4. For, though one of the chosen and holy twelve, yet he was an Israelite, of the Lord's nation, that Thomas who desired to put his fingers into the places of the wounds. The Lord censured him just as He did this ruler. To the ruler He said, "Except ye see signs and wonders, ye believe not;" and to Thomas He said, "Because thou hast seen, thou hast believed." He had come to the Galileans after the Samaritans, who had believed His word, before whom He wrought no miracles, whom He without anxiety quickly left, strong in faith, because by the presence of His divinity He had not left them. Now, then, when the Lord said to Thomas, "Come, reach hither thy hand, and be not faithless, but believing;" and he, having touched the places of the wounds, exclaimed, and said, "My Lord, and my God;" he is chided, and has it said to him, "Because thou hast seen, thou hast believed." Why, but "because a prophet has no honor in his own country?" But since this Prophet has honor among strangers, what follows? "Blessed are they that have not seen, and yet have believed."[1] We are the persons here foretold; and that which the Lord by anticipation praised, He has deigned to fulfill even in us. They saw Him, who crucified Him, and touched Him with their hands, and thus a few believed; we have not seen nor handled Him, we have heard and believed. May it be our lot, that the blessedness which He has promised may be made good in us: both here, because we have been preferred to His own country; and in the world to come, because we have been grafted in instead of the branches that were broken off!

5. For He showed that He would break off these branches, and ingraft this wild olive, when moved by the faith of the centurion, who said to Him, "I am not worthy that thou

---

[1] John xx. 29.

shouldest come under my roof; but only speak the word, and my child shall be healed: for I also am a man put under authority, having soldiers under me; and I say to one, Go, and he goeth; and to another, Come, and he cometh; and to my servant, Do this, and he doeth it. Jesus turned to those who followed Him, and said, Verily I say unto you, I have not found so great faith in Israel." Why not found so great faith in Israel? "Because a prophet has no honor in his own country." Could not the Lord have said to that centurion, what He said to this ruler, "Go, thy child liveth?" See the distinction: this ruler desired the Lord to come down to his house; that centurion declared himself to be unworthy. To the one it was said, "I will come and heal him;" to the other, "Go, thy son liveth." To the one He promised His presence; the other He healed by His word. The ruler sought His presence by force; the centurion declared himself unworthy of His presence. Here is a ceding to loftiness; there, a conceding to humility. As if He said to the ruler, "Go, thy son liveth;" do not weary me. "Except ye see signs and wonders, ye believe not;" thou desirest my presence in thy house, I am able to command by a word; do not wish to believe in virtue of signs: the centurion, an alien, believed me able to work by a word, and believed before I did it; you, "except ye see signs and wonders, believe not." Therefore, if it be so, let them be broken off as proud branches, and let the humble wild olive be grafted; nevertheless, let the root remain, while those are cut off, and these received in their place. Where does the root remain? In the patriarchs. For the people Israel is Christ's own country, since it is of them that He came according to the flesh; but the root of this tree is Abraham, Isaac, and Jacob, the holy patriarchs. And where are they? In rest with God, in great honor; so that it was into Abraham's bosom that the poor man, on being promoted, was raised after his departure from the body, and in Abraham's bosom was he seen from afar off by the proud rich man. Wherefore the root remains, the root is praised; but the proud branches deserved to be cut off, and to wither away; and by their cutting off, the humble wild olive has found a place.

6. Hear now how the natural branches are cut off, how the wild olive is grafted in, by means of the centurion himself, whom I have thought proper to mention for the sake of comparison with this ruler. "Verily I say unto you, I have not found so great faith in Israel; therefore I say unto you, that many

shall come from the east and from the west." How widely the wild olive took possession of the earth! This world was a bitter forest; but because of the humility, because of this "I am not worthy—many shall come from the east and from the west." And grant that they come, what shall become of them? For if they come, they are cut off from the forest; where are they to be ingrafted, that they may not wither? "And shall sit down," saith He, "with Abraham, and Isaac, and Jacob." At what banquet, in case thou dost not invite to ever living, but to much drinking? Where, "shall sit down? In the kingdom of heaven." And how will it be with them who came of the stock of Abraham? What will become of the branches with which the tree was full? What but to be cut off, that these may be grafted in? Show us that they shall be cut off: "But the children of the kingdom shall go into outer darkness." [1]

7. Therefore let the Prophet have honor among us, because He had no honor in His own country. He had no honor in His country, wherein He was formed; let Him have honor in the country which He has formed. For in that country was He, the Maker of all, made as to the form of a servant. For that city in which He was made, that Zion, that nation of the Jews He Himself made when He was with the Father as the Word of God: for "all things were made by Him, and without Him was nothing made." Of that man we have to-day heard it said: "One Mediator of God and men, the man Christ Jesus." [2] The Psalms also foretold, saying, "My mother is Sion, shall a man say." A certain man, the Mediator man between God and men, says, "My mother Sion." Why says, "My mother is Sion"? Because from it He took flesh, from it was the Virgin Mary, of whose womb He took upon Him the form of a servant; in which He deigned to appear most humble. "My mother is Sion," saith a man; and this man, who says, "My mother is Sion," was made in her, became man in her. For He was God before her, and became man in her. He who was made man in her, "Himself did found her; the Most High [3] was made man in her most low." Because "the Word was made flesh, and dwelt among us." "He Himself, the Most High, founded her." Now, because He founded this country, here let Him have honor. The country in which He was born rejected Him; let that country receive Him which He regenerated.

---

[1] Matt. viii. 5-12.   [2] 1 Tim. ii. 5.   [3] Ps. lxxxiv. 7.

TRACTATE XVII.

CHAPTER V. 1-18.

1. IT ought not to be a matter of wonder that a miracle was wrought by God; the wonder would be if man had wrought it. Rather ought we to rejoice than wonder that our Lord and Saviour Jesus Christ was made man, than that He performed divine works among men. It is of greater importance to our salvation what He was made for men, than what He did among men: it is more important that He healed the faults of souls, than that He healed the weaknesses of mortal bodies. But as the soul knew not Him by whom it was to be healed, and had eyes in the flesh whereby to see corporeal deeds, but had not yet sound eyes in the heart with which to recognise Him as God concealed in the flesh, He wrought what the soul was able to see, in order to heal that by which it was not able to see.

He entered a place where lay a great multitude of sick folk—of blind, lame, withered; and being the physician both of souls and bodies, and having come to heal all the souls of them that should believe, of those sick folk He chose one for healing, thereby to signify unity. If in doing this we regard Him with a commonplace mind, with the mere human understanding and wit, as regards power it was not a great matter that He performed; and also as regards goodness He performed too little. There lay so many there, and yet only one was healed, whilst He could by a word have raised them all up. What, then, must we understand but that the power and the goodness was doing what souls might, by His deeds, understand for their everlasting salvation, than what bodies might gain for temporal health? For that which is the real health of bodies, and which is looked for from the Lord, will be at the end, in the resurrection of the dead. What shall live then shall no more die; what shall be healed shall no more be sick; what shall be satisfied shall no more hunger and thirst; what shall be made new shall not grow old. But at this time, however, the eyes of the blind, that were opened by those acts of our Lord and Saviour Jesus Christ, were again closed in death; and limbs of the paralytics that received strength were loosened again in death; and whatever was for a time made whole in mortal limbs came to nought in the end: but the soul that believed passed to eternal life. Accordingly, to the soul that should believe,

whose sins He had come to forgive, to the healing of whose ailments He had humbled Himself, He gave a significant proof by the healing of this impotent man. Of the profound mystery of this thing and this proof, so far as the Lord deigns to grant us, while you are attentive and aiding our weakness by prayer, I will speak as I shall have ability. And whatever I am not able to do, that will be supplied to you by Him by whose help I do what I can.

2. Of this pool, which was surrounded with five porches, in which lay a great multitude of sick folk, I remember that I have very often treated; and most of you will with me recollect what I am about to say, rather than gain the knowledge of it for the first time. But it is by no means unprofitable to go back upon matters already known, that both they who know not may be instructed, and they who do know may be confirmed. Therefore, as being already known, these things must be touched upon briefly, not leisurely inculcated. That pool and that water seem to me to have signified the Jewish people. For that peoples are signified under the name of waters, the Apocalypse of John clearly indicates to us, where, after he had been shown many waters, and he had asked what they were, was answered that they were peoples.[1] That water, then—namely, that people—was shut in by the five books of Moses, as by five porches. But those books brought forth the sick, not healed them. For the law convicted, not acquitted sinners. Accordingly the letter, without grace, made men guilty, whom on confessing grace delivered. For this is what the apostle saith: "For if a law had been given which could have given life, verily righteousness should have been by the law." Why, then, was the law given? He goes on to say, "But the Scripture hath concluded all under sin, that the promise by faith of Jesus Christ might be given to them that believe."[2] What more evident? Have not these words expounded to us both the five porches, and also the multitude of sick folk? The five porches are the law. Why did not the five porches heal the sick folk? Because, "if there had been a law given which could have given life, verily righteousness should have

---

[1] Rev. xvii. 15.　　[2] Gal. iii. 21, 22.

been by the law." Why, then, did the porches contain those whom they did not heal? Because "the Scripture hath concluded all under sin, that the promise by faith of Jesus Christ might be given to them that believe."

3. What was done, then, that they who could not be healed in the porches might be healed in that water after being troubled? For on a sudden the water was seen troubled, and that by which it was troubled was not seen. Thou mayest believe that this was wont to be done by angelic virtue, yet not without some mystery being implied. After the water was troubled, the one who was able cast himself in, and he alone was healed: whoever went in after that one, did so in vain. What, then, is meant by this, unless it be that there came one, even Christ, to the Jewish people; and by doing great things, by teaching profitable things, troubled sinners, troubled the water by His presence, and roused it towards His own death? But He was hidden that troubled. For had they known Him, they would never have crucified the Lord of glory.[1] Wherefore, to go down into the troubled water means to believe in the Lord's death. There only one was healed, signifying unity: whoever came thereafter was not healed, because whoever shall be outside unity cannot be healed.

4. Now let us see what He intended to signify in the case of that one whom He Himself, keeping the mystery of unity, as I said before, deigned to heal out of so many sick folk. He found in the number of this man's years the number, so to speak, of infirmity: "He was thirty and eight years in infirmity." How this number refers more to weakness than to health must be somewhat more carefully expounded. I wish you to be attentive; the Lord will aid us, so that I may fitly speak, and that you may sufficiently hear. The number forty is commended to our attention as one consecrated by a kind of perfection. This, I suppose, is well known to you, beloved. The Holy Scriptures very often testify to the fact. Fasting was consecrated by this number, as you are well aware. For Moses fasted forty days, and Elias as many; and our Lord and Saviour Jesus Christ did Himself fulfill this number of fasting. By Moses is signified the law; by Elias, the prophets; by the Lord, the gospel. It was for this reason that these three appeared on that mountain, where He showed Himself to His disciples in the brightness of His countenance and vesture. For He appeared in the middle, between Moses and Elias, as the

gospel had witness from the law and the prophets.[2] Whether, therefore, in the law, or in the prophets, or in the gospel, the number forty is commended to our attention in the case of fasting. Now fasting, in its large and general sense, is to abstain from the iniquities and unlawful pleasures of the world, which is perfect fasting: "That, denying ungodliness and worldly lusts, we may live temperately, and righteously, and godly in this present world." What reward does the apostle join to this fast? He goes on to say: "Looking for that blessed hope, and the appearing of the glory of the blessed God, and our Saviour Jesus Christ."[3] In this world, then, we celebrate, as it were, the forty days' abstinence, when we live aright, and abstain from iniquities and from unlawful pleasures. But because this abstinence shall not be without reward, we look for "that blessed hope, and the revelation of the glory of the great God, and of our Saviour Jesus Christ." In that hope, when the reality of the hope shall have come to pass, we shall receive our wages, a *penny* (*denarius*). For the same is the wages given to the workers laboring in the vineyard,[4] as I presume you remember; for we are not to repeat everything, as if to persons wholly ignorant and inexperienced. A *denarius*, then, which takes its name from the number *ten*, is given, and this joined with the forty makes up fifty; whence it is that before Easter we keep the *Quadragesima* with labor, but after Easter we keep the *Quinquagesima* with joy, as having received our wages. Now to this, as if to the wholesome labor of a good work, which belongs to the number forty, there is added the *denarius* of rest and happiness, that it may be made the number fifty.

5. The Lord Jesus Himself showed this also far more openly, when He companied on earth with His disciples during forty days after His resurrection; and having on the fortieth day ascended into heaven, did at the end of ten days send the wages, the Holy Ghost. These were done in signs, and by a kind of signs were the very realities anticipated. By significant tokens are we fed, that we may be able to come to the enduring realities. We are workmen, and are still laboring in the vineyard: when the day is ended and the work finished, the wages will be paid. But what workman can hold out to the receiving of the wages, unless he be fed while he labors? Even thou thyself wilt not give thy workman only wages; wilt thou not also bestow on him that where with he may repair his strength in his labor? Surely thou feedest him to

---

whom thou art to give wages. In like manner also doth the Lord, in those significant tokens of the Scriptures, feed us while we labor. For if that joy in understanding holy mysteries be withdrawn from us, we faint in labor, and there will be none to come to the reward.

6. How, then, is work perfected in the number forty? The reason, it may be, is, because the law was given in ten precepts, and was to be preached throughout the whole world: which whole world, we are to mark, is made up of four quarters, east and west, south and north, whence the number ten, multiplied by four, comes to forty. Or, it may be, because the law is fulfilled by the gospel, which has four books: for in the gospel it is said, "I came not to destroy the law, but to fulfill it." Whether, then, it be for this reason or for that, or for some other more probable, which is hid from us, but not from more learned men; certain it is, however, that in the number forty a certain perfection in good works is signified, which good works are most of all practised by a kind of abstinence from unlawful lusts of the world, that is, by fasting in the general sense.

Hear also the apostle when he says, "Love is the fulfilling of the law."[1] Whence the love? By the grace of God, by the Holy Spirit. For we could not have it from ourselves, as if making it for ourselves. It is the gift of God, and a great gift it is: for, saith he, "the love of God is shed abroad in our hearts by the Holy Spirit, which is given to us."[2] Wherefore love completes the law, and most truly it is said, "Love is the perfecting of the law." Let us inquire as to this love, in what manner the Lord doth commend it to our consideration. Remember what I laid down: I want to explain the number thirty-eight of the years of that impotent man, why that number thirty-eight is one of weakness rather than of health. Now, as I was saying, love fulfils the law. The number forty belongs to the perfecting of the law in all works; but in love two precepts are committed to our keeping. Keep before your eyes, I beseech you, and fix in your memory, what I say; be ye not despisers of the word, that your soul may not become a trodden path, where the seed cast cannot sprout, "and the fowls of the air will come and gather it up." Apprehend it, and lay it up in your hearts. The precepts of love, given to us by the Lord, are two: "Thou shalt love the Lord thy God with all thy heart, and with all thy soul, and with all thy mind;" and, "Thou shalt love thy neighbor as thyself. On these two com-

mandments hang all the law and the prophets."[3] With good reason did the widow cast "two mites," all her substance, into the offerings of God: with good reason did the host take "two" pieces of money, for the poor man that was wounded by the robbers, for his making whole: with good reason did Jesus spent two days with the Samaritans, to establish them in love. Thus, whilst a certain good thing is generally signified by this number two, most especially is love in its twofold character set forth to us thereby. If, therefore, the number forty possesses the perfecting of the law, and the law is fulfilled only in the twin precepts of love, why dost thou wonder that he was weak and sick, who was short of forty by two?

7. Therefore let us now see the sacred mystery whereby this impotent man is healed by the Lord. The Lord Himself came, the Teacher of love, full of love, "shortening," as it was predicted of Him, "the word upon the earth,"[4] and showed that the law and the prophets hang on two precepts of love. Upon these hung Moses with his number forty, upon these Elias with his; and the Lord brought in this number in His testimony. This impotent man is healed by the Lord in person; but before healing him, what does He say to him? "Wilt thou be made whole?" The man answered that he had not a man to put him into the pool. Truly he had need of a "man" to his healing, but that "man" one who is also God. "For there is one God, and one Mediator between God and man, the man Christ Jesus."[5] He came, then, the Man who was needed: why should the healing be delayed? "Arise," saith He; "take up thy bed, and walk." He said three things: "Arise, Take up thy bed, and Walk." But that "Arise" was not a command to do a work, but the operation of healing. And the man, on being made whole, received two commands: "Take up thy bed, and Walk." I ask you, why was it not enough to say, "Walk?" Or, at any rate, why was it not enough to say, "Arise"? For when the man had arisen whole, he would not have remained in the place. Would it not be for the purpose of going away that he would have arisen? My impression is, that He who found the man lacking two things, gave him these two precepts: for, by ordering him to do two things, it is as if He filled up that which was lacking.

8. How, then, do we find the two precepts of love indicated in these two commands of the Lord? "Take up thy bed," saith He, "and walk." What the two precepts are, my

brethren, recollect with me. For they ought to be thoroughly familiar to you, and not merely to come into your mind when they are recited by us, but they ought never to be blotted out from your hearts. Let it ever be your supreme thought, that you must love God and your neighbor: "God with all thy heart, and with all thy soul, and with all thy mind; and thy neighbor as thyself." These must always be pondered, meditated, retained, practised, and fulfilled. The love of God comes first in the order of enjoying; but in the order of doing, the love of our neighbor comes first. For He who commanded thee this love in two precepts did not charge thee to love thy neighbor first, and then God, but first God, afterwards thy neighbor. Thou, however, as thou dost not yet see God, dost earn to see Him by loving thy neighbor; by loving thy neighbor thou purgest thine eye for seeing God, as John evidently says, "If thou lovest not thy brother whom thou seest, how canst thou love God, whom thou dost not see?"[1] See, thou art told, "Love God." If thou say to me, "Show me Him, that I may love Him;" what shall I answer, but what the same John saith: "No man hath seen God at any time"? And, that you may not suppose yourself to be wholly estranged from seeing God, he saith, "God is love; and he that dwelleth in love dwelleth in God."[2] Therefore love thy neighbor; look at the source of thy love of thy neighbor; there thou wilt see, as thou mayest, God. Begin, then, to love thy neighbor. "Break thy bread to the hungry, and bring into thy house him that is needy without shelter; if thou seest the naked, clothe him; and despise not those of the household of thy seed." And in doing this, what wilt thou get in consequence? "Then shall thy light break forth as the morning light."[3] Thy light is thy God, a "morning light" to thee, because He shall come to thee after the night of this world: for He neither rises nor sets, because He is ever abiding. He will be a morning light to thee on thy return, He who had set for thee on thy falling away from Him. Therefore, in this "Take up thy bed," He seems to me to have said, Love thy neighbor.

9. But why the love of our neighbor is set forth by the taking up of the bed, is still shut up, and, as I suppose, needs to be expounded: unless, perhaps, it offend us that our neighbor should be indicated by means of a bed, a stolid, senseless thing. Let not my neighbor be angry if he be set forth to us by a thing without soul and without feeling. The Lord Himself, even our Saviour Jesus Christ, is called the corner-stone, to build up two in Himself. He is called also a rock, from which water flowed forth: "And that rock was Christ."[4] What wonder, then, if Christ is called rock, that neighbor is called wood? Yet not any kind of wood whatever; as neither that was any kind of rock soever, but one from which water flowed to the thirsty; nor any kind soever of stone, but a corner-stone, which in itself coupled two walls coming from different directions. So neither mayest thou take thy neighbor to be wood of any kind soever, but a bed. Then what is there in a bed, pray? What, but that the impotent man was borne on it; but, when made whole, he carries the bed? What does the apostle say? "Bear ye one another's burdens, and so shall ye fulfill the law of Christ."[5] Now the law of Christ is love, and love is not fulfilled except we bear one another's burdens. "Forbearing," saith he, "one another in love, endeavoring to keep the unity of the Spirit in the bond of peace."[6] When thou wast weak thy neighbor bore thee; thou art made whole, bear thy neighbor. So wilt thou fill up, O man, that which was lacking to thee. "Take up thy bed, then." But when thou hast taken it up, stay not in the place; "walk." By loving thy neighbor, by caring for thy neighbor, dost thou perform thy going. Whither goest thou way, but to the Lord God, whom we ought to love with the whole heart, and with the whole soul, and with the whole mind? For we are not yet come to the Lord, but we have our neighbor with us. Bear him, then, when thou walkest, that thou mayest come to Him with whom thou desirest to abide. Therefore, "take up thy bed, and walk."

10. The man did this, and the Jews were offended. For they saw a man carrying his bed on the Sabbath-day, and they did not blame the Lord for healing him on the Sabbath, that He should be able to answer them, that if any of them had a beast fallen into a well, he would surely draw it out on the Sabbath-day, and save his beast; and so, now they did not object to Him that a man was made whole on the Sabbath-day, but that the man was carrying his bed. But if the healing was not to be deferred, should a work also have been commanded? "It is not lawful for thee," say they, to do what thou art doing, "to take up thy bed." And he, in defence, put the author of his healing before his censors, saying, "He that made me whole, the same said unto me, Take up thy bed, and

---

[1] 1 John iv. 20.   [2] 1 John iv. 16.   [3] Isa. lviii. 7, 8.   [4] 1 Cor. x. 4.   [5] Gal. vi. ..   [6] Eph. iv. 2.

walk." Should I not take injunction from him from whom I received healing? And they said, "Who is the man that said unto thee, Take up thy bed, and walk?"

11. "But he that was made whole knew not who it was" that had said this to him. "For Jesus," when He had done this, and given him this order, "turned away from him in the crowd." See how this also is fulfilled. We bear our neighbor, and walk towards God; but Him, to whom we are walking, we do not yet see: for that reason also, that man did not yet know Jesus. The mystery herein intimated to us is, that we believe on Him whom we do not yet see; and that He may not be seen, He turns aside in the crowd. It is difficult in a crowd to see Christ: a certain solitude is necessary for our mind; it is by a certain solitude of contemplation that God is seen. A crowd has noise; this seeing requires secrecy. "Take up thy bed"—being thyself borne, bear thy neighbor; "and walk," that thou mayest come to the goal. Do not seek Christ in a crowd: He is not as one of a crowd; He excels all crowd. That great fish first ascended from the sea, and He sits in heaven making intercession for us: as the great high priest He entered alone into that within the veil; the crowd stands without. Do thou walk, bearing thy neighbor: if thou hast learned to bear, thou, who wast wont to be borne. In a word, even now as yet thou knowest not Jesus, not yet seest Jesus: what follows thereafter? Since that man desisted not from taking up his bed and walking, "Jesus seeth him afterwards in the temple." He did not see Jesus in the crowd, he saw Him in the temple. The Lord Jesus, indeed, saw him both in the crowd and in the temple; but the impotent man does not know Jesus in the crowd, but he knows Him in the temple. The man came then to the Lord: saw Him in the temple, saw Him in a consecrated, saw Him in a holy place. And what does the Lord say to him? "Behold, thou art made whole; sin no more, lest some worse thing befall thee."

12. The man, then, after he saw Jesus, and knew Him to be the author of his healing, was not slothful in preaching Him whom he had seen: "He departed, and told the Jews that it was Jesus that had made him whole." He brought them word, and they were mad against him; he preached his own salvation, they sought not their own salvation.

13. The Jews persecuted the Lord Jesus because He did these things on the Sabbath-day. Let us hear what answer the Lord now made to the Jews. I have told you how He is wont to answer concerning the healing of men on the Sabbath-day, that they used not on the Sabbath-day to slight their cattle, either in delivering or in feeding them. What does He answer concerning the carrying of the bed? A manifest corporal work was done before the eyes of the Jews; not a healing of the body, but a bodily work, which appeared not so necessary as the healing. Let the Lord, then, openly declare that the sacrament of the Sabbath, even the sign of keeping one day, was given to the Jews for a time, but that the fulfillment of the sacrament had come in Himself. "My Father," saith He, "worketh hitherto, and I work." He sent a great commotion among them: the water is troubled by the coming of the Lord, but yet He that troubles is not seen. Yet one great sick one is to be healed by the troubled water, the whole world by the death of the Lord.

14. Let us see, then, the answer made by the Truth: "My Father worketh hitherto, and I work." Is it false, then, which the Scripture has said, that "God rested from all His works on the seventh day"? And does the Lord Jesus speak contrary to this Scripture ministered by Moses, whilst He Himself says to the Jews, "If ye believed Moses, ye would believe me; for He wrote of me"? See, then, whether Moses did not mean it to be significant of something that "God rested on the seventh day." For God had not become wearied in doing the work of His own creation, and needed rest as a man. How can He have been wearied, who made by a word? Yet is both that true, that "God rested from His works on the seventh day;" and this also is true that Jesus saith, "My Father worketh hitherto." But who can unfold it in words, man to men, weak to weak, unlearned to them that seek to learn; and if he chance to understand somewhat, unable to bring it forth and unfold it to men, who with difficulty, it may be, receive it, even if what is received can possibly be unfolded? Who, I say, my brethren, can unfold in words how God both works while at rest, and rests while working? I pray you to put this matter off while you are advancing on the way; for this seeing requires the temple of God, requires the holy place. Bear your neighbor, and walk. Ye shall see Him in that place where ye shall not require the words of men.

15. Perhaps we can more appropriately say this, that in the saying, "God rested on the seventh day," he signified by a great mystery the Lord and our Saviour Jesus Christ Himself, who spoke and said, "My Father worketh hitherto, and I work." For the Lord Jesus is, of course, God. For He is the Word of God, and you have heard that "in the begin-

ning was the Word;" and not any word what-soever, but "the Word was God, and all things were made by Him." He was perhaps signified as about to rest on the seventh day from all His works. For, read the Gospel, and see what great works Jesus wrought. He wrought our salvation on the cross, that all things foretold by the prophets might be ful-filled in Him. He was crowned with thorns; He hung on the tree; said, "I thirst," re-ceived vinegar on a sponge, that it might be fulfilled which was said, "And in my thirst they gave me vinegar to drink."[1] And when all His works were completed, on the sixth day of the week, He bowed His head and gave up the ghost, and on the Sabbath-day He rested in the tomb from all His works. Therefore it is as if He said to the Jews, "Why do ye expect that I should not work on the Sabbath? The Sabbath-day was or-dained for you for a sign of me. You observe the works of God: I was there when they were made, by me were they all made; I know them. 'My Father worketh hitherto.' The Father made the light, but He spoke that there should be light; if He spoke, it was by His Word He made it: His Word I was, I am; by me was the world made in those works, by me the world is ruled in these works. My Father worked when He made the world, and hitherto now worketh while He rules the world: therefore by me He made when He made, and by me He rules while He rules." This He said, but to whom? To men deaf, blind, lame, impotent, not acknowledging the physician, and as if in a frenzy they had lost their wits, wishing to slay Him.

16. Further, what said the evangelist as he went on? "Therefore the Jews sought the more to kill Him, because He not only broke the Sabbath, but said also that God was His Father;" not in any ordinary manner, but how? "Making Himself equal with God." For we all say to God, "Our Father which art in heaven;" we read also that the Jews said, "Seeing Thou art our Father."[2] Therefore it was not for this they were angry, because He said that God was His Father, but because He said it in quite another way

than men do. Behold, the Jews understand what the Arians do not understand. The Arians, in fact, say that the Son is not equal with the Father, and hence it is that the heresy was driven from the Church. Lo, the very blind, the very slayers of Christ, still understood the words of Christ. They did not understand Him to be Christ, nor did they understand Him to be the Son of God: but they did nevertheless understand that in these words such a Son of God was intimated to them as should be equal with God. Who He was they knew not; still they did acknowledge such a One to be declared, in that "He said God was His Father, making Himself equal with God." Was He not therefore equal with God? He did not make Himself equal, but the Father begat Him equal. Were He to make Himself equal, He would fall by rob-bery. For he who wished to make himself equal with God, whilst he was not so, fell, and of an angel became a devil,[3] and ad-ministered to man that cup of pride by which himself was cast down. For this fallen said to man, envying his standing, "Taste, and ye shall be as gods;"[3] that is, seize to your-selves by usurpation that which ye are not made, for I also have been cast down by rob-bery. He did not put forth this, but this is what he persuaded to. Christ, however, was begotten equal to the Father, not made; be-gotten of the substance of the Father. Whence the apostle thus declares Him: "Who, being in the form of God, thought it not robbery to be equal with God." What means "thought it not robbery"? He usurped not equality with God, but was in that equality in which He was begotten. And how were we to come to the equal God? "He emptied Himself, taking upon Him the form of a ser-vant."[5] But He emptied Himself not by losing what He was, but by taking to Him what He was not. The Jews, despising this form of a servant, could not understand the Lord Christ equal to the Father, although they had not the least doubt that He affirmed this of Himself, and therefore were they enraged: and yet He still bore with them, and sought the heal-ing of them, while they raged against Him.

---

[1] Ps. lxix. 22.　　　　[2] Isa. lxiii. 16.　　　　[3] Isa. xiv. 14.　　　[4] Gen. iii. 5.　　　[5] Phil. ii. 6.

TRACTATE XVIII.

CHAPTER V. 19.

1. JOHN the evangelist, among his fellows and companions the other evangelists, received this special and peculiar gift from the Lord (on whose breast he reclined at the feast, hereby to signify that he was drinking deeper secrets from His inmost heart), to utter those things concerning the Son of God which may perhaps rouse the attentive minds of the little ones, but cannot fill them, as yet not capable of receiving them; while to minds of somewhat larger growth, and coming to a certain age of inner manhood, he gives in these words something whereby they may both be exercised and fed. You have heard it when it was read, and you remember how this discourse arose. For yesterday it was read, that " therefore the Jews sought to kill Jesus, because He not only broke the Sabbath, but also said that God was His Father, making Himself equal with God." This that displeased the Jews, pleased the Father. This, without doubt, pleases them too that honor the Son as they honor the Father; for if it does not please them, they will not be pleasing. For God will not be greater because it pleases thee, but thou wilt be less if it displeases thee. Now against this calumny of theirs, coming either of ignorance or of malice, the Lord speaks not at all what they can understand, but that whereby they may be agitated and troubled, and, on being troubled, it may be, seek the Physician. And He uttered what should be written, that it might afterwards be read even by us. Now we have seen what happened in the hearts of the Jews when they heard these words; what happens in ourselves when we hear them, let us more fully consider. For heresies, and certain tenets of perversity, ensnaring souls and hurling them into the deep, have not sprung up except when good Scriptures are not rightly understood, and when that in them which is not rightly understood is rashly and boldly asserted. And so, dearly beloved, ought we very cautiously to hear those things for the understanding of which we are but little ones, and that, too, with pious heart and with trembling, as it is written, holding this rule of soundness, that we rejoice as in food in that which we have been able to understand, according to the faith with which we are imbued; and what we have not yet been able to understand, that we lay aside doubt-ing, and defer the understanding of it for a time; that is, even if we do not yet know what it is, that still we doubt not in the least that it is good and true. And as for me, brethren, you must consider who I am that undertake to speak to you, and what I have undertaken: for I have taken upon me to treat of things divine, being a man; of spiritual things, being carnal; of things eternal, being a mortal. Also from me, dearly beloved, far be vain presumption, if my conversation would be sound in the house of God, " which is the Church of the living God, the pillar and foundation of the truth."[1] In proportion to my measure I take what I put before you: where it is opened, I see with you; where it is shut, I knock with you.

2. Now the Jews were moved and indignant: justly, indeed, because a man dared to make himself equal with God; but unjustly in this, because in the man they understood not the God. They saw the flesh, the God they knew not; they observed the habitation, of the inhabitant they were ignorant. That flesh was a temple, within it dwelt God. It was not the flesh that Jesus made equal to the Father, it was not the form of a servant that He compared to the Lord; not that which He became for us, but that which He was when He made us. For who Christ is (I speak to Catholics) you know, because you have rightly believed; not Word only, nor flesh only, but the Word was made flesh to dwell among us. I recite again concerning the Word what you know: " In the beginning was the Word, and the Word was with God, and the Word was God:" here is equality with the Father. But " the Word was made flesh, and dwelt among us." Than this flesh the Father is greater. Thus the Father is both equal and greater; equal to the Word, greater than the flesh; equal to Him by whom He made us, greater than He who was made for us. By this sound catholic rule, which you ought particularly to know, which you who know it hold fast, from which your faith ought not in any case to slip, which is to be wrested from your heart by no arguments of men, let us measure the things we do understand; and the things which, it may be, we do not understand, let us defer, to be hereafter measured by this rule, when we

[1] 1 Tim. iii. 1

shall be competent to do this. We know Him, then, as equal to the Father, the Son of God, because we know Him in the beginning as God the Word. Why, then, sought the Jews to slay Him? "Because He not only broke the Sabbath, but also said that God was His Father, making Himself equal with God:" seeing the flesh, not seeing the Word. Let Him therefore speak against them, the Word through the flesh; let Him, the dweller within, speak for through His dwelling-place, that whoso can, shall know who He is that dwells within.

What saith He then to them? "Then answered Jesus, and said unto them," being indignant because He made Himself equal with God, "Verily, verily, I say unto you, The Son cannot do anything of Himself, but what He seeth the Father doing." What the Jews answered to these words is not written: and perhaps they said nothing. Certain, however, who wish to be esteemed Christians, are not silent, but from these words somehow conceive certain opinions in contradiction to us, which are not to be despised, both for their and for our sakes. The Arian heretics, namely, while they assert that the Son, who took upon Himself flesh, is less than the Father, not by the flesh, but before taking flesh, and not of the same substance as the Father, take a handle of misrepresentation from these words, and reply to us: "You see that the Lord Jesus, observing the Jews to be moved with indignation at his making himself equal to God the Father, subjoined such words as these, to show that he was not equal with God. For the Jews," say they, "were provoked against Christ, because he made himself equal with God; and Christ, wishing to cure them of this impression, and to show them that the Son is not equal to the Father, that is, to God, saith this, as if he said, Why are ye angry? Why are ye indignant? I am not equal to God, since 'the Son cannot do anything of himself, except what he seeth the Father doing.' Now," say they, "he who 'cannot do anything of himself, but what he seeth the Father doing,' is surely less, not equal."

4. In this distorted and depraved rule of his own heart, let the heretic hear us, not as yet chiding, but still as it were inquiring, and let him explain to us what he thinks. For, I suppose, whoever thou art (for we may regard him as here present in person), thou dost hold with us, that "in the beginning was the Word." I do hold it, saith he. And that "the Word was with God"? This too, saith he, I hold. Proceed then, and hold the stronger saying that follows, that "the Word was God." Even this, says he, I hold: but yet, this, God the greater; that, God the less. Now this somehow smells of the pagan: I thought I was speaking with a Christian. If there is God the greater, and God the less, then we worship two Gods, not one God. Why, saith he; dost not thou, too, affirm two Gods, equal the one to the other? This I do not assert: for I understand this equality as implying therein also undivided love; and if undivided love, tnen perfect unity. For if the love that God put in men doth make of many hearts of men one heart, and doth make many souls of men into one soul, as it is written of them that believed and mutually loved one another, in the Acts of the Apostles, "They had one soul and one heart toward God:"[1] if, therefore, my soul and thy soul become one soul, when we think the same thing and love one another, how much more must God the Father and God the Son be one God in the fountain of love!

5. But to these words, by which thy heart is disturbed, bend thy thought, and reflect with me on that which we were seeking out concerning the Word. We already hold that "the Word was God:" I join to this another thing, that, having said, "This was in the beginning with God," the evangelist immediately subjoined, "All things were made by Him." Now will I urge thee by questioning, now will I move thee against thyself, and sue thee against thyself: only keep this in memory concerning the Word, that "the Word was God, and all things were made by Him." Hear now the words by which thou wast moved to assert that the Son is less, forsooth, because He said, "The Son cannot of Himself do anything, but what He seeth the Father doing." Just so, saith he. Explain to me this a little: This is, I presume, how thou thinkest: that the Father doeth certain things, and the Son observes how the Father doeth, that He may also Himself be able to do those things which He seeth the Father doing. Thou hast set up two artisans, as it were: the Father and the Son just like master and learner, like as artisan fathers are wont to teach their sons their craft. Behold, I come down to thy carnal sense: for the moment I think as thou doest: let us see if this our conception finds an issue in harmony with the things which we have just now alike spoken and alike hold regarding the Word, that "the Word was God," and that "all things were made by Him." Suppose, then, the Father, as an artisan, doing certain works, and the Son as a learner, who

_____
[1] Acts iv. 32.

" cannot of Himself do anything, but what He seeth the Father doing:" He keenly watches, in a manner, the Father's hands, that, as He seeth Him fashioning aught, so He may Himself in like manner fashion something similar by His own works. But the Father here doeth all those things that He doeth, and wishes the Son to give heed to Him, and to do the like also Himself; by whom doeth the Father? Come! now is the time for thee to stand to thy former opinion, which thou didst recite with me, and didst hold with me, that " in the beginning was the Word, and the Word was with God, and the Word was God, and all things were made by Him." But thou, after holding with me, that all things were made by the Word, dost again, with thy carnal wit and childish fancy, imagine with thyself God making something, and the Word giving heed; so that when God has made, the Word also may make the like. Now, what does God make without the Word? For if He doeth aught, then were not all things made by the Word; thou hast given up the position which thou didst hold. But if all things were made by the Word, correct what thou didst understand amiss. The Father made, and made only by the Word: in what way does the Word give heed to see the Father making without the Word, what the Word may do in like manner? Whatever the Father hath made, He made it by the Word; else is it false that " all things were made by Him." But it is true that " all things were made by Him." Perhaps this did not seem enough for thee? Well, " and without Him was nothing made."

6. Withdraw, then, from this wisdom of the flesh, and let us inquire in what manner it is said, " The Son cannot of Himself do anything, but what He seeth the Father doing." Let us inquire, if we are worthy to apprehend. For I confess it is a great thing, and altogether difficult, to see the Father doing through the Son: not the Father and the Son doing each His particular works, but the Father doing every work whatsoever by the Son; so that not any works are done by the Father without the Son, or by the Son without the Father, because " all things were made by Him, and without Him was nothing made." These truths being most firmly established in the foundation of faith, what now is the nature of this " seeing "? Thou seekest, as I suppose, to know the Son doing: seek first to know the Son seeing. For what, in fact, saith He? " The Son cannot of Himself do anything, but what He seeth the Father doing." Note what He said, " but what He seeth the Father doing." The seeing comes first, the doing follows: He seeth in order to do. As for thee, why seekest thou at present to know how He doeth, whilst thou understandest not as yet how He seeth? Why runnest thou to that which comes later, leaving that which comes first? He declares Himself as seeing and doing, not doing and seeing; because " He cannot of Himself do anything, but what He seeth the Father doing." Wilt thou that I explain to thee how He doeth? Do thou explain to me how He seeth. If thou canst not explain this, neither can I that. If thou art not yet competent to understand this, neither am I to understand that. Wherefore let each of us seek, each knock, that each may merit to receive. Why dost thou, as if thou wert learned, unjustly blame me who am unlearned? I in respect of the doing, thou in respect of the seeing, being both unlearned, let us inquire of the Master, not childishly wrangle in His school. We have already, however, learned together that " all things were made by Him." Therefore it is manifest that it is not a different kind of works that the Father doeth, that, seeing them, the Son may do other works like them; but the very same doeth the Father by the Son, because all things were made by the Word. Now, as to *how* God doeth, who knows? How made He, I will not say the world, but thine own eye, in thy carnal attachment to which thou comparest visible things with invisible? For thou conceivest of God such things as thou art wont to see with these eyes. But if God might be seen with these eyes, He would not have said, " Blessed are the pure in heart, for they shall see God." Accordingly, thou hast an eye of the body to see an artificer, but thou hast not yet the eye of the heart to see God: hence, what thou art wont to see in an artificer, thou wouldest transfer to God. Leave earthly things on the earth; set thy heart on high.

7. What then, beloved, are we going to explain that which we have asked, how the Word seeth, how the Father is seen by the Word, what the seeing of the Word is? I am not so bold, so rash, as to promise to explain this, for myself or for you: however I estimate your measure, still I know my own. Therefore, if you please, not to delay it longer, let us run over the passage, and see how carnal hearts are troubled by the words of the Lord; to this end troubled, that they may not continue in that which they hold. Let this be wrested from them, as some toy is wrested from children, with which they amuse themselves to their hurt, that, as persons of larger growth, they may have more profitable things

planted in them, and may be able to make progress, instead of crawling on the earth. Arise, seek, sigh, pant with desire, and knock at what is shut. But if we do not yet desire, not yet earnestly seek, not yet sigh, we shall only be throwing pearls to all indiscriminately, or finding pearls ourselves, regardless of what kind. Wherefore, beloved, I would move a longing desire in your heart. Good character leads to right understanding: the kind of life leads to another kind of life. One kind of life is earthly, another is heavenly: there is a life of beasts, another of men, and another of angels. The life of beasts is excited with earthly pleasures, seeks earthly pleasures alone, and grovels after them with immoderate desire: the life of angels is alone heavenly; the life of men is midway between that of angels and of beasts. If man lives after the flesh, he is on a level with the beasts; if he lives after the Spirit, he joins in the fellowship of angels. When thou livest after the Spirit, examine even in the angelic life whether thou be small or well-grown. For if thou art still a little one, the angels say to thee, "Grow: we feed on bread; thou art nourished with milk, with the milk of faith, that thou mayest come to the meat of sight." But if there be still a longing for filthy pleasures, if the thoughts be still of deceit, if lies are not avoided, if perjuries be heaped on lies, shall a heart so foul dare to say, "Explain to me how the Word sees;" even if I be able to do so, even if I myself now see? And further, though not perhaps of this character myself, and I am nevertheless far from this vision, how must that man be weighed down with earthly desires, who is not yet rapt with this desire from above! There is a wide difference between loathing and desiring; and again, between desiring and enjoying. If thou livest as do the beasts, thou loathest: the angels have full enjoyment. If, on the other hand, thou livest not as the beast, thou hast no longer loathing: something thou desirest, and dost not receive; thou hast, by the very desire, begun the life of the angels. May it grow in thee, and be perfected in thee; and mayest thou receive this, not of me, but of Him who made both me and thee!

8. Yet the Lord also has not left us to chance, since, in that He said, "The Son cannot of Himself do anything, but what He seeth the Father doing," He meant us to understand that the Father doeth, not some works which the Son may see, and the Son doeth other works after He has seen the Father doing; but that both the Father and Son do the very same works. For He goes on to say, "For what things soever He doeth, these also doeth the Son in like manner." Not after the Father hath done works, doeth the Son other works in like manner; but, "whatever He doeth, these also the Son doeth in like manner." If these the Son doeth which the Father doeth, then it is by the Son that the Father doeth: if by the Son the Father doeth what He doeth, then the Father doeth not some, the Son others; but the works of the Father and of the Son are the same works. And how doeth the Son also the same? Both "the same," and "in like manner." In case you should think them the same, but in a different manner, the "same," saith He, and "in like manner." And how could they be the same and not in like manner? Take an example, which I presume is not too big for you: when we write letters they are first formed by our heart, then by our hand. Certainly: why otherwise have you all agreed, but because you perceived it to be so? It is as I have said, it is manifest to us all. The letters are made first by our heart, then by our body; the hand serves, the heart commands; both the heart and the hand make the same letters. Dost think the heart doeth some letters, the hand some others? The same indeed doeth the hand, but not in like manner: our heart forms them intelligibly, but our hand visibly. See how the same things are made, but not in like manner. Hence it was not enough for the Lord to say, "What things soever the Father doeth, these also the Son doeth;" He must add, "and in like manner." For what if thou shouldst understand this just as thou understandest whatever thy heart doeth, this also thy hand doeth, but in a different manner? Here, however, he added, "These also the Son doeth in like manner." If He both doeth these, and in like manner doeth, then awake; let the Jew be crushed, let the Christian believe, let the heretic be convinced: The Son is equal to the Father.

9. "For the Father loveth the Son, and showeth Him all things that Himself doeth." Here is that "showeth." "Showeth," as it were, to whom? Of course, as to one that sees. We return to that which we cannot explain, how the Word seeth. Behold, man was made by the Word; but man has eyes, ears, hands, divers members in the body: he is able by the eyes to see, by the ears to hear, by the hands to work; the members are diverse, their offices diverse. One member cannot do the office of another; yet, by reason of the unity of the body, the eye sees both for itself and for the ear, and the ear hears for itself and for the eye. Are we to

suppose that something like this holds good in the Word, seeing all things are by Him; and Scripture has said in the psalm, "Understand, ye brutish among the people; and ye fools, at length be wise. He that planted the ear, shall He not hear? And He that formed the eye, shall He not see?"[1] Hence, if the Word is He that formed the eye, for all things are by the Word; if the Word is He that planted the ear, for all things are by the Word: we cannot say the Word doth not hear, the Word doth not see; lest the psalm reprove us, and say, "Fools, at length be wise." Therefore, if the Word heareth and seeth, if the Son heareth and seeth, are we yet to search for eyes and ears in Him in separate places? Does He by one part hear, by another see; and cannot His ear do what His eye doth; and cannot His eye do what His ear can? Or is He not all sight, all hearing? Perhaps yes; nay, not perhaps, but truly yes; whilst, however, that seeing of His, and that hearing of His, is in a way far other than it is with us. Both to see and to hear exist together in the Word: seeing and hearing are not diverse things in Him; but hearing is sight, and sight is hearing.

10. And we, who see in one way, and hear in another way, how know we this? We return perhaps to ourselves, if we are not the transgressors to whom it is said, "Return, O transgressors, to your heart."[2] Return to your heart: why go from yourselves, and perish from yourselves? Why go the ways of solitude? You go astray by wandering: return ye. Whither? To the Lord. 'Tis quickly done: first return to thine own heart; thou hast wandered abroad an exile from thyself; thou knowest not thyself, and yet thou art asking by whom thou wast made! Return, return to thy heart, lift thyself away from the body: thy body is thy place of abode; thy heart perceives even by thy body. But thy body is not what thy heart is; leave even thy body, return to thy heart. In thy body thou didst find eyes in one place, ears in another place: dost thou find this in thy heart? Or hast thou not ears in thy heart? Else of what did the Lord say, "Whoso hath ears to hear, let him hear?"[3] Or hast thou not eyes in thy heart? Else of what saith the apostle, "The eyes of your heart being enlightened?"[4] Return to thy heart; see there what, it may be, thou canst perceive of God, for in it is the image of God. In the inner man dwelleth Christ, in the inner man art thou renewed after the image of God, in His own image recognize its Author. See how all the senses of the body bring intelligence to the heart within of what they have perceived abroad; see how many ministers the one commander within has and what it can do by itself even without these ministers. The eyes report to the heart things black and white; the ears report to the same heart pleasant and harsh sounds; to the same heart the nostrils announce sweet odors and stenches; to the same heart the taste announces things bitter and sweet; to the same heart the touch announces things smooth and rough; and the heart declares to itself things just and unjust. Thy heart sees and hears and judges all other things perceived by the senses; and, what the senses do not aspire to, discerns things just and unjust, things evil and good. Show me the eyes, ears, nostrils, of thy heart. Diverse are the things that are referred to thy heart, yet are there not diverse members there. In thy flesh, thou hearest in one place, seest in another; in thy heart, where thou seest, there thou hearest. If this be the image, how much more mightily He whose the image is! Therefore the Son both heareth and seeth; the Son is both the hearing itself and the seeing: to hear is to Him the same thing as "to be;" and to see is to Him the same thing as "to be." To see is not the same thing to thee as to be; for if thou lose thy sight, thou canst be; and if thou lose thy hearing, thou canst be.

11. Do we think we have knocked? Is there raised up within us something whereby we may even slightly conjecture whence light may come to us? It is my opinion, brethren, that when we speak of these things, and meditate upon them, we are exercising ourselves. And when we are exercising ourselves, and are as it were bent back again by our own weight to our customary thoughts, we are like weak-eyed persons, when they are brought forth to see the light, if perchance they had no sight at all before, and begin in some sort to recover their sight by the assiduous care of physicians. And when the physician would test the progress of recovery, he tries to show them something which they sought to see, but could not while they were blind: and while the eyesight is now somewhat recovered, they are brought forth to the light; and as they see it, are beaten back in a manner by the very glare; and they answer the physician, as he points out the object, This moment I did see, but now I cannot. What then does the physician? He brings them back to their usual ways, and applies the eye-salve to nourish the longing for seeing that which was seen only for a moment, so that by the very longing he may cure more completely; and if any stinging salves are applied for the recovery of sound-

---

[1] Ps. xciv. 8, 9. [2] Isa. xlvi. 8.
[3] Luke viii. 8. [4] Eph. i. 18.

ness, let the patient bear it bravely, and, inflamed with love of the light, say to himself, When will it be that with strong eyes I shall see what with sore and weak eyes I could not? He urges the physician, and begs him to heal him. Therefore, brethren, if, it may be, something like this has taken place in your hearts, if somehow you have raised your heart to see the Word, and, beaten back by its light, you have fallen back to your wonted ways; pray the Physician to apply sharp salves, the precepts of righteousness. There is that which thou mayest see, but not that whereby thou canst see. Thou didst not believe me before that there is that which thou mayest see: thou art now, as by the guidance of reason, brought to it: thou hast drawn near, strained thine eyes to see it, throbbed, and shrunk back. Thou knowest for certain that there is what thou mayest see, but that thou art not yet meet to see it. Therefore be healed. What are the eye-salves? Do not lie, do not swear falsely, do not commit adultery, do not steal, do not defraud. But thou art used to these, and it is with some pain thou art drawn away from old habits: this is what bites, but yet heals. For I tell thee freely, by fear of myself and of thee, if thou give up the healing, and scorn to become meet to enjoy this light, by weakness of thine eyes, thou wilt love darkness; and by loving darkness, wilt remain in darkness; and by remaining in darkness, wilt be cast even into outer darkness: there shall be weeping and gnashing of teeth. If the love of light has effected nothing in thee, let the fear of pain effect something.

12. I think I have spoken long enough, and yet I have not concluded the Gospel lesson: if I go on to declare what remains, I shall burden you, and I fear lest even what has been drawn may be lost; therefore let this be enough for you now, beloved. We are debtors, not now, but always as long as we live; because we live for you. However, do you, by good living, comfort this life of ours, so weak, toilsome, and full of peril in this world; do not afflict and wear us out by your evil manners. For if, when offended with your evil life, we flee from you and separate ourselves from you, and no longer come to you, will ye not complain, and say, And if we were sick, ye might care for us; and if we were weak, ye might have visited us? Behold, we do care for you; behold, we do visit you; but let it not be with us as you have heard from the apostle, "I fear lest I have bestowed labor upon you in vain."[1]

[1] Gal. iv. 11.

TRACTATE XIX.

CHAPTER V. 19–30.

IN the former discourse, so far as the subject impressed us, and so far as our poverty of understanding attained to, we have spoken by occasion of the words of the Gospel, where it is written: "The Son cannot do anything of Himself, but what He seeth the Father doing,"—what it is for the Son—that is, the Word, for the Son is the Word—"to see;" and as all things were made by the Word, how it is to be understood that the Son first sees the Father doing, and then only Himself also doeth the things which He has seen done, seeing that the Father has done nothing except by the Son. For "all things were made by Him, and without Him was nothing made. We have not, however, delivered to you anything as fully explained, and that because we have not understood anything thus clearly set forth. For, indeed, speech sometimes fails even where the understanding makes way; how much more doth speech suffer defect, where the understanding has nothing perfect! Now, therefore, as the Lord gives us, let us briefly run over the passage, and even to-day complete the due task. Should there perchance remain somewhat of time or of strength, we will reconsider (so far as it may be practicable for us and with you) what it is for the Word "to see" and "to be shown to;" since, in fact, all that is here spoken is such that, if understood according to man's sense, carnally, the soul full of vain fancies makes for us only certain images of the Father and the Son, just as of two men, the one showing, the other seeing; the one speaking, the other hearing,—all which are idols of the heart. And if now at length idols have been cast down from their own temples, how much more ought they to be cast down from Christian hearts!

2. "The Son," saith He, "cannot do anything of Himself, but what He sees the Father doing." This is true: hold this fast, while at the same time ye do not let slip what ye have gotten in the beginning of the Gospel, that "in the beginning was the Word, and the Word was with God, and the Word was God," and especially that "all things were made by Him." Join this that ye have now heard to that hearing, and let both agree together in your hearts. Thus, "The Son cannot of Himself do anything, except what He seeth the Father doing," is yet in such wise that what the Father doeth, He doeth only by the Son, because the Son is His Word: and, "In the beginning was the Word, and the Word was with God, and the Word was God;" also, "All things were made by Him." For what things soever He doeth, the Son also doeth in like manner; not other things, but these; and not in a different, but in like manner.

3. "For the Father loveth the Son, and showeth Him all things that Himself doeth." To that which He said above, "except what He seeth the Father doing," seems to belong this also, "He showeth Him all things that Himself doeth." But if the Father doth show what He doeth, and the Son cannot do except the Father hath shown, and if the Father cannot show unless He hath done, it will follow that it is not through the Son that the Father doeth all things; moreover, if we hold it fixed and unshaken, that the Father doeth all by the Son, then He shows the Son before He doeth. For if the Father doth show to the Son after He has done, that the Son may do the things shown, which being shown were already done, then doubtless something there is that the Father doeth without the Son. But the Father doeth not anything without the Son, because the Son of God is God's Word, and all things were made by Him. It remains, then, that possibly what the Father is about to do, He shows as about to be done, that it may be done by the Son. For if the Son doeth those things which the Father showeth as already done, surely it is not by the Son that the Father hath done the things which He thus showeth. For they could not be shown to the Son unless they were first done, and the Son would not be able to do them unless they were first shown; therefore were they made without the Son. But yet it is a true thing, "All things were made by Him;" therefore they were shown *before* they were made. But this we said must be put off, and returned to after briefly scanning the passage, if, as we said, some portion of time and of strength should remain to us for a reconsideration of the matters deferred.

4. Attend now to a wider and more difficult question. "And greater works than these," saith He, "will He show Him, that ye may marvel." "Greater than these." Greater than which? The answer readily occurs: than the cures of bodily diseases which ye have just heard: For the whole occasion of this discourse arose about the man who was thirty and eight years in infirmity, and was healed by the word of Christ; and in respect of this cure, the Lord could say, "Greater works than these He will show Him, that ye may marvel." For there are greater, and the Father will show them to the Son. It is not "hath shown," as of a thing past, but "will show," of a thing future; or, is about to show. Again a difficult question arises: Why, then, is there something with the Father that has not yet been shown to the Son? Is there something with the Father that was still hid from the Son when He spoke these words? For surely, if it be "will show," that is to say, "is about to show," then He has not yet shown; and He is about to show to the Son at the same time as to these persons, since it follows, "that ye may marvel." And this is a thing hard to see, how the Eternal Father doth show something, as it were in time, to the co-eternal Son, who knoweth all things that are with the Father.

5. But what are the greater works? For perhaps this is easy to understand. "For as the Father," saith He, "raiseth up the dead, and quickeneth them, even so the Son quickeneth whom He will." To raise the dead, then, are greater works than to heal the sick. But "as the Father raiseth the dead, and quickeneth them, so also the Son quickeneth whom He will." Hence, the Father some, the Son others? But all things are by Him: therefore the Son the same persons as the Father doth; since the Son doeth not other things and in a different manner, but "these" and in "like manner." Thus clearly it must be understood, and thus held. But keep in memory that "the Son quickeneth whom He will." Here, too, know not only the power of the Son, but also the will. Both the Son quickeneth whom He will, and also the Father quickeneth whom He will—the Son the same persons as the Father; and hence the power of the Father and of the Son is the same, and also the will is the same. What follows then? "For the Father judgeth not any man, but hath given all judgment to the Son, that all men may honor the Son, even as they honor the Father:" this He subjoined, as rendering a reason of the foregoing sentence. A great question comes before us; give it your earnest attention. The Son quickeneth whom He

will, the Father quickeneth whom He will; the son raiseth the dead, just as the Father raiseth the dead. And further, "the Father judgeth not any man." If the dead must be raised in the judgment, how can it be said that the Father raiseth the dead, if He judgeth not any man, since "He hath given all judgment to the Son"? But in that judgment the dead are raised; some rise to life, others to punishment. If the Son doeth all this, but the Father not, inasmuch as "He judgeth not any man, but hath given all judgment to the Son," it will appear contrary to what has been said, viz., "As the Father raiseth up the dead, and quickeneth them, so also the Son quickeneth whom He will." Consequently the Father and the Son raise together; if they raise together, they quicken together: hence they judge together. How, then, is that true, "For the Father judgeth not any man, but hath given all judgment to the Son"? Meanwhile let the questions now proposed engage your minds; the Lord will cause that, when solved, they will delight you. For so it is, brethren: every question, unless it stirs the mind to reflection, will not give delight when explained. May the Lord Himself then follow with us, in case He may perhaps reveal Himself somewhat in those matters which He foldeth up. For He foldeth up His light with a cloud; and it is difficult to fly like an eagle above every obscure mist with which the whole earth is covered, and to behold the most serene light in the words of the Lord. In case, then, He may perhaps dissipate our darkness with the heat of His rays, and deign to reveal Himself somewhat in the sequel, let us, deferring these questions, look at what follows.

6. "Whoso honoreth not the Son, honoreth not the Father that sent Him." This is a truth, and is plain. Since, then, "all judgment hath He given to the Son," as He said above, "that all may honor the Son, even as they honor the Father," what if there be those who honor the Father and honor not the Son? It cannot be, saith He: "Whoso honoreth not the Son, honoreth not the Father that sent Him." One cannot therefore say, I honored the Father, because I knew not the Son. If thou didst not yet honor the Son, neither didst thou honor the Father. For what is honoring the *Father*, unless it be in that He hath a Son? It is one thing when thou art taught to honor God in that He is God; but another thing when thou art taught to honor Him in that He is *Father*. When thou art taught to honor Him in that He is God, it is as the Creator, as the Almighty, as the Spirit supreme, eternal, invisible, unchangeable, that

thou art led to think of Him; but when thou art taught to honor Him in that He is *Father*, it is the same thing as to honor the Son; because *Father* cannot be said if there be not a Son, as neither can *Son* if there be not a Father. But lest, it may be, thou honorest the Father indeed as greater, but the Son as less,—as thou mayest say to me, "I do honor the Father, for I know that He has a Son; nor do I err in the name *Father*, for I do not understand Father without Son, and yet the Son also I honor as the less,"—the Son Himself sets thee right, and recalls thee, saying, "that all may honor the Son," not in a lower degree, but "as they honor the Father." Therefore, "whoso honoreth not the Son, honoreth not the Father that sent Him." "I," sayest thou, "wish to give greater honor to the Father, less to the Son." Therein thou takest away honor from the Father, wherein thou givest less to the Son. For, being thus minded, it must really seem to thee that the Father either would not or could not beget a Son equal to Himself: if He would not, He lacked the will; if He could not, He lacked the ability. Dost thou not therefore see that, being thus minded, wherein thou wouldst give greater honor to the Father, therein thou art reproachful to the Father? Wherefore, so honor the Son as thou honorest the Father, if thou wouldest honor both the Father and the Son.

7. "Verily, verily, I say unto you, Whoso heareth my word, and believeth on Him that sent me, hath eternal life, and cometh not into judgment, but is passed," not *is passing* now, but is already passed, "from death into life." And mark this, "Whoso heareth my word, and "—He says not, believeth me, but—"believeth Him that sent me." Let him hear the word of the Son, that he may believe the Father. Why heareth Thy word, and yet believeth another? When we hear any one's word, is it not him that utters the word we believe? is it not to him who speaks we lend our faith? What, then, did He mean, saying, "Whoso heareth my word, and believeth Him that sent me," if it be not this, because "His word is in me"? And what is "heareth my word," but "heareth me"? So, too, "believeth Him that sent me," because, believing Him, he believeth His word; but again, believing His word, he believeth me, because I am the Word of the Father. There is therefore peace in the Scriptures, and all things duly disposed, and in no way clashing. Cast away, then, contention from thy heart; understand the harmony of the Scriptures. Dost thou think that the Truth should speak things contrary to itself?

8. " Whoso heareth my word, and believeth Him that sent me, hath eternal life, and cometh not into judgment, but is passed from death unto life." You remember what we laid down above, that " as the Father raiseth up the dead, and quickeneth them, so also the Son quickeneth whom He will." He is beginning already to reveal Himself; and behold, even now, the dead are rising. For "whoso heareth my word, and believeth Him that sent me, hath eternal life, and will not come into judgment." Prove that he has risen again. " But is passed," saith He, " from death unto life." He that is passed from death unto life, has surely without any doubt risen again. For he could not pass from death to life, unless he were first in death and not in life; but when he will have passed, he will be in life, and not in death. He was therefore dead, and is alive again; he was lost, but is found.[1] Hence a resurrection does take place now, and men pass from a death to a life; from the death of infidelity to the life of faith; from the death of falsehood to the life of truth; from the death of iniquity to the life of righteousness. There is, therefore, that which is a resurrection of the dead.

9. May He open the same more fully, and dawn upon us as He begins to do! " Verily, verily, I say unto you, The hour is coming, and now is." We did look for a resurrection of the dead in the end, for so we have believed; yea, not we looked, but are manifestly bound to look for it: for it is not a false thing we believe, when we believe that the dead will rise in the end. When the Lord Jesus, then, was willing to make known to us *a* resurrection of the dead before *the* resurrection of the dead, it is not as that of Lazarus,[2] or of the widow's son,[3] or of the ruler of the synagogue's daughter,[4] who were raised to die again (for in their case there was *a* resurrection of the dead before *the* resurrection of the dead); but, as He says here, " hath," says He, " eternal life, and cometh not into judgment, but is passed from death into life." To what life? To life eternal. Not, then, as the body of Lazarus: for he indeed passed from the death of the tomb to the life of men, but not to life eternal, seeing he was to die again; whereas the dead, that are to rise again at the end of the world, will pass to eternal life. When our Lord Jesus Christ, then, our heavenly Master, the Word of the Father, and the Truth, was willing to represent to us *a* resurrection of the dead to eternal life before *the* resurrection of the dead to eternal life, " The hour cometh,"

saith He. Doubtless thou, imbued with a faith of the resurrection of the flesh, didst look for the hour of the end of the world, which, that thou shouldst not look for here, He added, " and now is." Therefore He saith not this, " The hour cometh," of that last hour, when " at the command and the voice of the archangel and the trump of God, the Lord Himself shall descend from heaven, and the dead in Christ shall rise first; then we who are alive and remain shall be caught up together with them in the clouds, to meet Christ in the air: and so shall we be ever with the Lord."[5] That hour will come, but is not now. But consider what this hour is: " The hour cometh, and now is." What happens in that hour? What, but a resurrection of the dead? And what kind of resurrection? Such that they who rise live for ever. This will be also in the last hour.

10. What then? How do we understand these two resurrections? Do we, it may be, understand that they who rise now will not rise then; that the resurrection of some is now, of some others then? It is not so. For we have risen in this resurrection, if we have rightly believed; and we ourselves, who have already risen, are looking for another resurrection in the end. Moreover, both now are we risen to eternal life, if we perseveringly continue in the same faith; and then, too, we shall rise to eternal life, when we shall be made equal with the angels.[6] But let Himself distinguish and open up what we have made bold to speak; how there happens to be a resurrection before a resurrection, not of different but of the same persons; nor like that of Lazarus, but into eternal life. He will open it clearly. Hear ye the Master, while dawning upon us, and as our Sun gliding in upon our hearts; not such as the eyes of flesh desire to look upon, but on whom the eyes of the heart fervently long to be opened. To Him, then, let us give ear: " Verily, verily, I say unto you, The hour cometh, and now is, when the dead "—you see that a resurrection is asserted—" shall hear the voice of the Son of God; and they that hear shall live." Why hath He added, " they that hear shall live "? Why, could they hear unless they lived? It would have been enough, then, to say, " The hour cometh, and now is, when the dead shall hear the voice of the Son of God." We should immediately understand them to be living, since they could not hear unless they lived. No, saith He, not because they live they hear; but by hearing they come to life again: " Shall hear, and they that hear

---

[1] Luke xv. 32.   [2] John xi. 43.
[3] Luke vi. 14.   [4] Matt. v. 41

[5] 1 Thess. iv. 15, 16   [6] Luke xx. 36.

shall live." What, then, is "shall hear," but "shall obey"? For, as to the hearing of the ear, not all who hear shall live. Many, indeed, hear and do not believe; by hearing and not believing, they obey not; by not obeying, they live not. And so here, they that "shall hear" are they that "shall obey." They that obey, then, shall live: let them be sure and certain of it, *shall live*. Christ, the Word of God, is preached to us; the Son of God, by whom all things were made, who, for the dispensation's sake, surely took flesh, was born of a virgin, was an infant in the flesh, a young man in the flesh, suffering in the flesh, dying in the flesh, rising again in the flesh, ascending in the flesh, promising a resurrection to the flesh, promising a resurrection to the mind—to the mind before the flesh, to the flesh after the mind. Whoso heareth and obeyeth, shall live; whoso heareth and obeyeth not, that is, heareth and despiseth, heareth and believeth not, shall not live. Why shall not live? Because he heareth not. What is "heareth not"? Obeyeth not. Thus, then, "they that hear shall live."

11. Turn your thoughts now to what we said had to be deferred, that it may now, if possible, be opened. Concerning this very resurrection He immediately subjoined, "For as the Father hath life in Himself, even so hath He given to the Son to have life in Himself." What means that, "The Father hath life in Himself"? Not elsewhere hath He life but in Himself. His living, in fact, is in Him, not from elsewhere, nor derived from another. He does not, as it were, borrow life, nor, as it were, become a partaker of life, of a life which is not what Himself is; but "hath life in Himself," so that the very life is to Him His very self. If I should be able yet further in some small measure to speak from this matter, by proposing examples for informing your understanding, will depend on God's help and the piety of your attention. God lives, and the soul also lives; but the life of God is unchangeable, the life of the soul is changeable. In God is neither increase nor decrease; but He is the same always in Himself, is ever as He is: not in one way now, in another way hereafter, in some other way before. But the life of the soul is exceedingly various: it lived foolish, it lives wise; it lived unrighteous, it lives righteous; now remembers, now forgets; now learns, now cannot learn; now loses what it had learned, now apprehends what it had lost. The life of the soul is changeable. And when the soul lives in unrighteousness, that is its death; when again it becomes righteous, it becomes partaker of another life, which is not what

itself is, inasmuch as by rising up to God, and cleaving to God, of Him it is justified. For it is said, "To him that believeth on Him that justifieth the ungodly, his faith is counted for righteousness."[1] By forsaking God, it becomes unrighteous; by coming to Him, it is made righteous. Does it not seem to thee as it were something cold, which, when brought near the fire, grows warm; when removed from the fire, grows cold? A something dark, which, brought near the light, grows bright; when removed from the light, grows dark? Something such is the soul: God is not any such thing. Moreover, man may say that he has light now in his eyes. Let thine eyes say then, if they can, as by a voice of their own, "We have light in ourselves." I answer: Not correctly do you say that you have light in yourselves: you have light, but in the heavens; you have light, but in the moon, in candles, if it happen to be night, not in yourselves: for, being shut, you lose what you perceive when open. Not in yourselves have you light; keep the light if you can when the sun is set: 'tis night, enjoy the light of night; keep the light when the candle is withdrawn; but since you remain in darkness when the candle is withdrawn, you have not light in yourselves. Consequently, to have light in oneself is not to need light from another. Behold, whoso understands wherein He shows that the Son is equal with the Father, when He saith, "As the Father hath life in Himself, so hath He given to the Son also to have life in Himself;" that there may be only this difference between the Father and the Son, that the Father hath life in Himself, which none gave Him, whilst the Son hath life in Himself which the Father gave.

12. But here also arises a cloud that must be scattered. Let us not lose heart, let us strive in earnest. Here are pastures of the mind; let us not disdain them, that we may live. Behold, sayest thou, thyself confessest that the Father hath given life to the Son, that He may have life in Himself, even as the Father hath life in Himself; that the Father not lacking, the Son may not lack; that as the Father is life, so the Son may be life; and both united one life, not two lives; because God is one, not two Gods; and this same *is to be life*. How, then, is the Father said to have *given* life to the Son? Not so as if the Son had been without life before, and received life from the Father that He might live; for if it were so, He would not have life in Himself. Behold, I was speaking of the soul. The soul exists; though it be not wise, though it

---

[1] Rom. iv. 5.

be not righteous, though it be not godly, it is soul. It is one thing for it to be soul, but another thing to be wise, to be righteous, to be godly. Something there is, then, in which it is not yet wise, not yet righteous, not yet godly. Nevertheless it is not therefore nothing, it is not therefore non-life; for it shows itself to be alive by certain of its own actions, although it does not show itself to be wise, godly, or righteous. For if it were not living it would not move the body, would not command the feet to walk, the hands to work, the eyes to look, the ears to hear; would not open the mouth for speaking, nor move the tongue to distinction of speech. So, then, by these operations it shows itself to have life, and to be something which is better than the body. But does it in any wise show itself by these operations to be wise, godly, or righteous? Do not the foolish, the wicked, the unrighteous walk, work, see, hear, speak? But when the soul rises to something which itself is not, which is above itself, and from which its being is, then it gets wisdom, righteousness, holiness, which so long as it was without, it was dead, and did not have the life by which itself should live, but only that by which the body was quickened. For that in the soul by which the body is quickened is one thing, that by which the soul itself is quickened is another. Better, certainly, than the body is the soul, but better than the soul itself is God. The soul, even if it be foolish, ungodly, unrighteous, is the life of the body. But since its own life is God, just as it supplies vigor, comeliness, activity, the functions of the limbs to the body, while it exists in the body; so, in like manner, while God, its life, is in the soul, He supplies to it wisdom, godliness, righteousness charity. Accordingly, what the soul supplies to the body, and what God supplies to the soul, are of a different kind: the soul quickens and is quickened. It quickens while dead, even if itself is not quickened. But when the word comes, and is poured into the hearers, and they not only hear, but are made obedient, the soul rises from its death to its life—that is, from unrighteousness, from folly, from ungodliness, to its God, who is to it wisdom, righteousness, light. Let it rise to Him, and be enlightened by Him. "Come near," saith he, "to Him." And what shall we have? "And be enlightened."[1] If, therefore, by "coming to" ye are enlightened, and by "departing from" ye become darkened, your light was not in yourselves, but in your God. Come to Him that ye may rise again: if ye depart from Him, ye shall die. If by coming to Him ye live, and by departing from Him ye die, your life was not in yourselves. For the same is your life which is your light. "Because with Thee is the fountain of life, and in Thy light we shall see light."[2]

13. Not, then, in like manner as the soul is one thing before it is enlightened, and becomes a better thing when it is enlightened, by participation of a better; not so, I say, was the Word of God, the Son of God, something else before He received life, that He should have life by participation; but He has life in Himself, and is consequently Himself the very life. What is it, then, that He saith, "hath given to the Son to have life in Himself"? I would say it briefly, He *begot* the Son. For it is not that He existed without life, and *received* life, but He *is* life by being begotten. The Father is life not by being begotten; the Son is life by being begotten. The Father is of no father; the Son is of God the Father. The Father in His being is of none, but in that He is Father, 'tis because of the Son. But the Son also, in that He is Son, 'tis because of the Father: in His being, He is of the Father. This He said, therefore: "hath given life to the Son, that He might have it in Himself." Just as if He were to say, "The Father, who is life in Himself, begot the Son, who should be life in Himself." Indeed, He would have this *dedit* (hath given) to be understood for the same thing as *genuit* (hath begotten). It is like as if we said to a person, "God hath given thee being." To whom? If to some one already existing, then He gave him not being, because he who could receive existed before it was given him. When, therefore, thou hearest it said, "He gave thee being," thou wast not in being to receive, but thou didst receive, that thou shouldst be by coming into existence. The builder gave to this house that it should be. But what did he give to it? He gave it to be a house. To what did he give? To this house. Gave it what? To be a house. How could he give to a house that it should be a house? For if the house was, to what *did he give* to be a house, when the house existed already? What, then, does that mean, "gave it to be a house"? It means, he brought to pass that it should be a house. Well, then, what gave He to the Son? Gave Him to be the Son, begot Him to be life—that is, "gave Him to have life in Himself" that He should be the life not needing life, that He may not be understood as having life by participation For if He had life by par-

ticipation, He might, by losing, be without life. Do not take, nor think, nor believe this to be possible respecting the Son. Wherefore the Father continues the life, the Son continues the life: the Father, life in Himself, not from the Son; the Son, life in Himself, but from the Father. Begotten of the Father, that He might live in Himself; but the Father, not begotten, life in Himself. Nor did He beget the Son less than Himself to become equal by growth. For surely He by whom, being perfect, the times were created, was not assisted by time towards His own perfection. Before all time, He is co-eternal with the Father. For the *Father* has never been without the Son; but the Father is eternal, therefore also the Son co-eternal. Soul, what of thee? Thou wast dead, didst lose life; hear then the Father through the Son. Arise, take to thee life, that in Him who has life in Himself thou mayest receive the life which is not in thee. He that giveth thee life, then, is the Father and the Son; and the first resurrection is accomplished when thou risest to partake of the life which thou art not thyself, and by partaking art made living. Rise from thy death to thy life, which is thy God, and pass from death to eternal life. For the Father hath eternal life in Himself; and unless He had begotten such a Son as had life in Himself, it could not be that as the Father raiseth up the dead, and quickeneth them, so also the Son should quicken whom He will.

14. But what of that resurrection of the body? For these who hear and live, whence live, except by hearing? For "the friend of the Bridegroom standeth and heareth Him, and rejoiceth greatly because of the Bridegroom's voice:"[1] not because of his own voice; that is to say, they hear and live by partaking, not by coming into being; and all that hear live, because all that obey live. Tell us something, O Lord, also of the resurrection of the flesh; for there have been those who denied it, asserting that this is the only resurrection which is wrought by faith. Of which resurrection the Lord has just now made mention, and inflamed our desire, because "the dead shall hear the voice of the Son of God, nd shall live." It is not *some* of those who hear shall live, and *others* shall die; but "all that hear shall live," because all that obey shall live. Behold, we see a resurrection of the mind; let us not therefore let go our faith of the resurrection of the flesh. And unless Thou, O Lord Jesus, declare to us this, whom shall we oppose to those who

assert the contrary? For truly all sects that have undertaken to engraft any religion upon men have allowed this resurrection of minds; otherwise, it might be said to them, If the soul rise not, why speakest thou to me? What meanest thou to do in me? If thou dost not make of the worse a better, why speakest thou? If thou dost not make a righteous of the unrighteous, why speakest thou? But if thou dost make righteous of the unrighteous, godly of the ungodly, wise of the foolish, thou confessest that my soul doth rise again, if I comply with thee and believe. So, then, all those that have founded any sect, even of false religion, while they wished to be believed, could not but admit this resurrection of minds: all have agreed concerning this; but many have denied the resurrection of the flesh, and affirmed that the resurrection had taken place already in faith. Such the apostle resisteth, saying, "Of whom is Hymeneus and Philetus, who concerning the truth have erred, saying that the resurrection hath taken place already, and overthrow the faith of some."[2] They said that the resurrection had taken place already, but in such manner that another was not to be expected; and they blamed people who were looking for a resurrection of the flesh, just as if the resurrection which was promised were already accomplished in the act of believing, namely, in the mind. The apostle censures these. Why does he censure them? Did they not affirm what the Lord spoke just now: "The hour cometh, and now is, when the dead shall hear the voice of the Son of God, and they that hear shall live"? But, saith Jesus to thee, it is of the life of minds that I am hitherto speaking: I am not yet speaking of the life of bodies; but I speak of the life of that which is the life of bodies, that is, of the life of souls, in which the life of bodies exists. For I know that there are bodies lying in the tombs; I know also that your bodies will lie in the tombs. I am not speaking of that resurrection, but I speak of this; in this, rise ye again, lest ye rise to punishment in that. But that ye may know that I speak also of that, what do I add? "For as the Father hath life in Himself, even so hath He given to the Son to have life in Himself." This life which the Father is, which the Son is, to what does it pertain? To the soul or to the body? It is not surely the body that is sensible of that life of wisdom, but the rational mind. For not every soul hath capacity to apprehend wisdom. A brute beast, in fact, has a soul, but the soul of the brute beast

---

[1] John iii. 29.

[2] 2 Tim. ii. 17, 18.

cannot apprehend wisdom. It is the human soul, then, that can perceive this life which the Father hath in Himself, and hath given to the Son to have in Himself; because that is "the true light which enlighteneth," not every soul, but "every man coming into this world." When, therefore, I speak to the mind itself, let it hear, that is, let it obey and live.

15. Wherefore, keep not silent, O Lord, concerning the resurrection of the flesh; lest men believe it not, and we continue reasoners, not preachers. But "as the Father hath life in Himself, even so hath He given to the Son to have life in Himself." Let them that hear, understand; let them believe that they may understand; let them obey that they may live. And that they may not suppose that the resurrection is finished here, let them hear this further: "and hath given Him authority to execute judgment also." Who hath given? The Father. To whom hath He given? To the Son; namely, to whom He gave to have life in Himself, to the same hath He given authority to execute judgment. "Because He is the Son of man." For this is the Christ, both Son of God and Son of man. "In the beginning was the Word, and the Word was with God, and the Word was God. This was in the beginning with God." Behold, how He hath given Him to have life in Himself! But because "the Word was made flesh, and dwelt among us," was made man of the Virgin Mary, He is the Son of man. What, therefore, hath He received as Son of man? Authority to execute judgment. What judgment? That in the end of the world. Then also there will be a resurrection, but a resurrection of bodies. So, then, God raiseth up souls by Christ, the Son of God; bodies He raiseth up by the same Christ, the Son of man. "Hath given Him authority." He should not have this authority did He not receive it; and He should be a man without authority. But the same who is Son of God is also Son of man. For by adhering to the unity of person, the Son of man with the Son of God is made one person, and the Son of God is the same person which the Son of man is. But what characteristic it has, and wherefore, must be distinguished. The Son of man has soul and body. The Son of God, which is the Word of God, has man, as the soul has body. And just as soul having body does not make two persons, but one man; so the Word, having man, maketh not two persons, but one Christ. What is man? A rational soul, having a body. What is Christ? The Word of God, having man. I see of what things I speak, who I

9

the speaker am, and to whom I am speaking.

16. Now hear concerning the resurrection of bodies, not me, but the Lord about to speak, on account of those who have risen again by a resurrection from death, by cleaving to life. To what life? To a life which knows not death. Why knows not death? Because it knows not mutability. Why knows not mutability? Because it is life in itself. "And hath given Him authority to execute judgment, because He is the Son of man." What judgment, what kind of judgment? "Marvel not at this" which I have said,—gave Him authority to execute judgment,—"for the hour is coming." He does not add, "and now is:" therefore He means to make known to us a certain hour in the end of the world. The hour is now that the dead rise, the hour will be in the end of the world that the dead rise: but that they rise now in the mind, then in the flesh; that they rise now in the mind by the Word of God, the Son of God; then in the flesh by the Word of God made flesh, the Son of man. For it will not be the Father Himself that will come to judgment, notwithstanding the Father doth not withdraw Himself from the Son. How, then, is it that the Father Himself will not come? In that He will not be seen in the judgment. "They shall look on Him whom they pierced."[1] That form which stood before the judge, will be Judge: that form will judge which was judged; for it was judged unjustly, it will judge justly. There will come the form of a servant, and that same will be apparent. For how could the form of God be made apparent to the just and to the unjust? If the judgment were to be only among the just, then the form of God might appear as to the just. But because the judgment is to be of the just and of the unjust, and that it is not permitted to the wicked to see God,—for "blessed are the pure in heart, for they shall see God,"[2]—such a Judge will appear as may be seen by those whom He is about to crown, and by those whom He is about to condemn. Hence the form of a servant will be seen, the form of God will be hid. The Son of God will be hid in the servant, and the Son of man will be manifest, because to Him "hath He given authority to execute judgment, because He is the Son of man." And because He alone will appear in the form of a servant, but the Father not, since He has not taken upon Him the form of a servant; for that reason He saith above: "The Father judgeth not any man, but hath given all judgment to

---

[1] John xix. 37.　　[2] Matt. v. 8.

the Son." Rightly then had it been deferred, that the propounder might Himself be the interpreter. For before it was hidden; now, as I think, it is already manifest, that "He gave Him authority to execute judgment," that "the Father judgeth not any man, but hath given all judgment to the Son:" because the judgment is to be by that form which the Father hath not. And what kind of judgment? "Marvel not at this, for the hour is coming:" not that which now is, for the souls to rise; but that which is to be, for the bodies to rise.

17. Let Him declare this more distinctly, that the heretical denier of the resurrection of the body may not find a pretext for sophistical cavil, although the meaning already shines out clearly. When it was said above, "The hour is coming," He added, "and now is;" but just now, "The hour is coming," He has not added, "and now is." Let Him, however, by the open truth, burst asunder all handles, all loops and pegs of sophistical attack, all the nooses of ensnaring objections. "Marvel not at this: for the hour is coming, in which all that are in the graves." What more evident? what more distinct? Bodies are in the graves; souls are not in the graves, either of just or of unjust. The soul of the just man was in the bosom of Abraham; the unjust man's soul was in hell, tormented: neither the one nor the other was in the grave. Above, when He saith, "The hour is coming, and now is," I beseech you give earnest heed. Ye know, brethren, that we get the bread of the belly with toil; with how much greater toil the bread of the mind! With labor you stand and hear, but with greater we stand and speak. If we labor for your sake, you ought to labor with us for your own sake. Above, then, when He said, "The hour is coming," and added, "and now is," what did He subjoin? "When the dead shall hear the voice of the Son of God, and they that hear shall live." He did not say, "All the dead shall hear, and they that hear shall live;" for He meant the unrighteous to be understood. And is it so, that all the unrighteous obey the gospel? The apostle says openly, "But not all obey the gospel."[1] But they that hear shall live, because all that obey the gospel shall pass to eternal life by faith: yet all do not obey; and this is now. But certainly, in the end, "All that are in the graves," both the just and the unjust, "shall hear His voice, and come forth." How is it He would not say, "and shall live"? All, indeed, will come forth, but all will not live.

For in that which He said above, "And they that hear shall live," He meant it to be understood that there is in that very hearing and obeying an eternal and blessed life, which not all that shall come forth from the graves will have. Here, then, both in the mention of graves, and by the expression of a "coming forth" from the graves, we openly understand a resurrection of bodies.

18. "All shall hear His voice, and shall come forth." And where is judgment, if all shall hear and all shall come forth? It is as if all were confusion; I see no distinguishing. Certainly Thou hast received authority to judge, because Thou art the Son of man: behold, Thou wilt be present in the judgment; the bodies will rise again; but tell us something of the judgment itself, that is, of the separation of the evil and the good. Hear this further, then: "They that have done good into the resurrection of life; they that have done evil into the resurrection of judgment." When above He spoke of a resurrection of minds and souls, did He make any distinction? No, for all "that hear shall live;" because by hearing, viz. by obeying, shall they live. But certainly not all will go to eternal life by rising and coming forth from the graves,— only they that have done well; and they that have done ill, to judgment. For here He has put judgment for punishment. There will also be a separation, not such as there is now. For now we are separated, not by place, but by character, affections, desires, faith, hope, charity. Now we live together with the unjust, though the life of all is not the same: in secret we are distinguished, in secret we are separated; as grain on the floor, not as grain in the granary. On the floor, grain is both separated and mixed: separated, because severed from the chaff; mixed, because not yet winnowed. Then there will be an open separation; a distinguishing of life just as of the character, a separation as there is in wisdom, so also will there be in bodies. They that have done well will go to live with the angels of God; they that have done evil, to be tormented with the devil and his angels. And the form of a servant will pass away. For to this end He had manifested Himself, that He might execute judgment. After the judgment, He shall go hence, will lead with Him the body of which He is the head, and deliver up the kingdom of God.[2] Then will openly be seen that form of God which could not be seen by the wicked, to whose vision the form of a servant must be shown. He says also in another place on this wise:

---

[1] Rom. x. 16.   [2] 1 Cor xv. 24.

" These shall go away into everlasting burning " (speaking of certain on the left), " but
the just into life eternal; "[1] of which life He
says in another place: "And this is eternal
life, that they may know Thee the one true
God, and Jesus Christ whom Thou hast
sent." [2] Then will He be there manifested,
" who, being in the form of God, thought it
not robbery to be equal with God." [3] Then
He will manifest Himself, as He has promised
to manifest Himself to them that love Him.
For " he that loveth me," saith He, " keepeth my commandments; and he that loveth
me shall be loved of my Father; and I will love
him, and will manifest myself to him."[4] He
was present in person with those to whom He
was speaking: but they saw the form of a
servant, they did not see the form of God.
They were being led on His own beast to His
dwelling to be healed; but now being healed,
they will see, because, saith He, " I will
manifest myself to him." How is He shown
equal to the Father? When He says to
Philip, " He that seeth me seeth my Father
also."[5]

19. " I cannot of myself do anything: as I
hear, I judge: and my judgment is just."
Else we might have said to Him, " Thou wilt
judge, and the Father will not judge, for ' all
judgment hath He given to the Son;' It is
not, therefore, according to the Father that
Thou wilt judge." Hence He added, " I
cannot of myself do anything: as I hear, I
judge: and my judgment is just; because I

seek not my own will, but the will of Him
that sent me." Undoubtedly the Son quickeneth whom He will. He seeketh not His
own will, but the will of Him that sent Him.
Not my own, my proper will; not mine, not
the Son of man's; not mine to resist God.
For men do their own will, not God's, when
they do what they list, not what God commands; but when they do what they list, so
as yet to follow God's will, they do not their
own will, notwithstanding they do what they
list to do. Do what thou art bidden willingly, and thus shalt thou both do what thou
willest, and also not do thine own will, but
His that biddeth.

20. What then? "As I hear, I judge."
The Son " heareth," and the Father " showeth " to Him, and the Son seeth the Father
doing. But we had deferred these matters,
in order to handle them, so far as might lie
in our abilities, with somewhat greater plainness and fullness, should time and strength
remain to us after finishing the perusal of
the passage. If I say that I am able to speak
yet further, you perhaps are not able to go
on hearing. Again, perhaps, in your eagerness to hear, you say, " We are able."
Better, then, that I should confess my weakness, that, being already fatigued, I am not
able to speak longer, than that, when you are
already satiated, I should continue to pour
into you what you cannot well digest. Then,
as to this promise, which I deferred until to-
day, should there be an opportunity, hold
me, with the Lord's help, your debtor until
to-morrow.

---

[1] Matt. xxv. 46.   [2] John xvii. 3.   [3] Phil. ii. 6.
[4] John xiv. 21.   [5] John xiv. 19.

TRACTATE XX.

CHAPTER V. 19.

1. THE words of our Lord Jesus Christ,
especially those recorded by the Evangelist
John,—who not without cause leaned on the
Lord's bosom, that he might drink in the
secrets of that higher wisdom, and by evan-
gelizing give forth again what by loving he
had drunk in,—are so secret and profound of
understanding, that they trouble all who are
perverse of heart, and exercise all who are in
heart upright. Wherefore, beloved, give
heed to these few words that have been read.
Let us see if in any wise we can, by His own
gift and help who has willed His words to be
recited to us, which at that time were heard

and committed to writing that they might now
be read, what He means in what ye have now
heard Him say: "Verily, verily, I say unto
you, The Son cannot of Himself do anything,
but what He seeth the Father doing: for
what things soever the Father doeth, these
same the Son also doeth in like manner."

2. Now you need to be reminded whence
this discourse arose, by reason of what precedes this passage, where the Lord had cured
a certain man among those who were lying in
the five porches of that pool of Solomon, and
to whom He had said, " Take up thy bed, and
go unto thy house." But this He had done

on the Sabbath; and hence the Jews, being troubled, were falsely accusing Him as a destroyer and transgressor of the law. He then said to them, " My Father worketh even until now, and I work." [1] For they, taking the observance of the Sabbath in a carnal sense, fancied that God had, as it were, slept after the labor of framing the world even to this day; and that therefore He had sanctified that day, from which He began to rest as from labor. Now, to our fathers of old there was ordained a sacrament of the Sabbath, [2] which we Christians observe spiritually, in abstaining from every servile work, that is, from every sin (for the Lord saith, " Every one that committeth sin is the servant of sin "), and in having rest in our heart, that is, spiritual tranquillity. And although in this life we strive after this rest, yet not until we have departed this life shall we attain to that perfect rest. But the reason why God is said to have rested is, that He made no creature after all was finished. Moreover, the Scripture called it rest, to admonish us that after good works we shall rest. For thus we have it written in Genesis, "And God made all things very good, and God rested on the seventh day," in order that thou, O man, considering that God Himself is said to have rested after good works, shouldest not expect rest for thyself, until after thou hast wrought good works; and even as God, after He made man in His own image and likeness, and in him finished all His works very good, rested on the seventh day, so mayest thou also not expect rest to thyself, except thou return to that likeness in which thou wast made, which likeness thou hast lost by sinning. For, in reality, God cannot be said to have toiled, who " said, and they were done." Who is there that, after such facility of work, desires to rest as if after labor? If He commanded and some one resisted Him, if He commanded and it was not done, and labored that it might be done, then justly He should be said to have rested after labor. But when in that same book of Genesis we read, "God said, Let there be light, and there was light; God said, Let there be a firmament, and the firmament was made," [3] and all the rest were made immediately at His word: to which also the psalm testifies, saying, " He spake, and they were made; He commanded, and they were created," [4]—how could He require rest after the world was made, as if to enjoy leisure after toil, He who in commanding never toiled? Consequently these sayings are mystical, and are laid down in this wise that we may be looking for rest after this life, provided we have done good works. Accordingly, the Lord, restraining the impudence and refuting the error of the Jews, and showing them that they did not think rightly of God, says to them, when they were offended at His working men's healing on the Sabbath, " My Father worketh until now, and I work: " do not therefore suppose that my Father so rested on the Sabbath, that thenceforth He doth not work; but even as He now worketh, so I also work. But as the Father without toil, so too the Son without toil. God " said, and they were done;" Christ said to the impotent man, " Take up thy bed, and go unto thy house," and it was done.

3. But the catholic faith has it, that the works of the Father and of the Son are not separable. This is what I wish, if possible, to speak to you, beloved; but, according to those words of the Lord, " he that is able to receive it, let him receive it." [5] But he that is not able to receive it, let him not charge it on me, but on his own dullness; and let him turn to Him that opens the heart, that He may pour in what He freely giveth. And, lastly, if any one may not have understood, because I have not declared it as I ought to have declared it, let him excuse the weakness of man, and supplicate the divine goodness. For we have within a Master, Christ. Whatever ye are not able to receive through your ear and my mouth, turn ye in your heart to Him who both teacheth me what to speak, and distributeth to you in what measure He deigns. He who knows what to give, and to whom to give, will help him that seeketh, and open to him that knocketh. And if so be that He give not, let no one call himself forsaken. For it may be that He delays to give something, but He leaves none hungry. If, indeed, He give not at the hour, He is exercising the seeker, He is not scorning the suitor. Look ye, then, and give heed to what I wish to say, even if I should not be able to say it. The catholic faith, confirmed by the Spirit of God in His saints, has this against all heretical perverseness, that the works of the Father and of the Son are inseparable. What is this that I have said? As the Father and the Son are inseparable, so also the works of the Father and of the Son are inseparable. How are the Father and the Son inseparable, since Himself said, " I and the Father are one?" [6] Because the Father and the Son are not two Gods, but one God, the Word and He whose the Word is, One and the Only One, Father and Son

bound together by charity, One God, and the Spirit of Charity also one, so that Father, Son, and Holy Spirit is made the Trinity. Therefore, not only of the Father and Son, but also of the Holy Spirit; as there is equality and inseparability of persons, so also the works are inseparable. I will tell you yet more plainly what is meant by "the works are inseparable." The catholic faith does not say that God the Father made something, and the Son made some other thing; but what the Father made, that also the Son made, that also the Holy Spirit made. For all things were made by the Word; when "He spake and they were done," it is by the Word they were done, by Christ they were done. For "in the beginning was the Word, and the Word was with God, and the Word was God: all things were made by Him." If all things were made by Him, "God said, Let there be light, and there was light; in the Word He made, by the Word He made.

4. Behold, then, we have now heard the Gospel, where He answered the Jews who were indignant "that He not only broke the Sabbath, but said also that God was His Father, making Himself equal with God.[1] For so it is written in the foregoing paragraph. When, therefore, the Son of God, the Truth, made answer to their erring indignation, saith He, "Verily, verily, I say unto you, The Son cannot of Himself do anything, but what He seeth the Father doing;" as if He said, "Why are ye offended because I have said that God is my Father, and that I make myself equal with God? I am equal in that wise that He begat me; I am equal in that wise that He is not from me, but I from Him." For this is implied in these words: "The Son cannot do anything of Himself, but what He seeth the Father doing." That is, whatever the Son hath to do, the doing it He hath of the Father. Why of the Father hath He the doing it? Because of the Father He hath it that He is Son. Why hath He it of the Father to be Son? Because of the Father He hath it that He is able, of the Father that He is. For, to the Son, both to be able and to be is the self-same thing. It is not so with man. Raise your hearts by all means from a comparison of human weakness, that lies far beneath; and should any of us perhaps reach to the secret, and, while awe-struck by the brilliance as it were of a great light, should discern somewhat, and not remain wholly ignorant; yet let him not imagine that he understands the whole, lest he should be-

come proud, and lose what knowledge he has gotten. With man, to be and to be able are different things. For sometimes the man is, and yet cannot what he wills; sometimes, again, the man is in such wise, that he can what he wills; therefore his being and his being able are different things. For if man's esse and posse were the same thing, then he could when he would. But with God it is not so, that His substance to be is one thing, and His power to be able another thing; but whatever is His, and whatever He is, is consubstantial with Him, because He is God: it is not so that in one way He is, in another way is able; He has the esse and the posse together, because He has to will and to do together. Since, then, the power of the Son is of the Father, therefore also the substance of the Son is of the Father; and since the substance of the Son is of the Father, therefore the power of the Son is of the Father. In the Son, power and substance are not different: the power is the self-same that the substance is; the substance to be, the power to be able. Accordingly, because the Son is of the Father, He said, "The Son cannot of Himself do anything." Because He is not Son from Himself, therefore He is not able from Himself.

5. He appears to have made Himself as it were less, when He said, "The Son cannot of Himself do anything, but what He seeth the Father doing." Hereupon heretical vanity lifts the neck; theirs, indeed, who say that the Son is less than the Father, of less authority, of less majesty, of less possibility, not understanding the mystery of Christ's words. But attend, beloved, and see how they are confounded in their carnal intellect by the words of Christ. And this is what I said a little before, that the word of God troubles all perverse hearts, just as it exercises pious hearts, especially that spoken by the Evangelist John. For they are deep words that are spoken by him, not random words, nor such as may be easily understood. So, a heretic, if he happen to hear these words, immediately rises and says to us, "Lo, the Son is less than the Father; hear the words of the Son, who says, 'The Son cannot do anything of Himself, but what He seeth the Father doing.'" Wait; as it is written, "Be meek to hear the word, that thou mayest understand."[2] Well, suppose that because I assert the power and majesty of the Father and of the Son to be equal, I was disconcerted at hearing these words, "The Son cannot do anything of Himself, but

what He seeth the Father doing." Well, I, being disconcerted at these words, will ask thee, who seemest to thyself to have instantly understood them, a question. We know in the Gospel that the Son walked upon the sea;[1] when saw He the Father walk upon the sea? Here now he is disconcerted. Lay aside, then, thy understanding of the words, and let us examine them together. What do we then? We have heard the words of the Lord: "The Son cannot of Himself do anything, but what He seeth the Father doing." The Son walked upon the sea, the Father never walked upon the sea. Yet certainly "the Son cannot of Himself do anything, but what He seeth the Father doing."

6. Return then with me to what I was saying, in case it is so to be understood that we may both escape from the question. For I see how I, according to the catholic faith, may escape without tripping or stumbling; whilst thou, on the other hand, shut in on every side, art seeking a way of escape. See by what way thou hast entered. Perhaps thou hast not understood this that I said, See by what way thou hast entered: hear Himself saying, "I am the door."[2] Not without cause, then, art thou seeking how thou mayest get out; and this only thou findest, that thou hast not entered by the door, but fell in over the wall. Therefore raise thyself up from thy fall how thou canst, and enter by the door, that thou mayest go in without stumbling, and go out without straying. Come by Christ, not bringing forward of thy own heart what thou mayest say; but what He shows, that speak. Behold how the catholic faith gets clear of this question. The Son walked upon the sea, planted the feet of flesh on the waves: the flesh walked, and the divinity directed. But when the flesh was walking and the divinity directing, was the Father absent? If absent, how doth the Son Himself say, "but the Father abiding in me, Himself doeth the works?"[3] If the Father, abiding in the Son, Himself doeth His works, then that walking upon the sea was made by the Father, and through the Son. Accordingly, that walking is an inseparable work of Father and Son. I see both acting in it. Neither the Father forsook the Son, nor the Son left the Father. Thus, whatever the Son doeth, He doeth not without the Father; because whatever the Father doeth, He doeth not without the Son.

7. We have got clear of this question. Mark ye that rightly we say the works of the Father, of the Son, and of the Holy Spirit are

inseparable. But as thou understandest it, lo, God made the light, and the Son saw the Father making light, according to thy carnal understanding, who wilt have it that He is less, because He said, "The Son cannot of Himself do anything, but what He seeth the Father doing." God the Father made light; what other light did the Son make? God the Father made the firmament, the heaven between waters and waters; and the Son saw Him, according to thy dull and sluggish understanding. Well, since the Son saw the Father making the firmament, and also said, "The Son cannot of Himself do anything, but what He seeth the Father doing," then show me the other firmament made by the Son. Hast thou lost the foundation? But they that are "built upon the foundation of the apostles and prophets, Jesus Christ Himself being the chief corner-stone," are brought into a state of peace in Christ;[4] nor do they strive and wander in heresy. Therefore we understand that the light was made by God the Father, but through the Son; that the firmament was made by God the Father, but through the Son. For "all things were made through Him, and without Him was nothing made." Cast out thine understanding, which ought not to be called understanding, but evidently foolishness. God the Father made the world; what other world did the Son make? Show me the Son's world. Whose is this world in which we are? Tell us, by whom made? If thou sayest, "By the Son, not by the Father," then thou hast erred from the Father; if thou sayest, "By the Father, not by the Son," the Gospel answers thee thus, "And the world was made by (through) Him, and the world knew Him not." Acknowledge Him, then, by whom the world was made, and be not among those who knew not Him that made the world.

8. Wherefore the works of the Father and of the Son are inseparable. Moreover, this, "The Son cannot do anything of Himself," would mean the same thing as if He were to say, "The Son is not from Himself." For if He is a Son, He was begotten; if begotten, He is from Him of whom He is begotten. Nevertheless, the Father begat Him equal to Himself. Nor was aught wanting to Him that begat; He who begat a co-eternal required not time to beget: who produced the Word of Himself, required not a mother to beget by; the Father begetting did not precede the Son in age, so that He should beget a Son younger than Himself. But perhaps some one may say, that after many ages God

---

begat a Son in His old age. Even as the Father is without age, so the Son is without growth; neither has the one grown old nor the other increased, but equal begat equal, eternal begat eternal. How, says some one, has eternal begat eternal? As a temporary flame generates a temporary light. The generating flame is coeval with the light which it generates: the generating flame does not precede in time the generated light; but from the moment the flame begins, from that moment the light begins. Show me flame without light, and I show thee God the Father without Son. Accordingly, "the Son cannot do anything of Himself, but what He seeth the Father doing," implies, that for the Son *to see* and *to be begotten* of the Father, is the same thing. His seeing and His substance are not different; nor are His power and substance different. All that He is, He is of the Father; all that He can is of the Father; because what He can and what He is is one thing, and all of the Father.

9. Moreover, He goes on in His own words, and troubles those that understand the matter amiss, in order to recall the erring to a right apprehension of it. After He had said, " The Son cannot of Himself do anything, but what He seeth the Father doing;" lest a carnal understanding of the matter should by chance creep in and turn the mind aside, and a man should imagine as it were two mechanics, one a master, the other a learner, attentively observing the master while making, say a chest, so that, as the master made the chest, the learner should make another chest according to the appearance which he looked upon while the master wrought; lest, I say, the carnal mind should frame to itself any such twofold notion in the case of the divine unity, going on, He saith, " For what things soever the Father doeth, these same also the Son doeth in like manner." It is not, the Father doeth some, the Son others like them, but the same in like manner. For He saith not, What things soever the Father doeth, the Son also doeth others the like; but saith He, " What things soever the Father doeth, these same also the Son doeth in like manner." What things the Father doeth, these also the Son doeth: the Father made the world, the Son made the world, the Holy Ghost made the world. If three Gods, then three worlds; if one God, the Father, the Son, and the Holy Ghost, then one world was made by the Father, through the Son, in the Holy Ghost. Consequently the Son doeth those things which also the Father doeth, and doeth not in a different manner; He both doeth these, and doeth them in like manner.

10. After He had said, " these doeth," why did He add, " in like manner doeth"? Lest another distorted understanding or error should spring up in the mind. Thou seest, for instance, a man's work: in man there is mind and body; the mind rules the body, but there is a great difference between body and mind: the body is visible, the mind is invisible: there is a great difference between the power and virtue of the mind and that of any kind of body whatever, be it even a heavenly body. Still the mind rules its own body, and the body doeth; and what the mind appears to do, this the body doeth also. Thus the body appears to do this same thing that the mind doeth, but not " in like manner." How doeth this same, but not in like manner? The mind frames a word in itself; it commands the tongue, and the tongue produces the word which the mind framed: the mind made, and the tongue made; the lord of the body made, and the servant made; but that the servant might make, it received of its lord what to make, and made while the lord commanded. The same thing was made by both, but was it in like manner? How not in like manner? says some one. See, the word that my mind formed, remains in me; that which my tongue made, passed through the smitten air, and is not. When thou hast said a word in thy mind, and uttered it by thy tongue, return to thy mind, and see that the word which thou hast made is there still. Has it remained on thy tongue, just as it has in thy mind? What was uttered by the tongue, the tongue made by sounding, the mind made by thinking; but what the tongue uttered has passed away, what the mind thought remains. Therefore the body made that which the mind made, but not in like manner. For the mind, indeed, made that which the mind may hold, but the tongue made what sounds and strikes the ear through the air. Dost thou chase the syllables, and cause them to remain? Well, not in such manner the Father and the Son; but " these same doeth," and " in like manner doeth." If God made heaven that remains, this heaven that remains the Son made. If God the Father made man that is mortal, the same man that is mortal the Son made. What things soever the Father made that endure, these things that endure made also the Son, because in like manner He made; and what things soever the Father made that are temporal, these same things that are temporal made also the Son, because He made not only the same, but also in like manner made. For the Father made by the Son, since by the Word the Father made all things.

11. Seek in the Father and Son a separation, thou findest none; no, not if thou hast mounted high; no, not even if thou hast reached something above thy mind. For if thou turnest about among the things which thy wandering mind makes for itself, thou talkest with thine own imaginations, not with the Word of God; thine own imaginations deceive thee. Mount also beyond the body, and understand the mind; mount also beyond the mind, and understand God. Thou reachest not unto God, unless thou hast passed beyond the mind; how much less thou reachest unto God, if thou hast tarried in the flesh! They who think of the flesh, how far are they from understanding what God is!—since they would not be there even if they knew the mind. Man recedes far from God when his thoughts are of the flesh; and there is a great difference between flesh and mind, yet a greater between mind and God. If thou art occupied with the mind, thou art in the midway: if thou directest thy attention beneath, there is the body; if above, there is God. Lift thyself up from the body, pass beyond even thyself. For observe what said the psalm, and thou art admonished how God must be thought of: "My tears," it saith, "were made to me my bread day and night, when it was said to me daily, Where is thy God?" As the pagans may say, "Behold our gods, where is your God?" They indeed show us what is seen; we worship what is not seen. And to whom can we show? To a man who has not sight with which to see? For anyhow, if they see their gods with their eyes, we too have other eyes with which to see our God: for "blessed are the pure in heart, for they shall see God."[1] Therefore, when he had said that he was troubled, when it was daily said to him, "Where is thy God?" "these things I remembered," saith he, "because it is daily said to me, Where is thy God?" And as if wishing to lay hold of his God, "These things," saith he, "I remembered, and poured out my soul above me."[2] Therefore, that I might reach unto my God, of whom it was said to me, "Where is thy God? I poured out my soul," not over my flesh, but "above me;" I transcended myself, that I might reach unto Him: for He is above me who made me; none reaches to Him but he that passes beyond himself.

12. Consider the body: it is mortal, earthy, weak, corruptible; away with it. Yes, perhaps thou sayest, but the body is temporal. Think then of other bodies, the heavenly; they are greater, better, more magnificent.

Look at them, moreover, attentively. They roll from east to west, they stand not; they are seen with the eyes, not only by man, but even by the beast of the field. Pass beyond them too. And how, sayest thou, pass beyond the heavenly bodies, seeing that I walk on the earth? Not in the flesh dost thou pass beyond them, but in the mind. Away with them too: though they shine ever so much, they are bodies; though they glitter from heaven, they are bodies. Come, now that perhaps thou thinkest thou hast not whither to go, after considering all these. And whither am I to go, sayest thou, beyond the heavenly bodies; and what am I to pass beyond with the mind? Hast thou considered all these? I have, sayest thou. By what means hast thou considered them? Let the being that considers appear in person. The being that considers all these, that discriminates, distinguishes, and in a manner weighs them in the balance of wisdom, is really the mind. Doubtless, then, better is the mind with which thou hast contemplated all these things, than these things which thou hast contemplated. This mind, then, is a spirit, not a body. Pass beyond it too. And that thou mayest see whither thou art to pass beyond, compare that mind itself, in the first place, with the flesh. Heaven forbid that thou shouldest deign so to compare it! Compare it with the brightness of the sun, of the moon, and of the stars; the brightness of the mind is greater. Observe, first, the swiftness of the mind; see whether the scintillation of the thinking mind be not more impetuous than the brilliance of the shining sun. With the mind thou seest the sun rising. How slow is its motion compared with thy mind! What the sun is about to do, thou canst think in a trice. It is about to come from the east to the west; to-morrow rises from another quarter. Where thy thought has done this, the sun still lags behind, and thou hast traversed the whole journey. A great thing, therefore, is the mind. But how do I say *is?* Pass beyond it also. For the mind, notwithstanding it be better than every kind of body, is itself changeable. Now it knows, now knows not; now forgets, now remembers; now wills, now wills not; now errs, now is right. Pass therefore beyond all changeableness; not only beyond all that is seen, but also beyond all that changes. For thou hast passed beyond the flesh which is seen; beyond heaven, the sun, moon, and stars, which are seen. Pass, too, beyond all that changes. For when thou hadst done with those things that are seen, and hadst come to thy mind, there thou didst find the changeableness of thy mind. Is God at all changeable?, Pass, then, beyond even thy mind. Pour out thy soul "above thee," that thou mayest reach unto God, of whom it is said to thee, "Where is thy God?"

13. Do not imagine that thou art to do something beyond a man's ability. The Evangelist John himself did this. He soared beyond the flesh, beyond the earth which he trod, beyond the seas which he looked upon, beyond the air in which the fowls fly, beyond the sun, the moon, the stars, beyond all the spirits unseen, beyond his own mind, by the very reason of his rational soul. Soaring beyond all these, pouring out his soul above him, whither did he arrive? What did he see? "In the beginning was the Word, and the Word was with God." If, therefore, thou seest no separation in the light, why seekest thou a separation in the work? See God, see His Word inhering to the Word speaking, that the speaker speaks not by syllables, but this his speaking is a shining out in the brightness of wisdom. What is said of the Wisdom itself? "It is the radiance of eternal light."[1] Observe the radiance of the sun. The sun is in the heaven, and spreads out its brightness over all lands and over all seas, and it is simply a corporal light.

If, indeed, thou canst separate the brightness from the sun, then separate the Word from the Father. I am speaking of the sun. One small, slender flame of a lamp, which can be extinguished by one breath, spreads its light over all that lies near it: thou seest the light generated by the flame spread out; thou seest its emission, but not a separation. Understand, then, beloved brethren, that the Father, and the Son, and the Holy Ghost are inseparably united in themselves; that this Trinity is one God; that all the works of the one God are the works of the Father, of the Son, and of the Holy Ghost. All the rest which follows, and which refers to the discourse of our Lord Jesus Christ, now that a discourse is due to you to-morrow also, be present that ye may hear.

[1] Wisd. vii. 26.

TRACTATE XXI.

CHAPTER V. 20–23

1. YESTERDAY, so far as the Lord vouchsafed to bestow, we discussed with what ability we could, and discerned according to our capacity, how the works of the Father and of the Son are inseparable; and how the Father doeth not some, the Son others, but that the Father doeth all things through the Son, as through His Word, of which it is written, "All things were made by Him, and without Him was nothing made." Let us to-day look at the words that follow. And of the same Lord let us pray for mercy, and hope that, if He deem it meet, we may understand what is true; but if we should not be able to do this, that we may not go into what is false. For it is better not to know than to go astray; but to know is better than not to know. Therefore, before all things, we ought to strive to know. Should we be able, to God be thanks; but should we not be able meanwhile to arrive at the truth, let us not go to falsehood. For we are bound to consider well what we are, and what we are treating of. We are men bearing flesh, walking in this life; and though now begotten again of the seed of the Word of God, yet in Christ renewed in such manner that we are not yet wholly rid of Adam. For truly our mortal and corruptible part that weighs down the soul[1] shows itself to be, and manifestly is, of Adam; but what in us is spiritual, and raises up the soul, is of God's gift and of His mercy, who has sent His only Son to partake our death with us, and to lead us to His own immortality. The Son we have for our Master, that we may not sin; and for our defender, if we have sinned and have confessed, and been converted; an intercessor for us, if we have desired any good of God; and the bestower of it with the Father, because Father and Son is one God. But He was speaking these things as man to men: God concealed, the man manifest, that He might make them gods that are manifest men; and the Son of God made Son of man, that He might make the sons of men sons of God. By what skill of His wisdom He doeth this, we perceive in His own words. For as a little one He speaks to little ones, but Himself little in such wise that He is also great, and we little, but in Him great. He speaks, in-

[1] Wisd. ix. 15.

deed, as one cherishing and nourishing children at the breast that grow by loving.

2. He had said, "The Son cannot of Himself do anything, but what He seeth the Father doing." We, however, understood it not that the Father doeth something separately, which when the Son seeth, Himself also doeth something of the same kind, after seeing His Father's work; but when He said, "The Son cannot of Himself do anything, but what He seeth the Father doing," we understood it that the Son is wholly of the Father—that His whole substance and His whole power are of the Father that begat Him. Bnt just now, when He had said that He doeth in like manner these things which the Father doeth, that we may not understand it to mean that the Father doeth some, the Son others, but that the Son with like power doeth the very same wnich the Father doeth, whilst the Father doeth through the Son, He went on, and said what we have heard read to-day: "For the Father loveth the Son, and showeth Him all things that Himself doeth." Again mortal thought is disturbed. The Father showeth to the Son what things Himself doeth; therefore, saith some one, the Father doeth separately, that the Son may be able to see what He doeth. Again, there occur to human thought, as it were, two artificers—as, for instance, a carpenter teaching his son his own art, and showing him whatever he doeth, that the son also may be able to do it. "Showeth Him," saith He, "all things that Himself doeth." Is it therefore so, that whilst He doeth, the Son doeth not, that He may be able to see the Father do? Yet, certainly, "all things were made by Him, and without Him was nothing made." Hence we see how the Father showeth the Son what He doeth, since the Father doeth nothing but what He doeth through the Son. What hath the Father made? He made the world. Hath He shown the world, when made, to the Son in such wise, that the Son also should make something like it? Then let us see the world which the Son made. Nevertheless, both "all things were made by Him, and without Him was nothing made," and also "the world was made by Him." ¹ If the world was made by Him, and all things were made by Him, and the Father doeth nothing save by the Son, where doth the Father show to the Son what He doeth, if it be not in the Son Himself, through whom He doeth? In what place can the work of the Father be shown to the Son, as though He were doing and sitting outside, and the Son attentively watching the Father's

hand how it maketh? Where is that inseparable Trinity? Where the Word, of which it is said that the same is "the power and the wisdom of God"? ² Where that which the Scripture saith of the same wisdom: "For it is the brightness of the eternal light?" ³ Where what was said of it again: "It powerfully reaches from the end even to the end, and ordereth all things sweetly"? ⁴ Whatever the Father doeth, He doeth through the Son: through His wisdom and his power He doeth; not from without doth He show to the Son what He may see, but in the Son Himself He showeth Him what He doeth.

3. What seeth the Father, or rather, what doth the Son see in the Father, that Himself also may do? Perhaps I may be able to speak it, but show me the man who can comprehend it; or perhaps I may be able to think and not speak it; or perhaps I may not be able even to think it. For that divinity excels us, as God excels men, as the immortal excels a mortal, as the eternal excels the temporal. May He inspire and endow us, and out of that fountain of life deign to bedew and to drop somewhat on our thirst, that we may not be parched in this wilderness! Let us say to Him, Lord, to whom we have learnt to say Father. We make bold to say this, because Himself willed it; if only we so live that He may not say to us, "If I am a Father, where is mine honor? if I am Lord, where is my fear?" Let us then say to Him, "Our Father." To whom do we say, "Our Father"? To the Father of Christ. He, then, who says "Our Father" to the Father of Christ, says to Christ, what else but "Our Brother"? Not, however, as He is the Father of Christ is He in like manner our Father; for Christ never so conjoined us as to make no distinction between Him and us. For He is the Son equal to the Father, the eternal Son with the Father, and co-eternal with the Father; but we became sons through the Son, adopted through the Only-begotten. Hence was it never heard from the mouth of our Lord Jesus Christ, when speaking to His disciples, that He said of the supreme God His Father, "Our Father;" but He said either "My Father" or "Your Father." But He said not "Our Father;" so much so, that in a certain place He used these two expressions: "I go to my God," saith He, "and to your God." Why did He not say, "Our God"? Further, He said, "My Father, and your Father;" He said not, "Our Father." He so joins as to distinguish, distinguishes so as not to disjoin. He wills us to be one in Him, but the Father and Himself one.

---

¹ John i. 3, 10.   ² 1 Cor. i. 24   ³ Wisd. vii. 26.   ⁴ Wisd. viii. 1.

4. How much soever then we may understand, and how much soever we may see, we shall not see as the Son seeth, even when we shall be made equal with the angels. For we are something even when we do not see; but what are we when we do not see, other than persons not seeing? And that we may see, we turn to Him whom we may see, and there is formed in us a seeing which was not before, although we were in being. For a man *is* when not seeing; and the same, when he doth see, is called a man seeing. For him, then, to see is not the same thing as to be a man; for if it were, he would not be man when not seeing. But since he is man when not seeing, and seeks to see what he sees not, he is one who seeks, and who turns to see; and when he has well turned and has seen, he becomes a man seeing, who was before a man not seeing. Consequently, to see is to him a thing that comes and goes; it comes to him when he turns to, and leaves him when he turns away. Is it thus with the Son? Far be it from us to think so. It was never so that He was Son, not seeing, and afterwards was made to see; but to see the Father is to Him the same thing as to be Son. For we, by turning away to sin, lose enlightenment; and by turning to God we receive enlightenment. For the light by which we are enlightened is one thing; we who are enlightened, another thing. But the light itself, by which we are enlightened, neither turns away from itself, nor loses its lucidity, because as light it exists. The Father, then, showeth a thing which He doeth to the Son, in such wise that the Son *seeth* all things in the Father, and *is* all things in the Father. For by seeing He was begotten; and by being begotten He seeth. Not, however, that at any time He was not begotten, and afterwards was begotten; nor that at any time He saw not, and afterwards saw. But in what consists His seeing, in the same consists His being, in the same His being begotten, in the same His continuing, in the same His unchanging, in the same His abiding without beginning and without end. Let us not therefore take it in a carnal sense that the Father sitteth and doeth a work, and showeth it to the Son; and the Son seeth the work that the Father doeth, and doeth another work in another place, or out of other materials. For "all things were made by Him, and without Him was nothing made." The Son is the Word of the Father. The Father said nothing which He did not say in the Son. For by speaking in the Son what He was about to do through the Son, He begat the Son through whom He made all things.

5. "And greater works than these will He show Him, that ye may marvel." Here again we are embarrassed. And who is there that may worthily investigate this so great a secret? But now, in that He has deigned to speak to us, Himself opens it. For He would not speak what He would not have us understand; and as He has deigned to speak, without doubt He has excited attention: for does He forsake any whom He has roused to give attentive hearing? We have said that it is not in a temporal sense that the Son knoweth,—that the knowledge of the Son is not one thing, and the Son Himself another; nor one thing His seeing, Himself another; but that the seeing itself is the Son, and the knowledge as well as the wisdom of the Father is the Son; and that that wisdom and seeing is eternal and co-eternal with Him from whom it is; that it is not something that varies by time, nor something produced that was not in being, nor something that vanishes away which did exist. What is it, then, that time does in this case, that He should say, "Greater works than these He will show Him"? "He will show," that is, "He is about to show." *Hath shown* is a different thing from *will show*: *hath shown*, we say of an act past; *will show*, of an act future. What shall we do here, then, brethren? Behold, He whom we had declared to be co-eternal with the Father, in whom nothing is varied by time, in whom is no moving through spaces either of moments or of places, of whom we had declared that He abides ever with the Father seeing, seeing the Father, and by seeing existing; He, I say, here again mentioning times to us, saith, "He will show Him greater works than these." Is He then about to show something to the Son, which the Son doth not as yet know? What, then, do we make of it? How do we understand this? Behold, our Lord Jesus Christ was above, is beneath. When was He above? When He said, "What things soever the Father doeth, these same also the Son doeth in like manner." Whence know we that He is now beneath? Hence: "Greater works than these He will show Him." O Lord Jesus Christ, our Saviour, Word of God, by which all things were made, what is the Father about to show Thee, that as yet Thou knowest not? What of the Father is hid from Thee? What in the Father is hid from Thee, from whom the Father is not hid? What greater works is He about to show Thee? Or greater than what works are they which He is to show Thee? For when He said, "Greater than these," we ought first to understand the works than which are they greater.

6. Let us again call to mind whence this discourse started. It was when that man

who was thirty-eight years in infirmity was healed, and Jesus commanded him, now made whole, to take up his bed and to go to his house. For this cause, indeed, the Jews with whom He was speaking were enraged. He spoke in words, as to the meaning He was silent; hinted in some measure at the meaning to those who understood, and hid the matter from them that were wroth. For this cause, I say, the Jews, being enraged because the Lord did this on the Sabbath, gave occasion to this discourse. Therefore let us not hear these things in such wise as if we had forgotten what was said above, but let us look back to that impotent man languishing for thirty-eight years suddenly made whole, while the Jews marvelled and were wroth. They sought darkness from the Sabbath more than light from the miracle. Speaking then to these, while they are indignant, He saith, "Greater works than these will He show Him." "Greater than these:" than which? What ye have seen, that a man, whose infirmity had lasted thirty-eight years, was made whole; greater than these the Father is about to show to the Son. What are greater works? He goes on, saying, "For as the Father raiseth the dead, and quickeneth them, so also the Son quickeneth whom He will." Clearly these are greater. Very much greater is it that a dead man should rise, than that a sick man should recover: these are greater. But when is the Father about to show these to the Son? Does the Son not know them? And He who was speaking, did He not know how to raise the dead? Had He yet to learn how to raise the dead to life—He, I say, by whom all things were made? He who caused that we should live, when we were not in being, had He yet to learn how we might be raised to life again? What, then, do His words mean?

7. But now He condescends to us, and He who a little before was speaking as God, now begins to speak as man. Notwithstanding, the same is man who is God, for God was made man; but was made what He was not, without losing what He was. The man therefore was added to the God, that He might be man who was God, but not that He should now henceforth be man and not be God. Let us then hear Him also as our brother whom we did hear as our Maker. Our Maker, because the Word in the beginning; our Brother, because born of the Virgin Mary: Maker, before Abraham, before Adam, before earth, before heaven, before all things corporeal and spiritual; but Brother, of the seed of Abraham, of the tribe of Judah, of the Israelitish virgin. If therefore we know Him who

speaks to us as both God and man, let us understand the words of God and of man; for sometimes He speaks to us such things as are applicable to the majesty, sometimes such as are applicable to the humility. For the self-same is high who was made low, that He might make us high who are low. What, then, saith He? "The Father will show" to me "greater than these, that ye may marvel." To us, therefore, He is about to show, not to Him. And since it is to us that the Father is to show, for that reason He said, "that ye may marvel." He has, in fact, explained what He meant in saying, "The Father will show" to me. Why did He not say, The Father will show to you; but, He will show to the Son? Because also we are members of the Son; and like as what we the members learn, He Himself in a manner learns in His members. How doth He learn in us? As He suffers in us. Whence may we prove that He suffers in us? From that voice out of heaven, "Saul, Saul, why persecutest thou me?"[1] Is it not Himself that will sit as Judge in the end of the world, and, setting the just on the right, and the wicked on the left, will say, "Come, ye blessed of my Father, receive the kingdom; for I was hungry, and ye gave me to eat"? And when they shall answer, "Lord, when saw we Thee hungry?" He will say to them, "Since ye gave to one of the least of mine, ye gave to me."[2] Let us at this time question Him, and let us say to Him, Lord, when wilt Thou be a learner, seeing Thou teachest all things? Immediately, indeed, He makes answer to us in our faith, When one of the least of mine doth learn, I learn.

8. Let us rejoice, then, and give thanks that we are made not only Christians, but Christ. Do ye understand, brethren, and apprehend the grace of God upon us? Marvel, be glad, we are made Christ. For if He is the head, we are the members: the whole man is He and we. This is what the Apostle Paul saith: "That we be no longer babes, tossed to and fro, and carried about with every wind of doctrine." But above he had said, "Until we all come together into the unity of faith, and to the knowledge of the Son of God, to the perfect man, to the measure of the age of the fullness of Christ."[3] The fullness of Christ, then, is head and members. Head and members, what is that? Christ and the Church. We should indeed be arrogating this to ourselves proudly, if He did not Himself deign to promise it, who saith by the same apostle, "But ye are the body of Christ, and members."[4]

---

[1] Acts ix. 4.   [2] Matt. xxv. 31-40.
[3] Eph. iv. 14.   [4] 1 Cor. xii. 27.

9. Whenever, then, the Father showeth to Christ's members, He showeth to Christ. A certain great but yet real miracle happens. There is a showing to Christ of what Christ knew, and it is shown to Christ through Christ. A marvelous and great thing it is, but the Scripture so saith. Shall we contradict the divine declarations? Shall we not rather understand them, and of His own gift render thanks to Him who freely bestowed it on us? What is this that I said, "is shown to Christ through Christ"? Is shown to the members through the head. Lo, look at this in thyself. Suppose that with thine eyes shut thou wouldest take up something, thy hand knows not whither to go; and yet thy hand is at any rate thy member, for it is not separated from thy body. Open thine eyes, now the hand sees whither it may go; while the head showed, the member followed. If, then, there could be found in thyself something such, that thy body showed to thy body, and that through thy body something was shown to thy body, then do not marvel that it is said there is shown to Christ through Christ. For the head shows that the members may see, and the head teaches that the members may learn; nevertheless one man, head and members. He willed not to separate Himself, but deigned to attach Himself to us. Far was He from us, yea, very far. What so far apart as the creature and the Creator? What so far apart as God and man? What so far as justice and iniquity? What so far as eternity and mortality? Behold, so far from us was the Word in the beginning, God with God, by whom all things were made. How, then, was He made near, that He might be what we are, and we in Him? "The Word was made flesh, and dwelt in (among) us."[1]

10. This, then, He is about to show us; this He showed to His disciples, who saw Him in the flesh. What is this? "As the Father raiseth the dead, and quickeneth them, so also the Son quickeneth whom He will." Is it that the Father some, the Son others? Surely all things were made by Him. What do we say, my brethren? Christ raised Lazarus; what dead man did the Father raise, that Christ might see how to raise Lazarus? When Christ raised Lazarus, did not the Father raise him? or was it the doing of the Son alone, without the Father? Read ye the passage itself, and see that He invokes the Father that Lazarus may rise again.[2] As a man, He calls on the Father; as God, He doeth with the Father. Therefore also Lazarus, who rose again, was raised both by the Father and by the Son, in the gift and grace of the Holy Spirit; and that wonderful work the Trinity performed. Let us not, therefore, understand this, "As the Father raiseth the dead, and quickeneth them, so also the Son quickeneth whom He will," in such wise as to suppose that some are raised and quickened by the Father, others by the Son; but that the Son raiseth and quickeneth the very same whom the Father raiseth and quickeneth; because "all things were made by Him, and without Him was nothing made." And to show that He has, though given by the Father, equal power, therefore He saith, "So also the Son quickeneth whom He will," that He might therein show His will; and lest any should say, "The Father raiseth the dead by the Son, but the Father as being powerful, and as having power, the Son as by another's power, as a servant does something, as an angel," He indicated His power when He saith, "So also the Son quickeneth whom He will." It is not so that the Father willeth other than the Son; but as the Father and the Son have one substance, so also one will.

11. And who are these dead whom the Father and the Son quicken? Are they the same of whom we have spoken—Lazarus, or that widow's son,[3] or the ruler of the synagogue's daughter?[4] For we know that these were raised by Christ the Lord. It is some other thing that He means to signify to us, —namely, the resurrection of the dead, which we all look for; not that resurrection which certain have had, that the rest might believe. For Lazarus rose to die again; we shall rise again to live for ever. Is it the Father that effects such a resurrection, or the Son? Nay verily, the Father in the Son. Consequently the Son, and the Father in the Son. Whence do we prove that He speaks of this resurrection? When He had said, "As the Father raiseth up the dead, and quickeneth them, so also the Son quickeneth whom He will." Lest we should understand here that resurrection which He performs for a miracle, not for eternal life, He proceeded, saying, "For the Father judgeth not any man, but all judgment hath He given to the Son." What is this? He was speaking of the resurrection of the dead, that "as the Father raiseth the dead, and quickeneth them, so also the Son quickeneth whom He will;" and immediately thereupon added as a reason, concerning the judgment, saying, "for the Father judgeth not any man, but all judgment hath He given to the Son." Why said He this, but to indicate that He had spoken of that resurrection of

---

[1] John i. 14.   [2] John xi. 41-44.   [3] Luke vii. 14.   [4] Luke viii. 54.

the dead which will take place in the judgment?

12. "For," saith He, "the Father judgeth no man, but all judgment hath He given to the Son." A little before we were thinking that the Father doeth something which the Son doeth not, when He said, "The Father loveth the Son, and showeth Him all things that Himself doeth;" as though the Father were doing, and the Son were seeing. In this way there was creeping in upon our mind a carnal conception, as if the Father did what the Son did not; but that the Son was looking on while the Father showed what He was doing. Then, as the Father was doing what the Son did not, just now we see the Son doing what the Father doeth not. How He turns us about, and keeps our mind busy! He leads us hither and thither, will not allow us to remain in one place of the flesh, that by changing He may exercise us, by exercising He may cleanse us, by cleansing He may render us capable of receiving, and may fill us when made capable. What have these words to do with us? What was He speaking? What is He speaking? A little before, He said that the Father showeth to the Son whatever He doeth. I did see, as it were, the Father doing, the Son waiting to see; presently again, I see the Son doing, the Father idle: "For the Father judgeth not any man, but all judgment hath He given to the Son." When, therefore, the Son is about to judge, will the Father be idle, and not judge? What is this? What am I to understand? What dost Thou say, O Lord? Thou art God the Word, I am a man. Dost Thou say that "the Father judgeth not any man, but hath given all judgment to the Son"? I read in another place that Thou sayest, "I judge not any man; there is one who seeketh and judgeth."[1] Of whom sayest Thou, "There is one who seeketh and judgeth," unless it be of the Father? He maketh inquisition for thy wrongs, and judgeth for them. How is it to be understood here that "the Father judgeth not any man, but all judgment hath He given to the Son"? Let us ask Peter; let us hear him speaking in his epistle: "Christ suffered for us," saith he, "leaving us an example that we should follow His steps; who did no sin, neither was guile found in His mouth; who, when He was reviled, reviled not again; when He suffered wrong, He threatened not, but committed Himself to Him that judgeth righteously."[2] How is it true that "the Father judgeth not any man, but hath given all judgment to the Son"? We are

here in perplexity, and being perplexed let us exert ourselves, that by exertion we may be purified. Let us endeavor as best we may, by His own gift, to penetrate the deep secrets of these words. It may be that we are acting rashly, in that we wish to discuss and to scrutinize the words of God. Yet why were they spoken, but to be known? Why did they sound forth, but to be heard? Why were they heard, but to be understood? Let Him greatly strengthen us, then, and bestow somewhat on us so far as He may deem worthy; and if we do not yet penetrate to the fountain, let us drink of the brook. Behold, John himself has flowed forth to us like a brook, conveyed to us the word from on high. He brought it low, and in a manner levelled it, that we may not dread the lofty One, but may draw nigh to Him that is low.

13. By all means there is a sense, a true and strong sense, if somehow we can grasp it, in which "the Father judgeth not any man, but hath given all judgment to the Son." For this is said because none will appear to men in the judgment but the Son. The Father will be hidden, the Son will be manifest. In what will the Son be manifest? In the form in which He ascended. For in the form of God He was hidden with the Father; in the form of a servant, manifest to men. Not therefore "the Father judgeth any man, but all judgment hath He given to the Son:" only the manifest judgment, in which manifest judgment the Son will judge, since the same will appear to them that are to be judged. The Scripture shows us more clearly that it is the Son that will appear. On the fortieth day after His resurrection He ascended into heaven, while His disciples were looking on; and they hear the angelic voice: "Men of Galilee," saith it, "why stand ye gazing up into heaven? This same that is taken up from you into heaven, shall so come in like manner as ye have seen Him going into heaven."[3] In what manner did they see Him go? In the flesh, which they touched, which they handled, the wounds even of which they proved by touching; in that body in which He went in and out with them for forty days, manifesting Himself to them in truth, not in falsity; not a phantom, or shadow, or ghost, but, as Himself said, not deceiving them, "Handle and see, for a spirit hath not flesh and bones, as ye see me have."[4] That body is now indeed worthy of a heavenly habitation, not being subject to death, nor mutable by the lapse of ages. It is not as it had grown to that age from infancy, so from the age of

---

[1] John viii. 15.   [2] 1 Pet. ii. 21-23.   [3] Acts i. 3-11.   [4] Luke xxiv. 39.

manhood declines to old age: He remains as He ascended, to come to those to whom He willed His word to be preached before He comes. Thus will He come in human form, and this form the wicked will see; both they on the right shall see it, and they that are separated to the left shall see it: as it is written, "They shall look on Him whom they pierced." [1] If they shall look on Him whom they pierced, they shall look on that same body which they struck through with the spear; for a spear does not pierce the Word. This body, therefore, will the wicked be able to look on which they were able to wound. God hidden in the body they will not see: after the judgment He will be seen by those who will be on the right hand. This, then, is what He means when He saith, "The Father judgeth not any man, but all judgment hath He given to the Son,"—that the Son will come to judgment manifest, apparent to men in human body; saying to those on the right, "Come, ye blessed of my Father, receive the kingdom;" and to those on the left, "Go into everlasting fire, which is prepared for the devil and his angels." [2]

14. Behold, that form of man will be seen by the godly and by the wicked, by the just and the unjust, by the believers and unbelievers, by those that rejoice and by those that mourn, by them that trusted and by them that are confounded: lo, seen it will be. When that form shall have appeared in the judgment, and the judgment shall have been finished, where it is said that the Father judgeth not any, but hath given all judgment to the Son, for this reason, that the Son will appear in the judgment in that form which He took from us. What shall be after this? When shall be seen the form of God, which all the faithful are thirsting to see? When shall be seen that Word which was in the beginning, God with God, by which all things were made? When shall be seen that form of God, of which the apostle saith, "Being in the form of God, He thought it not robbery to be equal with God"? [3] For great is that form, in which, moreover, the quality of the Father and Son is recognized; ineffable, incomprehensible, most of all to little ones. When shall this form be seen? Behold, on the right are the just, on the left are the unjust; all alike see the man, they see the Son of man, they see Him who was pierced, Him who was crucified they see: they see Him that was made low, Him who was born of the Virgin, the Lamb of the tribe of Judah they see. But when will they see the Word, God with God? He will be the very same even then, but the form of a servant will appear. The form of a servant will be shown to servants: the form of God will be reserved for sons. Wherefore let the servants be made sons; let them who are on the right hand go into the eternal inheritance promised of old, which the martyrs, though not seeing, believed, for the promise of which they poured out their blood without hesitation; let them go thither and see there. When shall they go thither? Let the Lord Himself say: "So those shall go into everlasting burning, but the righteous into life eternal." [4]

15. Behold, He has named eternal life. Has He told us that we shall there see and know the Father and Son? What if we shall live for ever, yet not see that Father and Son? Hear, in another place, where He has named eternal life, and expressed what eternal life is: "Be not afraid; I do not deceive thee; not without cause have I promised to them that love me, saying, 'He that hath my commandments, and keepeth them, he it is that loveth me; and he that loveth me, shall be loved of my Father, and I will love him, and will show myself to him.'" [5] Let us answer the Lord, and say, What great thing is this, O Lord our God? What great thing is it? Wilt Thou show Thyself to us? What, then, didst Thou not show Thyself to the Jews also? Did not they see Thee who crucified Thee? But Thou wilt show Thyself in the judgment, when we shall stand at Thy right hand; will not also they who will stand on Thy left see Thee? What is it that Thou wilt show Thyself to us? Do we, indeed, not see Thee now when Thou art speaking? He makes answer: I will show myself in the form of God; just now you see the form of a servant. I will not deceive thee, O faithful man; believe that thou shalt see. Thou lovest, and yet thou dost not see: shall not love itself lead thee to see? Love, persevere in loving; I will not disappoint thy love, saith He, I who have purified thy heart. For why have I purified thy heart, but to the end that God may be seen by thee? For "blessed are the pure in heart, for they shall see God." [6] "But this," saith the servant, as if disputing with the Lord, "Thou didst not express, when Thou didst say, 'The righteous shall go into life eternal;' Thou didst not say, They shall go to see me in the form of God, and to see the Father, with whom I am equal." Observe what He said elsewhere: "This is life eternal, that they may know Thee the one true God, and Jesus Christ whom Thou hast sent." [7]

---

[1] Zech. xii. 13.   [2] Matt. xxv. 34, 41.   [3] Phil. ii. 6.   [4] Matt. xxv. 46.   [5] John xiv. 21   [6] Matt. v. 8.   [7] John xvii. 3.

16. And immediately, then, after the judgment mentioned, all which the Father, not judging any man, hath given to the Son, what shall be? What follows? "That all may honor the Son, even as they honor the Father." The Jews honor the Father, despise the Son. For the Son was seen as a servant, the Father was honored as God. But the Son will appear equal with the Father, that all may honor the Son, even as they honor the Father. This we have, therefore, now in faith. Let not the Jew say, "I honor the Father; what have I to do with the Son?" Let him be answered, "He that honoreth not the Son, honoreth not the Father. Thou liest every way; thou blasphemest the Son, and dost wrong to the Father. For the Father sent the Son, and thou despisest Him whom the Father sent. How canst thou honor the sender, who blasphemest the sent?"

17. Behold, says some one, the Son has been sent; and the Father is greater, because He sent. Withdraw from the flesh; the old man suggests oldness in time. Let the ancient, the perpetual, the eternal, to thee the new, call off thy understanding from time to this. Is the Son less because He is said to have been sent? I hear of a sending, not a separation. But yet, saith he, among men we see that he who sends is greater than he who is sent. Be it so; but human affairs deceive a man; divine things purge him. Do not regard things human, in which the sender appears greater, the sent less; notwithstanding, things human themselves bear testimony against thee. Just as, for example, if a man wishes to ask a woman to wife, and, not being able to do this in person, sends a friend to ask for him. And there are many cases in which the greater is chosen to be sent by the less. Why, then, wouldst thou now raise a captious objection, because the one has sent, the other is sent? The sun sends out a ray, but does not separate it; the moon sends out her sheen, but does not separate it; a lamp sheds light, but does not separate it: I see there a sending forth, not a separation. For if thou seekest examples from human things, O heretical vanity, although, as I have said, even human things in some instances refute thee, and convict of error; yet consider how different it is in the case of things human, from which you wish to deduce examples for things divine. A man that sends remains himself behind, while only the man that is sent goes forward. Does the man who sends go with him whom he sends? Yet the Father, who sent the Son, has not departed from the Son. Hear the Lord Himself saying, "Behold, the hour is coming, when every one shall depart to his own, and ye will leave me alone; but I am not alone, because the Father is with me."[1] How has He, with whom He came, sent Him? How has He, from whom He has not departed, sent Him? In another place He said, "The Father abiding in me doeth the works."[2] Behold, the Father is in Him, works in Him. The Father sending has not departed from the Son sent, because the sent and the sender are one.

---

[1] John xvi. 32.   [2] John xiv. 10.

TRACTATE XXII

Chapter V. 24-30.

Upon the discourses delivered yesterday and the day before, follows the Gospel lesson of to-day, which we must endeavor to expound in due course, not indeed proportionably to its importance, but according to our ability: both because you take in, not according to the bountifulness of the gushing fountain, but according to your moderate capacity; and we too speak into your ears, not so much as the fountain gives forth, but so much as we are able to take in we convey into your minds,—the matter itself working more fruitfully in your hearts than we in your ears. For a great matter is treated of, not by great masters, nay, rather by very small; but He who, being great, for our sakes became small, gives us hope and confidence. For if we were not encouraged by Him, and invited to understand Him; if He abandoned us as contemptible, since we were not able to partake His divinity if He did not partake our mortality and come to us to speak His gospel to us; if He had not willed to partake with us what in us is abject and most small,—then we might think that He who took on Himself our smallness, had not been willing to bestow on us His own greatness. This I have said lest any should blame us as over-bold in handling these matters, or despair of himself that he should be able to understand, by God's gift, what the Son of God has deigned to speak to him. Therefore what He has deigned to speak to us, we ought to believe that He meant us to understand. But if we do not understand, He, being asked, gives understanding, who gave His Word unasked.

2. Lo, what these secrets of His words are, consider well. "Verily, verily, I say unto you, Whoso heareth my word, and believeth on Him that sent me, hath eternal life." Surely we are all striving after eternal life: and He saith, "Whoso heareth my word, and believeth Him that sent me, hath eternal life." Then, would He have us hear His word, and yet would He not have us understand it? Since, if in hearing and believing is eternal life, much more in understanding. But the *action* of piety is faith, the fruit of faith understanding, that we may come to eternal life, when there will be no reading of Gospel to us; but after all pages of reading and the voice of reader and preacher have been removed out of the way, He, who has at this time dispensed to us the gospel, will Himself appear to all that are His, now present with Him with purged heart and in an immortal body never more to die, cleansing and enlightening them, now living and seeing how that "in the beginning was the Word, and the Word was with God." Therefore let us consider at this time who we are, and ponder whom we hear. Christ is God, and He is speaking with men. He would have them to apprehend Him, let Him make them capable; He would have them see Him, let Him open their eyes. It is not, however, without cause that He speaks to us, but because that is true which He promises to us.

3. "Whoso heareth my words," saith He, "and believeth Him that sent me, hath eternal life, and shall not come into judgment, but is passed from death unto life." Where, when do we come from death to life, that we come not into judgment? In this life there is a passing from death to life; in this life, which is not yet life, there is a passing hence from death unto life. What is that passing? "Whoso heareth my words," He said, "and believeth Him that sent me." Observing these, thou believest and passest. And does a man pass while standing? Evidently; for in body he stands. in mind he passes. Where was he, whence he should pass, and whither does he pass? He passes from death to life. Look at a man standing, in whom all that is here said may happen. He stands, he hears; perhaps he did not be-

lieve, by hearing he believes: a little before he did not believe, just now he believes; he has made a passage, as it were, from the region of unbelief to the region of faith, by motion of the heart, not of the body, by a motion into the better; because they who again abandon faith move into the worse. Behold, in this life, which, just as I have said, is not yet life, there is a passing from death to life, so that there may not be a coming into judgment. But why did I say that it is not yet life? If this were life, the Lord would not have said to a certain man, "If thou wilt come into life, keep the commandments."[1] For He saith not to him, If thou wilt come into eternal life; He did not add *eternal*, but said only *life*. Therefore this life is not to be named life, because it is not a true life. What is true life, but that which is eternal life? Hear the apostle speaking to Timothy, when he says, "Charge them that are rich in this world, not to be high-minded, nor to trust in uncertain riches, but in the living God, who giveth us all things richly to enjoy; let them do good, be rich in good works, ready to distribute, to communicate." Why does he say this? Hear what follows: "Let them lay up in store for themselves a good foundation for the time to come, that they may lay hold of the true life."[2] If they ought to lay up for themselves a good foundation for the time to come, in order to lay hold of the true life, surely this in which they were is a false life. For why shouldest thou desire to lay hold of the true, if thou hast the true already? Is the true to be laid hold of? There must then be a departing from the false. And by what way must be the departing? Whither? Hear, believe; and thou makest the passage from death into life, and comest not into judgment.

4. What is this, "and thou comest not into judgment"? And who will be better than the Apostle Paul, who saith, "We must all appear before the judgment-seat of Christ, that every one may there receive what he has done in the body, whether it be good or evil"?[3] Paul saith, "We must all appear before the judgment-seat of Christ;" and darest thou promise to thyself that thou shalt not come into judgment? Be it far from me, sayest thou, that I should dare promise this to myself. But I believe Him that doth promise. The Saviour speaks, the Truth promises, Himself said to me, "Whoso heareth my words, and believeth Him that sent me, hath eternal life, and makes a passage from death unto life, and shall not come into

<hr>

[1] Matt. xix. 17.   [2] Tim. vi. 17–19.   [3] 2 Cor. v. 10.

judgment." I then have heard the words of my Lord, and I have believed; so now, when I was an unbeliever, I became a believer; even as He warned me, I passed from death to life, I come not into judgment; not by my presumption, but by His promise. Does Paul, however, speak contrary to Christ, the servant against his Lord, the disciple against his Master, the man against God; so that, when the Lord saith, "Whoso heareth and believeth, passeth from death to life," the apostle should say, "We must all appear before the judgment-seat of Christ"? Otherwise, if he comes not into judgment who appears before the judgment-seat, I know not how to understand it.

5. The Lord our God then reveals it, and by His Scriptures puts us in mind how it may be understood when judgment is spoken of. I exhort you, therefore, to give attention. Sometimes judgment means punishment, sometimes it means discrimination. According to that mode of speech in which judgment means discrimination, "we must all appear before the judgment-seat of Christ, that" a man "may there receive what things he has done in the body, whether it be good or ill." For this same is a discrimination, to distribute good things to the good, evil things to the evil. For if judgment were always to be taken in a bad sense, the psalm would not say, "Judge me, O God." Perhaps some one is surprised when he hears one say, "*Judge me*, O God." For man is wont to say, "Forgive me, O God;" "Spare me, O God." Who is it that says, "Judge me, O God"? Sometimes in the psalm this very verse even is placed in the pause,[1] to be given out by the reader and responded by the people. Does it not perhaps strike some man's heart so much that he is afraid to sing and to say to God, "Judge me, O God"? And yet the people sing it with confidence, and do not imagine that they wish an evil thing in that which they have learned from the divine word; even if they do not well understand it, they believe that what they sing is something good. And yet even the psalm itself has not left a man without an insight into the meaning of it. For, going on, it shows in the words that follow what kind of judgment it spoke of; that it is not one of condemnation, but of discrimination. For saith it, "Judge me, O God." What means "Judge me, O God, and discern my cause from an unholy nation"? According to this judgment of discerning, then, "we must all appear before the judgment-seat of Christ."

But again, according to the judgment of condemnation, "Whoso heareth my words," saith He, "and believeth Him that sent me, hath eternal life, and shall not come into judgment, but makes a passage from death to life." What is "shall not come into judgment?" Shall not come into condemnation. Let us prove from the Scriptures that *judgment* is put where *punishment* is understood; although also in this very passage, a little further on, you will hear the same term *judgment* put for nothing else than for condemnation and punishment. Yet the apostle says in a certain place, writing to those who abused the body, what the faithful among you know; and because they abused it, they were chastised by the scourge of the Lord. For he says to them, "Many among you are weak and sickly, and deeply sleep." For many therefore even died. And he went on: "For if we judged ourselves, we should not be judged by the Lord;" that is, if we reproved ourselves, we should not be reproved by the Lord. "But when we are judged, we are chastened by the Lord, that we may not be condemned with the world."[2] There are therefore those who are judged here according to punishment, that they may be spared there; there are those who are spared here, that they may be the more abundantly tormented there; and there are those to whom the very punishments are meted out without the scourge of punishment, if they be not corrected by the scourge of God; that, since here they have despised the Father that scourgeth, they may there feel the Judge that punisheth. Therefore there is a judgment into which God, that is, the Son of God, will in the end send the devil and his angels, and all the unbelieving and ungodly with him. To this judgment, he who, now believing, passes from death unto life, shall not come.

6. For, lest thou shouldest think that by believing thou art not to die according to the flesh, or lest, understanding it carnally, thou shouldest say to thyself, "My Lord has said to me, Whoso heareth my words, and believeth Him that sent me, is passed from death to life: I then have believed, I am not to die;" be assured that thou shalt pay that penalty, death, which thou owest by the punishment of Adam. For he, in whom we all then were, received this sentence, "Thou shalt surely die;"[3] nor can the divine sentence be made void. But after thou hast paid the death of the old man, thou shalt be received into the eternal life of the new man, and shalt pass from death to life. Mean-

---

[1] *Diapsalma.*   [2] 1 Cor. xi. 30, 32.   [3] Gen. ii. 17.

while, make the transition of life now. What is thy life? Faith: "The just doth live by faith."[1] The unbelievers, what of them? They are dead. Among such dead was he, in the body, of whom the Lord says, "Let the dead bury their dead."[2] So, then, even in this life there are dead, and there are living; all live in a sense. Who are dead? They who have not believed. Who are living? They who have believed. What is said to the dead by the apostle? "Arise, thou that sleepest." But, quoth an objector, he said sleep, not death. Hear what follows: "Arise, thou that sleepest, and come forth from the dead." And as if the sleeper said, Whither shall I go? "And Christ shall give thee light."[3] Christ having enlightened thee, now believing, immediately thou makest a passage from death to life: abide in that to which thou hast passed, and thou shalt not come into judgment.

7. Himself explains that already, and goes on, "Verily, verily, I say unto you." In case, because He said "is passed from death to life," we should understand this of the future resurrection, and willing to show that he who believes is passed, and that to pass from death to life is to pass from unbelief to faith, from injustice to justice, from pride to humility, from hatred to charity, He saith now, "Verily, verily, I say unto you, The hour cometh, and now is." What more evident? "And now is, when the dead shall hear the voice of the Son of God, and they that hear shall live." We have already spoken of these dead. What think we, my brethren? Are there no dead in this crowd that hear me? They who believe and act according to the true faith do live, and are not dead. But they who either do not believe, or believe as the devils believe, trembling,[4] and living wickedly, confessing the Son of God, and without charity, must rather be esteemed dead. This hour, however, is still passing. For the hour of which the Lord spoke will not be an hour of the twelve hours of a day. From the time when He spoke even to the present, and even to the end of the world, the same one hour is passing; of which hour John saith in his epistle, "Little children, it is the last hour."[5] Therefore, is now. Whoso is alive, let him live; whoso was dead, let him live; let him hear the voice of the Son of God, who lay dead; let him arise and live. The Lord cried out at the sepulchre of Lazarus, and he that was four days dead arose. He who stank in the grave came forth into the air. He was

buried, a stone was laid over him: the voice of the Saviour burst asunder the hardness of the stone; and thy heart is so hard, that that Divine Voice does not yet break it! Rise in thy heart; go forth from thy tomb. For thou wast lying dead in thy heart as in a tomb, and pressed down by the weight of evil habit as by a stone. Rise, and go forth. What is Rise, and go forth? Believe and confess. For he that has believed has risen; he that confesses is gone forth. Why said we that he who confesses is gone forth? Because he was hid before confessing; but when he does confess, he goes forth from darkness to light. And after he has confessed, what is said to the servants? What was said beside the corpse of Lazarus? "Loose him, and let him go." How? As it was said to His servants the apostles, "What things ye shall loose on earth, shall be loosed in heaven."[6]

8. "The hour cometh, and now is, when the dead shall hear the voice of the Son of God; and they that hear shall live." From what source shall they live? From life. From what life? From Christ. How do we prove that the source is Christ the life? "I am," saith He, "the way, the truth, and the life."[7] Dost thou wish to walk? "I am the way." Dost thou wish not to be deceived? "I am the truth." Wouldest thou not die? "I am the life." This saith thy Saviour to thee: There is not whither thou mayest go but to me; there is not whereby thou mayest go but by me. Therefore this hour is going on now, this act is clearly taking place, and does not at all cease. Men who were dead, rise; they pass over to life; at the voice of the Son of God they live; from Him they live, while persevering in the faith of Him. For the Son hath life, whence He has it that they that believe shall live.

9. And how hath He? Even as the Father hath. Hear Himself saying, "For as the Father hath life in Himself, so also hath He given to the Son to have life in Himself." Brethren, I shall speak as I shall be able. For these are those words that perplex the puny understanding. Why has He added, "in Himself"? It would suffice to say, "For as the Father hath life, so also hath He given to the Son to have life." He added, "in Himself:" for the Father "hath life in Himself," and the Son hath life in Himself. He meant us to understand something in that which He saith, "in Himself." And here a secret matter is shut up in this word; let there be knocking, that there may be an opening. O Lord, what is this that

---

[1] Hab. ii. 14; Rom. i. 17.   [2] Matt. viii. 22.
[3] Eph. i. 14.   [4] Jas. ii. 19.   [5] 1 John ii. 18.   [6] Matt. xviii. 18.   [7] John xiv. 6.

Thou hast said? Wherefore hast Thou added, "in Himself"? For did not Paul the apostle, whom Thou madest to live, have life? He had, said He. As for men that were dead to be made alive, and at Thy word to pass unto life by believing; when they shall have passed, will they not have life in Thee? They shall have life; for I said also a little before, "Whoso heareth my words, and believeth Him that sent me, hath eternal life." Therefore those that believe in Thee have life; and Thou hast not said, "in themselves." But when Thou speakest of the Father, "even as the Father hath life in Himself;" again, when Thou speakest of Thyself, Thou saidst, "So also hath He given to the Son to have life in Himself." Even as He hath, so gave He to have. Where hath He? "In Himself." Where gave He to have? "In Himself." Where hath Paul life? Not in himself, but in Christ. Where hast thou, believer? Not in thyself, but in Christ. Let us see whether the apostle says this: "Now I live; but not I, but Christ liveth in me."[1] Our life, as ours, that is, of our own personal will, will be only evil, sinful, unrighteous; but the life in us that is good is from God, not from ourselves; it is given to us by God, not by ourselves. But Christ hath life in Himself, as the Father hath, because He is the Word of God. With Him, it is not the case that He liveth now ill, now well; but as for man, he liveth now ill, now well. He who was living ill, was in his own life; he who is living well, is passed to the life of Christ. Thou art made a partaker of life; thou wast not that which thou hast received, but wast one who received: but it is not so with the Son of God, as if at first He was without life, and then received life. For if thus He received life, He would not have it in Himself. For, indeed, what is in Himself? That He should Himself be the very life.

10. I may perhaps declare that matter more plainly still. One lights a candle: that candle, for example, so far as regards the little flame which shines there—that fire has light in itself; but thine eyes, which lay idle and saw nothing, in the absence of the candle, now have light also, but not in themselves. Further, if they turn away from the candle, they are made dark; if they turn to it, they are illumined. But certainly that fire shines so long as it exists: if thou wouldst take the light from it, thou dost also at the same time extinguish it; for without the light it cannot remain. But Christ is light inex-

tinguishable and co-eternal with the Father, always bright, always shining, always burning: for if He were not burning, would it be said in the psalm, "Nor is there any that can hide himself from his heat?"[2] But thou wast cold in thy sin; thou turnest that thou mayest become warm; if thou wilt turn away, thou wilt become cold. In thy sin thou wast dark; thou turnest in order to be enlightened; if thou turnest away, thou wilt become dark. Therefore, because in thyself thou wast darkness, when thou shalt be enlightened, thou wilt *be* light, though in the light. For saith the apostle, "Ye were once darkness, but now light in the Lord."[3] When he had said, "but now light," he added, "in the Lord." Therefore in thyself darkness, "light in the Lord." In what way "light"? Because by participation of that light thou art light. But if thou wilt depart from the light by which thou art enlightened, thou returnest to thy darkness. Not so Christ, not so the Word of God. But how not? "As the Father hath life in Himself, so hath He given also to the Son to have life in Himself;" so that He lives, not by participation, but unchangeably, and is altogether Himself life. "So hath He given also to the Son to have life." Even as He hath, so has He given. What is the difference? For the one gave, the other received. Was He already in being when He received? Are we to understand that Christ was at any time in being without light, when Himself is the wisdom of the Father, of which it is said, "It is the brightness of the eternal light?"[4] Therefore what is said, "gave to the Son," is such as if it were said, "begat the Son;" for by begetting He gave. As He gave Him to be, so He gave Him to be life, so also gave Him to be life in Himself. What is that, to be life in Himself? Not to need life from elsewhere, but to be Himself the plenitude of life, out of which others believing should have life while they lived. "Hath given Him," then, "to have life in Himself." Hath given as to whom? As to His own Word, as to Him who "in the beginning was the Word, and the Word was with God."

11. *Afterwards*, because He was made man, what gave He to Him? "And hath given Him authority to execute judgment, because He is the Son of man." In that He is the Son of God, "As the Father hath life in Himself, so also hath He given to the Son to have life in Himself;" in that He is the Son of man, "He hath given Him authority of executing judgment." This is what I ex-

---

plained to you yesterday, my beloved, that in the judgment man will be seen, but God will not be seen; but after the judgment, God will be seen by those who have prevailed in the judgment, but by the wicked He will not be seen. Since, therefore, the man will be seen in the judgment in that form in which He will so come as He ascended, for that reason He had said above, "The Father judgeth not any man, but hath given all judgment to the Son." He repeats the same thing also in this place, when He says, "And hath given Him authority of executing judgment, because He is the Son of man." As if thou wert to say, "hath given Him authority of executing judgment." In what way? When He had not that authority of executing judgment? Since "in the beginning was the Word, and the Word was with God, and the Word was God;" since "all things were made by Him," did He not already have authority of executing judgment? Yes, but according to this, I say, "He gave Him authority of executing judgment, because He is the Son of man:" according to this, He received authority of judging "because He is the Son of man." For in that He is the Son of God, He always had this authority. He that was crucified, received; He who was in death, is in life: the Word of God never was in death, but is always in life.

12. Now, therefore, as to a resurrection, perhaps some one of us was saying: Behold, we have risen; he who hears Christ, and believes, and is passed from death to life, also will not come into judgment. The hour cometh, and now is, that whoso heareth the voice of the Son of God shall live: he was dead, he has heard; behold, he doth rise. What is this that is said, that there is to be a resurrection afterwards? Spare thyself, do not hasten the sentence, lest thou hurry after it. There is, indeed, this resurrection which comes to pass now; unbelievers were dead, the unrighteous were dead; the righteous live, they pass from the death of unbelief to the life of faith. But do not thence believe that there will not be a resurrection afterwards of the body; believe that there will be a resurrection of the body also. For hear what follows after the declaration of this resurrection which is by faith, lest any should think this to be the only resurrection, or fall into that desperation and error of men who perverted the thoughts of others, "saying that the resurrection is past already," of whom the apostle saith, "and they overthrow the faith of some."[1] For I believe that they

were saying to them such words as these: "Behold, when the Lord saith, 'And he that believeth in me is passed from death unto life;'" the resurrection has already taken place in believing men, who were before unbelievers: how can a second resurrection be meant?" Thanks to our Lord God, He supports the wavering, directs the perplexed, confirms the doubting. Hear what follows, now that thou hast not whereof to make to thyself the darkness of death. If thou hast believed, believe the whole. What whole, sayest thou, am I to believe? Hear what He saith: "Marvel not at this," namely, that He gave to the Son authority of making judgment. I say, in the end of the world, saith He. How in the end? "Do not marvel at this; for the hour cometh." Here He has not said, "and now is." In reference to that resurrection of faith, what did He say? "The hour cometh, and now is." In reference to that resurrection which He intimates there will be of dead bodies, He said, "The hour cometh;" He has not said, "and now is," because it is to come in the end of the world.

13. And whence, sayest thou, dost thou prove to me that He spoke about the resurrection itself? If thou hear patiently, thou wilt presently prove it to thyself. Let us go on then: "Marvel not at this; for the hour cometh, in which all that are in the graves." What more evident than this resurrection? A while ago, He had not said, "they that are in the graves," but, "The dead shall hear the voice of the Son of God; and they that hear shall live." He has not said, some shall live, others shall be damned; because all who believe shall live. But what does He say concerning the graves? "All that are in the graves shall hear His voice, and shall come forth." He said not, "shall hear and live." For if they have lived wickedly, and lay in the graves, they shall rise to death, not to life. Let us see, then, who shall come forth. Although, a little before, the dead by hearing and believing did live, there was no distinction there made: it was not said, The dead shall hear the voice of the Son of God; and when they shall have heard, some shall live, and some shall be damned; but, "all that hear shall live:" because they that believe shall live, they that have charity shall live, and none of them shall die. But concerning the graves, "They shall hear His voice, and come forth: they that have done well, to the resurrection of life; they that have done ill, to the resurrection of judgment." This is the judgment, that punishment of which He had said a while before,

---

[1] 2 Tim. ii. 18.

"Whoso believeth in me is passed from death to life," and shall not come into judgment.

14. "I cannot of myself do anything; as I hear I judge, and my judgment is just." If as Thou hearest Thou judgest, of whom dost Thou hear? If of the Father, yet surely "the Father judgeth not any man, but hath given all judgment to the Son.' When dost Thou, being in a manner the Father's herald, declare what Thou hearest? I speak what I hear, because what the Father is, that I am: for, indeed, speaking is my function; because I am the Father's Word. For this Christ says to thee. Thereupon, of thine. What is "As I hear I judge," but "As I am"? For in what manner does Christ hear? Let us inquire, brethren, I beg of you. Does Christ hear of the Father? How doth the Father speak to Him? Undoubtedly, if He speaks to Him, He uses words to Him; for every one who says something to any one, says it by a word. How doth the Father speak to the Son, seeing that the Son is the Father's Word? Whatever the Father says to us, He says it by His Word: the Word of the Father is the Son; by what other word, then, doth He speak to the Word Himself? God is one, has one Word, contains all things in one Word. What does that mean, then, "As I hear, I judge?" Just as I am of the Father, so I judge. Therefore "my judgment is just." If Thou doest nothing of Thyself, O Lord Jesus, as carnal men think; if Thou doest nothing of Thyself, how didst Thou say a while before, "So also the Son quickeneth whom He will"? Just now Thou sayest, Of myself I do nothing. But what does the Son declare, but that He is of the Father? He that is of the Father is not of Himself. If the Son were of Himself, He would not be the Son: He is of the Father. That the Father is, is not of the Son; that the Son is, is of the Father. Equal to the Father; but yet the Son of the Father, not the Father of the Son.

15. "Because I seek not my own will, but the will of Him that sent me." The Only Son saith, "I seek not my own will," and yet men desire to do their own will! To such a degree does He who is equal to the Father humble Himself; and to such a degree does He extol Himself, who lies in the lowest depth, and cannot rise except a hand is reached to Him! Let us then do the will of the Father, the will of the Son, the will of the Holy Ghost; because of this Trinity there is one will, one power, one majesty. Yet for that reason saith the Son, "I came not to do mine own will, but the will of Him that sent me;" because Christ is not of Himself, but of the Father. But what He had that He might appear as a man, He assumed of the creature which He himself formed.

TRACTATE XXIII.

Chapter V. 19–40.

1. In a certain place in the Gospel, the Lord says that the prudent hearer of His word ought to be like a man who, wishing to build a house, digs deeply until he comes to the foundation of stability on the rock, and there establishes in security what he builds against the violence of the flood; so that, when the flood comes, it may be rather beaten back by the strength of the building, than bring ruin on that house by the force of its pressure.[1] Let us regard the Scripture of God to be, as it were, the field where we wish to build something. Let us not be slothful, nor be content with the surface; let us dig deeply until we come to the rock: "And that rock was Christ."[2]

2. The passage read to-day has spoken to us of the witness of the Lord, that He does not hold the witness of men necessary, but has a greater witness than men; and He has told us what this witness is: "The works," saith He, "which I do bear witness of me." Then He added, "And the Father that sent me beareth witness of me." The very works also which He doeth, He says that He has received from the Father. The works, therefore, bear witness, the Father bears witness. Has John borne no witness? He did clearly bear witness, but as a lamp; not to satisfy friends, but to confound enemies: for it had been predicted long before by the person of the Father, "I have prepared a lamp for mine Anointed: I will clothe His enemies with confusion; but upon Him shall flourish

---

[1] Matt. vii. 24, 25.   [2] 1 Cor. x. 4.

my sanctification."[1] Be it that thou wert left in the dark in the night-time, thou didst direct thy attention to the lamp, thou didst admire the lamp, and didst exult at its light. But that lamp says that there is a sun, in which thou oughtest to exult; and though it burns in the night, it bids thee to be looking out for the day. Therefore it is not the case that there was no need of that man's testimony. For wherefore was he sent, if there was no need of him? But, on the contrary, lest man should stay at the lamp, and think the light of the lamp to be sufficient for him, therefore the Lord neither says that this lamp had been superfluous, nor yet doth He say that thou oughtest to stay at the lamp. The Scripture of God utters another testimony: there undoubtedly God hath borne witness to His Son, and in that Scripture the Jews had placed their hope,—namely, in the law of God, given by Moses His servant. "Search the Scripture," saith He, "in which ye think ye have eternal life: the same bears witness of me; and ye will not come to me that ye may have life." Why do ye think that in the Scripture ye have eternal life? Ask itself to whom does it bear witness, and understand what is eternal life. And because for the sake of Moses they were willing to reject Christ, as an adversary to the ordinances and precepts of Moses, He convicts those same men as by another lamp.

3. For, indeed, all men are lamps, since they can be both lighted and extinguished. Moreover, when the lamps are wise, they shine and glow with the Spirit; yet also, if they did burn and are put out, they even stink. The servants of God remain good lamps by the oil of His mercy, not by their own strength. The free grace of God, truly, is the oil of the lamps. " For I have labored more than they all," saith a certain lamp; and lest he should seem to burn by his own strength, he added, " But not I, but the grace of God that was with me."[2] All prophecy, therefore, before the coming of the Lord, is a lamp. Of this lamp the Apostle Peter says: " We have a more sure word of prophecy, to which ye do well giving heed, as unto a lamp shining in a dark place, until the day dawn, and the day-star arise in your hearts."[3] Accordingly the prophets are lamps, and all prophecy one great lamp. What of the apostles? Are not they, too, lamps? They are, clearly. He alone is not a lamp. For He is not lighted and put out; because " even as the Father hath life in Himself, so hath He given to the Son to

have life in Himself." The apostles also, I say, are lamps; and they give thanks because they were both lighted by the light of truth, and are burning with the spirit of charity, and supplied with the oil of God's grace. If they were not lamps, the Lord would not say to them, " Ye are the light of the world." For after He said, " Ye are the light of the world," He shows that they should not think themselves such a light as that of which it is said, " That was the true light, that enlighteneth every man coming into this world." But this was said of the Lord at that time when He was distinguished from John (the Baptist). Of John the Baptist, indeed, it had been said, " He was not the light, but that he might bear witness of the light."[4] And lest thou shouldst say, How was he not the light, of whom Christ says that " he was a lamp"?—I answer, In comparison of the other light, he was not light. For " that was the true light that enlighteneth every man coming into this world." Accordingly, when He said also to the disciples, " Ye are the light of the world," lest they should imagine that anything was attributed to them which was to be understood of Christ alone, and thus the lamps should be extinguished by the wind of pride, when He had said, " Ye are the light of the world," He immediately subjoined, "A city that is set on a hill cannot be hid; neither do men light a candle and put it under a bushel, but on a candlestick, that it may shine on all that are in the house." But what if He did not call the apostles the candle, but the lighters of a candle, which they were to put on a candlestick? Hear that He called themselves candle. " So let your light shine," saith He, " before men, that they, seeing your good works, may glorify," not you, but " your Father who is in heaven."[5]

4. Wherefore both Moses bore witness to Christ, and John bore witness to Christ, and all the other prophets and apostles bore witness to Christ. Before all these testimonies He places the testimony of His own works. Because through those men too, it was God and none other that bore witness to His Son. But yet in another way God bears testimony to His Son. God reveals His Son through the Son Himself, He reveals Himself through the Son. To Him, if a man shall have been able to reach, he shall need no lamps; and by truly digging deep, he will carry down his building to the rock.

5. The lesson of to-day, brethren, is easy; but on account of what was due yesterday

(for I know what I have delayed, not withdrawn, and the Lord has deigned to allow me even to-day to speak to you), recall to mind what you ought to demand, if perhaps, while preserving piety and wholesome humility, we may in some measure stretch out ourselves, not against God, but towards Him, and lift up our soul, pouring it out above us, like the Psalmist, to whom it was said, "Where is thy God?" "On these things," saith he, "I meditated, and poured out my soul above me."[1] Therefore let us lift up our soul to God, not against God; for this also is said, "To Thee, O Lord, I have lifted up my soul."[2] And let us lift it up with His own assistance, for it is heavy. And from what cause is it heavy? Because the body which is corrupt weighs down the soul, and the earthly tabernacle depresses the mind while meditating on many things.[3] Let us try, then, whether we may not be able to withdraw our mind from many things in order to concentrate it on one, and to raise it to one (which indeed we cannot do, as I have said, unless He assist us who wills our souls to be raised to Himself). And so we may apprehend in some measure how the Word of God, the only begotten of the Father, the co-eternal and equal with the Father, doeth not anything except what He seeth the Father doing, whilst yet the Father Himself doeth not anything but through the Son, who seeth Him doing. Since the Lord Jesus, as it seems to me,—willing here to make known some great matter to those that give attention to it, and to pour into those that are capable of receiving, and to rouse, on the other hand, the incapable to assiduity, in order that, while not yet understanding, they may by right living be made capable,—has intimated to us that the human soul and rational mind which is in man, not in the beast, is invigorated, enlightened, and made happy in no other way than by the very substance of God: that the soul itself gets somewhat by and of the body, and yet holds the body subject to it, while the senses of the body can be soothed and delighted by things bodily, and that because of this kind of fellowship of soul and body in this life, and in this mutual embrace of theirs, the soul is delighted when the bodily senses are soothed, and saddened when they are offended; while yet the happiness by which the soul itself is made happy cannot be realized but by a participation of that ever-living, unchangeable life, of that eternal substance, which is God: that as the soul, which is inferior to God, causes the body, which is inferior

to itself, to live, so that alone which is superior to the soul can cause that same soul to live happily. For the soul is higher than the body, and higher than the soul is God. It bestows something on its inferior, while there is something bestowed on itself by the superior. Let it serve its Lord, that it may not be trampled on by its own servant. This, brethren, is the Christian religion, which is preached through the whole world, while its enemies are dismayed; who, where they are conquered, murmur, and fiercely rage against it where they prevail. This is the Christian religion, that one God be worshipped, not many gods, because only one God can make the soul happy. It is made happy by participation of God. Not by participation of a holy soul does the feeble soul become happy, nor by participation of an angel does the holy soul become happy; but if the feeble soul seeks to be happy, let it seek that by which the holy soul is made happy. For thou art made happy, not of an angel, but the angel as well as thou of the same source.

6. These things being premised and firmly established,—that the rational soul is made happy only by God, that the body is enlivened only by the soul, and that the soul is a something intermediate between God and the body,—direct your thoughts to, and recollect with me, not the passage read to-day, of which we have spoken enough, but that of yesterday, which we have been turning over and handling these three days, and, to the best of our abilities, digging into until we should come to the rock. The Word Christ, Christ the Word of God with God, Christ the Word and the Word God, Christ and God and Word one God. To this press on; O soul, despising, or even transcending all things else, to this press on. There is nothing more powerful than this creature, which is called the rational mind, nothing more sublime: whatever is above this, is but the Creator. But I was saying that Christ is the Word, and Christ is the Word of God, and Christ the Word is God; but Christ is not only the Word, since "the Word became flesh, and dwelt among us:"[4] therefore Christ is both Word and flesh. For when "He was in the form of God, He thought it not robbery to be equal with God." And what of us in our low estate, who, feeble and crawling on the ground, were not able to reach unto God, were we to be abandoned? God forbid. "He emptied Himself, taking upon Him the form of a servant;"[5] not, therefore, by losing the form of God. He

---

[1] Ps. xlii   [2] Ps. xxv. 1   Wisd. ix. 15   [4] John i. 14.   [5] Phil. ii 6

became man who was God, by receiving what He was not, not by losing what He was: so God became man. There thou hast something for thy weakness, something for thy perfection. Let Christ raise thee by that which is man, lead thee by that which is God-man, and guide thee through to that which is God. And the whole preaching and dispensation by Christ is this, brethren, and there is not another, that souls may be raised again, and that bodies also may be raised again. For each of the two was dead; the body by weakness, the soul by iniquity. Because each was dead, each may rise again. What each? Soul and body. By what, then, can the soul rise again but by Christ God? By what the body, but by the man Christ? For there was also in Christ a human soul, a whole soul; not merely the irrational part of the soul, but also the rational, which is called mind. For there have been certain heretics, and they have been driven out of the Church, who fancied that the body of Christ did not have in it a rational mind, but, as it were, the animal life of a beast; since, without the rational mind, life is only animal life. But because they were driven out, and driven out by the truth, accept thou the whole Christ, Word, rational mind, and flesh. This is the whole Christ. Let thy soul rise again from iniquity by that which is God, thy body from corruption by that which is man. There, most beloved, hear ye what, so far as it appears to me, is the great profundity of this passage; and see how Christ here speaks to the effect, that the only reason why He came is, in order that souls may have a resurrection from iniquity, and bodies from corruption. I have already said by what our souls are raised, by the very substance of God; by what our bodies are raised, by the human dispensation of our Lord Jesus Christ.

7. "Verily, verily, I say unto you, The Son cannot of Himself do anything, but what He seeth the Father doing; for what things soever He has done, these also the Son doeth in like manner." Yes, the heaven, the earth, the sea; the things that are in heaven, on the earth, and in the sea; the visible and invisible, the animals on the land, the plants in the fields, the creatures that swim in the waters, that fly in the air, that shine in heaven; besides all these, angels, virtues, thrones, dominations, principalities, powers; "all were made by Him." Did God make all these, and show them when made to the Son, that He also should make another world full of all these? Certainly not. But, on the contrary, what does He say? "For what things soever He has made, these," not others, but "these also the Son doeth," not

differently, "but in like manner." "For the Father loveth the Son, and showeth Him all things which Himself doeth." The Father showeth to the Son that souls may be raised, for souls are raised up by the Father and the Son; nor can souls live except God be their life. If souls, then, cannot live unless God be their life, just as themselves are the life of bodies; what the Father shows to the Son, that is, what He doeth, He doeth through the Son. For it is not by doing that He shows to the Son, but by showing He doeth through the Son. For the Son sees the Father showing before anything is done; and from the Father's showing and the Son's vision, is done what is done by the Father through the Son. So are souls raised up, if they can see that conjunction of unity, the Father showing, the Son seeing, and the creature made by the Father's showing and the Son's seeing; and that thing made by the Father's showing and the Son's seeing, which is neither the Father nor the Son, but beneath the Father and the Son, whatever is made by the Father through the Son. Who sees this?

8. Behold, again we humble ourselves to carnal notions, and descend to you, if indeed we had at any time ascended somewhat from you. Thou wishest to show something to thy son, that he may do what thou doest; thou art about to do, and thus to show the thing. Therefore, what thou art about to do, in order to show it to thy son, thou doest not surely *by* thy son; but thou alone doest that thing which, when done, he may see, and do another such thing in like manner. This is not the case there; why goest thou on to thy own similitude, and blottest out the similitude of God within thee? There, the case is wholly otherwise. Find a case in which thou showest to thy son what thou doest before thou doest it; so that, after thou hast shown it, it will be by the son thou doest. Perhaps something like this now occurs to thee: Lo, sayest thou, I think to make a house, and I wish it to be built by my son: before I build it myself, I point out to my son what I mean to do: both he doeth, and I too by him to whom I pointed out my wish. Thou hast retreated, indeed, from the former similitude, but still thou liest in great dissimilitude. For, lo, before thou canst make the house, thou dost inform thy son, and point out to him what thou meanest to do; that, upon thy showing before thou makest, he may make what thou hast shown, and so thou mayest make by him: but thou wilt speak words to thy son, words will have to pass between thee and him; between the person showing and the person seeing, between speaker and hearer, flies articulate

sound, which is not what thou art, nor what he is. That sound, indeed, which goes out of thy mouth, and by the concussion of the air touches thy son's ear, and filling the sense of hearing, conveys thy thought to his heart; that sound, I say, is not thyself, nor thy son. A sign is given from thy mind to thy son's mind, but that sign not either thy mind or thy son's mind, but something else. Is it thus that we think the Father has spoken to the Son? Were there words between the Father and the Word? Then how is it? Or, whatever the Father would say to the Son, if He would say it by a word, the Son Himself is the Word of the Father, would He speak by a word to the Word? Or, since the Son is the great Word, had smaller words to pass between the Father and Son? Was it so, that some sound, as it were a temporal, fleeting creature, had to issue from the mouth of the Father, and strike upon the ear of the Son? Has God a body, that this should proceed, as it were, from His lips? And has the Word the ears of a body, into which sound may come? Lay aside all notions of corporeal forms, regard simplicity, if thou art single-minded. But how wilt thou be single-minded? If thou wilt not entangle thyself with the world. but disentangle thyself from the world. For by disentangling thyself, thou wilt be single-minded. And see, if thou canst, what I say; or if thou canst not, believe what thou dost not see. Thou speakest to thy son; thou speakest by a word: neither art thou, nor is thy son, the word that sounds.

9. I have, sayest thou, another method of showing; for so well instructed is my son, that he hears without my speaking, but I show him by a nod what to do. Lo, show him by a nod what thou wilt, yet certainly the mind holds within itself that which it would show. By what dost thou give this nod? With the body,—namely, with the lips, the look, the brows, the eyes, the hands. All these are not what thy mind is: these, too, are media; there was something understood by these signs which are not what thy mind is, not what the mind of thy son is; but all this which thou doest by the body is beneath thy mind, and beneath the mind of thy son: nor can thy son know thy mind, unless thou give him signs by the body. What, then, do I say? This is not the case there; there all is simplicity. The Father shows to the Son what He is doing, and by showing begets the Son. I see what I have said; but because I see also to whom I have said it, may such understanding be some time or other formed in you as to grasp it. If ye are not able now to comprehend what God is, comprehend at

least what God is not: you will have made much progress, if you think of God as being not something other than He is. God is not a body, not the earth, not the heaven, not the moon, or sun, or stars—not these corporeal things. For if not heavenly things, how much less is He earthly things! Put all body out of the question. Further, hear another thing: God is not a mutable spirit. For I confess,—and it must be confessed, for it is the Gospel that speaks it,—"God is a Spirit." But pass beyond all mutable spirit, beyond all spirit that now knows, now knows not; that now remembers, now forgets; that wills what before it willed not, that wills not what before it willed; either that suffers these mutabilities now or may suffer them: pass beyond all these. Thou findest not any mutability in God; nor aught that may have been one way before, and is otherwise now. For where thou findest alternation, there a kind of death has taken place: since, for a thing not to be what it was, is a death. The soul is said to be immortal; so indeed it is, because it ever lives, and there is in it a certain continuous life, but yet a mutable life. According to the mutability of this life, it may be said to be mortal; because if it lived wisely, and then becomes foolish, it dies for the worse; if it lived foolishly, and becomes wise, it dies for the better. For the Scripture teaches us that there is a death for the worse, and that there is a death for the better. In any case, they had died for the worse, of whom it said, "Let the dead bury their dead;"[1] and, "Awake, thou that sleepest, and arise from the dead, and Christ shall give thee light;"[2] and from this passage before us, "When the dead shall hear, and they that hear shall live." For the worse they had died; therefore do they come to life again. By coming to life they die for the better, because by coming to life again they will not be what they were; but for that to be, which was not, is death. But perhaps it is not called death if it is for the better? The apostle has called that death: "But if ye be dead with Christ from the elements of this world, why do ye judge concerning this world as if ye were still living?"[3] And again, "For ye are dead, and your life is hid with Christ in God." He wishes us to die that we may live, because we have lived to die. Whatever therefore dies, both from better to worse, and from worse to better, is not God; because neither can supreme goodness proceed to better, nor true eternity to worse. For true eternity is, where is nothing of time. But was there now

---

[1] Matt. viii. 22. [2] Eph. v. 14. [3] Col. ii. 20.

this, now that? Immediately time is admitted, it is not eternal. For that ye may know that God is not thus, as the soul is,—certainly the soul is immortal,—what, however, saith the apostle of God, "Who alone hath immortality," unless that he openly says this, He alone hath unchangeableness, because He alone hath true eternity? Therefore no mutability is there.

10. Recognize in thyself something which I wish to say within, in thyself; not within as if in thy body, for in a sense one may say, "in thyself." For there is in thee health, thy age whatever it be, but this in regard to the body. In thee is thy hand and thy foot; but there is one thing in thee, within; another thing in thee as in thy garment. But leave outside thy garment and thyself, descend into thyself, go to thy secret place, thy mind, and there see, if thou canst, what I wish to say. For if thou art far from thyself, how canst thou come near to God? I was speaking of God, and thou believedst that thou wouldst understand. I am speaking of the soul, I am speaking of thyself: understand this, there I will try thee. For I do not travel very far for examples, when I mean to give thee some similitude to thy God from thy own mind; because surely not in the body, but in that same mind, was man made after the image of God. Let us seek God in His own similitude; let us recognize the Creator in His own image. There within, if we can, let us find this that we speak of,—how the Father shows to the Son, and how the Son sees what the Father shows, before anything is made by the Father through the Son. But when I shall have spoken, and thou hast understood, thou must not think that spoken of to be something just such as our example, that thou mayest therein keep piety, which I wish to be kept by thee, and earnestly admonish thee to keep: that is, if thou art not able to comprehend what God is, do not think it a small matter for thee to know what He is not.

11. Behold, in thy mind, I see some two things, thy memory and thy thought, which is, as it were, the seeing faculty and the vision of thy soul. Thou seest something, and perceivest it by the eyes, and thou committest it to the care of the memory. There, within, is that which thou hast committed to thy memory, laid up in secret as in a storehouse, as in a treasury, as in a kind of secret chamber and inner cabinet. Thou thinkest of something else, thy attention is elsewhere; what thou didst see is in thy memory, but not seen by thee, because thy thought is bent on another thing. I prove this at once. I speak to you who know; I mention by name Carthage; all who know it have instantly seen Carthage within the mind. Are there as many Carthages as there are minds of you? You have all seen it by means of this name, by means of these syllables known to you, rushing forth from my mouth: your ears were touched; the sense of the soul was touched through the body, and the mind bent back from another object to this word, and saw Carthage. Was Carthage made there and then? It was there already, but latent in the memory. Why was latent there? Because thy mind was engaged on another matter; but when thy thought turned back to that which was in the memory, thence it was shaped, and became a kind of vision of the mind. Before, there was not a vision, but there was memory; the vision was made by the turning back of thought to memory. Thy memory, then, showed Carthage to thy thought; and that which was in it before thou didst direct thy mind to the memory, it exhibited to the attention of thy thought when turned upon it. Behold, a showing is effected by the memory, and a vision is produced in thought; and no words passed between, no sign was given from the body: thou didst neither nod, nor write, nor utter a sound; and yet thought saw what the memory showed. But both that which showed, and that to which it showed, are of the same substance. But yet, that thy memory might have Carthage in it, the image was drawn in through the eyes, for thou didst see what thou didst store up in thy memory. So hast thou seen the tree which thou rememberest; so the mountain, the river; so the face of a friend, of an enemy, of father, mother, brother, sister, son, neighbor; so of letters written in a book, of the book itself; so of this church: all these thou didst see, and didst commit to thy memory after they were seen; and didst, as it were, lay up there what thou mightst by thinking see at will, even when they should be absent from these eyes of the body. Thou sawest Carthage when thou wast at Carthage; thy soul received the image by the eyes; this image was laid up in thy memory; and thou, the person who wast present at Carthage, didst keep something within thee which thou mightst be able to see with thyself, even when thou shouldst not be there. All these things thou didst receive from without. What the Father shows to the Son, He does not receive from without: all comes to pass within, because there would be no creature at all without, unless the Father had made it by the Son. Every creature was made by God; before it was made it was not in being. It

was not therefore seen, after being made and retained in memory, that the Father might show it to the Son, as the memory might show to thought; but, on the contrary, the Father showed it to be made, the Son saw it to be made; and the Father made it by showing, because He made it by the Son seeing. And therefore we ought not to be surprised that it is said, "But what He seeth the Father doing," not *showing*. For by this it is intimated that, with the Father, *to do* and *to show* is the same thing; that hence we may understand that He doeth all things by the Son seeing. Neither is that showing, nor that seeing, temporal. Forasmuch as all times are made by the Son, they could not certainly be shown to Him at any point of time to be made. But the Father's showing begets the Son's seeing, just in the same manner as the Father begets the Son. For the showing produces the seeing, not the seeing the showing. And if we were able to look into this matter more purely and perfectly, perhaps we should find that the Father is not one thing, His showing another; nor the Son one thing, His seeing another. But if we have hardly apprehended this,—if we have hardly been able to explain how the memory exhibits to the thought what it has received from without,—how much less can we take in or explain how God the Father shows to the Son, what He has not from elsewhere, or that which is not other than Himself! We are only little ones: I tell you what God is not, I do not show you what God is. What shall we do, then, that we may apprehend what He is? Can ye do this by or through me? I say this to the little ones, both to you and to myself; there is by whom we can: we have just now sung, just now heard, "Cast thy care upon the Lord, and He will nourish thee."[1] The reason why thou art not able, O man, is because thou art a little one; being a little one, thou must be nourished; being nourished, thou wilt become full-grown; and what as a little one thou couldst not, thou shalt see when full-grown; but that thou mayest be nourished, "cast thy care upon the Lord, and He will nourish thee."

12. Therefore let us now briefly run over what remains, and do you see how the Lord makes known to us the things which I have been here commending to your attention. "The Father loveth the Son, and showeth Him all things which Himself doeth." Himself raiseth up souls, but by the Son, that the souls raised up may enjoy the substance of God, that is, of the Father and of the Son.

"And greater works than these He will show Him." Greater than which? Than healings of bodies. We have treated of this already, and must not linger upon it now. Greater is the resurrection of the body unto eternity than this healing of the body, wrought in that impotent man, to last only for a time. "And greater works than these He will show Him, that ye may marvel." "Will show," as if the act were temporal, therefore as to a man made in time, since God the Word is not made, He by whom all times were made. But Christ was made man in time. We know in what consulship the Virgin Mary brought forth Christ, conceived of the Holy Ghost. Wherefore He, by whom as God the times were made, was made man in time. Hence, just as in time, "He will show Him greater works," that is, the resurrection of bodies, "that ye may marvel" at the resurrection of bodies wrought by the Son.

13. He then returns to that resurrection of souls: "For as the Father raiseth the dead, and quickeneth them, so also the Son quickeneth whom He will;" but this according to the Spirit. The Father quickeneth, the Son quickeneth; the Father whom He will, the Son whom He will; but the Father quickeneth the same as the Son, because all things were made by Him. "For as the Father raiseth up the dead, and quickeneth them, so also the Son quickeneth whom He will." This is said of the resurrection of souls; but what of the resurrection of bodies? He returns, and says: "For the Father judgeth not any man, but all judgment hath He given to the Son." The resurrection of souls is effected by the eternal and unchangeable substance of the Father and Son. But the resurrection of bodies is effected by the dispensation of the Son's humanity, which dispensation is temporal, not co-eternal with the Father. Therefore, when He mentioned judgment, in which there should be a resurrection of bodies, He saith, "For the Father judgeth not any man, but all judgment hath He given to the Son;" but concerning the resurrection of souls, He saith, "Even as the Father raiseth the dead, and quickeneth them, so also the Son quickeneth whom He will." That, then, the Father and the Son together. But this concerning the resurrection of bodies: "The Father judgeth not any man, but hath given all judgment to the Son; that all may honor the Son, even as they honor the Father." This is referred to the resurrection of souls. "That all may honor the Son." How? "Even as they honor the Father." For the Son works the resurrection of souls in the same manner as the Father doth; the Son

quickeneth just as the Father doth. There-fore, in the resurrection of souls, "let all honor the Son as they honor the Father." But what of the honoring on account of the resurrection of the body? " Whoso honoreth not the Son, honoreth not the Father that sent Him." He said not *even as*, but *honoreth* and *honoreth*. For the man Christ is honored, but not *even as* God the Father. Why? Because, with respect to this, He said, " The Father is greater than I."[1] And when is the Son honored *even as* the Father is honored? When " in the beginning was the Word, and the Word was with God; and all things were made by Him." And hence, in this second honor-ing, what saith He? " Whoso honoreth not the Son, honoreth not the Father that sent Him." The Son was not sent, but because He was made man.

14. " Verily, verily, I say unto you." Again He returns to the resurrection of souls, that by continual repetition we may apprehend His meaning; because we could not keep up with His discourse hastening on as on wings. Lo, the Word of God lingers with us; lo, it doth, as it were, dwell with our infirmities. He returns again to the mention of the resur-rection of souls. " Verily, verily, I say unto you, Whoso heareth my word, and believeth Him that sent me, hath eternal life;" but hath it as from the Father. " For whoso heareth my word, and believeth Him that sent me, hath eternal life" from the Father, by believing the Father that sent the Son. " And shall not come into judgment, but is passed from death to life." But from the Father, whom he believes, is he quickened. What, dost Thou not quicken? See that the Son also "quickeneth whom He will." " Verily, verily, I say unto you, That the hour cometh when the dead shall hear the voice of the Son of God, and they that hear shall live." Here He did not say, they shall believe Him that sent me, and therefore shall live; but by hearing the voice of the Son of God, " they that hear," that is, they that obey the Son of God, " shall live." There-fore, both from the Father shall they live, when they will believe the Father; and from the Son shall they live, when they will hear the voice of the Son of God. Why shall they live both from the Father and from the Son? " For even as the Father hath life in Himself, so also hath He given to the Son to have life in Himself."

15. He has finished speaking of the resur-rection of souls; it remains to speak more evidently of the resurrection of bodies. " And hath given Him authority also to exe-cute judgment:" not only to raise up souls by faith and wisdom, but also to execute judgment. But why this? " Because He is the Son of man." Therefore the Father doeth something through the Son of man, which He doeth not from His own substance, to which the Son is equal: as, for instance, that He should be born, crucified, dead, and have a resurrection; for not any of these is contingent to the Father. In the same manner also the raising again of bodies. For the raising to life of souls the Father effects from His own substance, by the substance of the Son, in which the Son is equal to Him; because souls are made partakers of that un-changeable light, but not bodies; but the rais-ing again of bodies, the Father effects through the Son of man. For " He hath given Him au-thority also to execute judgment, because He is the Son of man;" according to that which He said above, " For the Father judgeth not any man." And to show that He said this of the resurrection of bodies, He goes on: " Mar-vel not at this, for the hour cometh:" not, *and now is;* but, "the hour cometh, in which all that are in the graves (this ye have already heard sufficiently explained yesterday) shall hear His voice, and come forth." Where? Into judgment: " They that have done well, into the resurrection of life; and they that have done evil, into the resurrection of judg-ment." And dost Thou do this alone, be-cause the Father hath given all judgment to the Son, and judgeth not any man? I, saith He, do it. But how doest Thou it? " I cannot of myself do anything; as I hear, I judge; and my judgment is just." When He was treating of the resurrection of souls, He did not say, *I hear;* but, *I see.* For *I hear* refers to the command of the Father as giving order. Therefore, now as a man, just as He than whom the Father is greater; as from the form of a servant, not from the form of God, " As I hear, I judge; and my judgment is just." Whence is the man's judgment a just one? My brethren, mark well: " Because I seek not my own will, but the will of Him that sent me."

[1] John xiv. 28.

TRACTATE XXIV.

Chapter VI. 1–14.

1. The miracles performed by our Lord Jesus Christ are indeed divine works, and incite the human mind to rise to the apprehension of God from the things that are seen. But inasmuch as He is not such a substance as may be seen with the eyes, and His miracles in the government of the whole world and the administration of the universal creation are, by their familiar constancy, slightly regarded, so that almost no man deigns to consider the wonderful and stupendous works of God, exhibited in every grain of seed; He has, agreeably to His mercy, reserved to Himself certain works, beyond the usual course and order of nature, which He should perform on fit occasion, that they, by whom His daily works are lightly esteemed, might be struck with astonishment at beholding, not indeed greater, but uncommon works. For certainly the government of the whole world is a greater miracle than the satisfying of five thousand men with five loaves; and yet no man wonders at the former; but the latter men wonder at, not because it is greater, but because it is rare. For who even now feeds the whole world, but He who creates the cornfield from a few grains? He therefore created as God creates. For, whence He multiplies the produce of the fields from a few grains, from the same source He multiplied in His hands the five loaves. The power, indeed, was in the hands of Christ; but those five loaves were as seeds, not indeed committed to the earth, but multiplied by Him who made the earth. In this miracle, then, there is that brought near to the senses, whereby the mind should be roused to attention, there is exhibited to the eyes, whereon the understanding should be exercised, that we might admire the invisible God through His visible works; and being raised to faith and purged by faith, we might desire to behold Him even invisibly, whom invisible we came to know by the things that are visible.

2. Yet it is not enough to observe these things in the miracles of Christ. Let us interrogate the miracles themselves, what they tell us about Christ: for they have a tongue of their own, if they can be understood. For since Christ is Himself the Word of God, even the act of the Word is a word to us. Therefore as to this miracle, since we have heard how great it is, let us also search how profound it is; let us not only be delighted with its surface, but let us also seek to know its depth. This miracle, which we admire on the outside, has something within. We have seen, we have looked at something great, something glorious, and altogether divine, which could be performed only by God: we have praised the doer for the deed. But just as, if we were to inspect a beautiful writing somewhere, it would not suffice for us to praise the hand of the writer, because he formed the letters even, equal and elegant, if we did not also read the information he conveyed to us by those letters; so, he who merely inspects this deed may be delighted with its beauty to admire the doer: but he who understands does, as it were, read it. For a picture is looked at in a different way from that in which a writing is looked at. When thou hast seen a picture, to have seen and praised it is the whole thing; when thou seest a writing, this is not the whole, since thou art reminded also to read it. Moreover, when thou seest a writing, if it chance that thou canst not read, thou sayest, "What do we think that to be which is here written?" Thou askest what it is, when already thou seest it to be something. He of whom thou seekest to be informed what it is that thou hast seen, will show thee another thing. He has other eyes than thou hast. Do you not alike see the form of the letters? But yet you do not alike understand the signs. Well, thou seest and praisest; but he sees, praises, reads and understands. Therefore, since we have seen and praised, let us also read and understand.

3. The Lord on the mount: much rather let us understand that the Lord on the mount is the Word on high. Accordingly, what was done on the mount does not, as it were, lie low, nor is to be cursorily passed by, but must be looked up to. He saw the multitude, knew them to be hungering, mercifully fed them: not only in virtue of His goodness, but also of His power. For what would mere goodness avail, where there was not bread with which to feed the hungry crowd? Did not power attend upon goodness, that crowd had remained fasting and hungry. In short, the disciples also, who were with the Lord, and hungry, themselves wished to feed the multitudes, that they might not remain empty, but had not wherewithal to feed

them. The Lord asked, whence they might buy bread to feed the multitude. And the Scripture saith: "But this He said, proving him;" namely, the disciple Philip of whom He had asked; "for Himself knew what He would do." Of what advantage then was it to prove him, unless to show the disciple's ignorance? And, perhaps, in showing the disciple's ignorance He signified something more. This will appear, then, when the sacrament of the five loaves itself will begin to speak to us, and to intimate its meaning: for there we shall see why the Lord in this act wished to exhibit the disciple's ignorance, by asking what He Himself knew. For we sometimes ask what we do not know, that, being willing to hear, we may learn; sometimes we ask what we do know, wishing to learn whether he whom we ask also knows. The Lord knew both the one and the other; knew both what He asked, for He knew what Himself would do; and He also knew in like manner that Philip knew not this. Why then did He ask, but to show Philip's ignorance? And why He did this, we shall, as I have said, understand afterwards.

4. Andrew saith: "There is a lad here, who has five loaves and two fishes, but what are these for so many?" When Philip, on being asked, had said that two hundred pennyworth of bread would not suffice to refresh that so great a multitude, there was there a certain lad, carrying five barley loaves and two fishes. "And Jesus saith, Make the men sit down. Now there was there much grass: and they sat down about five thousand men. And the Lord Jesus took the loaves, gave thanks;" He commanded, the loaves were broken, and put before the men that were set down. It was no longer five loaves, but what He had added thereto, who had created that which was increased. "And of the fishes as much as sufficed." It was not enough that the multitude had been satisfied, there remained also fragments; and these were ordered to be gathered up, that they should not be lost: "And they filled twelve baskets with the fragments."

5. To run over it briefly: by the five loaves are understood the five books of Moses; and rightly are they not wheaten but barley loaves, because they belong to the Old Testament. And you know that barley is so formed that we get at its pith with difficulty; for the pith is covered in a coating of husk, and the husk itself tenacious and closely adhering, so as to be stripped off with labor. Such is the letter of the Old Testament, invested in a covering of carnal sacraments: but yet, if we get at its pith, it feeds and satisfies us. A certain lad,

then, brought five loaves and two fishes. If we inquire who this lad was, perhaps it was the people Israel, which, in a childish sense, carried, not ate. For the things which they carried were a burden while shut up, but when opened afforded nourishment. And as for the two fishes, they appear to us to signify those two sublime persons, in the Old Testament, of priest and of ruler, who were anointed for the sanctifying and governing of the people. And at length Himself in the mystery came, who was signified by those persons: He at length came who was pointed out by the pith of the barley, but concealed by its husk. He came, sustaining in His one person the two characters of priest and ruler: of priest by offering Himself to God as a victim for us; of ruler, because by Him we are governed. And the things that were carried closed are now opened up. Thanks be to Him. He has fulfilled by Himself what was promised in the Old Testament. And He bade the loaves to be broken; in the breaking they are multiplied. Nothing is more true. For when those five books of Moses are expounded, how many books have they made by being broken up, as it were; that is, by being opened and laid out? But because in that barley the ignorance of the first people was veiled, of whom it is said, "Whilst Moses is read, the veil is upon their hearts;"[1] for the veil was not yet removed, because Christ had not yet come; not yet was the veil of the temple rent, while Christ is hanging on the cross: because, I say, the ignorance of the people was in the law, therefore that proving by the Lord made the ignorance of the disciple manifest.

6. Wherefore nothing is without meaning; everything is significant, but requires one that understands: for even this number of the people fed, signified the people that were under the law. For why were there five thousand, but because they were under the law, which is unfolded in the five books of Moses? Why were the sick laid at those five porches, but not healed? He, however, there cured the impotent man, who here fed multitudes with five loaves. Moreover, they sat down upon the grass; therefore understood carnally, and rested in the carnal. "For all flesh is grass."[2] And what were those fragments, but things which the people were not able to eat? We understand them to be certain matters of more hidden meaning, which the multitude are not able to take in. What remains then, but that those matters of more hidden meaning, which the multitude cannot take in, be entrusted to men

_____

[1] 2 Cor. iii. 15.   [2] Isa. xl. 6.

who are fit to teach others also, just as were the apostles? Why were twelve baskets filled? This was done both marvellously, because a great thing was done; and it was done profitably, because a spiritual thing was done. They who at the time saw it, marvelled; but we, hearing of it, do not marvel. For it was done that they might see it, but it was written that we might hear it. What the eyes were able to do in their case, that faith does in our case. We perceive, namely, with the mind, what we could not with the eyes: and we are preferred before them, because of us it is said, "Blessed are they who see not, and yet believe." [1] And I add that, perhaps, we have understood what that crowd did not understand. And we have been fed in reality, in that we have been able to get at the pith of the barley.

7. Lastly, what did those men who saw this miracle think? "The men," saith he, "when they had seen the sign which He had done, said, This is indeed a prophet." Perhaps they still thought Christ to be a prophet for this reason, namely, that they were sitting on the grass. But He was the Lord of the prophets, the fulfiller of the prophets, the sanctifier of the prophets, but yet a prophet also: for it was said to Moses, "I will raise up for them a prophet like unto thee." Like, according to the flesh, but not according to the majesty. And that this promise of the Lord is to be understood concerning Christ Himself, is clearly expounded and read in the Acts of the Apostles.[2] And the Lord says of Himself, "A prophet is not without honor, except in his own country."[3] The Lord is a prophet, and the Lord is God's Word, and no prophet prophesies without the Word of God: the Word of God is with the prophets, and the Word of God is a prophet. The former times obtained prophets inspired and filled by the Word of God: we have obtained the very Word of God for our prophet. But Christ is in such manner a prophet, the Lord of prophets, as Christ is an angel, the Lord of angels. For He is also called the Angel of great counsel.[4] Nevertheless, what says the prophet elsewhere? that not an ambassador, nor an angel, but Himself coming will save them;[5] that is, He will not send an ambassador to save them, nor an angel, but Himself will come. Who will come? The Angel himself? Certainly not by an angel will He save them, except that He is so an angel, as also Lord of angels. For angels signify messengers. If Christ brought no message, He would not be called an angel: if Christ prophesied nothing, He would not be called a prophet. He has exhorted us to faith and to laying hold of eternal life; He has proclaimed something present, foretold something future because He proclaimed the present, thence He was an angel or messenger; because He foretold the future, thence He was a prophet; and that, as the Word of God He was made flesh, thence He was Lord of angels and of prophets.

---

[1] John xx. 29.

[2] Acts vii. 37.
[4] Isa. ix. 6, LXX.

[3] John iv. 44.
[5] Isa. xxxv. 4.

TRACTATE XXV.

CHAPTER VI. 15-44.

1. FOLLOWING upon yesterday's lesson from the Gospel is that of to-day, upon which this day's discourse is due to you. When that miracle was wrought, in which Jesus fed the five thousand with five loaves, and the multitudes marveled and said that He was a great prophet that came into the world, then follows this: "When Jesus therefore knew that they came to seize Him, and to make Him king, He escaped again unto the mountain alone." It is therefore given to be understood that the Lord, when He sat on the mountain with His disciples, and saw the multitudes coming to Him, had descended from the mountain, and fed the multitudes on its lower parts. For how can it be that He should escape thither again, if He had not before descended from the mountain? There is something meant by the Lord's descending from on high to feed the multitudes. He fed them, and ascended.

2. But why did He ascend after He knew that they wished to seize Him and make Him a king? How then; was He not a king, that He was afraid to be made a king? He was certainly not such a king as would be made by men, but such as would bestow a kingdom on men. May it not be that Jesus, whose deeds are words, does here, too, signify some-

thing to us? Therefore in this, that they wished to seize Him and make Him a king, and that for this He escapes to the mountain alone, is this action in His case silent; does it speak nothing, does it mean nothing? Or was this seizing of Him perhaps an intention to anticipate the time of His kingdom? For He had come now, not to reign immediately, as He is to reign in the sense in which we pray, Thy kingdom come. He ever reigns, indeed, with the Father, in that He is the Son of God, the Word of God, the Word by which all things were made. But the prophets foretold His kingdom according to that wherein He is Christ made man, and has made His faithful ones Christians. There will consequently be a kingdom of Christians, which at present is being gathered together, being prepared and purchased by the blood of Christ. His kingdom will at length be made manifest, when the glory of His saints shall be revealed, after the judgment is executed by Him, which judgment He Himself has said above is that which the Son of man shall execute. Of which kingdom also the apostle has said: "When He shall have delivered up the kingdom to God, even the Father."[1] In reference to which also Himself says: "Come, ye blessed of my Father, receive the kingdom which is prepared for you from the beginning of the world."[2] But the disciples and the multitudes that believed on Him thought that He had thus come immediately to reign; hence, they wished to seize Him and to make Him a king; they wished to anticipate the time which He hid with Himself, to make it known in due time, and in due time to declare it in the end of the world.

3. That ye may know that they wished to make Him a king,—that is, to anticipate, and at once to have manifest the kingdom of Christ, whom it behoved first to be judged and then to judge,—when He was crucified, and they who hoped in Him had lost hope of His resurrection, having risen from the dead, He found two of them despairingly conversing together, and, with groaning, talking with one another of what had been done; and appearing to them as a stranger, while their eyes were held that He should not be recognized by them, He mixed with them as they held discourse: but they, narrating to Him the matter of their conversation, said that He was a prophet, mighty in deeds and in words, that had been slain by the chief priests; "And we," say they, "did hope that it was He that should have redeemed Israel."[3] Rightly you hoped: a true thing you hoped

for: in Him is the redemption of Israel. But why are ye in haste? Ye wish to seize it. The following, too, shows us that this was their feeling, that, when the disciples inquired of Him concerning the end, they said to Him, "Wilt Thou at this time be made manifest, and when will be the kingdom of Israel?" For they longed for it now, they wished it now; that is, they wished to seize Him, and to make Him king. But saith He to the disciples (for He had yet to ascend alone), "It is not for you to know the times or seasons which the Father hath put in His own power: but ye shall receive virtue from on high, the Holy Spirit coming upon you, and ye shall be witnesses to me in Jerusalem, and in all Judea and Samaria, and unto the ends of the earth."[4] You wish that I should manifest the kingdom now; let me first gather what I may manifest; you love elevation, and you shall obtain elevation, but follow me through humility. Thus it was also foretold of Him, "And the gathering of the peoples will surround Thee, and for this cause return Thou on high;"[5] that is, that the gatherings of the peoples may surround Thee, that Thou mayest gather many together, return Thou on high. Thus He did; He fed men, and ascended.

4. But why is it said, He escaped? For He could not be held against His will, nor seized against His will, since He could not be recognized against His will. But that you may know that this was done mystically, not of necessity, but of express purpose, you will presently see in the following: that He appeared to the same multitudes that sought Him, said many things in speaking with them, and discoursed much about the bread of heaven; when discoursing about bread, was He not with the same people from whom He had escaped lest He should be held of them? Then, could He not have so acted at that time that He should not be seized by them, just as afterwards when He was speaking with them? Something, therefore, was meant by His escaping. What means, He escaped? His loftiness could not be understood. For of anything which thou hast not understood thou sayest, "It has escaped me." Wherefore, "He escaped again unto the mountain alone,—the first-begotten from the dead, ascending above all heavens, and interceding for us."[6]

5. Meanwhile, He, the one great High Priest being above (He who has entered into that within the veil, the people standing without; for Him that priest under the old law, who did this once a year, did signify): He then be-

---

[1] 1 Cor. xv. 24.   [2] Matt. xxv. 34.   [3] Luke xxiv. 12-21.   [4] Acts i. 6-8.   [5] Ps. vii. 8.   [6] Col. i. 18; Rom. viii. 34.

ing above, what were the disciples enduring in the ship? For that ship prefigured the Church while He is on high. For if we do not, in the first place, understand this thing which that ship suffered respecting the Church, those incidents were not significant, but simply transient; but if we see the real meaning of those signs expressed in the Church, it is manifest that the actions of Christ are a kind of speeches. "But when it was late, saith he, His disciples went down to the sea; and when they had entered into a ship, they came over the sea to Capernaum." He declared that as finished quickly, which was done afterwards,—"They came over the sea to Capernaum." He returns to explain how they came; that they passed over by sailing across the lake. And whilst they were sailing to that place to which He has already said they had come, He explains by recapitulation what befell them. "It was now dark, and Jesus had not come to them." Rightly he said "dark," for the light had not come to them. "It was now dark, and Jesus had not come to them." As the end of the world approaches, errors increase, terrors multiply, iniquity increases, infidelity increases; the light, in short, which, by the Evangelist John himself, is fully and clearly shown to be charity, so much so that he says, "Whoso hateth his brother is in darkness;"[1] that light, I say, is very often extinguished; this darkness of enmity between brethren increases, daily increases, and Jesus is not yet come. How does it appear to increase? "Because iniquity will abound, and the love of many will begin to wax cold." Darkness increases, and Jesus is not yet come. Darkness increasing, love waxing cold, iniquity abounding,— these are the waves that agitate the ship; the storms and the winds are the clamors of revilers. Thence love waxes cold; thence the waves do swell, and the ship is tossed.

6. "And a great wind blowing, the sea rose." Darkness was increasing, discernment was diminishing, iniquity was growing. "When, therefore, they had rowed about twenty-five or thirty furlongs." Meanwhile they struggled onward, kept advancing; nor did those winds and storms, and waves and darkness effect either that the ship should not make way, or that it should break in pieces and founder; but amid all these evils it went on. For, notwithstanding iniquity abounds, and the love of many waxes cold, and the waves do swell, the darkness grows and the wind rages, yet the ship is moving forward; "for he that perseveres to the end, the same

shall be saved."[2] Nor is that number of furlongs to be lightly regarded. For it cannot really be that nothing is meant, when it is said that, "when they had rowed twenty-five or thirty furlongs, Jesus came to them." It were enough to say, "twenty-five," so likewise "thirty;" especially as it was an estimate, not an assertion of the narrator. Could the truth be aught endangered by a mere estimate, if he had said nearly thirty furlongs, or nearly twenty-five furlongs? But from twenty-five he made thirty. Let us examine the number twenty-five. Of what does it consist? of what is it made up? Of the quinary, or number five. That number five pertains to the law. The same are the five books of Moses, the same are those five porches containing the sick folk, the same are the five loaves feeding the five thousand men. Accordingly the number twenty-five signifies the law, because five by five—that is, five times five—make twenty-five, or the number five squared. But this law lacked perfection before the gospel came. Moreover, perfection is comprised in the number six. Therefore in six days God finished, or *perfected*, the world, and the same five are multiplied by six, that the law may be completed by the gospel, that six times five become thirty. To them that fulfill the law, therefore, Jesus comes. And how does He come? Walking upon the waves, keeping all the swellings of the world under His feet, pressing down all its heights. Thus it goes on, so long as time endures, so long as the ages roll. Tribulations increase, calamities increase, sorrows increase, all these swell and mount up: Jesus passeth on treading upon the waves.

7. And yet so great are the tribulations, that even they who have trusted in Jesus, and who strive to persevere unto the end, greatly fear lest they fail; while Christ is treading the waves, and trampling down the world's ambitions and heights, the Christian is sorely afraid. Were not these things foretold him? Justly "they were afraid," too, at seeing Jesus walking on the waves; like as Christians, though having hope in the world to come, are frequently disquieted at the crash of human affairs, when they see the loftiness of this world trampled down. They open the Gospel, they open the Scriptures, and they find all these things there foretold; that this is the Lord's doing. He tramples down the heights of the world, that He may be glorified by the humble. Concerning whose loftiness it is foretold: 'Thou shalt destroy strongest cities," and "the spears of the enemy have

---

[1] 1 John ii. 11.

[2] Matt. xxiv. 12.

come to an end, and Thou hast destroyed cities."[1] Why then are ye afraid, O Christians? Christ speaks: "It is I; be not afraid." Why are ye alarmed at these things? Why are ye afraid? I have foretold these things, I do them, they must necessarily be done. "It is I; be not afraid. Therefore they would receive Him into the ship." Recognizing Him and rejoicing, they are freed from their fears. "And immediately the ship was at the land to which they went." There is an end made at the land; from the watery to the solid, from the agitated to the firm, from the way to the goal.

8. "On the next day the multitude that stood on the other side of the sea," whence the disciples had come, "saw that there was none other boat there, save that one whereinto His disciples were entered, and that Jesus went not with His disciples into the boat, but that His disciples were gone away alone; but there came other boats from Tiberias, nigh unto the place where they did eat bread, giving thanks to the Lord: when, therefore, the multitudes saw that Jesus was not there, nor His disciples, they also took shipping, and came to Capernaum seeking Jesus." Yet they got some knowledge of so great a miracle. For they saw that the disciples had gone into the ship alone, and that there was not another ship there. But there came boats also from near to that place where they did eat bread; in these the multitudes followed Him. He had not then embarked with His disciples, and there was not another ship there. How, then, was Jesus on a sudden beyond the sea, unless that He walked upon the sea to show a miracle?

9. "And when the multitudes had found Him." Behold, He presents Himself to the people from whom He had escaped into the mountain, afraid that He should be taken of them by force. In every way He proves to us and gives us to know that all these things are said in a mystery, and done in a great sacrament (or mystery) to signify something important. Behold, that is He who had escaped the crowds unto the mountain; is He not speaking with the same crowds? Let them hold Him now; let them now make Him a king. "And when they had found Him on the other side of the sea, they said unto Him, Rabbi, when camest Thou hither?"

10. After the sacrament of the miracle, He introduces discourse, that, if possible, they who have been fed may be further fed, that He may with discourse fill their minds, whose bellies He filled with the loaves, provided they

take in. And if they do not, let that be taken up which they do not receive, that the fragments may not be lost. Wherefore let Him speak, and let us hear. " Jesus answered and said Verily, verily, I say unto you, ye seek me, not because ye saw the signs, but because ye have eaten of my loaves." Ye seek me for the sake of the flesh not for the sake of the spirit. How many seek Jesus for no other object but that He may bestow on them a temporal benefit! One has a business on hand, he seeks the intercession of the clergy; another is oppressed by one more powerful than himself, he flies to the church. Another desires intervention in his behalf with one with whom he has little influence. One in this way, one in that, the church is daily filled with such people. Jesus is scarcely sought after for Jesus' sake. "Ye seek me, not because ye have seen the signs, but because ye have eaten of my loaves. Labor not for the meat which perisheth, but for that which endureth unto eternal life." Ye seek me for something else, seek me for my own sake. For He insinuates the truth, that Himself is that meat: this shines out clearly in the sequel. "Which the Son of man will give you." Thou didst expect, I believe, again to eat bread, again to sit down, again to be gorged. But He had said, "Not the meat which perisheth, but that which endureth unto eternal life," in the same manner as it was said to that Samaritan woman: "If thou knewest who it is that asketh of thee drink, thou wouldest perhaps have asked of Him, and He would give thee living water." When she said, "Whence hast thou, since thou hast nothing to draw with, and the well is deep?" He answered the Samaritan woman: " If thou knewest who it is that asketh of thee drink, thou wouldst have asked of Him, and He would give thee water, whereof whoso drinketh shall thirst no more; for whoso drinketh of this water shall thirst again." And she was glad and would receive, as if no more to suffer thirst of body, being wearied with the labor of drawing water. And so, during a conversation of this kind, He comes to spiritual drink. Entirely in this manner also here.

11. Therefore "this meat, not that which perisheth, but that which endureth unto everlasting life, which the Son of man shall give unto you; for Him hath God the Father sealed." Do not take this Son of man as you take other sons of men, of whom it is said, "And the sons of men will trust in the protection of Thy wings."[2] This Son of man

---

is separated by a certain grace of the spirit; Son of man according to the flesh, taken out from the number of men: He is the Son of man. This Son of man is also the Son of God; this man is even God. In another place, when questioning His disciples, He saith: "Whom do men say that I, the Son of man, am? And they answered, Some John, some Elias, some Jeremias, or one of the prophets. And He said unto them, But whom say ye that I am? Peter answered, Thou art the Christ, the S n of the living God."[1] He declared Himself Son of man, Peter declared Him the Son of the living God. Most fitly did He mention that which in mercy He had manifested Himself to be; most fitly did the other mention that which He continues to be in glory. The Word of God commends to our attention His own humility: the man acknowledged the glory of his Lord. And indeed, brethren, I think that this is just. He humbled Himself for us, let us glorify Him. For not for Himself is He Son of man, but for us. Therefore was He Son of man in that way, when "the Word was made flesh, and dwelt among us." For to that end "God the Father sealed Him." What is to seal, but to put some particular mark? To seal is to impress some mark which cannot be confounded with the rest. To seal is to put a mark on a thing. When thou puttest a mark on anything, thou doest so lest it might be confused with other things, and thou shouldst not be able to recognize it. "The Father," then, "hath sealed Him." What is that, "hath sealed"? Bestowed on Him something peculiar, which puts Him out of comparison with all other men. For that reason it is said of Him, "God, even Thy God, hath anointed Thee with the oil of gladness above Thy fellows."[2] What is it then to seal, but to have Him excepted? This is the import of "above Thy fellows." And so, do not, saith He, despise me because I am the Son of man, but seek from me, "not the meat that perisheth, but that which endureth to eternal life." For I am the Son of man in such manner as not to be one of you: I am Son of man in such manner that God the Father sealed me. What does that mean, He "sealed me"? Gave me something peculiarly my own, that I should not be confounded with mankind, but that mankind should be delivered by me.

12. "They said therefore unto Him, What shall we do, that we may work the works of God?" For He had said to them, "Labor not for the meat which perisheth, but for that which endureth unto eternal life." "What shall we do?" they ask; by observing what, shall we be able to fulfill this precept? "Jesus answered and said unto them, This is the work of God, that ye believe on Him whom He has sent." This is then to eat the meat, not that which perisheth, but that which endureth unto eternal life. To what purpose dost thou make ready teeth and stomach? Believe, and thou hast eaten already. Faith is indeed distinguished from works, even as the apostle says, "that a man is justified by faith without the works of the law:"[3] there are works which appear good, without faith in Christ; but they are not good, because they are not referred to that end in which works are good; "for Christ is the end of the law for righteousness to every one that believeth."[4] For that reason, He willeth not to distinguish faith from work, but declared faith itself to be work. For it is that same faith that worketh by love.[5] Nor did He say, This is your work; but, "This is the work of God, that ye believe on Him whom He has sent;" so that he who glories, may glory in the Lord. And because He invited them to faith, they, on the other hand, were still asking for signs by which they might believe. See if the Jews do not ask for signs. "They said therefore unto Him, What sign doest thou, that we may see and believe thee? what dost thou work?" Was it a trifle that they were fed with five loaves? They knew this indeed, but they preferred manna from heaven to this food. But the Lord Jesus declared Himself to be such an one, that He was superior to Moses. For Moses dared not say of Himself that He gave, "not the meat which perisheth, but that which endureth to eternal life." Jesus promised something greater than Moses gave. By Moses indeed was promised a kingdom, and a land flowing with milk and honey, temporal peace, abundance of children, health of body, and all other things, temporal goods indeed, yet in figure spiritual; because in the Old Testament they were promised to the old man. They considered therefore the things promised by Moses, and they considered the things promised by Christ. The former promised a full belly on the earth, but of the meat which perisheth; the latter promised, "not the meat which perisheth, but that which endureth unto eternal life." They gave attention to Him that promised the more, but just as if they did not yet see Him do greater things. They considered therefore what sort of works Moses had done, and they wished

---

[1] Matt. xvi. 13-16.　　[2] Ps. xlv. 8.　　[3] Rom. iii. 28.　　[4] Rom. x. 4.　　[5] Gal. v. 6.

yet some greater works to be done by Him who promised them such great things. What, say they, doest thou, that we may believe thee? And that thou mayest know that they compared those former miracles with this, and so judged these miracles which Jesus did as being less; "Our fathers," say they, "did eat manna in the wilderness." But what is manna? Perhaps ye despise it. "As it is written, He gave them manna to eat." By Moses our fathers received bread from heaven, and Moses did not say to them, "Labor for the meat which perisheth not." Thou promisest "meat which perisheth not, but which endureth to eternal life;" and yet thou workest not such works as Moses did. He gave, not barley loaves, but manna from heaven.

13. "Then Jesus said unto them, Verily, verily, I say unto you, not Moses gave you bread from heaven, but my Father gave you bread from heaven. For the true bread is He that cometh down from heaven, and giveth life to the world." The true bread then is He that giveth life to the world; and the same is the meat of which I have spoken a little before,—"Labor not for the meat which perisheth, but for that which endureth unto eernal life." Therefore, both that manna signified this meat, and all those signs were signs of me. Ye have longed for signs of me; do ye despise Him that was signified? Not Moses then gave bread from heaven: God gives bread. But what bread? Manna, perhaps? No, but the bread which manna signified, namely, the Lord Jesus Himself. My Father giveth you the true bread. "For the bread of God is He that cometh down from heaven, and giveth life to the world. Then said they unto Him, Lord, evermore give us this bread." Like that Samaritan woman, to whom it was said, "Whoso drinketh of this water shall never thirst." She, immediately understanding it in reference to the body, and wishing to be rid of want, said, "Give me, O Lord, of this water;" in the same manner also these said, "O Lord, give us this bread;" which may refresh us, and yet not fail.

14. "And Jesus said unto them, I am the Bread of Life: he that cometh to me shall never hunger; and he that believeth on me shall never thirst." "He that cometh to me;" this is the same thing as "He that believeth on me;" and "shall never hunger" is to be understood to mean the same thing as "shall never thirst." For by both is signified that eternal sufficiency in which there is no want. You desire bread from heaven; you have it before you, and yet you do not eat. "But I said unto you, that ye

also have seen me, and ye believed not." But I have not on that account lost my people. "For hath your unbelief made the faith of God of none effect?"[1] For, see thou what follows: "All that the Father giveth me shall come to me; and him that cometh to me, I will not cast out of doors." What kind of within is that, whence there is no going out of doors? Noble interior, sweet retreat! O secret dwelling without weariness, without the bitterness of evil thoughts, without the solicitings of temptations and the interruptions of griefs! Is it not that secret dwelling whither shall enter that well-deserving servant, to whom the Lord will say, "Enter thou into the joy of thy Lord?"[2]

15. "And him that will come to me, I will not cast out. For I came down from heaven, not to do mine own will, but the will of Him that sent me." Is it for that reason that Thou wilt not cast out him that shall come unto Thee, because Thou hast descended from heaven, not to do Thine own will, but the will of Him that sent Thee? Great mystery! I beseech you, let us knock together; something may come forth to us which may feed us, according to that which has delighted us. That great and sweet secret dwelling-place: "He that will come to me." Give heed, give heed, and weigh the matter: "He that will come unto me, I will not cast out." Why? "Because I came down from heaven, not to do my own will, but the will of Him that sent me." Is it then the very reason why Thou castest not out him that cometh unto Thee, that Thou camest down from heaven, not to do Thy own will, but the will of Him that sent Thee? The very reason. Why do we ask whether it be the same? The same it is; Himself says it. For it would not be right in us to suspect Him to mean other than He says, "Whoso will come to me, I will not cast out." And, as if thou askedst, wherefore? He answered, "Because I came not to do my own will, but the will of Him that sent me." I am afraid that the reason why the soul went forth away from God is, that it was proud; nay, I do not doubt it. For it is written, "Pride is the beginning of all sin; and the beginning of man's pride is a falling away from God." It is written, it is firm and sure, it is true. And hence what is said of proud mortal man, clad in the tattered rags of the flesh, weighed down with the weight of a corruptible body, and withal extolling himself, and forgetting with what skin-coat he is clothed,—what, I ask, saith the Scripture to him?

---

[1] Rom. iii. 3. [2] Matt. xxv. 23.

"Why is dust and ashes proud?" Why proud! Let the Scripture tell why. "Because in his life he put forth his inmost parts."[1] What is "put forth," but "threw afar off"? This is to go forth away. For to enter within, is to long after the inmost parts; to put forth the inmost parts, is to go forth away. The proud man puts forth the inmost parts, the humble man earnestly desires the inmost parts. If we are cast out by pride, let us return by humility.

16. Pride is the source of all diseases, because pride is the source of all sins. When a physician removes a disorder from the body, if he merely cures the malady produced by some particular cause, but not the cause itself, he seems to heal the patient for a time, but while the cause remains, the disease will repeat itself. For example, to speak of this more expressly, some humor in the body produces a scurf or sores; there follows a high fever, and not a little pain; certain remedies are applied to repress the scurf, and to allay that heat of the sore; the remedies are applied, and they do good; thou seest the man who was full of sores and scurf healed; but because that humor was not expelled, it returns again to ulcers. The physician, perceiving this, purges away the humor, removes the cause, and there will be no more sores. Whence doth iniquity abound? From pride. Cure pride and there will be no more iniquity. Consequently, that the cause of all diseases might be cured, namely, pride, the Son of God came down and was made low. Why art thou proud, O man? God, for thee, became low. Thou wouldst perhaps be ashamed to imitate a lowly man; at any rate, imitate the lowly God. The Son of God came in the character of a man and was made low. Thou art taught to become humble, not of a man to become a brute. He, being God, became man; do thou, O man, recognize that thou art man. Thy whole humility is to know thyself. Therefore because God teaches humility, He said, "I came not to do my own will, but the will of Him that sent me." For this is the commendation of humility. Whereas pride doeth its own will, humility doeth the will of God. Therefore, "Whoso cometh to me, I will not cast him out." Why? "Because I came not to do my own will, but the will of Him that sent me." I came humble, I came to teach humility, I came a master of humility: he that cometh to me is made one body with me; he that cometh to me becomes humble; he who adhereth to me will be humble, because he doeth not his own will, but the will of God; and therefore he shall not be cast out, for when he was proud he was cast out.

17. See those inner things commended to us in the psalm: "But the sons of men will put their trust in the covering of Thy wings." See what it is to enter within; see what it is to flee for refuge to His protection; see what it is to run even under the Father's lash, for He scourgeth every son whom He receiveth. "But the sons of men shall put their trust under the cover of Thy wings." What is within? "They shall be filled with the plenteousness of Thy house," when Thou shalt have sent them within, entering into the joy of their Lord; "they shall be filled with the plenteousness of Thy house; and Thou shalt give them to drink of the stream of Thy pleasure. For with Thee is the fountain of life." Not away without Thee, but within with Thee, is the fountain of life. "And in Thy light we shall see light. Show Thy mercy upon them that know Thee, and Thy righteousness to them that are of upright heart." They who follow the will of their Lord, not seeking their own, but the things of the Lord Jesus Christ, they are the upright in heart, their feet shall not be moved. For "God is good to Israel, to the upright in heart. But, as for me, says he, my feet were almost moved." Why? "Because I was jealous at sinners, looking at the peace of sinners."[2] To whom is God good then, unless to the upright in heart? For God was displeasing to me when my heart was crooked. Why displeasing? Because He gave happiness to the wicked, and therefore my feet tottered, as if I had served God in vain. For this reason, then, my feet were almost moved, because I was not upright of heart. What then is upright in heart? Following the will of God. One man is prosperous, another man toils; the one lives wickedly and yet is prosperous, the other lives rightly and is distressed. Let not him that lives rightly and is in distress be angry; he has within what the prosperous man has not: let him therefore not be saddened, nor vex himself, nor faint. That prosperous man has gold in his own chest; this other has God in his conscience. Compare now gold and God, chest and conscience. The former has that which perishes, and has it where it will perish; the latter has God, who cannot perish, and has Him there whence He cannot be taken away: only if he is upright in heart; for then He enters within and goeth not out. For that reason, what said he? "For with Thee is the fountain of life:"

---

[1] Ecclus. x. 14, 15.

[2] Ps. lxxiii. 1, 2.

not with us. We must therefore enter within, that we may live; we must not be, as it were, content to perish, nor willing to be satisfied of our own, to be dried up, but we must put our mouth to the very fountain, where the water fails not. Because Adam wished to live by his own counsel, he, too, fell through him who had fallen before through pride, who invited him to drink of the cup of his own pride. Wherefore, because "with Thee is the fountain of life, and in Thy light we shall see light," let us drink within, let us see within. Why was there a going out thence? Hear why: "Let not the foot of pride come to me." Therefore he, to whom the foot of pride came, went out. Show that therefore he went out. "And let not the hands of sinners move me;" because of the foot of pride. Why sayest thou this? "They are fallen, all they that work iniquity." Where are they fallen? In their very pride. "They were driven out, and they could not stand"[1] If, then, pride drove them out who were not able to stand, humility sends them in who can stand for ever. For this reason, moreover, he who said, "The bones that were brought low shall rejoice,"[2] said before, "Thou shalt give joy and gladness to my hearing." What does he mean by, "to my hearing"? By hearing Thee I am happy; because of Thy voice I am happy; by drinking within I am happy. Therefore do I not fall; therefore "the bones that were brought low will rejoice;" therefore "the friend of the Bridegroom standeth and heareth Him;" therefore he stands, because he hears. He drinks of the fountain within, therefore he stands. They who willed not to drink of the fountain within, "there are they fallen: they were driven, they were not able to stand."

18. Thus, the teacher of humility came not to do His own will, but the will of Him that sent Him. Let us come to Him, enter in unto Him, be ingrafted into Him, that we may not be doing our own will, but the will of God: and He will not cast us out, because we are His members, because He willed to be our head by teaching us humility. Finally, hear Himself discoursing: "Come unto me, ye who labor and are heavy laden: take my yoke upon you, and learn of me; for I am meek and lowly of heart:" and when ye have learned this, "ye shall find rest for your souls,"[3] from which ye cannot be cast out; "because I am come down from heaven, not to do my own will, but the will of Him that sent me;" I teach humility; none but the humble can come unto me. Only pride casteth out; how can he go out who keeps humility and falls not away from the truth? So much as could be said about the hidden sense has now been said, brethren: this sense is hidden enough, and I know not whether I have drawn out and shaped in suitable words for you, why it is that He casteth not out him that cometh unto Him; because He came not to do His own will, but the will of Him that sent Him.

19. "And this," saith He, "is the will of the Father that sent, that of all that He hath given me I should lose nothing." He that keeps humility was given to Him; the same He receives: he that keeps not humility is far from the Master of humility. "That of all which He hath given me, I should lose nothing." "So it is not the will of your Father that one of these little ones should perish." Of the proud, there may perish; but of the little ones, none perisheth; because, "if ye will not become as this little one, ye shall not enter into the kingdom of heaven." "Of all that the Father hath given me, I should lose nothing, but I will raise it up again on the last day." See how here He delineates that twofold resurrection. "He that cometh unto me" immediately rises again, being made humble in my members; but I will raise him up again on the last day also according to the flesh. "For this is the will of my Father that sent me, that every one who seeth the Son, and believeth on Him, may have eternal life; and I will raise him up on the last day." He said above, "Whoso heareth my word, and believeth Him that sent me:" but now, "Whoso seeth the Son, and believeth on Him." He has not said, seeth the Son, and believeth on the Father; for to believe on the Son is the same thing as to believe on the Father. Because, "even as the Father hath life in Himself, so hath He given also to the Son to have life in Himself. That every one who seeth the Son, and believeth on Him, may have eternal life:" by believing and by passing unto life, just as by that first resurrection. And, because that is not the only resurrection, He saith, "And I will raise him up at the last day."

---

[1] Ps. xxxvi. 8-13.   [2] Ps. li. 10.   [3] Matt. xi. 28, 29.

TRACTATE XXVI.

CHAPTER VI. 41–59.

1. WHEN our Lord Jesus Christ, as we have heard in the Gospel when it was read, had said that He was Himself the bread which came down from heaven, the Jews murmured and said, "Is not Jesus the son of Joseph, whose father and mother we know? how is it then that he saith, I came down from heaven?" These Jews were far off from the bread of heaven, and knew not how to hunger after it. They had the jaws of their heart languid; with open ears they were deaf, they saw and stood blind. This bread, indeed, requires the hunger of the inner man: and hence He saith in another place, "Blessed are they that hunger and thirst after right-eousness, for they shall be satisfied."[1] But the Apostle Paul says that Christ is for us righteousness.[2] And, consequently, he that hungers after this bread, hungers after right-eousness,—that righteousness however which cometh down from heaven, the righteousness that God gives, not that which man works for himself. For if man were not making a righteousness for himself, the same apostle would not have said of the Jews: "For, being ignorant of the righteousness of God, and wishing to establish their own righteousness, they are not subject to the righteousness of God."[3] Of such were these who understood not the bread that cometh down from heaven; because being satisfied with their own right-eousness, they hungered not after the right-eousness of God. What is this, God's right-eousness and man's righteousness? God's righteousness here means, not that wherein God is righteous, but that which God bestows on man, that man may be righteous through God. But again, what was the righteousness of those Jews? A righteousness wrought of their own strength on which they presumed, and so declared themselves as if they were fulfillers of the law by their own virtue. But no man fulfills the law but he whom grace assists, that is, whom the bread that cometh down from heaven assists. "For the fulfill-ing of the law," as the apostle says in brief, "is charity."[4] Charity, that is, love, not of money, but of God; love, not of earth nor of heaven, but of Him who made heaven and earth. Whence can man have that love? Let us hear the same: "The love of God," saith he, "is shed abroad in our hearts by the Holy Spirit which is given unto us."[5] Where-fore, the Lord, about to give the Holy Spirit, said that Himself was the bread that came down from heaven, exhorting us to believe on Him. For to believe on Him is to eat the living bread. He that believes eats; he is sated invisibly, because invisibly is he born again. A babe within, a new man within. Where he is made new, there he is satisfied with food.

2. What then did the Lord answer to such murmurers? "Murmur not among your-selves." As if He said, I know why ye are not hungry, and do not understand nor seek after this bread. "Murmur not among your-selves: no man can come unto me, except the Father that sent me draw him." Noble ex-cellence of grace! No man comes unless drawn. There is whom He draws, and there is whom He draws not; why He draws one and draws not another, do not desire to judge, if thou desirest not to err. Accept it at once and then understand; thou art not yet drawn? Pray that thou mayest be drawn. What do we say here, brethren? If we are "drawn" to Christ, it follows that we believe against our will; so then is force applied, not the will moved. A man can come to Church unwill-ingly, can approach the altar unwillingly, par-take of the sacrament unwillingly: but he cannot believe unless he is willing. If we believed with the body, men might be made to believe against their will. But believing is not a thing done with the body. Hear the apostle: "With the heart man believeth unto righteousness." And what follows? "And with the mouth confession is made unto sal-vation."[6] That confession springs from the root of the heart. Sometimes thou hearest a man confessing, and knowest not whether he believes. But thou oughtest not to call him one confessing, if thou shouldest judge him to be one not believing. For to confess is this, to utter the thing that thou hast in thy heart: if thou hast one thing in thy heart, and another thing on thy tongue, thou art speak-ing, not confessing. Since, then, with the heart man believeth on Christ, which no man assuredly does against his will, and since he that is drawn seems to be as if forced against

---

[1] Matt. v. 6.   [2] 1 Cor. i. 30.
[3] Rom. x. 3.   [4] Rom. xiii. 10.   [5] Rom. v. 5.   [6] Rom. x. 10.

his will, how are we to solve this question, "No man cometh unto me, except the Father that sent me draw him"?.

3. If he is drawn, saith some one, he comes unwillingly. If he comes unwillingly, then he believes not; but if he believes not, neither does he come. For we do not run to Christ on foot, but by believing; nor is it by a motion of the body, but by the inclination of the heart that we draw nigh to Him. This is why that woman who touched the hem of His garment touched Him more than did the crowd that pressed Him. Therefore the Lord said, "Who touched me?" And the disciples wondering said, "The multitude throng Thee, and press Thee, and sayest Thou, Who touched me?"[1] And He repeated it, "Somebody hath touched me." That woman touched, the multitude pressed. What is "touched," except "believed"? Whence also He said to that woman that wished to throw herself at His feet after His resurrection: "Touch me not; for I am not yet ascended to the Father."[2] Thou thinkest me to be that alone which thou seest; "touch me not." What is this? Thou supposest that I am that alone which I appear to thee: do not thus believe; that is, "touch me not; for I am not yet ascended to the Father." To thee I am not ascended, for thence I never departed. She touched Him not while He stood on the earth; how then could she touch Him while ascending to the Father? Thus, however, thus He willed Himself to be touched; thus He is touched by those by whom He is profitably touched, ascending to the Father, abiding with the Father, equa to the Father.

4. Thence also He says here, if thou turn thy attention to it, "No man cometh to me except he whom the Father shall draw." Do not think that thou art drawn against thy will. The mind is drawn also by love. Nor ought we to be afraid, lest perchance we be censured in regard to this evangelic word of the Holy Scriptures by men who weigh words, but are far removed from things, most of all from divine things; and lest it be said to us, "How can I believe with the will if I am drawn?" I say it is not enough to be drawn by the will; thou art drawn even by delight. What is it to be drawn by delight? "Delight thyself in the Lord, and He shall give thee the desires of thy heart."[3] There is a pleasure of the heart to which that bread of heaven is sweet. Moreover, if it was right in the poet to say, "Every man is drawn by his own pleasure,"[4] —not necessity, but pleasure; not obligation,

but delight,—how much more boldly ought we to say that a man is drawn to Christ when he delights in the truth, when he delights in blessedness, delights in righteousness, delights in everlasting life, all which Christ is? Or is it the case that, while the senses of the body have their pleasures, the mind is left without pleasures of its own? If the mind has no pleasures of its own, how is it said, "The sons of men shall trust under the cover of Thy wings: they shall be well satisfied with the fullness of Thy house; and Thou shalt give them drink from the river of Thy pleasure. For with Thee is the fountain of life; and in Thy light shall we see light"?[5] Give me a man that loves, and he feels what I say. Give me one that longs, one that hungers, one that is travelling in this wilderness, and thirsting and panting after the fountain of his eternal home; give such, and he knows what I say. But if I speak to the cold and indifferent, he knows not what I say. Such were those who murmured among themselves. "He whom the Father shall draw," saith He, "cometh unto me."

5 But what is this, "Whom the Father shall draw," when Christ Himself draws? Why did He say, "Whom the Father shall draw"? If we must be drawn, let us be drawn by Him to whom one who loves says, "We will run after the odor of Thine ointment."[6] But let us, brethren, turn our minds to, and, as far as we can, apprehend how He would have us understand it. The Father draws to the Son those who believe on the Son, because they consider that God is His Father. For God begat the Son equal to Himself, so that he who ponders, and in his faith feels and muses that He on whom he has believed is equal to the Father, this same is drawn of the Father to the Son. Arius believed the Son to be creature: the Father drew not him; for he that believes not the Son to be equal to the Father, considers not the Father. What sayest thou, Arius? What, O heretic, dost thou speak? What is Christ? Not very God, saith he, but one whom very God has made. The Father has not drawn thee, for thou hast not understood the Father, whose Son thou deniest: it is not the Son Himself but something else that thou art thinking of. Thou art neither drawn by the Father nor drawn to the Son; for the Son is very different from what thou sayest. Photius said, "Christ is only a man, he is not also God." The Father hath not drawn him who thus believes. One whom the Father has drawn says: "Thou art Christ, Son of the living

---

[1] Luke viii. 45.   [2] John xx. 17.   [3] Ps. xxxvii. 4.
[4] *Trahit sua quemque voluptas.*—Virg. Ec. 2.
[5] Ps. xxxvi. 8.   [6] Cant. i. 3.

God." Not as a prophet, not as John, not as some great and just man, but as the only, the equal, " Thou art Christ, Son of the living God." See that he was drawn, and drawn by the Father. "Blessed art thou, Simon Bar-jonas: for flesh and blood hath not revealed it to thee, but my Father who is in heaven."[1] This revealing is itself the drawing. Thou holdest out a green twig to a sheep, and thou drawest it. Nuts are shown to a child, and he is attracted; he is drawn by what he runs to, drawn by loving it, drawn without hurt to the body, drawn by a cord of the heart. If, then, these things, which among earthly delights and pleasures are shown to them that love them, draw them, since it is true that "every man is drawn by his own pleasure," does not Christ, revealed by the Father, draw? For what does the soul more strongly desire than the truth? For what ought it to have a greedy appetite, with which to wish that there may be within a healthy palate for judging the things that are true, unless it be to eat and drink wisdom, righteousness, truth, eternity?

6. But where will this be? There better, there more truly, there more fully. For here we can more easily hunger than be satisfied, especially if we have good hope: for "Blessed," saith He, "are they that hunger and thirst after righteousness," that is here; "for they shall be filled," that is there. Therefore when He had said, "No man cometh unto me except the Father that sent me draw him," what did He subjoin? "And I will raise him up in the last day." I render unto him what he loves, what he hopes for: he will see what, not as yet by seeing, he has believed; he shall eat that which he hungers after; he shall be filled with that which he thirsts after. Where? In the resurrection of the dead; for "I will raise him up on the last day."

7. For it is written in the prophets, "And they shall all be taught of God." Why have I said this, O Jews? The Father has not taught you; how can ye know me? For all the men of that kingdom shall be taught of God, not learn from men. And though they do learn from men, yet what they understand is given them within, flashes within, is revealed within. What do men that proclaim tidings from without? What am I doing even now while I speak? I am pouring a clatter of words into your ears. What is that that I say or that I speak, unless He that is within reveal it? Without is the planter of the tree, within is the tree's Creator. He that planteth

and He that watereth work from without: this is what we do. But "neither he that planteth is anything, nor he that watereth; but God that giveth the increase."[2] That is, "they shall be all taught of God." All who? "Every one who has heard and learned of the Father cometh unto me." See how the Father draws: He delights by teaching, not by imposing a necessity. Behold how He draws: "They shall be all taught of God." This is God's drawing. "Every man that hath heard, and hath learned of the Father, cometh unto me." This is God's drawing.

8. What then, brethren? If every man who has heard and learned of the Father, the same cometh unto Christ, has Christ taught nothing here? What shall we say to this, that men who have not seen the Father as their teacher have seen the Son? The Son spake, but the Father taught. I, being a man, whom do I teach? Whom, brethren, but him who has heard my word? If I, being a man, do teach him who hears my word, the Father also teacheth him who hears His word. And if the Father teacheth him that hears His word, ask what Christ is, and thou wilt find the word of the Father. "In the beginning was the Word." Not in the beginning God made the Word, just as "in the beginning God made the heaven and the earth."[3] Behold how that He is not a creature. Learn to be drawn to the Son by the Father: that the Father may teach thee, hear His Word. What Word of Him, sayest thou, do I hear? "In the beginning was the Word" (it is not "was made," but "was"), "and the Word was with God, and the Word was God." How can men abiding in the flesh hear such a Word? "The Word was made flesh, and dwelt among us."

9. He Himself explains this also, and shows us His meaning when He said, "He that hath heard and learned of the Father cometh unto me." He forthwith subjoined what we were able to conceive: "Not that any man hath seen the Father, save he who is of God, he hath seen the Father." What is that which He saith? I have seen the Father, you have not seen the Father; and yet ye come not unto me unless ye are drawn by the Father. And what is it for you to be drawn by the Father but to learn of the Father? What is to learn of the Father but to hear of the Father? What is to hear of the Father but to hear the Word of the Father—that is, to hear me? In case, therefore, when I say to you, "Every man that hath heard and learned of the Father," you should say within

---

[1] Matt. xvi. 16, 17.　　　[2] 1 Cor. iii. 7.　　　[3] Gen. i. 1.

yourselves, But we have never seen the Father, how could we learn of the Father? hear from myself: "Not that any man hath seen the Father, save He who is of God, He hath seen the Father." I know the Father, I am from Him; but in that manner in which the Word is from Him where the Word is, not that which sounds and passes away, but that which remains with the speaker and attracts the hearer.

10. Let what follows admonish us: "Verily, verily, I say unto you, he that believeth on me hath eternal life." He willed to reveal Himself, what He was: He might have said in brief, He that believeth on me hath me. For Christ is Himself true God and eternal life. Therefore, he that believeth on me, saith He, goeth into me; and he that goeth into me, hath me. But what is the meaning of "to have me"? To have eternal life. Eternal life took death upon itself; eternal life willed to die; but of thee, not of itself; of thee it received that whereby it may die in thy behalf. Of men, indeed, He took flesh, but yet not in the manner of men. For having His Father in heaven, He chose a mother on earth; both there begotten without mother, and here born without father. Accordingly, life took upon itself death, that life might slay death. "For he that believeth on me," saith He, "hath eternal life:" not what is open, but what is hid. For eternal life is the Word, that "in the beginning was with God, and the Word was God, and the life was the light of men." The same eternal life gave eternal life also to the flesh which it assumed. He came to die; but on the third day He rose again. Between the Word taking flesh and the flesh rising again, death which came between was consumed.

11. "I am," saith He, "the bread of life." And what was the source of their pride? "Your fathers," saith He, "did eat manna in the wilderness, and are dead." What is it whereof ye are proud? "They ate manna, and are dead." Why they ate and are dead? Because they believed that which they saw; what they saw not, they did not understand. Therefore were they "your" fathers, because you are like them. For so far, my brethren, as relates to this visible corporeal death, do not we too die who eat the bread that cometh down from heaven? They died just as we shall die, so far, as I said, as relates to the visible and carnal death of this body. But so far as relates to that death, concerning which the Lord warns us by fear, and in which their fathers died: Moses ate manna, Aaron ate manna, Phinehas ate manna, and many ate manna, who were pleasing to the Lord, and they are not dead. Why? Because they understood the visible food spiritually, hungered spiritually, tasted spiritually, that they might be filled spiritually. For even we at this day receive visible food: but the sacrament is one thing, the virtue of the sacrament another. How many do receive at the altar and die, and die indeed by receiving? Whence the apostle saith, "Eateth and drinketh judgment to himself."[1] For it was not the mouthful given by the Lord that was the poison to Judas. And yet he took it; and when he took it, the enemy entered into him: not because he received an evil thing, but because he being evil received a good thing in an evil way. See ye then, brethren, that ye eat the heavenly bread in a spiritual sense; bring innocence to the altar. Though your sins are daily, at least let them not be deadly. Before ye approach the altar, consider well what ye are to say: "Forgive us our debts, even as we forgive our debtors."[2] Thou forgivest, it shall be forgiven thee: approach in peace, it is bread, not poison. But see whether thou forgivest; for if thou dost not forgive, thou liest, and liest to Him whom thou canst not deceive. Thou canst lie to God, but thou canst not deceive God. He knows what thou doest. He sees thee within, examines thee within, inspects within, judges within, and within He either condemns or crowns. But the fathers of these Jews were evil fathers of evil sons, unbelieving fathers of unbelieving sons, murmuring fathers of murmurers. For in no other thing is that people said to have offended the Lord more than in murmuring against God. And for that reason, the Lord, willing to show those men to be the children of such murmurers, thus begins His address to them: "Why murmur ye among yourselves," ye murmurers, children of murmurers? Your fathers did eat manna, and are dead; not because manna was an evil thing, but because they ate it in an evil manner.

12. "This is the bread which cometh down from heaven." Manna signified this bread; God's altar signified this bread. Those were sacraments. In the signs they were diverse; in the thing which was signified they were alike. Hear the apostle: "For I would not that ye should be ignorant, brethren," saith he, "that all our fathers were under the cloud, and all passed through the sea; and were all baptized unto Moses in the cloud and in the sea; and did all eat the same spiritual meat." Of course, the same spiritual meat; for corporally it was another: since they ate

---

[1] 1 Cor. xi. 29.   [2] Matt. vi. 12.

manna, we eat another thing; but the spiritual was the same as that which we eat. But "our" fathers, not the fathers of those Jews; those to whom we are like, not those to whom they were like. Moreover he adds: "And did all drink the same spiritual drink." They one kind of drink, we another, but only in the visible form, which, however, signified the same thing in its spiritual virtue. For how was it that they drank the "same drink"? "They drank," saith he, "of the spiritual Rock that followed them, and that Rock was Christ."[1] Thence the bread, thence the drink. The rock was Christ in sign; the real Christ is in the Word and in flesh. And how did they drink? The rock was smitten twice with a rod; the double smiting signified the two wooden beams of the cross. "This, then, is the bread that cometh down from heaven, that if any man eat thereof, he shall not die." But this is what belongs to the virtue of the sacrament, not to the visible sacrament; he that eateth within, not without; who eateth in his heart, not who presses with his teeth.

13. "I am the living bread, which came down from heaven." For that reason "living," because I came down from heaven. The manna also came down from heaven; but the manna was only a shadow, this is the truth. "If any man eat of this bread, he shall live for ever: and the bread that I will give is my flesh, for the life of the world." When did flesh comprehend this flesh which He called bread? That is called flesh which flesh does not comprehend, and for that reason all the more flesh does not comprehend it, that it is called flesh. For they were terrified at this: they said it was too much for them; they thought it impossible. "Is my flesh," saith He, "for the life of the world." Believers know the body of Christ, if they neglect not to be the body of Christ. Let them become the body of Christ, if they wish to live by the Spirit of Christ. None lives by the Spirit of Christ but the body of Christ. Understand, my brethren, what I mean to say. Thou art a man; thou hast both a spirit and a body. I call that a spirit which is called the soul; that whereby it consists that thou art a man, for thou consistest of soul and body. And so thou hast an invisible spirit and a visible body. Tell me which lives of the other: does thy spirit live of thy body, or thy body of thy spirit? Every man that lives can answer; and he that cannot answer this, I know not whether he lives: what doth every man that lives answer? My body, of course,

lives by my spirit. Wouldst thou then also live by the Spirit of Christ. Be in the body of Christ. For surely my body does not live by thy spirit. My body lives by my spirit, and thy body by thy spirit. The body of Christ cannnot live but by the Spirit of Christ. It is for this that the Apostle Paul, expounding this bread, says: "One bread," saith he, "we being many are one body."[2] O mystery of piety! O sign of unity! O bond of charity! He that would live has where to live, has whence to live. Let him draw near, let him believe; let him be embodied, that he may be made to live. Let him not shrink from the compact of members; let him not be a rotten member that deserves to be cut off; let him not be a deformed member whereof to be ashamed; let him be a fair, fit, and sound member; let him cleave to the body, live for God by God: now let him labor on earth, that hereafter he may reign in heaven.

14. The Jews, therefore, strove among themselves, saying, "How can this man give us his flesh to eat?" They strove, and that among themselves, since they understood not, neither wished to take the bread of concord: "for they who eat such bread do not strive with one another; for we being many are one bread, one body." And by this bread, "God makes people of one sort to dwell in a house."[3]

15. But that which they ask, while striving among themselves, namely, how the Lord can give His flesh to be eaten, they do not immediately hear: but further it is said to them, "Verily, verily, I say unto you, except ye eat the flesh of the Son of man, and drink His blood, ye will have no life in you." How, indeed, it may be eaten, and what may be the mode of eating this bread, ye are ignorant of; nevertheless, "except ye eat the flesh of the Son of man, and drink His blood, ye will not have life in you." He spoke these words, not certainly to corpses, but to living men. Whereupon, lest they, understanding it to mean this life, should strive about this thing also, He going on added, "Whoso eateth my flesh, and drinketh my blood, hath eternal life." Wherefore, he that eateth not this bread, nor drinketh this blood, hath not this life; for men can have temporal life without that, but they can noways have eternal life. He then that eateth not His flesh, nor drinketh His blood, hath no life in him; and he that eateth His flesh, and drinketh His blood, hath life. This epithet, *eternal*, which He used, answers to both. It is not so in the case of that food which we take for the purpose of sustaining

---

[1] 1 Cor. x. 1–4.   [2] 1 Cor. x. 17.   [3] Ps. lxviii. 6.

this temporal life. For he who will not take it shall not live, nor yet shall he who will take it live. For very many, even who have taken it, die; it may be by old age, or by disease, or by some other casualty. But in this food and drink, that is, in the body and blood of the Lord, it is not so. For both he that doth not take it hath no life, and he that doth take it hath life, and that indeed eternal life. And thus He would have this meat and drink to be understood as meaning the fellowship of His own body and members, which is the holy Church in his predestinated, and called, and justified, and glorified saints and believers. Of these, the first is already effected, namely, predestination; the second and third, that is, the vocation and justification, have taken place, are taking place, and will take place; but the fourth, namely, the glorifying, is at present in hope, but a thing future in realization. The sacrament of this thing, namely, of the unity of the body and blood of Christ, is prepared on the Lord's table in some places daily, in some places at certain intervals of days, and from the Lord's table it is taken, by some to life, by some to destruction: but the thing itself, of which it is the sacrament, is for every man to life, for no man to destruction, whosoever shall have been a partaker thereof.

16. But lest they should suppose that eternal life was promised in this meat and drink in such manner that they who should take it should not even now die in the body, He condescended to meet this thought; for when He had said, "He that eateth my flesh, and drinketh my blood, hath eternal life," He forthwith subjoined, "and I will raise him up on the last day." That meanwhile, according to the Spirit, he may have eternal life in that rest into which the spirits of the saints are received; but as to the body, he shall not be defrauded of its eternal life, but, on the contrary, he shall have it in the resurrection of the dead at the last day.

17. "For my flesh," saith He, "is meat indeed, and my blood is drink indeed." For whilst by meat and drink men seek to attain to this, neither to hunger nor thirst, there is nothing that truly affords this, except this meat and drink, which doth render them by whom it is taken immortal and incorruptible; that is, the very fellowship of the saints, where will be peace and unity, full and perfect. Therefore, indeed, it is, even as men of God understood this before us, that our Lord Jesus Christ has pointed our minds to His body and blood in those things, which from being many are reduced to some one thing. For a unity is formed by many grains forming together;

and another unity is effected by the clustering together of many berries.

18. In a word, He now explains how that which He speaks of comes to pass, and what it is to eat His body and to drink His blood. "He that eateth my flesh, and drinketh my blood, dwelleth in me, and I in him." This it is, therefore, for a man to eat that meat and to drink that drink, to dwell in Christ, and to have Christ dwelling in him. Consequently, he that dwelleth not in Christ, and in whom Christ dwelleth not, doubtless neither eateth His flesh [spiritually] nor drinketh His blood [although he may press the sacrament of the body and blood of Christ carnally and visibly with his teeth], but rather doth he eat and drink the sacrament of so great a thing to his own judgment, because he, being unclean, has presumed to come to the sacraments of Christ, which no man taketh worthily except he that is pure: of such it is said, "Blessed are the pure in heart, for they shall see God."[1]

19. "As the living Father hath sent me," saith He, "and I live by the Father; so he that eateth me, even he shall live by me." He says not: As I eat the Father, and live by the Father; so he that eateth me, the same shall live by me. For the Son, who was begotten equal, does not become better by participation of the Father; just as we are made better by participation of the Son, through the unity of His body and blood, which thing that eating and drinking signifies. We live then by Him, by eating Him; that is, by receiving Himself as the eternal life, which we did not have from ourselves. Himself, however, lives by the Father, being sent by Him, because "He emptied Himself, being made obedient even unto the death of the cross."[2] For if we take this declaration, "I live by the Father,"[3] according to that which He says in another place, "The Father is greater than I;" just as we, too, live by Him who is greater than we; this results from His being sent. The sending is in fact the emptying of Himself, and His taking upon Him the form of a servant: and this is rightly understood, while also the Son's equality of nature with the Father is preserved. For the Father is greater than the Son as man, but He has the Son as God equal,—whilst the same is both God and man, Son of God and Son of man, one Christ Jesus. To this effect, if these words are rightly understood, He spoke thus: "As the living Father hath sent me, and I live by the Father; so he that eateth me, even he shall live by me:" just as if He were to say, My emptying of myself (in that He

---

sent me) effected that I should live by the Father; that is, should refer my life to Him as the greater; but that any should live by me is effected by that participation in which he eats me. Therefore, I being humbled, do live by the Father, man being raised up, liveth by me. But if it was said, "I live by the Father," so as to mean, that He is of the Father, not the Father of Him, it was said without detriment to His equality. And yet further, by saying, "And he that eateth me, even he shall live by me," He did not signify that His own equality was the same as our equality, but He thereby showed the grace of the Mediator.

20. "This is the bread that cometh down from heaven;" that by eating it we may live, since we cannot have eternal life from ourselves. Not," saith He, "as your fathers did eat manna, and are dead: he that eateth this bread shall live forever." That those fathers are dead, He would have to be understood as meaning, that they do not live forever. For even they who eat Christ shall certainly die temporally; but they live forever, because Christ is eternal life.

TRACTATE XXVII.

CHAPTER VI. 60–72.

1. WE have just heard out of the Gospel the words of the Lord which follow the former discourse. From these a discourse is due to your ears and minds, and it is not unseasonable to-day; for it is concerning the body of the Lord which He said that He gave to be eaten for eternal life. And He explained the mode of this bestowal and gift of His, in what manner He gave His flesh to eat, saying, "He that eateth my flesh, and drinketh my blood, dwelleth in me, and I in him." The proof that a man has eaten and drank is this, if he abides and is abode in, if he dwells and is dwelt in, if he adheres so as not to be deserted. This, then, He has taught us, and admonished us in mystical words that we may be in His body, in His members under Himself as head, eating His flesh, not abandoning our unity with Him. But most of those who were present, by not understanding Him, were offended; for in hearing these things, they thought only of flesh, that which themselves were. But the apostle says, and says what is true, "To be carnally-minded is death."[1] The Lord gives us His flesh to eat, and yet to understand it according to the flesh is death; while yet He says of His flesh, that therein is eternal life. Therefore we ought not to understand the flesh carnally. As in these words that follow:

2. "Many therefore," not of His enemies, but "of His disciples, when they had heard this, said. This is a hard saying; who can hear it?" If His disciples accounted this saying hard, what must His enemies have thought? And yet so it behoved that to be said which should not be understood by all. The secret of God ought to make men eagerly attentive, not hostile. But these men quickly departed from Him, while the Lord said such things: they did not believe Him to be saying something great, and covering some grace by these words; they understood just according to their wishes, and in the manner of men, that Jesus was able, or was determined upon this, namely, to distribute the flesh with which the Word was clothed, piecemeal, as it were, to those that believe on Him. "This," say they, "is a hard saying; who can hear it?"

3. "But Jesus, knowing in Himself that His disciples murmured at it,"—for they so said these things with themselves that they might not be heard by Him; but He who knew them in themselves, hearing within Himself,—answered and said, "This offends you;" because I said, I give you my flesh to eat, and my blood to drink, this forsooth offends you. "Then what if ye shall see the Son of man ascending where He was before?" What is this? Did He hereby solve the question that perplexed them? Did He hereby uncover the source of their offense? He did clearly, if only they understood. For they supposed that He was going to deal out His body to them; but He said that He was to ascend into heaven, of course, whole: "When ye shall see the Son of man ascending where He was before;" certainly then, at least, you will see that not in the manner you suppose does He dispense His body; certainly then, at least, you will understand that His grace is not consumed by tooth-biting.

---

[1] Rom. vii. 6.

4. And He said, " It is the Spirit that quickeneth; the flesh profiteth nothing." Before we expound this, as the Lord grants us, that other must not be negligently passed over, where He says, " Then what if ye shall see the Son of man ascending where He was before ? " For Christ is the Son of man, of the Virgin Mary. Therefore Son of man He began to be here on earth, where He took flesh from the earth. For which cause it was said prophetically, " Truth is sprung from the earth."[1] Then what does He mean when He says, " When ye shall see the Son of man ascending where He was before " ? For there had been no question if He had spoken thus: " If ye shall see the Son of God ascending where He was before." But since He said, " The Son of man ascending where He was before," surely the Son of man was not in heaven before the time when He began to have a being on earth ? Here, indeed, He said, " where He was before," just as if He were not there at this time when He spoke these words. But in another place He says, " No man has ascended into heaven but He that came down from heaven, the Son of man who is in heaven."[2] He said not " was," but, saith He, " the Son of man who is in heaven." He was speaking on earth, and He declared Himself to be in heaven. And yet He did not speak thus: " No man hath ascended into heaven but He that came down from heaven," the Son of God, " who is in heaven." Whither tends it, but to make us understand that which even in the former discourse I commended to your minds, my beloved, that Christ, both God and man, is one person, not two persons, lest our faith be not a trinity, but a quaternity ? Christ, therefore, is one; the Word, soul and flesh, one Christ; the Son of God and Son of man, one Christ; Son of God always, Son of man in time, yet one Christ in regard to unity of person. In heaven He was when He spoke on earth. He was Son of man in heaven in that manner in which He was Son of God on earth; Son of God on earth in the flesh which He took, Son of man in heaven in the unity of person.

5. What is it, then, that He adds ? " It is the Spirit that quickeneth; the flesh profiteth nothing." Let us say to Him (for He permits us, not contradicting Him, but desiring to know), O Lord, good Master, in what way does the flesh profit nothing, whilst Thou hast said, " Except a man eat my flesh, and drink my blood, he shall not have life in him ? " Or does life profit nothing ? And why are we what we are, but that we may have eternal life, which Thou dost promise by Thy flesh ? Then what means " the flesh profiteth nothing " ? It profiteth nothing, but only in the manner in which they understood it. They indeed understood the flesh, just as when cut to pieces in a carcass, or sold in the shambles; not as when it is quickened by the Spirit. Wherefore it is said that " the flesh profiteth nothing," in the same manner as it is said that " knowledge puffeth up." Then, ought we at once to hate knowledge ? Far from it ! And what means "Knowledge puffeth up " ? Knowledge alone, without charity. Therefore he added, " but charity edifieth."[3] Therefore add thou to knowledge charity, and knowledge will be profitable, not by itself, but through charity. So also here, " the flesh profiteth nothing," only when alone. Let the Spirit be added to the flesh, as charity is added to knowledge, and it profiteth very much. For if the flesh profited nothing, the Word would not be made flesh to dwell among us. If through the flesh Christ has greatly profited us, does the flesh profit nothing ? But it is by the flesh that the Spirit has done somewhat for our salvation. Flesh was a vessel; consider what it held, not what it was. The apostles were sent forth; did their flesh profit us nothing ? If the apostles' flesh profited us, could it be that the Lord's flesh should have profited us nothing ? For how should the sound of the Word come to us except by the voice of the flesh ? Whence should writing come to us ? All these are operations of the flesh, but only when the spirit moves it, as if it were its organ. Therefore " it is the Spirit that quickeneth; the flesh profiteth nothing," as they understood the flesh, but not so do I give my flesh to be eaten.

9. Hence " the words," saith He, " which I have spoken to you are Spirit and life." For we have said, brethren, that this is what the Lord had taught us by the eating of His flesh and drinking of His blood, that we should abide in Him and He in us. But we abide in Him when we are His members, and He abides in us when we are His temple. But that we may be His members, unity joins us together. And what but love can effect that unity should join us together ? And the love of God, whence is it ? Ask the apostle: " The love of God," saith he, " is shed abroad in our hearts by the Holy Spirit which is given to us."[4] Therefore " it is the Spirit that quickeneth," for it is the Spirit that makes living members. Nor does the Spirit make

---

[1] Ps. lxxxv. 12.   [2] John iii. 13.   [3] 1 Cor. viii. 1.   [4] Rom. v. 5.

any members to be living except such as it finds in the body, which also the Spirit itself quickens. For the Spirit which is in thee, O man, by which it consists that thou art a man, does it quicken a member which it finds separated from thy flesh? I call thy soul thy spirit. Thy soul quickeneth only the members which are in thy flesh; if thou takest one away, it is no longer quickened by thy soul, because it is not joined to the unity of thy body. These things are said to make us love unity and fear separation. For there is nothing that a Christian ought to dread so much as to be separated from Christ's body. For if he is separated from Christ's body, he is not a member of Christ; if he is not a member of Christ, he is not quickened by the Spirit of Christ. "But if any man," saith the apostle, "have not the Spirit of Christ, he is none of His."[1] "It is the Spirit," then, "that quickeneth; the flesh profiteth nothing. The words that I have spoken to you are spirit and life." What means "are spirit and life"? They are to be understood spiritually. Hast thou understood spiritually? "They are spirit and life." Hast thou understood carnally? So also "are they spirit and life," but are not so to thee.

7. "But," saith He, "there are some among you that believe not." He said not, There are some among you that understand not; but He told the cause why they understand not "There are some among you that believe not," and therefore they understand not, because they believe not. For the prophet has said, "If ye believe not, ye shall not understand."[2] We are united by faith, quickened by understanding. Let us first adhere to Him through faith, that there may be that which may be quickened by understanding. For he who adheres not resists; he that resists believes not. And how can he that resists be quickened? He is an adversary to the ray of light by which he should be penetrated: he turns not away his eye, but shuts his mind. "There are," then, "some who believe not." Let them believe and open, let them open and be illumined. "For Jesus knew from the beginning who they were that believed, and who should betray Him." For Judas also was there. Some indeed, were offended; but he remained to watch his opportunity, not to understand. And because he remained for that purpose, the Lord kept not silence concerning him. He described him not by name, but neither was He silent about him; that all might fear though only one should perish. But after

He spoke, and distinguished those that believe from those that believe not, He clearly showed the cause why they believed not. "Therefore I said unto you," saith He, "that no man can come unto me except it were given to him of my Father." Hence to believe is also given to us; for certainly to believe is something. And if it is something great, rejoice that thou hast believed, yet be not lifted up; for "What hast thou that thou didst not receive?"[3]

8. "From that time many of His disciples went back, and walked no more with Him." Went back, but after Satan, not after Christ. For our Lord Christ once addressed Peter as Satan, rather because he wished to precede his Lord, and to give counsel that He should not die, He who had come to die, that we might not die for ever; and He says to him, "Get thee behind me, Satan; for thou savorest not the things that be of God, but the things that be of men."[4] He did not drive him back to go after Satan, and so called him Satan; but He made him go behind Himself, that by walking after his Lord he should not be a Satan. But these went back in the same manner as the apostle says of certain women: "For some are turned back after Satan."[5] They walked not further with Him. Behold, cut off from the body, for perhaps they were not in the body, they have lost life. They must be reckoned among the unbelieving, notwithstanding they were called disciples. Not a few, but "many went back." This happened, it may be, for our consolation. For sometimes it happens that a man may declare the truth, and that what he says may not be understood, and so they that hear it are offended and go away. Now the man regrets that he had spoken that truth, and he says to himself, "I ought not to have spoken so, I ought not to have said this." Behold, it happened to the Lord: He spoke, and lost many; He remained with few. But yet He was not troubled, because He knew from the beginning who they were that believed and that believed not. If it happen to us, we are sorely perplexed. Let us find comfort in the Lord, and yet let us speak words with prudence.

9. And now addressing the few that remained: "Then said Jesus to the twelve" (namely, those twelve who remained), "Will ye also," said He, "go away?" Not even Judas departed. But it was already manifest to the Lord why he remained: to us he was made manifest afterwards. Peter answered in behalf of all, one for many, unity for the

---

[1] Rom. viii. 9.   [2] Isa. vii. 9, LXX.   [3] 1 Cor. iv. 7.   [4] Matt. xvi. 23.   [5] 1 Tim. v. 15.

collective whole: "Then Simon Peter answered Him, Lord, to whom shall we go?" Thou drivest us from Thee; give us Thy other self. "To whom shall we go?" If we abandon Thee, to whom shall we go? "Thou hast the words of eternal life." See how Peter, by the gift of God and the renewal of the Holy Spirit, understood Him. How other than because he believed? "Thou hast the words of eternal life." For Thou hast eternal life in the ministration of Thy body and blood. "And we have believed and have known." Not have known and believed, but "believed and known." For we believed in order to know; for if we wanted to know first, and then to believe, we should not be able either to know or to believe What have we believed and known? "That Thou art Christ, the Son of God;" that is, that Thou art that very eternal life, and that Thou givest in Thy flesh and blood only that which Thou art.

10. Then said the Lord Jesus: "Have not I chosen you twelve, and one of you is a devil?" Therefore, should He have said, "I have chosen eleven:" or is a devil also chosen, and among the elect? Persons are wont to be called "elect" by way of praise: or was man elected because some great good was done by him, without his will and knowledge? This belongs peculiarly to God; the contrary is characteristic of the wicked. For as wicked men make a bad use of the good works of God; so, on the contrary, God makes a good use of the evil works of wicked men. How good it is that the members of the body are, as they can be disposed only by God, their author and framer! Nevertheless what evil use doth wantonness make of the eyes? What ill use doth falsehood make of the tongue? Does not the false witness first both slay his own soul with his tongue, and then, after he has destroyed himself, endeavor to injure another? He makes an ill use of the tongue, but the tongue is not therefore an evil thing; the tongue is God's work, but iniquity makes an ill use of that good work of God. How do they use their feet who run into crimes? How do murderers employ their hands? And what ill use do wicked men make of those good creatures of God that lie outside of them? With gold they corrupt judgment and oppress the innocent. Bad men make a bad use of the very light; for by evil living they employ even the very light with which they see into the service of their villanies. A bad man, when going to do a bad deed, wishes the light to shine for him, lest he stumble; he who has already stumbled and fallen within; that which he is afraid of in his body has already befallen him in his

12

heart. Hence, to avoid the tediousness of running through them separately, a bad man makes a bad use of all the good creatures of God: a good man, on the contrary, makes a good use of the evil deeds of wicked men. And what is so good as the one God? Since, indeed, the Lord Himself said, "There is none good, but the one God."[1] By how much He is better, then, by so much the better use He makes of our evil deeds. What worse than Judas? Among all that adhered to the Master, among the twelve, to him was committed the common purse; to him was allotted the dispensing for the poor. Unthankful for so great a favor, so great an honor, he took the money, and lost righteousness: being dead, he betrayed life: Him whom he followed as a disciple, he persecuted as an enemy. All this evil was Judas's; but the Lord employed his evil for good. He endured to be betrayed, to redeem us. Behold, Judas's evil was turned to good. How many martyrs has Satan persecuted! If Satan left off persecuting, we should not to-day be celebrating the very glorious crown of Saint Laurence. If then God employs the evil works of the devil himself for good, what the bad man effects, by making a bad use, is to hurt himself, not to contradict the goodness of God. The Master makes use of that man. And if He knew not how to make use of him, the Master contriver would not have permitted him to be. Therefore, He saith, "One of you is a devil," whilst I have chosen you twelve. This saying, "I have chosen you twelve," may be understood in this way, that twelve is a sacred number. For the honor of that number was not taken away because one was lost, for another was chosen into the place of the one that perished.[2] The number remained a sacred number, a number containing twelve: because they were to make known the Trinity throughout the whole world, that is, throughout the four quarters of the world. That is the reason of the three times four. Judas, then only cut himself off, not profaned the number twelve: he abandoned his Teacher, for God appointed a successor to take his place.

11. All this that the Lord spoke concerning His flesh and blood;—and in the grace of that distribution He promised us eternal life, and that He meant those that eat His flesh and drink His blood to be understood, from the fact of their abiding in Him and He in them; and that they understood not who believed not; and that they were offended through their understanding spiritual things

---

[1] Mark x. 10.   [2] Acts i. 26.

in a carnal sense; and that, while these were offended and perished, the Lord was present for the consolation of the disciples who remained, for proving whom He asked, "Will ye also go away?" that the reply of their steadfastness might be known to us, for He knew that they remained with Him;—let all this, then, avail us to this end, most beloved, that we eat not the flesh and blood of Christ merely in the sacrament, as many evil men do, but that we eat and drink to the participation of the Spirit, that we abide as members in the Lord's body, to be quickened by His Spirit, and that we be not offended, even if many do now with us eat and drink the sacraments in a temporal manner, who shall in the end have eternal torments. For at present Christ's body is as it were mixed on the threshing-floor: "But the Lord knoweth them that are His."[1] If thou knowest what thou threshest, that the substance is there hidden, that the threshing has not consumed what the winnowing has purged; certain are we, brethren, that all of us who are in the Lord's body, and abide in Him, that He also may abide in us, have of necessity to live among evil men in this world even unto the end. I do not say among those evil men who blaspheme Christ; for there are now few found who blaspheme with the tongue, but many who do so by their life. Among those, then, we must necessarily live even unto the end.

12. But what is this that He saith: "He that abideth in me, and I in him"? What, but that which the martyrs heard: "He that persevereth unto the end, the same shall be saved"?[2] How did Saint Laurence, whose feast we celebrate to-day, abide in Him? He abode even to temptation, abode even to tyrannical questioning, abode even to bitterest threatening, abode even to destruction; —that were a trifle, abode even to savage torture. For he was not put to death quickly, but tormented in the fire: he was allowed to live a long time; nay, not allowed to live a long time, but forced to die a slow, lingering death. Then, in that lingering death, in those torments, because he had well eaten and well drunk, as one who had feasted on that meat, as one intoxicated with that cup, he felt not the torments. For He was there who said, "It is the Spirit that quickeneth." For the flesh indeed was burning, but the Spirit was quickening the soul. He shrunk not back, and he mounted into the kingdom. But the holy martyr Xystus, whose day we celebrated five days ago, had said to him, "Mourn not, my son;" for Xystus was a bishop, he was a deacon. "Mourn not," said he; "thou shalt follow me after three days." He said three days, meaning the interval between the day of Saint Xystus's suffering and that of Saint Laurence's suffering, which falls on to-day. Three days is the interval. What comfort! He says not, "Mourn not, my son; the persecution will cease, and thou wilt be safe;" but, "do not mourn: whither I precede thou shalt follow; nor shall thy pursuit be deferred: three days will be the interval, and thou shalt be with me." He accepted the oracle, vanquished the devil, and attained to the triumph.

[1] 2 Tim. ii. 19.

[2] Matt. xxiv. 13.

TRACTATE XXVIII.

Chapter VII. 1–13.

1. In this chapter of the Gospel, brethren, our Lord Jesus Christ has most especially commended Himself to our faith in respect of His humanity. For indeed He always keeps in view, both in His words and deeds, that He should be believed to be God and man: God who made us, man who sought us; with the Father, always God; with us, man in time. For He would not have sought man whom He had made if Himself had not become that which He had made. But remember this, and do not let it slip from your hearts, that Christ became man in such manner that He ceased not to be God. While remaining God, He who made man took manhood. While, therefore, as man He concealed Himself, He must not be thought to have lost His power, but only to have offered an example to our infirmity. For He was detained when He willed to be, and He was put to death when he willed to be. But since there were to be His members, that is, His faithful ones, who would not have that power which He, our God, had; by His being hid, by His con-

cealing Himself as if He would not be put to death, He indicated that His members would do this, in which members He Himself in fact was. For Christ is not simply in the head and not in the body, but Christ whole is in the head and body. What, therefore, His members are, that He is; but what He is, it does not necessarily follow that His members are. For if His members were not Himself, He would not have said, "Saul, why persecutest thou me?"[1] For Saul was not persecuting Himself on earth, but His members, namely, His believers. He would not, however, say, my saints, my servants, or, in short, my brethren, which is more honorable; but, *me*, that is, my members, whose head I am.

2. With these preliminary remarks, I think that we shall not have to labor much for the meaning in this chapter; for that is often betokened in the head which was to be in the body. "After these things," saith he, "Jesus walked in Galilee: for He would not walk in Judea, because the Jews sought to kill Him." This is what I have said; He offered an example to our infirmity. He had not lost power, but He was comforting our weakness. For it would happen, as I have said, that some believer in Him would retreat into concealment, lest he should be found by the persecutors; and lest the concealment should be objected to him as a crime, that occurred first in the head, which should afterwards be confirmed in the member. For it is said, "He would not walk in Judea, beuse the Jews sought to kill Him," just as if Christ were not able both to walk among the Jews, and not be killed by them. For He manifested this power when He willed; for when they would lay hold of Him, as He was now about to suffer, "He said to them, Whom seek ye? They answered, Jesus. Then, said He, I am He," not concealing, but manifesting Himself. That manifestation, however, they did not withstand, but "going backwards, they fell to the ground."[2] And yet, because He had come to suffer, they rose up, laid hold of Him, led Him away to the judge, and slew Him. But what was it they did? That which a certain scripture says: "The earth was delivered into the hands of the ungodly."[3] The flesh was given into the power of the Jews; and this that thereby the bag, as it were, might be rent asunder, whence our purchase-price might run out.

3. "Now the Jews' feast of tabernacles was at hand." What the feast of tabernacles is, they who read the Scriptures know. They used on the holy day to make tabernacles, in likeness of the tabernacles in which they dwelt while they sojourned in the wilderness, after being led out of Egypt. This was a holy day, a great solemnity. The Jews were celebrating this, as being mindful of the Lord's benefits—they who were about to kill the Lord. On this holy day, then (for there were several holy days; but it was called a holy day with the Jews, though it was not one day, but several), "His brethren" spoke to the Lord Christ. Understand the phrase, "His brethren," as you know it must be taken, for it is not a new thing you hear. The blood relations of the Virgin Mary used to be called the Lord's brethren. For it was of the usage of Scripture to call blood relations and all other near kindred by the term brethren, which is foreign to our usage, and not within our manner of speech. For who would call an uncle or a sister's son "brother"? Yet the Scripture calls relatives of this kind "brothers." For Abraham and Lot are called brothers, while Abraham was Lot's uncle.[4] Laban and Jacob are called brothers, while Laban was Jacob's uncle.[5] When, therefore, you hear of the Lord's brethren, consider them the blood relations of Mary, who did not a second time bear children. For, as in the sepulchre, where the Lord's body was laid, neither before nor after did any dead lie; likewise, Mary's womb, neither before nor after conceived anything mortal.

4. We have said who the brethren were, let us hear what they said: "Pass over hence, and go into Judea, that thy disciples also may see thy work which thou doest." The Lord's works were not hid from the disciples, but to these men they were not apparent. They might have Christ for a kinsman, but through that very relationship they disdained to believe on Him. It is told us in the Gospel; for we dare not hold this as a mere opinion, you have just now heard it. They go on advising Him: "For no man doeth anything in secret, and he himself seeketh to be known openly: if thou do these things, show thyself to the world." And directly after it says: "For neither did His brethren believe in Him." Why did they not believe in Him? Because they sought human glory. For as to what His brethren appear to advise Him, they consult for His glory. Thou doest marvellous works, make thyself known; that is, appear to all, that thou mayest be praised by all. The flesh spoke to the flesh; but the flesh without God, to the flesh with God. It was the wisdom of the flesh speak-

ing to the Word which became flesh and dwelt among us.

5 What did the Lord answer to these things? Then saith Jesus to them: "My time is not yet come; but your time is always ready." What is this? Had not Christ's time yet come? Why then was Christ come, if His time had not yet come? Have we not heard the apostle say, "But when the fullness of time came, God sent His Son"?[1] If, therefore, He was sent in the fullness of time, He was sent when He ought to be sent, He came when it behoved that He should come. What means then, "My time is not yet come"? Understand, brethren, with what intention they spoke, when they appeared to advise Him as their brother. They were giving Him counsel to pursue glory; as advising in a worldly manner and with an earthly disposition, that He should not be unknown to fame, nor hide Himself in obscurity. This is what the Lord says in answer to those who were giving Him counsel of glory, "My time is not yet come;"—the time of my glory is not yet come. See how profound it is: they were advising Him as to glory; but He would have loftiness preceded by humility, and willed to prepare the way to elevation itself through humility. For those disciples, too, were of course seeking glory who wished to sit, one at His right hand and the other at His left: they thought only of the goal, and saw not by what way it must be reached; the Lord recalled them to the way, that they might come to their fatherland in due order. For the fatherland is on high, the way thither lies low. That land is the life of Christ, the way is Christ's death; that land is the habitation of Christ, the way is Christ's suffering. He that refuses the way, why seeks he the fatherland? In a word, to these also, while seeking elevation, He gave this answer: "Can ye drink the cup which I am about to drink?"[2] Behold the way by which you must come to that height which you desire. The cup He made mention of was indeed that of His humility and suffering.

6. Therefore also here: "My time is not yet come; but your time," that is the glory of the world, "is always ready." This is the time of which Christ, that is the body of Christ, speaks in prophecy: "When I shall have received the fit time, I will judge righteously."[3] For at present it is not the time of judging, but of tolerating the wicked. Therefore, let the body of Christ bear at present, and tolerate the wickedness of evil livers. Let it, however, have righteousness

now, for by righteousness it shall come to judgment. And what saith the Holy Scripture in the psalm to the members,—namely, that tolerate the wickedness of this world? "The Lord will not cast off His people." For, in fact, His people labors among the unworthy, among the unrighteous, among blasphemers, among murmurers, detractors, persecutors, and, if they are allowed, destroyers. Yes, it labors; but "the Lord will not cast off His people, and He will not forsake His inheritance until justice is turned into judgment."[4] "Until the justice," which is now in His saints, "be turned into judgment;" when that shall be fulfilled which was said to them, "Ye shall sit upon twelve thrones, judging the twelve tribes of Israel."[5] The apostle had righteousness, but not yet that judgment of which he says, "Know ye not that we shall judge angels?"[6] Be it now, therefore, the time for living rightly; the time for judging them that have lived ill shall be hereafter. "Until righteousness," saith he, "is turned into judgment." The time of judgment will be that of which the Lord has here said, "My time is not yet come." For there will be a time of glory, when He who came in humility will come in loftiness; He who came to be judged will come to judge; He who came to be slain by the dead will come to judge the quick and the dead. "God," saith the psalm, "will come manifest, our God, and He will not be silent."[7] What is "shall come manifest"? Because He came concealed. Then He will not be silent; for when He came concealed, "He was led as a sheep to the slaughter; and as a lamb before its shearer, He opened not His mouth."[8] He shall come, and shall not keep silence. "I was silent," saith He, "shall I always be silent?"[9]

7. But what is necessary at the present time for those who have righteousness? That which is read in that psalm: "Until righteousness is turned into judgment, and they that have it are upright of heart." You ask, perhaps, who are the upright in heart? We find in Scripture those to be upright in heart who bear the evils of the world, and do not accuse God. See, brethren, an uncommon thing is that which I speak of. For I know not how it is that, when any evil befalls a man, he runs to accuse God, when he ought to accuse himself. When thou gettest any good, thou praisest thyself; when thou sufferest any evil, thou accusest God. This is then the crooked heart, not the upright. When thou art cured of this distorting and

[1] Gal. iv. 4. [2] Matt. xx. 22. [3] Ps. lxxv. 2.

[4] Ps. xciv. 14. [5] Matt. xix. 28. [6] 1 Cor. vi. 3.
[7] Ps. l. 3. [8] Isa. liii. 7. [9] Isa. xlii. 14.

perversity, what thou didst use to do will be turned into the contrary. For what didst thou use to do before? Thou didst praise thyself in the good things of God, and didst accuse God in thine own evil things; with thy heart converted and made right, thou wilt praise God in His good things, and accuse thyself in thy own evil things. These are the upright in heart. In short, that man, who was not yet right in heart when the success of the wicked and the distress of the good grieved him, says, when he is corrected: "How good is the God of Israel to the upright in heart! But as for me," when I was not right in heart, "my feet were almost gone; my steps had well-nigh slipped." Why? . "Because I was envious at sinners, beholding the peace of sinners." I saw, saith he, the wicked prosperous, and I was displeased at God; for I did wish that God should not permit the wicked to be happy. Let man understand: God never does permit this; but a bad man is thought to be happy, for this reason, because men are ignorant of what happiness is. Let us then be right in heart: the time of our glory is not yet come. Let it be told to the lovers of this world, such as the brethren of the Lord were, "your time is always ready;" our time "is not yet come." For let us, too, dare to say this. And since we are the body of our Lord Jesus Christ, since we are His members, since we joyfully acknowledge our head, let us say it without hesitation; since, for our sakes, He deigned also Himself to say this. And when the lovers of this world revile us, let us say to them, "Your time is always ready; our time is not yet come." For the apostle has said to us, "For ye are dead, and your life is hid with Christ in God." When will our time come? "When Christ," saith he, "your life shall appear, then shall ye also appear with Him in glory."[2]

8. What said He further? "The world cannot hate you." What is this, but, The world cannot hate its lovers, the false witnesses? For you call the things that are evil, good; and the things that are good, evil. "But me it hateth, because I bear witness concerning it, that its works are evil. Go ye up to this feast." What means "to this"? Where ye seek human glory. What means "to this"? Where ye wish to prolong carnal joys, not to meditate on eternal joys. "I go not up to this feast, because my time is not yet full come." On this feast-day you seek human glory; but my time, that is, the time of my glory, is not yet come. That will

be my feast-day, not running before and passing over these days, but remaining for ever; that will be festivity, joy without end, eternity without a blot, serenity without a cloud. "When He had said these words unto them, He abode still in Galilee. But when His brethren were gone up, then went He also up unto the feast, not openly, but as it were in secret." Therefore "not to this feast-day," because His desire was not for temporal glory, but to teach something to profit, to correct men, to admonish them of an eternal feast-day, to turn away their love from this world, and to turn it to God. But what means this, "He went up as it were in secret to the feast"? This action of the Lord also is not without meaning. It appears to me that, even from this circumstance that He went up as it were in secret, He had intended to signify something; for the things that follow will show that He thus went up on the middle of the feast, that is, when those days were half over, to teach even openly. But he said, "As it were in secret," meaning, not to show Himself to men. It is not without meaning that Christ went up "as it were in secret" to that feast, because He Himself lay hid in that feast-day. What I have said as yet is also under cover of secrecy. Let it be manifested then, let the veil be lifted, and let that which was secret appear.

9. All things that were spoken to the ancient people Israel in the manifold Scripture of the holy law, what things they did, whether in sacrifices, or in priestly offices, or in feast-days, and, in a word, in what things soever they worshipped God, what things soever were spoken to and given them in precept, were shadows of things to come. Of what things to come? Things which find their fulfillment in Christ. Whence the apostl essays, "For all the promises of God are in Him yea;"[3] that is, they are fulfilled in Him. Again he says in another place, "All happened to them in a figure; but they were written for our sakes, upon whom the end of the ages is come."[4] And he said elsewhere, "For Christ is the end of the law;"[5] likewise in another place, "Let no man judge you in meat, or in drink, or in respect of an holy day, or of a new moon, or of Sabbath-days, which is a shadow of things to come."[6] If, therefore, all these things were shadows of things to come, also the feast of tabernacles was a shadow of things to come. Let us examine, then, of what thing to come was this feast-day a shadow. I have explained what this feast of tabernacles was: it was a celebration of taber-

---

[1] Ps. lxxiii. 1-3.   [2] Col. iii. 3, 4.

[3] 2 Cor. i. 20.   [4] 1 Cor. x. 1.
[5] Rom. x. 4.   [6] 1 Cor. ii. 16, 17.

nacles, because the people, after their deliverance from Egypt, while directing their course through the wilderness to the land of promise, dwelt in tents. Let us observe what it is, and we shall be that thing; we, I say, who are members of Christ, if such we are; but we are, He having made us worthy, not we having earned it for ourselves. Let us then consider ourselves, brethren: we have been led out of Egypt, where we were slaves to the devil as to Pharaoh; where we applied ourselves to works of clay, engaged in earthly desires, and where we toiled exceedingly. And to us, while laboring, as it were, at the bricks, Christ cried aloud, "Come unto me, all ye that labor and are heavy laden." Thence we were led out by baptism as through the Red Sea,—red because consecrated by the blood of Christ. All our enemies that pursued us being dead, that is, all our sins being blotted out, we have been brought over to the other side. At the present time, then, before we come to the land of promise, namely, the eternal kingdom, we are in the wilderness in tabernacles. They who acknowledge these things are in tabernacles; for it was to be that some would acknowledge this. For that man, who understands that he is a sojourner in this world, is in tabernacles. That man understands that he is travelling in a foreign country, when he sees himself sighing for his native land. But whilst the body of Christ is in tabernacles, Christ is in tabernacles; but at that time He was so, not evidently but secretly. For as yet the shadow obscured the light; when the light came, the shadow was removed. Christ was in secret: He was in the feast of tabernacles, but there hidden. At the present time, when these things are already made manifest, we acknowledge that we are journeying in the wilderness: for if we know it, we are in the wilderness. What is it to be in the wilderness? In the desert waste. Why in the desert waste? Because in this world, where we thirst in a way in which is no water. But yet, let us thirst that we may be filled. For, "Blessed are they that hunger and thirst after righteousness, for they shall be filled."[1] And our thirst is quenched from the rock in the wilderness: for "the Rock was Christ," and it was smitten with a rod that the water might flow. But that it might flow, the rock was smitten twice: because there are two beams of the cross.[2] All these things, then, which were done in a figure, are made manifest to us. And it is not without meaning that it was said of the Lord, "He went up to the feast-day, but not openly, but as it were in secret." For Himself in secret was the thing prefigured, because Christ was hid in that same festal-day; for that very festal-day signified Christ's members that were to sojourn in a foreign land.

10. "Then the Jews sought Him on the feast-day:" before He went up. For His brethren went up before Him, and He went not up then when they supposed and wished: that this too might be fulfilled which He said, "Not to this, that is, the first or second day, to which you wish me to go. But He went up afterwards, as the Gospel tells us, "on the middle of the feast;' that is, when as many days of that feast had passed as there remained. For they celebrated that same festival, so far as we can understand, on several successive days.

11. "They said, therefore, Where is he? And there was much murmuring among the people concerning Him." Whence the murmuring? Of strife. What was the strife? "Some said, He is a good man; but others said, Nay; but he deceiveth the people." We must understand this of all His servants: this is said now of them. For whoever becomes eminent in some spiritual grace, of him some will assuredly say, "He is a good man;" others, "Nay; but he deceiveth the people." Whence is this? "Because our life is hid with Christ in God."[3] On this account people may say during the winter, This tree is dead; for example, a fig tree, pear tree, or some kind of fruit tree, it is like a withered tree, and so long as it is winter it does not appear whether it is so or not. But the summer proves, the judgment proves. Our summer is the appearing of Christ: "God shall come manifest, our God, and He will not be silent;"[4] "fire shall go before Him:" that fire "shall burn up His enemies:"[5] that fire shall lay hold of the withered trees. For then shall the dry trees be apparent, when it shall be said to them, "I was hungry, and ye gave me not to eat;" but on the other side, namely, on the right, will be seen abundance of fruit, and magnificence of leaves; the green will be eternity. To those, then, as withered trees, it shall be said, "Go into everlasting fire. For behold," it saith, "the axe is laid to the root of the trees: every tree, therefore, that bringeth not forth good fruit shall be cut down, and cast into the fire."[6] Let them then say of thee, if thou art growing in Christ, let men say of thee, "He deceiveth the people." This is said of Christ Himself; it is said of the whole body

---

[1] Matt. v. 6.					[2] 1 Cor. x. 4; Num. xx. 11.

[3] Col. iii. 3.					[4] Ps. l. 3.
[5] Ps. xcvii. 3.					[6] Matt. iii. 10.

of Christ. Think of the body of Christ still in the world, think of it still on the threshing-floor; see how it is blasphemed by the chaff. The chaff and the grain are, indeed, threshed together; but the chaff is consumed, the corn is purged. What was said of the Lord then, avails for consolation, whenever it will be said of any Christian.

12. "Howbeit no man spake openly of Him for fear of the Jews." But who were they that did not speak of Him for fear of the Jews? Undoubtedly they who said, "He is a good man:" not they who said, "He deceiveth the people." As for them who said "He deceiveth the people," their din was heard like the noise of dry leaves. "He deceiveth the people," they sounded more and more loudly: "He is a good man," they whispered more and more constrainedly. But now, brethren, notwithstanding that glory of Christ which is to make us immortal is not yet come, yet now, I say, His Church so increases, He has deigned to spread it abroad through the whole world, that it is now only whispered. "He deceiveth the people;" and more and more loudly it sounds forth, "He is a good man."

TRACTATE XXIX.

CHAPTER VII. 14–18.

1. WHAT follows of the Gospel, and was read to-day, we must next in order look at, and speak from it as the Lord may grant us. Yesterday it was read thus far, that although they had not seen the Lord Jesus in the temple on the feast-day, yet they were speaking about Him: "And some said, He is a good man: but others said, Nay; but he seduceth the people." For this was said for the comfort of those who, afterwards preaching God's word, were to be seducers, and yet true men.[1] For if to seduce is to deceive, neither was Christ a seducer, nor His apostles, nor ought any Christian to be such; but if to seduce (to lead aside) is by persuading to lead one from something to something else, we ought to inquire into the *whence* and the *whither:* if from evil to good, the seducer is a good man; if from good to evil, the seducer is a bad man. In that sense, then, in which men are seduced from evil to good, would that all of us both were called, and actually were seducers!

2. Then afterwards the Lord went up to the feast, "about the middle of the feast, and taught." "And the Jews marvelled, saying, How knoweth this man letters, having never learned?" He who was in secret taught, He was speaking openly and was not restrained. For that hiding of Himself was for the sake of example; this showing Himself openly was an intimation of His power. But as He taught, "the Jews marvelled;" all indeed, so far as I think, marvelled, but all were not converted. And why this wondering? Because all knew where He was born, where He had been brought up; they had never seen Him learning letters, but they heard Him disputing about the law, bringing forward testimonies of the law, which none could bring forward unless he had read, and none could read unless he had learned letters: and therefore they marvelled. But their marvelling was made an occasion to the Master of insinuating the truth more deeply into their minds. By reason, indeed of their wondering and words, the Lord said something profound, and worthy of being more diligently looked into and discussed. On account of which I would urge you, my beloved, to earnestness, not only in hearing for yourselves, but also in praying for us.

3. How then did the Lord answer those that were marvelling how He knew letters which He had not learned? "My doctrine," saith He, "is not mine, but His that sent me." This is the first profundity. For He seems as if in a few words He had spoken contraries. For He says not, This doctrine is not mine; but, "My doctrine is not mine." If not Thine, how Thine? If Thine, how not Thine? For Thou sayest both: both, "my doctrines;" and, "not mine." For if He had said, This doctrine is not mine, there would have been no question. But now, brethren, in the first place, consider well the question, and so in due order expect the solution. For he who sees not the question proposed, how can he understand what is expounded? The subject of inquiry, then, is

---

[1] 2 Cor. vi. 8.

that which He says, "My, not mine·" this appears to be contrary; how "my," how "not mine"? If we carefully look at what the holy evangelist himself says in the beginning of his Gospel, "In the beginning was the Word, and the Word was with God, and the Word was God;" thence hangs the solution of this question. What then is the doctrine of the Father, but the Father's Word? Therefore, Christ Himself is the doctrine of the Father, if He is the Word of the Father. But since the Word cannot be of none, but of some one, He said both "His doctrine," namely, Himself, and also, "not His own," because He is the Word of the Father. For what is so much "Thine" as Thyself? And what so much not Thine as Thyself, if that Thou art is of another?

4. The Word then is God; and it is also the Word of a stable, unchangeable doctrine, not such as can be sounded by syllables and fleeting, but abiding with the Father, to which abiding doctrine let us be converted, being admonished by the transitory sounds of the voice. For that which is transitory does not so admonish us as to call us to transitory things. We are admonished to love God. All this that I have said were syllables; they smote through the air to reach your sense of hearing, and by sounding passed away: that, however, which I advise you ought not so to pass away, because He whom I exhort you to love passes not away; and when you, exhorted in transient syllables, shall have been converted, you shall not pass away, but shall abide with Him who is abiding. There is therefore in the doctrine this great matter, this deep and eternal thing which is permanent: whither all things that pass away in time call us, when they mean well and are not falsely put forward. For, in fact, all the signs which we produce by sounds do signify something which is not sound. For God is not the two short syllables "Deus," and it is not the two short syllables that we worship, and it is not the two short syllables that we adore, nor is it to the two short syllables that we desire to come—two syllables which almost cease to sound before they have begun to sound; nor in sounding them is there room for the second until the first has passed away. There remains, then, something great which is called "God," although the sound does not remain when we say the word "God." Thus direct your thoughts to the doctrine of Christ, and ye shall arrive at the Word of God; and when you have arrived at the Word of God, consider this, "The Word was God," and you will see that it was said truly, "my doctrine:" consider also whose the Word is, and

you will see that it was rightly said, "is not mine."

5. Therefore, to speak briefly, beloved, it seems to me that the Lord Jesus Christ said, "My doctrine is not mine," meaning the same thing as if He said, "I am not from myself." For although we say and believe that the Son is equal to the Father, and that there is not any diversity of nature and substance in them, that there has not intervened any interval of time between Him that begets and Him that is begotten, nevertheless we say these things, while keeping and guarding this, that the one is the Father, the other the Son. But Father He is not if He have not a Son, and Son He is not if He have not a Father: but yet the Son is God from the Father; and the Father is God, but not from the Son. The Father of the Son, not God from the Son: but the other is Son of the Father, and God from the Father. For the Lord Christ is called Light from Light. The Light then which is not from Light, and the equal Light which is not from Light, are together one Light not two Lights.

6. If we have understood this, thanks be to God; but if any has not sufficiently understood, man has done as far as he could: as for the rest, let him see whence he may hope to understand. As laborers outside, we can plant and water; but it is of God to give the increase. "My doctrine," saith He, "is not mine, but His that sent me." Let him who says he has not yet understood hear counsel. For since it was a great and profound matter that had been spoken, the Lord Christ Himself did certainly see that all would not understand this so profound a matter, and He gave counsel in the sequel. Dost thou wish to understand? Believe. For God has said by the prophet: "Except ye believe, ye shall not understand."[1] To the same purpose what the Lord here also added as He went on— "If any man is willing to do His will, he shall know concerning the doctrine, whether it be of God, or whether I speak from myself." What is the meaning of this, "If any man be willing to do His will"? But I had said, if any man believe; and I gave this counsel: If thou hast not understood, said I, believe. For understanding is the reward of faith. Therefore do not seek to understand in order to believe, but believe that thou mayest understand; since, "except ye believe, ye shall not understand." Therefore when I would counsel the obedience of believing toward the possibility of understanding, and say that our Lord Jesus Christ has added this very thing in

---

[1] Isa. vii. 9.

the following sentence, we find Him to have said, "If any man be willing to do His will, he shall know of the doctrine." What is "he shall know"? It is the same thing as "he shall understand." But what is "If any man be willing to do His will"? It is the same thing as to believe. All men indeed perceive that "shall know" is the same thing as "shall understand:" but that the saying, "If any man be willing to do His will," refers to believing, all do not perceive; to perceive this more accurately, we need the Lord Himself for expounder, to show us whether the doing of the Father's will does in reality refer to believing. But who does not know that this is to do the will of God, to work the work of God; that is, to work that work which is pleasing to Him? But the Lord Himself says openly in another place: "This is the work of God, that ye believe on Him whom He has sent."[1] "That ye believe on Him," not, that ye believe Him. But if ye believe *on* Him, ye believe Him; yet he that believes Him does not necessarily believe *on* Him. For even the devils believed Him, but they did not believe on Him. Again, moreover, of His apostles we can say, we believe Paul; but not, we believe on Paul: we believe Peter; but not, we believe on Peter. For, "to him that believeth on Him that justifieth the ungodly, his faith is counted unto him for righteousness."[2] What then is "to believe on Him"? By believing to love Him, by believing to esteem highly, by believing to go into Him and to be incorporated in His members. It is faith itself then that God exacts from us: and He finds not that which He exacts, unless He has bestowed what He may find. What faith, but that which the apostle has most amply defined in another place, saying, "Neither circumcision availeth anything, nor uncircumcision, but faith that worketh by love?"[3] Not any faith of what kind soever, but "faith that worketh by love:" let this faith be in thee, and thou shalt understand concerning the doctrine. What indeed shalt thou understand? That "this doctrine is not mine, but His that sent me;" that is, thou shalt understand that Christ the Son of God, who is the doctrine of the Father, is not from Himself, but is the Son of the Father.

7. This sentence overthrows the Sabellian heresy. The Sabellians have dared to affirm that the Son is the very same as He who is also the Father: that the names are two, but the reality one. If the names were two and reality one, it would not be said, "My doctrine is not mine." Anyhow, if Thy doctrine is not Thine, O Lord, whose is it, unless there be another whose it is? The Sabellians understand not what Thou saidst; for they see not the trinity, but follow the error of their own heart. Let us worshippers of the trinity and unity of Father, Son, and Holy Ghost, and one God, understand concerning Christ's doctrine, how it is not His. And He said that He spoke not from Himself for this reason, because Christ is the Son of the Father, and the Father is the Father of Christ; and the Son is from God the Father, God, but God the Father is God not from God the Son.

8. "He that speaketh of himself seeketh his own glory.' This will be he who is called Antichrist, " exalting himself," as the apostle says, "above all that is called God, and that is worshipped."[4] The Lord, declaring that this same it is that will seek his own glory, not the glory of the Father, says to the Jews: "I am come in my Father's name, and ye have not received me; another will come in his own name, him ye will receive."[5] He intimated that they would receive Antichrist, who will seek the glory of his own name, puffed up, not solid; and therefore not stable, but assuredly ruinous. But our Lord Jesus Christ has shown us a great example of humility: for doubtless He is equal with the Father, for " in the beginning was the Word, and the Word was with God, and the Word was God;" yea, doubtless, He Himself said, and most truly said, "Am I so long time with you, and ye have not known me, Philip? He that hath seen me hath seen the Father."[6] Yea, doubtless, Himself said, and most truly said, " I and the Father are one."[7] If, therefore, He is one with the Father, equal to the Father, God from God, God with God, co-eternal, immortal, alike unchangeable, alike without time, alike Creator and disposer of times; and yet because He came in time, and took the form of a servant, and in condition was found as a man,[8] He seeks the glory of the Father, not His own; what oughtest thou to do, O man, who, when thou doest anything good, seekest thy own glory; but when thou doest anything ill, dost meditate calumny against God? Consider thyself: thou art a creature, acknowledge thy Creator: thou art a servant, despise not thy Lord: thou art adopted, not for thy own merits; seek His glory from whom thou hast this grace, that thou art a man adopted; His, whose glory He sought who is from Him, the Only-begotten. "But He that seeketh His glory that sent Him, the same is true, and no unrighteousness is in Him." In Antichrist,

---

[1] John vi. 29.   [2] Rom. iv. 5.   [3] Gal. v. 6.

[4] 2 Thess. ii. 4.   [5] John v. 45.   [6] John xiv. 9.
[7] John x. 30.   [8] Phil. ii. 7.

however, there is unrighteousness, and he is not true; because he will seek his own glory, not His by whom he was sent: for, indeed, he was not sent, but only permitted to come. Let us all, therefore, that belong to the body of Christ, seek not our own glory, that we be not led into the snares of Antichrist. But if Christ sought His glory that sent Him, how much more ought we to seek the glory of Him who made us?

TRACTATE XXX.

Chapter VII. 19–24.

1. The passage of the holy Gospel of which we have before discoursed to you, beloved, is fo lowed by that of to-day, which has just now been read. Both the disciples and the Jews heard the Lord speaking; both men of truth and liars heard the Truth speaking; both friends and enemies heard Charity speaking; both good men and bad men heard the Good speaking. They heard, but He discerned; He saw and foresaw whom His discourse profited and would profit. Among those who were then, He saw; among us who were to be, He foresaw. Let us therefore hear the Gospel, just as if we were listening to the Lord Himself present: nor let us say, O happy they who were able to see Him! because there were many of them who saw, and also killed Him; and there are many among us who have not seen Him, and yet have believed. For the precious truth that sounded forth from the mouth of the Lord was both written for our sakes, and preserved for our sakes, and recited for our sakes, and will be recited also for the sake of our prosperity, even until the end of the world. The Lord is above; but the Lord, the Truth, is also here. For the body of the Lord, in which He rose again from the dead, can be only in one place; but His truth is everywhere diffused. Let us then hear the Lord, and let us also speak that which He shall have granted to us concerning His own words.

2. "Did not Moses," saith He, "give you the law, and yet none of you doeth the law? Why do ye seek to kill me?" For ye seek to kill me just for this reason, that none of you doeth the law; for if ye did do the law, ye would recognize Christ in its very letters, and ye would not kill Him when present with you. And they answered: "The crowd answered Him;" answered as a tumultuous crowd,[1] things not pertaining to order, but to confusion; in a word, the crowd was disturbed. See what answer it made: "Thou hast a devil: who seeks to kill thee?" As if it were not worse to say, "Thou hast a devil," than to kill Him. To Him, indeed, was it said, that He had a devil, who was casting out devils. What else can a turbulent disorderly crowd say? What else can filth stirred up do but stink? The crowd was disturbed, by what? By the truth. For the eyes that have not soundness cannot endure the brightness of the light.

3. But the Lord, manifestly not disturbed, but calm in His truth, rendered not evil for evil nor railing for railing;[2] although, if He were to say to these men, You have a devil, He would certainly be saying what was true. For they would not have said such things to the Truth, unless the falsehood of the devil had instigated them. What then did He answer? Let us calmly hear, and drink in the serene word: "I have done one work, and ye all marvel." As if He said, What if ye were to see all my works? For they were His works which they saw in the world, and yet they saw not Him who made them all: He did one thing, and they were disturbed because he made a man whole on the Sabbath-day. As if, indeed, when any sick man recovered his health on the Sabbath-day, it had been any other that made such a man whole than He who offended them, because He made one man whole on the Sabbath-day. For who else has made others whole than He who is health itself,—He who gives even to the beasts that health which He gave to this man? For it was bodily health. The health of the flesh is repaired, and the flesh dies; and when it is repaired, death is only put off, not taken away. However, even that same health, brethren, is from the Lord, through whomsoever it may be given: by whose care and ministry soever it may be imparted, it is given by Him from whom all health is, to whom it

---

[1] Turba.   [2] 1 Pet. iii. 9.

is said in the psalm, " O Lord, Thou wilt save men and beasts; as Thou hast multiplied Thy mercy, O God." For because Thou art God, Thy multiplied mercy reaches even to the safety of human flesh, reaches even to the safety of dumb animals; but Thou who givest health of flesh common to men and beasts, is there no health which Thou reservest for men? There is certainly another which is not only not common to men and beasts, but to men themselves is not common to good and bad. In a word, when he had there spoken of this health which men and cattle receive in common, because of that health which men, but only the good, ought to hope for, he added as he went on: " But the sons of men shall put their trust under the cover of Thy wings. They shall be fully satisfied with the fatness of Thy house; and Thou shalt give them drink from the torrent of Thy pleasure. For with Thee is the fountain of life; and in Thy light shall they see light."[1] This is the health which belongs to good men, those whom he called " sons of men;" whilst he had said above, " O Lord, Thou shalt save men and beasts." How then? Were not those men sons of men, that after he had said *men*, he should go on and say, *But the sons of men*: as if *men* and *sons of men* meant different things? Yet I do not believe that the Holy Spirit had said this without some indication of distinction. The term *men* refers to the first Adam, *sons of men* to Christ. Perhaps, indeed, *men* relate to the first man; but *sons of men* relate to the Son of man.

4. " I have done one work, and ye all marvel." And immediately He subjoined: " Moses therefore gave unto you circumcision." It was well done that ye received circumcision from Moses. " Not that it is of Moses, but of the fathers;" since it was Abraham that first received circumcision from the Lord.[2] " And ye circumcise on the Sabbath-day." Moses has convicted you: ye have received in the law to circumcise on the eighth day; ye have received in the law to cease from labor on the seventh day;[3] if the eighth day from the child's birth fall on the seventh day of the week, what will ye do? Will ye abstain from work to keep the Sabbath, or will ye circumcise to fulfill the sacrament of the eighth day? But I know, saith He, what ye do. " Ye circumcise a man." Why? Because circumcision relates to what is a kind of seal of salvation, and men ought not to abstain from the work of salvation on the Sabbath-day. Therefore be ye not " angry with me, because I have made a man

every whit whole on the Sabbath-day." " If," saith He, " a man on the Sabbath-day receiveth circumcision that the law should not be broken " (for it was something saving that was ordained by Moses in that ordinance of circumcision), why are ye angry at me for working a healing on the Sabbath-day?

5. Perhaps, indeed, that circumcision pointed to the Lord Himself, at whom they were indignant, because He worked cures and healing. For circumcision was commanded to be applied on the eighth day: and what is circumcision but the spoiling of the flesh? This circumcision, then, signified the removal of carnal lusts from the heart. Therefore not without cause was it given, and ordered to be made in that member; since by that member the creature of mortal kind is procreated. By one man came death, just as by one man the resurrection of the dead;[4] and by one man sin entered into the world, and death by sin.[5] Therefore every man is born with a foreskin, because every man is born with the vice of propagation; and God cleanses not, either from the vice with which we are born, or from the vices which we add thereto by ill living, except by the stony knife, the Lord Christ. For Christ was the Rock. Now they used to circumcise with stone knives, and by the name of rock they prefigured Christ: and yet when He was present with them they did not acknowledge Him, but besides, they sought to kill Him. But why on the eighth day, unless because after the seventh day of the week the Lord rose again on the Lord's day? Therefore Christ's resurrection, which happened on the third day indeed of His passion, but on the eighth day in the days of the week, that same resurrection it is that doth circumcise us. Hear of those that were circumcised with the real stone, while the apostle admonishes them: " If then ye be risen with Christ, seek those things which are above, where Christ is, sitting on the right hand of God; set your affection on things above, not on things on the earth."[6] He speaks to the circumcised: Christ has risen; He has taken away from you carnal desires, evil lusts, the superfluity with which you were born, and that far worse which you had added thereto by ill living; being circumcised by the Rock, why do you still set your affections on the earth? And finally, for that " Moses gave you the law, and ye circumcise a man on the Sabbath-day," understand that by this is signified the good work which I have done, in that I have made a man every whit whole on the Sabbath-day; because he was cured that

¹ Ps. xxxvi. 7-10.   ² Gen. xvii. 10.   ³ Ex. xx. 10.   ⁴ 1 Cor. xv. 21   ⁵ Rom. v. 12.   ⁶ Col. iii. 1, 2.

he might be whole in body, and also he believed that he might be whole in soul.

6. "Judge not according to personal appearance, but judge righteous judgment." What is this? Just now, you who by the law of Moses circumcise on the Sabbath-day are not angry with Moses; and because I made a man whole on the Sabbath-day you are angry with me. You judge by the person; give heed to the truth. I do not prefer myself to Moses, says the Lord, who was also the Lord of Moses. So consider us as you would two men, as both men; judge between us, but judge a true judgment; do not condemn him by honoring me, but honor me by understanding him. For this He said to them in another place: "If ye believed Moses ye would certainly believe me also, for he wrote of me."[1] But in this place He willed not to say this, Himself and Moses being as it were placed before these men for judgment. Because of Moses' law you circumcise, even when it happens to be the Sabbath-day, and will ye not that I should show the beneficence of healing during the Sabbath? For the Lord of circumcision and the Lord of the Sabbath is the same who is the Author of health; and they are servile works that ye are forbidden to do on the Sabbath; if ye really understand what servile works are, ye sin not. For he that committeth sin is the servant of sin. Is it a servile work to heal a man on the Sabbath-day? Ye do eat and drink (to infer somewhat from the admonition of our Lord Jesus Christ, and from His words); at any rate, why do ye eat and drink on the Sabbath, but because that what ye do pertains to health? By this ye show that the works of health are not in any wise to be omitted on the Sabbath. Therefore "do not judge by person, but judge righteous judgment." Consider me as ye would a man; consider Moses as a man: if ye will judge according to the truth, ye will condemn neither Moses nor me; and when ye know the truth ye will know me, because I am the Truth.

7. It requires great labor in this world, brethren to get clear of the vice which the Lord has noted in this place, so as not to judge by appearance, but to keep right judgment. The Lord, indeed, admonished the Jews, but He warned us also; them He convicted, us He instructed; them He reproved, us He encouraged. Let us not imagine that this was not said to us, simply because we were not there at that time. It was written, it is read; when it was recited we heard it; but we heard it as said to the Jews; let us not place ourselves behind ourselves and watch Him reproving enemies, while we ourselves do that which the truth may reprove in us. The Jews indeed judged by appearance, but for that reason they belong not to the New Testament, they have not the kingdom of heaven in Christ, nor are joined to the society of the holy angels; they sought earthly things of the Lord; for a land of promise, victory over enemies, fruitfulness of child-bearing, increase of children, abundance of fruit,—all which things were indeed promised to them by God, the True and the Good, promised to them, however, as unto carnal men,—all these things made for them the Old Testament. What is the Old Testament? The inheritance, as it were, belonging to the old man. We have been renewed, have been made a new man, because He who is the new man has come. What is so new as to be born of a virgin? Therefore, because there was not in Him what instruction might renew, because He had no sin, there was given Him a new origin of birth. In Him a new birth, in us a new man. What is a new man? A man renewed from oldness. Renewed unto what? Unto desiring heavenly things, unto longing for things eternal, unto earnestly seeking the country which is above and fears no foe, where we do not lose a friend nor fear an enemy; where we live with good affection, without any want; where no longer any advances, because none fails; where no man is born, because no man dies; where there is no hungering nor thirsting; where immortality is fullness, and truth our aliment. Having these promises, and pertaining to the New Testament, and being made heirs of a new inheritance, and co-heirs of the Lord Himself, we have a far different hope from theirs: let us not judge by appearance, but hold right judgment.

8. Who is he that judges not according to the person? He that loves equally. Equal love causes that persons be not accepted. It is not when we honor men in diverse measure according to their degrees that we ought to fear lest we are accepting persons. For where we judge between two, and at times between relations, sometimes it happens that judgment has to be made between father and son; the father complains of a bad son, or the son complains of a harsh father; we regard the honor which is due to the father from the son; we do not make the son equal to the father in honor, but we give him preference if he has a good cause: let us regard the son on an equality with the father in the truth, and thus shall we bestow the honor due, so that equity destroy not merit. Thus we profit by the words of the Lord, and that we may profit, we are assisted by His grace.

---

[1] John v. 46.

TRACTATE XXXI.

CHAPTER VII. 25–36.

1. YOU remember, beloved, in the former discourses,—for it was both read in the Gospel and also discussed by us according to our ability,—how that the Lord Jesus went up to the feast-day, as it were in secret, not because He feared lest He should be laid hold of,—He who had the power not to be laid hold of,—but to signify that even in that very feast which was celebrated by the Jews He Himself was hidden, and that the mystery of the feast was His own. In the passage read to-day then, that which was supposed to be timidity appeared as power; for He spoke openly on the feast-day, so that the crowds marvelled, and said that which we have heard when the passage was read: " Is not this he whom they sought to kill? And, lo, he speaketh openly, and they say nothing. Do the rulers know indeed that this is the Christ?" They who knew with what fierceness He was sought after, wondered by what power He was kept from being taken. Then, not fully understanding His power, they fancied it was the knowledge of the rulers, that these rulers knew Him to be the very Christ, and that for this reason they spared Him whom they had with so much eagerness sought out to be put to death.

2. Then those same persons who had said, " Did the rulers know that this is the Christ?" proposed a question among themselves, by which it appeared to them that He was not the Christ; for they said in addition, " But we know this man whence he is: but when Christ cometh, no man knoweth whence he is." As to how this opinion among the Jews arose, that " when Christ comes, no man knoweth whence He is " (for it did not arise without reason), if we consider the Scriptures, we find, brethren, that the Holy Scriptures have declared of Christ that " He shall be called a Nazarene."[1] Therefore they foretold whence He is. Again, if we seek the place of His nativity, as that whence He is by birth, neither was this hidden from the Jews, because of the Scriptures which had foretold these things. For when the Magi, on the appearing of a star, sought Him out to worship Him, they came to Herod and told him what they sought and what they meant: and he, having called together those who had knowledge of the law,

inquired of them where Christ should be born: they told him, " In Bethlehem of Judah," and also brought forward the prophetic testimony.[2] If, therefore, the prophets had foretold both the place where the origin of His flesh was, and the place where His mother would bring Him forth, whence did spring that opinion among the Jews which we have just heard, but from this, that the Scriptures had proclaimed beforehand, and had foretold both? In respect of His being man, the Scriptures foretold whence He should be; in respect of His being God, this was hidden from the ungodly, and it required godly men to discover it. Moreover, they said this, " When Christ comes, no man knoweth whence He is," because that which was spoken by Isaiah produced this opinion in them, viz. " And His generation, who shall tell?"[3] In short, the Lord Himself made answer to both, that they both did, and also did not know whence He was; that He might testify to the holy prophecy which before was predicted of Him, both as to the humanity of infirmity and also as to the divinity of majesty.

3. Hear, therefore, the word of the Lord, brethren; see how He confirmed to them both what they said, " We know this man whence he is," and also what they said, " When Christ cometh, no man knoweth whence He is. Then cried Christ in the temple, saying, Ye both know me, and ye know whence I am: and I am not come of myself, but He that sent me is true, whom ye know not." That is to say, ye both know me, and ye know me not; ye both know whence I am, and ye know not whence I am. Ye know whence I am: Jesus of Nazareth, whose parents also ye knew. For in this case, the birth of the Virgin alone was hidden, to whom, however, her husband was witness; for the same was able faithfully to declare this, who was also able as a husband to be jealous. Therefore, this birth of the Virgin excepted, they knew all that in Jesus pertains to man: His face was known, His country was known, His family was known; where He was born was to be known by inquiry. Rightly then did He say, " Ye both know me, and ye know whence I am," according to the flesh and form of man which He bore; but according to His

---

[1] Matt. ii. 23.   [2] Matt. ii. 6.   [3] Isa. viii. 8.

divinity, "And I am not come of myself, but He that sent me is true, whom ye know not;" but yet that ye may know Him, believe on Him whom He has sent, and ye will know Him. For, "No man has seen God at any time, except the only-begotten Son, who is in the bosom of the Father, He hath declared Him:"[1] and, "None knoweth the Father but the Son, and he to whom the Son wills to reveal Him."[2]

4. Lastly, when He had said, "But He that sent me is true, whom ye know not," in order to show them whence they might know that which they did not know, He subjoined, "I know Him." Therefore seek from me to know Him. But why is it that I know Him? "Because I am from Him, and He sent me." Gloriously has He shown both. "I am from Him," said He; because the Son is from the Father, and whatever the Son is, He is of Him whose Son He is. Hence we say that the Lord Jesus is God of God: we do not say that the Father is God of God, but simply God: and we say that the Lord Jesus is Light of Light; we do not say that the Father is Light of Light, but simply Light. Accordingly, to this belongs that which He said, "I am from Him." But as to my being seen of you in the flesh, "He sent me." When thou hearest "He sent me," do not understand a difference of nature to be meant, but the authority of Him that begets.

5. "Then they sought to take Him: but no man laid hands on Him, because His hour was not yet come;" that is, because He was not willing. For what is this. "His hour was not yet come"? The Lord was not born under fate. This is not to be believed concerning thee, much less concerning Him by whom thou wast made. If thy hour is His good will, what is His hour but His good will? He meant not therefore an hour in which He should be forced to die, but that in which He would deign to be put to death. But He was awaiting the time in which He should die, for He awaited also the time in which He should be born. The apostle, speaking of this time, says, "But when the fullness of time came, God sent His Son."[3] For this cause many say, Why did not Christ come before? To whom we must make answer, Because the fullness of time had not yet come, while He by whom the times were made sets their bounds; for He knew when He ought to come. In the first place, it was necessary that He should be foretold through a long series of times and years; for it was not something insignificant that was to come:

He who was to be ever held, had to be for a long time foretold. The greater the judge that was coming, the longer the train of heralds that preceded him. In short, when the fullness of time came, He also came who was to deliver us from time. For being delivered from time, we shall come to that eternity where there is no time: there it is not said, When shall the hour come? for the day is everlasting, a day which is neither preceded by a yesterday, nor cut off by a morrow. But in this world days roll on, some are passing away, others come; none abides; and the moments in which we are speaking drive out one another in turn, nor stands the first syllable for the second to sound. Since we began to speak we are somewhat older, and without doubt I am just now older than I was in the morning; thus, nothing stands, nothing remains fixed in time. Therefore ought we to love Him by whom the times were made, that we may be delivered from time and be fixed in eternity, where there is no more changeableness of times. Great, therefore, is the mercy of our Lord Jesus Christ, in that for our sakes He was made in time, by whom the times were made; that He was made among all things, by whom all things were made; that He became what He made. For He was made what He had made; for He was made man who had made man, lest what He had made should perish. According to this dispensation, the hour of His birth had now come, and He was born; but not yet had come the hour of His suffering, therefore not yet had He suffered.

6. In short, that ye may know that the words refer, not to the necessity of His dying, but to His power,—I speak this for the sake of some who, when they hear "His hour was not yet come," are determined on believing in fate, and their hearts become infatuated;—that ye may know, then, that it was His power of dying, recollect the passion, look at Him crucified. While hanging on the tree, He said, "I thirst." They, having heard this, offered to Him on the cross vinegar by a sponge on a reed. He received it, and said, "It is finished;" and, bowing His head, gave up the ghost. You see His power of dying, that He waited for this—until all things should be fulfilled that had been foretold concerning Him—to take place before His death. For the prophet had said, "They gave me gall for my meat; and in my thirst they gave me vinegar to drink."[4] He waited for all these things to be fulfilled: after they were completed, He said, "It is finished;"

---

[1] John i. 8.   [2] Matt. xi. 27.   [3] Gal. iv. 4.   [4] Ps. lxix. 21.

and He departed by power, because He came not by necessity. Hence some wondered more at this His power to die than at His ability to work miracles. For they came to the cross to take the bodies down from the tree, for the Sabbath was drawing near, and the thieves were found still living. The punishment of the cross was so much the harder because it tortured men so long, and all that were crucified were killed by a lingering death. But the thieves, that they might not remain on the tree, were forced to die by having their legs broken, that they might be taken down thence. The Lord, however, was found to be already dead,[1] and the men marvelled; and they who despised Him when living, so wondered at Him when dead, that some of them said, "Truly this was the Son of God."[2] Whence also that, brethren, where He says to those that seek Him, "I am He;" and they, going backward, all fell to the ground?[3] Consequently there was in Him supreme power. Nor was He forced to die at an hour; but He waited the hour on which His will might fittingly be done, not that on which necessity might be fulfilled against His will.

7. "But many of the people believed on Him." The Lord made whole the humble and the poor. The rulers were mad, and therefore they not only did not acknowledge the Physician, but even were eager to slay Him. There was a certain crowd of people which quickly saw its own sickness, and without delay recognized His remedy. See what that very crowd, moved by His miracles, said: "When Christ cometh will He do more signs than these?" Surely, unless there will be two Christs, this is the Christ. Consequently, in saying these things, they believed on Him.

8. But those rulers, having heard the assurance of the multitude, and that murmuring noise of the people in which Christ was being glorified, "sent officers to take Him." To take whom? Him not yet willing to be taken. Because then they could not take Him while He would not, they were sent to hear Him teaching. Teaching what? "Then said Jesus, Yet a little while I am with you." What ye wish to do now ye will do, but not just now; because I am not just now willing. Why am I now as yet unwilling? Because "yet a little while I am with you; and then I go unto Him that sent me." I must complete my dispensation, and in this manner come to my suffering.

9. "Ye shall seek me, and shall not find me: and where I am, thither ye cannot come." Here He has already foretold His resurrection; for they would not acknowledge Him when present, and afterwards they sought Him when they saw the multitude already believing on Him. For great signs were wrought, even when the Lord was risen again and ascended into heaven. Then mighty deeds were done by His disciples, but He wrought by them as He wrought by Himself: since, indeed, He had said to them, "Without me ye can do nothing."[4] When that lame man who sat at the gate rose up at Peter's voice, and walked on his feet, so that men marvelled, Peter spoke to them to this effect, that it was not by his own power that he did this, but in the virtue of Him whom they slew.[5] Many pricked in the heart said, "What shall we do?" For they saw themselves bound by an immense crime of impiety, since they slew Him whom they ought to have revered and worshipped; and this crime they thought inexpiable. A great wickedness indeed it was, the thought of which might make them despair; yet it did not behove them to despair, for whom the Lord, as He hung on the cross, deigned to pray. For He had said, "Father, forgive them; for they know not what they do."[8] He saw some who were His own among many who were aliens; for these He sought pardon, from whom at the time He was still receiving injury. He regarded not that He was being put to death by them, but only that He was dying for them. It was a great thing that was forgiven them, it was a great thing that was done by them and for them, so that no man should despair of the forgiveness of his sin when they who slew Christ obtained pardon. Christ died for us, but surely He was not put to death by us? But those men indeed saw Christ dying by their own villany; and yet they believed on Christ pardoning their villanies. Until they drank the blood they had shed, they despaired of their own salvation. Therefore said He this: "Ye shall seek me, and shall not find me: and where I am, ye cannot come;" because they were to seek Him after the resurrection, being pricked in their heart with remorse. Nor did He say "where I will be," but "where I am." For Christ was always in that place whither He was about to return; for He came in such manner that He did not depart from that place. Hence He says in another place, "No man has ascended into heaven, but He who came down from heaven, the Son of man who is in heaven."[7] He said not, who *was* in heaven. He spoke on the earth, and declared that He

---

[1] John xix. 28–33. [2] Matt. xxvii. 54. [3] John xviii. 6.

[4] John xv. 5.   [5] Acts iii. 2–16.
[6] Luke xxiii. 34.   [7] John iii. 13.

was at the same time in heaven. He came in such wise that He departed not thence; and He so returned as not to abandon us. What do ye marvel at? This is God's doing. For man, as regards his body, is in a place, and departs from a place; and when he comes to another place, he will not be in that place whence he came: but God fills all things, and is all everywhere; He is not held in places according to space. Nevertheless the Lord Christ was, as regards His visible flesh, on the earth: as regards His invisible majesty, He was in heaven and on earth; and therefore He says, "Where I am, thither ye cannot come." Nor did He say, "Ye shall not be able," but "ye are not able to come;" for at that time they were such as were not able. And that ye may know that this was not said to cause despair, He said something of the same kind also to His disciples: "Whither I go ye cannot come."[1] Yet while praying in their behalf, He said, "Father, I will that where I am they also may be with me."[2] And, finally, this He expounded to Peter, and says to him, "Whither I go thou canst not follow me now, but thou shalt follow me hereafter."[3]

10. "Then said the Jews," not to Him, but "to themselves, Whither will this man go, that we shall not find him? will he go unto the dispersion among the Gentiles, and teach the Gentiles?" For they knew not what they said; but, it being His will, they prophesied. The Lord was indeed about to go to the Gentiles, not by His bodily presence, but still with His feet. What were His feet? Those which Saul desired to trample upon by persecution, when the Head cried out to him, "Saul, Saul, why persecutest thou me?"[4] What is this saying that He said, "Ye shall seek me, and shall not find me: and where I am, thither ye cannot come?" Wherefore the Lord said this they knew not, and yet they did predict something that was to be without knowing it. For this is what the Lord said that they knew not the place, if place however it must be called, which is the bosom of the Father, from which Christ never departed; nor were they competent to conceive where Christ was, whence Christ never withdrew, whither He was to return, where He was all the while dwelling. How was it possible for the human heart to conceive this, least of all to explain it with the tongue? This, then, they in no wise understood; and yet by occasion of this they foretold our salvation, that the Lord would go to the dispersion of the Gentiles, and would fulfill that which they read but did not understand. "A

people whom I have not known served me, and by the hearing of the ear obeyed me."[5] They before whose eyes He was, heard Him not; those heard Him in whose ears He was sounded.

11. For of that Church of the Gentiles which was to come, the woman that had the issue of blood was a type: she touched and was not seen; she was not known and yet was healed. It was in reality a figure what the Lord asked: "Who touched me?" As if not knowing, He healed her as unknown: so has He done also to the Gentiles. We did not get to know Him in the flesh, yet we have been made worthy to eat His flesh, and to be members in His flesh. In what way? Because He sent to us. Whom? His heralds, His disciples, His servants, His redeemed whom He created, but whom He redeemed, His brethren also. I have said but little of all that they are: His own members, Himself; for He sent to us His own members, and He made us His members. Nevertheless, Christ has not been among us with the bodily form which the Jews saw and despised; because this also was said concerning Him, even as the apostle says: "Now I say that Christ was a minister of the circumcision for the truth of God, to confirm the promises made unto the fathers."[6] He owed it to have come to those by whose fathers and to whose fathers He was promised. For this reason He says also Himself: "I am not sent but unto the lost sheep of the house of Israel."[7] But what says the apostle in the following words? "And that the Gentiles might glorify God for His mercy." What, moreover, saith the Lord Himself? "Other sheep I have which are not of this fold.[8] He who had said, "I am not sent but unto the lost sheep of the house of Israel," how has He other sheep to which He was not sent, except that He intimated that He was not sent to show His bodily presence but to the Jews only, who saw and killed Him? And yet many of them, both before and afterwards, believed. The first harvest was winnowed from the cross, that there might be a seed whence another harvest might spring up. But at this present time, when roused by the fame of the gospel, and by its goodly odor, His faithful ones among all nations believe, He shall be the expectation of the Gentiles, when He shall come who has already come; when He shall be seen by all, He who was then not seen by some, by some was seen; when He shall come to judge who came to be judged; when He shall come to distinguish who came not to be distinguish-

---

[1] John xiii. 33.　　　　　[2] John xvii. 24.
[3] John xiii. 36.　　　　　[4] Acts ix. 4.
[5] Ps. xviii. 44.　　　　　[6] Rom. xv. 8.
[7] Matt. xv. 24.　　　　　[8] John x. 16.

ed. For Christ was not discerned by the ungodly, but was condemned with the ungodly; for it was said concerning Him, "He was accounted among the wicked."[1] The robber escaped, Christ was condemned. He who was loaded with criminal accusations received pardon; He who has released from their crimes all who confess Him, was condemned. Nevertheless even the cross itself, if thou considerest it well, was a judgment-seat; for the Judge being set up in the middle, one thief who believed was delivered, the other who reviled was condemned.[2] Already He signified what He is to do with the quick and the dead: some He will set on His right hand and others on His left. That thief was like those that shall be on the left hand, the other like those that shall be on the right. He was undergoing judgment, and He threatened judgment.

Isa. liii. 12.

[2] Luke xxii. 43.

TRACTATE XXXII.

CHAPTER VII. 37–39.

1. AMONG the dissensions and doubtings of the Jews concerning the Lord Jesus Christ, among other things which He said, by which some were confounded, others taught: "On the last day of that feast" (for it was then that these things were done) which is called the feast of tabernacles; that is, the building of tents, of which feast you remember, my beloved, that we have already discoursed, the Lord Jesus Christ calls, not by speaking in any way soever, but by crying aloud, that whoso thirsts may come to Him. If we thirst, let us come; and not by our feet, but by our affections; let us come, not by removing from our place, but by loving. Although, according to the inner man, he that loves does also move from a place. But it is one thing to move with the body, another thing to move with the heart: he migrates with the body who changes his place by a motion of the body; he migrates with the heart who changes his affection by a motion of the heart. If thou lovest one thing, and didst love another thing before, thou art not now where thou wast.

2. Accordingly, the Lord cries aloud to us: for, "He stood and cried out, if any man thirst, let him come unto me, and drink. He that believeth on me, as the Scripture saith, out of his belly shall flow rivers of living water." We are not obliged to delay to inquire what this meant, since the evangelist has explained it. For why the Lord said, "If any man thirst, let him come unto me, and drink;" and, "He that believeth on me, out of his belly shall flow rivers of living water;" the evangelist has subsequently explained, saying: "But this spake He of the Spirit which they that believe on Him should receive. For the Spirit was not yet given, because Jesus was not yet glorified." There is therefore an inner thirst and an inner belly, because there is an inner man. And that inner man is indeed invisible, but the outer man is visible; but yet better is the inner than the outer. And this which is not seen is the more loved; for it is certain that the inner man is loved more than the outer. How is this certain? Let every man prove it in himself. For although they who live ill may surrender their minds to the body, yet they do wish to live, and to live is the property of the mind only; and they who rule, manifest themselves more than those things that are ruled. Now it is minds that rule, bodies are ruled. Every man rejoices in pleasure, and receives pleasure by the body: but separate the mind from it, and nothing remains in the body to rejoice; and if there is joy of the body, it is the mind that rejoices. If it has joy of its dwelling, ought it not to have joy of itself? And if the mind has whereof it may have delight outside itself, does it remain without delights within? It is quite certain that a man loves his soul more than his body. But further, a man loves the soul even in another man more than the body. What is it that is loved in a friend, where the love is the purer and more sincere? What in the friend is loved—the mind, or the body? If fidelity is loved, the mind is loved; if benevolence is loved, the mind is the seat of benevolence: if this is what thou lovest in another, that he too loves thee, it is the mind thou lovest, because it is not the flesh, but the mind that loves. For therefore thou lovest, because he loves thee: ask why he loves thee, and then

13

see what it is thou lovest. Consequently, it is more loved, and yet is not seen.

3. I would say something further, by which it may more clearly appear to you, beloved, how much the mind is loved, and how it is preferred to the body. Those wanton lovers even, who delight in beauty of bodies, and are charmed by shapeliness of limbs, love the more when they are loved. For when a man loves, and finds that he is regarded with hatred, he feels more anger than liking. Why does he feel anger rather than liking? Because the love that he bestows is not given him in return. If, therefore, even the lovers of bodies desire to be loved in return, and this delights them more when they are loved, what shall we say of the lovers of minds? And if the lovers of minds are great, what shall we say of the lovers of God who makes minds beautiful? For as the mind gives grace to the body, so it is God that gives grace to the mind. For it is only the mind that causes that in the body by which it is loved; when the mind has left it, it is a corpse at which thou hast a horror; and how much soever thou mayest have loved its beautiful limbs, thou makest haste to bury it. Hence, the ornament of the body is the mind; the ornament of the mind is God.

4. The Lord, therefore, cries aloud to us to come and drink, if we thirst within; and He says that when we have drunk, rivers of living water shall flow from our belly. The belly of the inner man is the conscience of the heart. Having drunk that water then, the conscience being purged begins to live; and drinking in, it will have a fountain, will be itself a fountain. What is the fountain, and what the river that flows from the belly of the inner man? Benevolence, whereby a man will consult the interest of his neighbor. For if he imagines that what he drinks ought to be only for his own satisfying, there is no flowing of living water from his belly; but if he is quick to consult for the good of his neighbor, then he becomes not dry, because there is a flowing. We will now see what it is that they drink who believe in the Lord; because we surely are Christians, and if we believe, we drink. And it is every man's duty to know in himself whether or not he drinks, and whether he lives by what he drinks; for the fountain does not forsake us if we forsake not the fountain.

5. The evangelist explained, as I have said, whereof the Lord had cried out, to what kind of drink He had invited, what He had procured for them that drink, saying, "But this spake He of the Spirit, which they that believe on Him should receive: for the Spirit was not yet given, because Jesus was not yet glori-

fied." What spirit does He speak of, if not the Holy Spirit? For every man has in himself a spirit of his own, of which I spoke when I was commending to you the consideration of the mind. For every man's mind is his own spirit: of which the Apostle Paul says, "For what man knoweth the things of a man, but the spirit of the man which is in himself?" And then he added, "So also the things of God knoweth no man, but the Spirit of God."[1] None knows the things that are ours but our own spirit. I indeed do not know what are thy thoughts, nor dost thou know what are mine; for those things which we think within are our own, peculiar to ourselves; and his own spirit is the witness of every man's thoughts. "So also the things of God knoweth no man, but the Spirit of God." We with our spirit, God with His: so, however, that God with His Spirit knows also what goes on within us; but we are not able, without His own Spirit, to know what takes place in God. God, however, knows in us even what we know not in ourselves. For Peter did not know his own weakness, when he heard from the Lord that he would deny Him thrice: the sick man was ignorant of his own condition; the Physician knew him to be sick. There are then certain things which God knows in us, while we ourselves know them not. So far, however, as belongs to men, no man knows a man as he does himself: another does not know what is going on within him, but his own spirit knows it. But on receiving the Spirit of God, we learn also what takes place in God: not the whole, for we have not received the whole. We know many things from the pledge; for we have received a pledge, and the fullness of this pledge shall be given hereafter. Meanwhile, let the pledge console us in our pilgrimage here; because he who has condescended to bind himself to us by a pledge, is prepared to give us much. If such is the token, what must that be of which it is the token?

6. But what is meant by this which he says, "For the Spirit was not yet given, because Jesus was not yet glorified?" He is understood to say this in a sense that is evident. For the meaning is not that the Spirit of God, which was with God, was not in being; but was not yet in them who had believed on Jesus. For thus the Lord Jesus disposed not to give them the Spirit of which we speak, until after His resurrection; and this not without a cause. And perhaps if we inquire, He will favor us to find; and if we knock, He will open for us to enter. Piety knocks, not the

---

[1] 1 Cor. ii. 11.

hand though the hand also knocks, if it cease not from works of mercy. What then is the cause why the Lord Jesus Christ determined not to give the Holy Spirit until He should be glorified? which thing before we speak of as we may be able, we must first inquire, lest that should trouble any one, in what manner the Spirit was not yet in holy men, whilst we read in the Gospel concerning the Lord Himself newly born, that Simeon by the Holy Spirit recognized Him; that Anna the widow, a prophetess, also recognized Him;[1] that John, who baptized Him, recognized Him;[2] that Zacharias, being filled with the Holy Ghost, said many things; that Mary herself received the Holy Ghost to conceive the Lord.[3] We have therefore many preceding evidences of the Holy Spirit before the Lord was glorified by the resurrection of His flesh. Nor was it another spirit that the prophets also had, who proclaimed beforehand the coming of Christ. But still, there was to be a certain manner of this giving, which had not at all appeared before. For nowhere do we read before this, that men being gathered together had, by receiving the Holy Ghost, spoken in the tongues of all nations. But after His resurrection, when He first appeared to His disciples, He said to them: " Receive ye the Holy Ghost." Of this giving then it is said, "The Spirit was not given, because Jesus was not yet glorified. And He breathed upon their faces,"[4] He who with His breath enlivened the first man, and raised him up from the clay, by which breath He gave a soul to the limbs; signifying that He was the same who breathed upon their faces, that they might rise out of the mire and renounce their miry works. Then, after His resurrection, which the evangelist calls His glorifying, did the Lord first give the Holy Ghost to His disciples. Then having tarried with them forty days, as the book of the Acts of the Apostles shows, while they were seeing Him and companying with Him, He ascended into heaven in their sight. There at the end of ten days, on the day of Pentecost, He sent the Holy Ghost from above. Which having received, they, who had been gathered together in one place, as I have said, being filled withal, spoke in the tongues of all nations.

7. How then, brethren, because he that is baptized in Christ, and believes on Him, does not speak now in the tongues of all nations, are we not to believe that he has received the Holy Ghost? God forbid that our heart should be tempted by this faithlessness. Certain we are that every man receives: but only as much as the vessel of faith that he shall bring to the fountain can contain, so much does He fill of it. Since, therefore, the Holy Ghost is even now received by men, some one may say, Why is it that no man speaks in the tongues of all nations? Because the Church itself now speaks in the tongues of all nations. Before, the Church was in one nation, where it spoke in the tongues of all. By speaking then in the tongues of all, it signified what was to come to pass; that by growing among the nations, it would speak in the tongues of all. Whoso is not in this Church, does not now receive the Holy Ghost. For, being cut off and divided from the unity of the members, which unity speaks in the tongues of all, let him declare for himself; he has it not. For if he has it, let him give the sign which was given then. What do we mean by saying, Let him give the sign which was then given? Let him speak in all tongues. He answers me: How then, dost thou speak in all tongues? Clearly I do; for every tongue is mine, namely, of the body of which I am a member. The Church, spread among the nations, speaks in all tongues; the Church is the body of Christ, in this body thou art a member: therefore, since thou art a member of that body which speaks with all tongues, believe that thou too speakest with all tongues. For the unity of the members is of one mind by charity; and that unity speaks as one man spoke.

8. Consequently, we too receive the Holy Ghost if we love the Church, if we are joined together by charity, if we rejoice in the Catholic name and faith. Let us believe, brethren; as much as every man loves the Church of Christ, so much has he the Holy Ghost. For the Spirit is given, as the apostle saith, "to manifestation." To what manifestation? Just as the same apostle saith, " For to one is given by the Spirit the word of wisdom, to another the word of knowledge after the same Spirit, to another faith in the same Spirit, to another the gift of healing in one Spirit, to another the working of miracles in the same Spirit."[5] For there are many gifts given to manifestation, but thou, it may be, hast nothing of all those I have said. If thou lovest, it is not *nothing* that thou hast: if thou lovest unity, whoever has aught in that unity has it also for thee. Take away envy, and what I have is thine too. The envious temper puts men apart, soundness of mind unites them. In the body, the eye alone sees; but is it for itself alone that the eye sees? It

---

[1] Luke ii. 25-38.　　[2] John i. 26-34.
[3] Luke i. 35-79.　　[4] John xx. 22.　　[5] 1 Cor. xii. 7-9.

sees both for the hand and the foot, and for all the other members. If a blow be coming against the foot, the eye does not turn away from it, so as not to take precaution. Again, in the body, the hand alone works, but is it for itself alone the hand works? For the eye also it works: for if a coming blow comes, not against the hand, but only against the face, does the hand say, I will not move, because it is not coming to me? So the foot by walking serves all the members: all the other members are silent, and the tongue speaks for all. We have therefore the Holy Spirit if we love the Church; but we love ·the Church if we stand firm in its union and charity. For the apostle himself, after he had said that diverse gifts were bestowed on diverse men, just as the offices of the several members, saith, "Yet I show you a still more pre-eminent way;" and begins to speak of charity. This he put before tongues of men and angels, before miracles of faith, before knowledge and prophecy, before even that great work of mercy by which a man distributes to the poor all that he possesses; and, lastly, put it before even the martyrdom of the body: before all these so great things he put charity. Have it, and thou shalt have all: for without it, whatever thou canst have will profit nothing. But that thou mayest know that the charity of which we are speaking refers to the Holy Spirit (for the question now in hand in the Gospel is concerning the Holy Spirit), hear the apostle when he says, "The charity of God is shed abroad in our hearts by the Holy Spirit which is given to us." [1]

9. Why then was it the will of the Lord, seeing that the Spirit's benefits in us are the greatest, because by Him the love of God is shed abroad in our hearts, to give us that Spirit after His resurrection? Why did He signify by this? In order that in our resurrection our love may be inflamed, and may part from the love of the world to run wholly towards God. For here we are born and die: let us not love this world; let us migrate hence by love; by love let us dwell above, by that love by which we love God. In this sojourn of our life let us meditate on nothing else, but that here we shall not always be, and that by good living we shall prepare a place for ourselves there, whence we shall never migrate. For our Lord Jesus Christ, after that He is risen again, "now dieth no more;" "death," as the apostle says, "shall no more have dominion over Him." [2] Behold what we must love. If we live, if we believe on Him who is risen again, He will give us, not that which men love here who love not God, or love the more the less they love Him, but love this the less the more they love Him; but let us see what He has promised us. Not earthly and temporal riches, not honors and power in this world; for you see all these things given to wicked men, that they may not be highly prized by the good. Not, in short, bodily health itself, though it is He that gives that also, but that, as you see, He gives even to the beasts. Not long life; for what, indeed, is long that will some day have an end? It is not length of days that He has promised to His believers, as if that were a great thing, or decrepit old age, which all wish for before it comes, and all murmur at when it does come. Not beauty of person, which either bodily disease or that same old age which is desired drives away. One wishes to be beautiful, and also to live to be old: these two desires cannot agree together; if thou shalt be old, thou wilt not be beautiful; when old age comes, beauty will flee away; the vigor of beauty and the groaning of old age cannot dwell together in one body. All these things, then, are not what He promised us when He said, "He that believeth in me, let him come and drink, and out of his belly shall flow rivers of living water." He has promised us eternal life, where we shall have no fear, where we shall not be troubled, whence we shall have no migration, where we shall not die; where there is neither bewailing a predecessor deceased, nor a hoping for a successor. Accordingly, because such is what He has promised to us that love Him, and glow with the charity of the Holy Spirit, therefore He would not give us that same Spirit until He should be glorified, so that He might show in His body the life which we have not now, but which we hope for in the resurrection.

---

[1] Rom. v. 5.

[2] Rom. vi. 9

TRACTATE XXXIII.

CHAPTER VII. 40–53; VIII. 1–11.

1. YOU remember, my beloved, that in the last discourse, by occasion of the passage of the Gospel read, we spoke to you concerning the Holy Spirit. When the Lord had invited those that believe on Him to this drinking, speaking among those who meditated to lay hold of Him, and sought to kill Him, and were not able, because it was not His will: well, when He had spoken these things, there arose a dissension among the multitude concerning Him; some thinking that He was the very Christ, others saying that Christ shall not arise from Galilee. But they who had been sent to take Him returned clear of the crime and full of admiration. For they even gave witness to His divine doctrine, when those by whom they had been sent asked, " Why have ye not brought him?" They answered that they had never heard a man so speak: " For not any man so speaks." But He spake thus, because He was God and man. But the Pharisees, repelling their testimony, said to them: "Are ye also deceived?" We see, indeed, that you also have been charmed by his discourses. " Hath any one of the rulers or the Pharisees believed on him? But this multitude who know not the law are cursed." They who knew not the law believed on Him who had sent the law; and those men who were teaching the law despised Him, that it might be fulfilled which the Lord Himself had said, " I am come that they who see not may see, and they that see may be made blind." [1] For the Pharisees, the teachers of the law, were made blind, and the people that knew not the law, and yet believed on the author of the law, were enlightened.

2. "Nicodemus," however, "one of the Pharisees, who had come to the Lord by night,"—not indeed as being himself unbelieving, but timid; for therefore he came by night to the light, because he wished to be enlightened and feared to be known;—Nicodemus, I say, answered the Jews, " Doth our law judge a man before it hear him, and know what he doeth?" For they perversely wished to condemn before they examined. Nicodemus indeed knew, or rather believed, that if only they were willing to give Him a patient hearing, they would perhaps become like those who were sent to take Him, but

preferred to believe. They answered, from the prejudice of their heart, what they had answered to those officers, "Art thou also a Galilean?" That is, one seduced as it were by the Galilean. For the Lord was said to be a Galilean, because His parents were from the city of Nazareth. I have said " His parents" in regard to Mary, not as regards the seed of man; for on earth He sought but a mother, He had already a Father on high. For His nativity on both sides was marvellous: divine without mother, human without father. What, then, said those would-be doctors of the law to Nicodemus? " Search the Scriptures, and see that out of Galilee ariseth no prophet." Yet the Lord of the prophets arose thence. " They returned," saith the evangelist, " every man to his own house."

3. " Thence Jesus went unto the mount;" namely, to mount " Olivet,"—unto the fruitful mount, unto the mount of ointment, unto the mount of chrism. For where, indeed, but on mount Olivet did it become the Christ to teach? For the name of *Christ* is from *chrism;* χρισμα in the Greek, is called in Latin *unctio,* an *anointing.* And He has anointed us for this reason, because He has made us wrestlers against the devil. "And early in the morning He came again into the temple, and all the people came unto Him; and He sat down and taught them." And He was not taken, for He did not yet deign to suffer.

4. And now observe wherein the Lord's gentleness was tempted by His enemies. "And the scribes and Pharisees brought to Him a woman just taken in adultery: and they set her in the midst, and said to Him, Master, this woman has just been taken in adultery. Now Moses in the law commanded us, that such should be stoned: but what sayest thou? But this they said, tempting Him, that they might accuse Him." Why accuse Him? Had they detected Himself in any misdeed; or was that woman said to have been concerned with Him in any manner? What, then, is the meaning of " tempting Him, that they might accuse Him"? We understand, brethren, that a wonderful gentleness shone out pre-eminently in the Lord. They observed that He was very meek, very gentle: for of Him it had been previously foretold, " Gird Thy sword upon Thy thigh, O most Mighty; in Thy splendor and beauty

---

[1] John ix. 39.

urge on, march on prosperously, and reign, because of truth, and meekness, and righteousness."[1] Accordingly, as a teacher, He brought truth; as a deliverer, He brought gentleness; as a protector, He brought righteousness. That He was to reign on account of these things, the prophet had by the Holy Spirit foretold. When He spoke His truth was acknowledged; when He was not provoked to anger against His enemies, His meekness was praised. Whilst, therefore, in respect of these two,—namely, His truth and meekness,—His enemies were tormented with malice and envy; in respect of the third,—namely, righteousness,—they laid a stumbling-block for Him. In what way? Because the law had commanded the adulterers to be stoned, and surely the law could not command what was unjust: if any man should say other than the law had commanded, he would be detected as unjust. Therefore they said among themselves, "He is accounted true, he appears to be gentle; an accusation must be sought against him in respect of righteousness. Let us bring before him a woman taken in adultery; let us say to him what is ordered in the law concerning such: if he shall approve her being stoned, he will not show his gentleness; if he consent to let her go, he will not keep righteousness. But, say they, that he may not lose the reputation of gentleness, for which he is become an object of love to the people, without doubt he will say that she must be let go. Hence we find an opportunity of accusing him, and we charge him as being a transgressor of the law: saying to him, Thou art an enemy to the law; thou answerest against Moses, nay, against Him who gave the law through Moses; thou art worthy of death; thou too must be stoned with this woman." By these words and sentiments they might possibly be able to inflame envy against Him, to urge accusation, and cause His condemnation to be eagerly demanded. But this against whom? It was perversity against rectitude, falsehood against the truth, the corrupt heart against the upright heart, folly against wisdom. When did such men prepare snares, into which they did not first thrust their own heads? Behold, the Lord in answering them will both keep righteousness, and will not depart from gentleness. He was not taken for whom the snare was laid, but rather they were taken who laid it, because they believed not on Him who could pull them out of the net.

5. What answer, then, did the Lord Jesus make? How answered the Truth? How answered Wisdom? How answered that Righteousness against which a false accusation was ready? He did not say, Let her not be stoned; lest He should seem to speak against the law. But God forbid that He should say, Let her be stoned: for He came not to lose what He had found, but to seek what was lost. What then did He answer? See you how full it is of righteousness, how full of meekness and truth! "He that is without sin of you," saith He, "let him first cast a stone at her." O answer of Wisdom! How He sent them unto themselves! For without they stood to accuse and censure, themselves they examined not inwardly: they saw the adulteress, they looked not into themselves. Transgressors of the law, they wished the law to be fulfilled, and this by heedlessly accusing; not really fulfilling it, as if condemning adulteries by chastity. You have heard, O Jews, you have heard, O Pharisees, you have heard, O teachers of the law, the guardian of the law, but have not yet understood Him as the Lawgiver. What else does He signify to you when He writes with His finger on the ground? For the law was written with the finger of God; but written on stone because of the hard-hearted. The Lord now wrote on the ground, because He was seeking fruit. You have heard then, Let the law be fulfilled, let the adulteress be stoned. But is it by punishing her that the law is to be fulfilled by those that ought to be punished? Let each of you consider himself, let him enter into himself, ascend the judgment-seat of his own mind, place himself at the bar of his own conscience, oblige himself to confess. For he knows what he is: for "no man knoweth the things of a man, but the spirit of man which is in him." Each looking carefully into himself, finds himself a sinner. Yes, indeed. Hence, either let this woman go, or together with her receive ye the penalty of the law. Had He said, Let not the adulteress be stoned, He would be proved unjust: had He said, Let her be stoned, He would not appear gentle: let Him say what it became Him to say, both the gentle and the just, "Whoso is without sin of you, let him first cast a stone at her." This is the voice of Justice: Let her, the sinner, be punished, but not by sinners: let the law be fulfilled, but not by the transgressors of the law. This certainly is the voice of justice: by which justice, those men pierced through as if by a dart, looking into themselves and finding themselves guilty, "one after another all withdrew." The two were left alone, the wretched woman and Mercy. But the Lord, having struck them through with that dart of

justice, deigned not to heed their fall, but, turning away His look from them, " again He wrote with His finger on the ground."

6. But when that woman was left alone, and all they were gone out, He raised His eyes to the woman. We have heard the voice of justice, let us also hear the voice of clemency. For I suppose that woman was the more terrified when she had heard it said by the Lord, " He that is without sin of you, let him first cast a stone at her." But they, turning their thought to themselves, and by that very withdrawal having confessed concerning themselves, had left the woman with her great sin to Him who was without sin. And because she had heard this, " He that is without sin, let him first cast a stone at her," she expected to be punished by Him in whom sin could not be found. But He, who had driven back her adversaries with the tongue of justice, raising the eyes of clemency towards her, asked her, " Hath no man condemned thee?" She answered, " No man, Lord." And He said, " Neither do I condemn thee;" by whom, perhaps, thou didst fear to be condemned, because in me thou hast not found sin. " Neither will I condemn thee." What is this, O Lord? Dost Thou therefore favor sins? Not so, evidently. Mark what follows: " Go, henceforth sin no more." Therefore the Lord did also condemn, but condemned sins, not man. For if He were a patron of sin, He would say, Neither will I condemn thee; go, live as thou wilt: be secure in my deliverance; how much soever thou wilt sin, I will deliver thee from all punishment even of hell, and from the tormentors of the infernal world. He said not this.

7. Let them take heed, then, who love His gentleness in the Lord, and let them fear His truth. For " The Lord is sweet and right."[1] Thou lovest Him in that He is sweet; fear Him in that He is right. As the meek, He said, " I held my peace;" but as the just, He said, " Shall I always be silent?"[2] " The Lord is merciful and pitiful." So He is, certainly. Add yet further, " Long-suffering;" add yet further, "And very pitiful:" but fear what comes last, "And true."[3] For those whom He now bears with as sinners, He will judge as despisers. " Or despisest thou the riches of His long-suffering and gentleness; not knowing that the forbearance of God leadeth thee to repentance? But thou, after thy hardness and impenitent heart, treasurest up for thyself wrath against the day of wrath and the revelation of the righteous judgment of God; who will render to every man according to his deeds."[4] The Lord is gentle, the Lord is long-suffering, the Lord is pitiful; but the Lord is also just, the Lord is also true. He bestows on thee space for correction; but thou lovest the delay of judgment more than the amendment of thy ways. Hast thou been a bad man yesterday? To-day be a good man. Hast thou gone on in thy wickedness to-day? At any rate change to-morrow. Thou art always expecting, and from the mercy of God makest exceeding great promises to thyself. As if He, who has promised thee pardon through repentance, promised thee also a longer life. How knowest thou what to-morrow may bring forth? Rightly thou sayest in thy heart: When I shall have corrected my ways, God will put all my sins away. We cannot deny that God has promised pardon to those that have amended their ways and are converted. For in what prophet thou readest to me that God has promised pardon to him that amends, thou dost not read to me that God has promised thee a long life.

8. From both, then, men are in danger; both from hoping and despairing, from contrary things, from contrary affections. Who is deceived by hoping? He who says, God is good, God is merciful, let me do what I please, what I like; let me give loose reins to my lusts, let me gratify the desires of my soul. Why this? Because God is merciful, God is good, God is kind. These men are in danger by hope. And those are in danger from despair, who, having fallen into grievous sins, fancying that they can no more be pardoned upon repentance, and believing that they are without doubt doomed to damnation, do say with themselves, We are already destined to be damned, why not do what we please? with the disposition of gladiators destined to the sword. This is the reason that desperate men are dangerous: for, having no longer aught to fear, they are to be feared exceedingly. Despair kills these; hope, those. The mind is tossed to and fro between hope and despair. Thou hast to fear lest hope slay thee; and, when thou hopest much from mercy, lest thou fall into judgment: again, thou hast to fear lest despair slay thee, and, when thou thinkest that the grievous sins which thou hast committed cannot be forgiven thee, thou dost not repent, and thou incurrest the sentence of Wisdom, which says, " I also will laugh at your perdition."[5] How then does the Lord treat those who are in danger from both these maladies? To those who are in danger from hope, He says, " Be

---

[1] Ps. xxv. 8.   [2] Isa. xlii. 14.   [3] Ps. lxxxvi. 15.   [4] Rom. ii. 4-6.   [5] Prov. i. 26.

not slow to be converted to the Lord, neither put it off from day to day; for suddenly His anger will come, and in the time of vengeance, will utterly destroy thee."[1] To those who are in danger from despair, what does He say? "In what day soever the wicked man shall be converted, I will forget all his iniquities."[2] Accordingly, for the sake of those who are in danger by despair, He has offered us a refuge of pardon; and because of those who are in danger by hope, and are deluded by delays, He has made the day of death uncertain. Thou knowest not when thy last day may come. Art thou ungrateful because thou hast to-day on which thou mayest be improved? Thus therefore said He to the woman, "Neither will I condemn thee;" but, being made secure concerning the past, beware of the future. "Neither will I condemn thee:" I have blotted out what thou hast done; keep what I have commanded thee, that thou mayest find what I have promised.

[1] Ecclus. v. 8, 9.　　　　[2] Ezek. xviii. 21.

TRACTATE XXXIV.

Chapter VIII. 12.

1. What we have just heard and attentively received, as the holy Gospel was being read, I doubt not that all of us have also endeavored to understand, and that each of us according to his measure apprehended what he could of so great a matter as that which has been read; and while the bread of the word is laid out, no one can complain that he has tasted nothing. But again I doubt not that there is scarcely any who has understood the whole. Nevertheless, even should there be any who may sufficiently understand the words of our Lord Jesus Christ now read out of the Gospel, let him bear with our ministry, whilst, if possible, with His assistance, we may, by treating thereof, cause that either all or many may understand that which a few are joyful of having understood for themselves.

2. I think that what the Lord says, "I am the light of the world," is clear to those that have eyes, by which they are made partakers of this light: but they who have not eyes except in the flesh alone, wonder at what is said by the Lord Jesus Christ, "I am the light of the world." And perhaps there may not be wanting some one too who says with himself: Whether perhaps the Lord Christ is that sun which by its rising and setting causes the day? For there have not been wanting heretics who thought this. The Manicheans have supposed that the Lord Christ is that sun which is visible to carnal eyes, exposed and public to be seen, not only by men, but by the beasts. But the right faith of the Catholic Church rejects such a fiction, and perceives it to be a devilish doctrine: not only by believing acknowledges it to be such, but in the case of whom it can, proves it even by reasoning. Let us therefore reject this kind of error, which the Holy Church has anathematized from the beginning. Let us not suppose that the Lord Jesus Christ is this sun which we see rising from the east, setting in the west; to whose course succeeds night, whose rays are obscured by a cloud, which removes from place to place by a set motion: the Lord Christ is not such a thing as this. The Lord Christ is not the sun that was made, but He by whom the sun was made. For "all things were made by Him, and without Him was nothing made."

3. There is therefore a Light which made this light of the sun: let us love this Light, let us long to understand it, let us thirst for the same; that, with itself for our guide, we may at length come to it, and that we may so live in it that we may never die. This is indeed that Light of which prophecy long ago going before thus sang in the psalm: "O Lord, Thou shalt save men and beasts; even as Thy mercy is multiplied, O God." These are the words of the holy psalm: mark ye what the ancient discourse of holy men of God did premise concerning such a light. "Men," saith it, "and beasts Thou shalt save, O Lord; even as Thy mercy is multiplied, O God." For since Thou art God, and hast manifold mercy, the same multiplicity of Thy mercy reaches not only to men whom Thou hast created in Thine own image, but even to the beasts which Thou hast made subservient to men. For He who gives salvation to man, the same gives salvation also to the beast. Do not blush to think this of the Lord thy

God: nay, rather believe this and trust it, and see thou think not otherwise. He that saves thee, the same saves thy horse and thy sheep; to come to the very least, also thy hen: "Salvation is of the Lord,"[1] and God saves these. Thou art uneasy, thou questionest. I wonder why thou doubtest. Shall He disdain to save who deigned to create? Of the Lord is the saving of angels, of men, and of beasts: "Salvation is of the Lord." Just as no man is from himself, so no man is saved by himself. Therefore most truly and right well doth the psalm say, "O Lord, Thou shalt save men and beasts." Why? "Even as thy mercy is multiplied, O God." For Thou art God, Thou hast created, Thou savest: Thou gavest being, Thou givest to be in health.

4. Since, therefore, as the mercy of God is multiplied, men and beasts are saved by Him, have not men something else which God as Creator bestows on them, which He bestows not on the beasts? Is there no distinction between the living creature made after the image of God, and the living creature made subject to the image of God? Clearly there is: beyond that salvation common to us with the dumb animals, there is what God bestows on us, but not on them. What is this? Follow on in the same psalm: "But the sons of men shall hope under the covert of Thy wings." Having now a salvation in common with their cattle, "the sons of men shall hope under the covert of Thy wings." They have one salvation in fact, another in hope. This salvation which is at present is common to men and cattle; but there is another which men hope for; and which they who hope for receive, they who despair of receive not. For it saith, "The sons of men shall hope under covert of Thy wings." And they that perseveringly hope are protected by Thee, lest they be cast down from their hope by the devil: "Under covert of Thy wings they shall hope." If they shall hope, what shall they hope for, but for what the cattle shall not have? "They shall be fully drunk with the fatness of Thy house; and from the torrent of Thy pleasure Thou shalt give them drink." What sort of wine is that with which it is laudable to be drunk? What sort of wine is that which disturbs not the mind, but directs it? What sort of wine is that which makes perpetually sane, and makes not insane by drinking? "They shall be fully drunk." How? "With the fatness of Thy house; and from the torrent of Thy pleasure Thou shalt give them drink." How

so? "Because with Thee is the fountain of life." The very fountain of life walked on the earth, the same who said, "Whoso thirsts, let him come unto me." Behold the fountain! But we begin to speak about the light, and to handle the question laid down from the Gospel concerning the light. For we read how the Lord said, "I am the light of the world." Thence arose a question, lest any one, carnally understanding this, should fancy this light to mean the sun: we came thence to the psalm, which having considered, we found meanwhile that the Lord is the fountain of life. Drink and live. "With Thee," it saith, "is the fountain of life;" therefore, "under the shadow of Thy wings the sons of men hope," seeking to be full drunk with this fountain. But we were speaking of the Light. Follow on, then; for the prophet, having said, "With Thee is the fountain of life," went on to add, "In Thy light shall we see light,"—God of God, Light of Light. By this Light the sun's light was made; and the Light which made the sun, under which He also made us, was made under the sun for our sake. That Light which made the sun, was made, I say, under the sun for our sake. Do not despise the cloud of the flesh; with that cloud it is covered, not to be obscured, but to be moderated.

5. That unfailing Light, the Light of wisdom, speaking through the cloud of the flesh, says to men, "I am the light of the world; he that followeth me shall not walk in darkness, but shall have the light of life." How He has withdrawn thee from the eyes of the flesh, and recalled thee to the eyes of the heart! For it is not enough to say, "Whoso followeth me shall not walk in darkness, but shall have light;" He added too, "of life;" even as it was there said, "For with Thee is the fountain of life." See thus, my brethren, how the words of the Lord agree with the truth of that psalm: both there, the light is put with the fountain of life, and by the Lord it is said, "light of life." But for bodily use, *light* and *fountain* are different things: our mouths seek a fountain, our eyes light; when we thirst we seek a fountain, when we are in darkness we seek light; and if we chance to thirst in the night, we kindle a light to come to a fountain. Not so with God: light and fountain are the same thing: He who shines for thee that thou mayest see, the same flows for thee that thou mayest drink.

6. You see, then, my brethren, you see, if you see inwardly, what kind of light this is, of which the Lord says, "He that followeth me shall not walk in darkness." Follow the sun, and let us see if thou wilt not walk in

[1] Ps. iii. 9.

darkness. Behold, by rising it comes forth to thee; it goes by its course towards the west. Perhaps thy journey is towards the east: unless thou goest in a contrary direction to that in which it travels, thou wilt certainly err by following it, and instead of east wilt get to the west. If thou follow it by land, thou wilt go wrong; if the mariner follow it by sea, he will go wrong. Finally, it seems to thee, suppose, that thou must follow the sun, and thou also travellest thyself towards the west, whither it also travels; let us see after it has set if thou wilt not walk in darkness. See how, although thou art not willing to desert it, yet it will desert thee, to finish the day by necessity of its service. But our Lord Jesus Christ, even when He was not manifest to all through the cloud of His flesh, was yet at the same time holding all things by the power of His wisdom. Thy God is whole everywhere: if thou fall not off from Him, He will never fall away from thee.

7. Accordingly, "He that followeth me," saith He, "shall not walk in darkness, but shall have the light of life." What He has promised, He put in a word of the future tense; for He says not *has*, but "shall have the light of life." Yet He does not say, He that *shall follow* me; but, he that *does follow* me. What it is our duty to do, He put in the present tense; but what He has promised to them that do it, He has indicated by a word of the future tense. "He that followeth, shall have." That followeth now, shall have hereafter: followeth now by faith, shall have hereafter by sight. For, "whilst we are in the body," saith the apostle, "we are absent from the Lord: for we walk by faith, not by sight."[1] When shall we walk by sight? When we shall have the light of life, when we shall have come to that vision, when this night shall have passed away. Of that day, indeed, which is to arise, it is said. "In the morning I will stand near thee, and contemplate thee."[2] What means "in the morning"? When the night of this world is over, when the terrors of temptations are over, when that lion which goeth about roaring in the night, seeking whom it may devour, is vanquished. "In the morning I will stand near thee, and contemplate." Now what do we think, brethren, to be our duty for the present time, but what is again said in the psalm, "Every night through will I wash my couch; I will moisten my bed with my tears"?[3] Every night through, saith he, I will weep; I will burn with desire for the light. The Lord

sees my desire: for another psalm says to Him, "All my desire is before Thee; and my groaning is not hid from Thee."[4] Dost thou desire gold? Thou canst be seen; for, while seeking gold, thou wilt be manifest to men. Dost thou desire corn? Thou askest one that has it; whom also thou informest, while seeking to get at that which thou desirest. Dost thou desire God? Who sees, but God? From whom, then, dost thou seek God, as thou seekest bread, water, gold, silver, corn? From whom dost thou seek God, except from God? He is sought from Himself who has promised Himself. Let the soul extend her desire, and with more capacious bosom seek to comprehend that which "eye hath not seen, nor ear heard, nor hath entered into the heart of man."[5] Desire it we can, long for it we can, pant after it we can; but worthily conceive it, worthily unfold it in words, we cannot.

8. Wherefore, my brethren, since the Lord says briefly, "I am the light of the world: he that followeth me shall not walk in darkness, but shall have the light of life;" in these words He has commanded one thing, promised another; let us do what He has commanded, that we may not with shameless face demand what He has promised; that He may not say to us in His judgment, Hast thou done what I commanded, that thou shouldest expect what I promised? What hast Thou commanded, then, O Lord our God? He says to thee, That thou shouldest follow me. Thou hast sought counsel of life? Of what life, but of that of which it is said, "With Thee is the fountain of life"? A certain man heard it said to him, "Go, sell all that thou hast, and give to the poor, and thou shalt have treasure in heaven; and come, follow me." He followed not, but went away sorrowful; he sought the "good Master," went to Him as a teacher, and despised His teaching; he went away sorrowful, tied and bound by his lusts; he went away sorrowful, having a great load of avarice on his shoulders. He toiled and fretted; and yet he thought that He, who was willing to rid him of his load, was not to be followed but forsaken. But after the Lord has, by the gospel, cried aloud, "Come unto me, all ye that labor, and are heavy laden, and I will give you rest; take my yoke upon you, and learn of me, for I am meek and lowly in heart,"[6] how many, on hearing the gospel, have done what that rich man, on hearing from His own mouth, did not do? Therefore, let us do it now, let us follow the Lord; let us loose the

---

[1] 2 Cor. v. 6, 7.   [2] Ps. v. 4.   [3] Ps. vi. 6.   [4] Ps. xxxviii. 10.   [5] 1 Cor. ii. 9.   [6] Matt. xi. 29.

fetters by which we are hindered from following Him. And who is sufficient to loose such bonds, unless He help, to whom it is said, "Thou hast burst asunder my bonds"?[1] Of whom another psalm says, "The Lord looseth them that are in bonds; the Lord raiseth up them that are crushed and oppressed."[2]

9. And what do they follow, who have been loosed and raised up, but the Light from which they hear, "I am the light of the world: he that followeth me shall not walk in darkness"? For the Lord gives light to the blind. Therefore we, brethren, having the eye-salve of faith, are now enlightened. For His spittle did before mingle with the earth, by which the eyes of him who was born blind were anointed. We, too, have been born blind of Adam, and have need of Him to enlighten us. He mixed spittle with clay: "The Word was made flesh, and dwelt among us." He mixed spittle with earth; hence it was predicted, "Truth has sprung from the earth;"[3] and He said Himself, "I am the way, the truth, and the life." When we shall see face to face, we shall have the full fruition of the truth; for this also is promised to us. For who would dare hope for what God had not deigned either to promise or to give? We shall see face to face. The apostle says, "Now I know in part, now through a glass darkly; but then, face to face."[4] And the Apostle John says in his epistle, "Beloved, now are we the sons of God; and it has not yet appeared what we shall be: we know that, when He shall appear, we shall be like Him; for we shall see Him even as He is."[5] This is a great promise; if thou lovest, follow. I do love, sayest thou, but by what way am I to follow? If the Lord thy God had said to thee, "I am the truth and the life," in desiring truth and longing for life, thou mightest truly ask the way by which thou mightest come to these, and mightest say to thyself: A great thing is the truth, a great thing is the life, were there only the means whereby my soul might come thereto! Dost thou ask by what way? Hear Him say at the first, "I am the way." Before He said *whither*, He premised by what way: "I am," saith He, "the way." The way whither? "And the truth and the life." First, He told thee the way to come; then, whither to come. I am the way, I am the truth, I am the life. Remaining with the Father, the truth and life; putting on flesh, He became the way. It is not said to thee, Labor in finding a way to come to the truth and life; this is not said to thee. Slug-

gard, arise: the way itself has come to thee, and roused thee from thy sleep; if, however, it has roused thee, up and walk. Perhaps thou art trying to walk, and art not able, because thy feet ache. How come thy feet to ache? Have they been running over rough places at the bidding of avarice? But the word of God has healed even the lame. Behold, thou sayest, I have my feet sound, but the way itself I see not. He has also enlightened the blind.

10. All this by faith, so long as we are absent from the Lord, dwelling in the body; but when we shall have traversed the way, and have reached the home itself, what shall be more joyful than we? What shall be more blessed than we? Because nothing more at peace than we; for there will be no rebelling against a man. But now, brethren, it is difficult for us to be without strife. We have indeed been called to concord, we are commanded to have peace among ourselves; to this we must give our endeavor, and strain with all our might, that we may come at last to the most perfect peace; but at present we are at strife, very often with those whose good we are seeking. There is one who goes astray, thou wishest to lead him to the way; he resists, thou strivest with him: the pagan resists thee, thou disputest against the errors of idols and devils; a heretic resists, thou disputest against other doctrines of devils; a bad catholic is not willing to live aright, thou rebukest even thy brother within; he dwells with thee in the house, and seeks the paths of ruin; thou art inflamed with eager passion to put him right, that thou mayest render to the Lord a good account of both concerning him. How many necessities of strife there are on every side! Very often one is overcome with weariness, and says to himself, "What have I to do with bearing with gainsayers, bearing with those who render evil for good? I wish to benefit them, they are willing to perish; I wear out my life in strife; I have no peace; besides, I make enemies of those whom I ought to have as friends, if they regarded the good will of him that seeks their good: what business is it of mine to endure this? Let me return to myself, I will be kept to myself, I will call upon my God. Do return to thyself, thou findest strife there. If thou hast begun to follow God, thou findest strife there. What strife, sayest thou, do I find? "The flesh lusteth against the Spirit, and the Spirit against the flesh."[6] Behold thou art thyself, thou art alone, thou art with thyself; behold,

---

Ps. cxvi. 16.　　[2] Ps. xlvi. 8.　　[3] Ps. lxxxv. 11.
[1] Cor. xiii. 12.　　[5] 1 John iii. 2.　　[6] Gal. v. 17.

thou art bearing with no other person, but yet thou seest another law in thy members warring against the law of thy mind, and taking thee captive in the law of sin, which is in thy members. Cry aloud, then, and cry to God, that He may give thee peace from the inner strife: " O wretched man that I am, who shall deliver me from the body of this death? The grace of God through our Lord Jesus Christ." [1] Because, "He that followeth me," saith He, "shall not walk in darkness, but shall have the light of life." All strife ended, immortality shall follow; for "the last enemy, death, shall be destroyed." And what peace will this be? " This corruptible must put on incorruption, and this mortal must put on immortality." [2] To which that we may come (for it will then be in reality), let us now follow in hope Him who said, " I am the light of the world: he that followeth me shall not walk in darkness, but shall have the light of life."

---

[1] Rom. vii. 23-25.

[2] 1 Cor. xv. 26.

TRACTATE XXXV.

Chapter VIII. 13, 14.

1. You who were present yesterday, bear in mind that we were a long while discoursing of the words of our Lord Jesus Christ, where He says, "I am the light of the world: he that followeth me shall not walk in darkness, but shall have the light of life;" and if we wished to go on discoursing of that light, we might still speak a long time; for it would be impossible for us to expound the matter in brief. Therefore, my brethren, let us follow Christ, the light of the world, that we may not be walking in darkness. We must fear the darkness,—not the darkness of the eyes, but that of the moral character; and even if it be the darkness of the eyes, it is not of the outer, but of the inner eyes, of those by which we discern, not between white and black, but between right and wrong.

2. When our Lord Jesus Christ had spoken these things, the Jews answered, "Thou bearest record of thyself; thy record is not true." Before our Lord Jesus Christ came, He lighted and sent many prophetic lamps before Him. Of these was also John Baptist, to whom the great Light itself, which is the Lord Christ, gave a testimony such as was given to no other man; for He said, "Among them that are born of women, there hath not risen a greater than John the Baptist." [1] Yet this man, than whom none was greater among those born of women, said of the Lord Jesus Christ, " I indeed baptize you in water; but He that is coming is mightier than I, whose shoe I am not worthy to loose." [2] See how the lamps submits itself to the Day. The Lord Himself bears witness that the same John was indeed a lamp: "He was," saith He, "a burning and a shining lamp; and ye were willing for a season to rejoice in his light." [3] But when the Jews said to the Lord, " Tell us by what authority thou doest these things," He, knowing that they regarded John the Baptist as a great one, and that the same whom they regarded as a great one had borne witness to them concerning the Lord, answered them, " I also will ask you one thing; tell me, the baptism of John, whence is it? from heaven, or from men?" Thrown into confusion, they considered among themselves that, if they said, " From men," they might be stoned by the people, who believed John to be a prophet; if they said, "From heaven," He might answer them, " He whom ye confess to have been a prophet from heaven bore testimony to me, and ye have heard from him by what authority I do these things." They saw, then, that whichever of these two answers they made, they would fall into the snare, and they said, " We do not know." And the Lord answered them, " Neither tell I you by what authority I do these things." [4] " I tell you not what I know, because you will not confess what you know." Most justly, certainly, were they repulsed, and they departed in confusion; and that was fulfilled which God the Father says by the prophet in the psalm, " I have prepared a lamp for my Christ" (the lamp was John); "His enemies I will clothe with confusion." [5]

---

[1] Matt. xi. 11.   [2] John i. 26. 27.   [3] John v. 35.   [4] Matt. xxi. 23-27.   [5] Ps. cxxxii. 17, 18.

3. The Lord Jesus Christ, then, had the witness of prophets sent before Him, of the heralds that preceded the judge: He had witness from John; but He was Himself the greater witness which He bore to Himself. But those men with their feeble eyes sought lamps, because they were not able to bear the day; for that same Apostle John, whose Gospel we have in our hands, says in the beginning of his Gospel, concerning John the Baptist: " There was a man sent from God, whose name was John. He came for a witness, to bear witness of the light, that all men might believe through him. He was not the light, but was sent to bear witness of the light. That was the true light, that lighteth every man coming into the world." If " every man," therefore also lighteth John. Whence also the same John says, " We all have received out of His fullness." Wherefore discern ye these things, that your minds may profit in the faith of Christ, that ye be not always babes seeking the breasts and shrinking from solid food. You ought to be nourished and to be weaned by our holy mother the Church of Christ, and to come to more solid food by the mind, not by the belly. This discern ye then, that the light which enlighteneth is one thing, another that which is enlightened. For also our eyes are called lights;[1] and every man thus swears, touching his eyes, by these lights of his: " So may my lights live." This is a customary oath. Let these lights, if lights they are, be opened, and shine for thee in thy closed chamber, when the light is not there; they certainly cannot. Therefore, as these which we have in our face, and call lights, when they are both healthy and open, need the help of light from without,—which being removed or not brought in, though they are sound and are open, yet they do not see,—so our mind, which is the eye of the soul, unless it be irradiated by the light of truth, and wondrously shone upon by Him who enlightens and is not enlightened, will not be able to come to wisdom nor to righteousness. For to live righteously is for us the way itself. But how can he on whom the light does not shine but stumble in the way? And hence, in such a way, we have need of seeing, in such a way it is a great thing to see. Now Tobias had the eyes in his face closed, and the son gave his hand to the father; and yet the father, by his instruction, pointed out the way to the son.[2]

4. The Jews then answered, " Thou bearest witness of thyself; thy witness is not true." Let us see what they hear; let us also hear, yet not as they did: they despising, we believing; they wishing to slay Christ, we desiring to live through Christ. Let this difference distinguish our ears and minds from theirs, and let us hear what the Lord answers to the Jews. " Jesus answered and said to them, Though I bear witness of myself, my witness is true; because I know whence I came and whither I go." The light shows both other things and also itself. Thou lightest a lamp, for instance, to look for thy coat, and the burning lamp affords thee light to find thy coat; dost thou light the lamp to see itself when it burns ? A burning lamp is indeed capable at the same time of exposing to view other things which the darkness covered, and also of showing itself to thine eyes. So also the Lord Christ distinguished between His faithful ones and His Jewish enemies, as between light and darkness: as between those whom He illuminated with the ray of faith, and those on whose closed eyes He shed His light. So, too, the sun shines on the face of the sighted and of the blind; both alike standing and facing the sun are shone upon in the flesh, but both are not enlightened in the eyesight. The one sees, the other sees not: the sun is present to both, but one is absent from the present sun. So likewise the Wisdom of God, the Word of God, the Lord Jesus Christ, is everywhere present, because the truth is everywhere, wisdom is everywhere. One man in the east understands justice, another man in the west understands justice; is justice which the one understands a different thing from that which the other understands ? In body they are far apart, and yet they have the eyes of their minds on one object. The justice which I, placed here, see, if justice it is, is the same which the just man, separated from me in the flesh by ever so many days' journey, also sees, and is united to me in the light of that justice. Therefore the light bears witness to itself; it opens the sound eyes and is its own witness, that it may be known as the light. But how about the unbelievers ? Is it not present to them ? It is present also to them, but they have not eyes of the heart with which to see it. Hear the sentence fetched from the Gospel itself concerning them: "And the light shineth in darkness, and the darkness comprehended it not."[3] Hence the Lord saith, and saith truly, " Though I bear witness of myself, my witness is true; because I know whence I came and whither I go." He meant us to understand the Father here:

---

[1] *Lumina.*   [2] Tobit ii. 11.   [3] John i. 5.

the Son gave glory to the Father. Himself the equal glorifies Him by whom He was sent. How ought man to glorify Him by whom he was created!

5. "I know whence I came and whither I go." He who speaks to you in person has what He has not left, and yet He came; for by coming He departed not thence, nor has He forsaken us by returning thither. Why marvel ye? It is God: this cannot be done by man; it cannot be done even by the sun. When it goes to the west it leaves the east, and until it returns to the east, when about to rise, it is not in the east; but our Lord Jesus Christ both comes and is there, both returns and is here. Hear the evangelist himself speaking in another place, and, if thou canst, understand it; if not, believe it: "God," saith he, "no man hath ever seen, but the only-begotten Son, who is in the bosom of the Father, He hath declared Him." He said not *was* in the bosom of the Father, as if by coming He had quitted the Father's bosom. Here He was speaking, and yet He declared that He was there; and when about to depart hence, what said He? "Lo, I am with you always, even unto the end of the world."[1]

6. The witness of the light then is true, whether it be manifesting itself or other things; for without light thou canst not see light, and without light thou canst not see any other thing whatever that is not light. If light is capable of showing other things which are not lights, is it not capable of showing itself? Does not that discover itself, without which other things cannot be made manifest? A prophet spoke a truth; but whence had he it, unless he drew it from the fountain of truth? John spoke a truth; but whence he spoke it, ask himself: "We all," saith he, "have received of His fullness." Therefore our Lord Jesus Christ is worthy to bear witness to Himself. But in any case, my brethren, let us who are in the night of this world hear also prophecy with earnest attention: for now our Lord willed to come in humility to our weakness and the deep night-darkness of our hearts. He came as a man to be despised and to be honored, He came to be denied and to be confessed; to be despised and to be denied by the Jews, to be honored and confessed by us: to be judged and to judge; to be judged unjustly, to judge righteously. Such then He came that He behoved to have a lamp to bear witness to Him. For what need was there that John should, as a lamp, bear witness to the day, if the day itself could be looked upon by our weakness? But we could not look upon it: He became weak for the weak; by infirmity He healed infirmity; by mortal flesh He took away the death of the flesh; of His own body He made a salve for our eyes. Since, therefore, the Lord is come, and since we are still in the night of the world, it behoves us to hear also prophecies.

7. For it is from prophecy that we convince gainsaying pagans. Who is Christ? says the pagan. To whom we reply, He whom the prophets foretold. What prophets? asks he. We quote Isaiah, Daniel, Jeremiah, and other holy prophets: we tell him that they came long before Christ, by what length of time they preceded His coming. We make this reply then: Prophets came before Him, and they foretold His coming. One of them answers: What prophets? We quote for him those which are daily read to us. And, said he, Who are these prophets? We answer: Those who also foretold the things which we see come to pass. And he urges: You have forged these for yourselves, you have seen them come to pass, and have written them in what books you pleased, as if their coming had been predicted. Here in opposition to pagan enemies the witness of other enemies offers itself. We produce books written by the Jews, and reply: Doubtless both you and they are enemies of our faith. Hence are they scattered among the nations, that we may convince one class of enemies by another. Let the book of Isaiah be produced by the Jews, and let us see if it is not there we read, "He was led as a sheep to be slaughtered, and as a lamb before his shearer was dumb, so He opened not His mouth. In humility His judgment was taken away; by His bruises we are healed: all we as sheep went astray, and He was delivered up for our sins."[2] Behold one lamp. Let another be produced, let the psalm be opened, and thence, too, let the foretold suffering of Christ be quoted: "They pierced my hands and my feet, they counted all my bones: but they considered me and gazed upon me, they parted my garments among them, and upon my vesture they cast the lot. My praise is with Thee; in the great assembly will I confess to Thee. All the ends of the earth shall be reminded, and be converted to the Lord: all countries of the nations shall worship in His sight; for the kingdom is the Lord's, and He shall have dominion over the nations."[3] Let one enemy blush, for it is another enemy that gives me the book. But lo, out of the

---

[1] Matt. xxviii. 20.　　　[2] Isa. liii. 5-8.　　　[3] Ps. xxii. 17-29.

book produced by the one enemy, I have vanquished the other: nor let that same who produced me the book be left; let him produce that by which himself also may be vanquished. I read another prophet, and I find the Lord speaking to the Jews: "I have no pleasure in you, saith the Lord, nor will I accept sacrifice at your hands: for from the rising of the sun even to his going down, a pure sacrifice is offered to my name."[1] Thou dost not come, O Jew, to a pure sacrifice; I prove thee impure.

8. Behold, even lamps bear witness to the day, because of our weakness, for we cannot bear and look at the brightness of the day. In comparison, indeed, with unbelievers, we Christians are even now light; as the apostle says, "For ye were once darkness, but now light in the Lord: walk as children of light:"[2] and he says elsewhere, "The night is far spent, the day is at hand: let us therefore cast away the works of darkness, and put on us the armor of light; let us walkhon estly as in the day."[3] Yet that even the day in which we now are is still night, in comparison with the light of that to which we are to come, listen to the Apostle Peter: he says that a voice came to the Lord Christ from the excellent glory, "Thou art my beloved Son, in whom I am well pleased. This voice," said he, "which came from heaven, we heard, when we were with Him in the holy mount." But because we were not there, and have not then heard this voice from heaven, the same Peter says to us, "And we have a more sure word of prophecy." You have not heard the voice come from heaven, but you have a more sure word of prophecy. For the Lord Jesus Christ, foreseeing that there would be certain wicked men who would calumniate His miracles, by attributing them to magical arts, sent prophets before Him. For, supposing He was a magician, and by magical arts caused that He should be worshipped after His death, was He then a magician before He was born? Hear the prophets, O man dead, and breeding the worms of calumny, hear the prophets: I read, hear them who came before the Lord. "We have," saith the Apostle Peter, "a more sure word of prophecy, to which ye do well to give heed, as to a lamp in a dark place, until the day dawn, and the day-star arise in your hearts."[4]

9. When, therefore, our Lord Jesus Christ shall come, and, as the Apostle Paul also says, will bring to light the hidden things of darkness, and will make manifest the thoughts of the heart, that every man may have praise from God;[5] then, in presence of such a day, lamps will not be needed: no prophet shall then be read to us, no book of an apostle shall be opened; we shall not require the witness of John, we shall not need the Gospel itself. Accordingly all Scriptures shall be taken out of the way,—which, in the night of this world, were as lamps kindled for us that we might not remain in darkness,—when all these are taken away, that they may not shine as if we needed them, and the men of God, by whom these were ministered to us, shall themselves, together with us, behold that true and clear light. Well, what shall we see after these aids have been removed? Wherewith shall our mind be fed? Wherewith shall our gaze be delighted? Whence shall arise that joy which neither eye hath seen, nor ear heard, nor hath gone up into the heart of man? What shall we see? I beseech you, love with me, by believing run with me: let us long for our home above, let us pant for our home above, let us feel that we are strangers here. What shall we see then? Let the Gospel now tell us: "In the beginning was the Word, and the Word was with God, and the Word was God." Thou shalt come to the fountain from which a little dew has already besprinkled thee: thou shalt see that very light, from which a ray was sent aslant and through many windings into thy dark heart, in its purity, for the seeing and bearing of which thou art being purified. John himself says, and this I cited yesterday: "Beloved, we are the sons of God; and it hath not yet appeared what we shall be: we know that, when He shall appear, we shall be like Him, for we shall see Him even as He is."[6] I feel that your affections are being lifted up with me to the things that are above: but the body, which is corrupt, weighs down the soul; and, the earthly habitation depresses the mind while meditating many things.[7] I am about to lay aside this book, and you too are going to depart, every man to his own house. It has been good for us to have been in the common light, good to have been glad therein, good to have rejoiced therein; but when we part from one another, let us not depart from Him.

---

[1] Mal. i. 10, 11.   [2] Eph. v. 8.
[3] Rom. xiii. 12, 13.   [4] 2 Pet. i. 17-19.   [5] 1 Cor. iv. 5.   [6] 1 John iii. 2.   [7] Wisd. ix. 15.

TRACTATE XXXVI.

Chapter VIII. 15–18.

1. In the four Gospels, or rather in the four books of the one Gospel, Saint John the apostle, not undeservedly in respect of his spiritual understanding compared to the eagle, has elevated his preaching higher and far more sublimely than the other three; and in this elevating of it he would have our hearts likewise lifted up. For the other three evangelists walked with the Lord on earth as with a man; concerning His divinity they have said but little; but this evangelist, as if he disdained to walk on earth, just as in the very opening of his discourse he thundered on us, soared not only above the earth and above the whole compass of air and sky, but even above the whole army of angels and the whole order of invisible powers, and reached to Him by whom all things were made; saying, "In the beginning was the Word, and the Word was with God, and the Word was God. This was in the beginning with God. All things were made by Him, and without Him was nothing made." To this so great sublimity of his beginning all the rest of his preaching well agrees; and he has spoken concerning the divinity of the Lord as none other has spoken. What he had drank in, the same he gave forth. For it is not without reason that it is recorded of him in this very Gospel, that at supper he reclined on the Lord's bosom. From that breast then he drank in secret; but what he drank in secret he gave forth openly, that there may come to all nations not only the incarnation of the Son of God, and His passion and resurrection, but also what He was before His incarnation, the only Son of the Father, the Word of the Father, co-eternal with Him that begat, equal with Him by whom He was sent; but yet in that very sending made less, that the Father might be greater.

2. Whatever, then, you have heard stated in lowly manner concerning the Lord Jesus Christ, think of that economy by which He assumed flesh; but whatever you hear, or read, stated in the Gospel concerning Him that is sublime and high above all creatures, and divine, and equal and coeternal with the Father, be sure that this which you read appertains to the form of God, not to the form of the servant. For if you hold this rule, you who can understand it (inasmuch as you are not all able to understand it, but you are all bound to trust it),—if, I say, you hold this rule, as men walking in the light, you will fight against the calumnies of heretical darkness without fear. For there have not been wanting those who, in reading the Gospel, followed only those testimonies that concern the humility of Christ, and have been deaf to those which have declared His divinity; deaf for this reason, that they may be full of evil words. There have likewise been some, who, giving heed only to those which speak of the excellency of the Lord, even though they have read of His mercy in becoming man for our sakes, have not believed the testimonies, but accounted them false and invented by men; contending that our Lord Jesus Christ was only God, not also man Some in this way, some in that: both in error. But the catholic faith, holding from both the truths which each holds and preaching the truth which each believes, has both understood that Christ is God and also believed Him to be man: for each is written and each is true. Shouldst thou assert that Christ is only God, thou deniest the medicine whereby thou wast healed: shouldst thou assert that Christ is only man, thou deniest the power whereby thou wast created. Hold therefore both. O faithful soul and catholic heart, hold both, believe both, faithfully confess both. Christ is both God and also man. How is Christ God? Equal with the Father, one with the Father. How is Christ man? Born of a virgin, taking upon Himself mortality from man, but not taking iniquity.

3 These Jews then saw the man; they neither perceived nor believed Him to be God: and you have already heard how, among all the rest, they said to Him, "Thou bearest witness of thyself; thy witness is not true." You have also heard what He said in reply, as it was read to you yesterday, and according to our ability discussed. To-day have been read these words of His, "Ye judge after the flesh." Therefore it is, saith He, that you say to me, "Thou bearest witness of thyself; thy witness is not true," because you judge after the flesh, because you perceive not God; the man you see, and by persecuting the man, you offend God hidden in Him. "Ye," then, "judge after the flesh." Because I bear witness of myself, I therefore appear to you arrogant. For every

man, when he wishes to bear commendatory witness of himself, seems arrogant and proud. Hence it is written, "Let not thy own mouth praise thee, but let thy neighbor's" mouth praise thee.[1] But this was said to man. For we are weak, and we speak to the weak. We can speak the truth, but we can also lie; although we are bound to speak the truth, still we have it in our power to lie when we will. But far be it from us to think that the darkness of falsehood could be found in the splendor of the divine light. He spoke as the light, spoke as the truth; but the light was shining in the darkness, and the darkness comprehended it not: therefore they judged after the flesh. "Ye," saith He, "judge after the flesh."

4. "I judge not any man." Does not the Lord Jesus Christ, then, judge any man? Is He not the same of whom we confess that He rose again on the third day, ascended into heaven, there sits at the right hand of the Father, and thence shall come to judge the quick and the dead? Is not this our faith of which the apostle says, "With the heart man believeth unto righteousness, and with the mouth confession is made unto salvation?"[2] When, therefore, we confess these things, do we contradict the Lord? We say that He shall come a judge of the quick and the dead, whilst He says Himself, "I judge not any man." This question may be solved in two ways: Either that we may understand this expression, "I judge not any man," to mean, I judge not any man *now;* in accordance with what He says in another place, "I am not come to judge the world, but to save the world;" not denying His judgment here, but deferring it. Or, otherwise, surely that when He said, "Ye judge after the flesh," He sub-joined, "I judge not any man," in such man-ner that thou shouldst understand "after the flesh" to complete the sense. Therefore let no scruple of doubt remain in our heart against the faith which we hold and declare concerning Christ as judge. Christ is come, but first to save, then to judge: to adjudge to punishment those who would not be saved; to bring them to life who, by believing, did not reject salvation. Accordingly, the first dispensation of our Lord Jesus Christ is me-dicinal, not judicial; for if He had come to judge first, He would have found none on whom He might bestow the rewards of right-eousness. Because, therefore, He saw that all were sinners, and that none was exempt from the death of sin, His mercy had first to be craved, and afterwards His judgment

must be executed; for of Him the psalm had sung, "Mercy and judgment will I sing to Thee, O Lord."[3] Now, He says not "judg-ment and mercy," for if judgment had been first, there would be no mercy; but it is mercy first, then judgment. What is the mercy first? The Creator of man deigned to become man; was made what He had made, that the creature He had made might not perish. What can be added to this mercy? And yet He has added thereto. It was not enough for Him to be made man, He added to this that He was rejected of men; it was not enough to be rejected, He was dishon-ored; it was not enough to be dishonored, He was put to death; but even this was not enough, it was by the death of the cross. For when the apostle was commending to us His obedience even unto death, it was not enough for him to say, "He became obedient unto death;" for it was not unto death of any kind whatever: but he added, "even the death of the cross."[4] Among all kinds of death, there was nothing worse than that death. In short, that wherein one is racked by the most intense pains is called *cruciatus,* which takes its name from *crux,* a cross. For the crucified, hanging on the tree, nailed to the wood, were killed by a slow lingering death. To be crucified was not merely to be put to death; for the victim lived long on the cross, not because longer life was chosen, but because death itself was stretched out, that the pain might not be too quickly ended. He willed to die for us, yet it is not enough to say this; He deigned to be crucified, be-came obedient even to the death of the cross. He who was about to take away all death, chose the lowest and worst kind of death: He slew death by the worst of deaths. To the Jews who understood not, it was indeed the worst of deaths, but it was chosen by the Lord. For He was to have that very cross as His sign; that very cross, a trophy, as it were, over the vanquished devil, He was to put on the brow of believers, so that the apos-tle said, "God forbid that I should glory, save in the cross of our Lord Jesus Christ, by whom the world is crucified to me, and I to the world."[5] Nothing was then more intoler-able in the flesh, nothing is now more glori-ous on the brow. What does He reserve for His faithful one, when He has put such honor on the instrument of His own torture? Now is the cross no longer used among the Romans in the punishment of criminals, for where the cross of the Lord came to be honored, it was thought that even a guilty man would be

---

[1] Prov. xxvii. 2.   [2] Rom. x. 10.   [3] Ps. ci. 1.   [4] Phil. ii. 8.   [5] Gal. vi. 14.

honored if he should be crucified. Hence, He who came for this cause judged no man: He suffered also the wicked. He suffered unjust judgment, that He might execute righteous judgment. But it was of His mercy that He endured unjust judgment. In short, He became so low as to come ·to the cross; yea, laid aside His power, but published His mercy. Wherein did He lay aside His power? In that He would not come down from the cross, though He had the power to rise again from the sepulchre. Wherein did He publish His mercy? In that, when hanging on the cross, He said, "Father, forgive them; for they know not what they do." [1] Whether, then, it be that He said, "I judge not any man," because He had come not to judge the world, but to save the world; or, that, as I have mentioned, when He had said, "Ye judge after the flesh," He added, "I judge not any man," for us to understand that Christ judgeth not after the flesh, like as He was judged by men.

5. But that you may know that Christ is judge even now, hear what follows: "And if I judge, my judgment is true." Behold, thou hast Him as thy judge, but acknowledge Him as thy Saviour, lest thou feel the judge. But why has He said that His judgment is true? "Because," saith He, "I am not alone, but I and the Father that sent me." I have said to you, brethren, that this holy Evangelist John soars exceedingly high: it is with difficulty that he is comprehended. But we need to remind you, beloved, of the deeper mystery of this soaring. Both in the prophet Ezekiel, and in the Apocalypse of this very John whose Gospel this is, there is mentioned a fourfold living creature, having four characteristic faces; that of a man, of an ox, of a lion, and of an eagle. Those who have handled the mysteries of Holy Scripture before us have, for the most part, understood by this living creature, or rather, these four living creatures, the four evangelists. They have understood the lion as put for king, because he appears to be, in a manner, the king of beasts on account of his strength and terrible valor. This character is assigned to Matthew, because in the generations of the Lord he followed the royal line, showing how the Lord was, along the royal line, of the seed of David. But Luke, because he begins with the priesthood of Zacharias, mentioning the father of John the Baptist, is designated the ox; for the ox was an important victim in the sacrifice of the priests. To Mark is deservedly assigned the man Christ, because

neither has he said anything of the royal authority, nor did he begin with the priestly function, but only set out with the man Christ. All these have departed but little from the things of earth, that is, from those things which our Lord Jesus Christ performed on earth; of His divinity they have said very little, like men walking with Him on the earth. There remains the eagle; this is John, the preacher of sublime truths, and a contemplator with steady gaze of the inner and eternal light. It is said, indeed, that the young eagles are tested by the parent birds in this way: the young one is suspended from the talons of the male parent and directly exposed to the rays of the sun; if it looks steadily at the sun, it is recognized as a true brood; if its eye quivers, it is allowed to drop off, as a spurious brood. Now, therefore, consider how sublime are the things he ought to speak who is compared to the eagle; and yet even we, who creep on the earth, weak and hardly of any account among men, venture to handle and to expound these things; and imagine that we can either apprehend when we meditate them, or be apprehended when we speak.

6. Why have I said this? For perhaps after these words one may justly say to me: Lay aside the book then. Why dost thou take in hand what exceeds thy measure? Why trust thy tongue to it? To this I reply: Many heretics abound; and God has permitted them to abound to this end, that we may not be always nourished with milk and remain in senseless infancy. For inasmuch as they have not understood how the divinity of Christ is set forth to our acceptance, they have concluded according to their will: and by not discerning aright, they have brought in most troublesome questions upon catholic believers; and the hearts of believers began to be disturbed and to waver. Then immediately it became a necessity for spiritual men, who had not only read in the Gospel anything respecting the divinity of our Lord Jesus Christ, but had also understood it, to bring forth the armor of Christ against the armor of the devil, and with all their might to fight in most open conflict for the divinity of Christ against false and deceitful teachers; lest, while they were silent, others might perish. For whoever have thought either that our Lord Jesus Christ is of another substance than the Father is, or that there is only Christ, so that the same is Father, Son, and Holy Spirit; whoever also have chosen to think that He was only man, not God made man, or God in such wise as to be mutable in His Godhead, or God in such wise as not to

---

[1] Luke xxiii. 34.

be man; these have made shipwreck from the faith, and have been cast forth from the harbor of the Church, lest by their inquietude they might wreck the ships in their company. Which thing obliged that even we, though least and as regards ourselves wholly unworthy, but in regard of His mercy set in some account among His stewards, should speak to you what either you may understand and rejoice with me, or, if you cannot yet understand, by believing it you may remain secure in the harbor.

7. I will accordingly speak; let him who can, understand; and let him who cannot understand, believe: yet will I speak what the Lord saith, "Ye judge after the flesh; I judge not any man," either now, or after the flesh. "But even if I judge, my judgment is true." Why is Thy judgment true? "Because I am not alone," saith He, "but I and the Father that sent me." What then, O Lord Jesus? If Thou wert alone would Thy judgment be false: and is it because Thou art not alone, but Thou and the Father that sent Thee, that Thou judgest truly? How shall I answer? Let Himself answer: He saith, "My judgment is true." Why? "Because I am not alone, but I and the Father that sent me." If He is with Thee, how has He sent Thee? And has He sent Thee, and yet is He also with Thee? Is it so that having been sent, Thou hast not departed from Him? And didst Thou come to us, and yet abode there? How is this to be believed? how apprehended? To these two questions I answer: Thou sayest rightly, how is it to be apprehended; how believed, thou sayest not rightly. Rather, for that reason is it right to believe it, because it is not immediately to be apprehended; for if it were a thing to be immediately apprehended, there would be no need to believe it, because it would be seen. It is because thou dost not apprehend that thou believest; but by believing thou art made capable of apprehending. For if thou dost not believe, thou wilt never apprehend, since thou wilt remain less capable. Let faith then purify thee, that understanding may fill thee. "My judgment is true," saith He, "because I am not alone, but I and the Father that sent me." Therefore, O Lord our God, Jesus Christ, Thy sending is Thy incarnation. So I see, so I understand: in short, so I believe, in case it may smack of arrogance to say, so I understand. Doubtless the Lord Jesus Christ is even here; rather, *was* here as to His flesh, *is* here now as to His Godhead: He was both with the Father and had not left the Father. Hence, in that He is said to have been sent and to have

come to us, His incarnation is set forth to us, for the Father did not take flesh.

8. For there are certain heretics called Sabellians, who are also called Patripassians, who affirm that it was the Father Himself that had suffered. Do not thou so affirm, O Catholic; for if thou wilt be a Patripassian, thou wilt not be sane. Understand, then, that the incarnation of the Son is termed the sending of the Son; and do not believe that the Father was incarnate, but do not yet believe that He departed from the incarnate Son. The Son carried flesh, the Father was with the Son. If the Father was in heaven, the Son on earth, how was the Father with the Son? Because both Father and Son were everywhere: for God is not in such manner in heaven as not to be on earth. Hear him who would flee from the judgment of God, and found not a way to flee by: "Whither shall I go," saith he, "from Thy Spirit; and whither shall I flee from Thy face? If I ascend up into heaven, Thou art there." The question was about the earth; hear what follows: "If I descend unto hell, Thou art there."[1] If, then, He is said to be present even in hell, what in the universe remains where He is not present? For the voice of God with the prophet is, "I fill heaven and earth."[2] Hence He is everywhere, who is confined by no place. Turn not thou away from Him, and He is with thee. If thou wouldst come to Him, be not slow to love; for it is not with feet but with affections thou runnest. Thou comest while remaining in one place, if thou believest and lovest. Wherefore He is everywhere; and if everywhere, how not also with the Son? Is it so that He is not with the Son, while, if thou believest, He is even with thee?

9. How, then, is His judgment true, but because the Son is true? For this He said: "And if I judge, my judgment is true; because I am not alone, but I and the Father that sent me." Just as if He had said, "My judgment is true," because I am the Son of God. How dost Thou prove that Thou art the Son of God? "Because I am not alone, but I and the Father that sent me." Blush, Sabellian; thou hearest the *Son*, thou hearest the *Father*. Father is Father, Son is Son. He said not, I am the Father. and I the same am the Son; but He saith, "I am not alone." Why art Thou not alone? Because the Father is with me. "I am, and the Father that sent me;" thou hearest, "I am, and He that sent me." Lest thou lose sight of the person, distinguish the persons. Distin-

---

guish by understanding, do not separate by faithlessness; lest again, fleeing as it were Charybdis, thou rush upon Scylla. For the whirlpool of the impiety of the Sabellians was swallowing thee, to say that the Father is the same who is Son: just now thou hast learned, "I am not alone, but I and the Father that sent me." Thou dost acknowledge that the Father is Father, and that the Son is Son; thou dost rightly acknowledge: but do not say the Father is greater, the Son is less; do not say, the Father is gold, the Son is silver. There is one substance, one Godhead, one co-eternity, perfect equality, no unlikeness. For if thou only believe that Christ is another, not the same person that the Father is, but yet imagine that in respect of His nature He is somewhat different from the Father, thou hast indeed escaped Charybdis, but thou hast been wrecked on the rocks of Scylla. Steer the middle course, avoid each of the two perilous sides. Father is Father, Son is Son. Thou sayest now, Father is Father, Son is Son: thou hast fortunately escaped the danger of the absorbing whirl; why wouldst thou go unto the other side to say, the Father is this, the Son that? The Son is another person than the Father is, this thou sayest rightly; but that He is different in nature, thou sayest not rightly. Certainly the Son is another person, because He is not the same who is Father; and the Father is another person, because He is not the same who is Son: nevertheless, they are not different in nature, but the self-same is both Father and Son. What means the self-same? God is one. Thou hast heard, "Because I am not alone, but I and the Father that sent me:" hear how thou mayest believe Father and Son; hear the Son Himself, "I and the Father are one."[1] He said not, I am the Father; or, I and the Father *is* one person; but when He says, "I and the Father are one," hear both, both the *one, unum,* and the *are, sumus,* and thou shalt be delivered both from Charybdis and from Scylla. In these two words, in that He said *one,* He delivers thee from Arius; in that He said *are,* He delivers thee from Sabellius. If *one,* therefore not diverse; if *are,* therefore both Father and Son. For He would not say *are* of one person; but, on the other hand, He would not say *one* of diverse. Hence the reason why He says, "my judgment is true," is, that thou mayest hear it briefly, because I am the Son of God. But I would have thee in such wise believe that I am the Son of God, that thou mayest understand that the Father is with me: I am not Son in such

manner as to have left Him; I am not in such manner here that I should not be with Him; nor is He in such manner there as not to be with me: I have taken to me the form of a servant, yet have I not lost the form of God; therefore He saith, "I am not alone, but I and the Father that sent me."

10. He had spoken of judgment; He means to speak of testimony. "In your law," saith He, "it is written that the testimony of two men is true. I am one that bear witness of myself, and the Father that sent me beareth witness of me." He expounded the law to them also, if they were not unthankful. For it is a great question, my brethren, and to me it certainly appears to have been ordained in a mystery, where God said, "In the mouth of two or three witnesses every word shall stand."[2] Is truth sought by two witnesses? Clearly it is; so is the custom of mankind: but yet it may be that even two witnesses lie. The chaste Susanna was pressed by two false witnesses: were they not therefore false because they were two? Do we speak of two or of three? A whole people lied against Christ.[3] If, then, a people, consisting of a great multitude of men, was found a false witness, how is it to be understood that "in the mouth of two or three witnesses every word shall stand," unless it be that in this manner the Trinity is mysteriously set forth to us, in which is perpetual stability of truth? Dost thou wish to have a good cause? Have two or three witnesses,—the Father, Son, and Holy Ghost. In short, when Susanna, the chaste woman and faithful wife, was pressed by two false witnesses, the Trinity supported her in her conscience and in secret: that Trinity raised up from secrecy one witness, Daniel, and convicted the two.[4] Therefore, because it is written in your law that the witness of two men is true, receive our witness, lest ye feel our judgment. "For I," saith He, "judge not any man; but I bear witness of myself:" I defer judgment, I defer not the witness.

11. Let us, brethren, choose for ourselves God as our judge, God as our witness, against the tongues of men, against the weak suspicions of mankind. For He who is the judge disdains not to be witness, nor is He advanced in honor when He becomes judge; since He who is witness will also Himself be judge. In what way is He witness? Because He asks not another to learn from Him who thou art. In what way is He judge? Because He has the power of killing and making alive, of condemning and acquitting, of casting down

---

nto hell and of raising up into heaven, of joining to the devil and of crowning with the angels. Since, therefore, He has this power, He is judge. Now, because He requires not another witness that He may know thee; and that He who will hereafter judge thee is now seeing thee, there is no means whereby thou canst deceive Him when He begins to judge. For there is no furnishing thyself with false witnesses who can circumvent that judge when He shall begin to judge thee. This is what God says to thee: When thou despisedst, I did see it; and when thou believedst not, I did not frustrate my sentence. I delayed it, not removed it. Thou wouldst not hear what I enjoined, thou shalt feel what I foretold. But if thou hearest what I enjoined, thou shalt not feel the evils which I have foretold, but thou shalt enjoy the good things which I have promised.

12. Let it not by any means surprise any one that He says, "My judgment is true; because I am not alone, but I and the Father that sent me;" whilst He has said in another place, "The Father judgeth not any man, but all judgment hath He given to the Son." We have already discoursed on these same words of the evangelist, and we remind you now that this was not said because the Father will not be with the Son when He comes to judge, but because the Son alone will be apparent to the good and the bad in the judgment, in that form in which He suffered, and rose again, and ascended into heaven. For at that moment, indeed, as they were beholding Him ascending, the angelic voice sounded in the ears of His disciples, "So shall He come in like manner as ye have seen Him going into heaven;"[1] that is, in the form of man in which He was judged, will He judge, in order that also that prophetic utterance may be fulfilled, "They shall look upon Him whom they pierced."[2] But when the righteous go into eternal life, we shall see Him as He is; that will not be the judgment of the living and the dead, but only the reward of the living.

13. Likewise, let it not surprise you that He says, "In your law it is written that the testimony of two men is true," that any man should hence suppose that this was not also the law of God, because it is not said, *In the law of God:* let him know that, when it is said thus, *In your law,* it is just as if He said, "In the law which was given to you;" given by whom, except by God? Just as we say, "Our daily bread;" and yet we say, "Give us this day."

---

[1] Acts i. 11.   [2] Zech. xii. 10; John xix. 37.

TRACTATE XXXVII.

CHAPTER VIII. 19, 20.

1. WHAT in the holy Gospel is spoken briefly ought not briefly to be expounded, so that what is read may be understood. The words of the Lord are few, but great; to be valued not by number, but by weight: to be despised not because they are few, but to be sought because they are great. You who were present yesterday have heard, as we discoursed according to our ability from that which the Lord said, "Ye judge after the flesh; I judge not any man. But yet if I judge, my judgment is true; because I am not alone, but I and the Father that sent me. It is written in your law, that the testimony of two men is true. I am one that bear witness of myself, and the Father that sent me beareth witness of me." Yesterday, as I have said, from these words a discourse was delivered to your ears and to your minds. When the Lord had spoken these words, they who heard, "Ye judge after the flesh," manifested the truth of what they had heard. For they answered the Lord, as He spoke of God His Father, and said to Him, "Where is thy Father?" The Father of Christ they understood carnally, because they judged the words of Christ after the flesh. But He who spoke was openly flesh, but secretly the Word: man visible, God hidden. They saw the covering, and despised the wearer: they despised because they knew not; knew not, because they saw not; saw not, because they were blind; they were blind, because they believed not.

2. Let us see, then, what answer the Lord made to this. "Where," say they, "is thy Father?" For we have heard thee say, "I am not alone, but I and the Father that sent me:" we see thee alone, we do not see thy Father

with thee; how sayest thou that thou art not alone, but that thou art with thy Father? Else show us that thy Father is with thee. And the Lord answered them: Do ye know me, that I should show you the Father? This is indeed what follows; this is what He answered in His own words, the exposition of which we have already premised. For see what He said, " Ye neither know me nor my Father: if ye knew me, ye would perhaps know my Father also." Ye say then, " Where is thy Father?" As if already ye knew me; as if what you see were all that I am. Therefore because ye know not me, I do not show you my Father. Ye suppose me, in fact, to be a man; hence ye seek a man for my father, because " ye judge after the flesh." But because, according to what you see, I am one thing, and another thing according to what you see not, and that I as hidden from you speak of my Father as hidden, it is requisite that you should first know me, and then ye know my Father also.

3. " For if ye knew me, ye would perhaps know my Father also." He who knows all things is not in doubt when He says *perhaps*, but rebuking. Now see how this very word *perhaps*, which seems to be a word of doubting, may be spoken chidingly. Yea, a word expressive of doubt it is when used by man, for man doubts because he knows not; but when a word of doubting is spoken by God, from whom surely nothing is hid, it is unbelief that is reproved by that doubting, not the Godhead merely expressing an opinion. For men sometimes chidingly express doubt concerning things which they hold certain; that is, use a word of doubting, while in their heart they doubt not: just as thou wouldst say to thy slave, if thou wert angry with him, " Thou despisest me; but consider, perhaps I am thy master." Hence also the apostle, speaking to some who despised him, says: "And I think that I also have the Spirit of God." [1]   When he says, " I think," he seems to doubt; but he is rebuking, not doubting. And in another place the Lord Jesus Christ Himself, rebuking the future unbelief of mankind, saith: " When the Son of man cometh, will He, thinkest thou, find faith on the earth?" [2]

4. You now, as I think, understand how the word *perhaps* is used here, in case any weigher of words and poiser of syllables, as if to show his knowledge of Latin, finds fault with a word which the Word of God spoke; and by blaming the Word of God, remain not eloquent, but mute. For who is there that speaks as doth the Word which was in the beginning with God? Do not consider these words as we use them, and from these wish to measure that Word which is God. Thou hearest the Word indeed, and despisest it; hear God and fear Him: " In the beginning was the Word." Thou referrest to the usage of thy conversation, and sayest within thyself, What is a word? What mighty thing is a word? It sounds and passes away; after beating the air, it strikes the ear and is no more. Hear further: " The Word was with God;" remained, did not by sounding pass away. Perhaps thou still despisest it: " The Word was God." With thyself, O man, a word in thy heart is a different thing from sound; but the word that is with thee, in order to pass to me, requires sound for a vehicle as it were. It takes to itself sound, mounts it as a vehicle, runs through the air, comes to me and yet does not leave thee. But the sound, in order to come to me, left thee and yet did not stay with me. Now has the word that was in thy heart also passed away with the passing sound? Thou didst speak thy thought; and, that the thought which was hid with thee might come to me, thou didst sound syllables; the sound of the syllables conveyed thy thought to my ear; through my ear thy thought descended into my heart, the intermediate sound flew away: but that word which took to itself sound was with thee before thou didst sound it, and is with me, because thou didst sound it, without quitting thee. Consider this, thou nice weigher of sounds, whoever thou be. Thou despisest the Word of God, thou who comprehendest not the word of man.

5. He, then, by whom all things were made knows all things, and yet He rebukes by doubting: " If ye knew me ye would perhaps know my Father also." He rebukes unbelievers. He spoke a like sentence to the disciples, but there is not a word of doubting in it, because there was no occasion to rebuke unbelief. For this, "If ye knew me, ye would perhaps know my Father also," which He said to the Jews, He said also to the disciples, when Philip asked, or rather, demanded of Him, saying, " Lord, show us the Father, and it sufficeth us:" just as if he said, We already know Thee even ourselves; Thou hast been apparent to us; we have seen Thee; Thou hast deigned to choose us; we have followed Thee, have seen Thy marvels, heard Thy words of salvation, have taken Thy precepts upon us, we hope in Thy promises: Thou hast deigned to confer much upon us by Thy very presence: but still, while we know Thee, and we do not yet know the Father, we are inflamed with desire to see Him whom we do not yet know; and thus, be-

---

[1] 1 Cor. vii. 40.   [2] Luke xviii. 8.

cause we know Thee, but it is not enough until we know the Father, show us the Father, and it sufficeth us. And the Lord, that they might understand that they knew not what they thought they did already know, said, "Am I so long time with you, and ye know me not, Philip? he who hath seen me hath seen the Father."[1] Has this sentence a word of doubting in it? Did He say, He that hath seen me hath *perhaps* seen the Father? Why not? Because it was a believer that listened to Him, not a persecutor of the faith: hence did the Lord not rebuke, but teach. "Whoso hath seen me hath seen the Father also;" and here, "If ye knew me, ye would know my Father also," let us remove the word which indicates the unbelief of the hearers, and it is the same sentence.

6. Yesterday we commended it to your consideration, beloved, and said that the sentences of the Evangelist John, in which he narrates to us what he learned from the Lord, had not required to be discussed, were that possible, except the inventions of heretics had compelled us. Yesterday, then, we briefly intimated to you, beloved, that there are heretics who are called Patripassians, or Sabellians after their founder: these say that the same is the Father who is the Son; the names different, but the person one. When He wills, say they, He is Father; when He wills, He is Son: still He is one. There are likewise other heretics who are called Arians. They indeed confess that our Lord Jesus Christ is the only Son of the Father; the one, Father of the Son; the other, Son of the Father; that He who is Father is not Son, nor He who is Son is Father; they confess that the Son was begotten, but deny His equality. We, namely, the catholic faith, coming from the doctrine of the apostles planted in us, received by a line of succession, to be transmitted sound to posterity,—the catholic faith, I say, has, between both those parties, that is, between both errors, held the truth. In the error of the Sabellians, He is only one; the Father and Son is the same person: in the error of the Arians, the Father and the Son are indeed different persons; but the Son is not only a different person, but different in nature. Thou midway between these, what sayest thou? Thou hast shut out the Sabellian, shut out the Arian also. The Father is Father, the Son is Son; another person, not another in nature; for, "I and the Father are one," which, so far as I could, I pressed on your thoughts yesterday. When he hears that word, we *are*, let the Sabellian go away

confounded; when he hears the word *one*, let the Arian go away confounded. Let the catholic steer the bark of his faith between both, since in both he must be on his guard against shipwreck. Say thou, then, what the Gospel saith, "I and the Father are one." Not different in nature, because *one;* not one person, because *are.*

7. A little before He said, "My judgment is true; because I am not alone, but I and the Father that sent me:" as if He said, The reason why my judgment is true is, because I am the Son of God, because I speak the truth, because I am truth itself. Those men, understanding Him carnally, said, "Where is thy Father?" Now hear, O Arian: "Ye neither know me, nor my Father;" because, "If ye knew me, ye would know my Father also." What doth this mean, except "I and the Father are one"? When thou seest some person like some other,—give heed, beloved, it is a common remark; let not that appear to you difficult which you see to be customary,—when, I say, thou seest some person like another, and thou knowest the person to whom he is like, thou sayest in wonder, "How like this person is to that!" Thou wouldst not say *this* unless there were two. Here one who does not know the person to whom thou sayest the other is like remarks, "Is he so like him?" And thou answerest him: What? dost thou not know that person? Saith he, "No, I do not." Immediately thou, in order to make known to him the person whom he does not know by means of the person whom he observes before him, answerest, saying, Having seen this man, thou hast seen the other. Thou didst not, surely, assert that they are one person in saying this, or that they are not two; but made such answer because of the likeness: "If thou knowest the one, thou knowest the other; for they are very like, and there is no difference whatever between them." Hence also the Lord saith, "If ye knew me, ye would know my Father also;" not that the Son is the Father but like the Father. Let the Arian blush. Thanks be to the Lord that even the Arian is separate from the Sabellian error, and is not a Patripassian: he does not affirm that the Father assumed flesh and came to men, that the Father suffered, rose again, and somehow ascended to Himself; this he does not affirm; he acknowledges with me the Father to be Father, the Son to be Son. But, O brother, thou hast escaped that shipwreck, why go to the other? Father is Father, Son is Son; why dost thou affirm that the Son is unlike, that He is different, another substance? If He were unlike, would He say to

---

[1] John xiv. 8.

His disciples, "He that hath seen me hath seen the Father"? Would He say to the Jews, "If ye knew me, ye would know my Father also"? How would this be true, unless that other was also true, "I and the Father are one"?

8. "These words spake Jesus in the treasury, speaking in the temple:" great boldness, without fear. For He could not suffer if He did not will it, since He were not born if He did not will it. What follows then? "And no man laid hold of Him, because His hour was not yet come." Some, again, when they hear this, believe that the Lord Christ was subject to fate, and say: Behold, Christ is held by fate! O, if thy heart were not fatuous, thou wouldst not believe in fate. If *fate*, as some understand it, is derived from *fando*, that is from speaking, how can the Word of God be held by fate, whilst all things that are made are in the Word itself? For God has not ordained anything which He did not know beforehand; that which was made was in His Word. The world was made; both was made and was there. How both was made and was there? Because the house which the builder rears, was previously in his art; and there, a better house, without age, without decay: however, to show forth his art, he makes a house; and so, in a manner, a house comes forth from a house; and if the house should fall, the art remains. So were all things that are made with the Word of God; because God made all things in wisdom,[1] and all that He made were known to Him: for He did not learn because He made, but made because He knew. To us they are known, because they are made: to Him, if they had not been known, they would not have been made Therefore the Word went before. And what was before the Word? Nothing at all. For were there anything before it, it would not have been said, "In the beginning was the Word;" but, In the beginning was the Word made. In short, what says Moses concerning the world? "In the beginning God made the heavens and the earth." Made what was not: well, if He made what was not, what was there before? "In the beginning was the Word." And whence came heaven and earth? "All things were made by Him." Dost thou then put Christ under fate? Where are the fates? In heaven, sayest thou, in the order and changes of the stars. How then can fate rule Him by whom the heavens and the stars were made; whilst thy own will, if thou thinkest rightly, transcends even the stars? Or, because thou knowest that Christ's flesh

was under heaven, is that the reason why thou thinkest that Christ's power was put under the heavens?

9. Hear, thou fool: "His hour was not yet come;" not the hour in which He should be forced to die, but that in which He would deign to be put to death. For Himself knew when He should die: He considered all things that were foretold of Him, and awaited all to be finished that was foretold to be before His suffering; that when all should be fulfilled, then should come His suffering in set order, not by fatal necessity. In short, hear that you may prove. Among the rest that was prophesied of Him, it is also written: "They gave me gall for meat, and in my thirst they gave me vinegar to drink."[2] How this happened, we know from the Gospel. First, they gave Him gall; He received it, tasted it, and spat it out. Thereafter, as He hung on the cross, that all that was foretold might be fulfilled, He said, "I thirst." They took a sponge filled with vinegar, bound it to a reed, and put it to His mouth; He received it, and said, "It is finished." What did that mean? All things which were prophesied before my death are completed, then what do I here any longer? In a word, when He said "It is finished, He bowed His head, and gave up the ghost." Did the thieves, who were nailed beside Him, expire when they would? They were held by the bonds of flesh, for they were not the creators of the flesh; fixed by nails, they were a long time tormented, because they had not lordship over their weakness. The Lord, however, when He would, took flesh in a virgin's womb: came forth to men when He would; lived among men so long as He would; and when He would He quitted the flesh. This is the part of power, not of necessity. This hour, then, He awaited; not the fated, but the fitting and voluntary hour; that all might first be fulfilled which behoved to be fulfilled before His decease. How could he have been under necessity of fate, when He said in another place, "I have power to lay down my life, and I have power to take it again: no man taketh it from me, but I lay it down of myself and take it again?"[3] He showed this power when the Jews sought Him. "Whom seek ye?" saith He. "Jesus," said they. And He answered, "I am He." When they heard this voice, "they went back and fell to the ground."[4]

10. Says one, If he had this power, why, when the Jews insulted him on the cross and said, "If he be the Son of God let him come down from the cross," did he not come down,

---

[1] Ps. civ. 24.   [2] Ps. lxix. 22.   [3] John x. 18.   [4] John xviii. 6.

to show them his power by coming down? Because He was teaching us patience, therefore He deferred the demonstration of His power. For if He came down, moved as it were at their words, He would be thought to have been overcome by the sting of their insults. He did not come down; there He remained fixed, to depart when He would. For what great matter was it for Him to descend from the cross, when He could rise again from the sepulchre? Let us, then, to whom this is ministered, understand that the power of our Lord Jesus Christ, then concealed, will be made manifest in the judgment, of which it is said, "God will come manifest; our God, and He will not be silent."[1] Why is it said, "will come manifest"? Because He, our God,—namely, Christ,—came hidden, will come manifest. "And will not be silent:" why this "will not be silent"? Because at first He did keep silence. When? When He was judged; that this, too, might be ful-

filled which the prophet had foretold: "As a sheep He was led to the slaughter, and as a lamb before his shearer is dumb, so He opened not His mouth."[2] He would not have suffered did He not will to suffer: did He not suffer, that blood had not been shed; if that blood were not shed, the world would not be redeemed. Therefore let us give thanks to the power of His divinity, and to the compassion of His infirmity; both concerning the hidden power which the Jews did not recognize, whence it is now said to them, "Ye neither know me nor my Father," and also concerning the flesh assumed, which the Jews did not recognize, and yet knew His lineage: whence He said to them elsewhere, "Ye both know me, and ye know whence I am." Let us know both in Christ, both wherein He is equal to the Father and wherein the Father is greater than He. That is the Word, this is the flesh; that is God, this is man; but yet Christ is one, God and man.

[1] Ps. l. 3.

[2] Isa. liii. 7.

TRACTATE XXXVIII.

Chapter VIII. 21–25.

1. The lesson of the holy Gospel which preceded to-day's had concluded thus: that "the Lord spake, teaching in the treasury," what it pleased Him, and what you have heard; "and no one laid hands on Him, for His hour was not yet come."[1] Accordingly, on the Lord's day we made our subject of discourse what He Himself thought fit to give us. We indicated to your Charity why it was said, "His hour was not yet come," lest any in their impiety should have the effrontery to suspect Christ as laid under some fatal necessity. For the hour was not yet come when by His own appointment, in accordance with what was predicted regarding Him, He should not be forced to die unwillingly, but be ready to be slain.

2. But of His own passion itself, which lay not in any necessity He was under, but in His own power, all that He said in His discourse to the Jews was, "I go away." For to Christ the Lord's death was His proceeding to the place whence He had come, and from which He had never departed. "I go away,"

said He, "and ye shall seek me," not from any longing for me, but in hatred. For after His removal from human sight, He was sought for both by those who hated Him and those who loved Him; by the former in a spirit of persecution, by the latter with the desire of having Him. In the Psalms the Lord Himself says by the prophet, "A place of refuge hath failed me, and there is none that seeketh after my life;"[2] and again He says in another place in the Psalms, "Let them be confounded and ashamed who seek after my life."[3] He blamed the former for not seeking, He condemned the latter because they did. For it is wrong not to seek the life of Christ, that is, in the way the disciples sought it; and it is wrong to seek the life of Christ, that is, in the way the Jews sought it: for the former sought to possess it, these latter to destroy it. Accordingly, because these men sought it thus in a wrong way, with a perverted heart, what next did He add? "Ye shall seek me, and"—not to let you suppose that ye will seek me for good—"ye

[1] Chap. viii. 20.

[2] Ps. cxlii. 4.

[3] Ps. xl. 14.

shall die in your sin." This comes of seeking Christ wrongly, to die in one's sin; this of hating Him, through whom alone salvation could be found. For, while men whose hope is in God ought not to render evil even for evil, these men were rendering evil for good. The Lord therefore announced to them beforehand, and in His foreknowledge uttered the sentence, that they should die in their sin. And then He adds, "Whither I go, ye cannot come." He said the same to the disciples also in another place; and yet He said not to them, "Ye shall die in your sin." But what did He say? The same as to these men: "Whither I go, ye cannot come."[1] He did not take away hope, but foretold delay. For at the time when the Lord spake this to the disciples, they were not able to come whither He was going, yet were they to come afterwards; but these men never, to whom in His foreknowledge He said, "Ye shall die in your sin."

3. But on hearing these words, as is usual with those whose thoughts are carnal, who judge after the flesh, and hear and apprehend everything in a carnal way, they said, "Will he kill himself? because he said, Whither I go ye cannot come." Foolish words, and overflowing with stupidity! For why? could they not go whither He would have proceeded had He killed Himself? Were not they themselves to die? What, then, means, "Will he kill himself? because he said, Whither I go ye cannot come?" If He spake of man's death, what man is there that does not die? Therefore, by "whither I go" He meant, not the going to death, but whither He was going Himself after death. Such, then, was their answer, because they did not understand.

4. And what said the Lord to those who savored of the earth? "And He said unto them, Ye are from beneath." For this cause ye savor of the earth, because ye lick dust like serpents. Ye eat earth! What does it mean? Ye feed on earthly things, ye delight in earthly things, ye gape after earthly things, ye have no heart for what is above. "Ye are from beneath: I am from above. Ye are of this world: I am not of this world." For how could He be of the world, by whom the world was made? All that are of the world come after the world, because the world preceded; and so man is of the world. But Christ was first, and then the world; and since Christ was before the world, before Christ there was nothing: because "In the beginning was the Word; all things were made by Him."[2] He, therefore, was of that which is

above. But of what that is above? Of the air? Perish the thought! there the birds wing their flight. Of the sky that we see? Again I say, Perish the thought! it is there that the stars and sun and moon revolve. Of the angels? Neither is this to be understood: by Him who made all things were the angels also made. Of what, then, above is Christ? Of the Father Himself. Nothing is above that God who begat the Word equal with Himself, co-eternal with Himself, only-begotten, timeless, that by Him time's own foundations should be laid. Understand, then, Christ as from above, so as in thy thought to get beyond everything that is made,—the whole creation together, every material body, every created spirit, everything in any way subject to change: rise above all, as John rose, in order to reach this: "In the beginning was the Word, and the Word was with God, and the Word was God."

5. Therefore said He, "I am from above. Ye are of this world: I am not of this world. I said therefore unto you, that ye shall die in your sins." He has explained to us, brethren, what He wished to be understood by "ye are of this world." He said therefore in fact, "Ye are of this world," because they were sinners, because they were unrighteous, because they were unbelieving, because they savored of the earthly. For what is your opinion as regards the holy apostles? What difference was there between the Jews and the apostles? As great as between darkness and light, as between faith and unbelief, as between piety and impiety, as between hope and despair, as between love and avarice: surely the difference was great. What then? because there was such a difference, were the apostles not of the world? If thy thoughts turn to the manner of their birth, and whence they came, inasmuch as all of them had come from Adam, they were of this world. But what said the Lord Himself to them? "I have chosen you out of the world."[3] Those, then, who were of the world, became not of the world, and began to belong to Him by whom the world was made. But these men continued to be of the world, to whom it was said, "Ye shall die in your sins."

6. Let none then, brethren, say, I am not of this world. Whoever thou art as a man, thou art of this world; but He who made the world came to thee, and delivered thee from this world. If the world delights thee, thou wishest always to be unclean (*immundus*); but if this world no longer delight thee, thou art already clean (*mundus*). And yet, if through

---

[1] Chap. xiii. 33.   [2] Chap. i. 1, 3.   [3] Chap. xv. 19.

some infirmity the world still delight thee, let Him who cleanseth (*mundat*) dwell in thee, and thou too shalt be clean.[1] But if thou art once clean, thou wilt not continue in the world; neither wilt thou hear what was heard by the Jews, "Ye shall die in your sins." For we are all born with sin; we have all in living added to that wherein we were born, and have since become more of the world than when we were born of our parents. And where should we be, had He not come, who was wholly free from sin, to expiate all sin? And so, because in Him the Jews believed not, they deservedly heard [the sentence], "Ye shall die in your sins;" for in no way could ye, who were born with sin, be without sin; and yet, said He, if ye believe in me, although it is still true that ye were born with sin, yet in your sin ye shall not die. The whole misery, then, of the Jews was just this, not to have sin, but to die in their sins. From this it is that every Christian ought to seek to escape; because of this we have recourse to baptism; on this account do those whose lives are in danger from sickness or any other cause become anxious for help; for this also is the sucking child carried by his mother with pious hands to the church, that he may not go out into the world without baptism, and die in the sin wherein he was born. Most wretched surely the condition and miserable the lot of these men, who heard from those truth-speaking lips, "Ye shall die in your sins!"

7. But He explains whence this should befall them: "For if ye believe not that I am [He], ye shall die in your sins." I believe, brethren, that among the multitude who listened to the Lord, there were those also who should yet believe. But against all, as it were, had that most severe sentence gone forth, "Ye shall die in your sin;" and thereby even from those who should yet believe had hope been withdrawn: the others were roused to fury, they to fear, yea, to more than fear, they were brought now to despair. But He revived their hope; for He added, "If ye believe not that I am, ye shall die in your sins." Therefore if ye do believe that I am, ye shall not die in your sins. Hope was restored to the desponding, the sleeping were aroused, their hearts got a fresh awakening; and thereafter very many believed, as the Gospel itself attests in the sequel. For members of Christ were there, who had not yet become attached to the body of Christ; and among that people by whom He was crucified,

by whom He was hanged on a tree, by whom when hanging He was mocked, by whom He was wounded with the spear, by whom gall and vinegar were given Him to drink, were the members of Christ, for whose sake He said, "Father, forgive them, for they know not what they do." And what will a convert not be forgiven, if the shedding of Christ's blood is forgiven? What murderer need despair, if he was restored to hope by whom even Christ was slain? After this many believed; they were presented with Christ's blood as a gift, that they might drink it for their salvation, rather than be held guilty of shedding it. Who can despair? And if the thief was saved on the cross,—a murderer shortly before, a little afterwards accused, convicted, condemned, hanged, delivered,— wonder not. The place of his conviction was that of his condemnation; while that of his conversion was the place also of his deliverance.[2] Among this people, then, to whom the Lord was speaking, were those who should yet die in their sin: there were those also who should yet believe on Him who spake, and find deliverance from all their sin.

8. But look at this which is said by Christ the Lord: "If ye believe not that I am, ye shall die in your sins." What is this, "If ye believe not that I am?" "I am" what? There is nothing added; and because He added nothing, He left much to be inferred. For He was expected to say what He was, and yet He said it not. What was He expected to say? Perhaps, "If ye believe not that I am" Christ; "if ye believe not that I am" the Son of God; "if ye believe not that I am" the Word of the Father: "if ye believe not that I am" the founder of the world; "if ye believe not that I am" the former and re-former, the creator and re-creator, the maker and re-maker of man;—"if ye believe not that I am" this, "ye shall die in your sins." There is much implied in His only saying "I am;" for so also had God said to Moses, "I am who am." Who can adequately express what that AM means? God by His angel sent His servant Moses to deliver His people out of Egypt (you have read and know what you now hear; but I recall it to your minds); He sent him trembling, self-excusing, but obedient. And while thus excusing himself, he said to God, whom he understood to be speaking in the person of the angel: If the people say to me, And who is the God that hath sent thee? what shall I say to them? And the Lord answered him, "I am who am;" and added, "Thou shalt

---

[1] There is a play here on the words *mundus*, the world, and *mundus*, clean, with its compound *immundus*, and its cognate verb *mundare*. Such plays are frequent in St. Augustin.—TR.

[2] Luke xviii. 34-43.

say to the children of Israel, He who is hath sent me to you." There also He says not, I am God; or, I am the framer of the world; or, I am the creator of all things; or, I am the multiplier of the very people to be delivered: but only this, "I am who am;" and, "Thou shalt say to the children of Israel, He who is." He added not, Who is your God, who is the God of your fathers; but said only this: "He who is hath sent me to you." Perhaps it was too much even for Moses himself, as it is too much for us also, and much more so for us, to understand the meaning of such words, "I am who am;" and, "He who is hath sent me to you." And supposing that Moses comprehended it, when would those to whom he was sent comprehend it? The Lord therefore put aside what man could not comprehend, and added what he could; for He said also besides, "I am the God of Abraham, and the God of Isaac, and the God of Jacob."[1] This thou canst comprehend; for "I am who am," what mind can comprehend?

9. What then of us? Shall we venture to say anything on such words, "I am who am;" or rather on this, that you have heard the Lord saying, "If ye believe not that I am, ye shall die in your sins"? Shall I venture with these feeble and scarcely existing powers of mine to discuss the meaning of that which Christ the Lord hath said, "If ye believe not that I am"? I shall venture to ask the Lord Himself. Listen to me as one asking rather than discussing, inquiring rather than assuming, learning rather than teaching, and fail not yourselves also to be asking with me or through me. The Lord Himself, who is everywhere, is also at hand. Let Him hear the feeling that prompts to ask, and grant the fruit of understanding. For in what words, even were it so that I comprehend something, can I convey to your hearts what I comprehend? What voice is adequate? what eloquence sufficient? what powers of intelligence? what faculty of utterance?

10. I shall speak, then, to our Lord Jesus Christ; I shall speak and may He be pleased to hear me. I believe He is present, I am fully assured of it; for He Himself has said, "Lo, I am with you even to the end of the world."[2] O Lord our God, what is that which Thou saidst, "If ye believe not that I am"? For what is there that belongs not to the things Thou hast made? Does not heaven so belong? Does not the earth? Does not everything in earth and heaven? Does not man

himself to whom Thou speakest? Does not the angel whom Thou sendest? If all these are things made by Thee, what is that existence[3] Thou hast retained as something exclusively Thine own, which Thou hast given to none besides, that Thou mightest be such Thyself alone? For how do I hear "I am who am," as if there were none besides? and how do I hear "If ye believe not that I am"? For had they no existence who heard Him? Yea, though they were sinners, they were men. What then can I do? What that existence, let Him tell my heart, let Him tell, let Him declare it within; let the inner man hear, the mind apprehend this true existence; for such existence is always unvarying in character.[4] For a thing, anything whatever (I have begun as it were to dispute, and have left off inquiring. Perhaps I wish to speak what I have heard. May He grant enlargement to my hearing, and to yours, while I speak);—for anything, whatever in short be its excellence, if it is changeable, does not truly exist; for there is no true existence wherever non-existence has also a place. For whatever can be changed, so far as changed, it is not that which was: if it is no longer what it was, a kind of death has therein taken place; something that was there has been eliminated, and exists no more. Blackness has died out in the silvery locks of the patriarch, comeliness in the body of the careworn and crooked old man, strength in the body of the languishing, the [previous] standing posture in the body of one walking, walking in the body of one standing, walking and standing in the body of one reclining, speech in the tongue of the silent;—whatever changes, and is what it was not, I see there a kind of life in that which is, and death in that which was. In fine, when we say of one deceased, Where is that person? we are answered, He was. O Truth, it is thou [alone] that truly art! For in all actions and movements of ours, yea, in every activity of the creature, I find two times; the past and the future. I seek for the present, nothing stands still: what I have said is no longer present; what I am going to say is not yet come: what I have done is no longer present; what I am going to do is not yet come; the life I have lived is no longer present; the life I have still to live is not yet come. Past and future I find in every creature-movement: in truth, which is abiding, past and future I find not, but the present alone, and that unchangeably, which has no place in the creature. Sift the mutations of things, thou wilt find WAS and WILL BE:

---

[1] Ex. iii. 13-15.　　[2] Matt. xxviii. 20.　　[3] Esse.　　[4] Eodem modo.

think on God, thou wilt find the IS, where WAS and WILL BE cannot exist. To be so then thyself, rise beyond the boundaries of time. But who can transcend the powers of his being? May He raise us thither who said to the Father, "I will that they also be with me where I am." And so, in making this promise, that we should not die in our sins, the Lord Jesus Christ, I think, said nothing else by these words, "If ye believe not that I am;" yea, by these words I think He meant nothing else than this, "If ye believe not that I am" God, "ye shall die in your sins." Well, God be thanked that He said, "If ye believe not," and did not say, If ye comprehend not. For who can comprehend this? Or is it so, since I have ventured to speak and you have seemed to understand, that you have indeed comprehended somewhat of a subject so unspeakable? If then thou comprehendest not, faith sets thee free. Therefore also the Lord said not, If ye comprehend not that I am; but said what they were capable of attaining, "If ye believe not that I am, ye shall die in your sins."

11. And savoring as these men always did of the earth, and ever hearing and answering according to the flesh, what did they say to Him? "Who art thou?" For when thou saidst, "If ye believe not that I am," thou didst not tell us what thou wert. Who art thou, that we may believe? He answered "The Beginning." Here is the existence that [always] is. The beginning cannot be changed: the beginning is self-abiding and all-originating; that is, the beginning, to which it has been said, "But thou Thyself art the same, and Thy years shall not fail."[1] "The beginning," He said, "for so I also speak to you." Believe me [to be] the beginning, that ye may not die in your sins. For just as if by saying, "Who art thou?" they had said nothing else than this, What shall we believe thee to be? He replied, "The beginning;" that is, Believe me [to be] the "beginning." For in the Greek expression we discern what we cannot in the Latin. For in Greek the word "beginning" (*principium*, ἀρχή), is of the feminine gender, just as with us "law" (*lex*) is of the feminine gender, while it is of the masculine (νόμος) with them; or as "wisdom" (*sapientia*, σοφία) is of the feminine gender with both. It is the custom of speech, therefore, in different languages to

vary the gender of words, because in things themselves there is no place for the distinction of sex. For wisdom is not really female, since Christ is the Wisdom of God,[2] and Christ is termed of the masculine gender, wisdom of the feminine. When then the Jews said, "Who art thou?" He, who knew that there were some there who should yet believe, and therefore had said, Who art thou? that so they might come to know what they ought to believe regarding Him, replied, "The beginning:" not as if He said, I am the beginning; but as if He said, Believe me [to be] the beginning. Which, as I said, is quite evident in the Greek language, where beginning (ἀρχή) is of the feminine gender.[3] Just as if He had wished to say that He was the Truth, and to their question, "Who art thou?" had answered, *Veritatem*[4] [the Truth]; when to the words, "Who art thou?" He evidently ought to have replied, *Veritas*[5] [the Truth]; that is, I am the Truth. But His answer had a deeper meaning, when He saw that they had put the question, "Who art thou?" in such a way as to mean, Having heard from thee, "If ye believe not that I am,' what shall we believe thee to be? To this He replied, "The beginning:" as if He said, Believe me to be the beginning. And He added "for [as such] I also speak to you;" that is, having humbled myself on your account, I have condescended to such words. For if the beginning as it is in itself had remained so with the Father, as not to receive the form of a servant and speak as man with men; how could they have believed in Him, since their weak hearts could not have heard the Word intelligently without some voice that would appeal to their senses? Therefore, said He, believe me to be the beginning; for, that you may believe, I not only am, but also speak to you.[6] But on this subject I have still much to say to you; may it therefore please your Charity that we reserve what remains, and by His gracious aid deliver it tomorrow.

---

[1] Ps. cii. 27.

[2] 1 Cor. i. 24.

[3] The Greek is τὴν ἀρχήν, which to some has here the sound of an adverb, like the Latin *principio* and *primum*. So at least it sounded to Chrysostom. But Augustin's interpretation is favored by Ambrose, Bernard, etc.

[4] In the accusative case.   [5] In the nominative case.

[6] Augustin here makes Christ's speaking—His use of human language—the means whereby they should be able to know and believe Him to be the beginning, the Eternal Alpha. Had He not become man and spoken to them, but remained always hidden with the Father, and *silent*, they could never have had the means of knowing that *He* personally was the beginning, or believing *Him* such.—TR.

TRACTATE XXXIX.

Chapter VIII. 26, 27.

1. THE words of our Lord Jesus Christ, which He had addressed to the Jews, so regulating His discourse that the blind saw not, and believers' eyes were opened, are these, which have been read to-day from the holy Gospel: "Then said the Jews, Who art thou?" Because the Lord had said before, "If ye believe not that I am, ye shall die in your sins." [1] To this accordingly they rejoined, "Who art thou?" as if seeking to know on whom they ought to believe, so as not to die in their sin. He replied to those who asked Him : "Who art thou?" by saying, "The beginning, for [so] also I speak to you." If the Lord has called Himself the beginning, it may be inquired whether the Father also is the beginning. For if the Son who has a Father is the beginning, how much more easily must God the Father be understood as the beginning, who has indeed the Son whose Father He is, but has no one from whom He Himself proceedeth? For the Son is the Son of the Father, and the Father certainly is the Father of the Son; but the Son is called God of God,—the Son is called Light of Light; the Father is called Light, but not, of Light,—the Father is called God, but not, of God. If, then, God of God, Light of Light, is the beginning, how much more easily may we understand as such that Light, from whom the Light [cometh], and God, of whom is God? It seems, therefore, absurd, dearly beloved, to call the Son the beginning, and not to call the Father the beginning also.

2. But what shall we do? Are there, then, two beginnings? Let us beware of saying so. What then? if both the Father is the beginning and the Son the beginning, how are there not two beginnings? In the same way that we call the Father God, and the Son God, and yet say not that there are two Gods; and yet He who is the Father is not the Son, He who is the Son is not the Father; and the Holy Spirit, the Spirit of the Father and of the Son, is neither the Father nor the Son. Although, then, as Catholic ears have been taught in the bosom of mother Church, neither He who is the Father is the Son, nor He who is the Son is the Father, nor is the Holy Spirit, of the Father and of the Son, either the Son or the Father, yet we say not that there are three Gods; although, if we are asked of each apart, we must, of whichever we are questioned, confess that He is God.

3. But all this seems absurd to those who drag up familiar things to a level with things little known, visible things with invisible, and compare the creature to the Creator. For unbelievers sometimes question us and say: Whom you call the Father, do you call him God? We answer, God. Whom you call the Son, do you call him God? We answer, God. Whom you call the Holy Spirit, do you call him God? We answer, God. Then, say they, are the Father, and the Son, and the Holy Spirit three Gods? We answer, No. They are confounded, because they are not enlightened; they have their heart shut up, because they want the key of faith. Let us then, brethren, by an antecedent faith that heals the eye of our heart, receive without obscurity what we understand,—and what we understand not, believe without hesitation; let us not quit the foundation of faith in order to reach the summit of perfection. The Father is God, the Son is God, the Holy Spirit is God: and yet He is not the Father who is the Son, nor He the Son who is the Father, and the Holy Spirit, the Spirit of the Father and the Son, is neither the Father nor the Son. The Trinity is one God. The Trinity is one eternity, one power, one majesty;—three, but not [three] Gods. Let not the reviler answer me: "Three what, then? For," he adds, "if there are three, you must say, three what?" I reply: The Father, and the Son, and the Holy Spirit. "See," he says, "you have named three; but express what the three are?" Nay, count them yourself; for I make out three when I say, the Father, and the Son, and the Holy Spirit. For the Father is God as respects Himself, but [He is] the Father as respects the Son; the Son is God as respects Himself, but He is the Son as regards the Father.

4. What I say you may gather from daily analogies. So it is with one man and another, if the one be a father, the other his son. He is man as regards himself, but a father as regards his son; and the son man as respects himself, but a son as respects his father. For father is a name given relatively, and so with son; but these are two men. And certainly God the Father is Father in a

relative sense, that is, in relation to the Son; and God the Son is Son relatively, that is, in relation to the Father; but not as the former are two men are these two Gods. Why is it not so here? Because that belongs to one sphere and this to another; for this is divine. There is here something ineffable which cannot be explained in words, that there should both be, and not be, number. For see if there appear not a kind of number, Father, and Son, and Holy Ghost—the Trinity. If three, three what? Here number fails. And so God neither keeps apart from number, nor is comprehended by number. Because there are three, there is a kind of number. If you ask three what, number ceases. Hence it is said, "Great is our Lord, and great His power; and of His understanding there is no number."[1] When you have begun to reflect, you begin to number; when you have numbered, you cannot tell what you have numbered. The Father is Father, the Son is Son, the Holy Spirit is the Holy Spirit. What are these three, the Father, the Son, and the Holy Spirit? Are They not three Gods? No. Are They not three Almighties? No. Not three Creators of the world? No. Is the Father then almighty? Manifestly almighty. And is the Son then not almighty? Clearly the Son is also almighty. And is the Holy Spirit then not almighty? He, too, is almighty. Are there then three Almighties? No; only one Almighty. Only in Their relation to each other do They suggest number, not in Their essential existence. For though God the Father is, as respects Himself, God along with the Son and the Holy Spirit, there are not three Gods; and, though as respects Himself He is omnipotent, as well as the Son and the Holy Spirit, there are not three omnipotents; for in truth He is the Father not in respect to Himself, but to the Son; nor is the Son so in respect to Himself, but to the Father; nor is the Spirit so as regards Himself, in as far as He is called the Spirit of the Father and of the Son. I have no name to give the three, save the Father, the Son, and the Holy Spirit, one God, one Almighty. And so one beginning.

5. Take an illustration from the Holy Scriptures, whereby you may in some measure comprehend what I am saying. After our Lord Jesus Christ rose again, and was pleased to ascend into heaven, at the end of ten days He sent from thence the Holy Spirit, by whom those who were present in that one chamber were filled, and began to speak in the languages of all nations. The Lord's

murderers, terrified by the miracle, were pricked to the heart and sorrowed; sorrowing, were changed; and being changed, believed. There were added to the Lord's body, that is, to the number of believers, three thousand people. And so also by the working of another miracle there were added other five thousand. A considerable community was created, in which all, receiving the Holy Spirit, by whom spiritual love was kindled, were by their very love and fervor of spirit welded into one, and began in the very unity of fellowship to sell all that they had, and to lay the price at the apostles' feet, that distribution might be made to every one as each had need. And the Scripture says this of them, that "they were of one soul and one heart toward God."[2] Give heed then, brethren, and from this acknowledge the mystery of the Trinity, how it is we say, There is both the Father, and the Son, and the Holy Spirit, and yet there is one God. See! there were so many thousands of these, and yet there was one heart; there were so many thousands, and one soul. But where? In God. How much more so God Himself? Do I err at all in word when I call two men two souls, or three men three souls, or many men many souls? Surely I speak correctly. Let them approach God, and one soul belongs to all. If by approaching God many souls by love become one soul, and many hearts one heart, what of the very fountain of love in the Father and Son? Is it not still more so here that the Trinity is one God? For thence, of that Holy Spirit, does love come to us, as the apostle says: "The love of God is shed abroad in our hearts by the Holy Ghost, which is given unto us."[3] If then the love of God, shed abroad in our hearts by the Holy Ghost which is given unto us, makes many souls one soul, and many hearts one heart, how much rather are the Father and Son and Holy Spirit, one God, one light, and one beginning?

6. Let us hear, then, the Beginning who speaks to us: "I have," said He, "many things to say of you and to judge." You remember that He said, "I do not judge any one."[4] See, now He says, "I have many things to say of you and to judge." But, "I do not judge" is one thing: "I have to judge" is another; for He had come to save the world, not to judge the world.[5] In saying, "I have many things to say of you and to judge," He speaks of the future judgment. For therefore did He ascend, that He may come to judge the living and the dead. No one will judge more justly than He who was

---

[1] Ps. cxlvii. 5 (marg.).

[2] Acts ii. and iv. 32, etc.   [3] Rom. v. 5.
[4] Ver. 15.   [5] Chap. xii. 47.

unjustly judged. "Many things," said He, "have I to say of you and to judge; but He that sent me is true." See how the Son, His equal, gives glory to the Father. For He sets us an example, and says as it were in our hearts: O believer, if thou hearest my gospel, the Lord thy God saith to thee, when I, in the beginning God the Word with God, equal with the Father, co-eternal with Him that begat, give glory to Him whose Son I am, how canst thou be proud before Him, whose servant thou art?

7. "I have many things," He said, "to say of you and to judge: but He that sent me is true;" as if He had said, Therefore I judge the truth, because, as the Son of the True One, I am the truth. The Father true, the Son the truth,—which do we account the greater? Let us reflect, if we can, which is the greater, the True One or the Truth.[1] Take some other instances. Is a pious man, or piety, the more comprehensive? Surely piety itself; for the pious is derived from piety, not piety from the pious. For piety may still exist, though he who was pious became impious. He has lost his piety, but has taken nothing from piety itself. What also of comely and comeliness? Comeliness is more than comely; for comeliness gives existence to the comely, not the comely to comeliness. And so of chaste and chastity. Chastity is clearly something more than chaste. For if chastity had no existence, one would have no ground to be chaste; but though one may refuse to be chaste, chastity remains entire. If then the term piety implies more than the term pious, comeliness more than comely, chastity than chaste, shall we say that the Truth is more than the True One? If we say so, we shall begin to say that the Son is greater than the Father. For the Lord Himself says most distinctly, "I am the way, and the truth, and the life."[2] Therefore, if the Son is the truth, what is the Father but what the Truth Himself says, "He that sent me is true"? The Son is the truth, the Father true. I inquire which is the greater, but find equality. For the true Father is true not because He contained a part of that truth, but because He begat it entire.

8. I see I must speak more plainly. And, not to detain you long, let me treat only of this point to-day. When I have finished what,

with God's help, I wish to say, my discourse shall close. I have said this, then, to enlist your attention. Every soul, as being a thing, is mutable; and although a great creature, yet a creature; though superior to the body, yet made. Every soul, then, since it is changeable—that is, sometimes believes, sometimes disbelieves; at one time wishes, at another time refuses; at one time is adulterous, at another chaste; now good, and again wicked,—is changeable. But God is that which is, and so has retained as His own peculiar name, "I am who am."[3] Such also is the Son, when He says, "If ye believe not that I am;" and thereto pertains also, "Who art thou? The Beginning" (ver. 25). God therefore is unchangeable, the soul changeable. When the soul receives from God the elements of its goodness it becomes good by participation, just as by participation thine eye seeth. For it sees not when the light is withdrawn, while so long as it shares in the light it sees. Since then by participation the soul is made good, if it changes and becomes bad, the goodness remains that made it good. For there is a goodness of which it partook when good; and when it has turned to evil, that goodness continues entire. If the soul fall away and become evil, there is no lessening of goodness; if it return and become good, that goodness is not enlarged. Thine eye participates in this light, and thou seest. Is it shut? Then thou hast not diminished the light. Is it open? Thou hast not increased the light. By this illustration, brethren, understand that if the soul is pious, there is piety with God, of which the soul is partaker; if the soul is chaste, there is chastity with God, of which it partakes; if it is good, there is goodness with God, of which it partakes; if it is true, there is truth with God, of which the soul is partaker. Whereof if the soul is no partaker, every man is false;[4] and if every man may be false, no man is true of himself.[5] But the true Father is true of Himself,[5] for He begat the Truth. It is one thing to say, That man is true, for he has taken in the truth: it is another, God is true, for He begat the Truth. See then how God is true,—not by participating in, but by generating the Truth. I see you have understood me, and am glad. Let this suffice you to-day. The rest, according as He gives it, we shall expound when the Lord pleases.

---

[1] *Verax an veritas.*   [2] John xiv. 6.   [3] Ex. iii. 14.   [4] Ps. cxvi. 11.   [5] *De suo.*

TRACTATE XL.

Chapter VIII. 28–32.

1. OF the holy Gospel according to John, which you see in our hand, your Charity has already heard much, whereon by God's grace we have discoursed according to our ability, pressing on your notice that this evangelist, specially, has chosen to speak of the Lord's divinity, wherein He is equal with the Father and the only Son of God; and on that account he has been compared to the eagle, because no other bird is understood to take a loftier flight. Accordingly, to what follows in order, as the Lord enables us to treat of it, listen with all your attention.

2. We have spoken to you on the preceding passage, suggesting how the Father may be understood as True, and the Son as the Truth. But when the Lord Jesus said, "He that sent me is true," the Jews understood not that He spake to them of the Father. And He said to them, as you have just heard in the reading, "When ye have lifted up the Son of man, then shall ye know that I am, and [that] I do nothing of myself; but as the Father hath taught me, I speak these things." What means this? For it looks as if all He said was, that they would know who He was after His passion. Without doubt, therefore, He saw that some there, whom He Himself knew, whom with the rest of His saints He Himself in His foreknowledge had chosen before the foundation of the world, would believe after His passion. These are the very persons whom we are constantly commending, and with much entreaty setting forth for your imitation. For on the sending down of the Holy Spirit after the Lord's passion, and resurrection, and ascension, when miracles were being done in the name of Him whom, as if dead, the persecuting Jews had despised, they were pricked in their hearts; and they who in their rage slew Him were changed and believed; and they who in their rage shed His blood, now in the spirit of faith drank it; to wit, those three thousand, and those five thousand Jews[1] whom now He saw there, when He said, "When ye have lifted up the Son of man, then shall ye know that I am [He]." It was as if He had said, I let your recognition lie over till I have completed my passion: in your own order ye shall know who I am. Not that all who heard Him were only then to believe, that is, after the Lord's passion; for a little after it is said, "As He spake these words, many believed on Him;" and the Son of man was not yet lifted up. But the lifting up He is speaking of is that of His passion, not of His glorification; of the cross, not of heaven; for He was exalted there also when He hung on the tree. But that exaltation was His humiliation; for then He became obedient even to the death of the cross.[2] This required to be accomplished by the hands of those who should afterwards believe, and to whom He says, "When ye have lifted up the Son of man, then shall ye know that I am [He]." And why so, but that no one might despair, however guilty his conscience, when he saw those forgiven their homicide who had slain the Christ?

3. The Lord then, recognizing such in that crowd, said, "When ye have lifted up the Son of man, then shall ye know that I am [He]." You know already what "I am" signifies; and we must not be continually repeating, lest so great a subject beget distaste. Recall that, "I am who am," and "He who is hath sent me,"[3] and you will recognize the meaning of the words, "Then shall ye know that I am." But both the Father is, and the Holy Spirit is. To the same is belongs the whole Trinity. But because the Lord spake as the Son, in order that, when He says, "Then shall ye know that I am," there might be no chance of entrance for the error of the Sabellians, that is, of the Patripassians,—an error which I have charged you not to hold, but to beware of,—the error, I mean, of those who have said, The Father and Son are one and the same; two names, but one reality; —to guard them against that error, when the Lord said, "Then shall ye know that I am," that He might not be understood as Himself the Father, He immediately added, "And I do nothing of myself; but as my Father taught me, I speak these things." Already was the Sabellian beginning to rejoice over the discovery of a ground for his error; but immediately on showing himself as it were in the shade, he was confounded by the light of the following sentence. Thou thoughtest that He was the Father, because He said, "I am." Hear now that He is the Son: "And

---

[1] Acts ii. 37, 41; iv. 4.   [2] Phil. ii. 8.   [3] Ex. iii. 14.

15

I do nothing of myself." What means this, "I do nothing of myself"? Of myself I am not. For the Son is God, of [1] the Father; but the Father is God, yet not of the Son. The Son is God of God, and the Father is God, but not of God. The Son is light of light; and the Father is light, but not of light. The Son is, but there is [One] of whom He is; and the Father is, but there is none of whom He is.

4. Let not then, my brethren, His further words, "As my Father hath taught me, I speak these things," be the occasion of any carnal thought stealing into your minds. For human weakness cannot think, but as it is accustomed to act and to hear. Do not then set before your eyes as it were two men, one the father, the other the son, and the father speaking to the son; as any one of you may do, when you say something to your son, admonishing and instructing him how to speak, to charge his memory with what you have told him, and, having done so, to express it in words, to enunciate distinctly, and convey to the ears of others what he has apprehended with his own. Think not thus, lest you be fabricating idols in your heart. The human shape, the outlines of human limbs, the form of human flesh, the outward senses, stature and motions of the body, the functions of the tongue, the distinctions of sounds,—think not of such as existing in that Trinity, save as they pertain to the servant-form, which the only-begotten Son assumed, when the Word was made flesh to dwell among us.[2] Thereof I forbid thee not, human weakness, to think according to thy knowledge: nay, rather I require thee. If the faith that is in thee be true, think of Christ as such; but as such of the Virgin Mary, not of God the Father. He was an infant, He grew as a man, He walked as a man, He hungered, He thirsted as a man, He slept as a man; at last He suffered as a man, hung on the tree, was slain and buried as a man. In the same form He rose again; in the same, before the eyes of His disciples, He ascended into heaven; in the same will He yet come to judgment. For angel lips have declared in the Gospel, "He shall so come in like manner as ye have seen Him go into heaven." [3] When then you think of the servant-form in Christ, think of a human likeness, if you have faith; but when you think, "In the beginning was the Word, and the Word was with God, and the Word was God," [4] away with all human fashioning from your heart. Banish from your thoughts everything bounded by corporeal limits, in-

cluded in local measurement, or spread out in a mass, how great soever its size. Perish utterly such a figment from your heart. Think, if you can, on the beauty of wisdom, picture to yourself the beauty of righteousness. Has that a shape? a size? a color? It has none of these, and yet it is; for if it were not, it would neither be loved nor worthy of praise, nor be cherished in our heart and life as an object of honor and affection. But men here become wise; and whence would they so, had wisdom no existence? And further, O man, if thou canst not see thine own wisdom with the eyes of the flesh, nor think of it by the same mental imagery as thou canst of bodily things, wilt thou dare to thrust the shape of a human body on the wisdom of God?

5. What shall we say then, brethren? How spake the Father to the Son, seeing that the Son says, "As the Father taught me, I speak these things"? Did He speak to Him? When the Father taught the Son, did He use words, as you do when you teach your son? How could He use words to the Word! What words, many in number, could be used to the one Word? Did the Word of the Father approach His ears to the Father's mouth? Such things are carnal: banish them from your hearts. For this I say, if only you have understood my words, I certainly have spoken and my words have sounded, and by their sound have reached your ears, and through your sense of hearing have carried their meaning to your mind, if so be you have understood. Suppose that some person of Latin [5] speech has heard, but has only heard without understanding, what I have said. As regards the noise issuing from my mouth, he who has understood not has been a sharer therein just like yourselves. He has heard that sound; the same syllables have smote on his ears, but they have produced no effect on his mind. Why? Because he understood not. But if you have understood, whence comes your understanding? My words have sounded in the ear: have I kindled any light in the heart? Without doubt, if what I have said is true, and this truth you have not only heard, but also understood, two things have there been wrought (distinguish between them), hearing and intelligence. Hearing has been wrought by me, but by whom has understanding? I have spoken to the ear, that you might hear; who has spoken to your heart for understanding? Doubtless some one has also said something

---

[5] " Latin " here, as used by Augustin, would require to be translated " English," to give the exact force of the illustration in an *English* version.—Tr.

to your heart, that not only the noise of words might strike your ear, but something also of the truth might descend into your heart. Some one has spoken also to your heart, but you do not see him. If, brethren, you have understood, your heart also has been spoken to. Intelligence is the gift of God. And who, if you have understood, has spoken so in your heart, but He to whom the Psalm says, "Give me understanding, that I may learn Thy commandments?"[1] For example, the bishop has spoken. What has he said? some one asks. You repeat what he has spoken, and add, He has said the truth. Then another, who has not understood, says, What has he said, or what is it you are praising? Both have heard me; I have spoken to both; but to one of them God has spoken. If we may compare small things with great (for what are we to Him?), something, I know not what, of an incorporeal and spiritual kind God works in us, which is neither sound to strike the ear, nor color to be discerned by the eyes, nor smell to enter the nostrils, nor taste to be judged of by the mouth, nor anything hard or soft to be sensible to the touch; yet something there is which it is easy to feel,—impossible to explain. If then God, as I was saying, speaks in our hearts without sound, how speaks He to His Son? Thus then, brethren, think thus as much as you can, if, as I have said, we may in some measure compare small things with great: think thus. In an incorporeal way the Father spoke to the Son, because in an incorporeal way the Father begat the Son. Nor did He so teach Him as if He had begotten Him untaught; but to have taught Him is the same as to have begotten Him full of knowledge; and this, "The Father hath taught me," is the same as, The Father hath begotten me already knowing. For if, as few understand, the nature of the Truth is simple, to be is to the Son the same as to know. From Him therefore He has knowledge, from whom He has being.[2] Not that from Him He had first being, and afterwards knowledge; but as in begetting He gave Him to be, so in begetting He gave Him to know; for, as was said, to the simple nature of the Truth, being is not one thing and knowing another, but one and the same.

6. Thus then He spake to the Jews, and added, "And He that sent me is with me." He had already said this also before, but of this important point He is constantly reminding them,—"He sent me," and "He is with me." If then, O Lord, He is with Thee, not so much hath the One been sent by the other, but ye Both have come. And yet, while Both are together, One was sent, the Other was the sender; for incarnation is a sending, and the incarnation itself belongs only to the Son and not to the Father. The Father therefore sent the Son, but did not withdraw from the Son. For it was not that the Father was absent from the place to which He sent the Son. For where is not the Maker of all things? Where is He not, who said, "I fill heaven and earth"?[3] But perhaps the Father is everywhere, and the Son not so? Listen to the evangelist: "He was in this world, and the world was made by Him."[4] Therefore said He, "He that sent me," by whose power as Father I am incarnate, "is with me,—hath not left me." Why hath He not left me? "He hath not left me," He says, "alone; for I do always those things that please Him." That equality exists *always;* not from a certain beginning, and then onwards; but without beginning, without end. For Divine generation has no beginning in time, since time itself was created by the Only-begotten.

7. "As He spake these words, many believed on Him." Would that, while I speak also, many, who before this were otherwise disposed, understood and believed on Him! For perhaps there are some Arians in this large assembly. I dare not suspect that there are any Sabellians, who say that the Father Himself is one with the Son, seeing that heresy is too old, and has been gradually eviscerated. But that of the Arians seems still to have some movement about it, like that of a putrefying carcase, or certainly, at the most, like a man at the last gasp; and from this some still require deliverance, just as from that other many were delivered. This province, indeed, did not use to have such; but ever since the arrival of many foreigners, some of these have also found their way to our neighborhood. See then, while the Lord spake these words, many Jews believed on Him. May I see also that, while I am speaking, Arians are believing, not on me, but with me!

8. "Then said the Lord to those Jews who believed on Him, If ye continue in my word." "Continue," I say, for you are now initiated and have begun to be there. "If ye continue," that is, in the faith which is now begun in you who believe, to what will you attain? See the nature of the beginning, and whither it leads. You have loved the foundation, give heed to the summit, and out of this

---

[1] Ps. cxix. 73.   [2] *Ut noverit—ut sit.*   [3] Jer. xxiii. 24.   [4] Chap. i. 10.

low condition seek that other elevation. For faith has humility, but knowledge and immortality and eternity possess not lowliness, but loftiness; that is, upraising, all-sufficiency, eternal stability, full freedom from hostile assault, from fear of failure. That which has its beginning in faith is great, but is despised. In a building also the foundation is usually of little account with the unskilled. A large trench is made, and stones are thrown in every way and everywhere. No embellishment, no beauty are apparent there; just as also in the root of a tree there is no appearance of beauty. And yet all that delights you in the tree has sprung from the root. You look at the root and feel no delight: you look at the tree and admire it. Foolish man! what you admire has grown out of that which gave you no delight. The faith of believers seems a thing of little value,—you have no scales to weigh it. Hear then to what it attains, and see its greatness: as the Lord Himself says in another place, "If ye have faith as a grain of mustard seed."[1] What is there of less account than that, yet what is there pervaded with greater energy? What more minute, yet what more fervidly expansive? And so "ye" also, He says, "if ye continue in my word," wherein ye have believed, to what will ye be brought? "ye shall be my disciples indeed." And what does that benefit us? "and ye shall know the truth."

9. What, brethren, does He promise believers? "And ye shall know the truth." Why so? Had they not come to such knowledge when the Lord was speaking? If they had not, how did they believe? They believed, not because they knew, but that they might come to know. For we believe in order that we may know, we do not know in order that we may believe. For what we shall yet know, neither eye hath seen, nor ear heard, nor hath it entered the heart of man.[2] For what is faith, but to believe what you see not? Faith then is to believe what you see not; truth, to see what you have believed, as He Himself saith in a certain place. The Lord then walked on earth, first of all, for the creation of faith. He was man, He was made in a low condition. He was seen by all, but not by all was He known. By many was He rejected, by the multitude was He slain, by few was He mourned; and yet even by those who mourned Him, His true being was still unrecognized. All this is the beginning as it were of faith's lineaments and future upbuilding. As the Lord, referring thereto, saith in a certain place, "He that loveth me

keepeth my commandments; and he that loveth me shall be loved of my Father, and I will love him, and will manifest myself to him."[3] They certainly already saw the person to whom they were listening; and yet to them, if they loved Him, does He give it as a promise that they should see Him. So also here, "Ye shall know the truth." How so? Is that not the truth which Thou hast been speaking? The truth it is, but as yet it is only believed, not beheld. If you abide in that which is believed, you shall attain to that which is seen. Hence John himself, the holy evangelist, says in his epistle, "Dearly beloved, we are the sons of God; but it is not yet apparent what we shall be." We are so already, and something we shall be. What more shall we be than we are? Listen: "It is not yet apparent what we shall be: [but] we know that, when He shall appear, we shall be like Him." How? "For we shall see Him as He is."[4] A great promise, but the reward of faith. You seek the reward; then let the work precede. If you believe, ask for the reward of faith; but if you believe not, with what face can you seek the reward of faith? "If" then "ye continue in my word, ye shall be my disciples indeed," that ye may behold the very truth as it is, not through sounding words, but in dazzling light, wherewith He shall satisfy[5] us: as we read in the psalm, "The light of Thy countenance is impressed upon us."[6] We are God's money: we have wandered away as a coin from the treasury. The impression that was stamped upon us has been rubbed out by our wandering. He has come to refashion, for He it was that fashioned us at first; and He is Himself asking for His money, as Cæsar for his. Therefore He says, "Render unto Cæsar the things that are Cæsar's, and unto God the things that are God's:"[7] to Cæsar his money, to God yourselves. And then shall the truth be reproduced in us.

10. What shall I say to your Charity? Oh that our hearts were in some measure aspiring after that ineffable glory! Oh that we were passing our pilgrimage in sighs, and loving not the world, and continually pushing onwards with pious minds to Him who hath called us! Longing is the very bosom of the heart. We shall attain, if with all our power we give way to our longing. Such in our behalf is the object of the divine Scriptures, of the assembling of the people, of the celebration of the sacra-

---

[1] Matt. xvii. 20.   [2] Isa. lxiv, 4; 1 Cor. ii. 9.

[3] Chap. xiv. 21.   [4] 1 John iii 2.
[5] Or "impress;" *satiaverit,* or *signaverit.*
[6] Ps. iv. 6: Aug., with Vulg., translates נָסָה־עָלֵינוּ passively and indic., instead of active and imperat., as Engl. Vers.—Tr.
[7] Matt. xxii. 21.

ments, of holy baptism, of singing God's praise, and of this our own exposition,—that this longing may not only be implanted and germinate, but also expand to such a measure of capacity as to be fit to take in what eye hath not seen, nor ear heard, nor hath entered into the heart of man. But love with me. He who loves God is not much in love with money. And I have but touched on this infirmity, not venturing to say, He loves not money at all, but, He loves not money much; as if money were to be loved, but not in a great degree. Oh, were we loving God worthily, we should have no love at all for money! Money then will be thy means of pilgrimage, not the stimulant of lust; something to use for necessity, not to joy over as a means of delight. Love God, if He has wrought in thee somewhat of that which thou hearest and praisest. Use the world: let not the world hold thee captive. Thou art passing on the journey thou hast begun; thou hast come, again to depart, not to abide. Thou art passing on thy journey, and this life is but a wayside inn. Use money as the traveller at an inn uses table, cup, pitcher, and couch, with the purpose not of remaining, but of leaving them behind. If such you would be, you, who can stir up your hearts and hear me; if such you would be, you will attain to His promises. It is not too much for your strength, for mighty is the hand of Him who hath called you. He hath called you. Call upon Him, say to Him, Thou hast called us, we call upon Thee; see, we have heard Thee calling us, hear us calling upon Thee: lead us whither Thou hast promised; perfect what Thou hast begun; forsake not Thine own gifts; leave not Thine own field; let Thy tender shoots yet be gathered into Thy barn. Temptations abound in the world, but greater is He who made the world. Temptations abound, but he fails not whose hope reposes in Him in whom there is no deficiency.

11. I have been exhorting you, brethren, to this in such words, because the freedom of which our Lord Jesus Christ speaks belongs not to this present time. Look at what He added: "Ye shall be my disciples indeed; and ye shall know the truth, and the truth shall set you free." What means that— "shall set you free"? It shall make you freemen. In a word, the carnal, and fleshly-minded Jews—not those who had believed, but those in the crowd who believed not— thought that an injury was done them, because He said to them, "The truth shall make you free." They were indignant at being designated as slaves. And slaves truly they were; and He explains to them what slavery it is, and what is that future freedom which is promised by Himself. But of this liberty and of that slavery it were too long to speak to-day.

TRACTATE XLI.

CHAPTER VIII. 31–36.

1. OF what follows of the previous lesson, and has been read publicly to us to-day from the holy Gospel, I then deferred speaking, because I had already said much, and of that liberty into which the grace of the Saviour calleth us it was needful to treat in no cursory or negligent way. Of this, by the Lord's help, we purpose speaking to you to-day. For those to whom the Lord Jesus Christ was speaking were Jews, in a large measure indeed His enemies, but also in some measure already become, and yet to be, His friends; for some He saw there, as we have already said, who should yet believe after His passion. Looking to these, He had said, "When ye have lifted up the Son of man, then shall ye know that I am [He]."[1] There also were those who, when He so spake. straightway believed. To them He spake what we have heard to-day: "Then said Jesus to those Jews who believed on Him, If ye continue in my word, ye shall be my disciples indeed." By continuing ye shall be so; for as now ye are believers, by so continuing ye shall be beholders. Hence there follows, "And ye shall know the truth." The truth is unchangeable. The truth is bread, which refreshes our minds and fails not; changes the eater, and is not itself changed into the eater. The truth itself is the Word of God,

---

[1] Chap. viii. 28.

God with God, the only-begotten Son. This Truth was for our sake clothed with flesh, that He might be born of the Virgin Mary, and the prophecy fulfilled, "Truth has sprung from the earth."[1] This Truth then, when speaking to the Jews, lay hid in the flesh. But He lay hid not in order to be denied, but to be deferred [in His manifestation]; to be deferred, in order to suffer in the flesh; and to suffer in the flesh, in order that flesh might be redeemed from sin. And so our Lord Jesus Christ, standing full in sight as regards the infirmity of flesh, but hid as regards the majesty of Godhead, said to those who had believed on Him, when He so spake, "If ye continue in my word, ye shall be my disciples indeed." For he that endureth to the end shall be saved.[2] "And ye shall know the truth," which now is hid from you, and speaks to you. "And the truth shall free you." This word, *liberabit* [shall free], the Lord hath taken from *libertas* [freedom]. For *liberat* [frees, delivers] is properly nothing else but *liberum facit* [makes free]. As *salvat* [he saves] is nothing else but *salvum facit* [he makes safe]; as *he heals* is nothing else but *he makes whole; he enriches* is nothing else but *he makes rich;* so *liberat* [he frees] is nothing else but *liberum facit* [he makes free]. This is clearer in the Greek word.[3] For in Latin usage we commonly say that a man is delivered (*liberari*), in regard not to liberty, but only to safety, just as one is said to be delivered from some infirmity. So is it said customarily, but not properly. But the Lord made such use of this word in saying, "And the truth shall make you free (*liberabit*)," that in the Greek tongue no one could doubt that He spake of freedom.

2. In short, the Jews also so understood and "answered Him;" not those who had already believed, but those in that crowd who were not yet believers. "They answered Him, We are Abraham's seed, and were never in bondage to any man: how sayest thou, Ye shall be free?" But the Lord had not said, "Ye shall be free," but, "The truth shall make you free." That word, however, they, because, as I have said, it is clearly so in the Greek, understood as pointing only to freedom, and puffed themselves up as Abraham's seed, and said, "We are Abraham's seed, and were never in bondage to any man: how sayest thou, Ye shall be free?" O inflated skin! such is not magnanimity, but windy swelling. For even as regards freedom in this life, how was that the truth when you said, "We were never in bondage to any

man"? Was not Joseph sold?[4] Were not the holy prophets led into captivity?[5] And again, did not that very nation, when making bricks in Egypt, also serve hard rulers, not only in gold and silver, but also in clay?[6] If you were never in bondage to any man, ungrateful people, why is it that God is continually reminding you that He delivered you from the house of bondage?[7] Or mean you, perchance, that your fathers were in bondage, but you who speak were never in bondage to any man? How then were you now paying tribute to the Romans, out of which also you formed a trap for the Truth Himself, as if to ensnare Him, when you said, "Is it lawful to give tribute to Cæsar?" in order that, had He said, It is lawful, you might fasten on Him as one ill-disposed to the liberty of Abraham's seed; and if He said, It is not lawful, you might slander Him before the kings of the earth, as forbidding the payment of tribute to such? Deservedly were you defeated on producing the money, and compelled yourselves to concur in your own capture. For there it was told you, "Render to Cæsar the things that are Cæsar's, and to God the things that are God's," after your own reply, that the money-piece bore the image of Cæsar.[8] For as Cæsar looks for his own image on the coin, so God looks for His in man. Thus, then, did He answer the Jews. I am moved, brethren, by the hollow pride of men, because even of that very freedom of theirs, which they understood carnally, they lied when they said, "We were never in bondage to any man."

3. But to the Lord's own answer, let us give better and more earnest heed, lest we ourselves be also found bondmen. For "Jesus answered them, Verily, verily, I say unto you, that every one who committeth sin is the servant of sin." He is the servant— would that it were of man, and not of sin! Who will not tremble at such words? The Lord our God grant us, that is, both you and me, that I may speak in fitting terms of this freedom to be sought, and of that bondage to be avoided. "Amen, amen [verily, verily], I say unto you." The Truth speaks: and in what sense does the Lord our God claim it as His to say, "Amen, amen, I say unto you"? His charge is weighty in so announcing it. In some sort, if lawful to be said, His form of swearing is, "Amen, amen, I say unto you." *Amen* in a way may be interpreted, [It is] true [truly, verily]; and yet it is not interpreted, though it might have

1 Ps. lxxxv. 11.   2 Matt. x. 22.   3 ἐλευθερώσει.

4 Gen. xxxvii. 28.   5 2 Kings xxiv. (Ezek. i. 1, etc.—Tr.).
6 Ex. i. 14.   7 Ex. xiii. 3 ; Deut. v. 6, etc.
8 Matt. xxii. 15-21.

been said, What is true [verily] I say unto you. Neither the Greek translator nor the Latin has dared to do so; for this word *Amen* is neither Greek nor Latin, but Hebrew. So it has remained without interpretation, to possess honor as the covering of something hidden; not in order to be disowned, but that it might not, as a thing laid bare to the eye, fall into disrepute. And yet it is not once, but twice uttered by the Lord, "Amen, amen, I say unto you." And now learn from the very doubling, how much was implied in the charge before us.

4. What, then, is the charge given? Verily, verily, I say unto you, saith the Truth, who surely, though He had not said, Verily, I say, could not possibly lie. Yet [thereby] He impresses, inculcates His charge, arouses in a way the sleeping, makes them attentive, and would not be contemned. What does He say? "Verily, verily, I say unto you, that every one who committeth sin is the servant of sin." Miserable slavery! Men frequently, when they suffer under wicked masters, demand to get themselves sold, not seeking to be without a master, but at all events to change him. What can the servant of sin do? To whom can he make his demand? To whom apply for redress? Of whom require himself to be sold? And then at times a man's slave, worn out by the commands of an unfeeling master, finds rest in flight. Whither can the servant of sin flee? Himself he carries with him wherever he flees. An evil conscience flees not from itself; it has no place to go to; it follows itself. Yea, he cannot withdraw from himself, for the sin he commits is within. He has committed sin to obtain some bodily pleasure. The pleasure passes away; the sin remains. What delighted is gone; the sting has remained behind. Evil bondage! Sometimes men flee to the Church, and we generally permit them, uninstructed as they are—men, wishing to be rid of their master, who are unwilling to be rid of their sins. But sometimes also those subjected to an unlawful and wicked yoke flee for refuge to the Church; for, though free-born men, they are retained in bondage: and an appeal is made to the bishop. And unless he care to put forth every effort to save free-birth from oppression, he is accounted unmerciful. Let us all flee to Christ, and appeal against sin to God as our deliverer. Let us seek to get ourselves sold, that we may be redeemed by His blood. For the Lord says, "Ye were sold for nought, and ye shall be redeemed without money." [1]

Without price, that is, of your own; because of mine. So saith the Lord; for He Himself has paid the price, not in money, but His own blood. Otherwise we had remained both bondmen and indigent.

5. From this bondage, then, we are set free by the Lord alone. He who had it not, Himself delivers us from it; for He alone came without sin in the flesh. For the little ones whom you see carried in their mothers' hands cannot yet walk, and are already in fetters; for they have received from Adam what they are loosened from by Christ. To them also, when baptized, pertains that grace which is promised by the Lord; for He only can deliver from sin who came without sin, and was made a sacrifice for sin. For you heard when the apostle was read: "We are ambassadors," he says, "for Christ, as though God were exhorting you by us; we beseech you in Christ's stead,"—that is, as if Christ were beseeching you, and for what? —"to be reconciled unto God." If the apostle exhorts and beseeches us to be reconciled unto God, then were we enemies to God. For no one is reconciled unless from a state of enmity. And we have become enemies not by nature, but by sin. From the same source are we the servants of sin, that we are the enemies of God. God has no enemies in a state of freedom. They must be slaves; and slaves will they remain unless delivered by Him to whom they wished by their sins to be enemies. Therefore, says he, "We beseech you in Christ's stead to be reconciled unto God." But how are we reconciled, save by the removal of that which separates between us and Himself? For He says by the prophet, "He hath not made the ear heavy that it should not hear; but your iniquities have separated between you and your God." [2] And so, then, we are not reconciled, unless that which is in the midst is taken away, and something else is put in its place. For there is a separating medium, and, on the other hand, there is a reconciling Mediator. The separating medium is sin, the reconciling Mediator is the Lord Jesus Christ: "For there is one God and Mediator between God and men, the man Christ Jesus." [3] To take then away the separating wall, which is sin, that Mediator has come, and the priest has Himself become the sacrifice. And because He was made a sacrifice for sin, offering Himself as a whole burnt-offering on the cross of His passion, the apostle, after saying, "We beseech you in Christ's stead to be reconciled unto God,"—as if we had said, How shall

---

[1] Isa. lii. 3.   [2] Isa. lix. 1, 2.   [3] 1 Tim. ii. 5.

we be able to be reconciled ?—goes on to say, "He hath made Him," that is, Christ Himself, "who knew no sin, [to be] sin for us, that we may be the righteousness of God in Him:"[1] "Him," he says, Christ Himself our God, "who knew no sin." For He came in the flesh, that is, in the likeness of sinful flesh,[2] but not in sinful flesh, because He had no sin at all; and therefore became a true sacrifice for sin, because He Himself had no sin.

6. But perhaps, through some special perception of my own, I have said that *sin* is a sacrifice for sin. Let those who have read it be free to acknowledge it; let not those who have not read it be backward; let them not, I say, be backward to read, that they may be truthful in judging. For when God gave commandment about the offering of sacrifices for sin, in which sacrifices there was no expiation of sins, but the shadow of things to come, the self-same sacrifices, the self-same offerings, the self-same victims, the self-same animals, which were brought forward to be slain for sins, and in whose blood that [true] blood was prefigured, are themselves called *sins*[3] by the law; and that to such an extent that in certain passages it is written in these terms, that the priests, when about to sacrifice, were to lay their hands on the head of the sin, that is, on the head of the victim about to be sacrificed for sin. Such *sin*, then, that is, such a sacrifice for sin, was our Lord Jesus Christ made, "who knew no sin."

7. With efficacious merit does He deliver from this bondage of sin, who saith in the psalms: "I am become as a man without help, free among the dead."[4] For He only was free, because He had no sin. For He Himself says in the Gospel, "Behold, the prince of this world cometh," meaning the devil about to come in the persons of the persecuting Jews;—"behold," He says, "he cometh, and shall find nothing in me."[5] Not as he found some measure of sin in those whom he also slew as righteous; in me he shall find nothing. And just as if He were asked, If he shall find nothing in Thee, wherefore will he slay Thee? He further said, "But that all may know that I do the will of my Father, rise and let us go hence." I do not, He says, pay the penalty of death as a necessity of my sinfulness; but in the death I die, I do the will of my Father. And in this, I am doing rather than enduring it; for, were I unwilling, I should not have had

the suffering to endure. You have Him saying in another place, "I have power to lay down my life, and I have power to take it up again."[6] Here surely is one "free among the dead."

8. Since, then, every one that committeth sin is the servant of sin, listen to what is our hope of liberty. "And the servant," He says, "abideth not in the house for ever." The church is the house, the servant is the sinner. Many sinners enter the church. Accordingly He has not said, "The servant" is not in the house, but "abideth not in the house for ever." If, then, there shall be no servant there, who will be there? For "when" as the Scripture speaketh, "the righteous king sitteth on the throne, who will boast of having a clean heart? or who will boast that he is pure from his sin?"[7] He has greatly alarmed us, my brethren, by saying, "The servant abideth not in the house for ever." But He further adds, "But the Son abideth ever." Will Christ, then, be alone in His house? Will no people remain at His side? Whose head will He be, if there shall be no body? Or is the Son all this, both the head and the body? For it is not without cause that He has inspired both terror and hope: terror, in order that we should not love sin; and hope, that we should not be distrustful of the remission of sin. "Every one," He says, "that committeth sin is the servant of sin. And the servant abideth not in the house for ever." What hope, then, have we, who are not without sin? Listen to thy hope: "The Son abideth for ever. If the Son, therefore, shall make you free, then shall ye be free indeed." Our hope is this, brethren, to be made free by the free One; and that, in setting us free, He may make us His servants. For we were the servants of lust; but being set free, we are made the servants of love. This also the apostle says: "For, brethren, ye have been called unto liberty; only use not liberty for an occasion to the flesh, but by love serve one another."[8] Let not then the Christian say, I am free; I have been called unto liberty: I was a slave, but have been redeemed, and by my very redemption have been made free, I shall do what I please: no one may balk me of my will, if I am free. But if thou committest sin with such a will, thou art the servant of sin. Do not then abuse your liberty for freedom in sinning, but use it for the purpose of sinning not. For only if thy will is pious, will it be free. Thou wilt be free, if thou art a servant still,—free from sin, the servant of righteous-

---

[1] 2 Cor. v. 20, 21. [2] Rom. viii. 3.
[3] That is, "sin-offerings." *Peccata* is here used to correspond to the Hebrew אָשָׁם and חַטָּאת, which signify, the one, both *trespass* and *trespass-offering*, and the other, *sin* and *sin-offering*; indicating the thoroughness of the substitutionary idea.—Tr.
[4] Ps. lxxxviii. 4, 5.   [5] Chap. xiv. 30, 31.

[6] Chap. x. 18.   [7] Prov. xx. 8, 9.   [8] Gal. v. 13.

ness: as the apostle says, "When ye were the servants of sin, ye were free from righteousness. But now, being made free from sin, and become servants to God, ye have your fruit unto holiness, and the end everlasting life."[1] Let us be striving after the latter, and be doing the other.

9. The first stage of liberty is to be free from crimes. Give heed, my brethren, give heed, that I may not by any means mislead your understanding as to the nature of that liberty at present, and what it will be. Sift any one soever of the highest integrity in this life, and however worthy he may already be of the name of upright, yet is he not without sin. Listen to Saint John himself, the author of the Gospel before us, when he says in his epistle, "If we say that we have no sin, we deceive ourselves, and the truth is not in us."[2] He alone could say this who was "free among the dead:" of Him only could it be said, who knew no sin. It could be said only of Him, for He also "was in all points tempted like as we are, yet without sin."[3] He alone could say, "Behold, the prince of this world cometh, and shall find nothing in me." Sift any one else, who is accounted righteous, yet is he not in all respects without sin; not even such as was Job, to whom the Lord bore such testimony, that the devil was filled with envy, and demanded that he should be tempted, and was himself defeated in the temptation, to the end that Job might be proved.[4] And he was proved for this reason, not that the certainty of his carrying off the conqueror's wreath was unknown to God, but that he might become known as an object of imitation to others. And what says Job himself? "For who is clean? not even the infant whose life is but a day's span upon the earth."[5] But it is plain that many are called righteous without opposition, because the term is understood as meaning, free from crime; for in human affairs there is no just ground of complaint attaching to those who are free from criminal conduct. But crime is grievous sin, deserving in the highest measure to be denounced and condemned. Not, however, that God condemns certain sins, and justifies and praises certain others. He approves of none. He hates them all. As the physician dislikes the ailment of the ailing, and works by his healing measures to get the ailment removed and the ailing relieved; so God by his grace worketh in us, that sin may be consumed, and man made free. But when, you will be saying, is it consumed? If it is les-

sened, why is it not consumed? That is growing less in the life of those who are advancing onwards, which is consumed in the life of those who have attained to perfection.

10. The first stage of liberty, then, is to be free from crimes [sinful conduct]. And so the Apostle Paul, when he determined on the ordination of either elders or deacons, or whoever was to be ordained to the superintendence of the Church, says not, If any one is without sin; for had he said so, every one would be rejected as unfit, none would be ordained: but he says, "If any one is without crime" [E.V. blame],[6] such as, murder, adultery, any uncleanness of fornication, theft, fraud, sacrilege, and others of that sort. When a man has begun to be free from these (and every Christian man ought to be so), he begins to raise his head to liberty; but that is liberty begun, not completed. Why, says some one, is it not completed liberty? Because, "I see another law in my members warring against the law of my mind;" "for what I would," he says, "that do I not; but what I hate, that do I."[7] "The flesh," he says, "lusteth against the spirit, and the spirit against the flesh; so that ye do not the things that ye would."[8] In part liberty, in part bondage: not yet entire, not yet pure, not yet full liberty, because not yet eternity. For we have still infirmity in part, in part we have attained to liberty. Whatever has been our sin, was previously wiped out in baptism. But because all our iniquity has been blotted out, has there remained no infirmity? If there had not, we should be living here without sin. Yet who would venture to say so, but the proud, but the man unworthy of the Deliverer's mercy, but he who wishes to be self-deceived, and who is destitute of the truth? Hence, from the fact that some infirmity remains, I venture to say that, in what measure we serve God, we are free; in what measure we serve the law of sin, we are still in bondage. Hence says the apostle, what we began to say, "I delight in the law of God after the inward man."[9] Here then it is, wherein we are free, wherein we delight in the law of God; for liberty has joy. For as long as it is from fear that thou doest what is right, God is no delight to thee. Find thy delight in Him, and thou art free. Fear not punishment, but love righteousness. Art thou not yet able to love righteousness? Fear even punishment, that thou mayest attain to the love of righteousness.

11. In the measure then spoken of above, he felt himself to be already free, and there-

---

[1] Rom. vi. 20, 22.
[2] 1 John i. 8.
[3] Heb. iv. 15.
[4] Job i. 2.
[5] Job xiv. 4, 5; according to a reading of the Septuagint.
[6] 1 Tim. iii. 10; Tit. i. 6.
[7] Rom. vii. 13, 15.
[8] Gal. v. 17.
[9] Rom. vii. 22.

fore said, "I delight in the law of God after the inward man." I delight in the law, I delight in its requirements, I delight in righteousness itself. "But I see another law in my members"—this infirmity which remains —"warring against the law of my mind, and bringing me into captivity to the law of sin, which is in my members." On this side he feels his captivity, where righteousness has not been perfected; for where he delights in the law of God, he is not the captive but the friend of the law; and therefore free, because a friend. What then is to be done with that which so remains? What, but to look to Him who has said, "If the Son shall make you free, then shall ye be free indeed"? Indeed he also who thus spake so looked to Him: "O wretched man that I am," he says, "who shall deliver me from the body of this death? I thank God, through Jesus Christ our Lord." *Therefore* "if the Son shall make you free, ye shall be free indeed." And then he concluded thus: "So then, with the mind I myself serve the law of God; but with the flesh the law of sin."¹ *I myself*, he says; for there are not two of us contrary to each other, coming from different origins; but "with the mind I myself serve the law of God, and with the flesh the law of sin," so long as languor struggles against salvation.

12. But if with the flesh thou servest the law of sin, do as the apostle himself says: "Let not sin therefore reign in your mortal body, that ye should obey it in the lust thereof: neither yield ye your members as weapons of unrighteousness unto sin."² He says not, Let it not be; but, "Let it not reign." So long as sin must be in thy members, let its reigning power at least be taken away, let not its demands be obeyed. Does anger rise? Yield not up thy tongue to anger for the purpose of evil-speaking; yield not up thy hand or foot to anger for the purpose of striking. That irrational anger would not rise, were there no sin in the members. But take away its ruling power; let it have no weapons wherewith to fight against thee. Then also it will learn not to rise, when it begins to find the lack of weapons. "Yield not your members as weapons of unrighteousness unto sin," else will ye be entirely captive, and there will be no room to say, "With the mind I serve the law of God." For if the mind keep possession of the weapons, the members are not roused to the service of raging sin. Let the inward ruler keep possession of the citadel, because it stands there under a greater ruler, and is certain of assistance. Let it bridle anger;

let it restrain evil desire. There is within something that needs bridling, that needs restraining, that needs to be kept in command. And what did that righteous man wish, who with the mind was serving the law of God, but that there should be a complete deliverance from that which needed to be bridled? And this ought every one to be striving after who is aiming at perfection, that lust itself also, no longer receiving the obedience of the members, may every day be lessened in the advancing pilgrim. "To will," he says, "is present with me; but not so, how to perfect that which is good."³ Has he said, To *do* good is not present with me? Had he said so, hope would be wanting. He does not say, To do is not present with me, but, "To perfect is not present with me." For what is the perfecting of good, but the elimination and end of evil? And what is the elimination of evil, but what the law says, "Thou shalt not lust [covet]"?⁴ To lust not at all is the perfecting of good, because it is the eliminating of evil. This he said, "To perfect that which is good is not present with me," because his doing could not get the length of setting him free from lust. He labored only to bridle lust, to refuse consent to lust, and not to yield his members to its service. "To perfect," then, he says, "that which is good is not present with me." I cannot fulfill the commandment, "Thou shalt not lust." What then is needed? To fulfill this: "Go not after thy lusts."⁵ Do this meanwhile so long as unlawful lusts are present in thy flesh; "Go not after thy lusts." Abide in the service of God, in the liberty of Christ. With the mind serve the law of thy God. Yield not thyself to thy lusts. By following them, thou addest to their strength. By giving them strength, how canst thou conquer, when on thine own strength thou art nourishing enemies against thyself?

13. What then is that full and perfect liberty in the Lord Jesus, who said, "If the Son shall make you free, then shall ye be free indeed;" and when shall it be a full and perfect liberty? When enmities are no more; when "death, the last enemy, shall be destroyed." "For this corruptible must put on incorruption, and this mortal must put on immortality.—And when this mortal shall have put on immortality, then shall be brought to pass the saying that is written, Death is swallowed up in victory. O death, where is thy struggle?"⁶ What is this, "O death, where is thy struggle"? "The flesh *lusteth* against the spirit, and the spirit against the flesh,"

---

¹ Rom. vii. 23-25.   ² Rom. vi. 12, 13.

³ Rom. vii. 18.   ⁴ Ex. xx. 17.   ⁵ Ecclus. xviii. 30.
⁶ 1 Cor. xv. 26, 53-55. Struggle, "*contentio*."

but only when the flesh of sin was in vigor. "O death, where is [now] thy struggle?" Now shall we live, no more shall we die, in Him who died for us and rose again: "that they," he says, "who live, should no longer live unto themselves, but unto Him who died for them and rose again."[1] Let us be praying, as those who are wounded, for the physician; let us be carried into the inn to be healed. For it is He who promises salvation, who pitied the man left half-alive on the road by robbers. He poured in oil and wine, He healed the wounds, He put him on his beast, He took him to the inn, He commended him to the innkeeper's care. To what innkeeper? Perhaps to him who said, "We are ambassadors for Christ." He gave also two pence to pay for the healing of the wounded man.[2] And perhaps these are the two commandments, on which hang all the law and the prophets.[3] Therefore, brethren, is the Church also, wherein the wounded is healed meanwhile, the traveller's inn; but above the Church itself, lies the possessor's inheritance.

[1] 2 Cor. v. 15.   [2] Luke x. 30-35.   [3] Matt. xxii. 37-40.

TRACTATE XLII.

CHAPTER VIII. 37-47.

1. OUR Lord, in the form of a servant, yet not a servant, but even in servant-form the Lord (for that form of flesh was indeed servant-like; but though He was "in the likeness of sinful flesh,"[1] yet was He not sinful flesh) promised freedom to those who believed in Him. But the Jews, as if proudly glorying in their own freedom, refused with indignation to be made free, when they were the servants of sin. And therefore they said that they were free, because Abraham's seed. What answer, then, the Lord gave them to this, we have heard in the reading of this day's lesson. "I know," He said, "that ye are Abraham's children; but ye seek to kill me, because my word taketh no hold in you." I recognize you, He says; "Ye are the children of Abraham, but ye seek to kill me." I recognize the fleshly origin, not the believing heart. "Ye are the children of Abraham," but after the flesh. Therefore He says, "Ye seek to kill me, because my word taketh no hold in you." If my word were taken, it would take hold: if ye were taken, ye would be enclosed like fishes within the meshes of faith. What then means that—"taketh no hold in you"? It taketh not hold of your heart, because not received by your heart. For so is the word of God, and so it ought to be to believers, as a hook to the fish: it takes when it is taken. No injury is done to those who are taken; since they are taken for salvation, and not for destruction. Hence the Lord says to His disciples: "Come after me, and I shall make you fishers of men."[2] But such were not these; and yet they were the children of Abraham,—children of a man of God, unrighteous themselves. For they inherited the fleshly genus, but were become degenerate, by not imitating the faith of him whose children they were.

2. You have heard, indeed, the Lord saying, "I know that ye are Abraham's children." Hear what He says afterwards: "I speak that which I have seen with my Father; and ye do that which ye have seen with your father." He had already said, "I know that ye are Abraham's children." What is it, then, that they do? What He told them: "Ye seek to kill me." This they never saw with Abraham. But the Lord wishes God the Father to be understood when He says, "I speak that which I have seen with my Father." I have seen the truth: I speak the truth, because I am the Truth. For if the Lord speaks the truth which He has seen with the Father, He has seen Himself—He speaks Himself; because He Himself is the Truth of the Father, which He saw with the Father. For He is the Word—the Word which was with God. The evil, then, which these men do, and which the Lord chides and reprehends, where have they seen it? With their father. When we come to hear in what follows the still clearer statement who is their father, then shall we understand what kind of things they saw with such a father; for as yet He names not their father. A little above He referred to Abraham, but in regard to their fleshly origin, not their similarity of life. He is about to speak of that other father of theirs, who neither begat them

[1] Rom. viii. 3.   [2] Matt. iv. 19.

nor created them to be men. But still they were his children in as far as they were evil, not in as far as they were men; in what they imitated him, and not as created by him.

3. "They answered and said unto Him, Abraham is our father;" as if, Whàt hast thou to say against Abraham? or, If thou canst, dare to find fault with Abraham. Not that the Lord dared not find fault with Abraham; but Abraham was not one to be found fault with by the Lord, but rather approved. But these men seemed to challenge Him to say some evil of Abraham, and so to have some occasion for doing what they purposed. "Abraham is our father."

4. Let us hear how the Lord answered them, praising Abraham to their condemnation. "Jesus saith unto them, If ye are Abraham's children, do the works of Abraham. But now ye seek to kill me, a man that hath told you the truth, which I have heard of God: this did not Abraham." See, he was praised, they were condemned. Abraham was no manslayer. I say not, He implies, I am Abraham's Lord; though did I say it, I would say the truth. For He said in another place, "Before Abraham was, I am" (ver. 58); and then they sought to stone Him. He said not so. But meanwhile, as you see me, as you look upon me, as alone you think of me, I am a man. Wherefore, then, wish you to kill a man who is telling you what he has heard of God, but because you are not the children of Abraham? And yet He said above, "I know that ye are Abraham's children." He does not deny their origin, but condemns their deeds. Their flesh was from him, but not their life.

5. But we, dearly beloved, do we come of Abraham's race, or was Abraham in any sense our father according to the flesh? The flesh of the Jews draws its origin from his flesh, not so the flesh of Christians. We have come of other nations, and yet, by imitating him, we have become the children of Abraham. Listen to the apostle: "To Abraham and to his seed were the promises made. He saith not," he adds, "And to seeds, as of many; but as of one, And to thy seed, which is Christ. And if ye be Christ's, then are ye Abraham's seed, and heirs according to the promise."[1] We then have become Abraham's seed by the grace of God. It was not of Abraham's flesh that God made any co-heirs with him. He disinherited the former, He adopted the latter; and from that olive tree whose root is in the patriarchs, He cut off the proud natural branches, and engrafted the lowly wild olive.[2] And so, when the Jews came to John to be baptized, he broke out upon them, and addressed them, "O generation of vipers." Very greatly indeed did they boast of the loftiness of their origin, but he called them a generation of vipers,—not even of human beings, but of vipers. He saw the form of men, but detected the poison. Yet they had come to be changed,[3] because at all events to be baptized; and he said to them, "O generation of vipers, who hath warned you to flee from the wrath to come? Bring forth therefore fruits meet for repentance. And think not to say within yourselves, We have Abraham to our father; for God is able of these stones to raise up children unto Abraham."[4] If ye bring not forth fruits meet for repentance, flatter not yourselves about such a lineage. God is able to condemn you, without defrauding Abraham of children. For He has a way to raise up children to Abraham. Those who imitate his faith shall be made his children. "God is able of these stones to raise up children unto Abraham." Such are we. In our parents we were stones, when we worshipped stones for our god. Of such stones God has created a family to Abraham.

6. Why, then, does this empty and vain bragging exalt itself? Let them cease boasting that they are the children of Abraham. They have heard what they ought to have heard: "If ye are the children of Abraham," prove it by your deeds, not by words. "Ye seek to kill me, a man;"—I say not, meanwhile, the Son of God; I say not God; I say not the Word, for the Word dies not I say merely this that you see; for only what you see can you kill, and whom you see not can you offend. "This," then, "did not Abraham." "Ye do the works of your father." And as yet He says not who is that father of theirs.

7. And now what answer did they give Him? For they began somewhat to realize that the Lord was not speaking of carnal generation, but of their manner of life. And because it is the custom of the Scriptures, which they read, to call it, in a spiritual sense, fornication, when the soul is, as it were, prostituted by subjection to many false gods, they made this reply: "Then said they to Him, We be not born of fornication; we have one Father, even God." Abraham has now lost his importance. For they were repulsed as they ought to have been by the truth-speaking mouth; because such was Abraham, whose deeds they failed to imitate, and yet gloried

---

1 Gal. iii. 16, 29.

2 Rom. xi. 17.   3 In some editions, " to be cleansed."
4 Matt. iii. 7-9.

in his lineage. And they altered their reply, saying, I believe, with themselves, As often as we name Abraham, he goes on to say to us, Why do ye not imitate him in whose lineage ye glory? Such a man, so holy, just, and guileless, we cannot imitate. Let us call God our Father, and see what he will say to us.

8. Has falsehood indeed found something to say, and should not truth find its fitting reply? Let us hear what they say: let us hear what they hear. "We have one Father," they say, "even God. Then said Jesus unto them, If God were your Father, ye would [doubtless] love me; for I proceeded forth and came from God; neither came I of myself, but He sent me." Ye call God Father; recognize me, then, as at least a brother. At the same time He gave a stimulus to the hearts of the intelligent, by touching on that which He has a habit of saying, "I came not of myself: He sent me. I proceeded forth and came from God." Remember what we are wont to say: From Him He came; and from whom He came, with Him He came. The sending of Christ, therefore, is His incarnation. But as respects the proceeding forth of the Word from God, it is an eternal procession. Time holds not Him by whom time was created. Let no one be saying in his heart, Before the Word was, how did God exist? Never say, Before the Word of God was. God was never without the Word, because the Word is abiding, not transient; God, not a sound; by whom the heaven and earth were made, and which passed not away with those things that were made upon the earth. From Him, then, He proceeded forth as God, the equal, the only Son, the Word of the Father; and came to us, for the Word was made flesh that He might dwell among us. His coming indicates His humanity; His abiding, His divinity. It is His Godhead towards which, His humanity whereby, we make progress. Had He not become that whereby we might advance, we should never attain to Him who abideth ever.

9. "Why," He says, "do ye not understand my speech? Even because ye cannot hear my word." And so they could not understand, because they could not hear. And whence could they not hear, but just because they refused to be set right by believing? And why so? "Ye are of your father the devil." How long do ye keep speaking of a father? How often will ye change your fathers,—at one time Abraham, at another God? Hear from the Son of God whose children ye be: "Ye are of your father the devil."

10. Here, now, we must beware of the heresy of the Manicheans, which affirms that there is a certain principle of evil, and a certain family of darkness with its princes, which had the presumption to fight against God; but that God, not to let His kingdom be subdued by the hostile family, despatched against them, as it were, His own offspring, princes of His own [kingdom of] light; and so subdued that race from which the devil derives his origin. From thence, also, they say our flesh derives its origin, and accordingly think the Lord said, "Ye are of your father the devil," because they were evil, as it were, by nature, deriving their origin from the opposing family of darkness. So they err, so their eyes are blinded, so they make themselves the family of darkness, by believing a falsehood against Him who created them. For every nature is good; but man's nature has been corrupted by an evil will. What God made cannot be evil, if man were not [a cause of] evil to himself. But surely the Creator is Creator, and the creature a creature [a thing created]. The creature cannot be put on a level with the Creator. Distinguish between Him who made, and that which He made. The bench cannot be put on a level with the mechanic, nor the pillar with its builder; and yet the mechanic, though he made the bench, did not himself create the wood. But the Lord our God, in His omnipotence and by the Word, made what He made. He had no materials out of which to make all that He made, and yet He made it. For they were made because He willed it, they were made because He said it; but the things made cannot be compared with the Maker. If thou seekest a proper subject of comparison, turn thy mind to the only-begotten Son. How, then, were the Jews the children of the devil? By imitation, not by birth. Listen to the usual language of the Holy Scriptures. The prophet says to those very Jews, "Thy father was an Amorite, and thy mother a Hittite."[1] The Amorites were not a nation that gave origin to the Jews. The Hittites also were themselves of a nation altogether different from the race of the Jews. But because the Amorites and Hittites were impious, and the Jews imitated their impieties, they found parents for themselves, not of whom they were born, but in whose damnation they should share, because following their customs. But perhaps you inquire, Whence is the devil himself? From the same source certainly as the other angels. But the other angels continued in their obedi-

---

[1] Ezek. xvi. 3.

ence. He, by disobedience and pride, fell as an angel, and became a devil.

11. But listen now to what the Lord says: "Ye," said He, "are of your father the devil, and the lusts of your father ye will do." This is how ye are his children, because such are your lusts, not because ye are born of him. What are his lusts? "He was a murderer from the beginning." This it is that explains, "the lusts of your father ye will do." "Ye seek to kill me, a man that telleth you the truth." He, too, had ill-will to man, and slew man. For the devil, in his ill-will to man, assuming the guise of a serpent, spoke to the woman, and from the woman instilled his poison into the man. They died by listening to the devil,[1] whom they would not have listened to had they but listened to the Lord; for man, having his place between Him who created and him who was fallen, ought to have obeyed the Creator, not the deceiver. Therefore "he was a murderer from the beginning." Look at the kind of murder, brethren. The devil is called a murderer, not as armed with a sword, or girded with steel. He came to man, sowed his evil suggestions, and slew him. Think not, then, that thou art not a murderer when thou persuadest thy brother to evil. If thou persuadest thy brother to evil, thou slayest him. And to let thee know that thou slayest him, listen to the psalm: "The sons of men, whose teeth are spears and arrows, and their tongue a sharp sword."[2] Ye, then, "will do the lusts of your father;" and so ye go madly after the flesh, because ye cannot go after the spirit. "He was a murderer from the beginning;" at least in the case of the first of mankind. From the very time that murder [manslaughter] could possibly be committed, *he* was a murderer [manslayer]. Only from the time that man was made could manslaughter be committed. For man could not be slain unless man was previously made. Therefore, "*he* was a murderer from the beginning." And whence a murderer? "And he stood [abode] not in the truth." Therefore he was in the truth, and fell by not standing in it. And why "stood he not in the truth"? "Because the truth is not in him;" not as in Christ. In such a way is the truth [in Him], that Christ Himself *is* the Truth. If, then, he had stood in the truth, he would have stood in Christ; but "he abode not in the truth, because there is no truth in him."

12. "When he speaketh a lie, he speaketh of his own: for he is a liar, and the father of it."[3] What is this? You have heard the words of the Gospel: you have received them with attention. Here now, I repeat them, that you may clearly understand the subject of your thoughts. The Lord said those things of the devil which ought to have been said of the devil by the Lord. That "he was a murderer from the beginning" is true, for he slew the first man; "and he abode not in the truth," for he lapsed from the truth. "When he speaketh a lie," to wit, the devil himself, "he speaketh of his own;" for he is a liar, and its [his] father." From these words some have thought that the devil has a father, and have inquired who was the father of the devil. Indeed this detestable error of the Manicheans has found means down to this present time wherewith to deceive the simple. For they are wont to say, Suppose that the devil was an angel, and fell; and with him sin began as you say; but, Who was his father? We, on the contrary, reply, Who of us ever said that the devil had a father? And they, on the other hand, rejoin, The Lord saith, and the Gospel declares, speaking of the devil, "He was a murderer from the beginning, and abode not in the truth, because there is no truth in him. When he speaketh a lie, he speaketh of his own: for he is a liar, and *his* father."

13. Hear and understand. I shall not send thee far away [for the meaning]; understand it from the words themselves. The Lord called the devil the father of falsehood. What is this? Hear what it is, only revolve the words themselves, and understand. It is not every one who tells a lie that is the father of his lie. For if thou hast got a lie from another, and uttered it, thou indeed hast lied in giving utterance to the lie; but thou art not the father of that lie, because thou hast got it from another. But the devil was a liar of himself. He begat his own falsehood; he heard it from no one. As God the Father begat as His Son the Truth, so the devil, having fallen, begat falsehood as his son. Hearing this, recall now and reflect upon the words of the Lord. Ye catholic minds, consider what ye have heard; attend to what He says. "He"—who? The devil—"was a murderer from the beginning." We admit it, —he slew Adam. "And he abode not in the truth." We admit it,•for he lapsed from the

---

[3] In this and the following paragraph, Augustin deals with the rendering given to these words by the Manichæans in support of their heresy, stated in section 10. The words "*pater ejus*" (ὁ πατὴρ αὐτοῦ), taken by themselves, might of course mean either "his father" or "the father of it" [*i.e.* of falsehood]. Both the Greek idiom and the context require the latter; but the Manichæans adopted the former, and made the passage run, "for he [*i.e.* the devil] is a liar, and [so is] *his* father." Hence the question they are made to put afterwards, "Who was *his* [the devil's] father?" and our author's exposition of the passage.—Tr.

---

[1] Gen. iii. 1.　　　　[2] Ps. lvii. 4.

truth. "Because there is no truth in him." True: by falling away from the truth he has lost its possession. "When he speaketh a lie, he speaketh of his own: for he is a liar, and the father of it." He is both a liar, and the father of lies. For thou, it may be, art a liar, because thou utterest a lie; but thou art not its father. For if thou hast got what thou sayest from the devil, and hast believed the devil, thou art a liar, but not the father of the lie. But he, because he got not elsewhere the lie wherewith in serpent-form he slew man as if by poison, is the father of lies; just as God is Father of truth. Withdraw, then, from the father of lies: make haste to the Father of truth; embrace the truth, that you may enter into liberty.

14. Those Jews, then, spake what they saw with their father. And what was that but falsehood? But the Lord saw with His Father what He should speak: and what was that, but Himself? What, but the Word of the Father? What, but the truth of the Father, eternal itself, and co-eternal with the Father? He, then, "was a murderer from the beginning, and abode not in the truth, because there is no truth in him; when he speaketh a lie, he speaketh of his own, for he is a liar,"—and not only a liar, but also "the father of it;" that is, of the very lie that he speaks he is the father, for he himself begat his lie. "And because *I* tell you the truth, ye believe me not. Which of you convicteth me of sin," as I convict both you and your father? "If I say the truth, why do ye not believe me," but just because ye are the children of the devil?

15. "He that is of God heareth God's words: ye therefore hear them not, because ye are not of God." Here, again, it is not of their nature as men, but of their depravity, that you are to think. In this way they are of God, and yet not of God. By nature they are of God, in depravity they are not of God. Give heed, I pray you. In the gospel you have the remedy against the poisonous and impious errors of the heretics. For of these words also the Manicheans are accustomed to say, See, here there are two natures,[1]—the one good and the other bad; the Lord says it. What says the Lord? "Ye therefore hear me not, because ye are not of God." This is what the Lord says. What then, he rejoins, dost thou say to that? Hear what I say. They are both of God, and not of God. By nature they are of God: by depravity they are not of God; for the good nature which is of God sinned voluntarily by believing the

persuasive words of the devil, and was corrupted; and so it is seeking a physician, because no longer in health. That is what I say. But thou thinkest it impossible that they should be of God, and yet not of God. Hear why it is not impossible. They are of God, and yet not of God, in the same way as they are the children of Abraham, and yet not the children of Abraham. Here you have it. It is not as you say. Hearken to the Lord Himself; it is He that said to them, "I know that ye are the children of Abraham." Could there be any lie with the Lord? Surely not. Then is it true what the Lord said? It is true. Then it is true that they were the children of Abraham? It is true. But listen to Himself denying it. He who said, "Ye are the children of Abraham," Himself denied that they were the children of Abraham. "If ye are Abraham's children, do the deeds of Abraham. But now ye seek to kill me, a man that telleth you the truth, which I have heard from God: this did not Abraham. Ye do the works of your father," that is, of the devil. How, then, were they both Abraham's children, and yet not his children? Both states He showed in them. They were both Abraham's children in their carnal origin, and not his children in the sin of following the persuasion of the devil. So, also, apply it to our Lord and God, that they were both of Him, and not of Him. How were they of Him? Because He it was that created the man of whom they were born. How were they of Him? Because He is the Architect of nature,—Himself the Creator of flesh and spirit. How, then, were they not of Him? Because they had made themselves depraved. They were no longer of Him, because, imitating the devil, they had become the children of the devil.

16. Therefore came the Lord God to man as a sinner. Thou hast heard the two names, both *man* and *sinner*. As man, he is of God; as a sinner, he is not of God. Let the moral evil[2] in man be distinguished from his nature. Let that nature be owned, to the praise of the Creator; let the evil be acknowledged, that the physician may be called in to its cure. When the Lord then said, "He that is of God heareth the words of God: ye therefore hear them not, because ye are not of God." He did not distinguish the value of different natures, or find, beyond their own soul and body, any nature in men which had not been vitiated by sin; but foreknowing those who should yet believe, them He called *of God*,

---

[1] That is, *in man*. Compare section 10.—TR.

[2] *Vitium.*

because yet to be born again of God by the adoption of regeneration. To these apply the words, "He that is of God heareth the words of God." But that which follows, "Ye therefore hear them not, because ye are not of God," was said to those who were not only corrupted by sin (for this evil was common to all), but also foreknown as those who would not believe with the faith that alone could deliver them from the bondage of sin. On this account He foreknew that those to whom He so spake would continue in that which they derived from the devil, that is, in their sins, and would die in the impiety in which they resembled him; and would not come to the regeneration wherein they would be the children of God, that is, be born of the God by whom they were created as men. In accordance with this predestinating purpose did the Lord speak; and not that He had found any man amongst them who either by regeneration was already of God, or by nature was no longer of God.

TRACTATE XLIII.

CHAPTER VIII. 48–59.

1. IN that lesson of the holy Gospel which has been read to-day, from power we learn patience. For what are we as servants to the Lord, as sinners to the Just One, as creatures to the Creator? Howbeit, just as in what we are evil, we are so of ourselves; so in whatever respects we are good, we are so of Him, and through Him. And nothing does man so seek as he does power. He has great power in the Lord Christ; but let him first imitate His patience, that he may attain to power. Who of us would listen with patience if it were said to him, "Thou hast a devil"? as was said to Him, who was not only bringing men to salvation, but also subjecting devils to His authority.

2. For when the Jews had said, "Say we not well that thou art a Samaritan, and hast a devil?" of these two charges cast at Him, He denied the one, but not the other. For He answered and said, "I have not a devil." He did not say, I am not a Samaritan; and yet the two charges had been made. Although He returned not cursing with cursing, although He met not slander with slander, yet was it proper for Him to deny the one charge and not to deny the other. And not without a purpose, brethren. For Samaritan means keeper.[1] He knew that He was our keeper. For "He that keepeth Israel neither slumbereth nor sleepeth;"[2] and, "Except the Lord keep the city, they wake in vain who keep it."[3] He then is our Keeper who is our Creator. For did it belong to Him to redeem us, and would it not be His to preserve us? Finally, that you may know more fully the hidden reason[4] why He ought not to have denied that He was a Samaritan, call to mind that well-known parable, where a certain man went down from Jerusalem to Jericho, and fell among thieves, who wounded him severely, and left him half dead on the road. A priest came along and took no notice of him. A Levite came up, and he also passed on his way. A certain Samaritan came up—He who is our Keeper. He went up to the wounded man. He exercised mercy, and did a neighbor's part to one whom He did not account an alien.[5] To this, then, He only replied that He had not a devil, but not that He was not a Samaritan.

3. And then after such an insult, this was all that He said of His own glory: "But I honor," said He, "my Father, and ye dishonor me." That is, I honor not myself, that ye may not think me arrogant. I have One to honor; and did ye recognize me, just as I honor the Father, so would ye also honor me. I do what I ought; ye do not what ye ought.

4. "And I," said He, "seek not mine own glory: there is one that seeketh and judgeth." Whom does He wish to be understood but the Father? How, then, does He say in another place, "The Father judgeth no man, but hath committed all judgment unto the Son,"[6] while here He says, "I seek not mine own glory: there is one that seeketh and judgeth"? If, then, the Father judgeth,

---

[1] Samaria, Hebrew שֹׁמְרוֹן, literally, "a keep," from שָׁמַר to keep, to guard; hence, according to Augustin, "Samaritan," שֹׁמְרֹנִי, a keeper, a guardian.—TR.

[2] Ps. cxxi. 4.　　　　[3] Ps. cxxvii. 1.　　　　[4] *Mysterium.*　　[5] Luke x. 30–37.　　[6] Chap. v. 22.

how is it that He judgeth no man, but hath committed all judgment unto the Son?

5. In order to solve this point, attend. It may be solved by [quoting] a similar mode of speaking. Thou hast it written, "God tempteth not any man;"[1] and again thou hast it written, "The Lord your God tempteth you, to know whether you love Him."[2] Just the point in dispute, you see. For how *does God tempt not any man,* and how *does the Lord your God tempt you, to know whether ye love Him?* It is also written, "There is no fear in love; but perfect love casteth out fear;"[3] and in another place it is written, "The fear of the Lord is clean, enduring for ever."[4] Here also is the point in dispute. For how *does perfect love cast out fear,* if *the fear of the Lord,* which is clean, *endureth for ever?*

6. We are to understand, then, that there are two kinds of temptation: one, that deceives; the other, that proves. As regards that which deceives, *God tempteth not any man;* as regards that which proves, *the Lord your God tempteth you, that He may know whether ye love Him.* But here again, also, there arises another question, how *He tempteth that He may know,* from whom, prior to the temptation, nothing can be hid. It is not that God is ignorant; but it is said, *that He may know,* that is, that He may make you to know. Such modes of speaking are found both in our ordinary conversation, and in writers of eloquence. Let me say a word on our style of conversation. We speak of a blind ditch, not because it has lost its eyes, but because by lying hid it makes us blind to its existence. One speaks of "bitter lupins," that is, "sour;" not that they themselves are bitter, but because they occasion bitterness to those who taste them.[5] And so there are also expressions of this sort in Scripture. Those who take the trouble to attain a knowledge of such points have no trouble in solving them. And so "the Lord your God tempts you, that He may know." What is this, "that He may know"? That He may make you to know "if you love Him." Job was unknown to himself, but he was not unknown to God. He led the tempter into [Job], and brought him to a knowledge of himself.

7. What then of the two fears? There is a servile fear, and there is a clean [chaste] fear: there is the fear of suffering punishment, there is another fear of losing righteousness. That fear of suffering punishment

is slavish. What great thing is it to fear punishment? The vilest slave and the cruelest robber do so. It is no great thing to fear punishment, but great it is to love righteousness. Has he, then, who loves righteousness no fear? Certainly he has; not of incurring of punishment, but of losing righteousness. My brethren, assure yourselves of it, and draw your inference from that which you love. Some one of you is fond of money. Can I find any one, think you, who is not so? Yet from this very thing which he loves he may understand my meaning. He is afraid of loss: why is he so? Because he loves money. In the same measure that he loves money, is he afraid of losing it. So, then, some one is found to be a lover of righteousness, who at heart is much more afraid of its loss, who dreads more being stripped of his righteousness, than thou of thy money. This is the fear that is clean—this [the fear] that endureth for ever. It is not this that love makes away with, or casteth out, but rather embraces it, and keeps it with it, and possesses it as a companion. For we come to the Lord that we may see Him face to face. And there it is this pure fear that preserves us; for such a fear as that does not disturb, but reassure. The adulterous woman fears the coming of her husband, and the chaste one fears her husband's departure.

8. Therefore, as, according to one kind of temptation, "God tempteth not any man;" but according to another, "The Lord your God tempteth you;" and according to one kind of fear, "there is no fear in love; but perfect love casteth out fear;" but according to another, "the fear of the Lord is clean, enduring for ever;"—so also, in this passage, according to one kind of judgment, "the Father judgeth no man, but hath committed all judgment unto the Son;" and according to another, "I," said He, "seek not mine own glory: there is one that seeketh and judgeth."

9. This point may also be solved from the word itself. Thou hast penal judgment spoken of in the Gospel: "He that believeth not is judged[6] already;" and in another place, "The hour is coming, when those who are in the graves shall hear His voice, and shall come forth; they that have done good, unto the resurrection of life; and they that have done evil, unto the resurrection of judgment."[7] You see how He has put judgment for condemnation and punishment. And yet if judgment were always to be taken for condemnation, should we ever have heard in the

[1] Jas. i. 13.　　　　　　　[2] Deut. xiii. 3.
[3] 1 John iv. 18.　　　　[4] Ps. xix. 9.
[5] Virg. *Georg.* lib. i. 75: *Tristes lupinos non quia ipsi sunt tristes, sed quia gustati contristant, hoc est, tristes faciunt.*
16

[6] *Judicatus.* John iii. 18.　　　*Judicium.* John v. 28, 29.

psalm, "Judge me, O God"? In the former place, judgment is used in the sense of inflicting pain; here, it is used in the sense of discernment.[1] How so? Just because so expounded by him who says, "Judge me, O God." For read, and see what follows. What is this "Judge me, O God," but just what he adds, "and discern[2] my cause against an unholy nation"?[3] Because then it was said, "Judge me, O God, and discern [the true merits of] my cause against an unholy nation;" similarly now said the Lord Christ, "I seek not mine own glory: there is one that seeketh and judgeth." How is there "one that seeketh and judgeth"? There is the Father, who discerns and distinguishes between my glory and yours. For ye glory in the spirit of this present world. Not so do I, who say to the Father, "Father, glorify Thou me with that glory which I had with Thee before the world was."[4] What is "that glory"? One altogether different from human inflation. Thus doth the Father judge. And so to "judge" is to "discern."[1] And what does He discern? The glory of His Son from the glory of mere men; for to that end is it said, "God, Thy God, hath anointed Thee with the oil of gladness above Thy fellows."[5] For not because He became man is He now to be compared with us. We, as men, are sinful, He is sinless; we, as men, inherit from Adam both death and delinquency, He received from the Virgin mortal flesh, but no iniquity. In fine, neither because *we* wish it are we born, nor as long as we wish it do we live, nor in the way that we wish it do we die: but He, before He was born, chose of whom He should be born; at His birth He brought about the adoration of the Magi; He grew as an infant, and showed Himself God by His miracles, and surpassed man in His weakness. Lastly, He chose also the manner of His death, that is, to be hung on the cross, and to fasten the cross itself on the foreheads of believers, so that the Christian may say, "God forbid that I should glory, save in the cross of our Lord Jesus Christ."[6] On the very cross, when He pleased, He made His body be taken down, and departed; in the very sepulchre, as long as it pleased Him, He lay; and, when He pleased, He arose as from a bed. So, then, brethren, in respect to His very form as a servant (for who can speak of that other form as it ought to be spoken of, "In the beginning was the Word, and the Word was with God, and the

Word was God"?)—in respect, I say, to His very form as a servant, the difference is great between the glory of Christ and the glory of other men. Of that glory He spoke, when the devil-possessed heard Him say, "I seek not mine own glory: there is one that seeketh and judgeth."

10. But what sayest Thou, O Lord, of Thyself? "Verily, verily, I say unto you, If a man keep my saying, he shall never see death." Ye say, "Thou hast a devil." I call you to life: keep my word and ye shall not die. They heard, "He shall never see death who keepeth my word," and were angry, because already dead in that death from which they might have escaped. "Then said the Jews, Now we know that thou hast a devil. Abraham is dead, and the prophets; and thou sayest, If a man keep my saying, he shall never see death." See how Scripture speaks: "He shall not see," that is, "taste of death." "He shall see death —he shall taste of death." Who seeth? Who tasteth? What eyes has a man to see with when he dies? When death at its coming shuts up those very eyes from seeing aught, how is it said, "he shall not see death"? With what palate, also, and with what jaws can death be tasted, that its savor may be discovered? When it taketh every sense away, what will remain in the palate? But here, "he will see," and "he will taste," are used for that which is really the case, he will know by experience.

11. Thus spake the Lord (it is scarcely sufficient to say), as one dying to dying men; for "to the Lord also belong the issues from death,"[7] as saith the psalm. Seeing, then, He was both speaking to those destined to die, and speaking as one appointed to death Himself, what mean His words, "He who keepeth my saying shall never see death;" save that the Lord saw another death, from which He was come to deliver us—the second death, death eternal, the death of hell,[8] the death of damnation with the devil and his angels? *This* is real death; for that other is only a removal. What is that other death? The leaving of the body—the laying down of a heavy burden; provided another burden be not carried away, to drag the man headlong to hell. Of that real death then did the Lord say, "He who keepeth my saying shall never see death."

12. Let us not be frightened at that other death, but let us fear this one. But, what is very grievous, many, through a perverse fear of that other, have fallen into this. It has

---

[1] *Discretionem, discerne,*—legal terms, implying the judicial expiscation and discriminating of the real facts and merits of a case, by sifting the evidence and separating the true from the false.   [2] See previous note.   [3] Ps. xliii. 1.
[4] John xvii. 5.   [5] Ps. xlv. 7.   [6] Gal. vi. 14.   [7] Ps. lxviii. 20.   [8] *Gehennarum.*

been said to some, Adore idols; for if you do it not, you shall be put to death: or, as Nebuchadnezzar said, If you do not, you shall be thrown into the furnace of flaming fire. Many feared and adored. Shrinking from death, they died. Through fear of the death which cannot be escaped, they fell into that which they might happily have escaped, had they not, unhappily, been afraid of that which is inevitable. As a man, thou art born—art destined to die. Whither wilt thou go to escape death? What wilt thou do to escape it? That thy Lord might comfort thee in thy necessary subjection to death, of His own good pleasure He condescended to die. When thou seest the Christ lying dead, art thou reluctant to die? Die then thou must; thou hast no means of escape. Be it to-day, be it to-morrow; it is to be —the debt must be paid. What, then, does a man gain by fearing, fleeing, hiding himself from discovery by his enemy? Does he get exemption from death? No, but that he may die a little later. He gets not security against his debt, but asks a respite. Put it off as long as you please, the thing so delayed will come at last. Let us fear that death which the three men feared when they said to the king, "God is able to deliver us even from that flame; and if not," etc.[1] There was there the fear of that death which the Lord now threatens, when they said, But also if He be not willing openly to deliver us, He can crown us with victory in secret. Whence also the Lord, when on the eve of appointing martyrs and becoming the head-martyr Himself, said, "Be not afraid of them that kill the body, and after that have no more that they can do." How "have they no more that they can do"? What if, after having slain one, they threw his body to be mangled by wild beasts, and torn to pieces by birds? Cruelty seems still to have something it can do. But to whom is it done? He has departed. The body is there, but without feeling. The tenement lies on the ground, the tenant is gone. And so "after that they have no more that they can do;" for they can do nothing to that which is without sensation. "But fear Him who hath power to destroy both body and soul in hell fire."[2] Here is the death that He spake of when He said, "He that keepeth my saying shall never see death." Let us keep then, brethren, His own word in faith, as those who are yet to attain to sight, when the liberty we receive has reached its fullness.

13. But those men, indignant, yet dead, and predestinated to death eternal, answered with insults, and said, "Now we know that thou hast a devil. Abraham is dead, and the prophets." But not in that death which the Lord meant to be understood was either Abraham dead or the prophets. For these were dead, and yet they live: those others were alive, and yet they had died. For, replying in a certain place to the Sadducees, when they stirred the question of the resurrection, the Lord Himself speaks thus: "But as touching the resurrection of the dead, have ye not read how the Lord said to Moses from the bush, I am the God of Abraham, and the God of Isaac, and the God of Jacob? He is not the God of the dead, but of the living."[3] If, then, they live, let us labor so to live, that after death we may be able to live with them. "Whom makest thou thyself," they add, that thou sayest, "he shall never see death who keepeth my saying," when thou knowest that both Abraham is dead and the prophets?

14. "Jesus answered, If I glorify myself, my glory is nothing: it is my Father that glorifieth me." He said this on account of their saying, "Whom makest thou thyself?" For He refers His glory to the Father, of whom it is that He is God. From this expression also the Arians sometimes revile our faith, and say, See, the Father is greater; for at all events He glorifies the Son. Heretic, hast thou not read of the Son Himself also saying that He glorifies His Father?[4] If both He glorifieth the Son, and the Son glorifieth the Father, lay aside thy stubbornness, acknowledge the equality, correct thy perversity.

15. "It is," then, said He, "my Father that glorifieth me; of whom ye say, that He is your God: and ye have not known Him." See, my brethren, how He shows that God Himself is the Father of the Christ, who was announced also to the Jews. I say so for this reason, that now again there are certain heretics who say that the God revealed in the Old Testament is not the Father of Christ, but some prince or other, I know not what, of evil angels. There are Manicheans who say so; there are Marcionites who say so. There are also, perhaps, other heretics, whom it is either unnecessary to mention, or all of whom I cannot at present recall; yet there have not been wanting those who said this. Attend, then, that you may have something also to affirm against such. Christ the Lord calleth Him His Father whom they called their God, and did not know; for had they known [that God] Himself they would have received His Son. "But I," said He, "know

[1] Dan. iii. 16-18.
[2] "In the gehenna of fire." Matt. x. 28, and Luke xii. 4, 5.   [3] Matt. xxii. 31, 32 ; Ex. iii. 6.   [4] Chap. xvii. 4.

Him." To those judging after the flesh He might have seemed from such words to be self-assuming, because He said, "I know Him." But see what follows: "If I should say that I know Him not, I shall be a liar like unto you." Let not, then, self-assumption be so guarded against as to cause the relinquishment of truth. "But I know Him, and keep His saying." The saying of the Father He was speaking as Son; and He Himself was the Word of the Father, that was speaking to men.

16. "Your father Abraham rejoiced to see my day; and he saw, and was glad." Abraham's seed, Abraham's Creator, bears a great testimony to Abraham. "Abraham rejoiced," He says, "to see my day." He did not fear, but "rejoiced to see it." For in him there was the love that casteth out fear.[1] He says not, rejoiced *because* he saw; but "rejoiced that he might see." Believing, at all events, he rejoiced in hope to see with the understanding. "And he saw." And what more could the Lord Jesus Christ say, or what more ought He to have said? "And he saw," He says, "and was glad." Who can unfold this joy, my brethren? If those rejoiced whose bodily eyes were opened by the Lord, what joy was his who saw with the eyes of his soul the light ineffable, the abiding Word, the brilliance that dazzles the minds of the pious, the unfailing Wisdom, God abiding with the Father, and at some time to come in the flesh and yet not to withdraw from the bosom of the Father? All this did Abraham see. For in saying "my day," it may be uncertain of what He spake; whether the day of the Lord in time, when He should come in the flesh, or that day of the Lord which knows not a dawn, and knows no decline. But for my part I doubt not that father Abraham knew it all. And where shall I find it out? Ought the testimony of our Lord Jesus Christ to satisfy us? Let us suppose that we cannot find it out, for perhaps it is difficult to say in what sense it is clear that Abraham "rejoiced to see the day" of Christ, "and saw it, and was glad." And though we find it not, can the Truth have lied? Let us believe the Truth, and cherish no doubt of Abraham's merited rewards.[2] Yet listen to one passage that occurs to me meanwhile. When father Abraham sent his servant to seek a wife for his son Isaac, he bound him by this oath, to fulfill faithfully what he was commanded, and know also for himself what to do. For it was a great matter that was in hand when marriage was sought for Abraham's seed. But that the servant might apprehend what Abraham knew, that it was not offspring after the flesh he desired, nor anything of a carnal kind concerning his race that was referred to, he said to the servant whom he sent, "Put thy hand under my thigh, and swear by the God of heaven.[3] What connection has the God of heaven with Abraham's thigh? Already you understand the mystery:[4] by thigh is meant race. And what was that swearing, but the signifying that of Abraham's race would the God of heaven come in the flesh? Fools find fault with Abraham because he said, Put thy hand under my thigh. Those who find fault with Christ's flesh find fault with Abraham's conduct. But let us, brethren, if we acknowledge the flesh of Christ as worthy of veneration, despise not that thigh, but receive it as spoken of prophetically. For a prophet also was Abraham. Whose prophet? Of his own seed, and of his Lord. To his own seed he pointed in saying, "Put thy hand under my thigh." To his Lord he pointed in adding, "and swear by the God of heaven."

17. The angry Jews replied, "Thou art not yet fifty years old, and hast thou seen Abraham?" And the Lord: "Verily, verily, I say unto you, Before Abraham was made, I am."[5] Weigh the words, and get a knowledge of the mystery. "Before Abraham was made." Understand, that "was made" refers to human formation; but "am" to the Divine essence. "He was made," because Abraham was a creature. He did not say, Before Abraham was, I was; but, "Before Abraham was made," who was not made save by me, "I am." Nor did He say this, Before Abraham was made I was made; for "In the beginning God created the heaven and the earth;"[6] and "in the beginning was the Word."[7] "Before Abraham was made, I am." Recognize the Creator—distinguish the creature. He who spake was made the seed of Abraham; and that Abraham might be made, He Himself was before Abraham.

18. Hence, as if by the most open of all insults thrown at Abraham, they were now excited to greater bitterness. Of a certainty it seemed to them that Christ the Lord had uttered blasphemy in saying, "Before Abraham was made, I am." "Therefore took they up stones to cast at Him." To what could so great hardness have recourse, save to its like? "But Jesus" [acts] as man, as one in

---

[1] 1 John iv. 18.   [2] *Meritis.*

[3] Gen. xxiv. 2-4.   [4] *Sacramentum.*
[5] *Antequam Abraham fieret ego sum.* Greek, "πρὶν Ἀβραὰμ γενέσθαι, ἐγώ εἰμι."
[6] Gen. i. 1.   [7] Chap. i. 1.

the form of a servant, as lowly, as about to suffer, about to die, about to redeem us with His blood; not as He who *is*—not as the Word in the beginning, and the Word with God. For when they took up stones to cast at Him, what great thing were it had they been instantly swallowed up in the gaping earth, and found the inhabitants of hell in place of stones? It were not a great thing to God; but better was it that patience should be commended than power exerted. Therefore " He hid Himself " from them, that He might not be stoned. As man, He fled from the stones; but woe to those from whose stony hearts God has fled?

TRACTATE XLIV.

CHAPTER IX.

1. WE have just read the long lesson of the man born blind, whom the Lord Jesus restored to the light; but were we to attempt handling the whole of it, and considering, according to our ability, each passage in a way proportionate to its worth, the day would be insufficient. Wherefore I ask and warn your Charity not to require any words of ours on those passages whose meaning is manifest; for it would be too protracted to linger at each. I proceed, therefore, to set forth briefly the mystery of this blind man's enlightenment. All, certainly, that was done by our Lord Jesus Christ, both works and words, are worthy of our astonishment and admiration: His works, because they are facts; His words, because they are signs. If we reflect, then, on what is signified by the deed here done, that blind man is the human race; for this blindness had place in the first man through sin, from whom we all draw our origin, not only in respect of death, but also of unrighteousness. For if unbelief is blindness, and faith enlightenment, whom did Christ find a believer at His coming? seeing that the apostle, belonging himself to the family of the prophets, says: "And we also in times past were by nature the children of wrath, even as others." [1] If " children of wrath," then children of vengeance, children of punishment, children of hell. For how is it " by nature," save that through the first man sinning moral evil rooted itself in us as a nature? If evil has so taken root within us, every man is born mentally blind. For if he sees, he has no need of a guide. If he does need one to guide and enlighten him, then is he blind from his birth.

2. The Lord came: what did He do? He set forth a great mystery. " He spat on the ground," He made clay of His spittle; for the Word was made flesh. [2] "And He anointed the eyes of the blind man." The anointing had taken place, and yet he saw not. He sent him to the pool which is called Siloam. But it was the evangelist's concern to call our attention to the name of this pool; and he adds, " Which is interpreted, Sent." You understand now who it is that was sent; for had He not been sent, none of us would have been set free from iniquity. Accordingly he washed his eyes in that pool which is interpreted, Sent—he was baptized in Christ. If, therefore, when He baptized him in a manner in Himself, He then enlightened him; when He anointed Him, perhaps He made him a catechumen. [3] In many different ways indeed may the profound meaning of such a sacramental act be set forth and handled; but let this suffice your Charity. You have heard a great mystery. Ask a man, Are you a Christian? His answer to you is, I am not, if he is a pagan or a Jew. But if he says, I am; you inquire again of him, Are you a catechumen or a believer? If he reply, A catechumen; he has been anointed, but not yet washed. But how anointed? Inquire, and he will answer you. Inquire of him in whom he believes. In that very respect in which he is a catechumen he says, In Christ. See, I am speaking in a way both to the faithful and to catechumens. What have I said of the spittle and the clay? That the Word was made flesh. This even catechumens hear; but that to which they have been anointed is not all they need; let them hasten to the font if they are in search of enlightenment.

3. And now, because of certain points in

---

[2] Chap. i. 14.
[3] The name given to one who was under instruction for baptism, and for entrance into the full privileges of church membership.

the lesson before us, let us run over the words of the Lord, and of the whole lesson itself, rather than make them a theme of discourse. "As He passed out, He saw a man who was blind;" blind, not from any cause whatever, but "from his birth." "And His disciples asked Him, Rabbi." You know that "Rabbi" is Master. They called Him Master, because they desired to learn. The question, at all events, they proposed to the Lord as a master, "Who did sin, this man, or his parents, that he was born blind?" Jesus answered, "Neither hath this man sinned, nor his parents," that he was born blind. What is this that He has said? If no man is sinless, were the parents of this blind man without sin? Was he himself either born without original sin, or had he committed none in the course of his lifetime? Because his eyes were closed, had his lusts lost their wakefulness? How many evils are done by the blind? From what evil does an evil mind abstain, even though the eyes are closed? He could not see, but he knew how to think, and perchance to lust after something which his blindness hindered him from attaining, and so still in his heart to be judged by the searcher of hearts. If, then, both his parents had sin, and the man himself had sin, wherefore said the Lord, "Neither hath this man sinned, nor his parents," but only in respect to the point on which he was questioned, "that he was born blind"? For his parents had sin; but not by reason of the sin itself did it come about that he was born blind. If, then, it was not through the parents' sin that he was born blind, why was he born blind? Listen to the Master as He teaches. He seeks one who believes, to give him understanding. He Himself tells us the reason why that man was born blind: "Neither hath this man sinned," He says, "nor his parents: but that the works of God should be made manifest in him."

4. And then, what follows? "I must work the works of Him that sent me." See, here is that sent one [Siloam], wherein the blind man washed his face. And see what He said: "I must work the works of Him that sent me, while it is day." Recall to thy mind the way in which He gives universal glory to Him of whom He is:[1] for that One has the Son who is of Him; He Himself has no One of whom He is.[1] But wherefore, Lord, saidst Thou, "While it is day"? Hearken why He did so. "The night cometh when no man can work." Not even Thou, Lord. Will that night have such power that not even

Thou, whose work the night is, wilt be able to work therein? For I think, Lord Jesus, nay I do not think, but believe and hold it sure, that Thou wast there when God said, "Let there be light, and there was light."[2] For if He made it by the Word, He made it by Thee: and therefore it is said, "All things were made by Him; and without Him was nothing made."[3] "God divided between the light and the darkness: the light He called Day, and the darkness He called Night."[4]

5. What is that night wherein, when it comes, no one shall be able to work? Hear what the day is, and then thou wilt understand what the night is. But how shall we hear what the day is? Let Himself tell us: "As long as I am in this world, I am the light of the world." See, He Himself is the day. Let the blind man wash his eyes in the day, that he may behold the day. "As long," He says, "as I am in the world, I am the light of the world." Then will it be night of a kind unknown to me, when Christ will no longer be there; and so no one will be able to work. An inquiry remains, my brethren; patiently listen to me as I inquire. With you I inquire: with you shall I find Him to whom my inquiry is addressed. We are agreed; for it is expressly and definitely stated that the Lord proclaimed Himself in this place as the day, that is, the light of the world. "As long," He says, "as I am in this world, I am the light of the world." Therefore He Himself works. But how long is He in this world? Are we to think, brethren, that He was here then, and is here no longer? If we think so, then already, after the Lord's ascension, did that fearful night begin, when no one can work. If that night began after the Lord's ascension, how was it that the apostles wrought so much? Was that the night when the Holy Spirit came, and, filling all who were in one place, gave them the power of speaking in the tongues of every nation?[5] Was it night when that lame man was made whole at the word of Peter, or rather, at the word of the Lord dwelling in Peter?[6] Was it night when, as the disciples were passing by, the sick were laid in couches, that they might be touched at least by their shadow as they passed?[7] Yet, when the Lord was here, there was no one made whole by His shadow as He passed; but He Himself had said to the disciples, "Greater things than these shall ye do."[8] Yes, the Lord had said, "Greater things than these shall ye do;" but let not flesh and blood exalt itself:

---

[1] Or, "from whom He proceeds." The Son is of the Father, but the Father is of none.

[2] Gen. i. 3.   [3] Chap. i. 3.   [4] Gen. i. 4, 5.
[5] Acts ii. 1 6.   [6] Acts iii. 6-8.   [7] Acts v. 15.
[8] Chap. xiv. 12.

let such hear Him also saying, "Without me ye can do nothing."[1]

6. What then? What shall we say of that night? When will it be, when no one shall be able to work? It will be that night of the wicked, that night of those to whom it shall be said in the end, "Depart into everlasting fire, prepared for the devil and his angels." But it is here called night, not flame, nor fire. Hearken, then, why it is also night. Of a certain servant He says, "Bind ye him hand and foot, and cast him into outer darkness."[2] Let man, then, work while he liveth, that he may not be overtaken by that night when no man can work. It is now that faith is working by love; and if now we are working, then this is the day—Christ is here. Hear His promise, and think Him not absent. It is Himself who hath said, 'Lo, I am with you." How long? Let there be no anxiety in us who are alive; were it possible, with this very word we might place in perfect security the generations still to come. "Lo," He says, "I am with you always, even to the end of the world."[3] That day, which is completed by the circuit of yonder sun, has but few hours; the day of Christ's presence extends even to the end of the world. But after the resurrection of the living and the dead, when He shall say to those placed at His right hand, "Come, ye blessed of my Father, receive the kingdom;" and to those at His left, "Depart into everlasting fire, prepared for the devil and his angels;"[4] then shall be the night when no man can work, but only get back what he has wrought before. There is a time for working. another for receiving; for the Lord shall render to every one according to his works.[5] While thou livest, be doing, if thou art to be doing at all; for then shall come that appalling night, to envelope the wicked in its folds. But even now every unbeliever, when he dies, is received within that night: there is no work to be done there. In that night was the rich man burning, and asking a drop of water from the beggar's finger; he mourned, agonized, confessed, but no relief was vouchsafed. He even endeavored to do good; for he said to Abraham, "Father Abraham, send Lazarus to my brethren, that he may tell them what is being done here, lest they also come into this place of torment."[6] Unhappy man! when thou wert living, then was the time for working: now thou art already in the night, in which no man can work.

7. "When He had thus spoken, He spat on the ground, and made clay of the spittle, and He spread the clay upon his eyes, and said unto him, Go and wash in the pool of Siloam (which is, by interpretation, Sent). He went his way therefore, and washed, and came seeing." As these words are clear, we may pass them over.

8. "The neighbors therefore, and those who saw him previously, for he was a beggar, said, Is not this he who sat and begged? Some said, It is he: others, No; but he is like him." The opening of his eyes had altered his countenance. "He said, I am he." His voice utters its gratitude, that it might not be condemned as ungrateful. "Therefore said they unto him, How were thine eyes opened? He answered, The man who is called Jesus made clay, and anointed mine eyes, and said unto me, Go to the pool of Siloam, and wash: and I went and washed, and saw." See, he is become the herald of grace; see, he preaches the gospel; endowed with sight, he becomes a confessor. That blind man makes confession, and the heart of the wicked was troubled; for they had not in their heart what he had now in his countenance. "They said to him, Where is he who hath opened thine eyes? He said, I know not." In these words the man's own soul was like that of one only as yet anointed, but not yet seeing. Let us so put it, brethren, as if he had that anointing in his soul. He preaches, and knows not the Being whom he preaches.

9. "They brought to the Pharisees him who had been blind. And it was the Sabbath when Jesus made the clay, and opened his eyes. Then again the Pharisees also asked how he had received his sight. And he said unto them, He put clay upon mine eyes, and I washed, and do see. Therefore said some of the Pharisees;" not all, but some; for some were already anointed. What then said those who neither saw nor were anointed? "This man is not of God, because he keepeth not the Sabbath." He it was rather who kept it, who was without sin. For this is the spiritual Sabbath, to have no sin. In fact, brethren, it is of this that God admonishes us, when He commends the Sabbath to our notice: "Thou shalt do no servile work"[7] These are God's words when commending the Sabbath, "Thou shalt do no servile work." Now ask the former lessons, what is meant by servile work;[8] and listen to the Lord: "Every one that committeth sin is the servant of sin."[9] But these men, neither seeing, as I said, nor anointed, kept the Sabbath carnally, and profaned it spiritually. "Others

---

[1] Chap. xv. 5.　　[2] Matt. xxii. 13.　　[3] Matt. xxviii. 28.
[4] Matt. xxv. 34, 41.　　[5] Matt. xvi. 27.　　[6] Luke xvi. 24–28.　　[7] Lev. xxiii. 8.　　[8] Tract. xx. 2.　　[9] Chap. viii. 34.

said, How can a man that is a sinner do such miracles?" These were the anointed ones. "And there was a division among them." The day had divided between the light and the darkness. "They say then unto the blind man again, What sayest thou of him who hath opened thine eyes?" What is thy feeling about him? what is thine opinion? what is thy judgment? They sought how to revile the man, that he might be cast out of the synagogue, but be found by Christ. But he steadfastly expressed what he felt. For he said, "That he is a prophet." As yet, indeed, anointed only in heart, he does not thus far confess the Son of God, and yet he speaks not untruthfully. For the Lord saith of Himself, "A prophet is not without honor, save in his own country." [1]

10. "Therefore the Jews did not believe concerning him, that he had been blind, and received his sight, till they called the parents of him that received his sight;" that is, who had been blind, and had come to the possession of sight. "And they asked them, saying, Is this your son, who ye say was born blind? how then doth he now see? His parents answered them, and said, We know that this is our son, and that he was born blind: but how he now seeth, we know not; or who hath opened his eyes, we know not. And they said, Ask himself; he is of age, let him speak of himself." He is indeed our son, and we might justly be compelled to answer for him as an infant, because then he could not speak for himself: from of old he has had power of speech, only now he sees: we have been acquainted with him as blind from his birth, know him as having speech from of old, only now do we see him endowed with sight: ask himself, that you may be instructed; why seek to calumniate us? "These words spake his parents, because they feared the Jews: for the Jews had conspired already, that if any man did confess that He was Christ, he should be put out of the synagogue." It was no longer a bad thing to be put out of the synagogue. They cast out, but Christ received. "Therefore said his parents, He is of age, ask himself."

11. "Then again called they the man who had been blind, and said unto him, Give God the glory." What is that, "Give God the glory"? Deny what thou hast received. Such conduct is manifestly not to give God the glory, but rather to blaspheme Him. "Give God," they say, "the glory: we know that this man is a sinner. Then said he, If he is a sinner, I know not: one thing I know,

that whereas I was blind, now I see. Then said they to him, What did he to thee? how opened he thine eyes?" And he, indignant now at the hardness of the Jews, and as one brought from a state of blindness to sight, unable to endure the blind, "answered them, I have told you already, and ye have heard: wherefore would ye hear it again? Will ye also become his disciples?" What means, "Will ye also," but that I am one already? "Will ye also be so?" Now I see, but see not askance.

12. "They cursed him, and said, Thou art his disciple." Such a malediction be upon us, and upon our children! For a malediction it is, if thou layest open their heart, not if thou ponderest the words. "But we are Moses' disciples. We know that God spake unto Moses: as for this fellow, we know not from whence he is." Would ye had known that "God spake to Moses!" ye would have also known that God preached by Moses. For ye have the Lord saying, "Had ye believed Moses, ye would have also believed me; for he wrote of me." [2] Is it thus ye follow the servant, and turn your back against the Lord? But not even the servant do ye follow; for by him ye would be guided to the Lord.

13. "The man answered and said unto them, Herein is a marvellous thing, that ye know not from whence he is, and yet he hath opened mine eyes. Now we know that God heareth not sinners; but if any man is a worshipper of God, and doeth His will, him He heareth." He speaks still as one only anointed. For God heareth even sinners. For if God heard not sinners, in vain would the publican, casting his eyes on the ground, and smiting on his breast, have said, "Lord, be merciful to me a sinner." And that confession merited justification, as this blind man enlightenment. "Since the world began was it not heard that any man opened the eyes of one that was born blind. If this man were not of God, he could do nothing." With frankness, constancy, and truthfulness [he spoke]. For these things that were done by the Lord, by whom were they done but by God? Or when would such things be done by disciples, were not the Lord dwelling in them?

14. "They answered and said unto him, Thou wast wholly born in sins." What means this "wholly"? Even to blindness of the eyes. But He who has opened his eyes, also saves him wholly: He will grant a resurrection at His right hand, who gave enlight-

[1] Matt. xiii. 57.   [2] Chap. v. 46.

enment to his countenance. " Thou wast altogether born in sins, and dost thou teach us? And they cast him out." They had made him their master; many questions had they asked for their own instruction, and they ungratefully cast forth their teacher.

15. But, as I have already said before, brethren, when they expel, the Lord receiveth; for the rather that he was expelled, was he made a Christian. " Jesus heard that they had cast him out; and when He had found him, He said unto him, Dost thou believe on the Son of God?" Now He washes the face of his heart. " He answered and said," as one still only anointed, "Who is he, Lord, that I might believe on him? And Jesus said unto him, Thou hast both seen Him, and it is He that talketh with thee." The One is He that is sent; the other is one washing his face in Siloam, which is interpreted, Sent. And now at last, with the face of his heart washed, and a conscience purified, acknowledging Him not only as the son of man, which he had believed before, but now as the Son of God, who had assumed our flesh, " he said, Lord, I believe." It is but little to say, " I believe:" wouldst thou also see what he believes Him? " He fell down and worshipped Him."

16. "And Jesus said to him." Now is He, the day, discerning between the light and the darkness. " For judgment am I come into this world; that they who see not might see, and they who see might be made blind." What is this, Lord? A weighty subject of inquiry hast Thou laid on the weary; but revive our strength that we may be able to understand what Thou hast said. Thou art come " that they who see not may see:" rightly so, for Thou art the light: rightly so, for Thou art the day: rightly so, for Thou deliverest from darkness: this every soul accepts, every one understands. What is this that follows, "And those who see may be made blind?" Shall then, because Thou art come, those be made blind who saw? Hear what follows, and perhaps thou wilt understand.

17. By these words, then, were " some of the Pharisees " disturbed, " and said unto Him, Are we blind also?" Hear now what it is that moved them, "And they who see may be made blind." " Jesus said unto them, If ye were blind, ye should have no sin;" while blindness itself is sin. " If ye were blind," that is, if ye considered yourselves blind, if ye called yourselves blind, ye also would have recourse to the physician: " if " then in this way " ye were blind, ye should have no sin;" for I am come to take away sin. " But now ye say, We see; [therefore] your sin remaineth." Wherefore? Because by saying, " We see:" ye seek not the physician, ye remain in your blindness. This, then, is that which a little above we did not understand, when He said, " I am come, that they who see not may see;" for what means this, " that they who see not may see "? They who acknowledge that they do not see, and seek the physician, that they may receive sight. And they who see may be made blind:" what means this, " they who see may be made blind"? That they who think they see, and seek not the physician, may abide in their blindness. Such discerning therefore of one from another He called judgment, when He said, " For judgment I am come into this world," whereby He distinguishes the cause of those who believe and make confession from the proud, who think they see, and are therefore the more grievously blinded: just as the sinner, making confession, and seeking the physician, said to Him, " Judge me, O God, and discern my cause against the unholy nation,"[1]—namely, those who say, " We see," and their sin remaineth. But it was not that judgment He now brought into the world, whereby in the end of the world He shall judge the living and the dead. For in respect to this He had said, " I judge no man;"[2] seeing that He came the first time, " not to judge the world, but that the world through Him might be saved."[3]

---

[1] Ps. xliii. 1.   [2] Chap. viii. 15.   [3] Chap. iii. 17.

TRACTATE XLV

CHAPTER X. 1–10.

1. OUR Lord's discourse to the Jews began in connection with the man who was born blind and was restored to sight. Your Charity therefore ought to know and be advised that to-day's lesson is interwoven with that one. For when the Lord had said, " For judgment I am come into this world; that they who see not might see, and they who see might be made blind,"—which, on the occasion of its reading, we expounded according to our

ability,—some of the Pharisees said, "Are we blind also?" To whom He replied. "If ye were blind, ye should have no sin: but now ye say, We see; [therefore] your sin remaineth."[1] To these words He added what we have been hearing to-day when the lesson was read.

2. "Verily, verily, I say unto you, He that entereth not by the door into the sheepfold, but climbeth up some other way, the same is a thief and a robber." For they declared that they were not blind; yet could they see only by being the sheep of Christ. Whence claimed they possession of the light, who were acting as thieves against the day? Because, then, of their vain and proud and incurable arrogance, did the Lord Jesus subjoin these words, wherein He has given us also salutary lessons, if we lay them to heart. For there are many who, according to a custom of this life, are called good people,—good men, good women, innocent, and observers as it were of what is commanded in the law; paying respect to their parents, abstaining from adultery, doing no murder, committing no theft, giving no false witness against any one, and observing all else that the law requires—yet are not Christians; and for the most part ask boastfully, like these men, "Are we blind also?" But just because all these things that they do, and know not to what end they should have reference, they do to no purpose, the Lord has set forth in to-day's lesson the similitude of His own flock, and of the door that leads into the sheepfold. Pagans may say, then, We live well. If they enter not by the door, what good will that do them, whereof they boast? For to this end ought good living to benefit every one, that it may be given him to live for ever: for to whomsoever eternal life is not given, of what benefit is the living well? For they ought not to be spoken of as even living well, who either from blindness know not the end of a right life, or in their pride despise it. But no one has the true and certain hope of living always, unless he know the life, that it is Christ; and enter by the gate into the sheepfold.

3. Such, accordingly, for the most part seek to persuade men to live well, and yet not to be Christians. By another way they wish to climb up, to steal and to kill, not as the shepherd, to preserve and to save. And thus there have been certain philosophers, holding many subtle discussions about the virtues and the vices, dividing, defining, drawing out to their close the most acute processes of reasoning, filling books, brandishing their wisdom with rattling jaws; who would even dare to say to people, Follow us, keep to our sect, if you would live happily. But they had not entered by the door: they wished to destroy, to slay, and to murder.

4. What shall I say of such? Look, the Pharisees themselves were in the habit of reading, and in what they read, their voices re-echoed the Christ, they hoped He would come, and recognized Him not when present; they boasted, even they, of being amongst those who saw, that is, among the wise, and they disowned the Christ, and entered not in by the door. Therefore would such also, if they chanced to seduce any, seduce them to be slaughtered and murdered, not to be brought into liberty. Let us leave these also to themselves, and look at those who glory in the name of Christ Himself, and see whether even they perchance are entering in by the door.

5. For there are countless numbers who not only boast that they see, but would have it appear that they are enlightened by Christ; yet are they heretics. Have even they somehow entered by the gate? Surely not. Sabellius says, He who is the Son is Himself the Father; but if the Son, then is there no Father. He enters not by the door, who asserts that the Son is the Father. Arius says, The Father is one thing, the Son is another thing. He would say rightly if he said, Another person; but not another thing.[2] For when he says, Another thing, he contradicts Him who says in his hearing, "I and my Father are One."[3] Neither does he therefore enter by the door; for he preaches a Christ such as he fabricates for himself, not such as the truth declares Him. Thou hast the name, thou hast not the reality. Christ is the name of something; keep hold of the thing itself, if thou wouldst benefit by the name. Another, I know not from whence, says with Photinus,[4] Christ is mere man; He is not God. He enters not in by the door, for Christ is both man and God. But why need I make many references, and enumerate the many vanities of heretics? Keep hold of this, that Christ's sheepfold is the Catholic Church. Whoever would enter the sheepfold, let him enter by the door, let him preach the true Christ. Not only let him preach the true Christ, but seek Christ's glory, not his own; for many, by seeking their own glory, have scattered Christ's sheep, instead of gathering them. For Christ the Lord is a low gateway: he who

---

[1] Chap. ix. 39-41.

[2] Or, " substance :" *Alius, non aliud.*
[3] Ver. 38, *unum;* lit. " one thing or substance."
[4] Bishop of Sirmium, who published his heretical opinions about A.D. 343.

enters by this gateway must humble himself, that he may be able to enter with head unharmed. But he that humbleth not, but exalteth himself, wishes to climb over the wall; and he that climbeth over the wall, is exalted only to fall.

6. Thus far, however, the Lord Jesus speaks in covert language; not as yet is He understood. He names the door, He names the sheepfold, He names the sheep: all this He sets forth, but does not yet explain. Let us read on then, for He is coming to those words, wherein He may think proper to give us some explanation of what He has·said; from the explanation of which He will perhaps enable us to understand also what He has not explained. For He gives us what is plain, for food; what is obscure, for exercise. "He that entereth not by the door into the sheepfold, but climbeth up some other way." Woe to the wretch, for he is sure to fall! Let him then be humble, let him enter by the door: let him walk on the level ground, and he shall not stumble. "The same," He says, "is a thief and a robber." The sheep of another he desires to call his own sheep,—his own, that is, as carried off by stealth, for the purpose, not of saving, but of slaying them. Therefore is he a thief, because what is another's he calls his own; a robber, because what he has stolen he also kills. "But he that entereth in by the door is the shepherd of the sheep: to him the porter openeth." Concerning this porter we shall make inquiry, when we have heard of the Lord Himself what is the door and who is the shepherd. "And the sheep hear his voice: and he calleth his own sheep by name." For He has their names written in the book of life. "He calleth his own sheep by name." Hence, says the apostle, "The Lord knoweth them that are His."[1] "And he leadeth them out. And when he putteth forth his own sheep, he goeth before them, and the sheep follow him: for they know his voice. And a stranger do they not follow, but do flee from him: for they know not the voice of strangers." These are veiled words, full of topics of inquiry, pregnant with sacramental signs. Let us follow then, and listen to the Master as He makes some opening into these obscurities; and perhaps by the opening He makes, He will cause us to enter.

7. "This parable spake Jesus unto them; but they understood not what He spake unto them." Nor we also, perhaps. What, then, is the difference between them and us, before even we can understand these words? This,

that we on our part knock, that it may be opened unto us; while they, by disowning Christ, refused to enter for salvation, and preferred remaining outside to be destroyed. In as far, then, as we listen to these words with a pious mind, in as far as, before we understand them, we believe them to be true and divine, we stand at a great distance from these men. For when two persons are listening to the words of the gospel, the one impious, the other pious, and some of these are such as neither perhaps understands, the one says, It has said nothing; the other says, It has said the truth, and what it has said is good, but we do not understand it. This latter, because he believes, now knocks, that he may be worthy to have it opened up to him, if he continue knocking; but the other still hears the words, "If ye believe not, ye shall not understand."[2] Why do I draw your attention to this? Even for this reason, that when I have explained as I can these obscure words, or, because of their great abstruseness, I have either myself failed to arrive at an understanding of them, or wanted the faculty of explaining what I do understand, or every one has been so dull as not to follow me, even when I give the explanation, yet should he not despair of himself; but continue in faith, walk on in the way, and hear the apostle saying, "And if in anything ye be otherwise minded, God shall reveal even this unto you. Nevertheless whereto we have already attained, let us walk therein."[3]

8. Let us begin, then, with hearing His exposition of what we have heard Him propounding. "Then said Jesus unto them again, Verily, verily, I say unto you, I am the·door of the sheep." See, He has opened the very door which was shut in His former description. He Himself is the door. We have come to know it; let us enter, or rejoice that we are already within. "All that ever came are thieves and robbers." What is this, Lord, "All that ever came"? How so? hast Thou not come? But understand; I said, "All that ever came," meaning, of course, exclusive of myself.[4] Let us recollect then. Before His coming came the prophets: were they thieves and robbers? God forbid. They did not come apart from Him, for they came

1 2 Tim. ii. 19.

2 Isa. vii. 9, according to the Septuagint, which, however, can hardly be said here to give the meaning of the Hebrew text. Our English version gives a pretty correct translation of the latter. --Tr.
3 Phil. iii. 15, 16.
4 *Præter me: besides, apart from, myself.* These words are an explanation suggested by Augustin himself. The words, "πρὸ ἐμοῦ," "before me," of the received text, which are undoubtedly genuine, were wanting in the version here used by Augustin, just as in the Vulgate. It is supposed that the authors of these versions had been tempted to omit them, because of the use made of them by some early heretics to throw discredit on the Old Testament Scriptures.--Tr.

with Him. When about to come, He sent heralds, but retained possession of the hearts of His messengers. Do you wish· to know that they came with Him, who is Himself ever existent? Certainly He assumed human flesh at the time appointed. But what means that "ever"? "In the beginning was the Word."¹ With Him, therefore, came those who came with the word of God. "I am," said He, "the way, and the truth, and the life."² If He is the truth, with Him came those who were truthful. As many, therefore, as were apart from Him, were "thieves and robbers," that is, had come to steal and to destroy.

9. 'But the sheep did not hear them.' This is a more important point, "the sheep did not hear them." Before the advent of our Lord Jesus Christ, when He came in humility in the flesh, righteous men preceded, believing in the same way in Him who was to come, as we believe in Him who has come. Times vary, but not faith. For verbs themselves also vary with the tense, when they are variously declined. He is to come, has one sound; He has come, has another: there is a change in the sound between He is to come, and He has come:³ yet the same faith unites both,—both those who believed that He would come, and those who have believed that He is come. At different times, indeed, but by the one doorway of faith, that is, by Christ, do we see that both have entered. We believe that the Lord Jesus Christ was born of the Virgin, that He came in the flesh, suffered, rose again, ascended into heaven: all this, just as you hear verbs of the past tense, we believe to be already fulfilled. In that faith a partnership is also held with us by those fathers who believed that He would be born of the Virgin, would suffer, would rise again, would ascend into heaven; for to such the apostle pointed when he said, "But we having the same spirit of faith, according as it is written, I believed, and therefore have I spoken; we also believe, and therefore speak."⁴ The prophet said, "I believed, therefore have I spoken:"⁵ the apostle says, "We also believe, and therefore speak." But to let you know that their faith is one, listen to him saying, "Having the same spirit of faith, we also believe." So also in another place, "For I would not have you ignorant, brethren, how that all our fathers were under the cloud, and all passed through the sea: and were all baptized unto Moses in the cloud and in the sea; and did all eat the same spiritual meat, and did all

drink the same spiritual drink." The Red Sea signifies baptism; Moses, their leader through the Red Sea, signifies Christ; the people, who passed through, signify believers; the death of the Egyptians signifies the abolition of sins. Under different signs there is the same faith. It is with different signs as with different words [verbs]; for verbs change their sounds through the tenses, and verbs are indeed nothing else than signs. For they are words because of what they signify: take away the meaning from a word,⁶ and it becomes a senseless sound. All, therefore, have become signs. Was not the same faith theirs by whom these signs were employed, and by whom were foretold in prophecy the very things which we believe? Certainly it was: but they believed that they were yet to come, and we, that they have come. In like manner does he also say, "They all drank the same spiritual drink;" "the same spiritual," for it was not the same material [drink]. For what was it they drank? "For they drank of the spiritual Rock that followed them; and that Rock was Christ."⁷ See, then, how that while the faith remained, the signs were varied. There the rock was Christ; to us that is Christ which is placed on the altar of God. And they, as a great sacramental sign of the same Christ, drank the water flowing from the rock: what we drink is known to believers. If one's thoughts turn to the visible form, the thing is different; if to the meaning that addresses the understanding, they drank the same spiritual drink. As many, then, at that time as believed, whether Abraham, or Isaac, or Jacob, or Moses, or the other patriarchs or prophets who foretold of Christ, were sheep, and heard Christ. His voice, and not another's, did they hear. The Judge was present in the person of the Crier. For even when the judge speaks through the crier, the clerk⁸ does not make it, The crier said; but the judge said. But others there are whom the sheep did not hear, in whom Christ's voice had no place,—wanderers, uttering falsehoods, prating inanities, fabricating vanities, misleading the miserable.

10. Why is it, then, that I have said, This is a more important point? What is there about it obscure and difficult to understand? Listen, I beseech you. See, the Lord Jesus Christ Himself came and preached. Much more surely was that the Shepherd's voice which was uttered by the very mouth of the

---

⁶ Augustin seems here to use *verbum* sometimes in its grammatical, sometimes in its general, meaning.—Tr.
⁷ 1 Cor. x. 1-4.
⁸ *Exceptor :* the person employed to take down notes of the decisions, sentences, etc., in the public courts or assemblies.—Tr.

---

¹ Chap. i. 1.   ² Chap. xiv. 6.   ³ *Venturus ist, et venit.*
⁴ 2 Cor. iv. 13.   ⁵ Ps. cxvi. 10.

Shepherd. For if the Shepherd's voice came through the prophets, how much more did the Shepherd's own tongue give utterance to the Shepherd's voice? Yet all did not hear Him. But what are we to think? Those who did hear, were they sheep? Lo? Judas heard, and was a wolf: he followed, but, clad in sheep-skin, he was laying snares for the Shepherd. Some, again, of those who crucified Christ did not hear, and yet were sheep; for such He saw in the crowd when He said, "When ye have lifted up the Son of man, then shall ye know that I am He."[1] Now, how is this question to be solved? They that are not sheep do hear, and they that are sheep do not hear. Some, who are wolves, follow the Shepherd's voice; and some, that are sheep, contradict it. Last of all, the sheep slay the Shepherd. The point is solved; for some one in reply says, But when they did not hear, as yet they were not sheep, they were then wolves: the voice, when it was heard, changed them, and out of wolves transformed them into sheep; and so, when they became sheep, they heard, and found the Shepherd, and followed Him. They built their hopes on the Shepherd's promises, because they obeyed His precepts.

11. That question has been solved in a way, and perhaps satisfies every one. But I have still a subject of concern, and what concerns me I shall impart to you, that, in some sort inquiring together, I may through His revelation be found worthy with you to attain the solution. Hear, then, what it is that moves me. By the Prophet Ezekiel the Lord rebukes the shepherds, and among other things says of the sheep, "The wandering sheep have ye not recalled."[2] He both declares it *a wanderer*, and calls it *a sheep*. If, while wandering, it was a sheep, whose voice was it hearing to lead it astray? For doubtless it would not be straying were it hearing the shepherd's voice: but it strayed just because it heard another's voice; it heard the voice of the thief and the robber. Surely the sheep do not hear the voice of robbers. "Those that came," He said,—and we are to understand, *apart from me,*—that is, "those that came *apart from me* are thieves and robbers, and the sheep did not hear them." Lord, if the sheep did not hear them, how can the sheep wander? If the sheep hear only Thee, and Thou art the truth, whoever heareth the truth cannot certainly fall into error. But they err, and are called sheep. For if, in the very midst of their wandering, they were not called sheep, it

would not be said by Ezekiel, "The wandering sheep have ye not recalled." How is it at the same time a wanderer and a sheep? Has it heard the voice of another? Surely "the sheep did not hear them." Accordingly many are just now being gathered into Christ's fold, and from being heretics are becoming catholics. They are rescued from the thieves, and restored to the shepherds: and sometimes they murmur, and become wearied of Him that calls them back, and have no true knowledge of him that would murder them; nevertheless also, when, after a struggle, those have come who are sheep, they recognize the Shepherd's voice, and are glad they have come, and are ashamed of their wandering. When, then, they were glorying in that state of error as in the truth, and were certainly not hearing the Shepherd's voice, but were following another, were they sheep, or were they not? If they were sheep, how can it be the case that the sheep do not listen to aliens? If they were not sheep, wherefore the rebuke addressed to those to whom it is said, "The wandering sheep have ye not recalled"? In the case also of those already become catholic Christians, and believers of good promise, evils sometimes occur: they are seduced into error, and after their error are restored. When they were thus seduced, and were rebaptized, or after the companionship of the Lord's fold were turned back again into their former error, were they sheep, or were they not? Certainly they were catholics. If they were faithful catholics, they were sheep. If they were sheep, how was it that they could listen to the voice of a stranger when the Lord saith, "The sheep did not hear them"?

12. You hear, brethren, the great importance of the question. I say then, "The Lord knoweth them that are His."[3] He knoweth those who were foreknown, He knoweth those who were predestinated; because it is said of Him, "For whom He did foreknow, He also did predestinate to be conformed to the image of His Son, that He might be the firstborn among many brethren. Moreover, whom He did predestinate, them He also called; and whom He called, them He also justified; and whom He justified, them He also glorified. If God be for us, who can be against us?" Add to this: "He that spared not His own Son, but delivered Him up for us all, how hath He not with Him also freely given us all things?" But what "us"? Those who are foreknown, predestinated, justified, glorified; regarding

---

whom there follows, "Who shall lay anything to the charge of God's elect?"[1] Therefore "the Lord knoweth them that are His;" they are the sheep. Such sometimes do not know themselves, but the Shepherd knoweth them, according to this predestination, this foreknowledge of God, according to the election of the sheep before the foundation of the world: for so saith also the apostle, "According as He hath chosen us in Him before the foundation of the world."[2] According, then, to this divine foreknowledge and predestination, how many sheep are outside, how many wolves within! and how many sheep are inside, how many wolves without! How many are now living in wantonness who will yet be chaste! how many are blaspheming Christ who will yet believe in Him! how many are giving themselves to drunkenness who will yet be sober! how many are preying on other people's property who will yet freely give of their own! Nevertheless at present they are hearing the voice of another, they are following strangers. In like manner, how many are praising within who will yet blaspheme; are chaste who will yet be fornicators; are sober who will wallow hereafter in drink; are standing who will by and by fall! These are not the sheep. (For we speak of those who were predestinated,—of those whom the Lord knoweth that they are His.) And yet these, so long as they keep right, listen to the voice of Christ. Yea, these hear, the others do not; and yet, according to predestination, these are not sheep, while the others are.

13. There remains still the question, which I now think may meanwhile thus be solved. There is a voice of some kind,—there is, I say, a certain kind of voice of the Shepherd, in respect of which the sheep hear not strangers, and in respect of which those who are not sheep do not hear Christ. What a word is this! "He that endureth to the end, the same shall be saved."[3] No one of His own is indifferent to such a voice, a stranger does not hear it: for this reason also does He announce it to the former, that he may abide perseveringly with Himself to the end; but by one who is wanting in such persevering continuance with Him, such a word remains unheard. One has come to Christ, and has heard word after word of one kind and another, all of them true, all of them salutary; and among all the rest is also this utterance, "He that endureth to the end, the same shall be saved." He who has heard this is one of the sheep. But there was, perhaps, some one listening to it, who treated it with dislike,

with coldness, and heard it as that of a stranger. If he was predestinated, he strayed for the time, but he was not lost for ever: he returns to hear what he has neglected, to do what he has heard. For if he is one of those who are predestinated, then both his very wandering and his future conversion have been foreknown by God: if he has strayed away, he will return to hear that voice of the Shepherd, and to follow Him who saith, "He that endureth to the end, the same shall be saved." A good voice, brethren, it is; true and shepherd-like, the very voice of salvation in the tabernacles of the righteous.[4] For it is easy to hear Christ, easy to praise the gospel, easy to applaud the preacher: but to endure unto the end, is peculiar to the sheep who hear the Shepherd's voice. A temptation befalls thee, endure thou to the end, for the temptation will not endure to the end. And what is that end to which thou shalt endure? Even till thou reachest the end of thy pathway. For as long as thou hearest not Christ, He is thine adversary in the pathway, that is, in this mortal life. And what doth He say? "Agree with thine adversary quickly, while thou art in the way with him."[5] Thou hast heard, hast believed, hast agreed. If thou hast been at enmity, agree. If thou hast got the opportunity of coming to an agreement, keep not up the quarrel longer. For thou knowest not when thy way will be ended, and it is known to Him. If thou art a sheep, and if thou endurest to the end, thou shalt be saved: and therefore it is that His own despise not that voice, and strangers hear it not. According to my ability, as He gave me the power, I have either explained to you or gone over with you a subject of great profundity. If any have failed fully to understand, let him retain his piety, and the truth will be revealed: and let not those who have understood vaunt themselves as swifter at the expense of the slower, lest in their vaunting they turn out of the track, and the slower more easily attain the goal. But let all of us be guided by Him to whom we say, "Lead me, O Lord, in Thy way, and I will walk in Thy truth."[6]

14. By this, then, which the Lord hath explained, that He Himself is the door, let us find entrance to what He has set forth, but not explained. And indeed who it is that is the Shepherd, although He hath not told us in the lesson we have read to-day, yet in that which follows He very plainly tells us: "I am the good Shepherd." And although He had not said so, whom else but Himself ought

---

we to have understood in those words where He saith, " He that entereth in by the door is the Shepherd of the sheep. To Him the porter openeth: and the sheep hear His voice: and He calleth His own sheep by name, and leadeth them out. And when He putteth forth His own sheep, He goeth before them, and the sheep follow Him: for they know His voice " ? For who else calleth His own sheep by name, and leadeth them hence unto eternal life, but He who knoweth the names of those that are fore-ordained ? Hence He said to His disciples, " Rejoice that your names are written in heaven; "¹ for from this it is that He calleth them by name. And who else putteth them forth, save He who putteth away their sins, that, freed from their grievous fetters, they may be able to follow Him ? And who hath gone before them to the place whither they are to follow Him, but He who, rising from the dead, dieth no more; and death shall have no more dominion over Him;² and who, when He was manifest here in the flesh, said, " Father, I will that they also whom Thou hast given me be with me where I am " ?³ Hence it is that He saith, " I am the door: by me if any man enter in, he shall be saved, and shall go in and out, and find pasture." In this He clearly shows that not only the Shepherd, but the sheep also enter in by the door.

15. But what is this, " He shall go in and out, and find pasture " ? To enter indeed into the Church by Christ the door, is eminently good; but to go out of the Church, as this same John the evangelist saith in his epistle, " They went out from us, but they were not of us," ⁴ is certainly otherwise than good. Such a going out could not then be commended by the good Shepherd, when He said, "And he shall go in and out, and find pasture." There is therefore not only some sort of entrance, but some outgoing also that is good, by the good door, which is Christ. But what is that praiseworthy and blessed outgoing? I might say, indeed, that we enter when we engage in some inward exercise of thought; and go out, when we take to some active work without: and since, as the apostle saith, Christ dwelleth in our hearts by faith,⁵ to enter by Christ is to give ourselves to thought in accordance with that faith; but

to go out by Christ is, in accordance also with that same faith, to take to outside works, that is to say, in the presence of others. Hence, also, we read in a psalm, " Man goeth forth to his work;" ⁶ and the Lord Himself saith, " Let your works shine before men." ⁷ But I am better pleased that the Truth Himself, like a good Shepherd, and therefore a good Teacher, hath in a certain measure reminded us how we ought to understand His words, " He shall go in and out, and find pasture," when He added in the sequel, " The thief cometh not, but for to steal, and to kill, and to destroy: I am come that they might have life, and that they might have it more abundantly." For He seems to me to have meant, That they may have life in coming in, and have it more abundantly at their departure. For no one can pass out by the door—that is, by Christ—to that eternal life which shall be open to the sight, unless by the same door—that is, by the same Christ —he has entered His church, which is His fold, to the temporal life, which is lived in faith. Therefore, He saith, " I am come that they may have life," that is, faith, which worketh by love;⁸ by which faith they enter the fold that they may live, for the just liveth by faith: ⁹ " and that they may have it more abundantly," who, enduring unto the end, pass out by this same door, that is, by the faith of Christ; for as true believers they die, and will have life more abundantly when they come whither the Shepherd hath preceded them, where they shall die no more. Although, therefore, there is no want of pasture even here in the fold,—for we may understand the words " and shall find pasture " as referring to both, that is, both to their going in and their going out,—yet there only will they find the true pasture, where they shall be filled who hunger and thirst after righteousness,¹⁰—such pasture as was found by him to whom it was said, " To-day shalt thou be with me in paradise." ¹¹ But how He Himself is the door, and Himself the Shepherd, so that He also may in a certain respect be understood as going in and out by Himself, and who is the porter, it would be too long to inquire to-day, and, according to the grace given us by Himself, to unfold in the way of dissertation.

---

¹ Luke x. 20. ² Rom. vi. 9. ³ Chap. xvii. 24.
⁴ 1 John ii. 19. ⁵ Eph. iii. 17.

⁶ Ps. civ. 23. ⁷ Matt. v. 16. ⁸ Gal. v. 6.
⁹ Rom. i. 17. ¹⁰ Matt. v. 6. ¹¹ Luke xxiii. 43.

TRACTATE XLVI.

Chapter X. 11–13.

1. The Lord Jesus is speaking to His sheep —to those already so, and to those yet to become such—who were then present; for in the place where they were, there were those who were already His sheep, as well as those who were afterwards to become so: and He likewise shows to those then present and those to come, both to them and to us, and to as many also after us as shall yet be His sheep, who it is that had been sent to them. All, therefore, hear the voice of their Shepherd saying, "I am the good Shepherd." He would not add "good," were there not bad shepherds. But the bad shepherds are those who are thieves and robbers, or certainly hirelings at the best. For we ought to examine into, to distinguish, and to know, all the characters whom He has here depicted. The Lord has already unfolded two points, which He had previously set forth in a kind of covert form: we already know that He is Himself the door, and we know that He is Himself the Shepherd. Who the thieves and robbers are, was made clear in yesterday's lesson; and to-day we have heard of the hireling, as we have heard also of the wolf. Yesterday the porter was also introduced by name. Among the good, therefore, are the door, the doorkeeper, the shepherd, and the sheep: among the bad, the thieves and robbers, the hirelings, and the wolf.

2. We understand the Lord Christ as the door, and also as the Shepherd; but who is to be understood as the doorkeeper? For the former two, He has Himself explained: the doorkeeper He has left us to search out for ourselves. And what doth He say of the doorkeeper? "To him," He saith, "the porter [doorkeeper][1] openeth." To whom doth he open? To the Shepherd. What doth he open to the Shepherd? The door. And who is also the door? The Shepherd Himself. Now, if Christ the Lord had not Himself explained, had not Himself said, "I am the Shepherd," and "I am the door," would any of us have ventured to say that Christ is Himself both the Shepherd and the door? For had He said, "I am the Shepherd," and had not said, "I am the door," we should be setting ourselves to inquire what was the door, and perhaps, mistaken in our views, be still standing before the door. His grace and mercy have revealed to us the Shepherd, by His calling Himself so; have revealed to us also the door, when He declared Himself such; but He hath left us to search out the doorkeeper for ourselves. Whom, then, are we to call the doorkeeper? Whomsoever we fix upon, we must take care not to think of him as greater than the door itself; for in men's houses the doorkeeper is greater than the door. The doorkeeper is placed before the door, not the door before the doorkeeper; because the porter keepeth the door, not the door the porter. I dare not say that any one is greater than the door, for I have heard already what is the door: that is no longer unknown to me, I am not left to my own conjecture, and I have not got much room for mere human guess work: God hath said it, the Truth hath said it, and we cannot change what the Unchangeable hath uttered.

3. In respect, then, of the profound nature of this question, I shall tell you what I think: let each one make the choice that pleases him, but let him think of it reverently; as it is written, "Think of the Lord with goodness, and in simplicity of heart seek Him."[2] Perhaps we ought to understand the Lord Himself as the doorkeeper: for the shepherd and the door are in human respects as much different from each other as the doorkeeper and the door; and yet the Lord has called Himself both the Shepherd and the door. Why, then, may we not understand Him also as the doorkeeper? For if we look at His personal qualities,[3] the Lord Christ is neither a shepherd, in the way we are accustomed to know and to see shepherds; nor is He a door, for no artisan made Him: but if, because of some point of similarity, He is both the door and the Shepherd, I venture to say, He is also a sheep. True, the sheep is under the shepherd; yet He is both the Shepherd and a sheep. Where is He the Shepherd? Look, here thou hast it; read the Gospel: "I am the good Shepherd." Where is He a sheep? Ask the prophet: "He was led as a sheep to the slaughter."[4] Ask the friend of the bridegroom: "Behold the Lamb of God, that taketh away the sin of the world."[5] Moreover,

---

[1] Ostiarius.

[2] Wisdom i. 1.
[4] Isa. liii. 7.
[3] Proprietates.
[5] Chap. i. 29.

I am going to say something of a still more wonderful kind, in accordance with these points of similarity. For both the lamb, and the sheep, and the shepherd are friendly with one another, but from the lions as their foes the sheep are protected by their shepherds: and yet of Christ, who is both sheep and Shepherd, we have it said, "The Lion of the tribe of Judah hath prevailed."[1] All this, brethren, understand in connection with points of similarity, not with personal qualities. It is a common thing to see the shepherds sitting on a rock, and there guarding the cattle committed to their care. Surely the shepherd is better than the rock that he sits upon; and yet Christ is both the Shepherd and the rock. All this by way of comparison. But if thou askest me for His peculiar personal quality:[2] "In the beginning was the Word, and the Word was with God, and the Word was God."[3] If thou askest me for the personal quality peculiarly His own: The only Son, from everlasting to everlasting begotten of the Father, the equal of Him that begat, the Maker of all things, unchangeable with the Father, unchanged by the assuming of human form, man by incarnation, the Son of man, and the Son of God. All this that I have said is not figure, but reality.

4. Therefore, let us not, brethren, be disturbed in understanding Him, in harmony with certain resemblances, as Himself the door, and also the doorkeeper. For what is the door? The way of entrance. Who is the doorkeeeper? He who opens it. Who, then, is He that opens Himself, but He who unveils Himself to sight? See, when the Lord spoke at first of the door, we did not understand: so long as we did not understand, it was shut: He who opened it is Himself the doorkeeper. There is no need, then, of seeking any other meaning, no need; but perhaps there is the desire. If there is so, quit not the path, go not outside of the Trinity. If thou art in quest of some other impersonation of the doorkeeper, bethink thee of the Holy Spirit; for the Holy Spirit will not think it unmeet to be the doorkeeper, when the Son has thought it meet to be Himself the door. Look at the doorkeeper as perhaps the Holy Spirit: about Him the Lord saith to His disciples, "He shall guide you into all truth."[4] What is the door? Christ. What is Christ? The Truth. Who, then, openeth the door, but He who guideth into all truth?

5. But what are we to say of the hireling? He is not mentioned here among the good.

"The good Shepherd," He says, "giveth His life for the sheep. But he that is an hireling, and not the Shepherd, whose own the sheep are not, seeth the wolf coming, and leaveth the sheep, and fleeth; and the wolf catcheth them, and scattereth the sheep." The hireling does not here bear a good character, and yet in some respects is useful; nor would he be called an hireling, did he not receive hire from his employer. Who then is this hireling, that is both blameworthy and needful? And here, brethren, let the Lord Himself give us light, that we may know who the hirelings are, and be not hirelings ourselves. Who then is the hireling? There are some in office in the church, of whom the Apostle Paul saith, "Who seek their own, not the things that are Jesus Christ's." What means that, "Who seek their own"? Who do not love Christ freely, who do not seek after God for His own sake; who are pursuing after temporal advantages, gaping for gain, coveting honors from men. When such things are loved by an overseer, and for such things God is served, whoever such an one may be, he is an hireling who cannot count himself among the children. For of such also the Lord saith: "Verily, I say unto you, they have their reward."[5] Listen to what the Apostle Paul says of St. Timothy: "But I trust in the Lord Jesus to send Timothy shortly unto you, that I also may be of good comfort, when I know your circumstances; for I have no man like-minded, who will naturally[6] care for you. For all seek their own, not the things which are Jesus Christ's."[7] The shepherd mourned in the midst of hirelings. He sought some one who sincerely loved the flock of Christ, and round about him, amongst those who were with him at that time, he found not one. Not that there was no one then in the Church of Christ but the Apostle Paul and Timothy, who had a brother's[8] concern for the flock; but it so happened at the time of his sending Timothy, that he had none else of his sons about him; only hirelings were with him, "who sought their own, not the things which are Jesus Christ's." And yet he himself, with a brother's anxiety for the flock, preferred sending his son, and remaining himself amongst hirelings. Hirelings are also found among ourselves, but the Lord alone distinguisheth them. He that searcheth the heart, distinguisheth them; and yet sometimes we know them ourselves. For it was not without a purpose that the Lord Himself said also of the wolves: "By their fruits ye shall know

[1] Rev. v. 5.   [2] *Proprietatem.*
[3] Chap. i. 1.   [4] Chap. xvi. 13.
17
[5] Matt. vi. 5.   [6] *Germane*, like a brother.
[7] Phil. ii. 19-21.   [8] *Germane*, like a brother.

them." [1] Temptations put many to the question, and then their thoughts are made manifest; but many remain undiscovered. The Lord's fold must have as overseers, both those who are children and those who are hirelings. But the overseers, who are sons, are the shepherds. If they are shepherds, how is there but one Shepherd, save that all of them are members of the one Shepherd, to whom the sheep belong? For they are also members of Himself as the one sheep; because "as a sheep he was led to the slaughter."

6. But give heed to the fact that even the hirelings are needful. For many indeed in the Church are following after earthly profit, and yet preach Christ, and through them is heard the voice of Christ; and the sheep follow, not the hireling, but the Shepherd's voice speaking through the hireling. Hearken to the hirelings as pointed out by the Lord Himself: "The scribes," He saith, "and the Pharisees sit in Moses' seat: do what they say; but do not what they do." [2] What else said He but, Listen to the Shepherd's voice speaking through the hirelings? For sitting in Moses' seat, they teach the law of God; therefore God teacheth by them. But if they wish to teach their own things, hear them not, do them not. For certainly such seek their own, not the things which are Jesus Christ's; but no hireling has dared to say to Christ's people, Seek your own, not the things which are Jesus Christ's. For his own evil conduct he does not preach from the seat of Christ: he does injury by the evil that he does, not by the good that he says. Pluck the grapes, beware of the thorn. It is well; I see that you have understood; but for the sake of those that are slower, I shall repeat these words with greater plainness. How said I, Pluck the bunch of grapes, beware of the thorn; when the Lord saith, "Do men gather grapes of thorns, or figs of thistles"? That is quite true: and yet what I said is also true, Pluck the bunch of grapes, beware of the thorn. For sometimes the grape-cluster, springing from the root of the vine, finds its support in a common hedge; its branch grows, becomes embedded among thorns, and the thorn bears other fruit than its own. For the thorn has not been produced from the vine, but has become the resting-place of its runner. Make thine inquiries only at the roots. Seek for the thorn-root, thou wilt find it apart from the vine: seek the origin of the grape, and from the root of the vine it will be found to have sprung. And so, Moses' seat

was the vine; the morals of the Pharisees were the thorns. Sound doctrine cometh through the wicked, as the vine-branch in a hedge, a bunch of grapes among thorns. Gather carefully, so as in seeking the fruit not to tear thine hand; and while thou art to hear one speaking what is good, imitate him not when doing what is evil. "What they tell you, do,"—gather the grapes; "but what they do, do not,"—beware of the thorns. Even through hirelings listen to the voice of the Shepherd, but be not hirelings yourselves, seeing ye are members of the Shepherd. Yea, Paul himself, the holy apostle who said, "I have no one who hath a brother's concern about you; for all seek their own, not the things which are Jesus Christ's," draws a distinction in another place between hirelings and sons; and see what he saith: "Some preach Christ even of envy and strife, and some also of good will: some of love, knowing that I am set for the defence of the gospel; but some also preach Christ of contention, not sincerely, supposing to add affliction to my bonds." These were hirelings who disliked the Apostle Paul. And why such dislike, but just because they were seeking after temporal things? But mark what he adds: "What then? notwithstanding, every way, whether in pretence or in truth, Christ is preached: and I therein do rejoice, yea, and will rejoice." [3] Christ is the truth: let the truth be preached in pretense by hirelings, let it be preached in truth by the children: the children are waiting patiently for the eternal inheritance of the Father, the hirelings are longing for, and in a hurry to get, the temporal pay of their employer. For my part let me be shorn of the human glory, which I see such an object of envy to hirelings: and yet by the tongues both of hirelings and of children let the divine glory of Christ be published abroad, seeing that, "whether in pretense or in truth, Christ is preached."

7. We have seen who the hireling is also. Who, but the devil, is the wolf? And what was said of the hireling? "When he seeth the wolf coming, he fleeth: but the sheep are not his own, and he careth not for the sheep." Was the Apostle Paul such an one? Certainly not. Was Peter such an one? Far from it. Was such the character of the other apostles, save Judas, the son of perdition? Surely not. Were they shepherds then? Certainly they were. And how is there one Shepherd? I have already said they were shepherds, because members of the Shepherd. In that head they rejoiced, under that head

---

[1] Matt. vii. 16.   [2] Matt. xxiii. 2, 3.   [3] Phil. i. 15-18.

they were in harmony together, with one spirit they lived in the bond of one body; and therefore belonged all of them to the one Shepherd. If, then, they were shepherds, and not hirelings, wherefore fled they when suffering persecution? Explain it to us, O Lord. In an epistle, I have seen Paul fleeing: he was let down by the wall in a basket, to escape the hands of his persecutor.[1] Had he, then, no care of the sheep, whom he thus abandoned at the approach of the wolf? Clearly he had, but he commended them by his prayers to the Shepherd who was sitting in heaven; and for their advantage he preserved himself by flight, as he says in a certain place, "To abide in the flesh is needful for you."[2] For all had heard from the Shepherd Himself, "If they persecute you in one city, flee ye into another."[3] May the Lord be pleased to explain to us this point! Lord, Thou saidst to those whom Thou didst certainly wish to be faithful shepherds, and whom Thou didst form into Thine own members, "If they persecute you, flee." Doest Thou, then, injustice to them, when Thou blamest the hirelings who flee when they see the wolf coming! We ask Thee to tell us what meaning lies hid in the depths of the question. Let us knock, and the keeper of the door, which is Christ, will be here to reveal Himself.

8. Who is the hireling that seeth the wolf coming, and fleeth? He that seeketh his own, not the things which are Jesus Christ's. He is one that does not venture plainly to rebuke an offender.[4] Look, some one or other has sinned—grievously sinned; he ought to be rebuked, to be excommunicated: but once excommunicated, he will turn into an enemy, hatch plots, and do all the injury he can. At present, he who seeketh his own, not the things that are Jesus Christ's, in order not to lose what he follows after, the advantages of human friendship, and incur the annoyances of human enmity, keeps quiet and does not administer rebuke. See, the wolf has caught a sheep by the throat; the devil has enticed a believer into adultery: thou holdest thy peace — thou utterest no reproof. O hireling, thou hast seen the wolf coming and hast fled! Perhaps he answers and says: See, I am here; I have not fled. Thou hast fled, because thou hast been silent; thou hast been silent, because thou hast been afraid. The flight of the mind is fear. Thou stoodest with thy body, thou fleddest in thy spirit, which was not the conduct of him who said, "Though I be absent in the flesh, yet am I with you in the spirit."[5] For how did he flee in spirit, who, though absent in the flesh, yet in his letters reproved the fornicators? Our affections are the motions of our minds. Joy is expansion of the mind; sorrow, contraction of the mind; desire, a forward movement of the mind; and fear, the flight of the mind. For thou art expanded in mind when thou art glad; contracted in mind when thou art in trouble; thou movest forward in mind when thou hast an earnest desire; and thou fleest in mind when thou art afraid. This, then, is how the hireling is said to flee at the sight of the wolf. Why? "Because he careth not for the sheep." Why "careth he not for the sheep"? "Because he is an hireling." What is that, "he is an hireling"? He seeketh a temporal reward, and shall not dwell in the house for ever. There are still some things here to be inquired about and discussed with you, but it is not prudent to burden you. For we are ministering the Lord's food to our fellow-servants; we feed as sheep in the Lord's pastures, and are fed together. And just as we must not withhold what is needful, so our weak hearts are not to be overcharged with the abundance of provisions. Let it not then annoy your Charity that I do not take up to-day all that I think is still here to be discussed; but the same lesson will, in the Lord's name, be read over to us again on the preaching days, and be, with His help, more carefully considered.

---

[1] 2 Cor. xi. 33. [2] Phil. i. 24.
[3] Matt. x. 23. [4] 1 Tim. v. 20. [5] Col. ii. 5.

TRACTATE XLVII.

CHAPTER X. 14–21.

1. THOSE of you who hear the word of our God, not only with willingness, but also with attention, doubtless remember our promise. Indeed the same gospel lesson has also been read to-day which was read last Lord's day; because, having lingered over certain closely related topics, we could not discuss all that we owed to your powers of understanding. Accordingly, what has been already said and discoursed about we do not inquire into to-

day, lest by continual repetitions we should be prevented from reaching what has still to be spoken. You know now in the Lord's name who is the good Shepherd, and in what way good shepherds are His members, and therefore the Shepherd is one. You know who is the hireling we have to bear with; who the wolf, and the thieves, and the robbers we have to beware of; who are the sheep, and what is the door whereby both sheep and shepherd enter: how we are to understand the doorkeeper. You know also that every one who entereth not by the door is a thief and a robber, and cometh not but to steal, and to kill, and to destroy. All these sayings have, as I think, been sufficiently handled. To-day we ought to tell you, as far as the Lord enables us (for Jesus Christ our Saviour hath Himself told us that He is both the Shepherd and the door, and that the good Shepherd entereth in by the door), how it is that He entereth in by Himself. For if no one is a good shepherd but he that entereth by the door, and He Himself is pre-eminently the good Shepherd, and also Himself the door, I can understand it only in this way, that He entereth in by Himself to His sheep, and calleth them to follow Him, and they, going in and out, find pasture, which is to say, eternal life.

2. I proceed, then, without more delay. When I seek to get into you, that is, into your heart, I preach Christ: were I preaching something else, I should be trying to climb up some other way. Christ, therefore, is my gate to you: by Christ I get entrance, not to your houses, but to your hearts. It is by Christ I enter: it is Christ in me that you have been willingly hearing. And why is it you have thus willingly hearkened to Christ in me? Because you are the sheep of Christ, purchased with the blood of Christ. You acknowledge your own price, which is not paid by me, but is preached by my instrumentality. He, and only He, was the buyer, who shed precious blood—the precious blood of Him who was without sin. Yet made He precious also the blood of His own, for whom He paid the price of blood: for had He not made the blood of His own precious, it would not have been said, " Precious in the sight of the Lord is the death of His saints." [1] So also when He saith, " The good Shepherd giveth His life for the sheep," He is not the only one who has done such a deed; and yet if those who have done so are His members, He only Himself was the doer of it. For He was able to do so without them, but

whence had they the power apart from Him, who Himself had said, " Without me ye can do nothing " ? [2] But from the same source we can show what others also have done, for the apostle John himself, who preached the very gospel you have been hearing, has said in his epistle, " Just as Christ laid down His life for us, so ought we also to lay down our lives for the brethren." [3] " We ought," he says: He made us debtors who first set the example. To the same effect it is written in a certain place, " If thou sittest down to sup at a ruler's table, make wise observation of what is set before thee; and put to thy hand, knowing that it will be thy duty to make similar provision in turn." [4] You know what is meant by the ruler's table: you there find the body and blood of Christ; let him who comes to such a table be ready with similar provision. And what is such similar provision? *As He laid down His life for us, so ought we also*, for the edification of others, and the maintenance of the faith, [5] *to lay down our lives for the brethren.* To the same effect He said to Peter, whom He wished to make a good shepherd, not in Peter's own person, but as a member of His body: " Peter, lovest thou me? Feed my sheep." This He did once, again, and a third time, to the disciple's sorrow. And when the Lord had questioned him as often as He judged it needful, that he who had thrice denied might thrice confess Him, and had a third time given him the charge to feed His sheep, He said to him, " When thou wast young, thou girdedst thyself, and walkedst whither thou wouldest: but when thou shalt be old, thou shalt stretch forth thy hands, and another shall gird thee, and carry thee whither thou wouldest not." And the evangelist has explained the Lord's meaning: " But this spake He, signifying by what death he should glorify God." [6] " Feed my sheep " applies, then, to this, that thou shouldst lay down thy life for my sheep.

3. And now when He saith, " As the Father knoweth me, even so know I the Father," who can be ignorant of His meaning? For He knoweth the Father by Himself, and we by Him. That He hath knowledge by Himself, we know already: that we also have knowledge by Him, we have like-

---

[2] Chap. xv. 5.　　　　　　　[3] 1 John iii. 16.
[4] Prov. xxiii. 1, 2, according to the Septuagint, whose reading of verse 2 must have been somewhat different from that of the present Hebrew text, with which our English version pretty closely agrees: " And thou shalt put a knife to thy throat, if thou art a man of appetite " (*or perhaps,* " if thou hast control over thy appetite," אִם־בַּעַל נֶפֶשׁ אָתָּה). So somewhat similarly the Vulgate, which makes the last clause, " if thou hast power over thy life."—Tr.
[5] This clause, " for the edification," etc., is wanting in many of the mss.
[6] Chap. xxi. 15-19.

wise learned, for this also we have learned of Him. For He Himself hath said: "No one hath seen God at any time; but the only-begotten Son, who is in the bosom of the Father, He hath declared Him." [1] And so by Him do we also get this knowledge, to whom He hath declared Him. In another place also He saith: "No one knoweth the Son, but the Father; neither knoweth any one the Father, save the Son, and he to whomsoever the Son will reveal Him." [2] As He then knoweth the Father by Himself, and we know the Father by Him; so into the sheepfold He entereth by Himself, and we by Him. We were saying that by Christ we have a door of entrance to you; and why? Because we preach Christ. We preach Christ; and therefore we enter in by the door. But Christ preacheth Christ, for He preacheth Himself; and so the Shepherd entereth in by Himself. When the light shows the other things that are seen in the light, does it need some other means of being made visible itself? The light, then, exhibits both other things and itself. Whatever we understand, we understand with the intellect: and how, save by the intellect, do we understand the intellect itself? But does one in the same way with the bodily eye see both other things and [the eye] itself? For though men see with their eyes, yet their own eyes they see not. The eye of the flesh sees other things, itself it cannot [see]: but the intellect understands itself as well other things. In the same way as the intellect seeth itself, so also doth Christ preach Himself. If He preacheth Himself, and by preaching entereth into thee, He entereth into thee by Himself. And He is the door to the Father, for there is no way of approach to the Father but by Him. "For there is one God and one Mediator between God and men, the man Christ Jesus." [3] Many things are expressed by a word: all that I have just said, I have said, of course, by means of words. If I were wishing to speak also of a word itself, how could I do so but by the use of the word? And thus both many things are expressed by a word, which are not the same as the word, and the word itself can only be expressed by means of the word. By the Lord's help we have been copious in illustration. Remember, then, how the Lord Jesus Christ is both the door and the Shepherd: the door, in presenting Himself to view; the Shepherd, in entering in by Himself. And indeed, brethren, because He is the Shepherd, He hath given to His members to be so likewise.

For both Peter, and Paul, and the other apostles were, as all good bishops are, shepherds. But none of us calleth himself the door. This—the way of entrance for the sheep—He has retained as exclusively belonging to Himself. In short, Paul discharged the office of a good shepherd when he preached Christ, because he entered by the door. But when the undisciplined sheep began to create schisms, and to set up other doors before them, not of entrance to their joint assembly, but for falling away into divisions, saying, some of them, "I am of Paul;" others, "I am of Cephas;" others, "I of Apollos;" others, "I of Christ:" terrified for those who said, "I am of Paul,"—as if calling out to the sheep, Wretched ones, whither are you going? I am not the door,—he said, "Was Paul crucified for you? or were ye baptized in the name of Paul?" [4] But those who said, "I am of Christ," had found the door.

4. But of the one sheepfold and of the one Shepherd, you are now indeed being constantly reminded; for we have commended much the one sheepfold, preaching unity, that all the sheep should enter by Christ, and none of them should follow Donatus. Nevertheless, for what particular reason this was said by the Lord, is sufficiently apparent. For He was speaking among the Jews, and had been specially sent to the Jews, not for the sake of that class who were bound up in their inhuman hatred and persistently abiding in darkness, but for the sake of some in the nation whom He calls His sheep: of whom He saith, "I am not sent but to the lost sheep of the house of Israel." [5] He knew them even amid the crowd of His raging foes, and foresaw them in the peace of believing. What, then, does He mean by saying, "I am not sent but to the lost sheep of the house of Israel," but that He exhibited His bodily presence only to the people of Israel? He did not proceed Himself to the Gentiles, but sent: to the people of Israel He both sent and came in person, that those who proved despisers should receive the greater judgment, because favored also with the sight of His actual presence. The Lord Himself was there: there He chose a mother: there He wished to be conceived, to be born, to shed His blood: there are His footprints,[6] now objects of adoration where last He stood, and

---

1 Chap. i. 18.　　2 Matt. xi. 27.　　3 1 Tim. ii. 5.

4 1 Cor. i. 12, 13.　　5 Matt. xv. 24.
6 Of Christ's footprints on Mount Olivet, impressed on the ground, there is mention made in the works of Jerome, in the book on "Hebrew places," and in Bede, in the names of places in the Acts of the Apostles; as likewise in the sacred history of Sulpitius Severus, Book ii.—MIGNE. The text is somewhat uncertain, but indicates the existence of "holy places" in Augustin's day, and certain acts of worship performed in their honor.—TR.

whence He ascended to heaven: but to the Gentiles He only sent.

5. But perhaps some one thinks that, as He Himself came not to us, but sent, we have not heard His own voice, but only the voice of those whom He sent. Far from it: let such a thought be banished from your hearts; for He Himself was in those whom He sent. Listen to Paul himself whom He sent; for Paul was specially sent as an apostle to the Gentiles; and it is Paul who, terrifying them not with himself but with Him, saith, "Do ye wish to receive a proof of Him who speaketh in me, that is, of Christ?"[1] Listen also to the Lord Himself. "And other sheep I have," that is, among the Gentiles, "which are not of this fold," that is, of the people of Israel: "them also must I bring." Therefore, even when it is by the instrumentality of His servants, it is He and not another that bringeth them. Listen further: "They shall hear my voice." See here also, it is He Himself who speaks by His servants, and it is His voice that is heard in those whom He sends. "That there may be one fold, and one shepherd." Of these two flocks, as of two walls, is the corner-stone formed.[2] And thus is He both door and the corner-stone: all by way of comparison, none of them literally.

6. For I have said so before, and earnestly pressed it on your notice, and those who comprehend it are wise, yea, those who are wise do comprehend it; and yet let those who are not yet intellectually enlightened, keep hold by faith of what they cannot as yet understand. Christ is many things metaphorically, which strictly speaking[3] He is not. Metaphorically Christ is both a rock, and a door, and a corner-stone, and a shepherd, and a lamb, and a lion. How numerous are such similitudes, and as many more as would take too long to enumerate! But if you select the strict significations of things as you are accustomed to see them, then He is neither a rock, for He is not hard and senseless; nor a door, for no artisan made Him; nor a corner-stone, for He was not constructed by a builder; nor a shepherd, for He is no keeper of four-footed animals; nor a lion, as it ranks among the beasts of the forest; nor a lamb, as it belongs to the flock. All such, then, are by way of comparison. But what is He properly? "In the beginning was the Word, and the Word was with God, and the Word was God [God was the Word]." And what, as He appeared in human nature? "And the Word was made flesh, and dwelt among us [in us]."[4]

7. Hear also what follows. "Therefore doth my Father love me," He saith, "because I lay down my life, that I might take it again." What is this that He says? "Therefore doth my Father love me:" because I die, that I may rise again.[5] For the "I" is uttered with special emphasis: "Because _I_ lay down," He saith, "_I_ lay down my life," "_I_ lay down." What is that "I lay down"? I LAY it down. Let the Jews no longer boast: they might rage, but they could have no power: let them rage as they can; if I were unwilling to lay down my life, what would all their raging effect? By one answer of His they were prostrated in the dust: when they were asked, "Whom seek ye?" they said, "Jesus;" and on His saying to them, "I am He, they went backward, and fell to the ground."[6] Those who thus fell to the ground at one word of Christ when about to die, what will they do at the sound of His voice when coming to judgment? "I, I," I say, "lay down my life, that I may take it again." Let not the Jews boast, as if they had prevailed; He Himself laid down His life. "I laid me down [to sleep]," He says [elsewhere]. You know the psalm: "I laid me down and slept; and I awaked [rose up], for the Lord sustaineth me." What of that—"I lay down"? Because it was my pleasure, I did so. What does "I lay down" mean? I died. Was it not a lying down to sleep on His part, who, when He pleased, rose from the tomb as He would from a bed? But He loves to give glory to the Father, that He may stir us up to glorify our Creator. For in adding, "I arose, for the Lord sustaineth me;" think you there was here a kind of failing in His power, so that, while He had it in His own power to die, He had it not in His power to rise again? So, indeed, the words seem to imply when not more closely considered. "I lay down to sleep;" that is, I did so, because I pleased. "And I arose:" why? "Because the Lord sustaineth [will sustain] me."[7] What then? wouldst Thou not have power to rise of Thyself? If Thou hadst not the power, Thou wouldst not have said, "I have power to lay down my life, and I have power to take it again." But, as showing that not only did the Father raise the Son, but the Son also raised Himself,

---

[1] 2 Cor. xiii. 3.
[2] Eph. ii. 11-22.
[3] _Per proprietatem._
[4] Chap. i. 1, 14.

[5] Migne says that "there is, perhaps, in this passage something either superfluous or lacking." But there does not seem any real cause for such a supposition.—Tr.
[6] Chap. xviii. 4-6.
[7] Ps. iii. 5. It need scarcely be said that this psalm cannot bear the Messianic interpretation attached to it by Augustin, any more than Prov. xxiii. 1, 2, similarly applied in Sec. 2 of this lecture; and frequently elsewhere. But the accommodation at the will of the writer of all Old Testament Scripture equally to such a purpose was characteristic of the age.—Tr.

hear how, in another passage in the Gospel, He saith, " Destroy this temple, and in three days I will raise it up." And the evangelist adds: " But this He spake of the temple of is body."[1] For only that which died was restored to life. The Word is not mortal, His soul is not mortal. If even thine dieth not, could the Lord's be subject to death?

8. How can I know, thou wilt say, that mine dieth not? Slay it not thyself, and it cannot die. How, thou asketh, can I slay my soul? To say nothing meanwhile of other sins, " The mouth that lieth, slayeth the soul."[2] How, thou sayest, can I be sure that it dieth not? Listen to the Lord Himself giving security to His servant: " Be not afraid of them that kill the body, and after that have no more that they can do." But what in the plainest terms does He say? " Fear Him who hath power to slay both soul and body in hell."[3] Here you have the fact that it dieth, and that it doth not die. What is its dying? What is dying to thy flesh? Dying, to thy flesh, is the losing of its life: dying to thy soul, is the losing of its life. The life of thy flesh is thy soul: the life of thy soul is thy God. As the flesh dies in losing the soul, which is its life, so the soul dieth in losing God, who is its life. Of a certainty, then, the soul is immortal. Manifestly immortal, for it liveth even when dead. For what the apostle said of the luxurious widow, may also be said of the soul if it has lost its God, " she is dead while she liveth."[4]

9. How, then, does the Lord lay down His life [soul]?[5] Let us, brethren, inquire into this a little more carefully. The time is not so pressing as is usual on the Lord's day: we have leisure, and theirs will be the profit who have assembled to-day also to wait on the Word of God. " I lay down my life," He says. Who lays down? What lays He down? What is Christ? The Word and man. Not man as being flesh alone: but as man consists of flesh and soul, so, in Christ there is a complete humanity. For He would not have assumed the baser part, and left the better behind, seeing that the soul of man is certainly superior to the body. Since, then, there is entire manhood in Christ, what is Christ? The Word, I repeat, and man. What is the Word and man? The Word, soul, and flesh. Keep hold of that, for there has been no lack of heretics on this point also, expelled as they were some time ago from the catholic truth, but still persisting,

like thieves and robbers who enter not by the door, to lay their snares around the fold. These heretics are termed Apollinarians,[6] and have ventured to assert dogmatically that Christ is only the word and flesh, and contend that He did not assume a human soul. And yet some of them could not deny that there was a soul in Christ. See their intolerable absurdity and madness. They would have Him to possess an irrational soul, but deny Him a rational one. They allowed Him a mere animal, they deprived Him of a human, soul. But they took away Christ's reason by losing their own. Let it be otherwise with us, who have been nourished and established in the catholic faith. Accordingly, on this occasion I would remind your Charity, that, as in former lectures, we have given you sufficient instruction against the Sabellians and Arians,—the Sabellians, who say, The Father is the same as the Son—the Arians, who say, The Father is one being, the Son is another, as if the Father and Son were not of the same substance -- and also, provided you remember as you ought, against the Photinian heretics, who have asserted that Christ was mere man, and destitute of Godhead:[7] and against the Manicheans, who maintain that He was God only without any true humanity: we may, on this occasion, in speaking about the soul, give you some instruction also in opposition to the Apollinarians, who say that our Lord Jesus Christ had no human soul, that is, a rational intelligent soul,—that soul, I mean, by which, as men, we differ from the brutes.

10. In what sense, then, did our Lord say here, " I have power to lay down my soul [life]" ? Who lays down his soul, and takes it again? Is it as being the Word that Christ does so? Or is it the human soul He possesses that lays down and resumes its own existence? Or is it His fleshly nature that lays down its life and takes it again? Let us sift each of the three questions I have suggested, and choose that which conforms to the standard of truth. For if we say that the Word of God laid down His soul, and took it again, we should have to fear the entrance of a wicked thought, and have it said to us: Then there was a time when that soul was separated from the Word, and a time, after His assumption of that soul, when He was without a soul. I see, indeed, that the Word

---

[1] Chap. ii. 19, 21.　　　　　　　[2] Wisd. i. 11.
[3] Matt. x. 28, and Luke xii. 4, 5.　　　[4] 1 Tim. v. 6.
[5] The word *anima*, according to Augustin's explanation of it above, may be rendered in these sections either " soul " or " life." The original also is ψύχη.—TR.

[6] From Apollinaris, bishop of Alexandria, who held that the body which Christ assumed had only a sensitive, and not a rational soul, and that His divine nature supplied the place of the latter. His doctrines were condemned by the Council of Alexandria, A.D. 362, and he himself was deposed by the Council of Rome, A.D. 378.—TR.
[7] *Sine deo :* which, however, is wanting in all the MSS.

was once without a human soul, but only so, when "in the beginning was the Word, and the Word was with God, and the Word was God." But from the time that the Word was made flesh, to dwell amongst us,[1] and manhood was assumed by the Word, that is, our whole nature, soul and flesh, what more could His passion and death do than separate the body from the soul? It separated not the soul from the Word. For if the Lord died, yea, because He died (for He did so for us on the cross), doubtless His flesh breathed out that which was its life: for a short time the soul forsook the flesh, although destined by its own return to raise the flesh again to life. But I cannot say that the soul was separated from the Word. He said to the soul of the thief, "To-day shalt thou be with me in paradise."[2] He forsook not the believing soul of the robber, and did He abandon His own? Surely not; but when the Lord took that of the other into His keeping, He certainly retained His own in indissoluble union. If, on the other hand, we say that the soul laid down and reassumed itself, we fall into the greatest absurdity; for what was not separated from the Word, was inseparable from itself.

11. Let us turn, then, to what is true and easily understood. Take the case of any man, who does not consist of the word and soul and flesh, but only of soul and flesh; and let us inquire how any such man lays down his life. Can no ordinary man do so? Thou mayest say to me: No man has power to lay down his life [soul], and to take it again. But were not a man able to lay down his life, the Apostle John would not say, "As Christ laid down his life for us, even so ought we also to lay down our lives for the brethren."[3] Therefore may we also (if only we are filled with His courage, for without Him we can do nothing) lay down our lives for the brethren. When some holy martyr has laid down his life for the brethren, who laid it down, and what laid he down? If we understand this, we shall perceive in what sense it was said by Christ, "I have power to lay down my life." Art thou prepared, O man, to die for Christ? I am prepared, he replies. Let me repeat the question in other words. Art thou prepared to lay down thy life for Christ? And to these words he makes me the same reply, I am prepared, as he had, when I said, Art thou prepared to die? To lay down one's life [soul], is, then, the same as to die. But in whose behalf is the sacrifice in this case? For all men, when they die, lay down their life; but it is not all who lay it down for Christ. And no one has power to resume what he has laid down. But Christ both laid it down for us, and did so when it pleased Him; and when it pleased Him, He took it again. To lay down one's soul then, is to die. As also the Apostle Peter said to the Lord: "I will lay down my life [soul] for Thy sake;"[4] that is, I will die for Thy sake. View it, then, as referable to the flesh: the flesh layeth down its life, and the flesh taketh it again; not, indeed, the flesh by its own power, but by the power of Him that inhabiteth it. The flesh, then, layeth down its life in expiring. Look at the Lord Himself on the cross: He said, "I thirst:" those who were present dipped a sponge in vinegar, fastened it to a reed, and applied it to His mouth; then, having received it, He said, "It is finished;" meaning, All is fulfilled which had been prophesied regarding me as, prior to my death, still in the future. And because He had the power, when He pleased, to lay down His life, after He had said, "It is finished," what adds the evangelist? "And He bowed His head, and gave up the spirit."[5] This is to lay down the soul [life]. Only let your Charity attend to this. "He bowed His head, and gave up the spirit." Who gave up? what gave He up? He gave up the spirit; His flesh gave it up. What means, the flesh gave it up? The flesh sent it forth, breathed it out. For so, in becoming separated from the spirit, we are said to expire. Just as getting outside the paternal soil is to be expatriated, turning aside from the track is to deviate; so to become separated from the spirit is to expire; and that spirit is the soul [life]. Accordingly, when the soul quits the flesh, and the flesh remains without the soul, then is a man said to lay down his soul [his human life]. When did Christ lay down His life? When it pleased the Word. For sovereign authority resided in the Word; and therein lay the power to determine when the flesh should lay down its life, and when it should take it again.

12. If, then, the flesh laid down its life, how did Christ lay down His life? For the flesh is not Christ. Certainly in this way, that Christ is both flesh, and soul, and the Word; and yet these three things are not three Christs, but one. Ask thine own human nature, and from thyself ascend to what is above thee, and which, if not yet able to be understood, can at least be believed. For in the same way that one man is soul and body, is one Christ both the Word and man.

---

[1] Chap. i. 1, 14.   [2] Luke xxiii. 43.   [3] 1 John iii. 16.   [4] Chap. xiii. 37.   [5] Chap. xix. 28-30.

Consider what I have said, and understand. The soul and body are two things, but one man: the Word and man are two things, but one Christ. Apply, then, the subject to any man. Where is now the Apostle Paul? If one answer, At rest with Christ, he speaks truly. And likewise, should one reply, In the sepulchre at Rome, he is equally right. The one answer I get refers to his soul, the other to his flesh. And yet we do not say that there are two Apostle Pauls, one who rests in Christ, another who was laid in the sepulchre; although we may say that the Apostle Paul liveth in Christ, and that the same apostle lieth dead in the tomb. Some one dieth, and we say, He was a good man, and faithful; he is in peace with the Lord: and then immediately, Let us attend his obsequies, and lay him in the sepulchre. Thou art about to bury one whom thou hadst just declared to be in peace with God; for the latter regards the soul which blooms eternally, and the other the body, which is laid down in corruption. But while the partnership of the flesh and soul has received the name of man, the same name is now applied to either of them, singly and by itself.

13. Let no one, then, be perplexed, when he hears that the Lord has said, "I lay down my life, and I take it again." The flesh layeth it down, but by the power of the Word: the flesh taketh it again, but by the same power. Even His own name, the Lord Christ, was applied to His flesh alone. How can you prove it? says some one. We believe of a certainty not only in God the Father, but also in Jesus Christ His Son, our only Lord: and this that I have just said contains the whole, in Jesus Christ His Son, our only Lord. Understand that the whole is here: the Word, and soul, and flesh. At all events thou confessest what is also held by the same faith, that thou believest in that Christ who was crucified and buried. *Ergo,* thou deniest not that Christ was buried; and yet it was the burial only of His flesh. For had the soul been there, He would not have been dead: but if it was a true death, and its resurrection real, it was previously without life in the tomb; and yet it was Christ that was buried. And so the flesh apart from the soul was also Christ, for it was only the flesh that was buried. Learn the same likewise in the words of an apostle. "Let this mind," he says, "be in you, which was also in Christ Jesus: who, being in the form of God, thought it not robbery to be equal with God." Who, save Christ Jesus, as respects His na-

ture as the Word, is God with God? But look at what follows: "But emptied Himself, and took upon Him the form of a servant; being made in the likeness of men, and found in fashion as a man." And who is this, but the same Christ Jesus Himself? But here we have now all the parts, both the Word in that form of God which assumed the form of a servant, and the soul and the flesh in that form of a servant which was assumed by the form of God. "He humbled Himself, and became obedient unto death."[1] Now in His death, it was His flesh only that was slain by the Jews. For if He said to His disciples, "Fear not them that kill the body, but are not able to kill the soul,"[2] how could they do more in His own case than kill the body? And yet in the slaying of His flesh, it was Christ that was slain. Accordingly, when the flesh laid down its life, Christ laid it down; and when the flesh, in order to its resurrection, assumed its life, Christ assumed it. Nevertheless this was done, not by the power of the flesh, but of Him who assumed both soul and flesh, that in them these very things might receive fulfillment.

14. "This commandment," He says, "have I received of my Father." The Word received not the commandment in word, but in the only-begotten Word of the Father every commandment resides. But when the Son is said to receive of the Father what He possesses essentially in Himself, as it is said, "As the Father hath life in Himself, so hath He given to the Son to have life in Himself,"[3] while the Son is Himself the life, there is no lessening of His authority, but the setting forth of His generation. For the Father added not after-gifts as to a son whose state was imperfect at birth, but on Him whom He begat in absolute perfection He bestowed all gifts in begetting. In this manner He gave Him equality with Himself, and yet begat Him not in a state of inequality. But while the Lord thus spake, for the light was shining in the darkness, and the darkness comprehended it not,[4] "there was a dissension again created among the Jews for these sayings, and many of them said, He hath a devil, and is mad: why hear ye him?" This was the thickest darkness. Others said, "These are not the words of him that hath a devil; can a devil open the eyes of the blind?" The eyes of such were now begun to be opened.

[1] Phil. ii. 6-8.　　[2] Matt. x. 28.
[3] John v. 26.　　[4] Chap. i. 5.

TRACTATE XLVIII.

Chapter X. 22–42.

1. As I have already charged you, beloved, you ought steadfastly to bear in mind that Saint John the evangelist would not have us be always nourished with milk, but fed with solid food. Still, whoever is hardly able as yet to partake of the solid food of God's word, let him find nourishment in the milk of faith; and the word which he cannot understand, let him not hesitate to believe. For faith is the deserving: understanding, the reward. In the very labor of intent application the eye of our mind struggles[1] to get rid of the foul films of human mists, and be cleared up to the word of God. Labor, then, will not be declined if love is present; for you know that he who loves his labor is insensible to its pain. For no labor is grievous to those who love it. If cupidity on the part of the avaricious endures so great toils, what in our case will not love endure?

2. Listen to the Gospel: "And it was at Jerusalem the Encœnia."[2] Encœnia was the festival of the dedication of the temple. For in Greek *kainos* means *new;* and whenever there was some new dedication, it was called Encœnia.[3] And now this word is come into common use; if one puts on a new coat, he is said "encœniare" (to renovate, or to hold an *encœnia*). For the Jews celebrated in a solemn manner the day on which the temple was dedicated; and it was the very feast day when the Lord spake what has just been read.

3. "It was winter. And Jesus walked in the temple in Solomon's porch. Then came the Jews round about Him, and said unto Him, How long dost thou keep our mind in suspense? If thou be the Christ, tell us plainly." They were not desiring the truth, but preparing a calumny. "It was winter," and they were chill; because they were slow to approach that divine fire. For to approach is to believe: he who believes, approaches; who denies, retires. The soul is not moved by the feet, but by the affections. They had become icy cold to the sweetness of loving Him, and they burned with the desire of doing Him an injury. They were far away, while there beside Him. It was not with

them a nearer approach in believing, but the pressure of persecution. They sought to hear the Lord saying, I am Christ; and probably enough they only thought of the Christ in a human way. The prophets preached Christ; but the Godhead of Christ asserted in the prophets and in the gospel itself is not perceived even by heretics; and how much less by Jews, so long as the vail is upon their heart?[4] In short, in a certain place, the Lord Jesus, knowing that their views of the Christ were cast in a human mould, not in the Divine, taking His stand on the human ground, and not on that where along with the assumption of humanity He also continued Divine, He said to them, "What think ye of Christ? Whose Son is He?" Following their own opinion, they replied, "Of David." For so they had read, and this only they retained; because while they read of His divinity, they did not understand it. But the Lord, to pin them down to some inquiry touching the divinity of Him whose apparent weakness they despised, answered them: "How, then, doth David in spirit call Him Lord, saying, The Lord said unto my Lord, Sit Thou on my right hand, till I put Thine enemies under Thy feet? If David, then, in spirit call Him Lord, how is He his son?"[5] He did not deny, but questioned. Let no one think, on hearing this, that the Lord Jesus denied that He was the Son of David. Had Christ the Lord given any such denial, He would not have enlightened the blind who so addressed Him. For as He was passing by one day, two blind men, who were sitting by the wayside, cried out, "Have mercy upon us, thou Son of David." And on hearing these words He had mercy on them. He stood still, healed, enlightened them;[6] for He owned the name. The Apostle Paul also says, "Who was made of the seed of David according to the flesh;"[7] and in his Epistle to Timothy, "Remember that Jesus Christ was raised from the dead, [He that is] of the seed of David, according to my gospel."[8] For the Virgin Mary drew her origin, and hence our Lord also, from the seed of David.

4. The Jews made this inquiry of Christ,

---

[1] *Desudat*, struggles to sweating.
[2] *Encœnia*, ἐγκαίνια, from ἐν and καινός, *new.*
[3] It was a feast, however, instituted by Judas Maccabæus, to commemorate his purification of the temple, after its profanation by Antiochus.—Tr.

[4] 2 Cor. iii. 15.   [5] Matt. xxii. 42–45.   [6] Matt. xx. 30–34.
[7] Rom. i. 3.   [8] 2 Tim. ii. 8.

chiefly in order that, should He say, I am Christ, they might, in accordance with the only sense they attached to such a name, that He was of the seed of David, calumniate Him with aiming at the kingly power. There is more than this in His answer to them: they wished to calumniate Him with claiming to be the Son of David. He replied that He was the Son of God. And how? Listen: "Jesus answered them, I tell you, and ye believe not: the works that I do in my Father's name, they bear witness of me: but ye believe not; because ye are not of my sheep." Ye have already learned above (in Lecture XLV.) who the sheep are: be ye sheep. They are sheep through believing, sheep in following the Shepherd, sheep in not despising their Redeemer, sheep in entering by the door, sheep in going out and finding pasture, sheep in the enjoyment of eternal life. What did He mean, then, in saying to them, "Ye are not of my sheep"? That He saw them predestined to everlasting destruction, not won to eternal life by the price of His own blood.

5. "My sheep hear my voice, and I know them, and they follow me: and I give unto them eternal life." This is the pasture. If you recollect, He had said before, "And he shall go in and out, and find pasture." We have entered by believing—we go out at death.[1] But as we have entered by the door of faith, so, as believers, we quit the body; for it is in going out by that same door that we are able to find pasture. The good pasture is called eternal life; there no blade withereth—all is green and flourishing. There is a plant commonly said to be ever-living; there only is it found to live. "I will give," He says, "unto them," unto my sheep, "eternal life." Ye are on the search for calumnies, just because your only thoughts are of the life that is present.

6. "And they shall never perish:" you may hear the undertone, as if He had said to them, Ye shall perish for ever, because ye are not of my sheep. "No one shall pluck them out of my hand." Give still greater heed to this: "That which my Father gave me is greater than all."[2] What can the wolf do? What can the thief and the robber? They destroy none but those predestined to destruction. But of those sheep of which the apostle says, "The Lord knoweth them that are His;"[3] and "Whom He did foreknow, them He also did predestinate; and whom He did predestinate, them He also called; and whom He called, them He also justified; and whom He justified, them He also glorified;"[4]—there is none of such sheep as these that the wolf seizes, or the thief steals, or the robber slays. He, who knows what He gave for them, is sure of their number. And it is this that He says: "No one shall pluck them out of my hand;" and in reference also to the Father, "That which my Father gave me is greater than all." What did the Father give to the Son that was greater than all? To be His own only-begotten Son. What, then, means "gave"? Was He to whom He gave previously existent, or gave He in the act of begetting? For if He previously existed to whom He gave the gift of Sonship, there was a time when He was, and was not the Son. Far be it from us to suppose that the Lord Christ ever was, and yet was not the Son. Of us such a thing may be said: there was a time when we were the sons of men, but were not the sons of God. For we are made the sons of God by grace, but He by nature, for such was He born. And yet not so, as that one may say, He did not exist till He was born; for He, who was coeternal with the Father, was never unborn. Let him who is wise understand: and whoever understands not, let him believe and be nourished, and he will come to understanding. The Word of God was always with the Father, and always the Word; and because the Word, therefore the Son. So then, always the Son, and always equal. For it is not by growth but by birth that He is equal, who was always born, the Son of the Father, God of God, coeternal of the Eternal. But the Father is not God of[5] the Son: the Son is God of[5] the Father; therefore in begetting the Son, the Father "gave" Him to be God, in begetting He gave Him to be coeternal with Himself, in begetting He gave Him to be His equal. This is that which is greater than all. How is the

---

[1] The *pasture*, and the *going in and out*, refer rather to Christ's guidance and nourishment of His people in this present life.—TR.

[2] There is a considerable difference in these words, as rendered by Augustin, from that which is found in our English version: "My Father who gave them me is greater than all." The latter is certainly the more intelligible and suitable to the context. But the variation of the mss. between the two readings, "ὅ . . μεῖζον" and "ὅς . . μεῖζων," is somewhat remarkable. The far larger number are certainly in favor of the latter, as followed by our English Bibles, but the former is countenanced by some of the more important; while others which have ὅς have at the same time μεῖζον (neut.), and *vice versa*. Thus the Sinaitic reads ὅ (neut.), and μεῖζων (masc.); while the Alexandrian has ὅς (masc.), and μεῖζον (neut.). The Vulgate, and some of the other early versions, have Augustin's reading; but the Peshito (Syriac), which is the earliest of them all, supports the other, its literal rendering being, "For my Father, who gave to me, than all greater [is] He." Modern critics have generally adopted the masc. reading,—Griesbach, Bengel, and others, almost ignoring the other, and Stier dismissing it as wholly inadmissible; while Alford, in a very strange and unsatisfactory way, gives the neuter in his Greek text, and not a syllable of explanation in his notes. It seems to us that the transcriber had first let ὅ creep into the text, perhaps from the previous similar expression in chap. vi. 39; and then μεῖζον was made neuter by some other to agree with it. This is more likely than the reverse; and our English reading is every way more satisfactory than Augustin's.—TR.

[3] Tim. ii. 19.   [4] Rom. viii. 29, 30.   [5] De.

Son the life, and the possessor of life? What He has, He is: as for thee, thou art one thing, thou hast another. For example, thou hast wisdom, but art thou wisdom itself? In short, because thou thyself art not that which thou hast, shouldst thou lose what thou hast, thou returnest to the state of no longer having it: and sometimes thou re-acquirest, sometimes thou losest. As our eye has no light inherently in itself, it opens, and admits it; it shuts, and loses it. It is not thus that the Son of God is God—not thus that He is the Word of the Father; and not thus is He the Word, that passes away with the sound, but that which abides in its birth. In such a way hath He wisdom that He is Himself wisdom, and maketh men wise: and life, that He is Himself the life, and maketh others alive. This is that which is greater than all. The evangelist John himself looked to heaven and earth when wishing to speak of the Son of God; he looked, and rose above them all. He thought on the thousands of angelic armies above the heavens; he thought, and, like the eagle soaring beyond the clouds, his mind overpassed the whole creation: he rose beyond all that was great, and arrived at that which was greater than all; and said, "In the beginning was the Word." But because He, of[1] whom is the Word, is not of the Word, and the Word is of Him, whose Word He is; therefore He says, "That which the Father gave me," namely, to be His Word, His only-begotten Son, the brightness of His light, "is greater than all." Therefore, "No one," He says, "plucketh my sheep out of my hand. No one can pluck them out of my Father's hand."

7. "Out of my hand," and "out of my Father's hand." What is this, "No one plucketh them out of my hand," and "No one plucketh them out of my Father's hand"? Have the Father and Son one hand, or is the Son Himself, shall we say, the hand of His Father? If by hand we are to understand power, the power of Father and Son is one; for their Godhead is one. But if we mean hand in the way spoken of by the prophet, "And to whom is the arm of the Lord revealed?"[2] the Father's hand is the Son Himself, which is not to be so understood as if God had the human form, and, as it were, bodily members; but that all things were made by Him. For men also are in the habit of calling other men their hands, by whom they get done what they wish. And sometimes also the very work done by a man's hand is called his hand; as one is said to rec-

ognize his hand when he recognizes what he has written. Since, then, there are many ways of speaking of the hand of a man, who literally has a hand among the members of his body; how much rather must there be more than one way of understanding it, when we read of the hand of God, who has no bodily form? And in this way it is better here, by the hand of the Father and Son, to understand the power of the Father and the Son; lest, in taking here the hand of the Father as spoken of the Son, some carnal thought also about the Son Himself should set us looking for the Son as somehow to be similarly regarded as the hand of Christ. Therefore, "no one plucketh them out of my Father's hand;" that is, no one plucketh them from me.

8. But that there may be no more room for hesitation, hear what follows: "I and my Father are one." Up to this point the Jews were able to bear Him; they heard, "I and my Father are one," and they bore it no longer; and hardened in their own way, they had recourse to stones. "They took up stones to stone Him." The Lord, because He suffered not what He was unwilling to suffer, and only suffered what He was pleased to suffer, still addresses them while desiring to stone Him. "The Jews took up stones to stone Him. Jesus answered them, Many good works have I showed you from my Father; for which of those works do ye stone me? And they answered, For a good work we stone thee not, but for blasphemy, and because that thou, being a man, makest thyself God." Such was their reply to His words, "I and my Father are one." You see here that the Jews understood what the Arians understand not. For they were angry on this account, that they felt it could not be said, "I and my Father are one," save where there was equality of the Father and the Son.

9. But see what answer the Lord gave to their dull apprehension. He saw that they could not bear the brilliance of the truth, and He tempered it with words. "Is it not written in your law," that is, as given to you, "that I said, Ye are gods?"[3] And the Lord called all the Scriptures generally, the law: although elsewhere He speaks more definitely of the law, distinguishing it from the prophets; as it is said, "The law and the prophets were until John;"[4] and "On these two commandments hang all the law and the prophets."[5] Sometimes, however, He divided the same Scriptures into three parts, as where He saith, "All things must be fulfilled which

---

[1] *De.* [2] Isa. liii. 1. [3] Ps. lxxxii. 6. [4] Luke xvi. 16. [5] Matt. xxii. 40.

were written in the law, and the prophets, and the psalms, concerning me.."[1] But now He includes the psalms also under the name of the law, where it is written, "I said, Ye are gods. If He calleth them gods, to whom the word of God came, and the Scripture cannot be broken: say ye of Him, whom the Father hath sanctified, and sent into the world, Thou blasphemest; because I said, I am the Son of God?" If the word of God came to men, that they might be called gods, how can the very Word of God, who is with God, be otherwise than God? If by the word of God men become gods, if by fellowship they become gods, can He by whom they have fellowship not be God? If lights which are lit are gods, is the light which enlighteneth not God? If through being warmed in a way by saving fire they are constituted gods, is He who gives them the warmth other than God? Thou approachest the light and art enlightened, and numbered among the sons of God; if thou withdrawest from the light, thou fallest into obscurity, and art accounted in darkness; but that light approacheth not, because it never recedeth from itself. If, then, the word of God maketh you gods, how can the Word of God be otherwise than God? Therefore did the Father sanctify His Son, and send Him into the world. Perhaps some one may be saying: If the Father sanctified Him, was there then a time when He was not sanctified? He sanctified in the same way as He begat Him. For in the act of begetting He gave Him the power to be holy, because He begat Him in holiness. For if that which is sanctified was unholy before, how can we say to God the Father, "Hallowed be Thy name"?[2]

10. "If I do not the works of my Father, believe me not. But if I do, though ye will not believe me, believe the works; that ye may know and believe that the Father is in me, and I in Him." The Son says not, "the Father is in me, and I in Him," as men can say it. For if we think well, we are in God; and if we live well, God is in us: believers, by participating in His grace, and being illuminated by Himself, are in Him, and He in us. But not so is it with the only-begotten Son: He is in the Father, and the Father in Him; as one who is equal is in him whose equal he is. In short, we can sometimes say, We are in God, and God is in us; but can we say, I and God are one? Thou art in God, because God contains thee; God is in thee, because thou art become the temple of God: but because thou art in God, and God is in thee, canst thou say, He that seeth

me seeth God; as the Only-begotten said, "He that hath seen me, hath seen the Father also;"[3] and "I and the Father are one"? Recognize the prerogative of the Lord, and the privilege of the servant. The prerogative of the Lord is equality with the Father: the privilege of the servant is fellowship with the Saviour.

11. "Therefore they sought to apprehend Him." Would they had apprehended by faith and understanding, not in wrath and murder! For now, my brethren, when I speak thus, it is the weak one wishing to apprehend what is strong, the small what is great, the fragile what is solid; and it is we ourselves—both you who are of the same matter as I am, and I myself who speak to you—who all wish to apprehend Christ. And what is it to apprehend Him? [If] thou hast understood, thou hast apprehended. But not as did the Jews: thou hast apprehended in order to possess, they wished to apprehend in order to make away with Him. And because this was the kind of apprehension they desired, what did He do to them? "He escaped out of their hands." They failed to apprehend Him, because they lacked the hand of faith. The Word was made flesh; but it was no great task to the Word to rescue His own flesh from fleshy hands. To apprehend the Word in the mind, is the right apprehension of Christ.

12. "And He went away again beyond Jordan, into the place where John at first baptized; and there He abode. And many resorted unto Him, and said, John, indeed, did no miracle." You remember what was said of John, that he was a light, and bore witness to the day.[4] Why, then, say these among themselves, "John did no miracle"? John, they say, signalized himself by no miracle; he did not put devils to flight, he drove away no fever, he enlightened not the blind, he raised not the dead, he fed not so many thousand men with five or seven loaves, he walked not upon the sea, he commanded not the winds and the waves. None of these things did John, and in all he said he bore witness to this man. By lamp-light we may advance to the day. "John did no miracle: but all things that John spake of this man were true." Here are those who apprehended in a different way from the Jews. The Jews wished to apprehend one who was departing from them, these apprehended one who remained with them. In a word, what is it that follows? "And many believed on Him."

---

[1] Luke xxiv. 44.   [2] Matt. vi. 9.   [3] Chap. xiv. 9.   [4] Chap. v. 35, 33.

TRACTATE XLIX.

Chapter XI. 1–54.

1. Among all the miracles wrought by our Lord Jesus Christ, the resurrection of Lazarus holds a foremost place in preaching. But if we consider attentively who did it, our duty is to rejoice rather than to wonder. A man was raised up by Him who made man: for He is the only One of the Father, by whom, as you know, all things were made. And if all things were made by Him, what wonder is it that one was raised by Him, when so many are daily brought into the world by His power? It is a greater deed to create men than to raise them again from the dead. Yet He deigned both to create and to raise again; to create all, to resuscitate some. For though the Lord Jesus did many such acts, yet all of them are not recorded; just as this same St. John the evangelist himself testifies, that Christ the Lord both said and did many things that are not recorded;[1] but such were chosen for record as seemed to suffice for the salvation of believers. Thou hast just heard that the Lord Jesus raised a dead man to life; and that is sufficient to let thee know that, were He so pleased, He might raise all the dead to life. And, indeed, this very work has He reserved in His own hands till the end of the world. For while you have heard that by a great miracle He raised one from the tomb who had been dead four days, "the hour is coming," as He Himself saith, "in the which all that are in the graves shall hear *His* voice, and shall come forth." He raised one who was putrid, and yet in that putrid carcase there was still the form of limbs; but at the last day He will by a word reconstitute ashes into human flesh. But it was needful then to do only some such deeds, that we, receiving them as tokens of His power, may put our trust in Him, and be preparing for that resurrection which shall be to life and not to judgment. So, indeed, He saith, "The hour is coming, in the which all that are in the graves shall hear *His* voice, and shall come forth; they that have done good, unto the resurrection of life; and they that have done evil, unto the resurrection of damnation."[2]

2. We have, however, read in the Gospel of three dead persons who were raised to life by the Lord, and, let us hope, to some good purpose. For surely the Lord's deeds are not merely deeds, but signs. And if they are signs, besides their wonderful character, they have some real significance: and to find out this in regard to such deeds is a somewhat harder task than to read or hear of them. We were listening with wonder, as at the sight of some mighty miracle enacted before our eyes, in the reading of the Gospel, how Lazarus was restored to life. If we turn our thoughts to the still more wonderful works of Christ, every one that believeth riseth again: if we all consider, and understand that more horrifying kind of death, every one who sinneth dies.[3] But every man is afraid of the death of the flesh; few, of the death of the soul. In regard to the death of the flesh, which must certainly come some time, all are on their guard against its approach: this is the source of all their labor. Man, destined to die, labors to avert his dying; and yet man, destined to live for ever, labors not to cease from sinning. And when he labors to avoid dying, he labors to no purpose, for its only result will be to put off death for a while, not to escape it; but if he refrain from sinning, his toil will cease, and he shall live for ever. Oh that we could arouse men, and be ourselves aroused along with them, to be as great lovers of the life that abideth, as men are of that which passeth away! What will a man not do who is placed under the peril of death? When the sword was overhanging their heads, men have given up every means of living they had in reserve. Who is there that has not made an immediate surrender of all, to escape being slain? And, after all, he has perhaps been slain. Who is there that, to save his life, has not been willing at once to lose his means of living, and prefer a life of beggary to a speedy death? Who has had it said to him, Be off to sea if you would escape with your life, and has delayed to do so? Who has had it said to him, Set to work if you would preserve your life, and has continued a sluggard? It is but little that God requires of us, that we may live for ever: and we neglect to obey Him. God says not to thee, Lose all you have, that you may live a

---

[1] Chap. xx. 30. [2] Chap. v. 28, 29.

[3] Another reading of this sentence may be : " If we reflect, it is by a more wonderful work of Christ that every one who believeth rises again to life: if we reflect all, and understand, it is by a more horrible death that every sinner dieth."

little time oppressed with toil; but, Give to the poor of what you have, that you may live always exempt from labor. The lovers of this temporal life, which is theirs, neither when, nor as long as they wish, are our accusers; and we accuse not ourselves in turn, so sluggish are we, so lukewarm about obtaining eternal life, which will be ours if we wish it, and will be imperishable when we have it; but this death which we fear, notwithstanding all our reluctance, will yet be ours in possession.

3. If, then, the Lord in the greatness of His grace and mercy raiseth our souls to life, that we may not die for ever, we may well understand that those three dead persons whom He raised in the body, have some figurative significance of that resurrection of the soul which is effected by faith: He raised up the ruler of the synagogue's daughter, while still lying in the house;[1] He raised up the widow's young son, while being carried outside the gates of the city;[2] and He raised up Lazarus, when four days in the grave. Let each one give heed to his own soul: in sinning he dies: sin is the death of the soul. But sometimes sin is committed only in thought. Thou hast felt delight in what is evil, thou hast assented to its commission, thou hast sinned; that assent has slain thee: but the death is internal, because the evil thought had not yet ripened into action. The Lord intimated that He would raise such a soul to life, in raising that girl, who had not yet been carried forth to the burial, but was lying dead in the house, as if sin still lay concealed. But if thou hast not only harbored a feeling of delight in evil, but hast also done the evil thing, thou hast, so to speak, carried the dead outside the gate: thou art already without, and being carried to the tomb. Yet such an one also the Lord raised to life, and restored to his widowed mother. If thou hast sinned, repent, and the Lord will raise thee up, and restore thee to thy mother Church. The third example of death is Lazarus. A grievous kind of death it is, and is distinguished as a habit of wickedness. For it is one thing to fall into sin, another to form the habit of sinning. He who falls into sin, and straightway submits to correction, will be speedily restored to life; for he is not yet entangled in the habit, he is not yet laid in the tomb. But he who has become habituated to sin, is buried, and has it properly said of him, "he stinketh;" for his character, like some horrible smell, begins to be of the worst repute. Such are all who

are habituated to crime, abandoned in morals. Thou sayest to such an one, Do not so. But when wilt thou be listened to by one on whom the earth is thus heaped, who is breeding corruption, and pressed down with the weight of habit? And yet the power of Christ was not unequal to the task of restoring such an one to life. We know, we have seen, we see every day men changing the very worst of habits, and adopting a better manner of life than that of those who blamed them. Thou detestedst such a man: look at the sister of Lazarus herself (if, indeed, it was she who anointed the Lord's feet with ointment, and wiped with her hair what she had washed with her tears), who had a better resurrection than her brother; she was delivered from the mighty burden of a sinful character. For she was a notorious sinner; and had it said of her, "Her many sins are forgiven her, for she has loved much."[3] We see many such, we know many: let none despair, but let none presume in himself. Both the one and the other are sinful. Let thine unwillingness to despair take such a turn as to lead thee to make choice of Him in whom alone thou mayest well presume.

4. So then the Lord also raised Lazarus to life. You have heard what type of character he represents; in other words, what is meant by the resurrection of Lazarus. Let us now, therefore, read over the passage; and as there is much in this lesson clear already, we shall not go into any detailed exposition, so as to take up more thoroughly the necessary points. "Now a certain man was sick, [named] Lazarus, of Bethany, the town of Mary and Martha, his sisters." In the previous lesson you remember that the Lord escaped from the hands of those who sought to stone Him, and went away beyond Jordan, where John baptized.[4] When the Lord therefore had taken up His abode there, Lazarus fell sick in Bethany, which was a town lying close to Jerusalem.

5. "But Mary was she who anointed the Lord with ointment, and wiped His feet with her hair, whose brother Lazarus was sick. Therefore his sisters sent unto Him, saying." We now understand whither it was they sent, namely, where the Lord was; for He was

---

[1] Mark v. 41, 42.   [2] Luke vii. 14, 15.

[3] Luke vii. 37-47. Augustin is mistaken here, although his error has been followed by many ancient writers, and some in more recent times. The time, place, and circumstances make it impossible for the incident here referred to, to be the same as that which took place in Bethany immediately before our Lord's crucifixion. On that last occasion only was it Lazarus' sister, Mary, who anointed Jesus. Luke here speaks only of a woman that was a sinner. and there is little evidence to connect her with any of the other Scripture women, even with Mary of Magdala, as is often done, and who is first mentioned by Luke in a different connection in the following chapter (viii. 2).—Tr.
[4] Chap. x. 39, 40.

away, as you know, beyond the Jordan. They sent messengers to the Lord to tell Him that their brother was ill. He delayed to heal, that He might be able to raise to life. But what was the message sent by his sisters? "Lord, behold, he whom Thou lovest is sick." They did not say, Come; for the intimation was all that was needed for one who loved. They did not venture to say, Come and heal him: they ventured not to say, Command there, and it shall be done here. And why not so with them, if on these very grounds the centurion's faith was commended? For he said, "I am not worthy that Thou shouldest enter under my roof; but speak the word only, and my servant shall be healed." [1] No such words said these women, but only, "Lord, behold, he whom Thou lovest is sick." It is enough that Thou knowest; for Thou art not one that loveth and forsaketh. But says some one, How could a sinner be represented by Lazarus, and be so loved by the Lord? Let him listen to Him, when He says, "I came not to call the righteous, but sinners." [2] For had not God loved sinners, He would not have come down from heaven to earth.

6. "But when Jesus heard [that], He said, This sickness is not unto death, but for the glory of God, that the Son of God may be glorified." Such a glorifying of Himself did not add to *His* dignity, but benefited us. Hence He says, "is not unto death," because even that death itself was not unto death, but rather unto the working of a miracle whereby men might be led to faith in Christ, and so escape the real death. And mark how the Lord, as it were indirectly, called Himself God, for the sake of some who deny that the Son is God. For there are heretics who make such a denial, that the Son of God is God. Let them hearken here: "This sickness," He says, "is not unto death, but for the glory of God." For what glory? For the glory of what God? Hear what follows: "That the Son of God may be glorified." "This sickness," therefore, He says, "is not unto death, but for the glory of God, that the Son of God may be glorified thereby." By what? By that sickness.

7. "Now Jesus loved Martha, and her sister Mary, and Lazarus." The one sick, the others sad, all of them beloved: but He who loved them was both the Saviour of the sick, nay more, the Raiser of the dead and the Comforter of the sad. "When He heard therefore that he was sick, He abode then two days still in the same place." They sent Him word: He abode where He was: and the time ran on till four days were completed. And not in vain, were it only that perhaps, nay that certainly, even the very number of days has some sacramental significance. "Then after that He saith again to His disciples, Let us go into Judea:" where He had been all but stoned, and from which He had apparently departed for the very purpose to escape being stoned. For as man He departed; but returned as if in forgetfulness of all infirmity, to show His power. "Let us go," He said, "into Judea."

8. And now see how the disciples were terrified at His words. "The disciples say unto Him, Master, the Jews of late sought to stone Thee, and goest Thou thither again? Jesus answered, Are there not twelve hours in the day?" What means such an answer? They said to Him, "The Jews of late sought to stone Thee, and goest Thou thither again" to be stoned? And the Lord, "Are there not twelve hours in the day? If any man walk in the day, he stumbleth not, because he seeth the light of this world: but if he walk in the night, he stumbleth, because there is no light in him." He spoke indeed of the day, but to our understanding as if it were still the night. Let us call upon the Day to chase away the night, and illuminate our hearts with the light. For what did the Lord mean? As far as I can judge, and as the height and depth of His meaning breaks into light, He wished to argue down their doubting and unbelief. For they wished by their counsel to keep the Lord from death, who had come to die, to save themselves from death. In a similar way also, in another passage, St. Peter, who loved the Lord, but did not yet fully understand the reason of His coming, was afraid of His dying, and so displeased the Life, to wit, the Lord Himself: for when He was intimating to the disciples what He was about to suffer at Jerusalem at the hands of the Jews, Peter made reply among the rest, and said, "Far be it from Thee, Lord; pity Thyself: this shall not be unto Thee." And at once the Lord replied, "Get thee behind me, Satan: for thou savorest not the things that be of God, but those that be of men." And yet a little before, in confessing the Son of God, he had merited commendation: for he heard the words, "Blessed art thou, Simon Bar-jona: for flesh and blood hath not revealed it unto thee, but my Father who is in heaven." [3] To whom He had said, "Blessed art thou," He now says, "Get thee behind me, Satan;" because

---

[1] Matt. viii.   [2] Matt. ix. 13.   [3] Matt. xvi. 16-23.

it was not of himself that he was blessed. But of what then? " For flesh and blood hath not revealed it unto thee, but my Father who is in heaven." See, this is how thou art blessed, not from anything that is thine own, but from that which is mine. Not that I am the Father, but that all things which the Father hath are mine.[1] But if his blessedness came from the Lord's own working, from whose [working] came he to be Satan? He there tells us: for He assigned the reason of such blessedness, when He said, " Flesh and blood hath not revealed *this* unto thee, but my Father who is in heaven:" that is the cause of thy blessedness. But that I said, " Get thee behind me, Satan, hear also *its* cause. For thou savorest not the things that be of God, but those that be of men." Let no one then flatter himself: in that which is natural to himself he is Satan, in that which is of God he is blessed. For all that is of his own, whence comes it, but from his sin? Put away the sin, which is thine own. Righteousness, He saith, belongeth unto me. For what hast thou that thou didst not receive?[2] Accordingly, when men wished to give counsel to God, disciples to their Master, servants to their Lord, patients to their Physician, He reproved them by saying, "Are there not twelve hours in the day? If any man walk in the day, he stumbleth not." Follow me, if ye would not stumble: give not counsel to me, from whom you ought to receive it. To what, then, refer the words, "Are there not twelve hours in the day"? Just that to point Himself out as the day, He made choice of twelve disciples. If I am the day, He says, and you the hours, is it for the hours to give counsel to the day? The day is followed by the hours, not the hours by the day. If these, then, were the hours, what in such a reckoning was Judas? Was he also among the twelve hours? If he was an hour, he had light; and if he had light, how was the Day betrayed by him to death? But the Lord, in so speaking, foresaw, not Judas himself, but his successor. For Judas, when he fell, was succeeded by Matthias, and the duodenary number preserved.[3] It was not, then, without a purpose that the Lord made choice of twelve disciples, but to indicate that He Himself is the spiritual Day. Let the hours then attend upon the Day, let them preach the Day, be made known and illuminated by the Day, and by the preaching of the hours may the world believe in the Day. And so in a summary way it was just this that He said: Follow me, if ye would not stumble.

9. "And after that He saith unto them, Our friend Lazarus sleepeth; but I go, that I may awake him out of sleep." It was true what He said. To his sisters he was dead, to the Lord he was asleep. He was dead to men, who could not raise him again; but the Lord aroused him with as great ease from the tomb as one arouseth a sleeper from his bed. Hence it was in reference to His own power that He spoke of him as sleeping: for others also, who are dead, are frequently spoken of in Scripture as sleeping; as when the apostle says, " But I would not have you to be ignorant, brethren, concerning those who are asleep, that ye sorrow not, even as others who have no hope."[4] Therefore he also spoke of them as sleeping, because foretelling their resurrection. And so, all the dead are sleeping, both good and bad. But just as, in the case of those who sleep and waken day by day, there is a great difference as to what they severally see in their sleep: some experience pleasant dreams; others, dreams so frightful that the waking are afraid to fall asleep for fear of their recurrence: so every individual sleeps and wakens in circumstances peculiar to himself. And there is a difference as to the kind of custody one may be placed in, who is afterwards to be taken before the judge. For the kind of custody in which men are placed depends on the merits of the case: some are required to be guarded by lictors, an office humane and mild, and becoming a citizen; others are given up to subordinates;[5] some, again, are sent to prison: and in the prison itself all are not thrust together into its lowest dungeons, but dealt with in proportion to the merits and superior gravity of the charges. As, then, there are different kinds of custody among those engaged in official life, so there are different kinds of custody for the dead, and differing merits in those who rise again. The beggar was taken into custody, so was the rich man: but the one into Abraham's bosom; the other, where he thirsted, and found not a drop of water.[6]

10. Therefore, to make this the occasion of instructing your Charity, all souls have, when they quit this world, their different receptions. The good have joy; the evil, torments. But when the resurrection takes

---

[4] 1 Thess. iv. 13.
[5] *Optionibus*, assistants, underlings. In the MSS., it is written, but incorrectly, *optionibus*; for Varro, Isidorus, and others think the *optiones* were so called *ab optando*, as being doubtless *chosen* as assistants to the decuriones and military adjutants. They were also attached to various offices: and hence there were artisan *optiones*, and those belonging to official or prison life, in which last signification they are used here; as also in Ambrose's works (*Commentary on the Ephesians*, chap. 4) in these words: " Nor did Paul and Silas delay to baptize the jailor (*optionem carceris*)."
[6] Luke xvi. 22–24.

place, both the joy of the good will be fuller, and the torments of the wicked heavier, when they shall be tormented in the body. The holy patriarchs, prophets, apostles, martyrs, and good believers, have been received into peace; but all of them have still in the end to receive the fulfillment of the divine promises; for they have been promised also the resurrection of the flesh, the destruction of death, and eternal life with the angels. This we have all to receive together; for the rest, which is given immediately after death, every one, if worthy of it, receives when he dies. The patriarchs first received it—think only from what they rest; the prophets afterwards; more recently the apostles; still more lately the holy martyrs, and day by day the good and faithful. Thus some have now been in that rest for long, some not so long; others for fewer years, and others whose entrance therein is still less than recent. But when they shall wake from this sleep, they shall all together receive the fulfillment of the promise.

11. "Our friend Lazarus sleepeth; but I go, that I may awake him out of sleep. Then said His disciples"—according to their understanding they replied—"Lord, if he sleep, he shall do well." For the sleep of the sick is usually a sign of returning health. "Howbeit Jesus spake of his death, but they thought that He spake of the taking of rest in sleep. Then said Jesus unto them plainly,"—for He said somewhat obscurely, "He sleepeth;"—therefore He said plainly, "Lazarus is dead. And I am glad for your sakes that I was not there, to the intent ye may believe." I even know that he is dead, and I was not there: for he had been reported not as dead, but sick. But what could remain hid from Him who had created it, and into whose hands the soul of the dying man had departed? This is why He said, "I am glad for your sakes that I was not there, to the intent ye may believe;" that they might now begin to wonder that the Lord could assert his death, which He had neither seen nor heard of. For here we ought specially to bear in mind that as yet the disciples themselves, who already believed in Him, had their faith built up by miracles: not that a faith, utterly wanting till then, might begin to exist; but that what had previously come into being might be increased; although He made use of such an expression as if only then they would begin to believe. For He said not, "I am glad for your sakes," that your faith may be increased or confirmed; but, "that ye may believe;" which is to be understood as meaning, that your faith may be fuller and more vigorous.

12. "Nevertheless, let us go unto him. Then said Thomas, who is called Didymus, unto his fellow-disciples, Let us also go, that we may die with Him. Therefore Jesus came, and found that he had [lain] in the grave four days already." Much might be said of the four days, according to the wont of the obscure passages of Scripture, which bear as many senses as there is diversity of those who understand them. Let us express also our opinion of what is meant by one four days dead. For as in the former case of the blind man we understand in a way the human race, so in the case of this dead man many perhaps are also to be understood; for one thing may be signified by different figures. When a man is born, he is born already in a state of death; for he inherits sin from Adam. Hence the apostle says: "By one man sin entered into the world, and death by sin; and so that passed upon all men, wherein all have sinned."[1] Here you have one day of death, because man inherits it from the seed stock of death. Thereafter he grows, and begins to approach the years of reason that he may know the law of nature, which every one has had implanted in his heart: What thou wouldst not have done to thyself, do not to another. Is this learned from the pages of a book, and not in a measure legible in our very nature? Hast thou any desire to be robbed? Certainly not. See here, then, the law in thy heart: What thou art unwilling to suffer, be unwilling to do. This law also is transgressed by men; and here, then, we have the second day of death. The law was also divinely given through Moses, the servant of God; and therein it is said, "Thou shalt not kill; thou shalt not commit adultery; thou shalt not bear false witness; honor thy father and mother; thou shalt not covet thy neighbor's property; thou shalt not covet thy neighbor's wife."[2] Here you have the written law, and it also is despised: this is the third day of death. What remains? The gospel also comes, the kingdom of heaven is preached, Christ is everywhere published; He threatens hell, He promises eternal life; and that also is despised. Men transgress the gospel; and *this* is the fourth day of death. Now he deservedly stinketh. But is mercy to be denied to such? God forbid; for to raise such also from the dead, the Lord thinks it not unfitting to come.

13. "And many of the Jews had come to Martha and Mary, to comfort them concerning their brother. Then Martha, as soon as she heard that Jesus was coming, went and

---

[1] Rom. v. 12.　　[2] Ex. xx. 12-17.

met Him; but Mary sat [still] in the house. Then said Martha unto Jesus, Lord, if Thou hadst been here, my brother had not died. But I know that even now, whatsoever Thou wilt ask of God, God will give it Thee." She did not say, But even now I ask Thee to raise my brother to life again. For how could she know if such a resurrection would be of benefit to her brother? She only said, I know that Thou canst, and whatsoever Thou art pleased, Thou doest: for Thy doing it is dependent on Thine own judgment, not on my presumption. "But even now I know that, whatsoever Thou wilt ask of God, God will give it Thee."

14 "Jesus saith unto her, Thy brother shall rise again." This was ambiguous. For He said not, Even now I will raise thy brother; but, "Thy brother shall rise again. Martha saith unto Him, I know that he shall rise again in the resurrection, at the last day." Of that resurrection I am sure, but uncertain about this. "Jesus saith unto her, I am the resurrection." Thou sayest, My brother shall rise again at the last day: true; but by Him, through whom he shall rise then, can he rise even now, for "I," He says, "am the resurrection and the life." Give ear, brethren, give ear to what He says. Certainly the universal expectation of the bystanders was that Lazarus, one who had been dead four days,[1] would live again; let us hear, and rise again. How many are there in this audience who are crushed down under the weighty mass of some sinful habit! Perhaps some are hearing me to whom it may be said, "Be not drunk with wine, wherein is excess;"[2] and they say, We cannot. Some others, it may be, are hearing me, who are unclean, and stained with lusts and crimes, and to whom it is said, Refrain from such conduct, that ye perish not; and they reply, We cannot give up our habits. O Lord, raise them again. "I am," He says, "the resurrection and the life." The resurrection *because* the life.

15. "He that believeth in me, though he were dead, yet shall he live: and whosoever liveth and believeth in me shall never die." What meaneth this? "He that believeth in me, though he were dead," just as Lazarus is dead, "yet shall he live;" for He is not the God of the dead, but of the living. Such was the answer He gave the Jews concerning their fathers, long ago dead, that is, concerning Abraham, and Isaac, and Jacob: I am the God of Abraham, and the God of Isaac, and the God of Jacob: He is not the God of the

dead, but of the living; for all live unto Him."[3] Believe then, and though thou wert dead, yet shalt thou live: but if thou believest not, even while thou livest thou art dead. Let us prove this likewise, that if thou believest not, though thou livest thou art dead. To one who was delaying to follow Him, and saying, "Let me first go and bury my father," the Lord said, "Let the dead bury their dead; but come thou and follow me."[4] There was there a dead man requiring to be buried, there were there also dead men to bury the dead: the one was dead in the flesh, the others in soul. And how comes death on the soul? When faith is wanting. How comes death on the body? When the soul is wanting. Therefore thy soul's soul is faith. "He that believeth in me," says Christ, though he were dead in the flesh, yet shall he live in the spirit; till the flesh also rise again, never more to die. This is "he that believeth in me," though he die, "yet shall he live. And whosoever liveth" in the flesh, "and believeth in me," though he shall die in time on account of the death of the flesh, "shall never die," because of the life of the spirit, and the immortality of the resurrection. Such is the meaning of the words, "And whosoever liveth and believeth in me shall never die. Believest thou this? She saith unto Him, Yea, Lord, I have believed that Thou art the Christ, the Son of God, who hast come into the world." When I believed this, I believed that Thou art the resurrection, that Thou art the life: I believed that he that believeth in Thee, though he die, yet shall he live; and whosoever liveth and believeth in Thee, shall never die.

16. "And when she had so said, she went her way, and called Mary her sister silently, saying, The Master is come, and calleth for thee." It is worthy of notice the way in which the whispering of her voice was denominated silence. For how could she be silent, when she said, "The Master is come, and calleth for thee"? It is also to be noticed why it is that the evangelist has not said where, or when, or how the Lord called for Mary; namely, that in order to preserve the brevity of the narrative, it may rather be understood from the words of Martha.

17. "As soon as she heard that, she arose quickly, and came unto Him. For Jesus was not yet come into the town, but was still in that place where Martha met Him. The Jews, then, who were with her in the house, and comforted her, when they saw Mary, that she rose up hastily, and went out, followed her, saying, She goeth unto the grave, to weep there." What cause had the evangelist to

---

[1] That is (Augustin here would suggest the emblem) of one who was lying under the fourth and most terrible form of spiritual death referred to before.—TR.
[2] Eph. v. 18.

[3] Matt. xxii. 32, and Luke xx. 37, 38.   [4] Matt. viii. 21, 22.

tell us this? To show us what it was that occasioned the numerous concourse of people to be there when Lazarus was raised to life. For the Jews, thinking that her reason for hastening away was to seek in weeping the solace of her grief, followed her; that the great miracle of one rising again who had been four days dead, might have the presence of many witnesses.

18. "Then when Mary was come where Jesus was, and saw Him, she fell down at His feet, saying unto Him, Lord, if Thou hadst been here, my brother had not died. When Jesus therefore saw her weeping, and the Jews also weeping, who were with her, He groaned in the spirit, and troubled Himself,[1] and said, Where have ye laid him?" Something there is, did we but know it, that He has suggested to us by groaning in the spirit, and troubling Himself. For who could trouble Him, save He Himself? Therefore, my brethren, first give heed here to the power that did so, and then look for the meaning. Thou art troubled against thy will; Christ was troubled because He willed. Jesus hungered, it is true, but because He willed; Jesus slept, it is true, but because He willed; He was sorrowful, it is true, but because He willed; He died, it is true, but because He willed: in His own power it lay to be thus and thus affected or not. For the Word assumed soul and flesh, fitting on Himself our whole human nature in the oneness of His person. For the soul of the apostle was illuminated by the Word; so was the soul of Peter, the soul of Paul, of the other apostles, and the holy prophets,—the souls of all were illuminated by the Word; but of none was it said, "The Word was made flesh;"[2] of none was it said, "I and the Father are one."[3] The soul and flesh of Christ is one person with the Word of God, one Christ. And by this [Word] wherein resided the supreme power, was infirmity made use of at the beck of His will; and in this way "He troubled Himself."

19. I have spoken of the power: look now to the meaning. It is a great criminal that is signified by that four days' death and burial. Why is it, then, that Christ troubleth Himself, but to intimate to thee how thou oughtest to be troubled, when weighed down and crushed by so great a mass of iniquity? For here thou hast been looking to thyself, been seeing thine own guilt, been reckoning for thyself: I have done this, and God has spared me; I have committed this, and He hath borne with me; I have heard the gospel, and despised it; I have been baptized, and returned again to

the same course: what am I doing? whither am I going? how shall I escape? When thou speakest thus, Christ is already groaning; for thy faith is groaning. In the voice of one who groaneth thus, there comes to light the hope of his rising again. If such faith is within, there is Christ groaning; for if there is faith in us, Christ is in us. For what else says the apostle: "That Christ may dwell in your hearts by faith."[4] Therefore thy faith in Christ is Christ Himself in thy heart. This is why He slept in the ship; and why, when His disciples were in danger and already on the verge of shipwreck, they came to Him and awoke Him. Christ arose, laid His commands on the winds and waves, and there ensued a great calm.[5] So also with thee; the winds enter thy heart, that is, where thou sailest, where thou passest along this life as a stormy and dangerous sea; the winds enter, the billows rise and toss thy vessel. What are the winds? Thou hast received some insult, and art wroth: that insult is the wind; that anger, the waves. Thou art in danger, thou preparest to reply, to render cursing for cursing, and thy vessel is already nigh to shipwreck. Awake the Christ who is sleeping. For thou art in commotion, and making ready to render evil for evil, because Christ is sleeping in thy vessel. For the sleep of Christ in thy heart is the forgetfulness of faith. But if thou arousest Christ, that is, recallest thy faith, what dost thou hear said to thee by Christ, when now awake in thy heart? I [He says] have heard it said to me, "Thou hast a devil,"[6] and I have prayed for them. The Lord hears and suffers; the servant hears and is angry! But thou wishest to be avenged. Why so? I am already avenged. When thy faith so speaks to thee, command is exercised, as it were, over the winds and waves, and there is a great calm. As, then, to awaken Christ in the vessel is just to awaken faith; so in the heart of one who is pressed down by a great mass and habit of sin, in the heart of the man who has been a transgressor even of the holy gospel and a despiser of eternal punishment, let Christ groan, let such a man betake himself to self-accusation. Hear still more: Christ wept; let man bemoan himself. For why did Christ weep, but to teach man to weep? Wherefore did He groan and trouble Himself, but to intimate that the faith of one who has just cause to be displeased with himself ought to be in a sense groaning over the accusation of wicked works, to the end that the habit of sinning may give way to the vehemence of penitential sorrow?

1 As in margin of English Version.
2 Chap. i. 14.　　3 Chap. x. 30.　　4 Eph. iii. 17.　　5 Matt. viii. 24-26.　　6 Chap. vii. 30.

20. "And He said, Where have ye laid him?" Thou knewest that he was dead, and art Thou ignorant of the place of his burial? The meaning here is, that a man thus lost becomes, as it were, unknown to God. I have not ventured to say, Is unknown—for what is unknown to Him?—but, As it were unknown. And how do we prove this? Listen to the Lord, who will yet say in the judgment, "I know you not: depart from me."[1] What does that mean, "I know you not"? I see you not in that light of mine—in that righteousness which I know. So here, also, as if knowing nothing of such a sinner, He said, "Where have ye laid him?" Similar in character was God's voice in Paradise after man had sinned: "Adam, where art thou?"[2] "They say unto Him, Lord, come and see." What means this "see"? Have pity. For the Lord sees when He pities. Hence it is said to Him, "Look upon my humility [affliction] and my pain, and forgive all my sins."[4]

21. "Jesus wept. Then said the Jews, Behold how He loved him!" "Loved him," what does that mean? "I came not to call the righteous, but sinners to repentance."[3] "But some of them said, Could not this man, who opened the eyes of the blind, have caused that even this man should not die?" But He, who would do nought to hinder his dying, had something greater in view in raising him from the dead.

22. "Jesus therefore again groaning in Himself, cometh to the tomb." May His groaning have thee also for its object, if thou wouldst re-enter into life! Every man who lies in that dire moral condition has it said to him, "He cometh to the tomb." "It was a cave, and a stone had been laid upon it." Dead under that stone, guilty under the law. For you know that the law, which was given to the Jews, was inscribed on stone.[5] And all the guilty are under the law: the right-living are in harmony with the law. The law is not laid on a righteous man.[6] What mean then the words, "Take ye away the stone"? Preach grace. For the Apostle Paul calleth himself a minister of the New Testament, not of the letter, but of the spirit; "for the letter," he says, "killeth, but the spirit giveth life."[7] The letter that killeth is like the stone that crusheth. "Take ye away," He saith, "the stone." Take away the weight of the law; preach grace. "For if there had been a law given, which could have given life, verily righteousness should be by the law. But the Scripture hath con-

cluded all under sin, that the promise by faith of Jesus Christ might be given to them that believe."[8] Therefore "take ye away the stone."

23. "Martha, the sister of him that was dead, saith unto Him, Lord, by this time he stinketh: for he hath been [dead] four days.[9] Jesus saith unto her, Have I not said unto thee, that, if thou believest, thou shalt see the glory of God?" What does He mean by this, "thou shalt see the glory of God"? That He can raise to life even one who is putrid and hath been four days [dead]. "For all have sinned, and come short of the glory of God;"[10] and, "Where sin abounded, grace also did superabound."[11]

24. "Then they took away the stone. And Jesus lifted up His eyes, and said, Father, I thank Thee, that Thou hast heard me. And I knew that Thou hearest me always: but because of the people that stand by I said it, that they may believe that Thou hast sent me. And when He had thus spoken, He cried with a loud voice." He groaned, He wept, He cried with a loud voice. With what difficulty does one rise who lies crushed under the heavy burden of a habit of sinning! And yet he does rise: he is quickened by hidden grace within; and after that loud voice he riseth. For what followed? "He cried with a loud voice, Lazarus, come forth. And immediately he that was dead came forth, bound hand and foot with bandages;[12] and his face was bound about with a napkin." Dost thou wonder how he came forth with his feet bound, and wonderest not at this, that after four days' interment he rose from the dead? In both events it was the power of the Lord that operated, and not the strength of the dead. He came forth, and yet still was bound. Still in his burial shroud, he has already come outside the tomb. What does it mean? While thou despisest [Christ], thou liest in the arms of death; and if thy contempt reacheth the lengths I have mentioned, thou art buried as well: but when thou makest confession, thou comest forth. For what is this coming forth, but the open acknowledgment thou makest of thy state, in quitting, as it were, the old refuges of darkness? But the confession thou makest is effected by God, when He crieth with a loud voice, or in other words, calleth thee in abounding grace. Accordingly, when the dead man had come forth, still bound; confessing, yet guilty still; that his sins also might be taken away, the Lord said to His servants: "Loose him, and let him go." What does He mean by such words? What-

1 Matt. vii. 23.   2 Gen. iii. 9.   3 Ps. xxv. 18.
4 Matt. ix. 13.   5 Ex. xxxi. 18.   6 1 Tim. i. 9.
7 2 Cor. iii. 6.

8 Gal. iii. 21, 22.   9 Quatriduanus est.   10 Rom. iii. 23.
11 Rom. v. 20.   12 Institis: Gr. κειρίαις.

soever ye shall loose on earth shall be loosed in heaven.[1]

25. "Then many of the Jews who had come to Mary, and had seen the things which Jesus did, believed on Him. But some of them went away to the Pharisees, and told them what things Jesus had done." All of the Jews who had come to Mary did not believe, but many of them did. " But some of them," whether of the Jews who had come, or of those who had believed, " went away to the Pharisees, and told them what things Jesus had done:" whether in the way of conveying intelligence, in order that they also might believe, or rather in the spirit of treachery, to arouse their anger. But whoever were the parties, and whatever their motive, intelligence of these events was carried to the Pharisees.

26. " Then gathered the chief priests and the Pharisees a council, and said, What do we?" But they did not say, Let us believe. For these abandoned men were more occupied in considering what evil they could do to effect His ruin, than in consulting for their own preservation: and yet they were afraid, and took counsel of a kind together. For " they said, What do we? for this man doeth many miracles: if we let him thus alone, all men will believe on him; and the Romans shall come, and take away both our place and nation." They were afraid of losing their temporal possessions, and thought not of life eternal; and so they lost both. For the Romans, after our Lord's passion and entrance into glory, took from them both their place and nation, when they took the one by storm and transported the other: and now that also pursues them, which is said elsewhere, " But the children of the kingdom shall go into outer darkness."[2] But this was what they feared, that if all believed on Christ, there would be none remaining to defend the city of God and the temple against the Romans; just because they had a feeling that Christ's teaching was directed against the temple itself and their own paternal laws.

27. "And one of them, [named] Caiaphas, being the high priest that same year, said unto them, Ye know nothing at all, nor consider that it is expedient for us that one man should die for the people, and that the whole nation perish not. And this spake he not of himself; but being high priest that year, he prophesied." We are here taught that the Spirit of prophecy used the agency even of wicked men to foretell what was future; which, however, the evangelist attributes to the divine sacramental fact that he was pontiff, which is to say, the high priest. It may, however, be a question in what way he is called the high priest of that year, seeing that God appointed one person to be high priest, who was to be succeeded only at his death by another. But we are to understand that ambitious schemes and contentions among the Jews led to the appointment afterwards of more than one, and to their annual turn of service. For it is said also of Zacharias: "And it came to pass that, while he executed the priest's office before God in the order of his course, according to the custom of the priest's office, his lot was to burn incense when he went into the temple of the Lord."[3] From which it is evident that there were more than one, and that each had his turn: for it was lawful for the high priest alone to place the incense on the altar.[4] And perhaps also there were several in actual service in the same year, who were succeeded next year by several others, and that it fell by lot to one of them to burn incense. What was it, then, that Caiaphas prophesied? " That Jesus should die for the nation; and not for the nation only, but that also He should gather together in one the children of God that were scattered abroad." This is added by the evangelist; for Caiaphas prophesied only of the Jewish nation, in which there were sheep of whom the Lord Himself had said, " I am not sent but unto the lost sheep of the house of Israel."[5] But the evangelist knew that there were other sheep, which were not of this fold, but which had also to be brought, that there might be one fold and one shepherd.[6] But this was said in the way of predestination; for those who were still unbelieving were as yet neither His sheep nor the children of God.

28. " Then, from that day forth, they took counsel together for to put Him to death. Jesus therefore walked no more openly among the Jews; but went thence unto a country near to the wilderness, into a city called Ephraim, and there continued with His disciples." Not that there was any failure in His power, by which, had He only wished, He might have continued His intercourse with the Jews, and received no injury at their hands; but in His human weakness He furnished His disciples with an example of living, by which He might make it manifest that it was no sin in His believing ones, who are His members, to withdraw from the presence of their persecutors, and escape the fury of the wicked by concealment, rather than inflame it by showing themselves openly.

---

[1] Matt. xvi. 19. [2] Matt. viii. 12.

[3] Luke i. 8, 9 [4] Ex. xxx. 7.
[5] Matt. xv. 24. [6] Chap. x. 16.

TRACTATE L.

Chapter XI. 55–57; XII. 1–11.

1. Yesterday's lesson in the holy Gospel, on which we spake as the Lord enabled us, is followed by to-day's, on which we purpose to speak in the same spirit of dependence. Some passages in the Scriptures are so clear as to require a hearer rather than an expounder: over such we need not tarry, that we may have sufficient time for those which necessarily demand a fuller consideration.

2. "And the Jews' passover was nigh at hand." The Jews wished to have that feast-day crimsoned with the blood of the Lord. On it that Lamb was slain, who hath consecrated it as a feast-day for us by His own blood. There was a plot among the Jews about slaying Jesus: and He, who had come from heaven to suffer, wished to draw near to the place of His suffering, because the hour of His passion was at hand. Therefore "many went out of the country up to Jerusalem before the passover, to sanctify themselves." The Jews did so in accordance with the command of the Lord delivered by holy Moses in the law, that on the feast-day of the passover all should assemble from every part of the land, and be sanctified in celebrating the services of the day. But that celebration was a shadow of the future. And why a shadow? It was a prophetic intimation of the Christ to come, a prophecy of Him who on that day was to suffer for us: that so the shadow might vanish and the light come; that the sign might pass away, and the truth be retained. The Jews therefore held the passover in a shadowy form, but we in the light. For what need was there that the Lord should command them to slay a sheep on the very day of the feast, save only because of Him it was prophesied, "He is led as a sheep to the slaughter"?[1] The door-posts of the Jews were sealed with the blood of the slaughtered animal: with the blood of Christ are our foreheads sealed. And that sealing—for it had a real significance—was said to keep away the destroyer from the houses that were sealed:[2] Christ's seal drives away the destroyer from us, if we receive the Saviour into our hearts. But why have I said this? Because many have their door-posts sealed while there is no inmate abiding within: they find it easy to have Christ's seal in the forehead, and yet at heart refuse admission to His word. Therefore, brethren, I have said, and I repeat it, Christ's seal driveth from us the destroyer, if only we have Christ as an inmate of our hearts. I have stated these things, lest any one's thoughts should be turning on the meaning of these festivals of the Jews. The Lord therefore came as it were to the victim's place, that the true passover might be ours, when we celebrated His passion as the real offering of the lamb.

3. "Then sought they for Jesus:" but with evil intent. For happy are they who seek for Jesus in a way that is good. They sought for Him, with the intent that neither they nor we should have Him more: but in departing from them, He has been received by us. Some who seek Him are blamed, others who do so are commended; for it is the spirit animating the seeker that finds either praise or condemnation. Thence you have it also in the psalms, "Let them be confounded and put to shame that seek after my soul:"[3] such are those who sought with evil purpose. But in another place he says, "Refuge hath failed me, and there is no one that seeketh after my soul."[4] Those who sought, and those who did not, are blamed alike. Therefore let us seek for Christ, that He may be ours, that we may keep Him, and not that we may slay Him; for these men sought to get hold of Him, but only for the purpose of speedily getting quit of Him for ever. "Therefore they sought for Him, and spake among themselves: What think ye, that He will not come to the feast?"

4. "Now the chief priests and the Pharisees had given a commandment, that, if any man knew where He were, he should show it, that they might take Him." Let us for our parts show the Jews where Christ is. Would, indeed, that all the seed of those who had given commandment to have it shown them where Christ was, would but hear and apprehend! Let them come to the church and hear where Christ is, and take Him. They may hear it from us, they may hear it from the gospel. He was slain by their forefathers, He was buried, He rose again, He was recognized by the disciples, He ascended before their eyes into heaven, and there sitteth at

---

[1] Isa. liii. 7.   [2] Ex. xii. 22, 23.   [3] Ps. xl. 14.   [4] Ps. cxlii. 4, *marg.*

the right hand of the Father; and He who was judged is yet to come as Judge of all: let them hear, and hold fast. Do they reply, How shall I take hold of the absent? how shall I stretch up my hand into heaven, and take hold of one who is sitting there? Stretch up thy faith, and thou hast got hold. Thy forefathers held by the flesh, hold thou with the heart; for the absent Christ is also present. But for His presence, we ourselves were unable to hold Him. But since His word is true, "Lo, I am with you alway, even to the end of the world," [1] He is away, and He is here; He has returned, and will not forsake us; for He has carried His body into heaven, but His majesty He has never withdrawn from the world.

5. "Then Jesus, six days before the passover, came to Bethany, where Lazarus was who had been dead, whom Jesus raised from the dead. And there they made Him a supper; and Martha served: but Lazarus was one of them that reclined at the table." To prevent people thinking that the man had become a phantom, because he had risen from the dead, he was one of those who reclined at table; he was living, speaking, feasting: the truth was made manifest, and the unbelief of the Jews was confounded. The Lord, therefore, reclined at table with Lazarus and the others; and they were waited on by Martha, one of the sisters of Lazarus.

6. But "Mary," the other sister of Lazarus, "took a pound of ointment of pure nard, very precious, and anointed the feet of Jesus, and wiped His feet with her hair; and the house was filled with the odor of the ointment." Such was the incident, let us look into the mystery it imported. Whatever soul of you wishes to be truly faithful, anoint like Mary the feet of the Lord with precious ointment. That ointment was righteousness, and therefore it was [exactly] a pound weight: but it was ointment of pure nard [*nardi pistici*], very precious. From his calling it "pistici," [2] we ought to infer that there was some locality from which it derived its preciousness: but this does not exhaust its meaning, and it harmonizes well with a sacramental symbol. The root of the word ["pure"] in the Greek is by us called "faith." Thou wert seeking to work righteousness: the just shall live by faith.[3] Anoint the feet of Jesus: follow by a good life the Lord's footsteps. Wipe them with thy hair: what thou hast of superfluity,

give to the poor, and thou hast wiped the feet of the Lord; for the hair seems to be the superfluous part of the body. Thou hast something to spare of thy abundance: it is superfluous to thee, but necessary for the feet of the Lord. Perhaps on this earth the Lord's feet are still in need. For of whom but of His members is He yet to say in the end, "Inasmuch as ye did it to one of the least of mine, ye did it unto me"? [4] Ye spent what was superfluous for yourselves, but ye have done what was grateful to my feet.

7. "And the house was filled with the odor." The world is filled with the fame of a good character: for a good character is as a pleasant odor. Those who live wickedly and bear the name of Christians, do injury to Christ: of such it is said, that through them "the name of the Lord is blasphemed." [5] If through such God's name is blasphemed, through the good the name of the Lord is honored. Listen to the apostle, when he says, "We are a sweet savor of Christ in every place." As it is said also in the Song of Songs, "Thy name is as ointment poured forth." [6] Attend again to the apostle: "We are a sweet savor," he says, "of Christ in every place, both in them that are saved, and in them that perish. To the one we are the savor of life unto life, to the other the savor of death unto death: and who is sufficient for these things?" [7] The lesson of the holy Gospel before us affords us the opportunity of so speaking of that savor, that we on our part may give worthy utterance, and you diligent heed, to what is thus expressed by the apostle himself, "And who is sufficient for these things?" But have we any reason to infer from these words that we are qualified to attempt speaking on such a subject, or you to hear? We, indeed, are not so; but He is sufficient, who is pleased to speak by us what it may be for your profit to hear. The apostle, you see, is, as he calls himself, "a sweet savor:" but that sweet savor is "to some the savor of life unto life, and to others the savor of death unto death;" and yet all the while "a sweet savor" in itself. For he does not say, does he, To some we are a sweet savor unto life, to others an evil savor unto death? He called himself a sweet savor, not an evil; and represented himself as the same sweet savor, to some unto life, to others unto death. Happy they who find life in this sweet savor! but what misery can be greater than theirs, to whom the sweet savor is the messenger of death?

8. And who is it, says some one, that is

---

[1] Matt. xxviii. 20.
[2] The full expression is *nardi pistici pretiosi :* Gr. "νάρδου πιστικῆς πολυτίμου :" πιστικός from πίστις, *trustworthy*, hence, *genuine, pure ;*—though Aug. seems to indicate that it may also have had a geographical reference.—Tr.
[3] Rom. i. 17.

[4] Matt. xxv. 40.
[5] Rom. ii. 24.
[6] Song of Sol. i. 3.
[7] 2 Cor. ii. 14-16.

thus slain by the sweet savor? It is to this the apostle alludes in the words, "And who is sufficient for these things?" In what wonderful ways God brings it about that the good savor is fraught both with life to the good, and with death to the wicked; how it is so, so far as the Lord is pleased to inspire my thoughts (for it may still conceal a deeper meaning beyond my power to penetrate),—yet so far, I say, as my power of penetration has reached, you ought not to have the information withheld. The integrity of the Apostle Paul's life and conduct, his preaching of righteousness in word and exhibition of it in works, his wondrous power as a teacher and his fidelity as a steward, were everywhere noised abroad: he was loved by some, and envied by others. For he himself tells us in a certain place of some, that they preached Christ not sincerely, but of envy; "thinking," he says, "to add affliction to my bonds." But what does he add? "Whether in pretence or in truth, let Christ be preached."[1] They preach who love me, they preach who hate me; in that good savor the former live, in it the others die: and yet by the preaching of both let the name of Christ be proclaimed, with this excellent savor let the world be filled. Hast thou been loving one whose conduct evidenced his goodness? then in this good savor thou hast lived. Hast thou been envying such a one? then in this same savor thou hast died. But hast thou, pray, in thus choosing to die, converted this savor into an evil one? Turn from thine envious feelings, and the good savor will cease to slay thee.

9. And now, lastly, listen to what we have here, how this ointment was to some a sweet savor unto life, and to others a sweet savor unto death. When the pious Mary had rendered this grateful service to the Lord, straightway one of His disciples, Judas Iscariot, who was yet to betray Him, said, "Why was not this ointment sold for three hundred pence, and given to the poor?" Alas for thee, wretched man! the sweet savor hath slain thee. For the cause that led him so to speak is disclosed by the holy evangelist. But we, too, might have supposed, had not the real state of his mind been revealed in the Gospel, that the care of the poor might have induced him so to speak. Not so. What then? Hearken to a true witness: "This he said, not that he cared for the poor; but because he was a thief, and had the money bag, and bare[2] what was put therein." Did

he bear it about, or bear it away? For the common service he bore it, as a thief he bore it away.

10. Look now, and learn that this Judas did not become perverted only at the time when he yielded to the bribery of the Jews and betrayed his Lord. For not a few, inattentive to the Gospel, suppose that Judas only perished when he accepted money from the Jews to betray the Lord. It was not then that he perished, but he was already a thief, and a reprobate, when following the Lord; for it was with his body and not with his heart that he followed. He made up the apostolic number of twelve, but had no part in the apostolic blessedness: he had been made the twelfth in semblance, and on his departure, and the succession of another, the apostolic reality was completed, and the entireness of the number conserved.[3] What lesson then, my brethren, did our Lord Jesus Christ wish to impress on His Church, when it pleased Him to have one castaway among the twelve, but this, that we should bear with the wicked, and refrain from dividing the body of Christ? Here you have Judas among the saints,—that Judas, mark you! who was a thief, yea—do not overlook it—not a thief of any ordinary type, but a thief and a sacrilegist: a robber of money bags, but of such as were the Lord's; of money bags, but of such as were sacred. If there is a distinction made in the public courts between such crimes as ordinary theft and peculation,—for by peculation we mean the theft of public property; and private theft is not visited with the same sentence as public,—how much more severe ought to be the sentence on the sacrilegious thief, who has dared to steal, not from places of any ordinary kind, but to steal from the Church? He who thieves from the Church, stands side by side with the castaway Judas. Such was this man Judas, and yet he went in and out with the eleven holy disciples. With them he came even to the table of the Lord: he was permitted to have intercourse with them, but he could not contaminate them. Of one bread did both Peter and Judas partake, and yet what communion had the believer with the infidel? Peter's partaking was unto life, but that of Judas unto death. For that good bread was just like the sweet savor. For as the sweet savor, so also does the good bread give life to the good, and bring death to the wicked. "For he that eateth unworthily, eateth and drinketh judgment to himself:"[4] "judgment to himself," not to thee. If, then, it is judgment to himself, not to thee, bear as one that

[1] Phil. i. 16, 18.

[2] "ἐβάσταζεν," as used by John, may signify here, *carried*, *bore*, in a good sense; or *carried off* as a thief: for the latter sense, see chap. xx. 15.—TR.

[3] Acts i. 26. [4] 1 Cor. xi. 29.

is good with him that is evil, that thou mayest attain unto the rewards of the good, and be not hurled into the punishment of the wicked.

11. Lay to heart our Lord's example while living with man upon earth. Why had He a money bag, who was ministered unto by angels, save to intimate that His Church was destined thereafter to have her repository for money? Why gave He admission to a thief, save to teach His Church patiently to bear with thieves? But he who had formed the habit of abstracting money from the bag, did not hesitate for money received to sell the Lord Himself. But let us see what answer our Lord gave to such words. See, brethren: He does not say to him, Thou speakest so on account of thy thievishness. He knew him to be a thief, yet did not betray him, but rather endured him, and showed us an example of patience in tolerating the wicked in the Church. "Then said Jesus to him: Let her keep it against the day of my burial." [1] He announced that His own death was at hand.

12. But what follows? "For the poor ye have always with you, but me ye will not have always." We can certainly understand, "the poor ye have always;" what He has thus said is true. When were the poor wanting in the Church? "But me ye will not have always;" what does He mean by this? How are we to understand, "Me ye will not have always"? Don't be alarmed: it was addressed to Judas. Why, then, did He not say, thou wilt have, but, ye will have? Because Judas is not here a unit. One wicked man represents the whole body of the wicked; in the same way as Peter, the whole body of the good, yea, the body of the Church, but in respect to the good. For if in Peter's case there were no sacramental symbol of the Church, the Lord would not have said to him, "I will give unto thee the keys of the kingdom of heaven: whatsoever thou shalt loose on earth shall be loosed in heaven; and whatsoever thou shalt bind on earth shall be bound in heaven." [2] If this was said only to Peter, it gives no ground of action to the Church. But if such is the case also in the Church, that what is bound on earth is bound in heaven, and what is loosed on earth is loosed in heaven,—for when the Church excommunicates, the excommunicated person is bound in heaven; when one is re-

conciled by the Church, the person so reconciled is loosed in heaven:—if such, then, is the case in the Church, Peter, in receiving the keys, represented the holy Church. If, then, in the person of Peter were represented the good in the Church, and in Judas' person were represented the bad in the Church, then to these latter was it said, "But me ye will not have always." But what means the "not always;" and what, the "always"? If thou art good, if thou belongest to the body represented by Peter, thou hast Christ both now and hereafter: now by faith, by sign, by the sacrament of baptism, by the bread and wine of the altar. Thou hast Christ now, but thou wilt have Him always; for when thou hast gone hence, thou wilt come to Him who said to the robber, "To-day shalt thou be with me in paradise." [3] But if thou livest wickedly, thou mayest seem to have Christ now, because thou enterest the Church, signest thyself with the sign of Christ, art baptized with the baptism of Christ, minglest thyself with the members of Christ, and approachest His altar: now thou hast Christ, but by living wickedly thou wilt not have Him always.

13. It may be also understood in this way: "The poor ye will have always with you, but me ye will not have always." The good may take it also as addressed to themselves, but not so as to be any source of anxiety; for He was speaking of His bodily presence. For in respect of His majesty, His providence, His ineffable and invisible grace, His own words are fulfilled, "Lo, I am with you alway, even to the end of the world." [4] But in respect of the flesh He assumed as the Word, in respect of that which He was as the son of the Virgin, of that wherein He was seized by the Jews, nailed to the tree, let down from the cross, enveloped in a shroud, laid in the sepulchre, and manifested in His resurrection, "ye will not have Him always." And why? Because in respect of His bodily presence He associated for forty days with His disciples, and then, having brought them forth for the purpose of beholding and not of following Him, He ascended into heaven, [5] and is no longer here. He is there, indeed, sitting at the right hand of the Father; and He is here also, having never withdrawn the presence of His glory. In other words, in respect of His divine presence we always have Christ; in respect of His presence in the flesh it was rightly said to the disciples, "Me ye will not have always." In this respect the Church enjoyed His presence only for a few days: now it possesses Him by faith, without

---

[1] Augustin's words, *sinite illam, ut in diem sepulturæ meæ servet illud*, as rendered above, differ considerably from those of our English version, and are more difficult to understand; but they agree with by far the larger number of Greek MSS., which read, Ἄφες αὐτὴν ἵνα εἰς τὴν ἡμέραν τοῦ ἐνταφιασμοῦ μου τηρήσῃ αὐτό. Our English version, "Let her alone: against the day of my burying hath she kept this," is taken from MSS. which omit ἵνα, and have τετήρηκεν instead of τηρήσῃ.—Tr.
[2] Matt. xvi. 19.

[3] Luke xxiii. 43.   [4] Matt. xxviii. 20.   [5] Acts i. 3, 9, 10.

seeing Him with the eyes. In whichever way, then, it was said, "But me ye will not have always," it can no longer, I suppose, after this twofold solution, remain as a subject of doubt.

14. Let us listen to the other few points that remain: "Much people of the Jews therefore knew that He was there: and they came not for Jesus' sake only, but that they might see Lazarus, whom He had raised from the dead." They were drawn by curiosity, not by charity: they came and saw. Hearken to the strange scheming of human vanity. Having seen Lazarus as one raised from the dead,—for the fame of such a miracle of the Lord's had been accompanied everywhere with so much evidence of its genuineness, and it had been so openly performed, that they could neither conceal nor deny what had been done,—only think of the plan they hit upon. "But the chief priests consulted that they might put Lazarus also to death; because that by reason of him many of the Jews went away, and believed on Jesus." O foolish consultation and blinded rage! Could not Christ the Lord, who was able to raise the dead, raise also the slain? When you were preparing a violent death for Lazarus, were you at the same time denuding the Lord of His power? If you think a dead man one thing, a murdered man another, look you only to this, that the Lord made both, and raised Lazarus to life when dead, and Himself when slain.

TRACTATE LI.

CHAPTER XII. 12–26.

1. AFTER our Lord's raising of one to life, who had been four days dead, to the utter amazement of the Jews, some of whom believed on seeing it, and others perished in their envy, because of that sweet savor which is unto life to some, and to others unto death;[1] after He had sat down to meat with Lazarus—the one who had been dead and raised to life—reclining also at table, and after the pouring on His feet of the ointment which had filled the house with its odor; and after the Jews also had shown their own spiritual abandonment in conceiving the useless cruelty and the monstrously foolish and insane guilt of slaying Lazarus; —of all which we have spoken as we could, by the grace of the Lord, in previous discourses: let your Charity now notice how abundant before our Lord's passion was the fruit that appeared of His preaching, and how large was the flock of lost sheep of the house of Israel which had heard the Shepherd's voice.

2. For the Gospel, the reading of which you have just been listening to, says: "On the next day much people that were come to the feast, when they heard that Jesus was coming to Jerusalem, took branches of palm trees and went forth to meet Him, and cried, Hosanna: blessed is He that cometh in the name of the Lord as the King of Israel." The branches of palm trees are laudatory emblems, significant of victory, because the Lord was about to overcome death by dying, and by the trophy of His cross to triumph over the devil, the prince of death. The exclamation used by the worshipping[2] people is Hosanna, indicating, as some who know the Hebrew language affirm, rather a state of mind than having any positive significance;[3] just as in our own tongue[4] we have what are called interjections, as when in our grief we say, Alas! or in our joy, Ha! or in our admiration, O how fine! where O! expresses only the feeling of the admirer. Of the same class must we believe this word to be, as it has failed to find an interpretation both in Greek and Latin, like that other, "Whosoever shall say to his brother, Raca."[5] For this also is allowed to be an interjection, expressive of angry feelings.

3. But when it is said, "Blessed is He that cometh in the name of the Lord, [as] the

---

[1] 2 Cor. ii. 15.

[2] *Obsecrantis*, literally *suppliant*, which is scarcely suitable to the context.

[3] The "some" here referred to by Augustin could scarcely have had a very extensive knowledge of the Hebrew language, as the word *Hosanna*, though left untranslated, as a well-known exclamation of the Jews in their religious services, is part of the same quotation from Psalm cxviii. (see vers. 25, 26) with the words that follow in the text. The sacred writers gave the nearest equivalent in Greek letters (ὡσαννά, Hosanna) of the Hebrew הוֹשִׁיעָה נָּא Save now!—TR.

[4] In text, *in lingua latina*.

[5] Raca (Syriac רֵקָא, Chaldee רֵיקָא, Hebrew רֵיק, *empty*) was an insulting epithet of common use from an early period among the Babylonians, and in our Lord's day among the inhabitants of Syria and Palestine. It exactly answers to our *idiot*, or *numskull*, and is of frequent occurrence afterwards in the same sense in rabbinical writings.—TR.

King of Israel," by "in the name of the Lord" we are rather to understand "in the name of God the Father," although it might also be understood as *in His own name*, inasmuch as He is also Himself the Lord. As we find Scripture also saying in another place, "The Lord rained [upon Sodom fire] from the Lord."[1] But His own words are a better guide to our understanding, when He saith, "I am come in my Father's name, and ye receive me not: another will come in his own name, and him ye will receive."[2] For the true teacher of humility is Christ, who humbled Himself, and became obedient unto death, even the death of the cross.[3] But He does not lose His divinity in teaching us humility; in the one He is the Father's equal, in the other He is assimilated to us. By that which made Him the equal of the Father, He called us into existence; and by that in which He is like unto us, He redeemed us from ruin.

4. These, then, were the words of praise addressed to Jesus by the multitude, "Hosanna: blessed is He that cometh in the name of the Lord, the King of Israel." What a cross of mental suffering must the Jewish rulers have endured when they heard so great a multitude proclaiming Christ as their King! But what honor was it to the Lord to be King of Israel? What great thing was it to the King of eternity to become the King of men? For Christ's kingship over Israel was not for the purpose of exacting tribute, of putting swords into His soldiers' hands, of subduing His enemies by open warfare; but He was King of Israel in exercising kingly authority over their inward natures, in consulting for their eternal interests, in bringing into His heavenly kingdom those whose faith, and hope, and love were centred in Himself. Accordingly, for the Son of God, the Father's equal, the Word by whom all things were made, in His good pleasure to be King of Israel, was an act of condescension and not of promotion; a token of compassion, and not any increase of power. For He who was called on earth the King of the Jews, is in the heavens the Lord of angels.

5. "And Jesus, when He had found a young ass, sat thereon." Here the account is briefly given: for how it all happened may be found at full length in the other evangelists.[4] But there is appended to the circumstance itself a testimony from the prophets, to make it evident that He in whom was fulfilled all they read in Scripture, was entirely misunderstood by the evil-minded rulers of the Jews. Jesus, then, "found a young ass, and sat thereon; as it is written, Fear not, daughter of Zion: behold, thy King cometh, sitting on an ass's colt." Among that people, then, was the daughter of Zion to be found; for Zion is the same as Jerusalem. Among that very people, I say, reprobate and blind as they were, was the daughter of Zion, to whom it was said, "Fear not, daughter of Zion: behold, thy King cometh, sitting on an ass's colt." This daughter of Zion, who was thus divinely addressed, was amongst those sheep that were hearing the Shepherd's voice, and in that multitude which was celebrating the Lord's coming with such religious zeal, and accompanying Him in such warlike array. To her was it said, "Fear not:" acknowledge Him whom thou art now extolling, and give not way to fear when He comes to suffering; for by the shedding of His blood is thy guilt to be blotted out, and thy life restored. But by the ass's colt, on which no man had ever sat (for so it is found recorded in the other evangelists), we are to understand the Gentile nations which had not received the law of the Lord; by the ass, on the other hand (for both animals were brought to the Lord), that people of His which came of the nation of Israel, and was already so far subdued as to recognize its Master's crib.

6. "These things understood not His disciples at the first; but when Jesus was glorified," that is, when He had manifested the power of His resurrection, "then remembered they that these things were written of Him, and they had done these things unto Him," that is, they did nothing else but what had been written concerning Him. In short, mentally comparing with the contents of Scripture what was accomplished both prior to and in the course of our Lord's passion, they found this also therein, that it was in accordance with the utterance of the prophets that He sat on an ass's colt.

7. "The people, therefore, that was with Him when He called Lazarus out of his tomb, and raised him from the dead, bare record. For this cause the crowd also met Him, for that they heard that He had done this miracle. The Pharisees, therefore, said among themselves: Perceive ye that we prevail nothing? Behold, the whole world is gone after Him." Mob set mob in motion.[5] "But why art thou, blinded mob that thou art, filled with envy because the world has gone after its Maker?"

8. "And there were certain Gentiles among them that had come up to worship at the feast:

---

[1] Gen. xix. 24. [2] Chap. v. 43. [3] Phil. ii. 8.
[4] Matt. xxi. 1-16; Mark xi. 1-11; Luke xix. 29-48.

[5] *Turba turbavit turbam.*

the same came therefore to Philip, who was of Bethsaida of Galilee, and desired him, saying, Sir, we would see Jesus. Philip cometh and telleth Andrew: and again Andrew and Philip tell Jesus." Let us hearken to the Lord's reply. See how the Jews wish to kill Him, the Gentiles to see Him; and yet those, too, were of the Jews who cried, "Blessed is He that cometh in the name of the Lord, the King of Israel." Here, then, were they of the circumcision and they of the uncircumcision, like two house walls running from different directions and meeting together with the kiss of peace, in the one faith of Christ. Let us listen, then, to the voice of the Cornerstone: "And Jesus answered them, saying, The hour is come that the Son of man should be glorified." Perhaps some one supposes here that He spake of Himself as glorified, because the Gentiles wished to see Him. Such is not the case. But He saw the Gentiles themselves in all nations coming to the faith after His own passion and resurrection, because, as the apostle says, "Blindness in part has happened to Israel, until the fullness of the Gentiles should be come in."[1] Taking occasion, therefore, from those Gentiles who desired to see Him, He announces the future fullness of the Gentile nations, and promises the near approach of the hour when He should be glorified Himself, and when, on its consummation in heaven, the Gentile nations should be brought to the faith. To this it is that the prediction pointed, "Be Thou exalted, O God, above the heavens, and Thy glory above all the earth."[2] Such is the fullness of the Gentiles, of which the apostle saith, "Blindness in part is happened to Israel, till the fullness of the Gentiles come in."

9. But the height of His glorification had to be preceded by the depth of His passion. Accordingly, He went on to add, "Verily, verily, I say unto you, except a grain of wheat fall into the ground and die, it abideth alone; but if it die, it bringeth forth much fruit." But He spake of Himself. He Himself was the grain that had to die, and be multiplied; to suffer death through the unbelief of the Jews, and to be multiplied in the faith of many nations.

10. And now, by way of exhortation to follow in the path of His own passion, He adds, "He that loveth his life shall lose it," which may be understood in two ways: "He that loveth shall lose," that is, If thou lovest, be ready to lose; if thou wouldst possess life in Christ, be not afraid of death for Christ. Or

otherwise, "He that loveth his life shall lose it." Do not love for fear of losing; love it not here, lest thou lose it in eternity. But what I have said last seems better to correspond with the meaning of the Gospel, for there follow the words, "And he that hateth his life in this world shall keep it unto life eternal." So that when it is said in the previous clause, "He that loveth," there is to be understood *in this world*, he it is that shall lose it. "But he that hateth," that is, in this world, is he that shall keep it unto life eternal. Surely a profound and strange declaration as to the measure of a man's love for his own life that leads to its destruction, and of his hatred to it that secures its preservation! If in a sinful way thou lovest it, then dost thou really hate it; if in a way accordant with what is good thou hast hated it, then hast thou really loved it. Happy they who have so hated their life while keeping it, that their love shall not cause them to lose it. But beware of harboring the notion that thou mayest court self-destruction by any such understanding of thy duty to hate thy life in this world. For on such grounds it is that certain wrong-minded and perverted people, who, with regard to themselves, are murderers of a specially cruel and impious character, commit themselves to the flames, suffocate themselves in water, dash themselves against a precipice, and perish. This was no teaching of Christ's, who, on the other hand, met the devil's suggestion of a precipice with the answer, "Get thee behind me, Satan; for it is written, Thou shalt not tempt the Lord thy God."[3] To Peter also He said, signifying by what death he should glorify God, "When thou wast young, thou girdedst thyself, and walkedst whither thou wouldest: but when thou shalt be old, another shall gird thee, and carry thee whither thou wouldest not;"[4]— where He made it sufficiently plain that it is not by himself but by another that one must be slain who follows in the footsteps of Christ. And so, when one's case has reached the crisis that this condition is placed before him, either that he must act contrary to the divine commandment or quit this life, and that a man is compelled to choose one or other of the two by the persecutor who is threatening him with death, in such circumstances let him prefer dying in the love of God to living under His anger, in such circumstances let him hate his life in this world that he may keep it unto life eternal.

11. "If any man serve me, let him follow me." What is that, "let him follow me,"

---

[1] Rom. xi. 25.   [2] Ps. cviii. 5.   [3] Matt. iv. 7.   [4] Chap. xxi. 18, 19.

but just, let him imitate me? "Because Christ suffered for us," says the Apostle Peter, "leaving us an example that we should follow His steps."[1] Here you have the meaning of the words, "If any man serve me, let him follow me." But with what result? what wages? what reward? "And where I am," He says, "there shall also my servant be." Let Him be freely loved, that so the reward of the service done Him may be to be with Him. For where will one be well apart from Him, or when will one come to feel himself in an evil case in company with Him? Hear it still more plainly: "If any man serve me, him will my Father honor." And what will be the honor but to be with His Son? For of what He said before, "Where I am, there shall also my servant be," we may understand Him as giving the explanation, when He says here, "him will my Father honor." For what greater honor can await an adopted son than to be with the Only-begotten; not, indeed, as raised to the level of His Godhead, but made a partaker of His eternity?

12. But it becomes us rather to inquire what is to be understood by this serving of Christ to which there is attached so great a reward. For if we have taken up the idea that the serving of Christ is the preparation of what is needful for the body, or the cooking and serving up of food, or the mixing of drink and handing the cup to one at the supper table; this, indeed, was done to Him by those who had the privilege of His bodily presence, as in the case of Martha and Mary, when Lazarus also was one of those who sat at the table. But in that sort of way Christ was served also by the reprobate Judas; for it was he also who had the money bag; and although he had the exceeding wickedness to steal of its contents, yet it was he also who provided what was needful for the meal.[2] And so also, when our Lord said to him, "What thou doest, do quickly," there were some who thought that He only gave him orders to make some needful preparations for the feast-day, or to give something to the poor.[3] In no sense, therefore, was it of this class of servants that the Lord said, "Where I am, there shall also my servant be," and "If any man serve me, him will my Father honor;" for we see that Judas, who served in this way, became an object of reprobation rather than of honor. Why, then, go elsewhere to find out what this serving of Christ

implies, and not rather see its disclosure in the words themselves? for when He said, "If any man serve me, let him follow me," He wished it to be understood just as if He had said, If any man doth not follow me, he serveth me not. And those, therefore, are the servants of Jesus Christ, who seek not their own things, but the things that are Jesus Christ's.[4] For "let him follow me" is just this: Let him walk in my ways, and not in his own; as it is written elsewhere, "He that saith he abideth in Christ, ought himself also so to walk, even as He walked."[5] For he ought, if supplying food to the hungry, to do it in the way of mercy and not of boasting, seeking therein nothing else but the doing of good, and not letting his left hand know what his right hand doeth;[6] in other words, that all thought of self-seeking should be utterly estranged from a work of charity. He that serveth in this way serveth Christ, and will have it rightly said to him, "Inasmuch as ye did it unto one of the least of those who are mine, ye did it unto me."[7] And thus doing not only those acts of mercy that pertain to the body, but every good work, for the sake of Christ (for then will all be good, because "Christ is the end of the law for righteousness to every one that believeth"[8]), he is Christ's servant even to that work of special love, which is to lay down his life for the brethren, for that were to lay it down also for Christ. For this also will He say hereafter in behalf of His members: Inasmuch as ye did it for these, ye have done it for me. And certainly it was in reference to such a work that He was also pleased to make and to style Himself a servant, when He says, "Even as the Son of man came not to be ministered unto [served], but to minister [serve], and to lay down His life for many."[9] Every one, therefore, is the servant of Christ in the same way as Christ also is a servant. And he that serveth Christ in this way will be honored by His Father with the signal honor of being with His Son, and having nothing wanting to his happiness for ever.

13. Accordingly, brethren, when you hear the Lord saying, "Where I am, there shall also my servant be," do not think merely of good bishops and clergymen. But be yourselves also in your own way serving Christ, by good lives, by giving alms, by preaching His name and doctrine as you can; and every father of a family also, be acknowledging in this name the affection he owes as a parent to his family. For Christ's sake, and for the sake of life eternal, let him be warning, and

[1] 1 Pet. ii. 21.
[2] Chap. xii. 2-6. There is no ground in these verses for Augustin's notion that the expense of that supper was defrayed out of the funds in Judas' keeping. The whole account leaves the impression that it was provided by Lazarus and his sisters, although, strictly speaking, ἐποίησαν (ver. 2) leaves it undetermined.—Tr.
[3] Chap. xiii. 27, 29.

[4] Phil. ii. 21.　[5] 1 John ii. 6.　[6] Matt. vi. 3.
[7] Matt. xxv. 40.　[8] Rom. x. 4.　[9] Matt. xx. 28.

teaching, and exhorting, and correcting all his household; let him show kindliness, and exercise discipline; and so in his own house he will be filling an ecclesiastical and kind of episcopal office, and serving Christ, that he may be with Him for ever. For even that noblest service of suffering has been rendered by many of your class; for many who were neither bishops nor clergy, but young men and virgins, those advanced in years with those who were not, many married persons both male and female, many fathers and mothers of families, have served Christ even to the laying down of their lives in martyrdom for His sake, and have been honored by the Father in receiving crowns of exceeding glory.

TRACTATE LII.

CHAPTER XII. 27–36.

1. AFTER the Lord Jesus Christ, in the words of yesterday's lesson, had exhorted His servants to follow Him, and had predicted His own passion in this way, that unless a corn of wheat fall into the ground and die, it abideth alone; but if it die, it bringeth forth much fruit; and also had stirred up those who wished to follow Him to the kingdom of heaven, to hate their life in this world if their thought was to keep it unto life eternal,—He again toned down His own feelings to our infirmity and says, where our lesson to-day commenced, " Now is my soul[1] troubled." Whence, Lord, was Thy soul troubled? He had, indeed, said a little before, " He that hateth his life [soul] in this world shall keep it unto life eternal." Dost thou then love thy life in this world, and is thy soul troubled as the hour approacheth when thou shalt leave this world? Who would dare affirm this of the soul [life] of the Lord? We rather it was whom He transferred unto Himself; He took us into His own person as our Head, and assumed the feelings of His members; and so it was not by any others He was troubled, but, as was said of Him when He raised Lazarus, " He was troubled in Himself."[2] For it behoved the one Mediator between God and men, the man Christ Jesus, just as He has lifted us up to the heights of heaven, to descend with us also into the lowest depths of suffering.

2. I hear Him saying a little before, " The hour cometh that the Son of man should be glorified: if a corn of wheat die, it bringeth forth much fruit." I hear this also, " He that hateth his life in this world shall keep it unto life eternal." Nor am I permitted merely to admire, but commanded to imitate, and so, by the words that follow, " If any man serve me, let him follow me; and where I am, there shall also my servant be," I am all on fire to despise the world, and in my sight the whole of this life, however lengthened, becomes only a vapor; in comparison with my love for eternal things, all that is temporal has lost its value with me. And now, again, it is my Lord Himself, who by such words has suddenly transported me from the weakness that was mine to the strength that was His, that I hear saying, " Now is my soul troubled." What does it mean? How biddest Thou my soul follow Thee if I behold Thine own troubled? How shall I endure what is felt to be heavy by strength so great? What is the kind of foundation I can seek if the Rock is giving way? But methinks I hear in my own thoughts the Lord giving me an answer, saying, Thou shalt follow me the better, because it is to aid thy power of endurance that I thus interpose. Thou hast heard, as addressed to thyself, the voice of my fortitude; hear in me the voice of thy infirmity: I supply strength for thy running, and I check not thy hastening, but I transfer to myself thy causes for trembling, and I pave the way for thy marching along. O Lord our Mediator, God above us, man for us, I own Thy mercy! For because Thou, who art so great, art troubled through the good will of Thy love, Thou preservest, by the richness of Thy comfort, the many in Thy body who are troubled by the continual experience of their own weakness, from perishing utterly in their despair.

---

[1] The word *anima* used here, and frequently elsewhere, and corresponding to the Greek ψυχή, denotes " human life," in reference to its internal principle or substance ; and differs from " vita " (Gr. ζωή), as in the words following above, " unto eternal life " (*vitam*), which expresses rather the general idea of life in its existence, aggregate qualities, and duration. Our English word " soul," which best corresponds with *anima*, is, however, more restricted in the idea which it popularly suggests ; and hence, as in our English version of the Scriptures, the apparent confusion, which is unavoidable, in translating *anima* sometimes by " soul " and sometimes by " life."—TR.

[2] Chap. xi. 33: literally, as in margin of English Bible, " He troubled Himself."

3. In a word, let the man who would follow learn the road by which he must travel. Perhaps an hour of terrible trial has come, and the choice is set before thee either to do iniquity or endure suffering; the weak soul is troubled, on whose behalf the invincible soul [of Jesus] was voluntarily troubled; set then the will of God before thine own. For notice what is immediately subjoined by thy Creator and thy Master, by Him who made thee, and became Himself for thy teaching that which He made; for He who made man was made man, but He remained still the unchangeable God, and transplanted manhood into a better condition. Listen, then, to what He adds to the words, "Now is my soul troubled." "And what shall I say? Father, save me from this hour: but for this cause came I unto this hour. Father, glorify Thy name." He has taught thee here what to think of, what to say, on whom to call, in whom to hope, and whose will, as sure and divine, to prefer to thine own, which is human and weak. Imagine Him not, therefore, as losing aught of His own exalted position in wishing thee to rise up out of the depths of thy ruin. For He thought it meet also to be tempted by the devil, by whom otherwise He would never have been tempted, just as, had He not been willing, He would never have suffered; and the answers He gave to the devil are such as thou also oughtest to use in times of temptation.[1] And He, indeed, was tempted, but not endangered, that He might show thee, when in danger through temptation, how to answer the tempter, so as not to be carried away by the temptation, but to escape its danger. But when He here said, "Now is my soul troubled;" and also when He says, "My soul is sorrowful, even unto death;" and "Father, if it be possible, let this cup pass from me;" He assumed the infirmity of man, to teach him, when thereby saddened and troubled, to say what follows: "Nevertheless, Father, not as I will, but as Thou wilt."[2] For thus it is that man is turned from the human to the divine, when the will of God is preferred to his own. But to what do the words "Glorify Thy name" refer, but to His own passion and resurrection? For what else can it mean, but that the Father should thus glorify the Son, who in like manner glorifieth His own name in the similar sufferings of His servants? Hence it is recorded of Peter, that for this cause He said concerning him, "Another shall gird thee, and carry thee whither thou wouldest not." because He intended to signify "by what death

he should glorify God."[3] Therefore in him, too, did God glorify His name, because thus also does He glorify Christ in His members.

4. "Then came there a voice from heaven, [saying], I have both glorified it, and will glorify it again." "I have both glorified it," before I created the world, "and I will glorify it again," when He shall rise from the dead and ascend into heaven. It may also be otherwise understood. "I have both glorified it,"—when He was born of the Virgin, when He exercised miraculous powers; when the Magi, guided by a star in the heavens, bowed in adoration before Him; when He was recognized by saints filled with the Holy Spirit; when He was openly proclaimed by the descent of the Spirit in the form of a dove, and pointed out by the voice that sounded from heaven; when He was transfigured on the mount; when He wrought many miracles, cured and cleansed multitudes, fed so vast a number with a very few loaves, commanded the winds and the waves, and raised the dead;—"and I will glorify it again;" when He shall rise from the dead; when death shall have no longer dominion over Him; and when He shall be exalted over the heavens as God, and His glory over all the earth.

5. "The people therefore that stood by, and heard it, said that it thundered: others said, An angel spake to Him. Jesus answered and said, This voice came not because of me, but for your sakes." He thereby showed that the voice made no intimation to Him of what He already knew, but to those who needed the information. And just as that voice was uttered by God, not on His account, but on that of others, so His soul was troubled, not on His own account, but voluntarily for the sake of others.

6. Look at what follows: "Now," He says, "is the judgment of the world." What, then, are we to expect at the end of time? But the judgment that is looked for in the end will be the judging of the living and the dead, the awarding of eternal rewards and punishment. Of what sort, then, is the judgment now? I have already, in former lessons, as far as I could, put you in mind, beloved, that there is a judgment spoken of, not of condemnation, but of discrimination;[4] as it is written, "Judge me, O God, and plead [discern, discriminate] my cause against an unholy nation."[5] And many are the judgments of God; as it is said in the psalm, "Thy judgments are a great deep."[6]

---

[1] Matt. iv. 1-10.   [2] Matt. xxvi. 38, 39.

[3] Chap. xxi. 18, 19.
[4] Or, discernment, *discretio*; see Tract. XLIII. sec. 9.
[5] Ps. xliii. 1.   [6] Ps. xxxvi. 6.

And the apostle also says, "O the depth of the riches of the wisdom and the knowledge of God! how unsearchable are His judgments!"[1] To such judgments does that spoken of here by the Lord also belong, "Now is the judgment of this world;" while that judgment in the end is reserved, when the living and the dead shall at last be judged. The devil, therefore, had possession of the human race, and held them by the written bond of their sins as criminals amenable to punishment; he ruled in the hearts of unbelievers, and, deceiving and enslaving them, seduced them to forsake the Creator and give worship to the creature; but by faith in Christ, which was confirmed by His death and resurrection, and, by His blood, which was shed for the remission of sins, thousands of believers are delivered from the dominion of the devil, are united to the body of Christ, and under this great head are made by His one Spirit to spring up into new life as His faithful members. This it was that He called the judgment, this righteous separation, this expulsion of the devil from His own redeemed.

7. Attend, in short, to His own words. For just as if we had been inquiring what He meant by saying, "Now is the judgment of the world," He proceeded to explain it when He says, "Now shall the prince of this world be cast out." What we have thus heard was the kind of judgment He meant. Not that one, therefore, which is yet to come in the end, when the living and dead shall be judged, some of them set apart on His right hand, and the others on His left; but that judgment by which "the prince of this world shall be cast out." In what sense, then, was he within, and whither did He mean that he was to be cast out? Was it this: That he was in the world, and was cast forth beyond its boundaries? For had He been speaking of that judgment which is yet to come in the end, some one's thoughts might have turned to that eternal fire into which the devil is to be cast with his angels, and all who belong to him;—that is, not naturally, but through moral delinquency; not because he created or begat them, but because he persuaded and kept hold of them: some one, therefore, might have thought that that eternal fire was outside the world, and that this was the meaning of the words, "he shall be cast out." But as He says, "Now is the judgment of this world," and in explanation of His meaning, adds, "Now shall the prince of this world be cast out," we are thereby to understand

what is now being done, and not what is to be, so long afterwards, at the last day. The Lord, therefore, foretold what He knew, that after His own passion and glorification, many nations throughout the whole world, in whose hearts the devil was an inmate, would become believers, and the devil, when thus renounced by faith, is cast out.

8. But some one says, Was he then not cast out of the hearts of the patriarchs and prophets, and the righteous of olden time? Certainly he was. How, then, is it said, "Now he shall be cast out"? How else can we think of it, but that what was then done in the case of a very few individuals, was now foretold as speedily to take place in many and mighty nations? Just as also that other saying, "For the Spirit was not yet given, because that Jesus was not yet glorified,"[2] may suggest a similar inquiry, and find a similar solution. For it was not without the Holy Spirit that the prophets predicted the events of the future; nor was it so that the aged Simeon and the widowed Anna knew by the Holy Spirit the infant Lord;[3] and that Zacharias and Elisabeth uttered by the Holy Spirit so many predictions concerning Him, when He was not yet born, but only conceived.[4] But "the Spirit was not yet given;" that is, with that abundance of spiritual grace which enabled those assembled together to speak in every language,[5] and thus announce beforehand in the language of every nation the Church of the future: and so by this spiritual grace it was that nations were gathered into congregations, sins were pardoned far and wide, and thousands of thousands were reconciled unto God.

9. But then, says some one, since the devil is thus cast out of the hearts of believers, does he now tempt none of the faithful? Nay, verily, he does not cease to tempt. But it is one thing to reign within, another to assail from without; for in like manner the best fortified city is sometimes attacked by an enemy without being taken. And if some of his arrows are discharged, and reach us, the apostle reminds us how to render them harmless, when he speaks of the breastplate and the shield of faith.[6] And if he sometimes wounds us, we have the remedy at hand. For as the combatants are told, "These things I write unto you, that ye sin not:" so those who are wounded have the sequel to listen to, "And if any man sin, we have an Advocate with the Father, Jesus Christ, the righteous; and He is the propitiation for our sins."[7] And what do we pray for when we

---

[1] Rom. xi. 33.
19

[2] Chap. vii. 39.   [3] Luke ii. 25–38.   [4] Luke i. 41–45, 67–69.
[5] Acts ii. 4–6.   [6] 1 Thess. v. 8.   [7] 1 John ii. 1, 2.

say, "Forgive us our debts," but for the healing of our wounds? And what else do we ask, when we say, "Lead us not into temptation,"[1] but that he who thus lies in wait for us, or assails us from without, may fail on every side to effect an entrance, and be unable to overcome us either by fraud or force? Nevertheless, whatever engines of war he may erect against us, so long as he has no more a place in the heart that faith inhabits, he is cast out. But "except the Lord keep the city, the watchman waketh but in vain."[2] Presume not, therefore, about yourselves, if you would not have the devil, who has once been cast out, to be recalled within.

10. On the other hand, let us be far from supposing that the devil is called in any such way the prince of the world, as that we should believe him possessed of power to rule over the heaven and the earth. The world is so spoken of in respect of wicked men, who have overspread the whole earth; just as a house is spoken of in respect to its inhabitants, and we accordingly say, It is a good house, or a bad house; not as finding fault with, or approving of, the erection of walls and roofs, but the morals either of the good or the bad within it. In a similar way, therefore, it is said, "The prince of this world;" that is, the prince of all the wicked who inhabit this world. The world is also spoken of in respect to the good, who in like manner have overspread the whole earth; and hence the apostle says, "God was in Christ, reconciling the world unto Himself."[3] These are they out of whose hearts the prince of this world is ejected.

11. Accordingly, after saying, "Now shall the prince of this world be cast out," He added, "And I, if I be lifted up from the earth, will draw all things[4] after me." And what "all" is that, but those out of which the other is ejected? But He did not say, All men, but "all things;" for all men have not faith.[5] And, therefore, He did not allude to the totality of men, but to the creature in its personal integrity, that is, to spirit, and soul, and body; or all that which makes us the intelligent, living, visible, and palpable beings we are. For He who said, "Not a hair of your head shall perish,"[6] is He who draweth all things after Him. Or if by "all things" it is men that are to be understood, we can speak of all things that are foreordained to salvation: of all which He declared,

when previously speaking of His sheep, that not one of them would be lost.[7] And of a certainty all classes of men, both of every language and every age, and all grades of rank, and all diversities of talents, and all the professions of lawful and useful arts, and all else that can be named in accordance with the innumerable differences by which men, save in sin alone, are mutually separated, from the highest to the lowest, and from the king to the beggar, "all," He says, "will I draw after me;" that He may be their head, and they His members. But this will be, He adds, "if I be lifted up from the earth," that is, when I am lifted up; for He has no doubt of the future accomplishment of that which He came to fulfill. He here alludes to what He said before: "But if the corn of wheat die, it bringeth forth much fruit." For what else did He signify by His lifting up, than His suffering on the cross? an explanation which the evangelist himself has not omitted; for he has appended the words, "And this He said signifying what death He should die."

12. "The people answered Him, We have heard out of the law that Christ abideth for ever: and how sayest Thou, The Son of man must be lifted up? And who is this Son of man?" It had stuck to their memory that the Lord was constantly calling Himself the Son of man. For, in the passage before us, He does not say, If the Son of man be lifted up from the earth; but had called Himself so before, in the lesson which was read and expounded yesterday, when those Gentiles were announced who desired to see Him: "The hour is come that the Son of man should be glorified" (ver. 23). Retaining this, therefore, in their minds, and understanding what He now said, "When I am lifted up from the earth," of the death of the cross, they inquired of Him, and said, "We have heard out of the law that Christ abideth for ever; and how sayest Thou, The Son of man must be lifted up? who is this Son of man?" For if it is Christ, He, they say, abideth for ever; and if He abideth for ever, how shall He be lifted up from the earth, that is, how shall He die through the suffering of the cross? For they understood Him to have spoken of what they themselves were meditating to do. And so He did not dissipate for them the obscurity of such words by imparting wisdom, but by stimulating their conscience.

13. "Then said Jesus unto them, Yet a little[8] light is in you." And by this it is you understand that Christ abideth for ever.

---

[1] Matt. vi. 12, 13.   [2] Ps. cxxvii. 1.   [3] 2 Cor. v. 19.
[4] There are here two readings in the Greek MSS., πάντας (all men), and πάντα (all things), of which the former seems now the better approved; but the latter is that adopted by Augustin and the Vulgate.—TR.
[5] 2 Thess. iii. 2.   [6] Luke xxi. 18.

[7] Chap. x. 28.   [8] *Modicum lumen.*

"Walk, then, while ye have the light, lest darkness come upon you." Walk, draw near, come to the full understanding that Christ shall both die and shall live for ever; that He shall shed His blood to redeem us, and ascend on high to carry His redeemed along with Him. But darkness will come upon you, if your belief in Christ's eternity is of such a kind as to refuse to admit in His case the humiliation of death. "And he that walketh in darkness knoweth not whither he goeth." So may he stumble on that stone of stumbling and rock of offence which the Lord Himself became to the blinded Jews: just as to those who believed, the stone which the builders despised was made the head of the corner.[1] Hence, they thought Christ unworthy of their belief; because in their impiety they treated His dying with contempt, they ridiculed the idea of His being slain:

[1] 1 Pet. ii. 6-8.

and yet it was the very death of the grain of corn that was to lead to its own multiplication, and the lifting up of one who was drawing all things after Him. "While ye have the light," He adds, "believe in the light, that ye may be the children of light." While you have possession of some truth that you have heard, believe in the truth, that you may be born again in the truth.

14. "These things spake Jesus, and departed, and did hide Himself from them." Not from those who had begun to believe and to love Him, nor from those who had come to meet Him with branches of palm trees and songs of praise; but from those who saw and hated Him, for they saw Him not, but only stumbled on that stone in their blindness. But when Jesus hid Himself from those who desired to slay Him (as you need from forgetfulness to be often reminded), He had regard to our human weakness, but derogated not in aught from His own authority.

TRACTATE LIII.

CHAPTER XII. 37–43.

1. WHEN our Lord Christ, foretelling His own passion, and the fruitfulness of His death in being lifted up on the cross, said that He would draw all [things] after Him; and when the Jews, understanding that He spake of His death, put to Him the question how He could speak of death as awaiting Him, when they heard out of the law that Christ abideth for ever; He exhorted them, while still they had in them the little light, which had so taught them that Christ was eternal, to walk, to make themselves acquainted with the whole subject, lest they should be overtaken with darkness. And, when He had said this, He hid Himself from them. With these points you have been made acquainted in former Lord's day lessons and discourses.

2. The evangelist thereafter brings forward what has formed the brief subject of to-day's reading, and says, " But though He had done so many miracles before them, yet they believed not on Him: that the saying of Isaiah the prophet might be fulfilled, which he spake, Lord, who hath believed our report? and to whom hath the arm of the Lord been revealed?" Where he makes it sufficiently plain that the Son of God is Himself the arm of the Lord; not that the person of God the

Father is determined by the shape of human flesh, and that the Son is attached to Him as a member of His body; but because all things were made by Him, and therefore He is designated the arm of the Lord. For as it is with thine arm that thou workest, so the Word of God is styled His arm; because by the Word He elaborated the world. For why does a man, in order to do some work, stretch forth his arm, but because the doing of it does not straightway follow his word? And if he was endowed with such pre-eminent power that what he said was done without any movement of his body, then would his word be his arm. But the Lord Jesus, the only-begotten Son of God the Father, as He is no mere member of the Father's body, so is He no mere thinkable, and audible, and transitory word; for, as all things were made by Him, He was the word of God.

3. When, therefore, we hear that the Son of God is the arm of God the Father, let no carnal custom raise its distracting din in our ears; but as far as His grace enables us, let us think of that power and wisdom of God by which all things were made. Surely such an arm as that is neither held out by stretching, nor drawn in by contracting it. For He

is not one and the same with the Father, but He and the Father are one; and as equal with the Father, He is in all respects complete, as well as the Father: so that no room is left open for the abominable error of those who assert that the Father alone exists, but according to the difference of causes is Himself sometimes called the Son, sometimes the Holy Spirit; and so also from these words may venture to say, See, you perceive that the Father alone exists, if the Son is IIis arm: for a man and his arm are not two persons, but one. Not understanding nor considering how words are transferred from one thing to another, on account of some mutual likeness, even in our daily forms of speech about things the most familiar and visible; and how much the more must it be so, in order that things ineffable may find some sort of expression in our speech, things which, as they really exist, cannot be expressed in words at all? For even one man styles another his arm, by whom he is accustomed to transact his business: and if he is deprived of him, he says in his grief, I have lost my arm; and to him who has taken him away, he says, You have deprived me of my arm. Let them understand, then, the sense in which the Son is termed the arm of the Father, as that by which the Father hath executed all His works; that they may not, by failing to understand this, and continuing in the darkness of their error, resemble those Jews of whom it was said, "And to whom hath the arm of the Lord been revealed?"

4. And here we meet with the second question, to treat of which, indeed, in any adequate manner, to investigate all its mysterious windings, and throw them open to the light in a befitting way, I think within the scope neither of my own powers, nor of the shortness of the time, nor of your capacity. Yet, as we cannot allow ourselves so far to disappoint your expectations as to pass on to other topics without saying something on this, take what we shall be able to offer you: and wherein we fail to satisfy your expectations, ask the increase of Him who appointed us to plant and to water; for, as the apostle saith, "Neither is he that planteth anything, nor he that watereth; but God that giveth the increase."[1] There are some, then, who mutter among themselves, and sometimes speak out when they can, and even break forth into turbulent debate, saying: What did the Jews do, or what fault was it of theirs, if it was a necessity "that the saying of Isaiah the prophet should be fulfilled, which he spake,

Lord, who hath believed our report? and to whom hath the arm of the Lord been revealed?" To whom our answer is, that the Lord, in His foreknowledge of the future, foretold by the prophet the unbelief of the Jews; He foretold it, but did not cause it. For God does not compel any one to sin simply because He knows already the future sins of men. For He foreknew sins that were theirs, not His own; sins that were referable to no one else, but to their own selves. Accordingly, if what He foreknew as theirs is not really theirs, then had He no true foreknowledge: but as His foreknowledge is infallible, it is doubtless no one else, but they themselves, whose sinfulness God foreknew, that are the sinners. The Jews, therefore, committed sin, with no compulsion to do so on His part, to whom sin is an object of displeasure; but He foretold their committing of it, because nothing is concealed from His knowledge And accordingly, had they wished to do good instead of evil, they would not have been hindered; but in this which they were to do they were foreseen of Him who knows what every man will do, and what He is yet to render unto such an one according to his work.

5. But the words of the Gospel also, that follow, are still more pressing, and start a question of more profound import: for He goes on to say, "Therefore they could not believe, because that Isaiah said again, He hath blinded their eyes, and hardened their heart; that they should not see with their eyes, nor understand with their heart, and be converted, and I should heal them." For it is said to us: If they could not believe, what sin is it in man not to do what he cannot do? and if they sinned in not believing, then they had the power to believe, and did not use it. If, then, they had the power, how says the Gospel, "Therefore they could not believe, because that Isaiah said again, He hath blinded their eyes, and hardened their heart;" so that (which is of grave import) to God Himself is referred the cause of their not believing, inasmuch as it is He who "hath blinded their eyes, and hardened their heart"? For what is thus testified to in the prophetical Scriptures, is at least not spoken of the devil, but of God. For were we to suppose it said of the devil, that he "hath blinded their eyes, and hardened their heart;" we have to undertake the task of being able to show what blame was theirs in not believing, of whom it is said, "they could not believe." And then, what reply shall we give touching another testimony of this very prophet, which the Apostle Paul has adopted, when he says: "Israel

---

[1] 1 Cor. iii. 7.

hath not obtained that which he seeketh for; but the election hath obtained it, and the rest were blinded, according as it is written, God hath given them the spirit of remorse, eyes that they should not see, and ears that they should not hear, unto this day"?[1]

6. Such, as you have just heard, brethren, is the question that comes before us, and you can perceive how profound it is; but we shall give what answer we can. "They could not believe," because that Isaiah the prophet foretold it; and the prophet foretold it because God foreknew that such would be the case. But if I am asked why they could not, I reply at once, because they would not; for certainly their depraved will was foreseen by God, and foretold through the prophet by Him from whom nothing that is future can be hid. But the prophet, sayest thou, assigns another cause than that of their will. What cause does the prophet assign? That "God hath given them the spirit of remorse, eyes that they should not see, and ears that they should not hear; and hath blinded their eyes, and hardened their heart." This also, I reply, their will deserved. For God thus blinds and hardens, simply by letting alone and withdrawing His aid: and God can do this by a judgment that is hidden, although not by one that is unrighteous. This is a doctrine which the piety of the God-fearing ought to preserve unshaken and inviolable in all its integrity: even as the apostle, when treating of the same intricate question, says, "What shall we say then? is there unrighteousness with God? God forbid."[2] If, then, we must be far from thinking that there is unrighteousness with God, this only can it be, that, when He giveth His aid, He acteth mercifully; and, when He withholdeth it, He acteth righteously: for in all He doeth, He acteth not rashly, but in accordance with judgment. And still further, if the judgments of the saints are righteous, how much more those of the sanctifying and justifying God? They are therefore righteous, although hidden. Accordingly, when questions of this sort come before us, why one is dealt with in such a way, and another in such another way; why this one is blinded by being forsaken of God, and that one is enlightened by the divine aid vouchsafed to him: let us not take upon ourselves to pass judgment on the judgment of so mighty a judge, but tremblingly exclaim with the apostle, "O the depth of the riches both of the wisdom and knowledge of God! how unsearchable are His judgments, and His ways past finding out!"[3] As it is also said in the psalm, "Thy judgments are as a great deep."[4]

7. Let not then, brethren, the expectations of your Charity drive me to attempt the task of penetrating into such a deep, of sounding such an abyss, of searching into what is unsearchable. I own my own little measure of ability, and I think I have some perception of yours also, as equally small. This is too high for my stature, and too strong for my strength; and for yours also, I think. Let us, therefore, listen together to the admonition and to the words of Scripture: "Seek not out the things that are too high for thee, neither search the things that are above thy strength."[5] Not that such things are forbidden us, since the divine Master saith, "There is nothing hid that shall not be revealed:"[6] but if we walk up to the measure of our present attainments, then, as the apostle tells us, not only what we know not and ought to know, but also if we are minded to know anything else, God will reveal even this unto us.[7] But if we have reached the pathway of faith, let us keep to it with all constancy: let it be our guide to the chamber of the King, in whom are hid all the treasures of wisdom and knowledge.[8] For it was in no spirit of grudging that the Lord Jesus Christ Himself acted towards those great and specially chosen disciples of His, when He said, "I have many things to say unto you, but ye cannot bear them now."[9] We must be walking, making progress, and growing, that our hearts may become fit to receive the things which we cannot receive at present. And if the last day shall find us sufficiently advanced, we shall then learn what here we were unable to know.

8. If, however, any one considers himself able, and has confidence enough, to give a clearer and better exposition of the question before us, God forbid that I should not be still more ready to learn than to teach. Only let no one dare to defend the freedom of the will in any such way as to attempt depriving us of the prayer that says, "Lead us not into temptation;" and, on the other hand, let no one deny the freedom of the will, and so venture to find an excuse for sin. But let us give heed to the Lord, both in commanding and in offering His aid; in both telling us our duty, and assisting us to discharge it. For some He hath let be lifted up to pride through an overweening trust in their own wills, while others He hath let fall into carelessness

---

[1] Rom. xi. 7 ; Isa. vi. 10 : "spirit of *remorse*," as in margin of English Bible, where the text has "*blindness*."—TR.
[2] Rom. ix. 14.
[3] Rom. xi. 33.　[4] Ps. xxxvi. 6.　[5] Ecclus. iii. 22 (21).
[6] Matt. x. 26.　[7] Phil. iii. 15, 16.　[8] Col. ii. 3.
[9] Chap. xvi. 12.

through a contrary excess of distrust. The former say: Why do we ask God not to let us be overcome by temptation, when it is all in our own power? The latter say: Why should we try to live well, when the power to do so is in the hands of God? O Lord, O Father, who art in heaven, lead us not into any of these temptations; but "deliver us from evil!"[1] Listen to the Lord, when He says, "I have prayed for thee, Peter, that thy faith fail not;"[2] that we may never think of our faith as so lying in our free will that it has no need of the divine assistance. Let us listen also to the evangelist, when he says, "He hath given them power to become the sons of God;"[3] that we may not imagine it as altogether beyond our own power that we believe: but in both let us acknowledge His beneficent acting. For, on the one side, we have to give Him thanks that the power is bestowed; and on the other, to pray that our own little strength may not utterly fail. It is this very faith that worketh by love,[4] according to the measure thereof that the Lord hath given to every man;[5] that he that glorieth may glory, not in himself, but in the Lord.[6]

9. It is no wonder, then, that they could not believe, when such was their pride of will, that, being ignorant of the righteousness of God, they wished to establish their own: as the apostle says of them, "They have not submitted themselves unto the righteousness of God."[7] For it was not by faith, but as it were by works, that they were puffed up; and blinded by this very self-elation, they stumbled against the stone of stumbling. And so it is said, "they could not," by which we are to understand that they would not; in the same way as it was said of the Lord our God, "If we believe not, yet He abideth faithful, He cannot deny Himself."[8] It is said of the Omnipotent, "He cannot." And so, just as it is a commendation of the divine will that the Lord "cannot deny Himself," that they "could not believe" is a fault chargeable on the will of man.

10. And, look you! so also say I, that those who have such lofty ideas of themselves as to suppose that so much must be attributed to the powers of their own will, that they deny their need of the divine assistance in order to a righteous life, cannot believe on Christ. For the mere syllables of Christ's name, and the Christian sacraments, are of no profit, where faith in Christ is itself resisted. For faith in Christ is to believe in Him that justifieth the ungodly;[5] to believe in the Mediator, without whose interposition we cannot be reconciled unto God; to believe in the Saviour, who came to seek and to save that which was lost;[10] to believe in Him who said, "Without me ye can do nothing."[11] Because, then, being ignorant of that righteousness of God that justifieth the ungodly, he wishes to set up his own to satisfy the minds of the proud, such a man cannot believe on Christ. And so, those Jews "could not believe:" not that men cannot be changed for the better; but so long as their ideas run in such a direction, they cannot believe. Hence they are blinded and hardened; for, denying the need of divine assistance, they are not assisted. God foreknew this regarding these Jews who were blinded and hardened, and the prophet by His Spirit foretold it.

11. But when he added, "And they should be converted, and I should heal them," is there a "not" to be understood, that is, they should *not* be converted, connecting it with the clause before, where it is said, "that they should not see with their eyes and understand with their heart;" for here also it is certainly meant, "and should not understand"? For conversion itself is likewise a gift of His grace, as when it is said to Him, "Turn us, O God of Hosts."[12] Or may it be that we are to understand this also as actually taking place through the merciful experience of the divine method of healing, [namely this,] that, being of proud and perverse wills, and wishing to establish their own righteousness, they were left alone for the very purpose of being blinded; and thus blinded in order that they might stumble on the stone of stumbling, and have their faces filled with shame; and so, being thus humbled, might seek the name of the Lord, and no longer a righteousness of their own, that inflated their pride, but the righteousness of God, that justifieth the ungodly? For this very way turned out to the good of many of them, who were afterwards filled with remorse for wickedness, and believed on Christ; and on whose behalf He Himself had put up the prayer, "Father, forgive them, for they know not what they do."[13] And it is of that ignorance of theirs also that the apostle says, "I bear them record that they have a zeal of God, but not according to knowledge:" for he then goes on also to add, "For they, being ignorant of God's righteousness, and seeking to establish their own righteousness, have not submitted themselves unto the righteousness of God."[14]

---

[1] Matt. vi. 13. [2] Luke xxii. 32. [3] Chap. i. 12.
[4] Gal. v. 6. [5] Rom. xii. 3. [6] 1 Cor. i. 31.
[7] Rom. x. 3. [8] 2 Tim. ii. 13.

[9] Rom. iv. 5. [10] Luke xix. 10. [11] Chap. xv. 5.
[12] Ps. lxxx. 7. [13] Luke xxiii. 34. [14] Rom. x. 2, 3.

12. "These things said Isaiah, when he saw His glory, and spake of Him." What Isaiah saw, and how it refers to Christ the Lord, are to be read and learned in his book. For he saw Him, not as He is, but in some symbolical way to suit the form that the vision of the prophet had itself to assume. For Moses likewise saw Him, and yet we find him saying to Him whom he saw, "If I have found grace in Thy sight, show me now Thyself, that I may clearly see Thee;"[1] for he saw Him not as He is. But the time when this shall yet be our experience, that same Saint John the Evangelist tells us in his Epistle: "Dearly beloved, [now] are we the sons of God; and it hath not yet become manifest what we shall be: because we know that, when He shall appear, we shall be like Him; for we shall see Him as He is."[2] He might have said "for we shall see Him," without adding "as He is;" but because he knew that He was seen of some of the fathers and prophets, but not as He is, therefore after saying "we shall see Him," he added "as He is." And be not deceived, brethren, by any of those who assert that the Father is invisible, and the Son visible. This assertion is made by those who think that the latter is a creature, and whose understanding runs not in harmony with the words, "I and my Father one."[3] Accordingly, as respects the form of God wherein He is equal with the Father, the Son also is invisible: but, in order to be seen of men, He assumed the form of a servant, and being made in the likeness of men,[4] became visible to man. He showed Himself, therefore, even before His incarnation, to the eyes of men, as it pleased Him, in the creature-form at His command, but not as He is. Let us be purifying our hearts by faith, that we may be prepared for that ineffable and, so to speak, invisible vision. For "blessed are the pure in heart; for they shall see God."[5]

13. "Nevertheless among the chief rulers also many believed on Him; but, because of the Pharisees, they did not confess Him, lest they should be put out of the synagogue: for they loved the glory of men more than the glory of God." See how the evangelist marked and disapproved of some, who yet, he said, believed on Him: who, if ever they did advance though this gateway of faith, would thereby also overcome that love of human glory which had been overcome by the apostle, when he said, "God forbid that I should glory, save in the cross of our Lord Jesus Christ, by whom the world is crucified unto me, and I unto the world."[6] For to this end also did the Lord Himself, when derided by the madness of human pride and impiety, fix His cross on the foreheads of those who believed on Him, on that which is in a manner the abode of modesty, that faith may learn not to blush at His name, and love the glory of God more than the glory of men.

---

[1] Ex. xxxiii. 13.   [2] 1 John iii. 2.   [3] Chap. x. 30.   [4] Phil. ii. 7.   [5] Matt. v. 8.   [6] Gal. vi. 14.

TRACTATE LIV

CHAPTER XII. 44–50.

1. WHILST our Lord Jesus Christ was speaking among the Jews, and giving so many miraculous signs, some believed who were foreordained to eternal life, and whom He also called His sheep; but some did not believe, and could not believe, because that, by the mysterious yet not unrighteous judgment of God, they had been blinded and hardened, because forsaken of Him who resisteth the proud, but giveth grace unto the humble.[1] But of those who believed, there were some whose confession went so far, that they took branches of palm trees, and met Him as He approached, turning in their joy that very confession into a service of praise: while there were others, belonging to the chief rulers, who had not the boldness to confess their faith, lest they should be put out of the synagogue; and whom the evangelist has branded with the words, that "they loved the praise of men more than the praise of God" (ver. 43). Of those also who did not believe, there were some who would afterwards believe, and whom He foresaw, when He said, "When ye have lifted up the Son of man, then shall ye acknowledge that I am He:"[2] but there were some who would remain in the same unbelief, and be imitated by the Jewish nation of the

---

[1] Jas. iv. 6.   [2] Chap. viii. 28.

present day, which, being shortly afterwards crushed in war, according to the prophetic testimony which was written concerning Christ, has since been scattered almost through the whole world.

2. While matters were in this state, and His own passion was now at hand, "Jesus cried, and said," as our lesson to-day commences, "He that believeth on me, believeth not on me, but on Him that sent me; and he that seeth me, seeth Him that sent me." He had already said in a certain place, "My doctrine is not mine, but His that sent me."[1] Where we understood that He called His doctrine just what He is Himself, the Word of the Father; and in saying, "My doctrine is not mine, but His that sent me," implied this, that He was not of Himself, but had His being from another.[2] For He was God of God, the Son of the Father: but the Father is not God of God, but God, the Father of the Son. And now when He says, "He that believeth on me, believeth not on me, but on Him that sent me," how else are we to understand it, but that He appeared as man to men, while He remained invisible as God? And that none might think that He was no more than what they saw of Him, He indicated His wish to be believed on, as equal in character and rank with the Father, when He said, "He that believeth on me, believeth not on me," that is, merely on what he seeth of me, "but on Him that sent me," that is, on the Father. But he that believeth on the Father, must believe that He is the Father; and he that believeth on Him as the Father, must believe that He has a Son; and in this way, he that believeth on the Father, must believe on the Son. But let no one believe about the only-begotten Son just what they believe about those who are called the sons of God by grace and not by nature, as the evangelist says, "He gave them power to become the sons of God,"[3] and according to what the Lord Himself also mentioned, as declared in the law, "I said, Ye are gods; and all of you children of the Most High:"[4] because He said, "He that believeth on me, believeth not on me," to show that the whole extent of our faith in Christ should not be limited by His manhood. He therefore, He saith, believeth on me, who doth not believe on me merely according to what he seeth of me, but on Him that sent me: so that, believing thus on the Father, he may believe that He has a Son co-equal with Himself, and then attain to a true faith in me. For if one should think that He has sons only according to

grace, who are certainly no more than His creatures, and not the Word, but those made by the Word, and that He has no Son co-equal and co-eternal with Himself, ever born, alike incommutable, in nothing dissimilar and inferior, then he believes not on the Father who sent Him, for the Father who sent Him is no such conception as this.

3. And, accordingly, after saying, "He that believeth on me, believeth not on me, but on Him that sent me," that it might not be thought that He would have the Father so understood, as if He were the Father only of many sons regenerated by grace, and not of the only-begotten Word, His own co-equal, He immediately added, "And he that seeth me, seeth Him that sent me." Does He say here, He that seeth me, seeth not me, but Him that sent me, as He had said, "He that believeth me, believeth not on me, but on Him that sent me"? For He uttered the former of these words, that He might not be believed on merely as He then appeared, that is, as the Son of man; and the latter, that He might be believed on as the equal of the Father. He that believeth on me, believeth not merely on what He sees of me, but believeth on Him that sent me. Or, when he believeth on the Father, who begat me, His own co-equal, let him believe on me, not as he seeth me, but as [he believeth] on Him that sent me; for so far does the truth, that there is no distance between Him and me, reach, that He who seeth me, seeth Him that sent me. Certainly, Christ the Lord Himself sent His apostles, as their name implies: for as those who in Greek are called *angeli* are in Latin called *nuntii* [messengers], so the Greek *apostoli* [apostles] becomes the Latin *missi* [persons sent]. But never would any of the apostles have dared to say, "He that believeth on me, believeth not on me, but on Him that sent me;" for in no sense whatever would he say, "He that believeth on me." We believe an apostle, but we do not believe on him; for it is not an apostle that justifieth the ungodly. But to him that believeth on Him that justifieth the ungodly, his faith is counted for righteousness.[5] An apostle might say, He that receiveth me, receiveth Him that sent me; or, He that heareth me, heareth Him that sent me; for the Lord tells them so Himself: "He that receiveth you, receiveth me; and he that receiveth me, receiveth Him that sent me."[6] For the master is honored in the servant, and the father in the son: but then the father is as it were in the son, and the master as it were in

---

[1] Chap. vii. 16.   [2] Tract. XXIX., *haberet a quo esset.*
[3] Chap. i. 12.   [4] Chap. x. 34 ; Ps. lxxxii. 6.   [5] Rom. iv. 5.   [6] Matt. x. 40.

the servant. But the only-begotten Son could rightly say, " Believe on God, and believe on me;"¹ as also what He saith here, " He that believeth on me, believeth not on me, but on Him that sent me." He did not turn away the faith of the believer from Himself, but only would not have the believer continue in the form of a servant: because every one who believeth in the Father that sent Him, straightway believeth on the Son, without whom he knoweth that the Father hath no existence as such, and thus reacheth in his faith to the belief of His equality with the Father, in conformity with the words that follow, "And he that seeth me, seeth Him that sent me."

. 4. Attend to what follows: " I am come a light into the world, that whosoever believeth on me should not abide in darkness." He said in a certain place to His disciples, " Ye are the light of the world. A city that is set on a hill cannot be hid. Neither do men light a candle, and put it under a bushel, but on a candlestick; that it may give light to all that are in the house: so let your light shine before men, that they may see your good works, and glorify your Father who is in heaven:"² but He did not say to them, Ye are come a light into the world, that whosoever believeth on you should not abide in darkness. Such a statement, I maintain, can nowhere be met with. All the saints, therefore, are lights, but they are illuminated by Him through faith; and every one that becomes separated from Him will be enveloped in darkness. But that Light, which enlightens them, cannot become separated from itself; for it is altogether beyond the reach of change. We believe, then, the light that has thus been lit, as the prophet or apostle: but we believe him for this end, that we may not believe on that which is itself enlightened, but, with him, on that Light which has given him light; so that we, too, may be enlightened, not by him, but, along with him, by the same Light as he. And when He saith, " That whosoever believeth on me may not abide in darkness," He makes it sufficiently manifest that all have been found by Him in a state of darkness: but that they may not abide in the darkness wherein they have been found, they ought to believe on that Light which hath come into the world, for thereby was the world created.

5. "And if any man," He says, " hear my words, and keep them not, I judge him not." Remember what I know you have heard in former lessons; and if any of you have forgotten, recall it: and those of you who were absent then, but are present now, hear how it is that the Son saith, " I judge him not," while in another place He says, " The Father judgeth no man, but hath committed all judgment unto the Son;"³ namely, that thereby we are to understand, It is not now that I judge him. And why not now? Listen to the sequel: " For I am not come," He says, " to judge the world, but to save the world;" that is, to bring the world into a state of salvation. Now, therefore, is the season of mercy, afterwards will be the time for judgment: for He says, " I will sing to Thee, O Lord, of mercy and judgment."⁴

6. But see also what He says of that future judgment in the end: " He that despiseth me, and receiveth not my words, hath one that judgeth him: the word that I have spoken, the same shall judge him in the last day." He says not, He that despiseth me, and receiveth not my words, I judge him not at the last day; for had He said so, I do not see how it could have been else than contradictory of that other statement, when He says, " The Father judgeth no man, but hath committed all judgment unto the Son." But when He said, " He that despiseth me, and receiveth not my words, hath one to judge him," and, for the information of those who were waiting to hear who that one was, went on to add, " The word that I have spoken, the same shall judge him in the last day," He made it sufficiently manifest that He Himself would then be the judge. For it was of Himself He spake, Himself He announced, and Himself He set forth as the gate whereby He entered as the Shepherd to His sheep. In one way, therefore, will those be judged who have never heard that word, in another way those who have heard and despised. "For as many as have sinned without law," says the apostle, " shall also perish without law; and as many as have sinned in the law, shall be judged by the law."⁵

7. " For I have not," He says, " spoken of myself." He says that He has not spoken of Himself, because He is not of Himself. Of this we have frequently discoursed already; so that now, without any more instruction, we have simply to remind you of it as a truth with which you are familiar. " But the Father who sent me, He gave me a commandment what I should say, and what I should speak." We would not stay to elaborate this, did we know that we were now speaking with those with whom we have spoken on former occasions, and of these, not with all, but such only whose memories

---

have retained what they heard: but because there are perhaps some now present who did not hear, and some in a similar condition who have forgotten what they heard, on their account let those who remember what they have heard bear with our delay. How giveth the Father a commandment to His only Son? With what words doth He speak to the Word, seeing that the Son Himself is the only-begotten Word? Could it be by an angel, seeing that by Him the angels were created? Was it by means of a cloud, which, when it gave forth its sound to the Son, gave it not on His account, as He Himself also tells us elsewhere, but for the sake of others who were needing to hear it (ver. 29)? Could it be by any sound issuing from the lips, where bodily form was wanting, and where there is no such local distance separating the Son from the Father as to admit of any intervening air, to give effect, by its percussion, to the voice, and render it audible? Let us put away all such unworthy notions of that incorporeal and ineffable subsistence. The only Son is the Word and the Wisdom of the Father, and therein *are* all the commandments of the Father. For there was no time that the Son knew not the Father's commandment, so as to make it necessary for Him to possess in course of time what He possessed not before. For what He has received from the Father, He received in being born, and was given it in being begotten. For the life He is, and life He certainly received in being born, while yet there was no antecedent time when life was wanting to His personal existence. For, on the one hand, the Father *has* life, and *is* what He has: and yet He received it not, because He is not of any one. But the Son received life as the Father's gift, of whom He is: and so He Himself is what He has; for He has life, and is the life. Listen to Himself when He says, "As the Father hath life in Himself, so hath He given to the Son to have life in Himself." [1] Could He give it to one who was in being, and yet hitherto was destitute thereof? On the contrary, in the very begetting it, was given by Him who begat the life, and so life begat the life. And to show that He begat the life equal, and not inferior to Himself, it was said, "As *He* hath life in Himself, so hath He also given to the Son to have life in Himself." He gave life; for in begetting the life, what was it He gave Him, save to be the life? And as His nativity is itself eternal, there never was a time without that Son who is the life, and never was there a time when the Son

Himself was without the life; and as His nativity is eternal, so He, who was thus born, is eternal life. And so the Father gave not to the Son a commandment which He had not already; but, as I said, in the Wisdom of the Father, that is, in the word of the Father, are laid up all the Father's commandments. And yet the commandment is said to have been given Him, because He, to whom it is thus given, is not of Himself: and to give that to the Son which He never was without, is the same in meaning as to beget that Son who never was without existence.

8. There follow the words: "And I know that His commandment is life everlasting." If, then, the Son Himself is eternal life, and the Father's commandment the same, what else is expressed than this, I am the Father's commandment? And in like manner, in what He proceeds to say, "Whatsoever I speak, even as the Father said unto me, so I speak," let us not be taking the "said unto me" as if the Father used words in speaking to the only Word, or that the Word of God needed words from God. The Father spake to the Son in the same way as He gave life to the Son; not that He knew not the one, or had not the other, but just because He was the *Son.* What, then, do the words mean, "Even as He said unto me, so I speak;" but just, I speak the truth? So the former said as the Truthful One [2] what the latter thus spake as the Truth. The Truthful begat the Truth. What, then, could He now say to the Truth? For the Truth had no imperfection to be supplied by additional truth. He spake, therefore, to the Truth, because He begat the Truth. And in like manner the Truth Himself speaks what has been said to Him; but only to those who have understanding, and who are taught by Him as the God-begotten Truth. But that men might believe what they had not yet capacity to understand, words that were audible issued from His human lips; sounds passing rapidly away broke on the ear, and speedily completed the little term of their duration: but the truths themselves, of which the sounds are but signs, passed, as it were, into the memory of those who heard them, and have come down to us also by means of written characters as signs addressed to the eye. But it is not thus that the Truth speaks; He speaks inwardly to the souls of the intelligent; He needs no sound to instruct, but floods the mind with the light of understanding. And he, then, who in that light is able to behold the eternity of His birth, himself hears in the same way the Truth speaking, as He

---

[1] Chap. v. 26.

[2] *Verax.*

heard the Father telling Him what He should speak. He has awakened in us a great longing for that sweet experience of His presence within: but it is by daily growth that we ac-quire it; it is by walking that we grow, and it is by forward efforts we walk, so as to be able at last to attain it.

TRACTATE LV

CHAPTER XIII. 1–5.

1. THE Lord's Supper, as set forth in John, must, with His assistance, be unfolded in a becoming number of Lectures, and explained with all the ability He is pleased to grant us. "Now, before the feast of the passover, when Jesus knew that His hour was come that He should depart out of this world unto the Father, having loved His own who were in the world, He loved them unto the end." Pascha (passover) is not, as some think, a Greek noun, but a Hebrew: and yet there occurs in this noun a very suitable kind of accordance in the two languages. For inasmuch as the Greek word *paschein* means *to suffer*, therefore *pascha* has been supposed to mean suffering, as if the noun derived its name from His passion: but in its own language, that is, in Hebrew, pascha means passover;[1] because the pascha was then celebrated for the first time by God's people, when, in their flight from Egypt, they *passed over* the Red Sea.[2] And now that prophetic emblem is fulfilled in truth, when Christ is led as a sheep to the slaughter,[3] that by His blood sprinkled on our doorposts, that is, by the sign of His cross marked on our foreheads, we may be delivered from the perdition awaiting this world, as Israel from the bondage and destruction of the Egyptians;[4] and a most salutary transit we make when we pass over from the devil to Christ, and from this unstable world to His well-established kingdom. And therefore surely do we pass over to the ever-abiding God, that we may not pass away with this passing world. The apostle, in extolling God for such grace bestowed upon us, says: "Who hath delivered us from the power of darkness, and hath translated us into the kingdom of the Son of His love."[5] This name, then, of pascha, which, as I have said, is in Latin called *tran-situs* (pass over), is interpreted, as it were, for us by the blessed evangelist, when he says, "Before the feast of pascha, when Jesus knew that His hour was come that He should *pass* out of this world to the Father." Here you see we have both pascha and *pass*-over. Whence, and whither does He pass? Namely, "out of this world to the Father." The hope was thus given to the members in their Head, that they doubtless would yet follow Him who was "passing" before. And what, then, of unbelievers, who stand altogether apart from this Head and His members? Do not they also pass away, seeing that they abide not here always? They also do plainly pass away: but it is one thing to pass from the world, and another to pass away with it; one thing to pass to the Father, another to pass to the enemy. For the Egyptians also passed over [the sea]; but they did not pass through the sea to the kingdom, but in the sea to destruction.

2. "When Jesus knew," then, "that His hour was come that He should pass out of this world unto the Father, having loved His own who were in the world, He loved them unto the end." In order, doubtless, that they also, through that love of His, might pass from this world where they now were, to their Head who had passed hence before them. For what mean these words, "to the end," but just to Christ? "For Christ is the end of the law," says the apostle, "for righteousness to every one that believeth."[6] The end that consummates, not that consumes; the end whereto we attain, not wherein we perish. Exactly thus are we to understand the passage, "Christ our passover is sacrificed."[7] He is our end; into Him do we pass. For I see that these gospel words may also be taken in a kind of human sense, that Christ loved His own even unto death, so that this may be the meaning of "He loved them unto the end." This meaning is

---

[1] *Transitus*, transit, pass over.—TR.
[2] Ex. xiv. 29. A curious mistake of Augustin's to derive the name of the feast from Israel's *passing over* the Red Sea, instead of Jehovah's *passing over* the houses of the Israelites, when He smote the firstborn of Egypt! Compare Ex. xii. 11, 13, 23, 27.—TR.
[3] Isa. liii. 7.　　[4] Ex. xii. 23.　　[5] Col. i. 13.　　　　[6] Rom. x. 4.　　　　[7] 1 Cor. v. 7.

human, not divine:[1] for it was not merely up to this point that we were loved by Him, who loveth us always and endlessly. God forbid that He, whose death could not end, should have ended His love at death. Even after death that proud and ungodly rich man loved his five brethren;[2] and is Christ to be thought of as loving us only till death? God forbid, beloved. He would have come in vain with a love for us that lasted till death, if that love had ended there. But perhaps the words, "He loved them unto the end," may have to be understood in this way, That He so loved them as to die for them. For this He testified when He said, "Greater love hath no man than this, that a man lay down his life for his friends."[3] We have certainly no objection that "He loved them unto the end" should be so understood, that is, it was His very love that carried Him on to death.

3. "And the supper," he says, "having taken place,[4] and the devil having now put into the heart of Judas Iscariot, Simon's son, to betray Him, [Jesus] knowing that the Father had given all things into His hands, and that He has come from God, and is going to God; He riseth from supper, and layeth aside His garments; and took a towel, and girded Himself. After that He poureth water into a basin, and began to wash the disciples' feet, and to wipe them with the towel wherewith He was girded." We are not to understand by the supper having taken place, as if it were already finished and over; for it was still going on when the Lord rose and washed His disciples' feet. For He afterwards sat down again, and gave the morsel [sop] to His betrayer, implying certainly that the supper was not yet over, or, in other words, that there was still bread on the table. Therefore, by supper having taken place, is meant that it was now ready, and laid out on the table for the use of the guests.

4. But when he says, "The devil having now put into the heart of Judas Iscariot, Simon's son, to betray Him;" if one inquires, what was put into Judas' heart, it was doubtless this, "to betray Him." Such a putting [into the heart] is a spiritual suggestion: and entereth not by the ear, but through the thoughts; and thereby not in a way that is corporal, but spiritual. For what we call spiritual is not always to be understood in a commendatory way. The apostle knew of certain spiritual things [powers], of wicked-

ness in heavenly places, against which he testifies that we have to maintain a struggle;[5] and there would not be spiritual wickednesses, were there not also wicked spirits. For it is from a spiritual being that spiritual things get their name. But how such things are done, as that devilish suggestions should be introduced, and so mingle with human thoughts that a man accounts them his own, how can he know? Nor can we doubt that good suggestions are likewise made by a good spirit in the same unobservable and spiritual way; but it is matter of concern to which of these the human mind yields assent, either as deservedly left without, or graciously aided by, the divine assistance. The determination, therefore, had now been come to in Judas' heart by the instigation of the devil, that the disciple should betray the Master, whom he had not learned to know as his God. In such a state had he now come to their social meal, a spy on the Shepherd, a plotter against the Redeemer, a seller of the Saviour; as such was he now come, was he now seen and endured, and thought himself undiscovered: for he was deceived about Him whom he wished to deceive. But He, who had already scanned the inward state of that very heart, was knowingly making use of one who knew it not.

5. "[Jesus] knowing that the Father has given all things into His hands." And therefore also the traitor himself: for if He had him not in His hands, He certainly could not use him as He wished. Accordingly, the traitor had been already betrayed to Him whom he sought to betray; and he carried out his evil purpose in betraying Him in such a way, that good he knew not of was the issue in regard to Him who was betrayed. For the Lord knew what He was doing for His friends, and patiently made use of His enemies: and thus had the Father given all things into His hands, both the evil for present use, and the good for the final issue. "Knowing also that He has come from God, and is going to God:" neither quitting God when He came from Him, nor us when He returned.

6. Knowing, then, these things, "He riseth from supper, and layeth aside His garments; and took a towel, and girded Himself. After that He poureth water into a basin, and began to wash the disciples' feet, and to wipe them with the towel wherewith He was girded." We ought, dearly beloved, carefully to mark the meaning of the evangelist; because that, when about to speak of the pre-eminent

---

[1] That is, "applies to Christ's humanity, not His divinity." —Tr.
[2] Luke xvi. 27, 28.   [3] Chap. xv. 13.
[4] *Cœna facta;* δείπνου γενομένου. See Augustin's explanation below.—Tr.

[5] Eph. vi. 12.

humility of the Lord, it was his desire first to commend His majesty. It is in reference to this that he says, "Jesus knowing that the Father had given all things into His hands, and that He has come from God, and is going to God." It is He, therefore, into whose hands the Father had given all things, who now washes, not the disciples' hands, but their feet; and it was just while knowing that He had come from God, and was proceeding to God, that He discharged the office of a servant, not of God the Lord, but of man. And this also is referred to by the prefatory notice he has been pleased to make of His betrayer, who was now come as such, and was not unknown to Him; that the greatness of His humility should be still further enhanced by the fact that He did not esteem it beneath His dignity to wash also the feet of one whose hands He already foresaw to be steeped in wickedness.

7. But why should we wonder that He rose from supper, and laid aside His garments, who, being in the form of God, made Himself of no reputation?[1] And why should we wonder, if He girded Himself with a towel, who took upon Him the form of a servant, and was found in the likeness of a man?[2] Why wonder, if He poured water into a basin wherewith to wash His disciples' feet, who poured His blood upon the earth to wash away the filth of their sins? Why wonder, if with the towel wherewith He was girded He wiped the feet He had washed, who with the very flesh that clothed Him laid a firm pathway for the footsteps of His evangelists? In order, indeed, to gird Himself with the towel, He laid aside the garments He wore; but when He emptied Himself [of His divine glory] in order to assume the form of a servant, He laid not down what He had, but assumed that which He had not before. When about to be crucified, He was indeed stripped of His garments, and when dead was wrapped in linen clothes: and all that suffering of His is our purification. When, therefore, about to suffer the last extremities [of humiliation,] He here illustrated beforehand its friendly compliances; not only to those for whom He was about to endure death, but to him also who had resolved on betraying Him to death. Because so great is the beneficence of human humility, that even the Divine Majesty was pleased to commend it by His own example; for proud man would have perished eternally, had he not been found by the lowly God. For the Son of man came to seek and to save that which was lost.[3] And as he was lost by imitating the pride of the deceiver, let him now, when found, imitate the Redeemer's humility.

---

[1] Literally, "emptied Himself," as in the Greek.—TR.
[2] Phil. ii. 6, 7.

[3] Luke xix. 10.

TRACTATE LVI.

CHAPTER XIII. 6–10.

1. WHEN the Lord was washing the disciples' feet, "He cometh to Simon Peter; and Peter saith unto Him, Lord, dost Thou wash my feet?" For who would not be filled with fear at having his feet washed by the Son of God? Although, therefore, it was a piece of the greatest audacity for the servant to contradict his Lord, the creature his God; yet Peter preferred doing this to the suffering of his feet to be washed by his Lord and God. Nor ought we to think that Peter was one amongst others who so expressed their fear and refusal, seeing that others before him had suffered it to be done to themselves with cheerfulness and equanimity. For it is easier so to understand the words of the Gospel, because that, after saying, "He began to wash the disciples' feet, and to wipe them with the towel wherewith He was girded," it is then added, "Then cometh He to Simon Peter," as if He had already washed the feet of some, and after them had now come to the first of them all. For who can fail to know that the most blessed Peter was the first of the apostles? But we are not so to understand it, that it was after some others that He came to him; but that He began with him.[1] When, therefore, He began to wash the disciples' feet, He came to him with whom He began, namely, to Peter; and then Peter took fright at what any one of them

---

[1] It is curious to notice how Augustin here contradicts his previous and natural explanation of the passage, in order to uphold the primacy of Peter. It looks as if here he suddenly felt that his former words were rather adverse to the notion.—TR.

might have been frightened, and said, "Lord, dost Thou wash my feet?" What is implied in this "Thou"? and what in "my"? These are subjects for thought rather than for speech; lest perchance any adequate conception the soul may have formed of such words may fail of explanation in the utterance.

2. But "Jesus answered and said unto him, What I do thou knowest not now, but thou shalt know hereafter." And not even yet, terrified as he was by the sublimity of the Lord's action, does he allow it to be done, while ignorant of its purpose; but is unwilling to see, unable to endure, that Christ should thus humble Himself to his very feet. "Thou shalt never," he says, "wash my feet." What is this "never" [in æternum]? I will never endure, never suffer, never permit it: that is, a thing is not done "in æternum" which is never done. Then the Saviour, to terrify His reluctant patient with the danger of his own salvation, says, "If I wash thee not, thou shalt have no part with me." He speaks in this way, "If I wash thee not," when He was referring only to his feet; just as it is customary to say, You are trampling on me, when it is only the foot that is trampled on. And now the other, in a perturbation of love and fear, and more frightened at the thought that Christ should be withheld from him, than even to see Him humbled at his feet, exclaims, "Lord, not my feet only, but also my hands and my head." Since this, indeed, is Thy threat, that my bodily members must be washed by Thee, not only do I no longer withhold the lowest, but I lay the foremost also at Thy disposal. Deny me not having a part with Thee, and I deny Thee not any part of my body to be washed.

3. "Jesus saith to him, He that is washed needeth not save to wash his feet, but is clean every whit." Some one perhaps may be aroused at this, and say: Nay, but if he is every whit clean, what need has He even to wash his feet? But the Lord knew what He was saying, even though our weakness reach not into His secret purposes. Nevertheless, so far as He is pleased to instruct and teach us out of His law, up to the little measure of my apprehension, I would also, with His help, make some answer bearing on the depths of this question: and, first of all, I shall have no difficulty in showing that there is no self-contradiction in the manner of expression. For who may not say, as here, with the greatest propriety, He is all clean, except [1] his feet?— although he would speak with greater elegance

were he to say, He is all clean, save [1] his feet; which is equivalent in meaning. Thus, then, doth the Lord say, "He needeth not save to wash his feet, but is all clean." All, that is, except, or save [1] his feet, which he still needs to wash.

4. But what is this? what does it mean? and what is there in it we need to examine? The Lord says, The Truth declares that even he who has been washed has need still to wash his feet. What, my brethren, what think you of it? save that in holy baptism a man has all of him washed, not all save his feet, but every whit; and yet, while thereafter living in this human state, he cannot fail to tread on the ground with his feet. And thus our human feelings themselves, which are inseparable from our mortal life on earth, are like feet wherewith we are brought into sensible contact with human affairs; and are so in such a way, that if we say we have no sin, we deceive ourselves, and the truth is not in us.[2] And every day, therefore, is He who intercedeth for us [3] washing our feet: and that we, too have daily need to be washing our feet, that is, ordering aright the path of our spiritual footsteps, we acknowledge even in the Lord's prayer, when we say, "Forgive us our debts, as we also forgive our debtors."[4] For "if," as it is written, "we confess our sins," then verily is He, who washed His disciples' feet, "faithful and just to forgive us our sins, and to cleanse us from all unrighteousness,"[5] that is, even to our feet wherewith we walk on the earth.

5. Accordingly the Church, which Christ cleanseth with the washing of water in the word, is without spot and wrinkle,[6] not only in the case of those who are taken away immediately after the washing of regeneration from the contagious influence of this life, and tread not the earth so as to make necessary the washing of their feet, but in those also who have experienced such mercy from the Lord as to be enabled to quit this present life even with feet that have been washed. But although the Church be also clean in respect of those who tarry on earth, because they live righteously; yet have they need to be washing their feet, because they assuredly are not without sin. For this cause is it said in the Song of Songs, "I have washed my feet; how shall I defile them?"[7] For one so speaks when he is constrained to come to Christ, and in coming has to bring his feet into contact with the ground. But again, there is another question that arises. Is not Christ above?

---

1 Of course, it is a mere elegance in the Latinity to which Augustin here refers, as between *præter pedes* and *nisi pedes*, when

2 1 John i. 8.   3 Rom. viii. 34.   4 Matt. vi. 12.
5 1 John i. 9.   6 Eph. v. 26, 27.   7 Song of Sol. v. 3.

hath He not ascended into heaven, and sitteth He not at the Father's right hand? Does not the apostle expressly declare, "If ye, then, be risen with Christ, set your thoughts on those things which are above, where Christ is sitting on the right hand of God. Seek the things which are above, not things which are on earth?"[1] How is it, then, that to get to Christ we are compelled to tread the earth, since rather our hearts ought to be turned upwards toward the Lord, that we may be en-abled to dwell in His presence? You see, brethren, the shortness of the time to-day curtails our consideration of this question. And if you perhaps fail in some measure to do so, yet I for my part see how much clearing up it requires. And therefore I beg of you to suffer it rather to be adjourned, than to be treated now in too negligent and restricted a manner; and your expectations will not be defrauded, but only deferred. For the Lord who thus makes us your debtors, will be present to enable us also to pay our debts.

[1] Col. iii. 1, 2.

TRACTATE LVII.

CHAPTER XIII. 6–10 (continued), and SONG OF SOL. V. 2, 3.

IN WHAT WAY THE CHURCH SHOULD FEAR TO DEFILE HER FEET, WHILE PROCEEDING ON HER WAY TO CHRIST.

1. I HAVE not been unmindful of my debt, and acknowledge that the time of payment has now come. May He give me wherewith to pay, as He gave me cause to incur the debt. For He has given me the love, of which it is said, "Owe no man anything, but to love one another."[1] May He give also the word, which I feel myself owing to those I love. I put off your expectations till now for this reason, that I might explain as I could how it is we come to Christ along the ground, when we are commanded rather to seek the things which are above, not the things which are upon the earth.[2] For Christ is sitting above, at the right hand of the Father: but He is assuredly here also; and for that reason said also to Saul, as he was raging on the earth, "Why persecutest thou me?"[3] But the topic on which we were speaking, and which led to our entering on this inquiry, was our Lord's washing His disciples' feet, after the disciples themselves had already been washed, and needed not, save to wash their feet. And we there saw it to be understood that a man is indeed wholly washed in baptism; but while thereafter he liveth in this present world, and with the feet of his human passions treadeth on this earth, that is, in his life-intercourse with others, he contracts enough to call forth the prayer, "Forgive us our debts."[4] And thus from these also is he cleansed by Him who washed His disciples' feet,[5] and ceaseth not to make intercession for us.[6] And here occurred the words of the Church in the Song of Songs, when she saith, "I have washed my feet; how shall I defile them?" when she wished to go and open to that Being, fairer in form than the sons of men,[7] who had come to her and knocked, and asked her to open to Him. This gave rise to a question, which we were unwilling to compress into the narrow limits of the time, and therefore deferred till now, in what sense the Church, when on her way to Christ, may be afraid of defiling her feet, which she had washed in the baptism of Christ.

2. For thus she speaks: "I sleep, but my heart waketh: it is the voice of my Beloved[8] that knocketh at the gate." And then He also says: "Open to me, my sister, my nearest, my dove, my perfect one; for my head is filled with dew, and my hair with the drops of the night." And she replies: "I have put off my dress; how shall I put it on? I have washed my feet; how shall I defile them?"[9] O wonderful sacramental symbol! O lofty mystery! Does she, then, fear to defile her feet in coming to Him who washed the feet of His disciples? Her fear is genuine; for it is along the earth she has to come to Him, who is still on earth, because refusing to leave His own who are stationed here. Is it not He that saith, "Lo, I am with you always, even unto the end of the world"?[10] Is it not He that saith, "Ye shall see the heavens

[1] Rom. xiii. 8.
[2] Col. iii. 1, 2.
[3] Acts ix. 4.
[4] Matt. vi. 12.
[5] Chap. xiii. 5.   [6] Rom. viii. 34.   [7] Ps. xlv. 2.
[8] *Patruelis*, literally cousin (by the father's side).
[9] Song of Sol. v. 2, 3.   [10] Matt. xxviii. 20.

opened, and the angels of God ascending and descending upon the Son of man"?[1] If they ascend to Him because He is above, how do they descend to Him, but because He is also here? Therefore saith the Church: "I have washed my feet; how shall I defile them?" She says so even in the case of those who, purified from all dross, can say: "I desire to depart, and to be with Christ; nevertheless to abide in the flesh is more needful for you."[2] She says it in those who preach Christ, and open to Him the door, that He may dwell by faith in the hearts of men.[3] In such she says it, when they deliberate whether to undertake such a ministry, for which they do not consider themselves qualified, so as to discharge it blamelessly, and so as not, after preaching to others, themselves to become castaways.[4] For it is safer to hear than to preach the truth: for in the hearing, humility is preserved; but when it is preached, it is scarcely possible for any man to hinder the entrance of some small measure of boasting, whereby the feet at least are defiled.

3. Therefore, as the Apostle James saith, "Let every man be swift to hear, slow to speak."[5] As it is also said by another man of God, "Thou wilt make me to hear joy and gladness, and the bones Thou hast humbled will rejoice."[6] This is what I said: When the truth is heard, humility is preserved. And another says: "But the friend of the bridegroom standeth and heareth him, and rejoiceth greatly because of the bridegroom's voice."[7] Let us rejoice in the hearing that comes from the noiseless speaking of the truth within us. For although, when the sound is outwardly uttered, as by one that readeth, or proclaimeth, or preacheth, or disputeth, or commandeth, or comforteth, or exhorteth, or even by one that sings or accompanies his voice on an instrument, those who do so may fear to defile their feet, when they aim at pleasing men with the secretly active desire of human applause. Yet the one who hears such with a willing and pious mind, has no room for self-gratulation in the labors of others; and with no self-inflation, but with the joy of humility, rejoices because of the Master's words of truth. Accordingly, in those who hear with willingness and humility, and spend a tranquil life in sweet and wholesome studies, the holy Church will take delight, and may say, "I sleep, and my heart waketh." And what is this, "I sleep, and my heart waketh," but just I sit down quietly to listen? My leisure is not laid out in nour-

ishing slothfulness, but in acquiring wisdom. "I sleep, and my heart waketh." I am still, and see that Thou art the Lord:[8] for "the wisdom of the scribe cometh by opportunity of leisure; and he that hath little business shall become wise."[9] "I sleep, and my heart waketh:" I rest from troublesome business, and my mind turns its attention to divine concerns (or communications).[10]

4. But while the Church finds delightful repose in those who thus sweetly and humbly sit at her feet, here is one who knocks, and says: "What I tell you in darkness, that speak ye in light; and what ye hear in the ear, that preach ye upon the house-tops."[11] It is His voice, then, that knocks at the gate, and says: "Open to me, my sister, my neighbor, my dove, my perfect one; for my head is filled with dew, and my locks with the drops of the night." As if He had said, Thou art at leisure, and the door is closed against me: thou art caring for the leisure of the few, and through abounding iniquity the love of many is waxing cold.[12] The night He speaks of is iniquity: but His dew and drops are those who wax cold and fall away, and make the head of Christ to wax cold, that is, the love of God to fail. For the head of Christ is God.[13] But they are borne on His locks, that is, their presence is tolerated in the visible sacraments; while their senses never take hold of the internal realities. He knocks, therefore, to shake off this quiet from His inactive saints, and cries, "Open to me," thou who, through my blood, art become "my sister;" through my drawing nigh, "my neighbor;" through my Spirit, "my dove;" through my word which thou hast fully learned in thy leisure, "my perfect one:" open to me, go and preach me to others. For how shall I get in to those who have shut their door against me, without some one to open? and how shall they hear without a preacher?[14]

5. Hence it happens that those who love to devote their leisure to good studies, and shrink from encountering the troubles of toilsome labors, as feeling themselves unsuited to undertake and discharge such services with credit, would prefer, were it possible, to have the holy apostles and ancient preachers of the truth again raised up against that abounding of iniquity which hath so reduced the warmth of Christian love. But in regard to those who have already left the body, and put off the garment of the flesh (for they are not utterly parted), the Church replies, "I have put off my dress; how shall I put it on?" That

---

[1] Chap. i. 51.　　[2] Phil. i. 23, 24.　　[3] Eph. iii. 17.
[4] 1 Cor. ix. 27.　　[5] Jas. i. 19.　　[6] Ps. li. 8.
[7] Chap. iii. 29.

[8] Ps. xlvi. 10.　　[9] Ecclus. xxxviii. 24.
[10] Two readings, affectibus or affatibus.　　[11] Matt. x. 27.
[12] Matt. xxiv. 12　　[13] 1 Cor. xi. 3.　　[14] Rom. x. 14.

dress shall, indeed, yet be recovered; and in the persons of those who have meanwhile laid it aside, shall the Church again put on the garment of flesh: only not now, when the cold are needing to be warmed; but then, when the dead shall rise again. Realizing, then, her present difficulty through the scarcity of preachers, and remembering those members of her own who were so sound in word and holy in character, but are now disunited from their bodies, the Church says in her sorrow, "I have put off my dress; how shall I put it on?" How can those members of mine, who had such surpassing power, through their preaching, to open the door to Christ, now return to the bodies which they have laid aside?

6. And then, turning again to those who preach, and gather in and govern the congregations of His people, and so open as they can to Christ, but are afraid, amid the difficulties of such work, of falling into sin, she says, "I have washed my feet; how shall I defile them?" For whosoever offendeth not in word, the same is a perfect man. And who, then, is perfect? Who is there that offendeth not amid such an abounding of iniquity, and such a freezing of charity? "I have washed my feet; how shall I defile them?" At times I read and hear: "My brethren, be not many masters, seeing that ye shall receive the greater condemnation: for in many things we offend all."[1] "I have washed my feet; how shall I defile them?" But see, I rise and open. Christ, wash them. "Forgive us our debts," because our love is not altogether extinguished: for "we also forgive our debtors."[2] When we listen to Thee, the bones which have been humbled rejoice with Thee in the heavenly places.[3] But when we preach Thee, we have to tread the ground in order to open to Thee: and then, if we are blameworthy, we are troubled; if we are commended, we become inflated. Wash our feet, that were formerly cleansed, but have again been defiled in our walking through the earth to open unto Thee. Let this be enough to-day, beloved. But in whatever we have happened to offend, by saying otherwise than we ought, or have been unduly elated by your commendations, entreat that our feet may be washed, and may your prayers find acceptance with God.

[1] Jas. iii. 1, 2.   [2] Matt. vi. 12.   [3] Ps. li. 8.

TRACTATE LVIII.

Chapter XIII. 10–15.

1. We have already, beloved, as the Lord was pleased to enable us, expounded to you those words of the Gospel, where the Lord, in washing His disciples' feet, says, "He that is once washed needeth not save to wash his feet, but is clean every whit." Let us now look at what follows. "And ye," He says, "are clean, but not all." And to remove the need of inquiry on our part, the evangelist has himself explained its meaning, by adding: "For He knew who it was that should betray Him; therefore said He, Ye are not all clean." Can anything be clearer? Let us therefore pass to what follows.

2. "So, after He had washed their feet, and had taken His garments, and was set down again, He said unto them, Know ye what I have done to you?" Now it is that the blessed Peter gets that promise fulfilled: for he had been put off when, in the midst of his trembling and asserting, "Thou shalt never wash my feet," he received the answer, "What I do, thou knowest not now, but thou shalt know hereafter" (vers. 7, 8). Here, then, is that very hereafter; it is now time to tell what was a little ago deferred. Accordingly, the Lord, mindful of His foregoing promise to make him understand an act of His so unexpected, so wonderful, so frightening, and, but for His own still more terrifying rejoinder, impossible to be permitted, that the Master not only of themselves, but of angels, and the Lord not only of them, but of all things, should wash the feet of His own disciples and servants: having then promised to let him know the meaning of so important an act, when He said, "Thou shalt know afterwards," begins now to show them what it was that He did.

3. "Ye call me," He says, "Master and Lord: and ye say well; for so I am." "Ye say well," for ye only say the truth; I am indeed what ye say. There is a precept laid on man: "Let not thine own mouth praise thee, but the mouth of thy neighbor."[1] For

[1] Prov. xxvii. 2.

20

self-pleasing is a perilous thing for one who has to be on his guard against falling into pride. But He who is over all things, however much He commend Himself, cannot exalt Himself above His actual dignity: nor can God be rightly termed arrogant. For it is to our advantage to know Him, not to His; nor can any one know Him, unless that self-knowing One make Himself known. If He, then, by abstaining from self-commendation, wish, as it were, to avoid arrogance, He will deny us the power of knowing Him. And no one surely would blame Him for calling Himself Master, even though believing Him to be nothing more than a man; seeing He only makes profession of what even men themselves in the various arts profess to such an extent, without any charge of arrogance, that they are termed professors. But to call Himself also the Lord of His disciples,—of men who, in an earthly sense, were themselves also free-born,—who would tolerate it in a man? But it is God that speaks. Here no elation is possible to loftiness so great, no lie to the truth: the profit is ours to be the subjects of such loftiness, the servants of the truth. That He calls Himself Lord is no imperfection on His side, but a benefit on ours. The words of a certain profane [1] author are commended, when he says, "All arrogance is hateful, and specially disagreeable is that of talent and eloquence;" [2] and yet, when the same person was speaking of his own eloquence, he said, "I would call it perfect, were I to pronounce judgment; nor, in truth, would I greatly fear the charge of arrogance." [3] If, then, that most eloquent man had in truth no fear of being charged with arrogance, how can the truth itself have such a fear? Let Him call Himself Lord who is the Lord, let Him say what is true who is the Truth; so that I may not fail to learn that which is profitable, by His being silent about that which *is*. The most blessed Paul—certainly not himself the only-begotten Son of God, but the servant and apostle of that Son; not the Truth, but a partaker of the truth—declares with freedom and consistency, "And though I would desire to glory, I shall not be a fool; for I say the truth." [4] For it would not be in himself, but in the truth, which is superior to himself, that he was glorying both humbly and truly: for it is he also who has given the charge, that he that glorieth should glory in the Lord. [5] Could thus the lover of wisdom have no fear of being chargeable with foolishness, though he desired to glory? and would wisdom itself, in its glorying, have

any fear of such a charge? He had no fear of arrogance who said, "My soul shall make her boast in the Lord;" [6] and could the power of the Lord have any such fear in commending itself, in which His servant's soul is making her boast? "Ye call me," He says, "Master and Lord: and ye say well; for so I am." Therefore ye say well, that I am so: for if I were not what ye say, ye would be wrong to say so, even with the purpose of praising me. How, then, could the Truth deny what the disciples of the Truth affirm? How could that which was said by the learners be denied by the very Truth that gave them their learning? How can the fountain deny what the drinker asserts? how can the light hide what the beholder declares?

4. "If I, then," He says, "your Lord and Master, have washed your feet, ye also ought to wash one another's feet. For I have given you an example, that ye should do as I have done to you." This, blessed Peter, is what thou didst not know when thou wert not allowing it to be done. This is what He promised to let thee know afterwards, when thy Master and thy Lord terrified thee into submission, and washed thy feet. We have learned, brethren, humility from the Highest; let us, as humble, do to one another what He, the Highest, did in His humility. Great is the commendation we have here of humility: and brethren do this to one another in turn, even in the visible act itself, when they treat one another with hospitality; for the practice of such humility is generally prevalent, and finds expression in the very deed that makes it discernible. And hence the apostle, when he would commend the well-deserving widow, says, "If she is hospitable, if she has washed the saints' feet." [7] And wherever such is not the practice among the saints, what they do not with the hand they do in heart, if they are of the number of those who are addressed in the hymn of the three blessed men, "O ye holy and humble of heart, bless ye the Lord." [8] But it is far better, and beyond all dispute more accordant with the truth, that it should also be done with the hands; nor should the Christian think it beneath him to do what was done by Christ. For when the body is bent at a brother's feet, the feeling of such humility is either awakened in the heart itself, or is strengthened if already present.

5. But apart from this moral understanding of the passage, we remember that the way in

---

[1] *Sæcularis.*		[2] Cicero, *in Q. Cæcilium.*
[3] Cicero, *de Oratore.*	[4] 2 Cor. xii. 6.	[5] 1 Cor. i. 31.

[6] Ps. xxxiv. 2.			[7] 1 Tim. v. 10.
[8] Dan. iii. 88; that is, in the apocryphal piece called "*The Song of the Three Children,*" and which, as it has no place in the Hebrew Scriptures, is also omitted in our English version. Its place would fall between the 23d and 24th verses of chap. iii.—TR.

which we commended to your attention the grandeur of this act of the Lord's, was that, in washing the feet of disciples who were already washed and clean, the Lord instituted a sign, to the end that, on account of the human feelings that occupy us on earth, however far we may have advanced in our apprehension of righteousness, we might know that we are not exempt from sin; which He thereafter washes away by interceding for us, when we pray the Father, who is in heaven, to forgive us our debts, as we also forgive our debtors.[1] What connection, then, can such an understanding of the passage have with that which He afterwards gave Himself, when He explained the reason of His act in the words, "If I then, your Lord and Master, have washed your feet, ye also ought to wash one another's feet. For I have given you an example, that ye should do as I have done to you"? Can we say that even a brother may cleanse a brother from the contracted stain of wrongdoing? Yea, verily, we know that of this also we were admonished in the profound significance of this work of the Lord's, that we should confess our faults one to another, and pray for one another, even as Christ also maketh intercession for us.[2] Let us listen to the Apostle James, who states this precept with the greatest clearness when he says, "Confess your faults one to another, and pray one for another."[3] For of this also the Lord gave us the example. For if He who neither has, nor had, nor will have any sin, prays for our sins, how much more ought we to pray for one another's in turn! And if He forgives us, whom we have nothing to forgive; how much more ought we, who are unable to live here without sin, to forgive one another! For what else does the Lord apparently intimate in the profound significance of this sacramental sign, when He says, "For I have given you an example, that ye should do as I have done to you;" but what the apostle declares in the plainest terms, "Forgiving one another, if any man have a quarrel against any: even as Christ forgave you, so also do ye"?[4] Let us therefore forgive one another his faults, and pray for one another's faults, and thus in a manner be washing one another's feet. It is our part, by His grace, to be supplying the service of love and humility: it is His to hear us, and to cleanse us from all the pollution of our sins through Christ, and in Christ; so that what we forgive even to others, that is, loose on earth, may be loosed in heaven.

[1] Matt. vi. 12.   [2] Rom. viii. 34.   [3] Jas. v. 16.   [4] Col. iii. 13.

TRACTATE LIX.

Chapter XIII. 16–20.

1. We have just heard in the holy Gospel the Lord speaking, and saying, "Verily, verily, I say unto you, The servant is not greater than his lord, nor the apostle [he that is sent] greater than he that sent him: if ye know these things, blessed shall ye be if ye do them." He said this, therefore, because He had washed the disciples' feet, as the Master of humility both by word and example. But we shall be able, with His help, to handle what is in need of more elaborate handling, if we linger not at what is perfectly clear. Accordingly, after uttering these words, the Lord added, "I speak not of you all: I know whom I have chosen: but, that the Scripture may be fulfilled, He that eateth bread with me, shall lift up his heel upon me." And what is this, but that he shall trample upon me? We know of whom He speaks: it is Judas, that betrayer of His, who is referred to. He had not therefore chosen the person whom, by these words, He setteth utterly apart from His chosen ones. When I say then, He continues, "Blessed shall ye be if ye do them, I speak not of you all:" there is one among you who will not be blessed, and who will not do these things. "I know whom I have chosen." Whom, but those who shall be blessed in the doing of what has been commanded and shown as needful to be done, by Him who alone can make them blessed? The traitor Judas, He says, is not one of those that have been chosen. What, then, is meant by what He says in another place, "Have I not chosen you twelve, and one of you is a devil?"[1] Was it that he also was chosen for some purpose, for which he was really necessary; although not for the blessedness of

[1] Chap. vi. 70.

which He has just been saying, "Blessed shall ye be if ye do these things"? He speaketh not so of them all; for He knows whom He has chosen to be associated with Himself in blessedness. Of such he is not one, who ate His bread in order that he might lift up his heel upon Him. The bread they ate was the Lord Himself; he ate the Lord's bread in enmity to the Lord: they ate life, and he punishment. "For he that eateth unworthily," says the apostle, "eateth judgment unto himself."[1] "From this time,"[2] Christ adds, "I tell you before it come; that when it is come to pass, ye may believe that I am He:" that is, I am He of whom the Scripture that preceded has just said, "He that eateth bread with me, shall lift up his heel upon me."

2. He then proceeds to say: "Verily, verily, I say unto you, He that receiveth whomsoever I send, receiveth me; and he that receiveth me, receiveth Him that sent me." Did He mean us to understand that there is as little distance between one sent by Him, and Himself, as there is between Himself and God the Father? If we take it in this way, I know not what measurements of distance (which may God forbid!) we shall be adopting, in the Arian fashion. For they, when they hear or read these words of the Gospel, have immediate recourse to their dogmatic measurements, whereby they ascend not to life, but fall headlong into death. For they straightway say: The Son's messenger stands at the same relative distance from the Son, as expressed in the words, "He that receiveth whomsoever I send, receiveth me," as that in which the Son Himself stands from the Father, when He said, "He that receiveth me, receiveth Him that sent me." But if thou sayest so, thou forgettest, heretic, thy measurements. For if, because of these words of the Lord, thou puttest the Son at as great a distance from the Father as the messenger [apostle] from the Son, where dost thou purpose to place the Holy Spirit? Has it escaped thee, that ye are wont to place Him after the Son? He will therefore come in between the messenger and the Son; and much greater, then, will be the distance between the Son and His messenger, than between the Father and His Son. Or perhaps, to preserve that distinction between the Son and His messenger, and between the Father and His Son, at their equality of distance, will the Holy Spirit be equal to the Son?

But as little will ye allow this. And where, then, do ye think of placing Him, if ye place the Son as far beneath the Father, as ye place the messenger beneath the Son? Restrain, therefore, your foolhardy presumption; and do not be seeking to find in these words the same distance between the Son and His messenger as between the Father and His Son. But listen rather to the Son Himself, when He says, "I and my Father are one."[3] For there the Truth hath left you no shadow of distance between the Begetter and the Only-begotten; there Christ Himself hath erased your measurements, and the rock hath broken your staircase to pieces.

3. But now that the heretical slander has been disposed of, in what sense are we to understand these words of the Lord: "He that receiveth whomsoever I send, receiveth me; and he that receiveth me, receiveth Him that sent me"? For if we were inclined to understand the words, "He that receiveth me, receiveth Him that sent me," as expressing the oneness in nature of the Father and the Son; the sequence from the similar arrangement of words in the other clause, "He that receiveth whomsoever I send, receiveth me," would be the unity in nature of the Son and His messenger. And there might, indeed, be no impropriety in so understanding it, seeing that a twofold substance belongeth to the strong man, who hath rejoiced to run the race;[4] for the Word was made flesh,[5] that is, God became man. And accordingly He might be supposed to have said, "He that receiveth whomsoever I send, receiveth me," with reference to His human nature; "and he that receiveth me" as God, "receiveth Him that sent me." But in so speaking, He was not commending the unity of nature, but the authority of the Sender in Him who is sent. Let every one, therefore, so receive Him that is sent, that in His person he may give heed to Him who sent Him. If, then, thou lookest for Christ in Peter, thou wilt find the disciple's instructor; and if thou lookest for the Father in the Son, thou wilt find the Begetter of the Only-begotten: and so in Him who is sent, thou art not mistaken in receiving the Sender. What follows in the Gospel cannot be compressed within the shortness of the time remaining. And therefore, dearly beloved, let what has been said, if thought sufficient, be received in a healthful way, as pasture for the holy sheep; and if it is somewhat scanty, let it be ruminated over with ardent desire for more.

---

[1] 1 Cor. xi. 29.
[2] *A modo;* Greek, 'Aπ' ἄρτι; margin of English Bible, "From henceforth."—TR.

[3] Chap. x. 30.   [4] Ps. xix. 5.   [5] Chap. i. 14.

TRACTATE LX.

Chapter XIII. 21.

1. It is no light question, brethren, that meets us in the Gospel of the blessed John, when he says: "When Jesus had thus said, He was troubled in spirit, and testified, and said, Verily, verily, I say unto you, that one of you shall betray me." Was it for this reason that Jesus was troubled, not in flesh, but in spirit, that He was now about to say, "One of you shall betray me"? Did this occur then for the first time to His mind, or was it at that moment suddenly revealed to Him for the first time, and so troubled Him by the startling novelty of so great a calamity? Was it not a little before that He was using these words, "He that eateth bread with me will lift up his heel against me"? And had He not also, previously to that, said, "And ye are clean, but not all"? where the evangelist added, "For He knew who should betray Him:"[1] to whom also on a still earlier occasion He had pointed in the words, "Have not I chosen you twelve, and one of you is a devil?"[2] Why is it, then, that He "was now troubled in spirit," when "He testified, and said, Verily, verily, I say unto you, that one of you shall betray me"? Was it because now He had so to mark him out, that he should no longer remain concealed among the rest, but be separated from the others, that therefore "He was troubled in spirit"? Or was it because now the traitor himself was on the eve of departing to bring those Jews to whom he was to betray the Lord, that He was troubled by the imminency of His passion, the closeness of the danger, and the swooping hand of the traitor, whose resolution was foreknown? For some such cause it certainly was that Jesus "was troubled in spirit," as when He said, "Now is my soul troubled; and what shall I say? Father, save me from this hour; but for this cause came I unto this hour."[3] And accordingly, just as then His soul was troubled as the hour of His passion approached; so now also, as Judas was on the point of going and coming, and the atrocious villainy of the traitor neared its accomplishment, "He was troubled in spirit."

2. He was troubled, then, who had power to lay down His life, and had power to take it again.[4] That mighty power is troubled, the firmness of the rock is disturbed: or is it rather our infirmity that is troubled in Him? Assuredly so: let servants believe nothing unworthy of their Lord, but recognize their own membership in their Head. He who died for us, was also Himself troubled in our place. He, therefore, who died in power, was troubled in the midst of His power: He who shall yet transform[5] the body of our humility into similarity of form with the body of His glory, hath also transferred into Himself the feeling of our infirmity, and sympathizeth with us in the feelings of His own soul. Accordingly, when it is the great, the brave, the sure, the invincible One that is troubled, let us have no fear for Him, as if He were capable of failing: He is not perishing, but in search of us [who are]. Us, I say; it is us exclusively whom He is thus seeking, that in His trouble we may behold ourselves, and so, when trouble reaches us, may not fall into despair and perish. By His trouble, who could not be troubled save with His own consent, He comforts such as are troubled unwillingly.

3. Away with the reasons of philosophers, who assert that a wise man is not affected by mental perturbations. God hath made foolish the wisdom of this world;[6] and the Lord knoweth the thoughts of men, that they are vain.[7] It is plain that the mind of the Christian may be troubled, not by misery, but by pity: he may fear lest men should be lost to Christ; he may sorrow when one is being lost; he may have ardent desire to gain men to Christ; he may be filled with joy when such is being done; he may have fear of falling away himself from Christ; he may sorrow over his own estrangement from Christ; he may be earnestly desirous of reigning with Christ, and he may be rejoicing in the hope that such fellowship with Christ will yet be his lot. These are certainly four of what they call perturbations—fear and sorrow, love and gladness. And Christian minds may have sufficient cause to feel them, and evidence their dissent from the error of Stoic philosophers, and all resembling them: who indeed, just as they esteem truth to be vanity, regard

---

[1] Chap. xiii. 18, 10, 11.   [2] Chap. vi. 71.
[3] Chap. xii. 27.   [4] Chap. x. 18.

[5] Phil. iii. 21. The text has *transfiguravit* (pret.), "hath transformed," in this as well as in the next clause, "hath transferred," but here it is evidently a misprint for *transfigurabit* (fut.).—Tr.
[6] 1 Cor. i. 20.   [7] Ps. xciv. 11.

also insensibility as soundness; not knowing that a man's mind, like the limbs of his body, is only the more hopelessly diseased when it has lost even the feeling of pain.

4. But says some one: Ought the mind of the Christian to be troubled even at the prospect of death? For what comes of those words of the apostle, that he had a desire to depart, and to be with Christ,[1] if the object of his desire can thus trouble him when it comes? Our answer to this would be easy, indeed, in the case of those who also term gladness itself a perturbation [of the mind]. For what if the trouble he thus feels arises entirely from his rejoicing at the prospect of death? But such a feeling, they say, ought to be termed gladness, and not rejoicing.[2] And what is that, but just to alter the name, while the feeling experienced is the same? But let us for our part confine our attention to the Sacred Scriptures, and with the Lord's help seek rather such a solution of this question as will be in harmony with them; and then, seeing it is written, "When He had thus said, He was troubled in spirit," we will not say that it was joy that disturbed Him; lest His own words should convince us of the contrary when He says, "My soul is sorrowful, even unto death."[3] It is some such feeling that is here also to be understood, when, as His betrayer was now on the very point of departing alone, and straightway returning along with his associates, "Jesus was troubled in spirit."

5. Strong-minded, indeed, are those Christians, if such there are, who experience no trouble at all in the prospect of death; but for all that, are they stronger-minded than Christ? Who would have the madness to say so? And what else, then, does His being troubled signify, but that, by voluntarily assuming the likeness of their weakness, He comforted the weak members in His own body, that is, in His Church; to the end that, if any of His own are still troubled at the approach of death, they may fix their gaze upon Him, and so be kept from thinking themselves castaways on this account, and being swallowed up in the more grievous death of despair? And how great, then, must be that good which we ought to expect and hope for in the participation of His divine nature, whose very perturbation tranquillizes us, and whose infirmity confirms us? Whether, therefore, on this occasion it was by His pity for Judas himself thus rushing into ruin, or by the near approach of His own death, that He was troubled, yet there is no possibility of doubting that it was not through any infirmity of mind, but in the fullness of power, that He was troubled, and so no despair of salvation need arise in our minds, when we are troubled, not in the possession of power, but in the midst of our weakness. He certainly bore the infirmity of the flesh,—an infirmity which was swallowed up in His resurrection. But He who was not only man, but God also, surpassed by an ineffable distance the whole human race in fortitude of mind. He was not, then, troubled by any outward pressure of man, but troubled Himself; which was very plainly declared of Him when He raised Lazarus from the dead: for it is there written that He troubled Himself,[4] that it may be so understood even where the text does not so express it, and yet declares that He was troubled. For having by His power assumed our full humanity, by that very power He awoke in Himself our human feelings whenever He judged it becoming.

---

[1] Phil. i. 23. [2] *Gaudium, non lætitia.* [3] Matt. xxvi. 38. [4] Chap. xi. 33, *margin.*

TRACTATE LXI.

CHAPTER XIII. 21-26.

1. THIS short section of the Gospel, brethren, we have in this lesson brought forward for exposition, as thinking that we ought also to say something of the Lord's betrayer, as now plainly enough disclosed by the dipping and holding out to him of the piece of bread. Of that indeed which precedes, (namely), that Jesus, when about to point him out, was troubled in spirit, we have treated in our last discourse; but what I perhaps omitted to mention there, the Lord, by His own perturbation of spirit, thought proper to indicate this also, that it is necessary to bear with false brethren, and those tares that are among the wheat in the Lord's field until harvest-time, because that when we are compelled by

urgent reasons to separate some of them even before the harvest, it cannot be done without disturbance to the Church.   Such disturbance to His saints in the future, through schismatics and heretics, the Lord in a way foretold and prefigured in Himself, when, at the moment of that wicked man Judas' departure, and of his thereby bringing to an end, in a very open and decided way, his past intermingling with the wheat, in which he had long been tolerated, He was troubled, not in body, but in spirit.   For it is not spitefulness, but charity, that troubles His spiritual members in scandals of this kind; lest perchance, in separating some of the tares, any of the wheat should also be uprooted therewith.

2. "Jesus," therefore, "was troubled in spirit, and testified, and said: Verily, verily, I say unto you, that one of you shall betray me." "One of you," in number, not in merit; in appearance, not in reality; in bodily commingling, not by any spiritual tie; a companion by fleshly juxtaposition, not in any unity of the heart; and therefore not one who is of you, but one who is to go forth from you. For how else can this "one of you" be true, of which the Lord so testified, and said, if that is true which the writer of this very Gospel says in his Epistle, "They went out from us, but they were not of us; for if they had been of us, they would no doubt have continued with us"?[1] Judas, therefore, was not of them; for, had he been of them, he would have continued with them. What, then, do the words "One of you shall betray me" mean, but that one is going out from you who shall betray me? Just as he also, who said, "If they had been of us, they would no doubt have continued with us," had said before, "They went out from us." And thus it is true in both senses, "of us," and "not of us;" in one respect "of us," and in another "not of us;" "of us" in respect to sacramental communion, but "not of us" in respect to the criminal conduct that belongs exclusively to themselves.

3. "Then the disciples looked one on another, doubting of whom He spake." For while they were imbued with a reverential love to their Master, they were none the less affected by human infirmity in their feelings towards each other. Each one's own conscience was known to himself; but as he was ignorant of his neighbor's, each one's self-assurance was such that each was uncertain of all the others, and all the others were uncertain of that one.

4. "Now there was leaning on Jesus'

bosom, one of His disciples, whom Jesus loved." What he meant by saying "in His bosom," he tells us a little further on, where he says, "on the breast of Jesus." It was that very John whose Gospel is before us, as he afterwards expressly declares.[2] For it was a custom with those who have supplied us with the sacred writings, that when any of them was relating the divine history, and came to something affecting himself, he spoke as if it were about another; and gave himself a place in the line of his narrative becoming one who was the recorder of public events, and not as one who made himself the subject of his preaching. Saint Matthew acted also in this way, when, in coming in the course of his narrative to himself, he says, "He saw a publican named Matthew, sitting at the receipt of custom, and saith unto him, Follow me."[3] He does not say, He saw me, and said to me. So also acted the blessed Moses, writing all the history about himself as if it concerned another, and saying, "The Lord said unto Moses."[4] Less habitually was this done by the Apostle Paul, not however in any history which undertakes to explain the course of public events, but in his own epistles. At all events, he speaks thus of himself: "I knew a man in Christ fourteen years ago, (whether in the body, or whether out of the body, I cannot tell: God knoweth;) such an one caught up into the third heaven."[5] And so, when the blessed evangelist also says here, not, I was leaning on Jesus' bosom, but, "There was leaning one of the disciples," let us recognize a custom of our author's, rather than fall into any wonder on the subject. For what loss is there to the truth, when the facts themselves are told us, and all boastfulness of language is in a measure avoided? For thus at least did he relate that which most signally pertained to his praise.

5. But what mean the words, "whom Jesus loved"? As if He did not love the others, of whom this same John has said above, "He loved them to the end" (ver. 1); and as the Lord Himself, "Greater love hath no man than this, that a man lay down his life for his friends." And who could enumerate all the testimonies of the sacred pages, in which the Lord Jesus is exhibited as the lover, not only of this one, or of those who were then around Him, but of such also as were to be His members in the distant future, and of His universal Church? But there is some truth, doubtless, underlying these words, and having reference to the bosom on which the narrator was leaning. For what else can be in-

---

[1] 1 John ii. 19.

[2] Chap. xxi. 20–24.   [3] Matt. ix. 9.
[4] Ex. vi. 1.   [5] 2 Cor. xii. 2.

dicated by the *bosom* but some hidden truth? But there is another more suitable passage, where the Lord may enable us to say something about this secret that may prove sufficient.

6. "Simon Peter therefore beckons, and says to him."[1] The expression is noteworthy, as indicating that something was said not by any sound of words, but by merely beckoning with the head. " He beckons, and says;" that is, his beckoning is his speech. For if one is said to speak in his thoughts, as Scripture saith, " They said [reasoned] with themselves;"[2] how much more may he do so by

---

[1] The original MSS. give different readings of this verse. That followed by our English version is supported by the Codd. Alex. and Cantabr., which read, Νεύει οὖν τούτῳ Σίμων Πέτρος πυθέσθαι τίς ἂν εἴη περὶ οὗ λέγει. The Latin version used by Augustin reads, *Innuit ergo Simon Petrus, et dicit ei, Quis est de quo dicit*, and approaches nearly to that found in the Codd. Vat. and Ephr., which read, Νεύει οὖν τούτῳ Σ. Π., καὶ λέγει αὐτῷ, Εἰπὲ τίς ἐστιν περὶ οὗ λέγει—"Simon Peter therefore beckons to this one, and says to him, Say [ask], who is it of whom He speaks?" Of the early versions, the Syriac adopts the former, while the Vulgate resembles the latter. The Sinaitic gives a fuller reading, compounded of both the others. There is thus some doubt as to the original text; but the latter has some special arguments of an internal kind in its favor: such as the consideration that, from its peculiar and somewhat redundant form, *it* could hardly have been substituted in place of the former, which is smoother and more elegant, while the converse is perfectly supposable ; and also the weighty fact that John nowhere else makes use of the optative mood, as he would here (τίς ἂν εἴη), if the former reading—that followed by our English version—were the true one.—TR.

[2] Wisd. of Sol. ii. 1.

---

beckoning, which expresses outwardly by some sort of signs what had previously been conceived within ! What, then, did his beckoning mean? What else but that which follows? " Who is it of whom He speaks?" Such was the language of Peter's beckoning; for it was by no vocal sounds, but by bodily gestures, that he spake. " He then, having leaned back on Jesus' breast,"—surely the very bosom[3] of His breast this, the secret place of wisdom !—" saith unto Him, Lord, who is it? Jesus answered, He it is to whom I shall give a piece of bread, when I have dipped it. And when He had dipped the bread, he gave it to Judas Iscariot, the son of Simon. And after the bread, Satan entered into him." The traitor was disclosed, the coverts of darkness were revealed. What he got was good, but to his own hurt he received it, because, evil himself, in an evil spirit he received what was good. But we have much to say about that dipped bread which was presented to the false-hearted disciple, and about that which follows; and for these we shall require more time than remains to us now at the close of this discourse.

---

[3] *Pectoris sinus ;* the hollow, the inmost part of the breast.

TRACTATE LXII.

CHAPTER XIII. 26-31.

1. I KNOW, dearly beloved, that some may be moved, as the godly to inquire into the meaning of, and the ungodly to find fault with, the statement, that it was after the Lord had given the bread, that had been dipped, to His betrayer that Satan entered into him. For so it is written: "And when He had dipped the bread, He gave it to Judas Iscariot, the Son of Simon. And after the bread, then entered Satan into him." For they say, Was this the worth of Christ's bread, given from Christ's own table, that after it Satan should enter into His disciple? And the answer we give them is, that thereby we are taught rather how much we need to beware of receiving what is good in a sinful spirit. For the point of special importance is, not the thing that is received, but the person that receives it; and not the character of the thing that is given, but of him to whom it is given. For even good things are hurtful, and evil things are beneficial, according to the character of the

recipients. " Sin," says the apostle, " that it might appear sin, wrought death to me by that which is good."[1] Thus, you see, evil is brought about by the good, so long as that which is good is wrongly received. It is he also that says: " Lest I should be exalted unduly through the greatness of my revelations, there was given to me a thorn in my flesh, the messenger of Satan to buffet me. For which thing I besought the Lord thrice, that He would take it away from me; and He said unto me, My grace is sufficient for thee: for strength is made perfect in weakness."[2] And here, you see, good was brought about by that which was evil, when the evil was received in a good spirit. Why, then, do we wonder if Christ's bread was given to Judas, that thereby he should be made over to the devil; when we see, on the other hand, that Paul was visited by a messenger of the devil,

---

[1] Rom. vii. 13.   [2] 2 Cor. xii. 7-9.

that by such an instrumentality he might be perfected in Christ? In this way, both the good was injurious to the evil man, and the evil was beneficial to the good. Bear in mind the meaning of the Scripture, "Whosoever shall eat the bread or drink the cup of the Lord unworthily, shall be guilty of the body and blood of the Lord."[1] And when the apostle said this, he was dealing with those who were taking the body of the Lord, like any other food, in an undiscerning and careless spirit. If, then, he is thus taken to task who does not discern, that is, does not distinguish from the other kinds of food, the body of the Lord, what condemnation must be his, who in the guise of a friend comes as an enemy to His table! If negligence in the guest is thus visited with blame, what must be the punishment that will fall on the man that sells the very person who has invited him to his table! And why was the bread given to the traitor, but as an evidence of the grace he had treated with ingratitude?

2. It was after this bread, then, that Satan entered into the Lord's betrayer, that, as now given over to his power, he might take full possession of one into whom before this he had only entered in order to lead him into error. For we are not to suppose that he was not in him when he went to the Jews and bargained about the price of betraying the Lord; for the evangelist Luke very plainly attests this when he says: "Then entered Satan into Judas, who was surnamed Iscariot, being one of the twelve; and he went his way, and communed with the chief priests."[2] Here, you see, it is shown that Satan had already entered into Judas. His first entrance, therefore, was when he implanted in his heart the thought of betraying Christ; for in such a spirit had he already come to the supper. But now, after the bread, he entered into him, no longer to tempt one who belonged to another, but to take possession of him as his own.

3. But it was not then, as some thoughtless readers suppose, that Judas received the body of Christ. For we are to understand that the Lord had already dispensed to all of them the sacrament of His body and blood, when Judas also was present, as very clearly related by Saint Luke;[3] and it was after this that we come to the moment when, in accordance with John's account, the Lord made a full disclosure of His betrayer by dipping and holding out to him the morsel of bread, and intimating perhaps by the dipping of the bread the false pretensions of the other. For the dipping of a thing does not always imply its washing; but some things are dipped in order to be dyed. But if a good meaning is to be here attached to the dipping, his ingratitude for that good was deservedly followed by damnation.

4. But still, possessed as Judas now was, not by the Lord, but by the devil, and now that the bread had entered the belly, and an enemy the soul of this man of ingratitude: still, I say, there was this enormous wickedness, already conceived in his heart, waiting to be wrought out to its full issue, for which the damnable desire had always preceded. Accordingly, when the Lord, the living Bread, had given this bread to the dead, and in giving it had revealed the betrayer of the Bread, He said, "What thou doest, do quickly." He did not command the crime, but foretold evil to Judas, and good to us. For what could be worse for Judas, or what could be better for us, than the delivering up of Christ, —a deed done by him to his own destruction, but done, apart from him, in our behalf? "What thou doest, do quickly." Oh that word of One whose wish was to be ready rather than to be angry! That word! expressing not so much the punishment of the traitor as the reward awaiting the Redeemer! For He said, "What thou doest, do quickly," not as wrathfully looking to the destruction of the trust-betrayer, but in His own haste to accomplish the salvation of the faithful; for He was delivered for our offences,[4] and He loved the Church, and gave Himself for it.[5] And as the apostle also says of himself: "Who loved me, and gave Himself for me."[6] Had not, then, Christ given Himself, no one could have given Him up. What is there in Judas' conduct but sin? For in delivering up Christ he had no thought of our salvation, for which Christ was really delivered, but thought only of his money gain, and found the loss of his soul. He got the wages he wished, but had also given him, against his wish, the wages he merited. Judas delivered up Christ, Christ delivered Himself up: the former transacted the business of his own selling of his Master, the latter the business of our redemption. "What thou doest, do quickly," not because thou hast the power in thyself, but because He wills it who has all the power.

5. "Now no one of those at the table knew for what intent He spake this unto him. For some of them thought, because Judas had the money-bag, that Jesus said unto him, Buy those things which we have need of against

[1] 1 Cor. xi. 27.   [2] Luke xxii. 3, 4.   [3] Luke xxii. 19–21.   [4] Rom. iv. 25.   [5] Eph. v. 25.   [6] Gal. ii. 20.

the feast; or, that he should give something to the poor." The Lord, therefore, had also a money-box, where He kept the offerings of believers, and distributed to the necessities of His own, and to others who were in need. It was then that the custom of having church-money was first introduced, so that thereby we might understand that His precept about taking no thought for the morrow [1] was not a command that no money should be kept by His saints, but that God should not be served for any such end, and that the doing of what is right should not be held in abeyance through the fear of want. For the apostle also has this foresight for the future, when he says: "If any believer hath widows, let him give them enough, that the church may not be burdened, that it may have enough for them that are widows indeed." [2]

6. "He then, having received the morsel of bread, went immediately out: and it was night." And he that went out was himself the night. "Therefore when" the night "was gone out, Jesus said, Now is the Son of man glorified." The day therefore uttered speech unto the day, that is, Christ did so to His faithful disciples, that they might hear and love Him as His followers; and the night showed knowledge unto the night,[3] that is, Judas did so to the unbelieving Jews, that they might come as His persecutors, and make Him their prisoner. But now, in considering these words of the Lord, which were addressed to the godly, before His arrest by the ungodly, special attention on the part of the hearer is required; and therefore it will be more becoming in the preacher, instead of hurriedly considering them now, to defer them till a future occasion.

---

[1] Matt. vi. 34.   [2] 1 Tim. v. 16.   [3] Ps. xix. 2.

TRACTATE LXIII

Chapter XIII. 31, 32

1. LET us give our mind's best attention, and, with the Lord's help, seek after God. The language of the divine hymn is: "Seek God and your soul shall live."[1] Let us search for that which needs to be discovered, and into that which has been discovered. He whom we need to discover is concealed, in order to be sought after; and when found, is infinite, in order still to be the object of our search. Hence it is elsewhere said, "Seek His face evermore."[2] For He satisfies the seeker to the utmost of his capacity; and makes the finder still more capable, that he may seek to be filled anew, according to the growth of his ability to receive. Therefore it was not said, "Seek His face evermore," in the same sense as of certain others, who are "always learning, and never coming to a knowledge of the truth;"[3] but rather as the preacher saith, "When a man hath finished, then he beginneth;"[4] till we reach that life where we shall be so filled, that our natures shall attain their utmost capacity, because we shall have arrived at perfection, and no longer be aiming at more. For then all that can satisfy us will be revealed to our eyes. But here let us always be seeking, and let our re-ward in finding put no end to our searching. For we do not say that it will not be so always, because it is only so here; but that here we must always be seeking, lest at any time we should imagine that here we can ever cease from seeking. For those of whom it is said that they are "always learning, and never coming to a knowledge of the truth," are here indeed always learning; but when they depart this life they will no longer be learning, but receiving the reward of their error. For the words, "always learning, and never coming to a knowledge of the truth," mean, as it were, always walking, and never getting into the road. Let us, on the other hand, be walking always in the way, till we reach the end to which it leads; let us nowhere tarry in it till we reach the proper place of abode: and so we shall both persevere in our seeking, and be making some attainments in our finding, and, thus seeking and finding, passing on to that which remains, till the very end of all seeking shall be reached in that world where perfection shall admit of no further effort at advancement. Let these prefatory remarks, dearly beloved, make your Charity attentive to this discourse of our Lord's, which He addressed to the disciples before His passion: for it is profound in it-

---

[1] Ps. lxix. 32.   [2] Ps. cv. 4.
[3] 2 Tim. iii. 7.   [4] Ecclus. xviii. 7.

self; and where, in particular, the preacher purposes to expend much labor, the hearer ought not to be remiss in attention.

2. What is it, then, that the Lord says, after that Judas went out, to do quickly what he purposed doing, namely, betraying the Lord? What says the day when the night had gone out? What says the Redeemer when the seller had departed? "Now," He says, "is the Son of man glorified." Why "*now*"? It was not, was it, merely that His betrayer was gone out, and that those were at hand who were to seize and slay Him? Is it thus that He "is now glorified," to wit, that His deeper humiliation is approaching; that over Him are impending both bonds, and judgment, and condemnation, and mocking, and crucifixion, and death? Is this glorification, or rather humiliation? Even when He was working miracles, does not this very John say of Him, "The Spirit was not yet given, because that Jesus was not yet glorified"?[1] Even then, therefore, when He was raising the dead, He was not yet glorified; and is He glorified now, when drawing near in His own person unto death? He was not yet glorified when acting as God, and is He glorified in going to suffer as man? It would be strange if it were this that God, the great Master, signified and taught in such words. We must ascend higher to unveil the words of the Highest, who reveals Himself somewhat that we may find Him, and anon hides Himself that we may seek Him, and so press on step by step, as it were, from discoveries already made to those that still await us. I get here a sight of something that prefigures a great reality. Judas went out, and Jesus is glorified; the son of perdition went out, and the Son of man is glorified. He it was that had gone out, on whose account it had been said to them all, "And ye are clean, but not all" (ver. 10). When, therefore, the unclean one departed, all that remained were clean, and continued with their Cleanser. Something like this will it be when this world shall have been conquered by Christ, and shall have passed away, and there shall be no one that is unclean remaining among His people; when, the tares having been separated from the wheat, the righteous shall shine forth as the sun in the kingdom of their Father.[2] The Lord, foreseeing such a future as this, and in testimony that such was signified now in the separation of the tares, as it were, by the departure of Judas, and the remaining behind of the wheat in the persons of the holy apostles, said, "Now is the Son of man glorified:" as

if He had said, See, so will it be in that day of my glorification yet to come, when none of the wicked shall be present, and none of the good shall be wanting. His words, however, are not expressed in this way: Now is *prefigured* the glorification of the Son of man; but expressly, "Now is the Son of man glorified:" just as it was not said, The Rock signified Christ; but, "That Rock *was* Christ."[3] Nor is it said, The good seed signified the children of the kingdom, or, The tares signified the children of the wicked one; but what is said is, "The good seed, these are the children of the kingdom; and the tares, the children of the wicked one."[4] According, then, to the usage of Scripture language, which speaks of the signs as if they were the things signified, the Lord makes use of the words, "Now is the Son of man glorified;" indicating that in the completed separation of that arch sinner from their company, and in the remaining around Him of His saints, we have the foreshadowing of His glorification, when the wicked shall be finally separated, and He shall dwell with His saints through eternity.

3. But after saying, "Now is the Son of man glorified," He added, "and God is glorified in Him." For this is itself the glorifying of the Son of man, that God should be glorified in Him. For if He is not glorified in Himself, but God in Him, then it is He whom God glorifies in Himself. And just as if to give them this explanation, He furthers adds: "If God is glorified in Him, God shall also glorify Him in Himself." That is, "If God is glorified in Him," because He came not to do His own will, but the will of Him that sent Him; "and God shall glorify Him in Himself," in such wise that the human nature, in which He is the Son of man, and which was so assumed by the eternal Word, should also be endowed with an eternal immortality. "And," He says, "He shall straightway glorify Him;" predicting, to wit, by such an asseveration, His own resurrection in the immediate future, and not, as it were, ours in the end of the world. For it is this very glorification of which the evangelist had previously said, as I mentioned a little ago, that on this account the Spirit was not yet in their case given in that new way, in which He was yet to be given after the resurrection to those who believed, because that Jesus was not yet glorified: that is, mortality was not yet clothed with immortality, and temporal weakness transformed into eternal strength. This glorification may also be indicated in the

---

[1] Chap. vii. 39.   [2] Matt. xiii. 43.   [3] 1 Cor. x. 4.   [4] Matt. xiii. 38.

words, "Now is the Son of man glorified;" so that the word "now" may be supposed to refer, not to His impending passion, but to His closely succeeding resurrection, as if what was now so near at hand had actually been accomplished. Let this suffice your affection to-day; we shall take up, when the Lord permits us, the words that follow.

TRACTATE LXIV.

Chapter XIII. 33.

1. It becomes us, dearly beloved, to keep in view the orderly connection of our Lord's words. For after having previously said, but subsequently to Judas' departure, and his separation from even the outward communion of the saints, "Now is the Son of man glorified, and God is glorified in Him;"—whether He said so as pointing to His future kingdom, when the wicked shall be separated from the good, or that His resurrection was then to take place, that is, was not to be delayed, like ours, till the end of the world;—and having then added, "If God is glorified in Him, God shall also glorify Him in Himself, and shall straightway glorify Him," whereby without any ambiguity He testified to the immediate fulfillment of His own resurrection; He proceeded to say, "Little children, yet a little while I am with you." To keep them, therefore, from thinking that God was to glorify Him in such a way that He would never again be joined with them in earthly intercourse, He said, "Yet a little while I am with you:" as if He had said, Straightway indeed I shall be glorified in my resurrection; and yet I am not straightway to ascend into heaven, but "yet a little while I am with you." For, as we find it written in the Acts of the Apostles, He spent forty days with them after His resurrection, going in and out, and eating and drinking:[1] not indeed that He had any experience of hunger and thirst, but even by such evidences confirmed the reality of His flesh, which no longer needed, but still possessed the power, to eat and to drink. Was it, then, these forty days He had in view when He said, "Yet a little while I am with you," or something else? For it may also be understood in this way: "Yet a little while I am with you;" still, like you, I also am in this state of fleshly infirmity, that is, till He should die and rise again: for after He rose again He was with them, as has been said, for forty days in the full manifestation of His bodily presence; but He was no longer with them in the fellowship of human infirmity.

2. There is also another form of His divine presence unknown to mortal senses, of which He likewise says, "Lo, I am with you alway, even to the end of the world."[2] This, at least, is not the same as "yet a little while I am with you;" for it is not a little while until the end of the world. Or if even this is so (for time flies, and a thousand years are in God's sight as one day, or as a watch in the night,)[3] yet we cannot believe that He intended any such meaning on this occasion, especially as He went on to say, "Ye shall seek me, and as I said unto the Jews, Whither I go, ye cannot come." That is to say, after this little while that I am with you, "ye shall seek me, and whither I go, ye cannot come." Is it after the end of the world that, whither He goes, they will not be able to come? And where, then, is the place of which He is going to say a little after in this same discourse, "Father, I will that they also be with me where I am"?[4] It was not then of that presence of His with His own which He is maintaining with them till the end of the world that He now spake, when He said, "Yet a little while I am with you;" but either of that state of mortal infirmity in which He dwelt with them till His passion, or of that bodily presence which He was to maintain with them up till His ascension. Whichever of these any one prefers, he can do so without being at variance with the faith.

3. That no one, however, may deem that sense inconsistent with the true one, in which we say that the Lord may have meant the communion of mortal flesh which He held with the disciples till His passion, when He said, "Yet a little while I am with you;" let those words also of His after His resurrection, as found in another evangelist, be taken into consideration, when He said, "These are the words which I spake unto you, while I

[1] Acts i. 3.   [2] Matt. xxviii. 20.   [3] Ps. xc. 4.   [4] Chap. xvii. 24.

was yet with you:"[1] as if then He was no longer with them, even at the very time that they were standing by, seeing, touching, and talking with Him. What does He mean, then, by saying, "while I was yet with you," but, while I was yet in that state of mortal flesh wherein ye still remain? For then, indeed, He had been raised again in the same flesh; but He was no longer associated with them in the same mortality. And accordingly, as on that occasion, when now clothed in fleshly immortality, He said with truth, "while I was yet with you," to which we can attach no other meaning than, while I was yet with you in fleshly mortality; so here also, without any absurdity, we may understand His words, "Yet a little while I am with you," as if He had said, Yet a little while I am mortal like yourselves. Let us look, then, at the words that follow.

4. "Ye shall seek me: and as I said unto the Jews, Whither I go, ye cannot come; so say I to you now." That is, ye cannot come *now*. But when He said so to the Jews, He did not add the "now."[2] The former, therefore, were not able at that time to come where He was going, but they were so afterwards; because He says so a little afterwards in the plainest terms to the Apostle Peter. For, on the latter inquiring, "Lord, whither goest Thou?" He replied to him, "Whither I go thou canst not follow me now; but thou shalt follow me afterwards" (ver. 36). But what it means is not to be carelessly passed over.

For whither was it that the disciples could not then follow the Lord, but were able afterwards? If we say, to death, what time can be discovered when any one of the sons of men will find it impossible to die; since such, in this perishable body, is the lot of man, that therein life is not a whit easier than death? They were not, therefore, at that time less able to follow the Lord to death, but they were less able to follow Him to the life which is deathless. For thither it was the Lord was going, that, rising from the dead, He should die no more, and death should no more have dominion over Him.[3] For as the Lord was about to die for righteousness' sake, how could they have followed Him now, who were as yet unripe for the ordeal of martyrdom? Or, with the Lord about to enter the fleshly immortality, how could they have followed Him now, when, even though ready to die, they would have no resurrection till the end of the world? Or, on the point of going, as the Lord was, to the bosom of the Father, and that without any forsaking of them, just as He had never quitted that bosom in coming to them, how could they have followed Him now, since no one can enter on that state of felicity but he that is made perfect in love? And to show them, therefore, how it is that they may attain the fitness to proceed, where He was going before them, He says, "A new commandment I give unto you, that ye love one another" (ver. 34). These are the steps whereby Christ must be followed; but any fuller discourse thereon must be put off till another opportunity.

---

[1] Luke xxiv. 44.
[2] Scarcely an admissible use of the "now" (ἄρτι), which manifestly refers to the time of Jesus saying so to the disciples, and not to the period of their inability to come.—TR.

[3] Rom. vi. 9.

TRACTATE LXV.

CHAPTER XIII. 34, 35.

1. THE Lord Jesus declares that He is giving His disciples a new commandment, that they should love one another. "A new commandment," He says, "I give unto you, that ye love one another." But was not this already commanded in the ancient law of God, where it is written, "Thou shalt love thy neighbor as thyself"?[1] Why, then, is it called a new one by the Lord, when it is proved to be so old? Is it on this account a

new commandment, because He hath divested us of the old, and clothed us with the new man? For it is not indeed every kind of love that renews him that listens to it, or rather yields it obedience, but that love regarding which the Lord, in order to distinguish it from all carnal affection, added, "as I have loved you." For husbands and wives love one another, and parents and children, and all other human relationships that bind men together: to say nothing of the blameworthy and damnable love which is mutually

---

[1] Lev. xix. 18.

felt by adulterers and adulteresses, by fornicators and prostitutes, and all others who are
knit together by no human relationship, but
by the mischievous depravity of human life.
Christ, therefore, hath given us a new commandment, that we should love one another,
as He also hath loved us. This is the love
that renews us, making us new men, heirs of
the New Testament, singers of the new song.
It was this love, brethren beloved, that renewed also those of olden time, who were then
the righteous, the patriarchs and prophets, as
it did afterwards the blessed apostles: it is it,
too, that is now renewing the nations, and
from among the universal race of man, which
overspreads the whole world, is making and
gathering together a new people, the body of
the newly-married spouse of the only-begotten
Son of God, of whom it is said in the Song
of Songs, "Who is she that ascendeth, made
white?"¹ Made white indeed, because renewed; and how, but by the new commandment? Because of this, the members thereof
have a mutual interest in one another; and if
one member suffer, all the members suffer
with it; and one member be honored, all the
members rejoice with it.² For this they hear
and observe, "A new commandment I give
unto you, that ye love one another:" not as
those love one another who are corrupters, nor
as men love one another in a human way;
but they love one another as those who are
God's, and all of them sons of the Highest,
and brethren, therefore, of His only Son,
with that mutual love wherewith He loved
them, when about to lead them on to the goal
were all sufficiency should be theirs, and
where their every desire should be satisfied
with good things.³ For then there will be
nothing wanting they can desire, when God
will be all in all.⁴ An end like that has no
end. No one dieth there, where no one ar-
riveth save he that dieth to this world, not
that universal kind of death whereby the body
is bereft of the soul; but the death of the
elect, through which, even while still remaining in this mortal flesh, the heart is set on
the things which are above. Of such a death
it is that the apostle said, "For ye are dead,
and your life is hid with Christ in God."⁵
And perhaps to this, also, do the words refer,

"Love is strong as death."⁶ For by this
love it is brought about, that, while still held
in the present corruptible body, we die to this
world, and our life is hid with Christ in God;
yea, that love itself is our death to the world,
and our life with God. For if that is death
when the soul quits the body, how can it be
other than death when our love quits the
world? Such love, therefore, is strong as
death. And what is stronger than that which
bindeth the world?

2. Think not then, my brethren, that when
the Lord says, "A new commandment I give
unto you, that ye love one another," there is
any overlooking of that greater commandment, which requires us to love the Lord our
God with all our heart, and with all our soul,
and with all our mind; for along with this
seeming oversight, the words "that ye love
one another" appear also as if they had
no reference to that second commandment,
which says, "Thou shalt love thy neighbor as
thyself." For "on these two commandments," He says, "hang all the law and the
prophets."⁷ But both commandments may
be found in each of these by those who have
good understanding. For, on the one hand,
he that loveth God cannot despise His commandment to love his neighbor; and on the
other, he who in a holy and spiritual way loveth his neighbor, what doth he love in him
but God? That is the love, distinguished
from all mundane love, which the Lord specially characterized, when He added, "as I
have loved you." For what was it but God
that He loved in us? Not because we had
Him, but in order that we might have Him;
and that He may lead us on, as I said a little
ago, where God is all in all. It is in this way,
also, that the physician is properly said to
love the sick; and what is it he loves in them
but their health, which at all events he desires
to recall; not their sickness, which he comes
to remove? Let us, then, also so love one
another, that, as far as possible, we may by
the solicitude of our love be winning one another to have God within us. And this love
is bestowed on us by Him who said, "As I
have loved you, that ye also love one another." For this very end, therefore, did He
love us, that we also should love one another;
bestowing this on us by His own love to us,
that we should be bound to one another in
mutual love, and, united together as members
by so pleasant a bond, should be the body of
so mighty a Head.

3. "By this," He adds, "shall all men
know that ye are my disciples, if ye have love

---

¹ Song of Sol. viii. 5, where Augustin, in *dealbata*, follows the
Septuagint in their misreading and alteration of the original
מִן־הַמִּדְבָּר, "*from the wilderness*" (as in chap. iii. 6), into

מְחֻבֶּרֶת, מִתְחַבֶּגֶת, or some such participle. The Vulgate differs from Augustin, and reads correctly, *de deserto*, but interposes
between this and the next clause another participial expression,
deliciis affluens, abounding in delights. Our English version follows the original.—TR.

² 1 Cor. xii. 25, 26.   ³ Ps. ciii. 5.
⁴ 1 Cor. xv. 28.   ⁵ Col. iii. 3.

⁶ Song of Sol. viii. 6.   ⁷ Matt. xxii. 37-40.

one to another:" as if He said, Other gifts of mine are possessed in common with you by those who are not mine,—not only nature, life, perception, reason, and that safety which is equally the privilege of men and beasts; but also languages, sacraments, prophecy, knowledge, faith, the bestowing of their goods upon the poor, and the giving of their body to the flames: but because destitute of charity, they only tinkle like cymbals; they are nothing, and by nothing are they profited.[1] It is not, then, by such gifts of mine, however good, which may be alike possessed by those who are not my disciples, but " by this it is that all men shall know that ye are my disciples, that ye have love one to another." O thou spouse of Christ, fair amongst women ! O thou who ascendest in whiteness, leaning upon thy Beloved ! for by His light thou art made dazzling to whiteness, by His assistance thou art preserved from falling. How well becoming thee are the words in that Song of Songs, which is, as it were, thy bridal chant, " That there is love in thy delights " ![2] This it is that suffers not thy soul to perish with the ungodly; it is this that judges thy cause, and is strong as death, and is present in thy delights. How wonderful is the character of that death, which was all but swallowed up in penal sufferings, had it not been over and above absorbed in delights ! But here this discourse must now be closed; for we must make a new commencement in dealing with the words that follow.

[1] 1 Cor. xiii. 1-3.

[2] Song of Sol. vii. 6, according to the Septuagint. It is very doubtful, however, whether the LXX. themselves held the meaning drawn from their version by Augustin. It seems all to depend on where they inserted the point of interrogation (;) ; and the MSS. vary. The Vatican, that in common use, places it *after* ἀγάπη (love), which could hardly have been Augustin's reading. Other MSS. place it at the end of the verse, making the whole a single sentence, as in our English version. Augustin must have found the point immediately after ἡδύνθης (" thou art pleasant "), thus disjoining ἀγάπη from what precedes, and making it, with ἐν τρυφαῖς σου, a clause by itself. The Masoretic punctuation of the Hebrew gives some grounds for Augustin's reading : for there is a larger disjunctive accent over נָעַמְתְּ (" thou art pleasant "), indicating the central pause of the verse ; while the minor disjunctive under אַהֲבָה may only be intended to make up by emphasis for the abruptness of the language.—Tr.

TRACTATE LXVI.

Chapter XIII. 36-38.

1. While the Lord Jesus was commending to the disciples that holy love wherewith they should love one another, " Simon Peter saith unto Him, Lord, whither goest Thou ?" So, at all events, said the disciple to his Master, the servant to his Lord, as one who was prepared to follow. Just as for the same reason the Lord, who read in his mind the purpose of such a question, made him this reply: " Whither I go, thou canst not follow me now;" as if He said, In reference to the object of thy asking, thou canst not now. He does not say, Thou canst not; but " Thou canst not now." He intimated delay, without depriving of hope; and that same hope, which He took not away, but rather bestowed, in His next words He confirmed, by proceeding to say, " Thou shalt follow me afterwards." Why such haste, Peter ? The Rock (*petra*) has not yet solidified thee by His Spirit. Be not lifted up with presumption, " Thou canst not now;" be not cast now into despair, " Thou shalt follow afterwards." But what does he say to this ? " Why cannot I follow Thee now? I will lay down my life for Thy sake." He saw what was the kind of desire in his mind; but what the measure of his strength, he saw not. The weak man boasted of his willingness, but the Physician had an eye on the state of his health; the one promised, the Other foreknew: the ignorant was bold; He that foreknew all, condescended to teach. How much had Peter taken upon himself, by looking only at what he wished, and having no knowledge of what he was able ! How much had he taken upon himself, that, when the Lord had come to lay down His life for His friends, and so for him also, he should have the assurance to offer to do the same for the Lord; and while as yet Christ's life was not laid down for himself, he should promise to lay down his own life for Christ ! " Jesus " therefore " answered him, Wilt thou lay down thy life for my sake ?" Wilt thou do for me what I have not yet done for thee ? " Wilt thou lay down thy life for my sake ?" Canst thou go before, who art unable to follow ? Why dost thou presume so far ? what dost thou think of thyself ? what dost thou imagine thyself to be ? Hear what thou art: " Verily, verily, I say unto thee, The cock shall not crow, till

thou hast denied me thrice." See, that is how thou wilt speedily become manifest to thyself, who art now talking so loftily, and knowest not that thou art but a child. Thou promisest me thy death, and thou wilt deny me thy life. Thou, who now thinkest thyself able to die for me, learn to live first for thyself; for in fearing the death of thy flesh, thou wilt occasion the death of thy soul. Just as much as it is life to confess Christ, it is death to deny Him.

2. Or was it that the Apostle Peter, as some with a perverse kind of favor strive to excuse him,[1] did not deny Christ, because, when questioned by the maid, he replied that he did not know the man, as the other evangelists more expressly affirm? As if, indeed, he that denies the man Christ does not deny Christ; and so denies Him in respect of what He became on our account, that the nature He had given us might not be lost. Whoever, therefore, acknowledges Christ as God, and disowns Him as man, Christ died not for him; for as man it was that Christ died. He who disowns Christ as man, finds no reconciliation to God by the Mediator. For there is one God, and one Mediator between God and men, the man Christ Jesus.[2] He that denies Christ as man is not justified: for as by the disobedience of one man, many were made sinners; so also by the obedience of one man shall many be made righteous.[3] He that denies Christ as man, shall not rise again into the resurrection of life; for by man is death, and by man is also the resurrection of the dead: for as in Adam all die, even so in Christ shall all be made alive.[4] And by what means is He the Head of the Church, but by His manhood, because the Word was made flesh? that is, God, the Only-begotten of God the Father, became man. And how then can one be in the body of Christ who denies the man Christ? Or how can one be a member who disowns the Head? But why linger over a multitude of reasons when the Lord Himself undoes all the windings of human argumentation? For He says not, The cock shall not crow till thou hast denied the man; or, as He was wont to speak in His more familiar condescension with men, The cock shall not crow till thou hast thrice denied the Son of

man; but He says, "till thou hast denied me thrice." What is that "me," but just what He was? and what was He but Christ? Whatever of Him, therefore, he denied, he denied Himself, he denied the Christ, he denied the Lord his God. For Thomas also, his fellow-disciple, when he exclaimed, "My Lord and my God," did not handle the Word, but only His flesh; and laid not his inquisitive hands on the incorporeal nature of God, but on His human body.[5] And so he touched the man, and yet recognized his God. If, then, what the latter touched, Peter denied; what the latter invoked, Peter offended. "The cock shall not crow till thou hast denied me thrice." Although thou say, "I know not the man;" although thou say, "Man, I know not what thou sayest;" although thou say, "I am not one of His disciples;"[6] thou wilt be denying me. If, which it were sinful to doubt, Christ so spake, and foretold the truth, then doubtless Peter denied Christ. Let us not accuse Christ in defending Peter. Let infirmity acknowledge its sin; for there is no falsehood in the Truth. When Peter's infirmity acknowledged its sin, his acknowledgment was full; and the greatness of the evil he had committed in denying Christ, he showed by his tears. He himself reproves his defenders, and for their conviction, brings his tears forward as witnesses. Nor have we, on our part, in so speaking, any delight in accusing the first of the apostles; but in looking on him, we ought to take home the lesson to ourselves, that no man should place his confidence in human strength. For what else had our Teacher and Saviour in view, but to show us, by making the first of the apostles himself an example, that no one ought in any way to presume of himself? And that, therefore, really took place in Peter's soul, for which he gave cause in his body. And yet he did not go before in the Lord's behalf, as he rashly presumed, but did so otherwise than he reckoned. For before the death and resurrection of the Lord, he both died when he denied, and returned to life when he wept; but he died, because he himself had been proud in his presumption, and he lived again, because that Other had looked on him with kindness.

---

[1] See Ambrose, *on Luke* xxii. [2] 1 Tim. ii. 5.
[3] Rom. v. 19. [4] 1 Cor. xv. 21, 22.

[5] Chap. xx. 27, 28.
[6] Matt. xxvi. 34, 69-74, and Luke xxii. 55-60.

TRACTATE LXVII.

Chapter XIV. 1–3.

1. Our special attention, brethren, must be earnestly turned to God, in order that we may be able to obtain some intelligent apprehension of the words of the holy Gospel, which have just been ringing in our ears. For the Lord Jesus saith: "Let not your heart be troubled. Believe [1] in God, and believe [or, believe also] in me." That they might not as men be afraid of death, and so be troubled, He comforts them by affirming Himself also to be God. "Believe," He says, "in God, believe also in me." For it follows as a consequence, that if ye believe in God, ye ought to believe also in me: which were no consequence if Christ were not God. "Believe in God, and believe in" Him, who, by nature and not by robbery, is equal with God; for He emptied Himself; not, however, by losing the form of God, but by taking the form of a servant.[2] You are afraid of death as regards this servant form, "let not your heart be troubled," the form of God will raise it again.

2. But why have we this that follows, "In my Father's house are many mansions," but that they were also in fear about themselves? And therein they might have heard the words, "Let not your heart be troubled." For, was there any of them that could be free from fear, when Peter, the most confident and forward of them all, was told, "The cock shall not crow till thou hast denied me thrice"?[3] Considering themselves, therefore, beginning with Peter, as destined to perish, they had cause to be troubled: but when they now hear, "In my Father's house are many mansions: if it were not so, I would have told you; for I go to prepare a place for you," they are revived from their trouble, made certain and confident that after all the perils of temptations they shall dwell with Christ in the presence of God. For, albeit one is stronger than another, one wiser than another, one more righteous than another, "in the Father's house there are many mansions;" none of them shall remain outside that house, where every one, according to his deserts, is to receive a mansion. All alike have that penny, which the householder orders to be given to all that have wrought in the vineyard, making no distinction therein between those who have labored less and those who have labored more:[4] by which penny, of course, is signified eternal life, wherein no one any longer lives to a different length than others, since in eternity life has no diversity in its measure. But the many mansions point to the different grades of merit in that one eternal life. For there is one glory of the sun, another glory of the moon, and another glory of the stars: for one star differeth from another star in glory; and so also the resurrection of the dead. The saints, like the stars in the sky, obtain in the kingdom different mansions of diverse degrees of brightness; but on account of that one penny no one is cut off from the kingdom; and God will be all in all[5] in such a way, that, as God is love,[6] love will bring it about that what is possessed by each will be common to all. For in this way every one really possesses it, when he loves to see in another what he has not himself. There will not, therefore, be any envying amid this diversity of brightness, since in all of them will be reigning the unity of love.

3. Every Christian heart, therefore, must utterly reject the idea of those who imagine that there are many mansions spoken of, because there will be some place outside the kingdom of heaven, which shall be the abode of those blessed innocents who have departed this life without baptism, because without it they cannot enter the kingdom of heaven. Faith like this is not faith, inasmuch as it is not the true and catholic faith. Are you not so foolish and blinded with carnal imaginations as to be worthy of reprobation, if you should thus separate the mansion, I say not of Peter and Paul, or any of the apostles, but even of any baptized infant from the kingdom of heaven; do you not think yourselves deserving of reprobation in thus putting a separation between these and the house of God the Father? For the Lord's words are not, In the whole world, or, In all creation, or, In everlasting life and blessedness, there are many mansions; but He says, "In my Father's house are many mansions." Is not that the house where we have a building of God, a house not made with hands, eternal in the heavens?[7] Is not that the house whereof we sing to the Lord, "Blessed are they that

---

[1] A few of the mss. have "ye believe," after the Vulgate: the Greek verb also, πιστεύετε which occurs twice in this clause, is doubtful, signifying, ye believe, or, believe (imperative).—Migne.
[2] Phil. ii. 6, 7.   [3] Chap. xiii. 38.
[4] Matt. xx. 9.   [5] 1 Cor. xv. 41, 42, 28.
[6] 1 John iv. 8.   [7] 2 Cor. v. 1.

21

dwell in Thy house; they shall praise Thee for ever and ever"?[1] Will you then venture to separate from the kingdom of heaven the house, not of every baptized brother, but of God the Father Himself, to whom all we who are brethren say, "Our Father, who art in heaven,"[2] or divide it in such a way as to make some of its mansions inside, and some outside, the kingdom of heaven? Far, far be it from those who desire to dwell in the kingdom of heaven, to be willing to dwell in such folly with you: far be it, I say, that since every house of sons that are reigning can be nowhere else but in the kingdom, any part of the royal house itself should be outside the kingdom.

4. "And if I go," He says, "and prepare a place for you, I will come again, and receive you unto myself; that where I am, there ye may be also. And whither I go ye know, and the way ye know." O Lord Jesus, how goest Thou to prepare a place, if there are already many mansions in Thy Father's house, where Thy people shall dwell with Thyself? Or if Thou receivest them unto Thyself, how wilt Thou come again, who never withdrawest Thy presence? Such subjects as these, beloved, were we to attempt to explain them with such brevity as seems within the proper bounds of our discourse to-day, would certainly suffer in clearness from compression, and the very brevity would become itself a second obscurity; we shall therefore defer this debt, which the bounty of our Family-head will enable us to repay at a more suitable opportunity.

[1] Ps. lxxxiv. 4.   [2] Matt. vi. 9.

TRACTATE LXVIII.

ON THE SAME PASSAGE.

1. We acknowledge, beloved brethren, that we are owing you, and ought now to repay, what was left over for consideration, how we can understand that there is no real mutual contrariety between these two statements, namely, that after saying, "In my Father's house are many mansions: if it were not so, I would have told you, that I go to prepare a place for you;"—where He makes it clear enough that He said so to them for the very reason that there are many mansions there already, and there is no need of preparing any;[1]—the Lord again says: "And if I go and prepare a place for you, I will come again and receive you unto myself; that where I am, there ye may be also." How is it that He goes and prepares a place, if there are many mansions already? If there were not such, He would have said, "I go to prepare." Or if the place has still to be prepared, would He not then also properly have said, "I go to prepare"? Are these mansions in existence already, and yet needing still to be prepared? For if they were not in existence, He would have said, "I go to prepare." And yet, because their present state of existence is such as still to stand in need of preparation, He does not go to prepare them in the same sense as they already exist; but if He go and prepare them as they shall be hereafter, He will come again and receive His own to Himself; that where He is, there they may be also. How then are there mansions in the Father's house, and these not different ones but the same, which already exist in a sense in which they can admit of no preparation, and yet do not exist, inasmuch as they are still to be prepared? How are we to think of this, but in the same way as the prophet, who also declares of God, that He has [already] made that which is yet to be. For he says not, Who will make what is yet to be, but, "Who has made what is yet to be."[2] Therefore He has both made such things and is yet to make them. For they have not been

[1] The apparent contrariety that Augustin here deals with, partly arises from a mistaken interpretation of the second half of verse 2, as given above. His Latin version read, *si quo minus, dixissem vobis quia vado,* etc., and is a close verbal rendering of the original text, as found in several MSS.,—εἰ δὲ μή, εἶπον ἂν ὑμῖν, ὅτι πορεύομαι,—although some others omit the ὅτι. But while verbally exact, grammatical accuracy and a fair exegesis will admit of a pause after ὑμῖν (*vobis*), as the general sense of the passage requires. Ὅτι might thus be used in the sense of "because;" or, as it often is, as a particle introducing a direct statement.—Tr.

[2] Isa. xlv. 11, according to the Septuagint, whose reading, as usual, is followed by Augustin, although here a very manifest mistranslation of the Hebrew. The words are, "Thus saith Jehovah, the Holy One of Israel (ויצרו האירות שאלוני) and his Maker, Ask me of things to come," etc. This is the rendering really in accordance with the usual Hebrew idiom, with the sense of the passage itself, and with the frequent use of *Yotser* (Maker) by Isaiah. It is that also approved by the Masoretic pointing, and followed generally by the other translations, including the Vulgate, which has: *plastes ejus: ventura interrogate n.e,* etc. The LXX., however, makes *ha'othiyyoth* dependent on *yots'ro* (notwithstanding its own suffix), instead of the verb that follows, and reads, ὁ ποιήσας (αὐτὸν in some copies) τὰ ἐπερχόμενα, which Augustin renders in the text: *qui fecit quæ futura sunt.*--Tr.

made at all if He has not made them; nor will they ever be if He make them not Himself. He has made them therefore in the way of fore-ordaining them; He has yet to make them in the way of actual elaboration. Just as the Gospel plainly intimates when He chose His disciples, that is to say, at the time of His calling them;[1] and yet the apostle says, " He chose us before the foundation of the world,"[2] to wit, by predestination, not by actual calling. "And whom He did predestinate, them He also called;"[3] He hath chosen by predestination before the foundation of the world, He chooses by calling before its close. And so also has He prepared those mansions, and is still preparing them; and He who has already made the things which are yet to be, is now preparing, not different ones, but the very mansions He has already prepared: what He *has* prepared in predestination, He *is* preparing by actual working. Already, therefore, they *are*, as respects predestination; if it were not so, He would have said, I will go and prepare, that is, I will predestinate. But because they are not yet in a state of practical preparedness, He says, "And if I go and prepare a place for you, I will come again, and receive you unto myself."

2. But He is in a certain sense preparing the dwellings by preparing for them the dwellers. As, for instance, when He said, " In my Father's house are many dwellings," what else can we suppose the house of God to mean but the temple of God? And what that is, ask the apostle, and he will reply, " For the temple of God is holy, which [temple] ye are "[4] This is also the kingdom of God, which the Son is yet to deliver up to the Father; and hence the same apostle says, " Christ, the beginning, and then they that are Christ's in His presence; then [cometh] the end, when He shall have delivered up the kingdom to God, even the Father;"[5] that is, those whom He has redeemed by His blood, He shall then have delivered up to stand before His Father's face. This is that kingdom of heaven whereof it is said, " The kingdom of heaven is likened unto a man who sowed good seed in his field. But the good seed are the children of the kingdom;" and although now they are mingled with tares, at the end the King Himself shall send forth His angels, " and they shall gather out of His kingdom all things that offend. Then shall the righteous shine forth as the sun in the kingdom of their Father."[6] The kingdom will shine forth in the kingdom when [those that are]

the kingdom shall have reached the kingdom; just as we now pray when we say, " Thy kingdom come."[7] Even now, therefore, already is the kingdom called, but only as yet being called together. For if it were not now called, it could not be then said, " They shall gather out of His kingdom everything that offends." But the realm is not yet reigning. Accordingly it is already so far the kingdom, that when all offences shall have been gathered out of it, it shall then attain to sovereignty, so as to possess not merely the name of a kingdom, but also the power of government. For it is to this kingdom, standing then at the right hand, that it shall be said in the end, " Come, ye blessed of my Father, receive the kingdom;"[8] that is, ye who were the kingdom, but without the power to rule, come and reign; that what you formerly were only in hope, you may now have the power to be in reality. This house of God, therefore, this temple of God, this kingdom of God and kingdom of heaven, is as yet in the process of building, of construction, of preparation, of assembling. In it there will be mansions, even as the Lord is now preparing them; in it there are such already, even as the Lord has already ordained them.

3. But why is it that He went away to make such preparation, when, as it is certainly we ourselves that are the subjects in need of preparation, His doing so will be hindered by leaving us behind? I explain it, Lord, as I can: it was surely this Thou didst signify by the preparation of those mansions, that the just ought to live by faith.[9] For he who is sojourning at a distance from the Lord has need to be living by faith, because by this we are prepared for beholding His countenance.[10] For " blessed are the pure in heart, for they shall see God;"[11] and " He purifieth their hearts by faith."[12] The former we find in the Gospel, the latter in the Acts of the Apostles. But the faith by which those who are yet to see God have their hearts purified, while sojourning at a distance here, believeth what it doth not see; for if there is sight, there is no longer faith. Merit is accumulating now to the believer, and then the reward is paid into the hand of the beholder. Let the Lord then go and prepare us a place; let Him go, that He may not be seen; and let Him remain concealed, that faith may be exercised. For then is the place preparing, if it is by faith we are living. Let the believing in that place be desired, that the place desired may itself be possessed; the longing of love is the preparation of the mansion. Prepare thus, Lord,

---

[1] Luke vi. 13. [2] Eph. i. 4. [3] Rom. viii. 30.
[4] 1 Cor. iii. 17. [5] 1 Cor. xv. 23, 24. [6] Matt. xiii. 24, 38-43.

[7] Matt. vi. 10. [8] Matt. xxv. 34. [9] Rom. i. 17.
[10] 2 Cor. v. 6-8. [11] Matt. v. 8. [12] Acts xv. 9.

what Thou art preparing; for Thou art preparing us for Thyself, and Thyself for us, inasmuch as Thou art preparing a place both for Thyself in us, and for us in Thee. For Thou hast said, "Abide in me, and I in you."[1] As far as each one has been a partaker of Thee, some less, some more, such will be the diversity of rewards in proportion to the diversity of merits; such will be the multitude of mansions to suit the inequalities among their inmates; but all of them, none the less, eternally living, and endlessly blessed. Why is it that Thou goest away? Why is it Thou comest again? If I understand Thee aright, Thou withdrawest not Thyself either from the place Thou goest from, or from the place Thou comest from: Thou goest away by becoming invisible, Thou comest by again becoming manifest to our eyes. But unless Thou remainest to direct us how we may still be advancing in goodness of life, how will the place be prepared where we shall be able to dwell in the fullness of joy? Let what we have said suffice on the words which have been read from the Gospel as far as "I will come again, and receive you to myself." But the meaning of what follows, "That where I am, there ye may be also; and whither I go ye know, and the way ye know," we shall be in a better condition—after the question put by the disciple, that follows, and which we also may be putting, as it were, through him —for hearing, and more suitably situated for making the subject of our discourse.

[1] Chap. xv. 4.

TRACTATE LXIX.

CHAPTER XIV. 4–6.

1. WE have now the opportunity, dearly beloved, as far as we can, of understanding the earlier words of the Lord from the later, and His previous statements by those that follow, in what you have heard was His answer to the question of the Apostle Thomas. For when the Lord was speaking above of the mansions, of which He both said that they already were in His Father's house, and that He was going to prepare them; where we understood that those mansions already existed in predestination, and are also being prepared through the purifying by faith of the hearts of those who are hereafter to inhabit them, seeing that they themselves are the very house of God; and what else is it to dwell in God's house than to be in the number of His people, since His people are at the same time in God, and God in them? To make this preparation the Lord departed, that by believing in Him, though no longer visible, the mansion, whose outward form is always hid in the future, may now by faith be prepared; for this reason, therefore, He had said, "And if I go away and prepare a place for you, I will come again, and receive you to myself; that where I am, there ye may be also. And whither I go ye know, and the way ye know." In reply to this, "Thomas saith unto Him, Lord, we know not whither Thou goest; and how can we know the way?" Both of these the Lord had said that they knew; both of them this other declares that he does not know, to wit, the place to which, and the way whereby, He is going. But he does not know that he is speaking falsely; they knew, therefore, and did not know that they knew. He will convince them that they already know what they imagine themselves still to be ignorant of. "Jesus saith unto him, I am the way, and the truth, and the life." What, brethren, does He mean? See, we have just heard the disciple asking, and the Master instructing, and we do not yet, even after His voice has sounded in our ears, apprehend the thought that lies hid in His words. But what is it we cannot apprehend? Could His apostles, with whom He was talking, have said to Him, We do not know Thee? Accordingly, if they knew Him, and He Himself is the way, they knew the way; if they knew Him who is Himself the truth, they knew the truth; if they knew Him who is also the life, they knew the life. Thus, you see, they were convinced that they knew what they knew not that they knew.

2. What is it, then, that we also have not apprehended in this discourse? What else, think you, brethren, but just that He said, "And whither I go ye know, and the way ye know"? And here we have discovered that they knew the way, because they knew Him who is the way: the way is that by which we go; but is the way the place also to which we

go? And yet each of these He said that they knew, both whither He was going, and the way. There was need, therefore, for His saying, "I am the way," in order to show those who knew Him that they knew the way, which they thought themselves ignorant of; but what need was there for His saying, "I am the way, and the truth, and the life," when, after knowing the way by which He went, they had still to learn whither He was going, but just because it was to the truth and to the life He was going? By Himself, therefore, He was going to Himself. And whither go we, but to Him? and by what way go we, but by Him? He, therefore, went to Himself by Himself, and we by Him to Him; yea, likewise both He and we go thus to the Father. For He says also in another place of Himself, "I go to the Father;"[1] and here on our account He says, "No man cometh unto the Father but by me." And in this way, He goeth by Himself both to Himself and to the Father, and we by Him both to Him and to the Father. Who can apprehend such things save he who has spiritual discernment? and how much is it that even he can apprehend, although thus spiritually discerning? Brethren, how can you desire me to explain such things to you? Only reflect how lofty they are. You see what I am, I see what you are; in all of us the body, which is corrupted, burdens the soul, and the earthly tabernacle weigheth down the mind that museth upon many things.[2] Do we think we can say, "To Thee have I lifted up my soul, O Thou that dwellest in the heavens"?[3] But burdened as we are with so great a weight, under which we groan, how shall I lift up my soul unless He lift it with me who laid His own down for me? I shall speak then as I can, and let each of you who is able receive it. As He gives, I speak; as He gives, the receiver receiveth; and as He giveth, there is faith for him who cannot yet receive with understanding. For, saith the prophet, "If ye will not believe, ye shall not understand."[4]

3. Tell me, O my Lord, what to say to Thy servants, my fellow-servants. The Apostle Thomas had Thee before him in order to ask Thee questions, and yet could not understand Thee unless he had Thee within him;

I ask Thee because I know that Thou art over me; and I ask, seeking, as far as I can, to let my soul diffuse itself in that same region over me where I may listen to Thee, who usest no external sound to convey Thy teaching. Tell me, I pray, how it is that Thou goest to Thyself. Didst Thou formerly leave Thyself to come to us, especially as Thou camest not of Thyself, but the Father sent Thee? I know, indeed, that Thou didst empty Thyself; but in taking the form of a servant,[5] it was neither that Thou didst lay down the form of God as something to return to, or that Thou lost it as something to be recovered; and yet Thou didst come, and didst place Thyself not only before the carnal eyes, but even in the very hands of men. And how otherwise save in Thy flesh? By means of this Thou didst come, yet abiding where Thou wast; by this means Thou didst return, without leaving the place to which Thou hadst come. If, then, by such means Thou didst come and return, by such means doubtless Thou art not only the way for us to come unto Thee, but wast the way also for Thyself to come and to return. For when Thou didst return to the life, which Thou art Thyself, then of a truth that same flesh of Thine Thou didst bring from death unto life. The Word of God, indeed, is one thing, and man another; but the Word was made flesh, or became man. And so the person of the Word is not different from that of the man, seeing that Christ is both in one person; and in this way, just as when His flesh died, Christ died, and when His flesh was buried, Christ was buried (for thus with the heart we believe unto righteousness, and thus with the mouth do we make confession unto salvation[6]); so when the flesh came from death unto life, Christ came to life. And because Christ is the Word of God, He is also the life. And thus in a wonderful and ineffable manner He, who never laid down or lost Himself, came to Himself. But God, as was said, had come through the flesh to men, the truth to liars; for God is true, and every man a liar.[7] When, therefore, He withdrew His flesh from amongst men, and carried it up there where no liar is found, He also Himself—for the Word was made flesh—returned by Himself, that is, by His flesh, to the truth, which is none other but Himself. And this truth, we cannot doubt, although found amongst liars, He preserved even in death; for Christ was once dead, but never false.

4. Take an example, very different in character and wholly inadequate, yet in some lit-

---

[1] Chap. xvi. 10. [2] Wisd. ix. 15. [3] Ps. cxxiii. 1.
[4] Isa. vii. 9, according to LXX., which reads, ἐὰν μὴ πιστεύσητε, οὐδὲ μὴ συνῆτε. תַאֲמִינוּ, however, will scarcely admit the meaning of "understand" (συνῆτε). There is a play in the Hebrew upon the verb אָמַן, which is the one used in both clauses, first in the *Hiphil*, where it means *to cleave fast to, to show a firm trust in;* and secondly, in the *Niphal, to be held fast, to be confirmed in one's trust.* Hence the rendering of our English Bible is more correct: "If ye will not believe, surely ye shall not be established."—TR.

[5] Phil. ii. 7. [6] Rom. x. 10. [7] Rom. iii. 4.

tle measure helpful to the understanding of God, from things that are in peculiarly intimate subjection to God. See here in my own case, while as far as pertains to my mind I am just the same as yourselves, if I keep silence I am so to myself; but if I speak to you something suited to your understanding, in a certain sense I go forth to you without leaving myself, but at the same time approach you and yet quit not the place from which I proceed. But when I cease speaking, I return in a kind of way to myself, and in a kind of way I remain with you, if you retain what you have heard in the discourse I am deliver-ing. And if the mere image that God made is capable of this, what may not God, the very image of God, not made by, but born of God; whose body, wherein He came forth to us and returned from us, has not ceased to be, like the sound of my voice, but abides there, where it shall die no more, and death shall have no more dominion over it?[1] Much more, perhaps, might and ought to have been said on these words of the Gospel; but your souls ought not to be burdened with spiritual food, however pleasant, especially as the spirit is willing, but the flesh is weak.[2]

[1] Rom. vi. 9. [2] Matt. xxvi. 41.

TRACTATE LXX.

CHAPTER XIV. 7–10.

1. THE words of the holy Gospel, brethren, are rightly understood only if they are found to be in harmony with those that precede; for the premises ought to agree with the conclusion, when it is the Truth that speaks. The Lord had said before, "And if I go and prepare a place for you, I will come again and receive you unto myself; that where I am, there ye may be also:" and then had added, "And whither I go ye know, and the way ye know;" and showed that all He said was that they knew himself. What, therefore, the meaning was of His going to Himself by Himself,—for He also lets the disciples see that it is by Him that they are to come to Him,—we have already told you, as we could, in our last discourse. When He says, therefore, "That where I am, there ye may be also," where else were they to be but in Himself? In this way is He also in Himself, and they, therefore, are just where He is, that is, in Himself. Accordingly, He Himself is that eternal life which is yet to be ours, when He has received us unto Himself; and as He is that life eternal, so is it in Him, that where He is there shall we be also, that is to say, in Himself. "For as the Father hath life in Himself," and certainly that life which He has is in no wise different from what He is Himself as its possessor, "so hath He given to the Son to have life in Himself,"[1] inasmuch as He *is* the very life which He hath in Himself. But shall we then actually be what He is, (namely), the life, when we shall have begun our existence in that life, that is, in Himself? Certainly not, for He, by His very existence as the life, hath life, and is Himself what He hath; and as the life, is in Him, so is He in Himself: but we are not that life, but partakers of His life, and shall be there in such wise as to be wholly incapable of being in ourselves what He is, but so as, while ourselves not the life, to have Him as our life, who has Himself the life on this very account that He Himself is the life. In short, He both exists unchangeably in Himself and inseparably in the Father. But we, when wishing to exist in ourselves, were thrown into inward trouble regarding ourselves, as is expressed in the words, "My soul is cast down within me:"[2] and changing from bad to worse, cannot even remain as we were. But when by Him we come unto the Father, according to His own words, "No man cometh unto the Father but by me," and abide in Him, no one shall be able to separate us either from the Father or from Him.

2. Connecting, therefore, His previous words with those that follow, He proceeded to say, "If ye had known me, ye should certainly have known my Father also." This conforms to His previous words, "No man cometh unto the Father but by me." And then He adds: "And from henceforth ye know Him, and have seen Him." But Philip, one of the apostles, not understanding what he had just heard, said, "Lord, show us the Father, and it sufficeth us." And the

[1] Chap. v. 26. [2] Ps. xlii. 6.

Lord replied to him, "Have I been so long time with you, and yet have ye not known me, Philip? he that seeth me, seeth also the Father." Here you see He complains that He had been so long time with them, and yet He was not known. But had He not Himself said, "And whither I go ye know, and the way ye know;" and on their saying that they knew it not, had convinced them that they did know, by adding the words: "I am the way, and the truth, and the life"? How, then, says He now, "Have I been so long time with you, and have ye not known me?" when, in fact, they knew both whither He went and the way, on no other grounds save that they really knew Himself? But this difficulty is easily solved by saying that some of them knew Him, and others did not, and that Philip was one of those who did not know Him; so that, when He said, "And whither I go ye know, and the way ye know," He is understood as having spoken to those that knew, and not to Philip, who has it said to him, "Have I been so long time with you, and have ye not known me, Philip?" To such, then, as already knew the Son, was it now also said of the Father, "And from henceforth ye know Him, and have seen Him:" for such words were used because of the all-sided likeness subsisting between the Father and the Son; so that, because they knew the Son, they might henceforth be said to know the Father. Already, therefore, they knew the Son, if not all of them, those at least to whom it is said, "And whither I go ye know, and the way ye know;" for He is Himself the way. But they knew not the Father, and so have also to hear, "If ye have known me, ye have known my Father also;" that is, through me ye have known Him also. For I am one, and He another. But that they might not think Him unlike, He adds, "And from henceforth ye know Him, and have seen Him." For they saw His perfectly resembling Son, but needed to have the truth impressed on them, that exactly such as was the Son whom they saw, was the Father also whom they did not see. And to this points what is afterwards said to Philip, "He that seeth me, seeth also the Father." Not that He Himself was Father and Son, which is a notion of the Sabellians, who are also called Patripassians,[1] condemned by the Catholic faith; but that Father and Son are so alike, that he who knoweth one knoweth both. For we are accustomed to speak in this way of two who closely resemble each other, to those who are in the habit of seeing one of them, and wish to know what like the other is, so that we say, In seeing the one, you have seen the other. In this way, then, is it said "He that seeth me, seeth also the Father." Not, certainly, that He who is the Son is also the Father, but that the Son in no respect disagrees with the likeness of the Father. For had not the Father and Son been two persons, it would not have been said, "If ye have known me, ye have known my Father also." Such is certainly the case, for "no one," He says, "cometh unto the Father but by me: if ye have known me, ye have known my Father also;" because it is I, who am the only way to the Father, that will lead you to Him, that He also may Himself become known to you. But as I am in all respects His perfect image, "from henceforth ye know Him" in knowing me; "and have seen Him," if you have seen me with the spiritual eyesight of the soul.

3. Why, then, Philip, dost thou say, "Show us the Father, and it sufficeth us? Have I been so long time with you, and yet have ye not known me, Philip? He that seeth me, seeth the Father also." If it interests thee much to see this, believe at least what thou seest not. For "how," He says, "sayest thou, Show us the Father?" If thou hast seen me, who am His perfect likeness, thou hast seen Him to whom I am like. And if thou canst not directly see this, "believest thou not," at least, "that I am in the Father, and the Father in me?" But Philip might say here, "I see Thee indeed, and believe Thy full likeness to the Father; but is one to be reproved and rebuked because, when he sees one who bears a likeness to another, he wishes to see that other to whom he is like? I know, indeed, the image, but as yet I know only the one without the other; it is not enough for me, unless I know that other whose likeness he bears. Show us, therefore, the Father, and it sufficeth us." But the Master really reproved the disciple because He saw into the heart of his questioner. For it was with the idea, as if the Father were somehow better than the Son, that Philip had the desire to know the Father: and so he did not even know the Son, because believing that He was inferior to another. It was to correct such a notion that it was said, "He that seeth me, seeth the Father also. How sayest thou, Show us the Father?" I see the meaning of thy words: it is not the original likeness thou seekest to see, but it is that other thou thinkest the superior. "Believest thou not that I am in the Father, and the Father in me?" Why desirest thou to dis-

---

[1] That is, those who ascribed suffering to the Father; because the Sabellians, denying the distinct personality of the Son, and regarding Him as only a special revelation of God the Father, were chargeable, therefore, with holding that it was God the Father who really suffered and died on the cross.—TR.

cover some distance between those who are thus alike? why cravest thou the separate knowledge of those who cannot be separated? What, after this, He says not only to Philip, but to all of them together, must not now be thrust into a corner, in order that, by His help, it may be the more carefully expounded.

TRACTATE LXXI.

Chapter XIV. 10–14.

1. Give close attention, and try to understand, beloved; for while it is we who speak, it is He Himself who never withdraweth His presence from us who is our Teacher. The Lord saith, what you have just heard read, "The words that I speak unto you, I speak not of myself: but the Father, that dwelleth in me, He doeth the works." Even His words, then, are works? Clearly so. For surely he that edifies a neighbor by what he says, works a good work. But what mean the words, "I speak not of myself," but, I who speak am not of myself? Hence He attributes what He does to Him, of whom He, that doeth them, is. For the Father is not God [as born, etc.] of any one else, while the Son is God, as equal, indeed, to the Father, but [as born] of God the Father. Therefore the former is God, but not of God; and the Light, but not of light: whereas the latter is God of God, Light of Light.

2. For in connection with these two clauses, —the one where it is said, "I speak not of myself;" and the other, which runs, "but the Father that dwelleth in me, He doeth the works,"—we are opposed by two different classes of heretics, who, by each of them holding only to one clause, run off, not in one, but opposite directions, and wander far from the pathway of truth. For instance, the Arians say, See here, the Son is not equal to the Father, He speaketh not of Himself. The Sabellians, or Patripassians, on the other hand, say, See, He who is the Father is also the Son; for what else is this, "The Father that dwelleth in me, He doeth the works," but I that do them dwell in myself? You make contrary assertions, and that not only in the sense that any one thing is false, that is, contrary to truth, but in this also, when two things that are both false contradict one another. In your wanderings you have taken opposite directions; midway between the two is the path you have left. You are a far longer distance apart from each other than from the very way you have both forsaken.

Come hither, you from the one side, and you from the other: pass not across, the one to the other, but come from both sides to us, and make this the place of your mutual meeting. Ye Sabellians, acknowledge the Being you overlook; Arians, set Him whom you subordinate in His place of equality, and you will both be walking with us in the pathway of truth. For you have grounds on both sides that make mutual admonition a duty. Listen, Sabellian: so far is the Son from being the same as the Father, and so truly is He another, that the Arian maintains His inferiority to the Father. Listen, Arian: so truly is the Son equal to the Father, that the Sabellian declares Him to be identical with the Father. Do thou restore the personality thou hast abstracted, and thou, the full dignity thou hast lowered, and both of you stand together on the same ground as ourselves: because the one of you [who has been an Arian], for the conviction of the Sabellian, never lets out of sight the personality of Him who is distinct from the Father, and the other [who has been a Sabellian] takes care, for the conviction of the Arian, of not impairing the dignity of Him who is equal with the Father. For to both of you He cries, "I and my Father are one."[1] When He says "one," let the Arians listen; when He says, "we are," let the Sabellians give heed, and no longer continue in the folly of denying, the one, His equality [with the Father], the other, His distinct personality. If, then, in saying, "The words that I speak unto you, I speak not of myself," He is thereby accounted of a power so inferior, that what He doeth is not what He Himself willeth; listen to what He also said, "As the Father raiseth up the dead and quickeneth them, even so the Son quickeneth whom He will." And so likewise, if in saying, "The Father that dwelleth in me, He doeth the works," He is on that account not to be regarded as distinct in

---

[1] Chap. x. 30.

person from the Father, let us listen to His other words, "What things soever the Father doeth, these also doeth the Son likewise;"[1] and He will be understood as speaking not of one person twice over, but of two who are one. But just because their mutual equality is such as not to interfere with their distinct personality, therefore He speaketh not of Himself, because He is not of Himself; and the Father also, that dwelleth in Him, Himself doeth the works, because He, by whom and with whom He doeth them, is not, save of [the Father] Himself. And then He goes on to say, "Believe ye not that I am in the Father, and the Father in me? Or else believe me for the very works' sake." Formerly it was Philip only who was reproved, but now it is shown that he was not the only one there that needed reproof. "For the very works' sake," He says, "believe ye that I am in the Father, and the Father in me:" for had we been separated, we should have been unable to do any kind of work inseparably.

3. But what is this that follows? "Verily, verily, I say unto you, He that believeth on me, the works that I do shall he do also; and greater works than these shall he do; because I go unto my Father. And whatsoever ye shall ask in my name, that will I do, that the Father may be glorified in the Son. If ye shall ask anything in my name, I will do it." And so He promised that He Himself would also do those greater works. Let not the servant exalt himself above his Lord, or the disciple above his Master.[2] He says that they will do greater works than He doeth Himself; but it is all by His doing such in or by them, and not as if they did them of themselves. Hence the song that is addressed to Him, "I will love Thee, O Lord, my strength."[3] But what, then, are those greater works? Was it that their very shadow, as they themselves passed by, healed the sick?[4] For it is a mightier thing for a shadow, than for the hem of a garment, to possess the power of healing.[5] The one work was done by Christ Himself, the other by them; and yet it was He that did both. Nevertheless, when He so spake, He was commending the efficacious power[6] of His own words: for it was in this sense He had said, "The words that I speak unto you, I speak not of myself; but the Father that dwelleth in me, He doeth the works." What works was He then referring to, but the words He was speaking? They were hearing and believing, and their faith was the fruit of those very words: howbeit, when the disciples preached the gospel, it was not small numbers like themselves, but nations also that believed; and such, doubtless, are greater works. And yet He said not, Greater works than these shall ye do, to lead us to suppose that it was only the apostles who would do so; for He added, "He that believeth on me, the works that I do shall he do also; and greater works than these shall he do." Is the case then so, that he that believeth on Christ doeth the same works as Christ, or even greater than He did? Points like these are not to be treated in a cursory way, nor ought they to be hurriedly disposed of; and, therefore, as our present discourse must be brought to a close, we are obliged to defer their further consideration.

---

[1] Chap. v. 21, 19.   [2] Chap. xiii. 16.   [3] Ps. xviii. 1.   [4] Acts v. 15.   [5] Matt. xiv. 36.   [6] *Opera.*

TRACTATE LXXII

ON THE SAME PASSAGE.

1. It is no easy matter to comprehend what is meant by, or in what sense we are to receive, these words of the Lord, "He that believeth on me, the works that I do shall he do also:" and then, to this great difficulty in the way of our understanding, He has added another still more difficult, "And greater things than these shall he do." What are we to make of it? We have not found one who did such works as Christ did; and are we likely to find one who will do even greater? But we remarked in our last discourse, that it was a greater deed to heal the sick by the passing of their shadow, as was done by the disciples, than as the Lord Himself did by the touch of the hem of His garment; and that more believed on the apostles than on the Lord Himself, when preaching with His own lips; so that we might suppose works like these to be understood as greater: not that the disciple was to be greater than his Master, or the servant than his Lord, or the

adopted son than the Only-begotten, or man than God, but that by them He Himself would condescend to do these greater works, while telling them in another passage, "Without me ye can do nothing."[1] While He Himself, on the other hand, to say nothing of His other works, which are numberless, made them without any aid from themselves, and without them made this world; and because He Himself thought meet to become man, without them He made also Himself. But what have they [made or done] without Him, save sin? And last of all, He straightway also withdrew from the subject all that could cause us agitation; for after saying, "He that believeth on me, the works that I do shall he do also; and greater works than these shall he do;" He immediately went on to add, "Because I go unto the Father; and whatsoever ye shall ask in my name, that will I do." He who had said, "He will do," afterwards said, "I will do;" as if He had said, Let not this appear to you impossible; for he that believeth on me can never become greater than I am, but it is I who shall then be doing greater things than now; greater things by him that believeth on me, than by myself apart from him; yet it is I myself apart from him,[2] and I myself by him [that will do the works]: and as it is apart from him, it is not he that will do them; and as, on the other hand, it is by him, although not by his own self, it is he also that will do them. And besides, to do greater things by one than apart from one, is not a sign of deficiency, but of condescension. For what can servants render unto the Lord for all His benefits towards them?[3] And sometimes He hath condescended to number this also amongst His other benefits towards them, namely, to do greater works by them than apart from them. Did not that rich man go away sad from His presence, when seeking counsel about eternal life? He heard, and cast it away: and yet in after days the counsel that fell on his ears was followed, not by one, but by many, when the good Master was speaking by the disciples; He was an object of contempt to the rich man, when warned by Himself directly, and of love to those whom by means of poor men He transformed from rich into poor. Here, then, you see, He did greater works when preached by believers, than when speaking Himself to hearers.

2. But there is still something to excite

thought in His doing such greater works by the apostles; for He said not, as if merely with reference to them, The works that I do shall ye do also; and greater works than these shall ye do: but wishing to be understood as speaking of all that belonged to His family, said, "He that believeth on me, the works that I do shall he do also; and greater works than these shall he do." If, then, he that believeth shall do such works, he that shall do them not is certainly no believer: just as "He that loveth me, keepeth my commandments,"[4] implies, of course, that he who keepeth them not, loveth not. In another place, also, He says, "He that heareth these sayings of mine and doeth them, I will liken him unto a wise man, who buildeth his house upon a rock;"[5] and he, therefore, who is unlike this wise man, without doubt either heareth these sayings and doeth them not, or faileth even to hear them. "He that believeth in me," He says, "though he die, yet shall he live;"[6] and he, therefore, that shall not live, is certainly no believer now. In a similar way, also, it is said here, "He that believeth in me shall do [such works]:" he is, therefore, no believer who shall not do so. What have we here, then, brethren? Is it that one is not to be reckoned among believers in Christ, who shall not do greater works than Christ? It were hard, unreasonable, intolerable, to suppose so; that is, unless it be rightly understood. Let us listen, then, to the apostle, when he says, "To him that believeth on Him that justifieth the ungodly, his faith is counted for righteousness."[7] This is the work in which we may be doing the works of Christ, for even our very believing in Christ is the work of Christ. It is this He worketh in us, not certainly without us. Hear now, then, and understand, "He that believeth on me, the works that I do shall he do also:" I do them first, and he shall do them afterwards; for I do such works that he may do them also. And what are the works, but the making of a righteous man out of an ungodly one?

3. "And greater works than these shall he do." Than what, pray? Shall we say that one is doing greater works than all that Christ did who is working out his own salvation with fear and trembling?[8] A work which Christ is certainly working in him, but not without him; and one which I might, without hesitation, call greater than the heavens and the earth, and all in both within the compass of our vision. For both heaven and earth shall pass away,[9] but the salvation and justi-

[1] Chap. xv. 5.
[2] That is, here, "without any self-originating aid of his," as if he had any independent and meritorious share in the work. Augustin plays on the prepositions, *per* (*eum*), and *præter* (*eum*).—Tr.
[3] Ps. cxvi. 12.

[4] Chap. xiv. 21.   [5] Matt. vii. 24.   [6] Chap. xi. 25.
[7] Rom. iv. 5.   [8] Phil. ii. 12.   [9] Matt. xxiv. 35.

fication of those predestinated thereto, that is, of those whom He foreknoweth, shall continue forever. In the former there is only the working of God, but in the latter there is also His image. But there are also in the heavens, thrones, governments, principalities, powers, archangels, and angels, which are all of them the work of Christ; and is it, then, greater works also than these that he doeth, who, with Christ working in him, is a co-worker in his own eternal salvation and justification? I dare not call for any hurried decision on such a point: let him who can, understand, and let him who can, judge whether it is a greater work to create righteous beings than to make righteous the ungodly. For at least, if there is equal power employed in both, there is greater mercy in the latter. For "this is the great mystery of godliness which was manifested in the flesh, justified in the Spirit, seen of angels, preached unto the Gentiles, believed on in the world, received up into glory."[1] But when He said, "Greater works than these shall he do," there is no necessity requiring us to suppose that all of Christ's works are to be understood. For He spake, perhaps, only *of these* He was now doing; and the work He was doing at that time was uttering the words of faith, and of such works specially had He spoken just before when He said, "The words that I speak unto you, I speak not of myself: but the Father, that dwelleth in me, He doeth the works." His words, accordingly, were His works. And it is assuredly something less to preach the words of righteousness, which He did apart from us, than to justify the ungodly, which He does in such a way in us that we also are doing it ourselves. It remains for us to inquire how the words are to be understood, "Whatsoever ye shall ask in my name, I will do it." Because of the many things His believing ones ask, and receive not, there is no small question claiming our attention; but as this discourse must now be concluded, we must allow at least a little delay for its consideration and discussion.

---

[1] 1 Tim. iii. 16. On account of the well-known textual controversy among Biblicists, this passage, as quoted by Augustin, is so far valuable, as it shows us how he read and understood the point in dispute, namely, whether it is "GOD was manifested" (as in our English version), or, "WHO [which] was manifested," as here by Augustin; in other words, whether the original text read Θεός or ὅς before ἐφανερώθη. The evidence is almost equally divided between the two; and the difficulty is chiefly caused by the circumstance, that in the earliest MSS., the Uncial, ΘΕΟΣ (God) is usually written in a contracted form, consisting of the first and last letters, ΘΣ, which differs from the pronoun ὅς (who), written ΟΣ, merely by the little line inside the Θ, and another line over the contraction; both of which may have been unintentionally omitted at the time of copying, or purposely inserted at an after date. To us now, the question is of less importance, as, if the true reading be ὅς (who), its antecedent can only be Χριστός (Christ). [The R. V., in accordance with the oldest MSS. and the best critical edition, reads: "He who (ὅς) was manifested.—TR.

TRACTATE LXXIII.

AGAIN ON THE SAME PASSAGE.

1. THE Lord, by His promise, gave those whose hopes were resting on Himself a special ground of confidence, when He said, "For I go to the Father; and whatsoever ye shall ask in my name, I will do it." His proceeding, therefore, to the Father, was not with any view of abandoning the needy, but of hearing and answering their petitions. But what is to be made of the words, "Whatsoever ye shall ask," when we behold His faithful ones so often asking and not receiving? Is it, shall we say, for no other reason but that they ask amiss? For the Apostle James made this a ground of reproach when he said, "Ye ask and receive not, because ye ask amiss, that ye may consume it upon your lusts."[1] What one, therefore, wishes to receive, in order to turn to an improper use, God in His mercy rather refuses to bestow. Nay, more, if a man asks what would, if answered, only tend to his injury, there is surely greater cause to fear, lest what God could not withhold with kindness, He should give in His anger. Do we not see how the Israelites got to their own hurt what their guilty lusting craved? For while it was raining manna on them from heaven, they desired to have flesh to eat.[2] They disdained what they had, and shamelessly sought what they had not: as if it were not better for them to have asked not to have their unbecoming desires gratified with the food that was wanting, but to have their own dislike removed, and be made themselves to receive aright the food that was provided. For when evil becomes our delight, and what is good the reverse, we ought to be entreating God rather to win us back to the love of the good, than to grant us the evil. Not that it

---

[1] Jas. iv. 3   [2] Num. xi. 32

is wrong to eat flesh, for the apostle, speaking of this very thing, says, "Every creature of God is good, and nothing to be refused which is received with thanksgiving;"[1] but because, as he also says, "It is evil for that man who eateth with offense;"[2] and if so, with offense to man, how much more so if to God? to whom it was no light offense, on the part of the Israelites, to reject what wisdom was supplying, and ask for that which lust was craving: although they would not actually make the request, but murmured because it was wanting. But to let us know that the wrong lies not with any creature of God, but with obstinate disobedience and inordinate desire, it was not in swine's flesh that the first man found death, but in an apple;[3] and it was not for a fowl, but for a dish of pottage, that Esau lost his birthright.[4]

2. How, then, are we to understand "Whatsoever ye shall ask, I will do it," if there are some things which the faithful ask, and which God, even purposely on their behalf, leaves undone? Or ought we to suppose that the words were addressed only to the apostles? Surely not. For what He has got the length of now saying is in the very line of what He had said before: "He that believeth in me, the works that I do shall he do also; and greater works than these shall he do;" which was the subject of our previous discourse. And that no one might attribute such power to himself, but rather to make it manifest that even these greater works were done by Himself, He proceeded to say, "For I go to the Father; and whatsoever ye shall ask in my name, I will do it." Was it the apostles only that believed on Him? When, therefore, He said, "He that believeth on me," He spake to those, among whom we also by His grace are included, who by no means receive everything that we ask. And if we turn our thoughts even to the most blessed apostles, we find that he who labored more than they all, yet not he, but the grace of God that was with him,[5] besought the Lord thrice that the messenger of Satan might depart from him, and received not what he had asked.[6] What shall we say, beloved? Are we to suppose that the promise here made, "Whatsoever ye shall ask in my name, I will do it," was not fulfilled by Him even to the apostles? And to whom, then, will ever His promise be fulfilled, if therein He has deceived His own apostles?

3. Wake up, then, believer, and give careful heed to what is stated here, "*in my name:*" for in these words He does not say, "whatso-

ever ye shall ask" in any way; but, "in my name." How, then, is He called, who promised so great a blessing? Christ Jesus, of course: Christ means King, and Jesus means Saviour! for certainly it is not any one who is a king that will save us, but only the Saviour-King; and therefore, whatsoever we ask that is adverse to the interests of salvation, we do not ask in the name of the Saviour. And yet He is the Saviour, not only when He does what we ask, but also when He refuses to do so; since by not doing what He sees to be contrary to our salvation, He manifests Himself the more fully as our Saviour. For the physician knows which of his patient's requests will be favorable, and which will be adverse, to his safety; and therefore yields not to his wishes when asking what is prejudicial, that he may effect his recovery. Accordingly, when we wish Him to do whatsoever we ask, let it not be in any way, but in His name, that is, in the name of the Saviour, that we present our petition. Let us not, then, ask aught that is contrary to our own salvation; for if He do that, He does it not as the Saviour, which is the name He bears to His faithful disciples. For He who condescends to be the Saviour of the faithful, is also a Judge to condemn the ungodly. Whatsoever, therefore, any one that believeth on Him shall ask in that name which He bears to those who believe on Him, He will do it; for He will do it as the Saviour. But if one that believeth on Him asketh something through ignorance that is injurious to his salvation, he asketh it not in the name of the *Saviour;* for His Saviour He will no longer be if He do aught to impede his salvation. And hence, in such a case, in not doing what He is entreated to do, His way is kept the clearer for doing what His name imports. And on that account, not only as the Saviour, but also as the good Master, He taught us, in the very prayer He gave us, what we should ask, in order that, whatsoever we shall ask, He may do it; and that we, too, might thereby understand that we cannot be asking in the Master's name anything that is inconsistent with the rule of His own instructions.

4. There are some things, indeed, which, although really asked in His name, that is, in harmony with His character as both Saviour and Master, He doeth not at the time we ask them, and yet He faileth not to do them. For when we pray that the kingdom of God may come, it does not imply that He is not doing what we ask, because we do not begin at once to reign with Him in the everlasting kingdom: for what we ask is delayed, but not denied. Nevertheless, let us not fail in pray-

ing, for in so doing we are as those that sow the seed; and in due season we shall reap.[1] And even when we are asking aright, let us ask Him at the same time not to do what we ask amiss; for there is reference to this also in the Lord's Prayer, when we say, "Lead us not into temptation."[2] For surely the temptation is no slight one if thine own request be hostile to thy cause. But we must not listen with indifference to the statement that the Lord (to prevent any from thinking that what He promised to do to those that asked, He

would do without the Father, after saying, "Whatsoever ye shall ask in my name, I will do it") immediately added, "That the Father may be glorified in the Son: if ye shall ask anything in my name, I will do it." In no respect, therefore, does the Son act without the Father, since He so acts for the very purpose that in Him the Father may be glorified. The Father, therefore, acts in the Son, that the Son may be glorified in the Father: and the Son acts in the Father, that the Father may be glorified in the Son; for the Father and the Son are one.

[1] Gal. vi. 9   [2] Matt. vi. 9-13.

TRACTATE LXXIV.

Chapter XIV. 15-17.

1. WE have heard, brethren, while the Gospel was read, the Lord saying: "If ye love me, keep my commandments: and I will ask the Father, and He shall give you another Comforter [Paraclete], that He may abide with you for ever; [even] the Spirit of truth; whom the world cannot receive, because it seeth Him not, neither knoweth Him: but ye shall know Him; for He shall dwell with you, and shall be in you."[1] There are many points which might form the subject of inquiry in these few words of the Lord; but it were too much for us either to search into all that is here for the searching, or to find out all that we here search for. Nevertheless, as far as the Lord is pleased to grant us the power, and in proportion to our capacity and yours, attend to what we ought to say and you to hear, and receive, beloved, what we on our part are able to give, and apply to Him for that wherein we fail. It is the Spirit, the Comforter, that Christ has promised to His apostles; but let us notice the way in which He gave the promise. "If ye love me," He says, "keep my commandments: and I will ask the Father, and He shall give you another Comforter, that He may abide with you for ever; [even] the Spirit of truth." We have here, at all events, the Holy Spirit in the Trinity, whom the catholic faith ac-

knowledges to be consubstantial and co-eternal with Father and Son: He it is of whom the apostle says, "The love of God is shed abroad in our hearts by the Holy Spirit, who is given unto us."[2] How, then, doth the Lord say, "If ye love me, keep my commandments: and I will ask the Father, and He shall give you another Comforter;" when He saith so of the Holy Spirit, without [having] whom we can neither love God nor keep His commandments? How can we love so as to receive Him, without whom we cannot love at all? or how shall we keep the commandments so as to receive Him, without whom we have no power to keep them? Or can it be that the love wherewith we love Christ has a prior place within us, so that, by thus loving Christ and keeping His commandments, we become worthy of receiving the Holy Spirit, in order that the love, not of Christ, which had already preceded, but of God the Father, may be shed abroad in our hearts by the Holy Spirit, who is given unto us? Such a thought is altogether wrong. For he who believes that he loveth the Son, and loveth not the Father, certainly loveth not the Son, but some figment of his own imagination. And besides, this is the apostolic declaration, "No one saith, Lord Jesus,[3] but in the Holy Spirit:[4] and who is it that calleth Him Lord Jesus but he that loveth Him, if he so call Him in the way the apostle intended to be understood? For many

[1] Augustin has *cognoscetis* for the second "know," and *scit* for that immediately preceding. The Greek text, however, has γινώσκω in both places, and in the *present* tense. He has also *manebit et in vobis erit*. The tense of μενει, whether *present* or *future*, depends simply on the place of the accent, μένει, or μενεῖ: while, as between the two readings ἐστιν and ἔσται, the preponderance of MS. authority seems in favor of the latter; although the *present* γινώσκετε in the principal clause would be more naturally followed by an equally *proleptic* present in those which follow.—TR.

[2] Rom. v. 5.
[3] Or, "Jesus is Lord." The weight of authority is clearly in favor of the reading followed by Augustin—λέγει, Κύριος Ἰησοῦς, giving the direct utterance of the speaker; and not the indirect accusative, Κύριον Ἰησοῦν, followed by our English version.—TR.
[4] 1 Cor. xii. 3.

call Him so with their lips, but deny Him in their hearts and works; just as He saith of such, "For they profess that they know God, but in works they deny Him."[1] If it is by works He is denied, it is doubtless also by works that His name is truly invoked. "No one," therefore, "saith, Lord Jesus," in mind, in word, in deed, with the heart, the lips, the labor of the hands,—no one saith, Lord Jesus, but in the Holy Spirit; and no one calls Him so but he that loveth. And accordingly the apostles were already calling Him Lord Jesus: and if they called Him so, in no way that implied a feigned utterance, with the mouth confessing, in heart and works denying Him; if they called Him so in all truthfulness of soul, there can be no doubt they loved. And how, then, did they love, but in the Holy Spirit? And yet they are commanded to love Him and keep His commandments, previous and in order to their receiving the Holy Spirit: and yet, without having that Spirit, they certainly could not love Him and keep His commandments.

2. We are therefore to understand that he who loves has already the Holy Spirit, and by what he has becomes worthy of a fuller possession, that by having the more he may love the more. Already, therefore, had the disciples that Holy Spirit whom the Lord promised, for without Him they could not call Him Lord; but they had Him not as yet in the way promised by the Lord. Accordingly they both had, and had Him not, inasmuch as they had Him not as yet to the same extent as He was afterwards to be possessed. They had Him, therefore, in a more limited sense: He was yet to be given them in an ampler measure. They had Him in a hidden way, they were yet to receive Him in a way that was manifest; for this present possession had also a bearing on that fuller gift of the Holy Spirit, that they might come to a conscious knowledge of what they had. It is in speaking of this gift that the apostle says: "Now we have received, not the spirit of this world, but the spirit which is of God, that we may know the things that are freely given to us of God."[2] For that same manifest bestowal of the Holy Spirit the Lord made, not once, but on two separate occasions. For close on the back of His resurrection from the dead He breathed on them and said, "Receive ye the Holy Spirit."[3] And because He then gave [the Spirit], did He on that account fail in afterwards sending Him according to His promise? Or was it not the very same Spirit who was both then breathed upon

them by Himself, and afterwards sent by Him from heaven?[4] And so, why that same giving on His part which took place publicly, also took place twice, is another question: for it may be that this twofold bestowal of His in a public way took place because of the two commandments of love, that is, to our neighbor and to God, in order that love might be impressively intimated as pertaining to the Holy Spirit. And if any other reason is to be sought for, we cannot at present allow our discourse to be improperly prolonged by such an inquiry: provided, however, it be admitted that, without the Holy Spirit, we can neither love Christ nor keep His commandments; while the less experience we have of His presence, the less also can we do so; and the fuller our experience, so much the greater our ability. Accordingly, the promise is no vain one, either to him who has not [the Holy Spirit], or to him who has. For it is made to him who has not, in order that he may have; and to him who has, that he may have more abundantly. For were it not that He was possessed by some in smaller measure than by others, St. Elisha would not have said to St. Elijah, "Let the spirit that is in thee be in a twofold measure in me.[5]

3. But when John the Baptist said, "For God giveth not the Spirit by measure,"[6] he was speaking exclusively of the Son of God, who received not the Spirit by measure; for in Him dwelleth all the fullness of the Godhead.[7] And no more is it independently of the grace of the Holy Spirit that the Mediator between God and men is the man Christ Jesus:[8] for with His own lips He tells us that the prophetical utterance had been fulfilled in Himself: "The Spirit of the Lord is upon me; because He hath anointed me, and hath sent me to preach the gospel to the poor."[9] For His being the Only-begotten, the equal of the Father, is not of grace, but of nature; but the assumption of human nature into the personal unity of the Only-begotten is not of nature, but of grace, as the Gospel acknowledges itself when it says, "And the child grew, and waxed strong, being filled with wisdom, and the grace of God was in Him."[10] But to others He is given by measure,—a measure ever enlarging until each has received his full complement up to the limits of his own perfection. As we are also reminded by the apostle, "Not to think of ourselves more highly than we ought to think, but to think soberly; according as God hath dealt to every man the measure of faith."[11] Nor is it the

---

[1] Tit. i. 16.   [2] 1 Cor. ii, 12.   [3] Chap. xx. 22.

[4] Acts ii. 4.   [5] 2 Kings ii. 9.   [6] Chap. iii. 34.
[7] Col. ii. 9.   [8] 1 Tim. ii. 5.   [9] Luke iv. 18-21.
[10] Luke ii. 42.   [11] Rom. xii. 3.

Spirit Himself that is divided, but the gifts bestowed by the Spirit: for there are diversities of gifts, but the same Spirit.[1]

4. But when He says, "I will ask the Father, and He shall give you another Paraclete," He intimates that He Himself is also a paraclete. For paraclete is in Latin called *advocatus* (advocate); and it is said of Christ, "We have an advocate with the Father, Jesus Christ the righteous."[2] But He said that the world could not receive the Holy Spirit, in much the same sense as it is also said, "The minding of the flesh is enmity against God: for it is not subject to the law of God; neither indeed can be;"[3] just as if we were to say, Unrighteousness cannot be righteous. For in speaking in this passage of the world, He refers to those who love the world; and such a love is not of the Father.[4] And thus the love of this world, which gives us enough to do to weaken and destroy its power within us, is in direct opposition to the love of God, which is shed abroad in our hearts by the Holy Spirit who is given unto us. "The world," therefore, "cannot receive Him, because it seeth Him not, neither knoweth Him." For worldly love possesseth not those invisible eyes, whereby, save in an invisible way, the Holy Spirit cannot be seen.

5. But ye," He adds, "shall know Him; for He shall dwell with you, and be in you." He will be in them, that He may dwell with them; He will not dwell with them to the end that He may be in them: for the being anywhere is prior to the dwelling there. But to prevent us from imagining that His words, "He shall dwell with you," were spoken in the same sense as that in which a guest usually dwells with a man in a visible way, He explained what "He shall dwell with you" meant, when He added the words, "He shall be in you." He is seen, therefore, in an invisible way: nor can we have any knowledge of Him unless He be in us. For it is in a similar way that we come to see our conscience within us: for we see the face of another, but we cannot see our own; but it is our own conscience we see, not another's. And yet conscience is never anywhere but within us: but the Holy Spirit can be also apart from us, since He is given that He may also be in us. But we cannot see and know Him in the only way in which He may be seen and known, unless He be in us.

---

[1] 1 Cor. xii. 4.
[2] 1 John ii. 1.
[3] Rom. viii. 7, *marg.*
[4] 1 John ii. 16.

TRACTATE LXXV.

CHAPTER XIV. 18–21.

1. AFTER the promise of the Holy Spirit, lest any should suppose that the Lord was to give Him, as it were, in place of Himself, in any such way as that He Himself would not likewise be with them, He added the words: "I will not leave you orphans; I will come to you." *Orphani* [Greek] are *pupilli* [parentless children] in Latin. The one is the Greek, the other the Latin name of the same thing: for in the psalm where we read, "Thou art the helper of the fatherless" [in the Latin version, *pupillo*], the Greek has *orphano.*[1] Accordingly, although it was not the Son of God that adopted sons to His Father, or willed that we should have by grace that same Father, who is His Father by nature, yet in a sense it is paternal feelings toward us that He Himself displays, when He declares, "I will not leave you orphans; I will come to you." In the same way He calls us also the children of the bridegroom, when He says, "The time will come, when the bridegroom shall be taken away from them, and then shall the children of the bridegroom fast."[2] And who is the bridegroom, but Christ the Lord?

2. He then goes on to say, "Yet a little while, and the world seeth me no more." How so? the world saw Him then; for under the name of the world are to be understood those of whom He spake above, when saying of the Holy Spirit, "Whom the world cannot receive, because it seeth Him not, neither knoweth Him." He was plainly visible to the carnal eyes of the world, while manifest in the flesh; but it saw not the Word that lay hid in the flesh: it saw the man, but it saw not God: it saw the covering, but not the Being within. But as, after the resurrection, even His very flesh, which He exhibited both to the sight and to the handling of His own,

---

[1] Ps. x. 14.
[2] Matt. ix. 15.

He refused to exhibit to others, we may in this way perhaps understand the meaning of the words, "Yet a little while, and the world seeth me no more; but ye shall see me: because I live, ye shall live also."

3. What is meant by the words, "Because I live, ye shall live also"? Why did He speak in the present tense of His own living, and in the future of theirs, but just by way of promise that the life also of the resurrection-body, as it preceded in His own case, would certainly follow in theirs? And as His own resurrection was in the immediate future, He put the word in the present tense to signify its speedy approach: but of theirs, as delayed till the end of the world, He said not, ye live; but, "ye shall live." With elegance and brevity, therefore, by means of two words, one of them in the present tense and the other in the future, He gave the promise of two resurrections, to wit, His own in the immediate future, and ours as yet to come in the end of the world. "Because I live," He says, "ye shall live also:" because He liveth, therefore shall we live also. For as by man is death, by man also is the resurrection of the dead. For as in Adam all die, even so in Christ shall all be made alive.[1] As it is only through the former that every one is liable to death, it is only through Christ that any one can attain unto life. Because we did not live, we are dead; because He lived, we shall live also. We were dead to Him, when we lived to ourselves; but, because He died in our behalf, He liveth both for Himself and for us. For, because He liveth, we shall live also. For while we were able of ourselves to attain unto death, it is not of ourselves also that life can come into our possession.

4. "In that day," He says, "ye shall know that I am in my Father, and ye in me, and I in you." In what day, but in that whereof He said, "Ye shall live also"? For then will it be that we can see what we believe. For even now is He in us, and we in Him: this we believe now, but then shall we also know it; although what we know even now by faith, we shall know then by actual vision. For as long as we are in the body, as it now is, to wit, corruptible, and encumbering to the soul,

we live at a distance from the Lord; for we walk by faith, not by sight.[2] Then accordingly it will be by sight, for we shall see Him as He is.[3] For if Christ were not even now in us, the apostle would not say, "And if Christ be in you, the body is dead indeed because of sin; but the spirit is life because of righteousness."[4] But that we are also in Him even then, He makes sufficiently clear, when He says, "I am the vine, ye are the branches."[5] Accordingly in that day, when we shall be living the life, whereby death shall be swallowed up, we shall know that He is in the Father, and we in Him, and He in us; for then shall be completed that very state which is already in the present begun by Him, that He should be in us, and we in Him.

5. "He that hath my commmandments," He adds, "and keepeth them, he it is that loveth me." He that hath [them] in his memory, and keepeth them in his life; who hath them orally, and keepeth them morally; who hath them in the ear, and keepeth them in deed; or who hath them in deed, and keepeth them by perseverance;—"he it is," He says, "that loveth me." By works is love made manifest as no fruitless application of a name. "And he that loveth me," He says, "shall be loved of my Father, and I will love him, and will manifest myself to him." But what is this, "I *will* love"? Is it as if He were then only to love, and loveth not at present? Surely not. For how could the Father love us apart from the Son, or the Son apart from the Father? Working as They do inseparably, how can They love apart?[6] But He said, "I will love him," in reference to that which follows, "and I will manifest myself to him." "I will love, and will manifest;" that is, I will love to the very extent of manifesting. For this has been the present aim of His love, that we may believe, and keep hold of the commandment of faith; but then His love will have this for its object, that we may see, and get that very sight as the reward of our faith: for we also love now, by believing in that which we shall see hereafter; but then shall we love in the sight of that which now we believe.

---

[1] 1 Cor. xv. 21, 22.
[2] 2 Cor. v. 7.   [3] 1 John iii. 2.   [4] Rom. viii. 10.
[5] Chap. xv. 5.   [6] *Separabiliter.*

TRACTATE LXXVI.

CHAPTER XIV. 22–24.

1. WHILE the disciples thus question, and Jesus their Master replies to them, we also, as it were, are learning along with them, when we either read or listen to the holy Gospel. Accordingly, because the Lord had said, "Yet a little while, and the world seeth me no more; but ye shall see me," Judas—not indeed His betrayer, who was surnamed Iscariot, but he whose epistle is read among the canonical Scriptures—asked Him of this very matter: "Lord, how is it that Thou wilt manifest Thyself unto us, and not unto the world?" Let us, too, be as it were questioning disciples with them, and listen to our common Master. For Judas the holy, not the impure, the follower, but not the persecutor of the Lord, has inquired the reason why Jesus was to manifest Himself to His own, and not to the world; why it was that yet a little while, and the world should not see Him, but they should see Him.

2. "Jesus answered and said unto him, If a man love me, he will keep my word: and my Father will love him, and we will come unto him, and make our abode with him. He that loveth me not, keepeth not my sayings." Here we have set forth the reason why He is to manifest Himself to His own, and not to that other class whom He distinguishes by the name of the world; and such is the reason also why the one loveth Him, and the other loveth Him not. It is the very reason, whereof it is declared in the sacred psalm, "Judge me, O God, and plead my cause against an unholy nation."[1] For such as love are chosen, because they love: but those who have not love, though they speak with the tongues of men and angels, are become a sounding brass and a tinkling cymbal; and though they had the gift of prophecy, and knew all mysteries and all knowledge, and had all faith so that they could remove mountains, they are nothing; and though they distributed all their substance, and gave their body to be burnt, it profiteth them nothing.[2] The saints are distinguished from the world by that love which maketh the one-minded[3] to dwell [together] in a house[4]　In this house

Father and Son make their abode, and impart that very love to those whom They shall also honor at last with this promised self-manifestation; of which the disciple questioned his Master, that not only those who then listened might learn it from His own lips, but we also from his Gospel. For he had made inquiry about the manifestation of Christ, and heard [in reply] about His loving and abiding. There is therefore a kind of inward manifestation of God, which is entirely unknown to the ungodly, who receive no manifestation of God the Father and the Holy Spirit: of the Son, indeed, there might have been such, but only in the flesh; and that, too, neither of the same kind as the other, nor able under any form to remain with them, save only for a little while; and even that, for judgment, not for rejoicing; for punishment, not for reward.

3. We have now, therefore, to understand, so far as He is pleased to unfold it, the meaning of the words, "Yet a little while, and the world seeth me no more; but ye shall see me." It is true, indeed, that after a little while He was to withdraw even His body, in which the ungodly also were able to see Him, from their sight; for none of *them* saw Him after His resurrection. But since it was declared on the testimony of angels, "He shall so come in like manner as ye have seen Him go into heaven;"　and our faith stands to this, that He will come in the same body to judge the living and the dead; there can be no doubt that He will then be seen by the world, meaning by the name, those who are aliens from His kingdom. And, on this account, it is far better to understand Him as having intended to refer at once to that epoch, when He said, "Yet a little while, and the world seeth me no more," when in the end of the world He shall be taken away from the sight of the damned, that for the future He may be seen only of those with whom, as

---

with the context, "who setteth the solitary in families," or rather, "who maketh the solitary [lit. those standing alone] to dwell in a house," *marg.;* that is, if יְחִיד might not even here retain its

proper meaning of "*only one,*" and, hence, "*beloved one.*" At all events, the word thus used, and its place in the context (see especially the preceding verse), may warrant the combination of both meanings,—that those who are "ones standing alone," friendless, cast off from others, in a human sense, are יְחִידִים, "*only ones,*"

"*beloved ones*" in the heavenly Father's sight, to whom He extends a special protection, and provideth a *home.*—TR.
5 Acts i. 11.

---

[1] Ps. xliii. 1.　　[2] 1 Cor. xiii. 1–3.　　3 *Unanimes.*
4 Ps. lxviii. 6: according to Augustin's translation and adaptation of the words מוֹשִׁיב יְחִידִים בַּיְתָה, and which the Vulgate

has also rendered somewhat similarly, *qui inhabitare facit unius moris in domo.* The English version is rather more accordant

those that love Him, the Father and Himself are making their abode. But He said, "a little while," because that which appears tedious to men is very brief in the sight of God: for of this same "little while" our evangelist, John, himself says, "Little children, it is the last time."[1]

4. But further, lest any should imagine that the Father and Son only, without the Holy Spirit, make their abode with those that love Them, let him recall what was said above of the Holy Spirit, "Whom the world cannot receive, because it seeth Him not, neither knoweth Him: but ye shall know Him; for He shall dwell with you, and shall be in you" (ver. 17). Here you see that, along with the Father and the Son, the Holy Spirit also taketh up His abode in the saints; that is to say, within them, as God in His temple. The triune God, Father, and Son, and Holy Spirit, come to us while we are coming to Them: They come with help, we come with obedience; They come to enlighten, we to behold; They come to fill, we to contain: that our vision of Them may not be external, but inward; and Their abiding in us may not be transitory, but eternal. The Son doth not manifest Himself in such a way as this to the world: for the world is spoken of in the passage before us as those, of whom He immediately adds, "He that loveth me not, keepeth not my sayings." These are such as never see the Father and the Holy Spirit: and see the Son for a little while, not to their attainment of bliss, but to their condemnation; and even Him, not in the form of God, wherein He is equally invisible with the Father and the Holy Spirit, but in human form, in which it was His will to be an object of contempt in suffering, but of terror in judging the world.

5. But when He added, "And the saying which ye have heard is not mine, but the Father's who sent me," let us not be filled with wonder or fear: He is not inferior to the Father, and yet He is not, save of the Father: He is not unequal in Himself, but He is not of Himself. For it was no false word He uttered when He said, "He that loveth me not, keepeth not my sayings." He called them, you see, His own sayings; does He, then, contradict Himself when He said again, "And the saying which ye have heard is not mine"? And, perhaps, it was on account of some intended distinction that, when He said *His own*, He used "sayings" in the plural; but when He said that "the saying," that is, the Word, was not His own, but the Father's, He wished it to be understood of Himself. For in the beginning was the Word, and the Word was with God, and the Word was God.[2] For as the Word, He is certainly not His own, but the Father's: just as He is not His own image, but the Father's; and is not Himself His own Son, but the Father's. Rightly, therefore, does He attribute whatever He does, as equal, to the Author of all, of whom He has this very prerogative, that He is in all respects His equal.

[1] 1 John ii. 18.

[2] Chap. i. 1.

TRACTATE LXXVII.

Chapter XIV. 25-27.

1. In the preceding lesson of the holy Gospel, which is followed by the one that has just been read, the Lord Jesus had said that He and the Father would come to those who loved Them, and make Their abode with them. But He had also already said above of the Holy Spirit, "But ye shall know Him; for He shall dwell with you, and shall be in you" (ver. 17): by which we understood that the divine Trinity dwelleth together in the saints as in His own temple. But now He saith, "These things have I spoken unto you while [still] dwelling with you." That dwelling, therefore, which He promised in the future, is of one kind; and this, which He declares to be present, is of another. The one is spiritual, and is realized inwardly by the mind; the other is corporal, and is exhibited outwardly to the eye and the ear. The one brings eternal blessedness to those who have been delivered, the other pays its visits in time to those who await deliverance. As regards the one, the Lord never withdraws from those who love Him: as regards the other, He comes and goes. "These things," He says, "have I spoken unto you, while [still] dwelling with you;" that is, in His bodily presence, wherein He was visibly conversing with them.

2. "But the Comforter," He adds, "[which

is] the Holy Ghost, whom the Father will send in my name, He shall teach you all things, and bring all things to your remembrance, whatsoever I have said unto you." Is it, then, that the Son speaks, and the Holy Spirit teaches, so that we merely get hold of the words that are uttered by the Son, and then understand them by the teaching of the Spirit? as if the Son could speak without the Holy Spirit, or the Holy Spirit teach without the Son: or is it not rather that the Son also teacheth and the Spirit speaketh, and, when it is God that speaketh and teacheth anything, that the Trinity itself is speaking and teaching? And just because it is a Trinity, its persons required to be introduced individually, so that we might hear it in its distinct personality, and understand its inseparable nature.[1] Listen to the Father speaking in the passage where thou readest, "The Lord said unto me, Thou art my Son:"[2] listen to Him also teaching, in that where thou readest, "Every man that hath heard, and hath learned of the Father, cometh unto me."[3] The Son, on the other hand, thou hast just heard speaking; for He saith of Himself, "Whatsoever I have said unto you:" and if thou wouldst also know Him as a Teacher, bethink thyself of the Master, when He saith, "One is your Master, even Christ."[4] Furthermore, of the Holy Spirit, whom thou hast just been told of as a Teacher in the words, "He shall teach you all things," listen to Him also speaking, where thou readest in the Acts of the Apostles, that the Holy Spirit said to the blessed Peter, "Go with them, for I have sent them."[5] The whole Trinity, therefore, both speaketh and teacheth: but were it not also brought before us in its individual personality, it would certainly altogether surpass the power of human weakness to comprehend it. For as it is altogether inseparable in itself, it could never be known as the Trinity, were it always spoken of inseparably; for when we speak of the Father, and the Son, and the Holy Spirit, we certainly do not pronounce them simultaneously, and yet in themselves they cannot be else than simultaneous. But when He added, "He will bring to your remembrance," we ought also to understand that we are commanded not to forget that these pre-eminently salutary admonitions are part of that grace which the Holy Spirit brings to our remembrance.

3. "Peace," He said, "I leave with you, my peace I give unto you." It is here we read in the prophet, "Peace upon peace:"

peace He leaves with us when going away, His own peace He will give us when He cometh in the end. Peace He leaveth with us in this world, His own peace He will give us in the world to come. His own peace He leaveth with us, and abiding therein we conquer the enemy. His own peace He will give us when, with no more enemies to fight, we shall reign as kings. Peace He leaveth with us, that here also we may love one another: His own peace will He give us, where we shall be beyond the possibility of dissension. Peace He leaveth with us, that we may not judge one another of what is secret to each, while here on earth: His own peace will He give us, when He "will make manifest the counsels of the heart; and then shall every man have praise of God."[6] And yet in Him and from Him it is that we have peace, whether that which He leaveth with us when going to the Father, or that which He will give us when we ourselves are brought by Him to the Father. And what is it He leaveth with us, when ascending from us, save His own presence, which He never withdraweth? For He Himself is our peace who hath made both one.[7] It is He, therefore, that becomes our peace, both when we believe that He is, and when we see Him as He is.[8] For if, so long as we are in this corruptible body that burdens the soul, and are walking by faith, not by sight, He forsaketh not those who are sojourning at a distance from Himself;[9] how much more, when we have attained to that sight, shall He fill us with Himself?

4. But why is it that, when He said, "Peace I leave with you," He did not add, "my;" but when He said, "I give unto you," He there made use of it? Is "my" to be understood even where it is not expressed, on the ground that what is expressed once may have a reference to both? Or may it not be that here also we have some underlying truth that has to be asked and sought for, and opened up to those who knock thereat? For what, if by His own peace He meant such to be understood as that which He possesses Himself? whereas the peace, which He leaves us in this world, may more properly be termed our peace than His. For He, who is altogether without sin, has no elements of discord in Himself; while the peace we possess, meanwhile, is such that in the midst of it we have still to be saying, "Forgive us our debts."[10] A certain kind of peace, accordingly, we do possess, inasmuch as we delight in the law of God after the inward man: but it is not a full peace, for we see another law

---

[1] Eam [Trinitatem] distincte audire, inseparabiliter intelligere.
[2] Ps. ii. 7.   [3] Chap. vi. 45
[4] Matt. xxiii. 10.   [5] Acts x. 20.

[6] 1 Cor. iv. 5.   [7] Eph. ii. 14.   [8] 1 John iii. 2.
[9] 2 Cor. v. 6, 7.   [10] Matt. vi. 12

in our members warring against the law of our mind.[1]   In the same way we have peace in our relations with one another, just because, in mutually loving, we have a mutual confidence in one another: but no more is such a peace as that complete, for we see not the thoughts of one another's hearts; and we have severally better or worse opinions in certain respects of one another than is warranted by the reality.   And so that peace, although left us by Him, is our peace: for were it not from Him, we should not be possessing it, such as it is; but such is not the peace He has Himself.   And if we keep what we received to the end, then such as He has shall we have, when we shall have no elements of discord of our own, and we shall have no secrets hid from one another in our hearts.   But I am not ignorant that these words of the Lord may be taken so as to seem only a repetition of the same idea, "Peace I leave with you, my peace I give unto you:" so that after saying "peace," He only repeated it in saying "my peace;" and what He had meant in saying "I leave with you," He simply repeated in saying "I give unto you."   Let each one understand it as he pleases; but it is my delight, as I believe it is yours also, my beloved brethren, to keep such hold of that peace

here, where our hearts are making common cause against the adversary, that we may be ever longing for the peace which there will be no adversary to disturb.

5. But when the Lord proceeded to say, "Not as the world giveth, give I unto you," what else does He mean but, Not as those give who love the world, give I unto you? For their aim in giving themselves peace is that, exempt from the annoyance of lawsuits and wars, they may find enjoyment, not in God, but in the friendship of the world; and although they give the righteous peace, in ceasing to persecute them, there can be no true peace where there is no real harmony, because their hearts are at variance.   For as one is called a consort who unites his lot (*sortem*) with another, so may he be termed concordant whose heart has entered into a similar union.[2]   Let us, therefore, beloved, with whom Christ leaveth peace, and to whom He giveth His own peace, not after the world's way, but in a way worthy of Him by whom the world was made, that we should be of one heart with Himself, having our hearts run into one, that this one heart, set on that which is above, may escape the corruption of the earth.

---

[1] Rom. vii. 22, 23.

[2] *Consors dicitur, qui sortem jungit—concors dicendus, qui corda jungit.*

TRACTATE LXXVIII.

Chapter XIV. 27, 28.

1. We have just heard, brethren, these words of the Lord, which He addressed to His disciples: "Let not your heart be troubled, neither let it be afraid.   Ye have heard how I said unto you, I go away, and come unto you: if ye loved me, ye would surely rejoice, because I go unto the Father; for the Father is greater than I."   Their hearts might have become filled with trouble and fear, simply because of His going away from them, even though intending to return; lest, possibly, in the very interval of the shepherd's absence, the wolf should make an onset on the flock. But as God, He abandoned not those from whom He departed as man: and Christ Himself is at once both man and God.   And so He both went away in respect of His visible humanity, and remained as regards His Godhead: He went away as regards the nature which is subject to local limitations, and re-

mained in respect of that which is ubiquitous. Why, then, should their heart be troubled and afraid, when His quitting their eyesight was of such a kind as to leave unaltered His presence in their heart?   Although even God, who has no local bounds to His presence, may depart from the hearts of those who turn away from Him, not with their feet, but their moral character; just as He comes to such as turn to Him, not with their faces, but in faith, and approach Him in the spirit, and not in the flesh.   But that they might understand that it was only in respect of His human nature that He said, "I go and come to you," He went on to say, "If ye loved me, ye would surely rejoice, because I go unto the Father; for the Father is greater than I."   And so, then, in that very respect wherein the Son is not equal to the Father, in that was He to go to the Father, just as from Him is He hereafter to come to judge the quick and the dead: while in so far as the Only-begotten is equal to Him that begat, He never withdraws from the Father; but with Him is everywhere perfectly equal in that Godhead which knows of no local limitations. For "being as He was in the form of God," as the apostle says, " He thought it not robbery to be equal with God." For how could that nature be robbery, which was His, not by usurpation, but by birth? " But He emptied Himself, taking upon Him the form of a servant;"[1] and so, not losing the former, but assuming the latter, and emptying Himself in that very respect wherein He stood forth before us here in a humbler state than that wherein He still remained with the Father. For there was the accession of a servant-form, with no recession of the divine: in the assumption of the one there was no consumption of the other. In reference to the one He says, " The Father is greater than I;" but because of the other, " I and my Father are one."[2]

2. Let the Arian attend to this, and find healing in his attention; that wrangling may not lead to vanity, or, what is worse, to insanity. For it is the servant-form which is that wherein the Son of God is less, not only than the Father, but also than the Holy Spirit; and more than that, less also than Himself, for He Himself, in the form of God, is greater than Himself. For the man Christ does not cease to be called the Son of God, a name which was thought worthy of being applied even to His flesh alone as it lay in the tomb. And what else than this do we confess, when we declare that we believe in the only-begotten Son of God, who, under Pontius Pilate, was crucified, and buried? And what of Him was buried, save the flesh without the spirit? And so in believing in the Son of God, who was buried, we surely affix the name, Son of God, even to His flesh, which alone was laid in the grave. Christ Himself, therefore, the Son of God, equal with the Father because in the form of God, inasmuch as He emptied Himself, without losing the form of God, but assuming that of a servant, is greater even than Himself; because the unlost form of God is greater than the assumed form of a servant. And what, then, is there to wonder at, or what is there out of place, if, in reference to this servant-form, the Son of God says, " The Father is greater than I;" and in speaking of the form of God, the self-same Son of God declares, " I and my Father are one "? For one they are, inasmuch as " The Word was God;" and greater is the Father, inasmuch

as " the Word was made flesh."[3] Let me add what cannot be gainsaid by Arians and Eunomians:[4] in respect of this servant-form, Christ as a child was inferior also to His own parents, when, according to Scripture, " He was subject "[5] as an infant to His seniors. Why, then, heretic, seeing that Christ is both God and man, when He speaketh as man, dost thou calumniate God? He in His own person commends our human nature; dost thou dare in Him to asperse the divine? Unbelieving and ungrateful as thou art, wilt thou degrade Him who made thee, just for the very reason that He is declaring what He became because of thee? For equal as He is with the Father, the Son, by whom man was made, became man, in order to be less than the Father: and had He not done so, what would have become of man?

3. May our Lord and Master bring home clearly to our minds the words, " If ye loved me, ye would surely rejoice, because I go unto the Father; for the Father is greater than I." Let us, along with the disciples, listen to the Teacher's words, and not, with strangers, give heed to the wiles of the deceiver. Let us acknowledge the twofold substance of Christ; to wit, the divine, in which he is equal with the Father, and the human, in respect of which the Father is greater. And yet at the same time both are not two, for Christ is one; and God is not a quaternity, but a Trinity. For as the rational soul and the body form but one man, so Christ, while both God and man, is one; and thus Christ is God, a rational soul, and a body. In all of these we confess Him to be Christ, we confess Him in each. Who, then, is He that made the world? Christ Jesus, but in the form of God. Who is it that was crucified under Pontius Pilate? Christ Jesus, but in the form of a servant. And so of the several parts whereof He consists as man. Who is He who was not left in hell? Christ Jesus, but only in respect of His soul. Who was to rise on the third day, after being laid in the tomb? Christ Jesus, but solely in reference to His flesh. In reference, then, to each of these, He is likewise called Christ And yet all of them are not two, or three, but one Christ. On this account, therefore, did He say, " If ye loved me, ye would surely rejoice, because I go unto the Father;" for human nature is worthy of congratulation, in being so assumed by the only-begotten Word as to

---

[1] Phil. ii. 6, 7.　　　　[2] Chap. x. 30.

[3] Chap. i. 1, 14.
[4] The *Eunomians* were a branch of the Arians, only slightly differing in some of their tenets regarding the essential inferiority to God, and the creaturehood of the Son and the Holy Spirit. As a sect, they belong to the fourth century, and derived their name from Eunomius, bishop of Cyzicus.—TR.
[5] Luke ii. 51.

be constituted immortal in heaven, and, earthy in its nature, to be so sublimated and exalted, that, as incorruptible dust, it might take its seat at the right hand of the Father. In such a sense it is that He said He would go to the Father. For in very truth He went unto Him, who was always with Him. But His going unto Him and departing from us were neither more nor less than His transforming and immortalizing that which He had taken upon Him from us in its mortal condition, and exalting that to heaven, by means of which He lived on earth in man's behalf. And who would not draw rejoicing from such a source, who has such love to Christ that he can at once congratulate his own nature as already immortal in Christ, and cherish the hope that he himself will yet become so through Christ?

TRACTATE LXXIX.

CHAPTER XIV. 29–31.

1. OUR Lord and Saviour, Jesus Christ, had said unto His disciples, "If ye loved me, ye would surely rejoice, because I go unto the Father; for the Father is greater than I." And that He so spake in His servant-form, and not in that of God, wherein He is equal with the Father, is well known to faith as it resides in the minds of the pious, not as it is feigned by the scornful and senseless. And then He added, "And now I have told you before it come to pass, that, when it is come to pass, ye might believe." What can He mean by this, when the fact rather is, that a man ought, before it comes to pass, to believe that which demands his belief? For it forms the very encomium of faith when that which is believed is not seen. For what greatness is there in believing what is seen, as in those words of the same Lord, when, in reproving a disciple, He said, "Because thou hast seen, thou hast believed; blessed are they that see not, and yet believe."[1] And I hardly know whether any one can be said to believe what he sees; for this same faith is thus defined in the epistle addressed to the Hebrews: "Now faith is the substance of those that hope,[2] the assurance[3] of things not seen." Accordingly, if faith is in things that are believed, and that, too, in things which are not seen,[4] what mean these words of the Lord, "And now I have told you before it come to pass, that, when it is come to pass, ye might believe"? Ought He not rather to have said, And now I have told you before it come to pass, that ye may believe what, when it is come to pass, ye shall see? For even he who was told, "Because thou hast seen, thou hast believed," did not believe only what he saw; but he saw one thing, and believed another: for he saw Him as man, and believed Him to be God. He perceived and touched the living flesh, which he had seen in the act of dying, and he believed in the Deity infolded in that flesh. And so he believed with the mind what he did not see, by the help of that which was apparent to his bodily senses. But though we may be said to believe what we see, just as every one says that he believes his own eyes, yet that is not to be mistaken for the faith which is built up by God in our souls; but from things that are seen, we are brought to believe in those which are invisible. Wherefore, beloved, in the passage before us, when our Lord says, "And now I have told you before it come to pass, that, when it is come to pass, ye might believe;" by the words, "when it is come to pass," He certainly means, that they would yet see Him after His death, alive, and ascending to His Father; at the sight of which they should then be compelled to believe that He was indeed the Christ, the Son of the living God, seeing He could do such a thing, even after predicting it, and also could predict it before He did it: and this they should then believe, not with a new, but with an augmented faith; or at least [with a faith] that had been impaired[5] by His death, and was now repaired[5] by His resurrection. For it was not that they had not previously also believed Him to be the Son of God, but when His own predictions were actually fulfilled in Him, that faith, which was still weak at the time of His here speaking to them, and at the time of His death almost ceased to exist, sprang up again into new life and increased vigor.

---

[1] Chap. xx. 29.
[2] Text, *sperantium*, although many MSS. have *sperandorum*, or *sperandarum*, "things hoped for."
[3] *Convictio.*
[4] Heb. xi. 1
[5] *Defecta—refecta.*

2. But what says He next? "Hereafter I will not talk much with you; for the prince of this world cometh;" and who is that, but the devil? "And hath nothing in me;" that is to say, no sin at all. For by such words He points to the devil, as the prince, not of His creatures, but of sinners, whom He here designates by the name of *this world*. And as often as the name of the world is used in a bad sense, He is pointing only to the lovers of such a world; of whom it is elsewhere recorded, "Whosoever will be a friend of this world, becomes the enemy of God."[1] Far be it from us, then, so to understand the devil as prince of the world, as if he wielded the government of the whole world, that is, of heaven and earth, and all that is in them; of which sort of world it was said, when we were lecturing on Christ the Word, "And the world was made by Him."[2] The whole world, therefore, from the highest heavens to the lowest earth, is subject to the Creator, not to the deserter; to the Redeemer, not to the destroyer; to the Deliverer, not to the enslaver; to the Teacher, not to the deceiver. And in what sense the devil is to be understood as the prince of the world, is still more clearly unfolded by the Apostle Paul, who, after saying, "We wrestle not against flesh and blood," that is, against men, went on to say, "but against principalities and powers, and the world-rulers of this darkness."[3] For in the very next word he has explained what he meant by "world," when he added, "of this darkness;" so that no one, by the name of the world, should understand the whole creation, of which in no sense are fallen angels the rulers. "Of this darkness," he says, that is, of the lovers of this world: of whom, nevertheless, there were some elected, not from any deserving of their own, but by the grace of God, to whom he says, "Ye were sometimes darkness; but now are ye light in the Lord."[4] For all have been under the rulers of this darkness, that is, [under the rulers] of wicked men, or darkness, as it were, in subjection to darkness: but "thanks be to God, who hath delivered us," says the same apostle, "from the power of darkness, and hath translated us into the kingdom of the Son of His love."[5] And in Him the prince of this world, that is, of this darkness, had nothing; for neither did He come with sin as God, nor had His flesh any hereditary taint of sin in its procreation by the Virgin. And, as if it were said to Him, Why, then, dost Thou die, if Thou hast no sin to merit the punishment of death? He immediately added, "But that the world may know that I love the Father, and as the Father gave me commandment, even so I do: arise, let us go hence." For He was sitting at table with those who were similarly occupied. But "let us go," He said, and whither, but to the place where He, who had nothing in Him deserving of death, was to be delivered up to death? But He had the Father's commandment to die, as the very One of whom it had been foretold, "Then I paid for that which I took not away;"[6] and so appointed to pay death to the full, while owing it nothing, and to redeem us from the death that was our due. For Adam had seized on sin as a prey, when, deceived, he presumptuously stretched forth his hand to the tree, and attempted to invade the incommunicable name of that Godhead which was disallowed him, and with which the Son of God was endowed by nature, and not by robbery.

---

[1] Jas. iv. 4.   [2] Chap. i. 10.
[3] Eph. vi. 12: Augustin, *rectores mundi tenebrarum harum;* original, τοὺς κοσμοκράτορας τοῦ σκότους τούτου.

[4] Eph. v. 8.   [5] Col. i. 12, 13.   [6] Ps. lxix. 4.

TRACTATE LXXX.

Chapter XV. 1–3.

1. THIS passage of the Gospel, brethren, where the Lord calls Himself the vine, and His disciples the branches, declares in so many words that the Mediator between God and men, the man Christ Jesus,[1] is the head of the Church, and that we are His members. For as the vine and its branches are of one nature, therefore, His own nature as God being different from ours, He became man, that in Him human nature might be the vine, and we who also are men might become branches thereof. What mean, then, the words, "I am the true vine"? Was it to the literal vine, from which that metaphor was drawn, that

---

[1] 1 Tim. ii. 5.

He intended to point them by the addition of "true"? For it is by similitude, and not by any personal propriety, that He is thus called a vine; just as He is also termed a sheep, a lamb, a lion, a rock, a corner-stone, and other names of a like kind, which are themselves rather the *true* ones, from which these are drawn as similitudes, not as realities. But when He says, "I am the true vine," it is to distinguish Himself, doubtless, from that [vine] to which the words are addressed: "How art thou turned into sourness,[1] as a strange vine?"[2] For how could that be a true vine which was expected to bring forth grapes and brought forth thorns?[3]

2. "I am," He says, "the true vine, and my Father is the husbandman. Every branch in me that beareth not fruit, He taketh away; and every one that beareth fruit, He purgeth it, that it may bring forth more fruit." Are, then, the husbandman and the vine one? Christ is the vine in the same sense as when He said, "The Father is greater than I;"[4] but in that sense wherein He said, "I and my Father are one," He is also the husbandman. And yet not such a one as those, whose whole service is confined to external labor; but such, that He also supplies the increase from within. "For neither is he that planteth anything, neither he that watereth; but God that giveth the increase." But Christ is certainly God, for the Word was God; and so He and the Father are one: and if the Word was made flesh,—that which He was not before,—He nevertheless still remains what He was. And still more, after saying of the Father, as of the husbandman, that He taketh away the fruitless branches, and pruneth the fruitful, that they may bring forth more fruit, He straightway points to Himself as also the purger of the branches, when He says, "Now ye are clean through the word which I have spoken unto you." Here, you see, He is also the pruner of the branches—a work which belongs to the husbandman, and not to the vine; and more than that, He maketh the branches His workmen. For although they give not the increase, they afford some help; but not of themselves: "For without me," He says, "ye can do nothing.'" And listen, also, to their own confession: "What, then, is Apollos? and what is Paul? but ministers by whom ye believed, even as the Lord gave

to every man. I have planted, Apollos watered." And this, too, "as the Lord gave to every man;" and so not of themselves. In that, however, which follows, "but God gave the increase,"[5] He works not by them, but by Himself; for work like that exceeds the lowly capacity of man, transcends the lofty powers of angels, and rests solely and entirely in the hands of the Triune Husband-man. "Now ye are clean," that is, clean, and yet still further to be cleansed. For, had they not been clean, they could not have borne fruit; and yet every one that beareth fruit is purged by the husbandman, that he may bring forth more fruit. He bears fruit because he is clean; and to bear more, he is cleansed still further. For who in this life is so clean as not to be in need of still further and further cleansing? seeing that, "if we say that we have no sin, we deceive ourselves, and the truth is not in us; but if we confess our sins, He is faithful and just to forgive us our sins, and to cleanse us from all unrighteousness;" to cleanse in very deed the clean, that is, the fruitful, that they may be so much the more fruitful, as they have been made the cleaner.

3. "Now ye are clean through the word which I have spoken unto you." Why does He not say, Ye are clean through the baptism wherewith ye have been washed, but "through the word which I have spoken unto you," save only that in the water also it is the word that cleanseth? Take away the word, and the water is neither more nor less than water. The word is added to the element, and there results the Sacrament, as if itself also a kind of visible word. For He had said also to the same effect, when washing the disciples' feet, "He that is washed needeth not, save to wash his feet, but is clean every whit."[6] And whence has water so great an efficacy, as in touching the body to cleanse the soul, save by the operation of the word; and that not because it is uttered, but because it is believed? For even in the word itself the passing sound is one thing, the abiding efficacy another. "This is the word of faith which we preach," says the apostle, "that if thou shalt confess with thy mouth that Jesus is the Lord, and shalt believe in thine heart that God hath raised Him from the dead, thou shalt be saved. For with the heart man believeth unto righteousness, and with the mouth confession is made unto salvation."[7] Accordingly, we read in the Acts of the Apostles, "Purifying their hearts by faith;"[8] and, says the blessed Peter in his epistle, "Even as

---

[1] Hebrew סוֹרֵי, pass. part. of סוּר, to depart [from God], and so, perhaps, "*stragglers*," i.e. "*straggling branches* of [a strange vine];" or, as in English version, "*degenerate branches*," rather than as in text, where Augustin gives, *in amaritudinem, vitis aliena*, following the LXX., which reads, "εἰς πικρίας ἡ ἄμπελος ἡ ἀλλοτρία." The Vulgate is better: *in pravum, vinea aliena.*—Tr.
[2] Jer. ii. 21.   [3] Isa. v. 4.   [4] Chap. xiv. 28.

[5] 1 Cor. iii. 5-7.   [6] Chap. xiii. 10.
[7] Rom. x. 10.   [8] Acts xv. 9.

baptism doth also now save us, not the putting away of the filth of the flesh, but the answer[1] of a good conscience." "This is the word of faith which we preach," whereby baptism, doubtless, is also consecrated, in order to its possession of the power to cleanse. For Christ, who is the vine with us, and the husbandman with the Father, "loved the Church, and gave Himself for it." And then read the apostle, and see what he adds: "That He might sanctify it, cleansing it with the washing of water by the word."[2]

[1] Literally, "questioning," *interrogatio*, 1 Pet. iii. 21.
[2] Eph. v. 25, 26.

The cleansing, therefore, would on no account be attributed to the fleeting and perishable element, were it not for that which is added, "by the word." This word of faith possesses such virtue in the Church of God, that through the medium of him who in faith presents, and blesses, and sprinkles it, He cleanseth even the tiny infant, although itself unable as yet with the heart to believe unto righteousness, and to make confession with the mouth unto salvation. All this is done by means of the word, whereof the Lord saith, "Now ye are clean through the word which I have spoken unto you."

TRACTATE LXXXI.

CHAPTER XV. 4–7.

1. JESUS called Himself the vine, and His disciples the branches, and His Father the husbandman; whereon we have already discoursed as we were able. But in the present passage, while still speaking of Himself as the vine, and of His branches, or, in other words, of the disciples, He said, "Abide in me, and I in you." They are not in Him in the same kind of way that He is in them. And yet both ways tend to their advantage, and not to His. For the relation of the branches to the vine is such that they contribute nothing to the vine, but from it derive their own means of life; while that of the vine to the branches is such that it supplies their vital nourishment, and receives nothing from them. And so their having Christ abiding in them, and abiding themselves in Christ, are in both respects advantageous, not to Christ, but to the disciples. For when the branch is cut off, another may spring up from the living root; but that which is cut off cannot live apart from the root.

2. And then He proceeds to say: "As the branch cannot bear fruit of itself, except it abide in the vine; no more can ye, except ye abide in me." A great encomium on grace, my brethren,—one that will instruct the souls of the humble, and stop the mouths of the proud. Let those now answer it, if they dare, who, ignorant of God's righteousness, and going about to establish their own, have not submitted themselves unto the righteousness of God.[1] Let the self-complacent answer it, who think they have no need of God for

[1] Rom. x. 3.

the performance of good works. Fight they not against such a truth, those men of corrupt mind, reprobate concerning the faith,[2] whose reply is only full of impious talk, when they say: It is of God that we have our existence as men, but it is of ourselves that we are righteous? What is it you say, you who deceive yourselves, and, instead of establishing freewill, cast it headlong down from the heights of its self-elevation through the empty regions of presumption into the depths of an ocean grave? Why, your assertion that man of himself worketh righteousness, *that* is the height of your self-elation. But the Truth contradicts you, and declares, "The branch cannot bear fruit of itself, except it abide in the vine." Away with you now over your giddy precipices, and, without a spot whereon to take your stand, vapor away at your windy talk. These are the empty regions of your presumption. But look well at what is tracking your steps, and, if you have any sense remaining, let your hair stand on end. For whoever imagines that he is bearing fruit of himself is not in the vine, and he that is not in the vine is not in Christ, and he that is not in Christ is not a Christian. Such are the ocean depths into which you have plunged.

3. Ponder again and again what the Truth has still further to say: "I am the vine," He adds, "ye are the branches: he that abideth in me, and I in him, the same bringeth forth much fruit; for without me ye can do nothing." For just to keep any from supposing that the branch can bear at least some little

[2] 2 Tim. iii. 8.

fruit of itself, after saying, "the same bringeth forth much fruit," His next words are not, Without me ye can do but little, but "ye can do nothing." Whether then it be little or much, without Him it is impracticable; for without Him nothing can be done. For although, when the branch beareth little fruit, the husbandman purgeth it that it may bring forth more; yet if it abide not in the vine, and draw its life from the root, it can bear no fruit whatever of itself. And although Christ would not have been the vine had He not been man, yet He could not have supplied such grace to the branches had He not also been God. And just because such grace is so essential to life, that even death itself ceases to be at the disposal of free-will, He adds, "If any one abide not in me, he shall be cast forth as a branch, and wither; and they shall gather him, and cast him into the fire, and he is burned." The wood of the vine, therefore, is in the same proportion the more contemptible if it abide not in the vine, as it is glorious while so abiding; in fine, as the Lord likewise says of them in the prophet Ezekiel, when cut off, they are of no use for any purpose of the husbandman, and can be applied to no labor of the mechanic.[1] The branch is suitable only for one of two things, either the vine or the fire: if it is not in the vine, its place will be in the fire; and that it may escape the latter, may it have its place in the vine.

4. "If ye abide in me," He says, "and my words abide in you, ye shall ask what ye will, and it shall be done unto you." For abiding thus in Christ, is there aught they can wish but what will be agreeable to Christ? So abiding in the Saviour, can they wish anything that is inconsistent with salvation? Some things, indeed, we wish because we are in Christ, and other things we desire because still in this world. For at times, in connection with this our present abode, we are inwardly prompted to ask what we know not it would be inexpedient for us to receive. But God forbid that such should be given us if we abide in Christ, who, when we ask, only does what will be for our advantage. Abiding, therefore, ourselves in Him, when His words abide in us we shall ask what we will, and it shall be done unto us. For if we ask, and the doing follows not, what we ask is not connected with our abiding in Him, nor with His words which abide in us, but with that craving and infirmity of the flesh which are not in Him, and have not His words abiding in them. For to His words, at all events, belongs that prayer which He taught, and in which we say, "Our Father, who art in heaven."[2] Let us only not fall away from the words and meaning of this prayer in our petitions, and whatever we ask, it shall be done unto us. For then only may His words be said to abide in us, when we do what He has commanded us, and love what He has promised. But when His words abide only in the memory, and have no place in the life, the branch is not to be accounted as in the vine, because it draws not its life from the root. It is to this distinction that the word of Scripture has respect, "and to those that remember His commandments to do them."[3] For many retain them in their memory only to treat them with contempt, or even to mock at and assail them. It is not in such as have only some kind of contact, but no connection, that the words of Christ abide; and to them, therefore, they will not be a blessing, but a testimony against them; and because they are present in them without abiding in them, they are held fast by them for the very purpose of being judged according to them at last.

---

[1] Ezek. xv. 5.   [2] Matt. vi. 9.   [3] Ps. ciii. 18.

TRACTATE LXXXII.

CHAPTER XV. 8–10.

1. THE Saviour, in thus speaking to the disciples, commends still more and more the grace whereby we are saved, when He says, "Herein is my Father glorified,[1] that ye bear very much fruit, and be made my disciples." Whether we say *glorified*, or *made bright*, both are the rendering given us of one Greek verb, namely *doxazein* (δοξάζειν). For what is doxa (δόξα) in Greek, is in Latin glory. I have thought it worth while to mention this, because the apostle says, "If Abraham was justified by works, he hath glory, but not before God."[2] For this is the glory *before God*,

---

[1] *Clarificatus*, literally, "clarified," or made bright, clear, to men's eyes. See immediately afterwards in text.

[2] Rom. iv. 2.

whereby God, and not man, is glorified, when he is justified, not by works, but by faith, so that even his doing well is imparted to him by God; just as the branch, as I have stated above,[1] cannot bear fruit of itself. For if herein God the Father is glorified, that we bear much fruit, and be made the disciples of Christ, let us not credit our own glory therewith, as if we had it of ourselves. For of Him is such a grace, and accordingly therein the glory is not ours, but His. Hence also, in another passage, after saying, "Let your light so shine before men that they may see your good works;" to keep them from the thought that such good works were of themselves, He immediately added, "and may glorify your Father who is in heaven."[2] For herein is the Father glorified, that we bear much fruit, and be made the disciples of Christ. And by whom are we so made, but by Him whose mercy hath forestalled us? For we are His workmanship, created in Christ Jesus unto good works.[3]

2. "As the Father hath loved me," He says, "so have I loved you: continue ye in my love." Here, then, you see, is the source of our good works. For whence should we have them, were it not that faith worketh by love?[4] And how should we love, were it not that we were first loved? With striking clearness is this declared by the same evangelist in his epistle: "We love God because He first loved us."[5] But when He says, "As the Father hath loved me, so have I loved you," He indicates no such equality between our nature and His as there is between Himself and the Father, but the grace whereby the Mediator between God and men is the man Christ Jesus.[6] For He is pointed out as Mediator when He says, "The Father—me, and I—you." For the Father, indeed, also loveth us, but in Him; for herein is the Father glorified, that we bear fruit in the vine, that is, in the Son, and so be made His disciples.

3. "Continue ye," He says, "in my love." How shall we continue? Listen to what follows: "If ye keep my commandments, ye shall abide in my love." Love brings about the keeping of His commandments; but does the keeping of His commandments bring about love? Who can doubt that it is love which precedes? For he has no true ground for keeping the commandments who is destitute of love. And so, in saying, "If ye keep my commandments, ye shall abide in my love," He shows not the source from which love springs, but the means whereby it is manifested. As if He said, Think not that

ye abide in my love if ye keep not my commandments; for it is only if ye have kept them that ye shall abide. In other words, it will thus be made apparent that ye shall abide in my love if ye keep my commandments. So that no one need deceive himself by saying that he loveth Him, if he keepeth not His commandments. For we love Him just in the same measure as we keep His commandments; and the less we keep them, the less we love. And although, when He saith, "Continue ye in my love," it is not apparent what love He spake of; whether the love we bear to Him, or that which He bears to us: yet it is seen at once in the previous clause. For He had there said, "So have I loved you;" and to these words He immediately adds, "Continue ye in my love:" accordingly, it is that love which He bears to us. What, then, do the words mean, "Continue ye in my love," but just, continue ye in my grace? And what do these mean, "If ye keep my commandments, ye shall abide in my love," but, hereby shall ye know that ye shall abide in the love which I bear to you, if ye keep my commandments? It is not, then, for the purpose of awakening His love to us that we first keep His commandments; but this, that unless He loves us, we cannot keep His commandments. This is a grace which lies all disclosed to the humble, but is hid from the proud.

4. But what are we to make of that which follows: "Even as I have kept my Father's commandments, and abide in His love"? Here also He certainly intended us to understand that fatherly love wherewith He was loved of the Father. For this was what He has just said, "As the Father hath loved me, so have I loved you;" and then to these He added the words, "Continue ye in my love;" in that, doubtless, wherewith I have loved you. Accordingly, when He says also of the Father, "I abide in His love," we are to understand it of that love which was borne Him by the Father. But then, in this case also, is that love which the Father bears to the Son referable to the same grace as that wherewith we are loved of the Son: seeing that we on our part are sons, not by nature, but by grace; while the Only-begotten is so by nature and not by grace? Or is this even in the Son Himself to be referred to His condition as man? Certainly so. For in saying, "As the Father hath loved me, so have I loved you," He pointed to the grace that was His as Mediator. For Christ Jesus is the Mediator between God and men, not in respect to His Godhead, but in respect to His manhood.[7]

---

[1] Tract. LXXXI. sec. 2.   [2] Matt. v. 16.   [3] Eph. ii. 10.
[4] Gal. v. 6.   [5] 1 John iv. 19.   [6] 1 Tim. ii. 5.

[7] *Non in quantum Deus, sed in quantum homo est.*

And certainly it is in reference to this His human nature that we read, "And Jesus increased in wisdom and age, and in favor [grace] with God and men." [1] In harmony, therefore, with this, we may rightly say that while human nature belongs not to the nature of God, yet such human nature does by grace belong to the person of the only-begotten Son of God; and that by grace so great, that there is none greater, yea, none that even approaches equality. For there were no merits that preceded that assumption of humanity, but all His merits began with that very assumption. The Son, therefore, abideth in the love wherewith the Father hath loved Him, and so hath kept His commandments. For what are we to think of Him even as man, but that God is His lifter up? [2] for the Word was God, the Only-begotten, co-eternal with Him that begat; but that He might be given to us as Mediator, by grace ineffable, the Word was made flesh, and dwelt among us. [3]

---

[1] Luke ii. 52.   [2] Ps. iii. 3.   [3] Chap. i. 1, 14.

TRACTATE LXXXIII.

Chapter XV. 11, 12.

1. You have just heard, beloved, the Lord saying to His disciples, "These things have I spoken unto you, that my joy might be in you, and that your joy might be full." And what else is Christ's joy in us, save that He is pleased to rejoice over us? And what is this joy of ours which He says is to be made full, but our having fellowship with Him? On this account He had said to the blessed Peter, "If I wash thee not, thou shalt have no part with me." [1] His joy, therefore, in us is the grace He hath bestowed upon us: and that is also our joy. But over it He rejoiced even from eternity, when He chose us before the foundation of the world. [2] Nor can we rightly say that His joy was not full; for God's joy was never at any time imperfect. But that joy of His was not in us: for we, in whom it could be, had as yet no existence; and even when our existence commenced, it began not to be in Him. But in Him it always was, who in the infallible truth of His own foreknowledge rejoiced that we should yet be His own. Accordingly, He had a joy over us that was already full, when He rejoiced in foreknowing and foreordaining us: and as little could there be any fear intermingling in that joy of His, lest there should be any possible failure in what He foreknew would be done by Himself. Nor, when He began to do what He foreknew that He would do, was there any increase to His joy as the expression of His blessedness; otherwise His making of us must have added to His blessedness. Be such a supposition, brethren, far from our thoughts; for the blessedness of God was neither less without us, nor became greater because of us. His joy, therefore, over our salvation, which was always in Him, when He foreknew and foreordained us, began to be *in us* when He called us; and this joy we properly call our own, as by it we, too, shall yet be blessed: but this joy, as it is ours, increases and advances, and presses onward perseveringly to its own completion. Accordingly, it has its beginning in the faith of the regenerate, and its completion in the reward when they rise again. Such is my opinion of the purport of the words, "These things have I spoken unto you, that my joy might be in you, and that your joy might be made full:" that *mine* "might be in you;" that *yours* "might be made full." For mine was always full, even before ye were called, when ye were foreknown as those whom I was afterwards to call; but it finds its place in you also, when ye are transformed into that which I have foreknown regarding you. And "that yours may be full:" for ye shall be blessed, what ye are not as yet; just as ye are now created, who had no existence before.

2. "This," He says, "is my injunction, that ye love one another, as I have loved you." Whether we call it injunction or commandment, [3] both are the rendering of the same Greek word, *entolé* (ἐντολή). But He had already made this same announcement on a former occasion, when, as ye ought to remember, I repounded it to you to the best of my ability. [4] For this is what He says there, "A new commandment I give unto you, that ye love one another; as I have loved you,

---

[1] Chap. xiii. 8.   [2] Eph. i. 4.   [3] *Præceptum, sive mandatum.*   [4] See Tract. LXV.

that ye also love one another." [1] And so the repetition of this commandment is its commendation: only that there He said, "A new commandment I give unto you;" and here, "This is my commandment:" *there*, as if there had been no such commandment before; and *here*, as if He had no other commandment to give them. But there it is spoken of as "new," to keep us from persevering in our old courses; here, it is called "mine," to keep us from treating it with contempt.

3. But when He said in this way here, "This is my commandment," as if there were none else, what are we to think, my brethren? Is, then, the commandment about that love, wherewith we love one another, His only one? Is there not also another that is still greater, —that we should love God? Or has God in very truth given us such a charge about love alone, that we have no need of searching for others? There are three things at least that the apostle commends when he says, "But now abide faith, hope, charity, these three; but the greatest of these is charity." [2] And although in charity, that is, in love, are comprehended the two commandments; yet it is here declared to be the greatest only, and not the sole one. Accordingly, what a host of commandments are given us about faith, what a multitude about hope! who is there that could collect them together, or suffice to number them? But let us ponder the words of the same apostle: "Love is the fullness of the law." [3] And so, where there is love, what can be wanting? and where it is not, what is there that can possibly be profitable? The devil believes, [4] but does not love: no one

loveth who doth not believe. One may, indeed, hope for pardon who does not love, but he hopes in vain; but no one can despair who loves. Therefore, where there is love, there of necessity will there be faith and hope; and where there is the love of our neighbor, there also of necessity will be the love of God. For he that loveth not God, how loveth he his neighbour as himself, seeing that he loveth not even himself? Such an one is both impious and iniquitous; and he that loveth iniquity, manifestly loveth not, but hateth his own soul. [5] Let us, therefore, be holding fast to this precept of the Lord, to love one another; and then all else that is commanded we shall do, for all else we have contained in this. But this love is distinguished from that which men bear to one another as such; for in order to mark the distinction, it is added, "as I have loved you." And wherefore is it that Christ loveth us, but that we may be fitted to reign with Christ? With this aim, therefore, let us also be loving one another, that we may manifest the difference of our love from that of others, who have no such motive in loving one another, because the love itself is wanting. But those whose mutual love has the possession of God Himself for its object, will truly love one another; and, therefore, even for the very purpose of loving one another, they love God. There is no such love as this in all men; for few have this motive for their love one to another, that God may be all in all. [6]

---

[5] Ps. xi. 5. Augustin here, as usual, along with the Vulgate, follows the Septuagint in what is clearly a mistranslation of the Hebrew text, which is correctly rendered grammatically in our English version, though not exactly according to the Masoretic punctuation. שֹׂנֵא נַפְשׁוֹ (fem.) shows that "his soul" is the subject, and not the object of the hatred.—Tr.   [6] 1 Cor. xv. 28.

---

[1] Chap. xiii. 34.   [2] 1 Cor. xiii. 13.
[3] Rom. xiii. 10.   [4] Jas. ii. 19.

TRACTATE LXXXIV.

CHAPTER XV. 13.

1. THE Lord, beloved brethren, hath defined that fullness of love which we ought to bear to one another, when He said: "Greater love hath no man than this, that a man lay down his life for his friends." Inasmuch, then, as He had said before, "This is my commandment, that ye love one another, as I have loved you;" and appended to these words what you have just been hearing, "Greater love hath no man than this, that a man lay down his life for his friends;" there

follows from this as a consequence, what this same Evangelist John says in his epistle, "That as Christ laid down His life for us, even so we also ought to lay down our lives for the brethren;" [1] loving one another in truth, as He hath loved us, who laid down His life for us. Such also is doubtless the meaning of what we read in the Proverbs of Solomon: "If thou sittest down to supper at

---

[1] 1 John iii. 16.

the table of a ruler, consider wisely what is set before thee; and so put to thy hand, knowing that thou art bound to make similar preparations."[1]   For what is the table of the ruler, but that from which we take the body and blood of Him who laid down His life for us? And what is it to sit thereat, but to approach in humility? And what is it to consider intelligently what is set before thee, but worthily to reflect on the magnitude of the favor? And what is it, so to put to thy hand, as knowing that thou art bound to make similar preparations, but as I have already said, that, as Christ laid down His life for us, so we also ought to lay down our lives for the brethren? For as the Apostle Peter also says, "Christ suffered for us, leaving us an example, that we should follow His steps."[2] This is to make similar preparations. This it was that the blessed martyrs did in their burning love; and if we celebrate their memories in no mere empty form, and, in the banquet whereat they themselves were filled to the full, approach the table of the Lord, we must, as they did, be also ourselves making similar preparations. For on these very grounds we do not commemorate them at that table in the same way, as we do others who now rest in peace, as that we should also pray for them, but rather that they should do so for us, that we may cleave to their footsteps; because they have actually attained that fullness of love, than which, our Lord hath told us, there cannot be a greater. For such tokens of love they exhibited for their brethren, as they themselves had equally received at the table of the Lord.

2. But let us not be supposed to have so spoken as if on such grounds we might possibly arrive at an equality with Christ the Lord, if for His sake we have undergone witness-bearing even unto blood. *He* had power to lay down His life, and to take it again;[3] but we have no power to live as long as we wish; and die we must, however unwilling: *He*, by dying, straightway slew death in Himself; we, by His death, are delivered from death: *His* flesh saw no corruption;[4] ours, after corruption, shall in the end of the world be clothed by Him with incorruption: *He* had no need of us, in order to work out our salvation; we, without Him, can do nothing: *He* gave Himself as the vine, to us the branches; we, apart from Him, can have no life. Lastly, although brethren die for brethren, yet no martyr's blood is ever shed for the remission of the sins of brethren, as was

the case in what He did for us; and in this respect He bestowed not on us aught for imitation, but something for congratulation. In as far, then, as the martyrs have shed their blood for the brethren, so far have they exhibited such tokens of love as they themselves perceived at the table of the Lord. (One might imitate Him in dying, but no one could, in redeeming.)[5] In all else, then, that I have said, although it is out of my power to mention everything, the martyr of Christ is far inferior to Christ Himself. But if any one shall set himself in comparison, I say, not with the power, but with the innocence of Christ, and (I would not say) in thinking that he is healing the sins of others, but at least that he has no sins of his own, even so far is his avidity overstepping the requirements of the method of salvation; it is a matter of considerable moment for him, only he attains not his desire. And well it is that he is admonished in that passage of the Proverbs, which immediately goes on to say, " But if thy greed is too great, be not desirous of his dainties; for it is better that thou take nothing thereof, than that thou shouldst take more than is befitting. For such things," it is added, "have a life of deceit," that is, of hypocrisy. For in asserting his own sinlessness, he cannot prove, but only pretend, that he is righteous. And so it is said, " For such have a deceiving life." There is only One who could at once have human flesh and be free from sin. Appropriately are we commanded that which follows; and such a word and proverb is well adapted to human weakness, when it is said, " Lay not thyself out, seeing thou art poor, against him that is rich." For the rich man is Christ, who was never obnoxious to punishment either through hereditary or personal debt and is righteous Himself, and justifies others. Lay not thyself out against Him, thou who art so poor, that thou art manifestly to the eyes of all the daily beggar that thou art in thy prayer for the remission of sins. " But keep thyself," he says, " from thine own counsel' [" cease from thine own wisdom "—E. V.]. From what, but from this delusive presumption? For He, indeed, inasmuch as He is not only man but also God, can never be chargeable with evil. " For if thou turn thine eye upon Him, He will nowhere be visible." " Thine eye," that is, the human eye, wherewith thou distinguishest that which is human; " if thou turn it upon Him, He will nowhere be visible," because

---

[1] Prov. xxiii. 1, 2: see *below*, and also Tract. XLVII. sec. 2, note 4.
[2] 1 Pet. ii. 21.   [3] Chap. x. 18.   [4] Acts ii. 31.

[5] This parenthesized sentence is found, according to Migne, inserted here in six MSS. In three others it occurs immediately before the second following sentence, beginning, " But if any one," etc. In other MSS. it is wanting; and Migne omits it from the text. —TR.

He cannot be seen with such organs of sight as are thine. "For He will provide Himself wings like an eagle's, and will depart to the house of His overseer,"[1] from which, at all events, He came to us, and found us not such as He Himself was who came. Let us therefore love one another, even as Christ hath loved us, and given Himself for us.[2] "For greater love hath no man than this, that a man lay down his life for his friends." And let us be imitating Him in such a spirit of reverential obedience, that we shall never have the boldness to presume on a comparison between Him and ourselves.

[1] The whole of this passage, taken from Proverbs xxiii. 3-5, as well as verses 1 and 2, quoted in sec. 1 of this Lecture, and in Tract. XLVII. sec. 2 (where see note 4), departs so widely from the Hebrew text, and even from the Septuagint (which is itself considerably astray), that it is hardly possible to account for the differences; and we refrain from attempting it. The text had evidently been felt to be obscure from very early times, especially for those who were unacquainted with the Hebrew; and hence transformations, omissions, and interpolations of words, and even of sentences, on the part of copyists and commentators, had resulted in the very various readings of different versions. The passage as given by Augustin is a good example of his ingenuity in spiritualizing the statements of Scripture.—TR.

[2] Gal. ii. 20.

TRACTATE LXXXV.

CHAPTER XV. 14, 15.

1. WHEN the Lord Jesus had commended the love which He manifested toward us in dying for us, and had said, "Greater love hath no man than this, that a man lay down his life for his friends," He added, "Ye are my friends, if ye do whatsoever I command you." What great condescension! when one cannot even be a good servant unless he do his lord's commandments; the very means, which only prove men to be good servants, He wished to be those whereby His friends should be known. But the condescension, as I have termed it, is this, that the Lord condescends to call those His friends whom He knows to be His servants. For, to let us know that it is the duty of servants to yield obedience to their master's commands, He actually in another place reproaches those who are servants, by saying, "And why call ye me, Lord, Lord, and do not the things that I say?"[1] Accordingly, when ye say Lord, prove what you say by doing my commandments. Is it not to the obedient servant that He is yet one day to say, "Well done, thou good servant; because thou hast been faithful over a few things, I will make thee ruler over many things: enter thou into the joy of thy Lord"?[2] One, therefore, who is a good servant, can be both servant and friend.

2. But let us mark what follows. "Henceforth I call you not servants; for the servant knoweth not what his lord doeth." How, then, are we to understand the good servant to be both servant and friend, when He says, "Henceforth I call you not servants; for the servant knoweth not what his lord doeth"?

He introduces the name of friend in such a way as to withdraw that of servant; not as if to include both in the one term, but in order that the one should succeed to the place vacated by the other. What does it mean? Is it this, that even in doing the Lord's commandments we shall not be servants? Or this, that then we shall cease to be servants, when we have been good servants? And yet who can contradict the Truth, when He says, "Henceforth I call you not servants?" and shows why He said so: "For the servant," He adds, "knoweth not what his lord doeth." Is it that a good and tried servant is not likewise entrusted by his master with his secrets? What does He mean, then, by saying, "The servant knoweth not what his lord doeth"? Be it that "he knoweth not what he doeth," is he ignorant also of what he commands? For if he were so, how can he serve? Or how is he a servant who does no service? And yet the Lord speaks thus: "Ye are my friends, if ye do whatsoever I command you. Henceforth I call you not servants." Truly a marvellous statement! Seeing we cannot serve the Lord but by doing His commandments, how is it that in doing so we shall cease to be servants? If I be not a servant in doing His commandments, and yet cannot be in His service unless I so do, then, in my very service, I am no longer a servant.

3. Let us, brethren, let us understand, and may the Lord enable us to understand, and enable us also to do what we understand. And if we know this, we know of a truth what the Lord doeth; for it is only the Lord that so enables us, and by such means only do we attain to His friendship. For just as there

[1] Luke vi. 46.   [2] Matt. xxv. 21.

are two kinds of fear, which produce two classes of fearers; so there are two kinds of service, which produce two classes of servants. There is a fear, which perfect love casteth out;[1] and there is another fear, which is clean, and endureth for ever.[2] The fear that lies not in love, the apostle pointed to when he said, " For ye have not received the spirit of service again to fear."[3] But he referred to the clean fear when he said, " Be not high-minded, but fear."[4] In that fear which love casteth out, there has also to be cast out the service along with it: for both were joined together by the apostle, that is, the service and the fear, when he said, " For ye have not received the spirit of service again to fear." And it was the servant connected with this kind of service that the Lord also had in His eye when He said, " Henceforth I call you not servants; for the servant knoweth not what his lord doeth." Certainly not the servant characterized by the clean fear, to whom it is said, " Well done, thou good servant: enter thou into the joy of thy lord;" but the servant who is characterized by the fear which love casteth out, of whom He elsewhere saith, " The servant abideth not in the house for ever, but the Son abideth ever."[5] Since, therefore, He hath given us power to become the sons of God,[6] let us not be servants, but sons: that, in some wonderful and indescribable but real way, we may as servants have the power not to be servants; servants, indeed, with that clean fear which distinguishes the servant that enters into the joy of his lord, but not servants with the fear that has to be cast out, and which marketh him that abideth not in the house for ever. But let us bear in mind that it is the Lord that enableth us to serve so as not to be servants. And this it is that is unknown to the servant, who knoweth not what his Lord doeth; and who, when he doeth any good thing, is lifted up as if he did it himself, and not his Lord; and so, glories not in the Lord, but in himself, thereby deceiving himself, because glorying, as if he had not received.[7] But let us, beloved, in order that we may be the friends of the Lord, know what our Lord doeth. For it is He who makes us not only men, but also righteous, and not we ourselves. And who but He is the doer, in leading us to such a knowledge? For " we have received not the spirit of this world, but the Spirit which is of God, that we might know the things that are freely given to us of God."[8] Whatever good there is, is freely given by Him. And so because this also is good, by Him who graciously imparteth all good is this gift of knowing likewise bestowed; that, in respect of all good things whatever, he that glorieth may glory in the Lord.[9] But the words that follow, " But I have called you friends; for all things that I have heard of my Father I have made known unto you," are so profound, that we must by no means compress them within the limits of the present discourse, but leave them over till another.

---

[1] 1 John iv. 18.　[2] Ps. xix. 9.　[3] Rom. viii. 15.
[4] Rom. xi. 20.　[5] Chap. viii. 35.　[6] Chap. i. 12.

[7] 1 Cor. iv. 7.　[8] 1 Cor. ii. 12.　[9] 1 Cor. i. 31.

TRACTATE LXXXVI.

CHAPTER XV. 15, 16.

1. IT is a worthy subject of inquiry how these words of the Lord are to be understood, " But I have called you friends; for all things that I have heard of my Father I have made known unto you." For who is there that dare affirm or believe that any man knoweth all things that the only-begotten Son hath heard of the Father; when there is no one that can comprehend even how He heareth any word of the Father, being as He is Himself the only Word of the Father? Nay more, is it not the case that a little afterwards, in this same discourse, which He delivered to the disciples between the Supper and His passion, He said, " I have yet many things to say unto you, but ye cannot bear them now "?[1] How, then, are we to understand that He made known unto the disciples all that He had heard of the Father, when there are many things that He saith not, just because He knows that they cannot bear them now? Doubtless what He is yet to do He says that He has done as the same Being who hath made those things which are yet to be.[2] For as He says by the prophet, " They pierced my hands and my feet,"[3] and not, They will yet pierce; but

---

[1] Chap. xvi. 12.　[2] Isa. xlv. 11.　[3] Ps. xxii. 16.

speaking as it were of the past, and yet predicting what was still in the future: so also in the passage before us He declares that He has made known to the disciples all, that He knows He will yet make known in that fullness of knowledge, whereof the apostle says, " But when that which is perfect is come, then that which is in part shall be done away." For in the same place he adds: " Now I know in part, but then shall I know, even as also I am known: and now through a glass in a riddle, but then face to face." [1] For the same apostle also says that we have been saved by the washing of regeneration,[2] and yet declares in another place, " We are saved by hope: but hope that is seen is no hope; for what a man seeth, why doth he yet hope for? But if we hope for that we see not, then do we with patience wait for it." [3] To a similar purpose it is also said by his fellow-apostle Peter, " In whom, though now seeing Him not, ye believe; and in whom, when ye see Him, ye shall rejoice with a joy unspeakable and glorious: receiving the reward of faith, even the salvation of your souls." [4] If, then, it is now the season of faith, and faith's reward is the salvation of our souls; who, in that faith which worketh by love,[5] can doubt that the day must come to an end, and at its close the reward be received; not only the redemption of our body, whereof the Apostle Paul speaketh,[6] but also the salvation of our souls, as we are told by the Apostle Peter? For the felicity springing from both is at this present time, and in the existing state of mortality, a matter rather of hope than of actual possession. But this it concerns us to remember, that our outward man, to wit the body, is still decaying; but the inward, that is, the soul, is being renewed day by day.[7] Accordingly, while we are waiting for the immortality of the flesh and salvation of our souls in the future, yet with the pledge we have received, it may be said that we are saved already; so that knowledge of all things which the Only-begotten hath heard of the Father we are to regard as a matter of hope still lying in the future, although declared by Christ as something He had already imparted.

2. " Ye have not chosen me," He says, " but I have chosen you." Grace such as that is ineffable. For what were we so long as Christ had not yet chosen us, and we were therefore still destitute of love? For he who hath chosen Him, how can he love Him? Were we, think you, in that condition which is sung of in the psalm: " I had rather be an abject in the house of the Lord, than dwell in the tents of wickedness "? [8] Certainly not. What were we then, but sinful and lost? We had not yet come to believe on Him, in order to lead to His choosing us; for if it were those who already believed that He chose, then was He chosen Himself, prior to His choosing. But how could He say, " Ye have not chosen me," save only because His mercy anticipated us? [9] Here surely is at fault the vain reasoning of those who defend the foreknowledge of God in opposition to His grace, and with this view declare that we were chosen before the foundation of the world,[10] because God foreknew that we should be good, but not that He Himself would make us good. So says not He, who declares, " Ye have not chosen me." For had He chosen us on the ground that He foreknew that we should be good, then would He also have foreknown that we would not be the first to make choice of Him. For in no other way could we possibly be good: unless, forsooth, one could be called good who has never made good his choice. What was it then that He chose in those who were not good? For they were not chosen because of their goodness, inasmuch as they could not be good without being chosen. Otherwise grace is no more grace, if we maintain the priority of merit. Such, certainly, is the election of grace, whereof the apostle says: " Even so then at this present time also there is a remnant saved according to the election of grace." To which he adds: " And if by grace, then is it no more of works; otherwise grace is no more grace." [11] Listen, thou ungrateful one, listen: " Ye have not chosen me, but I have chosen you." Not that thou mayest say, I am chosen because I already believed. For if thou wert believing in Him, then hadst thou already chosen Him. But listen: " Ye have not chosen me." Not that thou mayest say, Before I believed I was already doing good works, and therefore was I chosen. For what good work can be prior to faith, when the apostle says, " Whatsoever is not of faith is sin "? [12] What, then, are we to say on hearing such words, " Ye have not chosen me," but that we were evil, and were chosen in order that we might be good through the grace of Him who chose us? For it is not by grace, if merit preceded: but it is of grace; and therefore that grace did not find, but effected the merit.

3. See then, beloved, how it is that He chooseth not the good, but maketh those whom He has chosen good. " I have chosen

[1] 1 Cor. xiii. 10, 12.   [2] Tit. iii. 5.   [3] Rom. viii. 24, 25.
[4] 1 Pet. i. 8, 9.   [5] Gal. v. 6.   [6] Rom. viii. 23.
[7] 2 Cor. iv. 16.   23

[8] Ps. lxxxiv. 10.   [9] Ps. lix. 10.   [10] Eph. i. 4
[11] Rom. xi. 5, 6.   [12] Rom. xiv. 23.

you," He saith, "and appointed you that ye should go and bring forth fruit, and [that] your fruit should remain." And is not that the fruit, whereof He had already said, "Without me ye can do nothing"?[1] He hath chosen therefore, and appointed that we should go and bring forth fruit; and no fruit, accordingly, had we to induce His choice of us. "That ye should go," He said, "and bring forth fruit." We go to bring forth, and He Himself is the way wherein we go, and wherein He hath appointed us to go. And so His mercy hath anticipated us in all.

[1] Chap. xv. 5.

"And that your fruit," He saith, "should remain; that whatsoever ye shall ask of the Father in my name, He may give it you." Accordingly let love remain; for He Himself is our fruit. And this love lies at present in longing desire, not yet in fullness of enjoyment; and whatsoever with that longing desire we shall ask in the name of the only-begotten Son, the Father giveth us. But what is not expedient for our salvation to receive, let us not imagine that we ask that in the Saviour's name: but we ask in the name of the Saviour only that which really belongs to the way of salvation.

TRACTATE LXXXVII.

Chapter XV. 17–19.

1. In the Gospel lesson which precedes this one, the Lord had said: "Ye have not chosen me, but I have chosen you, and appointed you, that ye should go and bring forth fruit, and [that] your fruit should remain; that whatsoever ye shall ask of the Father in my name, He may give it you." On these words you remember that we have already discoursed, as the Lord enabled us. But here, that is, in the succeeding lesson which you have heard read, He says: "These things I command you, that ye love one another." And thereby we are to understand that this is our fruit, of which He had said, "I have chosen you, that ye should go and bring forth fruit, and [that] your fruit should remain." And what He subjoined, "That whatsoever ye shall ask of the Father in my name, He may give it you," He will certainly give us if we love one another; seeing that this very thing He has also given us, in choosing us when we had no fruit, because we had chosen Him not; and appointing us that we should bring forth fruit,—that is, that we should love one another,—a fruit that we cannot have apart from Him, just as the branches can do nothing apart from the vine. Our fruit, therefore, is charity, which the apostle explains to be, "Out of a pure heart, and a good conscience, and faith unfeigned."[1] So love we one another, and so love we God. For it would be with no true love that we loved one another, if we loved not God. For every one loves his neighbor as himself if he loves God; and if he loves not God, he loves not himself. For on these two commandments of love hang all the law and the prophets:[2] this is our fruit. And it is in reference, therefore, to such fruit that He gives us commandment when He says, "These things I command you, that ye love one another." In the same way also the Apostle Paul, when wishing to commend the fruit of the Spirit in opposition to the deeds of the flesh, posited this as his principle, saying, "The fruit of the Spirit is love;" and then, as if springing from and bound up in this principle, he wove the others together, which are "joy, peace, long-suffering, kindness, goodness, faith, meekness, temperance."[3] For who can truly rejoice who loves not good as the source of his joy? Who can have true peace, if he have it not with one whom he truly loves? Who can be long-enduring through persevering continuance in good, save through fervent love? Who can be kind, if he love not the person he is aiding? Who can be good, if he is not made so by loving? Who can be sound in the faith, without that faith which worketh by love? Whose meekness can be beneficial in character, if not regulated by love? And who will abstain from that which is debasing, if he love not that which dignifies? Appropriately, therefore, does the good Master so frequently commend love, as the only thing needing to be commended, without which all other good things can be of no avail, and which cannot be possessed

[1] 1 Tim. i. 5.   [2] Matt. xxii. 40.   [3] Gal. v. 22.

without bringing with it those other good things that make a man truly good.

2. But alongside of this love we ought also patiently to endure the hatred of the world. For it must of necessity hate those whom it perceives recoiling from that which is loved by itself. But the Lord supplies us with special consolation from His own case, when, after saying, "These things I command you, that ye love one another," He added, "If the world hate you, know that it hated me before [it hated] you." Why then should the member exalt itself above the head? Thou refusest to be in the body if thou art unwilling to endure the hatred of the world along with the Head. "If ye were of the world," He says, "the world would love its own." He says this, of course, of the whole Church, which, by itself, He frequently also calls by the name of the world: as when it is said, "God was in Christ, reconciling the world unto Himself."[1] And this also: "The Son of man came not to condemn the world, but that the world through Him might be saved."[2] And John says in his epistle: "We have an advocate with the Father, Jesus Christ the righteous: and He is the propitiation for our sins; and not for ours only, but also [for those] of the whole world."[3] The whole world then is the Church, and yet the whole world hateth the Church. The world therefore hateth the world, the hostile that which is reconciled, the condemned that which is saved, the polluted that which is cleansed.

3. But that world which God is in Christ reconciling unto Himself, which is saved by Christ, and has all its sins freely pardoned by Christ, has been chosen out of the world that is hostile, condemned, and defiled. For out of that mass, which has all perished in Adam, are formed the vessels of mercy, whereof that world of reconciliation is composed, that is hated by the world which belongeth to the vessels of wrath that are formed out of the same mass and fitted to destruction.[4] Finally, after saying, "If ye were of the world, the world would love its own," He immediately added, "But because

ye are not of the world, but I have chosen you out of the world, therefore the world hateth you." And so these men were themselves also of that world, and, that they might no longer be of it, were chosen out of it, through no merit of their own, for no good works of theirs had preceded; and not by nature, which through free-will had become totally corrupted at its source: but gratuitously, that is, of actual grace. For He who chose the world out of the world, effected for Himself, instead of finding, what He should choose: for "there is a remnant saved according to the election of grace. And if by grace," he adds, "then is it no more of works: otherwise grace is no more grace."[5]

4. But if we are asked about the love which is borne to itself by that world of perdition which hateth the world of redemption; we reply, it loveth itself, of course, with a false love, and not with a true. And hence, it loves itself falsely, and hates itself truly. For he that loveth wickedness, hateth his own soul.[6] And yet it is said to love itself, inasmuch as it loves the wickedness that makes it wicked; and, on the other hand, it is said to hate itself, inasmuch as it loves that which causes it injury. It hates, therefore, the true nature that is in it, and loves the vice: it hates what it is. as made by the goodness of God, and loves what has been wrought in it by free-will. And hence also, if we rightly understand it, we are at once forbidden and commanded to love it: thus, we are forbidden, when it is said to us, "Love not the world;"[7] and we are commanded, when it is said to us, "Love your enemies."[8] These constitute the world that hateth us. And therefore we are forbidden to love in it that which it loves in itself; and we are enjoined to love in it what it hates in itself, namely, the workmanship of God, and the various consolations of His goodness. For we are forbidden to love the vice that is in it, and enjoined to love the nature, while it loves the vice in itself, and hates the nature: so that we may both love and hate it in a right manner. whereas it loves and hates itself perversely.

[1] 2 Cor. v. 19.   [2] John iii. 17.
[3] 1 John ii. 1, 2.   [4] Rom. ix. 21, 23.

[5] Rom. xi. 5, 6.
[6] Ps. xi. 5. See Tract. LXXXIII. sec. 3, note 4.
[7] 1 John ii. 15.   [8] Luke vi. 27.

TRACTATE LXXXVIII.

Chapter XV. 20, 21.

1. The Lord, in exhorting His servants to endure with patience the hatred of the world, proposes to them no greater and better example than His own; seeing that, as the Apostle Peter says, "Christ suffered for us, leaving us an example, that we should follow His steps." [1] And if we really do so, we do it by His assistance, who said, "Without me ye can do nothing." But further, to those to whom He had already said, "If the world hate you, know that it hated me before [it hated] you," He now also says in the word you have just been hearing, when the Gospel was read, "Remember my word that I said unto you, The servant is not greater than his lord: if they have persecuted me, they will also persecute you; if they have kept my saying, they will keep yours also." Now in saying, "The servant is not greater than his lord," does He not clearly indicate how He would have us understand what He had said above, "Henceforth I call you not servants"? [2] For, you see, He calleth them servants. For what else can the words imply, "The servant is not greater than his lord: if they have persecuted me, they will also persecute you"? It is clear, therefore, that when it is said, "Henceforth I call you not servants," He is to be understood as speaking of that servant [3] who abideth not in the house for ever,[4] but is characterized by the fear which love casteth out;[5] whereas, when it is here said, "The servant is not greater than his lord: if they have persecuted me, they will also persecute you," that servant is meant who is distinguished by the clean fear which endureth for ever.[6] For this is the servant who is yet to hear, "Well done, thou good servant: enter thou into the joy of thy Lord."[7]

2. "But all these things," He says, "will they do unto you for my name's sake, because they know not Him that sent me." And what are "all these things" that "they will do," but what He has just said, namely, that they will hate and persecute you, and despise your word? For if they kept not their word, and yet neither hated nor persecuted them; or if they even hated, but did not persecute them: it would not be *all these things* that they did. But "all these things will they do unto

you for my name's sake,"—what else is that but to say, they will hate me in you, they will persecute me in you; and your word, just because it is mine, they will not keep? For "all these things will they do unto you for my name's sake:" not for yours, but *mine*. So much the more miserable, therefore, are those who do such things on account of that name, as those are blessed who suffer such things in its behalf: as He Himself elsewhere saith, "Blessed are they that suffer persecution for righteousness' sake."[8] For that is on my account, or "for my name's sake;" because, as we are taught by the apostle, "He is made of God unto us wisdom, and righteousness, and santification, and redemption; that, according as it is written, He that glorieth, let him glory in the Lord."[9] For the wicked do such things to the wicked, but not for righteousness' sake; and therefore both are alike miserable, those who do, and those who suffer them. The good also do such things to the wicked: where, although the former do so for righteousness' sake, yet the latter suffer them not on the same behalf.

3. But some one says, If, when the wicked persecute the good for the name of Christ, the good suffer for righteousness' sake, then surely it is for righteousness' sake that the wicked do so to them; and if such is the case, then also, when the good persecute the wicked for righteousness' sake, it is for righteousness' sake likewise that the wicked suffer. For if the wicked can assail the good with persecution for the name of Christ, why cannot the wicked suffer persecution at the hands of the good on the same account; and what is that, but for righteousness' sake? For if the good act not so on the same account as that on which the wicked suffer, because the good do so for righteousness' sake, while the wicked suffer for unrighteousness, so then neither can the wicked act so on the same account as that for which the good suffer, because the wicked do so by unrighteousness, while the good suffer for righteousness' sake. And how then will that be true, "All these things will they do unto you for my name's sake," when the former do it not for the name of Christ, that is, for righteousness' sake, but because of their own iniquity? Such a question is solved in this way, if only we understand the words,

---

[1] 1 Pet. ii. 21.   [2] Chap. xv. 15, xiii. 16.
[3] See above, Tract. LXXXV. sec. 3.   [4] Chap. viii. 35.
[5] 1 John iv. 18.   [6] Ps. xix. 9.   [7] Matt. xxv. 21.   [8] Matt. v. 10.   [9] 1 Cor. i. 30, 31.

'All these things will they do unto you for my name's sake,'' as referring entirely to the righteous, as if it had been said, All these things will ye suffer at their hands for my name's sake, so that the words, "they will do unto you," are equivalent to these, Ye will suffer at their hands. But if "for my name's sake'' is to be taken as if He had said, For my name's sake which they hate in you, so also may the other be taken for that righteousness' sake which they hate in you; and in this way the good, when they institute persecution against the wicked, may be rightly said to do so both for righteousness' sake, in their love for which they persecute the wicked, and for that wickedness' sake which they hate in the wicked themselves; and so also the wicked may be said to suffer both for the iniquity that is punished in their persons, and for the righteousness which is exercised in their punishment.

4. It may also be inquired, if the wicked also persecute the wicked, just as ungodly princes and judges, while they were the persecutors of the godly, certainly also punished murderers and adulterers, and all classes of evil-doers whom they ascertained to be acting contrary to the public laws, how are we to understand the words of the Lord, "If ye were of the world, the world would love its own"? (ver. 19.) For those whom it punisheth cannot be loved by the world, which, we see, generally punisheth the classes of crimes mentioned above, save only that the world is both in those who punish such crimes, and in those that love them. Therefore that world, which is to be understood as existing in the wicked and ungodly, both hateth its own in respect of that section of men in whose case it inflicts injury on the criminal, and loveth its own in respect of that other section in whose case it shows favor to its own partners in criminality. Hence, "All these things will they do unto you for my name's sake," is said either in reference to that for the sake of which ye suffer, or to that on account of which they themselves so deal with you, because that which is in you they both hate and persecute. And He added, "Because they know not Him that sent me." This is to be understood as spoken of that knowledge of which it is also elsewhere recorded, "But to know Thee is perfect intelligence."[1] For those who with such a knowledge know the Father, by whom Christ was sent, can in no wise persecute those whom Christ is gathering; for they also themselves are being gathered by Christ along with the others.

[1] Wisd. vi. 16.

TRACTATE LXXXIX.

CHAPTER XV. 22, 23.

1. THE Lord had said above to His disciples, "If they have persecuted me, they will also persecute you; if they have kept my saying, they will keep yours also. But all these things will they do unto you for my name's sake, because they know not Him that sent me." And if we inquire of whom He so spake, we find that He was led on to these words from what He had said before, "If the world hate you, know ye that it hated me before [it hated] you;" and now in adding, "If I had not come and spoken unto them, they had not had sin," He more expressly pointed to the Jews. Of them, therefore, He also uttered the words that precede, for so does the context itself imply. For it is of the same parties that He said, "If I had not come and spoken unto them, they had not had sin;" of whom He also said, "If they have persecuted me, they will also persecute you; if they have kept my saying, they will keep yours also; but all these things will they do unto you for my name's sake, because they know not Him that sent me;" for it is to these words that He also subjoins the following: "If I had not come and spoken unto them, they had not had sin." The Jews, therefore, persecuted Christ, as the Gospel very clearly indicates, and Christ spake to the Jews, not to other nations; and it is they, therefore, that He meant to be understood by the world, that hateth Christ and His disciples; and, indeed, not those alone, but even these latter were shown by Him to belong to the same world. What, then, does He mean by the words, "If I had not come and spoken unto them, they had not had sin"? Was it that the Jews were without sin before Christ came to them in the flesh? Who, though he were the greatest fool, would say so? But it is

some great sin, and not every sin, that He would have to be understood, as it were, under the general designation. For this is the sin wherein all sins are included; and whosoever is free from it, has all his sins forgiven him: and this it is, that they believed not on Christ, who came for the very purpose of enlisting their faith. From this sin, had He not come, they would certainly have been free. His advent has become as much fraught with destruction to unbelievers, as it is with salvation to those that believe; for He, the Head and Prince of the apostles, has Himself, as it were, become what they declared of themselves, "to some, indeed, the savour of life unto life; and to some the savour of death unto death." [1]

2. But when He went on to say, "But now they have no excuse for their sin," some may be moved to inquire whether those to whom Christ neither came nor spake, have an excuse for their sin. For if they have not, why is it said here that these had none, on the very ground that He did come and speak to them? And if they have, have they it to the extent of thereby being barred from punishment, or of receiving it in a milder degree? To these inquiries, with the Lord's help and to the best of my capacity, I reply, that such have an excuse, not for every one of their sins, but for this sin of not believing on Christ, inasmuch as He came not and spake not to them. But it is not in the number of such that those are to be included, to whom He came in the persons of His disciples, and to whom He spake by them, as He also does at present; for by His Church He has come, and by His Church He speaks to the Gentiles. For to this are to be referred the words that He spake, "He that receiveth you, receiveth me;" [2] and, "He that despiseth you, despiseth me." [3] "Or would ye," says the Apostle Paul, "have a proof of Him that speaketh in me, namely Christ." [4]

3. It remains for us to inquire, whether those who, prior to the coming of Christ in His Church to the Gentiles and to their hearing of His Gospel, have been, or are now being, overtaken by the close of this life, can have such an excuse? Evidently they can, but not on that account can they escape damnation. "For as many as have sinned without the law, shall also perish without the law; and as many as have sinned in the law, shall be judged by the law." [5] And these words of the apostle, inasmuch as his saying, "they shall perish," has a more terrible sound than when he says, "they shall be judged,"

seem to show that such an excuse can not only avail them nothing, but even becomes an additional aggravation. For those that excuse themselves because they did not hear, "shall perish without the law."

4. But it is also a worthy subject of inquiry, whether those who met the words they heard with contempt, and even with opposition, and that not merely by contradicting them, but also by persecuting in their hatred those from whom they heard them, are to be reckoned among those in regard to whom the words, "they shall be judged by the law," convey somewhat of a milder sound. But if it is one thing to perish without the law, and another to be judged by the law; and the former is the heavier, the latter the lighter punishment: such, without a doubt, are not to have their place assigned in that lighter measure of punishment; for, so far from sinning in the law, they utterly refused to accept the law of Christ, and, as far as in them lay, would have had it altogether annihilated. But those that sin in the law, are such as are in the law, that is, who accept it, and confess that it is holy, and the commandment holy, and just, and good; [6] but fail through infirmity in fulfilling what they cannot doubt is most righteously enjoined therein. These are they in regard to whose fate there may perhaps be some distinction made from the perdition of those who are without the law: and yet if the apostle's words, "they shall be judged by the law," are to be understood as meaning, they shall not perish, what a wonder if it were so! For his discourse was not about infidels and believers to lead him to say so, but about Gentiles and Jews, both of whom, certainly, if they find not salvation in that Saviour who came to seek that which was lost, [7] shall doubtless become the prey of perdition; although it may be said that some shall perish in a more terrible, others in a more mitigated sense; in other words, that some shall suffer a heavier, and others a lighter penalty in their perdition. For he is rightly said to perish as regards God, whoever is separated by punishment from that blessedness which He bestows on His saints, and the diversity of punishments is as great as the diversity of sins; but the mode thereof is accounted too deep by divine wisdom for human guessing to scrutinize or express. At all events, those to whom Christ came, and to whom He spake, have not, for their great sin of unbelief, any such excuse as may enable them to say, We saw not, we heard not: whether it be that such an excuse would not be sustained by Him whose judg-

---

[1] 2 Cor. ii. 16.　　[2] Matt. x. 40.　　[3] Luke x. 16.
[4] 2 Cor. xiii. 3.　　[5] Rom. ii. 12.　　[6] Rom. vii. 12.　　[7] Luke xix. 10.

ments are unsearchable, or whether it would, and that, if not for their entire deliverance from damnation, at least for its partial alleviation.

5. "He that nateth me," He says, "hateth my Father also." Here it may be said to us, Who can hate one whom he knows not? And certainly before saying, "If I had not come and spoken unto them, they had not had sin," He had said to His disciples, "These things will they do unto you, because they know not Him that sent me." How, then, do they both know not, and hate? For if the notion they have formed of Him is not that which He is in Himself, but some unknown conjecture of their own, then certainly it is not Himself they are found to hate, but that figment which they devise or rather suspect in their error. And yet, were it not that men could hate that which they know not, the Truth would not have asserted both, namely, that they both know not, and hate His Father. But such a possibility, if by the Lord's help we are able to show it, cannot be demonstrated at present, as this discourse must now be brought to a close.

TRACTATE XC.

Chapter XV. 23.

1. The Lord says, as you have just been hearing, "He that hateth me, hateth my Father also;" and yet He had said a little before, "These things will they do unto you, because they know not Him that sent me." A question therefore arises that cannot be overlooked, how they can hate one whom they know not? For if it is not God as He really is, but something else, I know not what, that they suspect or believe Him to be, and hate this; then assuredly it is not God Himself that they hate, but the thing they conceive in their own erroneous suspicion or baseless credulity; and if they think of Him as He really is, how can they be said to know Him not? It may be the case, indeed, with regard to men, that we frequently love those whom we have never seen; and in this way it can, on the other hand, be none the less impossible that we should hate those whom we have never seen. The report, for instance, whether good or bad, about some preacher, leads us not improperly to love or to hate the unknown. But if the report is truthful, how can one, of whom we have got such true accounts, be spoken of as unknown? Is it because we have not seen his face? And yet, though he himself does not see it, he can be known to no one better than to himself. The knowledge of any one, therefore, is not conveyed to us in his bodily countenance, but only lies open to our apprehension when his life and character are revealed. Otherwise no one would be able to know himself, because unable to see his own face. But surely he knows himself more certainly than he is known to others, inasmuch as by inward inspection he can the more certainly see what he is conscious of, what he desires, what he is living for; and it is when these are likewise laid open to us, that he becomes truly known to ourselves. And as these, accordingly, are commonly brought to us regarding the absent, or even the dead, either by hearsay or correspondence, it thus comes about that people whom we have never seen by face (and yet of whom we are not entirely ignorant), we frequently either hate or love.

2. But in such cases our credulity is frequently at fault; for sometimes even history, and still more ordinary report, turns out to be false. Yet, it ought to be our concern, in order not to be misled by an injurious opinion, seeing we cannot search into the consciences of men, to have a true and certain sentiment about things themselves. I mean, that in regard to this or that man, if we know not whether he is immodest or modest, we should at all events hate immodesty and love modesty: and if in regard to some one or other we know not whether he is unjust or just, we should at any rate love justice and abhor injustice; not such things as we erroneously fancy to ourselves, but such as we believingly perceive according to God's truth, the one to be desired, the other to be shunned; so that, when in regard to things themselves we do desire what ought to be desired, and utterly avoid what ought to be avoided, we may find pardon for the mistaken feelings which we at times, yea, at all times, entertain regarding the actual state of others which is hidden from our eyes. For this, I think, has to do with human temptation, without which we cannot

pass through this life, so that the apostle said, " No temptation should befall you but such as is common to man."[1]   For what is so common to man as inability to inspect the heart of man; and therefore, instead of scrutinizing its inmost recesses, to suspect for the most part something very different from what is going on therein?   And although in these dark regions of human realities, that is, of other people's inward thoughts, we cannot clear up our suspicions, because we are only men, yet we ought to restrain our judgments, that is, all definite and fixed opinions, and not judge anything before the time, until the Lord come, and bring to light the hidden things of darkness, and make manifest the counsels of the hearts; and then shall every man have praise of God.[2]   When, therefore, we are falling into no error in regard to the thing itself, so that there is an accordance with right in our reprobation of vice and approbation of virtue; surely, if a mistake is committed in connection with individuals, a temptation so characteristic of man is within the scope of forgiveness.

3. But amid all these darknesses of human hearts, it happens as a thing much to be wondered at and mourned over, that one, whom we account unjust, and who nevertheless is just, and in whom, without knowing it, we love justice, we sometimes avoid, and turn away from, and hinder from approaching us, and refuse to have life and living in common with him; and, if necessity compel the infliction of discipline, whether to save others from harm or bring the person himself back to rectitude, we even pursue him with a salutary harshness; and so afflict a good man as if he were wicked, and one whom unknowingly we love.   This takes place if one, for example's sake, who is modest is believed by us to be the opposite.   For, beyond doubt, if I love a modest person, he is himself the very object that I love; and therefore I love the man himself, and know it not.   And if I hate an immodest person, it is on that account, not him that I hate: for he is not the thing that I hate; and yet to that object of my love, with whom my heart makes continual abode in the love of modesty, I am ignorantly doing an injury, erring as I do, not in the distinction I make between virtue and vice, but in the thick darkness of the human heart.   Accordingly, as it may so happen that a good man may unknowingly hate a good man, or rather loves him without knowing it (for the man himself he loves in loving that which is good; for what the other is, is the very thing that he loves); and without knowing it, hates not the man himself, but that which he supposes him to be: so may it also be the case that an unjust man hates a just man, and, while he opines that he loves one who is unjust like himself, unknowingly loves the just man; and yet so long as he believes him to be unjust, he loves not the man himself, but that which he imagines him to be.   And as it is with another man, so is it also with God.   For, to conclude, had the Jews been asked if they loved God, what other answer would they have given but that they did love Him, and that not with any intentional falsehood, but because erroneously fancying that they did so?   For how could they love the Father of the truth, who were filled with hatred to the truth itself?   For they do not wish their own conduct to be condemned, and it is the truth's task to condemn such conduct; and thus they hated the truth as much as they hated their own punishment, which the truth awards to such.   But they know not that to be the truth which lays its condemnation on such as they: therefore they hate that which they know not; and hating it, they certainly cannot but also hate Him of whom it is born.   And in this way, because they know not the truth, by whose judgment they are condemned, as that which is born of God the Father; of a surety also they both know not, and hate [the Father] Himself.   Miserable men! who, because wishing to be wicked, deny that to be the truth whereby the wicked are condemned.   For they refuse to own that to be what it is, when they ought themselves to refuse to be what they are ; in order that, while it remains the same, they may be changed, lest by its judgment they fall into condemnation.

---

[1] 1 Cor. x. 13.   [2] 1 Cor. iv. 5.

TRACTATE XCI.

Chapter XV. 24, 25.

1. The Lord had said, "He that hateth me, hateth my Father also." For of a certainty he that hateth the truth must also hate Him of whom the truth is born ; on which subject we have already spoken, as we were granted ability. And then He added the words on which we have now to discourse: "If I had not done among [in] them the works which none other man did, they had not had sin." To wit, that great sin whereof He also says before, "If I had not come and spoken unto them, they had not had sin." Their sin was that of not believing on Him who thus spake and wrought. For they were not without sin before He so spake to them and did such works among them; but this sin of theirs, in not believing on Him, is thus specially mentioned because really inclusive in itself of all sins besides. For had they been clear of this one, and believed on Him, all else would also have been forgiven.

2. But what is meant when, after saying, "If I had not done among them works," He immediately added, "which none other man did"? Of a certainty, among all the works of Christ, none seem to be greater than the raising of the dead; and yet we know that the same was done by the prophets of olden time. For Elias did so;[1] and Elisha also, both when alive in the flesh,[2] and when he lay buried in his sepulchre. For when certain men, who were carrying a dead person, had fled thither for refuge from an onset of their enemies, and had laid him down therein, he instantly came again to life.[3] And yet there were some works that Christ did which none other man did: as, when He fed the five thousand men with five loaves, and the four thousand with seven;[4] when He walked on the waters, and gave Peter power to do the same;[5] when He changed the water into wine;[6] when He opened the eyes of a man that was born blind,[7] and many besides, which it would take long to mention. But we are answered, that others also have done works which even He did not, and which no other man has done. For who else save Moses smote the Egyptians with so many and mighty plagues,[8] as when He led the people through the parted waters of the sea,[9] when he obtained manna for them from heaven in their hunger,[10] and water from the rock in their thirst?[11] Who else save Joshua the son of Nun[12] divided the stream of the Jordan for the people to pass over,[13] and by the utterance of a prayer to God bridled and stopped the revolving sun?[14] Who save Samson ever quenched his thirst with water flowing forth from the jawbone of a dead ass?[15] Who save Elias was carried aloft in a chariot of fire?[16] Who save Elisha, as I have just mentioned, after his own body was buried, restored the dead body of another to life? Who else besides Daniel lived unhurt amid the jaws of famishing lions, that were shut up with him?[17] And who else save the three men Ananias, Azariah, and Mishael, ever walked about unharmed in flames that blazed and did not burn?[18]

3. I pass by other examples, as these I consider to be sufficient to show that some of the saints have done wonderful works, which none other man did. But we read of no one whatever of the ancients who cured with such power so many bodily defects, and bad states of the health, and troubles of mortals. For, to say nothing of those individual cases which He healed, as they occurred, by the word of command, the Evangelist Mark says in a certain place: "And at even, when the sun had set, they brought unto Him all that were diseased, and them that were possessed with devils. And all the city was gathered together at the door. And He healed many that were sick of divers diseases, and cast out many devils."[19] And Matthew, in giving us the same account, has also added the prophetic testimony, when he says: "That it might be fulfilled which was spoken by Isaiah the prophet, saying, Himself took our infirmities, and bare our sickness."[20] In another passage also it is said by Mark: "And whithersoever He entered, into villages, or cities, or country, they laid the sick in the streets, and besought Him that they might touch if it were but the border of His garment: and as many as touched Him were made whole."[21] None other man did such things *in* them. For so are we to understand the words *in them*, not

---

[1] 1 Kings xvii. 21, 22.　　[2] 2 Kings iv. 35.　　[3] 2 Kings xiii. 21.
[4] Matt. xiv. 15-21, and xv. 32-38.　　[5] Matt. xiv. 25-29.
[6] John ii. 9.　　[7] John ix. 7.
[8] Ex. vii.-xii.　　[9] Ex. xiv. 21-29.
[10] Ex. xvi.　　[11] Ex. xvii. 6.
[12] "Jesus Nave": Ἰησοῦς (υἱὸς) Ναυῆ, Sept., Josh. i. 1.
[13] Josh. iii.　　[14] Josh. x. 12-14.　　[15] Judg. xv. 19.
[16] 2 Kings ii. 11.　　[17] Dan. vi. 22.　　[18] Dan. iii. 23-27.
[19] Mark. i. 32-34.　　[20] Matt. viii. 17.　　[21] Mark vi. 56.

among them, or in their presence; but directly *in them*, because He healed them. For He wished them to understand the works as those which not only occasioned admiration, but conferred also manifest healing, and were benefits which they ought surely to have requited with love, and not with hatred. He transcends, indeed, the miracles of all besides, in being born of a virgin, and in possessing alone the power, both in His conception and birth, to preserve inviolate the integrity of His mother: but that was done neither before their eyes nor in them. For the knowledge of the truth of such a miracle was reached by the apostles, not through any onlooking that they had in common with others, but in the course of their separate discipleship. Moreover, the fact that on the third day He restored Himself to life from the very tomb, in the flesh wherein He had been slain, and, never thereafter to die, with it ascended into heaven, even surpasses all else that He did: but just as little was this done either in the Jews or before their eyes; nor had it yet been done, when He said, "If I had not done among them the works which none other man did."

4. The works, then, are doubtless those miracles of healing in connection with their bodily complaints which He exhibited to such an extent as no one before had furnished amongst them: for these they saw, and it is in reproaching them therewith that He proceeds to say, "But now have they both seen and hated both me and my Father: but [this cometh to pass] that the word might be ful-filled that is written in their law, They hated me without a cause [gratuitously]." He calls it, their law, not as invented by them, but given to them: just as we say, " Our daily bread;" which, nevertheless, we ask of God in conjoining the words "Give us."[1] But one hates gratuitously who neither seeks advantage from the hatred nor avoids inconvenience: so do the wicked hate the Lord; and so also is He loved by the righteous, that is to say, gratuitously [gratis, freely,] inasmuch as they expect no other gifts beyond Himself, for He Himself will be all in all. But whoever would be disposed to look for something more profound in the words of Christ, "If I had not done among them the works which none other man did" (for although such were done by the Father, or the Holy Spirit, yet no one else did them, for the whole Trinity is one and the same in substance), he will find that it was He who did it even when some man of God did something similar. For in Himself He can do everything by Himself; but without Him no one can do anything. For Christ with the Father and the Holy Spirit are not three Gods, but one God, of whom it is written, " Blessed be the Lord God of Israel, who only doeth wondrous things."[2] No one else, therefore, really himself did the works which He did amongst them; for any one else who did any such works, did them only through His doing. But He Himself did them without any doing on their part.

---

[1] Matt. vi. 11.   [2] Ps. lxxii. 18.

TRACTATE XCII.

CHAPTER XV. 26, 27.

1. THE Lord Jesus, in the discourse which He addressed to His disciples after the supper, when Himself in immediate proximity to His passion, and, as it were, on the eve of departure, and of depriving them of His bodily presence while continuing His spiritual presence to all His disciples till the very end of the world, exhorted them to endure the persecutions of the wicked, whom He distinguished by the name of the world: and from which He also told them that He had chosen the disciples themselves, that they might know it was by the grace of God they were what they were, and by their own vices they had been what they had been. And then His own persecutors and theirs He clearly signified to be the Jews, that it might be perfectly apparent that they also were included in the appellation of that damnable world that persecuteth the saints. And when He had said of them that they knew not Him that sent Him, and yet hated both the Son and the Father, that is, both Him who was sent and Him who sent Him,—of all which we have already treated in previous discourses,—He reached the place where it is said, "This cometh to pass, that the word might be fulfilled that is written in their law, They hated

me without a cause." And then He added, as if by way of consequence, the words whereon we have undertaken at present to discourse : " But when the Comforter is come, whom I will send unto you from the Father, even the Spirit of truth, who proceedeth from the Father, He shall bear witness of me: and ye also shall bear witness, because ye have been with me from the beginning." But what connection has this with what He had just said, " But now have they both seen and hated both me and my Father: but that the word might be fulfilled that is written in their law, They hated me without a cause"? Was it that the Comforter, when He came, even the Spirit of truth, convicted those, who thus saw and hated, by a still clearer testimony? Yea, verily, some even of those who saw, and still hated, He did convert, by this manifestation of Himself, to the faith that worketh by love.[1] To make this view of the passage intelligible, we recall to your mind that so it actually befell. For when on the day of Pentecost the Holy Spirit fell upon an assembly of one hundred and twenty men, among whom were all the apostles; and when they, filled therewith, were speaking in the language of every nation; a goodly number of those who had hated, amazed at the magnitude of the miracle (especially when they perceived in Peter's address so great and divine a testimony borne in behalf of Christ, as that He, who was slain by them and accounted amongst the dead, was proved to have risen again, and to be now alive), were pricked in their hearts and converted; and so became aware of the beneficent character of that precious blood which had been so impiously and cruelly shed, because themselves redeemed by the very blood which they had shed.[2] For the blood of Christ was shed so efficaciously for the remission of all sins, that it could wipe out even the very sin of shedding it. With this therefore in His eye, the Lord said, " They hated me without a cause: but when the Comforter is come, He shall bear witness of me;" saying, as it were, They hated me, and slew me when I stood visibly before their eyes; but such shall be the testimony borne in my behalf by the Comforter, that He will bring them to believe in me when I am no longer visible to their sight.

2. "And ye also," He says, " shall bear witness, because ye have been with me from the beginning." The Holy Spirit shall bear witness, and so also shall ye. For, just because ye have been with me from the beginning,

ye can preach what ye know; which ye cannot do at present, because the fullness of that Spirit is not yet present within you. " He therefore shall testify of me, and ye also shall bear witness:" for the love of God shed abroad in your hearts by the Holy Spirit, who shall be given unto you,[3] will give you the confidence needful for such witnessbearing. And that certainly was still wanting to Peter, when, terrified by the question of a lady's maid, he could give no true testimony; but, contrary to his own promise, was driven by the greatness of his fear thrice to deny Him.[4] But there is no such fear in love, for perfect love casteth out fear.[5] In fine, before the Lord's passion, his slavish fear was questioned by a bond-woman; but after the Lord's resurrection, his free love by the very Lord of freedom:[6] and so on the one occasion he was troubled, on the other tranquillized; there he denied the One he had loved, here he loved the One he had denied. But still even then that very love was weak and straitened, till strengthened and expanded by the Holy Spirit. And then that Spirit, pervading him thus with the fullness of richer grace, kindled his hitherto frigid heart to such a witness-bearing for Christ, and unlocked those lips that in their previous tremor had suppressed the truth, that, when all on whom the Holy Spirit had descended were speaking in the tongues of all nations to the crowds of Jews collected around, he alone broke forth before the others in the promptitude of his testimony in behalf of the Christ, and confounded His murderers with the account of His resurrection. And if any one would enjoy the pleasure of gazing on a sight so charming in its holiness, let him read the Acts of the Apostles:[7] and there let him be filled with amazement at the preaching of the blessed Peter, over whose denial of his Master he had just been mourning; there let him behold that tongue, itself translated from diffidence to confidence, from bondage to liberty, converting to the confession of Christ the tongues of so many of His enemies, not one of which he could bear when lapsing himself into denial. And what shall I say more? In him there shone forth such an effulgence of grace, and such a fullness of the Holy Spirit, and such a weight of most precious truth poured from the lips of the preacher, that he transformed that vast multitude of Jews who were the adversaries and murderers of Christ into men that were ready to die for His name, at whose hands he himself was formerly afraid to die with his Master. All

---

[1] Gal. v. 6   [2] Acts ii. 2.   [3] Rom. v. 5.   [4] Matt. xxvi. 69-74.   [5] 1 John iv. 18.   [6] John xxi. 15.   [7] Acts ii.-v.

this did that Holy Spirit when sent, who had previously only been promised. And it was these great and marvellous gifts of His own that the Lord foresaw, when He said, "They have both seen and hated both me and my Father: that the word might be fulfilled that is written in their law, They hated me without a cause. But when the Comforter is come, whom I will send unto you from the Father, even the Spirit of truth, who proceedeth from the Father, He shall testify of me: and ye also shall bear witness." For He, in bearing witness Himself, and inspiring such witnesses with invincible courage, divested Christ's friends of their fear, and transformed into love the hatred of His enemies.

TRACTATE XCIII.

CHAPTER XVI. 1–4.

1. IN the words preceding this chapter of the Gospel, the Lord strengthened His disciples to endure the hatred of their enemies, and prepared them also by His own example to become the more courageous in imitating Him: adding the promise, that the Holy Spirit should come to bear witness of Him, and also that they themselves could become His witnesses, through the effectual working of His Spirit in their hearts. For such is His meaning when He saith, "He shall bear witness of me, and ye also shall bear witness." That is to say, because He shall bear witness, ye also shall bear witness: He in your hearts, you in your voices; He by inspiration, you by utterance: that the words might be fulfilled, "Their sound hath gone forth into all the earth."[1] For it would have been to little purpose to have exhorted them by His example, had He not also filled them with His Spirit. Just as we see that the Apostle Peter, after having heard His words, when He said, "The servant is not greater than his lord: if they have persecuted me, they will also persecute you;"[2] and seen that already fulfilled in Him, wherein, had example been sufficient, he ought to have imitated the patient endurance of his Lord, yet succumbed and fell into denial, as utterly unable to bear what He saw his Master enduring. But when he really received the gift of the Holy Spirit, he preached Him whom he had denied; and whom he had been afraid to confess, he had no fear now in openly proclaiming. Already, indeed, had he been sufficiently taught by example to know what was proper to be done; but not yet was he inspired with the power to do what he knew: he had got instruction to stand, but not the strength to keep him from falling. But after this was supplied by the Holy Spirit, he preached Christ even to the death, whom, in his fear of death, he had previously denied. And so the Lord in this succeeding chapter, on which we have now to address you, saith, "These things have I spoken unto you, that ye should not be offended." As it is sung in the psalm, "Great peace have they who love Thy law, and nothing shall offend them."[3] Properly enough, therefore, with the promise of the Holy Spirit, by whose operation in their hearts they should be made His witnesses, He added, "These things have I spoken unto you, that ye should not be offended." For when the love of God is shed abroad in our hearts by the Holy Spirit given unto us,[4] they have great peace who love God's law, so that nothing may offend them.

2. And then He expressly declares what they were to suffer: "They shall put you out of the synagogues." But what harm was it for the apostles to be expelled from the Jewish synagogues, as if they were not to separate themselves therefrom, although no one expelled them? Doubtless He meant to announce with reprobation, that the Jews would refuse to receive Christ, from whom they as certainly would refuse to withdraw; and so it would come to pass that the latter, who could not exist without Him, would also be cast out along with Him by those who would not have Him as their place of abode. For certainly, as there was no other people of God than that seed of Abraham, they would, had they only acknowledged and received Christ, have remained as the natural branches in the olive tree;[5] nor would the churches of Christ have been different from the synagogues of the Jews, for they would have been one and the same, had they also desired to abide in Him. But having refused, what remained but that,

---

[1] Ps. xix. 4.　　　　[2] Chap. xv. 20.　　　　[3] Ps. cxix. 165.　　　　[4] Rom. v. 5.　　　　[5] Rom. xi. 17.

continuing themselves out of Christ, they put out of the synagogues those who would not abandon Christ? For having received the Holy Spirit, and so become His witnesses, they would certainly not belong to the class of whom it is said: "Many of the chief rulers of the Jews believed on Him; but for fear of the Jews they dared not confess Him, lest they should be put out of the synagogue: for they loved the praise of men more than the praise of God."[1] And so they believed on Him, but not in the way He wished them to believe when He said: "How can ye believe, who expect honor one of another, and seek not the honor that cometh from God only?"[2] It is, therefore, with those disciples who so believe in Him, that, filled with the Holy Spirit, or, in other words, with the gift of divine grace, they no longer belong to those who, "ignorant of the righteousness of God, and going about to establish their own, have not submitted themselves to the righteousness of God;"[3] nor to those of whom it is said, "They loved the praise of men more than the praise of God:" that the prophecy harmonizes, which finds its fulfillment in their own case: "They shall walk, O Lord, in the light of Thy countenance: and in Thy name shall they rejoice all the day; and in Thy righteousness shall they be exalted: for Thou art the glory of their strength."[4] Rightly enough is it said to such, "They shall cast you out of the synagogues;" that is, they who "have a zeal for God, but not according to knowledge;" because, "ignorant of God's righteousness, and going about to establish their own,"[5] they expel those who are exalted, not in their own righteousness, but in God's, and have no cause to be ashamed at being expelled by men, since He is the glory of their strength.

3. Finally, to what He had thus told them, He added the words: "But the hour cometh, that whosoever killeth you will think that he doeth God service: and these things will they do unto you, because they have not known the Father, nor me." That is to say, they have not known the Father, nor His Son, to whom they think they will be doing service in slaying you. Words which the Lord added in the way of consolation to His own, who should be driven out of the Jewish synagogues. For it is in thus announcing beforehand what evils they would have to endure for their testimony in His behalf, that He said, "They will put you out of the synagogues." Nor does He say, And the hour cometh, that whosoever killeth you will think that he doeth

God service. What then? "*But* the hour cometh:" just in the way He would have spoken, were He foretelling them of something good that would follow such evils. What, then, does He mean by the words, "They will put you out of the synagogues: but the hour cometh"? As if He would have gone on to say this: They, indeed, will scatter you, *but* I will gather you; or, They shall, indeed, scatter you, *but* the hour of your joy cometh. What, then, has the word which He uses, "*but* the hour cometh," to do here, as if He were going on to promise them comfort after their tribulation, when apparently He ought rather to have said, in the form of continuous narration,[6] *And* the hour cometh? But He said not, And it cometh, although predicting the approach of one tribulation after another, instead of comfort after tribulation. Could it have been that such a separation from the synagogues would so discompose them, that they would prefer to die, rather than remain in this life apart from the Jewish assemblies? Far surely would those be from such discomposure, who were seeking, not the praise of men, but of God. What, then, of the words, "They will put you out of the synagogues: but the hour cometh;" when apparently He ought rather to have said, *And* the hour cometh, "that whosoever killeth you will think that he doeth God service"? For it is not even said, But the hour cometh that they shall kill you, as if implying that their comfort for such a separation would be found in the death that would befall them; but "The hour cometh," He says, "that whosoever killeth you will think that he doeth God service." On the whole, I do not think He wished to convey any further meaning than that they might understand and rejoice that they themselves would gain so many to Christ, by being driven out of the Jewish congregations, that it would be found insufficient to expel them, and they would not suffer them to live for fear of all being converted by their preaching to the name of Christ, and so turned away from the observance of Judaism, as if it were the very truth of God. For so ought we to understand the reference of His words to the Jews, when He said of them, "They will put you out of the synagogues." For the witnesses, in other words, the martyrs of Christ, were likewise slain by the Gentiles: they, however, thought not that it was to the true God, but to their own false deities, that they were doing service when they so acted. But every Jew that slew the preachers of Christ reckoned that he was doing God serv-

---

[1] Chap. xii. 42, 43.   [2] Chap. v. 44.   [3] Rom. x. 3.
[4] Ps. lxxxix. 15-17.   [5] Rom. x. 2, 3.   [6] *Indicativo modo.*

ice; believing as he did that all who were converted to Christ were deserting the God of Israel. For it was also by the same reasoning that they were incited to the murder of Christ Himself: because their own words on this subject have also been put on record. "Ye perceive that the whole world is gone after him:"[1] "If we let him live, the Romans will come, and take away both our place and nation." And those of Caiaphas: "It is expedient for us that one man should die for the people, and not that the whole nation should perish."[2] And accordingly in this address He sought by His own example to stimulate His disciples, to whom He had just been saying, "If they have persecuted me, they will also persecute you;"[3] that as in slaying Him they thought they had done God a service, so also would it be in reference to them.

4. Such, then, is the meaning of these words: "They will put you out of the synagogues;" but have no fear of solitude: inasmuch as, when separated from their assembly, you will assemble so many in my name, that they, in very fear lest the temple, that was with them, and all the sacraments of the old law, should be deserted, will slay you: actually, in thus shedding your blood, full of the notion that they are doing God service. An illustration surely of the apostle's words, "They have a zeal for God, but not according to knowledge;"[4] when they imagine that they are doing God service in slaying His servants. Appalling mistake! Is it thus thou wouldst please God by striking down the Godpleaser; and is the living temple of God by thy blows laid level with the ground, that God's temple of stone may not be deserted? Accursed blindness! But it is in part that it has happened to Israel, that the fullness of the Gentiles might come in: in part, I say,

and not totally, has it happened. For not all, but only some of the branches have been broken off, that the wild olive might be ingrafted.[5] For just at the time when the disciples of Christ, filled with the Holy Spirit, were speaking in the tongues of all nations, and performing many divine miracles, and scattering divine utterances on every side, Christ, even though slain, was so beloved, that His disciples, when expelled from the congregations of the Jews, gathered into a congregation of their own a vast multitude of those very Jews, and had no fear of being left to solitude.[6] Whereupon, accordingly, the others, reprobate and blind, being inflamed with wrath, and having a zeal of God, but not according to knowledge, and believing that they were doing God service, put them to death. But He, who was slain for them, gathered those together; just as He had also, before He was slain, instructed them in what was to happen, lest their minds, left ignorant and unprepared, should be cast into trouble by evils, however transient, that were unexpected and unprovided for; but rather by knowing of them beforehand, and sustaining them with patience, might be led onward to everlasting blessing. For that such was the cause of His making these announcements to them beforehand, is shown also by His words that followed: "But these things have I told you, that, when their time shall come, ye may remember that I told you of them." Their hour was an hour of darkness, a midnight hour. But the Lord commanded His loving-kindness in the daytime, and made them sing of it in the night:[7] when the Jewish night threw no confusion of darkness into the day of the Christians, separated as it was from themselves; and when that which could slay the flesh had no power to darken their faith.

---

[1] Chap. xii. 19.   [2] Chap. xi. 48, 50
[3] Chap. xv. 20.   [4] Rom. x. 2.

[5] Rom. xi. 25, 17.   [6] Acts ii.-iv.   [7] Ps. xlii. 8.

TRACTATE XCIV.

CHAPTER XVI. 4-7.

1. WHEN the Lord Jesus had foretold His disciples the persecutions they would have to suffer after His departure, He went on to say: "And these things I said not unto you at the beginning, because I was with you; but now I go my way to Him that sent me." And here the first thing we have to look at is,

whether He had not previously foretold them of the sufferings that were to come. And the three other evangelists make it sufficiently clear that He had uttered such predictions prior to the approach of the supper:[1] which

---

[1] Matt. xxiv. 9; Mark xiii. 9-13; and Luke xxi. 12-17.

was over, according to John, when He spake, and added, "And these things I said not unto you at the beginning, because I was with you." Are we, then, to settle such a question in this way, that they, too, tell us that He was near His passion when He said these things? Then it was not when He was with them at the beginning, that He so spake, for He was on the very eve of departing, and proceeding to the Father: and so also, even according to these evangelists, it is strictly true what is here said, "And these things I said not unto you at the beginning." But what are we to do with the credibility of the Gospel according to Matthew, who relates that such announcements were made to them by the Lord, not only when He was on the eve of sitting down with His disciples to the passover supper, but also at the beginning, when the twelve apostles are for the first time expressed by name, and sent forth on the work of God?[1] What, then, is the meaning of what He says here, "And these things I said not unto you at the beginning, because I was with you;" but that what He says here of the Holy Spirit who was to come to them, and to bear witness, when they should have such ills to endure, this He said not unto them at the beginning, because He was with themselves?

2. The Comforter then, or Advocate (for both form the interpretation of the Greek word, paracléte), had become necessary on Christ's departure: and therefore He had not spoken of Him at the beginning, when He was with them, because His own presence was their comfort; but on the eve of His own departure it behoved Him to speak of His coming, by whom it would be brought about that with love shed abroad in their hearts they would preach the word of God with all boldness; and with Him inwardly bearing witness with them of Christ, they also should bear witness, and feel it to be no cause of stumbling when their Jewish enemies put them out of the synagogues, and slew them, with the thought that they were doing God service; because the charity beareth all things,[2] which was to be shed abroad in their hearts by the gift of the Holy Spirit.[3] In this, therefore, is the whole meaning to be found, that He was to make them His martyrs, that is, His witnesses through the Holy Spirit; so that by His effectual working within them, they would endure the hardships of all kinds of persecution, and, set aglow at that divine fire, lose none of their warmth in the love of preaching. "These things," therefore, He says, "have I told you, that, when their time shall

come, ye may remember that I told you of them" (ver. 4). These things, I say, I have told you, not merely because ye shall have to endure such things, but because, when the Comforter is come, He shall bear witness of me, that ye may not keep them back through fear, and by whom ye yourselves shall also be enabled to bear witness. "And these things I said not unto you at the beginning, because I was with you," and I myself was your comfort through my bodily presence exhibited to your human senses, and which, as infants, ye were able to comprehend.

3. "But now I go my way to Him that sent me; and none of you," He says, "asketh me, Whither goest Thou?" He means that His departure would be such that none would ask Him of that which they should see taking place in broad daylight before their eyes: for previously to this they had asked Him whither He was going, and had been answered that He was going whither they themselves could not then come.[4] Now, however, He promises that He will go away in such a manner that none of them shall ask Him whither He goes. For a cloud received Him when He ascended up from their side; and of His going into heaven they made no verbal inquiry, but had ocular evidence.[5]

4. "But because I have said these things unto you," He adds, "sorrow hath filled your heart." He saw, indeed, what effect these words of His were producing in their hearts; for having not yet within them the spiritual consolation, which they were afterwards to have by the Holy Spirit, what they still saw objectively in Christ they were afraid of losing; and because they could have no doubt they were about to lose Him whose announcements were always true, their human feelings were saddened, because their carnal view of Him was to be left a blank. But He knew what was most expedient for them, because that inward sight, wherewith the Holy Spirit was yet to comfort them, was undoubtedly superior; not by bringing a human body into the bodies of those who saw, but by infusing Himself into the hearts of those who believed. And then He adds, "Nevertheless I tell you the truth, it is expedient for you that I go away. For if I go not away, the Comforter will not come unto you; but if I depart, I will send Him unto you:" as if He had said, It is expedient for you that this form of a servant be taken away from you; as the Word made indeed flesh I dwell among you; but I would not that ye should continue to love me carnally, and, content with such milk, desire to

---

1 Matt. x. 17.　　2 1 Cor. xiii. 7.　　3 Rom. v. 5.　　4 Chap. xiii. 36.　　5 Acts i. 9-11.

remain infants always. "It is expedient for you that I go away: for if I go not away, the Comforter will not come unto you." If I withdraw not the tender nutriment wherewith I have nourished you, ye will acquire no keen relish of solid food; if ye adhere in a carnal way to the flesh, ye will not have room for the Spirit. For what is this, "If I go not away, the Comforter will not come unto you; but if I depart, I will send Him unto you"? Was it that He could not send Him while located here Himself? Who would venture to say so? Neither was it, that where He was, thence the Other had withdrawn, or that He had so come from the Father as that He did not still abide with the Father. And still further, how could He, even when having His own abode on earth, be unable to send Him, who we know came and remained upon Him at His baptism;[1] yea, more, from whom we know that He was never separable? What does it mean, then, "If I go not away, the Comforter will not come unto you;" but that ye cannot receive the Spirit so long as ye continue to know Christ after the flesh? Hence one who had already been made a partaker of the Spirit says, "Though we have known Christ after the flesh, yet now henceforth know we [Him] no more."[2] For now even the very flesh of Christ he did not know in a carnal way, when brought to a spiritual knowledge of the Word that had been made flesh. And such, doubtless, did the good Master wish to intimate, when He said, "If I go not away, the Comforter will not come unto you; but if I depart, I will send Him unto you."

5. But with Christ's bodily departure, both the Father and the Son, as well as the Holy Spirit, were spiritually present with them. For had Christ departed from them in such a sense that it would be in His place, and not along with Him, that the Holy Spirit would be present in them, what becomes of His promise when He said, "Lo, I am with you alway, even to the end of the world;"[3] and, I and the Father "will come unto him, and will make Our abode with him;"[4] seeing that He also promised that He would send the Holy Spirit in such a way that He would be with them for ever? In this way it was, on the other hand, that seeing they were yet out of their present carnal or animal condition to become spiritual, with undoubted certainty also were they yet to have in a more comprehensive way both the Father, and the Son, and the Holy Spirit. But in no one are we to believe that the Father is present without the Son and the Holy Spirit, or the Father and the Son without the Holy Spirit, or the Son without the Father and the Holy Spirit, or the Holy Spirit without the Father and the Son, or the Father and the Holy Spirit without the Son; but wherever any one of Them is, there also is the Trinity, one God. But here the Trinity had to be suggested in such a way that, although there was no diversity of essence, yet the personal distinction of each one separately should be presented to notice; where those who have a right understanding can never imagine a separation of natures.

6. But that which follows, "And when He is come, He will convince the world of sin, and of righteousness, and of judgment: of sin, indeed, because they believe not on me; but of righteousness, because I go to the Father, and ye shall see me no more; and of judgment, because the prince of this world is judged" (vers. 8–11); as if it were sin simply not to believe on Christ; and as if it were very righteousness not to see Christ; and as if that were the very judgment, that the prince of this world, that is, the devil, is judged: all this is very obscure, and cannot be included in the present discourse, lest brevity only increase the obscurity; but must rather be deferred till another occasion for such explanation as the Lord may enable us to give.

---

[1] Chap. i. 32.   [2] 2 Cor. v. 16.   [3] Matt. xxviii. 20.   [4] Chap. xiv. 23.

TRACTATE XCV.

CHAPTER XVI. 8–11.

1. THE Lord, when promising that He would send the Holy Spirit, said, "When He is come, He will reprove the world of sin, and of righteousness, and of judgment." What does it mean? Is it that the Lord Christ did not reprove the world of sin, when He said, "If I had not come and spoken unto them, they had not had sin; but now they have no cloak for their sin"? And that no one may take it into his head to say that this applied

properly to the Jews, and not to the world, did He not say in another place, " If ye were of the world, the world would love his own " ? [1] Did He not reprove it of righteousness, when He said, " O righteous Father, the world hath not known Thee " ? [2] And did He not reprove it of judgment when He declared that He would say to those on the left hand, " Depart ye into everlasting fire, prepared for the devil and his angels " ? [3] And many other passages are to be found in the holy evangel, where Christ reproveth the world of these things. Why is it, then, He attributeth this to the Holy Spirit, as if it were His proper prerogative ? Is it that, because Christ spake only among the nation of the Jews, He does not appear to have reproved the world, inasmuch as one may be understood to be reproved who actually hears the reprover; while the Holy Spirit, who was in His disciples when scattered throughout the whole world, is to be understood as having reproved not one nation, but the world ? For mark what He said to them when about to ascend into heaven: " It is not for you to know the times or the moments, which the Father hath put in His own power. But ye shall receive the power of the Holy Spirit, that cometh upon you: and ye shall be witnesses unto me in Jerusalem, and in all Judea, and in Samaria, and unto the uttermost part of the earth." [4] Surely this is to reprove the world. But would any one venture to say that the Holy Spirit reproveth the world through the disciples of Christ, and that Christ Himself doth not, when the apostle exclaims, " Would ye receive a proof of Him that speaketh in me, namely Christ ? " [5] And so those, surely, whom the Holy Spirit reproveth, Christ reproveth likewise. But in my opinion, because there was to be shed abroad in their hearts by the Holy Spirit that love [6] which casteth out the fear, [7] that might have hindered them from venturing to reprove the world which bristled with persecutions, therefore it was that He said, " He shall reprove the world: " as if He would have said, He shall shed abroad love in your hearts, and, having your fear thereby expelled, ye shall have freedom to reprove. We have frequently said, however, that the operations of the Trinity are inseparable; [8] but the Persons needed to be set forth one by one, that not only without separating Them, but also without confounding Them together, we may have a right understanding both of Their Unity and Trinity.

2. He next explains what He has said " of sin, and of righteousness, and of judgment." " Of sin indeed," He says, " because they have believed not on me." For this sin, as if it were the only one, He has put before the others; because with the continuance of this one, all others are retained, and in the removal of this, the others are remitted. " But of righteousness," He adds, " because I go to the Father, and ye shall see me no more." And here we have to consider in the first place, if any one is rightly reproved of sin, how he may also be rightly reproved of righteousness. For if a sinner ought to be reproved just because he is a sinner, will any one imagine that a righteous man is also to be reproved because he is righteous ? Surely not. For if at any time a righteous man also is reproved, he is rightly reproved on this account, that, according to Scripture, " There is not a just man upon earth, that doeth good, and sinneth not." And accordingly, when a righteous man is reproved, he is reproved of sin, and not of righteousness. Since in that divine utterance also, where we read, " Be not made righteous over-much," [9] there is notice taken, not of the righteousness of the wise man, but of the pride of the presumptuous. The man, therefore, that becomes " righteous over-much," by that very excess becomes unrighteous. For he makes himself righteous over-much who says that he has no sin, or who imagines that he is made righteous, not by the grace of God, but by the sufficiency of his own will: nor is he righteous through living righteously, but is rather self-inflated with the imagination of being what he is not. By what means, then, is the world to be reproved of righteousness, if not by the righteousness of believers ? Accordingly, it is convinced of sin, because it believeth not on Christ; and it is convinced of the righteousness of those who do believe. For the very comparison with believers is itself a reproving of unbelievers. And this the exposition itself sufficiently indicates. For in wishing to open up what He has said, He adds, " Of righteousness, because I go to the Father, and ye shall see me no more." He does not say, And they shall see me no more; that is, those of whom He had said, " because they have believed not on me." Of them He spake, when expounding what He denominated sin, in the words, " because they have believed not on me; " but when expounding what He called righteousness, whereof the world is convicted, He turned to those to whom He was speaking, and said, " because I go to the Father, and ye shall see me no more." Wherefore it

---

[1] Chap. xv. 22, 19.   [2] Chap. xvii. 25.   [3] Matt. xxv. 41.
[4] Acts i. 7, 8.   [5] 2 Cor. xiii. 3.   [6] Rom. v. 5.
[7] 1 John iv. 18.   [8] Tract. XX.   [9] Eccles. vii. 20, 16.

is of its own sins, but of others' righteousness, that the world is convicted, just as darkness is reproved by the light: "For all things," says the apostle, "that are reproved, are made manifest by the light."[1] For the magnitude of the evil chargeable on those who do not believe, may be made apparent not only by itself, but also by the goodness of those who do believe. And since the cry of unbelievers usually is, How can we believe what we do not see? so the righteousness of unbelievers just required this very definition, "Because I go to the Father, and ye shall see me no more." For blessed are they who see not, and yet do believe.[2] For of those also who saw Christ, the faith in Him that met with commendation was not that they believed what they saw, namely, the Son of man; but that they believed what they did not see, namely, the Son of God. But after His servant-form was itself also withdrawn from their view, then in every respect was the word truly fulfilled, "The just liveth by faith."[3] For "faith," according to the definition in the Epistle to the Hebrews, "is the confidence of those that hope,[4] the conviction of things that are not seen."

3. But how are we to understand, "Ye shall see me no more"? For He saith not, I go to the Father, and ye shall not see me, so as to be understood as referring to the interval of time when He would not be seen, whether short or long, but at all events terminable; but in saying, "Ye shall see me no more," as if a truth announced beforehand that they would never see Christ in all time coming. Is this the righteousness we speak of, never to see Christ, and yet to believe on Him; seeing that the faith whereby the just liveth is commended on the very ground of believing that the Christ whom it seeth not meanwhile, it shall see some day? Once more, in reference to this righteousness, are we to say that the Apostle Paul was not righteous when confessing that He had seen Christ after His ascension into heaven,[5] which was undoubtedly the time of which He had already said, "Ye shall see me no more"? Was Stephen, that hero of surpassing renown, not righteous in the spirit of this righteousness, who, when they were stoning him, exclaimed, "Behold, I see the heavens opened, and the Son of man standing on the right hand of God"?[6] What, then, is meant by "I go to the Father, and ye shall see me no more," but just this, As I am while with you now? For at that time He was still mortal in the likeness of sinful flesh.[7] He could suffer hunger and thirst, be wearied, and sleep; and this Christ, that is, Christ in such a condition, they were no more to see after He had passed from this world to the Father; and such, also, is the righteousness of faith, whereof the apostle says, "Though we have known Christ after the flesh, yet now henceforth know we Him no more."[8] This, then, He says, will be your righteousness whereof the world shall be reproved, "because I go to the Father, and ye shall see me no more:" seeing that ye shall believe in me as in one whom ye shall not see; and when ye shall see me as I shall be then, ye shall not see me as I am while with you meanwhile; ye shall not see me in my humility, but in my exaltation; nor in my mortality, but in my eternity; nor at the bar, but on the throne of judgment: and by this faith of yours, in other words, your righteousness, the Holy Spirit will reprove an unbelieving world.

4. He will also reprove it "of judgment, because the prince of this world is judged." Who is this, save he of whom He saith in another place, "Behold, the prince of the world cometh, and shall find nothing in me;"[9] that is, nothing within his jurisdiction, nothing belonging to him; in fact, no sin at all? For thereby is the devil the prince of the world. For it is not of the heavens and of the earth, and of all that is in them, that the devil is prince, in the sense in which the world is to be understood, when it is said, "And the world was made by Him;" but the devil is prince of that world, whereof in the same passage He immediately afterwards subjoins the words, "And the world knew Him not;"[10] that is, unbelieving men, wherewith the world through its utmost extent is filled: among whom the believing world groaneth, which He, who made the world, chose out of the world; and of whom He saith Himself, "The Son of man came not to judge the world, but that the world through Him might be saved."[11] He is the judge by whom the world is condemned, the helper whereby the world is saved: for just as a tree is full of foliage and fruit, or a field of chaff and wheat, so is the world full of believers and unbelievers. Therefore the prince of this world, that is, the prince of the darkness thereof, or of unbelievers, out of whose hands that world is rescued, to which it is said, "Ye were at one time darkness, but now are ye light in the Lord:"[12] the prince of this world, of whom He elsewhere saith, "Now is the prince of this world cast out,"[13] is assuredly judged, inas-

---

[1] Eph. v. 13.   [2] Chap. xx. 29.
[3] Rom. i. 17; Hab. ii. 4; and Heb. xi. 1.
[4] *Sperantium substantia.*   [5] 1 Cor. xv. 8.
[6] Acts vii. 56.

[7] Rom. viii. 3.   [8] 2 Cor. v. 16.   [9] Chap. xiv. 30.
[10] Chap. i. 10.   [11] Chap. i. 17.   [12] Eph. v. 8.
[13] Chap. xii. 31.

much as he is irrevocably destined to the judgment of everlasting fire. And so of this judgment, by which the prince of the world is judged, is the world reproved by the Holy Spirit; for it is judged along with its prince, whom it imitates in its own pride and impiety. "For if God," in the words of the Apostle Peter, "spared not the angels that sinned, but thrust them into prisons of infernal darkness, and gave them up to be reserved for punishment in the judgment,"[1] how is the world otherwise than reproved of this judgment by the Holy Spirit, when it is in the Holy Spirit that the apostle so speaketh? Let men, therefore, believe in Christ, that they be not convicted of the sin of their own unbelief, whereby all sins are retained: let them make their way into the number of believers, that they be not convicted of the righteousness of those, whom, as justified, they fail to imitate: let them beware of that future judgment, that they be not judged with the prince of the world, whom, judged as he is, they continue to imitate. For the unbending pride of mortals can have no thought of being spared itself, as it is thus called to think with terror of the punishment that overtook the pride of angels.

[1] 2 Pet. ii. 4.

TRACTATE XCVI.

CHAPTER XVI. 12, 13.

1. IN this portion of the holy Gospel, where the Lord says to His disciples, "I have yet many things to say unto you, but ye cannot bear them now," there meets us first this subject of needful inquiry, how it was that He said a little before, "All things that I have heard of my Father I have made known unto you,"[1] and yet says here, "I have yet many things to say unto you, but ye cannot bear them now." But how it was that He spake of what He had not yet done as if it were done, just as the prophet testifies that God has made those things which are still to come, when He says, "Who hath made those things which are still to come,"[2] we have already explained as well as we could when dealing with those words themselves. Now, however, you are perhaps wishing to know what those things were which the apostles were then unable to bear. But which of us would venture to assert his own present capacity for what they wanted the ability to receive? And on this account you are neither to expect me to tell you things which perhaps I could not comprehend myself were they told me by another; nor would you be able to bear them, even were I talented enough to let you hear of things that are above your comprehension. It may be, indeed, that some among you are fit enough already to comprehend things which are still beyond the grasp of others; and if not all about which the divine Master said, "I have yet many things to say unto you," yet perhaps some of them: but what they were which He Himself thus omitted to tell them, it would be rash to have even the wish to presume to say. For at that time the apostles were not yet fitted even to die for Christ, when He said to them, "Ye cannot follow me now," and when the very foremost of them, Peter, who had presumptuously declared that he was already able, met with a different experience from what he anticipated:[3] and yet afterwards a countless number both of men and women, boys and girls, youths and maidens, old and young, were crowned with martyrdom; and the sheep were found able for that which, when the Lord spake these words, the shepherds were still unable to bear. Ought, then, those sheep to have been asked, in that extremity of trial, when required to contend for the truth even unto death, and to shed their blood for the name or doctrine of Christ;—ought they, I say, to have been asked, Which of you would venture to account himself ready for martyrdom, for which Peter was still unfitted, even when taught face to face by the Lord Himself? In the same way, therefore, one may say that Christian people, even when desiring to hear, ought not to be told what those things are of which the Lord then said, "I have yet many things to say unto you, but ye cannot bear them now." If the apostles were still unable, much more so are ye: although it may be that many now can bear what Peter then

[1] Chap. xv. 15.　　[2] Isa. xlv. 11, Septuagint.　　[3] Chap. xiii. 36-38.

could not, in the same way as many are able to be crowned with martyrdom which at that time was still beyond the power of Peter, more especially that now the Holy Spirit has been sent, as He was not then, of whom He went on immediately to add the words, "Howbeit when He, the Spirit of truth, is come, He will teach you all truth," thereby showing of a certainty that they could not bear what He had still to say, because the Holy Spirit had not yet come upon them.

2. Well, then, let us grant that it is so, that many can now bear those things when the Holy Spirit has been sent, which could not then, prior to His coming, be borne by the disciples: do we on that account know what it is that He would not say, as we should know it were we reading or hearing it as uttered by Himself? For it is one thing to know whether we or you could bear it; but quite another to know what it is, whether able to be borne or not. But when He Himself was silent about such things, which of us could say, It is this or that? Or if he venture to say it, how will he prove it? For who could manifest such vanity or recklessness as when saying what he pleased to whom he pleased, even though true, to affirm without any divine authority that it was the very thing which the Lord on that occasion refused to utter? Which of us could do such a thing without incurring the severest charge of rashness,—a thing which gets no countenance from prophetic or apostolic authority? For surely if we had read any such thing in the books confirmed by canonical authority, which were written after our Lord's ascension, it would not have been enough to have read such a statement, had we not also read in the same place that this was actually one of those things which the Lord was then unwilling to tell His disciples, because they were unable to bear them. As if, for example, I were to say that the words which we read at the opening of this Gospel, " In the beginning was the Word, and the Word was with God, and the Word was God; the same was in the beginning with God:" and those which follow, because they were written afterwards, and yet without any mention of their being uttered by the Lord Jesus when He was here in the flesh, but were written by one of His apostles, to whom they were revealed by His Spirit, were some of those which the Lord would not then utter, because the disciples were unable to bear them; who would listen to me in making so rash a statement? But if in the same passage where we read the one we were also to read the other, who would not give due credence to such an apostle?

3. But it seems to me also very absurd to say that the disciples could not then have borne what we find recorded, about things invisible and of profoundest import, in the apostolic epistles, which were written in after days, and of which there is no mention that the Lord uttered them when His visible presence was with them. For why could they not bear then what is now read in their books, and borne by every one, even though not understood? Some things there are, indeed, in the Holy Scriptures which unbelieving men both have no understanding of when they read or hear them, and cannot bear when they are read or heard: as the pagans, that the world was made by Him who was crucified; as the Jews, that He could be the Son of God, who broke up their mode of observing the Sabbath; as the Sabellians, that the Father, and Son, and Holy Spirit are a Trinity; as the Arians, that the Son is equal to the Father, and the Holy Spirit to the Father and Son; as the Photinians, that Christ is not only man like ourselves, but God also, equal to God the Father; as the Manicheans, that Christ Jesus, by whom we must be saved, condescended to be born in the flesh and of the flesh of man: and all others of divers perverse sects, who can by no means bear whatever is found in the Holy Scriptures and in the Catholic faith that stands out in opposition to their errors, just as we cannot bear their sacrilegious vaporings and mendacious insanities. For what else is it not to be able to bear, but not to retain in our minds with calmness and composure? But what of all that has been written since our Lord's ascension with canonical truth and authority, is it not read and heard with equanimity by every believer, and catechumen also, before in his baptism he receive the Holy Spirit, even although it is not yet understood as it ought to be? How then, could not the disciples bear any of those things which were written after the Lord's ascension, even though the Holy Spirit was not yet sent to them, when now they are all borne by catechumens prior to their reception of the Holy Spirit? For although the sacramental privileges of believers are not exhibited to them, it does not therefore happen that they cannot bear them; but in order that they may be all the more ardently desired by them, they are honorably concealed from their view.

4. Wherefore, beloved, you need not expect to hear from us what the Lord then refrained from telling His disciples, because they were still unable to bear them: but rather seek to grow in the love that is shed abroad in your hearts by the Holy Spirit who is given unto

you;[1] that, fervent in spirit, and loving spiritual things, you may be able, not by any sign apparent to your bodily eyes, or any sound striking on your bodily ears, but by the inward eyesight and hearing, to become acquainted with that spiritual light and that spiritual word which carnal men are unable to bear. For that cannot be loved which is altogether unknown. But when what is known, in however small a measure, is also loved, by the self-same love one is led on to a better and fuller knowledge. If, then, you grow in the love which the Holy Spirit spreads abroad in your hearts, "He will teach you all truth;" or, as other codices have it, "He will guide you in all truth:"[2] as it is said, "Lead me in Thy way, O Lord, and I will walk in Thy truth."[3] So shall the result be, that not from outward teachers will you learn those things which the Lord at that time declined to utter, but be all taught of God;[4] so that the very things which you have learned and believed by means of lessons and sermons supplied from without regarding the nature of God, as incorporeal, and unconfined by limits, and yet not rolled out as a mass of matter through infinite space, but everywhere whole and perfect and infinite, without the gleaming of colors, without the tracing of bodily outlines, without any markings of letters or succession of syllables,—your minds themselves may have the power to perceive. Well, now, I have just said something which is perhaps of that same character, and yet you have received it; and you have not only been able to bear it, but have also listened to it with pleasure. But were that inward Teacher, who, while still speaking in an external way to the disciples, said, "I have still many things to say unto you, but ye cannot bear them now," wishing to speak inwardly to us of what I have said of the incorporeal nature of God in the same way as He speaks to the angels, who always behold the face of the Father,[5] we should still be unable to bear them. Accordingly, when He says, "He will teach you all truth," or "will guide you into all truth," I do not think the fulfillment is possible in any one's mind in this present life

(for who is there, while living in this corruptible and soul-oppressing body,[6] that can know all truth, when even the apostle says, "We know in part"?), but because it is effected by the Holy Spirit, of whom we have now received the earnest,[7] that we shall attain also to the actual fullness of knowledge: whereof it is said by the same apostle, "But then face to face;" and, "Now I know in part, but then shall I know even as also I am known;"[8] not as a thing which he knows fully in this life, but which, as a thing that would still be future on to the attainment of that perfection, the Lord promised us through the love of the Spirit, when He said, "He will teach you all truth," or "will guide you unto all truth."

5. As these things are so, beloved, I warn you in the love of Christ to beware of impure seducers and sects of obscene filthiness, whereof the apostle says, "But it is a shame even to speak of those things which are done of them in secret:"[9] lest, when they begin to teach their horrible impurities, which no human ear whatever can bear, they declare them to be the very things whereof the Lord said, "I have yet many things to say unto you, but ye cannot bear them now;" and assert that it is the Holy Spirit's agency that makes such impure and detestable things possible to be borne. The evil things which no human modesty whatever can endure are of one kind, and of quite another are the good things which man's little understanding is unable to bear: the former are wrought in unchaste bodies, the latter are beyond the reach of all bodies; the one is perpetrated in the filthiness of the flesh, the other is scarcely perceivable by the pure mind. "Be ye therefore renewed in the spirit of your mind,"[10] and "understand what is the will of God, which is good, and acceptable, and perfect;"[11] that, "rooted and grounded in love, ye may be able to comprehend, with all saints, what is the length, and breadth, and height, and depth, even to know the love of Christ which passeth knowledge, that ye may be filled with all the fullness of God."[12] For in such a way will the Holy Spirit teach you all truth, when He shall shed abroad that love ever more and more largely in your hearts.

---

[1] Rom. v. 5.
[2] Ὁδηγήσει ὑμᾶς εἰς τὴν ἀλήθειαν πᾶσαν, or ἐν τῇ ἀληθείᾳ πάσῃ.
[3] Ps. lxxxvi. 11.　　[4] Chap. vi. 45.　　[5] Matt. xviii. 10.

[6] Wisd. ix. 15.　　[7] 2 Cor. i. 22.　　[8] 1 Cor. xiii. 9, 12.
[9] Eph. v. 12.　　[10] Eph. iv. 23.　　[11] Rom. xii. 2.
[12] Eph. iii. 17-19.

TRACTATE XCVII.

CHAPTER XVI. 12, 13 (*continued*).

1. THE Holy Spirit, whom the Lord promised to send to His disciples, to teach them all the truth which, at the time He was speaking to them, they were unable to bear: of the which Holy Spirit, as the apostle says, we have now received "the earnest,"[1] an expression whereby we are to understand that His fullness is reserved for us till another life: that Holy Spirit, therefore, teacheth believers also in the present life, as far as they can severally apprehend what is spiritual; and enkindles a growing desire in their breasts, according as each one makes progress in that love, which will lead him both to love what he knows already, and to long after what still remains to be known: so that those very things which he has some notion of at present, he may know that he is still ignorant of, as they are yet to be known in that life which eye hath not seen, nor ear heard, nor the heart of man hath perceived.[2] But were the inner Master wishing at present to say those things in such a way of knowing, that is, to unfold and make them patent to our mind, our human weakness would be unable to bear them. Whereof you remember, beloved, that I have already spoken, when we were occupied with the words of the holy Gospel, where the Lord says, "I have yet many things to say unto you, but ye cannot bear them now." Not that in these words of the Lord we should be suspecting an over-fastidious concealment of no one knows what secrets, which might be uttered by the Teacher, but could not be borne by the learner, but those very things which in connection with religious doctrine we read and write, hear and speak of, as within the knowledge of such and such persons, were Christ willing to utter to us in the self-same way as He speaks of them to the holy angels, in His own Person as the only-begotten Word of the Father, and co-eternal with Him, where are the human beings that could bear them, even were they already spiritual, as the apostles still were not when the Lord so spake to them, and as they afterwards became when the Holy Spirit descended? For, of course, whatever may be known of the creature, is less than the Creator Himself, who is the supreme and true and unchangeable God. And yet who keeps silence about Him? Where is His name not found in the mouths of readers, disputants, inquirers, respondents, adorers, singers, all sorts of haranguers, and lastly even of blasphemers themselves? And although no one keeps silence about Him, who is there that apprehends Him as He is to be understood, although He is never out of the mouths and the hearing of men? Who is there, whose keenness of mind can even get near Him? Who is there that would have known Him as the Trinity, had not He Himself desired so to become known? And what man is there that now holds his tongue about that Trinity; and yet what man is there that has any such idea of it as the angels? The very things, therefore, that are incessantly being uttered off-hand and openly about the eternity, the truth, the holiness of God, are understood well by some, and badly by others: nay rather, are understood by some, and not understood at all by others. For he that understands in a bad way, does not understand at all. And in the case even of those by whom they are understood in a right sense, by some they are perceived with less, by others with greater mental vividness, and by none on earth are apprehended as they are by the angels. In the very mind, therefore, that is to say, in the inner man, there is a kind of growth, not only in order to the transition from milk to solid food, but also to the taking of food itself in still larger and larger measure. But such growth is not in the way of a space-covering mass of matter, but in that of an illuminated understanding; because that food is itself the light of the understanding. In order, then, to your growth and apprehension of God, and in order that your apprehension may keep full pace with your ever-advancing growth, you ought to be addressing your prayer, and turning your hope, not to the teacher whose voice only reaches your ears, that is, who plants and waters only by outside labor, but to Him who giveth the increase.[3]

2. Accordingly, as I have admonished you in my last sermon, take heed, those of you specially who are still children and have need of a milk diet, of turning a curious ear to men, who have found occasion for self-deception and the deceiving of others in the words of

[1] 2 Cor. i. 22.   [2] 1 Cor. ii. 9.   [3] 1 Cor. iii. 6.

the Lord, "I have yet many things to say unto you, but ye cannot bear them now," in order to the discovery of that which is unknown, while you still have minds that are incompetent to discriminate between the true and the false; and most especially on account of the obscene lewdnesses which Satan has instilled, by God's permission, into unstable and carnal souls, for this end, that His judgments may everywhere be objects of terror, and that pure discipline may best manifest its sweetness in contrast with the impurities of wickedness; and that honor may be given to Him, and fear and modesty of demeanor assumed by every one, who has either been kept from falling into such evils by His kingly power, or been raised out of them by His uplifting hand. Beware, with fear and prayer, of rushing into that mystery of Solomon's, where "the woman that is foolish and brazen-faced, and become destitute of bread," invites the passers-by with the words, "Come and make a pleasant feast on hidden bread, and the sweetness of stolen waters."[1] For the woman thus spoken of is the vanity of the impious, who, utterly senseless as they are, fancy that they know something, just as was said of that woman, that she had "become destitute of bread;" who, though destitute of a single loaf, promises loaves; in other words, though ignorant of the truth, she promises the knowledge of the truth. But it is bread of a hidden character she promises, and which she declares is partaken of with pleasure, as well as the sweetness of stolen waters; in order that what is publicly forbidden to be uttered or believed in the Church, may be listened to and acted upon with willingness and relish. For by such secrecy profane teachers give a kind of seasoning to their poisons for the curious, that thereby they may imagine that they learn something great, because counted worthy of holding a secret, and may imbibe the more sweetly the folly which they regard as wisdom, the hearing of which, as a thing prohibited, they are represented as stealing.

3. Hence the system of magical arts commends its nefarious rites to those who are deceived, or ready to be so, by a sacrilegious curiosity. Hence, also, those unlawful divinations by the inspection of the entrails

of slain animals, or of the cries and flights of birds, or of multiform demoniacal signs, are distilled by converse with abandoned wretches into the ears of persons who are on the brink of destruction. And it is because of these unlawful and punishable secrets that the woman mentioned above is styled not merely "foolish," but also "audacious." But such things are alien not only to the reality, but to the very name of our religion. And what shall we say of this foolish and brazen-faced woman seasoning, as she does, so many wicked heresies, and serving up so many detestable fables with Christian forms of expression? Would that they were only such as are found in theatres, whether as the subjects of song or dancing, or turned into ridicule by a mimicking buffoonery; and not, some of them, such as makes us grieve at the foolishness, while wondering at the audacity that could have contrived them, against God! And yet all these utterly senseless heretics, who wish to be styled Christians, attempt to color the audacities of their devices, which are perfectly abhorrent to every human feeling, with the chance presented to them of that gospel sentence uttered by the Lord, "I have yet many things to say unto you, but ye cannot bear them now:" as if these were the very things which the apostles could not then bear, and as if the Holy Spirit had taught them what the unclean spirit, with all the length he can carry his audacity, blushes to teach and to preach in broad daylight.

4. It is such whom the apostle foresaw through the Holy Spirit, when he said: "For the time will come when they will not endure sound doctrine; but after their own lusts shall they heap to themselves teachers, having itching ears; and they shall turn away their ears from the truth, and shall be turned unto fables."[2] For that mentioning of secrecy and theft, whereof it is said, "Partake with pleasure of hidden bread and the sweetness of stolen waters," creates an itching in those who listen with ears that are lusting after spiritual fornication, just as by a kind of itching also of desire in the flesh the soundness of chastity is corrupted. Hear, therefore, how the apostle foresaw such things, and gave salutary admonition about avoiding them, when he said, "Shun profane novelties of words; for they increase unto much ungodliness, and their speech insinuates itself as doth a cancer."[3] He did not say novelties of words merely; but added, "profane."

---

[1] Prov. ix. 13-17, according to the Septuagint, where, in verse 13, פְּתַיּוּת is rendered ἐνδεὴς ψωμοῦ, "in want of a morsel of bread," as if from פַּת or פָּתוּת, a morsel. The form of the word, however, as well as the Masoretic pointing, shows its connection with פְּתִי in the sense of "simplicity" or "folly" personified. And again in verse 17, the LXX. have partly inverted the Hebrew order of the words, and translate יִמְתָּקוּ ("are sweet") in its active sense of "taste with relish" (or pleasure), as if it were מְתֻקּוֹ, Imperative; and read יִנְעַם ("is sweet") in the last clause, as if it were נְעַם or נֹעַם, "sweet," or "sweetness:" hence Augustin's rendering above. The Vulgate corresponds more nearly with the Hebrew and our English version.—TR.

[2] 2 Tim. iv. 3. 4.
[3] 2 Tim. ii. 16, 17. Augustin translates κενοφωνίας ("babblings," "empty utterances," vaniloquia, Vulgate) as if it read καινοφωνίας, "novelties of words."—TR.

For there are also novelties of words in perfect harmony with religious doctrine, as is told us in Scripture of the very name of Christians, when it began to be used. For it was in Antioch that the disciples were first called Christians after the Lord's ascension, as we read in the Acts of the Apostles:[1] and certain houses were afterwards called by the new names of hospices[2] and monasteries; but the things themselves existed prior to their names, and are confirmed by religious truth, which also forms their defense against the wicked. In opposition also to the impiety of Arian heretics, they coined the new term, Patris Homousios;[3] but there was nothing new signified by such a name; for what is called Homousios is just this: "I and my Father are one,"[4] to wit, of one and the same substance. For if every novelty were profane, as little should we have it said by the Lord, "A new commandment I give unto you;"[5] nor would the Testament be called New, nor the new song be sung throughout the whole earth. But there is profanity in the novelties of words, when it is said by "the foolish and audacious woman, Come and enjoy the tasting of hidden bread, and the sweetness of stolen waters." From such enticing words of false science the apostle also gives his prohibitory warning, in the passage where he says, "O Timothy, keep that which is committed to thy trust, avoiding profane novelties

of expression, and oppositions of science falsely so called; which some professing, have erred concerning the faith."[6] For there is nothing that these men so love as to profess science, and to deride as utter silliness faith in those verities which the young are enjoined to believe.

5. But some one will say, Have spiritual men nothing in the matter of doctrine, which they are to say nothing about to the carnal, but to speak out upon to the spiritual? If I shall answer, They have not, I shall be immediately met with the words of the Apostle Paul in his Epistle to the Corinthians: "I could not speak unto you as unto spiritual, but as unto carnal. As unto babes in Christ I have given you milk to drink, and not meat to eat: for hitherto ye were not able; neither yet now are ye able; for ye are yet carnal;"[7] and with these, "We speak wisdom among them that are perfect;" and with these also, "Comparing spiritual things with spiritual: but the natural man perceiveth not the things of the Spirit of God; for they are foolishness unto him."[8] The meaning of all this, in order that these words of the apostle may no longer lead to the hankering after secrets through the profane novelties of verbiage, and that what ought always to be shunned by the spirit and body of the chaste may not be asserted as only unable to be borne by the carnal, we shall, with the Lord's permission, make the subject of dissertation in another discourse, so that for the time we may bring the present to a close.

---

[1] Acts xi. 26.
[2] *Xenodochia*, houses of entertainment for strangers.
[3] "Of the same essence (or substance) with the Father," as applied to Christ.
[4] Chap. x. 30.   [5] Chap. xiii. 34.

[6] 1 Tim. vi. 20, 21.   [7] 1 Cor. iii. 1, 2.   [8] 1 Cor. ii. 6, 13, 14.

TRACTATE XCVIII

CHAPTER XVI. 12, 13 (*continuea*).

1. FROM the words of our Lord, where He says, "I have yet many things to say unto you, but ye cannot bear them now," there arose a difficult question, which I recollect to have put off, that it might be handled afterwards at greater leisure, because my last discourse had reached its proper limits, and required to be brought to a close. And now, accordingly, as we have time to redeem our promise, let us take up its discussion as the Lord Himself shall grant us ability, who put it into our heart to make the proposal. And the question is this: Whether spiritual men have aught in doctrine which they should with-

hold from the carnal, but declare to the spiritual. For if we shall say, They have not, we shall meet with the reply, What, then, is to be made of the words of the apostle in writing to the Corinthians: "I could not speak unto you as unto spiritual, but as unto carnal. As unto babes in Christ, I have given you milk to drink, and not meat to eat: for hitherto ye were not able; neither yet now are ye able; for ye are yet carnal?"[1] But if we say, They have, we have cause to fear and take heed, lest under such a pretext

---

[1] 1 Cor. iii. 1, 2.

detestable doctrines be taught in secret, and under the name of spiritual, as things which cannot be understood by the carnal, may seem not only capable of being whitewashed by plausible excuses, but deserving also to be lauded in preaching.

2. In the first place, then, your Charity ought to know that it is Christ Himself as crucified, wherewith the apostle says that he has fed those who are babes as with milk; but His flesh itself, in which was witnessed His real death, that is, both His real wounds when transfixed and His blood when pierced, does not present itself to the minds of the carnal in the same manner as to that of the spiritual, and so to the former it is milk, and to the latter it is meat; for if they do not hear more than others, they understand better. For the mind has not equal powers of perception even for that which is equally received by both in faith. And so it happens that the preaching of Christ crucified, by the apostle, was at once to the Jews a stumbling-block, and to the Gentiles foolishness; and to those who are called, both Jews and Greeks, the power of God, and the wisdom of God;"[1] but to the carnal, as babes who held it only as a matter of faith, and to the spiritual, as those of greater capacity, who perceived it as a matter of understanding; to the former, therefore, as a milk-draught, to the latter as solid food: not that the former knew it in one way out in the world at large, and the latter in another way in their secret chambers; but that what both heard in the same measure when it was publicly spoken, each apprehended in his own measure. For inasmuch as Christ was crucified for the very purpose of shedding His blood for the remission of sins, and of divine grace being thereby commended in the passion of His Only-begotten, that no one should glory in man, what understanding had they of Christ crucified who were still saying, " I am of Paul " ?[2] Was it such as Paul himself had, who could say, " But God forbid that I should glory, save in the cross of our Lord Jesus Christ "?[3] In regard, therefore, even to Christ crucified, he himself found food in proportion to his own capacity, and nourished them with milk in accordance with their infirmity. And still further, knowing that what he wrote to the Corinthians might doubtless be understood in one way by those who were still babes, and differently by those of greater capacity, he said, " If any one among you is a prophet, or spiritual, let him acknowledge that the things that I write unto you are the commandment of the Lord: but

if any man be ignorant, let him be ignorant."[4] Assuredly he would have the knowledge of the spiritual to be substantial, wherever not only faith had found a suitable abode, but a certain power of understanding was possessed; and whereby such believed those very things which as spiritual they likewise acknowledged. But " let him be ignorant," he says, who " is ignorant;" because it was not yet revealed to him to know that which he believes. When this takes place in a man's mind, he is said to be known of God; for it is God who endows him with this power of understanding, as it is elsewhere said, " But now, knowing God, or rather, being known of God."[5] For it was not then that God first knew those who were foreknown and chosen before the foundation of the world;[6] but then it was that He made them to know Himself.

3. Having ascertained this, therefore, at the outset, that the very things, which are equally heard by the spiritual and the carnal, are received by each according to the slender measure of his own capacity,—by some as babes, by others as those of riper years,—by one as milk nourishment, by another as solid food,—there seems no necessity for any matters of doctrine being retained in silence as secrets, and concealed from infant believers, as things to be spoken of apart to those who are older, or possessed of a riper understanding; and let us regard it as needful to act thus, just because of the words of the apostle, " I could not speak unto you as unto spiritual, but as unto carnal." For even this very statement of his, that he knew nothing among them but Jesus Christ and Him crucified,[7] he could not speak unto them as unto spiritual, but as unto carnal; because even that they were not able to receive as spiritual. But all who were spiritual among them received with spiritual understanding the very same truths which the others only heard as carnal; and in this way may we understand the words, " I could not speak unto you as unto spiritual, but as unto carnal," as if he said, What I did speak, ye could not receive as spiritual, but as carnal. For " the natural man " —that is, the man whose wisdom is of a mere human kind, and is called natural [literally, soulish] from the soul, and carnal from the flesh, because the complete man consists of soul and flesh—" perceiveth not the things of the Spirit of God;"[8] that is, the measure of grace bestowed on believers by the cross of Christ, and thinks that all that is effected by that cross is to provide us with an example for our imitation in contending even to death

---

[1] 1 Cor. i. 23, 24.   [2] 1 Cor. i. 12.
[3] Gal. vi. 14.

[4] 1 Cor. xiv. 37, 38.   [5] Gal. iv. 9.   [6] Eph. i. 4.
[7] 1 Cor. ii. 2.   [8] 1 Cor. ii. 14.

for the truth. For if men of this type, who have no desire to be aught else than men, knew how it is that Christ crucified is "made of God unto us wisdom, and righteousness, and sanctification, and redemption, that, according as it is written, He that glorieth, let him glory in the Lord."[1] they would doubtless no longer glory in man, nor say in a carnal spirit, "I am of Paul, and I of Apollos, and I of Cephas;" but in a spiritual way, "I am of Christ."[2]

4. But the question is still further raised by what we read in the Epistle to the Hebrews: "When now for the time ye ought to be teachers, ye have need again to be taught which be the first principles of the oracles of God; and are become such as have need of milk, and not of strong meat. For every one that useth milk hath no experience in the word of righteousness; for he is a babe. But strong meat belongeth to them that are perfect, even those who by habit have their senses exercised to distinguish good from evil."[3] For here we see, as if clearly defined, what he calls the strong meat of the perfect; and which is the same as that which he writes to the Corinthians, "We speak wisdom among them that are perfect."[4] But who it was that he wished in this passage to be understood as perfect, he proceeded to indicate in the words, "Even those who by habit have their senses exercised to distinguish good from evil." Those, therefore, who, through a weak and undisciplined mind, are destitute of this power, will certainly, unless enabled by what may be called the milk of faith to believe both the invisible things which they see not, and the comprehensible things which they do not yet comprehend, be easily seduced by the promise of science to vain and sacrilegious fables: so as to think both of good and evil only under corporeal forms, and to have no idea of God Himself save as some sort of body, and be able only to view evil as a substance; while there is rather a kind of falling away from the immutable Substance in the case of all mutable substances, which were made out of nothing by the immutable and supreme substance itself, which is God. And assuredly whoever not only believes, but also through the exercised inner senses of his mind understands, and perceives, and knows this, there is no longer cause for fear that he will be seduced by those who, while accounting evil to be a substance uncreated by God, make God Himself a mutable substance, as is done by the Manicheans, or any other

pests, if such there be, that fall into similar foily.

5. But to those who are still babes in mind, and who as carnal, the apostle says, require to be nourished with milk, all discoursing on such a subject, wherein we deal not only with the believing, but also with the understanding and the knowing of what is spoken, must be burdensome, as being still unable to perceive such things, and be more fitted to oppress than to feed them. Whence it comes to pass that the spiritual, while not altogether silent on such subjects to the carnal, because of the Catholic faith which is to be preached to all, yet do not so handle them as, in their wish to simplify them to understandings that are still deficient in capacity, to bring their discourse on the truth into disrepute, rather than the truth that is in their discourse within the perceptions of their hearers. Accordingly in his Epistle to the Colossians he says: "And though I be absent in the flesh, yet am I with you in the spirit, joying and beholding your order, and that which is lacking[5] in your faith in Christ."[6] And in that to the Thessalonians: "Night and day," he says, "praying more abundantly, that we might see your face, and might perfect that which is lacking in your faith."[7] Here we are, of course, to understand those who were under such primary catechetical instruction, as implied their nourishment with milk and not with strong meat; of the former of which there is mention made in the Epistle to the Hebrews of an abundant supply for such as nevertheless he would now have had to be feeding on solid food. Accordingly he says: "Therefore leaving the word of the beginning of Christ, let us have regard to the completion; not laying again the foundation of repentance from dead works, and of faith toward God, of the doctrine of the baptismal font, and of the laying on of hands, and of resurrection of the dead, and of eternal judgment."[8] This is the copious supply of milk, without which even they cannot live, who have already indeed their reason sufficiently in use to enable them to believe, but who cannot distinguish good from evil, so as to be not only a matter of faith, but also of understanding (which belongs to the department of solid food). But when he includes doctrine also in his description of the milk, it is that which has been delivered to us in the Creed and the Lord's Prayer.

6. But let us be far from supposing that there is any contrariety between this milk and

---

[1] Cor. i. 30, 31. [2] 1 Cor. i. 12. [3] Heb. v. 12-14.
[1] Cor. ii. 6.

[5] In place of τὸ στερέωμα, solidity, steadfastness, Augustin reads τὸ ὑστέρημα, that which is lacking. So also in his epistle to Paulinus, which is marked 149 (in Migne's edition of Augustin).
[6] Col. ii. 5. [7] 1 Thess. iii. 10. [8] Heb. vi. 1, 2.

the food of spiritual things that has to be received by the sound understanding, and which was wanting to the Colossians and Thessalonians, and had still to be supplied. For the supply of the deficiency implies no disapproval of that which existed. For even in the very food that we take, so far is there from being any contrariety between milk and solid food, that the latter itself becomes milk, in order to make it suitable to babes, whom it reaches through the medium of the mother's or the nurse's body; so did also mother Wisdom herself, who is solid food in the lofty sphere of angels, condescend in a manner to become milk for babes, when the Word became flesh, and dwelt among us.[1] But the man Christ Himself, who in His true flesh, true cross, true death, and true resurrection is called the pure milk of babes, is, when rightly understood by the spiritual, found to be the Lord of angels. Accordingly, babes are not to be so fed with milk as always to remain without understanding the Godhead of Christ; nor are they to be so withdrawn from milk as to turn their backs on His manhood. And the same thing may also be stated in another way in this manner: they are neither so to be fed with milk as never to understand Christ as Creator, nor so to be withdrawn from milk as ever to turn their backs on Christ as Mediator. In this respect, indeed, the similitude of maternal milk and solid food scarcely harmonizes with the reality as thus stated, but rather that of a foundation: for when the child is weaned, so as to be withdrawn from the nourishment of infancy, he never looks again amongst solid food for the breasts which he sucked; but Christ crucified is both milk to sucklings and meat to the more advanced. And the similitude of a foundation is on this account the more suitable, because, for the completion of the structure, the building is added without the foundation being withdrawn.

7. And since this is the case, do you, whoever you be, who are doubtless many of you still babes in Christ, be making advances towards the solid food of the mind, not of the belly. Grow in the ability to distinguish good from evil, and cleave more and more to the Mediator, who delivers you from evil; which does not admit of a local separation from you, but rather of being healed within you. But whoever shall say to you, Believe not Christ to be truly man, or that the body of any man or animal whatever was created by the true God, or that the Old Testament was given by the true God, and anything else of the same

sort, for such things as these were not told you previously, when your nourishment was milk, because your heart was still unfit for the apprehension of the truth: such an one provides you not with meat, but with poison. For therefore it was that the blessed apostle, in addressing those who appeared to him already perfect, even after calling himself imperfect, said, "Let us, therefore, as many as be perfect, be thus minded: and if in anything ye be otherwise minded, God shall reveal even this unto you." And that they might not rush into the hands of seducers, whose desire would be to turn them away from the faith by promising them the knowledge of the truth, and suppose such to be the meaning of the apostle's words, "God shall reveal even this unto you," he forthwith added, "Nevertheless, whereto we have already attained, let us walk by the same rule."[2] If, then, thou hast come to some understanding of what is not at variance with the rule of the Catholic faith, whereto thou hast attained as the way that is guiding thee to thy fatherland; and hast so understood it as to feel it a duty to dismiss all doubts whatever on the subject: add to the building, but do not abandon the foundation. And surely of such a character ought to be any teaching given by elders to those who are babes, as not to involve the assertion that Christ the Lord of all, and the prophets and apostles, who are much farther advanced in age than themselves, had in any respect spoken falsely. And not only ought you to avoid the babbling seducers of the mind, who prate away at their fables and falsehoods, and in such vanities make the promise, forsooth, of profound science contrary to the rule of faith, which we have accepted as Catholic; but avoid those also as a still more insidious pest than the others, who discuss truthfully enough the immutability of the divine nature, or the incorporeal creature, or the Creator, and fully prove what they affirm by the most conclusive documents and reasonings, and yet attempt to turn you away from the one Mediator between God and men. For such are those of whom the apostle says, "Because that, when they knew God, they glorified Him not as God."[3] For what advantage is it to have a true understanding of the immutable Good to one who has no hold of Him by whom there is deliverance from evil? And let not the admonition of the most blessed apostle by any means lose its place in your hearts: "If any man preach any other gospel unto you than that ye have received, let him be accursed."[4] He does not

---

[1] Chap. i. 1, 14. [2] Phil. iii. 15, 16. [3] Rom. i. 21. [4] Gal. i. 9.

say, More than ye have received; but, ' Other than ye have received." For had he said the former, he would be prejudging himself, inasmuch as he desired to come to the Thessalonians to supply what was lacking in their faith. But one who supplies, adds to what was deficient, without taking away what existed; while he that transgresses the rule of faith, is not progressing in the way, but turning aside from it.

8. Accordingly, when the Lord says, " I have yet many things to say unto you, but ye cannot bear them now," He means that what they were still ignorant of had afterwards to be supplied to them, and not that what they had already learned was to be subverted. And He, indeed, as I have already shown in a former discourse, could so speak, because the very things which He had taught them, had He wished to unfold them to them in the same way as they are conceived in regard to Him by the angels, their still remaining human weakness would be unable to bear. But any spiritual man may teach another man what he knows, provided the Holy Spirit grant him an enlarged capacity for profiting, wherein also the teacher himself may get some further increase, in order that both may be taught of God. [1] Although even among the spiritual themselves there are some, doubtless, who are of greater capacity and in a better condition than others; so that one of them attained even to things of which it is not lawful for a man to speak. Taking advantage of which, there have been some vain individuals, who, with a presumption that betrays the grossest folly, have forged a Revelation of Paul, crammed with all manner of fables, which has been rejected by the orthodox Church; affirming it to be that whereof he had said that he was caught up into the third heavens, and there heard unspeakable words " which it is not lawful for a man to utter." [2] Nevertheless, the audacity of such might be tolerable, had he said that he heard words which it is not as yet lawful for a man to utter; but when he said, " which it is not lawful for a man to utter," who are they that dare to utter them with such impudence and nonsuccess? But with these words I shall now bring this discourse to a close; whereby I would have you to be wise indeed in that which is good, but untainted by that which is evil.

[1] Chap. vi. 45.　　　[2] 2 Cor. xii. 2, 4.

TRACTATE XCIX.

Chapter XVI. 13.

1. What is this that the Lord said of the Holy Spirit, when promising that He would come and teach His disciples all truth, or guide them into all truth: " For He shall not speak of Himself; but whatsoever He shall hear, that shall He speak " ? For this is similar to what He said of Himself, " I can of mine own self do nothing: as I hear, I judge." [1] But when expounding that, we said that it might be taken as referring to His human nature; [2] so that He seemed as the Son to announce beforehand that His own obedience, whereby He became obedient even unto the death of the cross, [3] would have its place also in the judgment, when He shall judge the quick and the dead; for He shall do so for the very reason that He is the Son of man. Wherefore He said, " The Father judgeth no man, but hath committed all judgment unto the Son;" for in the judgment He will appear, not in the form of God, wherein He is equal to the Father, and cannot be seen by the wicked, but in the form of man, in which He was made even a little lower than the angels; although then He will come in glory, and not in His original humility, yet in a way that will be conspicuous both to the good and to the bad. Hence He says further: "And He hath given Him authority to execute judgment also, because He is the Son of man." [4] In these words of His own it is made clear that it is not that form that will be presented in the judgment, wherein He was when He thought it not robbery to be equal with God; but that which He assumed when He made Himself of no reputation. [5] For He emptied Himself in assuming the form of a servant; [6] in which, also, for the purpose of executing judgment, He seems to have commended His obedience, when He said, " I can of mine own self do nothing: as I hear, I

[4] Chap. v. 22, 27.
[5] Literally, "when He emptied Himself."
[6] Phil. ii. 6, 7.

[1] Chap. v. 30.　　　[2] Tracts. XIX.-XXII.　　　[3] Phil. ii. 8.

judge." For Adam, by whose disobedience, as that of one man, many were made sinners, did not judge as he heard; for he prevaricated what he heard, and of his own self did the evil that he did; for he did not the will of God, but his own: while this latter, by whose obedience, as that also of one man, many are made righteous,[1] was not only obedient even unto the death of the cross, in respect of which He was judged as alive from the dead; but promised also that He would be showing obedience in the very judgment itself, wherein He is yet to act as judge of the quick and the dead, when He said, " I can of mine own self do nothing: as I hear, I judge." But when it is said of the Holy Spirit, " For He shall not speak of Himself; but whatsoever He shall hear, that shall He speak," shall we dare to harbor the notion that it was so said in reference to any human nature of His, or the assumption of any creature-form? For it was the Son alone in the Trinity who assumed the form of a servant, a form which in His case was fitted into the unity of His person, or, in other words, that the one person, Jesus Christ, should be the Son of God and the Son of man; and so that we should be kept from preaching a quaternity instead of the Trinity, which God forbid that we should do. And it is on account of this one personality as consisting of two substances, the divine and the human, that He sometimes speaks in accordance with that wherein He is God, as when He says, " I and my Father are one;"[2] and sometimes in accordance with His manhood, as in the words, " For the Father is greater than I;"[3] in accordance with which also we have understood those words of His that are at present under discussion, " I can of mine own self do nothing: as I hear, I judge." But in reference to the person of the Holy Spirit, a considerable difficulty arises how we are to understand the words, " For He shall not speak of Himself; but whatsoever He shall hear, that shall He speak;" since in it there exists not one substance of Godhead and another of humanity, or of any other creature whatsoever.

2. For the fact that the Holy Spirit appeared in bodily form, as a dove,[4] was a sight begun and ended at the time: just as also, when He descended upon the disciples, there were seen upon them cloven tongues as of fire, which also sat upon every one of them.[5] Any one, therefore, who says that the dove was connected with the Holy Spirit in the unity of His person, as that it and Godhead (for the Holy Spirit is God) should go to consti-

tute the one person of the Holy Spirit, is compelled also to affirm the same thing of that fire; and so may understand that he ought to assert neither. For those things in regard to the substance of God, which needed at any time to be represented in some outward way, and so exhibited themselves to men's bodily senses, and then passed away, were formed for the moment by divine power from the subservient creation, and not from the dominant nature itself; which, ever abiding the same, excites into action whatever it pleases; and, itself unchangeable, changes all things else at its pleasure. In the same way also did that voice from the cloud actually strike upon the bodily ears, and on that bodily sense which is called the hearing;[6] and yet in no way are we to believe that the Word of God, which is the only-begotten Son, is defined, because He is called the Word, by syllables and sounds: for when a sermon is in course of delivery, all the sounds cannot be pronounced simultaneously; but the various individual sounds come, as it were, in their own order to the birth, and succeed those which are dying away, so that all that we have to say is completed only by the last syllable. Very different from this, surely, is the way in which the Father speaketh to the Son, that is to say, God to God, His Word. But this, so far as it can be understood by man, is a matter for the understanding of those who are fitted for the reception of solid food, and not of milk. Since, therefore, the Holy Spirit became not man by any assumption of humanity, and became not an angel by any assumption of angelic nature, and as little entered into the creature-state by the assumption of any creature-form whatever, how, in regard to Him, are we to understand those words of our Lord, " For He shall not speak of Himself; but whatsoever He shall hear, that shall He speak"? A difficult question; yea, too difficult. May the Spirit Himself be present, that, at least up to the measure of our power of thinking on such a subject, we may be able to express our thoughts, and that these, according to the little measure of my ability, may find entrance into your understanding.

3. You ought, then, to be informed in the first place, and, those of you who can, to understand, and the others, who cannot as yet understand, to believe, that in that substantial essence, which is God, the senses are not, as if through some material structure of a body, distributed in their appropriate places; as, in the mortal flesh of all animals there is in one place sight, in another hearing, in another

[1] Rom. v. 19. [2] Chap. x. 30. [3] Chap. xiv. 28.
[4] Matt. iii. 16. [5] Acts ii. 3. [6] Luke ix. 35.

taste, in another smelling, and over the whole the sense of touch. Far be it from us to believe so in the case of that incorporeal and immutable nature. In it, therefore, hearing and seeing are one and the same thing. In this way smelling also is said to exist in God; as the apostle says, "As Christ also hath loved us, and hath given Himself for us an offering and a sacrifice to God for a sweet-smelling savor."[1] And taste may be included, in accordance with which God hateth the bitter in temper, and spueth out of His mouth those who are lukewarm, and neither cold nor hot:[2] and Christ our God[3] saith, "My meat is to do the will of Him that sent me."[4] There is also that divine sense of touch, in accordance with which the spouse saith of the bridegroom: "His left hand is under my head, and his right hand shall embrace me."[5] But these are not in God's case in different parts of the body. For when He is said to know, all are included: both seeing, and hearing, and smelling, and tasting, and touching; without any alteration of His substance, and without the existence of any material element which is greater in one place and smaller in another: and when there are any such thoughts of God in those even who are old in years, they are the thoughts only of a childish mind.

4. Nor need you wonder that the ineffable knowledge of God, whereby He is cognizant of all things, is, because of the various modes of human speech designated by the names of all those bodily senses; since even our own mind, in other words, the inner man,—to which, while itself exercising its knowing faculty in one uniform way, the different subjects of its knowledge are communicated by those five messengers, as it were, of the body, when it understands, chooses, and loves the unchangeable truth,—is said both to see the light, whereof it is said, "That was the true light;" and to hear the word, whereof it is said, "In the beginning was the Word;"[6] and to be susceptible of smell, of which it is said, "We will run after the smell of thy ointments;"[7] and to drink of the fountain, whereof it is said, "With Thee is the fountain of life;"[8] and to enjoy the sense of touch, when it is said, "But it is good for me to cleave unto God;"[9] in all of which it is not different things, but the one intelligence, that is expressed by the names of so many senses. When, therefore, it is said of the Holy Spirit, "For He shall not speak of Himself; but whatsoever He shall hear, that shall He

speak," so much the more is a simple nature, which is simple [uncompounded] in the truest sense, to be either understood or believed, which in its extent and sublimity far surpasses the nature of our minds. For there is mutability in our mind, which comes by learning to the perception of what it was previously ignorant of, and loses by unlearning what it formerly knew; and is deceived by what has a similarity to truth, so as to approve of the false in place of the true, and is hindered by its own obscurity as by a kind of darkness from arriving at the truth. And so that substance is not in the truest sense simple, to which being is not identical with knowing; for it can exist without the possession of knowledge. But it cannot be so with that divine substance, for it is what it has. And on this account it has not knowledge in any such way as that the knowledge whereby it knows should be to it one thing, and the essence whereby it exists another; but both are one. Nor ought that to be called both, which is simply one. "As the Father hath life in Himself," and He Himself is not something different from the life that is in Him; "so hath He given to the Son to have life in Himself,"[10] that is, hath begotten the Son, that He also should Himself be the life. Accordingly we ought to accept what is said of the Holy Spirit, "For he shall not speak of Himself; but whatsoever He shall hear, that shall He speak," in such a way as to understand thereby that He is not of Himself. Because it is the Father only who is not of another. For the Son is born of the Father, and the Holy Spirit proceedeth from the Father; but the Father is neither born of, nor proceedeth from, another. And yet surely there should not on that account occur to human thought any idea of disparity in the supreme Trinity; for both the Son is equal to Him of whom He is born, and the Holy Spirit to Him from whom He proceedeth. But what difference there is in such a case between proceeding and being born, would be too lengthy to make the subject of inquiry and dissertation, and would make our definition liable to the charge of rashness, even after we had discussed it; for such a thing is of the utmost difficulty, both for the mind to comprehend in any adequate way, and even were it so that the mind has attained to any such comprehension, for the tongue to explain, however able the one that presides as a teacher, or he that is present as a hearer. Accordingly, "He shall not speak of Himself;" because He is not of Himself.

---

[1] Eph. v. 2.   [2] Rev. iii. 16.   [3] *Deus Christus.*
[4] Chap. iv. 34.   [5] Song of Sol. ii. 6.   [6] Chap. i. 9, 1.
[7] Song of Sol. i. 4, Septuagint.   [8] Ps. xxxvi. 9.
[9] Ps. lxxiii. 28.

[10] Chap. v. 26.

"But whatsoever He shall hear, that shall He speak:" He shall hear of Him from whom He proceedeth. To Him hearing is knowing; but knowing is being, as has been discussed above. Because, then, He is not of Himself, but of Him from whom He proceedeth, and of whom He has essence, of Him He has knowledge; from Him, therefore, He has hearing, which is nothing else than knowledge.

5. And be not disturbed by the fact that the verb is put in the future tense. For it is not said, whatsoever He hath heard, or, whatsoever He heareth; but, "whatsoever He shall hear, that shall He speak." For such hearing is everlasting, because the knowing is everlasting. But in the case of what is eternal, without beginning and without end, in whatever tense the verb is put, whether in the past, or present, or future, there is no falsehood thereby implied. For although to that immutable and ineffable nature, there is no proper application of Was and Will be, but only Is: for that nature alone *is* in truth, because incapable of change; and to it therefore was it exclusively suited to say, "I Am That I Am," and "Thou shalt say unto the children of Israel, He Who Is hath sent me unto you:"[1] yet on account of the changeableness of the times amid which our mortal and changeable life is spent, there is nothing false in our saying, both it was, and will be, and is. It was in past, it is in present, it will be in future ages. It was, because it never was wanting; it will be, because it will never be wanting; it is, because it always is. For it has not, like one who no longer survives, died with the past; nor, like one who abideth not, is it gliding away with the present; nor, as one who had no previous existence, will it rise up with the future. Accordingly, as our human manner of speaking varies with the revolutions of time, He, who through all times was not, is not, and will not by any possibility be found wanting, may correctly be spoken of in any tense whatever of a verb. The Holy Spirit, therefore, is always hearing, because He always knows: *ergo*, He both knew, and knows, and will know; and in the same way He both heard, and hears, and will hear; for, as we have already said, to Him hearing is one with knowing, and knowing with Him is one with being. From Him, therefore, He heard, and hears, and will hear, of whom He is; and of Him He is, from whom He proceeds.

6. Some one may here inquire whether the Holy Spirit proceedeth also from the Son.

For the Son is Son of the Father alone, and the Father is Father of the Son alone; but the Holy Spirit is not the Spirit of one of them, but of both. You have the Lord Himself saying, "For it is not ye that speak, but the Spirit of your Father that speaketh in you;"[2] and you have the apostle, "God hath sent forth the spirit of His Son into your hearts."[3] Are there, then, two, the one of the Father, the other of the Son? Certainly not. For there is "one body," he said, when referring to the Church; and presently added, "and one Spirit." And mark how he there makes up the Trinity. "As ye are called," he says, "in one hope of your calling." "One Lord," where he certainly meant Christ to be understood; but it remained that he should also name the Father: and accordingly there follows, "One faith, one baptism, one God and Father of all, who is above all, and through all, and in you all."[4] And since, then, just as there is one Father, and one Lord, namely, the Son, so also there is one Spirit; He is doubtless of both: especially as Christ Jesus Himself saith, "The Spirit of your Father that dwelleth in you;" and the apostle declares, "God hath sent forth the Spirit of His Son into your hearts." You have the same apostle saying in another place, "But if the Spirit of Him that raised up Jesus from the dead dwell in you," where he certainly intended the Spirit of the Father to be understood; of whom, however, he says in another place, "But if any man have not the Spirit of Christ, he is none of His."[5] And many other testimonies there are, which plainly show that He, who in the Trinity is styled the Holy Spirit, is the Spirit both of the Father and of the Son.

7. And for no other reason, I suppose, is He called in a peculiar way the Spirit; since though asked concerning each person in His turn, we cannot but admit that the Father and the Son are each of them a Spirit; for God is a Spirit,[6] that is, God is not carnal, but spiritual. By the name, therefore, which they each also hold in common, it was requisite that He should be distinctly called, who is not the one nor the other of them, but in whom what is common to both becomes apparent. Why, then, should we not believe that the Holy Spirit proceedeth also from the Son, seeing that He is likewise the Spirit of the Son? For did He not so proceed, He could not, when showing Himself to His disciples after the resurrection, have breathed upon them, and said, "Receive ye the Holy Spirit."[7] For what else was signified by

---

[1] Ex. iii. 14.

[2] Matt. x. 20.   [3] Gal. iv. 6.   [4] Eph. iv. 4-6.
[5] Rom. viii. 11, 9.   [6] Chap. iv. 24.   [7] Chap. xx. 22.

such a breathing upon them, but that from Him also the Holy Spirit proceedeth? And of the same character also are His words regarding the woman that suffered from the bloody flux: "Some one hath touched me; for I perceive that virtue is gone out of me." [1] For that the Holy Spirit is also designated by the name of virtue, is both clear from the passage where the angel, in reply to Mary's question, "How shall this be, seeing I know not a man?" said, "The Holy Ghost shall come upon thee, and the power [virtue] of the highest shall overshadow thee;" [2] and our Lord Himself when giving His disciples the promise of the Spirit, said, "But tarry ye in the city, until ye be endued with power [virtue] from on high;" [3] and on another occasion, "Ye shall receive the power [virtue] of the Holy Ghost coming upon you, and ye shall be witnesses unto me." [4] It is of this virtue that we are to believe, that the evangelist says, "Virtue went out of Him, and healed them all." [5]

8. If, then, the Holy Spirit proceedeth both from the Father and from the Son, why said the Son, "He proceedeth from the Father"? [6] Why, do you think, but just because it is to Him He is wont to attribute even that which is His own, of whom He Himself also is? Hence we have Him saying, "My doctrine is not mine, but His that sent me." [7] If, therefore, in such a passage we are to understand that as His doctrine, which nevertheless He declared not to be His own, but the Father's, how much more in that other passage are we to understand the Holy Spirit as proceeding from Himself, where His words, "He proceedeth from the Father," were uttered so as not to imply, He proceedeth not from me? But from Him, of whom the Son has it that He is God (for He is God of God), He certainly has it that from Him also the Holy Spirit proceedeth: and in this way the Holy Spirit has it of the Father Himself, that He should also proceed from the Son, even as He proceedeth from the Father.

9. In connection with this, we come also to some understanding of the further point, that is, so far as it can be understood by such beings as ourselves, why the Holy Spirit is not said to be born, but to proceed: since, if He also were called by the name of Son, He could not avoid being called the Son of both, which is utterly absurd. For no one is a son of two, unless of a father and mother. But it would be utterly abhorrent to entertain the suspicion of any such intervention between God the Father and God the Son. For not even a son of human parents proceedeth at the same time from father and from mother: but at the time that he proceedeth from the father into the mother, it is not then that he proceedeth from the mother; and when he cometh forth from the mother into the light of day, it is not then that he proceedeth from the father. But the Holy Spirit proceedeth not from the Father into the Son, and then proceedeth from the Son to the work of the creature's sanctification; but He proceedeth at the same time from both: although this the Father hath given unto the Son, that He should proceed from Him also, even as He proceedeth from Himself. And as little can we say that the Holy Spirit is not the life, seeing that the Father is the life, and the Son is the life. And in the same way as the Father, who hath life in Himself, hath given to the Son also to have life in Himself; so hath He also given that life should proceed from Him, even as it also proceedeth from Himself. [8] But we come now to the words of our Lord that follow, when He saith: "And He will show you things to come. He shall glorify me; for He shall receive of mine, and shall show it unto you. All things that the Father hath are mine: therefore, said I, that He shall take of mine, and shall show it unto you." But as the present discourse has already been protracted to some length, they must be left over for another.

---

[1] Luke viii. 46.   [2] Luke i. 34, 35.   [3] Luke xxiv. 49.
[4] Acts i. 8, *marg.*   [5] Luke vi. 19.   [6] Chap. xv. 26
[7] Chap. vii. 16.

[8] This passage from sec. 8, Augustin has transferred into Book XV. "On the Trinity," chap. 27.

TRACTATE C.

CHAPTER XVI. 13–15 (*continued*).

1. WHEN our Lord gave the promise of the coming of His Holy Spirit, He said, "He shall teach you all truth," or, as we read in some copies, "He shall guide you into all truth. For He shall not speak of Himself; but whatsoever He shall hear, that shall He speak." On these Gospel words we have already discoursed as the Lord enabled us; and now give your attention to those that follow. "And He will show you," He said, "things to come." Over this, which is perfectly plain, there is no need to linger; for it contains no question that demands from us any regular exposition. But the words that He proceeds to add, "He shall make me clearly known;[1] for He shall receive of mine, and shall show it unto you," are not to be carelessly passed over. For by the words, "He shall make me clearly known," we may understand, that by shedding abroad [God's] love in the hearts of believers, and making them spiritual, He showed them how it was that the Son was equal to the Father, whom previously they had only known according to the flesh, and as men themselves had thought of Him only as man. Or at least that, filled themselves through that very love with boldness, and divested of all fear, they might proclaim Christ unto men; and so His fame be spread abroad through the whole world. So that He said, "He shall make me clearly known," as if meaning, He shall free you from fear, and endow you with a love that will so inflame your zeal in preaching me, that you will send forth the odor, and commend the honor of, my glory throughout the world. For what they were to do in the Holy Spirit, He said that the Spirit Himself would also do, as is implied in the words, "For it is not ye that speak, but the Spirit of your Father that speaketh in you."[2] The Greek word, indeed, which is δοξάσει, has been rendered by the Latin interpreters in their respective translations, *clarificabit* ("shall make clearly known") by one, and *glorificabit* ("shall glorify") by another: for the idea expressed in Greek by the one term δόξα, from which is derived the verb δοξάσει, may be interpreted both by *claritas* (brightness) and *gloria* (glory). For by glory every one becomes bright, and glorious by brightness; and hence

what is signified by both words, is one and the same thing. And, as the most famous writers of the Latin tongue in olden time have defined it, glory is the generally diffused and accepted fame of any one accompanied with praise. But when this happened in the world in regard to Christ, we are not to suppose that it was the bestowing of any great thing on Christ, but on the world. For to praise what is good is not of benefit to that which receives, but to those who give the commendation.

2. But there is also a false glory, when the praise given is the result of a mistake, whether in regard to things or to persons, or to both. For men are mistaken in regard to things, when they think that to be good which is evil; and in regard to persons, when they think one to be good who is evil; and in regard to both, when what is actually a vice is esteemed a virtue; and when he who is praised for something is destitute of what he is supposed to have, whether he be good or evil. To credit vain-glorious persons[3] with the things they profess, is surely a huge vice, and not a virtue; and yet you know how common is the laudatory fame of such; for, as Scripture says, "The sinner is praised in the desires of his soul, and he who practises iniquity is blessed."[4] Here those who praise are not mistaken in the persons, but in the things; for that is evil which they believe to be good. But those who are morally corrupted with the evil of prodigality are undoubtedly such as those who praise them do not simply suspect, but perceive them to be. But further, if one feign himself a just man, and be not so, but, as regards all that he seems to do in a praiseworthy way in the sight of men, does it not for God's sake, that is, for the sake of true righteousness, but makes glory from men the only glory he seeks and hankers after; while those with whom his extolled fame is generally accepted think of him only as living in a

---

[3] *Histrionibus*, literally, play-actors.
[4] Ps. x. 3. Augustin here, as usual, follows the Septuagint. הֻלַּל (praise), however, is not passive, but, instead of its usual accusative, takes עַל with the subject of praise, and is rendered with sufficient accuracy in the English version. בֵּרֵךְ, also, must be translated *actively*, with "the covetous," or "the defrauder," as its *nominative :* and the verse should thus read, "The wicked boasteth of his soul's desire, and the defrauder blesseth [and] blasphemeth Jehovah." It would be natural enough in the defrauder to do both.—TR.

praiseworthy way for God's sake,—they are not mistaken in the thing, but are deceived in the person. For that which they believe to be good, is good; but the person whom they believe to be good, is the reverse. But if, for example, skill in magical arts be esteemed good, and any one, so long as he is believed to have delivered his country by those same arts whereof all the while he is utterly ignorant, attain amongst the irreligious to that generally accepted renown which is defined as glory, those who so praise err in both respects; to wit, both in the thing, for they esteem that good which is evil; and in the person, for he is not at all what they suppose him. But when, in regard to any one who is righteous by God's grace and for God's sake, in other words, truly righteous, there is on account of that very righteousness a generally accepted fame of a laudatory kind, then the glory is indeed a true one; and yet we are not to suppose that thereby the righteous man is made blessed, but rather those who praise him are to be congratulated, because they judge rightly, and love the righteous. And how much more, then, did Christ the Lord, by His own glory, benefit, not Himself, but those whom He also benefited by His death?

3. But that is not a true glory which He has among heretics, with whom, nevertheless, He appears to have a generally accepted fame accompanied with praise. Such is no true glory, because in both respects they are mistaken, for they both think that to be good which is not good, and they suppose Christ to be what Christ is not. For to say that the only-begotten Son is not equal to Him that begat, is not good: to say that the only-begotten Son of God is man only, and not God, is not good: to say that the flesh of the Truth is not true flesh, is not good. Of the three doctrines which I have stated, the first is held by the Arians, the second by the Photinians, and the third by the Manicheans. But inasmuch as there is nothing in any of them that is good, and Christ has nothing to do with them, in both respects they are in the wrong; and they attach no true glory to Christ, although there may appear to be amongst them a generally accepted fame regarding Christ of a laudatory character. And accordingly all heretics together, whom it would be too tedious to enumerate, who have not right views regarding Christ, err on this account, that their views are untrue regarding both good things and evil. The pagans, also, of whom great numbers are lauders of Christ, are themselves also mistaken in both respects, saying, as they do, not in accordance with the truth of God, but rather with their own conjectures, that He was a magician. For they reproach Christians as being destitute of skill; but Christ they laud as a magician, and so betray what it is that they love: Christ indeed they do not love, since what they love is that which Christ never was. And thus, then, in both respects they are in error, for it is wicked to be a magician; and as Christ was good, He was not a magician. Wherefore, as we have nothing to say in this place of those who malign and blaspheme Christ,—for it is of His glory we speak, wherewith He was glorified in the world,—it was only in the holy Catholic Church that the Holy Spirit glorified Him with His true glory. For elsewhere, that is, either among heretics or certain pagans, the glory He has in the world cannot be a true one, even where there is a generally accepted fame of Him accompanied with praise. His true glory, therefore, in the Catholic Church is celebrated in these words by the prophet: "Be thou exalted, O God, above the heavens; and Thy glory above all the earth."[1] Accordingly, that after His exaltation the Holy Spirit was to come, and to glorify Him, the sacred psalm, and the Only-begotten Himself, promised as an event of the future, which we see accomplished.

4. But when He says, "He shall receive of mine, and shall show it unto you," listen thereto with Catholic ears, and receive it with Catholic minds. For not surely on that account, as certain heretics have imagined, is the Holy Spirit inferior to the Son; as if the Son received from the Father, and the Holy Spirit from the Son, in reference to certain gradations of natures. Far be it from us to believe this, or to say it, and from Christian hearts to think it. In fine, He Himself straightway solved the question, and explained why He said so. "All things that the Father hath are mine: therefore, said I, that He shall take of mine, and shall show it unto you." What would you more? The Holy Spirit thus receives of the Father, of whom the Son receives; for in this Trinity the Son is born of the Father, and from the Father the Holy Spirit proceedeth. He, however, who is born of none, and proceedeth from none, is the Father alone. But in what sense it is that the only-begotten Son said, "All things that the Father hath are mine" (for it certainly was not in the same sense as when it was said to that son, who was not only begotten, but the elder of two, "Thou art ever with me; and all that I have is thine,")[2] will have our careful consideration, if the Lord

---

[1] Ps. cviii. 5.　　　[2] Luke xv. 31.

so will, in connection with the passage where the Only-begotten saith to the Father, "And all mine are Thine, and Thine are mine;"[1]

[1] Chap xvii. 10.

so that our present discourse may be here brought to a close, as the words that follow require a different opening for their discussion.

TRACTATE CI.

CHAPTER XVI. 16–23.

1. THESE words of the Lord, when He says, "A little while, and ye shall no more see me: and again a little while, and ye shall see me; because I go to the Father," were so obscure to the disciples, before what He thus says was actually fulfilled, that they inquired among themselves what it was that He said, and had to confess themselves utterly ignorant. For the Gospel proceeds, "Then said some of His disciples among themselves, What is this that He saith unto us, A little while, and ye shall not see me: and again a little while, and ye shall see me; and, Because I go to the Father? They said therefore, What is this that He saith, A little while? we know not what He saith." This is what moved them, that He said, "A little while, and ye shall not see me: and again a little while, and ye shall see me." For in what precedes, because He had not said, "A little while," but only, "I go to the Father and ye shall see me no more,"[1] He appeared to them to have spoken, as it were, quite plainly, and they had no inquiry among themselves regarding it. But now, what was then obscure to them, and was shortly afterwards revealed, is already perfectly manifest to us: for after a little while He suffered, and they saw Him not; again, after a little while He rose, and they saw Him. But how the words are to be taken that He used, "Ye shall no more see me," inasmuch as by the word "more"[2] He wished it to be understood that they would not see Him afterwards, we have explained at the passage where He said, The Holy Spirit "shall convince of righteousness, because I go to the Father, and ye shall see me no more;"[3] meaning thereby, that they would never afterwards see Christ in His present state of subjection to death.

2. "Now Jesus knew," as the evangelist proceeds to say, "that they were desirous to ask Him, and said unto them, Ye inquire among yourselves of that I said, A little while, and ye shall not see me: and again a little while, and ye shall see me. Verily verily, I say unto you, That ye shall weep and lament, but the world shall rejoice; and ye shall be sorrowful, but your sorrow shall be turned into joy:" which may be understood in this way, that the disciples were thrown into sorrow over the death of the Lord, and straightway were filled with joy at His resurrection; but the world, whereby are signified the enemies that slew Christ, were, of course, in a state of rapture over the murder of Christ, at the very time when the disciples were filled with sorrow. For by the name of the world the wickedness of this world may be understood; in other words, those who are the friends of this world. As the Apostle James says in his epistle, "Whosoever will be a friend of this world, is become the enemy of God;"[4] for the effect of that enmity to God was, that not even His Only-begotten was spared.

3. And then He goes on to say, "A woman when she is in travail hath sorrow, because her hour is come: but as soon as she is delivered of the child, she remembereth no more the anguish, for joy that a man is born into the world. And ye now therefore have sorrow; but I will see you again, and your heart shall rejoice, and your joy no man taketh from you." Nor does the metaphor here employed seem difficult to understand; for its key is at hand in the exposition given by Himself of its meaning. For the pangs of parturition are compared to sorrow, and the birth itself to joy; which is usually all the greater when it is not a girl but a boy that is born. But when He said, "Your joy no man taketh from you," for their joy was Jesus Himself, there is implied what was said by the apostle, "Christ, being raised from the dead, dieth no

[1] Chap. xvi. 10.
[2] The English version has here, "Ye shall not see me," reading οὐ in the original, with the Alexandrine Codex. Several of the others, however (including the Sinaitic), have οὐκέτι ("no more"), rendered by Augustin *jam non*, which has thus the greater weight of authority on its side.—TR.
[3] Above, Tract. XCV.
[4] Jas. iv. 4.

more; and death shall have no more dominion over Him.",

4. Hitherto in this section of the Gospel, whereon we are discoursing to-day, the tenor of everything has been, I may say, of easy understanding: a much closer attention is needful in connection with the words that follow. For what does He mean by the words, "And in that day ye shall ask me nothing"? The verb to ask, used here, means not only to beg of, but also to question; and the Greek Gospel, of which this is a translation, has a word that may also be understood in both senses, so that by it the ambiguity is not removed;[2] and even though it were so, every difficulty would not thereby disappear. For we read that the Lord Christ, after He rose again, was both questioned and petitioned. He was asked by the disciples, on the eve of His ascension into heaven, when He would be manifested, and when the kingdom of Israel would come;[3] and even when already in heaven, He was petitioned [asked] by St. Stephen to receive his spirit.[4] And who dare either think or say that Christ ought not to be asked, sitting as He does in heaven, and yet was asked while He abode on earth? or that He ought not to be asked in His state of immortality, although it was men's duty to ask Him while still in His state of subjection to death? Nay, beloved, let us ask Him to untie with His own hands the knot of our present inquiry, by so shining into our hearts that we may perceive what He saith.

5. For I think that His words, "But I will see you again, and your heart shall rejoice, and your joy no man taketh from you," are not to be referred to the time of His resurrection, and when He showed them His flesh to be looked at and handled;[5] but rather to that of which He had already said, "He that loveth me, shall be loved of my Father; and I will love him, and will manifest myself to him."[6] For He had already risen, He had already shown Himself to them in the flesh, and He was already sitting at the right hand of the Father, when that same Apostle John, whose Gospel this is, says in his epistle, "Beloved, now are we the sons of God; and it doth not yet appear what we shall be: but we know that, when He shall be manifested, we shall be like Him; for we shall see Him as He is."[7] That vision belongs not to this life, but to the future; and is not temporal, but eternal. "And this is life eternal," in the words of Him who is that life, "that they might know Thee the only true God, and

Jesus Christ, whom Thou hast sent."[8] Of this vision and knowledge the apostle says, "Now we see through a glass, in a riddle; but then face to face: now I know in part; but then shall I know even as also I am known."[9] At present the Church is in travail with the longing for this fruit of all her labor, but then she shall bring to the birth in its actual contemplation; now she travails in birth with groaning, then shall she bring forth in joy; now she travails in birth through her prayers, then shall she bring forth in her praises. Thus, too, is it a male child; since to such fruit in the contemplation are all the duties of her present conduct to be referred. For He alone is free; because He is desired on His own account, and not in reference to aught besides. Such conduct is in His service; for whatever is done in a good spirit has a reference to Him, because it is done on His behalf; while He, on the other hand, is got and held in possession on His own account, and not on that of aught besides. And there, accordingly, we find the only end that is satisfying to ourselves. He will therefore be eternal; for no end can satisfy us, save that which is found in Him who is endless. With this was Philip inspired, when he said, "Show us the Father, and it sufficeth us." And in that showing the Son gave promise also of His own presence, when He said, "Believest thou not that I am in the Father, and the Father in me?"[10] Of that, therefore, which alone sufficeth us, we are very appropriately informed, "Your joy no man taketh from you."

6. On this point, also, in reference to what has been said above, I think we may get a still better understanding of the words, "A little while, and ye shall no more see me: and again a little while, and ye shall see me." For the whole of that space over which the present dispensation extends, is but a little while; and hence this same evangelist says in his epistle, "It is the last hour."[11] For in this sense also He added, "Because I go to the Father," which is to be referred to the preceding clause, where He saith, "A little while, and ye shall no more see me;" and not to the subsequent, where He saith, "And again a little while, and ye shall see me." For by His going to the Father, He was to bring it about that they should not see Him. And on this account, therefore, His words did not mean that He was about to die, and to be withdrawn from their view till His resurrection; but that He was about to go to the Father, which He did after His resurrec-

---

[1] Rom. vi. 9.   [2] Greek, ἐρωτήσετε.   [3] Acts i. 6.
[4] Acts vii. 59.   [5] Chap. xx. 27.   [6] Chap. xiv. 21.
[7] 1 John iii. 2.

[8] Chap. xvii. 3.   [9] 1 Cor. xiii. 12.
[10] Chap. xiv. 8, 10   [11] 1 John ii. 18.

tion, and when, after holding intercourse with them for forty days, He ascended into heaven.[1]　He therefore addressed the words, "A little while, and ye shall no more see me," to those who saw Him at the time in bodily form; because He was about to go to the Father, and never thereafter to be seen in that mortal state wherein they now beheld Him when so addressing them.　But the words that He added, "And again a little while, and ye shall see me," He gave as a promise to the Church universal: just as to it, also, He gave the other promise, "Lo, I am with you always, even to the end of the world."[2]　The Lord is not slack concerning His promise: a little while, and we shall see Him, where we shall have no more any requests to make, any questions to put; for nothing shall remain to be desired, nothing lie hid to be inquired about.　This little while appears long to us, because it is still in continuance; when it is over, we shall then feel what a little while it was.　Let not, then, our joy be like that of the world, whereof it is said, "But the world shall rejoice;" and yet let not our sorrow in travailing in birth with such a desire be unmingled with joy; but, as the apostle says, be "rejoicing in hope, patient in tribulation;"[3] for even the woman in travail, to whom we are compared, has herself more joy over the offspring that is soon to be, than sorrow over her present pains. But let us here close our present discourse, for the words that follow contain a very trying question, and must not be unduly curtailed, so that they may, if the Lord will, obtain a more befitting explanation.

---

[1] Acts i. 3, 9.　　　[2] Matt. xxviii. 20.　　　[3] Rom. xii. 12.

TRACTATE CII.

CHAPTER XVI. 23–28.

1. WE have now to consider these words of the Lord, "Verily, verily, I say unto you, If ye shall ask anything of the Father in my name, He will give it you."　It has already been said in the earlier portions of this discourse of our Lord's, on account of those who ask some things of the Father in Christ's name and receive them not, that there is nothing asked of the Father in the Saviour's name that is asked in contrariety to the method of salvation.[1]　For it is not the sound of the letters and syllables, but what the sound itself imports, and what is rightly and truly to be understood by that sound, that He is to be regarded as declaring, when He says, "in my name."　Hence, he who has such ideas of Christ as ought not to be entertained of the only Son of God, asketh not in His name, even though he may not abstain from the mention of Christ in so many letters and syllables; since it is only in His name he asketh, of whom he is thinking when he asketh.　But he who has such ideas of Him as ought to be entertained, asketh in His name, and receiveth what he asketh, if he asketh nothing that is contrary to his own everlasting salvation.　And he receiveth it when he ought to receive it.　For some things are not refused, but are delayed till they can be given at a suitable time.　In this way, surely, we are to understand His words, "He will give you," so that thereby we may know that those benefits are signified which are properly applicable to those who ask.　For all the saints are heard effectively[2] in their own behalf, but are not so heard in behalf of all besides, whether friends or enemies, or any others: for it is not said in a general kind of way, "He will give;" but, "He will give you."

2. "Hitherto," He says, "ye have not asked anything in my name.　Ask, and ye shall receive, that your joy may be full." This that He calls a full joy is certainly no carnal joy, but a spiritual one; and when it shall be so great as to be no longer capable of any additions to it, it will then doubtless be full.　Whatever, then, is asked as belonging to the attainment of this joy, is to be asked in the name of Christ, if we understand the grace of God, and if we are truly in quest of a blessed life.　But if aught different from this is asked, there is nothing asked: not that the thing itself is nothing at all, but that in comparison with what is so great, anything else that is coveted is virtually nothing.

---

[1] Above, Tract. LXXIII.　　　[2] *Exaudiuntur*, heard and answered.

For, of course, the man is not actually nothing, of whom the apostle says, "He who thinketh himself to be something, when he is nothing."[1] But surely in comparison with the spiritual man, who knows that by the grace of God he is what he is, he who makes vain assumptions is nothing. In this way, then, may the words also be rightly understood, "Verily, verily, I say unto you, if ye shall ask anything of the Father in my name, He will give [it] you;" that by the words, "if anything," should not be understood anything whatever, but anything that is not really nothing in connection with the life of blessedness. And what follows, "Hitherto ye have not asked anything in my name," may be understood in two ways: either, that ye have not asked in my name, because a name that ye have not known as it is yet to be known; or, ye have not asked anything, since in comparison with that which ye ought to have asked, what ye have asked is to be accounted as nothing. In order, then, that they may ask in His name, not that which is nothing, but a full joy (since anything different from this that they ask is virtually nothing), He addresses to them the exhortation, "Ask, and ye shall receive, that your joy may be full;" that is, ask this in my name, that your joy may be full, and ye shall receive. For His saints, who persevere in asking such a good thing as this, will in no wise be defrauded by the mercy of God.

3. "These things," said He, "have I spoken to you in proverbs: but the hour cometh, when I shall no more speak unto you in proverbs, but I shall show you plainly of my Father." I might be disposed to say that this hour, whereof He speaketh, must be understood as that future period when we shall see openly, as the blessed Paul says, "face to face;" that what He says, "These things have I spoken to you in proverbs," is one with what has been said by the same apostle, "Now we see through a glass, in a riddle:"[2] and "I will show you," because the Father shall be seen through the instrumentality of the Son, is akin to what He says elsewhere, "Neither knoweth any man the Father, save the Son, and [he] to whom the Son shall be pleased to reveal Him."[3] But such a sense seems to be interfered with by that which follows: "At that day ye shall ask in my name." For in that future world, when we have reached the kingdom where we shall be like Him, for we shall see Him as He is,[4] what shall we then have to ask, when our desire shall be satisfied with good things?[5]

As it is also said in another psalm: "I shall be satisfied when Thy glory shall be revealed."[6] For petition has to do with some kind of want, which can have no place there where such abundance shall reign.

4. It remains, therefore, for us, so far as my capacity to apprehend it goes, to understand Jesus as having promised that He would cause His disciples, from being carnal and natural, to become spiritual, although not yet such as we shall be, when a spiritual body shall also be ours; but such as was he who said, "We speak wisdom among them that are perfect;"[7] and, "I could not speak unto you as unto spiritual, but as unto carnal;"[8] and, "We have received, not the spirit of the world, but the Spirit who is of God; that we might know the things that are freely given to us of God. Which things also we speak, not in the words which man's wisdom teacheth, but which the Spirit teacheth; comparing spiritual things with spiritual. But the natural[9] man perceiveth not the things of the Spirit of God." And thus the natural man, perceiving not the things of the Spirit of God, hears in such a way whatever is told him of the nature of God, that he can conceive of nothing else but some bodily form, however spacious or immense, however lustrous and magnificent, yet still a body: and therefore he holds as proverbs all that is said of the incorporeal and immutable substance of wisdom; not that he accounts them as proverbs, but that his thoughts follow the same direction as those who habitually listen to proverbs without understanding them. But when the spiritual man begins to discern all things, and he himself is discerned by no man, he perceives, even though in this life it still be through a glass and in part, not by any bodily sense, and not by any imaginative conception which catches at or devises the likenesses of all sorts of bodies, but by the clearest understanding of the mind, that God is not material, but spiritual: in such a way does the Son show us openly of the Father, that He, who thus shows, is also Himself seen to be of the same substance. And then it is that those who ask, ask in His name; for in the sound of that name they understand

---

[6] Ps. xvii. 15. So the Septuagint translate בְּהָקִיץ תְּמוּנָתֶךָ אֶשְׂבְּעָה. The *Hiphil* intransitive form הֵקִיץ is used, however, only of "awaking" out of sleep, not of "appearing," or "being manifested;" and תְּמוּנָה properly means, *appearance, form, likeness*, although "*glory*" may in the present connection be implied: so that while the rendering of the Septuagint may be grammatically defensible, "I shall be satisfied when Thy glory is manifested," yet the strict meaning of the words, the context, and the accentuation, favor that of the English version, "I shall be satisfied, on awaking, with Thy likeness."—Tr.

---

[1] Gal. vi. 3. [2] 1 Cor. xiii. 12. [3] Matt. xi. 27.
[4] 1 John iii. 2. [5] Ps. ciii. 5.

[7] 1 Cor. ii. 6. [8] 1 Cor. iii. 1. [9] *Animalis.*

nothing else than what the reality is that is called by that name, and harbor not, in vanity or infirmity of mind, the fiction of the Father being in one place, and the Son in another, standing before the Father and making request in our behalf, with the material substances of both occupying each its own place, and the Word pleading verbally for us with Him whose Word He is, while a definite space interposes between the mouth of the speaker and the ears of the hearer; and other such absurdities which those who are natural, and at the same time carnal, fabricate for themselves in their hearts. For any such thing, suggested by the experience of bodily habits, as occurs to spiritual men when thinking of God, they deny and reject, and drive away, like troublesome insects, from the eyes of their mind; and resign themselves to the purity of that light by whose testimony and judgment they prove these bodily images that thrust themselves on their inward vision to be altogether false. These are able to a certain extent to think of our Lord Jesus Christ, in respect of His manhood, as addressing the Father on our behalf; but in respect to His Godhead, as hearing [and answering] us along with the Father. And this I am of opinion that He indicated, when He said, "And I say not that I will pray the Father for you." But the intuitive perception of this, how it is that the Son asketh not the Father, but that Father and Son alike listen to those who ask, is a height that can be reached only by the spiritual eye of the mind.

5. "For the Father Himself," He says, "loveth you, because ye have loved me." Is it the case, then, that He loveth, because we love; or rather, that we love, because He loveth? Let this same evangelist give us the answer out of his own epistle: "We love Him," he says, "because He first loved us."[1] This, then, was the efficient cause of our loving, that we were loved. And certainly to love God is the gift of God. He it was that gave the grace to love Him, who loved while still unloved. Even when displeasing Him we were loved, that there might be that in us whereby we should become pleasing in His sight. For we could not love the Son unless we loved the Father also. The Father loveth us, because we love the Son; seeing it is of the Father and Son we have received [the power] to love both the Father and the Son: for love is shed abroad in our hearts by the Spirit of both,[2] by which Spirit we love both the Father and the Son, and whom we love along with the Father and the Son. God, therefore, it was that wrought this religious love of ours whereby we worship God; and He saw that it is good, and on that account He Himself loved that which He had made. But He would not have wrought in us something He could love, were it not that He loved ourselves before He wrought it.

6. "And ye have believed," He adds, "that I came out from God. I came forth from the Father, and am come into the world: again I leave the world, and go to the Father." Clearly we have believed. For surely it ought not to be accounted a thing incredible because of this, that in coming to the world He came forth in such a sense from the Father that He did not leave the Father behind; and that, on leaving the world, He goes to the Father in such a sense that He does not actually forsake the world. For He came forth from the Father because He is of the Father; and He came into the world, in showing to the world His bodily form, which He had received of the Virgin. He left the world by a bodily withdrawal, He proceeded to the Father by His ascension as man, but He forsook not the world in the ruling activity of His presence.

---

[1] 1 John iv. 19.

[2] Rom. v. 5.

TRACTATE CIII.

Chapter XVI. 29–33.

1. The inward state of Christ's disciples, when before His passion He talked with them as with children of great things, but in such a way as befitted the great things to be spoken to children, because, having not yet received the Holy Spirit, as they did after His resurrection, either by His own breathing upon them, or by descent from above, they had a mental capacity for the human rather than the divine,—is everywhere declared through the Gospel by numerous testimonies; and of a piece therewith, is what they said in the lesson before us. For, says the evangelist, "His disciples say unto Him: Lo, now

speakest Thou plainly, and utterest no proverb. Now we are sure that Thou knowest all things, and needest not that any man should ask Thee: by this we believe that Thou camest forth from God." The Lord Himself had said shortly before, "These things have I spoken unto you in proverbs: the hour cometh, when I shall no more speak to you in proverbs." How, then, say they, "Lo, now speakest Thou plainly, and utterest no proverb"? Was the hour, indeed, already come, when He had promised that He would no more speak unto them in proverbs? Certainly that such an hour had not yet come, is shown by the continuation of His words, which run in this way: "These things," said He, "have I spoken unto you in proverbs: the hour cometh, when I shall no more speak unto you in proverbs, but I shall show you plainly of my Father. At that day ye shall ask in my name: and I say not unto you, that I will pray the Father for you: for the Father Himself loveth you, because ye have loved me, and have believed that I came out from God. I came forth from the Father, and have come into the world: again, I leave the world, and go to the Father" (vers. 25–28). Seeing that throughout all these words He is still promising that hour when He shall no more speak in proverbs, but shall show them openly of the Father; the hour, when He says that they will ask in His name, and that He will not pray the Father for them, on the ground that the Father Himself loveth them, and that they also have loved Christ, and have believed that He came forth from the Father, and was come into the world, and was again about to leave the world and go to the Father: when thus that hour is still the subject of promise when He was to speak without proverbs, why say they, "Lo, now speakest Thou plainly, and utterest no proverb;" but just because those things, which He knows to be proverbs to those who have no understanding, they are still so far from understanding, that they do not even understand that they do not understand them? For they were babes, and had as yet no spiritual discernment of what they heard regarding things that had to do not with the body, but with the spirit.

2. And still further admonishing them of their age as still small and infirm in regard to the inner man, "Jesus answered them: Do ye now believe? Behold the hour cometh, yea, is now come, that ye shall be scattered every man to his own, and shall leave me alone. And yet I am not alone, because the Father is with me." He had said shortly before, "I leave the world, and go to the Father;" now He says, "The Father is with me." Who goes to him who is with him? This is a word to him that understandeth, a proverb to him that understandeth not: and yet in such way that what at present is unintelligible to babes, is in some sort sucked in; and even though it yield them not solid food, which they cannot as yet receive, it denies them not at least a milky diet. It was from this diet that they drew the knowledge that He knew all things, and needed not that any one should ask Him: and, indeed, why they said this, is a topic worthy of inquiry. For one would think they ought rather to have said, Thou needest not to ask any one; not, "That any one should ask Thee." They had just said, "We are sure that Thou knowest all things:" and surely He that knoweth all things is accustomed rather to be questioned by those who do not know, that in reply to their questions they may hear what they wish from Him who knoweth all things; and not to be Himself the questioner, as if wishing to know something, when He knoweth all things. What, then, are we to understand by this, that, when apparently they ought to have said to Him, whom they knew to be omniscient, Thou needest not to ask any man, they considered it more befitting to say, "Thou needest not that any man should ask Thee"? Yea, is it not the case that we read of both being done; to wit, that the Lord both asked, and was asked questions? But this latter is speedily answered: for this was needful not for Him, but for those rather whom He questioned, or by whom He was questioned. For He never questioned any for the purpose of learning anything from them, but for the purpose rather of teaching them. And for those who put questions to Him, as desirous of learning something of Him, it was assuredly needful to be made acquainted with some things by Him who knew everything. And doubtless on the same account also it was that He needed not that any man should ask Him. As it is the case that we, when questioned by those who wish to get some information from us, discover by their very questionings what it is that they wish to know, we therefore need to be questioned by those whom we wish to teach, in order that we may be acquainted with their inquiries that call for an answer: but He, who knew all things, had no need even of that, and as little need had He of discovering by their questions what it was that any one desired to know of Him, for before a question was put, He knew the intention of him who was to put it. But He suffered Himself to be questioned on this account, that He might

show to those who were then present, or to those who should either hear the things that were to be spoken or read them when written, what was the character of those by whom He was questioned; and in this way we might come to know both the frauds that were powerless to impose upon Him, and the ways of approach that would turn to our profit in His sight. But to foresee the thoughts of men, and thus to have no need that any one should ask Him, was no great matter for God, but great enough for the babes, who said to Him, " By this we believe that Thou camest forth from God." A much greater thing it was, for the understanding of which He wished to have their minds expanded and enlarged, that, on their saying, and saying truly, " Thou camest forth from God," He replied, " The Father is with me;" in order that they should not think that the Son had come forth from the Father in any sense that would lead them to suppose that He had also withdrawn from His presence.

3. And then, in bringing to a close this weighty and protracted discourse, He said, " These things have I spoken unto you, that in me ye might have peace. In the world ye shall have tribulation; but be of good cheer, I have overcome the world." The beginning of such tribulation was to be found in that whereof, in order to show that they were infants, to whom, as still wanting in intelligence, and mistaking one thing for another, all the great and divine things He had said were little better than proverbs, He had previously said, " Do ye now believe? Behold, the hour cometh, yea, is now come, that ye shall be scattered, every man to his own." Such, I say, was the beginning of the tribulation, but not in the same measure of their perseverance. For in adding, " and ye shall leave me alone," He did not mean that they would be of such a character in the subsequent tribulation, which they should have to endure in the world after His ascen-

sion, as thus to desert Him; but that in Him they should have peace by still abiding in Him. But on the occasion of His apprehension, not only did they outwardly abandon His bodily presence, but they mentally abandoned their faith. And to this it is that His words have reference, " Do ye now believe? Behold, the hour cometh, that ye shall be scattered to your own, and shall leave me:" as if He had said, You will then be so confounded as to leave behind you even what you now believe. For they fell into such despair and such a death, so to speak, of their old faith, as was apparent in the case of Cleophas, who, after His resurrection, unaware that he was speaking with Himself, and narrating what had befallen Him, said, " We trusted that it had been He who should have redeemed Israel." [1] That was the way in which they then left Him, abandoning even the very faith wherewith they had formerly believed in Him. But in that tribulation, which they encountered after His glorification and they themselves had received the Holy Spirit, they did not leave Him: and though they fled from city to city, from Himself they did not flee; but in order that, while having tribulation in the world, they might have peace in Him, instead of being fugitives from Him, it was rather Himself that they made their refuge. For in receiving the Holy Spirit, there was wrought in them the very state described to them now in the words, " Be of good cheer, I have overcome the world." They were of good cheer, and they conquered. But in whom, save in Him? For He had not overcome the world, were it still to overcome His members. Hence said the apostle, " Thanks be unto God, who giveth us the victory;" and immediately added, " through our Lord Jesus Christ:" [2] through Him who had said to His own, " Be of good cheer, I have overcome the world."

---

[1] Luke xxiv. 21.   [2] 1 Cor. xv. 57

TRACTATE CIV.

CHAPTER XVII. 1.

1. BEFORE these words, which we are now, with the Lord's help, to make the subject of discourse, Jesus had said, " These things have I spoken unto you, that in me ye might have peace;" which we are to consider as referring, not to the later words uttered by Him imme-

diately before, but to all that He had addressed to them, whether from the time that He began to account them disciples, or at least from the time after supper when He commenced this admirable and lengthened discourse. He gave them, indeed, such a reason for speaking to them, that either all He ever spake to them may with the utmost propriety be referred to that end, or those especially, as His last words, which He now spake when on the eve of dying for them, after that he who was to betray Him had quitted their company. For He gave this as the cause of His discourse, that in Him they might have peace, just as it is wholly on this account that we are Christians. For this peace will have no temporal end, but will itself be the end of every pious intention and action that are ours at present. For its sake we are endowed with His sacraments, for its sake we are instructed by His works and sayings, for its sake we have received the earnest of the Spirit, for its sake we believe and hope in Him, and according to His gracious giving are enkindled with His love: by this peace we are comforted in all our distresses, by it we are delivered from them all: for its sake we endure with fortitude every tribulation, that in it we may reign in happiness without any tribulation. Fitly therewith did He bring His words to a close, which were proverbs to the disciples, who as yet had little understanding, but would afterwards understand them, when He had given them the Holy Spirit of promise, of whom He had said before: These things have I spoken unto you, being yet present with you. But the Comforter, the Holy Ghost, whom the Father will send in my name, He shall teach you all things, and bring all things to your remembrance, whatsoever I have said unto you."[1] Such, doubtless, was to be the hour, wherein He promised that He would no more speak unto them in proverbs, but show them openly of the Father. For these same words of His, when revealed by the Holy Spirit, were no more to be proverbs to those who had understanding. For when the Holy Spirit was speaking in their hearts, there was not to be silence on the part of the only-begotten Son, who had said that in that hour He would show them plainly of the Father, which, of course, would no longer be a proverb to them when now endowed with understanding. But even this also, how it is that both the Son of God and the Holy Spirit speak at once in the hearts of their spiritual ones, yea the Trinity itself, which is ever inseparably at work, is a word to those who have, but a proverb to those who are without, understanding.

2. When, therefore, He had told them on what account He had spoken all things, namely, that in Him they might have peace while having distress in the world, and had exhorted them to be of good cheer, because He had overcome the world; having thus finished His discourse to them, He then directed His words to the Father, and began to pray. For so the evangelist proceeds to say: "These things spake Jesus, and lifted up His eyes to heaven, and said: Father, the hour is come; glorify Thy Son." The Lord, the Only-begotten and co-eternal with the Father, could in the form of a servant and out of the form of a servant, if such were needful, pray in silence; but in this other way He wished to show Himself as one who prayed to the Father, that He might remember that He was still our Teacher. Accordingly, the prayer which He offered for us, He made also known to us; seeing that it is not only the delivering of discourses to them by so great a Master, but also the praying for them to the Father, that is a means of edification to disciples. And if so to those who were present to hear what was said, it is certainly so also to us who were to have the reading of it when written. Wherefore in saying this, "Father, the hour is come; glorify Thy Son," He showed that all time, and every occasion when He did anything or suffered anything to be done, were arranged by Him who was subject to no time: since those things, which were individually future in point of time, have their efficient causes in the wisdom of God, wherein there are no distinctions of time. Let it not, then, be supposed that this hour came through any urgency of fate, but rather by the divine appointment. It was no necessary law of the heavenly bodies that tied to its time the passion of Christ; for we may well shrink from the thought that the stars should compel their own Maker to die. It was not the time, therefore, that drove Christ to His death, but Christ who selected the time to die: who also fixed the time, when He was born of the Virgin, with the Father, of whom He was born independently of time. And in accordance with this true and salutary doctrine, the Apostle Paul also says, "But when the fullness of the time was come, God sent forth His Son;"[2] and God declares by the prophet, "In an acceptable time have I heard Thee, and in a day of salvation have I helped thee;"[3] and yet again the apostle, "Behold, now is the accepted time; behold, now is the day of salvation."[4] He then may say, "Father, the hour is come," who has arranged every hour with the Father: saying, as it were, "Father, the hour," which we fixed together for the sake of men and of my glorification among them, "is come, glorify Thy Son, that Thy Son also may glorify Thee."

3. The glorification of the Son by the

[1] Chap. xiv. 25, 26.   [2] Gal. iv. 4.   [3] Isa. xlix. 8.   [4] 2 Cor. vi. 2.

Father is understood by some to consist in this, that He spared Him not, but delivered Him up for us all.[1] But if we say that He was glorified by His passion, how much more was He so by His resurrection! For in His passion our attention is directed more to His humility than to His glory, in accordance with the testimony of the apostle, who says, "He humbled Himself, and became obedient unto death, even the death of the cross:" and then he goes on to say of His glorification, "Wherefore God also hath highly exalted Him, and given Him a name which is above every name: that in the name of Jesus every knee should bow, of things in heaven, and things in earth, and things under the earth; and that every tongue should confess that the Lord Jesus Christ is in the glory of God the Father." This is the glorification of our Lord Jesus Christ, that took its commencement from His resurrection. His humility accordingly begins in the apostle's discourse with the passage where he says, "He emptied Himself, and took upon Him the form of a servant;" and reaches "even to the death of the cross." But His glory begins with the clause where he says, "Wherefore God also hath exalted Him;" and reaches on to the words, "is in the glory of God the Father."[2] For even the noun itself, if the language of the Greek codices be examined, from which the apostolic epistles have been translated into Latin, which in the latter is read, glory, is in the former read, δόξα: whence we have the verb derived in Greek for the purpose of saying here, δόξασον (glorify), which the Latin translator renders by "*clarifica*" (make illus-

---

[1] Rom. viii. 32.
[2] Phil. ii. 7-11. So Augustin, with a few others of the early fathers, incorrectly renders the last clause instead of that given by our English version, which is alone grammatically and textually correct: "That Jesus Christ is Lord, to the glory (εἰς δόξαν) of God the Father."—Tr.

trious), although he might as well have said "*glorifica*" (glorify), which is the same in meaning. And for the same reason, in the apostle's epistle where we find "*gloria*," "*claritas*" might have been used; for by so doing, the meaning would have been equally preserved. But not to depart from the sound of the words, just as "*clarificatio*" (the making lustrous) is derived from "*claritas*" (lustre), so is "*glorificatio*" (the making glorious) from "*gloria*" (glory). In order, then, that the Mediator between God and men, the man Christ Jesus, might be made lustrous or glorious by His resurrection, He was first humbled by suffering; for had He not died, He would not have risen from the dead. Humility is the earning of glory; glory, the reward of humility. This, however, was done in the form of a servant; but He was always in the form of God, and always shall His glory continue: yea, it was not in the past as if it were no more so in the present, nor shall it be, as if it did not yet exist; but without beginning and without end, His glory is everlasting. Accordingly, when He says, "Father, the hour is come; glorify Thy Son," it is to be understood as if He said, The hour is come for sowing the seed-corn of humility, delay not the fruit of my glory. But what is the meaning of the words that follow: "That Thy Son may glorify Thee"? Was it that God the Father likewise endured the humiliation of the body or of suffering, out of which He must needs be raised to glory? If not, how then was the Son to glorify Him, whose eternal glory could neither appear diminished through human form, nor be enlarged in the divine? But I will not confine such a question within the present discourse, or draw the latter out to greater length by such a discussion.

TRACTATE CV.

Chapter XVII. 1-5.

1. THAT the Son was glorified by the Father in His form of a servant, which the Father raised from the dead and set at His own right hand, is indicated by the event itself, and is nowhere doubted by the Christian. But as He not only said, "Father, glorify Thy Son," but likewise added, "that Thy Son may glorify Thee," it is worthy of inquiry how it was that the Son glorified the Father, seeing that the eternal glory of the Father neither suffered diminution in any human form, nor could be increased in respect of its own divine perfection. In itself, indeed, the glory of the Father could neither be diminished nor enlarged; but without any doubt it was less among men when God was known only in

Judea:[1] and as yet children[2] praised not the name of the Lord from the rising of the sun to its going down.[2] But inasmuch as this was effected by the gospel of Christ, to wit, that the Father became known through the Son to the Gentiles, assuredly the Son also glorified the Father. Had the Son, however, only died, and not risen again, He would without doubt have neither been glorified by the Father, nor have glorified the Father; but now having been glorified through His resurrection by the Father, He glorifies the Father by the preaching of His resurrection. For this is disclosed by the very order of the words: "Glorify," He says, "Thy Son, that Thy Son may glorify Thee;" saying, as it were, Raise me up again, that by me Thou mayest become known to all the world.

2. And then expanding still further how it was that the Father should be glorified by the Son, He says: "As Thou hast given Him power over all flesh, that He should give eternal life to all that Thou hast given Him." By all flesh, He meant every man, signifying the whole by a part; as, on the other hand, the whole man is signified by the superior part, when the apostle says, "Let every soul be subject to the higher powers."[3] For what else did He mean by "every soul," save every man? And this, therefore, that power over all flesh was given to Christ by the Father, is to be understood in respect of His humanity; for in respect of His Godhead all things were made by Himself, and in Him were created all things in heaven and in earth, visible and invisible.[4] "As," then, He says, "Thou hast given Him power over all flesh," so may Thy Son glorify Thee, in other words, make Thee known to all flesh whom Thou hast given Him. For Thou hast so given, "that He should give eternal life to all that Thou hast given Him."

3. "And this," He adds, "is eternal life, that they may know Thee, the only true God, and Jesus Christ, whom Thou hast sent." The proper order of the words is, "That they may know Thee and Jesus Christ, whom Thou hast sent, as the only true God." Consequently, therefore, the Holy Spirit is also understood, because He is the Spirit of the Father and Son, as the substantial and consubstantial love of both. For the Father and Son are not two Gods, nor are the Father and Son and Holy Spirit three Gods; but the Trinity itself is the one only true God. And yet the Father is not the same as the Son, nor

the Son the same as the Father, nor the Holy Spirit the same as the Father and the Son; for the Father and Son and Holy Spirit are three [persons], yet the Trinity itself is one God. If, then, the Son glorifies Thee in the same manner " as Thou hast given Him power over all flesh," and hast so given, " that He should give eternal life to all that Thou hast given Him," and "this is life eternal, that they may know Thee;" in this way, therefore, the Son glorifies Thee, that He makes Thee known to all whom Thou hast given Him. Accordingly, if the knowledge of God is eternal life, we are making the greater advances to life, in proportion as we are enlarging our growth in such a knowledge. And we shall not die in the life eternal; for then, when there shall be no death, the knowledge of God shall be perfected. Then will be effected the full effulgence of God, because then the completed glory, as expressed in Greek by δόξα. For from it we have the word δόξασον, that is used here, and which some Latins have interpreted by "clarifica" (make effulgent), and some by "glorifica" (glorify). But by the ancients, glory, from which men are styled glorious, is thus defined: Glory is the widely-spread fame of any one accompanied with praise. But if a man is praised when the fame regarding him is believed, how will God be praised when He Himself shall be seen? Hence it is said in Scripture, " Blessed are they that dwell in Thy house; they will be praising Thee for ever and ever."[5] There will God's praise continue without end, where there shall be the full knowledge of God; and because the full knowledge, therefore also the complete effulgence or glorification.

4. But God is first of all glorified here, while He is being made known to men by word of mouth, and preached through the faith of believers. Wherefore, He says, "I have glorified Thee on the earth: I have finished the work which Thou gavest me to do." He does not say, Thou orderedst; but, "Thou gavest:" where the evident grace of it is commended to notice. For what has the human nature even in the Only-begotten, that it has not received? Did it not receive this, that it should do no evil, but all good things, when it was assumed into the unity of His person by the Word, by whom all things were made? But how has He finished the work which was committed unto Him to do, when there still remains the trial of the passion wherein He especially furnished His martyrs with the example they were to follow,

---

[1] Ps. lxxvi. 1.
[2] Ps. cxiii. 3, 1: *pueri*, from the LXX. παῖδες. The Hebrew is עֶבֶד, "servants."—Tr.

[3] Rom. xiii. 1.   [4] Col. i. 16.   [5] Ps. lxxxiv. 4.

whereof, says the apostle Peter, "Christ suffered for us, leaving us an example, that we should follow His steps:"[1] but just that He says He has finished, what He knew with perfect certainty that He would finish? Just as long before, in prophecy, He used words in the past tense, when what He said was to take place very many years afterwards: "They pierced," He says, "my hands and my feet, they counted[2] all my bones;"[2] He says not, They will pierce, and, They will count. And in this very Gospel He says, "All things that I have heard of my Father, I have made known unto you;"[3] to whom He afterward declares, "I have yet many things to say unto you, but ye cannot bear them now."[4] For He, who has predestinated all that is to be by sure and unchangeable causes, has done whatever He is to do: as it was also declared of Him by the prophet, "Who hath made the things that are to be."[5]

5. In a way similar, also, to this, He proceeds to say: "And now, O Father, glorify thou me with Thine own self with the glory which I had with Thee before the world was." For He had said above, "Father, the hour is come; glorify Thy Son, that Thy Son may glorify Thee:" in which arrangement of the words He had shown that the Father was first to be glorified by the Son, in order that the Son might glorify the Father. But now He said, "I have glorified Thee on the earth: I have finished the work which Thou gavest me to do; and now glorify Thou me;" as if He Himself had been the first to glorify the Father, by whom He then demands to be glorified. We are therefore to understand that He used both words above in accordance with that which was future, and in the order in which they were future, "Glorify Thy Son, that Thy Son may glorify Thee:" but that He now used the word in the past tense of that which was still future, when He said, "I have glorified Thee on the earth: I have finished the work which Thou gavest me to do." And then, when He said, "And now, O Father, glorify Thou me with Thine own self," as if He were afterwards to be glorified by the Father, whom He Himself had first glorified; what did He intimate but that, when He said above, "I have glorified Thee on the earth," He had so spoken as if He had done what He was still to do; but that here

He demanded of the Father to do that whereby the Son should yet do so; in other words, that the Father should glorify the Son, by means of which glorification of the Son, the Son also was yet to glorify the Father? In fine, if, in connection with that which was still future, we put the verb also in the future tense, where He has used the past in place of the future tense, there will remain no obscurity in the sentence: as if He had said, "I will glorify Thee on the earth: I will finish the work which Thou hast given me to do; and now, O Father, glorify Thou me with Thine own self." In this way it is as plain as when He says, "Glorify Thy Son, that Thy Son may glorify Thee:" and this is indeed the whole sentence, save that here we are told also the manner of that same glorification, which there was left unnoticed; as if the former were explained by the latter to those whose hearts it was able to stir, how it was that the Father should glorify the Son, and most of all how the Son also should glorify the Father. For in saying that the Father was glorified by Himself on the earth, but He Himself by the Father with the Father's very self, He showed them assuredly the manner of both glorifications. For He Himself glorified the Father on earth by preaching Him to the nations; but the Father glorified Him with His own self in setting Him at His own right hand. But on that very account, when He says afterward in reference to the glorifying of the Father, "I have glorified Thee," He preferred putting the verb in the past tense, in order to show that it was already done in the act of predestination, and what was with perfect certainty yet to take place was to be accounted as already done; namely, that the Son, having been glorified by the Father with the Father, would also glorify the Father on the earth.

6. But this predestination He still more clearly disclosed in respect of His own glorification, wherewith He was glorified by the Father, when He added, "With the glory which I had, before the world was, with Thee." The proper order of the words is, "which I had with Thee before the world was." To this apply His words, "And now glorify Thou me;" that is to say, as then, so also now: as then, by predestination; so also now, by consummmation: do Thou in the world what had already been done with Thee before the world: do in its own time what Thou hast determined before all times. This, some have imagined, should be so understood as if the human nature, which was assumed by the Word, were converted into the Word, and the man were changed into God; yea,

---

[1] 1 Pet. ii. 21.
[2] Ps. xxii. 16, 17. *Dinumeraverunt* (*they* counted), in accordance with a reading of the Septuagint—that found in the printed text—ἐξηρίθμησαν. A better reading, however, is also found in MSS., ἐξηρίθμησα, conforming in person, though not in tense, to the Hebrew אֲסַפֵּר (I may count).—TR.

[3] Chap. xv. 15.　　[4] Chap. xvi. 12.
[5] Isa. xlv. 11, according to the Septuagint. See note, Tract. LXVIII. sec. 1.

were we reflecting with some care on the opinions they have advanced, as if the humanity were lost in the Godhead. For no one would go the length of saying that out of such a transmutation of the humanity the Word of God is either doubled or increased, so that either what was one should now be two, or what was less should now be greater. Accordingly, if with His human nature changed and converted into the Word, the Word of God will still be as great as He was, and what He was, where is the humanity, if it is not lost?

7. But to this opinion, which I certainly do not see to be conformable to the truth, there is nothing to urge us, if, when the Son says, "And now, O Father, glorify Thou me with Thine own self, with the glory which I had with Thee before the world was," we understand the predestination of the glory of His human nature, as thereafter, from being mortal, to become immortal with the Father; and that this had already been done by predestination before the world was, as also in its own time it was done in the world. For if the apostle has said of us, "According as He hath chosen us in Him before the foundation of the world,"[1] why should it be thought incongruous with the truth, if the Father glorified our Head at the same time as He chose us in Him to be His members? For we were chosen in the same way as He was glorified; inasmuch as before the world was, neither we nor the Mediator between God and men, the *man* Christ Jesus,[2] were yet in existence. But He who, in as far as He is His Word, of His own self "made even those things which are yet to come," and "calleth those things which are not as though they were,"[3] certainly, in respect of His manhood as Mediator between God and men, was Himself glorified on our behalf by God the Father before the foundation of the world, if it be so that we also were then chosen in Him. For what saith the apostle? "And we know that all things work together for good to them that love God, to them who are the called according to His purpose. For whom He did foreknow, He also did predestinate to be conformed to the image of His Son, that He might be the first-born among many brethren: and whom He did predestinate, them He also called."[4]

8. But perhaps we shall have some fear in saying that He was predestinated, because the apostle seems to have said so only in reference to our being made conformable to His image. As if, indeed, any one, faithfully considering the rule of faith, were to deny that the Son of God was predestinated, who yet cannot deny that He was man. For it is rightly said that He was not predestinated in respect of His being the Word of God, God with God. For how could He be predestinated, seeing He already was what He was, without beginning and without ending, everlasting? But that, which as yet was not, had to be predestinated, in order that it might come to pass in its time, even as it was predestinated so to come before all times. Accordingly, whoever denies predestination of the Son of God, denies that He was also Himself the Son of man. But, on account of those who are disputatious, let us also on this subject listen to the apostle in the exordium of his epistles. For both in the first of his epistles, which is that to the Romans, and in the beginning of the epistle itself, we read: "Paul, a servant of Jesus Christ, called [to be] an apostle, separated unto the gospel of God, which He had promised afore by His prophets in the Holy Scriptures, concerning His Son, who was made for Him of the seed of David according to the flesh, who was predestinated[5] the Son of God in power, according to the Spirit of holiness, by the resurrection from the dead."[5] In respect, then, of this predestination also, He was gloried before the world was, in order that His glory might be, by the resurrection from the dead, with the Father, at whose right hand He sitteth. Accordingly, when He saw that the time of this, His predestinated glorification, was now come, in order that what had already been done in predestination might also be done now in actual accomplishment, He said in His prayer, "And now, O Father, glorify Thou me with Thine own self with the glory which I had with Thee before the world was:" as if He had said, The glory which I had with Thee, that is, that glory which I had with Thee in Thy predestination, it is time that I should have with Thee also in sitting at Thy right hand. But as the discussion of this question has already kept us long, what follows must be taken into consideration in another discourse.

---

[1] Eph. i. 4.   [2] 1 Tim. ii. 5.
[3] Rom. iv. 17.   [4] Rom. viii. 28-30.

[5] Rom. i. 1-4: ὁρισθέντος, *determined, declared*, not "*predestinated*," which is a mistake of the Latin version used by Augustin.—Tr.

TRACTATE CVI.

CHAPTER XVII. 6-8.

1. IN this discourse we purpose speaking, as He gives us grace, on these words of the Lord which run thus: " I have manifested Thy name unto the men whom Thou gavest me out of the world." If He said this only of those disciples with whom He had supped, and to whom, before beginning His prayer, He had said so much, it can have nothing to do with that clarification, or, as others have translated it, glorification, whereof He was previously speaking, and whereby the Son clarifies or glorifies the Father. For what great glory, or what like glory, was it to become known to twelve, or rather eleven mortal creatures? But if, in saying, " I have manifested Thy name unto the men whom Thou gavest me out of the world," He wished all to be understood, even those who were still to believe on Him, as belonging to His great Church which was yet to be made up of all nations, and of which it is said in the psalm, " I will confess to Thee in the great Church [congregation];"[1] it is plainly that glorification wherewith the Son glorifies the Father, when He makes His name known to all nations and to so many generations of men. And what He says here, " I have manifested Thy name unto the men whom Thou gavest me out of the world," is similar to what He had said a little before, " I have glorified Thee upon the earth " (ver. 4); putting both here and there the past for the future, as One who knew that it was predestinated to be done, and therefore saying that He had done what He had still to do, though without any uncertainty, in the future.

2. But what follows makes it more credible that His words, " I have manifested Thy name to the men whom Thou gavest me out of the world," were spoken by Him of those who were already His disciples, and not of all who were yet to believe on Him. For after these words, He added: " Thine they were, and Thou gavest them me; and they have kept Thy word. Now they have known that all things, whatsoever Thou hast given me, are of Thee: for I have given unto them the words which Thou gavest me; and they have received them, and have known surely that I came out from Thee, and they have believed that Thou didst send me." Al-

though all these words also might have been said of all believers still to come, when that which was now a matter of hope had been turned into fact, inasmuch as they were words that still pointed to the future; yet we are impelled the more to understand Him as uttering them only of those who were at that time His disciples, by what He says shortly afterwards: " While I was with them, I kept them in Thy name: those that Thou gavest me I have kept, and none of them is lost, but the son of perdition; that the Scripture might be fulfilled " (ver. 12); meaning Judas, who betrayed Him, for He was the only one of the apostolic twelve that perished. And then He adds, "And now come I to Thee," from which it is manifest that it was of His own bodily presence that He said, " While I was with them, I kept them," as if already that presence were no longer with them. For in this way He wished to intimate His own ascension as in the immediate future, when He said, "And now come I to Thee:" going, that is, to the Father's right hand; whence He is hereafter to come to judge the quick and the dead in the self-same bodily presence, according to the rule of faith and sound doctrine: for in His spiritual presence He was still, of course, to be with them after His ascension, and with the whole of His Church in this world even to the end of time.[2] We cannot, therefore, rightly understand of whom He said, " While I was with them, I kept them," save as those only who believed on Him, whom He had already begun to keep by His bodily presence, but was now to leave without it, in order that He might keep them with the Father by His spiritual presence. Thereafter, indeed, He also unites with them the rest of His disciples, when He says, " Neither pray I for these alone, but for those also who shall believe on me through their word." Where He shows still more clearly that He was not speaking before of all who belonged to Him, in the passage where He saith, " I have manifested Thy name unto the men whom Thou gavest me," but of those only who were listening to Him when He so spake.

3. From the very outset, therefore, of His prayer, when " He lifted up His eyes to

---

[1] Ps. xxxv. 18.

[2] Matt. xxviii. 20.

heaven, and said, Father, the hour is come; glorify Thy Son, that Thy Son also may glorify Thee," on to what He said a little afterwards, "And now, O Father, glorify Thou me with Thine own self with the glory which I had with Thee before the world was," He wished all His disciples to be understood, to whom He makes the Father known, and thereby glorifies Him. For after saying, "That Thy Son may glorify Thee," He straightway showed how that was to be done, by adding, "As Thou hast given Him power over all flesh, that He should give eternal life to as many as Thou hast given Him: and this is life eternal, that they might know Thee the only true God, and Jesus Christ, whom Thou hast sent." For the Father cannot be glorified through any knowledge attained by men, unless He also be known by whom He is glorified, that is to say, by whom He is made known to the nations of the world. The glorification of the Father is not that which was displayed in connection with the apostles only, but that which is displayed in all men, of whom as His members Christ is the head. For the words cannot be understood as applied to the apostles only, "As Thou hast given Him power over all flesh, that He should give eternal life to as many as Thou hast given Him;" but to all, assuredly, on whom, as believing on Him, eternal life is bestowed.

4. Accordingly, let us now see what He says about those disciples of His who were then listening to Him. "I have manifested," He says. "Thy name unto the men whom Thou gavest me." Did they not, then, know the name of God when they were Jews? And what of that which we read, "God is known in Judah; His name is great in Israel"?[1] Therefore, "I have manifested Thy name unto *these* men whom Thou gavest me out of the world," and who are now hearing my words: not that name of Thine whereby Thou art called God, but that whereby Thou art called my Father: a name that could not be manifested without the manifestation of the Son Himself. For this name of God, by which He is called, could not but be known in some way to the whole creation, and so to every nation, before they believed in Christ. For such is the energy of true Godhead, that it cannot be altogether and utterly hidden from any rational creature, so long as it makes use of its reason. For, with the exception of a few in whom nature has become outrageously depraved, the whole race of man acknowledges God as the maker of this world.

In respect, therefore, of His being the maker of this world that is visible in heaven and earth around us, God was known unto all nations even before they were indoctrinated into the faith of Christ. But in this respect, that He was not, without grievous wrong being done to Himself, to be worshipped alongside of false gods, God was known in Judah alone. But in respect of His being the Father of this Christ, by whom He taketh away the sin of the world, this name of His, previously kept secret from all, He now made manifest to those whom the Father Himself had given Him out of the world. But how had He done so, if the hour were not yet come, of which He had formerly said that the hour would come, "when I shall no more speak unto you in proverbs, but I shall show you plainly of my Father"?[2] Can it be supposed that the proverbs themselves contained such a plain anouncement? Why, then, is it said, "I will declare to you openly," but just because that "in proverbs" is not "openly"? But when it is no longer concealed in proverbs, but uttered in plain words, then without a doubt it is spoken openly. How, then, had He manifested what He had not as yet openly declared? It must be understood, therefore, in this way, that the past tense is put for the future, like those other words, "All things that I have heard of my Father, I have made known unto you:"[3] as something He had not yet done, but spake of as if He had, because His doing of it He knew to be infallibly pre-determined.

5. But what are we to make of the words. "Whom Thou gavest me out of the world"? For it is said of them that they were not of the world. But this they attained to by regeneration, and not by generation. And what, also, of that which follows, "Thine they were, and Thou gavest them me"? Was there a time when they belonged to the Father, and not to His only-begotten Son; and had the Father once on a time anything apart from the Son? Surely not. Nevertheless, there was a time when God the Son had something, which that same Son as man possessed not; for He had not yet become man of an earthly mother, when He possessed all things in common with the Father. Wherefore in saying, "Thine they were," there is thereby no self-disruption made by God the Son, apart from whom there was nothing ever possessed by the Father; but it is His custom to attribute all the power He possesses to Him, of whom He Himself is, who has the power. For of whom He has it that He is, of

---

[1] Ps. lxxvi. 1.   [2] Chap. xvi. 25.   [3] Chap. xv. 15.

Him He has it that He is able; and both together He always had, for He never had being without having ability. Accordingly, whatever the Father could [do], always side by side with Him could the Son; since He, who never had being without having ability, was never without the Father, as the Father never was without Him. And thus, as the Father is eternally omnipotent, so is the Son co-eternally omnipotent; and if all-powerful, certainly all-possessing.[1] For such rather, if we would speak exactly, is the word by which we translate what is called by the Greeks παντοκράτωρ; which our writers would not interpret by the term omnipotent, seeing that παντοκράτωρ is all-possessing, were it not that they felt it to be equivalent in meaning. What, then, could the eternal all-possessing ever have, that the co-eternal all-possessing had not likewise? In saying, therefore, "And Thou gavest them me," He intimated that it was as man He had received this power to have them; seeing that He, who was always omnipotent, was not always man. Accordingly, while He seems rather to have attributed it to the Father, that He received them from Him, since all that is, is of Him, of whom He is; yet He also gave them to Himself, that is, Christ, God with the Father, gave men to the manhood of Christ, which had not its being with the Father. Finally, He who says in this place, "Thine they were, and Thou gavest them me," had already said in a previous passage to the same disciples, "I have chosen you out of the world."[2] Here, then, let every carnal thought be crushed and annihilated. The Son says that the men were given Him by the Father out of the world, to whom He says elsewhere, "I have chosen you out of the world." Those whom God the Son chose along with the Father out of the world, the very same Son as man received out of the world from the Father; for the Father had not given them to the Son had He not chosen them. And in this way, as the Son did not thereby set the Father aside, when He said, "I have chosen you out of the world," seeing that they were simultaneously chosen by the Father also: as little did He thereby exclude Himself, when He said, "Thine they were," for they were equally also the property of the Son. But now that same Son as man received those who belonged not to Himself, because He also as God received a servant-form which was not originally His own.

6. He proceeds to say, "And they have kept Thy word: now they have known that all things, whatsoever Thou hast given me, are of Thee;" that is, they have known that I am of Thee. For the Father gave all things at the very time when He begat Him who was to have all things. "For I have given unto them," He says, "the words which Thou gavest me; and they have received them;" that is, they have understood and kept hold of them. For the word is received when it is perceived by the mind. "And they have known truly," He adds, "that I came out from Thee, and they have believed that Thou didst send me." In this last clause we must also supply "truly;" for when He said, "They have known truly," He intended its explanation by adding, "and they have believed." That, therefore, "they have believed truly" which "they have known truly;" just as "I came out from Thee" is the same as "Thou didst send me." When, therefore, He said, "They have known truly," lest any might suppose that such a knowledge was already acquired by sight, and not by faith, He subjoined the explanation, "And they have believed," so that we should supply "truly," and understand the saying, "They have known truly," as equivalent to "They have believed truly:" not in the way which He intimated shortly before, when He said, "Do ye now believe? The hour cometh, and is now come, that ye shall be scattered, every man to his own, and shall leave me alone."[3] But "they have believed truly," that is, in the way it ought to be believed, without constraint, with firmness, constancy, and fortitude: no longer now to go to their own, and leave Christ alone. As yet, indeed, the disciples were not of the character He here describes in words of the past tense, as if they were so already, but as thereby declaring beforehand what sort they were yet to be, namely, when they had received the Holy Spirit, who, according to the promise, should teach them all things. For how was it, before they received the Spirit, that they kept that word of His which He spake regarding them, as if they had done so, when the chief of them thrice denied Him,[4] after hearing from His lips the future fate of the man who denied Him before men?[5] He had given them, therefore, as He said, the words which the Father gave Him; but when at length they received them spiritually, not in an outward way with their ears, but inwardly in their hearts, then they truly received them, for then they truly knew them; and they truly knew them, because they truly believed.

7. But what human language will suffice to

---

[1] *Omnitenens.*   [2] Chap. xv. 19.   [3] Chap. xvi. 31, 32.   [4] Matt. xxvi. 69-74.   [5] Matt. x. 33.

26

explain how the Father gave those words to the Son? The question, of course, will appear easier if we suppose Him to have received such words in His capacity as the Son of man. And yet, although thus born of the Virgin, who will undertake to relate when and how it was that He learned them, since even that very generation which He had of the Virgin who will venture to declare? But if our idea be that He received these words of the Father in His capacity as begotten of, and co-eternal with, the Father, let us then exclude all such thoughts of time as if He existed previous to His possessing them, and so received the possession of that which He had not before; for whatever God the Father gave to God the Son, He gave in the act of begetting. For the Father gave those things to the Son without which He could not be the Son, in the same manner as He gave Him being itself. For how otherwise would He give any words to the Word, wherein in an ineffable way He hath spoken all things? But now, in reference to what follows, you must defer your expectations till another discourse.

TRACTATE CVII.

Chapter XVII. 9–13.

1. When the Lord was speaking to the Father of those whom He already had as disciples, He said this also among other things: "I pray for them. I pray not for the world, but for those whom Thou hast given me." By the world, He now wishes to be understood those who live according to the lust of the word, and stand not in the gracious lot of such as were to be chosen by Him out of the world. Accordingly it is not for the world, but for those whom the Father hath given Him, that He expresses Himself as praying: for by the very fact of their having already been given Him by the Father, they have ceased to belong to that world for which He refrains from praying.

2. And then He adds, "For they are Thine." For the Father did not lose those whom He gave, in the act of giving them to the Son; since the Son still goes on to say, "And all mine are Thine, and Thine are mine." Where it is sufficiently apparent how it is that all that belongs to the Father belongs also to the Son; in this way, namely, that He Himself is also God, and, of the Father born, is the Father's equal: and not as was said to one of the two sons, to wit, the elder, "Thou art ever with me; and all that I have is thine."[1] For that was said of all those creatures which are inferior to the holy rational creature, and are certainly subordinate to the Church; wherein its universal character is understood as including those two sons, the elder and the younger, along with all the holy angels, whose equals we shall be in the kingdom of Christ and of God:[2] but here it was said, "And all mine are Thine, and Thine are mine," with this meaning, that even the rational creature is itself included, which is subject only to God, so that all beneath it are also subject to Him. As it then belongs to God the Father, it would not at the same time be the Son's likewise, were He not equal to the Father: for to it He was referring when He said, " I pray not for the world, but for those whom Thou hast given me: for they are Thine, and all mine are Thine, and Thine are mine." Nor is it morally admissible that the saints, of whom He so spake, should belong to any save to Him by whom they were created and sanctified: and for the same reason, everything also that is theirs must of necessity be His also to whom they themselves belong. Accordingly, since they belong both to the Father and to the Son, they demonstrate the equality of those to whom they equally belong. But when He says, speaking of the Holy Ghost, "All things that the Father hath are mine; therefore said I, that He shall take of mine, and shall show it unto you,"[3] He referred to those things which concern the actual deity of the Father, and in which He is equal to Him, in having all that He has. And no more was it of the creature, which is subject to the Father and the Son, that the Holy Spirit was to receive that whereof He said, "He shall

---

[1] Luke xv. 31.   [2] Luke xx. 36.   [3] Chap. xvi. 15.

receive of mine;" but most certainly of the Father, from whom the Spirit proceedeth, and of whom also the Son is born.

3. He proceeds: "And I am glorified in them." He now speaks of His glorification as already accomplished, although it was still future; while a little before He was demanding of the Father its accomplishment. But whether this be the same glorification, whereof He had said, "And now, O Father, glorify Thou me with Thine own self with the glory which I had with Thee before the world was," is certainly a point worthy of examination. For if "with Thee," how can it be "in them"? Is it when this very knowledge is imparted to them, and, through them, to all who believe them as His witnesses? In such a way we may clearly understand Christ as having said of the apostles, that He was glorified in them; for in saying that it was already accomplished, He showed that it was already foreordained, and only wished what was future to be regarded as certain.

4. "And now," He adds, "I am no more in the world, and these are in the world." If your thoughts turn to the very hour in which He was speaking, both were still in the world; to wit, He Himself, and those of whom He was so speaking: for it is not in respect of the tendency of heart and life that we can or ought to understand it, so that they should be described as still in the world, on the ground that they still savored of the earthly; and that He was no longer in the world, because divine in the disposition of His mind. For there is one word used here, which makes any such understanding altogether inadmissible; because He does not say, And I am not in the world; but, "I am no more in the world:" thereby showing that He Himself had been in the world, but was no more so. And are we then at liberty to believe that He at one time savored of the worldly, and, delivered at length from such a mistake, no longer retained the old disposition? Who would venture to shut himself up in so profane a meaning. It remains, therefore, that in the same sense in which He Himself also was previously in the world, He declared that He was no longer in the world, that is to say, in His bodily presence; in other words, showing thereby that His own absence from the world was now in the immediate future, and theirs later, when He said that He was no longer here, and that they were so, although both He and they were still present. For He thus spake, as a man in harmony with men, in accordance with the prevailing custom of human speech. Do we not say every day, he is no longer here, of one who is on the very point

of departure? And such in particular is the way we are wont to speak of those who are at the point of death. And besides all else, the Lord Himself, as if foreseeing the thoughts that might possibly be excited in those who were afterwards to read these words, added, "And I come to Thee:" explaining thereby in some measure why He said, "I am no more in the world."

5. Accordingly He commends to the Father's care those whom He was about to leave by His bodily absence, saying: "Holy Father, keep through Thine own name those whom Thou hast given me." That is to say, as man He prays to God in behalf of His disciples, whom He has received from God. But attend to what follows: "That they may be one," He says, "even as we." He does not say, That they may be one with us, or, that they and we may be one, as we are one; but He says, "That they may be one, even as we:" meaning, of course, that in their nature they may be one, even as we are one in ours, Which certainly would not be spoken with truth, unless in this respect, that He, as God, is of the same nature as the Father also, in accordance with what He has said elsewhere, "I and the Father are one;"[1] and not with what He also is as man, for in this respect He said, "The Father is greater than I."[2] But since one and the same person is God and man, we are to understand the manhood in respect of His asking; but the Godhead, in as far as He Himself, and He whom He asks, are one. But there is still a passage in what follows, where we must have a more careful discussion of this subject.

6. But here He proceeds: "While I was with them, I kept them in Thy name." Since I am coming, He says, to Thee, keep them in Thy name, in which I myself have kept them while I was with them. In the Father's name, the Son as man kept His disciples, when placed side by side with them in human presence; but the Father also, in the name of the Son, kept those whom He heard and answered when praying in the name of the Son. For to them had it also been said by the Son Himself: "Verily, verily, I say unto you, whatsoever ye shall ask the Father in my name, He will give it you."[3] But we are not to take this in any such carnal way, as that the Father and Son keep us in turn, with an alternation in the guardianship of both in guarding us, as if one succeeded when the other departed; for we are guarded all at once by the Father, and Son, and Holy Spirit, who is the one true and blessed God.

---

[1] Chap. x. 30.   [2] Chap. xiv. 28.   [3] Chap. xvi. 23.

But Scripture does not exalt us save by descending to us: as the Word, by becoming flesh, came down to lift us up, and fell not so as to remain Himself in the depths. If we have known Him who thus descendeth, let us rise with Him who lifteth us up; and let us understand, when He speaks thus, that He is marking a distinction in the persons, without making any separation of the natures. While, therefore, the Son in bodily presence was keeping His disciples, the Father was not waiting the Son's departure in order to succeed to the guardianship, but both were keeping them by Their spiritual power; and when the Son withdrew from them His bodily presence, He retained along with the Father the spiritual guardianship. For when the Son also as man assumed the office of their guardian, He did not withdraw them from the Father's guardianship; and when the Father gave them to the guardianship of the Son, in the very giving He acted not apart from Him to whom He gave them, but gave them to the Son as man, yet not apart from that same Son Himself as God.

7. The Son therefore goes on to say: "Those that Thou gavest me, I have kept, and none of them is lost, but the son of perdition; that the Scripture might be fulfilled."

The betrayer of Christ was called the son of perdition, as foreordained to perdition, according to the Scripture, where it is specially prophesied of him in the 109th[1] Psalm.

8. "And now," He says, "come I to Thee; and these things I speak in the world, that they may have my joy fulfilled in themselves." See! He says that He speaketh in the world, when He had said only a little before, "I am no more in the world:" the reason of which we have there explained, or rather have shown that He Himself explained it. Accordingly, on the one hand, as He had not yet departed, He was still here; and because He was on the very point of departure, in a kind of way He was no more here. But what this joy is whereof He says, "That they may have my joy fulfilled in themselves," has already been elucidated above, where He says, "That they may be one, even as we are." This joy of His that is bestowed on them by Him, was to be fulfilled, He says, in them; and for that very end declared that He had spoken in the world. This is that peace and blessedness in the world to come, for the attaining of which we must live temperately, and righteously, and godly in the present.

_____

[1] Augustin: "108th" (Vulg.).

TRACTATE CVIII

Chapter XVII. 14–19.

1. While the Lord is still speaking to the Father, and praying for His disciples, He says: "I have given them Thy saying; and the world hath hated them." That hatred they had not yet experienced in those sufferings of their own, which afterwards overtook them; but He speaks thus in His usual way, foretelling the future in words of the past tense. And then, subjoining the reason of their being hated by the world, He says, "Because they are not of the world, even as I am not of the world." This was conferred on them by regeneration; for by generation they were of the world, as He had already said to them, "I have chosen you out of the world."[1] It was therefore a gracious privilege bestowed upon them, that they, like Himself, should not be of the world, through the deliverance which He was giving them from the world. He, however, was never of the world; for even in respect of His servant-form He was born of that Holy Spirit of whom they

were born again. For if on that account they were no more of the world, because born again of the Holy Spirit; on the same account He was never of the world, because born of the Holy Spirit.

2. "I pray not," He adds, "that thou shouldest take them out of the world, but that Thou shouldest keep them from the evil." For they still accounted it necessary to be in the world, although they were no longer of it. Then He repeats the same statement: "They are not of the world, even as I am not of the world. Sanctify them in the truth." For so are they kept from the evil, as He had previously prayed that they might be. But it may be inquired how they were no more of the world, if they were not yet sanctified in the truth; or, if they already were, why He requests that they should be so. Is it not because even those who are sanctified still continue to make progress in the same sanctification, and grow in holiness; and do not so without the aid of God's grace, but by His sanctifying of their progress, even as He

_____

[1] Chap. xv. 19.

sanctified their outset? And hence the apostle likewise says: "He who hath begun a good work in you, will perform it until the day of Jesus Christ."[1] The heirs therefore of the New Testament are sanctified in that truth which was adumbrated in the purifications of the Old Testament; and when they are sanctified in the truth, they are in other words sanctified in Christ, who said in truth, "I am the way, and the truth, and the life."[2] As also when He said, "The truth shall make you free," in explanation of His words, He added soon after, "If the Son shall make you free, ye shall be free indeed;"[3] in order to show that what He had previously called the truth, He a minute afterwards denominates the Son. And what else did He mean by the words before us, "Sanctify them in the truth," but, Sanctify them in me?

3. Finally, He proceeds, and doing so fails not to suggest the same with increasing clearness: "Thy speech (sermo) is truth." What else did He mean than "I am the truth"? For the Greek Gospel has λόγος, which is also the word that is found in the passage where it is said, "In the beginning was the Word, and the Word was with God, and the Word was God." And that Word at least we know to be the only begotten Son of God, which "was made flesh, and dwelt among us."[4] Hence also there might have been put here, as it actually has been put in certain copies, "Thy Word is truth;" just as in some copies that other passage is written, "In the beginning was the speech." But in the Greek without any variation it is λόγος in both cases. The Father therefore sanctifies in the truth, that is, in His own Word, in His Only begotten, His own heirs and His (the Son's) co-heirs.

4. But now He still goes on to speak of the apostles, for He proceeds to add, "As Thou hast sent me into the world, even so have I also sent them into the world." Whom did He so send but His apostles? For even the very name of apostles, which is a Greek word, signifies in Latin nothing more than, those that are sent. God, therefore, sent His Son, not in sinful flesh, but in the likeness of sinful flesh;[5] and His Son sent those who, born themselves in sinful flesh, were sanctified by Him from the defilement of sin.

5. But since, on the ground that the Mediator between God and men, the man Christ Jesus, has become Head of the Church, they are His members; therefore He says in the words that follow, "And for their sakes I sanctify myself." For what means He by the words, "And for their sakes I sanctify myself," but I sanctify them in myself, since they also are [part of] myself?[6] For those of whom He so speaks are, as I have said, His members; and the head and body are one Christ, as the apostle teaches when he says of the seed of Abraham, "And if ye be Christ's, then are ye Abraham's seed," after having said before, "He saith not, And to seeds, as in many, but as in one, And to thy seed, which is Christ."[7] If, then, the seed of Abraham is Christ, what else is declared to those to whom he says, "Then are ye Abraham's seed," but then are ye Christ? Of the same character is what this very apostle said in another place: "Now I rejoice in my sufferings for you, and fill up that which is lacking of the afflictions of Christ in my flesh."[8] He said not, of my afflictions, but "of Christ's;" for he was a member of Christ, and in his persecutions, such as it behoved Christ to suffer in the whole of His body, he also was filling up his own share of His afflictions. And to be assured of the certainty of this in the present passage, give heed to what follows. For after saying, "And for their sakes I sanctify myself," to let us understand that He thereby meant that He would sanctify them in Himself, He immediately added, "That they also may be sanctified in the truth." And what else is this but in me, in accordance with the fact that the truth is that Word in the beginning which is God? In whom also the Son of man was Himself sanctified from the beginning of His creation, when the Word was made flesh, for the Word and the man became one person. Then accordingly He sanctified Himself in Himself, that is, Himself the man in Himself the Word; for the Word and the man is one Christ, who sanctifies the manhood in the Word. But in behalf of His members He says, "And for their sakes I,"—that is, that the benefit may be also theirs, for they too are [included in the] I, just as it benefited me in myself, because I am man apart from them—"I sanctify myself," that is, I sanctify them as if it were my own self in me, since in me they also are I. "That they also may be sanctified in the truth." For what else mean the words "they *also*," but ["they"] *in the same way* as I; "in the truth," and that "truth" am I? After this He now begins to speak not only of the apostles, but also of the rest of His members, which we shall treat of, as grace may be granted us, in another discourse.

---

[1] Phil. i. 6.   [2] Chap. xiv. 6.   [3] Chap. viii. 32-36.
[4] Chap. i. 1, 14.   [5] Rom. viii. 3.

[6] *Cum et ipsi sint ego.*   [7] Gal. iii. 29, 16.   [8] Col. i. 24.

TRACTATE CIX.

Chapter XVII. 20.

1 The Lord Jesus, in the now close proximity of His passion, after praying for His disciples, whom He also named apostles, with whom He had partaken of that last supper from which His betrayer had taken his departure on being revealed by the sop of bread, and with whom, after the latter's departure, and before beginning His prayer in their behalf, He had already spoken at length, conjoined all others also who were yet to believe on Him, and said to the Father, "Neither pray I for these alone," that is, for the disciples who were with Him at the time, "but for them also," He adds, "who shall believe on me through their word." Whereby He wished all His own to be understood: not only such as were then in the flesh, but those also who were yet to come. For all that have since believed on Him have doubtless believed, and shall yet believe till He come, through the word of the apostles; for to themselves He had said, "And ye also shall bear witness, because ye have been with me from the beginning;"[1] and by them was the gospel ministered even before it was written, and every one assuredly who believeth on Christ believeth the gospel. Accordingly, those who He says should believe on Him through their word, are not to be understood as referring only to such as heard the apostles themselves while they lived in the flesh; but others also after their decease, and we, too, born long afterwards, have believed on Christ through their word. For they that were then with Him preached to the others what they had heard from Him; and so their word, that we too might believe, has found its way to us, and wherever His Church exists, and shall yet reach down to posterity, whoever and wherever they be who shall hereafter believe on Him.

2. In this prayer, therefore, Jesus may seem to have omitted praying for some of His own, unless we carefully examine His words in the prayer itself. For if He prayed first for those, as we have already shown, who were then with Him, and afterwards for those also who should believe on Him through their word, it may be said that He prayed not for those who were neither with Him when He so spake, nor afterwards believed

through their word, but had done so at some previous time either of themselves, or in some other supposable manner. For was Nathanael with Him at that time?[2] Was Joseph of Arimathea, who begged His body from Pilate, and of whom this same evangelist John testifies that he was already His disciple?[3] Were His mother, Mary, and other women who, we know from the Gospel, had been prior to that time His disciples? Were those with Him then, of whom this evangelist John frequently says, "Many believed on Him"?[4] For whence came the multitude of those who, with branches of trees, partly preceded and partly followed Him as He sat on the ass, saying, "Blessed is He that cometh in the name of the Lord;" and along with them the children of whom He Himself declared that the prophecy had been uttered, "Out of the mouth of babes and of sucklings Thou hast perfected praise"?[5] Whence the five hundred brethren, to all of whom at once He would not have appeared after His resurrection[6] had they not previously believed on Him? Whence that hundred and nine who, with the eleven, were a hundred and twenty, when, being assembled together after His ascension, they waited and received the promise of the Holy Spirit?[7] Whence came all these, save from those of whom it was said, "Many believed on Him"? For them, therefore, the Saviour did not at this time pray, seeing it was for those He prayed who were then with Him, and for others not who had already, but who were yet to believe on Him through their word. But these were certainly not with Him on that occasion, and had already believed on Him at some previous period. I say nothing of the aged Simeon, who believed on Him when an infant; of Anna the prophetess;[8] of Zachariah and Elisabeth, who prophesied of Him before He was born of the Virgin;[9] of their son John, His forerunner, the friend of the Bridegroom, who both recognized Him in the Holy Spirit, and preached Him in His absence, and pointed Him out when He was present to the

---

[2] The interrogative particle, *numquid*, beginning this and the following sentences, implies a negative answer. If Nathanael were identified with Bartholomew, the answer would be affirmative.—Tr.

[3] Chap. xix. 38.   [4] Chap. ii. 23, iv. 39, vii. 31, viii. 30, x. 42.
[5] Matt. xxi. 9; Ps. viii. 2.   [6] 1 Cor. xv. 6.
[7] Acts i. 15, and ii. 4.   [8] Luke ii. 25-38.
[9] Luke i. 41-45, 67-79.

---

[1] Chap. xv. 27.

recognition of others;[1]—I say nothing of these, as it might be replied that He ought not to have prayed for such when dead, who had gone hence with their great merits, and having met with a welcome reception were now at rest; for a similar answer is also given in connection with the righteous of olden time. For which of them could have been saved from the damnation awaiting the whole mass of perdition, which has been caused by one man, had he not believed, through the revelation of the Spirit, in the one Mediator between God and men as yet to come in the flesh? But behoved He to pray for the apostles, and not to pray for so many who were still alive, but were not then with Him, and had already at some previous period been brought to the faith? Who is there that would say so?

3. We are therefore to understand that their faith in Him was not yet such as He wished it to be, inasmuch as even Peter himself, to whom, on making the confession, "Thou art the Christ, the Son of the living God," He had borne so excellent a testimony, was disposed rather to hinder Him from dying than to believe in His resurrection when dead, and hence was called immediately thereafter by the same of Satan.[2] Those, accordingly, are found to be the greater in faith who were long since deceased, and yet, through the revelation of the Spirit, had no manner of doubt that Christ would rise again, than those who, after attaining to the belief that He should redeem Israel, at the sight of His death lost all the hope they previously possessed regarding Him. The best thing for us, therefore, to believe is, that after His resurrection, when the Holy Spirit was bestowed, and the apostles taught and confirmed, and from its outset constituted teachers in the Church, others, through their word, attained the proper faith in Christ, or, in other words, that they then got firm hold of the faith of His resurrection. And in this way also, that all those who seemed to have already believed on Him really belonged to the number of those for whom He prayed, when He said, "Neither pray I for these alone, but for them also who shall believe on me through their word."

4. But we have still in reserve for the further solution of this question the blessed apostle, and that robber who was a villain in wickedness, but a believer on the cross. For the Apostle Paul tells us that he was made an apostle not of men, nor by man, but by Jesus Christ: and speaking of his own gospel,

he says, "For I neither received it of man, neither did I learn it, but by the revelation of Jesus Christ."[3] How then was he among those of whom it is said, "They shall believe on me through their word"? On the other hand, the robber believed at the very time when in the case of the teachers themselves such faith as they previously possessed had utterly failed. Not even he, therefore, believed on Christ through their word, and yet his faith was such that he confessed that He whom he saw nailed to the cross would not only rise again, but would also reign, when he said, "Remember me when Thou comest into Thy kingdom."[4]

5. Accordingly it remains that if we are to believe that the Lord Jesus, in this prayer, prayed for all of His own who either then were or should thereafter be in this life, which is a state of trial upon earth,[5] we must so understand the expression, "through their word," as to believe that it here signified the word of faith itself which they preached in the world, and that it was called their word because it was primarily and principally preached by them. For it was already in the course of being preached by them in the earth when Paul received that same word of theirs by the revelation of Jesus Christ. Whence also it came about that he compared the Gospel with them, lest by any means he had run, or should run, in vain; and they gave him their right hand because in him also they found, although not given him by them, their own word which they were already preaching, and in which they were now established.[6] And in regard to this word of the resurrection of Christ, it is said by the same apostle, "Whether it were I, or they, so we preach, and so ye believed;"[7] and again, "This is the word of faith," he says, "which we preach, that if thou shalt confess with thy mouth that Jesus is the Lord, and shalt believe in thine heart that God hath raised Him from the dead, thou shalt be saved."[8] And in the Acts of the Apostles we read that in Christ, God hath marked out [the ground of] faith unto all men, in that He hath raised Him from the dead.[9] Accordingly, this word of faith, because principally and primarily preached by the apostles who adhered to Him, was called their word. Not, however, on that account does it cease to be the word of God because it is called their word; for

3 Gal. i. 1, 12.   4 Luke xxiii. 42.
5 Job vii. 1: *Tentatio super terram,* עֲבָא עַל־אָרֶץ; English version, "An appointed time (*marg.,* warfare) upon earth." Rev. Ver. puts "warfare" into the text, and "time of service" on the margin.
6 Gal. ii. 2, 9.   7 1 Cor. xv. 11.
8 Rom. x. 8, 9.   9 Acts xvii. 31.

1 Chap. i. 19-36, and iii. 26-36. 2 Matt. xvi. 16, 23.

the same apostle says that the Thessalonians received it from him "not as the word of men, but, as it is in truth, the word of God." [1] "Of God," for the very reason that it was freely given by God; but called "their word," because primarily and principally committed to them by God to be preached. In the same way also the thief mentioned above had in the matter of his own faith their word, which was called theirs precisely because the preaching of it primarily and principally pertained to the office they filled. And once more, when murmuring arose among the Grecian widows in reference to the serving of the tables, previous to the time when Paul was brought to the faith of Christ, the reply given by the apostles, who before then had adhered to the Lord, was: "It is not good that we should leave the word of God, and serve tables." [2] Then it was that they provided for the ordination of deacons, that they themselves might not be drawn aside from the duty of preaching the word. Hence that was properly enough called their word which is the word of faith, whereby all, from whatever quarter they had heard it, believed on Christ, or, as yet to hear it, should thereafter believe. In this prayer, therefore, all whom He redeemed, whether then alive or thereafter to live in the flesh, were prayed for by our Redeemer when, praying for the apostles who were then with Him, He also conjoined those who were yet to believe on Him through their word. But what, after such conjunction, He then proceeds to say, must be reserved for discussion in another discourse.

[1] 1 Thess. ii. 13.

[2] Acts vi. 1–4.

TRACTATE CX.

CHAPTER XVII. 21–23.

1. AFTER the Lord Jesus had prayed for His disciples whom He had with Him at the time, and had conjoined with them others who were also His own, by saying, "Neither pray I for these alone, but for them also who shall believe on me through their word," as if we were inquiring what or wherefore He prayed for them, He straightway subjoined, "That they all may be one; as Thou, Father, [art] in me, and I in Thee, that they also may be one in us." And a little above, while still praying for the disciples alone who were then with Him, He said, "Holy Father, keep in Thine own name those whom Thou hast given me,. that they may be one, as we are" (ver. 11). It is the same thing, therefore, that He now also prayed for in our behalf, as He did at that time in theirs, namely, that all—to wit, both we and they—may be one. And here we must take particular notice that the Lord did not say that we all may be one, but, "that they all may be one; as Thou Father, in me, and I in Thee" (where is to be understood *are one*, as is more clearly expressed afterwards); because He had also said before of the disciples who were with Him, "That they may be one, as we are." The Father, therefore, is in the Son, and the Son in the Father, in such a way as to be one, because they are of one substance; but while we may indeed be in them, we cannot be one with them; for they and we are not of one substance, in as far as the Son is God along with the Father. But in as far as He is man, He is of the same substance as we are. But at present He wished rather to call attention to that other statement which He made use of in another place, "I and the Father are one," [1] where He intimated that His own nature was the same with that of the Father. And accordingly, though the Father and Son, or even the Holy Spirit, are in us, we must not suppose that they are of one nature with ourselves. And hence they are in us, or we are in them, in this sense, that they are one in their own nature, and we are one in ours. For they are in us, as God in His temple; but we are in them, as the creature in its Creator.

2. But then after saying, "That they also may be one in us," He added, "That the world may believe that Thou hast sent me." What does He mean by this? Is it that the world will then be brought to the faith, when we shall all be one in the Father and Son? Is not such a state the everlasting peace, and the reward of faith, rather than faith itself? For we shall be one not in order to our believing, but because we have believed. But although in this life, because of the common

[1] Chap. x. 30.

faith itself, all who believe in one are one, according to the words of the apostle, " For ye are all one in Christ Jesus ;"¹ even thus we are one, not in order to our believing, but because we do believe. What, then, is meant by the words, " That they all may be one, that the world may believe"? This, doubtless, that the " all " are themselves the believing world. For those who shall be one are not of one class, and the world that is thereafter to believe on this very ground that these shall be one, of another ; since it is perfectly certain that He says, " That they all may be one," of those of whom He had said before, " Neither pray I for these alone, but for those also who shall believe on me through their word," immediately adding as He does, " That they all may be one." And this " all," what is it but the world ; not certainly that which is hostile, but that which is believing? For you see here that He who had said, " I pray not for the world," now prayeth for the world that it may believe. For there is a world whereof it is written, " That we might not be condemned with this world."² For that world He prayeth not, for He is fully aware to what it is predestinated. And there is a world whereof it is written, " For the Son of man came not to condemn the world, but that the world through Him might be saved ;"³ and hence the apostle also says, " God was in Christ, reconciling the world unto Himself."⁴ For this world it is that He prayeth, in saying, " That the world may believe that Thou hast sent me." For through this faith the world is reconciled unto God when it believes in the Christ whom God has sent. How, then, are we to understand Him when He says, " That they also may be one in us, that the world may believe that Thou hast sent me," but just in this way, that He did not assign the cause of the world believing to the fact that those others are one, as if it believed on the ground that it saw them to be one; for the world itself here consisteth of all who by their own believing become one; but in His prayer He said, " That the world may believe," just as in His prayer He also said, " That they all may be one;" and still further in the same prayer, " That they also may be one in us." For the words, " they all may be one," are equivalent to " the world may believe," since it is by believing that they become one, perfectly one; that is, those who, although one by nature, had ceased to be so by their mutual dissensions. In fine, if the verb which He uses, " I pray," be understood in the third clause, or rather, to

make the whole fuller, be everywhere supplied, the explanation of this sentence will be all the clearer : I pray " that they all may be one ; as Thou, Father, in me, and I in Thee ;" I pray " that they also may be one in us ;" I pray " that the world may believe that Thou hast sent me." And, mark, He added the words " in us " in order that we may know that our being made one in that love of unchanging faithfulness is to be attributed to the grace of God, and not to ourselves : just as the apostle, after saying, " For ye were at one time darkness, but now are ye light," that none might attribute the doing of this to themselves, added, " in the Lord."⁵

3. Furthermore, our Saviour in thus praying to the Father showed Himself to be man; while He now also shows that He Himself, as being God along with the Father, doeth that which He prayeth for, when He says, " And the glory which Thou gavest me, I have given them." And what was that glory but immortality, which human nature was henceforth to receive in Him ? For not even He Himself had as yet received it, but in His own customary way, on account of the absolute fixedness of predestination, He intimates what is future in verbs of the past tense, because being now on the point of being glorified, or in other words, raised up again by the Father, He Himself is going to raise us up to the same glory in the end. What we have here is similar to what He says elsewhere, " As the Father raiseth up the dead, and quickeneth them, even so the Son quickeneth whom He will." And "whom," but just the same as the Father ? " For what things soever the Father doeth," not other things, but " these also doeth the Son," not in a different way, but " in like manner."⁶ And in this way He also raised up even His own self. For to this effect he said, " Destroy this temple, and in three days I will raise it up again."⁷ Accordingly the glory of immortality, which He says had been given Him by the Father, He must be also understood as having bestowed upon Himself, although He does not say it. For on this very account He more frequently says that the Father alone doeth, what He Himself also doeth along with the Father, that everything whatever He may attribute to Him of whom He is. But sometimes also He is silent about the Father, and says that He Himself doeth what He only doeth along with the Father: that we may thereby understand that the Son is not to be separated from the working of the Father, when He is silent about Himself, and ascribes

some work or other to the Father; as, on the other hand, the Father is not separated from the working of the Son, when the Son is said, without any mention being made of [the Father] Himself, to be doing some work in which nevertheless both are equally engaged. When, therefore, in some work of the Father, the Son says nothing of His own working, He commends humility, that He may become the source of sounder health to us; but when, in turn, in the case of some work of His own, He says nothing of the working of the Father, He commends His own equality, that we may not suppose Him to be inferior. In this way, then, and in this passage, He neither estranges Himself from the Father's working, although He has said, "The glory which Thou gavest me;" for He also gave it to Himself: nor does He estrange the Father from His own working, although saying, "I have given to them;" for the Father also gave it to them. For the works not only of the Father and the Son, but also of the Holy Spirit, are inseparable. But just as, because of His praying the Father in behalf of all His people, it was His own pleasure that this should be done, "that they all may be one;" so also on the ground of His own beneficence, as expressed in the words, "The glory which Thou gavest me, I have given them," the doing of that was none the less His pleasure; for He immediately added, "That they may be one, as we also are one."

4. And then He added: "I in them, and Thou in me, that they may be made perfect in one." Here He briefly intimated Himself as the Mediator between God and men. Nor was this said in any such way as if the Father were not in us, or we were not in the Father; since He had also said in another place, "We will come unto him, and make our abode with him;"[1] and a little before in this present passage He had not said, "I in them, and Thou in me," as He said now; or, They in me, and I in Thee; but, "Thou in me, and I in Thee, and they in us." Accordingly, when He now says, "I in them, and Thou in me," the words take this form in reference to the person of the Mediator, like that other expression used by the apostle, "Ye are Christ's, and Christ is God's."[2] But in adding, "That they may be made perfect in one," He showed that the reconciliation, which is effected by the Mediator, is carried to the very length of bringing us to the enjoyment of that perfect blessedness, which is thenceforth incapable of further addition. Hence the words that follow, "That the world may know that Thou

hast sent me," are not, I think, to be taken as if He had again said, "That the world may believe;" for sometimes, to know, is also used in the same sense as to believe, as it is in the words He uttered some time before: "And they have known truly that I came out from Thee, and they have believed that Thou didst send me." He expressed the same thing by the later words, "they have believed," as He had done by the earlier, "they have known." But inasmuch as He here speaks of the consummation, the knowledge must be taken for such, as it shall then be by sight, and not, as it now is, by faith. For an order seems to have been preserved in reference to what He said a little before, "that the world may believe;" while here it is, "that the world may know." For although He said there, "that they all may be one," and "may be one in us," yet He did not say, "they may be made perfect in one," and so subjoined the words, "that the world may believe that Thou hast sent me;" but here He said, "That they may be made perfect in one," and then added, not, "that the world may believe," but, "that the world may know that Thou hast sent me." For so long as we believe what we do not see, we are not yet made perfect, as we shall be when we have merited the sight of that which we believe. Most correctly, therefore, did He say in that previous place, "That the world may believe," and here "That the world may know;" yet both there and here, "that Thou hast sent me;" that we may know, so far as belongs to the inseparable love of the Father and the Son, that at present we only believe what we are on the way, by believing, to know. And had He said, That they may know that Thou hast sent me, it would be just of the same force as what He actually does say, "that the world may know." For they are the world that abideth not in enmity, as doth the world that is foreordained to damnation; but one that out of an enemy has been transformed into a friend, and on whose account "God was in Christ reconciling the world unto Himself." Therefore said He, "I in them, and Thou in me;" as if He had said, I in those to whom Thou hast sent me; and Thou in me, reconciling the world unto Thyself through me.

5. In close relation to these come also His further words: "And Thou hast loved them as thou hast loved me." That is to say, in the Son the Father loveth us, because in Him He hath chosen us before the foundation of the world.[3] For He who loveth the Only-begotten, certainly loveth also His members which, through His in-

---

[1] Chap. xiv. 23.　　　[2] 1 Cor. iii. 23.　　　[3] Eph. i. 4.

strumentality, He engrafted into Him by adoption. But we are not on this account equal to the only-begotten Son, by whom we have been created and re-created, that it is said, " Thou hast loved them as [Thou hast] also [loved] me." For one does not always intimate equality when he says, As this, so also that other; but sometimes only, Because this is, so also is the other ; or, That the one is, in order that the other may be also. For who could say that the apostles were sent by Christ into the world in exactly the same way as He Himself was sent by the Father? For, to say nothing of other differences, which it would be tedious to mention, they at all events were sent when they were already men ; but He was sent in order that He might be man ; and yet He said above, " As Thou hast sent me into the world, even so have I sent them into the world ;" as if He had said, Because Thou hast sent me, I have sent them. So also in the passage before us He says, "Thou hast loved them, as Thou hast loved me ;" which is nothing else than this, Thou hast loved them because that Thou hast also loved me. For He could not but love the members of the Son, seeing that He loveth the Son Himself; nor is there any other reason for loving His members, save that He loveth Himself. But He loveth the Son as regards His Godhead, because He begat Him equal with Himself; He loveth Him also in regard to what He is as man, because the only-begotten Word was Himself made flesh, and on account of the Word is the flesh of the Word dear to Him; but He loveth us, inasmuch as we are the members of Him whom He loveth; and in order that we might be so, He loved us on this account before we existed.

6. The love, therefore, wherewith God loveth, is incomprehensible and immutable. For it was not from the time that we were reconciled unto Him by the blood of His Son that He began to love us; but He did so before the foundation of the world, that we also might be His sons along with His Only-begotten, before as yet we had any existence of our own. Let not the fact, then, of our having been reconciled unto God through the death of His Son be so listened to or so understood, as if the Son reconciled us to Him in this respect, that He now began to love those whom He formerly hated, in the same way as enemy is reconciled to enemy, so that thereafter they become friends, and mutual love takes the place of their mutual hatred ; but we were reconciled unto Him who already loved us, but with whom we were at enmity because of our sin. Whether I say the truth on this, let the apostle testify, when he says :

" God commendeth His love toward us, in that, while we were yet sinners, Christ died for us."[1] He, therefore, had love toward us even when we were practising enmity against Him and working iniquity ; and yet to Him it is said with perfect truth, " Thou hatest, O Lord, all workers of iniquity."[2] Accordingly, in a wonderful and divine manner, even when He hated us, He loved us ; for He hated us, in so far as we were not what He Himself had made ; and because our own iniquity had not in every part consumed His work, He knew at once both how, in each of us, to hate what we had done, and to love what He had done. And this, indeed, may be understood in the case of all regarding Him to whom it is truly said, " Thou hatest nothing that Thou hast made."[3] For He would never have wished anything that He hated to exist, nor would aught that the Omnipotent had not wished exist at all, were it not that in what He hated there was also something that He loved. For He justly hateth and reprobateth vice as utterly repugnant to the principle of His procedure, yet He loveth even in the persons of the vitiated what is susceptible either of His own beneficence through healing, or of His judgment by condemnation. In this way God at the same time hateth nothing of what He has made; for as the Creator of natures, and not of vices, it was not He who made the evil that He hateth ; and of these same evils, all is good that He really doeth, either by mercifully healing them, or by judicially regulating them. Seeing, then, that He hateth nothing that He hath made, who can worthily describe how much He loveth the members of His Only-begotten, and how much more the Only-begotten Himself, in whom are hid all things visible and invisible, which were ordained in their various classes, and which He loves in fullest harmony with such ordination? For the members of His Only-begotten He is leading on by the liberality of His grace to an equality with the holy angels; while the Only-begotten Himself, being Lord of all, is doubtless Lord of angels, being by nature, as God, the equal not of angels, but rather of the Father Himself; while through grace, in respect of which He is man, how can He otherwise than surpass all angelic excellence, seeing that in Him human flesh and the Word constitute but one personality?

7. Nevertheless there are not wanting some who place us likewise before the angels; because, they say, Christ died for us and not for angels. But what else is such a notion

---

[1] Rom. v. 8, 9.   [2] Ps. v. 5.   [3] Wisd. xi. 25.

than the desire to glory over our very impiety? For "Christ," as the apostle says, "in due time died for the ungodly."[1] Where it is not any desert of ours, but the mercy of God, that is commended. For what can be the character of the man who wishes himself to be lauded, because he has become so abominably diseased through his own wickedness, that he can only be healed by the death of his physician? That surely is not the glory of our deserts, but the medicine of our diseases. Or do we prefer ourselves to the angels on this account, that, while there are angels also who have sinned, there has been no such labor expended on their healing? As if something that was at least small in amount had been undertaken for them, and what was greater for us. But had even such been the case, it might still be a subject of inquiry whether it was so because we had once stood in a position of superior excellence, or because we were now lying in a more desperate condition. But knowing as we do that the Creator of all good has imparted no grace for the reparation of angelic evils, why do we not rather draw the inference that their fault was judged all the more damnable, that the nature of those who committed it was of a loftier sublimity? For to the same extent as they less than we ought to have fallen into sin, were they superior in nature to us. But now in offending against the Creator they became all the more detestably ungrateful for His beneficence, that they were created capable of exercising the greater beneficence; nor was it enough for them to become deserters from Him, but they must also become our deceivers. This, therefore, is the great goodness of which we are to be made the subjects by Him, who hath loved us even as He hath loved Christ, that, for His sake, whose members He wished us to be, we may be equal to the holy angels,[2] to whom we were created with an inferiority of nature, and have by our sin fallen into such greater depths of unworthiness, as to make it incumbent that we should be in some sort their associates.

[1] Rom. v. 6.

[2] Luke xx. 36.

TRACTATE CXI.

CHAPTER XVII. 24-26.

1. THE Lord Jesus raises up His people to a great hope, than which there could not possibly be a greater. Listen and rejoice in hope, that, since the present is not a life to be loved, but to be tolerated, you may have the power of patient endurance amid all its tribulation.[1] Listen, I say, and weigh well to what it is that our hopes are exalted. Christ Jesus saith, The Son of God, the Only-begotten, who is co-eternal and equal with the Father, saith: He, who for our sakes became man, but became not, like every man besides, a liar,[2] saith: the Way, the Life, the Truth saith:[3] He who overcame the world, saith of those for whom He overcame it: listen, believe, hope, desire what He saith: "Father," He says, "I will that they also whom Thou hast given me be with me where I am." Who are these who He says were given Him by the Father? Are they not those of whom He says in another place, "No man cometh unto me, unless the Father, who hath sent me, draw him"?[4] We already know if we have made any beneficial progress in this Gospel, how it is that the things which He says the Father doeth, He Himself doeth likewise along with the Father. They are those, therefore, whom He has received from the Father, whom He Himself has also chosen out of the world, and chosen that they may be no more of the world, even as He also is not of the world; and yet that they also may be a world that believeth and knoweth that Christ has been sent by God the Father that the world might be delivered from the world, and so, as a world that was to be reconciled unto God, might not be condemned with the world that lieth in enmity. For so He says in the beginning of this prayer: "Thou hast given Him power over all flesh," that is, over every man, "that He should give eternal life to as many as Thou hast given Him." Here He makes it clear that He has indeed received power over all men, that, as the future Judge of quick and dead, He may deliver whom He pleases, and condemn whom He pleases; but that these were given Him that to all of them He should give eternal life. For so He

[1] Rom. xii. 12.   [2] Ps. cxvi. 11.
[3] Chap. xiv. 6.   [4] Chap. vi. 44.

says: " That He should give eternal life to as many as Thou hast given Him." Accordingly they were not given Him that from them He should withhold eternal life; although over them also the power has been given Him, inasmuch as He has received it over all flesh, in other words, over every man. In this way the world that has been reconciled will be delivered from the hostile world, when He putteth into exercise His power over it, to send it away into death eternal; but the other He maketh His own that He may give it everlasting life. Accordingly, to every one, without fail, of His own sheep the Good Shepherd, as to every one of His members the great Head, hath promised this reward, that where He is, there also we shall be with Him; nor can that be otherwise which the omnipotent Son declared to be His will to the omnipotent Father. For there also is the Holy Spirit, equally eternal, equally God, the one Spirit of the two, the substance of the will of both. For the words that we read of Him as uttering on the eve of His passion, " Yet not, Father, as I will, but as Thou wilt," [1] as if the Father has or had one will, and the Son another, are the echo of our infirmity, however faith-pervaded, which our Head transfigured in His own person, when He likewise bare our iniquities. But that the will of the Father and the Son is one, of both of whom also there is but one Spirit, by including whom we come to the knowledge of the Trinity, let piety believe, even though our infirmity meanwhile permitteth us not to understand.

2. But as we have already, in a way proportionate to the brevity of our discourse, spoken of the objects of the promise, and of its own stability; let us now look at this one point, as far as we are able, what it is that He was pleased to promise when He said, " I will that they also whom Thou hast given me be with me where I am." As far as pertains to the creaturehood wherein He was made of the seed of David according to the flesh, [2] not even He Himself was yet, where He would afterwards be: but He could say in this way, " where I am," to let us understand that He was soon to ascend into heaven, so that He spake of Himself as being already there, where He was presently to be. He could do so also in the same way as He had said on a former occasion, when speaking to Nicodemus, " No man ascendeth into heaven, save He that came down from heaven, even the Son of man who is in heaven." [3] For there also He did not say, Will be, but " is," because of the oneness of person, wherein God is at once man, and man God. He

promised, therefore, that we should be in heaven; for thither the servant-form, which He received of the Virgin, has been elevated, and set at the right hand of the Father. Because of the same blessed hope the apostle also says: " But God, who is rich in mercy, for His great love wherewith He loved us, even when we were dead in sins, hath quickened us together with Christ; by whose grace we are saved; and hath raised us up together, and made us sit together in heavenly places in Christ Jesus." [4] And so accordingly we may understand the Lord to have said, " That where I am, there they may be also." He, indeed, said of Himself that He was there already; but of us He merely declared that He wished us to be there with Him, without any indication that we were there already. But what the Lord said that He wished to be done, the apostle spake of as already accomplished. For he said not, He will yet raise us up, and make us sit in heavenly places; but, " hath raised us up, and made us sit in heavenly places:" for it is not without good grounds, but in believing assurance, that he reckons as already done what he is certain will yet be done. But if it is in respect of the form of God, wherein He is equal to the Father, that we would be inclined to understand His words, " I will that they also be with me, where I am," let our mind get quit of every thought of material images: whatever the soul has had presented to it, that is endowed with length, or breadth, or thickness, tinted by the light with any sort of bodily hue, or diffused through local space of any kind, whether finite or infinite, let it, as far as possible, turn away from all such notions the glance of its contemplation on the inward bent of its thoughts. And let us not be making inquiries as to where the Son, the Father's co-equal, is, since no one has yet found out where He is not. But if any one would inquire, let him inquire rather how he may be with Him; not everywhere as He is, but wherever He may be. For when He said to the man that was expiating his crimes on the tree, and making confession unto salvation, " To-day shalt thou be with me in paradise," [5] in respect to His human nature His own soul was on that very day to be in hell, [6] His flesh in the sepulchre; but as respected His Godhead He was certainly also in paradise. And therefore the soul of the thief, absolved from his by-gone crimes, and already in the blessed enjoyment of His grace, although it could not be everywhere as He was, yet could on that very day be also with Him in paradise, from which He, who is always everywhere, had not withdrawn. On this account, doubtless, it was not enough for Him to say, "I will that they also be where I am;" but He added, "with me." For to be with Him is the chief good. For even the miserable can be where He is, since wheresoever any are, there is He also; but the blessed only are with Him, because it is only of Him that they can be blessed. Was it not truly said to God, "If I ascend into heaven, Thou art there; and if I go down into hell, Thou art present?"[1] or is not Christ after all that Wisdom of God which "penetrateth everywhere because of its purity"?[2] But the light shineth in darkness; and the darkness comprehendeth it not.[3] And similarly, to take a kind of illustration from what is visible, although greatly unlike, as the blind man, even though he be where the light is, is yet not himself with the light, but is really absent from that which is present; so the unbeliever and profane, or even the believer and pious, because not yet competent to gaze on the light of wisdom, although he cannot be anywhere that Christ is not there likewise, yet is not himself with Christ, I mean in actual sight. For we cannot doubt that the true believer is with Christ by faith; because in reference to this He saith, "He that is not with me is against me."[4] But when He said to God the Father, "I will that they also whom Thou hast given me be with me where I am," He spake exclusively of that sight wherein we shall see Him as He is.[5]

3. Let no one disturb the clearness of the meaning by any cloudy contradiction; but let what follows furnish its testimony to the words that precede. For after saying, "I will that they also be with me where I am," He went on immediately to add, "That they may behold my glory, which Thou gavest me: for Thou lovedst me before the foundation of the world." "That they may behold," He said; not, that they may believe. This is faith's wages,[6] not faith itself. For if faith has been correctly defined in the Epistle to the Hebrews as "the assurance [conviction] of things that are not seen,"[7] why may not the wages of faith be defined, the beholding of things which were hoped for in faith? For when we shall see the glory which the Father hath given the Son, even though we may understand what is spoken of in this passage, not as that [glory] which the Father gave His co-equal Son in begetting Him, but as that which He gave Him, when become the Son of man, after the death of the cross;—when, I say, we shall see that glory of the Son, then of a cer-

tainty shall take place the judgment of the quick and the dead, and then shall the wicked be taken away that he may not behold the glory of the Lord;[8] and what [glory], save that of His Godhead? For blessed are the pure in heart, for they shall see God:[9] and because the wicked are not pure in heart, therefore they shall not see. Then shall they go away into everlasting punishment; for so shall the wicked be taken away, that he may not behold the glory of the Lord: but the righteous shall go into life eternal.[10] And what is life eternal? "That they may know Thee, the only true God, and Jesus Christ, whom Thou hast sent" (ver. 3): not, indeed, as those knew Him, who although impure in heart, yet were able to see Him as He sat in judgment in His glorified servant-form; but as He is yet to be known by the pure in heart, as the only true God, the Son along with the Father and Holy Spirit, because the Trinity itself is the only true God. If, then, it is in reference to His Godhead as the Son of God, equal and co-eternal with the Father, that we take the words, "I will that they also be with me where I am," we shall be with Christ in the Father; but He in His own way, we in ours, wherever we may be in body. For if localities are to be understood, and such as contain incorporeal beings, and everything has a place where it is, the eternal place of Christ where He always is, is the Father Himself, and the place of the Father is the Son; for "I," He said, "am in the Father, and the Father in me;"[11] and in this prayer, "As Thou, Father, art in me, and I in Thee:" and they are our place, because there follows, "That they also may be one in us:" and we are God's place, inasmuch as we are His temple; even as He, who died for us and liveth for us, also prayeth for us, that we may be one in them; because "His [dwelling] place was made in peace,"[12] and His habitation in Zion,"[12] which we are. But who is qualified to think on such places or what is in them, apart from the idea of space-defined capacities and material masses? Yet no little progress is made, if at least, when any such idea presents itself to the eye of the mind, it is denied, rejected, and reprobated: and a certain kind of light is, as far as possible, thought of, in which such things are perceived as deserving only to be denied, rejected, and reprobated; and the certainty of that light is known and loved, so that from thence an upward movement is begun in us, and an effort made

---

[1] Ps. cxxxix. 8.　[2] Wisd. vii. 24.　[3] Chap. i. 5.
[4] Matt. xii. 30.　[5] 1 John iii. 2.　[6] *Merces.*
[7] Heb. xi. 1.

[8] Isa. xxvi. 10.　[9] Matt. v. 8.
[10] Matt. xxv. 46.　[11] Chap. xiv. 10.
[12] Ps. lxxvi. 2: *in pace,* בְשָׁלֵם ; rather as in English version, "in Salem" (Jerusalem).—TR.

to reach into places farther within: and when the mind through its own infirmity and still inferior purity has failed to penetrate them, it is driven back again, not without the sighings of love and the tears of ardent longing, and continues to bear in patience until it is purified by faith, and prepared by the holiness of the inward life to be able to take up its abode therein.

4. How, then, shall we not be with Christ where He is, when we shall be with Him in the Father in whom He is? On this, also, the apostle is not without something to say to us, although we are not yet in possession of the reality, but only cherishing the hope. For he says, " If ye be risen with Christ, seek those things which are above, where Christ sitteth on the right hand of God: set your affections on things above, not on things on the earth. For ye have died," he adds, " and your life is hid with Christ in God." Here, you see, our life is meanwhile in faith and hope with Christ, where He is; because it is with Christ in God. That, you see, is as if already accomplished for which He prayed, when He said, " I will that they also be with me where I am;" but now only by faith. And when will it be accomplished by actual sight? " When Christ," he says, " [who is] your life, shall appear, then shall ye also appear with Him in glory."[1] Then shall we appear as that which we then shall be; for it shall then be apparent that it was not without good grounds that we believed and hoped we should become so, before it actually took place. He will do this, to whom the Son, after saying, " That they may behold my glory, which Thou gavest me," immediately added, " For Thou lovedst me before the foundation of the world." For in Him He loved us also before the foundation of the world, and then foreordained what He was to do in the end of the world.

5. " O righteous Father," He saith, " the world hath not known Thee." Just because Thou art righteous it hath not known Thee. It is as that world which has been predestined to condemnation really deserved, that it hath not known Him; while the world which He hath reconciled unto Himself through Christ hath known Him not of merit, but by grace. For what else is the knowing of Him, but eternal life? which, while He undoubtedly withheld it from the condemned world, He bestowed on the reconciled. On that very account, therefore, the world hath not known Thee, because Thou art righteous, and hast rendered unto it according to its deserts, that it should not know Thee: while on the same account the reconciled world hath known Thee, because Thou art merciful, and, not for any merit of its own, but by grace, hast supplied it with the needed help to know Thee. And then there follows, " But I have known Thee." He is the Fountain of grace, who is by nature God, and, by grace ineffable, man also of the Holy Spirit and the Virgin: and then on His own behalf, because the grace of God is through Jesus Christ our Lord, He adds, "And these have known that Thou hast sent me." Such is the reconciled world. But it is because Thou hast sent me that they have known: by grace, therefore, have they known.

6. "And I have made known to them," He says, " Thy name, and will make it known." I have made it known by faith, I will make it known by sight: I have made it known to those whose present sojourn in a strange land has its appointed end, I will make it known to those whose reign as kings shall be endless. " That the love," He adds, " wherewith [literally, which] Thou hast loved me,[2] may be in them, and I in them. (The form of speech is unusual, " the love, *which Thou hast loved me*, may be in them, and I in them;" for the common way of speaking is, the love wherewith thou hast loved me. Here, of course, it is a translation from the Greek: but there are similar forms also in Latin; as we say, He served a faithful service, He served as a soldier a strenuous soldier-service; when apparently we ought to have said, He served with a faithful service, he served as a soldier with a strenuous soldier-service. But such as the form of expression is, " the love which Thou hast loved me;" one similar to it is also used by the apostle, " I have fought a good fight;"[3] he does not say, *in* a good fight, which would be the more usual and perhaps correcter form of expression.) But how else is the love wherewith the Father loved the Son in us also, but because we are His members and are loved in Him, since He is loved in the totality of His person, as both Head and members? Therefore He added, " and I in them;" as if saying, Since I am also in them. For in one sense He is in us as in His temple; but in another, because we are also Himself, seeing that, in accordance with His becoming man, that He might be our Head, we are His body. The Saviour's prayer is finished, His passion begins; let us, therefore, also finish the present discourse, that we may treat of His passion, as He granteth us grace, in others to follow.

[2] *Quam dilexisti me.* The part which follows, which we have enclosed within parentheses, may be omitted by the English reader, as it only deals with the Latin idiom.—Tr.

[3] 2 Tim. iv. 7.

TRACTATE CXII.

CHAPTER XVIII. 1–12.

1. WHEN the grand and lengthened discourse was concluded which the Lord delivered after supper, and on the eve of shedding His blood for us, to the disciples who were then with Him, and had added the prayer addressed to His Father, the evangelist John began thereafter the narrative of His passion in these words: "When Jesus had so spoken, He went forth with His disciples over the brook Cedron, where was a garden, into the which He entered, and His disciples. And Judas also, who betrayed Him, knew the place; for Jesus oft-times resorted thither with His disciples." What he here relates of the Lord entering the garden with His disciples did not take place immediately after He had brought the prayer to a close, of which he says, "When Jesus had spoken these words:" but certain other incidents were interposed, which are passed over by the present evangelist and found in the others; just as in this one are found many things on which the others are similarly silent in their own narratives. But any one who desires to know how they all agree together, and the truth which is advanced by one is never contradicted by another, may seek for what he wants, not in these present discourses, but in other elaborate treatises;[1] but he will master the subject not by standing and listening, but rather by sitting down and reading, or by giving his closest attention and thought to one who does so. Yet let him believe before he know, whether he be able also to come to such a knowledge in this life, or find it impossible through some existing entanglements, that there is nothing written by any one evangelist, as far as regards those who have been received by the Church into canonical authority, that can be contrary to his own or another's equally veracious narrative. At present, therefore, let us look at the narrative of the blessed John, which we have undertaken to expound, without any comparison with the others, and without lingering over anything in it that is already sufficiently clear; so that where it is needful to do so, we may the better answer the demand. Let us, therefore, not take His words, "When Jesus had spoken these words, He went forth with His disciples over the brook Cedron, where was a garden, into the which He entered, and His disciples," as if it were immediately after the utterance of these words that He entered the garden; but let the clause, "When Jesus had spoken these words," bear this meaning, that we are not to suppose Him entering the garden before He had brought these words to a close.

2. "Judas also," he says, "who betrayed Him, knew the place;[2] for Jesus oft-times resorted thither with His disciples." There, accordingly, the wolf, clad in a sheep's skin, and tolerated among the sheep by the profound counsel of the Father of the family, learned where he might opportunely scatter the slender flock, and lay his coveted snares for the Shepherd. "Judas then," he adds, "having received a cohort, and officers from the chief men and the Pharisees, cometh thither with lanterns, and torches, and weapons." It was a cohort, not of Jews, but of soldiers. We are therefore to understand it as having been received from the governor, as if for the purpose of securing the person of a criminal, and by preserving the forms of legal power, to deter any from venturing to resist his captors: although at the same time so great a band had been assembled, and came armed in such a way as either to terrify or even attack any one who should dare to make a stand in Christ's defense. For only in so far was His power concealed and prominence given to His weakness, that these very measures were deemed necessary by His enemies to be taken against Him, for whose hurt nothing would have sufficed but what was pleasing to Himself; in His own goodness making a good use of the wicked, and doing what was good in regard to the wicked, that He might transform the evil into the good, and distinguish between the good and the evil.

3. "Jesus, therefore," as the evangelist proceeds to say, "knowing all things that should come upon Him, went forth and saith unto them, Whom seek ye? They answered

---

[1] Augustin refers to his books "On the Harmony of the Evangelists."

[2] The text runs thus: *Sciebat, inquit, et Judas, qui tradebat eum, locum. Ordo verborum est, Sciebat locum, qui tradebat eum;* which could not be intelligibly translated into English. —TR.

Him, Jesus of Nazareth. Jesus saith unto them, I am [He]. And Judas also, who betrayed Him, stood with them. As soon then as He had said unto them, I am He, they went backward, and fell to the ground." Where now were the military cohort, and the servants of the chief men and the Pharisees? where the terror and protection of weapons? His own single voice uttering the words, "I am [He]," without any weapon, smote, repelled, prostrated that great crowd, with all the ferocity of their hatred and terror of their arms. For God lay hid in that human flesh; and eternal day was so obscured in those human limbs, that with lanterns and torches He was sought for to be slain by the darkness. "I am [He]," He says; and He casteth the wicked to the ground. What will He do when He cometh as judge, who did this when giving Himself up to be judged? What will be His power when He cometh to reign, who had this power when He came to die? And now everywhere through the gospel Christ is still saying, "I am [He];" and the Jews are looking for antichrist, that they may go backward and fall to the ground, as those who have abandoned what is heavenly, and are hankering after the earthly. It was for the very purpose of apprehending Jesus that His persecutors accompanied the traitor: they found the One they were seeking, for they heard, "I am [He]." Why, then, did they not seize Him, but went backward and fell, but just because so He pleased, who could do whatever He pleased? But had He never permitted them to apprehend Him, they would certainly not have done what they came to do, but no more would He be doing what He came to do. They, verily, in their mad rage, sought for Him to put Him to death; but He, too, in giving Himself to death, was seeking for us. Accordingly, having thus shown His power to those who had the will, but not the power, to hold Him; let them now hold Him that He may work His own will with those who know it not.

4. "Then asked He them again, Whom seek ye? And they said, Jesus of Nazareth. Jesus answered, I have told you that I am [He]. If therefore ye seek me, let these go their way: that the saying might be fulfilled which He spake, That of those whom Thou hast given me I have lost none." "If ye seek me," He says, "let these go their way." He sees His enemies,[1] and they do what He bids them: they let those go their way, whom He would not have perish. But were they not afterwards to die? How then, if they died now, should He lose them, were it not that as yet they did not believe in Him, as all believe who perish not?

5. "Then Simon Peter, having a sword, drew it, and smote the high priest's servant, and cut off his right ear. And the servant's name was Malchus." This is the only evangelist who has given us the very name of this servant, as Luke is the only one who tells us that the Lord touched his ear and healed him.[2] The interpretation of Malchus is, one who is destined to reign. What, then, is signified by the ear that was cut off in the Lord's behalf, and healed by the Lord, but the renewed hearing that has been pruned of its oldness, that it may henceforth be in the newness of the spirit, and not in the oldness of the letter?[3] Who can doubt that he, who had such a thing done for him by Christ, was yet destined to reign with Christ? And his being found as a servant, pertains also to that oldness that gendereth to bondage, which is Agar.[4] But when healing came, liberty also was shadowed forth. Peter's deed, however, was disapproved of by the Lord, and He prevented Him from proceeding further by the words: "Put up thy sword into the sheath: the cup which my Father hath given me, shall I not drink it?" For in such a deed that disciple only sought to defend his Master, without any thought of what it was intended to signify. And he had therefore to be exhorted to the exercise of patience, and the event itself to be recorded as an exercise of understanding. But when He says that the cup of suffering was given Him by the Father, we have precisely the same truth as that which was uttered by the apostle: "If God be for us, who can be against us? He that spared not His own Son, but gave Him up for us all."[5] But the originator of this cup is also one with Him who drank it; and hence the same apostle likewise says, "Christ loved us, and gave Himself for us an offering and a sacrifice to God of a sweet-smelling savor."[6]

6. "Then the cohort, and the tribune, and the officers of the Jews, took Jesus, and bound Him." They took Him to whom they had never found access: for He continued the day, while they remained as darkness; neither had they given heed to the words, "Come unto Him, and be enlightened."[7] For had they so approached Him, they would have taken Him, not with their hands for the purpose of murder, but with their hearts for the purpose of a welcome reception. Now, however, when they laid hold of Him in this way, their distance from Him was vastly in-

---

1 Thomas Aquinas in the *Casena* reads here, *He commands his enemies*, and not altogether unsuitably.—MIGNE.
27

2 Luke xxii. 51.   3 Rom. vii. 6   4 Gal. iv. 24.
5 Rom. viii. 31, 32.   6 Eph. v. 2.   7 Ps. xxxiv. 5.

creased: and they bound Him by whom they themselves ought rather to have been loosed. And perhaps there were those among them who then fastened their fetters on Christ, and yet were afterwards delivered by Him, and could say, "Thou hast loosed my bonds."[1] Let this be enough for to-day; we shall deal, God willing, with what follows in another discourse.

[1] Ps. cxvi. 16.

TRACTATE CXIII.

Chapter XVIII. 13–27.

1. AFTER that His persecutors had, through the treason of Judas, taken and bound the Lord, who loved us, and gave Himself for us,[1] and whom the Father spared not, but gave Him up for us all:[2] that we may understand that there was no praise due to Judas for the usefulness of his treachery, but damnation for the willfulness of his wickedness: "They led Him," as John the evangelist tells us, "to Annas first." Nor does he withhold the reason for so doing: "For he was father-in-law to Caiaphas, who was the high priest that same year. Now Caiaphas was he," he says, "who gave counsel to the Jews, that it was expedient that one man should die for the people." And properly enough Matthew, when wishing to say the same in fewer words, tells us that He was led to Caiaphas;[3] for He was also taken in the first place to Annas, simply because he was his father-in-law; and where we have only to understand that such was the very thing that Caiaphas wished to be done.

2. "But Jesus was followed," he says, "by Simon Peter, and another disciple." Who that other disciple is, we cannot affirm with confidence, because it is left unnoticed here. But it is in this way that John usually refers to himself, with the addition, "whom Jesus loved."[4] Perhaps, therefore, it is he also in the present case; but whoever it is, let us look at what follows. "And that disciple," he says, "was known unto the high priest, and went in with Jesus into the palace of the high priest; but Peter stood at the door without. Then went out that other disciple, who was known unto the high priest, and spake unto her that kept the door, and brought in Peter. Then saith the damsel that kept the door unto Peter, Art thou also one of this man's disciples? He saith, I am not." Lo, the pillar of greatest strength has at a single breath of air trembled to its foundations. Where is now all that boldness of the promiser, and his overweening confidence in himself beforehand? What now of those words, when he said, "Why cannot I follow Thee now? I will lay down my life for Thy sake."[5] Is this the way to follow the Master, to deny his own discipleship? is it thus that one's life is laid down for the Lord, when one is frightened at a maid-servant's voice, lest it should compel us to the sacrifice? But what wonder, if God foretold what was true, and man presumptuously imagined what was false? Assuredly in this denial of the Apostle Peter, which had now entered on its first stage, we ought to take notice that not only is Christ denied by one who says that He is not Christ, but by him also who, while really a Christian, himself denies that he is so. For the Lord said not to Peter, Thou shalt deny that thou art my disciple; but, "Thou shalt deny me."[6] Him, therefore, he denied, when he denied that he was His disciple. And what else did such a form of denial imply, but that of his own Christianity? For although the disciples of Christ were not yet called by such a name, —because it was after His ascension, in Antioch, first that the disciples began to be called Christians,[7]—yet the thing itself, that afterwards assumed such a name, already existed, those who were afterwards called Christians were already disciples; and this common name, like the common faith, they transmitted to their posterity. He, therefore, who denied that he was Christ's disciple, denied the reality of the thing, of which the being called a Christian was only the name. How many afterwards, not to speak of old men and women, whose satiated feelings as regards the present life might more easily enable them to brave death for the confession of Christ; and not merely the youth of

[1] Eph. v. 2.   [2] Rom. viii. 32.
[3] Matt. xxvi. 57.   [4] Chap. xiii. 23, and xix. 26.   [5] Chap. xiii. 37.   [6] Matt. xxvi. 34.   [7] Acts xi. 26

both sexes, when of an age at which the exercise of fortitude seems to be fairly required; but even boys and girls could do—even as an innumerable company of holy martyrs with brave hearts and by a violent death entered the kingdom of heaven—what at that moment he was unable to do, who received the keys of that kingdom.[1]   It is here we see why it was said, "Let these go their way," when He, who hath redeemed us by His own blood, gave Himself for us; that the saying which He spake might be fulfilled, "Of those whom Thou hast given me I have lost none."   For assuredly, had Peter gone hence after denying the Christ, what else would have awaited him but destruction?

3. "And the servants and officers stood beside the fire of burning coals, for it was cold, and warmed themselves."   Though it was not winter, it was cold: which is sometimes wont to be the case even at the vernal equinox. "And Peter was standing with them, and warming himself.   The high priest then asked Jesus of His disciples, and of His doctrine. Jesus answered him, I spake openly to the world; I always taught in the synagogue, and in the temple, whither all the Jews resort, and in secret have I said nothing.   Why askest thou me? ask those who heard me, what I have said unto them: behold, they know what I said."   A question occurs that ought not to be passed over, how it is that the Lord Jesus said, "I spake openly to the world;" and in particular that which He afterwards added, "In secret have I said nothing."   Did He not, even in that latest discourse which He delivered to the disciples after supper, say to them, "These things have I spoken unto you in proverbs; but the hour cometh, when I shall no more speak unto you in proverbs, but I shall show you plainly of my Father?"[2] If, then, He spake not openly even to the more intimate company of His disciples, but gave the promise of a time when He would speak openly, how was it that He spake openly to the world?   And still further, as is also testified on the authority of the other evangelists, to those who were truly His own, in comparison with others who were not His disciples, He certainly spake with much greater plainness when He was alone with them at a distance from the multitudes; for then He unfolded to them the parables, which He had uttered in obscure terms to others.   What then is the meaning of the words, "In secret have I said nothing"?   It is in this way we are to understand His saying, "I spake openly to the world;" as if He had said, There were

many that heard me.   And that word "openly" was in a certain sense openly, and in another sense not openly.   It was openly, because many heard Him; and again it was not openly, because they did not understand Him.   And even what He spake to His disciples apart, He certainly spake not in secret. For who speaketh in secret. that speaketh before so many persons; as it is written, "At the mouth of two or three witnesses shall every word be established:"[3] especially if that be spoken to a few which he wisheth to become known to many through them; as the Lord Himself said to the few whom He had as yet, "What I tell you in darkness, that speak ye in light; and what ye hear in the ear, that preach ye upon the house-tops"?[4]   And accordingly the very thing that seemed to be spoken by Himself in secret, was in a certain sense not spoken in secret; for it was not so spoken to remain unuttered by those to whom it was spoken; but rather so in order to be preached in every possible direction.   A thing therefore may be uttered at once openly, and not openly; or at the same time in secret, and yet not in secret, as it is said, "That seeing, they may see, and not see."[5]   For how "may they see," save only because it is openly, and not in secret; and again, how is it that the same parties "may not see," save that it is not openly, but in secret?   Howbeit the very things which they had heard without understanding, were such as could not with justice or truth be turned into a criminal charge against Him: and as often as they tried by their questions to find something whereof to accuse Him, He gave them such replies as utterly discomfited all their plots, and left no ground for the calumnies they devised. Therefore He said, "Why askest thou me? ask those who heard me, what I have said unto them: behold, they know what I said."

4. "And when He had thus spoken, one of the officers who stood by gave Jesus a blow with his open hand, saying, Answerest thou the high priest so?   Jesus answered him, If I have spoken evil, bear witness of the evil; but if well, why smitest thou me?"   What could be truer, meeker, juster, than such an answer?   For it is His [reply], from whom the prophetic voice had issued before, "Make for thy goal (literally, take aim), and advance prosperously and reign, because of truth, and meekness, and righteousness."[6]   If we con-

---

[3] Deut. xix. 15.   [4] Matt. x. 27.   [5] Mark. iv. 12.
[6] Ps. xlv. 4.   In the Hebrew text, at the close of verse 4 and beginning of verse 5 (Eng. Ver. verses 3 and 4), there is a repetition of the word הֲדָרְךָ, which in both cases is rendered in our English Version, "and [in] Thy majesty."   By the Septuagint, however, and the Vulgate, and here by Augustin, the latter of the two has been differently read as a verb, as if pointed וְהַדְרֵךְ,

---

[1] Matt. xvi. 19.   [2] Chap. xvi. 25.

sider who it was that received the blow, might we not well feel the wish that he who struck it were either consumed by fire from heaven, or swallowed up by the gaping earth, or seized and carried off by devils, or visited with some other or still heavier punishment of this kind? For what one of all these could not He, who made the world, have commanded by His power, had He not wished rather to teach us the patience that overcometh the world? Some one will say here, Why did He not do what He Himself commanded?[1] for to one that smote Him, He ought not to have answered thus, but to have turned to him the other cheek. Nay, more than this, did He not answer truthfully, and meekly, and righteously, and at the same time not only prepare His other cheek to him who was yet again to smite it, but His whole body to be nailed to the tree? And hereby He rather showed, what needed to be shown, namely, that those great precepts of His are to be fulfilled not by bodily ostentation, but by the preparation of the heart. For it is possible that even an angry man may visibly hold out his other cheek. How much better, then, is it for one who is inwardly pacified to make a truthful answer, and with tranquil mind hold himself ready for the endurance of heavier sufferings to come? Happy is he who, in all that he suffers unjustly for righteousness' sake, can say with truth, "My heart is ready, O God, my heart is ready;" for this it is that gives cause for that which follows: "I will sing and give praise;"[2] which Paul and Barnabas[3] could do even in the cruellest of bonds.

5. But let us return to what follows in the Gospel narrative. "And Annas sent Him bound unto Caiaphas the high priest." To him, according to Matthew's account, He was led at the outset, because he was the high priest that year. For both the pontiffs are to be understood as in the habit of acting year by year alternately, that is, as chief priests; and these were at that time Annas

and Caiaphas, as recorded by the evangelist Luke, when telling of the time when John, the Lord's forerunner, began to preach the kingdom of heaven and to gather disciples. For he speaks thus: "Under the high priests Annas and Caiaphas, the word of the Lord came upon John, the son of Zacharias, in the wilderness,"[4] etc. Accordingly these two pontiffs fulfilled their years in turn: and it was the year of Caiaphas when Christ suffered. And so, according to Matthew, when He was apprehended, He was taken to him; but first, according to John, they came with Him to Annas; not because he was his colleague, but his father-in-law. And we must suppose that it was by Caiaphas' wish that it was so done; or that their houses were so situated, that Annas could not properly be overlooked by them as they passed on their way.

6. But the evangelist, after saying that Annas sent Him bound unto Caiaphas, returns to the place of his narrative, where he had left Peter, in order to explain what had taken place in Annas' house in regard to his threefold denial. "But Peter was standing," he says, "and warming himself." He thus repeats what he had already stated before; and then adds what follows. "They said therefore unto him, Art thou also one of his disciples? He denied, and said, I am not." He had already denied once; this is the second time. And then, that the third denial might also be fulfilled, "one of the servants of the high priest, being his kinsman whose ear Peter cut off, saith, Did I not see thee in the garden with him? Peter then denied again, and immediately the cock crew." Behold, the prediction of the Physician is fulfilled, the presumption of the sick man is brought to the light. For there is no performance of what the latter had asserted, "I will lay down my life for Thy sake;" but a performance of what the former had predicted, "Thou shalt thrice deny me."[5] But with the completion of Peter's threefold denial, let the present discourse be also now completed, that hereafter we may make a fresh start with the consideration of what was done respecting the Lord before Pontius Pilate the governor.

---

in the sense of "Bend thy bow," "Take aim," with the acc. omitted. Our English Version combines the next two verbs צְלַח רְכַב,

"ride prosperously," while in the above the distinction is preserved, "advance prosperously, ride (as a king, reign)."—Tr.

[1] Matt. v. 39.　　　　　　　　[2] Ps. lvii. 7.
[3] Here probably we should read *Silas*, according to Acts xvi. 25.—Migne.

[4] Luke iii. 2.　　　　[5] Chap. xiii. 38.

TRACTATE CXIV

1. LET us now consider, so far as indicated by the evangelist John, what was done with, or in regard to, our Lord Jesus Christ, when brought before Pontius Pilate the governor. For he returns to the place of his narrative, where he had left it, to explain the denial of Peter. He had already, you know, said, "And Annas sent Him bound unto Caiaphas the high priest:" and having returned from where he had dismissed Peter as he was warming himself at the fire in the hall, after completing the whole of his denial, which was thrice repeated, he says, "Then they bring Jesus unto Caiaphas[1] into the hall of judgment (pretorium);" for he had said that He was sent to Caiaphas by his colleague and father-in-law Annas. But if to Caiaphas, why into the hall of judgment? Nothing else is thereby meant to be understood than the place where Pilate the governor dwelt. And therefore, either for some urgent reason Caiaphas had proceeded from the house of Annas, where both had met to give Jesus a hearing, to the governor's pretorium, and had left the hearing of Jesus to his father-in-law; or Pilate had made his pretorium in the house of Caiaphas, which was so large as to contain separate apartments for its own master, and the like for the judge.

2. "And it was morning; and they themselves," that is, those who brought Jesus, "went not into the judgment hall," to wit, into that part of the house which Pilate occupied, supposing it to be Caiaphas' house. And then in explanation of the reason why they went not into the judgment hall, he says, "lest they should be defiled; but that they might eat the passover." For it was the commencement of the days of unleavened bread: on which they accounted it defilement to enter the abode of one of another nation. Impious blindness! Would they, forsooth, be defiled by a stranger's abode, and not be defiled by their own wickedness? They were afraid of being defiled by the pretorium of a foreign judge, and had no fear of defilement from the blood of an innocent brother: not to say more than this meanwhile, which was enough to fix guilt on the conscience of the wicked. For the additional fact, that it was the Lord who was led to death by their impiety, and the giver of life that was on the way to be slain, may be charged, not to their conscience, but to their ignorance.

3. "Pilate then went out unto them, and said, What accusation bring ye against this man? They answered and said unto him, If he were not a malefactor, we would not have delivered him up unto thee." Let the question be put to, and the answer come from, those who had been delivered from foul spirits, from the sickly who had been healed, the lepers who had been cleansed, the deaf who were hearing, the dumb who were speaking, the blind who were seeing, the dead who were raised to life, and, above all, the foolish who were become wise, whether Jesus were a malefactor. But these things were said by those of whom He Himself had already foretold by the prophet, "They rewarded me evil for good."[2]

4. "Then said Pilate unto them, Take ye him, and judge him according to your law. The Jews therefore said unto him. It is not lawful for us to put any man to death." What is this that their insane cruelty saith? Did not they put Him to death, whom they were here presenting for the very purpose? Or does the cross, forsooth, fail to kill? Such is the folly of those who do not pursue, but persecute wisdom. What then mean the words, "It is not lawful for us to put any man to death"? If He is a malefactor, why is it not lawful? Did not the law command them not to spare malefactors, especially (as they accounted Him to be) those who seduced them from their God?[3] We are, however, to understand that they said that it was not lawful for them to put any man to death, on account of the sanctity of the festal day, which they had just begun to celebrate, and on account of which they were afraid of being defiled even by entering the pretorium. Had you become so hardened, false Israelites? Were you by your excessive malice so lost to all

---

[1] This reading of the text is also found in "The Harmony of the Evangelists," Book iii. chap. 7; but the true biblical reading is now ascertained to be, ἀπὸ τοῦ Καιάφα, "from Caiaphas."—MIGNE.

[2] Ps. xxxv. 12.

[3] Deut. xiii. 5. Augustin evidently attaches a wrong meaning to the words, *Nobis non licet interficere quenquam;* as if these Jews thereby insinuated that they did not themselves wish Christ's death: unaware, seemingly, of the fact, that, on their subjugation by the Romans, their own rulers were still allowed to try minor offenses, but were deprived of the power of inflicting capital punishment; and that, consequently, it was because they were actually bent on putting Him to death, and no less penalty would satisfy them, that they thus brought Him before the Roman governor.—TR.

sense, as to imagine that you were unpolluted by the blood of the innocent, because you gave it up to be shed by another? Was even Pilate himself going to slay Him with his own hands, when made over by you into his power for the very purpose? If you did not wish Him to be slain; if you did not lay snares for Him; if you did not get Him to be betrayed to you for money; if you did not lay hands upon Him, and bind Him, and bring Him there; if you did not with your own hands present Him, and with your voices demand Him to be slain,—then boast that He was not put to death by you. But if in addition to all these former deeds of yours, you also cried out, "Crucify, crucify [him];"[1] then hear what it is against you that the prophet proclaims: "The sons of men, whose teeth are spears and arrows, and their tongue a sharp sword."[2] These, look you, are the spears, the arrows, the sword, wherewith you slew the righteous, when you said that it was not lawful for you to put any man to death. Hence it is also that when for the purpose of apprehending Jesus the chief priests did not themselves come, but sent; yet the evangelist Luke says in the same passage of his narrative, "Then said Jesus unto those who were come to him, [namely] the chief priests, and captains of the temple, and elders, Be ye come out, as against a thief," etc?[3] As therefore the chief priests went not in their own persons, but by those whom they had sent, to apprehend Jesus, what else was that but coming themselves in the authority of their own order? and so all, who cried out with impious voices for the crucifixion of Christ, slew Him, not, indeed, directly with their own hands, but personally through him who was impelled to such a crime by their clamor.

5. But when the evangelist John adds, "That the saying of Jesus might be fulfilled, which He spake, signifying what death He should die:" if we would understand such words as referring to the death of the cross, as if the Jews had said, "It is not lawful for us to put any man to death," for this reason that it was one thing to be put to death, and another to be crucified: I do not see how such can be understood as a consequence, seeing that this was their answer to the words that Pilate had just addressed to them, "Take ye him, and judge him according to your law." If it were so, could they not then have taken Him, and crucified Him themselves, had they desired by any such form of punishment to avoid the putting of Him to death? But who is there that may not see the absurdity of allowing those to crucify any one, who were not allowed to put any one to death? Nay more, did not the Lord Himself call that same death of His, that is, the death of the cross, a putting to death, as we read in Mark, where he says, "Behold, we go up to Jerusalem; and the Son of man shall be delivered unto the chief priests, and unto the scribes; and they shall condemn Him to death, and shall deliver Him to the Gentiles: and they shall mock Him, and shall spit upon Him, and shall scourge Him, and shall put Him to death, and the third day He shall rise again"?[4] There is no doubt, therefore, that in so speaking the Lord signified what death He should die: not that He here meant the death of the cross to be understood, but that the Jews were to deliver Him up to the Gentiles, or, in other words, to the Romans. For Pilate was a Roman, and had been sent by the Romans into Judea as governor. That, then, this saying of Jesus might be fulfilled, namely, that, being delivered up to them, He should be put to death by the Gentiles, as Jesus had foretold would happen; therefore when Pilate, who was the Roman judge, wished to hand Him back to the Jews, that they might judge Him according to their law, they refused to receive Him, saying, "It is not lawful for us to put any man to death." And so the saying of Jesus was fulfilled, which He foretold concerning His death, that, being delivered up by the Jews, He should be put to death by the Gentiles: whose crime was less than that of the Jews, who sought by this method to make themselves appear averse to His being put to death, to the end that, not their innocence, but their madness might be made manifest.

---

[1] Chap. xix. 6.   [2] Ps. lvii. 4.   [3] Luke xxii. 52.

[4] Mark x. 33, 34.

TRACTATE CXV.

CHAPTER XVIII. 33-40.

1. WHAT Pilate said to Christ, or what He replied to Pilate, has to be considered and handled in the present discourse. For after the words had been addressed to the Jews, "Take ye him, and judge him according to your law," and the Jews had replied, "It is not lawful for us to put any man to death," Pilate entered again into the judgment hall, and called Jesus, and said unto Him, Art thou the King of the Jews? And Jesus answered, Sayest thou this thing of thyself, or did others tell it thee of me?" The Lord indeed knew both what He Himself asked, and what reply the other was to give; but yet He wished it to be spoken, not for the sake of information to Himself, but that what He wished us to know might be recorded in Scripture. "Pilate answered, Am I a Jew? Thine own nation, and the chief priests, have delivered thee unto me: what hast thou done? Jesus answered, My kingdom is not of this world. If my kingdom were of this world, then would my servants fight, that I should not be delivered to the Jews: but now is my kingdom not from hence." This is what the good Master wished us to know; but first there had to be shown us the vain notion that men had regarding His kingdom, whether Gentiles or Jews, from whom Pilate had heard it; as if He ought to have been punished with death on the ground of aspiring to an unlawful kingdom; or as those in the possession of royal power usually manifest their ill-will to such as are yet to attain it, as if, for example, precautions were to be used lest His kingdom should prove adverse either to the Romans or to the Jews. But the Lord was able to reply to the first question of the governor, when he asked Him, "Art thou the King of the Jews?" with the words, "My kingdom is not of this world," etc.; but by questioning him in turn, whether he said this thing of himself, or heard it from others, He wished by his answer to show that He had been charged with this as a crime before him by the Jews: laying open to us the thoughts of men, which were all known to Himself, that they are but vain;[1] and now, after Pilate's answer, giving them, both Jews and Gentiles, all the more reasonable and fitting a reply, "My kingdom is not of this world."

But had He made an immediate answer to Pilate's question, His reply would have appeared to refer to the Gentiles only, without including the Jews, as entertaining such an opinion regarding Him. But now when Pilate replied, "Am I a Jew? Thine own nation, and the chief priests, have delivered thee to me;" he removed from himself the suspicion of being possibly supposed to have spoken of his own accord, in saying that Jesus was the king of the Jews, by showing that such a statement had been communicated to him by the Jews. And then by saying, "What hast thou done?" he made it sufficiently clear that this was charged against Him as a crime: as if he had said, If thou deniest such kingly claims, what hast thou done to cause thy being delivered unto me? As if there would be no ground for wonder that one should be delivered up to a judge for punishment, who proclaimed himself a king; but if no such assertion were made, it became needful to inquire of Him, what else, if anything, He had done, that He should thus deserve to be delivered unto the judge.

2. Hear then, ye Jews and Gentiles; hear, O circumcision; hear, O uncircumcision; hear, all ye kingdoms of the earth: I interfere not with your government in this world, "My kingdom is not of this world." Cherish ye not the utterly vain terror that threw Herod the elder into consternation when the birth of Christ was announced, and led him to the murder of so many infants in the hope of including Christ in the fatal number,[2] made more cruel by his fear than by his anger: "My kingdom," He said, "is not of this world." What would you more? Come to the kingdom that is not of this world; come, believing, and fall not into the madness of anger through fear. He says, indeed, prophetically of God the Father, "Yet have I been appointed king by Him upon His holy hill of Zion;"[3] but that hill of Zion is not of this world. For what is His kingdom, save those who believe in Him, to whom He says, "Ye are not of the world, even as I am not of the world"? And yet He wished them to be in the world: on that very account saying of them to the Father, "I pray not that Thou shouldest take them out of the world, but that

[1] Ps. xciv. 11.   [2] Matt. ii. 3, 16.   [3] Ps. ii. 6.

Thou shouldest keep them from the evil."[1] Hence also He says not here, "My kingdom is not" in this world; but, "is not of this world." And when He proved this by saying, "If my kingdom were of this world, then would my servants fight, that I should not be delivered to the Jews," He saith not, "But now is my kingdom not" here, but, "is not from hence." For His kingdom is here until the end of the world, having tares intermingled therewith until the harvest; for the harvest is the end of the world, when the reapers, that is to say, the angels, shall come and gather out of His kingdom everything that offendeth;[2] which certainly would not be done, were it not that His kingdom is here. But still it is not from hence; for it only sojourns as a stranger in the world: because He says to His kingdom, "Ye are not of the world, but I have chosen you out of the world."[3] They were therefore of the world, so long as they were not His kingdom, but belonged to the prince of this world. Of the world therefore are all mankind, created indeed by the true God, but generated from Adam as a vitiated and condemned stock; and there are made into a kingdom no longer of the world, all from thence that have been regenerated in Christ. For so did God rescue us from the power of darkness, and translate us into the kingdom of the Son of His love:[4] and of this kingdom it is that He saith, "My kingdom is not of this world;" or, "My kingdom is not from hence."

3. "Pilate therefore said unto Him, Art thou a king then? Jesus answered, Thou sayest that I am a king." Not that He was afraid to confess Himself a king, but "Thou sayest" has been so balanced that He neither denies Himself to be a king (for He is a king whose kingdom is not of this world), nor does He confess that He is such a king as to warrant the supposition that His kingdom is of this world. For as this was the very idea in Pilate's mind when he said, "'Art thou a king then?" so the answer he got was, "Thou sayest that I am a king." For it was said, "Thou sayest," as if it had been said, Carnal thyself, thou sayest it carnally.

4. Thereafter He adds, "To this end was I born, and for this cause came I into the world, that I should bear witness unto the truth." * *[5] Whence it is evident that He here referred to His own temporal nativity, when by becoming incarnate He came into the world, and not to that which had no beginning, whereby He was God through whom the Father created the world. For this, then, that is, on this account, He declared that He was born, and to this end He came into the world, to wit, by being born of the Virgin, that He might bear witness unto the truth. But because all men have not faith,[6] He still further said, "Every one that is of the truth heareth my voice." He heareth, that is to say, with the ears of the inward man, or, in other words, He obeyeth my voice, which is equivalent to saying, He believeth me. When Christ, therefore, beareth witness unto the truth, He beareth witness, of course, unto Himself; for from His own lips are the words, "I am the truth;"[7] as He said also in another place, "I bear witness of myself."[8] But when He said, "Every one that is of the truth heareth my voice," He commendeth the grace whereby He calleth according to His own purpose. Of which purpose the apostle says, "We know that all things work together for good to them that love God, to those who are called according to the purpose of God,"[9] to wit, the purpose of Him that calleth, not of those who are called; which is put still more clearly in another place in this way, "Labor together in the gospel according to the power of God, who saveth us and calleth us with His holy calling, not according to our works, but according to His own purpose and grace."[10] For if our thoughts turn to the nature wherein we have been created, inasmuch as we were all created by the Truth, who is there that is not of the truth? But it is not all to whom it is given of the truth to hear, that is, to obey the truth, and to believe in the truth; while in no case certainly is there any preceding of merit, lest grace should cease to be grace. For had He said, Every one that heareth my voice is of the truth, then it would be supposed that he was declared to be of the truth because he conforms to the truth; it is not this, however, that He says, but, "Every one that is of the truth heareth my voice." And in this way he is not of the truth simply because he heareth His voice; but only on this account he heareth, because he is of the truth, that is, because this is a gift bestowed on him of the truth. And what else is this, but that by

[1] Chap. xvii. 16, 15.   [2] Matt. xiii. 38-41.
[3] Chap. xv. 19.   [4] Col. i. 13.
[5] The verse quoted reads in Latin, *Ego in hoc natus sum, et ad hoc veni*," etc.; and in reference to the words, *in hoc*, Augustin goes on to say, in the passage marked * * . "We are not to lengthen the syllable [vowel] of this pronoun when He says, *In hoc natus sum*, as if He meant to say, In this thing was I born; but to shorten it, as if He had said, *Ad hanc rem natus sum, vel ad hoc natus sum* (for this thing was I born), just as He says, *Ad hoc veni in mundum* (for this came I into the world). For in the Greek Gospel there is no ambiguity in this expression," the Greek having εἰς τοῦτο. This passage is interesting only to Latin scholars, as showing that in ordinary *parlance* they marked, in Augustin's time, the distinction between *hoc* of the abl. and *hoc* of the nom. or acc.—Tr.
[6] 2 Thess. iii. 2.   [7] Chap. xiv. 6.   [8] Chap. viii. 18.
[9] Rom. viii. 28.   [10] 2 Tim. i. 8, 9.

Christ's gracious bestowal he believeth on Christ?

5. "Pilate said unto Him, What is truth?" Nor did he wait to hear the answer; but "when he had said this, he went out again unto the Jews, and said unto them, I find in him no fault. But ye have a custom that I should release unto you one at the passover: will ye therefore that I release unto you the King of the Jews?" I believe when Pilate said, "What is truth?" there immediately occurred to his mind the custom of the Jews, according to which he was wont to release unto them one at the passover; and therefore he did not wait to hear Jesus' answer to his question, What is truth? to avoid delay on recollecting the custom whereby He might be released unto them during the passover— a thing which it is clear he greatly desired. It could not, however, be torn from his heart that Jesus was the King of the Jews, but was fixed there, as in the superscription, by the truth itself, whereof he had just inquired what it was. "But on hearing this, they all cried again, saying, Not this man, but Barabbas. Now Barabbas was a robber." We blame you not, O Jews, for liberating the guilty during the passover, but for slaying the innocent; and yet unless that were done, the true passover would not take place. But a shadow of the truth was retained by the erring Jews, and by a marvellous dispensation of divine wisdom the truth of that same shadow was fulfilled by deluded men; because in order that the true passover might be kept, Christ was led as a sheep to the sacrificial slaughter. Hence there follows the account of the injurious treatment received by Christ at the hands of Pilate and his cohort; but this must be taken up in another discourse.

TRACTATE CXVI.

Chapter XIX. 1–16.

1. On the Jews crying out that they did not wish Jesus to be released unto them at the passover, but Barabbas the robber; not the Saviour, but the murderer; not the Giver of life, but the destroyer,—"then Pilate took Jesus and scourged Him." We must believe that Pilate acted thus for no other reason than that the Jews, glutted with the injuries done to Him, might consider themselves satisfied, and desist from madly pursuing Him even unto death. With a similar intention was it that, as governor, he also permitted his cohort to do what follows, or even perhaps ordered them, although the evangelist is silent on the subject. For he tells us what the soldiers did thereafter, but not that Pilate ordered it. "And the soldiers," he says, "platted a crown of thorns, and put it on His head, and they clothed Him with a purple robe. And they came to Him and said, Hail, King of the Jews! And they smote Him with their hands." Thus were fulfilled the very things which Christ had foretold of Himself; thus were the martyrs moulded for the endurance of all that their persecutors should be pleased to inflict; thus, by concealing for a time the terror of His power, He commended to us the prior imitation of His patience; thus the kingdom which was not of this world overcame that proud world, not by the ferocity of fighting, but by the humility of suffering; and thus the grain of corn that was yet to be multiplied was sown amid the horrors of shame, that it might come to fruition amid the wonders of glory.

2. "Pilate went forth again, and saith unto them, Behold, I bring him forth, that ye may know that I find no fault in him. Then came Jesus forth, wearing the crown of thorns and the purple robe. And he saith unto them, Behold the man!" Hence it is apparent that these things were done by the soldiers not without Pilate's knowledge, whether it was that he ordered them or only permitted them, namely, for the reason we have stated above, that His enemies might all the more willingly drink in the sight of such derisive treatment, and cease to thirst further for His blood. Jesus goes forth to them wearing the crown of thorns and the purple robe, not resplendent in kingly power, but laden with reproach; and the words are addressed to them, Behold the man! If you hate your king, spare him now when you see him sunk so low; he has been scourged, crowned with thorns, clothed with the garments of derision, jeered at with the bitterest insults, struck with the open hand; his ignominy is at the boiling point, let your ill-will sink to zero. But there is no such cooling on the part of the latter, but rather a further increase of heat and vehemence.

3. "When the chief priests, therefore, and

attendants saw Him, they cried out, saying, Crucify, crucify him. Pilate saith unto them, Take ye him and crucify him; for I find no fault in him. The Jews answered him, We have a law, and by the law he ought to die, because he made himself the Son of God." Behold another and still greater ground of hatred. The former, indeed, seemed but a small matter, as that shown towards the usurpation, by an unlawful act of daring, of the royal power; and yet of neither did Jesus falsely claim possession, but each of them is truly His as both the only-begotten Son of God, and by Him appointed King upon His holy hill of Zion; and both might He now have shown to be His, were it not that in proportion to the greatness of His power, He preferred to manifest the corresponding greatness of His patience.

4. "When Pilate, therefore, heard that saying, he was the more afraid; and entered again into the judgment hall, and saith unto Jesus, Whence art thou? But Jesus gave him no answer." It is found, in comparing the narratives of all the evangelists, that this silence on the part of our Lord Jesus Christ took place more than once, both before the chief priests and before. Herod, to whom, as Luke intimates, Pilate had sent Him for a hearing, and before Pilate himself;[1] so that it was not in vain that the prophecy regarding Him had preceded, "As the lamb before its shearer was dumb, so He opened not His mouth,"[2] especially on those occasions when He answered not His questioners. For although He frequently replied to questions addressed to Him, yet because of those in regard to which He declined making any reply, the metaphor of the lamb is supplied, in order that in His silence He might be accounted not as guilty, but innocent. When, therefore, He was passing through the process of judgment, wherever He opened not His mouth it was in the character of a lamb that He did so; that is, not as one with an evil conscience who was convicted of his sins, but as one who in His meekness was sacrificed for the sins of others.

5. "Then saith Pilate unto Him, Speakest thou not unto me? knowest thou not that I have power to crucify thee, and have power to release thee? Jesus answered: Thou wouldest have no power against me, except it were given thee from above: therefore he that delivered me unto thee hath the greater sin." Here, you see, He replied; and yet wherever He replied not, it is not as one who

is criminal or cunning, but as a lamb; that is, in simplicity and innocence He opened not His mouth. Accordingly, where He made no answer, He was silent as a sheep; where He answered, He taught as the Shepherd. Let us therefore set ourselves to learn what He said, what He taught also by the apostle, that "there is no power but of God;"[3] and that he is a greater sinner who maliciously delivereth up to the power the innocent to be slain, than the power itself, if it slay him through fear of another power that is greater still. Of such a sort, indeed, was the power which God had given to Pilate, that he should also be under the power of Cæsar. Wherefore "thou wouldest have," He says, "no power against me," that is, even the little measure thou really hast, "except" this very measure, whatever its amount, "were given thee from above." But knowing as I do its amount, for it is not so great as to render thee altogether independent, "therefore he that delivered me unto thee hath the greater sin." He, indeed, delivered me to thy power at the bidding of envy, whilst thou art to exercise thy power upon me through the impulse of fear. And yet not even through the impulse of fear ought one man to slay another, especially the innocent; nevertheless to do so by an officious zeal is a much greater evil than under the constraint of fear. And therefore the truth-speaking Teacher saith not, "He that delivered me to thee," he only hath sin, as if the other had none; but He saith, "hath the greater sin," letting him understand that he himself was not exempt from blame. For that of the latter is not reduced to nothing because the other is greater.

6. "Hence Pilate sought to release Him." What is to be understood by the word here used, "hence,"[4] as if he had not been seeking to do so before? Read what precedes, and thou wilt find that he had already for some time been seeking to release Jesus. By the original word,[4] therefore, we are to understand, on this account, that is, for this reason, that he might not contract sin by slaying an innocent man who had been delivered into his hands, even though his sin would be less than that of the Jews, who delivered Him to him to be put to death. "From thence,"[4] therefore, that is, for this reason, that he might not commit such a sin, "he sought" not now for the first time, but from the beginning, "to release Him."

7. "But the Jews cried out, saying, If thou let this man go, thou art not Cæsar's

---

[1] Matt. xxvi. 63, xxvii. 14; Mark xiv. 61, xv. 5; Luke xxiii. 7–9; John xix. 9.
[2] Isa. liii. 7.

[3] Rom. xiii. 1.
[4] *Exinde:* Greek, ἐκτούτου; literally, "therefrom."—Tr.

friend: whosoever maketh himself a king, speaketh against Cæsar." They thought to inspire Pilate with greater fear by terrifying him about Cæsar, in order that he might put Christ to death, than formerly when they said, "We have the law, and by the law he ought to die, because he made himself the Son of God." It was not their law, indeed, that impelled him through fear to the deed of murder, but rather it was his fear of the Son of God that held him back from the crime. But now he could not set Cæsar, who was the author of his own power, at nought, in the same way as the law of another nation.

8. As yet, however, the evangelist proceeds to say: "But when Pilate heard these sayings, he brought Jesus forth, and sat down before the tribunal, in a place that is called the Pavement,[1] but in the Hebrew, Gabbatha. And it was the preparation[2] of the passover, and about the sixth hour." The question, at what hour the Lord was crucified, because of the testimony supplied by another evangelist, who says, "And it was the third hour, and they crucified Him,"[3] we shall consider as we can, if the Lord please, when we are come to the passage itself where His crucifixion is recorded.[4] When Pilate, therefore, had sat down before the tribunal, " he saith unto the Jews, Behold your king! But they cried out, Away with him, away with him, crucify him. Pilate said unto them, Shall I crucify your king?" As yet he tries to overcome the terror with which they had inspired him about Cæsar, by seeking to break them from their purpose on the ground of the ignominy it brought on themselves, with the words, " Shall I crucify your king?" when he failed to soften them on the ground of the ignominy done to Christ; but by and by he is overcome by fear.

9. For " the chief priests answered, We have no king but Cæsar. Then delivered he Him therefore unto them to be crucified." For he would have every appearance of acting against Cæsar if, on their declaration that they had no king but Cæsar, he were wishing to impose on them another king by releasing without punishment one whom for these very attempts they had delivered unto him to be put to death. " Therefore he delivered Him unto them to be crucified." But was it, then, anything different that he had previously desired when he said, " Take ye him, and crucify him;" or even earlier still, " Take ye him, and judge him according to your law?" And why did they show so great reluctance, when they said, " It is not lawful for us to put any man to death,"[5] and were in every way urgent to have Him slain not by themselves, but by the governor, and therefore refused to receive Him for the purpose of putting Him to death, if now for the same purpose they actually do receive Him? Or if such be not the case, why was it said, " Then delivered he Him therefore unto them to be crucified?" Or is it of any importance? Plainly it is. For it was not said, " Then delivered he Him therefore unto them " that they might crucify Him, but " that He might be crucified," that is, that He might be crucified by the judicial sentence and power of the governor. But it is for this reason that the evangelist has said that He was delivered to them, that he might show that they were implicated in the crime from which they tried to hold themselves aloof; for Pilate would have done no such thing, save to implement what he perceived to be their fixed desire. The words, however, that follow, "And they took Jesus, and led Him away," may now refer to the soldiers, the attendants of the governor. For it is more clearly stated afterwards, " When the soldiers therefore had crucified Him,"[6] although the evangelist properly does so even when he attributes the whole to the Jews, for they it was that received what they had with the utmost greediness demanded, and they it was that did all that they compelled to be done. But the events that follow must be made the subject of consideration in another discourse.

---

[1] *Lithostrotos.*
[3] Mark xv. 25.
[2] *Parasceve;* Greek, παρασκευή.
[4] See below, Tract. CXVII. secs. 1, 2.
[5] Chap. xviii. 31.
[6] Chap. xix. 23.

TRACTATE CXVII.

CHAPTER XIX. 17-22.

1. ON Pilate's judgment and condemnation before the tribunal, they took the Lord Jesus Christ, about the sixth hour, and led Him away. "And He, bearing His cross, went forth into the place that is called Calvary, but in Hebrew, Golgotha; where they crucified Him." What else, then, is the meaning of the evangelist Mark saying, "And it was the third hour, and they crucified Him,"[1] but this, that the Lord was crucified at the third hour by the tongues of the Jews, at the sixth hour by the hands of the soldiers? That we may understand that the fifth hour was now completed, and there was some beginning made of the sixth, when Pilate took his seat before the tribunal, which is expressed by John as "about[2] the sixth hour;" and when He was led forth, and nailed to the tree with the two robbers, and the events recorded were enacted beside His cross, the completion of the sixth hour was fully reached, being the hour from which, on to the ninth, the sun was obscured, and the darkness took place, we have it jointly attested on the authority of the three evangelists, Matthew, Mark, and Luke.[3] But as the Jews attempted to transfer the crime of slaying Christ from themselves to the Romans, that is to say, to Pilate and his soldiers, therefore Mark suppresses the hour at which Christ was crucified by the soldiers, and which then began to enter upon the sixth, and remembers rather to give an express place to the third hour, at which they are understood to have cried out before Pilate, "Crucify, crucify him" (verse 6), that it not only may be seen that the former crucified Jesus, namely, the soldiers who hung Him on the tree at the sixth hour, but the Jews also, who at the third hour cried out to have Him crucified.

2. There is also another solution of this question, that we should not here understand the sixth hour of the day, because John says not, And it was about the sixth hour of the day, or about the sixth hour, but says, "And it was the parasceve of the passover, about the sixth hour" (ver. 14). And parasceve is in Latin præparatio (preparation); but the Jews are fonder of using the Greek words in observances of this sort, even those of them who speak Latin rather than Greek. It was therefore the preparation of the passover. But "our passover, Christ," as the apostle says, "has been sacrificed;"[4] and if we reckon the preparation of this passover from the ninth hour of the night (for then the chief priests seem to have given their verdict for the sacrifice of the Lord, when they said, "He is guilty of death,"[5] and when the hearing of His case was still proceeding in the high priest's house: whence there is a kind of harmony in understanding that therewith began the preparation of the true passover, whose shadow was the passover of the Jews, that is, of the sacrificing of Christ, when the priests gave their sentence that He was to be sacrificed), certainly from that hour of the night, which is conjectured to have been then the ninth, on to the third hour of the day, when the evangelist Mark testifies that Christ was crucified, there are six hours, three of the night, and three of the day. Hence in the case of this parasceve of the passover, that is, the preparation of the sacrifice of Christ, which began with the ninth hour of the night, it was about the sixth hour; that is to say, the fifth hour was completed, and the sixth had already begun to run, when Pilate ascended the tribunal: for that same preparation, which had begun with the ninth hour of the night, still continued till the sacrifice of Christ, which was the event in course of preparation, was completed, which took place at the third hour, according to Mark, not of the preparation, but of the day; while it was also the sixth hour, not of the day, but of the preparation, by reckoning, of course, six hours from the ninth hour of the night to the third of the day. Of these two solutions of this difficult question let each choose the one that pleases him. But one will judge better what to choose who reads the very elaborate discussions on "The Harmony of the Evangelists."[6] And if other solutions of it can also be found, the stability of gospel truth will have a more cumulative defense against the calumnies of unbelieving and profane vanity. And now, after these brief discussions, let us return to the narrative of the evangelist John.

3. "And they took Jesus," he says, "and

---

[1] Mark xv. 25. [2] Quasi.
[3] Matt. xxvii. 45; Mark xv. 33; and Luke xxiii. 44.
[4] 1 Cor. v. 7. [5] Matt. xxvi. 66.
[6] "On the Harmony of the Evangelists," Book iii. chap. xiii. secs. 40-50.

led Him away; and He, bearing His cross, went forth unto the place that is called Calvary, in the Hebrew, Golgotha; where they crucified Him." Jesus, therefore, went to the place where He was to be crucified, bearing His cross. A grand spectacle! but if it be impiety that is the onlooker, a grand laughing-stock; if piety, a grand mystery: if impiety be the onlooker, a grand demonstration of ignominy; if piety, a grand bulwark of faith: if it is impiety that looketh on, it laughs at the King bearing, in place of His kingly rod, the tree of His punishment; if it is piety, it sees the King bearing the tree for His own crucifixion, which He was yet to affix even on the foreheads of kings, exposed to the contemptuous glances of the impious in connection with that wherein the hearts of saints were thereafter to glory. For to Paul, who was yet to say, " But God forbid that I should glory, save in the cross of our Lord Jesus Christ,"[1] He was commending that same cross of His by carrying it on His own shoulders, and bearing the candelabrum of that light that was yet to burn, and not to be placed under a bushel.[2] " Bearing," therefore, " His cross, He went forth into the place that is called Calvary, in the Hebrew, Golgotha; where they crucified Him, and two others with Him on either side one, and Jesus in the midst." These two, as we have learned in the narrative of the other evangelists, were thieves with whom He was crucified, and between whom He was fixed,[3] whereof the prophecy sent before had declared, "And He was numbered among the transgressors."[4]

4. "And Pilate wrote a title also, and put it on the cross, and the writing was, Jesus of Nazareth, the King of the Jews. This title then read many of the Jews: for the place where Jesus was crucified was nigh to the city: and it was written in Hebrew, Greek, and Latin, The King of the Jews." For these three languages were conspicuous in that place beyond all others: the Hebrew on account of the Jews, who gloried in the law of God; the Greek, because of the wise men among the Gentiles; and the Latin, on account of the Romans, who at that very time were exercising sovereign power over many and almost all countries.

5. " Then said the chief priests of the Jews unto Pilate Write not, The King of the Jews; but that he said, I am King of the Jews. Pilate answered, What I have written I have written." Oh the ineffable power of the working of God, even in the hearts of the

ignorant! Was there not some hidden voice that sounded through Pilate's inner man with a kind, if one may so say, of loud-toned silence, the words that had been prophesied so long before in the very letter of the Psalms, " Corrupt not the inscription of the title"?[5] Here, then, you see, he corrupted it not; what he has written he has written. But the high priests, who wished it to be corrupted, what did they say? " Write not, The King of the Jews; but that he said, I am King of the Jews." What is it, madmen, that you say? Why do you oppose the doing of that which you are utterly unable to alter? Will it by any such means become the less true that Jesus said, " I am King of the Jews"? If that cannot be tampered with which Pilate has written, can that be tampered with which the truth has uttered? But is Christ king only of the Jews, or of the Gentiles also? Yes, of the Gentiles also. For when He said in prophecy, " I am set king by Him upon His holy hill of Zion, declaring the decree of the Lord," that no one might say, because of the hill of Zion, that He was set king over the Jews alone, He immediately added, " The Lord said unto me, Thou art my Son; this day have I begotten Thee. Ask of me, and I will give Thee the Gentiles for Thine inheritance, and the uttermost parts of the earth for Thy possession."[6] Whence He Himself, speaking now with His own lips among the Jews, said, " Other sheep I have which are not of this fold; them also I must bring, and they shall hear my voice, and there shall be one flock and one Shepherd."[7] Why then would we have some great mystery[8] to be understood in this superscription, wherein it was written, " King of the Jews," if Christ is king also of the Gentiles? For this reason, because it was the wild olive tree that was made partaker of the fatness of the olive tree, and not the olive tree that was made partaker of the bitterness of the wild olive tree.[9] For inasmuch as the title, " King of the Jews," was truthfully written regarding Christ, who are they that are to be understood as the Jews but the seed of Abraham, the children of the promise, who are also the children of God? For " they," saith the apostle, " who are the children of the flesh, these are not the children of God; but the children of the promise are counted for the seed."[10] And the Gentiles were those to whom he said, " But if ye be Christ's, then are ye Abraham's seed, and heirs according to the promise."[11] Christ therefore is king of the

---

1 Gal. vi. 14.   2 Matt. v. 15.
3 Matt. xxvii. 38; Mark xv. 27; and Luke xxiii. 33.
4 Isa. liii. 12.

5 Ps. lvii., lviii.   6 Ps. ii. 6-8.   7 Chap. x. 16.
8 *Sacramentum.*   9 Rom. xi. 17.   10 Rom. ix. 7, 8.
11 Gal. iii. 29.

Jews, but of those who are Jews by the circumcision of the heart, in the spirit, and not in the letter; whose praise is not of men, but of God;[1] who belong to the Jerusalem that is free, our eternal mother in heaven, the spiritual Sarah, who casteth out the bondmaid and her children from the house of liberty.[2] And therefore what Pilate wrote he wrote, because what the Lord said He said.

[1] Rom. ii. 29.

[2] Gal. iv. 22-31.

TRACTATE CXVIII.

Chapter XIX. 23, 24.

1. The things that were done beside the Lord's cross, when at length He was now crucified, we would take up, in dependence on His help, in the present discourse. "Then the soldiers, when they had crucified Him, took His garments, and made four parts, to every soldier a part; and also His coat: now the coat was without seam, woven from the top throughout. They said therefore among themselves, Let us not rend it, but cast lots for it, whose it shall be: that the scripture might be fulfilled, which saith, They parted my raiment among them, and for my vesture they did cast lots." It was done as the Jews wished; not that it was they themselves, but the soldiers who obeyed Pilate, who himself acted as judge, that crucified Jesus: and yet if we reflect on their wills, their plots, their endeavors, their delivering up, and, lastly, on their extorting clamors, it was the Jews certainly, more than any else, who crucified Jesus.

2. But we must not speak in a mere cursory way of the partition and dividing by lot of His garments. For although all the four evangelists make mention thereof, yet the others do so more briefly than John: and their notice of it is obscure, while his is in the plainest manner possible. For Matthew says, "And after they crucified Him, they parted His garments, casting lots."[1] Mark: "And they crucified Him, and parted His garments, casting lots upon them, what every man should take."[2] Luke: "And they parted His raiment, and cast lots."[3] But John has told us also how many parts they made of His garments, namely, four, that they might take one part apiece. From which it is apparent that there were four soldiers, who obeyed the governor's orders in crucifying Him. For he plainly says: "Then the soldiers, when they had crucified Him, took His garments, and made four parts, to every soldier a part; and likewise the coat," where there is understood, *they took:* so that the meaning is, they took His garments, and made four parts, to every soldier a part; and they took also His coat. And he so spake, that we might see that there was no lot cast on His other garments; but His coat, which they took along with the others, they did not similarly divide. For in regard to it he proceeds to explain, "Now the coat was without seam, woven from the top throughout." And then telling us why they cast lots on it, he says, "They said therefore among themselves, Let us not rend it, but cast lots for it, whose it shall be." Hence it is clear that in the case of the other garments they had equal parts, so that there was no need to cast lots: but that as regards this one, they could not have had a part each without rending it, and thereby possessing themselves only of useless fragments of it; to prevent which, they preferred letting it come to one of them by lot. The account given by this evangelist is also in harmony with the testimony of prophecy, which he likewise immediately subjoins, saying, "That the scripture might be fulfilled which saith, They parted my raiment among them, and for my vesture they did cast lots." For He says not, they cast lots, but "they parted:" nor does He say, casting lots they parted; but while making no mention whatever of the lot in regard to the rest of the garments, He afterwards said, "and for my vesture they did cast lots," in reference solely to the coat that remained. On which I shall speak as He Himself enables me, after I have first refuted the calumny, which may possibly arise, as if the evangelists disagreed with one another, by showing that the words of none of the others are inconsistent with the narrative of John.

3. For Matthew, in saying, "They parted His garments, casting lots," wished it to be

[1] Matt. xxvii. 35.   Mark xv. 24.   [3] Luke xxiii. 34.

understood, that in the whole affair of parting the garments, the coat was also included, on which they cast lots; for in course of parting all the garments, of which it also was one, on it alone they cast lots. To the same purpose also are the words of Luke: "Parting His garments, they cast lots;" for in the process of parting they came to the coat, whereon the lot was cast, that the entire parting of His garments among them might be completed. And what difference is there whether it is said, "Parting they cast lots," according to Luke; or, "They parted, casting the lot," according to Matthew: unless it be that Luke, in saying "lots," used the plural for the singular number,—a form of speech that is not unusual in the Holy Scriptures, although some copies are found to have "lot,"[1] and not "lots"? Mark, therefore, is the only one who seems to have introduced any kind of difficulty; for in saying, "Casting the lot upon them, what every man should take," his words seem to imply, as if the lot was cast on all the garments, and not on the coat alone. But here also brevity is the cause of the obscurity; for the words, "Casting the lot upon them," are as if it were said, Casting the lot when they were in the process of division; which was also the case. For the partition of all His garments would not have been complete, had it not been declared by lot which of them also should get possession of the coat, so as thereby to bring any contention on the part of the dividers to an end, or rather prevent any such from arising. In saying, therefore, "What every man should take," so far as that has to do with the lot, we must not take it as referring to all the garments that were divided; for the lot was cast, who should take the coat: whereof having omitted to describe the particular form, and how, in the equal division that was made of the parts, it remained by itself, in order, without being rent, to be awarded by lot, he therefore made use of the expression, "what every man should take," in other words, who it was that should take it: as if the whole were thus expressed, They parted His garments, casting the lot upon them, who should take the coat, which had remained over in addition to their equal shares of the rest.

4. Some one, perhaps, may inquire what is signified by the division that was made of His garments into so many parts, and of the casting of lots for the coat. The raiment of the Lord Jesus Christ parted into four, symbolized His quadripartite Church, as spread abroad over the whole world, which consists of four quarters, and equally, that is to say, harmoniously, distributed over all these quarters. On which account He elsewhere says, that He will send His angels to gather His elect from the four winds:[2] and what is that, but from the four quarters of the world, east, west, north, and south? But the coat, on which lots were cast, signifies the unity of all the parts, which is contained in the bond of charity. And when the apostle is about to speak of charity, he says, "I show you a more excellent way;"[3] and in another place, "To know also the love of Christ, which far excelleth knowledge;"[4] and still further elsewhere, "And above all these things charity, which is the bond of perfectness."[5] If, then, charity both has a more excellent way, and far excelleth knowledge, and is enjoined above all things, it is with great propriety that the garment, by which it is signified, is represented as woven from the top.[6] And it was without seam, that its sewing might never be separated; and came into the possession of one man, because He gathereth all into one. Just as in the case of the apostles, who formed the exact number of twelve, in other words, were divisible into four parts of three each, when the question was put to all of them, Peter was the only one that answered, "Thou art the Christ, the Son of the living God;" and to whom it was said, "I will give unto thee the keys of the kingdom of heaven,"[7] as if he alone received the power of binding and loosing: seeing, then, that one so spake in behalf of all, and received the latter along with all, as if personifying the unity itself; therefore one stands for all, because there is unity in all. Whence, also, after here saying, "woven from the top," he added, "throughout."[8] And this also, if referred to its meaning, implies that no one is excluded from a share thereof, who is discovered to belong to the whole: from which whole, as the Greek language indicates, the Church derives her name of Catholic. And by the casting of lots, what else is commended but the grace of God? For in this way in the person of one it reached to all, since the lot satisfied them all, because the grace of God also in its unity reacheth unto all; and when the lot is cast, the award is decided, not by the merits of each individual, but by the secret judgment of God.

5. And yet let no one say that such things had no good signification because they were done by the bad, that is to say, not by those who followed Christ, but by those who perse-

---

2 Matt. xxiv. 31.   3 1 Cor. xii. 31.   4 Eph. iii. 19.
5 Col. iii. 14.   6 *Desuper.*
7 Matt. xvi. 15, 16, 19.   8 *Per totum.*

cuted Him.   For what could we have to say of the cross itself, which every one knows was in like manner made and fastened to Christ by enemies and sinners? And yet it is to it we may rightly understand the words of the apostle to be applicable, " what is the breadth, and the length, and the height, and the depth." [1] For its breadth lies in the transverse beam, on which the hands of the Crucified are extended; and signifies good works in all the breadth of love: its length extends from the transverse beam to the ground, and is that whereto the back and feet are affixed; and signifies perseverance through the whole length of time to the end: its height is in the summit, which rises upwards above the transverse beam; and signifies the supernal goal, to which all works have reference, since all things that are done well and perseveringly, in respect of their breadth and length, are to be done also with due regard to the exalted character of the divine rewards: its depth is found in the part that is fixed into the ground; for there it is both concealed and invisible, and yet from thence spring up all those parts that are outstanding and evident to the senses; just as all that is good in us proceeds from the depths of the grace of God, which is beyond the reach of human comprehension and judgment.   But even though the cross of Christ signified no more than what was said by the apostle, "And they who are Jesus Christ's have crucified the flesh with the passions and lusts," [2] how great a good it is! And yet it does not this, unless the good spirit be lusting against the flesh, seeing that it was the opposing, or, in other words, the evil spirit that constructed the cross of Christ. And lastly, as every one knows, what else is the sign of Christ but the cross of Christ? For unless that sign be applied, whether it be to the foreheads of believers, or to the very water out of which they are regenerated, or to the oil with which they receive the anointing chrism, or to the sacrifice that nourishes them, none of them is properly administered.   How then can it be that no good is signified by that which is done by the wicked, when by the cross of Christ, which the wicked made, every good thing is sealed to us in the celebration of His sacraments?   But here we stop; and what follows we shall consider at another time in the course of dissertation, as God shall grant us assistance.

[1] Eph. iii. 18.

[2] Gal. v. 24.

TRACTATE CXIX.

CHAPTER XIX. 24–30.

1. THE Lord being now crucified, and the parting of His garments having also been completed by the casting of the lot, let us look at what the evangelist John thereafter relates.   "And these things," he says, " the soldiers did.   Now there stood by the cross of Jesus His mother, and His mother's sister, Mary [the wife] of Cleophas, and Mary Magdalene.   When Jesus therefore saw His mother, and the disciple standing by whom He loved, He saith unto His mother, Woman, behold thy son !   Then saith He to the disciple, Behold thy mother !   And from that hour the disciple took her unto his own home."   This, without a doubt, was the hour whereof Jesus, when about to turn the water into wine, had said to His mother, " Woman, what have I to do with thee? mine hour is not yet come." [1]   This hour, therefore, He had foretold, which at that time had not yet arrived, when it should be His to acknowledge her at the point of death, and with reference to which He had been born as a mortal man. At that time, therefore, when about to engage in divine acts, He repelled, as one unknown, her who was the mother, not of His divinity, but of His [human] infirmity; but now, when in the midst of human sufferings, He commended with human affection [the mother] by whom He had become man.   For then, He who had created Mary became known in His power; but now, that which Mary had brought forth was hanging on the cross. [2]

2. A passage, therefore, of a moral character is here inserted.   The good Teacher does what He thereby reminds us ought to be done, and by His own example instructed His disciples that care for their parents ought to be a matter of concern to pious children: as if that tree to which the members of the

[1] Chap. ii. 4.

[2] See Tract. VIII.

dying One were affixed were the very chair of office from which the Master was imparting instruction. From this wholesome doctrine it was that the Apostle Paul had learned what he taught in turn, when he said, "But if any provide not for his own, and especially for those of his own house, he hath denied the faith, and is worse than an infidel."[1] And what are so much home concerns to any one, as parents to children, or children to parents? Of this most wholesome precept, therefore, the very Master of the saints set the example from Himself, when, not as God for the handmaid whom He had created and governed, but as a man for the mother, of whom He had been created, and whom He was now leaving behind, He provided in some measure another son in place of Himself. And why He did so, He indicates in the words that follow: for the evangelist says, "And from that hour the disciple took her unto his own," speaking of himself. In this way, indeed, he usually refers to himself as the disciple whom Jesus loved: who certainly loved them all, but him beyond the others, and with a closer familiarity, so that He even made him lean upon His bosom at supper;[2] in order, I believe, in this way to commend the more highly the divine excellence of this very gospel, which He was thereafter to preach through his instrumentality.

3. But what was this "his own," unto which John took the mother of the Lord? For he was not outside the circle of those who said unto Him, "Lo, we have left all, and followed Thee." No, but on that same occasion he had also heard the words, Every one that hath forsaken these things for my sake, shall receive an hundred times as much in this world.[3] That disciple, therefore, had an hundredfold more than he had cast away, whereunto to receive the mother of Him who had graciously bestowed it all. But it was in that society that the blessed John had received an hundredfold, where no one called anything his own, but they had all things in common; even as it is recorded in the Acts of the Apostles. For the apostles were as if having nothing, and yet possessing all things.[4] How was it, then, that the disciple and servant received unto his own the mother of his Lord and Master, where no one called anything his own? Or, seeing we read a little further on in the same book, "For as many as were possessors of lands or houses sold them, and brought the prices of them, and laid them down at the apostles' feet: and distribution was made unto every man according as he had need,"[5] are we not to understand that such distribution was made to this disciple of what was needful, that there was also added to it the portion of the blessed Mary, as if she were his mother; and ought we not the rather so to take the words, "From that hour the disciple took her unto his own," that everything necessary for her was entrusted to his care? He received her, therefore, not unto his own lands, for he had none of his own; but to his own dutiful services, the discharge of which, by a special dispensation, was entrusted to himself.

4. He then adds: "After this, Jesus knowing that all things were now accomplished, that the scripture might be fulfilled, saith, I thirst. Now there was set a vessel full of vinegar: and they filled a sponge with vinegar, and fixed it upon hyssop, and put it to His mouth. When Jesus therefore had received the vinegar, He said, It is finished: and He bowed His head, and gave up the ghost." Who has the power of so adjusting what he does, as this Man had of arranging all that He suffered? But this Man was the Mediator between God and men; the Man of whom we read in prophecy, He is man also, and who shall acknowledge Him? for the men who did such things acknowledged not this Man as God. For He who was manifest as man, was hid as God: He who was manifest suffered all these things, and He Himself also, who was hid, arranged them all. He saw, therefore, that all was accomplished that required to be done before He received the vinegar, and gave up the ghost; and that this also might be accomplished which the scripture had foretold, "And in my thirst they gave me vinegar to drink,"[6] He said, "I thirst:" as if it were, One thing still you have failed to do, give me what you are. For the Jews were themselves the vinegar, degenerated as they were from the wine of the patriarchs and prophets; and filled like a full vessel with the wickedness of this world, with hearts like a sponge, deceitful in the formation of its cavernous and tortuous recesses. But the hyssop, whereon they placed the sponge filled with vinegar, being a lowly herb, and purging the heart, we fitly take for the humility of Christ Himself; which they thus enclosed, and imagined they had completely ensnared. Hence we have it said in the psalm, "Thou shalt purge me with hyssop, and I shall be cleansed."[7] For it is by Christ's humility that we are cleansed; because, had He not humbled Himself, and became obedient unto the death of the cross,[8]

---

[1] 1 Tim. v. 8.
[2] Chap. xiii. 23.
[3] Matt. xix. 27, 29.
[4] 2 Cor. vi. 10.
[5] Acts iv. 32-35.
[6] Ps. lxix. 21.
[7] Ps. li. 7.
[8] Phil. ii. 8.

His blood certainly would not have been shed for the remission of sins, or, in other words, for our cleansing.

5. Nor need we be disturbed with the question, how the sponge could be applied to His mouth when He was lifted up from the earth on the cross. For as we read in the other evangelists, what is omitted by this one, it was fixed on a reed,[1] so that such drink as was contained in the sponge might be raised to the highest part of the cross. By the reed, however, the scripture was signified, which was fulfilled by this very act. For as a tongue is called either Greek or Latin, or any other, significant of the sound, which is uttered by the tongue; so the reed may give its name to the letter which is written with a reed. We most usually, however, call those tongues that express the sounds of the human voice: while in calling scripture a reed, the very rareness of the thing only enhances the mystical nature of that which it symbolizes. A wicked people did such things, a compassionate Christ suffered them. They who did

them, knew not what they did; but He who suffered, not only knew what was done, and why it was so, but also wrought what was good through those who were doing what was evil.

6. "When Jesus therefore had received the vinegar, He said, It is finished." What, but all that prophecy had foretold so long before? And then, because nothing now remained that still required to be done before He died, as if He, who had power to lay down His life and to take it up again,[2] had at length completed all for whose completion He was waiting, "He bowed His head, and gave up the ghost." Who can thus sleep when he pleases, as Jesus died when He pleased? Who is there that thus puts off his garment when he pleases, as He put off His flesh at His pleasure? Who is there that thus departs[3] when he pleases, as He departed this life[3] at His pleasure? How great the power, to be hoped for or dreaded, that must be His as judge, if such was the power He exhibited as a dying man!

---

[1] Matt. xxvii. 48, and Mark xv. 36.

[2] Chap. x. 18.　　　[3] *Abit . . . obiit.*

TRACTATE CXX.

CHAPTER XIX. 31–42, and XX. 1–9.

1. AFTER that the Lord Jesus had accomplished all that He foreknew required accomplishment before His death, and had, when it pleased Himself, given up the ghost, what followed thereafter, as related by the evangelist, let us now consider. "The Jews therefore," he says, "because it was the preparation (*parasceve*), that the bodies should not remain upon the cross on the Sabbath-day (for that Sabbath-day was an high day), besought Pilate that their legs might be broken, and that they might be taken away." Not that their legs might be taken away, but the persons themselves whose legs were broken for the purpose of effecting their death, and permitting them to be detached from the tree, lest their continuing to hang on the crosses should defile the great festal day by the horrible spectacle of their day-long torments.

2. "Then came the soldiers, and brake the legs of the first, and of the other who was crucified with Him. But when they came to Jesus, and saw that He was dead already, they brake not His legs: but one of the

soldiers with a spear laid open[1] His side, and forthwith came thereout blood and water." A suggestive[2] word was made use of by the evangelist, in not saying pierced, or wounded His side, or anything else, but "opened;"[1] that thereby, in a sense, the gate of life might be thrown open, from whence have flowed forth the sacraments of the Church, without which there is no entrance to the life which is the true life. That blood was shed for the remission of sins; that water it is that makes up the health-giving cup, and supplies at once the laver of baptism and water for drinking. This was announced beforehand, when Noah was commanded to make a door in the side of the ark,[3] whereby the animals might enter which were not destined to perish in the flood, and by which the Church was prefigured. Because of this, the first woman was formed from the side of the man when asleep,[4] and was called Life, and the mother of all living.[5] Truly it pointed to a great good, prior to the

---

[1] *Aperuit.*　　[2] *Vigilan*　　[3] Gen. vi. 16.
[4] Gen. ii. 22.　　[5] Gen. iii. 20.

great evil of the transgression (in the guise of one thus lying asleep).[1]   This second Adam bowed His head and fell asleep on the cross, that a spouse might be formed for Him from that which flowed from the sleeper's side.   O death, whereby the dead are raised anew to life !   What can be purer than such blood ? What more health-giving than such a wound ?

3. "And he that saw it," he says, " bare record, and his record is true; and he knoweth that he saith true, that ye also might believe." He said not, That ye also might know, but " that ye might believe; " for he knoweth who hath seen, that he who hath not seen might believe his testimony.   And believing belongs more to the nature of faith than seeing.   For what else is meant by believing than giving to faith a suitable reception ?   " For these things were done," he adds, " that the scripture should be fulfilled, A bone of Him ye shall not break.   And again, another scripture saith, They shall look on Him whom they pierced."   He has furnished two testimonies from the Scriptures for each of the things which he has recorded as having been done.   For to the words, " But when they came to Jesus, and saw that He was dead already, they brake not His legs," belongeth the testimony, "A bone of Him ye shall not break: " an injunction which was laid upon those who were commanded to celebrate the passover by the sacrifice of a sheep in the old law, which went before as a shadow of the passion of Christ.   Whence " our passover has been offered, even Christ,"[2] of whom the prophet Isaiah also had predicted, " He shall be led as a lamb to the slaughter."[3]   In like manner to the words which he subjoined, " But one of the soldiers laid open His side with a spear," belongeth the other testimony, " They shall look on Him whom they pierced; " where Christ is promised in the very flesh wherein He was afterwards to come to be crucified.

4. "And after this, Joseph of Arimathea (being a disciple of Jesus, but secretly for fear of the Jews) besought Pilate that he might take away the body of Jesus: and Pilate gave him leave.   He came therefore, and took the body of Jesus.   And there came also Nicodemus, who came to Jesus by night at first, bringing a mixture of myrrh and aloes, about an hundred pound weight."   We are not to explain the meaning by saying, " first bringing a mixture of myrrh," but by attaching the word " first " to the preceding clause.   For Nicodemus had at first come to

Jesus by night, as recorded by this same John in the earlier portions of his Gospel.[4] By the statement given us here, therefore, we are to understand that Nicodemus came to Jesus, not then only, but then for the first time; and that he was a regular comer afterwards, in order by hearing to become a disciple; which is certified, nowadays at least, to almost all nations in the revelation of the body of the most blessed Stephen.[5]   " Then took they the body of Jesus, and wound it in linen clothes with the spices, as the manner of the Jews is to bury."   The evangelist, I think, was not without a purpose in so framing his words, " as the manner of the Jews is to bury; " for in this way, unless I am mistaken, he has admonished us that, in duties of this kind, which are observed to the dead, the customs of every nation ought to be preserved.

5. " Now in the place where He was crucified there was a garden; and in the garden a new sepulchre, wherein was never man yet laid."   As in the womb of the Virgin Mary no one was conceived before Him, and no one after Him, so in this sepulchre there was no one buried before Him, and no one after Him.   " There laid they Jesus therefore, because of the Jews' preparation; for the sepulchre was nigh at hand."   He would have us to understand that the burial was hurried, lest the evening should overtake them; when it was no longer permitted to do any such thing, because of the preparation, which the Jews among us are more in the habit of calling in Latin, cœna pura (the pure meal).

6. "And on the first of the week came Mary Magdalene early, when it was yet dark, unto the sepulchre, and saw the stone taken away from the sepulchre."   The first of the week[6] is what Christian practice now calls the Lord's day, because of the resurrection of the Lord.[7]   " She ran, therefore, and came to Simon Peter and to the other disciple whom Jesus loved, and saith unto them, They have taken the Lord out of the sepulchre, and we know not where they have laid Him."   Some of the Greek codices have, " They have taken my Lord," which may likely enough have been said by the stronger than ordinary affection of love and handmaid relationship; but we have not found it in the several codices to which we have had access.

---

[1] This last clause is found only in three of the Augustinian MSS.
[2] 1 Cor. v. 7.   [3] Isa. liii. 7.

[4] Chap. iii. 1, 2.
[5] This revelation, whereby the body of Nicodemus was discovered, is referred to the close of the year 415, by those who trust in the authority of the Presbyter Lucian, in a small book written on the subject.—MIGNE.
[6] Una Sabbati.
[7] Augustin here adds, quem Matthæus solus in Evangelistis primam Sabbati nominavit (Matt. xxviii. 1), contrasting primam with una.

7. " Peter therefore went forth, and that other disciple, and came to the sepulchre. So they ran both together: and that other disciple did outrun Peter, and came first to the sepulchre." The repetition here is worthy of notice and of commendation for the way in which a return is made to what had previously been omitted, and yet is added just as if it followed in due order. For after having already said, " they came to the sepulchre," he goes back to tell us how they came, and says, " so they ran both together," etc. Where he shows that, by outrunning his companion, there came first to the sepulchre that other disciple, by whom he means himself, while he relates all[1] as if speaking of another.

8. "And he stooping down," he says, " saw the linen clothes lying; yet went he not in. Then cometh Simon Peter following him, and went into the sepulchre, and saw the linen clothes lying, and the napkin, which had been about His head, not lying with the linen clothes, but folded up in one place by itself." Do we suppose these things have no meaning? I can suppose no such thing. But we hasten on to other points, on which we are compelled to linger by the need there is for investigation, or some other kind of obscurity. For in such things as are self-manifest, the inquiry into the meaning even of individual details is, indeed, a subject of holy delight, but only for those who have leisure, which is not the case with us.

9. "Then went in also that other disciple who had come first to the sepulchre." He came first, and entered last. This also of a certainty is not without a meaning, but I am without the leisure needful for its explanation. "And he saw, and believed." Here some, by not giving due attention, suppose that John believed that Jesus had risen again; but there is no indication of this from the words that follow. For what does he mean by immediately adding, " For as yet they knew not the scripture, that He must rise again from the dead " ? He could not then have believed that He had risen again, when he did not know that it behoved Him to rise again. What then did he see ? what was it that he believed ? What but this, that he saw the sepulchre empty, and believed what the woman had said, that He had been taken away from the tomb ? " For as yet they knew not the scripture, that He must rise again from the dead." Thus also when they heard of it from the Lord Himself, although it was uttered in the plainest terms, yet from their custom of hearing Him speaking by parables, they did not understand, and believed that something else was His meaning. But we shall put off what follows till another discourse.

[1] Some editions here insert into the text, *More sanctæ Scripturæ*, "after the manner of Holy Scripture." Others enclose it within brackets.—MIGNE.

TRACTATE CXXI.

Chapter XX. 10–29.

1. MARY MAGDALENE had brought the news to His disciples, Peter and John, that the Lord was taken away from the sepulchre; and they, when they came thither, found only the linen clothes wherewith the body had been shrouded; and what else could they believe but what she had told them, and what she had herself also believed? " Then the disciples went away again unto their own" (home); that is to say, where they were dwelling, and from which they had run to the sepulchre. " But Mary stood without at the sepulchre weeping." For while the men returned, the weaker sex was fastened to the place by a stronger affection. And the eyes, which had sought the Lord and had not found Him, had now nothing else to do but weep, deeper in their sorrow that He had been taken away from the sepulchre than that He had been slain on the tree; seeing that in the case even of such a Master, when His living presence was withdrawn from their eyes, His remembrance also had ceased to remain. Such grief, therefore, now kept the woman at the sepulchre. "And as she wept, she stooped down, and looked into the sepulchre." Why she did so I know not. For she was not ignorant that He whom she sought was no longer there, since she had herself also carried word to the disciples that He had been taken from thence; while they, too, had come to the sepulchre, and had sought the Lord's body, not merely by looking, but also by entering, and had not found it. What then does it mean, that, as she wept, she stooped down, and looked again into the sepulchre?

Was it that her grief was so excessive that she hardly thought she could believe either their eyes or her own? Or was it rather by some divine impulse that her mind led her to look within? For look she did, "and saw two angels in white, sitting, the one at the head, and the other at the feet, where the body of Jesus had lain." Why is it that one was sitting at the head, and the other at the feet? Was it, since those who in Greek are called angels are in Latin *nuntii* [in English, news-bearers], that in this way they signified that the gospel of Christ was to be preached from head to foot, from the beginning even to the end? "They say to her, Woman, why weepest thou? She saith unto them, Because they have taken away my Lord, and I know not where they have laid Him." The angels forbade her tears: for by such a position what else did they announce, but that which in some way or other was a future joy? For they put the question, "Why weepest thou?" as if they had said, Weep not. But she, supposing they had put the question from ignorance, unfolded the cause of her tears. "Because," she said, "they have taken away my Lord:" calling her Lord's inanimate body her Lord, meaning a part for the whole; just as all of us acknowledge that Jesus Christ, the only Son of God, our Lord, who of course is at once both the Word and soul and flesh, was nevertheless crucified and buried, while it was only His flesh that was laid in the sepulchre. "And I know not," she added, "where they have laid Him." This was the greater cause of sorrow, because she knew not where to go to mitigate her grief. But the hour had now come when the joy, in some measure announced by the angels, who forbade her tears, was to succeed the weeping.

2. Lastly, "when she had thus said, she turned herself back, and saw Jesus standing, and knew not that it was Jesus. Jesus saith unto her, Woman, why weepest thou? whom seekest thou? She, supposing Him to be the gardener, saith unto Him, Sir, If thou hast borne Him hence, tell me where thou hast laid Him, and I will take Him away. Jesus saith unto her, Mary. She turned herself, and saith unto Him, Rabboni, which is to say, Master." Let no one speak ill of the woman because she called the gardener, Sir (*domine*), and Jesus, Master. For there she was asking, here she was recognizing; there she was showing respect to a person of whom she was asking a favor, here she was recalling the Teacher of whom she was learning to discern things human and divine. She called one lord (sir), whose handmaid she was not, in order by him to get at the Lord to whom she

belonged. In one sense, therefore, she used the word Lord when she said, "They have taken away my Lord; and in another, when she said, Sir (lord), if thou hast borne Him hence." For the prophet also called those lords who were mere men, but in a different sense from Him of whom it is written, "The Lord is His name."[1] But how was it that this woman, who had already turned herself back to see Jesus, when she supposed Him to be the gardener, and was actually talking with Him, is said to have again turned herself, in order to say unto Him "Rabboni," but just because, when she then turned herself in body, she supposed Him to be what He was not, while now, when turned in heart, she recognized Him to be what He was.

3. "Jesus saith unto her, Touch me not: for I am not yet ascended to my Father: but go to my brethren, and say unto them, I ascend unto my Father, and your Father; to my God, and your God." There are points in these words which we must examine with brevity indeed, but with somewhat more than ordinary attention. For Jesus was giving a lesson in faith to the woman, who had recognized Him as her Master, and called Him so in her reply; and this gardener was sowing in her heart, as in His own garden, the grain of mustard seed. What then is meant by "Touch me not"? And just as if the reason of such a prohibition would be sought, He added, "for I am not yet ascended to my Father." What does this mean? If, while standing on earth, He is not to be touched, how could He be touched by men when sitting in heaven? For certainly, before He ascended, He presented Himself to the touch of the disciples, when He said, as testified by the evangelist Luke, "Handle me, and see; for a spirit hath not flesh and bones, as ye see me have;"[2] or when He said to Thomas the disciple, "Reach hither thy finger, and behold my hands; and put forth thy hand, and thrust it into my side." And who could be so absurd as to affirm that He was willing indeed to be touched by the disciples before He ascended to the Father, but refused it in the case of women till after His ascension? But no one, even had any the will, was to be allowed to run into such folly. For we read that women also, after His resurrection and before His ascension to the Father, touched Jesus, among whom was Mary Magdalene herself; for it is related by Matthew that Jesus met them, and said, "All hail. And they approached, and held Him by the feet, and worshipped Him."[3] This was

---

[1] Ps. lxviii. 4.   [2] Luke xxiv. 39.   [3] Matt. xxviii. 9.

passed over by John, but declared as the truth by Matthew. It remains, therefore, that some sacred mystery must lie concealed in these words; and whether we discover it or utterly fail to do so, yet we ought to be in no doubt as to its actual existence. Accordingly, either the words, "Touch me not, for I am not yet ascended to my Father," had this meaning, that by this woman the Church of the Gentiles was symbolized, which did not believe on Christ till He had actually ascended to the Father, or that in this way Christ wished Himself to be believed on; in other words, to be touched spiritually, that He and the Father are one. For He has in a manner ascended to the Father, to the inward perception of him who has made such progress in the knowledge of Christ that he acknowledges Him as equal with the Father: in any other way He is not rightly touched, that is to say, in any other way He is not rightly believed on. But Mary might have still so believed as to account Him unequal with the Father, and this certainly is forbidden her by the words, "Touch me not;" that is, Believe not thus on me according to thy present notions; let not your thoughts stretch outwards to what I have been made in thy behalf, without passing beyond to that whereby thou hast thyself been made. For how could it be otherwise than carnally that she still believed on Him whom she was weeping over as a man? "For I am not yet ascended," He says, "to my Father:" there shalt thou touch me, when thou believest me to be God, in no wise unequal with the Father. "But go to my brethren, and say unto them, I ascend unto my Father, and your Father." He saith not, Our Father: in one sense, therefore, is He mine, in another sense, yours; by nature mine, by grace yours. "And my God, and your God." Nor did He say here, Our God: here, therefore, also is He in one sense mine, in another sense yours: my God, under whom I also am as man; your God, between whom and you I am mediator.

4. "Mary Magdalene came and told the disciples, I have seen the Lord, and He hath spoken these things unto me. Then the same day at evening, being the first day of the week, when the doors were shut where the disciples were assembled for fear of the Jews, came Jesus, and stood in the midst, and saith unto them, Peace be unto you. And when He had so said, He showed unto them His hands and His side." For nails had pierced His hands, a spear had laid open His side: and there the marks of the wounds are preserved for healing the hearts of the doubting.

But the shutting of doors presented no obstacle to the matter of His body, wherein Godhead resided. He indeed could enter without their being opened, by whose birth the virginity of His mother remained inviolate. "Then were the disciples glad when they saw the Lord. Then said He unto them again, Peace be unto you." Reiteration is confirmation; for He Himself gives by the prophet a promised peace upon peace.[1] "As the Father hath sent me," He adds, "even so send I you." We know the Son to be equal to the Father; but here we recognize the words of the Mediator. For He exhibits Himself as occupying a middle position when He says, He me, and I you. "And when He had said this, He breathed on them, and said unto them, Receive ye the Holy Ghost." By breathing on them He signified that the Holy Spirit was the Spirit, not of the Father alone, but likewise His own. "Whose soever sins," He continues, "ye remit, they are remitted unto them; and whose soever ye retain, they are retained." The Church's love, which is shed abroad in our hearts by the Holy Spirit, discharges the sins of all who are partakers with itself, but retains the sins of those who have no participation therein. Therefore it is, that after saying "Receive ye the Holy Ghost," He straightway added this regarding the remission and retention of sins.

5. "But Thomas, one of the twelve, who is called Didymus, was not with them when Jesus came. The other disciples therefore said unto him, We have seen the Lord. But he said unto them, Except I shall see in His hands the print of the nails, and put my finger into the place of the nails, and put my hand into His side, I will not believe. And after eight days, again His disciples were within, and Thomas with them. Then came Jesus, the doors being shut, and stood in the midst, and said, Peace be unto you. Then saith He to Thomas, Reach hither thy finger, and behold my hands; and reach hither thy hand, and put it into my side: and be not faithless, but believing. Thomas answered and said unto Him, My Lord and my God." He saw and touched the man, and acknowledged the God whom he neither saw nor touched; but by the means of what he saw and touched, he now put far away from him every doubt, and believed the other. "Jesus saith unto him, Because thou hast seen me, thou hast believed." He saith not, Thou hast touched me, but, "Thou hast seen me," because sight is a kind of general sense. For sight is also habitually named in connec-

---

[1] Isa. xxvi. 3, *margin.*

tion with the other four senses: as when we say, Listen, and see how well it sounds; smell it, and see how well it smells; taste it, and see how well it savors; touch it, and see how hot it is. Everywhere has the word, *See*, made itself heard, although sight, properly speaking, is allowed to belong only to the eyes. Hence here also the Lord Himself says, "Reach hither thy finger, and behold my hands:" and what else does He mean but, Touch and see? And yet he had no eyes in his finger. Whether therefore it was by looking, or also by touching, "Because thou hast seen me," He says, "thou hast believed." Although it may be affirmed that the disciple dared not so to touch, when He offered Himself for the purpose; for it is not written, And Thomas touched Him. But whether it was by gazing only, or also by touching that he saw and believed, what follows rather proclaims and commends the faith of the Gentiles: "Blessed are they that have not seen, and yet have believed." He made use of words in the past tense, as One who, in His predestinating purpose, knew what was future, as if it had already taken place. But the present discourse must be kept from the charge of prolixity: the Lord will give us the opportunity to discourse at another time on the topics that remain.

TRACTATE CXXII.

CHAPTER XX. 30, 31, and XXI. 1–11.

1. AFTER telling us of the incident in connection with which the disciple Thomas had offered to his touch the places of the wounds in Christ's body, and saw what he would not believe, and believed, the evangelist John interposes these words, and says: "And many other signs truly did Jesus in the presence of His disciples, which are not written in this book: but these are written that ye may believe that Jesus is the Christ, the Son of God; and that believing ye may have life through His name." This paragraph indicates, as it were, the end of the book; but there is afterwards related how the Lord manifested Himself at the sea of Tiberias, and in the draught of fishes made special reference to the mystery of the Church, as regards its future character, in the final resurrection of the dead. I think, therefore, it is fitted to give special prominence thereto, that there has been thus interposed, as it were, an end of the book, and that there should be also a kind of preface to the narrative that was to follow, in order in some measure to give it a position of greater eminence. The narrative itself begins in this way: "After these things Jesus showed Himself again to the disciples at the sea of Tiberias; and on this wise showed He (Himself). There were together Simon Peter, and Thomas called Didymus, and Nathanael of Cana in Galilee, and the sons of Zebedee, and two other of His disciples. Simon Peter saith unto them, I go a fishing. They say unto him, We also go with thee."

2. The inquiry is usually made in connection with this fishing of the disciples, why Peter and the sons of Zebedee returned to what they were before being called by the Lord; for they were fishers when He said to them, "Come after me, and I will make you fishers of men."[1] And they put such reality into their following of Him then, that they left all in order to cleave to Him as their Master: so much so, that when the rich man went away from Him in sorrow, because of His saying to him, "Go sell that thou hast, and give to the poor, and thou shalt have treasure in heaven, and come follow me," Peter said unto Him, "Lo, we have forsaken all, and followed Thee."[2] Why is it then that now, by the abandonment as it were of their apostleship, they become what they were, and seek again what they had forsaken, as if forgetful of the words they had once listened to, "No man, putting his hand to the plough, and looking back, is fit for the kingdom of heaven"?[3] Had they done so when Jesus was lying in the grave, before He rose from the dead,—which of course they could not have done, as the day whereon He was crucified kept them all in closest attention till His burial, which took place before evening; while the next day was the Sabbath, when it was unlawful for those who observed the ancestral custom to work at all; and on the third day the Lord rose again, and re-

---

[1] Matt. iv. 19.   [2] Matt. xix. 21, 22, 27.   [3] Luke ix. 62.

called them to the hope which they had not yet begun to entertain regarding Him;—yet had they then done so, we might suppose it had been done under the influence of that despair which had taken possession of their minds. But now, after His restoration to them alive from the tomb, after the most evident truth of His revivified flesh offered to their eyes and hands, not only to be seen, but also to be touched and handled; after inspecting the very marks of the wounds, even to the confession of the Apostle Thomas, who had previously declared that he would not otherwise believe; after the reception by His breathing on them of the Holy Spirit, and after the words poured from His lips into their ears, "'As the Father hath sent me, even so send I you: whose soever sins ye remit, they are remitted unto them; and whose soever ye retain, they are retained:" they suddenly become again what they had been, fishers, not of men, but of fishes.

3. We have therefore to give those who are disturbed by this the answer, that they were not prohibited from seeking necessary sustenance by their manual craft, when lawful in itself, and warranted so long as they preserved their apostleship intact, if at any time they had no other means of gaining a livelihood. Unless any one have the boldness to imagine or to affirm, that the Apostle Paul attained not to the perfection of those who left all and followed Christ, seeing that, in order not to become a burden to any of those to whom he preached the gospel, he worked with his own hands for his support:[1] wherein we find rather the fulfillment of his own words, "I labored more abundantly than they all;" and to which he added, "yet not I, but the grace of God that was with me:"[2] to make it manifest that this also was to be imputed to the grace of God, that both with mind and body he was able to labor so much more abundantly than they all, that he neither ceased from preaching the gospel, nor drew, like them, his present support out of the gospel; while he was sowing it much more widely and fruitfully through multitudes of nations where the name of Christ had never previously been proclaimed. Whereby he showed that living, that is, deriving their subsistence, by the gospel, was not imposed on the apostles as a necessity, but conferred on them as a power. And of this power the same apostle makes mention when he says: "If we have sown to you spiritual things, is it a great thing if we reap your carnal things? If others are partakers of this power among you, are not we

rather? But," he adds, "we have not used this power." And a little afterwards he says: "They who serve the altar are partakers with the altar: even so hath the Lord ordained, that they who preach the gospel should live of the gospel; but I have used none of these things." It is clear enough, therefore, that it was not enjoined on the apostles, but put in their power, not to find their living otherwise than by the gospel, and of those to whom by preaching the gospel they sowed spiritual things, to reap their carnal things; that is, to take their bodily support, and, as the soldiers of Christ, to receive the wages due to them, as from the inhabitants of provinces subject to Christ.[3] Hence that same illustrious soldier had said a little before, in reference to this matter, "Who goeth a warfare any time at his own charges?"[4] Which he nevertheless did himself; for he labored more abundantly than they all. If, then, the blessed Paul—that he might not use with them the power which he certainly possessed along with the other preachers of the gospel, but went a warfare at his own charges, that the Gentiles, who were utterly averse to the name of Christ, might not take offense at his teaching, as something offered them for a money equivalent,—in a way very different from that in which he had been educated, learned an altogether new art, that while the teacher supports himself with his own hands, none of his hearers might be burdened; how much rather did the blessed Peter, who had beforetimes been a fisherman, do what he was already acquainted with, if at that present time he found no other means of gaining a livelihood?

4. But some one will reply, And why did he not find them, when the Lord had promised, saying, "Seek first the kingdom and righteousness of God, and all these things shall be added unto you"?[5] Precisely also in this very way did the Lord fulfill His promise. For who else placed there the fishes that were to be caught, but He, who, we are bound to believe, threw them into the penury that compelled them to go a fishing, for no other reason than that He wished to show them the miracle He had prepared, that so He might both feed the preachers of His gospel, and at the same time enhance that gospel itself, by the great mystery which He was about to impress on their minds by the number of the fishes? And on this subject we also ought now to be telling you what He Himself has set before us.

5. "Simon Peter," therefore, "saith, I go

[1] 2 Thess. iii. 8.　　　[2] 1 Cor. xv. 10.

[3] *Sicut a provincialibus Christi.*
[4] 1 Cor. ix. 11-15, 7.　　　[5] Matt. vi. 33.

a fishing." Those who were with him "say unto him, We also go with thee. And they went forth, and entered into a ship; and that night they caught nothing. But when the morning was now come, Jesus stood on the shore; but the disciples knew not that it was Jesus. Then Jesus saith unto them, Children, have ye any meat? They answered Him, No. He saith unto them, Cast the net on the right side of the ship, and ye shall find. They cast therefore, and now they were not able to draw it for the multitude of fishes. Therefore that disciple whom Jesus loved saith unto Peter, It is the Lord. When Simon Peter heard that it was the Lord, he girt his coat unto him, for he was naked, and did cast himself into the sea. And the other disciples came in a little ship (for they were not far from the land, but as it were two hundred cubits), dragging the net with fishes. As soon then as they were come to land, they saw a fire of coals laid, and a fish laid thereon, and bread. Jesus saith unto them, Bring of the fish which ye have now caught. Simon Peter went up, and drew the net to land full of great fishes, an hundred and fifty and three: and for all there were so many, yet was not the net broken."

6. This is a great mystery in the great Gospel of John; and to commend it the more forcibly to our attention, the last chapter has been made its place of record. Accordingly, inasmuch as there were seven disciples taking part in that fishing, Peter, and Thomas, and Nathaneal, and the two sons of Zebedee, and two others whose names are withheld, they point, by their septenary number, to the end of time. For there is a revolution of all time in seven days. To this also pertains the statement, that when the morning was come, Jesus stood on the shore; for the shore likewise is the limit of the sea, and signifies therefore the end of the world. The same end of the world is shown also by the act of Peter, in drawing the net to land, that is, to the shore. Which the Lord has Himself elucidated, when in a certain other place He drew His similitude from a fishing net let down into the sea: "And they drew it," He said, "to the shore." And in explanation of what that shore was, He added, "So will it be in the end of the world." [1]

7. That, however, is a parable in word, not one embodied in outward action; and just as in the passage before us the Lord indicated by an outward action the kind of character the Church would have in the end of the world, so in the same way, by that other fish-ing, He indicated its present character. In doing the one at the commencement of His preaching and this latter after His resurrection, He showed thereby in the former case that the capture of fishes signified the good and bad presently existing in the Church; but in the latter, the good only, whom it will contain everlastingly, when the resurrection of the dead shall have been completed in the end of this world. Furthermore, on that previous occasion Jesus stood not, as here, on the shore, when He gave orders for the taking of the fish, but "entered into one of the ships, which was Simon's, and prayed him that he would thrust out a little from the land; and He sat down therein, and taught the crowds. And when He had left speaking, He said unto Simon, Launch out into the deep, and let down your nets for a draught." There also they put the fishes that were caught into the ship, and did not, as here, draw the net to the shore. By these signs, and any others that may be found, on the former occasion the Church was prefigured as it exists in this world, and on the other, as it shall be in the end of the world: the one accordingly took place before, and the other subsequently to the resurrection of the Lord; because there we were signified by Christ as called, and here as raised from the dead. On that occasion the nets are not let down on the right side, that the good alone might not be signified, nor on the left, lest the application should be limited to the bad; but without any reference to either side, He says, "Let down your nets for a draught," that we may understand the good and bad as mingled together: while on this He says, "Cast the net on the right side of the ship," to signify those who stood on the right hand, the good alone. There the net was broken on account of the schisms that were meant to be signified; but here, as then there will be no more schisms in that supreme peace of the saints, the evangelist was entitled to say, "And for all they were so great," that is, so large, "yet was not the net broken;" as if with reference to the previous time when it was broken, and a commendation of the good that was here in comparison with the evil that preceded. There the multitude of fishes caught was so great, that the two vessels were filled and began to sink,[2] that is, were weighed down to the point of sinking; for they did not actually sink, but were in extreme jeopardy. For whence exist in the Church the great evils under which we groan, save from the impossibility of withstanding the enormous

---

[1] Matt. xiii. 48, 49.   [2] Luke v. 3-7.

multitude that, almost to the entire subversion of discipline, gain an entrance, with their morals so utterly at variance with the pathway of the saints? Here, however, they cast the net on the right side, "and now they were not able to draw it for the multitude of fishes." What is meant by the words, "Now they were not able to draw it," but this, that those who belong to the resurrection of life, that is to say, to the right hand, and depart this life within the nets of the Christian name,, will be made manifest only on the shore, in other words, when they shall rise from the dead at the end of the world? Accordingly, they were not able to draw the nets so as to discharge into the vessel the fishes they had caught, as was done with all of those wherewith the net was broken, and the boats laden to sinking. But the Church possesses those right-hand ones after the close of this life in the sleep of peace, lying hid as it were in the deep, till the net reach the shore whither it is being drawn, as it were two hundred cubits. And as on that first occasion it was done by two vessels, with reference to the circumcision and the uncircumcision; so in this place, by the two hundred cubits, I am of opinion that there is symbolized, with reference to the elect of both classes, the circumcision and the uncircumcision, as it were two separate hundreds; because the number that passes to the right hand is represented summarily by hundreds. And last of all, in that former fishing the number of fishes is not expressed, as if the words were there acted on that were uttered by the prophet, "I have declared and spoken; they are multiplied beyond number:"[1] while here there are none beyond calculation, but the definite number of a hundred and fifty-three; and of the reason of this number we must now, with the Lord's help, give some account.

8. For if we determine on the number that should indicate the law, what else can it be but ten? For we have absolute certainty that the Decalogue of the law, that is, those ten well-known precepts, were first written by the finger of God on two tables of stone.[2] But the law, when it is not aided by grace, maketh transgressors, and is only in the letter, on account of which the apostle specially declared, "The letter killeth, but the spirit giveth life."[3] Let the spirit then be added to the letter, lest the letter kill him whom the spirit maketh not alive, and let us work out the precepts of the law, not in our own strength, but by the grace of the Saviour. But when grace is added to the law, that is, the spirit to the let-

ter, there is, in a kind of way, added to ten the number of seven. For this number, namely seven, is testified by the documents of holy writ given us for perusal, to signify the Holy Spirit. For example, sanctity or sanctification properly pertains to the Holy Spirit, whence, as the Father is a spirit, and the Son a spirit, because God is a spirit,[4] so the Father is holy and the Son holy, yet the Spirit of both is called peculiarly by the name of the Holy Spirit. Where, then, was there the first distinct mention of sanctification in the law but on the seventh day? For God sanctified not the first day, when He made the light; nor the second, when He made the firmament; nor the third, when He separated the sea from the land, and the land brought forth grass and timber; nor the fourth, wherein the stars were created; nor the fifth, wherein were created the animals that live in the waters or fly in the air; nor the sixth, when the terrestrial living soul and man himself were created; but He sanctified the seventh day, wherein He rested from all His works.[5] The Holy Spirit, therefore, is aptly represented by the septenary number. The prophet Isaiah likewise says, "The Spirit of God shall rest on Him;" and thereafter calls our attention to that Spirit in His septenary work or grace, by saying, "The spirit of wisdom and understanding, the spirit of counsel and might, the spirit of knowledge and piety; and He shall be filled with the spirit of the fear of God."[6] And what of the Revelation? Are they not there called the seven Spirits of God,[7] while there is only one and the same Spirit dividing to every one severally as He will?[8] But the septenary operation of the one Spirit was so called by the Spirit Himself, whose own presence in the writer led to their being spoken of as the seven Spirits. Accordingly, when to the number of ten, representing the law, we add the Holy Spirit as represented by seven, we have seventeen; and when this number is used for the adding together of every several number it contains, from 1 up to itself, the sum amounts to one hundred and fifty-three. For if you add 2 to 1, you have 3 of course; if to these you add 3 and 4, the whole makes 10; and then if you add all the numbers that follow up to 17, the whole amounts to the foresaid number; that is, if to 10, which you had reached by adding all together from 1 to 4, you add 5, you have 15; to these add 6, and the result is 21; then add 7, and you have 28; to this add 8, and 9, and 10, and you get 55; to this add 11, and 12, and 13, and you have 91; and

---

[1] Ps. xl. 5. [2] Deut. ix. 10. [3] 2 Cor. iii. 6. [4] Chap. iv. 24. [5] Gen. i., ii. 3. [6] Isa. xi. 2, 3. [7] Rev. iii. 1. [8] 1 Cor. xii. 11.

to this again add 14, 15, and 16, and it comes to 136; and then add to this the remaining number of which we have been speaking, namely, 17, and it will make up the number of fishes. But it is not on that account merely a hundred and fifty-three saints that are meant as hereafter to rise from the dead unto life eternal, but thousands of saints who have shared in the grace of the Spirit, by which grace harmony is established with the law of God, as with an adversary; so that through the life-giving Spirit the letter no longer kills, but what is commanded by the letter is fulfilled by the help of the Spirit, and if there is any deficiency it is pardoned. All therefore who are sharers in such grace are symbolized by this number, that is, are symbolically represented. This number has, besides, three times over, the number of fifty, and three in addition, with reference to the mystery of the Trinity; while, again, the number of fifty is made up by multiplying 7 by 7, with the addition of 1, for 7 times 7 make 49. And the 1 is added to show that there is one who is expressed by seven on account of His sevenfold operation; and we know that it was on the fiftieth day after our Lord's ascension that the Holy Spirit was sent, for whom the disciples were commanded to wait according to the promise.[1]

9. It was not, then, without a purpose that these fishes were described as so many in number, and so large in size, that is, as both an hundred and fifty-three, and large. For so it is written, "And He drew the net to land full of great fishes, an hundred and fifty and three." For when the Lord said, "I am not come to destroy the law, but to fulfill," because about to give the Spirit, through whom the law might be fulfilled, and to add thereby, as it were, seven to ten; after interposing a few other words He proceeded, "Whosoever therefore shall break one of these least commandments, and shall teach men so, he shall be called the least in the kingdom of heaven: but whosoever shall do and teach them, the same shall be called great in the kingdom of heaven." The latter, therefore, may possibly belong to the number of great fishes. But he that is the least, who undoes in deed what he teaches in word, may be in such a church as is signified by that first capture of fishes, which contains both good and bad, for it also

is called the kingdom of heaven, as He says, "The kingdom of heaven is like unto a net that was cast into the sea, and gathered of ever kind;"[2] where He wishes the good as well as the bad to be understood, and of whom He declares that they are yet to be separated on the shore, to wit, at the end of the world. And lastly, to show that those least ones are reprobates who teach by word of mouth the good which they undo by their evil lives, and that they will not be even the least, as it were, in the life that is eternal, but will have no place there at all; after saying, "He shall be called the least in the kingdom of heaven," He immediately added, "For I say unto you, That except your righteousness shall exceed [the righteousness] of the scribes and Pharisees, ye shall not enter into the kingdom of heaven."[3] Such, doubtless—these scribes and Pharisees—are those who sit in Moses' seat, and of whom He says, "Do ye what they say, but do not what they do; for they say, and do not."[4] They teach in sermons what they undo by their morals. It therefore follows that he who is least in the kingdom of heaven, as the Church now exists, shall not enter into the kingdom of heaven, as the Church shall be hereafter; for by teaching what he himself is in the habit of breaking, he can have no place in the company of those who do what they teach, and therefore will not be in the number of great fishes, seeing it is he "who shall do and teach that shall be called great in the kingdom of heaven." And because he will be great here, therefore shall he be there, where he that is least shall not be. Yea, so great will they certainly be there, that he who is less there is greater than the greatest here.[5] And yet those who are great here, that is, who do the good that they teach in that kingdom of heaven into which the net gathereth good and bad, shall be greater still in that eternal state of the heavenly kingdom,—those, I mean, who are indicated by the fishes here as belonging to the right hand and to the resurrection of life. We have still to discourse, as God shall grant us ability, on the meal that the Lord took with those seven disciples, and on the words He spake after the meal, as well as on the close of the Gospel itself; but these are topics that cannot be included in the present lecture.

---

[1] Acts i. 4 ; ii. 2-4.
[2] Matt. xiii. 47.
[4] Matt. xxiii. 2, 3.
[3] Matt. v. 17-20.
[5] Matt. xi. 11.

TRACTATE CXXIII.

Chapter XXI. 12–19.

1. With this third manifestation of Himself by the Lord to His disciples after His resurrection, the Gospel of the blessed Apostle John is brought to a close, of which we have already lectured through the earlier part as we were able, on to the place where it is related that an hundred and fifty-three fishes were taken by the disciples to whom He showed Himself, and for all they were so large, yet were not the nets broken. What follows we have now to take into consideration, and to discuss as the Lord enables us, and as the various points may appear to demand. When the fishing was over, " Jesus saith unto them, Come [and] dine. And none of those who sat down dared to ask Him, Who art Thou? knowing that it was the Lord." If, then, they knew, what need was there to ask? and if there was no need, wherefore is it said, " they dared not," as if there were need, but, from some fear or other, they dared not? The meaning here, therefore, is: so great was the evidence of the truth that Jesus Himself had appeared to these disciples, that not one of them dared not merely to deny, but even to doubt it; for had any of them doubted it, he ought certainly to have asked. In this sense, therefore, it was said, " No one dared to ask Him, Who art Thou?" as if it were, No one dared to doubt that it was He Himself.

2. "And Jesus cometh, and taketh bread, and giveth them, and fish likewise." We are likewise told here, you see, on what they dined; and of this dinner we also will say something that is sweet and salutary, if we, too, are made by Him to partake of the food. It is related above that these disciples, when they came to the land, " saw a fire of coals laid, and a fish laid thereon, and bread." Here we are not to understand that the bread also was laid upon the coals, but only to supply, *They saw.* And if we repeat this verb in the place where it ought to be supplied, the whole may read thus: They saw coals laid, and fish laid thereon, and they saw bread. Or rather in this way: They saw coals laid, and fish laid thereon; they saw also bread. At the Lord's command they likewise brought of the fishes which they themselves had caught; and although their doing so might not be actually stated by the historian, yet there has been no silence in regard to the Lord's command. For He says, " Bring of the fishes which ye have now caught." And when we have such certainty that He gave the order, will any suppose that they failed to obey it? Of this, therefore, the Lord prepared the dinner for these His seven disciples, namely, of the fish which they had seen laid upon the coals, with an addition thereto from those which they had caught, and of the bread which we are told with equal distinctness that they had seen. The fish roasted is Christ having suffered; He Himself also is the bread that cometh down from heaven.[1] With Him is incorporated the Church, in order to the participation in everlasting blessedness. For this reason is it said, " Bring of the fish which ye have now caught," that all of us who cherish this hope may know that we ourselves, through that septenary number of disciples whereby our universal community may in this passage be understood as symbolized, partake in this great sacrament, and are associated in the same blessedness. This is the Lord's dinner with His own disciples, and herewith John, although having much besides that he might say of Christ, brings his Gospel, with profound thought and an eye to important lessons, to a close. For here the Church, such as it will be hereafter among the good alone, is signified by the draught of an hundred and fifty-three fishes; and to those who so believe, and hope, and love, there is demonstrated by this dinner their participation in such super-eminent blessedness.

3. " This was now," he says, " the third time that Jesus showed Himself to His disciples after that He was risen from the dead." And this we are to refer not to the manifestations themselves, but to the days (that is to say, taking the first day when He rose again, and the [second] eight days after, when the disciple Thomas saw and believed, and [the third] on this day when He so acted in connection with the fishes, although how many days afterwards it was that He did so we are not told); for on that first day He was seen more than once, as is shown by the collated testimonies of all the evangelists: but, as we have said, it is in accordance with the days that His manifestations are to be calculated,

[1] Chap. vi. 41.

making this the third; for that [manifestation] is to be reckoned the first, and all one and the same, as included in one day, however often and to however many He showed Himself on the day of His resurrection; the second eight days afterwards, and this the third, and thereafter as often as He pleased on to the fortieth day, when He ascended into heaven, although all of them have not been recorded in Scripture.

4. "So when they had dined, He saith to Simon Peter, Simon, [son] of John, lovest thou me more than these? He saith unto Him, Yea, Lord; Thou knowest that I love Thee. He saith unto him, Feed my lambs. He saith to him again, Simon, [son] of John, lovest thou me? He saith unto Him, Yea, Lord; Thou knowest that I love Thee. He saith unto Him, Feed my lambs. He saith unto him the third time, Simon, [son] of John, lovest thou me? Peter was grieved because He said unto him the third time, Lovest thou me? And he said unto Him, Lord, Thou knowest all things; Thou knowest that I love Thee. He saith unto him, Feed my sheep. Verily, verily, I say unto thee, When thou wast young thou girdedst thyself, and walkedst whither thou wouldest: but when thou shalt be old, thou shalt stretch forth thy hands, and another shall gird thee, and carry thee whither thou wilt not. And this spake He, signifying by what death he should glorify God." Such was the end reached by that denier and lover; elated by his presumption, prostrated by his denial, cleansed by his weeping, approved by his confession, crowned by his suffering, this was the end he reached, to die with a perfected love for the name of Him with whom, by a perverted forwardness, he had promised to die. He would do, when strengthened by His resurrection, what in his weakness he promised prematurely. For the needful order was that Christ should first die for Peter's salvation, and then that Peter should die for the preaching of Christ. The boldness thus begun by human temerity was an utter inversion of the order that had been instituted by the Truth. Peter thought to lay down his life for Christ,[1] the one to be delivered in behalf of the Deliverer, seeing that Christ had come to lay down His life for all His own, including Peter also, which, you see, was now done. Now and henceforth a true, because graciously bestowed, strength of heart may be assumed for incurring death itself for the name of the Lord, and not a false one presumptuously usurped through an erroneous estimate of ourselves. Now there is no need that we should any more fear the passage out of the present life, because in the Lord's resurrection we have a foregoing illustration of the life to come. Now thou hast cause, Peter, to be no longer afraid of death, because He liveth whom thou didst mourn when dead, and whom in thy carnal love thou didst try to hinder from dying in our behalf.[2] Thou didst dare to step in before the Leader, and thou didst tremble before His persecutor: now that the price has been paid for thee, it is thy duty to follow the Buyer, and follow Him even to the death of the cross. Thou hast heard the words of Him whom thou hast already proved to be truthful; He Himself hath foretold thy suffering, who formerly foretold thy denial.

5. But first the Lord asks what He knew, and that not once, but a second and a third time, whether Peter loved Him; and just as often He has the same answer, that He is loved, while just as often He gives Peter the same charge to feed His sheep. To the threefold denial there is now appended a threefold confession, that his tongue may not yield a feebler service to love than to fear, and imminent death may not appear to have elicited more from the lips than present life. Let it be the office of love to feed the Lord's flock, if it was the signal of fear to deny the Shepherd. Those who have this purpose in feeding the flock of Christ, that they may have them as their own, and not as Christ's, are convicted of loving themselves, and not Christ, from the desire either of boasting, or wielding power, or acquiring gain, and not from the love of obeying, serving, and pleasing God. Against such, therefore, there stands as a wakeful sentinel this thrice inculcated utterance of Christ, of whom the apostle complains that they seek their own, not the things that are Jesus Christ's.[3] For what else mean the words, "Lovest thou me? Feed my sheep," than if it were said, If thou lovest me, think not of feeding thyself, but feed my sheep as mine, and not as thine own; seek my glory in them, and not thine own; my dominion, and not thine; my gain, and not thine; lest thou be found in the fellowship of those who belong to the perilous times, lovers of their own selves, and all else that is joined on to this beginning of evils? For the apostle, after saying, "For men shall be lovers of their own selves," proceeded to add, "Lovers of money, boastful, proud, blasphemers, disobedient to parents, unthankful, wicked, irreligious, without affection, false accusers, incontinent, implacable, with-

---

out kindness, traitors, heady, blinded;[1] lovers of pleasures more than of God; having a form of godliness, but denying the power thereof."[2] All these evils flow from that as their fountain which he stated first, "lovers of their own selves." With great propriety, therefore, is Peter addressed, "Lovest thou me?" and found replying, "I love Thee:" and the command applied to him, "Feed my lambs," and this a second and a third time. We have it also demonstrated here that love and liking are one and the same thing; for the Lord also in the last question said not, *Diligis me?* but, *Amas me?* Let us, then, love not ourselves, but Him; and in feeding His sheep, let us be seeking the things which are His, not the things which are our own. For in some inexplicable way, I know not what, every one that loveth himself, and not God, loveth not himself; and whoever loveth God, and not himself, he it is that loveth himself. For he that cannot live by himself will certainly die by loving himself; he therefore loveth not himself who loves himself to his own loss of life. But when He is loved by whom life is preserved, a man by not loving himself only loveth the more, when it is for this reason that he loveth not himself, [namely] that he may love Him by whom he lives. Let not those, then, who feed Christ's sheep be "lovers of their own selves," lest they feed them as if they were their own, and not His, and wish to make their own gain of them, as "lovers of money;" or to domineer over them, as "boastful;" or to glory in the honors which they receive at their hands, as "proud;" or to go the length even of originating heresies, as "blasphemers;" and not to give place to the holy fathers, as those who are "disobedient to parents;" and to render evil for good to those who wish to correct them, because unwilling to let them perish, as "unthankful;" to slay their own souls and those of others, as "wicked;" to outrage the motherly bowels of the Church, as "irreligious;" to have no sympathy with the weak, as those who are "without affection;" to attempt to traduce the character of the saints, as "false accusers;" to give loose reins to the basest lusts, as "incontinent;" to make lawsuits their practice, as "implacable;" to know nothing of loving service, as those who are "without kindness;" to make known to the enemies of the godly what they are well aware ought to be kept secret, as "traitors;" to disturb human modesty by shameless discussions, as "heady;" to understand neither what they say nor whereof

they affirm,[3] as "blinded;" and to prefer carnal delights to spiritual joys, as those who are "lovers of pleasures more than lovers of God." For these and such like vices, whether all of them meet in a single individual, or whether some dominate in one and others in another, spring up in some form or another from this one root, when men are "lovers of their own selves." A vice which is specially to be guarded against by those who feed Christ's sheep, lest they be seeking their own, not the things that are Jesus Christ's, and be turning those to the use of their own lusts for whom the blood of Christ was shed. Whose love ought, in one who feedeth His sheep, to grow up unto so great a spiritual fervor as to overcome even the natural fear of death, that makes us unwilling to die even when we wish to live with Christ. For the Apostle Paul also says that he had a desire to be dissolved, and to be with Christ,[4] and yet he groans, being burdened, and wishes not to be unclothed, but clothed upon, that mortality may be swallowed up of life.[5] And so to His present lover the Lord said, "When thou shalt be old, thou shalt stretch forth thy hands, and another shall gird thee, and carry thee whither thou wouldest not. For this He said to him, signifying by what death he should glorify God." "Thou shalt stretch forth thy hands," He said; in other words, thou shalt be crucified. But that thou mayest come to this, "another shall gird thee, and carry thee," not whither thou wouldest, but "whither thou wouldest not." He told him first what would happen, and then how it should come to pass. For it was not after being crucified, but when actually about to be crucified, that he was carried whither he would not; for after being crucified he went his way, not whither he would not, but rather whither he would. And though when set free from the body he wished to be with Christ, yet, were it only possible, he had a desire for eternal life apart from the grievousness of death, to which grievous experience he was unwillingly carried, but from it [when all was over] he was willingly carried away; unwillingly he came to it, but willingly he conquered it, and left this feeling of infirmity behind that makes every one unwilling to die,—a feeling so permanently natural, that even old age itself was unable to set the blessed Peter free from its influence, even as it was said unto him, "When thou shalt be old," thou shalt be led "whither thou wouldest not." For our consolation the Saviour Himself transfigured also the same feeling in His own person when He

---

[1] *Cæcati.*   [2] 2 Tim. iii. 1-5.   [3] 1 Tim. i. 7.   [4] Phil. i. 23.   [5] 2 Cor. v. 4.

said, "Father, if it be possible, let this cup pass from me;"[1] and He certainly had come to die without having any necessity, but only the willingness to die, with power to lay down His life, and with power to take it again. But however great be the grievousness of death, it ought to be overcome by the power of that love which is felt to Him who, being our life, was willing to endure even death in our behalf. For if there were no grievousness, even of the smallest kind, in death, the glory of the martyrs would not be so great. But if the good Shepherd, who laid down His own life for His sheep,[2] has raised up so many martyrs for Himself out of the very sheep, how much more ought those to contend to death for the truth, and even to blood against sin, who are entrusted by Him with the feeding, that is, with the teaching and governing of these very sheep? And on this account, along with the preceding example of His own passion, who can fail to see that the shepherds ought all the more to set themselves closely to imitate the Shepherd, if He was so imitated even by many of the sheep under whom, as the one Shepherd and in the one flock, the shepherds themselves are likewise sheep? For He made all those His sheep for [all of] whom He died, because He Himself also became a sheep that He might suffer for all.

[1] Matt. xxvi. 39.   [2] Chap. x. 18, 11.

TRACTATE CXXIV.

Chapter XXI. 19–25.

1. It is no unimportant question why the Lord, when He manifested Himself for the third time to the disciples, said unto the Apostle Peter, "Follow me;" but of the Apostle John, "Thus I wish him to remain[1] till I come, what is that to thee?" To the discussion or solution of this question, according as the Lord shall grant us ability, we devote the last discourse of this work. When the Lord, then, had announced beforehand to Peter by what death he was to glorify God, "He saith unto him, Follow me. Then Peter, turning about, seeth the disciple whom Jesus loved following; who also leaned on His breast at supper, and said, Lord, which is he that shall betray Thee? Peter, therefore, seeing him, saith to Jesus, Lord, and what [of] this man? Jesus saith unto him, Thus do I wish him to remain till I come, what is that to thee? Follow thou me. Then went this saying abroad among the brethren, that that disciple dieth not: yet Jesus said not unto him, He dieth not; but, Thus do I wish him to remain till I come, what is that to thee?" You see the great extent in this Gospel of a question which, by its depth, must exercise in no ordinary way the mind of the inquirer. For why is it said to Peter, "Follow me," and not to the others who were likewise present? Surely the disciples followed Him also as their Master. But if it is to be understood only in reference to his suffering, was Peter the only one that suffered for the truth of Christianity? Was there not present there amongst those seven, another son of Zebedee, the brother of John, who, after His ascension, is plainly recorded to have been slain by Herod?[2] But some one may say that, as James was not crucified, it was properly enough said to Peter, "Follow me," inasmuch as he underwent not only death, but, like Christ, even the death of the cross. Be it so, if no other explanation can be found that is more satisfactory. Why, then, was it said of John, "Thus do I wish him to remain till I come, what is that to thee?" and the words repeated, "Follow thou me," as if that other, therefore, were not to follow, seeing He wished him to remain till He comes. Who can readily believe that anything else was meant than what the brethren who lived at the time believed, namely, that that disciple was not to die, but to abide in this life till Jesus came? But John himself removed such an idea, by giving a flat contradiction to the report that the Lord had said so. For why should he add, "Jesus saith not, He dieth not," save to prevent what was false from taking hold of the hearts of men?

2. But let any one who so listeth still refuse his assent, and declare that what John asserts is true enough, that the Lord said not that that disciple dieth not, and yet that this is the meaning of such words as He is here

[1] Sic *eum volo manere donec veniam.*   [2] Acts xii. 2.

recorded to have used; and further assert that the Apostle John is still living, and maintain that he is sleeping rather than lying dead in his tomb at Ephesus. Let him employ as an argument the current report that there the earth is in sensible commotion, and presents a kind of heaving appearance, and assert whether it be steadfastly or obstinately that this is occasioned by his breathing. For we cannot fail to have some who so believe, if there is no want of those also who affirm that Moses is alive; because it is written that his sepulchre could not be found,[1] and that he appeared with the Lord on the mountain along with Elias,[2] of whom we read that he did not die, but was translated.[3] As if Moses' body could not have been hid somewhere in such a way as that its position should altogether escape discovery by men, and be raised up therefrom by divine power at the time when Elias and he were seen with Christ; just as at the time of Christ's passion many bodies of the saints arose, and after His resurrection appeared, according to Scripture, to many in the holy city.[4] But still, as I began to say, if some deny the death of Moses, whom Scripture itself, in the very passage where we read that his sepulchre could nowhere be found, explicitly declares to have died; how much more may occasion be taken from these words where the Lord says, "Thus do I wish him to stay till I come," to believe that John is sleeping, but still alive, beneath the ground? Of whom we have also the tradition (which is found in certain apocryphal scriptures), that he was present, in good health, when he ordered a sepulchre to be made for him; and that, when it was dug and prepared with all possible care, he laid himself down there as in a bed, and became immediately defunct: yet as those think who so understand these words of the Lord, not really defunct, but only lying like one in such a condition; and, while accounted dead, was actually buried when asleep, and that he will so remain till the coming of Christ, making known meanwhile the fact of his life by the bubbling up of the dust, which is believed to be forced by the breath of the sleeper to ascend from the depths to the surface of the grave. I think it quite superfluous to contend with such an opinion. For those may see for themselves who know the locality whether the ground there does or suffers what is said regarding it, because, in truth, we too have heard of it from those who are not altogether unreliable witnesses.

3. Meanwhile let us yield to the opinion,

which we are unable to refute by any certain evidence, lest we stir up still another question that may be put to us, Why the very ground should seem in a kind of way to live and breathe upon the interred corpse? But can so great a question as the one before us be settled on such grounds as these, if by a great miracle, such as can be wrought by the Almighty, the living body lies so long asleep beneath the ground, till the coming of the end of the world? Nay, rather, does there not arise a wider and more difficult one, why Jesus bestowed on the disciple, whom He loved beyond the others to such an extent that he was counted worthy to recline on His breast, the gift of a protracted sleep in the body, when He delivered the blessed Peter, by the eminent glory of martyrdom, from the burden of the body itself, and vouchsafed to him what the Apostle Paul said that he desired, and committed to writing, namely, "to be let loose, and to be with Christ"?[5] But if, what is rather to be believed, Saint John declared that the Lord said not, "He dieth not," for the very purpose that no such meaning might be attached to the words which He used; and his body lieth in its sepulchre lifeless like those of others deceased; it remains, if that really takes place which report has spread abroad regarding the soil, which grows up anew, though continually carried away, that it is either so done for the purpose of commending the preciousness of his death, seeing it wants the commendation of martyrdom (for he suffered not death at a persecutor's hand for the faith of Christ), or on some other account that is concealed from our knowledge. Still there remains the question, why the Lord said of one who was destined to die, "Thus I wish him to remain till I come."

4. And who, besides, would not be disposed, in the case of these two apostles, Peter and John, to make this further inquiry, why the Lord loved John better, when He Himself was better loved by Peter? For wherever John has something to say of himself, in order that the reference may be understood without any mention of his name, he adds this, that Jesus loved him, as if he were the only one so loved, that he might be distinguished by this mark from the others, who were all of them certainly loved by Christ: and what else, when he so spake, did he wish to be understood but that he himself was more abundantly loved? and far be it that he should utter a falsehood. And what greater proof could Jesus have given of His

---

[1] Deut. xxxiv. 6.
[3] 2 Kings ii. 11.

[2] Matt. xvii. 3.
[4] Matt. xxvii. 52, 53.

[5] Phil. i. 23.

own greater love to him than that this man, who was only a partner with the rest of his fellow-disciples in the great salvation, should be the only one that leaned on the breast of the Saviour Himself? And further, that the Apostle Peter loved Christ more than the others, may be adduced from many documentary evidences; but to go no further after others, it is plainly enough apparent in the lesson almost immediately preceding the present, in connection with that third manifestation of the Lord, when He put to him the question, "Lovest thou me more than these?" He knew it, of course, and yet asked, in order that we also, who read the Gospel, might know Peter's love to Christ, both from the questions of the One and the answers of the other. But when Peter only replied, "I love Thee," without adding, "more than these," his answer contained all that he knew of himself. For he could not know how much He was loved by any other, not being able to look into that other's heart. But by saying in the earliest of his answers, "Yea, Lord, Thou knowest," he stated in clear enough terms, that it was with perfect knowledge of all that the Lord asked what He asked. The Lord therefore knew, not only that Peter loved Him, but also that he loved Him more than the others. And yet if we propose to ourselves, in the way of inquiry, which of the two is the better, he that loveth Christ more or he that loveth Him less, who will hesitate to answer, he is the better that loveth Him more? If, on the other hand, we propose this question, which of the two is the better, he that is loved less or he that is loved more by Christ, without any doubt we shall reply that he is the better who is loved the more by Christ. In the comparison therefore which I drew first, Peter is superior to John; but in the latter, John is preferred to Peter. Accordingly, we have a third to propose in this form: Which of the two disciples is the better, he that loveth Christ less than his fellow-disciple [does], and is loved more than his fellow-disciple by Christ? or he who is loved less than his fellow-disciple by Christ, while he, more than his fellow-disciple, loveth Christ? Here it is that the answer plainly halts, and the question grows in magnitude. As far, however, as my own wisdom goes, I might easily reply, that he is the better who loveth Christ the more, but he the happier who is loved the more by Christ; if only I could thoroughly see how to defend the justice of our Deliverer in loving him the less by whom He is loved the more, and him the more by whom He is loved the less.

5. I shall therefore, in the manifested

mercy of Him whose justice is hidden, set about the discussion, in order to the solution of a question of such importance, in accordance with the strength which He may graciously bestow: for hitherto it has only been proposed, not expounded. Let this, then, be the commencement of its exposition, namely, that we bear in mind that in this corruptible body, which burdens the soul,[1] we live a miserable life. But we who are now redeemed by the Mediator, and have received the earnest of the Holy Spirit, have a blessed life in prospect, although we possess it not as yet in reality. But a hope that is seen is not hope; for what a man seeth, why doth he yet hope for? But if we hope for that we see not, then do we with patience wait for it.[2] And it is in the evils that every one suffers, not in the good things that he enjoys, that he has need of patience. The present life, therefore, whereof it is written, "Is not the life of man a term of trial upon earth?"[3] in which we are daily crying to the Lord, "Deliver us from evil,"[4] a man is compelled to endure, even when his sins are forgiven him, although it was the first sin that caused his falling into such misery. For the penalty is more protracted than the fault; lest the fault should be accounted small, were the penalty to end with itself. On this account it is also, either for the demonstration of our debt of misery, or for the amendment of our passing life, or for the exercise of the necessary patience, that man is kept through time in the penalty, even when he is no longer held by his sin as liable to everlasting damnation. This is the truly lamentable but unblameable condition of the present evil days we pass in this mortal state, even while in it we look with loving eyes to the days that are good. For it comes from the righteous anger of God, whereof the Scriptures say, "Man, that is born of woman, is of few days and full of anger:"[5] for the anger of God is not like that of man, the disturbance of an excited man, but the calm fixing of righteous punishment. In this anger of His, God restraineth not, as it is written, His tender mercies;[6] but, besides other consolations to the miserable, which He ceaseth not to bestow on mankind, in the fullness of time, when He knew that such had to be done, He sent His only-begotten Son,[7] by whom He created all things, that He might become man while remaining God, and so be the Mediator between God and men, the man Christ Jesus:[8] that those who believe in Him, being absolved by

---

[1] Wisd. ix. 15. [2] Rom. viii. 24, 25. [3] Job vii. 1.
[4] Matt. vi. 13. [5] Job xiv. 1. [6] Ps. lxxvii. 9.
[7] Gal. iv. 4. [8] 1 Tim. ii. 5.

the laver of regeneration from the guilt of all their sins,—to wit, both of the original sin they have inherited by generation, and to meet which, in particular, regeneration was instituted, and of all others contracted by evil conduct,—might be delivered from perpetual condemnation, and live in faith and hope and love while sojourning in this world, and be walking onward to His visible presence amid its toilsome and perilous temptations on the one hand, but the consolations of God, both bodily and spiritual, on the other, ever keeping to the way which Christ has become to them. And because, even while walking in Him, they are not exempt from sins, which creep in through the infirmities of this life, He has given them the salutary remedies of alms whereby their prayers might be aided, when He taught them to say, "Forgive us our debts, as we also forgive our debtors."¹ So does the Church act in blessed hope through this troublous life; and this Church, symbolized in its generality, was personified in the Apostle Peter, on account of the primacy of his apostleship. For, as regards his proper personality, he was by nature one man, by grace one Christian, by still more abounding grace one, and yet also, the first apostle; but when it was said to him, "I will give unto thee the keys of the kingdom of heaven, and whatsoever thou shalt bind on earth, shall be bound in heaven; and whatsoever thou shalt loose on earth, shall be loosed in heaven," he represented the universal Church, which in this world is shaken by divers temptations, that come upon it like torrents of rain, floods and tempests, and falleth not, because it is founded upon a rock (*petra*), from which Peter received his name. For *petra* (rock) is not derived from Peter, but Peter from *petra;* just as Christ is not called so from the Christian, but the Christian from Christ. For on this very account the Lord said, "On this rock will I build my Church," because Peter had said, "Thou art the Christ, the Son of the living God."² On this rock, therefore, He said, which thou hast confessed. I will build my Church. For the Rock (*Petra*) was Christ ;³ and on this foundation was Peter himself also built. For other foundation can no man lay than that is laid, which is Christ Jesus.⁴ The Church, therefore, which is founded in Christ received from Him the keys of the kingdom of heaven in the person of Peter, that is to say, the power of binding and loosing sins. For what the Church is essentially in Christ, such representatively is Peter in the rock (*petra*); and in this representation Christ is to be understood as the Rock, Peter as the Church. This Church, accordingly, which Peter represented, so long as it lives amidst evil, by loving and following Christ is delivered from evil. But its following is the closer in those who contend even unto death for the truth. But to the universality⁵ [of the Church] is it said, "Follow me," even as it was for the same universality that Christ suffered: of whom this same Peter saith, "Christ suffered for us, leaving us an example, that we should follow His footsteps."⁶ This, then, you see is why it was said to him, "Follow me." But there is another, an immortal life, that is not passed in the midst of evil: there we shall see face to face what is seen here through a glass and in a riddle,⁷ even when much progress is made in the beholding of the truth. There are two states of life, therefore, preached and commended to herself from heaven, that are known to the Church, whereof the one is in faith, the other in sight; one in the temporal sojourn in a foreign land, the other in the eternity of the [heavenly] abode; one in labor, the other in repose; one on the way, the other in the fatherland; one in active work, the other in the wages of contemplation; one declines from evil and makes for good, the other has no evil to decline from, and has great good to enjoy; the one fights with a foe, the other reigns without a foe; the one is brave in the midst of adversities, the other has no experience of adversity; the one is bridling its carnal lusts, the other has full scope for spiritual delights; the one is anxious with the care of conquering, the other secure in the peace of victory; the one is helped in temptations, the other, free from all temptations, rejoices in the Helper Himself; the one is occupied in relieving the indigent, the other is there, where no indigence is found; the one pardons the sins of others, that its own may be pardoned to itself, the other neither has anything to pardon nor does aught for which pardon has to be asked; the one is scourged with evils that it may not be elated with good things, the other is free from all evil by such a fullness of grace that, without any temptation to pride, it may cleave to that which is supremely good; the one discerneth both good and evil, the other has only that which is good presented to view: therefore the one is good, but miserable as yet; the other, better and blessed. This one was signified by the Apostle Peter, that other by John. The whole of the one is passed here to the end of this world, and there finds its

---

¹ Matt. vi. 12.   ² Matt. xvi. 16-19.
³ 1 Cor. x. 4.   ⁴ 1 Cor. iii. 11.   ⁵ *Universitati.*   ⁶ 1 Pet. ii. 21.   ⁷ 1 Cor.

termination, the other is deferred for its completion till after the end of this world, but has no end in the world to come. Hence it is said to the latter, "Follow me;" but of the former, "Thus I will that he tarry till I come, what is that to thee? follow thou me." For what means this last? So far as my wisdom goes, so far as I comprehend, what is it but this, Follow thou me by imitating me in the endurance of temporal evils; let him remain till I come to restore everlasting good? And this may be expressed more clearly in this way: Let perfected action, informed by the example of my passion, follow me; but let contemplation only begun remain [so] till I come, to be perfected when I come. For the godly plenitude of patience, reaching forward even unto death, followeth Christ; but the fullness of knowledge tarrieth till Christ come, to be manifested then. For here the evils of this world are endured in the land of the dying, while there shall be seen the good things of the Lord in the land of the living. For in saying, "I wish him to tarry till I come," we are not to understand Him as meaning to remain on, or abide permanently, but to wait; seeing that what is signified by him shall certainly not be fulfilled now, but when Christ is come. But what is signified by him to whom it was said, "Follow thou me," unless it be done now, will never attain to the expected end. And in this life of activity, the more we love Christ the more easily are we delivered from evil. But He loveth us less as we now are, and therefore delivers from it, that we may not be always such as we are. There, however, He loveth us more; for we shall not have aught about us to displease Him, or aught that He will have to separate us from: nor is it for aught else that He loveth us here but that He may heal and translate us from everything He loveth not. Here, therefore, [He loveth us] less, where He would not have us remain; there in larger measure, whither He would have us to be passing, and out of that wherein He would not that we should perish. Let Peter therefore love Him, that we may obtain deliverance from our present mortality; let John be loved by Him, that we may be preserved in the immortality to come.

6. But by this line of argument we have shown why Christ loved John more than Peter, not why Peter loved Christ more than John. For if Christ loveth us more in the world to come, where we shall live unendingly with Him, than in the present, from which we are in the course of being rescued, that we may be always in the other, it does not follow on that account that we shall love Him

less when better ourselves; since we can in no possible way be better ourselves, save by loving Him more. Why was it, then, that John loved Him less than Peter, if he signified that life, wherein He must be more abundantly loved, but because on that very account it was said, "I will that he tarry," that is wait, "till I come;" for we have not yet the love itself, which will then be greater far, but are expecting that future, that we may have it when He shall come? Just as in his own epistle the same apostle declares, "It has not yet appeared what we shall be: but we know that, when He shall appear, we shall be like Him; for we shall see Him as He is."[1] Then accordingly shall we love the more that which we shall see. But the Lord Himself, in His predestinating knowledge, loveth more that future life of ours that is yet to come, such as He knows it will be hereafter in us, in order that by so loving us He may draw us onward to its possession. Wherefore, as all the ways of the Lord are mercy and truth,[2] we know our present misery, because we feel it; and therefore we love more the mercy of the Lord, which we wish to be exhibited in our deliverance from misery, and we ask and experience it daily, especially in the remission of sins: this it is that was signified by Peter, as loving more, but less beloved; because Christ loveth us less in our misery than in our blessedness. But the contemplation of the truth, such as it then shall be, we love less, because as yet we neither know nor possess it: this was signified by John as loving less, and therefore waiting both for that state itself, and for the perfecting in us of that love to Him, to which He is entitled, till the Lord come; but loved the more, because that it is, which is symbolized by him, that maketh him blessed.

7. Let no one, however, separate these distinguished apostles. In that which was signified by Peter, they were both alike; and in that which was signified by John, they will both be alike hereafter. In their representative character, the one was following, the other tarrying; but in their personal faith they were both of them enduring the present evils of the misery here, both of them expecting the future good things of the blessedness to come. And such is the case, not with them alone, but with the holy universal Church, the spouse of Christ, who has still to be rescued from the present trials, and to be preserved in the future happiness. And these two states of life were symbolized by Peter and John, the one by the one, the other by

---

[1] 1 John iii. 2.   [2] Ps. xxv. 10.

the other; but in this life they both of them walked for a time by faith, and the other they shall both of them enjoy eternally by sight. For the whole body of the saints, therefore, inseparably belonging to the body of Christ, and for their safe pilotage through the present tempestuous life, did Peter, the first of the apostles, receive the keys of the kingdom of heaven for the binding and loosing of sins; and for the same congregation of saints, in reference to the perfect repose in the bosom of that mysterious life to come, did the evangelist John recline on the breast of Christ. For it is not the former alone, but the whole Church, that bindeth and looseth sins; nor did the latter alone drink at the fountain of the Lord's breast, to emit again in preaching, of the Word in the beginning, God with God, and those other sublime truths regarding the divinity of Christ, and the Trinity and Unity of the whole Godhead, which are to be yet beheld in that kingdom face to face, but meanwhile till the Lord's coming are only to be seen in a mirror and in a riddle; but the Lord has Himself diffused this very gospel through the whole world, that every one of His own may drink thereat according to his own individual capacity. There are some who have entertained the idea—and those, too, who are no contemptible handlers of sacred eloquence—that the Apostle John was more loved by Christ on the ground that he never married a wife, and lived in perfect chastity from early boyhood.[1] There is, indeed, no distinct evidence of this in the canonical Scriptures: nevertheless it is an idea that contributes not a little to the suitableness of the opinion expressed above, namely, that that life was signified by him, where there will be no marriage.

8. "This is the disciple who testifieth of these things, and wrote these things; and we know that his testimony is true. And there are also," he adds, "many other things which Jesus did, the which, if they should be written every one, I suppose that even the world itself could not contain the books that should be written." We are not to suppose that in regard to local space the world would be unable to contain them; for how could they be written in it if it could not bear them when written? but perhaps it is that they could not be comprehended by the capacity of the readers: although, while our faith in certain things themselves remains unharmed, the words we use about them may not unfrequently appear to exceed belief. This will not take place when anything that was obscure or dubious is in course of exposition by the setting forth of its ground and reason, but only when that which is clear of itself is either magnified or extenuated, without any real departure from the pathway of the truth to be intimated; for the words may outrun the thing itself that is indicated only in such a way, that the will of him that speaketh, but without any intention to deceive, may be apparent, so that, knowing how far he will be believed, he, orally, either diminishes or magnifies his subject beyond the limit to which credit will be given. This mode of speaking is called by the Greek name hyperbole, by the masters not only of Greek, but also of Latin literature. And this mode is found not only here, but in several other parts also of the divine literature: as, "They set their mouths against the heavens;"[2] and, "The top of the hair of such as go on in their trespasses;"[3] and many others of the same kind, which are no more wanting in the sacred Scriptures than other tropes or modes of speaking. Of these I might give a more elaborate discussion, were it not that, as the evangelist here terminates his Gospel, I am also compelled to bring my discourse to a close.

---

[1] Jerome, Book I., *Against Jovinian.*   [2] Ps. lxxiii. 9.   [3] Ps. lxviii. 21.

ST. AUGUSTIN:

TEN HOMILIES

ON

THE FIRST EPISTLE OF JOHN.

TRANSLATED BY

REV. H. BROWNE, M.A.,

CANON OF WALTHAM AND PRINCIPAL OF THE CHICHESTER DIOCESAN COLLEGE.

REVISED, WITH ADDITIONAL NOTES,

BY

REV. JOSEPH H. MYERS, D.D.

INTRODUCTION.

THIS first Epistle of John, probably written at Ephesus near the close of the first century, the last utterance of the Spirit of inspiration, breathes the calmness of an assured hope, and that fullness of joy of which the Apostle would have his readers to be made partakers. While strongly refuting error, it is not so much an argument as an intuition, an open vision of the divine truths announced.

It was evidently written in a time of external quiet for the Church, but of special exposure to errors and perils from within. The nature of the principal error is plain,—the denial that Jesus is the Christ (1 John ii: 22). Precisely this heresy was taught at Ephesus by Cerinthus in the old age of the Apostle; he alleged that Jesus was a man eminent for wisdom and holiness; that after his baptism Christ descended into him, and before the crucifixion left Jesus and returned to heaven. Over against this cardinal error, the Apostle announces the manifestation of the Son of God in the flesh,—the Incarnation of that Eternal Life which was with God from the beginning. This divine fact is shown in its own self-evidencing light, and is so presented as to render the epistle a "possession forever," of incalculable value to the Church. In our day, also, by separating Jesus the Son of Man from Christ the Son of God, the one Divine-Human Lord and Saviour of man is denied and rejected. The great words, fellowship, light, life, love, so often recurring in the Epistle, are filled with new meanings as vehicles of the message of God, as conveying the thoughts of God.

As regards the plan of the Epistle, it has been often asserted till lately that it was supposed to be but fragmentary, a series of aphorisms. Augustin, however, without formally announcing a plan as discovered by him in the Epistle, not only frequently affirms in his exposition that charity or love is the Apostle's main theme, but so conducts the discussion, gathering his arguments and illustrations around this central thought, as to render it evident that in his view the purpose and plan of the Apostle is to set forth love in its essence and its scope, and that he intends to make this thought dominant in every part. Westcott, in his admirable commentary (2nd edition, 1886), does not draw out a plan, but gives striking and comprehensive views of the object and scope of the Epistle.

Braune, in Lange's commentary, makes two main divisions, besides the introduction and conclusion: chief topic for the first division: i. 5–ii. 28, *God is Light;* for the second part: *Whosoever is born of God doeth righteousness.*

Huther (4th edition, 1880) suggests a three-fold division, first: i. 5–ii. 12–28, *against indifference to truth and love of the world;* second: ii. 29–iii. 22, *a life of brotherly love alone is in agreement with the nature of the child of God;* third: iii. 23–v. 17, pointing to *faith in Jesus Christ, the Son of God, as the foundation of the Christian Life.* As thus distributed (by Huther) "the conclusion of each part points to the joy of which the Christian partakes in fellowship with God."

Objections have been urged to any division proposed, as being inadequate; but the great divine facts of *fellowship with God, fullness of joy in Him,* and an *Eternal Life of love through the Son of God,* are leading topics. This is obvious; they are often recurred to, are frequently conjoined, and in their grandeur surpass our range and reach of thought, while satisfying the aspirations of the soul.

In these discourses of Augustin, on the first Epistle of John, we have a nearly complete text of the Epistle,—the exposition of the last 18 verses not being extant. He followed the old Itala, one of the most ancient (Latin) versions of the New Testament. Variations between the text on which he comments and the best Greek text (as given by Westcott and Hort), when of importance, are indicated in this revised edition of the translation of his homilies. In comparing the Oxford translation, word by word, with the original,—Benedictine (Migne's) edition,—several omissions, twelve at least, have been discovered; and though brief, some of them are of considerable importance: these are supplied in the present edition.

The translator copied, only too faithfully, the very form of the Latin sentences: to change them throughout and to remove all the archaisms in his English, might have seemed an undue reflection on a work executed for the most part with extraordinary fidelity.

After many alterations in phraseology, probably enough still remains in the translation of the original antique flavor to satisfy the taste of those who are ever disposed to say: "the old is better."

As regards any allegorizing tendency here and there manifested in the exposition, it may suffice to say that it is small in Augustin, as compared with very many of great fame.

If now and then he seems to mistake in interpretation (as in Homily VII.), not considering that in the Greek such propositions as "God is love," are not convertible, the subject ὁ θεός being marked by the article, and the predicate indicated by not having the article, let it be remembered that some exegetical canons of the kind were unknown in his time.

These expository discourses by the most illustrious of the Fathers of the Western Church, while often exhibiting great critical acumen, were not intended to be models in exegesis. They are familiar, homiletical talks, racy and vivid in style, couched in the plainest and most pointed language, and all aglow with the most fervent love.

Whatever St. John was in this respect, Augustin was clearly a polemic; but where can be found a more ardent lover of the brethren, nay of all men, even the worst? Not the least striking and touching of his utterances are those in which he discloses the breadth and depth of his charity toward enemies, and affirms such principles and such conduct to be necessarily and invariably found in all those who are Christians indeed.—J. H. M.

CONTENTS OF HOMILIES.

TEN HOMILIES

ON THE EPISTLE OF JOHN

TO THE PARTHIANS.

THE PROLOGUE.

YE remember, holy brethren, that the Gospel according to John, read in orderly course of lessons, is the subject on which we usually discourse: but because of the now intervening solemnity of the holy days, on which there must be certain lessons recited in the Church, which so come every year that they cannot be other than they are:[2] the order which we had undertaken is of necessity for a little while intermitted, not wholly omitted. But when I was thinking what matter of discourse upon the Scriptures, agreeably with the cheerfulness of these days, I might undertake with you, as the Lord shall vouchsafe to grant, during the present week, being such an one as might be finished in these seven or eight days; the Epistle of blessed John occurred to me: that whereas we have for a while intermitted the reading of his Gospel, we may in discoursing upon his Epistle not go from his side: the rather, as in this same Epistle, which is very sweet to all who have a healthy taste of the heart to relish the Bread of God, and very meet to be had in remembrance in God's Holy Church, charity is above all commended He has spoken many words, and nearly all are about charity.[3] He that hath in himself that which he is to hear, must needs rejoice at that which he heareth. For so shall this reading be to that man, as oil upon flame; if that be there which may be nourished, it is nourished and groweth and abideth. Again, to some it ought to be as flame to fuel; that if he did not burn, by added discourse he may be

---

[1] In this designation of St. John's first Epistle, the manuscript copies of St. Augustin all agree, both here and in the incidental mention, *Quæst. Evang.* ii. 39, of St. John's *Epistola ad Parthos ;* and that there is no error of transcription is further proved by the fact, that the present work appears in the Indiculus of Possidius under the title, *In Epistolam Joannis ad Parthos Tractatus decem.* And yet St. Augustin neither in these Tractates nor in any other of his extant works explains or comments upon this peculiar address. In the Latin Church, since Augustin, it frequently occurs in authors and in MSS. of the Vulgate. According to Venerable Bede, " Many ecclesiastical authors, and among them St. Athanasius, Bishop of the Church of Alexandria, witness that the first Epistle of St. John was written *ad Parthos.*" (Cave, *Hist. Lit.* i. 614). But there is no indication elsewhere that St. Athanasius was acquainted with this superscription, and with the exception of a few very modern MSS. which have πρὸς πάρθους in the subscription to the second Epistle, it seems to be unknown to the Greek Church. The tradition according to which St. John preached the Gospel in Parthia rests (so far as appears) on no ancient authority, and perhaps has no other foundation than the superscription itself : which may have originated either, as some critics have supposed, in an abbreviated form of πρὸς παρθένους, "To the Virgins," or, as Gieseler suggests, in τοῦ παρθένου, as the designation of St. John himself, "The Epistle of John the Virgin;" an epithet which has gone with his name from very early times. In favor of this explanation it may be remarked, that Griesbach's Codex, 30, has for the superscription of the Apocalypse, τοῦ ἁγίου ἐνδοξοτάτου ἀποστόλου καὶ εὐαγγελιστοῦ παρθένου ἠγαπημένου ἐπιστηθίου Ἰωάννου θεολόγου : " The Apocalypse of the holy, most glorious Apostle and Evangelist, 'the Virgin,' the Beloved, who lay in the bosom (of the Lord), John the Theologus."
[Most recent critics and commentators adopt the plausible conjecture of Gieseler that the title originated in the mistake of a transcriber for τοῦ παρθένου. Other conjecturers : *Ad Spartos, Ad Pattimios, Ad Sparsos,* are not worth considering. See the commentaries of Huther, Haupt, Braune, Westcott, and Plummer.— P. S.]

[2] From S. Aug. *Serm.* ccxxxii. 1, and ccxxxix. 1, it appears to have been the custom, that during seven or eight days after Easter Sunday, the history of the Resurrection from all four Evangelists should furnish the Gospel Lessons: but not always in the same order, St. Luke being sometimes read before St. Mark. And in fact the second of these Homilies, which one of the oldest MSS. assigns to Easter Monday, appears from the opening of it to have been preached on the day which had for its Lesson the narrative of St. Luke concerning the two disciples to whom Christ appeared on the way to Emmaus.—BEN. Ed.

[3] Some MSS. have in the title of these Homilies the addition, *De Caritate.*

set on fire. For in some that which is there, is nourished: in some it is kindled, if it be not there: that we all may rejoice in one charity. But where charity, there peace; and where humility, there charity. Now let us hear himself: and at his words, what the Lord suggests, that let us speak also to you, that ye may well understand.

HOMILY I.

1 JOHN I. 1.—II. 11.

"That which was from the beginning, which we have heard, and which we have seen with our eyes, and our hands have handled, of the Word of life: and the life was manifested, and we have seen, and bear witness, and show unto you that eternal life, which was with the Father, and was manifested unto us: the things which we have seen and heard declare we unto you, that ye also may have fellowship with us: and that our fellowship may be [1] with the Father, and with His Son Jesus Christ. And these things write we unto you, that your joy may be full. This then is the message which we have heard of Him, and declare unto you, that God is light, and in Him is no darkness at all. If we say that we have fellowship with Him, and walk in darkness, we lie, and do not the truth: if we walk in the light, as He is in the light, we have fellowship one with another, and the blood of Jesus Christ His Son shall cleanse [2] us from all sin. If we say that we have no sin, we deceive ourselves, and the truth is not in us. If we confess our sins, He is faithful and just to forgive us our sins, and to cleanse us from all unrighteousness. If we say that we have not sinned, we make Him a liar, and His word is not in us. My little children, these things write I unto you, that ye sin not. And if any man sin, we have an Advocate with the Father, Jesus Christ the righteous: and He is the propitiation for our sins: not for our's only, but also for the sins of the whole world. And in this we do know Him, if we keep His commandments. He that saith he knoweth Him, and keepeth not His commandments, is a liar, and the truth is not in him. But whoso keepeth His word, in him verily is the love of God perfected. In this we know that we are in Him, if in Him we be perfect. He that saith he abideth in Him ought himself also so to walk, even as He walked. Beloved, I write no new commandment unto you, but an old commandment which ye had from the beginning. The old commandment is the word which ye have heard. Again, a new commandment I write unto you, which thing is true in Him and in you: because the darkness is past, and the true light now shineth. He that saith he is in the light, and hateth his brother, is in darkness even until now. He that loveth his brother abideth in the light, and there is none occasion of stumbling in him. For he that hateth his brother is in darkness, and walketh in darkness, and knoweth not whither he goeth, because the darkness hath blinded his eyes."

1. "THAT which was from the beginning, which we have heard, which we have seen with our eyes, [3] and our hands have handled, of the word of life." Who is he that with hands doth handle the Word, except because "The Word was made flesh, and dwelt in us"? Now this Word which was made flesh that it might be handled, began to be flesh, of the Virgin Mary: but not then began the Word, for the Apostle saith, "That which was from the beginning." See whether his epistle does not bear witness to his gospel, where ye lately heard, "In the beginning was

[1] ["Our fellowship is."—J. H. M.]
[2] [Gr. καθαρίζει, cleanses.— J.H.M.]
[3] Ὅ ἐθεασάμεθα. "Which we have looked upon." Vulg. quod perspeximus. Aug. om.

the Word, and the Word was with God.[1] Perchance, "Concerning the word of life" one may take as a sort of expression concerning Christ, not the very body of Christ which was handled with hands. See what follows: "And the Life was manifested." Christ therefore is "the word of life." And whereby manifested? For it was "from the beginning," only not manifested to men: but it was manifested to angels, who saw it and fed on it as their bread. But what saith the Scripture? "Man did eat angels' bread."[2] Well then, "the Life was manifested" in the flesh; because it exhibited in manifestation, that that which can be seen by the heart only, should be seen by the eyes also, that it might heal the hearts. For only by the heart is the Word seen: but the flesh is seen by the bodily eyes also. We had wherewith to see the flesh, but had not wherewith to see the Word: "the Word was made flesh," which we might see, that so that in us might be healed wherewith we might see the Word.

2. "And we have seen and are witnesses."[3] Perhaps some of the brethren who are not acquainted with the Greek do not know what the word "witnesses" is in Greek: and yet it is a term much used by all, and had in religious reverence; for what in our tongue we call "witnesses," in Greek are "martyrs." Now where is the man that has not heard of martyrs, or where the Christian in whose mouth the name of martyrs dwelleth not every day? and would that it so dwelt in the heart also, that we should imitate the sufferings of the martyrs, not persecute them with our cups![4] Well then, "We have seen and are witnesses," is as much as to say, We have seen and are martyrs. For it was for bearing witness of that which they had seen, and bearing witness of that which they had heard from them who had seen, that, while their testimony itself displeased the men against whom it was delivered, the martyrs suffered all that they did suffer. The martyrs are God's witnesses. It pleased God to have men for His witnesses, that men also may have God to be their witness. "We have seen," saith he, "and are witnesses." Where have they seen? In the manifestation. What meaneth, in the

manifestation? In the sun, that is, in this light of day. And how should He be seen in the sun who made the sun, except as "in the sun He hath set His tabernacle; and Himself as a bridegroom going forth out of his chamber, exulted as a giant to run His course?"[5] He before the sun,[6] who made the sun, He before the day-star, before all the stars, before all angels, the true Creator, ("for all things were made by Him, and without Him was nothing made,") that He might be seen by eyes of flesh which see the sun, set His very tabernacle in the sun, that is, showed His flesh in manifestation of this light of day: and that Bridegroom's chamber was the Virgin's womb, because in that virginal womb were joined the two, the Bridegroom and the bride, the Bridegroom the Word, and the bride the flesh; because it is written, "And they twain shall be one flesh;"[7] and the Lord saith in the Gospel, "Therefore they are no more twain but one flesh.[8] And Esaias remembers right well that they are two: for speaking in the person of Christ he saith, "He hath set a mitre upon me as upon a bridegroom, and adorned me with an ornament as a bride."[9] One seems to speak, yet makes Himself at once Bridegroom and Bride; because "not two, but one flesh:" because "the Word was made flesh, and dwelt in us." To that flesh the Church is joined, and so there is made the whole Christ, Head and body.

3. "And we are witnesses, and show unto you that eternal life, which was with the Father, and was manifested unto us:" i.e., manifested among us: which might be more plainly expressed, manifested to us. "The things," therefore, "which we have seen and heard, declare we unto you."[10] Those saw the Lord Himself present in the flesh, and heard words from the mouth of the Lord, and told them to us. Consequently we also have heard, but have not seen. Are we then less happy than those who saw and heard? And how does he add, "That ye also may have fellowship with us"? Those saw, we have not seen, and yet we are fellows; because we hold the faith in common. For there was one who did not believe even upon seeing, and would needs handle, and so believe, and said, "I will not believe except I thrust my fingers into the place of the nails, and touch His scars."[11] And He did give Himself for a time to be handled by the hands of men, who always giveth Himself to be seen by the sight of the angels; and that disciple did handle, and exclaimed, "My Lord, and my

1 John i. 1.   2 Ps. lxxviii. 25.   3 1 John i. 2.
4 Edd. *Non calcibus persequamur:* "not virtually trample upon, or kick at them, persecuting the martyrs afresh by turning their festivals into luxurious orgies;" or "not merely walk after them." Morel. *Elem. Crit.* p. 208, cited by Ed. Par, proposes *calicibus persequamur:* Complaining of these excesses. S. Aug. says, *Enarr. in Psa.* 69, sec. 2: *Adhuc illi inimici martyrum quia voce et ferro non possunt, eos sua luxuria persequuntur. Atque utinam Paganos tantum doleremus! ... Videmus etiam portantes in fronte signum Ejus, simul in ipsa fronte portare impudentiam luxuriarum, diebusque et solemnitatibus martyrum non exultare, sed insultare.* On Ps. 59 (al. 60) sec. 15, he has, *modò eos ebriosi calicibus persequuntur,* and one Oxford MS. reads so here. Compare *infra,* Hom. iv. 4.

5 Ps. xix. 4, 5.   6 *Ante luciferum.* Ps. cx. 3.
7 Gen. ii. 24.   8 Matt. xix. 6.
9 Isa lxi. 10. *Enarr. in Ps.* ci. sec. 2.
10 1 John i. 3.   11 John xx. 25-29.

God!" Because he touched the Man, he confessed the God. And the Lord, to console us who, now that He sitteth in heaven, cannot touch Him with the hand, but only reach Him with faith, said to him, "Because thou hast seen, thou hast believed; blessed are they that have not seen, and yet believe. We are here described, we designated. Then let the blessedness take place in us, of which the Lord predicted that it should take place; let us firmly hold that which we see not; because those tell us who have seen. "That ye also," saith he, "may have fellowship with us." And what great matter is it to have fellowship with men? Do not despise it; see what he adds: "and our fellowship may be[1] with God the Father, and Jesus Christ His Son. And these things,"saith he, "we write unto you, that your joy may be full."[2] Full joy he means in that fellowship, in that charity, in that unity.

4. "And this is the message which we have heard of Him, and declare unto you."[3] What is this? Those same have seen, have handled with their hands, the Word of life: He "was from the beginning," and for a time was made visible and palpable, the Only-begotten Son of God. For what thing did He come, or what new thing did He tell us? What was it His will to teach? Wherefore did He this which He did, that the Word should be made flesh, that "God over all things"[4] should suffer indignities from men, that He should endure to be smitten upon the face by the hands which Himself had made? What would He teach? What would He show? What would He declare? Let us hear: for without the fruit of the precept the hearing of the story, how Christ was born, and how Christ suffered, is a mere pastime of the mind, not a strengthening of it. What great thing hearest thou? With what fruit thou hearest, see to that. What would He teach? What declare? Hear. That "God is light," saith he, "and there is no darkness in Him at all."[5]

Hitherto, he hath named indeed the light, but the words are dark: good is it for us that the very light which he hath named should enlighten our hearts, and we should see what he hath said. This it is that we declare, that "God is light, and there is no darkness in Him at all." Who would dare to say that there is darkness in God? Or what is the light? Or what darkness? Lest haply he speaks of such things as pertain to these eyes of ours. "God is light." Saith some man, "The sun also is light, and the moon also is light, and a candle is light." It ought to be something far greater than these, far more excellent, and far more surpassing. How much God is distant from the creature, how much the Maker from the making, how much Wisdom from that which is made by Wisdom, far beyond all things must this light needs be. And haply we shall be near to it, if we get to know what this light is, and apply ourselves unto it, that by it we may be enlightened; because in ourselves we are darkness, and only when enlightened by it can we become light, and not be put to confusion by it, being put to confusion by ourselves. Who is he that is put to confusion by himself? He that knows himself to be a sinner. Who is he that by it is not put to confusion? He who by it is enlightened. What is it to be enlightened by it? He that now sees himself to be darkened by sins, and desires to be enlightened by it, draws near to it: whence the Psalm saith, "Draw near unto Him, and be ye enlightened; and your faces shall not be ashamed."[6] But thou shalt not be shamed by it, if, when it shall show thee to thyself that thou art foul, thine own foulness shall displease thee, that thou mayest perceive its beauty. This it is that He would teach.

5. And may it be that we say this overhastily? Let the apostle himself make this plain in what follows. Remember what was said at the outset of our discourse, that the present epistle commendeth charity: "God is light," saith he, "and in Him is no dark-

---

[1] *Et societas nostra sit.* So Vulg. Mill cites one MS. ἢ μετὰ τοῦ πατρός.
[2] 1 John i. 4.   [3] 1 John i. 5.
[4] Rom. ix. 5. *Deus super omnia:* so *de Trin.* ii. 23, c. Faust. iii. 3, 6, *Propos. ex Ep. ad Rom. Exp.* 59, *super omnes Deus.* S. Aug. constantly refers this clause to Christ. So S. Iren. iii. 18 (*D. super omnes*), Tertull. adv. Prax. 13, 15; Origen (Lat.) *Comm. in Ep. ad Rom.* vii. 13; St. Cypr. *adv. Jud.* ii. 6; St. Hilar. *de Trin.* viii. 37; St. Ambros *de Sp. Sa.* i. 3, sec. 39; in all these it is *De super omnia* or *super omnia Deus.*
[5] 1 John i. 5. [*God is Light; God is Love.*—The Apostle gives in these two great words indications of the Divine essence, so far as it can be conveyed or suggested in human language. He had before said (John iv. 24), narrating the words of the Lord Jesus, "*God is spirit*" (not, *a* spirit). In this epistle he declares to us that *God is light*, and *God is love.*

God is light, not "*a* light" (Luther) or even "the light," but "light" in the most absolute sense. In the text, Augustin forcibly employs this language in reference to sins; they, he says, are "our darkness." In the phrase of the apostle we may recognize a declaration altogether unrestricted and absolute with respect to the essence of God. Surely, He cannot be fully or adequately apprehended

by man. Yet, He communicates Himself. He is revealed in His works; in them "the invisible things" of Him are clearly seen. His pure and glorious light shines; darkness confines; light is diffusive, without limit: by the light emanating from Him, alone, is God seen (Philo).

But God, adds the apostle, is *love.* Love has its source in God. It belongs to His essence, to His very nature. Like light it is diffusive; in its self-communication it begets love. Love discloses to us the personality of God. His love meets with returns from personal beings to whom it comes and whom it enters; he that loveth is born of God and knoweth God. Apart from creation God is love, and before creation He had in Himself the perfect object of love; in the unity of the One God, in the communion of the Father and the Son, and the perfect response of love in and by the Holy Spirit (the activity of love is affirmed in Scripture of each person of the Holy Trinity), uniting both in the society and fellowship of love.

Such love, manifested in the Gospel, encourages us to draw nigh in confidence to Him who is Love, and who may be loved. —J. H. M.]
[6] Ps. xxxiv. 5.

ness at all." And what said he above? "That ye may have fellowship with us, and our fellowship may be with God the Father, and with His Son Jesus Christ." But moreover, if "God be light, and in Him is no darkness at all, and we *must* have fellowship with Him," then from us also must the darkness be driven away, that there may be light created in us, for darkness cannot have fellowship with light. To this end, see what follows: "If we say that we have fellowship with Him, and walk in darkness, we lie."[1] Thou hast also the Apostle Paul saying, "Or what fellowship hath light with darkness?"[2] Thou sayest thou hast fellowship with God, and thou walkest in darkness; "and God is light, and in Him is no darkness at all:" then how should there be fellowship between light and darkness? At this point therefore a man may say to himself, What shall I do? how shall I be light? I live in sins and iniquities. There steals upon him, as it were, a desperation and sadness. There is no salvation save in the fellowship of God. "God is light, and in Him is no darkness at all." But sins are darkness, as the Apostle saith of the devil and his angels, that they are "rulers of this darkness."[3] He would not call them rulers of darkness, save as rulers of sins, having lordship over the wicked. Then what are we to do, my brethren? Fellowship[4] with God must be had, other hope of life eternal is none; now "God is Light, and in Him is no darkness at all:" now iniquities are darkness; by iniquities we are pressed down, that we cannot have fellowship with God: what hope have we then? Did I not promise to speak something during these days, that shall cause gladness? Which if I make not good, this is sadness. "God is Light, and in Him is no darkness at all;" sins are darkness: what shall become of us? Let us hear, whether peradventure He will console, lift up, give

hope, that we faint not by the way. For we are running, and running to our own country; and if we despair of attaining, by that very despair we fail. But He whose will it is that we attain, that He may keep us safe in our own land, feedeth us in the way. Hear we then: "If we say that we have fellowship with Him and walk in darkness, we lie, and do not the truth." Let us not say that we have fellowship with Him, if we walk in darkness. "If we walk in the light, as He is in the light, we have fellowship one with another."[5] Let us walk in the light, as He is in the light, that we may be able to have fellowship with Him. And what are we to do about our sins? Hear what follows, "And the blood of Jesus Christ His Son shall purge[6] us from all sin."[7] Great assurance hath God given! Well may we celebrate the Passover, wherein was shed the blood of the Lord, by which we are cleansed "from all sin!" Let us be assured: the "handwriting which was against us,"[8] the bond of our slavery, the devil held, but by the blood of Christ it is blotted out. "The blood," saith he, "of His Son shall purge us from all sin." What meaneth, "from all sin"? Mark: lo even now, in the name of Christ whom these[9] here have now confessed, who are called infants,[10] have all their sins been cleansed. They came in old, they went out new. How, came in old, went out new? Old men they came in, infants they went out. For the old life is old age with all its dotage, but the new life is the infancy of regeneration. But what are we to do? The past sins are pardoned, not only to these but to us; and after the pardon and abolition of all sins, by living in this world in the midst of temptations, some haply have been contracted. Therefore what he can, let man do; let him confess himself to be what he is, that he may be cured by Him who always is what He is: for He always was and is; we were not and are.

6. For see what He saith; "If we say that we have no sin, we deceive ourselves, and the truth is not in us."[11] Consequently, if thou hast confessed thyself a sinner, the truth is in thee: for the Truth itself is light. Thy life hath not yet shone in perfect brightness, because there are sins in thee; but yet thou hast already begun to be enlightened, because there is in thee the confession of sins. For see what follows: "If we confess our sins,[12] He is faithful and just to forgive us our sins, and to purge us from all iniquity."[13] Not

---

[1] 1 John i. 6.   [2] 2 Cor. vi. 14.   [3] Eph. vi. 12.
[4] [*Fellowship.*—The primary object of the apostle's communication in this epistle (1 John i. 3), is that his readers may have fellowship with the apostolic body, and, in connection with them, fellowship with the Father and with His Son, Jesus Christ.
St. John's message contemplates both a human and a Divine fellowship. The union among believers is described and emphasized, and he points also to the manifold blessings that flow from the Divine fellowship. The fruits of this revelation—of the disclosures of the love of God,—the apostle intimates are not for that age only, but for all who should afterwards believe ; a thought which Augustin brings out in the text by adducing the history of Thomas (John xx. 24–29), and the consolation administered to him by the Lord, with the wider comfort for all His disciples : "Blessed are they that have not seen, and yet believe."
The life, "even the life eternal," is manifested in this joyous fellowship, which is set forth by St. John in different forms of expression; it is reciprocal. "Hereby we know that we abide in Him and He in us" (1 John iv. 13). Again, it is presented as the abiding of man in God: "By this we know that we are in Him" (ii. 5). "We know that the Son of God hath come, and we are in Him is true" (v. 20). Again, the twofold fellowship (human and Divine), is represented as the abiding of God (or Christ) in man. "If we love one another, God abideth in us" (iv. 12). Among the results of this Divine-human fellowship, the apostle names, *confidence, growing purity* and *love* (ii. 28 ; iii. 3, 10).—J. H. M.]

[5] 1 John i. 7.   [6] [Gr. present, καθαρίζει, cleanseth.]
[7] *Delicto*.   [8] Col. ii. 14.
[9] The newly baptized.   [10] Neophytes.
[11] 1 John i. 8.   [12] *Delicta*.   [13] 1 John i. 9.

only the past, but haply if we have contracted any from this life; because a man, so long as he bears the flesh, cannot but have some at any rate light sins. But these which we call light, do not thou make light of. If thou make light of them when thou weighest them, be afraid when thou countest them. Many light make one huge sin: many drops fill the river; many grains make the lump. And what hope is there? Before all, confession: lest any think himself righteous, and, before the eyes of God who seeth that which is, man, that was not and is, lift up the neck. Before all, then, confession; then, love: for of charity what is said? "Charity covereth a multitude of sins."[1] Now let us see whether he commendeth charity in regard of the sins which subsequently overtake us: because charity alone extinguisheth sins. Pride extinguisheth charity: therefore humility strengtheneth charity; charity extinguisheth sins. Humility goes along with confession, the humility by which we confess ourselves sinners: this is humility, not to say it with the tongue, as if only to avoid arrogancy, lest we should displease men if we should say that we are righteous. This do the ungodly and insane: "I know indeed that I am righteous, but what shall I say before men? If I shall call myself righteous, who will bear it, who tolerate? let my righteousness be known unto God: I however will say that I am a sinner, but only that I may not be found odious for arrogancy." Tell men what thou art, tell God what thou art. Because if thou tell not God what thou art, God condemneth what He shall find in thee. Wouldest thou not that He condemn thee? Condemn thou. Wouldest thou that He forgive? do thou acknowledge, that thou mayest be able to say unto God, "Turn Thy face from my sins."[2] Say also to Him those words in the same Psalm, "For I acknowledge mine iniquity." "If we confess our sins, He is faithful and just to forgive us our sins, and to purge us from all iniquity. If we say that we have not sinned, we make Him a liar, and His word is not in us."[3] If thou shalt say, I have not sinned, thou makest Him a liar, while thou wishest to make thyself true. How is it possible that God should be a liar, and man true, when the Scripture saith the contrary, "Every man a liar, God alone true"?[4] Consequently, God true through Himself, thou true through God; because through thyself, a liar.

7. And lest haply he should seem to have given impunity for sins, in that he said, "He is faithful and just to cleanse us from all iniquity;" and men henceforth should say to themselves, Let us sin, let us do securely what we will, Christ purgeth us, is faithful and just, purgeth us from all iniquity: He taketh from thee an evil security, and putteth in an useful fear. To thine own hurt thou wouldest be secure; thou must be solicitous. For "He is faithful and just to forgive us our sins," provided thou always displease thyself, and be changing until thou be perfected. Accordingly, what follows? "My little children, these things I write unto you, that ye sin not."[5] But perchance sin overtakes us from our mortal life: what shall be done then? What? shall there be now despair? Hear: "And if any man sin, we have an advocate with the Father, Jesus Christ the righteous: and He is the propitiator for our sins."[6] He then is the advocate; do thou thine endeavor not to sin: if from the infirmity of this life sin shall overtake thee, see to it straightway, straightway be displeased, straightway condemn it; and when thou hast condemned, thou shalt come assured unto the Judge. There hast thou the advocate: fear not to lose thy cause in thy confession. For if oft-times in this life a man commits his cause to an eloquent tongue, and is not lost; thou committest thyself to the Word, and shalt thou be lost? Cry, "We have an advocate with the Father."

8. See John himself observing humility. Assuredly he was a righteous and a great man, who from the Lord's bosom drank in the secrets of His mysteries; he, the man who by drinking from the Lord's bosom indited[7] of His Godhead, "In the beginning was the Word, and the Word was with God:" he, being such a man as this, saith not, Ye have an advocate with the Father; but, "If any man sin, an advocate," saith he, "have we." He saith not, ye have; nor saith, ye have me; nor saith, ye have Christ Himself: but he puts Christ, not himself, and saith, also, "We have," not, ye have. He chose rather to put himself in the number of sinners that he might have Christ for his advocate, than to put himself in Christ's stead as advocate, and to be found among the proud that shall be condemned. Brethren, Jesus Christ the righteous, even Him have we for our advocate with the Father; "He," even He, "is the propitiation for our sins." This whoso hath held fast, hath made no heresy; this whoso hath held fast, hath made no schism. For whence came schisms? When men say, "we" are righteous, when men say, "we" sanctify the unclean, "we"

---

[1] 1 Pet. iv. 8.   [2] Ps. li. 9, 3.
[3] 1 John i. 9, 10.   [4] Rom. iii. 4.

[5] 1 John ii. 1.   [6] 1 John ii. 1, 2.   [7] *Ructavit.*

justify the ungodly; " we" ask, " we" obtain. But what saith John ? "And if any man sin, we have an advocate with the Father, Jesus Christ the righteous." But some man will say: then do the saints not ask for us ? Then do bishops and rulers not ask for the people ? Yea, but mark the Scriptures, and see that rulers also commend themselves to the prayers of the people. Thus the apostle saith to the congregation, " Praying withal for us also." [1] The apostle prayeth for the people, the people prayeth for the apostle. We pray for you, brethren: but do ye also pray for us. Let all the members pray one for another; let the Head intercede for all. Therefore it is no marvel that he here goes on and shuts the mouths of them that divide the Church of God. For he that has said, " We have Jesus Christ the righteous, and He is the propitiation for our sins:" having an eye to those who would divide themselves, and would say, "Lo, here is Christ, lo, there;" [2] and would show Him in a part who bought the whole and possesses the whole, he forthwith goes on to say, " Not our sins only, but also the sins of the whole world." What is this, brethren ? Certainly "we have found it in the fields of the woods," [3] we have found the Church in all nations. Behold, Christ " is the propitiation for our sins; not ours only, but also the sins of the whole world." Behold, thou hast the Church throughout the whole world; do not follow false justifiers who in truth are cutters off. Be thou in that mountain which hath filled the whole earth: because " Christ is the propitiation for our sins; not only ours, but also the sins of the whole world," which He hath bought with His blood.

9. "And in this," saith he, " we do know Him,[4] if we keep His commandments." [5] What commandments ? " He that saith, I know Him, and keepeth not His commandments, is a liar, and the truth is not in him." But still thou askest, What commandments ? " But whoso," saith he, " keepeth His word, in him verily is the love of God perfected." [6] Let us see whether this same commandment be not called love. For we were asking, what commandments ? and he saith, " But whoso keepeth His word, in him verily is the love of God perfected." Mark the Gospel, whether this be not the commandment: " A new commandment," saith the Lord, " give I unto you, that ye love one another.[7]—In

this we know that we are in Him, if in Him we be perfected." [8] Perfected in love, he calls them: what is perfection of love ? To love even enemies, and love them for this end, that they may be brethren. For not a carnal love ought ours to be. To wish a man temporal weal, is good; but though that fail, let the soul be safe. Dost thou wish life to any that is thy friend ? Thou doest well. Dost thou rejoice at the death of thine enemy ? Thou doest ill. But haply both to thy friend the life thou wishest him is not for his good, and to thine enemy the death thou rejoicest at hath been for his good. It is uncertain whether this present life be profitable to any man or unprofitable: but the life which is with God without doubt is profitable. So love thine enemies as to wish them to become thy brethren; so love thine enemies as that they may be called into thy fellowship. For so loved He who, hanging on the cross, said, " Father, forgive them, for they know not what they do." [9] For he did not say, Father let them live long, me indeed they kill, but let them live. He was casting out from them the death which is for ever and ever, by His most merciful prayer, and by His most surpassing might. Many of them believed, and the shedding of the blood of Christ was forgiven them. At first they shed it while they raged; now they drank it while they believed. " In this we know that we are in Him, if in Him we be made perfect." Touching the very perfection of love of enemies, the Lord admonishing, saith, " Be ye therefore perfect, as your Heavenly Father is perfect.[10] He," therefore, " that saith he abideth in Him, ought himself also so to walk, even as He walked." [11] How, brethren ? what doth he advise us ? " He that saith he abideth in Him," i.e., in Christ, " ought himself also so to walk even as He walked." Haply the advice is this, that we should walk on the sea ? That be far from us ! It is this then, that we walk in the way of righteousness. In what way ? I have already mentioned it. He was fixed upon the cross, and yet was He walking in this very way: this way is the way of charity, " Father, forgive them, for they know not what they do." If, therefore, thou have learned to pray for thine enemy, thou walkest in the way of the Lord.

10. " Dearly beloved, I write unto you no new commandment, but the old commandment which ye had from the beginning." [12] What commandment calls he " old ? Which

---

[1] Col. iv. 3.			[2] Matt. xxiv. 23.			[3] Ps. cxxxii. 6.
[4] *In hoc cognoscimus eum, si:* but all the Greek copies, ἐν τούτῳ γινώσκομεν ὅτι ἐγνώκαμεν αὐτόν, ἐάν. Vulg. *In hoc scimus quoniam cognovimus eum, si.*
[5] 1 John ii. 3, 4.		[6] 1 John ii. 5.		[7] John xiii. 34.
30

[8] 1 John ii. 5. *Si in ipso perfecti fuerimus.* Augustin and two or three Latin MSS.: an addition unknown to the Greek and to the other copies of the Latin.
[9] Luke xxiii. 34.				[10] Matt. v. 48.
[11] 1 John ii. 6.				[12] 1 John ii. 7.

ye had," saith he, "from the beginning. Old" then, in this regard, that ye have already heard it: otherwise he will contradict the Lord, where He saith, "A new commandment give I unto you, that ye love one another." [1] But why an "old" commandment? Not as pertaining to the old man. But why? "Which ye had from the beginning. The old commandment is the word which ye have heard." Old then, in this regard, that ye have already heard it. And the selfsame he showeth to be new, saying, "Again, a new commandment write I unto you." [2] Not another, but the selfsame which he hath called old, the same is also new. Why? "Which thing is true in Him and in you." Why old, ye have already heard: i.e., because ye knew it already. But why new? "Because the darkness is past, and the true light now shineth." Lo, whence it is new: because the darkness pertains to the old man, but the light to the new man. What saith the Apostle Paul? "Put ye off the old man, and put ye on the new." [3] And again what saith he? "Ye were sometime darkness, but now light in the Lord." [4]

11. "He that saith he is in the light"— now he is making all clear that he has been saying—"he that saith he is in the light, and hateth his brother, is in darkness even until now." [5] What! my brethren, how long shall we say to you, "Love your enemies"? [6] See whether, what is worse, ye do not hate your brethren. If ye loved only your brethren, ye would be not yet perfect: but if ye hate [7] your brethren, what are ye, where are ye? Let each look to his own heart: let him not keep hatred against his brother for any hard word; on account of earthly contention let him not become earth. For whoso hates his brother, let him not say that he walks in the light. "He that saith he is in the light, and hateth his brother, is in darkness even until now." Thus, some man who was a pagan has become a Christian; mark well: behold he was in darkness, while he was a pagan: now is he made henceforth a Christian; thanks be to God, say all joyfully; the apostle is read, where he saith joyfully, "For ye were sometime darkness, but now light in the Lord." [8] Once he worshipped idols, now he worships God; once he worshipped the things he made, now he worships Him that made him. He is changed: thanks be to God, say all Christians with joyful greeting.

Why? Because henceforth he is one that adores the Father and the Son and the Holy Ghost; one that detests demons and idols. Yet still is John solicitous about our convert: while many greet him with joy, by him he is still looked upon with apprehension. Brethren, let us gladly welcome a mother's solicitude. Not without cause is the mother solicitous about us when others rejoice: by the mother, I mean charity: for she dwelt in the heart of John, when he spake these words. Wherefore, but because there is something he fears in us, even when men now hail us with joy? What is it that he fears? "He that saith he is in the light"—What is this? He that saith now he is a Christian,—"and hateth his brother, is in darkness even until now." Which there is no need to expound: but to be glad of it, if it be not so, or to bewail it, if it be.

12. "He that loveth his brother abideth (*manet*) in the light, and there is none occasion of stumbling in him." [9]—I beseech you by Christ: God is feeding us, we are about to refresh our bodies in the name of Christ; they both are in some good measure refreshed, and are to be refreshed: let the mind be fed. Not that I am going to speak for a long time, do I say this; for behold, the lesson is now coming to an end: but lest haply of weariness we should hear less attentively than we ought that which is most necessary.—"He that loveth his brother abideth in the light, and there is no scandal," or "none occasion of stumbling, in him." Who are they that take scandal or make scandal? They that are offended in Christ, and in the Church. They that are offended in Christ, are as if burnt by the sun, those in the Church as by the moon. But the Psalm saith, "The sun shall not burn thee by day, neither the moon by night: [10] i.e., if thou hold fast charity, neither in Christ shalt thou have occasion of falling, nor in the Church; neither Christ shalt thou forsake, nor the Church. For he that forsakes the Church, how is he in Christ who is not in the members of Christ? How is he in Christ who is not in the body of Christ? Those therefore take scandal, or, occasion of falling, who forsake Christ or the Church. Whence do we understand that the Psalm in saying, "By day shall the sun not burn thee, nor the moon by night," saith it of this, that the burning means scandal, or occasion of stumbling? In the first place mark the similitude itself. Just as the person whom something is burning saith, I cannot bear it, I cannot away with it, and draws back; so those persons

---

[1] John xiii. 34.   [2] 1 John ii. 8.   [3] Col. iii. 9, 10.
[4] Eph. v. 8.   [5] 1 John ii. 9.   [6] Matt. v. 44.
[7] *Si autem oditis.* So ed. Erasm. and four mss. cited in ed. Louvain, which however has in the text *oderitis.* One ms. cited *ibid.* has, *Si autem odistis.* Edd. Lugd. and Ven. have *si autem auditis,* "if ye are called brethren." Four Oxf. mss. *oditis.*
[8] Eph. v. 8.

[9] 1 John ii. 10.   Ps. cxxi. 6.

who cannot bear some things in the Church, and withdraw themselves either from the name of Christ or from the Church, are taking scandal. For see how those took scandal as from the sun, those carnal ones to whom Christ preached of His flesh, saying, "He that eateth not the flesh of the Son of Man and drinkech His blood, shall have no life in him."[1] Some seventy persons[2] said, "This is an hard saying," and went back from Him, and there remained the twelve. All those the sun burnt, and they went back, not being able to bear the force of the Word. There remained therefore the twelve. And lest haply men should imagine that they confer a benefit upon Christ by believing on Christ, and not that the benefit is conferred by Him upon them; when the twelve were left, the Lord said to them, "Will ye also go?" That ye may know that I am necessary to you, not ye to me. But those whom the sun had not burnt, answered by the voice of Peter: "Lord, Thou hast the word[3] of eternal life; whither shall we go?" But who are they that the Church as the moon burneth by night? They that have made schisms. Hear the very word used in the apostle: "Who is offended, and I burn not?"[4] In what sense then is it, that there is no scandal or occasion of stumbling in him that loveth his brother? Because he that loveth his brother, beareth all things for unity's sake; because it is in the unity of charity that brotherly love exists. Some one, I know not who, offendeth thee: whether it be a bad man, or as thou supposest a bad man, or as thou pretendest a bad man: and dost thou desert so many good men? What sort of brotherly love is that which hath appeared in these[5] persons? While they accuse the Africans, they have deserted the whole world! What, were there no saints in the whole world? Or was it possible they should be condemned by you unheard? But oh! if ye loved your brethren, there would be none occasion of stumbling in you. Hear thou the Psalm, what it saith: "Great peace have they

that love Thy law, and there is to them none occasion of stumbling."[6] Great peace it saith there is for them that love the law of God, and that is why there is to them none occasion of stumbling. Those then who take scandal, or, occasion of stumbling, destroy peace. And of whom saith he that they take not and make not occasion of stumbling? They that love God's law. Consequently they are in charity. But some man will say, "He said it of them that love God's law, not of the brethren." Hear thou what the Lord saith: "A new commandment give I unto you, that ye love one another."[7] What is the Law but commandment? Moreover, how is it they do not take occasion of stumbling, but because they forbear one another? As Paul saith, "Forbearing one another in love, studying to keep the unity of the Spirit in the bond of peace."[8] And to show that this is the law of Christ, hear the same apostle commending this very law. "Bear ye one another's burdens," saith he, "and so shall ye fulfill the law of Christ."[9]

12. "For he that hateth his brother is in darkness, and walketh in darkness, and knoweth not whither he goeth."[10] A great thing, my brethren: mark it, we beseech you. "He that hateth his brother walketh in darkness, and knoweth not whither he goeth, because the darkness hath blinded his eyes." What so blind as these who hate their brethren? For that ye may know that they are blind, they have stumbled at a Mountain. I say the same things often, that they may not slip out of your memory. The Stone which was "cut out of the Mountain without hands," is it not Christ, who came of the kingdom of the Jews, without the work of man?[11] Has not that Stone broken in pieces all the kingdoms of the earth, that is, all the dominations of idols and demons? Has not that Stone grown, and become a great mountain, and filled the whole earth? Do we point with the finger to this Mountain in like manner as the moon on its third day[12] is pointed out to men? For example, when they wish people to see the new moon, they say, Lo, the moon! lo, where it is! and if there be some there who are not sharpsighted, and say, Where? then the finger is put forth that they may see it. Sometimes when they are ashamed to be thought blind,

---

[1] John vi. 54–69.
[2] So in Epist. 173, sec. 30, Augustin writes, *Attendis enim et sæpe repetis, sicut audio, quod in Evangelio scriptum est recessisse a Domino septuaginta discipules . . . . . cæterisque duodecim qui remanserant fuisse responsum, Numquid et vos vultis abire?* The notion entertained by some of the Ancients and, as it seems, by St. Augustin, that the disciples who took offense at our Lord's discourse in the synagogue of Capernaum were the Seventy, may have been derived from the Hypotyposes of St. Clem. Alex. (comp. Euseb. H. E. i. 12) or one of the Clementines. (Thus S. Epiphanius *Hær.* 51, p. 186, 188, relates from some such authority, that the Evangelists Mark and Luke were of the number of the Seventy, and of those who were offended; and that they were reclaimed to the faith, the one by St. Peter, the other by St. Paul.) But the notion, from whatever quarter it came, seems to have no foundation in Scripture, since it is sufficiently evident that the mission of the Seventy, Luke x. 1, was subsequent to the first miracle of feeding, John vi.; Luke ix. 12.
[3] *Verbum.*　　　[4] 2 Cor. xi. 29.　　　[5] Donatists.

[6] Ps. cxix. 165.　　　[7] John xiii. 34.　　　[8] Eph. iv. 2, 3.
[9] Gal. vi. 2.　　　[10] 1 John ii. 11.
[11] *Supra*, Hom. in Ev. iv. 4; Dan. ii. 34, 35.
[12] *Luna tertia:* i.e. the moon at its first appearance: for the first phasis in Africa as in Egypt usually took place on the third day after conjunction. See the passages cited from Geminus in the *Uranolog.* vii. 39, B. Horapoll, *Hieroglyph.* i. 66, in Mr. Greswell's *Dissertations on the Harmony of the Gospels*, vol. i. p. 323, note.

they say they have seen what they have not seen. Do we in this way point out the Church, my brethren? Is it not open? Is it not manifest? Has it not possessed all nations? Is not that fulfilled which so many years before was promised to Abraham, that in his seed should all nations be blessed?[1] It was promised to one believer, and the world is filled with thousands of believers. Behold here the mountain filling the whole face of the earth! Behold the city of which it is said, "A city set upon a mountain cannot be hid!"[2] But those stumble at the mountain, and when it is said to them, Go up; "There is no mountain," say they, and dash their heads against it sooner than seek a habitation there. Esaias was read yesterday; whosoever of you was awake not with his eyes only but with his ear, and not the ear of the body but the ear of the heart, noted this; "In the last days shall the mountain of the house of the Lord be manifest, prepared upon the top of the mountains."[3] What so manifest as a mountain? But there are even mountains unknown, because they are situated in one part of the earth. Which of you knows Mount Olympus? Just as the people who dwell there do not know our Giddaba. These mountains are in different parts of the earth. But not so that Mountain, for it hath filled the whole face of the earth, and of it is said, "Prepared upon the top of the mountains." It is a Mountain above the tops of all mountains. "And," saith he, "to it shall be gathered all nations." Who can fail to be aware of this Mountain? Who breaks his head by stumbling against it? Who is ignorant of the city set upon a mountain? But marvel not that it is unknown by these who hate the brethren, because they walk in darkness and know not whither they go, because the darkness hath blinded their eyes. They do not see the Mountain: I would not have thee marvel; they have no eyes. How is it they have no eyes? Because the darkness hath blinded them. How do we prove this? Because they hate the brethren, in that, while they are offended at Africans, they separate themselves from the whole earth: in that they do not tolerate for the peace of Christ those whom they defame, and do tolerate for the sake of Donatus[4] those whom they condemn.

---

[1] Gen. xxii. 18.   [2] Matt. v. 14.   [3] Is. ii. 2.

[4] See on Ps. xxxvii. Ser. 2

HOMILY II.

1 JOHN II. 12–17.

"I write unto you, little children, because your sins are forgiven through His name. I write unto you, fathers, because ye have known Him that is from the beginning. I write unto you, young men, because ye have overcome the wicked one. I write unto you, children, because ye have known the Father. I write[1] unto you, fathers, because ye have known Him that is from the beginning. I write unto you, young men, because ye are strong, and the word of God abideth in you, and ye have overcome the wicked one. Love not the world, neither the things that are in the world. If any man love the world, the love of the Father is not in him. For all that is in the world, is the lust of the flesh, and the lust of the eyes, and the pride of life, which is not of the Father, but is of the world. And the world passeth away, and the lust thereof: but he that doeth the will of God abideth for ever (even as God also abideth for ever).

1. ALL things that are read from the Holy Scriptures in order to our instruction and salvation, it behoves us to hear with earnest heed. Yet most of all must those things be commended to our memory, which are of most force against heretics; whose insidious designs cease not to circumvent all that are weaker and more negligent. Remember that our Lord and Saviour Jesus Christ both died for us, and rose again; died, to wit, for our offenses, rose again for our justification.[2] Even as ye have just heard concerning the

---

[1] [Have written, A. V.]   [2] Rom. iv. 25.

two disciples whom He met with in the way, how "their eyes were holden that they should not know Him:"[1] and He found them despairing of the redemption that was in Christ, and deeming that now He had suffered and was dead as a man, not accounting that as Son of God He ever liveth; and deeming too that He was so dead in the flesh as not to come to life again, but just as one of the prophets: as those of you who were attentive have just now heard their own words. Then "He opened to them the Scriptures, beginning at Moses," and going through all the prophets, showing them that all He had suffered had been foretold, lest they should be more staggered if the Lord should rise again, and the more fail to believe Him, if these things had not been told before concerning Him. For the firmness of faith is in this, that all things which came to pass in Christ were foretold. The disciples, then, knew Him not, save "in the breaking of bread." And truly he that eateth and drinketh not judgment to himself in the breaking of bread doth know Christ.[2] Afterward also those eleven "thought they saw a spirit." He gave Himself to be handled by them, who also gave Himself to be crucified; to be crucified by enemies, to be handled by friends: yet the Physician of all, both of the ungodliness of those, and of the unbelief of these. For ye heard when the Acts of the Apostles were read, how many thousands of Christ's slayers believed.[3] If those believed afterwards who had killed, should not those believe who for a little while doubted? And yet even in regard of them, (a thing which ye ought especially to observe, and to commit to your memory, because that which shall make us strong against insidious errors, God has been pleased to put in the Scriptures, against which no man dares to speak, who in any sort wishes to seem a Christian), when He had given Himself to be handled by them, that did not suffice Him, but He would also confirm by means of the Scriptures the heart of them that believe: for He looked forward to us who should be afterwards; seeing that in Him we have nothing that we can handle, but have that which we may read. For if those believed only because they held and handled, what shall we do? Now, Christ is ascended into heaven; He is not to come save at the end, to judge the quick and the dead. Whereby shall we believe, but by that whereby it was His will that even those who handled Him should be confirmed? For He opened to them the Scriptures and showed them that

it behoved Christ to suffer, and that all things should be fulfilled which were written of Him in the Law of Moses, and the Prophets, and the Psalms. He embraced in His discourse the whole ancient text of the Scriptures. All that there is of those former Scriptures tells of Christ; but only if it find ears. He also "opened their understanding that they might understand the Scriptures." Whence we also must pray for this, that He would open our understanding.

2. But what did the Lord show written of Him in the Law of Moses, and the Prophets, and the Psalms? What did He show? Let Himself say. The evangelist has put this briefly, that we might know what in all that great compass of the Scriptures we ought to believe and to understand. Certainly there are many pages, and many books; the contents of them all is this which the Lord briefly spake to His disciples. What is this? That "it behoved Christ to suffer, and to rise again the third day." Thou hast it now concerning the Bridegroom, that "it behoved Christ to suffer, and to rise again:" the Bridegroom has been set forth to us. Concerning the Bride, let us see what He saith; that thou, when thou knowest the Bridegroom and the Bride, mayest not without reason come to the marriage. For every celebration is a celebration of marriage: the Church's nuptials are celebrated. The King's Son is about to marry a wife, and that King's Son is Himself a King: and the guests frequenting the marriage are themselves the Bride. Not, as in a carnal marriage, some are guests, and another is she that is married; in the Church they that come as guests, if they come to good purpose, become the Bride. For all the Church is Christ's Bride, of which the beginning and first fruits is the flesh of Christ: there was the Bride joined to the Bridegroom in the flesh. With good reason when He would betoken that same flesh, He brake bread, and with good reason "in the breaking of bread," the eyes "of the disciples were opened, and they knew Him." Well then, what did the Lord say was written of Him in the Law and Prophets and Psalms? That "it behoved Christ to suffer." Had He not added, "and to rise again," well might those mourn whose eyes were holden; but "to rise again" is also foretold. And wherefore this? Why did it behove Christ to suffer and to rise again? Because of that Psalm which we especially commended to your attention on the fourth day, the first station, of last week.[4] Why did it behove

---

[1] Luke xxiv. 13-28.   [2] 1 Cor. xi. 29.   [3] Acts ii. 41.   [4] Tertull. *de Jejun.*, sec. 14; *de Orat.*, sec. 14.

Christ to suffer and to rise again? For this reason: "All the ends of the earth shall be reminded and converted unto the Lord, and all the kindreds of the nations shall worship before Him."[1] For that ye may know that it behoved Christ to suffer and to rise again; in this place also what hath He added, that after setting forth the Bridegroom He might also set forth the Bride? "And that there be preached," saith He, "in His name, repentance and remission of sins throughout all nations, beginning at Jerusalem." Ye have heard, brethren; hold it fast. Let no man doubt concerning the Church, that it is "throughout all nations:" let no man doubt that it began at Jerusalem, and hath filled all nations. We know the field where the Vine is planted: but when it is grown we know it not, because it has taken up the whole. Whence did it begin? "At Jerusalem." Whither has it come? To "all nations." A few remain: it shall possess all. In the mean time, while it is taking possession of all, it has seemed good to the Husbandman to cut off some unprofitable branches, and they have made heresies and schisms. Let not the branches that are cut off induce you to be cut off: rather exhort ye them that are cut off that they be graffed in again. It is manifest that Christ hath suffered, is risen again, and is ascended into heaven: made manifest also is the Church, because there is "preached in His name repentance and remission of sins throughout all nations." Whence did it begin? "Beginning at Jerusalem." The man hears this; foolish and vain, and (how shall I express it?) worse than blind! so great a mountain, and he does not see it; a candle set upon a candlestick, and he shuts his eyes against it!

3. When we say to them, If ye be Catholic Christians, communicate with that Church from which the Gospel is spread abroad over the whole earth: communicate with that Jerusalem:[2] when this we say to them, they make answer to us, we do not communicate with that city where our King was slain, where our Lord was slain: as though they hate the city where our Lord was slain. The Jews slew Him whom they found on earth, these scorn[3] Him that sitteth in heaven! Which are the worse; those who despised Him because they thought Him man, or those who scorn the sacraments of Him whom now they confess to be God? But they hate, forsooth, the city in which their Lord was slain! Pious men, and merciful! they much grieve that Christ was slain, and in men they slay

Christ! But He loved that city, and pitied it: from it He bade the preaching of Him begin, "beginning at Jerusalem." He made there the beginning of the preaching of His name: and thou shrinkest back with horror from having communion with that city![4] No marvel that being cut off thou hatest the root. What said He to His disciples? "Sit ye still in the city, because I send my promise[5] upon you." Behold what the city is that they hate! Haply they would love it, if Christ's murderers dwelt in it. For it is manifest that all Christ's murderers, i.e., the Jews, are expelled from that city.[6] That which had in it them that were fierce against Christ, hath now them that adore Christ. Therefore do these men hate it, because Christians are in it. There was it His will that His disciples should tarry, and there that He should send to them the Holy Ghost. Where had the Church its commencement, but where the Holy Ghost came from heaven, and filled the hundred and twenty sitting in one place? That number twelve was made tenfold. They sat, an hundred and twenty persons, and the Holy Ghost came, "and filled the whole place, and there came a sound, as it were the rushing of a mighty wind, and there were cloven tongues like as of fire." Ye have heard the Acts of the Apostles: this was the lesson read to-day:[7] "They began to speak with tongues as the Spirit gave them utterance." And all who were on the spot, Jews who were come from divers nations, recognised each his own tongue, and marvelled that those unlearned and ignorant men had on the sudden learned not one or two tongues, but the tongues of all nations whatsoever. There, then, where all tongues sounded, there was it betokened that all tongues should believe. But these men, who much love Christ, and therefore refuse to communicate with the city which killed Christ, so honor Christ as to affirm that He is left to two tongues, the Latin and the Punic, i.e. African. Christ possess only two tongues! For there are but these two tongues on the side of Donatus, more they have not. Let us awake, my brethren, let us rather see the gift of the Spirit of God, and let us believe the things spoken before concerning Him, and let us see fulfilled the things spoken before in the Psalm: "There are neither speeches nor discourses,[8] but their voices are heard among them.[9] And lest haply the case

---

[1] Ps. xxii. 27.   [2] S. Aug. *Ep. c. Donat. de Unit. Eccl.* sec. 26. [3] *Supra*, Hom. in Ev. xi. sec. 13.

[4] [The words, "Jerusalem, the city," the preacher appears, in this passage, to use interchangeably and sometimes confusedly for the Church—*e.g.*, "all Christ's murderers are expelled from that city," meaning that such are not in the Church.—J. H. M.]
[5] Acts i. 15 ; ii. 1-12.   [6] Enarr. in Ps. lxii. sec. 18; lxiv. sec. 1.
[7] The Acts of the Apostles were read in the seven weeks from Easter to Pentecost. *Supra*, Hom. in Ev. vi. sec. 18.
[8] *Loquelæ nec sermones.*   [9] Ps. xix. 3-4.

be so that the tongues themselves came to one place, and not rather that the gift of Christ came to all tongues, hear what follows: "Into all the earth is their sound gone out, and unto the ends of the world their words." Wherefore this? Because "in the sun hath He set His tabernacle," i.e., in the open light. His tabernacle, His flesh: His tabernacle, His Church: "in the sun" it is set; not in the night, but in the day. But why do those not acknowledge it? Return to the lesson at the place where it ended yesterday, and see why they do not acknowledge it: "He that hateth his brother, walketh in darkness, and knoweth not whither he goeth, because the darkness hath blinded his eyes." For us then, let us see what follows, and not be in darkness. How shall we not be in darkness? If we love the brethren. How is it proved that we love the brotherhood? By this, that we do not rend unity, that we hold fast charity.

4. "I write unto you, little children, because your sins are forgiven you through His name."[1] Therefore, "little children,"[2] because in forgiveness of sins ye have your birth. But through whose name are sins forgiven? Through Augustin's? No, therefore neither through the name of Donatus. Be it thy concern to see who is Augustin, or who Donatus: no, not through the name of Paul, not through the name of Peter. For to them that divided unto themselves the Church, and out of unity essayed to make parties, the mother charity in the apostle travailing in birth with her little ones, exposeth her own bowels, with words doth as it were rend her breasts, bewaileth her children whom she seeth borne out dead, recalleth unto the one Name them that would needs make them many names, repelleth them from the love of her that Christ may be loved, and saith, "Was Paul crucified for you? Or were ye baptized in the name of Paul?"[3] What saith he? "I would not that ye be mine, that so ye may be with me: be ye with me; all we are His who died for us, who was crucified for us": whence here also it is said, "Your sins are forgiven you through His name," not through the name of any man.

5. "I write unto you, fathers."[4] Why first sons? "Because your sins are forgiven you through His name," and ye are regenerated into a new life, therefore sons. Why fathers? "Because ye have known Him that is from the beginning:" for the beginning hath relation unto fatherhood. Christ new in flesh, but ancient in Godhead. How ancient think we? how many years old? Think

we, of greater age[5] than His mother? Assuredly of greater age than His mother, for "all things were made by Him."[6] If all things, then did the Ancient make the very mother of whom the New should be born. Was He, think we, before His mother only? Yea, and before His mother's ancestors is His antiquity. The ancestor of His mother was Abraham; and the Lord saith, "Before Abraham I am."[7] Before Abraham, say we? The heaven and earth, ere man was, were made. Before these was the Lord, nay rather also is. For right well He saith, not, Before Abraham I was, but, "Before Abraham I AM." For that of which one says, "was," is not; and that of which one says, "will be," is not yet: He knoweth not other than to be. As God, He knoweth "to be:" "was," and "will be," He knoweth not. It is one day there, but a day that is for ever and ever. That day yesterday and to-morrow do not set in the midst between them: for when the 'yesterday' is ended, the 'to-day' begins, to be finished by the coming 'to-morrow.' That one day there is a day without darkness, without night, without spaces, without measure, without hours. Call it what thou wilt: if thou wilt, it is a day; if thou wilt, a year; if thou wilt, years. For it is said of this same, "And thy years shall not fail."[8] But when is it called a day? When it is said to the Lord, "To-day have I begotten Thee."[9] From the eternal Father begotten, from eternity begotten, in eternity begotten: with no beginning, no bound, no space of breadth; because He is what is, because Himself is "He that Is." This His name He told to Moses: "Thou shalt say unto them, HE THAT Is hath sent me unto you."[10] Why speak then of "before Abraham"? why, before Noe? why, before Adam? Hear the Scripture: "Before the day-star have I begotten Thee."[11] In fine, before heaven and earth. Wherefore? Because "all things were made by Him, and without Him was nothing made."[12] By this know ye the "fathers:" for they become fathers by acknowledging "That which is from the beginning."

6. "I write unto you, young men." There are sons, are fathers, are young men: sons, because begotten; fathers, because they acknowledge the Beginning; why young men? "Because ye have overcome the wicked one." In the sons, birth: in the fathers, antiquity: in the young men, strength. If the wicked one is "overcome" by the young men, he

---

1 1 John ii. 12.   2 *Filioli*, τεκνία.
3 1 Cor. i. 13.   4 1 John ii. 13.

5 *Major*.   6 John i. 3.   7 John viii. 58.
8 Ps. cii. 27. 9 Ps. ii. 7. 10 Ex. iii. 14.
11 Ps. cx. 3. 12 John i. 3.

fights with us. Fights, but not conquers.[1] Wherefore? Because we are strong, or because He is strong in us who in the hands of the persecutors was found weak? He hath made us strong, who resisted not His persecutors. "For He was crucified of weakness, but He liveth by the power of God."[2]

7. "I write[3] unto you,[4] children."[5] Whence children? "Because ye have known the Father. I write unto you fathers:" he enforceth this, and repeateth,[6] "Because ye have known Him that is from the beginning." Remember that ye are fathers: if ye forget "Him that is from the beginning," ye have lost your fatherhood. "I write unto you, young men." Again and again consider that ye are young men: fight, that ye may overcome: overcome, that ye may be crowned: be lowly, that ye fall not in the fight. "I write unto you, young men, because ye are strong, and the word of God abideth in you, and ye have overcome the wicked one."

8. All these things, my brethren,—"because we have known That which is from the beginning, because we are strong, because we have known the Father,"—do all these, while they in a manner commend[7] knowledge, not commend charity? If we have known, let us love: for knowledge without charity saveth not. "Knowledge[8] puffeth up, charity edifieth."[9] If ye have a mind to confess and not love, ye begin to be like the demons. The demons confessed the Son of God, and said, "What have we to do with Thee?"[10] and were repulsed. Confess and embrace. For those feared for their iniquities; love ye Him that forgiveth your iniquities. But how can we love God, if we love the world? He prepareth us therefore to be inhabited by charity.[11] There are two loves: of the world, and of God: if the love of the world inhabit, there is no way for the love of God to enter in: let the love of the world make way, and the love of God inhabit; let the better have

place. Thou lovedst the world: love not the world: when thou hast emptied thine heart of earthly love, thou shalt drink in love Divine: and thenceforth beginneth charity to inhabit thee, from which can nothing of evil proceed. Hear ye therefore his words, how he goes to work in the manner of one that makes a clearance. He comes upon the hearts of men as a field that he would occupy: but in what state does he find it? If he finds a wood, he roots it up; if he finds the field cleared, he plants it. He would plant a tree there, charity. And what is the wood he would root up? Love of the world. Hear him, the rooter up of the wood! "Love not the world," (for this comes next,) "neither the things that are in the world; if any man love the world, the[12] love of the Father is not in him."[13]

9. Ye have heard that "if any man love the world, the love of the Father is not in him." Let not any say in his heart that this is false, brethren: God saith it; by the Apostle the Holy Ghost hath spoken; nothing more true: "If any man love the world, the love of the Father is not in him." Wouldest thou have the Father's love, that thou mayest be joint-heir with the Son? Love not the world. Shut out the evil love of the world, that thou mayest be filled with[14] the love of God. Thou art a vessel; but as yet thou art full. Pour out what thou hast, that thou mayest receive what thou hast not. Certainly,[15] our brethren are now born again of water and of the Spirit: we also some years ago were born again of water and of the Spirit. Good is it for us that we love not the world, lest the sacraments remain in us unto damnation, not as means of strengthening[16] unto salvation. That which strengthens unto salvation is, to have the root of charity, to have the "power of godliness," not "the form" only.[17] Good is the form, holy the form: but what avails the form, if it hold not the root? The branch that is cut off, is it not cast into the fire? Have the form, but in the root. But in what way are ye rooted so that ye be not rooted up? By holding charity, as saith the Apostle Paul, "rooted and grounded in charity."[18] How shall charity be rooted there, amid the overgrown wilderness of the love of the world? Make clear riddance of the woods. A mighty seed ye are about to put in: let there not be that in the field which shall choke the seed. These are the uprooting words which he hath said: "Love not the world, neither the things that

---

[1] *Pugnat, non expugnat.*   [2] 2 Cor. xiii. 4.
[3] Vulg. *scribo* throughout, but some copies *scripsi*, representing the true reading in the Greek, ἔγραψα, in the last clause of v. 13, and in both clauses of v 14.
[4] *Pueri, παιδία.*   [5] 1 John 13.
[6] The Benedictine editors remark that the Vulgate does not repeat this clause, *Scribo vobis, patres—a principio est*, and that it is absent from the Greek. This remark applies to the Complutensian Greek text, and the edited Latin Vulgate. Of extant Gr. mss., only Mill's Cod. Basil, 3 (Wetstein, 4), of the 15th century, omits the clause: and this, as Wetstein reports, not in v. 14, but in the preceding verse, χράφω ὑμῖν, πατέρες—ἀρχῆς.
[7] *Cognitionem.*   [8] *Scientia.*
[9] 1 Cor. viii. 1.   [10] Matt. viii. 29.
[11] *Sed quomodo poterimus amare Deum, si amamus mundum? Parat nos ergo inhabitari charitate*, and so Bodl. 813. The ed. of Erasmus has,—*separat nos a charitate Dei:* "—if we love the world? It separates us from the charity of God." And so 3 Oxf. mss. Ed. Lugdun., *si amamus mundum? Si amamus mundum, separat nos a charitate Dei. Parat nos ergo inhabitare charitatem:* "—if we love the world? If we love the world, it separates, &c. He prepares us therefore to inhabit charity."—Ed. Par.

[12] *Dilectio.*   [13] 1 John ii. 15.   [14] *Amore Dei.*
[15] The newly baptized.   [16] *Firmamenta.*
[17] 2 Tim. iii. 5.   [18] Eph. iii. 17.

are in the world. If any man love the world, the love of the Father is not in him."[1]

10. "For all that is in the world, is[2] the lust of the flesh, and the lust of the eyes, and the pride[3] of life,"[4] three things he hath said, which[2] are not of the Father, but are of the world. And the world passeth away, and the lust thereof: but he that doeth the will of God abideth for ever, even as He abideth for ever."[5] Why am I not to love what God made? What wilt thou? Whether wilt thou love the things of time, and pass away with time; or not love the world, and live to eternity with God? The river of temporal things hurries one along: but like a tree sprung up beside the river is our Lord Jesus Christ.[6] He assumed flesh, died, rose again, ascended into heaven. It was His will to plant Himself, in a manner, beside the river of the things of time. Art thou rushing down the stream to the headlong deep? Hold fast the tree. Is love of the world whirling thee on? Hold fast Christ. For thee He became temporal, that thou mightest become eternal; because He also in such sort became temporal, that He remained still eternal. Something was added to Him from time, not anything went from His eternity. But thou wast born temporal, and by sin wast made temporal: thou wast made temporal by sin, He was made temporal by mercy in remitting sins. How great the difference, when two are in a prison, between the criminal and him that visits him! For upon a time a person comes to his friend and enters in to visit him, and both seem to be in prison; but they differ by a wide distinction. The one, his cause presses down: the other, humanity has brought thither. So in this our mortal state, we were held fast by our guiltiness, He in mercy came down: He entered in unto the captive, a Redeemer not an oppressor. The Lord for us shed His blood, redeemed us, changed our hope. As yet we bear the mortality of the flesh, and take the future immortality upon trust: and on the sea we are tossed by the waves, but we have the anchor of hope already fixed upon the land.

11. But let us "not love the world, neither the things that are in the world. For the things that are in the world, are the lust of the flesh, and the lust of the eyes, and the pride of life." These three are they: lest haply any man say, "The things that are in the world, God made: i.e. heaven and earth,

the sea: the sun, the moon, the stars, all the garniture of the heavens. What is the garniture of the sea? all creeping things. What of the earth? animals, trees, flying creatures. These are 'in the world,' God made them. Why then am I not to love what God hath made?" Let the Spirit of God be in thee, that thou mayest see that all these things are good: but woe to thee if thou love the things made, and forsake the Maker of them! Fair are they to thee: but how much fairer He that formed them! Mark well, beloved. For by similitudes ye may be instructed: lest Satan steal upon you, saying what he is wont to say, Take your enjoyment in the creature of God; wherefore made He those things but for your enjoyment? And men drink themselves drunken, and perish, and forget their own Creator: while not temperately but lustfully they use the things created, the Creator is despised. Of such saith the apostle: "They worshipped and served the creature rather than the Creator, Who is blessed for ever."[7] God doth not forbid thee to love[8] these things, howbeit, not to[9] set thine affections upon them for blessedness, but to approve and praise them to this end, that thou mayest love thy Creator. In the same manner, my brethren, as if a bridegroom should make a ring for his bride, and she having received the ring, should love it more than she loves the bridegroom who made the ring for her: would not her soul be found guilty of adultery in the very gift of the bridegroom, albeit she did but love what the bridegroom gave her? By all means let her love what the bridegroom gave: yet should she say, "This ring is enough for me, I do not wish to see his face now:" what sort of woman would she be? Who would not detest such folly? who not pronounce her guilty of an adulterous mind? Thou lovest gold in place of the man, lovest a ring in place of the bridegroom: if this be in thee, that thou lovest a ring in place of thy bridegroom, and hast no wish to see thy bridegroom; that he has given thee an earnest, serves not to pledge thee to him, but to turn away thy heart from him! For this the bridegroom gives earnest, that in his earnest he may himself be loved. Well then, God gave thee all these things: love Him that made them. There is more that He would fain give thee, that is, His very Self that made these things. But if thou love these—what though God made them—and neglect the Creator and love the world; shall not thy love be accounted adulterous?[10]

---

[1] 1 John ii. 15.
[2] ["Is," better omitted; also "which."]
[3] *Ambitio sæculi.*   [4] 1 John ii. 16, 17.
[5] The last clause, *sicut et Deus manet in æternum,* is peculiar to the Latin authorities, S. Cyprian *ad Quir.* 3, 11, *quomodo et,* &c. and others in Griesbach. It is not received by the Vulgate.
[6] Ps. i. 3.

[7] Rom. i. 25.   [8] *Amare.*   [9] *Diligere.*
[10] *Et amaveris mundum: nonne tuus amor adulterinus ae-putabitur?*—MSS. *et amaveris mundum, delinquis* ("and love

12. For "the world" is the appellation given not only to this fabric which God made, heaven and earth, the sea, things visible and invisible: but the inhabitants of the world are called the world, just as we call a "house" both the walls and them that inhabit therein. And sometimes we praise a house, and find fault with the inhabitants. For we say, A good house; because it is marbled and beautifully [1] ceiled: and in another sense we say, A good house: no man there suffers wrong, no acts of plunder, no acts of oppression, are done there. Now we praise not the building, but those who dwell within the building: yet we call it "house," both this and that. For all lovers of the world, because by love they inhabit the world, just as those inhabit heaven, whose heart is on high while in the flesh they walk on earth: I say then, all lovers of the world are called the world. The same have only these three things, "lust of the flesh, lust of the eyes, vain glory of life." For they lust to eat, drink, cohabit: to use these pleasures. Not surely, that there is no allowed measure in these things? or that when it is said, Love not these things, it means that ye are not to eat, or not to drink, or not to beget children? This is not the thing said. Only, let there be measure, because of the Creator, that these things may not bind you by your loving of them: lest ye love that for enjoyment, which ye ought to have for use. But ye are not put to the proof except when two things are propounded to you, this or that: Wilt thou righteousness or gains? I have not wherewithal to live, have not wherewithal to eat, have not wherewithal to drink. But what if thou canst not have these but by iniquity? Is it not better to love that which thou losest not, than to lose thyself by iniquity? Thou seest the gain of gold, the loss of faith thou seest not. This then, saith he to us, is "the lust of the flesh," *i.e.* the lusting after those things which pertain to the flesh, such as food, and carnal cohabitation, and all other such like.

13 ."And the lust of the eyes:" by "the lust of the eyes," he means all curiosity. Now how wide is the scope of curiosity! This it is that works in spectacles, in theatres, in sacraments of the devil, in magical arts, in dealings [2] with darkness: none other than curiosity. Sometimes it tempts even the servants of God, so that they wish as it were to work a miracle, to tempt God whether He will hear

their prayers in working of miracles; it is curiosity: this is "lust of the eyes;" it "is not of the Father." If God hath given the power, do the miracle, for He hath put it in thy way to do it: for think not that those who have not done miracles shall not pertain to the kingdom of God. When the apostles were rejoicing that the demons were subject to them, what said the Lord to them? "Rejoice not in this, but rejoice because your names are written in heaven." [3] In that would He have the apostles to rejoice, wherein thou also rejoicest. Woe to thee truly if thy name be not written in heaven! Is it woe to thee if thou raise not the dead? is it woe to thee if thou walk not on the sea? is it woe to thee if thou cast not out demons? If thou hast received power to do them, use it humbly, not proudly. For even of certain false prophets the Lord hath said that "they shall do signs and prodigies." [4] Therefore let there be no "ambition of the world:" *Ambitio sæculi*, is Pride. The man wishes to make much of himself in his honors: he thinks himself great, whether because of riches, or because of some power.

14. These three there are, and thou canst find nothing whereby human cupidity can be tempted, but either by the lust of the flesh, or the lust of the eyes, or the pride of life. By these three was the Lord tempted of the devil.[5] By the lust of the flesh He was tempted when it was said to Him, "If thou be the Son of God, speak to these stones that they become bread," when He hungered after His fast. But in what way repelled He the tempter, and taught his soldier how to fight? Mark what He said to him: "Not by bread alone doth man live, but by every word of God." He was tempted also by the lust of the eyes concerning a miracle, when He said to Him, "Cast thyself down: for it is written, He shall give his angels charge concerning thee: and in their hands they shall bear thee up, lest at any time thou dash thy foot against a stone." He resisted the tempter, for to do the miracle, would only have been to seem either to have yielded, or to have done it from curiosity; for He wrought when He would, as God, howbeit as healing the weak. For if He had done it then, He might have been thought to wish only to do a miracle. But lest men should think this, mark what He answered; and when the like temptation shall happen to thee, say thou also the same: "Get thee behind me, Satan; for it is written, Thou shalt not tempt the Lord thy God:" that is, if I do this I shall tempt God. He

the world, thou art delinquent'"), (and so four in the Bodl. Library). Edd. Am. Bad. Er. *et amaveris mundum, amittis Creatorem qui fecit mundum* (" and love the world, thou lettest go the Creator who made the world ')--Ben.
[1] *Laqueata.*   [2] *Malefictis.*   [3] Luke x. 20.   [4] Matt. xxiv. 24.   [5] Matt. iv. 1-10.

said what He would have thee to say. When the enemy suggests to thee, " What sort of man, what sort of Christian, art thou? As yet hast thou done one miracle? or by thy prayers have the dead been raised, or hast thou healed the fevered? if thou wert truly of any moment, thou wouldest do some miracle:" answer and say: "It is written, Thou shalt not tempt the Lord thy God:" therefore I will not tempt God, as if I should belong to God if I do a miracle, and not belong if I do none: and what becomes then of His words, " Rejoice, because your names are written in heaven"? By " pride of life " how was the Lord tempted? When he carried Him up to an high place, and said to Him, "All these will I give thee, if thou wilt fall down and worship me." By the loftiness of an earthly kingdom he wished to tempt the King of all worlds: but the Lord who made heaven and earth trod the devil under foot. What great matter for the devil to be conquered by the Lord? Then what did He in the answer He made to the devil but teach thee the answer He would have thee to make? "It is written, Thou shalt worship the Lord thy God, and Him only shalt thou serve." Holding these things fast, ye shall not have the concupiscence of the world: by not having

concupiscence of the world, neither shall the lust of the flesh, nor the lust of the eyes, nor the pride of life, subjugate you: and ye shall make place for Charity when she cometh, that ye may love God. Because if love of the world be there, love of God will not be there. Hold fast rather the love of God, that as God is for ever and ever, so ye also may remain for ever and ever: because such is each one as is his love. Lovest thou earth? thou shalt be earth. Lovest thou God? what shall I say? thou shalt be a god? I dare not say it of myself, let us hear the Scriptures: "I have said, Ye are gods, and all of you sons of the Most High."[1] If then ye would be gods and sons of the Most High, " Love not the world, neither the things that are in the world. If any man love the world, the love of the Father is not in him. For all the things that are in the world, is the lust of the flesh, and the lust of the eyes, and the pride of life, which is not of the Father, but is of the world:"[2] *i.e.* of men, lovers of the world. "And the world passeth away, and the lusts thereof: but he that doeth the will of God abideth for ever, even as God also abideth for ever."

---

[1] Ps. lxxxii. 6.   [2] 1 John ii. 15-17.

HOMILY III.

1 John II. 18–27.

" Children, it is the last hour: and as ye have heard that antichrist shall come, even now are there many antichrists; whereby we know that it is the last hour. They went out from us, but they were not of us: if they had been of us, they would no doubt have continued with us: but they went out, that they might be made manifest that they were not all of us. But ye have an unction from the Holy One, and know all things.[1] I write unto you, not because ye know not the truth, but because ye know it, and that no lie is of the truth. Who is a liar but he that denieth that Jesus is the Christ? [He is antichrist, that denieth the Father and the Son.][2] Whosoever denieth the Son, the same hath neither the Father nor the Son: and he that acknowledgeth the Son hath both the Father and the Son. Let that therefore abide in you, which ye have heard from the beginning. If that which ye have heard from the beginning shall remain in you, ye also shall continue in the Son, and in the Father. And this is the promise that He hath promised us, even eternal life. These things have I written unto you concerning them that seduce you; that ye may know that ye have an unction, and that the unction which ye have received of him may abide in you. And ye need not that any man teach you; because His unction teacheth you of all things."

---

[1] See sec. 5, note.   [2] Omitted in the Exposition.

1. "Children,[1] it is the[2] last hour." In this lesson he addresses the children that they may make haste to grow, because "it is the last hour." Age or stature[3] of the body is not at one's own will. A man does not grow in respect of the flesh when he will, any more than he is born when he will: but where the being born rests with the will, the growth also rests with the will. No man is "born of water and the Spirit,[4] except he be willing. Consequently if he will, he grows or makes increase: if he will, he decreases. What is it to grow? To go onward[5] by proficiency. What is it to decrease? To go backward[6] by deficiency. Whoso knows that he is born, let him hear that he is an infant; let him eagerly cling to the breasts of his mother, and he grows apace. Now his mother is the Church; and her breasts are the two Testaments of the Divine Scriptures. Hence let him suck the milk of all the things that as signs of spiritual truths were done in time for our eternal salvation,[7] that being nourished and strengthened, he may attain to the eating of solid meat, which is, "In the beginning was the Word, and the Word was with God, and the Word was God."[8] Our milk is Christ in His humility; our meat, the self-same Christ equal with the Father. With milk He nourisheth thee, that He may feed thee with bread: for with the heart spiritually to touch Christ is to know that He is equal with the Father.

2. Therefore it was that He forbade Mary to touch Him, and said to her, "Touch me not; for I am not yet ascended unto the Father."[9] What is this? He gave Himself to be handled by the disciples. and did He shun Mary's touch? Is not He the same that said to the doubting disciple, "Reach hither thy fingers, and feel the scars"?[10] Was He at that time ascended to the Father? Then why doth He forbid Mary, and saith, "Touch me not; for I am not yet ascended to the Father?" Or are we to say, that He feared not to be touched by men, and feared to be touched by women? The touch of Him cleanseth all flesh. To whom He willed first to be manifested, by them feared He to be handled? Was not His resurrection announced by women to the men, that so the serpent should by a sort of counterplot be overcome? For because he first by the woman announced death to man, there-

fore to men was also life announced by a woman. Then why was He unwilling to be touched, but because He would have it to be understood of that spiritual touch? The spiritual touch takes place from a pure heart. That person does of a pure heart reach Christ with his touch who understands Him coequal with the Father. But whoso does not yet understand Christ's Godhead, that person reaches but unto the flesh, reaches not unto the Godhead. Now what great matter is it, to reach only unto that which the persecutors reached unto, who crucified Him? But that is the great thing, to understand the Word God with God, in the beginning, by whom all things were made: such as He would have Himself to be known when He said to Philip, "Am I so long time with you, and have ye not known me, Philip? He that seeth me, seeth also the Father."[11]

3. But lest any be sluggish to go forward, let him hear: "Children, it is the last hour." Go forward, run, grow; "it is the last hour." This same last hour is long; yet it is the last. For he has put "hour" for "the last time;" because it is in the last times that our Lord Jesus Christ is to come.[12] But some will say, How the last times? how the last hour? Certainly antichrist will first come, and then will come the day of judgment. John perceived these thoughts: lest people should in a manner become secure, and think it was not the last hour because antichrist was to come, he said to them, "And as ye have heard that antichrist is to come, now are there come many antichrists." Could it have many antichrists, except it were "the last hour"?

4. Whom has he called antichrists? He goes on and expounds. "Whereby we know that it is the last hour." By what? Because "many antichrists are come. They went out from us;" see the antichrists! "They went out from us:" therefore we bewail the loss. Hear the consolation. "But they were not of us." All heretics, all schismatics went out from us, that is, they go out from the Church; but they would not go out, if they were of us. Therefore, before they went out they were not of us. If before they went out they were not of us, many are within, are not gone out, but yet are antichrists. We dare to say this: and why, but that each one while he is within may not be an antichrist? For he is about to describe and mark the antichrists, and we shall see them now. And each person ought to question his own conscience, whether he be an antichrist. For antichrist in our tongue means, contrary to

---

[1] *Pueri*, παιδία.   [2] [Or "a," Westcott.—J. H. M.]   [3] *Aetas.*
[4] John iii. 5.   [5] *Proficere.*   [6] *Deficere.*
[7] *Omnium sacramentorum temporaliter pro æterna salute nostra gestorum : i.e.* of the historical facts of both Testaments understood in their inward and spiritual relation to Christ.
[8] John i. 1.   [9] *Supra*, Hom. cxxi. and xxvi.
[10] John xx. 17, 27.

[11] John xiv. 9.   [12] Epist. 199, *de Fine Sæc.*, sec. 17.

Christ.[1] Not, as some take it, that antichrist is to be so called because he is to come *ante Christum*, before Christ, *i.e.* Christ to come after him: it does not mean this, neither is it thus written, but *Antichristus, i.e.* contrary to Christ. Now who is contrary to Christ ye already perceive from the apostle's own exposition, and understand that none can go out but antichrists; whereas those who are not contrary to Christ, can in no wise go out. For he that is not contrary to Christ holds fast in His body, and is counted therewith as a member. The members are never contrary one to another. The entire body consists of all the members. And what saith the apostle concerning the agreement of the members? " If one member suffer, all the members suffer with it; and if one member be glorified, all the members rejoice with it."[2] If then in the glorifying of a member the other members rejoice with it, and in its suffering all the members suffer, the agreement of the members hath no antichrist. And there are those who inwardly are in such sort in the body of our Lord Jesus Christ—seeing His body is yet under cure, and the soundness will not be perfect save in the resurrection of the dead— are in such wise in the body of Christ, as bad humors. When these are vomited up, the

body is relieved: so too when bad men go out, then the Church is relieved. And one says, when the body vomits and casts them out, These humors went out of me, but they were not of me. How were not of me? Were not cut out of my flesh, but oppressed my breast while they were in me.

5. " They went out from us; but," be not sad, " they were not of us." How provest thou this? If they had been of us, they would doubtless have continued with us. Hence therefore ye may see, that many who are not of us, receive with us the Sacraments, receive with us baptism, receive with us what the faithful know they receive, Benediction, the Eucharist,[3] and whatever there is in Holy Sacraments: the communion of the very altar they receive with us, and are not of us. Temptation proves that they are not of us. When temptation comes to them as if blown by a wind they fly abroad; because they were not grain. But all of them will fly abroad, as we must often tell you, when once the fanning of the Lord's threshing-floor shall begin in the day of judgment. " They went out from us, but they were not of us; if they had been of us, they would no doubt have continued with us." For would ye know, beloved, how most certain this saying is, that they who haply have gone out and return, are not antichrists, are not contrary to Christ? Whoso are not antichrists, it cannot be that they should continue without. But of his own will is each either an antichrist or in Christ. Either we are among the members, or among the bad humors. He that changeth himself for the better, is in the body, a member: but he that continues in his badness, is a bad humor; and when he is gone out, then they who were oppressed will be relieved. " They went out from us, but they were not of us; for if they had been of us, they would no doubt have continued with us: but (they went out), that they might be made manifest that they were not all of us." That he has added, " that they might be made manifest," is, because even when they are within they are not of us; yet they are not manifest, but by going out are made manifest. "And ye have an unction from the Holy One, that ye may be manifest to your own selves.[4] The spiritual unction is the Holy Spirit Himself, of which

---

[1] So ἀντικείμενος 2 Thess. 2, 3, and so the word seems to be interpreted by Tertull. *de Præscr. Hær.* 4, *Antichristi—Christi rebelles.* And this is alleged by Theophylact as the traditional interpretation of the Greek Church : πάντως ὁ ψεύστης ἐναντίος ὢν τῇ ἀληθείᾳ ἤτοι τῷ Χριστῷ ἀντίχριστός ἐστι. "Certainly 'Antichrist' is the Liar opposed to the Truth, *i.e.* to Christ." So Œcumenius. But by earlier authorities it is taken in the sense of " false-Christ," or, one that gives himself out for Christ with denial of Jesus Christ. Thus in the *Acta Martyrum: Dicit autem Apostolus: Si Satanas,* &c. *Unde et Antichristus Quasi-Christus.* "The Apostle saith : If Satan be transfigured as an angel of light, it is no great matter if his ministers be transfigured." Whence also " Antichrist" means " seeming-Christ." And St. Hippolyt. *Portuensis de Antichristo,* 6, κατὰ πάντα ἐξομοιοῦσθαι βούλεται ὁ πλάνος τῷ υἱῷ τοῦ Θεοῦ. "In all things the deceiver will needs make himself like the Son of God." See Mr. Greswell's *Exposition of the Parables,* i. p. 372. ff.

[*Antichrist.*—Huther confirms (Meyer, Com. on N. T., 14th part, 4th German edition) Augustin's definition. "That ἀντι expresses not substitution but antagonism is now generally and justly acknowledged;" but he adds, "ὁ ἀιτίχριστος does not mean the enemy of Christ, in general, but the one opposed to Christ, or the '*opposition Christ*,' *i.e.* the enemy of Christ, who, under the lying pretense of being the true Christ, endeavors to destroy the work of Christ." "One who assuming the guise of Christ, opposes Christ." (Westcott.)

When Huther remarks in reference to the view held by Neander and others, who distinguish, in the apostle's representation of Antichrist, *form and idea,* viz.:—that evil will gradually increase more and more in its contest against Christ, until it has reached its summit, when it will be completely vanquished by the power of Christ ; and, as regards *form,* that this highest energy of evil will appear in *one person ;* "of this distinction Scripture gives no suggestion ;" yet, as there appears an intimation of distinct and successive Antichrists (1 John ii. 18, 22 ; 2 John vii.), and the Antichrist of whom the Apostle's readers "had heard," had not yet come personally, Westcott's interpretation of ii. 18, seems not unreasonable : " Antichrist may be the personification of the principle shown in different Antichrists ; or, the person whose appearance is prepared by these particular forms of evil."

Whatever may be thought of Augustin's application of the apostle's description to separatists in his day. that there have been many Antichrists, 1st and 2nd John teach very plainly : and most important, is St. John's description of the " master falsehood," the " denial of true manhood and true Godhead in Christ, which involves the denial of the essential relations of Fatherhood and Sonship in the Divine Nature.—J. H. M.]

[2] 1 Cor. xii. 26.

[3] Two MSS. *Benedictionem Eucharistiæ,* " the Benediction of the Eucharist."—BEN. (So Bodl. 242 and 455,—and 813 by correction.)

[4] *Ut ipsi vobis manifesti sitis.* As there is no trace of this reading in either the Greek or Latin authorities, it is perhaps not meant to stand as part of the text, though represented as such by the Benedictines. In the following clause Aug. seems to recognize the reading οἴδατε πάντες, *dicit omnes cognoscere bonos et malos.*

the Sacrament is in the visible unction.[1] Of this unction of Christ he saith, that all who have it know the bad and the good; and they need not to be taught, because the unction itself teacheth them.

6. " I write unto you not because ye know not the truth, but because ye know it, and that no lie is of the truth."[2] Behold, we are admonished how we may know antichrist. What is Christ? Truth. Himself hath said " I am the Truth."[3] But " no lie is of the truth." Consequently, all who lie are not yet of Christ. He hath not said that some lie is of the truth, and some lie not of the truth. Mark the sentence. Do not fondle yourselves, do not flatter yourselves, do not deceive yourselves, do not cheat yourselves: " No lie is of the truth." Let us see then how antichrists lie, because there is more than one kind of lying. " Who is a liar, but he that denieth that Jesus is the Christ?" One is the meaning of the word " Jesus," another the meaning of the word " Christ:" though it be one Jesus Christ our Saviour, yet " Jesus" is His proper name. Just as Moses was so called by his proper name, as Elias, as Abraham: so as His proper name our Lord hath the name " Jesus:" but " Christ" is the name of His[4] sacred character. As when we say, Prophet, as when we say, Priest; so by the name Christ we are given to understand the Anointed, in whom should be the redemption of the whole people. The coming of this Christ was hoped for by the people of the Jews: and because He came in lowliness, He was not acknowledged; because the stone was small, they stumbled at it and were broken. But "the stone grew, and became a great mountain;"[5] and what saith the Scripture? "Whosoever shall stumble at this stone shall be broken;[6] and on whomsoever this stone shall come, it will grind him to powder." We must mark the difference of the words: it saith, he that stumbleth shall be broken; but he on whom it shall come, shall be ground to powder. At the first, because He came lowly, men stumbled at Him: because He shall come lofty to judgment, on whomsoever He shall come, He will grind him to powder. But not that man will He grind to powder at His future coming, whom He broke not when He came. He that stumbled not at the lowly, shall not dread the lofty. Briefly ye have heard it, brethren: he that stumbled not at the lowly, shall not dread the lofty. For to all bad men is Christ a stone of stumbling; whatever Christ saith is bitter to them.

7. For hear and see. Certainly all who go out from the Church, and are cut off from the unity of the Church, are antichrists; let no man doubt it: for the apostle himself hath marked them, " They went out from us, but they were not of us; for if they had been of us, they would no doubt have continued with us." Therefore, whoso continue not with us, but go out from us, it is manifest that they are antichrists. And how are they proved to be antichrists? By lying. "And who is a liar, but he that denieth that Jesus is the Christ?"[7] Let us ask the heretics: where do you find a heretic that denies that Jesus is the Christ? See now, my beloved, a great mystery.[8] Mark what the Lord God may have inspired us withal, and what I would fain work into your minds. Behold, they went out from us, and turned Donatists: we ask them whether Jesus be the Christ; they instantly confess that Jesus is the Christ. If then that person is an antichrist, who denies that Jesus is the Christ, neither can they call us antichrists, nor we them; therefore, neither they went out from us, nor we from them. If then we have not gone out one from another, we are in unity: if we be in unity, what means it that there are two altars in this city? what, that there are divided houses, divided marriages? that there is a common bed, and a divided Christ? He admonishes us, he would have us confess what is the truth:—either they went out from us, or we from them. But let it not be imagined that we have gone out from them. For we have the testament of the Lord's inheritance, we recite it, and there we find, " I will give Thee the nations for Thine inheritance, and for Thy possessions the ends of the earth."[9] We hold fast Christ's inheritance; they hold it not, for they do not communcate with the whole earth, do not communicate with the [10] universal body redeemed by the blood of the Lord. We have the Lord Himself rising from the dead, who presented Himself to be felt by the hands of the doubting disciples: and while they yet doubted, He said to them, " It behoved Christ to suffer, and to rise from the dead the third day: and that repentance and remission of sins should be preached in His name "[11]—Where? which way? to what persons?—"through all nations, beginning at Jerusalem." Our minds are set at rest concerning the unity of the inheritance! Whoso does not communicate with this inheritance, is gone out.

8. But let us not be made sad: " They

---

[1] *Infra*, sec. 12.　[2] 1 John ii. 21.　[3] John xiv. 6.
[4] *Sacramenti*.　[5] Dan. ii. 35.　[6] *Conquassabitur*.

[7] 1 John ii. 22　[8] *Magnum sacramentum*, sec. 13, note 3.
[9] Ps. ii. 8　[10] *Universitate*.　[11] Luke xxiv. 46, 47.

went out from us, but they were not of us; for if they had been of us, they would no doubt have continued with us."[1] If then they went out from us, they are antichrists; if they are antichrists, they are liars; if they are liars, they deny that Jesus is the Christ. Once more we come back to the difficulty of the question. Ask them one by one; they confess that Jesus is the Christ. The difficulty that hampers us comes of our taking what is said in the Epistle in too narrow a sense. At any rate ye see the question; this question puts both us and them to a stand, if it be not understood. Either we are antichrists, or they are antichrists; they call us antichrists, and say that we went out from them; we say the like of. them. But now this epistle has marked out the antichrists by this cognizance: "Whosoever denies that Jesus is the Christ," that same "is an antichrist." Now therefore let us enquire who denies; and let us mark not the tongue, but the deeds. For if all be asked, all with one mouth confess that Jesus is the Christ. Let the tongue keep still for a little while, ask the life. If we shall find this, if the Scripture itself shall tell us that denial is a thing done not only with the tongue, but also with the deeds, then assuredly we find many antichrists, who with the mouth profess Christ, and in their manners dissent from Christ. Where find we this in Scripture? Hear Paul the Apostle; speaking of such, he saith, "For they confess that they know God, but in their deeds deny Him."[2] We find these also to be antichrists: whosoever in his deeds denies Christ, is an antichrist. I listen not to what he says, but I look what life he leads. Works speak, and do we require words? For where is the bad man that does not wish to talk well? But what saith the Lord to such? "Ye hypocrites, how can ye speak good things, while ye are evil?"[3] Your voices ye bring into mine ears: I look into your thoughts. I see an evil will there, and ye make a show of false fruits. I know what I must gather, and whence; I do not "gather figs of thistles," I do not gather "grapes of thorns;" for "every tree is known by its fruit."[4] A more lying antichrist is he who with his mouth professes that Jesus is the Christ, and with his deeds denies Him. A liar in this, that he speaks one thing, and does another.

9. Now therefore, brethren, if deeds are to be questioned, not only do we find many antichrists gone out; but many not yet manifest, who have not gone out at all. For as many as the Church hath within it that are perjured, defrauders,[5] addicted to black arts, consulters of fortune-tellers, adulterers, drunkards, usurers, boy-stealers,[6] and all the other vices that we are not able to enumerate; these things are contrary to the doctrine of Christ, are contrary to the word of God. Now the Word of God is Christ: whatever is contrary to the Word of God is in Antichrist. For Antichrist means, "contrary to Christ." And would ye know how openly these resist Christ? Sometimes it happens that they do some evil, and one begins to reprove them; because they dare not blaspheme Christ, they blaspheme His ministers by whom they are reproved: but if thou show them that thou speakest Christ's words, not thine own, they endeavor all they can to convict thee of speaking thine own words, not Christ's: if however it is manifest that thou speakest Christ's words, they go even against Christ, they begin to find fault with Christ: "How," say they, "and why did He make us such as we are?" Do not persons say this every day, when they are convicted of their deeds? Perverted by a depraved will, they accuse their Maker. Their Maker cries to them from heaven, (for the same made us, who new-made us:) What made I thee? I made man, not avarice; I made man, not robbery; I made man, not adultery. Thou hast heard that my works praise me. Out of the mouth of the Three Children, it was the hymn itself that kept them from the fires."[7] The works of the Lord praise the Lord, the heaven, the earth, the sea, praise Him; praise Him all things that are in the heaven, praise Him angels, praise Him stars, praise Him lights, praise Him whatever swims, whatever flies, whatever walks, whatever creeps; all these praise the Lord. Hast thou heard there that avarice praises the Lord? Hast thou heard that drunkenness praises the Lord? That luxury praises, that frivolity praises Him? Whatever thou hearest not in that hymn give praise to the Lord, the Lord made not that thing. Correct what thou hast made, that what God made in thee may be saved. But if thou wilt not, and lovest and embracest thy sins, thou art contrary to Christ. Be thou within, be thou without, thou art an antichrist; be thou within, be thou without, thou art chaff. But why art thou not without? Because thou hast not fallen in with a wind to carry thee away.

10. These things are now manifest, my brethren. Let no man say, I do not worship

[1] 1 John ii. 19.   [2] Tit. i. 16.
[3] Matt. xii. 34.   [4] Matt. xii. 7, 16.

[5] *Maleficos.*   [6] *Mangones.*
[7] Song of the Three Holy Children. *Ex ore trium puerorum ipse hymnus erat qui ab ignibus defendebat.*

Christ, but I worship God His Father. "Every one that denieth the Son, hath neither the Son nor the Father; and he that confesseth the Son, hath both the Son and the Father." [1] He speaks to you that are grain: and let those who were chaff, hear, and become grain. Let each one, looking well to his own conscience, if he be a lover of the world, be changed; let him become a lover of Christ, that he be not an antichrist. If one shall tell him that he is an antichrist, he is wroth, he thinks it a wrong done to him; perchance, if he is told by him that strives with him[2] that he is an antichrist, he threatens an action at law.[3] Christ saith to him, Be patient; if thou hast been falsely spoken of, rejoice with me, because I also am falsely spoken of by the antichrists: but if thou art truly spoken of, come to an understanding with thine own conscience; and if thou fear to be called this, fear more to be it.

11. "Let that therefore abide in you, which ye have heard from the beginning. If that which ye have heard from the beginning shall abide in you, ye also shall abide in the Son, and in the Father. And this is the promise that He hath promised us."[4] For haply thou mightest ask about the wages, and say, Behold, "that which I have heard from the beginning I keep safe in me, I comply therewith; perils, labors, temptations, for the sake of this continuance, I bear up against them all: with what fruit? what wages? what will He hereafter give me, since in this world I see that I labor among temptations? I see not here that there is any rest: mere mortality weigheth down the soul, and the corruptible body presseth it down to lower things: but I bear all things, that "that which I have heard from the beginning"[5] may "remain" in me; and that I may say to my God, "Because of the words of Thy lips have I kept hard ways."[6] Unto what wages then? Hear, and faint not. If thou wast fainting in the labors, upon the promised wages be strong. Where is the man that shall work in a vineyard, and shall let slip out of his heart the reward he is to receive? Suppose him to have forgotten, his hands fail. The remembrance of the promised wages makes him per-

severing in the work: and yet he that promised it is a man who can deceive thine expectation. How much more strong oughtest thou to be in God's field, when He that promised is the Truth, Who can neither have any successor, nor die, nor deceive him to whom the promise was made! And what is the promise? Let us see what He hath promised. Is it gold which men here love much, or silver? Or possessions, for which men lavish gold, however much they love gold? Or pleasant lands, spacious houses, many slaves, numerous beasts? Not these are the wages, so to say, for which he exhorts us to endure in labor. What are these wages called? ".eternal life." Ye have heard, and in your joy ye have cried out: love that which ye have heard, and ye are delivered from your labors into the rest of eternal life. Lo, this is what God promises; "eternal life."[7] Lo, this what God threatens; eternal fire. What to those set on the right hand? "Come, ye blessed of my Father, receive the kingdom prepared for you from the beginning of the world."[8] To those on the left, what? "Go into eternal fire, prepared for the devil and his angels." Thou dost not yet love that: at least fear this.

12. Remember then, my brethren, that Christ hath promised us eternal life: "This," saith he, "is the promise which He hath promised us, even eternal life. These things have I written unto you concerning them which seduce you."[9] Let none seduce you unto death: desire the promise of eternal life. What can the world promise? Let it promise what you will, it makes the promise perchance to one that to-morrow shall die. And with what face wilt thou go hence to Him that abideth for ever? "But a powerful man threatens me, so that I must do some evil." What does he threaten? Prisons, chains, fires, torments, wild beasts: aye, but not eternal fire? Dread that which One Almighty threatens; love that which One Almighty promises; and all the world becomes vile in our regard, whether it promise or terrify. "These things have I written unto you concerning them which seduce you; that ye may know that ye have an unction, and the unction which we have received from Him may abide in you." [10] In the unction we have the sacramental sign [of a thing unseen], the virtue itself is invisible;[11] the invisible unction

[1] 1 John ii. 23. *Omnis qui negat Filium, nec Filium nec Patrem habet: et qui confitetur Filium, Filium et Patrem habet.* St. Cyprian, *Testimon. adv. Jud.* ii. 27. *Qui negat Filium, neque Patrem habet: qui confitetur Filium, et Filium et Patrem habet:* and just so St. Hilar. *de Trin.* vi. 42. For the Greek, the clause ὁ ὁμολογῶν τὸν υἱὸν καὶ τὸν πατέρα ἔχει is abundantly authenticated by numerous MSS., Vers. Syr. and Aeth., St. Cyril, *Al. in Joann.* ix. sec. 40: and the mission by some MSS. and Œcumen. Theophyl. is sufficiently explained by the similar ending of this and the former clause. The addition *et Filium* in the latter clause seems to be peculiar to the Latin, and *nec Filium* in the former to Augustin's copies.
[2] *Litigante.*   [3] *Inscriptionem.*   [4] 1 John ii. 24, 25.
[5] Wisd. ix. 15.   [6] Ps. xvii. 4, LXX. and Vulg.

[7] Matt. xxv. 34.   [8] Matt. xxv. 41.   [9] 1 John ii. 25, 26.
[10] 1 John ii. 26, 27. *Ut sciatis quia unctionem habetis, et unctio quam accepimus ab eo permaneat in nobis.* This reading, which is not found in the Greek copies, may have originated in the attempt to explain a difficult construction. The Vulgate keeps close to the Greek: *Et vos unctionem quam accepistis ab eo maneat in vobis.*
[11] *Unctionis sacramentum est, virtus ipsa invisibilis: i.e. the*

is the Holy Ghost; the invisible unction is that charity, which, in whomsoever it be, shall be as a root to him: however burning the sun, he cannot wither. All that is rooted is nourished by the sun's warmth, not withered.

13. "And ye have no need that any man teach you, because His[1] unction teacheth you concerning all things."[2] Then to what purpose is it that " we," my brethren, teach you? If " His unction teacheth you concerning all things," it seems we labor without a cause. And what mean we, to cry out as we do? Let us leave you to His unction, and let His unction teach you. But this is putting the question only to myself: I put it also to that same apostle: let him deign to hear a babe that asks of him: to John himself I say, Had those the unction to whom thou wast speaking? Thou hast said, " His unction teacheth you concerning all things." To what purpose hast thou written an Epistle like this? what teaching didst " thou " give them? what instruction? what edification? See here now, brethren, see a mighty mystery.[3] The sound of our words strikes the ears, the Master is within. Do not suppose that any man learns ought from man. We can admonish by the sound of our voice; if there be not One within that shall teach, vain is the noise we make. Aye, brethren, have ye a mind to know it? Have ye not all heard this present discourse? and yet how many will go from this place untaught! I, for my part, have spoken to all; but they to whom that Unction within speaketh not, they whom the Holy Ghost within teacheth

not, those go back untaught. The teachings of the master from without are a sort of aids and admonitions. He that teacheth the hearts, hath His chair in heaven. Therefore saith He also Himself in the Gospel: " Call no man your master upon earth; One is your Master, even Christ."[4] Let Him therefore Himself speak to you within, when not one of mankind is there: for though there be some one at thy side, there is none in thine heart. Yet let there not be none in thine heart:[5] let Christ be in thine heart: let His unction be in the heart, lest it be a heart thirsting in the wilderness, and having no fountains to be watered withal. There is then, I say, a Master within that teacheth: Christ teacheth; His inspiration teacheth. Where His inspiration and His unction is not, in vain do words make a noise from without. So are the words, brethren, which we speak from without, as is the husbandman to the tree: from without he worketh, applieth water and diligence of culture; let him from without apply what he will, does he form the apples? does he clothe the nakedness of the wood with a shady covering of leaves? does he do any thing like this from within? But whose doing is this? Hear the husbandman, the apostle: both see what we are, and hear the Master within: " I have planted, Apollos hath watered; but God gave the increase: neither he that planteth is any thing, neither he that watereth, but He that giveth the increase, even God."[6] This then we say to you: whether we plant, or whether we water, by speaking we are not any thing; but He that giveth the increase, even God: that is, " His unction which teacheth you concerning all things."

---

unction or chrism which we receive is a *sacramentum*, a thing in which, as Aug. defines the term, " *aliud videtur, aliud intelligitur*, one thing is seen, another understood." " *Aliud est sacramentum, aliud virtus sacramenti*," *supra* Hom. xxvi. 11.

[1] *Unctio ipsius*, Vulg. *ejus*, representing the reading τὸ αὐτοῦ χρίσμα: but the truer reading, τὸ αὐτὸ χρίσμα, seems to be recognized in the opening of Hom. iv., *ipsa unctio docet vos de omnibus.*

[2] 1 John ii. 27.

[3] *Jam hic videte magnum sacramentum :* as above, sec. 7; meaning in both places, that whereas the apostle's words seem at first sight to be contradicted by facts, his true meaning lies deeper, and involves a spiritual truth of great importance.

[4] Matt. xxiii. 8, 9.

[5] *Et non sit nullus in corde tuo.* Three MSS. *et non sit ullus in corde tuo* [" and let there not be any in thine heart, (only) let Christ be in thine heart"]. One MS.: *et nullus in corde tuo;* another: *et nullus sit in corde tuo* [with the same meaning]. BEN. Bodl. MSS. vary, no two reading alike. One, " *et ne sit ullus.*" The reading most like St. Aug. would be, " *et ne sit nullus,*" " and lest there be none."

[6] 1 Cor. iii. 6, 7.

HOMILY IV.

1 JOHN II. 27; III. 8.

" And it is true, and lieth not. Even as it hath taught you, abide in it. And now, little children, abide in Him; that, when He shall appear, we may have confidence, and not be put to shame by Him at His coming. If ye know that He is righteous, know ye that every one that doeth righteousness is born of Him. Behold, what manner of love the Father hath bestowed upon us, that we should be called and should be the sons of God:

therefore the world knoweth us not, because it knew not Him, us also the world knoweth not. Beloved, now are we the sons of God, and it is not yet manifested what we shall be. We know that, when He shall appear, we shall be like Him; for we shall see Him as He is. And every man that hath this hope in Him purifieth himself, even as He is pure. Whosoever committeth sin committeth also iniquity. Sin is iniquity. And ye know that He was manifested to take away sin; and in Him is no sin. Whosoever abideth in Him sinneth not: whosoever sinneth hath not seen Him, neither known Him. Little children, let no man seduce you. He that doeth righteousness is righteous, even as He is righteous. He that committeth sin is of the devil; for the devil sinneth from the beginning. For this purpose the Son of God was manifested; that He might destroy the works of the devil.''

1. YE remember, brethren, that yesterday's lesson was brought to a close at this point, that " ye have no need that any man teach you, but the unction itself teacheth you concerning all things." Now this, as I am sure ye remember, we so expounded to you, that we who from without speak to your ears, are as workmen applying culture from without to a tree, but we cannot give the increase nor form the fruits: but only He that created and redeemed and called you, He, dwelling in you by faith and the Spirit, must speak to you within, else vain is all our noise of words. Whence does this appear? From this: that while many hear, not all are persuaded of that which is said, but only they to whom God speaks within. Now they to whom He speaks within, are those who give place to Him: and those give place to God, who " give not place to the devil." [1] For the devil wishes to inhabit the hearts of men, and speak there the things which are able to seduce. But what saith the Lord Jesus? " The prince of this world is cast out." [2] Whence cast? out of heaven and earth? out of the fabric of the world? Nay, but out of the hearts of the believing. The invader being cast out, let the Redeemer dwell within: because the same redeemed, who created. And the devil now assaults from without, not conquers Him that hath possession within. And he assaults from without, by casting in various temptations: but that person consents not thereto, to whom God speaks within, and the unction of which ye have heard.

2. "And it is true," namely, this same unction; i. e. the very Spirit of the Lord which teacheth men, cannot lie: " and is not false.[3] Even as it hath taught you, abide ye in the same. And now, little children, abide ye in Him, that when He shall be manifested, we may have boldness in His sight, that we be not put to shame by Him at His coming." [4] Ye see, brethren: we believe on Jesus whom we have not seen: they announced Him, that saw, that handled, that heard the word out of His own mouth; and that they might persuade all mankind of the truth thereof, they were sent by Him, not dared to go of themselves. And whither were they sent? Ye heard while the Gospel was read, " Go, preach the Gospel to the whole creation which is under heaven." [5] Consequently, the disciples were sent " every where:" with signs and wonders to attest that what they spake, they had seen. And we believe on Him whom we have not seen, and we look for Him to come. Whoso look for Him by faith, shall rejoice when He cometh: those who are without faith, when that which now they see not is come, shall be ashamed. And that confusion of face shall not be for a single day and so pass away, in such sort as those are wont to be confounded, who are found out in some fault, and are scoffed at by their fellow-men. That confusion shall carry them that are confounded to the left hand, that to them it may be said, " Go into everlasting fire, prepared for the devil and his angels." [6] Let us abide then in His words, that we be not confounded when He cometh. For Himself saith in the Gospel to them that had believed on Him: " If ye shall abide in my word, then are ye verily my disciples." [7] And, as if they had asked, With what fruit? "And," saith He, " ye shall know the truth, and the truth shall make you free." For as yet our salvation is in hope, not in deed: for we do not already possess that which is promised, but we hope for it to come. And " faithful is He that promised;" [8] He deceiveth not thee: only do thou not faint, but wait for the promise. For He, the Truth, cannot deceive. Be not thou a liar, to profess one thing and do another; keep thou the faith, and He keeps His promise. But if thou keep not the faith, thine own self, not He that promised, hath defrauded thee.

1 Eph. v. 27.   2 John xii. 31.
3 Mendax. Gr. ψεῦδος. Vulg. Mendacium. In the following clause et om. as καὶ in Cod. Alex. In ipsa, Gr. ἐν αὐτῷ, taken as referred to χρίσμα, " in the unction" (Lat. two MSS. in ipso.) Vulg. in eo, " in Christ."

4 1 John iii. 27, 28.   5 Mark xvi. 15. Universæ. creaturæ.
6 Matt. xxv. 31.   7 John viii. 31, 32.   8 Heb. x. 23.

3. "If ye know that He is righteous, know ye[1] that every one that doeth righteousness is born of Him."[2] The righteousness which at present is ours is of faith. Perfect righteousness is not, save only in the angels: and scarce in angels, if they be compared with God: yet if there be any perfect righteousness of souls and spirits which God hath created, it is in the angels, holy, just, good, by no lapse turned aside, by no pride falling, but remaining ever in the contemplation of the Word of God, and having nothing else sweet unto them save Him by whom they were created; in them is perfect righteousness: but in us it has begun to be, of faith, by the Spirit. Ye heard when the Psalm was read, "Begin[3] ye to the Lord in confession."[4] "Begin," saith it; the beginning of our righteousness is the confession of sins. Thou hast begun not to defend thy sin; now hast thou made a beginning of righteousness: but it shall be perfected in thee when to do nothing else shall delight thee, when "death shall be swallowed up in victory,"[5] when there shall be no itching of lust, when there shall be no struggling with flesh and blood, when there shall be the palm of victory, the triumph over the enemy; then shall there be perfect righteousness. At present we are still fighting: if we fight we are in the lists;[6] we smite and are smitten; but who shall conquer, remains to be seen. And that man conquers, who even when he smites presumes not on his own strength, but relies upon God that cheers him on. The devil is alone when he fights against us. If we are with God, we overcome the devil: for if thou fight alone with the devil, thou wilt be overcome. He is a skillful enemy: how may palms has he won! Consider to what he has cast us down! That we are born mortal, comes of this, that he in the first place cast down from Paradise our very original. What then is to be done, seeing he is so well practised? Let the Almighty be invoked to thine aid against the devices of the devil. Let Him dwell in thee, who cannot be overcome, and thou shalt securely overcome him who is wont to overcome. But to overcome whom? Those in whom God dwelleth not. For, that ye may know it, brethren; Adam being in Paradise despised the commandment of God, and lifted up the neck, as if he desired to be his own master, and were loath to be subject to the will of God: so he fell from that immortality,

from that blessedness. But there was a certain man, a man now well skilled, though a mortal born, who even as he sat on the dunghill, putrifying with worms, overcame the devil: yea, Adam himself then overcame: even he, in Job; because Job was of his race. So then, Adam, overcome in Paradise, overcame on the dunghill. Being in Paradise, he gave ear to the persuasion of the woman which the devil had put into her: but being on the dunghill he said to Eve, "Thou hast spoken as one of the foolish women."[7] There he lent an ear, here he gave an answer: when he was glad, he listened, when he was scourged, he overcame. Therefore, see what follows, my brethren, in the Epistle: because this is what it would have us lay to heart, that we may overcome the devil indeed, but not of ourselves. "If ye know that He is righteous," saith it, "know ye that every one that doeth righteousness is born of Him:" of God, of Christ. And in that he hath said, "Is born of Him," he cheers us on. Already therefore, in that we are born of Him, we are perfect.

4. Hear. "Behold what manner of love the Father hath given us, that we should be called sons of God, and be[8] (such).[9] For whoso are called sons, and are not sons, what profiteth them the name where the thing is not? How many are called physicians, who know not how to heal! how many are called watchers, who sleep all night long! So, many are called Christians, and yet in deeds are not found such; because they are not this which they are called, that is, in life, in manners, in faith, in hope, in charity. But what have ye heard here, brethren? "Behold, what manner of love the Father hath bestowed upon us, that we should be called, and should be, the sons of God: therefore the world knoweth us not, because it hath not known Him, us also the world knoweth not."[10] There is a whole world Christian, and a whole world ungodly; because throughout the whole world there are ungodly, and throughout the whole world there are godly: those know not these. In what sense, think we, do they not know them? They deride them that live good lives. Mark well and

---

[1] *Scitote* Vulg. Gr. γινώσκετε as imperative, "hence learn ye to know that, &c." Were it indicative, "to know that He is righteous is to know that, &c." probably οἴδατε would have been repeated as in 5, 15, ἂν οἴδαμεν—οἴδαμεν.
[2] 1 John iii. 29.
[3] *Incipite,* LXX. ἐξάρξατε. Vulg. *præcinite.*
[4] Ps. cxlvii. 7.   [5] 1 Cor. xv. 24.   [6] *Stadium.*

[7] Job ii. 10.   1 John iii. 1.
[9] *Vocemur et simus.* Vulg. *nominemur et simus.* Cod. Alex. and other authorities, κληθῶμεν καὶ ἐσμὲν (received by Lachmann). Mill in l. cites as from Augustin, but without specifying the place: *Qui vocantur et non sunt, quid prodest illis nomen?* [The very words of this passage.] *Verum hic loquitur de nomine quod a Deo tribuitur: hic non est discrimen inter dici et esse.* [Which looks rather like an expression of dissent, by Mill himself or some other.]
["καὶ ἐσμεν," Westcott and Hort, "and such we are," Rev.V. These closing words of ch. iii. 1, wanting in Auth. V.—J.H.M.]
[10] *Et nos non cognoscit mundus:* a reading of which there are no traces in the MSS.: it seems to be an expository gloss: "therefore (because we are sons of God) the world knoweth us not. Namely, because the world knew not Him, it knows not us."

see: for haply there are such also among you. Each one of you who now lives godly, who despises worldly things, who does not choose to go to spectacles, who does not choose to make himself drunken as it were by solemn custom, yea, what is worse, under countenance of holy days to make himself unclean; the man who does not choose to do these things, how is he derided by those who do them![1] Would he be scoffed at if he were known? But why is he not known? "The world knoweth Him not." Who is "the world"? Those inhabiters of the world. Just as we say, "a house;" meaning, its inhabitants. These things have been said to you again and again, and we forbear to repeat them to your disgust. By this time, when ye hear the word "world," in a bad signification, ye know that ye must understand it to mean only lovers of the world; because through love they inhabit, and by inhabiting have become entitled to the name. Therefore the world hath not known us, because it hath not known Him. He walked here Himself, the Lord Jesus Christ in the flesh; He was God, He was latent in weakness.[2] And wherefore was He not known? Because He reproved all sins in men. They, through loving the delights of sins, did not acknowledge the God: through loving that which the fever prompted, they did wrong to the Physician.

5. For us then, what are we? Already we are begotten of Him; but because we are such in hope, he saith, "Beloved, now are we sons of God." Now already? Then what is it we look for, if already we are sons of God? "And not yet," saith he, "is it manifested what[3] we shall be." But what else shall we be than sons of God? Hear what follows: "We know that, when He shall appear, we shall be like Him, because we shall see Him as He is." Understand, my beloved. It is a great matter: "We know that, when He shall appear, we shall be like Him; for we shall see Him as He is." In the first place mark, what is called "Is." Ye know what it is that is so called. That which is called "Is," and not only is called but is so, is unchangeable; It ever remaineth, It cannot be changed, It is in no part corruptible: It hath neither proficiency, for It is perfect; nor hath deficiency, for It is eternal. And what

is this? "In the beginning was the Word, and the Word was with God, and the Word was God."[4] And what is this? "Who being in the form of God, thought it not robbery to be equal with God."[5] To see Christ in this sort, Christ in the form of God, Word of God, Only-Begotten of the Father, equal with the Father, is to the bad impossible. But in regard that the Word was made flesh, the bad also shall have power to see Him: because in the day of judgment the bad also will see Him; for He shall so come to judge, as He came to be judged. In the selfsame form, a man, but yet God: for "cursed is every one that putteth his trust in man."[6] A man, He came to be judged, a man, He will come to judge. And if He shall not be seen, what is this that is written, "They shall look on Him whom they pierced?"[7] For of the ungodly it is said, that they shall see and be confounded. How shall the ungodly not see, when He shall set some on the right hand, others on the left? To those on the right hand He will say, "Come, ye blessed of my Father, receive the kingdom:"[8] to those on the left He will say, "Go into everlasting fire." They will see but the form of a servant, the form of God they will not see. Why? because they were ungodly; and the Lord Himself saith, "Blessed are the pure in heart, for they shall see God."[9] Therefore, we are to see a certain vision, my brethren, "which neither eye hath seen, nor ear hath heard, nor hath entered into the heart of man:"[10] a certain vision, a vision surpassing all earthly beautifulness, of gold, of silver, of groves and fields; the beautifulness of sea and air, the beautifulness of sun and moon, the beautifulness of the stars, the beautifulness of angels: surpassing all things: because from it are all things beautiful.

6. What then shall "we" be, when we shall see this? What is promised to us? "We shall be like Him, for we shall see Him as He is." The tongue hath done what it could, hath sounded the words: let the rest be thought by the heart. For what hath even John himself said in comparison of That which Is, or what can be said by us men, who are so far from being equal to his merits? Return we therefore to that unction of Him, return we to that unction which inwardly teacheth that which we cannot speak: and because ye cannot at present see, let your part and duty be in desire. The whole life of a good Christian is an holy desire.[11] Now

---

[1] Supra: add Ep. 29, ad Alypium.
[2] Ed. Ben. places the colon before in carne: "in the flesh He was God, &c." But [Aug. several times uses ambulare, without an object.—J. H. M.] ambulabat seems to require an object to complete the sense, and the antithesis between erat and latebat is more emphatic when in carne is given to the former clause. So Bodl. 150, Laud. 116.
[3] Quid erimus. Vulg. τί ἐσόμεθα. Enarr. in Psa. xxxvii. 2, § 8, quod erimus, ὅ τι: so St. Jerome in Epist. Epiphan. "the thing which we shall be is not yet made manifest."

[4] John i. 1.   [5] Phil. ii. 6.   [6] Jer. xvii. 5.
[7] John xix. 37.   [8] Matt. xxv. 41.   [9] Matt. v. 8.
[10] 1 Cor. ii. 9.
[11] ["Longing." The word of that other Church father,—before Augustin's day,—who thanked God that from his youth up he had been a "man of longings," vir desidiorum.—J. H. M.]

what thou longest for, thou dost not yet see: howbeit by longing, thou art made capable, so that when that is come which thou mayest see, thou shalt be filled. For just as, if thou wouldest fill a bag,[1] and knowest how great the thing is that shall be given, thou stretchest the opening of the sack or the skin, or whatever else it be; thou knowest how much thou wouldest put in, and seest that the bag is narrow; by stretching thou makest it capable of holding more: so God, by deferring our hope, stretches our desire; by the desiring, stretches the mind; by stretching, makes it more capacious. Let us desire therefore, my brethren, for we shall be filled. See Paul widening, as it were,[2] his bosom, that it may be able to receive that which is to come. He saith, namely, "Not that I have already received, or am already perfect: brethren, I deem not myself to have apprehended."[3] Then what art thou doing in this life, if thou have not yet apprehended? "But this one thing [I do]; forgetting the things that are behind, reaching forth to the things that are before,[4] upon the strain I follow on unto the prize of the high calling." He says he reaches forth, or stretches himself, and says that he follows "upon the strain." He felt himself too little to take in that "which eye hath not seen, nor ear heard, neither hath entered into the heart of man."[5] This is our life, that by longing we should be exercised. But holy longing exercises us just so much as we prune off our longings from the love of the world. We have already said, "Empty out that which is to be filled." With good thou art to be filled: pour out the bad. Suppose that God would fill thee with honey: if thou art full of vinegar, where wilt thou put the honey? That which the vessel bore in it must be poured out: the vessel itself must be cleansed; must be cleansed, albeit with labor, albeit with hard rubbing, that it may become fit for that thing, whatever it be. Let us say honey, say gold, say wine; whatever we say it is, being that which cannot be said, whatever we would fain say, It is called—God. And when we say "God," what have we said? Is that one syllable the whole of that we look for? So then, whatever we have had power to say is beneath Him: let us stretch ourselves unto Him, that when He shall come, He may fill us. For "we shall be like Him; because we shall see Him as He is."

7. "And every one that hath this hope in Him." Ye see how he hath set us our place, in "hope." Ye see how the Apostle Paul agreeth with his fellow-apostle, "By hope we are saved. But hope that is seen, is not hope: for what, a man seeth, why doth he hope for? For if what we see we not, we hope for, by patience we wait for it."[6] This very patience exerciseth desire. Continue thou, for He continueth: and persevere thou in walking, that thou mayest reach the goal: for that to which thou tendest will not remove. See: "And every one that hath this hope in Him, purifieth[7] himself even as He is pure."[8] See how he has not taken away free-will, in that he saith, "purifieth himself." Who purifieth us but God? Yea, but God doth not purify thee if thou be unwilling. Therefore, in that thou joinest thy will to God, in that thou purifiest thyself. Thou purifiest thyself, not by thyself, but by Him who cometh to inhabit thee. Still, because thou doest somewhat therein by the will, therefore is somewhat attributed to thee. But it is attributed to thee only to the end thou shouldest say, as in the Psalm, "Be thou my helper, forsake me not."[9] If thou sayest, "Be thou my helper," thou doest somewhat: for if thou be doing nothing, how should He be said to "help" thee?

8. "Every one that doeth sin, doeth also iniquity."[10] Let no man say, Sin is one thing, iniquity another: let no man say, I am a sinful man, but not [11] a doer of iniquity. For, "Every one that doeth sin, doeth also iniquity. Sin is iniquity." Well then, what are we to do concerning sins and iniquities? Hear what He saith: "And ye know that He was manifested to take away sin; and sin in Him is not."[12] He, in Whom sin is not, the same is come to take away sin. For were there sin in Him, it must be taken away from Him, not He take it away Himself. "Whosoever abideth in Him, sinneth not."[13] In so far as he abideth in Him, in so far sinneth not. "Whosoever sinneth hath not seen Him, neither known Him." A great question this: "Whosoever sinneth hath not seen Him, neither known Him." No marvel. We have not seen Him, but are to see; have not known Him, but are to know: we believe on One we have not known. Or haply, by faith we have known, and by actual beholding[14] have not yet known? But then in faith we have both seen and known. For if faith doth not yet see, why are we said to have been enlightened? There is an enlightening by faith, and an enlightening by sight. At present, while we are on pilgrimage, "we walk by faith, not by sight,"[15]

---

[1] Sinum.   [2] Sinum.   [3] Phil. iii. 13, 14.
[4] Secundum intentionem. Gr. κατὰ σκοπόν.   [5] 1 Cor. ii. 9.
[6] Rom. viii. 24, 25.   [7] Castificat.   [8] Castus.
[9] Ps. xxvii. 11.   [10] 1 John iii. 4. Lawlessness.
[11] Iniquus.   [12] 1 John iii. 5.   [13] 1 John iii. 6.
[14] Specie.   [15] 2 Cor. v. 7.

or, actually beholding. Therefore also our righteousness is "by faith, not by sight." Our righteousness shall be perfect, when we shall see by actual beholding.[1] Only, in the meanwhile, let us not leave that righteousness which is of faith, since "the just doth live by faith,"[2] as saith the apostle. "Whosoever abideth in Him, sinneth not." For, "whosoever sinneth, hath not seen Him, neither known Him." That man who sins, believes not: but if a man believes, so far as pertains to his faith, he sinneth not.

9. "Little children, let no man seduce you. He that doeth righteousness is righteous, as He is righteous."[3] What? on hearing that we are "righteous as He is righteous," are we to think ourselves equal with God? Ye must know what means that "as:" thus he said a while ago, "Purifieth himself even as He is pure." Then is our purity like and equal to the purity of God, and our righteousness to God's righteousness? Who can say this? But the word "as," is not always wont to be used in the sense of equality. As, for example, if, having seen this large church,[4] a person should wish to build a smaller church, but with the same relative dimensions: as, for example, if this be one measure in width and two measures in length, he too should build his church one measure in width and two measures in length: in that case one sees that he has built it "as" this is built. But this church has, say, a hundred cubits in length, the other thirty: it is at once "as" this, and yet unequal. Ye see that this "as" is not always referred to parity and equality. For example, see what a difference there is between the face of a man and its image from a mirror: there is a face in the image, a face in the body: the image exists in imitation, the body in reality. And what do we say? Why, "as" there are eyes here, so also there; "as" ears here, so ears also there. The thing is different, but the "as" is said of the resemblance. Well then, we also have in us the image of God; but not that which the Son equal with the Father hath: yet except we also, according to our measure, were "as" He, we should in no respect be said to be like Him. "He purifieth us," then, "even as He is pure:" but He is pure from eternity, we pure by faith. We are "righteous even as He is righteous;" but He is so in His immutable perpetuity, we righteous by believing on One we do not see, that so we may one day see Him. Even when our righteousness shall be perfect, when we shall be equal to the angels, not even then

shall it be equalled with Him. How far then is it from Him now, when not even then it shall be equal!

10. "He that doeth sin, is of the devil, because the devil sinneth from the beginning."[5] "Is of the devil:" ye know what he means: by imitating the devil. For the devil made no man, begat no man, created no man: but whoso imitates the devil, that person, as if begotten of him, becomes a child of the devil; by imitating him, not literally by being begotten of him. In what sense art thou a child of Abraham? not that Abraham begat thee? In the same sense as the Jews, the children of Abraham, not imitating the faith of Abraham, are become children of the devil: of the flesh of Abraham they were begotten, and the faith of Abraham they have not imitated. If then those who were thence begotten were put out of the inheritance, because they did not imitate, thou, who art not begotten of him, art made a child, and in this way shalt be a child of him by imitating him. And if thou imitate the devil, in such wise as he became proud and impious against God, thou wilt be a child of the devil: by imitating, not that he created thee or begat thee.

11. "Unto this end was the Son of God manifested." Now then, brethren, mark! All sinners are begotten of the devil, as sinners. Adam was made by God: but when he consented to the devil, he was begotten of the devil; and he begat all men such as he was himself. With lust itself we were born; even before we add our sins, from that condemnation we have our birth. For if we are born without any sin, wherefore this running with infants to baptism that they may be released? Then mark well, brethren, the two birth-stocks,[6] Adam and Christ: two men are; but one of them, a man that is man; the other, a Man that is God. By the man that is man we are sinners; by the Man that is God we are justified. That birth hath cast down unto death; this birth hath raised up unto life: that birth brings with it sin; this birth setteth free from sin. For to this end came Christ as Man, to undo[7] the sins of men. "Unto this end was the Son of God manifested, that He may undo the works of the devil."

12. The rest I commend to your thoughts, my beloved, that I may not burden you. For the question we labor to solve is even this —that we call ourselves sinners: for if any man shall say that he is without sin, he is a liar. And in the Epistle of this same John we have found it written, "If we say that we

---

have no sin, we deceive ourselves." [1] For ye should remember what went before: " If we say that we have no sin, we deceive ourselves, and the truth is not in us." And yet, on the other hand, in what follows thou art told, " He that is begotten of God sinneth not: he that doeth sin hath not seen Him, neither known Him.—Every one that doeth sin is of the devil:" sin is not of God: this affrights us again. In what sense are we begotten of God, and in what sense do we con-

fess ourselves sinners ? Shall we say, because we are not begotten of God ? And what do these Sacraments in regard to infants ? What hath John said ? " He that is begotten of God, sinneth not." And yet again the same John hath said, " If we say that we have no sin, we deceive ourselves, and the truth is not in us !" A great question it is, and an embarrassing one; and may I have made you intent upon having it solved, my beloved. To-morrow, in the name of the Lord, what He will give, we will discourse thereof.

HOMILY V.

1 John III. 9–18.

" Whosoever is born of God doth not commit sin; for his seed remaineth in him: and he cannot sin, because he is born of God. In this the children of God are manifest, and the children of the devil: whosoever is not righteous is not of God, neither he that loveth not his brother. For this is the message that ye heard from the beginning, that we should love one another. Not as Cain, who was of the wicked one, and slew his brother. And wherefore slew he him? Because his own works were evil, and his brother's righteous. Marvel not, my brethren, if the world hate us. We know that we have passed from death unto life, because we love the brethren. He that loveth not abideth in death. Whosoever hateth his brother is a murderer: and ye know that no murderer hath eternal life abiding in him. In this we know love, that He laid down His life for us: and we ought to lay down our lives for the brethren. But whoso hath this world's good, and seeth his brother have need, and shutteth up his bowels of compassion from him, how can the love of God dwell in him? My little children, let us not love only in word and in tongue; but in deed and in truth."

1. HEAR intently, I do beseech you, because it is no small matter that we have to cope withal: and I doubt not, because ye were intent upon it yesterday, that ye have with even greater intentness of purpose come together to-day. For it is no slight question, how he saith in this Epistle, " Whosoever is born of God, sinneth not," [1] and how in the same Epistle he hath said above, " If we say that we have no sin, we deceive ourselves, and the truth is not in us." [2] What shall the man do, who is pressed by both sayings out of the same Epistle? If he shall confess himself a sinner, he fears lest it be said to him, Then art thou not born of God; because it is written, " Whosoever is born of God, sinneth not." But if he shall say that

he is just and that he hath no sin, he receives on the other side a blow from the same Epistle, " If we say that we have no sin, we deceive ourselves, and the truth is not in us." Placed then as he is in the midst, what he can say and what confess, or what profess, he cannot find. To profess himself to be without sin, is full of peril; and not only full of peril, but also full of error: " We deceive ourselves," saith he, " and the truth is not in us, if we say that we have no sin." But oh that thou hadst none, and saidst this ! for then wouldest thou say truly, and in uttering the truth wouldest have not so much as a vestige of wrong to be afraid of. But, that thou doest ill if thou say so, is because it is a lie that thou sayest. " The truth," saith he, " is not in us, if we say that we have no sin." He saith not, " Have not had;"

---

lest haply it should seem to be spoken of the past life. For the man here hath had sins; but from the time that he was born of God, he has begun not to have sins. If it were so, there would be no question to embarrass us. For we should say, We have been sinners, but now we are justified: we have had sin, but now we have none. He saith not this: but what saith he? "If we say that we have no sin, we deceive ourselves, and the truth is not in us." And then after a while he says on the other hand, "Whosoever is born of God sinneth not." Was John himself not born of God? If John was not born of God, John, of whom ye have heard that he lay in the Lord's bosom; does any man dare engage for himself that in him has taken place that regeneration which it was not granted to that man to have, to whom it was granted to lie in the bosom of the Lord? The man whom the Lord loved more than the rest,[1] him alone had He not begotten of the Spirit?

2. Mark now these words. As yet, I am urging it upon you, what straits we are put to, that by putting your minds on the stretch, that is, by your praying for us and for yourselves, God may make enlargement, and give us an outlet: lest some man find in His word an occasion of his own perdition, that word which was preached and put in writing only for healing and salvation. "Every man," saith he, "that doeth sin, doeth also iniquity." Lest haply thou make a distinction, "Sin is iniquity." Lest thou say, A sinner I am, but not a doer of iniquity, "Sin is iniquity." And ye know that to this end was He manifested, that He should take away sin; and there is no sin in Him." And what doth it profit us, that He came without sin? "Every one that sinneth not, abideth in Him: and every one that sinneth, hath not seen Him, neither known Him. Little children, let no man seduce you. He that doeth righteousness is righteous, even as He is righteous." This we have already said, that the word "as" is wont to be used of a certain resemblance, not of equality. "He that doeth sin is of the devil, because the devil sinneth from the beginning." This too we have already said, that the devil created no man, nor begat any, but his imitators are, as it were, born of him. "To this end was the Son of God manifested, that He should undo[2] the works of the devil." Consequently, to undo (or loose) sins, He that hath no sin. And then follows: "Every one that is born of God doth not commit sin; for

his seed remaineth in him: and he cannot sin, because he is born of God:"[3] he has drawn the cord tight!—Belike, it is in regard of some one sin that he hath said, "Doth not sin," not in regard of all sin: that in this that he saith, "Whoso is born of God, doth not sin," thou mayest understand some one particular sin, which that man who is born of God cannot commit:[4] and such is that sin that, if one commit it, it confirms the rest. What is this sin? To do contrary to the commandment. What is the commandment? "A new commandment give I unto you, that ye love one another."[5] Mark well! This commandment of Christ is called, "love." By this love sins are loosed. If this love be not kept, the not holding it is at once a grievous sin, and the root of all sins.

3. Mark well, brethren; we have brought forward somewhat in which, to them that have good understanding, the question is solved. But do we only walk in the way with them that run more swiftly? Those that walk more slowly must not be left behind. Let us turn the matter every way, in such words as we can, in order that it may be brought within reach of all. For I suppose, brethren, that every man is concerned for his own soul, who does not come to Church without cause, who does not seek temporal things in the Church, who does not come here to transact secular business; but comes here in order that he may lay hold upon some eternal thing, promised unto him, whereunto he may attain: he must needs consider how he shall walk in the way, lest he be left behind, lest he go back, lest he go astray, lest by halting he do not attain. Whoever therefore is in earnest, let him be slow, let him be swift, yet let him not leave the way. This then I have said, that

---

3 1 John iii. 9.
4 ["*Cannot sin*," &c.—Augustin maintains that the one sin which the Christian cannot commit is violation of charity; he cannot do otherwise than love, and do acts that flow from love, if he be a Christian. No doubt this indicates a great truth, for love expresses the inner essence of the believer's life and character. But the strong language of the apostle is not met by this partial statement.
  Better acknowledge the apparent contradiction between "does not commit sin," "cannot sin," and "if we say, we have no sin, we deceive ourselves." The apostle does not solve the problem. Meyer, who discards many explanations of the first two phrases,—as, sinning knowingly and wilfully, committing mortal sins and many others specified by him, thinks that the solution lies in the fact simply that the apostle desires to emphasize the contrast between born of God and a sinner. He does not show how emphasizing a contrast explains a contradiction (which he discovers in the passage). Jonathan Edwards and Ezek. Hopkins, following many others with whom Westcott coincides, judge that the alleged impossibility of sinning relates to total character, or prevailing habit; the Christian may be surprised, overtaken, beguiled by sin, but fights against sin, does not consent to sin with his whole heart; "he does not wish sin." It has been added that as to his nature—renewed; as to the new life—life from the Spirit of God,—his divine sonship and sin are irreconcilable contraries. In part, these suggestions and definitions may meet the difficulty which the apostle, doubtless wishing to present a high ideal of the life of one born from above, leaves for practical solution by those who have passed from death unto life.—J. H. M.]
5 John xiii. 34.

in saying, "Whosoever is born of God sinneth not," it is probable he meant it of some particular sin: for else it will be contrary to that place: "If we say that we have no sin, we deceive ourselves, and the truth is not in us." In this way then the question may be solved. There is a certain sin, which he that is born of God cannot commit; a sin, which not being committed, other sins are loosed, and being committed, other sins are confirmed. What is this sin? To do contrary to the commandment of Christ, contrary to the New Testament.[1] What is the new commandment? "A new commandment give I unto you, that ye love one another."[2] Whoso doeth contrary to charity and contrary to brotherly love, let him not dare to glory and say that he is born of God: but whoso is in brotherly love, there are certain sins which he cannot commit, and this above all, that he should hate his brother. And how fares it with him concerning his other sins, of which it is said, "If we say that we have no sin, we deceive ourselves, and the truth is not in us?" Let him hear that which shall set his mind at rest from another place of Scripture; "Charity covereth a multitude of sins."[3]

4. Charity therefore we commend; charity this Epistle commendeth. The Lord, after His resurrection, what question put He to Peter, but, "Lovest thou me?"[4] And it was not enough to ask it once; a second time also He put none other question, a third time also none other. Although when it came to the third time, Peter, as one who knew not what was the drift of this, was grieved because it seemed as if the Lord did not believe him; nevertheless both a first time and a second, and a third He put this question. Thrice fear denied, thrice love confessed. Behold Peter loveth the Lord. What is he to do for the Lord? For think not that he in the Psalm did not feel himself at a loss what to do: "What shall I render unto the Lord for all the benefits He hath done unto me?"[5] He that said this in the Psalm, marked what great things had been done for him by God; and sought what he should render to God, and could find nothing. For whatever thou wouldest render, from Him didst thou receive it to render. And what did he find to offer in return? That which, as we said, my brethren, he had received from Him, that only found he to offer in return. "I will receive the cup of salvation, and will call upon the name of the Lord." For who had given

him the cup of salvation, but He to whom he wished to offer in return? Now to receive the cup of salvation, and call upon the name of the Lord, is to be filled with charity; and so filled, that not only thou shalt not hate thy brother, but shalt be prepared to die for thy brother. This is perfect charity, that thou be prepared to die for thy brother. This the Lord exhibited in Himself, who died for all, praying for them by whom He was crucified, and saying, "Father, forgive them, for they know not what they do."[6] But if He alone hath done this, He was not a Master, if He had no disciples. Disciples who came after Him have done this.[7] Men were stoning Stephen, and he knelt down and said, "Lord, lay not this sin to their charge."[8] He loved them that were killing him; since for them also he was dying. Hear also the Apostle Paul: "And I myself," saith he, "will be spent for your souls."[9] For he was among those for whom Stephen, when by their hands he was dying, besought forgiveness. This then is perfect charity. If any man shall have so great charity that he is prepared even to die for his brethren, in that man is perfect charity. But as soon as it is born, is it already quite perfect? That it may be made perfect, it is born; when born, it is nourished; when nourished, it is strengthened; when strengthened, it is perfected; when it has come to perfection, what saith it? "To me to live is Christ, and to die is gain. I wished to be dissolved, and to be with Christ; which is far better: nevertheless to abide in the flesh is needful for you."[10] For their sakes he was willing to live, for whose sakes he was prepared to die.

5. And that ye may know that it is this perfect charity which that man violates not, and against which that man sins not, who is born of God; this is what the Lord saith to Peter; "Peter lovest thou me?" And he answers, "I love." He saith not, If thou love me, shew kindness to me. For when the Lord was in mortal flesh, He hungered, He thirsted: at that time when He hungered and thirsted, He was taken in as a guest; those who had the means, ministered unto Him of their substance, as we read in the Gospel. Zacchæus entertained Him as his guest: he was saved from his disease by entertaining the Physician. From what disease? The disease of avarice. For he was very rich, and the chief of the publicans. Mark the man made whole from the disease of avarice: "The half of my goods I give to the poor; and if I have taken any thing from

---

[1] [Translator here follows Eras.; Bened. (Migne) omits "of Christ, contrary to the New Testament," and omits "new" in next sentence.—J. H. M.]
[2] John xiii. 34.   [3] 1 Pet. iv. 8.
[4] John xxi. 15-17.   [5] Ps. cxvi. 12, 13.
[6] Luke xxiii. 34.   [7] Serm. clxxxiii. 3, 4.   [8] Acts vii. 59.
[9] 2 Cor. xii. 15.   [10] Phil. i. 21-24.

any man, I will restore him fourfold." [1] That he kept the other half, was not to enjoy it, but to pay his debts. Well, he at that time entertained the Physician as his guest, because there was infirmity of the flesh in the Lord, to which men might show this kindness; and this, because it was His will to grant this very thing to them that did Him kind service; for the benefit was to them that did the service, not to Him. For, could He to whom angels ministered require these men's kindness? Not even His servant Elias, to whom He sent bread and flesh by the ravens upon a certain occasion,[2] had need of this; and yet that a religious widow might be blessed, the servant of God is sent, and he whom God in secret did feed, is fed by the widow. But still, although by the means of these servants of God, those who consider their need get good to themselves, in respect of that reward most manifestly set forth by the Lord in the Gospel: "He that receiveth a righteous man in the name of a righteous man shall receive a righteous man's reward: and he that receiveth a prophet in the name of a prophet shall receive a prophet's reward: and whosoever shall give to drink unto one of these little ones a cup of cold water only in the name of a disciple, verily I say unto you, He shall in no wise lose his reward:" [3] although, then, they that do this, do it to their own good: yet neither could this kind office be done to Him when about to ascend [4] into Heaven. What could Peter, who loved Him, render unto Him? Hear what. "Feed my sheep:" i.e. do for the brethren, that which I have done for thee. I redeemed all with my blood: hesitate not to die for confession of the truth, that the rest may imitate you.

6. But this, as we have said, brethren, is perfect charity. He that is born of God hath it. Mark, my beloved, see what I say. Behold, a man has received the Sacrament of that birth, being baptized; he hath the Sacrament, and a great Sacrament, divine, holy, ineffable. Consider what a Sacrament! To make him a new man by remission of all sins! Nevertheless, let him look well to the heart, whether that be thoroughly done there, which is done in the body; let him see whether he have charity, and then say, I am born of God. If however he have it not, he has indeed the soldier's mark upon him, but he roams as a deserter. Let him have charity; otherwise let him not say that he is born of God. But he says, I have the Sacrament. Hear the Apostle: "If I know all mysteries,[5] and have all faith, so that I can remove mountains, and have not charity, I am nothing." [6]

7. This, if ye remember, we gave you to understand in beginning to read this Epistle, that nothing in it is so commended as charity. Even if it seems to speak of various other things, to this it makes its way back, and whatever it says, it will needs bring all to bear upon charity. Let us see whether it does so here. Mark: "Whosoever is born of God doth not commit sin." We ask, what sin? because if thou understand all sin, it will be contrary to that place, "If we say that we have no sin, we deceive ourselves, and the truth is not in us." Then let him say what sin; let him teach us; lest haply I may have rashly said that the sin here is the violation of charity, because he said above, "He that hateth his brother is in darkness, and walketh in darkness, and knoweth not whither he goeth, because the darkness hath blinded his eyes." [7] But perhaps he has said something in what comes afterwards, and has mentioned charity by name? See that this circuit of words hath this end, hath this issue. "Whosoever is born of God, sinneth not, because His seed remaineth in him." [8] The "seed" of God, i.e. the word of God: whence the apostle saith, "I have begotten you through the Gospel. And he cannot sin, because he is born of God." [9] Let him tell us this, let us see in what we cannot sin. "In this are manifested the children of God and the children of the devil. Whosoever is not righteous is not of God, neither he that loveth not his brother." [10] Aye, now indeed it is manifest of what he speaks: "Neither he that loveth not his brother." Therefore, love alone puts the difference between the children of God and the children of the devil. Let them all sign themselves with the sign of the cross of Christ; let them all respond, Amen; let all sing Alleluia; let all be baptized, let all come to church, let all build the walls of churches: there is no discerning of the children of God from the children of the devil, but only by charity. They that have charity are born of God: they that have it not, are not born of God. A mighty token, a mighty distinction! Have what thou wilt; if this alone thou have not, it profiteth thee nothing: other things if thou have not, have this, and thou hast fulfilled the law. "For he that loveth another hath fulfilled the law," saith the apostle: and, "Charity is the fulfilling of the law." [11] I take this to be the pearl which the merchant man in the Gospel is described to have been seeking, who

---

[1] Luke xix. 8.　[2] 1 Kings xvii. 4–9.　[3] Matt. x. 41, 42.
[4] *Ascensuro.*—BEN.　[5] *Sacramenta.*

[6] 1 Cor. xiii. 2.　[7] 1 John ii. 11.　[8] 1 John iii. 9.
[9] 1 Cor. iv. 15.　[10] 1 John iii. 10.　[11] Rom. xiii. 8, 10.

"found one pearl, and sold all that he had, and bought it." [1] This is the pearl of price, Charity, without which whatever thou mayest have, profiteth thee nothing: which if alone thou have, it sufficeth thee. Now, with faith thou seest, then with actual beholding [2] thou shalt see. For if we love when we see not, how shall we embrace it when we see ! But wherein must we exercise ourselves ? In brotherly love. Thou mayest say to me, I have not seen God: canst thou say to me, I have not seen man ? Love thy brother. For if thou love thy brother whom thou seest, at the same time thou shalt see God also; be· cause thou shalt see Charity itself, and within dwelleth God.

8. "Whosoever is not righteous is not of God, neither he that loveth not his brother." [3] "For this is the message:" mark how he confirms it: "For this is the message which we heard from the beginning, that we should love one another." He has made it manifest to us that it is of this he speaks; whoso acts against this commandment, is in that accursed sin, into which those fall who are not born of God. "Not as Cain, who was of that wicked one, and slew his brother. And wherefore slew he him? Because his own works were evil, and his brother's righteous." [4] Therefore, where envy is, brotherly love cannot be. Mark, my beloved. He that envieth, loveth not. The sin of the devil is in that man; because the devil through envy cast man down. For he fell, and envied him that stood. He did not wish to cast man down that he himself might stand, but only that he might not fall alone. Hold fast in your mind from this that he has subjoined, that envy cannot exist in charity. Thou hast it openly, when charity was praised, "Charity envieth not." [5] There was no charity in Cain; and had there been no charity in Abel, God would not have accepted his sacrifice. For when they had both offered, the one of the fruits of the earth, the other of the offspring of the flock; what think ye, brethren, that God slighted the fruits of the earth, and loved the offspring of the flock ? God had not regard to the hands, but saw in the heart: and whom He saw offer with charity, to his sacrifice He had respect; whom He saw offer with envy, from his sacrifice He turned away His eyes. By the good works, then, of Abel, he means only charity: by the evil works of Cain he means only his hatred of his brother. It was not enough that he hated his brother and envied his good works; because he would not imitate, he would kill. And hence it

appeared that he was a child of the devil, and hence also that the other was God's righteous one. Hence then are men discerned, my brethren. Let no man mark the tongue, but the deeds and the heart. If any do not good for his brethren, he shews what he has in him. By temptations are men proved.

9. "Marvel not, brethren, if the world hate us." [6] Must one often be telling you what "the world" means? Not the heaven, not the earth, nor these visible works which God made; but lovers of the world. By often saying these things, to some I am burdensome: but I am so far from saying it without a cause, that some may be questioned whether I said it, and they cannot answer. Let then, even by thrusting it upon them, something stick fast in the hearts of them that hear. What is "the world"? The world, when put in a bad sense, is, lovers of the world: the world, when the word is used in praise, is heaven and earth, and the works of God that are in them; whence it is said, "And the world was made by Him." [7] Also, the world is the fullness of the earth, as John himself hath said, "Not only for our sins is He the propitiator, but (for the sins) of the whole world:" [8] he means, "of the world," of all the faithful scattered throughout the whole earth. But the world in a bad sense, is, lovers of the world. They that love the world, cannot love their brother.

10. "If the world hate us: we know "—What do we know?—"that we have passed from death unto life "—How do we know? "Because we love the brethren." [9] Let none ask man: let each return to his own heart: if he find there brotherly love, let him set his mind at rest, because he is "passed from death unto life." Already he is on the right hand: let him not regard that at present his glory is hidden: when the Lord shall come, then shall he appear in glory. For he has life in him, but as yet in winter; the root is alive, but the branches, so to say, are dry: within is the substance that has the life in it, within are the leaves of trees, within are the fruits: but they wait for the summer. Well then, "we know that we have passed from death unto life, because we love the brethren. He that loveth not, abideth in death." Lest ye should think it a light matter, brethren, to hate, or, not to love, hear what follows: "Every one that hateth his brother, is a murderer." [10] How now? if any made light of hating his brother, will he also in his heart make light of murder ? He does not stir his hands to kill a man; yet he is already held

---

[1] Matt. xiii. 46.　　[2] *Cum specie.*　　[3] 1 John iii. 10, 11.
[1] John iii. 12.　　[5] 1 Cor. xiii. 4.

[6] 1 John iii. 13.　Gr. ὑμᾶς; Vulg. *vos.*　[7] John i. 10.
[8] 1 John ii. 2.　　[9] 1 John iii. 14.　　[10] 1 John iii. 15.

by God a murderer; the other lives, and yet this man is already judged as his slayer! "Every one that hateth his brother is a murderer: and ye know that no murderer hath eternal life abiding in him."

11. "In this know we love:"[1] he means, perfection of love, that perfection which we have bidden you lay to heart: "In this know we love, that He laid down His life for us: and we ought to lay down our lives for the brethren." Lo here, whence that came: "Peter, lovest thou me? Feed My sheep."[2] For, that ye may know that He would have His sheep to be so fed by him, as that he should lay down his life for the sheep, straightway said He this to him: "When thou wast young, thou girdedst thyself, and walkedst whither thou wouldest: but when thou shalt be old, thou shalt stretch forth thy hands, and another shall gird thee, and carry thee whither thou wouldest not. This spake He," saith the evangelist, "signifying by what death he should glorify God;" so that to whom He had said, "Feed my sheep," the same He might teach to lay down his life for His sheep.

12. Whence beginneth charity, brethren? Attend a little: to what it is perfected, ye have heard; the very end of it, and the very measure of it is what the Lord hath put before us in the Gospel: "Greater love hath no man," saith He, "than that one lay down his life for his friends."[3] Its perfection, therefore, He hath put before us in the Gospel, and here also it is its perfection that is put before us: but ye ask yourselves, and say to yourselves, When shall it be possible for us to have "this" charity? Do not too soon despair of thyself. Haply, it is born and is not yet perfect; nourish it, that it be not choked. But thou wilt say to me, And by what am I to know it? For to what it is perfected, we have heard; whence it begins, let us hear. He goes on to say: "But whoso hath this world's good, and seeth his brother have hunger,[4] and shutteth up his bowels of compassion from him, how can the love of God dwell in him?"[5] Lo, whence charity begins withal![6] If thou art not yet equal to

the dying for thy brother, be thou even now equal to the giving of thy means to thy brother. Even now let charity smite thy bowels, that not of vainglory thou shouldest do it, but of the innermost [7]marrow of mercy; that thou consider him, now in want. For if thy superfluities thou canst not give to thy brother, canst thou lay down thy life for thy brother? There lies thy money in thy bosom, which thieves may take from thee; and though thieves do not take it, by dying thou wilt leave it, even if it leave not thee while living: what wilt thou do with it? Thy brother hungers, he is in necessity: belike he is in suspense, is distressed by his creditor: he is thy brother, alike ye are bought, one is the price paid for you, ye are both redeemed by the blood of Christ: see whether thou have mercy, if thou have this world's means. Perchance thou sayest, "What concerns it me? Am I to give my money, that he may not suffer trouble?" If this be the answer thy heart makes to thee, the love of the Father abideth not in thee. If the love of the Father abide not in thee, thou art not born of God. How boastest thou to be a Christian? Thou hast the name, and hast not the deeds. But if the work shall follow the name, let any call thee pagan, show thou by deeds that thou art a Christian. For if by deeds thou dost not show thyself a Christian, all men may call thee a Christian yet; what doth the name profit thee where the thing is not forthcoming? "But whoso hath this world's good, and seeth his brother have need,[8] and shutteth up his bowels of compassion from him, how can the love of God dwell in him?" And then he goes on: "My little children, let us not love in word, neither in tongue but in deed and in truth."[9]

13. I suppose the thing is now made manifest to you, my brethren: this great and most concerning secret and mystery.[10] What is the force of charity, all Scripture doth set forth; but I know not whether any where it be more largely set forth than in this Epistle. We pray you and beseech you in the Lord, that both what ye have heard ye will keep in

---

[1] 1 John iii. 16.   [2] John xxi. 15-19.   [3] John xv. 13.
[4] *Esurientem.*   [5] 1 John iii. 17.

[6] [*Love : beneficence.*—Augustin throughout these homilies amply vindicates his own declaration that the epistle on which he is commenting relates largely to charity; and his glowing words not only exhibit love as one star in the constellation of Christian graces, but as a deep and joyous principle and centre of life, "a well of water" within, from which refreshing streams of beneficence will spontaneously gush forth.

He controverts those in his day who taught that it was enough to have the truth, to possess right opinions, and that such need not be forward in sacrificing aught for the truth's sake, or to help their brethren. And in kindly reproof of such indolent and ignorant 'self seeking, he points the earnest believer to whom comes the lofty utterance of the apostle, lay down life, if need be, for thy brother, and who shrinks from such a test, to a lower evidence

of the Christ-like mind, within the reach of all, and from which all may go up higher—"help thy brother in his necessity, relieve his wants ; if not ready to do this for the brother before your eyes, how can you pretend love to the unseen Father and Friend?"

As the apostle's reprehension of errorists in his day is applicable in refutation of many false opinions rife in our times, so his and Augustin's fervent commendation of the surpassing excellence of love, and the absolute need, for the believer, of uniformly and constantly manifesting it in act and life, can never be superfluous, can never grow old.

Indifferentism as to doctrine, and careless coldness with respect to the sufferings of others, against both of which St. John lifts up his voice, if not peculiar to our day and nation, are yet deplorable evils among us, demanding energetic and practical protests from those who love the truth and love man.—J. H. M.]

[7] *Adipe.*   [8] *Egentem.*
[9] 1 John iii. 18.   [10] *Sacramentum.*

memory, and to that which is yet to be said, until the epistle be finished, will come with earnestness, and with earnestness hear the same. But open ye your heart for the good seed: root out the thorns, that that which we are sowing in you be not choked, but rather that the harvest may grow, and that the Husbandman may rejoice and make ready the barn for you as for grain, not the fire as for the chaff

HOMILY VI.

1 John III. 19.—IV. 3.

"And herein we know that we are of the truth, and assure our hearts before Him. For if our heart think ill of us, God is greater than our heart, and knoweth all things. Beloved, if our heart think not ill of us, then have we confidence toward God. And whatsoever we ask, we shall receive of Him, because we keep His commandments, and do in His sight those things that please Him. And this is His commandment, That we should believe on the name of His Son Jesus Christ, and love one another, as He gave us commandment. And he that keepeth His commandments shall dwell in Him, and He in him. And herein we know that He abideth in us, by the Holy Spirit which He hath given us. Dearly beloved, believe not every spirit, but try the spirits whether they are of God: because many false prophets are gone out into this world. In this is known the Spirit of God: every spirit that confesseth that Jesus Christ is come in the flesh is of God: and every spirit that confesseth not that Jesus Christ is come in the flesh is not of God: and this is the antichrist, of whom ye have heard that he should come; and even now already is he in this world."

1. IF ye remember, brethren, yesterday we closed our sermon at this sentence,[1] which without doubt behooved and does behoove to abide in your heart, seeing it was the last ye heard. " My little children, let us not love only in word and in tongue; but in deed and in truth." Then he goes on: "And herein we know that we are of the truth, and assure our hearts before Him."[2] " For if our heart[3] think ill of us, God is greater than our heart, and knoweth all things." He had said," Let us not love only in word and in tongue, but in work and in truth:" we are asked, In what work, or in what truth, is he known that loveth God, or loveth his brother? Above he had said up to what point charity is perfected: what the Lord saith in the Gospel, " Greater love than this hath no man, that one lay down his life for his friends,"[4] this same had the apostle also said: "As He laid down His life for us, we ought also to lay down our lives for the brethren."[5] This is the perfection of charity, and greater can not at all be found. But because it is not perfect in all, and that man ought not to despair in whom it is not perfect, if that be already born which may be perfected: and of course if born, it must be nourished, and by certain nourishments of its own must be brought unto its proper perfection: therefore, we have asked concerning the commencement of charity, where it begins, and there have straightway found: " But whoso hath this world's goods, and seeth his brother have need, and shutteth up his bowels of compassion from him, how dwelleth the love of the Father in him?"[6] Here then hath this charity, my brethren, its beginning: to give of one's superfluities to him that hath need to him that is in any distress; of one's temporal abundance to deliver his brother from temporal tribulation. Here is the first rise of charity. This, being thus begun, if thou shalt nourish with the word of God and hope of the life to come, thou wilt come at last unto that perfection, that thou shalt be ready to lay down thy life for thy brethren.

2. But, because many such things are done by men who seek other objects, and who love not the brethren; let us come back to the tes-

---

[1] 1 John iii. 18-20.
[2] [Better, "judge ill," *i.e.*, condemn.—J. H. M.]
[3] *Male senserit.*　　[4] John xv. 13.　　[5] 1 John iii. 16.　　[6] 1 John iii. 17.

timony of conscience. How do we prove that many such things are done by men who love not the brethren? How many in heresies and schisms call themselves martyrs! They seem to themselves to lay down their lives for their brethren. If for the brethren they laid down their lives, they would not separate themselves from the whole brotherhood. Again, how many there are who for the sake of vainglory bestow much, give much, and seek therein but the praise of men and popular glory, which is full of windiness, and possesses no stability! Seeing, then, there are such, where shall be the proof of brotherly charity? Seeing he wished it to be proved, and hath said by way of admonition, "My little children, let us not love only in word and in tongue; but in deed and in truth;" we ask, in what work, in what truth? Can there be a more manifest work than to give to the poor? Many do this of vainglory, not of love. Can there be a greater work than to die for the brethren? This also, many would fain be thought to do, who do it of vainglory to get a name, not from bowels of love. It remains, that that man loves his brother, who before God, where God alone seeth, assures his own heart, and questions his heart whether he does this indeed for love of the brethren; and his witness is that eye which penetrates the heart, where man cannot look. Therefore Paul the Apostle, because he was ready to die for the brethren, and said, "I will myself be spent for your souls,"[1] yet, because God only saw this in his heart, not the mortal men to whom he spake, he saith to them, "But to me it is a very small thing that I should be judged of you or at man's bar."[2] And the same apostle shows also in a certain place, that these things are oft done of empty vainglory, not upon the solid ground of love: for speaking of the praises of charity he saith, "If I distribute all my goods to the poor, and if I deliver up my body to be burned, but have not charity, it profiteth me nothing."[3] Is it possible for a man to do this without charity? It is. For they that have divided unity, are persons that have not charity. Seek there, and ye shall see many giving much to the poor; shall see others prepared to welcome death, insomuch that where there is no persecutor they cast themselves headlong: these doubtless without charity do this. Let us come back then to conscience, of which the apostle saith: "For our glorying is this, the testimony of our conscience."[4] Let us come back to conscience,

of which the same saith, "But let each prove his own work, and then he shall have glorying in himself and not in another."[5] Therefore, let each one of us "prove his own work," whether it flow forth from the vein of charity, whether it be from charity as the root that his good works sprout forth as branches. "But let each prove his own work, and then he shall have glorying in himself and not in another," not when another's tongue bears witness to him, but when his own conscience bears it.

3. This it is then that he enforces here. "In this we know that we are of the truth, when in deed and in truth" we love, "not only in words and in tongue: and [6] assure our heart before Him."[7] What meaneth, "before Him?" Where He seeth. Whence the Lord Himself in the Gospel saith: "Take heed that ye do not your righteousness before men, to be seen of them: otherwise ye have no reward with your Father which is in heaven."[8] And what meaneth, "Let not thy left hand know what thy right hand doeth:" except that the right hand means a pure conscience, the left hand the lust of the world?[9] Many through lust of the world do many wonderful things: the left hand worketh, not the right. The right hand ought to work, and without knowledge of the left hand, so that lust of the world may not even mix itself therewith when by love we work aught that is good. And where do we get to know this? Thou art before God: question thine heart, see what thou hast done, and what therein was thine aim; thy salvation, or the windy praise of men. Look within, for man cannot judge whom he cannot see. If "we assure our heart," let it be "before Him." Because "if our heart think ill of us," i.e. accuse us within, that we do not the thing with that mind it ought to be done withal, "greater is God than our heart, and knoweth all things." Thou hidest thine heart from man: hide it from God if thou canst! How shalt thou hide it from Him, to whom it is said by a sinner, fearing and confessing, "Whither shall I go from Thy Spirit? and from Thy face whither shall I flee?"[10] He sought a way to flee, to escape the judgment of God, and found none. For where is God not? "If I shall ascend," saith he, "into heaven, Thou art there: if I shall descend

---

[1] 2 Cor. xii. 15. [2] 1 Cor. iv. 3.
[3] 1 Cor. xiii. 3. [4] 2 Cor. i. 12.

[5] Gal. vi. 4.   [6] *Persuademus.*   [7] 1 John iii. 19.
[8] Matt. vi. 1-3. *Infra,* Hom. viii. 19, Serm. cxlix. 10-13.
[9] Comp. *de Serm. Dom. in Monte,* ii. 6-9, where having discussed and rejected several other explanations, St. Augustin rests in the interpretation, that "the left hand" denotes the carnal will looking aside to earthly rewards and the praise of men : "the right hand," the singleness of heart which looks straight forward to the will and commandment of God. Serm. cxlix. 15; *Enarr.* in Psa. 65, sec. 2.
[10] Ps. cxxxix. 7, 8.

into hell, Thou art there." Whither wilt thou go? whither wilt thou flee? Wilt thou hear counsel? If thou wouldest flee from Him, flee to Him. Flee to Him by confessing, not from Him by hiding: hide thou canst not, but confess thou canst. Say unto Him, "Thou art my place to flee unto;"[1] and let love be nourished in thee, which alone leadeth unto life. Let thy conscience bear thee witness that thy love is of God. If it be of God, do not wish to display it before men; because neither men's praises lift thee unto heaven, nor their censures put thee down from thence. Let Him see, who crowneth thee: be He thy witness, by whom as judge thou art crowned. "Greater is God than our heart, and knoweth all things."

4. "Beloved, if our heart think not ill of us, we have confidence towards God:"[2]—What meaneth, "If our heart think not ill"? If it make true answer to us, that we love and that there is[3] genuine love in us: not feigned but sincere; seeking a brother's salvation, expecting no emolument from a brother, but only his salvation—"we have confidence toward God: and whatsoever we ask, we shall receive of Him, because we keep His commandments."[4]—Therefore, not in the sight of men, but where God Himself seeth, in the heart—"we have confidence," then, "towards God: and whatsoever we ask, we shall receive of Him:" howbeit, because we keep His commandments. What are "His commandments"? Must we be always repeating? "A new commandment give I unto you, that ye love one another."[5] It is charity itself that he speaks of, it is this that he enforces. Whoso then shall have brotherly charity, and have it before God, where God seeth, and his heart being interrogated under righteous examination make him none other answer than that the genuine root of charity is there for good fruits to come from; that man hath confidence with God, and whatsoever he shall ask, he shall receive of Him, because he keepeth His commandments.

5. Here a question meets us: for it is not this or that man, or thou or I that come in question,—for if I have asked any thing of God and receive it not, any person may easily say of me, "He hath not charity:" and of any man soever of this present time, this may easily be said; and let any think what he will, a man of man:—not we, but those come more in question, those men of whom it is on all hands known that they were saints when they wrote, and that they are now with God. Where is the man that hath charity, if Paul

had it not, who said, "Our mouth is open unto you, O ye Corinthians, our heart is enlarged; ye are not straitened in us:"[6] who said," I will myself be spent for your souls:" and so great grace was in him, that it was manifested that he had charity. And yet we find that he asked and did not receive. What say we, brethren? It is a question: look attentively to God: it is a great question, this also. Just as, where it was said of sin, "He that is born of God sinneth not:" we found this sin to be the violating of charity, and that this was the thing strictly intended in that place: so too we ask now what it is that he would say. For if thou look but to the words, it seems plain: if thou take the examples into the account, it is obscure. Than the words here nothing can be plainer. "And whatsoever we ask, we shall receive of Him, because we keep His commandments, and do those things that are pleasing in His sight." "Whatsoever we ask," saith he, "we shall receive of Him." He hath put us sorely to straits. In the other place also he would put us to straits, if he meant all sin: but then we found room to expound it in this, that he meant it of a certain sin, not of all sin; howbeit of a sin which "whosoever is born of God committeth not:" and we found that this same sin is none other than the violation of charity. We have also a manifest example from the Gospel, when the Lord saith, "If I had not come, they had not had sin."[7] How? Were the Jews innocent when He came to them, because He so speaks? Then if He had not come, would they have had no sin? Then did the Physician's presence make one sick, not take away the fever? What madman even would say this? He came not but to cure and heal the sick. Therefore when He said, "If I had not come, they had not had sin," what would He have to be understood, but a certain sin in particular? For there was a sin which the Jews would not have had. What sin? That they believed not on Him, that when he had come they despised Him. As then He there said "sin," and it does not follow that we are to understand all sin, but a certain sin: so here also not all sin, lest it be contrary to that place where he saith, "If we say that we have no sin, we deceive ourselves, and the truth is not in us:"[8] but a certain sin in particular, that is, the violation of charity. But in this place he hath bound us more tightly: "If we shall ask," he hath said, "if our heart accuse us not, and tell us in answer, in the sight of God, that true love is in us;" "Whatsoever we ask, we shall receive of Him."

---

[1] Ps. xxxii. 7.   [2] 1 John iii. 21.   [3] Germana.
[4] 1 John iii. 21, 22.   [5] John xiii. 34.   [6] 2 Cor. vi. 11, 12; id. xii. 15.   [7] John xv. 22.   [8] 1 John i. 8.

6. Well now: I have already told you, my beloved brethren, let no man turn toward us. For what are we? or what are ye? What, but the Church of God which is known to all? And, if it please Him, in that Church are we; and those of us who by love abide in it, there let us persevere, if we would show the love we have. But then the apostle Paul, what evil are we to think of him? He not love the brethren! He not have within himself the testimony of his conscience in the sight of God! Paul not have within him that root of charity whence all good fruits proceeded! What madman would say this? Well then: where find we that the apostle asked and did not receive? He saith himself: "Lest I should be exalted above measure through the abundance of the revelations, there was given to me a thorn in the flesh, an angel of Satan to buffet me. For which thing I besought the Lord thrice, that He would take it from me. And He said unto me, My grace is sufficient for thee: for strength is made perfect in weakness."[1] Lo, he was not heard in his prayer that the "angel of Satan" should be taken from him. But wherefore? Because it was not good for him. He was heard, then, for salvation, when he was not heard according to his wish. Know, my beloved, a great[2] mystery: which we urge upon your consideration on purpose that it may not slip from you in your temptations. The saints are in all things heard unto salvation: they are always heard in that which respects their eternal salvation; it is this that they desire: because in regard of this, their prayers are always heard.

7. But let us distinguish God's different ways of hearing prayer. For we find some not heard for their wish, heard for salvation: and again some we find heard for their wish, not heard for salvation. Mark this difference, hold fast this example of a man not heard for his wish but heard for salvation. Hear the apostle Paul; for what is the hearing of prayer unto salvation, God Himself showed him: "Sufficient for thee," saith He, "is my grace; for strength is perfected in weakness." Thou hast besought, hast cried, hast thrice cried: the very cry thou didst raise once for all I heard, I turned not away mine ears from thee; I know what I should do: thou wouldest have it taken away, the healing thing by which thou art burned; I know the infirmity by which thou art burdened. Well then: here is a man who was heard for salvation, while as to his will he was not heard. Where find we persons heard for

their will, not heard for salvation? Do we find, think we, some wicked, some impious man, heard of God for his will, not heard for salvation? If I put to you the instance of some man, perchance thou wilt say to me, "It is thou that callest him wicked, for he was righteous; had he not been righteous, his prayer would not have been heard by God." The instance I am about to allege is of one, of whose iniquity and impiety none can doubt. The devil himself: he asked for Job, and received.[3] Have ye not here also heard concerning the devil, that "he that committeth sin is of the devil"?[4] Not that the devil created, but that the sinner imitates. Is it not said of him, "He stood not in the truth"?[5] Is not even he "that old serpent," who, through the woman pledged the first man in the drink of poison?[6] Who even in the case of Job, kept for him his wife, that by her the husband might be, not comforted, but tempted? The devil asked for a holy man, to tempt him; and he received: the apostle asked that the thorn in the flesh might be taken from him, and he received not. But the apostle was more heard than the devil. For the apostle was heard for salvation, though not for his wish: the devil was heard for his wish, but for damnation. For that Job was yielded up to him to be tempted, was in order that by his standing the proof the devil should be tormented. But this, my brethren, we find not only in the Old Testament books, but also in the Gospel. The demons besought the Lord, when He expelled them from the man, that they might be permitted to go into the swine. Should the Lord not have power to tell them not to approach even those creatures? For, had it not been His will to permit this, they were not about to rebel against the King of heaven and earth. But with a view to a certain mystery, with a certain[7] ulterior meaning, He let the demons go into the swine: to show that the devil hath dominion in them that lead the life of swine.[8] Demons then were heard in their request; was the apostle not heard? Or rather (what is truer) shall we say, The apostle was heard, the demons not heard? Their will was effected; his weal was perfected.

8. Agreeably with this, we ought to understand that God, though He give not to our will, doth give for our salvation. For sup-

[1] 2 Cor. xii. 7-9.   [2] Sacramentum.

[3] Job. i. 11, 12.   [4] 1 John iii. 3, 8.   [5] John viii. 44.
[6] Gen. iii. 1-6.   [7] Certa dispensatione.
[8] Luke viii. 32. Dimisit, not misit: so, Expulsa et in porcos permissa dæmonia: "the demons cast out from the man and allowed to go into the swine." Quæst. Evang. ii. 13. Quod in porcos in montibus pascentes ire permissa sunt, &c. "That they were allowed to go into the swine feeding upon the mountains, betokens unclean and proud men over whom through the worship of idols the demons have dominion."

pose the thing thou have asked be to thine hurt, and the Physician knows that it is to thine hurt; what then? It is not to be said that the physician does not give ear to thee, when, perhaps, thou askest for cold water, and if it is good for thee, he gives it immediately, if not good, he gives it not. Had he no ears for thy request, or rather, did he give ear for thy weal, even when he gainsaid thy will? Then let there be in you charity, my brethren; let it be in you, and then set your minds at rest: even when the thing ye ask for is not given you, your prayer is granted, only, ye know it not. Many have been given into their own hands, to their own hurt: of whom the apostle saith, "God gave them up to their own hearts' lusts."[1] Some man hath asked for a great sum of money; he hath received, to his hurt. When he had it not, he had little to fear; no sooner did he come to have it, than he became a prey to the more powerful. Was not that man's request granted to his own hurt, who would needs have that for which he should be sought after by the robber, whereas, being poor, none sought after him? Learn to beseech God that ye may commit it to the Physician to do what He knows best. Do thou confess the disease, let Him apply the means of healing. Do thou only hold fast charity. For He will needs cut, will needs burn; what if thou criest out, and art not spared for thy crying under the cutting, under the burning and the tribulation, yet He knows how far the rottenness reaches.[2] Thou wouldest have Him even now take off His hands, and He considers only the deepness of the sore; He knows how far to go. He does not attend to thee for thy will, but he does attend to thee for thy healing. Be ye sure, then, my brethren, that what the apostle saith is true: "For we know not what we should pray for as we ought: but the Spirit itself maketh intercession for us with groanings which cannot be uttered: for He maketh intercession for the saints."[3] How is it said, "The Spirit itself intercedeth for the saints," but as meaning the charity which is wrought in thee by the Spirit? For therefore saith the same apostle: "The charity of God is shed abroad in our hearts by the Holy Spirit which is given unto us."[4] It is charity that groans, it is charity that prays: against it He who gave it cannot shut His ears. Set your minds at rest: let charity ask, and the ears of God are there. Not that which thou wishest is done, but that is done which is advantageous. Therefore, "what-

ever we ask," saith he, "we shall receive of Him." I have already said, If thou understand it to mean, "for salvation," there is no question: if not for salvation, there is a question, and a great one, a question that makes thee an accuser of · the apostle Paul. "Whatever we ask, we receive of Him, because we keep His commandments, and do these things that are pleasing in His sight:" within, where He seeth.

9. And what are those commandments? "This," saith he, "is His commandment, That we should believe on the name of His Son Jesus Christ, and love one another."[5] Ye see that this is the commandment: ye see that whoso doeth aught against this commandment, doeth the sin from which "every one that is born of God" is free. "As He gave us commandment:" that we love one another. "And he that keepeth His commandment"[6]—ye see that none other thing is bidden us than that we love one another—"And he that keepeth His commandment shall abide[7] in Him, and He in him. "And in this we know that He abideth in us, by the Spirit which He hath given us. Is it not manifest that this is what the Holy Ghost works in man, that there should be in him love and charity? Is it not manifest, as the Apostle Paul saith, that "the love of God is shed abroad in our hearts by the Holy Ghost which is given us"?[8] For [our apostle] was speaking of charity, and was saying that we ought in the sight of God to interrogate our own heart. "But if our heart think not ill of us:" i.e. if it confess that from the love of our brother is done in us whatever is done in any good work. And then besides, in speaking of the commandment, he says this: "This is His commandment, That we should believe on the name of His Son Jesus Christ, and love one another, as He gave us commandment." "And he that doeth His commandment abideth[9] in Him, and He in him. In this we know that He abideth in us, by the Spirit which He hath given us."[10] If in truth thou find that thou hast charity, thou hast the Spirit of God in order to understand: for a very necessary thing it is.

10. In the earliest times, "the Holy Ghost fell upon them that believed: and they spake with tongues," which they had not learned, "as the Spirit gave them utterance."[11] These were signs adapted to the time. For there behooved to be that betokening of the Holy Spirit in all tongues, to shew that the Gospel of God was to run through all tongues over

---

1 Rom. i. 24.   2 *Enarr* in Ps. cxxx. sec. 1; Serm. cccliv. 7.
3 Rom. viii. 26, 27.   4 Rom. v. 5.
32

5 1 John iii. 23.   6 1 John iii. 24.
7 *Manebit.*   8 Rom. v. 5.
9 [Abideth. R. V.—J. H. M.]
10 [He gave us. R. V.—J. H. M.]   11 Acts ii. 4.

the whole earth. That thing was done for a betokening, and it passed away. In the laying on of hands now, that persons may receive the Holy Ghost, do we look that they should speak with tongues? Or when we laid the hand on these infants,[1] did each one of you look to see whether they would speak with tongues, and, when he saw that they did not speak with tongues, was any of you so wrong-minded as to say, These have not received the Holy Ghost; for, had they received, they would speak with tongues as was the case in those times? If then the witness of the presence of the Holy Ghost be not now given through these miracles, by what is it given, by what does one get to know that he has received the Holy Ghost? Let him question his own heart. If he love his brother, the Spirit of God dwelleth in him. Let him see, let him prove himself before the eyes of God, let him see whether there be in him the love of peace and unity, the love of the Church that is spread over the whole earth. Let him not rest only in his loving the brother whom he has before his eyes, for we have many brethren whom we do not see, and in the unity of the Spirit we are joined to them. What marvel that they are not with us? We are in one body, we have one Head, in heaven. Brethren, our two eyes do not see each other; as one may say, they do not know each other. But in the charity of the bodily frame do they not know each other? For, to shew you that in the charity which knits them together they do know each other; when both eyes are open, the right may not rest on some object, on which the left shall not rest likewise. Direct the glance of the right eye without the other, if thou canst. Together they meet in one object, together they are directed to one object: their aim is one, their places diverse. If then all who with thee love God have one aim with thee, heed not that in the body thou are separated in place; the eyesight of the heart ye have alike fixed on the light of truth. Then if thou wouldest know that thou hast received the Spirit, question thine heart: lest haply thou have the sacrament, and have not the virtue of the sacrament. Question thine heart. If love of thy brethren be there, set thy mind at rest. There cannot be love without the Spirit of God: since Paul cries, "The love of God is shed abroad in your hearts by the Holy Spirit which is given unto us."[2]

11. "Beloved, believe not every spirit."[3] Because he had said, "In this we know that He abideth in us, by the Spirit which He hath given us." But how this same Spirit is known, mark this: "Beloved, believe not every spirit, but prove the spirits whether they be from God." And who is he that proves the spirits? A hard matter has he put to us, my brethren! It is well for us that he should tell us himself how we are to discern them. He is about to tell us: fear not: but first see; mark: see that hereby is expressed the very thing that vain heretics[4] taunt us withal. Mark, see what he says, "Beloved, believe not every spirit, but prove the spirits whether they be from God." The Holy Spirit is spoken of in the Gospel by the name of water; where the Lord "cried and said, If any man thirst, let him come unto me, and drink. He that believeth on me, out of his belly shall flow rivers of living water."[5] But the evangelist has expounded of what He said this: for he goes on to say, "But this spake He of the Spirit, which they that believed on Him should receive." Wherefore did not the Lord baptize many? But what saith he? "For the Holy Ghost was not yet given; because that Jesus was not yet glorified." Then seeing those had baptism, and had not yet received the Holy Ghost, whom on the day of Pentecost the Lord sent from heaven, the glorifying of the Lord was first waited for, so that the Spirit might be given. Even before He was glorified, and before He sent the Spirit, He yet invited men to prepare themselves for the receiving of the water of which He said, "Whoso thirsteth, let him come and drink;" and, "He that believeth on me, out of his belly shall flow rivers of living water." What meaneth, "Rivers of living water"? What is that water? Let no man ask me; ask the Gospel. "But this," saith it, "He said of the Spirit, which they should receive that should believe on Him." Consequently, the water of the sacrament is one thing: another, the water which betokens the Spirit of God. The water of the sacrament is visible: the water of the Spirit invisible. *That* washes the body, and betokens that which is done in the soul. By *this* Spirit the soul itself is cleansed and fed. This is the Spirit of God, which heretics and all that cut themselves off from the Church, cannot have. And whosoever do not openly cut themselves off, but by iniquity are cut off, and being within, whirl about as chaff and are not grain; these have not this Spirit. This Spirit is denoted by the Lord under the name of water: and we have heard from this epistle, "Believe not every spirit;" and those words of Solomon

---

bear witness, " From strange water keep thee far." [1] What meaneth, " water "? Spirit. Does water always signify spirit? Not always: but in some places it signifies the Spirit, in some places it signifies baptism, in some places signifies peoples,[2] in some places signifies counsel: thus thou findest it said in a certain place, " Counsel is a fountain of life to them that possess it." [3] So then, in divers places of the Scriptures, the term " water " signifies divers things. Now however by the term water ye have heard the Holy Spirit spoken of, not by an interpretation of ours, but by witness of the Gospel, where it saith, " But this said He of the Spirit, which they should receive that should believe on Him." If then by the name of water is signified the Holy Spirit, and this epistle saith to us, " Believe not every spirit, but prove the spirits, whether they be of God;" let us understand that of this it is said, " From strange water keep thee far, and from a strange fountain drink thou not." [1] What meaneth, " From a strange fountain drink thou not "? A strange spirit believe thou not.

12. There remains then the test by which it is to be proved to be the Spirit of God. He has indeed set down a sign, and this, belike, difficult: let us see, however. We are to recur to that charity; it is that which teacheth us, because it is the unction. However, what saith he here? " Prove the spirits, whether they be from God: because many false prophets have gone out into this world." Now there are all heretics and all schismatics. How then am I to prove the spirit? He goes on: " In this is known [4] the Spirit of God." Wake up the ears of your heart. We were at a loss; we were saying, Who knows? who discerns? Behold, he is about to tell the sign. " Hereby is known the Spirit of God: every spirit that confesseth that Jesus Christ is come in the flesh is of God: and every spirit that confesseth not that Jesus Christ is come in the flesh is not of God: and this is the antichrist, of whom ye have heard that he should come; and even now already is he in this world." [5] Our ears, so to say, are on the alert for discerning of the spirits; and we have been told something, such that thereby we discern not a whit the more. For what saith he? " Every spirit that confesseth that Jesus Christ came in the flesh, is of God." Then is the spirit that is among the heretics, of God, seeing they " confess that Jesus Christ came in the

flesh "? Aye, here perchance they lift themselves up against us, and say: Ye have not the Spirit from God; but we confess " that Jesus Christ came in the flesh: " but the apostle here hath said that those have not the Spirit of God, who confess not " that Jesus Christ came in the flesh." Ask the Arians: they confess " that Jesus Christ came in the flesh: " ask the Eunomians; they confess " that Jesus Christ came in the flesh: " ask the Macedonians; they confess " that Jesus Christ came in the flesh: " put the question to the Cataphryges; they confess " that Jesus Christ came in the flesh: " put it to the Novatians; they confess " that Jesus Christ came in the flesh." Then have all these heresies the Spirit of God? Are they then no false prophets? Is there then no deception there, no seduction there? Assuredly they are antichrists; for " they went out from us, but were not of us."

13. What are we to do then? By what to discern them? Be very attentive; let us go together in heart, and knock. Charity herself keeps watch; for it is none other than she that shall knock, she also that shall open: anon ye shall understand in the name of our Lord Jesus Christ. Already ye have heard that it was said above, " Whoso denieth that Jesus Christ is come in the flesh, the same is an antichrist." There also we asked, Who denies? because neither do we deny, nor do those deny. And we found that some do in their deeds deny;[6] and we brought testimony from the apostle, who saith, " For they confess that they know God, but in their deeds deny Him." [7] Thus then let us now also make the enquiry in the deeds not in the tongue. What is the spirit that is not from God? That " which denieth that Jesus Christ is come in the flesh." And what is the spirit that is from God? That " which confesseth that Jesus Christ is come in the flesh." Who is he that confesseth that Jesus Christ is come in the flesh? Now, brethren, to the mark! let us look to the works, not stop at the noise of the tongue. Let us ask *why* Christ came in the flesh, so we get at the persons who deny that He is come in the flesh. If thou stop at tongues, why, thou shalt hear many a heresy confessing that Christ is come in the flesh: but the truth convicteth those men. Wherefore came Christ in the flesh? Was He not God? Is it not written of Him, " In the beginning was the Word, and the Word was with God, and the Word was God? " [8] Was it not He that did feed angels, is it not He that doth feed

---

[1] Prov. ix. 18 ; LXX.
[2] Rev. xvii. 15.　　　　[3] Prov. xvi. 22.
[4] *Cognoscitur*, so Vulg. representing the reading of some MSS. γινώσκεται. But the best authorities have γινώσκετε.
[5] 1 John iv. 2, 3.

[6] *Supra*, Hom. iii. 7-9.　　[7] Tit. i. 16.　　[8] John i. 1.

angels? Did He not in such sort come hither, that He departed not thence? Did He not in such sort ascend, that He forsook not us? Wherefore then came He in the flesh? Because it behooved us to have the hope of resurrection shown unto us. God He was, and in flesh He came; for God could not die, flesh could die; He came then in the flesh, that He might die for us. But how died He for us? "Greater charity than this hath no man, that a man lay down his life for his friends."[1] Charity therefore brought Him to the flesh. Whoever therefore has not charity denies that Christ is come in the flesh. Here then do thou now question all heretics. Did Christ come in the flesh? "He did come; this I believe, this I confess." Nay, this thou deniest. "How do I deny? Thou hearest that I say it!" Nay, I convict thee of denying it. Thou sayest with the voice, deniest with the heart; sayest in words, deniest in deeds. "How," sayest thou, "do I deny in deeds?" Because the end for which Christ came in the flesh, was, that He might die for us. He died for us, because therein He taught much charity. "Greater charity than this hath no man, that a man lay down his life for his friends." Thou hast not charity, seeing thou for thine own honor dividest unity. Therefore by this understand ye the spirit that is from God. Give the earthen vessels a tap, put them to the proof, whether haply they be cracked and give a dull sound: see whether they ring full and clear, see whether charity be there. Thou takest thyself away from the unity of the whole earth, thou dividest the Church by schisms, thou rendest the Body of Christ. He came in the flesh, to gather in one, thou makest an outcry to scatter abroad. This then is the Spirit of God, which saith that Jesus is come in the flesh, which saith, not in tongue but in deeds, which saith, not by making a noise but by loving. And that spirit is not of God, which denies that Jesus Christ is come in the flesh; denies, here also, not in tongue but in life; not in words but in deeds. It is manifest therefore by what we may know the brethren. Many within are in a sort within; but none without except he be indeed without.

14. Nay, and that ye may know that he has referred the matter to deeds, he saith, "And every spirit, *qui solvit Christum*, which does away with Christ that He came in the flesh,[2] is not of God." A doing away

in deeds is meant. What has he shown thee? "That denieth:" in that he saith, "doeth away" (or, "unmaketh"). He came to gather in one, thou comest to unmake. Thou wouldest pull Christ's members asunder. How can it be said that thou deniest not that Christ is come in the flesh, who rendest asunder the Church of God which He hath gathered together? Therefore thou goest against Christ; thou art an antichrist. Be thou within, or be thou without, thou art an antichrist: only, when thou art within, thou art hidden; when thou art without, thou art made manifest. Thou unmakest Jesus and deniest that He came in the flesh; thou art not of God. Therefore He saith in the Gospel: "Whoso shall break[3] one of these least commandments, and shall teach so, shall be called least in the kingdom of heaven."[4] What is this breaking? What this teaching? A breaking in the deeds and a teaching as it were in words.[5] "Thou that preachest men should not steal, dost thou steal?"[6] Therefore he that steals breaks or undoes the commandment in his deed, and as it were teaches so: "he shall be called least in the kingdom of heaven," *i.e.* in the Church of this present

printed Vulg. has, *Omnis spiritus qui solvit Christum ex Deo non est.* In Serm. 182 and 183, preached some time later on this text, Aug. reads it, *Omnis sp. qui non confitetur* (and, *qui negat*) *Jesum Christum in carne venisse.* S. Cypr. *Test. adv. Jud.* ii. 18, *qui autem negat in carne venisse, de Deo non est.* S. Iren. iii. 18, in the ancient Latin version, *Et omnis sp. qui solvit Jesum Christum, non est ex Deo.* Tertull. *adv. Marcion.* v. 16, *præcursores antichristi spiritus, negantes Christum in carne venisse et solventes Jesum, sc. in Deo creatore.* De *jejun. adv.* Psych. 1, *non quod alium Deum prædicent . . . , nec quod Jesum Christum solvant.* De *carne Christi,* 24. *Qui negat Christum in carne venisse, hic antichristus est:* where he says, the apostle "by clearly marking one Christ, shakes those who argue for a Christ multiform, making Christ one, Jesus another, &c." Leo Ep. x. 5, *ad Flavian,* seems to have read in the Gr. διαιροῦν. Other Latin authorities for the reading *qui solvit* are cited by Mill. *in loc.* Socrates H. E. vii. 32, affirms, that in the old mss. the reading was πᾶν πνεῦμα ὃ λύει τὸν Ἰησοῦν ἀπὸ τοῦ Θεοῦ οὐκ ἔστι: adding, that the expression was expunged from the old copies by those who would fain separate the Godhead from the Man of the Incarnation, οἱ χωρίζειν ἀπὸ τοῦ τῆς οἰκονομίας ἀνθρώπου βουλόμενοι τὴν θεότητα. (Valesius *in loc.* suggests that Socrates may have read in his mss. ὃ λύει τὸν Ἰησοῦν ἀπὸ τοῦ Θεοῦ, ἐκ τοῦ Θεοῦ οὐκ ἔστι: Matthäi, that he wrote, ὃ μὴ ὁμολογεῖ, τουτεστιν, ὃ λύει.) But no extant mss. acknowledge the reading: and the Greek Fathers headed by S. Polycarp *ad Philipp.* sec. 7 (πᾶς ὃς ἂν μὴ ὁμολογῇ Ἰ.Χ. ἐν σαρκὶ ἐληλυθέναι,) bear witness to the received text: only Cyril. *de recta Fide ad Reginas* being cited by Mill for the reading λύει. This reading may (as Mill has suggested, comp. Grot. *in loc.*) have originated in a marginal gloss, directed against the Gnostics. Thus in a scholion edited by Matthäi it is said: "For the precursors of Antichrist were the heresies, whose characteristic mark it is by the means of false prophets and spirits λύειν τὸν Ἰησοῦν, to unmake Jesus, by not confessing that He is come in the flesh."

3 *Solverit.*   4 Matt. v. 19.

5 S. Aug. *de Serm. Dom. in Monte,* i. 21. *Qui ergo solverit et docuerit homines . . . i.e., secundum id quod solvit, non secundum id quod invenit et legit . . . Qui autem fecerit et docuerit sic* (οὕτως for οὗτος) h. e. *secundum id quod non solvit.* Here he takes *docuerit sic* in the sense of teaching men by and agreeably with the practice of the teacher, which is that of breaking the commandments: "whosoever shall break one of these least commandments and in that way shall teach men," *solverit et secundum suam solutionem docuerit.* But *supra,* Hom. *in Ev.* cxxii. 9, he seems to make it parallel with Matt. xxiii. 3, "they say and do not:" *qui docent bona loquendo quæ solvunt male vivendo.* Comp. Serm. cclii. 3. His full meaning appears to be, that together with the good teaching in words, there goes a sort of teaching (*quasi docet*) not in words but in the deeds.

6 Rom. ii. 21.

1 John xv. 13.

2 *Qui solvit Christum in carne venisse.* Edd. *Erasm. Lugd.* and *Ven.* omit *in carne venisse,* but the Louvain editors attest that they are found in the mss. of Augustin. Ed. Par. (Bodl. mss. ext. Laud. 116, a late one, have them). *Infra,* Hom. vii. 2. *Omnis qui solvit J.C., et negat eum in carne venisse.* The

time.[1] Of him it is said, "What they say do ye; but what they do, that do not ye.[2] But he that shall do, and shall teach so, shall be called great in the kingdom of heaven." From this, that He has here said, *fecerit*, "shall do," while in opposition to this He has there said *solverit*, meaning *non fecerit*, "shall not do, and shall teach so"—to break, then, is, not to do—what doth He teach us, but that we should interrogate men's deeds, not take their words upon trust? The obscurity of the things compels us to speak much at length, chiefly that that which the Lord deigns to reveal may be brought within reach even of the brethren of slower understanding, because all were bought by the blood of Christ. And I am afraid the epistle itself will not be finished during these days as I promised: but as the Lord will, it is better to reserve the remainder, than to overload your hearts with too much food.

---

[1] So in Serm. cclii. 3: *de Civ. D.* xx. 9; but otherwise explained above, Tract. cxxii. 9.
[2] Matt. xxiii. 3.

HOMILY VII.

1 John IV. 4-12.

"Now are ye of God, little children, and have overcome him: because greater is He that is in you, than he that is in this world. They are of the world: therefore speak they of the world, and the world heareth them. We are of God: he that knoweth God heareth us; he that is not of God heareth not us. From this know we the spirit of truth, and [the spirit] of error. Dearly beloved, let us love one another: for love is of God; and every one that loveth is born of God, and knoweth God. He that loveth not knoweth not God; for God is love. In this was manifested the love of God in us, that God sent His only-begotten Son into this world, that we may live through Him. Herein is love, not that we loved, but that He loved us, and sent His Son to be the Atoner[1] for our sins. Dearly beloved, if God so loved us, we ought also to love one another. No man hath seen God at any time."

1. So is this world to all the faithful seeking their own country, as was the desert to the people Israel. They wandered indeed as yet, and were seeking their own country: but with God for their guide they could not wander astray. Their way was God's bidding.[2] For where they went about during forty years, the journey itself is made up of a very few stations, and is known to all. They were retarded because they were in training, not because they were forsaken. That therefore which God promiseth us is ineffable sweetness and a good,[3] as the Scripture saith, and as ye have often heard by us rehearsed, which "eye hath not seen, nor ear heard, neither hath entered into the heart of man."[4] But by temporal labors we are exercised, and by temptations of this present life are trained. Howbeit, if ye would not die of thirst in this wilderness, drink charity. It is the fountain which God has been pleased to place here that we faint not in the way: and we shall more abundantly drink thereof, when we are come to our own land. The Gospel has just been read; now to speak of the very words with which the lesson ended, what other thing heard ye but concerning charity? For we have made an agreement with our God in prayer, that if we would that He should forgive us our sins, we also should forgive the sins which may have been committed against us.[5] Now that which forgiveth is none other than charity. Take away charity from the heart; hatred possesseth it, it knows not how to forgive. Let charity be there, and she fearlessly forgiveth, not being straitened. And this whole epistle which we have undertaken to expound to you, see whether it commendeth aught else than this one thing, charity. Nor need we fear lest by much speaking thereof it come to be hateful. For what is there to love, if charity come to be hateful? It is by charity that other things come to be rightly loved; then how must

---

[1] *Litatorem.*
[2] *Jussio Dei:* so the mss. but the printed copies, *visio Dei.* Ben. (Bodl. 455, and Laud. 116, "*visio;*" Bodl. 813, so with "*jussio*" over the line; the rest "*jussio.*")
[3] Isa. lxiv. 4.　　　[4] 1 Cor. ii. 9.

[5] Matt. vi. 12.

itself be loved! Let not that then which ought never to depart from the heart, depart from the tongue.

2. "Now," saith he, "are ye of God little children, and have overcome him:"[1] whom but Antichrist? For above he had said, "Whosoever unmaketh[2] Jesus Christ and denieth that He is come in the flesh is not of God." Now we expounded, if ye remember, that all those who violate charity deny Jesus Christ to have come in the flesh. For Jesus had no need to come but because of charity: as indeed the charity we are commending is that which the Lord Himself commendeth in the Gospel, "Greater love than this can no man have, that a man lay down his life for his friends."[3] How was it possible for the Son of God to lay down His life for us without putting on flesh in which He might die? Whosoever therefore violates charity, let him say what he will with his tongue, his life denies that Christ is come in the flesh; and this is an antichrist, wherever he may be, whithersoever he have come in. But what saith the apostle to them who are citizens of that country for which we sigh? "Ye have overcome him." And whereby have they overcome? "Because greater is He that is in you, than he that is in this world." Lest they should attribute the victory to their own strength, and by arrogance of pride should be overcome, (for whomsoever the devil makes proud, he overcomes,) wishing them to keep humility, what saith he? "Ye have overcome him." Every man now, at hearing this saying, "Ye have overcome," lifts up the head, lifts up the neck, wishes himself to be praised. Do not extol thyself; see who it is that in thee hath overcome. Why hast thou overcome? "Because greater is He that is in you, than he that is in the world." Be humble, bear thy Lord; be thou the beast for Him to sit on. Good is it for thee that He should rule, and He guide. For if thou have not Him to sit on thee, thou mayest lift up the neck, mayest strike out the heels: but woe to thee without a ruler, for this liberty sendeth thee among the wild beasts to be devoured!

3. "These are of the world."[4] Who? The antichrists. Ye have already heard who they be. And if ye be not such, ye know them, but whosoever is such, knows not. "These are of the world: therefore speak they of the world, and the world heareth them." Who are they that "speak of the world"? Mark who are against charity. Behold, ye have heard the Lord saying,

"If ye forgive men their trespasses, your heavenly Father will forgive you also your trespasses. But if ye forgive not men their trespasses, neither will your Father forgive your trespasses."[5] It is the sentence of Truth: or if it be not Truth that speaks, gainsay it. If thou art a Christian and believest Christ, He hath said, "I am the truth." This sentence is true, is firm. Now hear men that "speak of the world." "And wilt thou not avenge thyself? And wilt thou let him say that he has done this to thee? Nay: let him feel that he has to do with a man." Every day are such things said. They that say such things, "of the world speak they, and the world heareth them." None say such things but those that love the world, and by none are such things heard but by those who love the world. And ye have heard that to love the world and neglect charity is to deny that Jesus came in the flesh. Or say if the Lord Himself in the flesh did that? if, being buffeted, He willed to be avenged? if, hanging on the cross, He did not say, "Father, forgive them, for they know not what they do"?[6] But if He threatened not, who had power; why dost thou threaten, why art thou inflated with anger, who art under power of another? He died because it was His will to die, yet He threatened not; thou knowest not when thou shalt die, and dost thou threaten?

4. "We are of God."[7] Let us see why; see whether it be for any other thing than charity. "We are of God: he that knoweth God heareth us; he that is not of God heareth not us. Hereby know we the spirit of truth, and of error:" namely by this, that he that heareth us hath the spirit of truth; he that heareth not us, hath the spirit of error. Let us see what he adviseth, and let us choose rather to hear him advising in the spirit of truth, and not antichrists, not lovers of the world, not the world. If we are born of God, "beloved,"[8] he goes on — see above from what: "We are of God: he that knoweth God heareth us; he that is not of God heareth not us. Hereby know we the spirit of truth, and of error:" aye, now, he makes us eagerly attentive: to be told that he who knows God, hears; but he who knows not, hears not; and that this is the discerning between the spirit of truth and the spirit of error: well then, let us see what he is about to advise; in what we must hear him —"Beloved, let us love one another."[8] Why? because a man adviseth? "Because love is of God." Much hath he commended love, in that he hath said, "Is of

God:" but he is going to say more; let us eagerly hear. At present he hath said, "Love is of God; and every one that loveth is born of God, and knoweth God. He that loveth not knoweth not God."[1] Why? "For God is love" [Love is God].[2] What more could be said, brethren? If nothing were said in praise of love throughout the pages of this epistle, if nothing whatever throughout the other pages of the Scriptures, and this one only thing were all we were told by the voice of the Spirit of God, "For Love is God;" nothing more ought we to require.

5. Now see that to act against love is to act against God. Let no man say, "I sin against man when I do not love my brother, (mark it!) and sin against man is a thing to be taken easily; only let me not sin against God. How sinnest thou not against God, when thou sinnest against love? "Love is God." Do "we" say this? If we said, "Love is God," haply some one of you might be offended and say, What hath he said? What meant he to say, that "Love is God"? God "gave" love, as a gift God bestowed love. "Love is of God: Love IS God." Look, here have ye, brethren, the Scriptures of God: this epistle is canonical; throughout all nations it is recited, it is held by the authority of the whole earth, it hath edified the whole earth. Thou art here told by the Spirit of God, "Love is God." Now if thou dare, go against God, and refuse to love thy brother!

6. In what sense then was it said a while ago, "Love is of God;" and now, "Love IS God?" For God is Father and Son and Holy Ghost: the Son, God of God, the Holy Ghost, God of God; and these three, one God, not three Gods. If the Son be God, and the Holy Ghost God, and that person loveth in whom dwelleth the Holy Ghost: therefore "Love is God;" but "IS God," because "Of God." For thou hast both in the epistle; both, "Love is of God," and, "Love is God." Of the Father alone the Scripture hath it not to say, that He is "of God:" but when thou hearest that expression, "Of God," either the Son is meant, or the Holy Ghost. Because while the apostle saith, "The love of God is shed abroad in our hearts by the Holy Spirit which is given unto us:"[3] let us understand that He who subsisteth in love is the Holy Ghost. For it is even this Holy Ghost, whom the bad cannot receive, even He is that Fountain of which the Scripture saith, "Let the fountain of thy water be thine own, and let no stranger partake with thee."[4] For all who love not God, are strangers, are antichrists. And though they come to the churches, they cannot be numbered among the children of God; not to them belongeth that Fountain of life. To have baptism is possible even for a bad man; to have prophecy is possible even for a bad man. We find that king Saul had prophecy: he was persecuting holy David, yet was he filled with the spirit of prophecy, and began to prophesy.[5] To receive the sacrament of the body and blood of the Lord is possible even for a bad man: for of such it is said, "He that eateth and drinketh unworthily, eateth and drinketh judgment to himself."[6] To have the name of Christ is possible even for a bad man; i.e. even a bad man can be called a Christian: as they of whom it is said, "They polluted the name of their God."[7] I say, to have all these sacraments is possible even for a bad man; but to have charity, and to be a bad man, is not possible. This then is the peculiar gift, this the "Fountain" that is singly one's "own." To drink of this the Spirit of God exhorteth you, to drink of Himself the Spirit of God exhorteth you.

7. "In this was manifested the love of God in us."[8] Behold, in order that we may love God, we have exhortation. Could we love Him, unless He first loved us? If we were slow to love, let us not be slow to love in return. He first loved us; not even so do we love. He loved the unrighteous, but He did away the unrighteousness: He loved the unrighteous, but not unto unrighteousness did He gather them together: He loved the sick, but He visited them to make them whole. "Love," then, "is God." "In this was manifested the love of God in us, because that God sent His only-begotten Son into the world, that we may live through Him." As the Lord Himself saith: "Greater love than this can no man have, that a man lay down his life for his friends:"[9] and there was proved the love of Christ towards us, in that He died for us: how is the love of the Father towards us proved? In that He "sent His only Son" to die for us: so also the apostle Paul saith: "He that spared not His own Son, but delivered Him up for us all, how hath He not with Him also freely given us all

---

[1] 1 John iv. 7, 8.
[2] Deus dilectio est: Augustin here expounds it, "Love is God;" it is "of God" and "is God," (as "the Word was with God and was God:") this is clear from sec. 6 and Hom.viii.14, "For He has not hesitated to say, Deus charitas est, Charity is God." In the theological exposition de Trin. xv. 27, he takes it in the usual sense, "God is Love" (as "God is Spirit"). In the Greek the proposition is not convertible. ἀγάπη being marked as the predicate by the absence of the article while θεὸς has it: ὁ θεὸς ἀγάπη ἐστίν.

[3] Rom. v. 5.   [4] Prov. v. 16, 17.   [5] 1 Sam. xix.
[6] 1 Cor. xi. 29. [7] Ezek. xxxvi. 20.   [8] 1 John iv. 9.
[9] John xv. 13.

things?"[1] Behold the Father delivered up Christ; Judas delivered Him up; does it not seem as if the thing done were of the same sort? Judas is "*traditor*," one that delivered up, [or, a traitor]: is God the Father that? God forbid! sayest thou. I do not say it, but the apostle saith, "He that spared not His own Son, but "*tradidit Eum*" delivered Him up for us all." Both the Father delivered Him up, and He delivered up Himself. The same apostle saith: "Who loved me, and delivered Himself up for me."[2] If the Father delivered up the Son, and the Son delivered up Himself, what has Judas done? There was a "*traditio*" (delivering up) by the Father; there was a "*traditio*" by the Son; there was a "*traditio*" by Judas: the thing done is the same, but what is it that distinguishes the Father delivering up the Son, the Son delivering up Himself, and Judas the disciple delivering up his Master? This: that the Father and the Son did it in love, but Judas did this[3] in treacherous betrayal. Ye see that not what the man does is the thing to be considered; but with what mind and will he does it. We find God the Father in the same deed in which we find Judas; the Father we bless, Judas we detest. Why do we bless the Father, and detest Judas? We bless charity, detest iniquity. How great a good was conferred upon mankind by the delivering up of Christ! Had Judas this in his thoughts, that therefore he delivered Him up? God had in His thoughts our salvation by which we were redeemed; Judas had in his thoughts the price for which he sold the Lord. The Son Himself had in His thoughts the price He gave for us, Judas in his the price he received to sell Him. The diverse intention therefore makes the things done diverse. Though the thing be one, yet if we measure it by the diverse intentions, we find the one a thing to be loved, the other to be condemned; the one we find a thing to be glorified, the other to be detested. Such is the force of charity. See that it alone discriminates, it alone distinguishes the doings of men.

8. This we have said in the case where the things done are similar. In the case where they are diverse, we find a man by charity made fierce;[4] and by iniquity made winningly gentle. A father beats a boy, and a boy-stealer caresses. If thou name the two things, blows and caresses, who would not choose the caresses, and decline the blows? If thou mark the persons, it is charity that beats, iniquity that caresses. See what we are insisting upon; that the deeds of men are only discerned by the root of charity. For many things may be done that have a good appearance, and yet proceed not from the root of charity. For thorns also have flowers: some actions truly seem rough, seem savage; howbeit they are done for discipline at the bidding of charity. Once for all, then, a short precept is given thee: Love, and do what thou wilt: whether thou hold thy peace, through love hold thy peace; whether thou cry out, through love cry out; whether thou correct, through love correct; whether thou spare, through love do thou spare: let the root of love be within, of this root can nothing spring but what is good.

9. "In this is love—in this was manifested the love of God toward us, because that God sent his only-begotten Son into this world, that we may live through Him.—In this is love, not that we loved God, but that He loved us:"[5] we did not love Him first: for to this end loved He us, that we may love Him: "And sent His Son to be the Atoner for our sins: "*litatorem*," *i.e.* one that sacrifices. He sacrificed for our sins. Where did He find the sacrifice? Where did He find the victim which he would offer pure? Other He found none; His own self He offered. "Beloved, if God so loved us we ought also to love one another.[6] Peter," saith He, "lovest thou me?" And he said, "I love." "Feed my sheep."

10. "No man hath seen God at any time:"[7] He is a thing invisible; not with the eye but with the heart must He be sought. But just as if we wished to see the sun, we should purge the eye of the body; wishing to see God, let us purge the eye by which God can be seen. Where is this eye? Hear the Gospel: "Blessed are the pure in heart, for they shall see God."[8] But let no man imagine God to himself according to the lust of his eyes. For so he makes unto himself either a huge form, or a certain incalculable magnitude which, like the light which he sees with the bodily eyes, he makes extend through all directions; field after field of space he gives it all the bigness he can; or, he represents to himself like as it were an old man of venerable form. None of these things do thou imagine. There is something thou mayest imagine, if thou wouldest see God; "God is love." What sort of face hath love? what form hath it? what stature? what feet? what hands hath it? no man can say. And yet it hath feet, for these carry men to church: it hath hands; for these reach forth to the poor: it hath eyes; for thereby we consider the

[1] Rom. viii. 32.   [2] Gal. ii. 20.   [5] 1 John iv. 9, 10.   [6] 1 John iv. 11.
[3] *In proditione.*   [4] *Sævientem.*   [7] 1 John iv. 12.   [8] Matt. v. 8.

needy: "Blessed is the man," it is said, "who considereth the needy and the poor."[1] It hath ears, of which the Lord saith, "He that hath ears to hear let him hear."[2] These are not members distinct by place, but with the understanding he that hath charity sees the whole at once. Inhabit, and thou shalt be inhabited; dwell, and thou shalt be dwelt in. For how say you, my brethren? who loves what he does not see? Now why, when charity is praised, do ye lift up your hands, make acclaim, praise? What have I shown you? What I produced, was it a gleam of colors? What I propounded, was it gold and silver? Have I dug out jewels from hid treasures? What of this sort have I shown to your eyes? Is my face changed while I speak? I am in the flesh; I am in the same form in which I came forth to you; ye are in the same form in which ye came hither: charity is praised, and ye shout applause. Certainly ye see nothing. But as it pleases you when ye praise, so let it please you that ye may keep it in your heart. For mark well what I say, brethren; I exhort you all, as God enables me, unto a great treasure. If there were shown you a beautiful little vase, embossed,[3] inlaid with gold, curiously wrought, and it charmed your eyes, and drew towards it the eager desire of your heart, and you were pleased with the hand of the artificer, and the weight of the silver, and the splendor of the metal; would not each one of you say, "O, if I had that vase!" And to no purpose ye would say it, for it would not rest with you to have it. Or if one should wish to have it, he might think of stealing it from another's house. Charity is praised to you; if it please you, have it, possess it: no need that ye should rob any man, no need that ye should think of buying it; it is to be had freely, without cost. Take it, clasp it; there is nothing sweeter. If such it be when it is but spoken of, what must it be when one has it?

11. If any of you perchance wish to keep charity, brethren, above all things do not imagine it to be an abject and sluggish thing; nor that charity is to be preserved by a sort of gentleness, nay not gentleness, but tameness and listlessness.[4] Not so is it preserved. Do not imagine that thou then lovest thy servant when thou dost not beat him, or that thou then lovest thy son when thou givest him not discipline, or that thou then lovest thy neighbor when thou dost not rebuke him: this is not charity, but mere feebleness. Let charity be fervent to correct, to amend: but if there be good manners, let them delight thee; if bad, let them be amended, let them be corrected. Love not in the man his error, but the man: for the man God made, the error the man himself made. Love that which God made, love not that which the man himself made. When thou lovest that, thou takest away this: when thou esteemest that, thou amendest this. But even if thou be severe[5] at any time, let it be because of love, for correction. For this cause was charity betokened by the Dove which descended upon the Lord.[6] That likeness of a dove, the likeness in which came the Holy Ghost, by whom charity should be shed forth into us: wherefore was this? The dove hath no gall: yet with beak and wings she fights for her young; hers is a fierceness without bitterness. And so does also a father; when he chastises his son, for discipline he chastises him. As I said, the kidnapper, in order that he may sell, inveigles the child with bitter endearments; a father, that he may correct, does without gall chastise. Such be ye to all men. See here, brethren, a great lesson, a great rule: each one of you has children, or wishes to have; or if he has altogether determined to have no children after the flesh, at least spiritually he desires to have children:—what father does not correct his son? what son does not his father discipline? And yet he seems to be fierce[7] with him. It is the fierceness of love, the fierceness of charity: a sort of fierceness without gall after the manner of the dove, not of the raven. Whence it came into my mind, my brethren, to tell you, that those violaters of charity are they that have made the schism: as they hate charity itself, so they hate also the dove. But the dove convicts them: it comes forth from heaven, the heavens open, and it abideth on the head of the Lord. Wherefore this? That John may hear, "This is He that baptizeth."[8] Away, ye robbers; away, ye invaders of the possession of Christ! On your own possessions, where ye will needs be lords, ye have dared to fix the titles of the great Owner. He recognizes His own titles; He vindicates to Himself His own possession. He does not cancel the titles, but enters in and takes possession. So in one that comes to the Catholic Church, his baptism is not cancelled, that the title of the commander[9] be not cancelled: but what is done in the Catholic Church? The title is acknowledged; the Owner enters in under His own titles, where the robber was entering in under titles not his own.

1 Ps. xli. 1.	2 Luke viii. 8.	3 *Anaglyphum.*
4 Ep. cliii. 17, c. litt.; Petil. ii. 67: Serm. clxxi. 5.
5 *Sævis.*	6 Hom. in Ev. vi. p. 82; Matt. iii. 16.
7 *Sævire.*	8 John i. 33.
9 ["Captain (ἀςχηῖος) of their salvation." Heb. ii. 10.—J. H. M.]

HOMILY VIII.

1 JOHN IV. 12–16.

"If we love one another, God abideth[1] in us, and His love will be perfected in us. In this know we that we abide in Him, and He in us, because He hath given us of His Spirit. And we have seen and are witnesses that the Father sent the Son to be the Saviour of the world. Whosoever shall confess that Jesus is the Son of God, God abideth in him, and he in God. And we have known and believed the love that God hath to us. God is love; and he that abideth in love abideth in God, and God abideth in him."

1. LOVE is a sweet word, but sweeter the deed. To be always speaking of it, is not in our power: for we have many things to do, and divers businesses draw us different ways, so that our tongue has not leisure to be always speaking of love: as indeed our tongue could have nothing better to do. But though we may not always be speaking of it, we may always keep it. Just as it is with the *Alleluia* which we sing at this present time,[1] are we always doing this? Not one hour, I do not say for the whole space of it, do we sing Alleluia, but barely during a few moments of one hour, and then give ourselves to something else. Now *Alleluia*, as ye already know, means, Praise ye the Lord. He that praises God with his tongue, cannot be always doing this: he that by his life and conduct praises God, can be doing it always. Works of mercy, affections of charity, sanctity of piety, incorruptness of chastity, modesty of sobriety, these things are always to be practiced: whether we are in public, or at home; whether before men, or in our chamber; whether speaking, or holding our peace; whether occupied upon something, or free from occupation: these are always to be kept, because all these virtues which I have named are within. But who is sufficient to name them all? There is as it were the army of an emperor seated within in thy mind. For as an emperor by his army does what he will, so the Lord Jesus Christ, once beginning to dwell in our inner man, (*i.e.* in the mind through faith), uses these virtues as His ministers. And by these virtues which cannot be seen with eyes, and yet when they are named are praised—and they would not be praised except they were loved, not loved except they were seen; and if not loved except seen, they are seen with another eye, that is, with the inward beholding of the heart—by these invisible virtues, the members are visibly put in motion: the feet to walk, but whither? whither they are moved by the good will which as a soldier serves the good emperor: the hands to work; but what? that which is bidden by charity which is inspired within by the Holy Ghost. The members then are seen when they are put in motion; He that orders them within is not seen: and who He is that orders them within is known almost alone to Him that orders, and to him who within is ordered.

2. For, brethren, ye heard just now when the Gospel was read, at least if ye had for it the ear not only of the body but also of the heart. What said it? "Take heed that ye do not your righteousness before men, to be seen of them."[2] Did He mean to say this, that whatever good things we do, we should hide them from the eyes of men,[3] and fear to be seen? If thou fearest spectators thou wilt not have imitators: thou oughtest therefore to be seen. But thou must not do it to the end thou mayest be seen. Not there should be the end of thy joy, not there the goal of thy rejoicing, that thou shouldest account thyself to have gotten the whole fruit of thy good work, when thou art seen and praised. This is nothing. Despise thyself when thou art praised, let Him be praised in thee who worketh by thee. Therefore do not for thine own praise work the good thou doest: but to the praise of Him from whom thou hast the power to do good. From thy-

---

[1] In Augustin's time and later, it was the usage of the Latin Churches (derived, as St. Gregory relates, lib. ix. Ep. 12, from the Church of Jerusalem) to sing the "Alleluia" on Easter Sunday, and during the whole Quinquagesima, or seven weeks from Easter to Whit-sunday. But it was not everywhere restricted to that time: Aug. *Epist.* (*ad Januar.*) 55, 32. *Ut Alleluia per solos dies quinquaginta cantetur in Ecclesia, non usquequaque observatur: nam et aliis diebus varie cantatur alibi atque alibi: ipsis autem diebus ubique.* Comp. *ibid.* 28. *Enarr.* in Psa. cvi. sec. 1, where this usage is said to rest upon an ancient tradition : in Psa. cxlviii. sec. 1, and xxi. sec. 24, that it is observed throughout the whole world: Serm. ccx. 8; cclii. 9. S. Hieronym. *Præf.* in Psa. l. and *c. Vigilant.* 1 (*exortus est subito Vigilantius qui dicat nunquam nisi in Pascha Alleluia cantandum: i.e.,*Vig. wished it to be sung only on Easter day).

[2] Matt. vi. 1.
[3] *De Serm. Dom. in Monte,* ii. 1, ff., Serm. cxlix. 10–13 ; *De Civ. Dei,* v. 14 ; *Enarr.* in Ps. lxv. sec 2.

self thou hast the ill doing, from God thou hast the well doing. On the other hand, see perverse men, how preposterous they are. What they do well, they will needs ascribe to themselves; if they do ill, they will needs accuse God. Reverse this distorted and preposterous proceeding, which puts the thing, as one may say, head downwards, which makes that undermost which is uppermost,[1] and that upwards which is downwards. Dost thou want to make God undermost and thyself uppermost? Thou goest headlong, not elevatest thyself; for He is always above. What then? thou well, and God ill? nay rather, say this, if thou wouldest speak more truly, I ill, He well; and what I do well from Him is the well-doing: for from myself whatever I do is ill. This confession strengthens the heart, and makes a firm foundation of love. For if we ought to hide our good works lest they be seen of men, what becomes of that sentence of the Lord in the sermon which He delivered on the mount? Where He said this, there He also said a little before, "Let your good works shine before men."[2] And He did not stop there, did not there make an end, but added, "And glorify your Father which is in Heaven." And what saith the apostle? "And I was unknown by face unto the Churches of Judea which were in Christ: but they heard only, That he which persecuted us in times past, now preacheth the faith which once he destroyed. And in me they glorified God."[3] See how he also, in regard that he became so widely known, did not set the good in his own praise, but in the praise of God. And as for him, in his own person, that he was one who laid waste the Church, a persecutor, envious, malignant, it is himself that confesses this, not we that reproach him therewith. Paul loves to have his sins spoken of by us, that He may be glorified who healed such a disease. For it was the hand of the Physician that cut and healed the greatness of the sore. That voice from heaven prostrated the persecutor, and raised up the preacher; killed Saul, and quickened Paul.[4] For Saul was the persecutor of a holy man; thence had this man his name, when he persecuted the Christians:[5] afterward of Saul he became Paul. What does the name *Paulus* mean? Little. Therefore when he was Saul, he was proud, lifted up; when he was Paul, he was lowly, little. Thus we say, I will see thee "*paulo post*," *i.e.*

after a little while.[6] Hear that he was made little: "For I am the least of the apostles;[7] and, To me the least of all saints," he saith in another place. So was he among the apostles as the hem of the garment: but the Church of the Gentiles touched it, as did the woman which had the flux, and was made whole.[8]

3. Then, brethren, this I would say, this I do say, this if I might I would not leave unsaid: Let there be in you now these works, now those, according to the time, according to the hours, according to the days. Are you always to be speaking? always to keep silence? always to be refreshing the body? always to be fasting? always to be giving bread to the needy? always to be clothing the naked? always to be visiting the sick? always to be bringing into agreement them that disagree? always to be burying the dead? No: but now this, now that. These things are taken in hand, and they stop: but that which as emperor commands all the forces within neither hath beginning nor ought to stop. Let charity within have no intermission: let the offices of charity be exhibited according to the time. Let "brotherly love" then, as it is written, let "brotherly love continue."[9]

4. But perchance it will have struck some of you all along, while we have been expounding to you this epistle of blessed John, why it is only "brotherly" love that he so emphatically commends. "He that loveth his brother," saith he: and, "a commandment is given us that we love one another."[10] Again and again it is of brotherly love that he speaks: but the love of God, *i.e.* the love with which we ought to love God, he has not so constantly named; howbeit, he has not altogether left it unspoken. But concerning love of an enemy, almost throughout the epistle, he has said nothing. Although he vehemently preaches up and commends charity to us, he does not tell us to love our enemies, but tells us to love our brethren. But just now, when the Gospel was read, we heard, "For if ye love them that love you, what reward shall ye have? Do not even the publicans this?"[11] How is it then that John

[1] *Quod susum faciens jusum ; quod deorsum faciens sursum. Jusum vis facere Deum, et te susum? Infra,* x. 8, *Jusum me honoras, susum me calcas.* Several mss. have *sursum deorsum* for *susum jusum.*—Ben. Laud. 116 and 136, and also Bodl. 813, as first written, have *susum, jusum.*

[2] Matt. v. 16.   [3] Gal. i. 22–24.
[4] Serm. clxviii. 6.   [5] 1 Sam. xix.

[6] So Serm. ci. 1; clxviii. 7; cclxxix. 5; cccxv. 7; *Lib. de Sp. et Litt.* vii. sec. 12. But *Confess.* viii. 4, sec. 9, it is remarked, without reference to the etymology, that the change of name from Saul to Paul was designed to commemorate the conversion of Sergius Paulus, Acts xiii. 7, 12; Origen *Præf. in Ep. ad Rom.* "Some have thought that the Apostle took the name of Paulus, the Proconsul, whom at Cyprus he had subjected to the faith of Christ: that as kings are wont to assume a title from the nations they have conquered, as Parthicus and Gothicus from Parthians and Goths, so the Apostle took the appellation Paulus from the Paulus whom he had subjugated. Which we do not think is altogether to be set aside." St. Jerome *Comm. in Ep. ad Philem.* "As Scipio took the name Africanus as conqueror of Africa, so the Apostle took the name Paulus by way of trophy, &c."

[7] 1 Cor. xv. 9; Eph. iii. 8.   [8] Matt. ix. 20–22.
[9] Heb. xiii. 1.   [10] 1 John ii. 10; iii. 23.   [11] Matt. v. 46.

the apostle, as the thing of great concern to us in order to a certain perfection, commends brotherly love; whereas the Lord saith it is not enough that we love our brethren, but that we ought to extend that love so that we may reach even to enemies? He that reaches even unto enemies does not overleap the brethren. It must needs, like fire, first seize upon what is nearest, and so extend to what is further off. A brother is nearer to thee than any chance person. Again, that person has more hold upon thee whom thou knowest not, who yet is not against thee, than an enemy who is also against thee. Extend thy love to them that are nearest, yet do not call this an extending: for it is almost loving thyself, to love them that are close to thee. Extend it to the unknown, who have done thee no ill. Pass even them: reach on to love thine enemies. This at least the Lord commands. Why has the apostle here said nothing about loving an enemy.

5. All love,[1] whether that which is called carnal, which is wont to be called not "*dilectio*" but "*amor*:" (for the word "*dilectio*" is wont to be used of better objects, and to be understood of better objects:) yet all love, dear brethren, hath in it a wishing well to those who are loved. For we ought not so to love, nor are we able so to love, (whether "*diligere*" or "*amare*:" for this latter word the Lord used when He said, "*Petra, amas me?*" "Peter, lovest thou me?") we ought not so to love[2] men, as we hear gluttons say, I love thrushes. Thou askest why he loves them? That he may kill, that he may consume. He says he loves, and to this end loves he them, that they may cease to be; to this end loves he them, that he may make away with them. And whatever we love in the way of food, to this end love we it, that it may be consumed and we recruited. Are men to be so loved as to be consumed? But there is a certain friendliness of well wishing, by which we desire at some time or other to do good to those whom we love. How if there be no good that we can do? The benevolence, the wishing well, of itself sufficeth him that loves. For we ought not to wish men to be wretched, that we may be enabled to practise works of mercy. Thou givest bread to the hungry: but better it were that none hungered, and thou hadst none to give to. Thou clothest the naked: oh that all were clothed, and this need existed not! Thou buriest the dead: oh that it were come at last, that life where none shall die! Thou reconcilest the quarrelling: oh that it were

here at last, that eternal peace of Jerusalem, where none shall disagree! For all these are offices done to necessities. Take away the wretched; there will be an end to works of mercy. The works of mercy will be at an end: shall the ardor of charity be quenched? With a truer touch of love thou lovest the happy man, to whom there is no good office thou canst do; purer will that love be, and far more unalloyed. For if thou have done a kindness to the wretched, perchance thou desirest to lift up thyself over against him, and wishest him to be subject to thee, who hast done the kindness to him. He was in need, thou didst bestow; thou seemest to thyself greater because thou didst bestow, than he upon whom it was bestowed. Wish him thine equal, that ye both may be under the One Lord, on whom nothing can be bestowed.

6. For in this the proud soul has passed bounds, and, in a manner, become avaricious. For, "The root of all evils is avarice;"[3] and again it is said, "The beginning of all sin is pride."[4] And we ask, it may be, how these two sentences agree: "The root of all evils is avarice;" and, "The beginning of all sin is pride." If pride is the beginning of all sin, then is pride the root of all evils. Now certainly, "the root of all evils is avarice." We find that in pride there is also avarice, (or grasping;) for man has passed bounds: and what is it to be avaricious? to go beyond that which sufficeth. Adam fell by pride: "the beginning of all sin is pride," saith it: did he fall by grasping? What more grasping, than he whom God could not suffice? In fact, my brethren, we read how man was made after the image and likeness of God: and what said God of him? "And let him have power over the fishes of the sea, and over the fowl of the heaven, and over all cattle which move upon the earth."[5] Said He, Have power over men? "Have power," saith He: He hath given him natural power: "have power" over what? "over the fishes of the sea, the fowl of the heaven, and all moving things which move upon the earth." Why is this power over these things a natural power? Because man hath the power from this; that he was made after the image of God. And in what was he made after God's image? In the intellect, in the mind, in the inner man; in that he understands truth, distinguishes between right and wrong, knows by whom he was made, is able to understand his Creator, to praise his Creator: he hath this intelligence, who hath prudence. Therefore

---

[1] *Dilectio.*　　　　[2] *Amare.*　　　　[3] 1 Tim. vi. 10.　　　[4] Ecclus. x. 15.　　　[5] Gen. i. 26.

when many by evil lusts wore out in themselves the image of God, and by perversity of their manners extinguished the very flame, so to say, of intelligence, the Scripture cried aloud to them, "Become not ye as the horse and mule which have no understanding."[1] That is to say, I have set thee above the horse and mule; thee, I made after mine image, I have given thee power over these. Why? Because they have not the rational mind: but thou by the rational mind art capable of truth, understandest what is above thee: be subject to Him that is above thee, and beneath thee shall those things be over which thou was set. But because by sin man deserted Him whom he ought to be under, he is made subject to the things which he ought to be above.

7. Mark what I say: God, man, beasts: to wit, above thee, God; beneath thee, the beasts. Acknowledge Him that is above thee, that those that are beneath thee may acknowledge thee.[2] Thus, because Daniel acknowledged God above him, the lions acknowledged him above them. But if thou acknowledge not Him that is above thee, thou despisest thy superior, thou becomest subject to thine inferior. Accordingly, how was the pride of the Egyptians quelled? By the means of frogs and flies.[3] God might have sent lions: but a great man may be scared by a lion. The prouder they were, the more by the means of things contemptible and feeble was their wicked neck broken. But Daniel, lions acknowledge, because he was subject to God. What? the martyrs who were cast to the wild beasts to fight with them, and were torn by the teeth of savage creatures, were they not under God? or were those three men servants of God, and the Maccabees not servants of God? The fire acknowledged as God's servants the three men, whom it burned not, neither hurt their garments;[4] and did it not acknowledge the Maccabees?[5] It acknowledged the Maccabees; it did, my brethren, acknowledge them also. But there was need of a scourge, by the Lord's permission: He hath said in Scripture, "He scourgeth every son whom He receiveth."[6] For think ye, my brethren, the iron would have pierced into the vitals[7] of the Lord unless He had permitted it, or that He would have hung fastened to the tree, unless it had been His will? Did not His own creature acknowledge Him? Or did He set an ensample of patience to His faithful ones? Ye see then, God delivered some visibly, some He delivered not visibly: yet all He spiritually delivered, spiritually deserted none. Visibly He seemed to have deserted some, some He seemed to have rescued. Therefore rescued He some, that thou mayest not think that He had not power to rescue. He has given proof that He has the power, to the end that where he doth it not, thou mayest understand a more secret will, not surmise difficulty of doing. But what, brethren? When we shall have come out of all these snares of mortality, when the times of temptation shall have passed away, when the river of this world shall have fleeted by, and we shall have received again that "first robe,"[8] that immortality which by sinning we have lost, "when this corruptible shall have put on incorruption," that is, this flesh shall have put on incorruption, "and this mortal shall have put on immortality;"[9] the now perfected sons of God, in whom is no more need to be tempted, neither to be scourged, shall all creatures acknowledge: subjected to us shall all things be, if we here be subjected to God.

8. So then ought the Christian to be, that he glory not over other "men." For God hath given it thee to be over the beasts, i.e. to be better than the beasts. This hast thou by nature; thou shalt always be better than a beast. If thou wish to be better than another man, thou wilt begrudge him when thou shalt see him to be thine equal. Thou oughtest to wish all men to be thine equals; and if by wisdom thou surpass any, thou oughtest to wish that he also may be wise. As long as he is slow, he learns from thee; as long as he is untaught, he hath need of thee; and thou art seen to be the teacher, he the learner; therefore thou seemest to be the superior, because thou art the teacher; he the inferior, because the learner. Except thou wish him thine equal, thou wishest to have him always a learner. But if thou wish to have him always a learner, thou wilt be an envious teacher. If an envious teacher, how wilt thou be a teacher? I pray thee, do not teach him thine enviousness. Hear the apostle speaking of the bowels of charity: "I would that all were even as I."[10] In what sense did he wish all to be his equals? In this was he superior to all, that by charity he wished all to be his equals. I say then, man

[1] Ps. xxxii. 9.   [2] Dan. vi. 22.   [3] Ex. viii.
[4] Dan. iii. 50.   [5] 2 Macc. vii.   [6] Heb. xii. 6.   [7] Viscera.

[8] Luke xv. 22, stolam primam. S. Aug. de Gen. ad litt. vi. 38. "That 'first robe' is either the righteousness from which man fell; or, if it signify the clothing of bodily immortality, this also he lost, when by reason of sin he could not attain thereto:" and sec. 31. "Why is 'the first robe' brought forth to him, but as he receives again the immortality which Adam lost?" Tertullian: vestem prestinam, priorem: "the former robe, which he had of old . . . the clothing of the Holy Spirit." Theophylact. τὴν στολὴν τὴν ἀρχαίαν . . . τὸ ἔνδυμα τῆς ἀφθαρσίας, "the original robe, the clothing of incorruption."
[9] 1 Cor. xv. 44-49.   [10] 1 Cor. vii. 7.

has past bounds; he would needs be greedy of more than his due, would be above men, he that was made above the beasts: and this is pride.

9. And see what great works pride does. Lay it up in your hearts, how much alike, how much as it were upon a par, are the works it doeth, and the works of charity. Charity feeds the hungry, and so does pride: charity, that God may be praised; pride, that itself may be praised. Charity clothes the naked, so does pride: charity fasts, so does pride: charity buries the dead, so does pride. All good works which charity wishes to do, and does; pride, on the other hand, drives at the same, and, so to say, keeps her horses up to the mark. But charity is between her and it, and leaves not place for ill-driven pride; not ill-driving, but ill-driven. Woe to the man whose charioteer is pride, for he must needs go headlong! But that, in the good that is done, it may not be pride that sets us on, who knows? who sees it? where is it? the works we see: mercy feeds, pride also feeds; mercy takes in the stranger, pride also takes in the stranger; mercy intercedes for the poor, pride also intercedes. How is this? In the works we see no difference. I dare to say somewhat, but not I; Paul hath said it: charity dies, that is, a man having charity confesses the name of Christ, suffers martyrdom: pride also confesses, suffers also martyrdom. The one hath charity, the other hath not charity. But let him that hath not charity hear from the apostle: " If I distribute all my goods to the poor, and if I give my body to be burned, and have not charity, it profiteth me nothing.[1] So then the divine Scripture calls us off from the display of the face outwardly to that which is within; from this surface which is vaunted before men, it calls us off to that which is within. Return to thy own conscience, question it. Do not consider what blossoms outwardly, but what root there is in the ground. Is lust rooted there? A show there may be of good deeds, truly good works there cannot be. Is charity rooted there? Have no fear: nothing evil can come of that. The proud caresses, love[2] is severe. The one clothes, the other smites. For the one clothes in order to please men, the other smites in order to correct by discipline. More accepted is the blow of charity than the alms of pride. Come then within, brethren; and in all things, whatsoever ye do, look unto God your witness. See, if He seeth, with what mind ye do it. If your heart accuse you not that ye

do it for the sake of display, it is well: fear ye not. But when ye do good, fear not lest another see you. Fear thou lest thou do it to the end that thou mayest be praised: let the other see it, that God may be praised. For if thou hidest it from the eyes of man, thou hidest it from the imitation of man, thou withdrawest from God His praise. Two are there to whom thou doest the alms: two hunger; one for bread, the other for righteousness. Between these two famishing souls: —as it is written, " Blessed are they that hunger and thirst after righteousness, for they shall be filled: "[3]—between these two famishing persons thou the doer of the good work art set; if charity does the work by occasion of the one, therein it hath pity on both, it would succor both. For the one craves what he may eat, the other craves what he may imitate. Thou feedest the one, give thyself as a pattern to the other; so hast thou given alms to both: the one thou hast caused to thank thee for killing his hunger, the other thou hast made to imitate thee by setting him an example.

10. Shew mercy then, as men of merciful hearts; because in loving enemies also, ye love brethren. Think not that John has given no precept concerning love of our enemy, because he has not ceased to speak of brotherly love. Ye love brethren. " How," sayest thou, " do we love brethren?" I ask wherefore thou lovest an enemy. Wherefore dost thou love him? That he may be whole in this life? what if it be not expedient for him? That he may be rich? what if by his very riches he shall be blinded? That he may marry a wife? what if he shall have a bitter life of it? That he may have children? what if they shall be bad? Uncertain therefore are these things which thou seemest to wish for thine enemy, in that thou lovest him; they are uncertain. Wish for him that he may have with thee eternal life; wish for him that he may be thy brother: when thou lovest him, thou lovest a brother. For thou lovest in him not what he is, but what thou wishest that he may be. I once said to you, my beloved, if I mistake not: There is a log of timber lying in sight; a good workman has seen the log, not yet planed, just as it was hewn from the forest, he has taken a liking to it, he would make something out of it. For indeed he did not love it to this end that it should always remain thus. In his art he has seen what it shall be, not in his liking what it is; and his liking is for the thing he will make of it, not

---

for the thing it is. So God loved us sinners. We say that God loved sinners: for He saith, " They that are whole need not the Physician, but they that are sick."[1] Did He love us sinners to the end we should still remain sinners? As timber from the wood our Carpenter saw us, and had in His thoughts the building He would make thereof, not the unwrought timber that it was. So too thou seest thine enemy striving against thee, raging, biting with words, exasperating with contumelies, harassing with hatred: thou hast regard to this in him, that he is a man. Thou seest all these things that are against thee, that they were done by man; and thou seest in him that he was made by God. Now that he was made man, was God's doing: but that he hates thee, is his doing; that he has ill-will at thee, is his doing. And what sayest thou in thy mind? Lord, be merciful to him, forgive him his sins, strike terror into him, change him. Thou lovest not in him what he is, but what thou wishest him to be. Consequently, when thou lovest an enemy, thou lovest a brother. Wherefore, perfect love is the loving an enemy: which perfect love is in brotherly love. And let no man say that John the apostle has admonished us somewhat less, and the Lord Christ somewhat more. John has admonished us to love the brethren; Christ has admonished us to love even enemies. Mark to what end Christ hath bidden thee to love thine enemies. That they may remain always enemies? If He bade it for this end, that they should remain enemies, thou hatest,[2] not lovest. Mark how He Himself loved, *i.e.* because He would not that they should be still the persecutors they were, He said, " Father, forgive them, for they know not what they do."[3] Whom He willed to be forgiven, them He willed to be changed: whom He willed to be changed, of enemies He deigned to make brethren, and did in truth make them so. He was killed, was buried, rose again, ascended into heaven: sent the Holy Ghost to His disciples: they began with boldness to preach His name, they did miracles in the name of Him that was crucified and slain: those slayers of the Lord saw them; and they who in rage had shed His blood, by believing drank it.

11. These things have I said, brethren, and somewhat at length: yet because charity was to be more earnestly commended to you, beloved, in this way was it to be commended. For if there be no charity in you, we have said nothing. But if it be in you, we have as it were cast oil upon the flames. And in

whom it was not, perchance by words it hath been kindled. In one; that which was there hath grown; in another, that hath begun to be, which was not. To this end therefore have we said these things, that ye be not slow to love your enemies. Does any man rage against thee? he rages, pray thou; he hates, pity thou. It is the fever of his soul that hates thee: he will be whole, and will thank thee. How do physicians love them that are sick? Is it the sick that they love? If they love them as sick, they wish them to be always sick. To this end love they the sick; not that they should still be sick, but that from being sick they should be made whole. And how much have they very often to suffer from the frenzied! What contumelious language! Very often they are even struck by them. He attacks the fever, forgives the man. And what shall I say, brethren? does he love his enemy? Nay, he hates his enemy, the disease; for it is this that he hates, and loves the man by whom he is struck: he hates the fever. For by whom or by what is he struck? by the disease, by the sickness, by the fever. He takes away that which strives against him, that there may remain that from which he shall have thanks. So do thou. If thine enemy hate thee, and unjustly hate thee; know that the lust of the world reigns in him, therefore he hates thee. If thou also hate him, thou on the other hand renderest evil for evil. What does it, to render evil for evil? I wept for one sick man who hated thee; now bewail I thee, if thou also hatest. But he attacks thy property; he takes from thee I know not what things which thou hast on earth: therefore hatest thou him, because he puts thee to straits on earth. Be not thou straitened, remove thee to heaven above; there shalt thou have thine heart where there is wide room, so that thou mayest not be straitened in the hope of life eternal. Consider what the things are that he takes from thee: not even them would he take from thee, but by permission of Him who " scourgeth every son whom He receiveth."[3] He, this same enemy of thine, is in a manner the instrument[4] in the hands of God, by which thou mayest be healed. If God knows it to be good for thee that he should despoil thee, He permits him; if He knows it to be good for thee that thou shouldest receive blows, He permits him to smite thee: by the means of Him He careth for thee: wish thou that he may be made whole.

12. " No man hath seen God at any time." See, beloved: " If we love one another, God

---

will dwell in us, and His love will be perfected in us."[1] Begin to love; thou shalt be perfected. Hast thou begun to love? God has begun to dwell in thee: love Him that has begun to dwell in thee, that by more perfect indwelling He may make thee perfect. "In this we know that we dwell in Him and He in us, because He hath given us of His Spirit."[2] It is well: thanks be to God! We come to know that He dwelleth in us. And whence come we to know this very thing, to wit, that we do know that He dwelleth in us? Because John himself has said this: "Because He hath given us of His Spirit." Whence know we that He hath given us of His Spirit? This very thing, that He hath given thee of His Spirit, whence comest thou to know it? Ask thine own bowels: if they are full of charity, thou hast the Spirit of God. Whence know we that by this thou knowest that the Spirit of God dwelleth in thee? "Because the love of God is shed abroad in our hearts by the Holy Spirit which is given unto us."[3]

13. "And we have seen, and are witnesses, that God hath sent His Son to be the Saviour of the world."[4] Set your minds at rest, ye that are sick: such a Physician is come, and do ye despair? Great were the diseases, incurable were the wounds, desperate was the sickness. Dost thou note the greatness of thine ill, and not note the omnipotence of the Physician? Thou art desperate, but He is omnipotent; Whose witnesses are these that first were healed, and that announce the Physician: yet even they are made whole in hope rather than in the reality. For so saith the apostle: "For by hope we are saved."[5] We have begun therefore to be made whole in faith: but our wholeness shall be perfected "when this corruptible shall have put on incorruption, and this mortal shall have put on immortality."[6] This is hope, not the reality. But he that rejoiceth in hope shall hold the reality also: whereas he that hath not the hope, shall not be able to attain unto the reality.

14. "Whosoever shall confess that Jesus is the Son of God, God dwelleth in him and he in God."[7] Now we may say it in not many words; "Whosoever shall confess;"

not in word but in deed, not with tongue but with the life. For many confess in words, but in deeds deny. "And we have known and believed the love which God hath in us."[8] And again, by what hast thou come to know this? "Love is God." He hath already said it above, behold he saith it again. Love could not be more exceedingly commended to thee than that it should be called GOD. Haply thou wast ready to despise a gift of God. And dost thou despise *God?* "Love is God: and he that dwelleth in love dwelleth in God, and God dwelleth in him." Each mutually inhabiteth the other; He that holdeth, and he that is holden. Thou dwellest in God, but that thou mayest be holden: God inhabiteth thee, but that He may hold thee, lest thou fall. Lest haply thou imagine that thou becomest an house of God in such sort as thine house supports thy flesh: if the house in which thou art withdraw itself from under thee, thou fallest; but if thou withdraw thyself, God falleth not. When thou forsakest Him, He is none the less; when thou hast returned unto Him, He is none the greater.[9] Thou art healed, on Him thou wilt bestow nothing; thou art made clean, thou art new-made, thou art set right: He is a medicine to the unhealthy, is a rule for the crooked, is light for the bedarkened, is an habitation for the deserted. All therefore is conferred on thee: see thou imagine not that ought is conferred upon God by thy coming unto Him: no, not so much as a slave. Shall God, forsooth, not have servants if thou like not, if all like not? God needs not the servants, but the servants need God: therefore saith the Psalm, "I have said unto the Lord, thou art my God."[10] He is the true Lord. And what saith it? "For of my goods Thou hast no need." Thou needest the good thou hast by thy servant. Thy servant needeth the good he hath by thee, that thou mayest feed him; thou also needest the good thou hast by thy servant, that he may

---

[1] 1 John iv. 12.   [2] 1 John iv. 13.   [3] Rom. v. 5.
[4] 1 John iv. 14.   [5] 1 John viii. 24.   [6] 1 Cor. xv. 53.
[7] 1 John iv. 15. [*Life;* "*the Life eternal.*'—The Epistle begins and ends with Life, announced and promised (the word occurs thirteen times in the one hundred and ten verses). The intermediate presentation of Love, as the grand efflux from the inner, spiritual life, gives the main theme of St. John, and it is of this that Augustin delights to speak in these discourses.
The life of an intelligent being is in conscious dependence on God. In the fullest sense, "in Him we live."
Death and life are among the striking contrasts named in the epistle: "the death," "the life,"--"the death that is truly death, the life that is truly life."
This life is in Christ. He not only brings it and imparts it, but He *is* "our Life." The living and life-giving Christ is manifested

in this epistle, and also the death that exists where there is no union, by love, to Him.
The Life, *eternal* (to distinguish it from the life that now is, the life bounded by sense and time), is not mere prolongation of existence. We must use sensuous images in order to apprehend the idea, but we are to remember that they are not realities in the spiritual order.
The life which Christ gives, enabling men to have life in Him, cannot exist apart from Himself; His seal remains in them, and He abides in them.
The "life eternal," while future as to its full realization, is present, is begun here and now. "He that believeth on the Son *hath* eternal life;" and its possession is matter of actual knowledge to those who have this life; "we *know* that we abide in Him and He in us" (1 John v. 13).
It is a life which unites heaven and earth, bringing into this stage of being "the powers of the world to come."
A life that satisfies, while it enkindles desire and aspiration: it gives strength to bear present ills in the joyous and assured hope of "a life beyond life."]--J. H. M.
[8] 1 John iv. 16.   [9] Hom. in Ev. xi. 5.
[10] Ps. xvi. 2.

help thee. Thou canst not draw water for thyself, canst not cook for thyself, canst not run before thy horse, canst not tend thy beast. Thou seest that thou needest the good thou hast by thy servant, thou needest his attendance. Therefore thou art not a true lord, while thou hast need of an inferior. He is the true Lord, who seeks nothing from us; and woe to us if we seek not Him! He seeks nothing from us: yet He sought us, when we sought not Him. One sheep had strayed; He found it, He brought it back on His shoulders rejoicing.[1] And was the sheep

necessary for the Shepherd, and not rather the Shepherd necessary for the sheep?—The more I love to speak of charity, the less willing am I that this epistle should be finished. None is more ardent in the commending of charity. Nothing more sweet is preached to you, nothing more wholesome drunk by you: but only thus if by godly living ye confirm in you the gift of God. Be not ungrateful for His so great grace, who, though He had one Only Son, would not that He should be alone a Son; but, that He might have brethren, adopted unto Him those who should with Him possess life eternal.

[1] Luke xv. 4, 5.

HOMILY IX.

1 JOHN IV. 17–21.

"Herein is love made perfect in us, that we may have boldness in the day of judgment: because as He is, so are we in this world. There is no fear in love; but perfect love casteth out fear: because fear hath torment. He that feareth is not made perfect in love. Let us love Him, because He first loved us. If a man say, I love God, and hateth his brother, he is a liar: for he that loveth not his brother whom he seeth, how can he love God whom he seeth not? And this commandment have we from Him, That he who loveth God love his brother also."

1. YE remember, beloved, that of the epistles of John the apostle the last past remains to be handled by us and expounded to you, as the Lord vouchsafes. Of this debt then we are mindful: and ye ought to be mindful of your claim. For indeed this same charity, which in this epistle is chiefly and almost alone commended, at once maketh us most faithful in paying our debts, and you most sweet in exacting your rights. I have said, most sweet in exacting, because where charity is not, he that exacts is bitter: but where charity is, both he that exacts is sweet, and he of whom it is exacted, although he undertakes some labor, yet charity makes the very labor to be almost no labor, and light. Do we not see how, even in dumb and irrational animals, where the love is not spiritual but carnal and natural, with great affection the mother yields herself to her young ones when they will have the milk which is their right: and however impetuously the suckling rushes at the teats, yet that is better for the mother than that it should not suck nor exact that which of love is due? Often we see great calves driving their heads at the cow's udders

with a force that almost lifts up the mother's body, yet does she not kick them off; nay, if the young one be not there to suck, the lowing of the dam calls for it to come to the teats. If then there be in us that spiritual charity of which the apostle saith, "I became small in the midst of you even as a nurse cherishing her young ones;"[1] we love you the more when ye are exacting. We like not the sluggish, because for the languid ones we are afraid. We have been obliged, however, to intermit the continuous reading of this epistle, because of certain stated lessons coming between, which must needs be read on their holy days, and the same preached upon. Let us now come back to the order which was interrupted; and what remains, holy brethren, receive ye with all attention. I know not whether charity could be more magnificently commended to us, than that it should be said, "Charity is God."[2] Brief praise, yet mighty praise: brief in utterance, mighty in meaning! How soon is it said, "Love is God!" This also is short: if thou

33

[1] 1 Thess. ii. 7.　　　[2] 1 John iv. 16.

count it, it is one: if thou weigh it, how great is it! "Love is God, and he that dwelleth," saith he, "in love, dwelleth in God, and God dwelleth in him." Let God be thy house, and be thou an house of God; dwell in God, and let God dwell in thee. God dwelleth in thee, that He may hold thee: thou dwellest in God, that thou mayest not fall; for thus saith the apostle of this same charity, "Charity never falleth."[1] How should He fall whom God holdeth?

2. "Herein is our love made perfect in us, that we may have boldness in the day of judgment: because as He is, so are we in this world."[2] He tells how each may prove himself, what progress charity has made in him; or rather what progress he has made in charity. For if charity is God, God is capable neither of proficiency nor of deficiency: that charity is said to be making proficiency in thee, means only that thou makest proficiency in it. Ask therefore what proficiency thou hast made in charity, and what thine heart will answer thee, that thou mayest know the measure of thy profiting. For he has promised to show us in what we may know Him, and hath said, "In this is love made perfect in us." Ask, in what? "That we have boldness in the day of judgment." Whoso hath boldness in the day of judgment, in that man is charity made perfect. What is it to have boldness in the day of judgment? Not to fear lest the day of judgment should come. There are men who do not believe in a day of judgment; these cannot have boldness in a day which they do not believe will come. Let us pass these: may God awaken them, that they may live; why speak we of the dead? They do not believe that there will be a day of judgment; they neither fear nor desire what they do not believe. Some man has begun to believe in a day of judgment: if he has begun to believe, he has also begun to fear. But because he fears as yet, because he hath not yet boldness in the day of judgment, not yet is charity in that man made perfect. But for all that, is one to despair? In whom thou seest the beginning, why despairest thou of the end? What beginning do I see? (sayest thou.) That very fear. Hear the Scripture: "The fear of the Lord is the beginning of wisdom."[3] Well then, he has begun to fear the day of judgment: by fearing let him correct himself, let him watch against his enemies, i.e. his sins; let him begin to come to life again inwardly, and to mortify his members which are upon the earth, as the apostle saith, "Mortify your

members which are upon the earth."[4] By the members upon earth he means spiritual wickedness:[5] for he goes on to expound it, "Covetousness, uncleanness,"[6] and the rest which he there follows out. Now in proportion as this man who has begun to fear the day of judgment, mortifies his members which are upon the earth, in that proportion the heavenly members rise up and are strengthened. But the heavenly members are all good works. As the heavenly members rise up, he begins to desire that which once he feared. Once he feared lest Christ should come and find in him the impious whom He must condemn; now he longs for Him to come, because He shall find the pious man whom He may crown. Having now begun to desire Christ's coming, the chaste soul which desires the embrace of the Bridegroom renounces the adulterer, becomes a virgin within by faith, hope, and charity. Now hath the man boldness in the day of judgment: he fights not against himself when he prays, "Thy kingdom come."[7] For he that fears lest the kingdom of God should come, fears lest his prayer be heard. How can he be said to pray, who fears lest his prayer be heard? But he that prays with boldness of charity, wishes now that He may come. Of this same desire said one in the Psalm, "And thou, Lord, how long? Turn, Lord, and deliver my soul."[8] He groaned at being so put off. For there are men who with patience submit to die; but there are some perfect who with patience endure to live. What do I mean? When a person still desires this life, that person, when the day of death comes, patiently endures death: he struggles against himself that he may follow the will of God, and in his mind desires that which God chooseth, not what man's will chooseth: from desire of the present life there comes a reluctance against death, but yet he takes to him patience and fortitude, that he may with an even mind meet death; he dies patiently. But when a man desires, as the apostle saith, "to be dissolved and to be with Christ,"[9] that person, not patiently dies, but patiently lives, delightedly dies. See the apostle patiently living, i.e. how with patience he here, not loves life, but endures it. "To be dissolved," saith he, "and to be with Christ, is far better: but to continue in the flesh is necessary for your sakes." Therefore, brethren, do your endeavor, settle it inwardly with yourselves to make this your concern, that ye may desire the day of judgment. No otherwise is charity proved to be

---

[1] I Cor. xiii. 8. Lit. πίπτει.
[3] Prov. i. 7; xv. 13.
[2] I John iv. 17.

[4] Col. iii. 5.
[6] Eph. vi. 12.
[8] Ps. vi. 4, 5.
[5] *Spiritualia nequitiæ.*
[7] Matt. vi. 10.
[9] Phil. i. 23, 24.

perfect, but only when one has begun to desire that day. But that man desires it, who hath boldness in it, whose conscience feels no alarm in perfect and sincere charity.

3. "In this is His love perfected in us, that we may have boldness in the day of judgment." Why shall we have boldness? "Because as He is are we also in this world." Thou hast heard the ground of thy boldness: "Because as He is," saith the apostle, "are we also in this world." Does he not seem to have said something impossible? For is it possible for man to be as God? I have already expounded to you that "*as*" is not always said of equality, but is said of a certain resemblance. For how sayest thou, *As I have ears, so* has my image? Is it quite *so?* and yet thou sayest "*so, as.*" If then we were made after God's image, why are we not *so as* God? Not unto equality, but relatively to our measure. Whence then are we given boldness in the day of judgment? "Because as He is, are we also in this world." We must refer this to the same charity, and understand what is meant. The Lord in the Gospel saith, "If ye love them that love you, what reward shall ye have? do not the publicans this?"[1] Then what would He have *us* do? "But I say unto you, Love your enemies, and pray for them that persecute you." If then He bids us love our enemies, whence brings He an example to set before us? From God Himself: for He saith, "That ye may be the children of your Father which is in heaven." How doth God this? He loveth His enemies, "Who maketh His sun to rise upon the good and the bad, and raineth upon the just and the unjust." If this then be the perfection unto which God inviteth us, that we love our enemies as He loved His; this is our boldness in the day of judgment, that "as He is, so are we also in this world:" because, as He loveth His enemies in making His sun to rise upon good and bad, and in sending rain upon the just and unjust, so we, since we cannot bestow upon them sun and rain, bestow upon them our tears when we pray for them.

4. Now therefore concerning this same boldness, let us see what he says. Whence do we understand that charity is perfect? "There is no fear in charity."[2] Then what say we of him that has begun to fear the day of judgment? If charity in him were perfect, he would not fear. For perfect charity would make perfect righteousness, and he would have nothing to fear: nay rather he would have something to desire; that iniquity may pass away, and God's kingdom come. So then, "there is no fear in charity." But in what charity? Not in charity begun: in what then? "But perfect charity," saith he, "casteth out fear." Then let fear make the beginning, because "the fear of the Lord is the beginning of wisdom." Fear, so to say, prepares a place for charity. But when once charity has begun to inhabit, the fear which prepared the place for it is cast out. For in proportion as this increases, that decreases: and the more this comes to be within, is the fear cast out. Greater charity, less fear; less charity, greater fear. But if no fear, there is no way for charity to come in. As we see in sewing, the thread is introduced by means of the bristle;[3] the bristle first enters, but except it come out the thread does not come into its place: so fear first occupies the mind, but the fear does not remain there, because it enters only in order to introduce charity. When once there is the sense of security in the mind, what joy have we both in this world and in the world to come! Even in this world, who shall hurt us, being full of charity? See how the apostle exults concerning this very charity: "Who shall separate us from the charity of Christ? shall tribulation, or distress, or persecution, or famine, or nakedness, or peril, or sword?"[4] And Peter saith: "And who is he that will harm you, if ye be followers[5] of that which is good?—There is no fear in love; but perfect love casteth out fear: because fear hath torment."[6] The consciousness of sins torments the heart: justification has not yet taken place. There is that in it which itches, which pricks. Accordingly in the Psalm what saith he concerning this same perfection of righteousness? "Thou hast turned for me my mourning into joy: Thou hast put off my sackcloth, and girded me with gladness; to the end that my glory may sing to thee, and that I be not pricked."[7] What is this, "That I be not pricked?" That there be not that which shall goad my conscience. Fear doth goad: but fear not thou: charity enters in, and she heals the wound that fear inflicts. The fear of God so wounds as doth the leech's knife;[8] it takes away the rottenness, and seems to make the wound greater. Behold, when the rottenness was in the body, the wound was less, but perilous: then comes the knife; the wound smarted less than it smarts now while the leech is cutting it. It smarts more while he is operating upon it than it would if it were

---

[1] Matt. v. 44-46.　　　[2] 1 John iv. 18.

[3] *Per setam.*
[5] 1 John iv. 18. *Æmulatores.*
[7] Ps. xxx. 11, 12. *Non compungar.*
[4] Rom. viii. 35.
[6] 1 Pet. iii. 13.
[8] *Ferramentum.*

not operated upon; it smarts more under the healing operation, but only that it may never smart when the healing is effected. Then let fear occupy thine heart, that it may bring in charity; let the cicatrice succeed to the leech's knife. He is such an Healer, that the cicatrices do not even appear: only do thou put thyself under His hand. For if thou be without fear, thou canst not be justified. It is a sentence pronounced by the Scriptures; "For he that is without fear, cannot be justified."[1] Needs then must fear first enter in, that by it charity may come. Fear is the healing operation: charity, the sound condition. "But he that feareth is not made perfect in love." Why? "Because fear hath torment;" just as the cutting of the surgeon's knife hath torment.

5. But there is another sentence, which seems contrary to this if it have not one that understands.[2] Namely, it is said in a certain place of the Psalms, "The fear of the Lord is chaste, enduring forever."[3] He shows us an eternal fear, but *a chaste*. But if he there shows us an eternal fear, does this epistle perchance contradict him, when it saith, "There is no fear in love, but perfect love casteth out fear?" Let us interrogate both utterances of God. One is the Spirit, though the books two, though the mouths two, though the tongues two. For this is said by the mouth of John, that by the mouth of David: but think not that the Spirit is more than one. If one breath fills two pipes [of the double-flute], cannot one Spirit fill two hearts, move two tongues? But if two pipes filled by one breathing sound in unison, can two tongues filled with the Spirit or Breathing of God make a dissonance? There is then an unison there, there is a harmony, only it requires one that can hear. Behold, this Spirit of God hath breathed into and filled two hearts, hath moved two tongues: and we have heard from the one tongue, "There is no fear in love; but perfect love casteth out fear;" we have heard from the other, "The fear of the Lord is chaste, enduring for ever." How is this? The notes seem to jar. Not so: rouse thine ears: mark the melody. It is not without cause that in the one place there is added that word, chaste, in the other it is not added: but because there is one fear which is called chaste, and there is another fear which is not called chaste. Let us mark the difference between these two fears, and so understand the harmony of the flutes. How are we to understand, or how to distinguish? Mark, my beloved. There

are men who fear God, lest they be cast into hell, lest haply they burn with the devil in everlasting fire. This is the fear which introduces charity: but it comes that it may depart. For if thou as yet fearest God because of punishments, not yet dost thou love Him whom thou in such sort fearest. Thou dost not desire the good things, but art afraid of the evil things. Yet because thou art afraid of the evil things, thou correctest thyself and beginnest to desire the good things. When once thou hast begun to desire the good, there shall be in thee the chaste fear. What is the chaste fear? The fear lest thou lose the good things themselves. Mark! It is one thing to fear God lest He cast thee into hell with the devil, and another thing to fear God lest He forsake thee. The fear by which thou fearest lest thou be cast into hell with the devil, is not yet chaste; for it comes not from the love of God, but from the fear of punishment: but when thou fearest God lest His presence forsake thee, thou embracest Him, thou longest to enjoy God Himself.

6. One cannot better explain the difference between these two fears, the one which charity casteth out, the other chaste, which endureth for ever, than by putting the case of two married women, one of whom, you may suppose, is willing to commit adultery, delights in wickedness, only fears lest she be condemned by her husband. She fears her husband: but because she yet loves wickedness, that is the reason why she fears her husband. To this woman, the presence of her husband is not grateful but burdensome; and if it chance she live wickedly, she fears her husband, lest he should come. Such are they that fear the coming of the day of judgment. Put the case that the other loves her husband, that she feels that she owes him chaste embraces, that she stains herself with no uncleanness of adultery; she wishes for the presence of her husband. And how are these two fears distinguished? The one woman fears, the other also fears. Question them: they seem to make one answer: question the one, Dost thou fear thine husband? she answers, I do. Question the other, whether she fears her husband; she answers, I do fear him. The voice is one, the mind diverse. Now then let them be questioned, Why? The one saith, I fear my husband, lest he should come: the other saith, I fear my husband, lest he depart from me. The one saith, I fear to be condemned: the other, I fear to be forsaken. Let the like have place in the mind of Christians, and thou findest a fear which love casteth out, and another fear, chaste, enduring for ever.

---

[1] Ecclus. i. 28.   [2] *Supra*, Hom. xliii.   [3] Ps. xix. 9.

7. Let us speak then first to these who fear God, just in the manner of that woman who delights in wickedness; namely, she fears her husband lest he condemn her; to such let us first speak. O soul, which fearest God lest He condemn thee, just as the woman fears who delights in wickedness; fears her husband, lest she be condemned by her husband: as thou art displeased at this woman, so be displeased at thyself. If perchance thou hast a wife, wouldest thou have thy wife fear thee thus, that she be not condemned by thee? that delighting in wickedness, she should be repressed only by the weight of the fear of thee, not by the condemnation of her iniquity? Thou wouldest have her chaste, that she may love thee, not that she may fear thee. Show thyself such to God, as thou wouldest have thy wife be to thee. And if thou hast not yet a wife, and wishest to have one, thou wouldest have her such. And yet what are we saying, brethren? That woman, whose fear of her husband is, to be condemned by her husband, perhaps does not commit adultery, lest by some means or other it come to her husband's knowledge, and he deprive her of this temporal light of life: now the husband can be deceived and kept in ignorance; for he is but human, as she is who can deceive him. She fears him, from whose eyes she can be hid: and dost thou not fear the face ever upon thee of thine Husband? "The countenance of the Lord is against them that do evil."[1] She catches at her husband's absence, and haply is incited by the delight of adultery; and yet she saith to herself, I will not do it: he indeed is absent, but it is hard to keep it from coming in some way to his knowledge. She restrains herself, lest it come to the knowledge of a mortal man, one who, it is also possible, may never know it, who, it is also possible, may be deceived, so that he shall esteem a bad woman to be good, esteem her to be chaste who is an adulteress: and dost thou not fear the eyes of Him whom no man can deceive? thou not fear the presence of Him who cannot be turned away from thee? Pray God to look upon thee, and to turn His face away from thy sins; "Turn away Thy face from my sins."[2] But whereby dost thou merit that He should turn away His face from thy sins, if thou turn not away thine own face from thy sins? For the same voice saith in the Psalm: "For I acknowledge mine iniquity, and my sin is ever before me."[3] Acknowledge thou, and He forgives.[4]

8. We have addressed that soul which hath

as yet the fear which endureth not for ever, but which love shuts out and casts forth: let us address that also which hath now the fear which is chaste, enduring for ever. Shall we find that soul, think you, that we may address it? think you, is it here in this congregation? is it, think you, here in this chancel?[5] think you, is it here on earth? It cannot but be, only it is hidden. Now is the winter: within is the greenness in the root. Haply we may get at the ears of that soul. But wherever that soul is, oh that I could find it, and instead of its giving ear to me, might myself give ear to it! It should teach me something, rather than learn of me! An holy soul, a soul of fire, and longing for the kingdom of God: that soul, not I address, but God Himself doth address, and thus consoleth while patiently it endures to live here on earth: "Thou wouldest that I should even now come, and I know that thou wishest I should even now come: I know what thou art, such that without fear thou mayest wait for mine advent; I know that is a trouble to thee: but do thou even longer wait, endure; I come, and come quickly." But to the loving soul the time moves slowly. Hear her singing, like a lily as she is from amid the thorns; hear her sighing and saying, "I will sing, and will understand in a faultless[6] way: when will thou come unto me?"[7] But in a faultless way well may she not fear; because "perfect love casteth out fear." And when He is come to her embrace, still she fears, but[8] in the manner of one that feels secure. What does she fear? She will beware and take heed to herself against her own iniquity, that she sin not again: not lest she be cast into the fire, but lest she be forsaken by Him. And there shall be in in her—what? the "chaste fear, enduring for ever." We have heard the two flutes sounding in unison. That speaks of fear, and this speaks of fear: but that, of the fear with which the soul fears lest she be condemned; this, of the fear with which the soul fears lest she be forsaken.[9] That is the fear which charity casteth out: this, the fear that endureth for ever.

9. "Let us love,[10] because He first loved us."[11] For how should we love, except He had first loved us? By loving we became

5 *Exedra*. In Eusebius, this term denotes certain outer buildings of the Church, such as the baptistery, &c. *Hist. Ecc.* x. 4. *Vales. ad Ens. de Vit. Const.* iii. 50; Bingham, *Antiq.* viii. 3, sec. 1. But in St. Augustin it evidently means that part of the church in which the Bishop had his seat, the *sanctuarium*, or chancel; and with this agrees the use of the term in Vitruvius, *v. Forcellini s. v. Comp. de Civ. Dei*, xxii. 8, and Epist. (*ad Alyp.*) xxix. 8. Here the meaning is, Is such a soul present in this church? among the laity? among the clergy?
6 *Immaculata*. 7 Ps. ci. 1, 2. 8 *Securiter*.
9 *Enarr. ii.* in Ps. xxvi. sec. 9; xlix. sec. 3.
10 ἀγαπῶμεν. 11 1 John iv. 19.

1 Ps. xxxiv. 16.   2 Ps. li. 9.   3 Ps. li. 3.
4 *Agnosce tu, et ille ignoscit*.

friends : but He loved us as enemies, that we might be made friends. He first loved us, and gave us the gift of loving Him. We did not yet love Him : by loving we are made beautiful. If a man deformed and ill-featured love a beautiful woman, what shall he do? Or what shall a woman do, if, being deformed and ill-featured and black-complexioned, she love a beautiful man? By loving can she become beautiful? Can he by loving become handsome? He loves a beautiful woman, and when he sees himself in a mirror, he is ashamed to lift up his face to her his lovely one of whom he is enamored. What shall he do that he may be beautiful? Does he wait for good looks to come? Nay rather, by waiting old age is added to him, and makes him uglier. There is nothing then to do, there is no way to advise him, but only that he should restrain himself, and not presume to love unequally: or if perchance he does love her, and wishes to take her to wife, in her let him love chastity, not the face of flesh. But our soul, my brethren, is unlovely by reason of iniquity: by loving God it becomes lovely. What a love must that be that makes the lover beautiful! But God is always lovely, never unlovely, never changeable. Who is always lovely first loved us; and what were we when He loved us but foul and unlovely? But not to leave us foul; no, but to change us, and of unlovely make us lovely. How shall we become lovely? By loving Him who is always lovely. As the love increases in thee, so the loveliness increases: for love is itself the beauty of the soul. "Let us love, because He first loved us." Hear the apostle Paul: "But God showed His love in us, in that while we were yet sinners, Christ died for us:"[1] the just for the unjust, the beautiful for the foul. How find we Jesus beautiful? "Thou art beauteous in loveliness surpassing the sons of men; grace is poured upon thy lips."[2] Why so? Again see why it is that He is fair; "Beauteous in loveliness surpassing the sons of men:" because "In the beginning was the Word, and the Word was with God, and the Word was God."[3] But in that He took flesh, He took upon Him, as it were, thy foulness, i.e. thy mortality, that He might adapt Himself to thee, and become suited to thee, and stir thee up to the love of the beauteousness within. Where then in Scripture do we find Jesus uncomely and deformed, as we have found Him comely and "beauteous in loveliness surpassing the sons of men?" where find we Him also deformed? Ask Esaias:

"And we saw Him, and He had no form nor comeliness."[4] There now are two flutes which seem to make discordant sounds: howbeit one Spirit breathes into both. By this it is said, "Beauteous in loveliness surpassing the sons of men:" by that it is said in Esaias, "We saw Him, and He had no form nor comeliness." By one Spirit are both flutes filled, they make no dissonance. Turn not away thine ears, apply the understanding. Let us ask the apostle Paul, and let him expound to us the unison of the two flutes. Let him sound to us the note, "Beauteous in loveliness surpassing the sons of men.—Who, being in the form of God, thought it not robbery to be equal with God."[5] Let him sound to us also the note, "We saw Him, and He had no form nor comeliness.—He made Himself of no reputation, taking upon Him the form of a servant, made in the likeness of men, and in fashion found as man. He had no form nor comeliness," that He might give thee form and comeliness. What form? what comeliness? The love which is in charity:[6] that loving, thou mayest run;[7] running, mayest love. Thou art fair now: but stay not thy regard upon thyself, lest thou lose what thou hast received; let thy regards terminate in Him by whom thou wast made fair. Be thou fair only to the end He may love thee. But do thou direct thy whole aim to Him, run thou to Him, seek His embraces, fear to depart from Him; that there may be in thee the chaste fear, which endureth for ever. "Let us love, because He first loved us."

10. "If any man say, I love God."[8] What God?[9] wherefore love we? "Because He first loved us," and gave us to love. He loved us ungodly, to make us godly; loved us unrighteous, to make us righteous; loved us sick, to make us whole. Ask each several man; let him tell thee if he love God. He cries out, he confesses: I love, God knoweth. There is another question to be asked. "If any man say, I love God, and hateth his brother, he is a liar." By what provest thou that he is a liar? Hear. "For he that loveth not his brother whom he seeth, how can he love God whom he seeth not?" What then? does he that loves a brother, love God also? He must of necessity love God, must of necessity love Him that is Love itself. Can one love his brother, and not love Love? Of necessity he must love Love. What then? because he loves Love, does it follow that he loves God? Certainly it does follow. In

---

[1] Rom. v. 8, 9.   [2] Ps. xlv. 2.   [3] John i. 1.

[4] Is. liii. 2.   [5] Phil. ii. 6, 7.   [6] *Dilectionem charitatis.*
[7] Cant. i. 4.   [8] 1 John iv. 20.
[9] *Quem Deum?* Ben. Ed. Louvain. reads it, *Quem? Deum.* But then the preceding *Deum* would be better omitted. "*If any man say, I love*—Whom? *God.*"

loving Love, he loves God. Or hast thou forgotten what thou saidst a little while ago, "Love is God"?[1] If "Love is God," whoso loveth Love, loveth God. Love then thy brother, and feel thyself assured. Thou canst not say, "I love my brother, but I do not love God." As thou liest, if thou sayest "I love God," when thou lovest not thy brother, so thou art deceived when thou sayest, I love my brother, if thou think that thou lovest not God. Of necessity must thou who lovest thy brother, love Love itself: but "Love is God:" therefore of necessity must he love God, whoso loveth his brother. But if thou love not the brother whom thou seest, how canst thou love God whom thou seest not? Why does he not see God? Because he has not Love itself. That he does not see God, is, because he has not love: that he has not love, is, because he loves not his brother. The reason then why he does not see God, is, that he has not Love. For if he have Love, he sees God, for "Love is God:" and that eye is becoming more and more purged by love, to see that Unchangeable Substance, in the presence of which he snall always rejoice, which he shall enjoy to everlasting, when he is joined with the angels. Only, let him run now, that he may at last have gladness in his own country. Let him not love his pilgrimage, not love the way: let all be bitter save Him that calleth us, until we hold Him fast, and say what is said in the Psalm: "Thou hast destroyed all that go a-whoring from Thee"[2]—and who are they that go a-whoring? they that go away and love the world: but what shalt thou do? he goes on and says:— "but for me it is good to cleave to God." All my good is, to cling unto God, freely. For if thou question him and say, For what dost thou cling to Him? and he should say, That He may give me—Give thee what? It is He that made the heaven, He that made the earth: what shall He give thee? Already thou are cleaving to Him: find something better, and He shall give it thee.

11. "For he that loveth not his brother whom he seeth, how can he love God whom he seeth not? And this commandment have we from Him, that he who loveth God love his brother also."[3] Marvellous fine talk it was, that thou didst say, "I love God," and hatest thy brother! O murderer, how lovest thou God? Hast thou not heard above in this very epistle, "He that hateth his brother is a murderer"?[4] Yea, but I do verily love God, however I hate my brother. Thou dost verily not love God, if thou hate thy brother. And now I make it good by another proof. This same apostle hath said, "He gave us commandment that we should love one another." How canst thou be said to love Him whose commandment thou hatest? Who shall say, I love the emperor, but I hate his laws? In this the emperor understands whether thou love him, that his laws be observed throughout the provinces. Our Emperor's law, what is it? "A new commandment give I unto you, that ye love one another."[5] Thou sayest then, that thou lovest Christ: keep His commandment, and love thy brother. But if thou love not thy brother, how canst thou be said to love Him whose commandment thou despisest?— Brethren, I am never satiated in speaking of charity in the name of the Lord. In what proportion ye have an insatiable desire of this thing, in that proportion we hope the thing itself is growing in you, and casting out fear, that so there may remain that chaste fear which is for ever permanent. Let us endure the world, endure tribulations, endure the stumbling-blocks of temptations. Let us not depart from the way; let us hold the unity of the Church, hold Christ, hold charity. Let us not be plucked away from the members of His Spouse, not be plucked away from faith, that we may glory in His coming: and we shall securely abide in Him, now by faith, then by sight, of whom we have so great earnest, even the gift of the Holy Spirit.

---

[1] 1 John iv. 8, 16.   [2] Ps. lxxiii. 27, 28.   [3] 1 John iv. 20, 21.   [4] 1 John iii. 15.   [5] John xiii. 34.

HOMILY X.

1 John V. 1-3.

"Whosoever believeth that Jesus is the Christ is born of God: and every one that loveth Him that begat Him, loveth Him also that is begotten of Him. By this we know that we love the children of God, because we love God, and do His commandments. For this is the love of God that we keep His commandments."

1. I suppose ye remember, those of you who were present yesterday, to what place in the course of this epistle our exposition has reached: namely, "He that loveth not his brother whom he seeth, how can he love God whom he seeth not? And this commandment have we from Him, That he who loveth God, love his brother also."[1] Thus far we discoursed. Let us see then what comes next in order. "Whosoever believeth that Jesus is the Christ is born of God."[2] Who is he that believeth not that Jesus is the Christ? He that does not so live as Christ commanded. For many say, "I believe:" but faith without works saveth not. Now the work of faith is Love, as Paul the apostle saith, "And faith which worketh by love."[3] Thy past works indeed, before thou didst believe, were either none, or if they seemed good, were nothing worth. For if they were none, thou wast as a man without feet, or with sore feet unable to walk: but if they seemed good, before thou didst believe, thou didst run indeed, but by running aside from the way thou wentest astray instead of coming to the goal. It is for us, then, both to run, and to run in the way. He that runs aside from the way, runs to no purpose, or rather runs but to toil. He goes the more astray, the more he runs aside from the way. What is the way by which we run? Christ hath told us, "I am the Way."[4] What the home to which we run? "I am the Truth." By Him thou runnest, to Him thou runnest, in Him thou restest. But, that we might run by Him, He reached even unto us: for we were afar off, foreigners in a far country. Not enough that we were in a far country, we were feeble also that we could not stir. A Physician, He came to the sick: a Way, He extended Himself to them that were in a far country. Let us be saved by Him, let us walk in Him. This it is to "believe that Jesus is the Christ," as Christians believe, who are not Christians only in name, but in deeds and in life, not as the devils believe. For "the devils also believe and tremble,"[5] as the Scripture tells us. What more could the devils believe, than that they should say, "We know who thou art, the Son of God?"[6] What the devils said, the same said Peter also. When the Lord asked them who He was, and whom did men say that He was, the disciples made answer to Him, "Some say that thou art John the Baptist; some, Elias; and others, Jeremias, or one of the prophets. He saith unto them, But whom say ye that I am? And Peter answered and said, Thou art the Christ, the Son of the Living God."[7] And this he heard from the Lord: "Blessed art thou, Simon Bar-jona; for flesh and blood hath not revealed it unto thee, but my Father which is in heaven." See what praises follow this faith. "Thou art Peter, and upon this rock I will build my Church." What meaneth, "Upon this rock I will build my Church"? Upon this faith; upon this that has been said, "Thou art the Christ, the Son of the Living God. Upon this rock," saith He, "I will build my Church." Mighty praise! So then, Peter saith, "Thou art the Christ, the Son of the Living God:" the devils also say, "We know who thou art, the Son of God, the Holy One of God." This Peter said, this also the devils: the words the same, the mind not the same. And how is it clear that Peter said this with love? Because a Christian's faith is with love, but a devil's without love. How without love? Peter said this, that he might embrace Christ; the devils said it, that Christ might depart from them. For before they said, "We know who thou art, the Son of God, they said, "What have we to do with thee? Why art thou come to destroy us before the time?" It is one thing then to confess Christ that thou mayest hold Christ, another thing to confess Christ that thou mayest drive Christ from thee. So then ye see, that in the sense in which he here saith, "Whoso believeth," it is a faith of

---

[1] 1 John iv. 20, 21.
[3] Gal. v. 6.
[2] 1 John v. 1.
[4] John xiv. 6.
[5] James ii. 19.
[7] Matt. xvi. 13-18.
[6] Matt. viii. 29; Mark i. 24.

one's own, not as one has a faith in common with many. Therefore, brethren, let none of the heretics say to you, "We also believe." For to this end have I given you an instance from the case of devils, that ye may not rejoice in the words of believing, but search well the deeds of the life.

2. Let us see then what it is to believe in Christ; what to believe that Jesus, He is the Christ. He proceeds: " Whosoever believeth that Jesus is the Christ, is born of God." But what is it to believe that? "And every one that loveth Him that begat Him, loveth Him also that is begotten of Him." To faith he hath straightway joined love, because faith without love is nothing worth. With love, the faith of a Christian; without love, the faith of a devil: but those who believe not, are worse than devils, more stupid than devils. Some man will not believe in Christ: so far, he is not even upon a par with devils. A person does now believe in Christ, but hates Christ: he hath the confession of faith in the fear of punishment, not in love of the crown: thus the devils also feared to be punished. Add to this faith love, that it may become a faith such as the Apostle Paul speaks of, a " faith which worketh by love:"[1] thou hast found a Christian, found a citizen of Jerusalem, found a fellow-citizen of the angels, found a pilgrim sighing in the way: join thyself to him, he is thy fellow-traveller, run with him, if indeed thou also art this. "Every one that loveth Him that begat Him, loveth Him also that is begotten of Him." Who " begat"? The Father. Who " is begotten "? The Son. What saith he then? "Every one that loveth the Father, loveth the Son."

3. " In this we know that we love the sons of God."[2] What is this, brethren? Just now he was speaking of the Son of God, not of sons of God: lo, here one Christ was set before us to contemplate, and we were told, " Whosoever believeth that Jesus is the Christ is born of God: and every one that loveth Him that begat," i. e. the Father, " loveth Him also that is begotten of Him," i. e. the Son, our Lord Jesus Christ. And he goes on: " In this we know that we love the sons of God;" as if he had been about to say, " In this we know that we love the Son of God." He has said, " the sons of God," whereas he was speaking just before of the Son of God—because the sons of God are the Body of the Only Son of God, and when He is the Head, we the members, it is one Son of God. Therefore, he that loves the sons of God, loves the Son of God, and he that

loves the Son of God, loves the Father; nor can any love the Father except he love the Son, and he that loves the sons, loves also the Son of God. What sons of God? The members of the Son of God. And by loving he becomes himself a member, and comes through love to be in the frame of the body of Christ, so there shall be one Christ, loving Himself. For when the members love one another, the body loves itself. " And whether one member suffer, all the members suffer with it; or one member be honored, all the members rejoice with it."[3] And then he goes on to say, " Now ye are the body of Christ, and members." John was speaking just before of brotherly love, and said, " He that loveth not his brother whom he seeth, how can he love God whom he seeth not?"[4] But if thou lovest thy brother, haply thou lovest thy brother and lovest not Christ? How should that be, when thou lovest members of Christ? When therefore thou lovest members of Christ, thou lovest Christ; when thou lovest Christ, thou lovest the Son of God; when thou lovest the Son of God, thou lovest also the Father. The love therefore cannot be separated into parts. Choose what thou wilt love; the rest follow thee. Suppose thou say, I love God alone, God the Father. Thou liest: if thou lovest, thou lovest Him not alone; but if thou lovest the Father, thou lovest also the Son. Behold, sayest thou, I love the Father, and I love the Son: but this only, the Father God and the Son God, our Lord Jesus Christ, who ascended into heaven, and sitteth at the right hand of the Father, that Word by which all things were made, and " the Word was made flesh, and dwelt in us:" this alone I love. Thou liest; for if thou lovest the Head, thou lovest also the members; but if thou lovest not the members, neither lovest thou the Head. Dost thou not quake at the voice uttered by the Head from Heaven on behalf of His members, " Saul, Saul, why persecutest thou ME?"[5] The persecutor of His members He called His persecutor: His lover, the lover of His members. Now what are His members, ye know, brethren: none other than the Church of God. " In this we know that we love the sons of God, in that we love God." And how? Are not the sons of God one thing, God Himself another? But he that loves God, loves His precepts. And what are the precepts of God? " A new commandment give I unto you, that ye love one another."[6] Let none excuse himself by another love, for another love; so and so

[1] Gal. v. 6. [2] 1 John iv. 2. [3] 1 Cor. xii. 26, 27. [4] 1 John iv. 20.
[5] Acts ix. 4. [6] John xiii. 34.

only is it with this love: as the love itself is compacted in one, so all that hang by it doth it make one, and as fire melts them down into one. It is gold: the lump is molten and becomes some one thing. But unless the fervor of charity be applied, of many there can be no melting down into one. "That we love God," by this "know we that we love the sons of God."

4. And by what do we know that we love the sons of God? By this, "that we love God, and do His commandments." We sigh here, by reason of the hardness of doing the commandments of God. Hear what follows. O man, at what toilest thou in loving? In loving avarice. With toil is that loved which thou lovest: there is no toil in loving God. Avarice will enjoin thee labors, perils, sore hardships and tribulations; and thou wilt do its bidding. To what end? That thou mayest have that with which thou shalt fill thy chest, and lose thy peace of mind. Thou didst feel thyself haply more secure before thou hadst it, than since thou didst begin to have. See what avarice has enjoined thee. Thou hast filled thine house, and art in dread of robbers; hast gotten gold, lost thy sleep. See what avarice has enjoined thee. Do, and thou didst. What does God enjoin thee! Love me. Thou lovest gold, thou wilt seek gold, and perchance not find it: whoso seeks me, I am with him. Thou wilt love honor, and perchance not attain unto it: who ever loved me, and did not attain? God saith to thee, thou wouldest make thee a patron, or a powerful friend: thou seekest a way to his favor by means of another inferior. Love me, saith God to thee: favor with me is not had by making interest with some other: thy love itself makes me present to thee. What sweeter than this love, brethren? It is not without reason that ye heard just now in the Psalm, "The unrighteous told me of delights,[1] but not as is Thy law, O Lord."[2] What is the Law of God? The commandment of God. What is the commandment of God? That "new commandment," which is called new because it maketh new: "A new commandment give I unto you, that ye love one another."[3] Hear because this is the law of God. The apostle saith, "Bear ye one another's burdens, and so shall ye fulfill the law of Christ."[4] This, even this, is the consummation of all our works; Love. In it is the end: for this we run: to it we run; when we are come to it, we shall rest.

5. Ye have heard in the Psalm, "I have seen the end of all perfection.[5] He hath said, I have seen the end of all perfection: what had he seen? Think we, had he ascended to the peak of some very high and pointed mountain, and looked out thence and seen the compass of the earth, and the circles of the round world, and therefore said, "I have seen the end of all perfection"? If this be a thing to be praised, let us ask of the Lord eyes of the flesh so sharp-sighted, that we shall but require some exceeding high mountain on earth, that from its summit we may see the end of all perfection. Go not far: lo, I say to thee, it is here; ascend the mountain, and see the end. Christ is the Mountain; come to Christ: thou seest thence the end of all perfection. What is this end? Ask Paul: "But the end of the commandment is charity, from a pure heart, and a good conscience, and faith unfeigned:"[6] and in another place, "Charity is the fullness," or fulfillment, "of the law." What so finished and terminated as "fullness"? For, brethren, the apostle here uses *end* in a way of praise. Think not of consumption, but of consummation. For it is in one sense that one says, I have finished my bread, in another, I have finished my coat. I have finished the bread, by eating it: the coat, by making it. In both places the word is "end," "finish:" but the bread is finished by its being consumed, the coat is finished by being made: the bread, so as to be no more; the coat, so as to be complete. Therefore in this sense take ye also this word, *end*, when the Psalm is read and ye hear it said, "On the end, a Psalm of David."[7] Ye are for ever hearing this in the Psalms, and ye should know what ye hear. What meaneth, "On the end"?—"For Christ is the end of the law unto every one that believeth."[8] And what meaneth, "Christ is the end"? Because Christ is God, and "the end of the commandment is charity," and "Charity is God:" because Father and Son and Holy Ghost are One. There is He the End to thee; elsewhere He is the Way. Do not stick fast in the way, and so never come to the end. Whatever else thou come to, pass beyond it, until thou come to the end. What is the end? It is good for me to "hold me fast in God."[9] Hast thou laid fast hold on God? thou hast finished the way: thou shalt abide in thine own country. Mark well! Some man seeks money: let not it be the end to thee: pass on, as a traveller in a strange land. But if thou love it, thou art entangled

---

[1] *Delectationes*, LXX. ἀδολεσχίας. Vulg. *fabulationes.*
[2] Ps. cxix. 85.   [3] John xiii. 34.
[4] Gal. vi. 2.

[5] *Consummationis.* Ps. cxix. 96.
[6] 1 Tim. i. 5.   [7] *Enarr.* in Ps. iv. 1, etc.
[8] Rom. xiii. 10.   [9] Ps. lxxiii. 28.

by avarice; avarice will be shackles to thy feet: thou canst make no more progress. Pass therefore this also: seek the end. Thou seekest health of the body: still do not stop there. For what is it, this health of the body, which death makes an end of, which sickness debilitates, a feeble, mortal, fleeting thing? Seek that, indeed, lest haply ill-health hinder thy good works: but for that very reason, the end is not there, for it is sought in order to something else. Whatever is sought in order to something else, the end is not there: whatever is loved for its own sake, and freely, the end is there. Thou seekest honors; perchance seekest them in order to do something, that thou mayest accomplish something, and so please God: love not the honor itself, lest thou stop there. Seekest thou praise? If thou seek God's, thou doest well; if thou seek thine own, thou doest ill; thou stoppest short in the way. But behold, thou art loved, art praised: think it not joy when in thyself thou art praised; be thou praised in the Lord, that thou mayest sing, " In the Lord shall my soul be praised." [1] Thou deliverest some good discourse, and thy discourse is praised. Let it not be praised as thine, the end is not there. If thou set the end there, there is an end of thee: but an end, not that thou be perfected, but that thou be consumed. Then let not thy discourse be praised as coming from thee, as being thine. But how praised? As the Psalm saith, " In God will I praise the discourse, in God will I praise the word." [2] Hereby shall that which there follows come to pass in thee: " In God have I hoped, I will not fear what man can do unto me." [3] For when all things that are thine are praised in God, no fear lest thy praise be lost, since God faileth not. Pass therefore this also.

6. See, brethren, how many things we pass, in which is not the end. These we use as by the way; we take as it were our refreshment at the halting places on our journey, and pass on.[4] Where then is the end? " Beloved, we are sons of God, and it hath not yet appeared what we shall be;" [5] here is this said, in this epistle. As yet then, we are on the way; as yet, wherever we come, we must pass on, until we attain unto some end. " We know that when He shall appear, we shall be like Him, for we shall see Him as He is. That is the end; there perpetual praising, there Alleluia [6] always without fail. This then is the end he has spoken of in the Psalm: " I have seen the end of all perfection:" [7]

and as though it were said to him, What is the end thou hast seen? " Thy commandment, exceeding broad." This is the end: the breadth of the commandment. The breadth of the commandment is charity, because where charity is, there are no straits. In this breadth, this wide room, was the apostle when he said, " Our mouth is open to you, O ye Corinthians, our heart is enlarged: ye are not straitened in us." [8] In this, then, is " Thy commandment exceeding broad." What is the broad commandment? "A new commmandment give I unto you, that ye love one another." Charity, then, is not straitened. Wouldest thou not be straitened here on earth? Dwell in the broad room. For whatever man may do to thee, he shall not straiten thee; because thou lovest that which man cannot hurt: lovest God, lovest the brotherhood, lovest the law of God, lovest the Church of God: it shall be for ever. Thou laborest here on earth, but thou shalt come to the promised enjoyment. Who can take from thee that which thou lovest? If no man can take from thee that which thou lovest, secure thou sleepest: or rather secure thou watchest, lest by sleeping thou lose that which thou lovest. For not without reason is it said, " Enlighten mine eyes, lest at any time I sleep in death." [9] They that shut their eyes against charity, fall asleep in the lusts of carnal delights. Be wakeful, therefore. For then are the delights, to eat, to drink, to wanton in luxury, to play, to hunt; these vain pomps all evils follow. Are we ignorant that they are delights? who can deny that they delight? But more beloved is the law of God. Cry against such persuaders: " The unrighteous have told me of delights: but not so as is thy law, O Lord." [10] This delight remaineth. Not only remaineth as the goal to which thou mayest come, but also calleth thee back when thou fleest.

7. " For this is the love of God, that we keep His commandments." [11] Already ye have heard, " On these two commandments hang all the law and the prophets." See how He would not have thee divide thyself over a multitude of pages: " On these two commandments hang all the law and the prophets." On what two commandments? " Thou shalt love the Lord thy God with all thy heart, and with all thy soul, and with all thy mind. And, thou shalt love thy neighbor as thyself. On these two commandments hang all the law and the prophets." [12] See here of what commandments this whole epis-

1 Ps. xxxiv. 2.　　　2 Ps. lvi. 10. (*Enarr.* in v. 4, sec. 7.)
3 Ps. lvi. 11.　　　4 *Supra.*　　　5 'ohn iii. 2.
6 *Supra.*　　　7 Ps. cxix. 96.

8 2 Cor. vi. 11, 12.　　　9 Ps. xiii. 3.　　　10 Ps. cxix. 85.
11 1 John iv. 3.　　　12 Matt. xxii. 37-40.

tle talks. Therefore hold fast love, and set your minds at rest. Why fearest thou lest thou do evil to some man? Who does evil to the man he loves? Love[1] thou: it is impossible to do this without doing good. But it may be, thou rebukest? Kindness[2] does it, not fierceness. But it may be thou beatest? For discipline thou dost this; because thy kindness of love[3] will not let thee leave him undisciplined. And indeed there come somehow these different and contrary results, that sometimes hatred uses winning ways, and charity shows itself fierce. A person hates his enemy, and feigns friendship for him: he sees him doing some evil, he praises him: he wishes him to go headlong, wishes him to go blind over the precipice of his lusts, haply never to return; he praises him, "For the sinner is praised in the desires of his soul;"[4] he applies to him the unction of adulation; behold, he hates, and praises. Another sees his friend doing something of the same sort; he calls him back; if he will not hear, he uses words even of castigation, he scolds, he quarrels:[5] there are times when it comes to this, that one must even quarrel! Behold, hatred shows itself winningly gentle, and charity quarrels! Stay not thy regard upon the words of seeming kindness, or the seeming cruelty of the rebuke; look into the vein[6] they come from; seek the root whence they proceed. The one is gentle and bland that he may deceive, the other quarrels that he may correct. Well then, it is not for us, brethren, to enlarge your heart: obtain from God the gift to love one another. Love all men, even your enemies, not because they are your brethren, but that they may be your brethren; that ye may be at all times on fire with brotherly love, whether toward him that is become thy brother, or towards thine enemy, so that, by being beloved, he may become thy brother. Wheresoever ye love a brother, ye love a friend. Now is he with thee, now is he knit to thee in unity, yea catholic unity. If thou art living aright, thou lovest a brother made out of an enemy. But thou lovest some man who has not yet believed Christ, or, if he have believed, believes as do the devils: thou rebukest his vanity. Do thou love, and that with a brotherly love: he is not yet a brother, but thou lovest to the end he may be a brother. Well then, all our love is a brotherly love, towards Christians, towards all His members. The discipline of charity, my brethren, its strength, flowers, fruit, beauty, pleasantness, food, drink, meat, embracing, hath in it no satiety. If it so delight

us while in a strange land, in our own country how shall we rejoice!

8. Let us run then, my brethren, let us run, and love Christ. What Christ? Jesus Christ. Who is He? The Word of God. And how came He to the sick? "The Word was made flesh, and dwelt in us."[7] It is complete then, which the Scripture foretold, "Christ must suffer, and rise again the third day from the dead."[8] His body, where is it? His members, where toil they? Where must thou be, that thou mayest be under thine Head? "And that repentance and remission of sins be preached in His name through all nations, beginning at Jerusalem."[9] There let thy charity be spread abroad. Christ saith, and the Psalm, i.e. the Spirit of God, "Thy commandment is exceeding broad:" and forsooth some man will have charity to be confined to Africa! Extend thy charity over the whole earth if thou wilt love Christ, for Christ's members are over all the earth. If thou lovest but a part, thou art divided: if thou art divided, thou art not in the body; if thou art not in the body, thou art not under the Head. What profiteth it thee that thou believest[10] and blasphemest? Thou adorest Him in the Head, blasphemest Him in the Body. He loves His Body. If thou hast cut thyself off from His Body, the Head hath not cut itself off from its Body. To no purpose dost thou honor me, cries thine Head to thee from on high, to no purpose dost thou honor me. It is all one as if a man would kiss thine head and tread upon thy feet: perchance with nailed boots he would crush thy feet, while he will clasp thy head and kiss it: wouldest thou not cry out in the midst of the words with which he honors thee, and say, What art thou doing, man? thou treadest on me. Thou wouldest not mean, Thou treadest on my head; for the head he honored; but more would the head cry out for the members trodden upon, than for itself because it was honored. Does not the head itself cry out, I will none of thine honor; do not tread on me? Now say if thou canst, How have I trodden upon thee? say that to the head: I wanted to kiss thee, I wanted to embrace thee. But seest thou not, O fool, that what thou wouldest embrace does in virtue of a certain unity, which knits the whole frame together, reach to that which thou treadest upon? Above[11] thou honorest me, beneath[12] thou treadest upon me. That on which thou treadest pains more than that which thou honorest rejoiceth. In what sort does the tongue cry out? "It hurts me."

---

[1] Dilige.   [2] Amor.   [3] Amor ipsius dilectionis.
[4] Ps. x. 3.   [5] Litigat.   [6] Venam, supra.

[7] John i. 14.   [8] Luke xxiv. 46.   [9] Luke xxiv. 47.
[10] Credis in Bened.   [11] Susum.   [12] Jusum.

It saith not, "It hurts my foot," but, "It hurts me," saith it. O tongue, who has touched thee? who has struck? who has goaded? who has pricked? No man, but I am knit together with the parts that are trodden upon. How wouldest thou have me not be pained, when I am not separate?

9. Our Lord Jesus Christ, then, ascending into heaven on the fortieth day, did for this reason commend to us His Body where it would continue to lie, because He saw that many would honor Him for that He is ascended into heaven: and saw that their honoring Him is useless if they trample upon His members here on earth. And lest any one should err, and, while he adored the Head in heaven should trample upon the feet on earth, He told us where would be His members. For being about to ascend, He spake His last words on earth: after those same words He spake no more on earth. The Head about to ascend into heaven commended to us His members on earth and departed. Thenceforth thou findest not Christ speaking on earth; thou findest Him speaking, but from heaven. And even from heaven, why? Because His members on earth were trodden upon. For to the persecutor Saul He said from on high, "Saul, Saul, why persecutest thou me?"[1] I am ascended into heaven, but still I lie on earth: here I sit at the right hand of the Father, but there I yet hunger, thirst, and am a stranger. In what manner then did He commend to us His Body, when about to ascend into heaven? When the disciples asked Him, saying, "Lord, wilt thou at this time present[2] thyself, and when shall be the kingdom of Israel?"[3] He made answer, now at the point to depart, "It is not for you to know the time which the Father hath put in His own power: but ye shall receive strength of the Holy Ghost coming upon you, and ye shall be witnesses to me." See where His Body is spread abroad, see where He will not be trodden upon: "Ye shall be witnesses to me, unto Jerusalem, and unto Judea, and even unto all the earth." Lo, where I lie that am ascending! For I ascend, because I am the Head: my Body lies yet beneath. Where lies? Throughout the whole earth. Beware thou strike not, beware thou hurt not, beware thou trample not: these be the last words of Christ about to go into heaven. Look at a sick man languishing on his bed, lying in his house, and worn out with sickness, at death's door, his soul as it were even now between his teeth: who, anxious, it may be, about something that is dear to him,

which he greatly loves, and it comes into his mind, calls his heirs, and says to them, I pray you, do this. He, as it were, detains his soul by a violent effort, that it may not depart ere those words be made sure. When he has dictated those last words, he breathes out his soul, he is borne a corpse to the sepulchre. His heirs, how do they remember the last words of the dying man? How, if one should stand up and say to them, Do it not: what would they say? "What? shall I not do that which my father, in the act of breathing out his soul, commanded me with his last breath, the last word of his that sounded in my ears when my father was departing this life? Whatever other words of his I may not regard, his last have a stronger hold upon me: since which I never saw him more, never more heard speech of his. Brethren, think with Christian hearts; if to the heirs of a man, his words spoken when about to go to the tomb are so sweet, so grateful, so weighty, what must we account of the last words of Christ, spoken not when about to go back to the tomb, but to ascend into heaven! As for the man who lived and is dead, his soul is hurried off to other places, his body is laid in the earth, and whether these words of his be done or not, makes no difference to him: he has now something else to do, or something else to suffer: either in Abraham's bosom he rejoices, or in eternal fire he longs for a drop of water, while his corpse lies there senseless in the sepulchre; and yet the last words of the dying man are kept. What have those to look for, who keep not the last words of Him that sitteth in heaven, who seeth from on high whether they be despised or not despised? The words of Him, who said, "Saul, Saul, why persecutest thou ME?" who keeps account, unto the judgment, of all that He seeth His members suffer?

10. And what have we done, say they? We are the persecuted, not the persecutors. Ye are the persecutors, O wretched men. In the first place, in that ye have divided the Church. Mightier the sword of the tongue than the sword of steel. Agar, Sarah's maid, was proud, and she was afflicted by her mistress for her pride. That was discipline, not punishment.[4] Accordingly, when she had gone away from her mistress, what said the angel to her? "Return to thy mistress."[5] Then, O carnal soul, like a proud bondwoman, suppose thou have suffered any trouble for discipline' sake, why ravest thou? "Return to thy mistress," hold fast the peace of the Church.[6] Lo, the gospels are pro-

---

[1] Acts ix 4.
[3] Acts i. 6-8.

[2] *Præsentaberis, Supra.*

[4] *Supra.*   [5] Gen. xvi. 4-9.   [6] *Dominicam pacem.*

duced, we read where the Church is spread abroad: men dispute against us, and say to us, "Betrayers!"[1] Betrayers of what? Christ commendeth to us His Church, and thou believest not: shall I believe thee, when thou revilest my parents? Wouldest thou that I should believe thee about the "betrayers"? Do thou first believe Christ. What is worth believing? Christ is God, thou art man: which ought to be believed first? Christ has spread His Church abroad over all the earth: I say it—despise me: the gospel speaks—beware. What saith the gospel? "It behoved Christ to suffer, and to rise again from the dead on the third day, and that repentance and remission of sins should be preached in His name."[2] Where remission of sins, there the Church is. How the Church? Why, to her it was said, "To thee I will give the keys of the kingdom of heaven, and whatsoever thou shalt loose on earth shall be loosed in heaven, and whatsoever thou shalt bind on earth shall be bound in heaven."[4] Where is this remission of sins spread abroad? "Through all nations, beginning at Jerusalem." Lo, believe Christ! But, because thou art well aware that if thou shalt believe Christ, thou wilt not have anything to say about "betrayers," thou wilt needs have me to believe thee when thou speakest evil against my parents, rather than thyself believe what Christ foretold!

* * * * * * *

[The remainder of the Homily is wanting in all the manuscripts. It seems also that St. Augustin was hindered from completing the exposition of the entire epistle, as he had undertaken to do: at least Possidius specifies this work under the title, "*In Epist. Joannis ad Parthos Tractatus decem*," and it is scarcely likely that the whole of the fifth chapter was expounded in this tenth Homily. —Of the "Sermons," there are none upon the remaining part of this epistle: the following extracts from other works of St. Augustin will supply what will be most desiderated: namely, his exposition of the text on "the Three Witnesses," of "the sin unto death," and of the twentieth verse].

Contra Maximinum, lib. ii. c. 22 §. 3.

1. *Joann.* v. 7. 8. *Tres sunt testes; spiritus, et aqua, et sanguis; et tres unum sunt.*[4]

I would not have thee mistake that place in the epistle of John the apostle where he saith, "There are three witnesses: the Spirit, and the water, and the blood: and the three are one." Lest haply thou say that the Spirit and the water and the blood are diverse substances, and yet it is said, "the three are one:" for this cause I have admonished thee, that thou mistake not the matter. For these are mystical expressions,[5] in which the point always to be considered is, not what the actual things are, but what they denote as signs: since they are signs of things, and what they are in their essence is one thing, what they are in their signification another. If then we understand the things signified, we do find these things to be of one substance. Thus, if we should say, the rock and the water are one, meaning by the Rock, Christ; by the water, the Holy Ghost: who doubts that rock and water are two different substances? yet because Christ and the Holy Spirit are of one and the same nature, therefore when one says, the rock and the water are one, this can be rightly taken in this behalf, that these two things of which the nature is diverse, are signs of other things of which the nature is one. Three things then we know to have issued from the Body of the Lord when He hung upon the tree: first, the spirit: of which it is written, "And He bowed the head and gave up the spirit:"[6] then, as His side was pierced by the spear, "blood and water." Which three things if we look at as they are in themselves, they are in substance several and distinct, and therefore they are not one. But if we will inquire into the things signified by these, there not unreasonably comes into our thoughts the Trinity itself, which is the One, Only, True, Supreme God, Father and Son and Holy Ghost, of whom it could most truly be said, "There are Three Witnesses, and the Three are One:" so that by the term *Spirit* we should understand God the Father to be signified; as indeed it was concerning the worshipping of Him that the Lord was speaking, when He said, "God is a Spirit:"[7] by the term, *blood*, the Son; because "the Word was made flesh:"[8] and by the term *water*, the Holy Ghost; as, when Jesus spake of the water which He would give to them that thirst, the evangelist saith, "But this said He of the Spirit which they that believed on Him were to receive."[9] Moreover, that the Father, Son, and Holy Ghost are "Witnesses," who that believes the Gospel can doubt, when the Son saith, "I am one that bear witness of myself, and the Father that sent me, He beareth witness of me."[10] Where, though the Holy Ghost is not men-

---

[1] *Traditores.*   [2] Luke xxiv. 47.   [3] Matt. xvi. 19.
[4] The clause of "the Three Heavenly Witnesses," v. 7, appears to be wholly unknown to St. Augustin: a circumstance left unexplained by Mill, who asserts that copies which had the clause "abounded in Africa" in the interval between St. Cyprian and the close of the fifth century.

[5] *Sacramenta.*   [6] John xix. 30, 34.   [7] John iv. 24.
[8] John i. 14.   [9] John vii. 39.   [10] John viii. 18.

tioned, yet He is not to be thought separated from them. Howbeit neither concerning the Spirit hath He kept silence elsewhere, and that He too is a witness hath been sufficiently and openly shown. For in promising Him He said, "He shall bear witness of me."[1] These are the "Three Witnesses, and the Three are One, because of one substance. But whereas, the signs by which they were signified came forth from the Body of the Lord, herein they figured the Church preaching the Trinity, that it hath one and the same nature: since these Three in threefold manner signified are One, and the Church that preacheth them is the Body of Christ. In this manner then the three things by which they are signified came out from the Body of the Lord: like as from the Body of the Lord sounded forth the command to "baptize the nations in the Name of the Father and of the Son and of the Holy Ghost."[2] "In the name:" not, In the names: for "these Three are One," and One God is these Three. And if in any other way this depth of mystery which we read in John's epistle can be expounded and understood agreeably with the Catholic faith, which neither confounds nor divides the Trinity, neither believes the substances diverse nor denies that the persons are three, it is on no account to be rejected. For whenever in Holy Scriptures in order to exercise the minds of the faithful any thing is put darkly, it is to be joyfully welcomed if it can be in many ways but not unwisely expounded.

De Sermone Domini in Monte, lib. i. 22, § 73.

1 *Joann.* v. 16. *Si quis scit peccare fratrem suum peccatum non ad mortem, postulabit, et dabit illi Dominus vitam qui peccat non ad mortem; est autem peccatum ad mortem; non pro illo dico ut roget.*

But what presses harder upon the present question [in the Lord's command of praying for enemies and persecutors] is that saying of the apostle John, "If any man know that his brother sinneth a sin not unto death, he shall ask, and the Lord will give life to that man who sinneth not unto death: but there is a sin unto death: not for that do I say that he should ask." For it manifestly shows that there are some "brethren" whom we are not commanded to pray for, whereas the Lord bids us pray even for our persecutors. Nor can this question be solved except we acknowledge, that there are some sins in brethren that are worse than the sin of enemies in persecuting. That "brethren" mean Chris-

tians, may be proved by many texts of Holy Writ; the plainest, however, is that of the apostle which he puts thus: "For the unbelieving husband is sanctified in the wife, and the unbelieving wife is sanctified in the brother."[3] For he has not added *our;* but thought it plain enough, when by the term *brother* he spake of the Christian that should have an unbelieving wife. And accordingly he says just afterwards, "But if the unbelieving depart, let her depart: but a brother or sister is not put under servitude in a matter of this sort." The "sin," therefore, of a brother, "unto death," I suppose to be when, after the acknowledging of God through the grace of our Lord Jesus Christ, one fights against the brotherhood, and is set on by the fire-brands of hatred[4] against the very grace through which he was reconciled to God.[5] But "a sin not unto death" is when a person, not having alienated his love from his brother, yet through some infirmity of mind may have failed to exhibit the due offices of brotherhood. Wherefore, on the one hand, the Lord on the cross said, "Father, forgive them, for they know not what they do,"[6] since they had not yet, by being made partakers of the grace of the Holy Spirit, entered into the fellowship of holy brotherhood; and blessed Stephen in the Acts of the Apostles prays for them who are stoning him;[7] because they had not yet believed Christ, and were not fighting against that grace of communion. On the other hand, the apostle Paul does not pray for Alexander, and the reason I suppose, is, that this man was a brother, and had sinned "unto death," *i.e.* by opposing the brotherhood in a spirit of hatred.[8] Whereas for such as had not broken off the bonds of love, but had given way through fear, he prays that they may be forgiven. For so he says: "Alexander the coppersmith did me much evil: the Lord reward him according to his works: of whom be thou ware also; for he hath greatly withstood our words."[9] Then he subjoins for whom he prays, saying, "At my first answer no man

---

[1] John xv. 26.   [2] Matt. xxviii. 19.

[3] 1 Cor. vii. 14, 15.   [4] *Invidentiæ.*
[5] In the *Retractations*, i. 7, he remarks on this passage: "I have not positively affirmed it to be so, for I have said, 'I suppose:' still it should have been added, 'if in this so wicked perversity of mind he departs this life:' since we have certainly no right to despair of any ever so wicked man so long as he is in this life, and it cannot be unwise to pray for that man of whom we do not despair." Comp. *Serm.* lxxi. 21.
[6] Luke xxiii. 34.   [7] Acts vii. 59.
[8] So the traditional interpretation of the Greeks in Œcumenius. "This 'alone' is 'the sin unto death,' *viz.* sin which has no thought of repentance: which sin Judas being diseased withal, was brought to eternal death." Especially (he adds) the sin of an unforgiving spirit, impenitently persisted in : "For the ways of the resentful are unto death," saith Solomon (Prov. xii. 28, LXX.). So Theophylact.—The *Scholia ap Matthäi,* p. 146, 230: "'The sin unto death' is, when a person having sinned is callous in impenitence." Comp. S. Hilar. *Tr. in Ps.* cxl. sec. 8.
[9] 2 Tim. iv. 14-16.

stood with me, but all men forsook me: I pray God that it may not be laid to their charge." This difference of sins it is that distinguishes Judas with his treason from Peter with his denial. Not that to him who repenteth there is to be no forgiveness: lest we go against that sentence of the Lord, in which He commands always to forgive the brother who asks his brother's forgiveness:[1] but that the mischief of that sin is, that the man cannot submit to the humiliation of begging for pardon, even when he is forced by his evil conscience both to acknowledge and to publish his sin. For when Judas had said, "I have sinned, in that I have betrayed the innocent blood,"[2] he went and hanged himself in desperation, rather than pray for forgiveness in humiliation. Wherefore it makes a great difference, what sort of repentance God forgives. For many are much quicker than others to confess that they have sinned, and are angry with themselves in such sort that they vehemently wish they had not sinned, while yet they cannot lay down their pride, and submit to have the heart humbled and broken so as to implore pardon: a state of mind which one may well believe to be, for the greatness of their sin, a part of their already begun damnation.

And this, perhaps, it is "to sin against the Holy Ghost:"[3] *i.e.* through malice and envy to fight against brotherly charity after receiving the grace of the Holy Spirit: that sin which the Lord saith hath no forgiveness, either here or in the world to come. . . . . . For the Lord in saying to the Pharisees, "Whosoever shall speak an evil word against the Son of Man,"[4] &c., may have meant to warn them to come to the grace of God, and having received it, not to sin as they have now sinned. For now they have spoken an evil word against the Son of Man, and it may be forgiven them, if they be converted and believe and receive the Holy Spirit: which when they have received, if they will then have ill-will against the brotherhood and oppose the grace they have received, there is no forgiveness for them, either in this world or in the world to come.

Liber de Correptione et Gratia, § 35.

By this grace such is the liberty they receive, that although as long as they live here they have to fight against the lusts of sins, and are overtaken by some sins for which they

must daily pray, "Forgive us our debts," yet they no longer serve the sin which is unto death, of which the apostle John saith, "There is a sin unto death, I do not say that he shall ask for that." Concerning which sin (since it is not expressed) many different opinions may be formed: but I affirm that sin to be the forsaking until death[5] the "faith which worketh by love."

Contra Maximinum, lib. ii. c. 14, § 2, 3.

1 *Joann.* v. 20. "*Ut simus in vero Filio ejus Jesu Christo; ipse est verus Deus et vita æterna.*"[6]

When ye read, "That we may be in His true Son Jesus Christ," think of the "true Son" of God. But this Son ye in no wise think to be the true Son of God, if ye deny Him to be begotten of the substance of the Father. For was He already Son of Man and by gift of God became Son of God, begotten indeed of God, but by grace, not by nature? Or, though not Son of Man, yet was He some sort of creature which, by God's changing it, was converted into Son of God? If you mean nothing of this sort, then was He either begotten of nothing, or of some substance. But thou hast relieved us from all fear of having to suppose that you affirm the Son of God to be of nothing, for thou hast declared that this is not your meaning. Therefore, He is of some substance. If not of the substance of the Father, then of what? Tell me. But ye cannot find any other . . . Consequently, the Father and the Son are of one and the same substance. This is the *Homöusion* . . . . In the Scriptures both you and

---

1 Luke xvii. 3.   2 Matt. xxvii. 4, 5.
3 Comp. Serm. lxxi. Scholl. *ap Matthäi*, p. 230. "By 'the sin unto death,' he means the blasphemy against the Holy Ghost, *i.e.*, against the Godhead," p. 147. "Some say that it is the blasphemy against the Holy Ghost, the sin of misbelief (κακοπιστίας)."
4 Matt. xii. 24-33.

5 So in the *Retractations, supra,* note b. *Si in hac tam scelerata mentis perversitate finierit hanc vitam:* "unto death," in the sense, "until death."
6 St. Hilary *de Trin.* vi.43, cites the passage with additions, of which there are no traces in the MSS. and other authorities; *Quia scimus quod Filius Dei venit et concarnatus est propter nos, et passus est, et resurgens de mortuis assumpsit nos, et dedit nobis intellectum optimum, ut intelligamus verum, et simus in vero filio ejus Jesu Christo: hic est verus [Deus om.], et vita æterna, et resurrectio nostra:* and it is remarkable that his contemporary Faustinus (the Luciferian) in his work *de Trinitate,* gives the passage *totidem verbis,* except that it is doubtful whether he read *verus Deus,* and that after *resurrectio nostra* he adds *in ipso.*—Vulg. *et simus in vero Filio ejus. Hic est verus Deus, et vita æterna.* In the Greek, the second ἐν τῷ is omitted by St. Cyril, Alex. St. Basil, *adv. Eunom.* and others; and this is the received reading of the Latins.—There is no certain evidence to show how the text was interpreted by the ante-Nicene Fathers. St. Athanasius *Orat. c. Arian.* iii. 24, sec. 4; 25, sec. 16; iv. 9, *init.* and St. Basil *adv. Eunom.* iv. p. 294, unhesitatingly refer the οὗτος to the nearest antecedent: "And we are in Him the True," (even) "in His Son Jesus Christ: this" (Jesus Christ) "is the True God and eternal Life:" and the Latin Fathers from St. Hilary and St. Ambrose downward allege the text as an explicit declaration of the true Godhead of the Son.—St. Epiphanius *Ancorat.* c. 4, seems to have read in his copy, οὗτος ἐστιν ὁ ἀληθινὸς καὶ ζωὴ αἰώνιος, omitting Θεὸς (as Hilary): for he says: "And though the epithet 'Very God' (θεὸς ἀληθινὸς) is not added," *i. e.* though this οὗτος, meaning Jesus Christ, is not expressly called the true God (as in v. 20, where he seems to have had in his copy the reading ἀληθινὸν Θεόν), "we do but accumulate madness if we dare to blaspheme and to say that the Son is not Very God. For it is enough that in the One [who is so called] we take in the whole Trinity, and from the Father [as Very God] understand the Son also to be Very God."

we read, "That we may be in His true Son Jesus Christ; He is the true God and Eternal Life." Let both parties yield to such weighty evidence. Tell us then, whether this "true Son" of God, discriminated as He is by the property of this name from those who are sons by grace,[1] be of no substance or of some substance. Thou sayest, "I do not say that He is of no substance, lest I should say that He is of nothing." He is therefore of some substance: I ask, of what? If not of the substance of the Father, seek another. If thou findest not another, as indeed thou canst find none at all, then acknowledge it to be the Father's, and confess the Son Homö-usios, "of one substance with the Father." Flesh is begotten of flesh, the Son of flesh is begotten of the substance of the flesh. Set aside corruption, reject from the eye of the mind all carnal passions, and behold "the invisible things of God understood by the means of the things that are made."[2] Be-lieve that the Creator who hath given flesh power to beget flesh, who hath given parents power of the substance of the flesh to gener-ate "true sons" of flesh, much more had power to beget a "true Son" of His own sub-stance, and to have one substance with the true Son, the spiritual incorruption remaining and carnal corruption being altogether alien therefrom.[3]

Collatio cum Maximino, § 14.

If He is begotten, He is Son: if He is Son, He is the "true Son," because Only-Begotten. For we also are called sons: He Son by nature, we sons by grace . . . To say that because He is begotten, He is of another nature, is to deny that He is the "true Son." Now we have the Scripture: "That we may be in His true Son Jesus Christ; He is the true God and Eternal Life."[4] Why "true God"? because "true Son" of God. For if He has given to animals this property, that

what they beget shall be none other than what they themselves are: man begets man, dog begets dog, and should God not beget God? If then He is of the same substance, why callest thou Him less? Is it because when a human father begets a son, though human beget human, yet greater begets less? If so, then let us wait for Christ to grow as human beings grow whom human beings beget![5] But if Christ, ever since He was begotten (and this was not in time but from eternity), is what He is, and yet is less than the Father, at that rate the human condition is the better of the two: for a human being at any rate can grow, and has the property of sooner or later attaining to the age, to the strength of the father; but He never: then how is He a "true Son"?

De Trinitate, lib. i. 6, § 9.

And if the Son be not of the same sub-stance as the Father, then is He a made sub-stance: if a made substance, then not "all things were made by Him:" but, "all things were made by Him;"[6] therefore, He is of one and the same substance with the Father. And therefore, not only God, but *True* (or, Very) *God*. Which the same John doth most openly affirm in his epistle: *Scimus quod Filius Dei venerit et dederit nobis intellectum ut cognoscamus verum Deum, et simus in vero Filio ejus Jesu Christo. Hic est verus Deus et vita æterna."* "We know that the Son of God is come; and hath given us an under-standing that we may (learn to) know the True God,[7] and may be in His true Son Jesus Christ. This is the True God and Eternal Life."

10. Hence also by consequence we under-stand, that what the apostle Paul saith, "Who only hath immortality,"[8] he saith not merely of the Father, but of the One and Only God, which the Trinity itself is. For neither is the "Eternal Life" itself mortal in respect of any mutability: and consequently, since the Son of God "is Eternal Life," He also is to be understood together with the Father, where it is said, "Who only hath immortality.

---

[1] Serm. cxl. 3. "Seek in the Epistle of this same John what he hath said of Christ. 'Believe' (*credamus*) saith he, 'on His true Son Jesus Christ, He is the True God and Eternal Life!' What meaneth, 'True God and Eternal Life?' The 'True Son' of God is 'the True God and Eternal Life.' Why has he said, 'On His True Son?' Because God hath many sons, therefore He was to be distinguished by adding that He was the 'True Son.' Not just by saying that He is the Son, but by adding, as I said, that He is the 'True Son': He was to be distinguished because of the many sons whom God hath. For we are sons by grace, He by Nature. We, made such by the Father through Him; He, what the Father is, Himself is also: what God is, are we also?"
[2] Rom. i. 20.   [3] Serm. cxxxix. 3, 4.
[4] C. Serm. Arian, sec. 1.

[5] C. Maximin. i. 5.   [6] John i. 2.
[7] So τὸν ἀληθινὸν Θεόν. St. Basil, St. Cyril. *Al. Vers. Arab. Aeth. Cod. Al.* (ΛΛΗΘΕΙΝΟΝΘΝ, which abbreviated manner of writing may explain the omission) and several other MSS. Beda, *verum Deum. Facundus: quod est verum* (τὸ ἀληθινόν).
[8] 1 Tim. i. 16.

ST. AUGUSTIN:

TWO BOOKS

OF

SOLILOQUIES.

TRANSLATED BY

REV. CHARLES C. STARBUCK, A.M.,

ANDOVER, MASS.

PREFACE TO SOLILOQUIES.

THE two books of the *Soliloquia* were, by the statement of the author himself (Lib. I. 17), written in his thirty-third year. They were therefore written immediately after his baptism, evidently in the rural retreat of Cassiacum, in Upper Italy, belonging to his friend Verecundus, to which we know that he retreated for awhile after he had been received into the Church. It is therefore his earliest Christian work. And as it is early, so it is raw. His new-found faith struggles to justify itself through an intricate course of reasoning, in which he confuses helplessly the forms of logic with the substance of truth. However, though crude, his essential characteristics appear distinctly in it ; his power of reasoning, his wide observation of fundamental facts, and of mental processes and experiences, his love of his friends, and above all of Alypius, his ardent aspirations after supernal light, his deep devotion, which, however, has not availed to subdue the artificialities of rhetoric into childlike simplicity.

He expresses in the work a longing for continued support to his tender faith from Ambrose, who, however, is described as having temporarily withdrawn into some Trans-alpine seclusion, where Augustin complains that he hardly knows how to reach him even by a letter.

He appears in the work as yet undetermined as to the form and course of his future life. The vast services he was to render the Church do not appear even to glimmer on his mind. Indeed, the life of leisure. devoted only, with some chosen friends, to the abstract contemplation of God, which forms his ideal, shows how very faintly penetrated he yet was by the Christian idea of serviceableness, as, in fact, there is in the *Soliloquia* very little that is distinctively Christian, either in doctrine or experience. But all the greatness of his following life lies shut up in his pliancy to the will of God, here expressed, and in his conviction that the God whom Christ reveals is the one true God.

In his *Retractationes* he recalls a few sentences of this work, one, which he seems to regard as inadvertently so expressed as to be capable of a Sabellian turn ; another, which he regards as savoring too much of a Gnostic or Neo-Platonic abhorrence of matter ; and another, in which he treats the effects of mental discipline as Plato does, supposing it to bring out into distinctness knowledge already possessed and forgotten. In the *Retractationes* he gives the true explanation, namely, that the mind is so constituted, that by the light of the Eternal Reason present in it, it is capable according to its measure of apprehending truths of which it had never before laid hold.

I have endeavored, in the rendering, to avail myself, wherever requisite, of the elder idioms of our tongue, which appear more germane, both to the matter and manner of St. Augustin, than the unmellowed English of the nineteenth century.

CONTENTS OF THE SOLILOQUIES.

TWO BOOKS OF SOLILOQUIES.

BOOK I.

As I had been long revolving with myself matters many and various, and had been for many days sedulously inquiring both concerning myself and my chief good, or what of evil there was to be avoided by .me: suddenly some one addresses me, whether I myself, or some other one, within me or without, I know not. For this very thing is what I chiefly toil to know. There says then to me, let us call it REASON,—Behold, assuming that you had discovered somewhat, to whose charge would you commit it, that you might go on with other things? *A.* To the memory, no doubt. *R.* But is the force of memory so great as to keep safely everything that may have been wrought out in thought? *A.* It hardly could, nay indeed it certainly could not. *R.* Therefore you must write. But what are you to do, seeing that your health recoils from the labor of writing? nor will these things bear to be dictated, seeing they consent not but with utter solitude. *A.* True. Therefore I am wholly at a loss what to say. *R.* Entreat of God health and help, that you may the better compass your desires, and commit to writing this very petition, that you may be the more courageous in the offspring of your brain. Then, what you discover sum up in a few brief conclusions. Nor care just now to invite a crowd of readers; it will suffice if these things find audience among the few of thine own city.

2. O God, Framer of the universe, grant me first rightly to invoke Thee; then to show myself worthy to be heard by Thee; lastly, deign to set me free. God, through whom all things, which of themselves were not, tend to be. God, who withholdest from perishing even that which seems to be mutually destructive.

God, who, out of nothing, hast created this world, which the eyes of all perceive to be most beautiful. God, who dost not cause evil, but causest that it be not most evil. God, who to the few that flee for refuge to that which truly is, showest evil to be nothing. God, through whom the universe, even taking in its sinister side, is perfect. God, from whom things most widely at variance with Thee effect no dissonance, since worser things are included in one plan with better. God, who art loved, wittingly or unwittingly, by everything that is capable of loving. God, in whom are all things, to whom nevertheless neither the vileness of any creature is vile, nor its wickedness harmful, nor its error erroneous. God, who hast not willed that any but the pure should know the truth. God, the Father of truth, the Father of wisdom, the Father of the true and crowning life, the Father of blessedness, the Father of that which is good and fair, the Father of intelligible light, the Father of our awakening and illumination, the Father of the pledge by which we are admonished to return to Thee.

3. Thee I invoke, O God, the Truth, in whom and from whom and through whom all things are true which anywhere are true. God, the Wisdom, in whom and from whom and through whom all things are wise which anywhere are wise. God, the true and crowning Life, in whom and from whom and through whom all things live, which truly and supremely live. God, the Blessedness, in whom and from whom and through whom all things are blessed, which anywhere are blessed. God, the Good and Fair, in whom and from whom and through whom all things are good and fair, which anywhere are good

and fair. God, the intelligible Light, in whom and from whom and through whom all things intelligibly shine, which anywhere intelligibly shine. God, whose kingdom is that whole world of which sense has no ken. God, from whose kingdom a law is even derived down upon these lower realms. God, from whom to be turned away, is to fall: to whom to be turned back, is to rise again: in whom to abide, is to stand firm. God, from whom to go forth, is to die: to whom to return, is to revive: in whom to have our dwelling, is to live. God, whom no one loses, unless deceived: whom no one seeks, unless stirred up: whom no one finds, unless made pure. God, whom to forsake, is one thing with perishing; towards whom to tend, is one thing with living: whom to see is one thing with having. God, towards whom faith rouses us, hope lifts us up, with whom love joins us. God, through whom we overcome the enemy, Thee I entreat. God, through whose gift it is, that we do not perish utterly. God, by whom we are warned to watch. God, by whom we distinguish good from ill. God, by whom we flee evil, and follow good. God, through whom we yield not to calamities. God, through whom we faithfully serve and benignantly govern. God, through whom we learn those things to be another's which aforetime we accounted ours, and those things to be ours which we used to account as belonging to another. God, through whom the baits and enticements of evil things have no power to hold us. God, through whom it is that diminished possessions leave ourselves complete. God, through whom our better good is not subject to a worse. God, through whom death is swallowed up in victory. God, who dost turn us to Thyself. God, who dost strip us of that which is not, and arrayest us in that which is. God, who dost make us worthy to be heard. God, who dost fortify us. God, who leadest us into all truth. God, who speakest to us only good, who neither terrifiest into madness nor sufferest another so to do. God, who callest us back into the way. God, who leadest us to the door of life. God, who causest it to be opened to them that knock. God, who givest us the bread of life. God, through whom we thirst for the draught, which being drunk we never thirst. God, who dost convince the world of sin, of righteousness, and of judgment. God, through whom it is that we are not commoved by those who refuse to believe. God, through whom we disapprove the error of those, who think that there are no merits of souls before Thee. God, through whom it comes that we are not in bondage to the weak and beggarly

elements. God, who cleansest us, and preparest us for Divine rewards, to me propitious come Thou.

4. Whatever has been said by me, Thou the only God, do Thou come to my help, the one true and eternal substance, where is no discord, no confusion, no shifting, no indigence, no death. Where is supreme concord, supreme evidence, supreme steadfastness, supreme fullness, and life supreme. Where nothing is lacking, nothing redundant. Where Begetter and Begotten are one. God, whom all things serve, that serve, to whom is compliant every virtuous soul. By whose laws the poles revolve, the stars fulfill their courses, the sun vivifies the day, the moon tempers the night: and all the framework of things, day after day by vicissitude of light and gloom, month after month by waxings and wanings of the moon, year after year by orderly successions of spring and summer and fall and winter, cycle after cycle by accomplished concurrences of the solar course, and through the mighty orbs of time, folding and refolding upon themselves, as the stars still recur to their first conjunctions, maintains, so far as this merely visible matter allows, the mighty constancy of things. God, by whose everduring laws the stable motion of shifting things is suffered to feel no perturbation, the thronging course of circling ages is ever recalled anew to the image of immovable quiet: by whose laws the choice of the soul is free, and to the good rewards and to the evil pains are distributed by necessities settled throughout the nature of everything. God, from whom distil even to us all benefits, by whom all evils are withheld from us. God, above whom is nothing, beyond whom is nothing, without whom is nothing. God, under whom is the whole, in whom is the whole, with whom is the whole. Who hast made man after Thine image and likeness, which he discovers, who has come to know himself. Hear me, hear me, graciously hear me, my God, my Lord, my King, my Father, my Cause, my Hope, my Wealth, my Honor, my House, my Country, my Health, my Light, my Life. Hear, hear, hear me graciously, in that way, all Thine own, which though known to few is to those few known so well.

5. Henceforth Thee alone do I love, Thee alone I follow, Thee alone I seek, Thee alone am I prepared to serve, for Thou alone art Lord by a just title, of Thy dominion do I desire to be. Direct, I pray, and command whatever Thou wilt, but heal and open my ears, that I may hear Thine utterances. Heal and open my eyes, that I may behold Thy significations of command. Drive delusion

from me, that I may recognize Thee. Tell me whither I must tend, to behold Thee, and I hope that I shall do all things Thou mayest enjoin. O Lord, most merciful Father, receive, I pray, Thy fugitive; enough already, surely, have I been punished, long enough have I served Thine enemies, whom Thou hast under Thy feet, long enough have I been a sport of fallacies. Receive me fleeing from these, Thy house-born servant, for did not these receive me, though another Master's, when I was fleeing from Thee? To Thee I feel I must return: I knock; may Thy door be opened to me; teach me the way to Thee. Nothing else have I than the will: nothing else do I know than that fleeting and falling things are to be spurned, fixed and everlasting things to be sought. This I do, Father, because this alone I know, but from what quarter to approach Thee I do not know. Do Thou instruct me, show me, give me my provision for the way. If it is by faith that those find Thee, who take refuge with Thee, then grant faith: if by virtue, virtue: if by knowledge, knowledge. Augment in me, faith, hope, and charity. O goodness of Thine, singular and most to be admired!

7. *A.* Behold I have prayed to God. *R.* What then wouldst thou know? *A.* All these things which I have prayed for. *R.* Sum them up in brief. *A.* God and the soul, that is what I desire to know. *R.* Nothing more? *A.* Nothing whatever. *R.* Therefore begin to inquire. But first explain how, if God should be set forth to thee, thou wouldst be able to say, It is enough. *A.* I know not how He is to be so set forth to me as that I shall say, It is enough: for I believe not that I know anything in such wise as I desire to know God. *R.* What then are we to do? Dost thou not judge that first thou oughtest to know, what it is to know God sufficiently, so that arriving at that point, thou mayst seek no farther? *A.* So I judge, indeed: but how that is to be brought about, I see not. For what have I ever understood like to God, so that I could say, As I understand this, so would I fain understand God? *R.* Not having yet made acquaintance with God, whence hast thou come to know that thou knowest nothing like to God? *A.* Because if I knew anything like God, I should doubtless love it: but now I love nothing else than God and the soul, neither of which I know. *R.* Do you then not love your friends? *A.* Loving them, how can I otherwise than love the soul? *R.* Do you then love gnats and bugs similarly? *A.* The animating soul I said I loved, not animals. *R.* Men are then either not your friends, or you do not love them. For every

man is an animal, and you say that you do not love animals. *A.* Men are my friends, and I love them, not in that they are animals, but in that they are men, that is, in that they are animated by rational souls, which I love even in highwaymen. For I may with good right in any man love reason, even though I rightly hate him, who uses ill that which I love. Therefore I love my friends the more, the more worthily they use their rational soul, or certainly the more earnestly they desire to use it worthily.

8. *R.* I allow so much: but yet if any one should say to thee, I will give thee to know God as well as thou dost know Alypius, wouldst thou not give thanks, and say, It is enough? *A.* I should give thanks indeed: but I should not say, It is enough. *R.* Why, I pray? *A.* Because I do not even know God so well as I know Alypius, and yet I do not know Alypius well enough. *R.* Beware then lest shamelessly thou wouldest fain be satisfied in the knowledge of God, who hast not even such a knowledge of Alypius as satisfies. *A. Non sequitur.* For, comparing it with the stars, what is of lower account than my supper? and yet what I shall sup on to-morrow I know not: but in what sign the moon will be, I need take no shame to profess that I know. *R.* Is it then enough for thee to know God as well as thou dost know in what sign the moon will hold her course to-morrow? *A.* It is not enough, for this I test by the senses. But I do not know whether or not either God, or some hidden cause of nature may suddenly change the moon's ordinary course, which if it came to pass, would render false all that I had presumed. *R.* And believest thou that this may happen? *A.* I do not believe. But I at least am seeking what I may know, not what I may believe. Now everything that we know, we may with reason perhaps be said to believe, but not to know everything which we believe. *R.* In this matter therefore you reject all testimony of the senses? *A.* I utterly reject it. *R.* That friend of yours then, whom you say you do not yet know, is it by sense that you wish to know him or by intellectual perception? *A.* Whatever in him I know by sense, if indeed anything is known by sense, is both mean and sufficiently known. But that part which bears affection to me, that is, the mind itself, I desire to know intellectually. *R.* Can it, indeed, be known otherwise? *A.* By no means. *R.* Do you venture then to call your friend, your inmost friend, unknown to you? *A.* Why not venture? For I account most equitable that law of friendship, by which it is prescribed, that as one is to bear no less, so he is to bear no

more affection to his friend than to himself. Since then I know not myself, what injury does he suffer, whom I declare to be unknown to me, above all since (as I believe) he does not even know himself? *R.* If then these things which thou wouldst fain know, are of such a sort as are to be intellectually attained, when I said it was shameless in thee to crave to know God, when thou knowest not even Alypius, thou oughtest not to have urged to me the similitude of thy supper and the moon, if these things, as thou hast said, appertain to sense.

9. But let that go, and now answer to this: if those things which Plato and Plotinus have said concerning God are true, is it enough for thee to know God as they knew him? *A.* Even allowing that those things which they have said are true, does it follow at once that they knew them? For many copiously utter what they do not know, as I myself have said that I desired to know all those things for which I prayed, which I should not desire if I knew them already: yet I was none the less able to enumerate them all. For I have enumerated not what I intellectually comprehended, but things which I have gathered from all sides and entrusted to my memory, and to which I yield as ample a faith as I am able: but to know is another thing. *R.* Tell me, I pray, do you at least know in geometry what a line is? *A.* So much I certainly know. *R.* Nor in professing so do you stand in awe of the Academicians? *A.* In no wise. For they, as wise men, would not run the risk of erring: but I am not wise. Therefore as yet I do not shrink from professing the knowledge of those things which I have come to know. But if, as I desire, I should ever have attained to wisdom, I will do what I may find her to suggest. *R.* I except not thereto: but, I had begun to inquire, as you know a line, do you also know a ball, or, as they say, a sphere? *A.* I do. *R.* Both alike, or one more, one less? *A.* Just alike. I am altogether certain of both. *R.* Have you grasped these by the senses or the intellect? *A.* Nay, I have essayed the senses in this matter as a ship. For after they had carried me to the place I was aiming for, and I had dismissed them, and was now, as it were, left on dry ground, where I began to turn these things over in thought, the oscillations of the senses long continued to swim in my brain. Wherefore it seems to me that it would be easier to sail on dry land, than to learn geometry by the senses, although young beginners seem to derive some help from them. *R.* Then you do not hesitate to call whatever acquaintance you have with such things,

Knowledge? *A.* Not if the Stoics permit, who attribute knowledge only to the Wise Man. Certainly I maintain myself to have the perception of these things, which they concede even to folly: but neither am I at all in any great fear of the stoics: unquestionably I hold those things which thou hast questioned me of in knowledge: proceed now till I see to what end thou questionest me of them. *R.* Be not too eager, we are not pressed for time. But give strict heed, lest you should make some rash concession. I would fain give thee the joy of things wherein thou fearest not to slip, and dost thou enjoin haste, as in a matter of no moment? *A.* God grant the event as thou forecastest it. Therefore question at thy will, and rebuke me more sharply if I err so again.

10. *R.* It is then plain to you that a line cannot possibly be longitudinally divided into two? *A.* Plainly so. *R.* What of a cross-section? *A.* This, of course, is possible to infinity. *R.* But is it equally apparent that if, beginning with the centre, you make any sections you please of a sphere, no two resulting circles will be equal? *A.* It is equally apparent. *R.* What are a line and a sphere? Do they seem to you to be identical, or somewhat different? *A.* Who does not see that they differ very much? *R.* If then you know this and that equally well, while yet, as you acknowledge, they differ widely from each other, there must be an indifferent knowledge of different things. *A.* Who ever disputed it? *R.* You, a little while ago. For when I asked thee what way of knowing God was in thy desire, such that thou couldst say, It is enough, thou didst answer that thou couldst not explain this, because thou hadst no perception held in such a way as that in which thou didst desire to perceive God, for thou didst know nothing like God. What then? Are a line and sphere alike? *A.* Absurd. *R.* But I had asked, not what you knew such as God, but what you knew so as you desire to know God. For you know a line in such wise as you know a sphere, although the properties of a line are not those of a sphere. Wherefore answer whether it would suffice you to know God in such wise as you know that geometrical ball; that is, to be equally without doubt concerning God as concerning that.

11. *A.* Pardon me, however vehemently thou urge and argue, yet I dare not say that I wish so to know God as I know these things. For not only the objects of the knowledge, but the knowledge itself appears to be unlike. First, because the line and the ball are not so unlike, but that one science includes the knowl-

edge of them both: but no geometrician has ever professed to teach God. Then, if the knowledge of God and of these things were equivalent, I should rejoice as much to know them as I am persuaded that I should rejoice if God were known by me. But now I hold these things in the deepest disdain in comparison with Him, so that sometimes it seems to me that if I understood Him, and that in that manner in which He can be seen, all these things would perish out of my knowledge: since even now by reason of the love of Him they scarce come into my mind. *R.* Allow that thou wouldst rejoice more and much more in knowing God than in knowing these things, yet not by a different perception of the things; unless we are to say that thou beholdest with a different vision the earth and the serenity of the skies, although the aspect of this latter soothes and delights thee far more than of the former. But unless your eyes are deceived, I believe that, if asked whether you are as well assured that you see earth as heaven, you ought to answer yes, although you are not as much delighted by the earth and her beauty as by the beauty and magnificence of heaven. *A.* I am moved, I confess, by this similitude, and am brought to allow that by how much earth differs in her kind from heaven, so much do those demonstrations of the sciences, true and certain as they are, differ from the intelligible majesty of God.

12. *R.* Thou art moved to good effect. For the Reason which is talking with thee promises so to demonstrate God to thy mind, as the sun demonstrates himself to the eyes. For the senses of the soul are as it were the eyes of the mind; but all the certainties of the sciences are like those things which are brought to light by the sun, that they may be seen, the earth, for instance, and the things upon it: while God is Himself the Illuminator. Now I, Reason, am that in the mind, which the act of looking is in the eyes. For to have eyes is not the same as to look; nor again to look the same as to see. Therefore the soul has need of three distinct things: to have eyes, such as it can use to good advantage, to look, and to see. Sound eyes, that means the mind pure from all stain of the body, that is, now remote and purged from the lusts of mortal things: which, in the first condition, nothing else accomplishes for her than Faith. For what cannot yet be shown forth to her stained and languishing with sins, because, unless sound, she cannot see, if she does not believe that otherwise she will not see, she gives no heed to her health. But what if she believes that the

case stands as I say, and that, if she is to see at all, she can only see on these terms, but despairs of being healed; does she not utterly contemn herself and cast herself away, refusing to comply with the prescriptions of the physician? *A.* Beyond doubt, above all because by sickness remedies must needs be felt as severe. *R.* Then Hope must be added to Faith. *A.* So I believe. *R.* Moreover, if she both believes that the case stands so, and hopes that she could be healed, yet loves not, desires not the promised light itself, and thinks that she ought meanwhile to be content with her darkness, which now, by use, has become pleasant to her; does she not none the less reject the physician? *A.* Beyond doubt. *R.* Therefore Charity must needs make a third. *A.* Nothing so needful. *R.* Without these three things therefore no mind is healed, so that it can see, that is, understand its God.

13. When therefore the mind has come to have sound eyes, what next? *A.* That she look. *R.* The mind's act of looking is Reason; but because it does not follow that every one who looks sees, a right and perfect act of looking, that is, one followed by vision, is called Virtue; for Virtue is either right or perfect Reason. But even the power of vision, though the eyes be now healed, has not force to turn them to the light, unless these three things abide. Faith, whereby the soul believes that thing, to which she is asked to turn her gaze, is of such sort, that being seen it will give blessedness; Hope, whereby the mind judges that if she looks attentively, she will see; Charity, whereby she desires to see and to be filled with the enjoyment of the sight. The attentive view is now followed by the very vision of God, which is the end of looking; not because the power of beholding ceases, but because it has nothing further to which it can turn itself: and this is the truly perfect virtue, Virtue arriving at its end, which is followed by the life of blessedness. Now this vision itself is that apprehension which is in the soul, compounded of the apprehending subject and of that which is apprehended: as in like manner seeing with the eyes results from the conjunction of the sense and the object of sense, either of which being withdrawn, seeing becomes impossible.

14. Therefore when the soul has obtained to see, that is, to apprehend God, let us see whether those three things are still necessary to her. Why should Faith be necessary to the soul, when she now sees? Or Hope, when she already grasps? But from Charity not only is nothing diminished, but rather it receives large increase. For when the soul has

once seen that unique and unfalsified Beauty, she will love it the more, and unless she shall with great love have fastened her gaze thereon, nor any way declined from the view, she will not be able to abide in that most blessed vision. But while the soul is in this body, even though she most fully sees, that is, apprehends God; yet, because the bodily senses still have their proper effect, if they have no prevalency to mislead, yet they are not without a certain power to call in doubt, therefore that may be called Faith whereby these dispositions are resisted, and the opposing truth affirmed. Moreover, in this life, although the soul is already blessed in the apprehension of God; yet, because she endures many irksome pains of the body, she has occasion of hope that after death all these incommodities will have ceased to be. Therefore neither does Hope, so long as she is in this life, desert the soul. But when after this life she shall have wholly collected herself in God, Charity remains whereby she is retained there. For neither can she be said to have Faith that those things are true, when she is solicited by no interruption of falsities; nor does anything remain for her to hope, whereas she securely possesses the whole. Three things therefore pertain to the soul, that she be sane, that she behold, that she see. And other three, Faith, Hope, Charity, for the first and second of those three conditions are always necessary: for the third in this life all; after this life, Charity alone.

15. Now listen, so far as the present time requires, while from that similitude of sensible things I now teach also something concerning God. Namely, God is intelligible, not sensible, intelligible also are those demonstrations of the schools; nevertheless they differ very widely. For as the earth is visible, so is light; but the earth, unless illumined by light, cannot be seen. Therefore those things also which are taught in the schools, which no one who understands them doubts in the least to be absolutely true, we must believe to be incapable of being understood, unless they are illuminated by somewhat else, as it were a sun of their own. Therefore as in this visible sun we may observe three things: that he is, that he shines, that he illuminates: so in that God most far withdrawn whom thou wouldst fain apprehend, there are these three things: that He is, that He is apprehended, and that He makes other things to be apprehended. These two, God and thyself, I dare promise that I can teach thee to understand. But give answer how thou receivest these things, as probable, or as true? A. As probable certainly; and, as I must own,

I have been hoping more: for excepting those two illustrations of the line and the globe, nothing has been said by thee which I should dare to say that I know. R. It is not to be wondered at: for nothing has been yet so set forth, as that it exacts of thee perception.

16. But why do we delay? Let us set out: but first let us see (for this comes first) whether we are in a sound state. A. Do thou see to it, if either in thyself or in me that hast any discernment of what is to be found; I will answer, being inquired of, to my best knowledge. R. Do you love anything besides the knowledge of God and yourself? A. I might answer, that I love nothing besides, having regard to my present feelings; but I should be safer to say that I do not know. For it hath often chanced to me, that when I believed I was open to nothing else, something nevertheless would come into the mind which stung me otherwise than I had presumed. So often, when something, conceived in thought, disturbed me little, yet when it came in fact it disquieted me more than I supposed: but now I do not see myself sensible to perturbation except by three things; by the fear of losing those whom I love, by the fear of pain, by the fear of death. R. You love, therefore, both a life associated with those dearest to you, and your own good health, and your bodily life itself: or you would not fear the loss of these. A. It is so, I acknowledge. R. Now therefore, the fact that all your friends are not with you, and that your health is not very firm, occasions you some uneasiness of mind. For that I see to be implied. A. Thou seest rightly; I am not able to deny it. R. How if you should suddenly feel and find yourself sound in health, and should see all whom you love and who love each other, enjoying in your company liberal ease? would you not think it right to give way in reasonable measure even to transports of joy? A. In a measure, undoubtedly. Nay, if these things, as thou sayest, bechanced me suddenly, how could I contain myself? how could I possibly even dissemble joy of such a sort? R. As yet, therefore, you are tossed about by all the diseases and perturbations of the mind. What shamelessness, then, that with such eyes you should wish to see such a Sun! A. Thy conclusion then is, that I am utterly ignorant how far I am advanced in health, how far disease has receded, or how far it remains. Suppose me to grant this.

17. R. Do you not see that these eyes of the body, even when sound, are often so smitten by the light of this visible sun, as to be compelled to turn away and to take

refuge in their own obscurity? Now you are proposing to yourself what you are moved to seek, but are not proposing to yourself what you desire to see: and yet I would discuss this very thing with you, what advance you think we have made. Are you without desire of riches? *A.* This at least no longer chiefly. For, being now three and thirty years of age, for almost these fourteen years last past I have ceased to desire them, nor have I sought anything from them, if by chance they should be offered, beyond the necessities of life and such a use of them as agrees with the state of a freeman. A single book of Cicero has thoroughly persuaded me, that riches are in no wise to be craved, but that if they come in our way, they are to be with the utmost wisdom and caution administered. *R.* What of honors? *A.* I confess that it is only lately, and as it were yesterday, that I have ceased to desire these. *R.* What of a wife? Are you not sometimes charmed by the image of a beautiful, modest, complying maiden, well lettered, or of parts that can easily be trained by you, bringing you too (being a despiser of riches) just so large a dowry as will relieve your leisure of all burden on her account? It is implied, moreover, that you have good hope of coming to no grief through her. *A.* However much thou please to portray her and adorn her with all manner of gifts, I have determined that nothing is so much to be avoided by me as such a bed-fellow: I perceive that nothing more saps the citadel of manly strength, whether of mind or body, than female blandishments and familiarities. Therefore, if (which I have not yet discovered) it appertains to the office of a wise man to desire offspring, whoever for this reason only comes into this connection, may appear to me worthy of admiration, but in no wise a model for imitation: for there is more peril in the essay, than felicity in the accomplishment. Wherefore, I believe, I am contradicting neither justice nor utility in providing for the liberty of my mind by neither desiring, nor seeking, nor taking a wife. *R.* I inquire not now what thou hast determined, but whether thou dost yet struggle, or hast indeed already overcome desire itself. For we are considering the soundness of thine eyes. *A.* Nothing of the kind do I any way seek, nothing do I desire; it is even with horror and loathing that I recall such things to mind. What more wouldst thou? And day by day does this benefit grow upon me: for the more I grow in the hope of beholding that supernal Beauty with the desire of which I glow, the more my love and delight is wholly converted thereto. *R.* What of

pleasant viands? How much do you care for them? *A.* Those things which I have determined not to eat, tempt me not. As to those which I have not cut off, I allow that I take pleasure in their present use, yet so that without any disturbance of mind, either the sight or the taste of them may be withdrawn. And when they are entirely absent, no craving of them dares intrude itself to the disturbance of my thoughts. But no need to inquire concerning food or drink, or baths: so much of these do I seek to have, as is profitable for the confirmation of health.

18. *R.* Thou hast made great progress: yet those things which remain in order to the seeing of that light, very greatly impede. But I am aiming at something which appears to me very easy to be shown; that either nothing remains to us to be subdued, or that we have made no advance at all, and that the taint of all those things which we believed cut away remains. For I ask of thee, if thou wert persuaded that thou couldst live with the throng of those dearest to thee in the study and pursuit of wisdom on no other terms than as possessed of an estate ample enough to meet all your joint necessities; would you not desire and seek for wealth? *A.* I should. *R.* How, if it should also be clear, that you would be to many a master of wisdom, if your authority in teaching were supported by civil honor, and that even these your familiars would not be able to put a bridle on their cravings except as they too were in honor, and that this could only accrue to them through your honors and dignity? would not honor then be a worthy object of desire, and of strenuous pursuit? *A.* It is as thou sayest. *R.* I do not consider the question of a wife; for perhaps no such necessity could arise of marrying one: although if it were certain that by her ample patrimony all those could be sustained whom thou wouldst fain have live at ease with thee in one place, and that moreover with her cordial consent, especially if she were of a family of such nobility as that through her those honors which you have just granted, in our hypothesis, to be necessary, could easily be attained, I do not know that it would be any part of your duty to contemn these advantages, thus obtained. *A.* But how could I hope for such things?

19. *R.* You speak as if I were now inquiring what you hope. I am not inquiring what, denied, delights not, but what delights, obtained. For an extinguished plague is one thing, a dormant plague another. And, as some wise men say, all pools are so unsound, that they always smell of every foul thing, although you do not always perceive this, but

only when you stir them up. And there is a wide difference whether a craving is suppressed by hopelessness of compassing it, or is expelled by saneness of soul. *A.* Although I am not able to answer thee, never wilt thou, for all this, persuade me that in this affection of mind in which I now perceive myself to be, I have advantaged nothing. *R.* This, doubtless, appears so to thee, because although thou mightest desire these things, yet they would not seem to thee objects of desire on their own account, but for ulterior ends. *A.* That is what I was endeavoring to say: for when I desired riches, I desired them for this reason, that I might be rich. And those honors, the lust of which I have declared myself to have but even now thoroughly overcome, I craved by a mere delight in some intrinsic splendor I imputed to them; and nothing else did I expect in a wife, when I expected, than the reputable enjoyment of voluptuousness. Then there was in me a veritable craving for those things; now I utterly contemn them all: but if I cannot except through these find a passage to those things which in effect I desire, I do not pursue them as things to be embraced, but accept them as things to be allowed. *R.* A thoroughly excellent distinction: for neither do I impute unworthiness to the desire of any lower things that are sought on account of something else.

20. But I ask of thee, why thou dost desire, either that the persons whom thou affectest should live, or that they should live with thee. *A.* That together and concordantly we might inquire out God and our souls. For so, whichever first discovers aught, easily introduces his companions into it. *R.* What if these will not inquire? *A.* I would persuade them into the love of it. *R.* What if you could not, be it that they suppose themselves to have already found, or think that such things are beyond discovery, or that they are entangled in cares and cravings of other things? *A.* We will use our best endeavors, I with them, and they with me. *R.* What if even their presence impedes you in your inquiries? would you not choose and endeavor that they should not be with you, rather than be with you on such terms? *A.* I own it is as thou sayest. *R.* It is not therefore on its own account that you crave either their life or presence, but as an auxiliary in the discovery of wisdom? *A.* I thoroughly agree to that. *R.* Further: if you were certain that your own life were an impediment to your comprehension of wisdom, should you desire its continuance? *A.* I should utterly eschew it. *R.* Furthermore: if thou wert taught,

that either in this body or after leaving it thou couldst equally well attain unto wisdom, wouldst thou care whether it was in this or another life that thou didst enjoy that which thou supremely affectest? *A.* If I ascertained that I was to experience nothing worse, which would lead me back from the point to which I had made progress, I should not care. *R.* Then thy present dread of death rests on the fear of being involved in some worse evil, whereby the Divine cognition may be borne away from thee. *A.* Not solely such a possible loss do I dread, if I have any right understanding of the fact, but also lest access should be barred me into those things which I am now eager to explore; although what I already possess, I believe will remain with me. *R.* Therefore not for the sake of this life in itself, but for the sake of wisdom thou dost desire the continuance of this life. *A.* It is the truth.

21. *R.* We have pain of body left, which perhaps moves thee of its proper force. *A.* Nor indeed do I grievously dread even that for any other reason than that it impedes me in my research. For although of late I have been grievously tormented with attacks of toothache, so that I was not suffered to revolve aught in my mind except such things as I have been engaged in learning; while, as the whole intensity of my mind was requisite for new advances, I was entirely restrained from making these: yet it seemed to me, that if the essential refulgence of Truth would disclose itself to me, I should either not have felt that pain, or certainly would have made no account of it. But although I have never had anything severer to bear, yet, often reflecting how much severer the pains are which I might have to bear, I am sometimes forced to agree with Cornelius Celsus, who says that the supreme good is wisdom, and the supreme evil bodily pain. For since, says he, we are composed of two parts, namely, mind and body, of which the former part, the mind, is the better, the body the worse; the highest good is the best of the better part, and the chiefest evil the worst of the inferior; now the best thing in the mind is wisdom, and the worst thing in the body is pain. It is concluded, therefore, and as I fancy, most justly, that the chief good of man is to be wise, and his chief evil, to suffer pain. *R.* We will consider this later. For perchance Wisdom herself, towards which we strive, will bring us to be of another mind. But if she should show this to be true, we will then not hesitate to adhere to this your present judgment concerning the highest good and the deepest ill.

22. Now let us inquire concerning this,

what sort of lover of wisdom thou art, whom thou desirest to behold with most chaste view and embrace, and to grasp her unveiled charms in such wise as she affords herself to no one, except to her few and choicest votaries. For assuredly a beautiful woman, who had kindled thee to ardent love, would never surrender herself to thee, if she had discovered that thou hadst in thy heart another object of affection; and shall that most chaste beauty of Wisdom exhibit itself to thee, unless thou art kindled for it alone? *A.* Why then am I still made to hang in wretchedness, and put off with miserable pining? Assuredly I have already made it plain that I love nothing else, since what is not loved for itself is not loved. Now I at least love Wisdom for herself alone, while as to other things, it is for her sake that I desire their presence or absence, such as life, ease, friends. But what measure can the love of that beauty have in which I not only do not envy others, but even long for as many as possible to seek it, gaze upon it, grasp it and enjoy it with me; knowing that our friendship will be the closer, the more thoroughly conjoined we are in the object of our love?

23. *R.* Such lovers assuredly it is, whom Wisdom ought to have. Such lovers does she seek, the love of whom has in it nothing but what is pure. But there are various ways of approach to her. For it is according to our soundness and strength that each one comprehends that unique and truest good. It is a certain ineffable and incomprehensible light of minds. Let this light of the common day teach us, as well as it can, concerning the higher light. For there are eyes so sound and keen, that, as soon as they are first opened, they turn themselves unshrinkingly upon the sun himself. To these, as it were, the light itself is health, nor do they need a teacher, but only, perchance, a warning. For these to believe, to hope, to love is enough. But others are smitten by that very effulgence which they vehemently desire to see, and when the sight of it is withdrawn often return into darkness with delight. To whom, although such as that they may reasonably be called sound, it is nevertheless dangerous to insist on showing what as yet they have not the power to behold. These therefore should be first put in training, and their love for their good is to be nourished by delay. For first certain things are to be shown to them which are not luminous of themselves, but may be seen by the light, such as a garment, a wall, or the like. Then something which, though still not shining of itself, yet in the light flames out more gloriously, such as gold

or silver, yet not so brilliantly as to injure the eyes. Then perchance this familiar fire of earth is to be cautiously shown, then the stars, then the moon, then the brightening dawn, and the brilliance of the luminous sky. Among which things, whether sooner or later, whether through the whole succession, or with some steps passed over, each one accustoming himself according to his strength, will at last without shrinking and with great delight behold the sun. In some such way do the best masters deal with those who are heartily devoted to Wisdom, and who, though seeing but dimly, yet have already eyes that see. For it is the office of a wise training to bring one near to her in a certain graduated approach, but to arrive in her presence without these intermediary steps is a scarcely credible felicity. But to-day, I think we have written enough; regard must be had to health.

24. And, another day having come, *A.* Give now, I pray, if thou canst, that order. Lead by what way thou wilt, through what things thou wilt, how thou wilt. Lay on me things ever so hard, ever so strenuous, and, if only they are within my power, I doubt not that I shall perform them if only I may thereby arrive whither I long to be. *R.* There is only one thing which I can teach thee; I know nothing more. These things of sense are to be utterly eschewed, and the utmost caution is to be used, lest while we bear about this body, our pinions should be impeded by the viscous distilments of earth, seeing we need them whole and perfect, if we would fly from this darkness into that supernal Light: which deigns not even to show itself to those shut up in this cage of the body, unless they have been such that whether it were broken down or worn out it would be their native airs into which they escaped. Therefore, whenever thou shalt have become such that nothing at all of earthly things delights thee, at that very moment, believe me, at that very point of time thou wilt see what thou desirest. *A.* When shall that be, I entreat thee? For I think not that I am able to attain to this supreme contempt, unless I shall have seen that in comparison with which these things are worthless.

25. *R.* In this way too the bodily eye might say: I shall not love the darkness, when I shall have seen the sun. For this too seems, as it were, to pertain to the right order though t is far otherwise. For it loves darkness, for the reason that it is not sound; but the sun, unless sound, it is not able to see. And in this the mind is often at fault, that it thinks itself and boasts itself sound; and complains, as if with good ight,

because it does not yet see. But that supernal Beauty knows when she should show herself. For she herself discharges the office of physician, and better understands who are sound than the very ones who are rendered sound. But we, as far as we have emerged, seem to ourselves to see; but how far we were plunged in darkness, or how far we had made progress, we are not permitted either to think or feel, and in comparison with the deeper malady we believe ourselves to be in health. See you not how securely yesterday we had pronounced, that we were no longer detained by any evil thing, and loved nothing except Wisdom; and sought or wished other things only for her sake? To thee how low, how foul, how execrable those female embraces seemed, when we discoursed concerning the desire of a wife! Certainly in the watches of this very night, when we had again been discoursing together of the same things, thou didst feel how differently from what thou hadst presumed those imaginary blandishments and that bitter sweetness tickled thee; far, far less indeed, than is the wont, but also far otherwise than thou hadst thought: so that that most confidential physician of thine set forth to thee each thing, both how far thou hast come on under his care, and what remains to be cured.

26. *A.* Peace, I pray thee, peace. Why tormentest thou me? Why diggest thou so remorselessly and descendest so deep? Now I weep intolerably, henceforth I promise nothing, I presume nothing; question me not concerning these things. Most true is what thou sayest, that He whom I burn to see Himself knows when I am in health; let Him do what pleaseth Him: when it pleaseth Him let Him show Himself; I now commit myself wholly to His clemency and care. Once for all do I believe that those so affected towards Him He faileth not to lift up. I will pronounce nothing concerning my health, except when I shall have seen that Beauty. *R.* Do nothing else, indeed. But now refrain from tears, and gird up thy mind. Thou hast wept most sore, and to the great aggravation of that trouble of thy breast. *A.* Wouldest thou set a measure to my tears, when I see no measure of my misery? or dost thou bid me consider the disease of my body, when I in my inmost self am wasted away with pining consumption? But, I pray thee, if thou availest aught over me, essay to lead me through some shorter ways, so that, at least by some neighbor nearness of that Light, such as, if I have made any advance whatever, I shall be able to endure, I may be made ashamed of withdrawing my eyes into that

darkness which I have left; if indeed I can be said to have left a darkness which yet dares to dally with my blindness.

27. *R.* Let us conclude, if you will, this first volume, that in a second we may attempt some such way as may commodiously offer itself. For this disposition of yours must not fail to be cherished by reasonable exercise. *A.* I will in no wise suffer this volume to be ended, unless thou open to me at least a gleam from the nearness of that Light whither I am bound. *R.* Thy Divine Physician yields so far to thy wish. For a certain radiance seizes me, inviting me to conduct thee to it. Therefore be intent to receive it. *A.* Lead, I entreat thee, and snatch me away whither thou wilt. *R.* Thou art sure that thou art minded to know the soul, and God? *A.* That is all my desire. *R.* Nothing more? *A.* Nothing at all. *R.* What, do you not wish to comprehend Truth? *A.* As if I could know these things except through her. *R.* Therefore she first is to be known, through whom these things can be known. *A.* I refuse not. *R.* First then let us see this, whether, as Truth and True are two words, you hold that by these two words two things are signified, or one thing. *A.* Two things, I hold. For, as Chastity is one thing, and that which is chaste, another, and many things in this manner; so I believe that Truth is one thing, and that which, being declared, is true, is another. *R.* Which of these two do you esteem most excellent? *A.* Truth, as I believe. For it is not from that which is chaste that Chastity arises, but that which is chaste from Chastity. So also, if anything is true, it is assuredly from Truth that it is true.

28. *R.* What? When a chaste person dies, do you judge that Chastity dies also? *A.* By no means. *R.* Then, when anything perishes that is true, Truth perishes not. *A.* But how should anything true perish? For I see not. *R.* I marvel that you ask that question: do we not see thousands of things perish before our eyes? Unless perchance you think this tree, either to be a tree, but not a true one, or if so to be unable to perish. For even if you believe not your senses, and are capable of answering, that you are wholly ignorant whether it is a tree; yet this, I believe, you will not deny, that it is a true tree, if it is a tree: for this judgment is not of the senses, but of the intelligence. For if it is a false tree, it is not a tree; but if it is a tree, it cannot but be a true one. *A.* This I allow. *R.* Then as to the other proposition; do you not concede that a tree is of such a sort of things, as that it originates and perishes? *A.* I cannot deny it. *R.* It is con-

cluded therefore, that something which is true perishes. *A.* I do not dispute it. *R.* What follows? Does it not seem to thee that when true things perish Truth does not perish, as Chastity dies not when a chaste person dies? *A.* I now grant this too, and eagerly wait to see what thou art laboring to show. *R.* Therefore attend. *A.* I am all attention.

29. *R.* Does this proposition seem to you to be true: Whatever is, is compelled to be somewhere? *A.* Nothing so entirely wins my consent. *R.* And you confess that Truth is? *A.* I confess it. *R.* Then we must needs inquire where it is; for it is not in a place, unless perchance you think there is something else in a place than a body, or think that Truth is a body. *A.* I think neither of these things. *R.* Where then do you believe her to be? For she is not nowhere, whom we have granted to be. *A.* If I knew where she was, perchance I should seek nothing more. *R.* At least you are able to know where she is not? *A.* If thou pass in review the places, perchance I shall be. *R.* It is not, assuredly, in mortal things. For whatever is, cannot abide in anything, if that does not abide in which it is: and that Truth abides, even though true things perish, has just been conceded. Truth, therefore, is not in mortal things. But Truth is, and is not nowhere. There are therefore things immortal. And nothing is true in which Truth is not. It results therefore that nothing is true, except those things which are immortal. And every false tree is not a tree, and false wood is not wood, and false silver is not silver, and everything whatever which is false, is not. Now everything which is not true, is false. Nothing therefore is rightly said to be, except things immortal. Do you diligently consider this little argument, lest there should be in it any point which you think impossible to concede. For if it is sound, we have almost accomplished our whole business, which in the other book will perchance appear more plainly.

30. *A.* I thank thee much, and will diligently and cautiously review these things in my own mind, and moreover with thee, when we are in quiet, if no darkness interfere, and, which I vehemently dread, inspire in me delight in itself. *R.* Steadfastly believe in God, and commit thyself wholly to Him as much as thou canst. Be not willing to be as it were thine own and in thine own control; but profess thyself to be the bondman of that most clement and most profitable Lord. For so will He not desist from lifting thee to Himself, and will suffer nothing to occur to thee, except what shall profit thee, even though thou know it not. *A.* I hear, I believe, and as much as I can I yield compliance; and most intently do I offer a prayer for this very thing, that I may have the utmost power, unless perchance thou desirest something more of me. *R.* It is well meanwhile, thou wilt do afterwards what He Himself, being now seen, shall require of thee.

BOOK II.

1. *A.* Long enough has our work been intermitted, and impatient is Love, nor have tears a measure, unless to Love is given what is loved: wherefore, let us enter upon the Second Book. *R.* Let us enter upon it. *A.* Let us believe that God will be present. *R.* Let us believe indeed, if even this is in our power. *A.* Our power He Himself is. *R.* Therefore pray most briefly and perfectly, as much as thou canst. *A.* God, always the same, let me know myself, let me know Thee. I have prayed. *R.* Thou who wilt know thyself, knowest thou that thou art? *A.* I know. *R.* Whence knowest thou? *A.* I know not. *R.* Feelest thou thyself to be simple, or manifold? *A.* I know not. *R.* Knowest thou thyself to be moved? *A.* I know not. *R.* Knowest thou thyself to think? *A.* I know. *R.* Therefore it is true that thou thinkest. *A.* True. *R.* Knowest thou thyself to be immortal? *A.* I know not. *R.* Of all these things which thou hast said that thou knowest not, which dost thou most desire to know? *A.* Whether I am immortal. *R.* Therefore thou lovest to live? *A.* I confess it. *R.* How will the matter stand when thou shalt have learned thyself to be immortal? Will it be enough? *A.* That will indeed be a great thing, but that to me will be but slight. *R.* Yet in this which is but slight how much wilt thou rejoice? *A.* Very greatly. *R.* For nothing then wilt thou weep? *A.* For nothing at all. *R.* What if this very life should be found such, that in it it is permitted thee to know nothing more than thou knowest? Wilt thou refrain from tears? *A.* Nay verily, I

will weep so much that life should cease to be. *R.* Thou dost not then love to live for the mere sake of living, but for the sake of knowing. *A.* I grant the inference. *R.* What if this very knowledge of things should itself make thee wretched? *A.* I do not believe that that is in any way possible. But if it is so, no one can be blessed; for I am not now wretched from any other source than from ignorance of things. And therefore if the knowledge of things is wretchedness, wretchedness is everlasting. *R.* Now I see all which you desire. For since you believe no one to be wretched by knowledge, from which it is probable that intelligence renders blessed; but no one is blessed unless living, and no one lives who is not: thou wishest to be, to live and to have intelligence; but to be that thou mayest live, to live that thou mayest have intelligence. Therefore thou knowest that thou art, thou knowest that thou livest, thou knowest that thou dost exercise intelligence. But whether these things are to be always, or none of these things is to be, or something abides always, and something falls away, or whether these things can be diminished and increased, all things abiding, thou desirest to know. *A.* So it is. *R.* If therefore we shall have proved that we are always to live, it will follow also that we are always to be. *A.* It will follow. *R.* It will then remain to inquire concerning intellection.

2. *A.* I see a very plain and compendious order. *R.* Let this then be the order, that you answer my questions cautiously and firmly. *A.* I attend. *R.* If this world shall always abide, it is true that this world is always to abide? *A.* Who doubts that? *R.* What if it shall not abide? is it not then true that the world is not to abide? *A.* I dispute it not. *R.* How, when it shall have perished, if it is to perish? will it not then be true, that the world has perished? For as long as it is not true that the world has come to an end, it has not come to an end: it is therefore self-contradictory, that the world is ended and that it is not true that the world is ended. *A.* This too I grant. *R.* Furthermore, does it seem to you that anything can be true, and not be Truth? *A.* In no wise. *R.* There will therefore be Truth, even though the frame of things should pass away. *A.* I cannot deny it. *R.* What if Truth herself should perish? will it not be true that Truth has perished? *A.* And even that who can deny? *R.* But that which is true cannot be, if Truth is not. *A.* I have just conceded this. *R.* In no wise therefore can Truth fail. *A.* Proceed as thou hast begun, for than this deduction nothing is truer.

3. *R.* Now I will have you answer me, does the soul seem to you to feel and perceive, or the body? *A.* The soul. *R.* And does the intellect appear to you to appertain to the soul? *A.* Assuredly. *R.* To the soul alone, or to something else? *A.* I see nothing else besides the soul, except God, in which I believe intellect to exist. *R.* Let us now consider that. If any one should tell you that wall was not a wall, but a tree, what would you think? *A.* Either that his senses or mine were astray, or that he called a wall by the name of a tree. *R.* What if he received in sense the image of a tree, and thou of a wall? may not both be true? *A.* By no means; because one and the same thing cannot be both a tree and a wall. For however individual things might appear different to us as individuals, it could not be but that one of us suffered a false imagination. *R.* What if it is neither tree nor wall, and you are both in error? *A.* That, indeed, is possible. *R.* This one thing therefore you had past by above. *A.* I confess it. *R.* What if you should acknowledge that anything seemed to you other than it is, are you then in error? *A.* No. *R.* Therefore that may be false which seems, and he not be in error to whom it seems. *A.* It may be so. *R.* It is to be allowed then that he is not in error who sees falsities, but he who assents to falsities. *A.* It is assuredly to be allowed. *R.* And this falsity, wherefore is it false? *A.* Because it is otherwise than it seems. *R.* If therefore there are none to whom it may seem, nothing is false. *A.* The inference is sound. *R.* Therefore the falsity is not in the things, but in the sense; but he is not beguiled who assents not to false things. It results that we are one thing, the sense another; since, when it is misled, we are able not to be misled. *A.* I have nothing to oppose to this. *R.* But when the soul is misled, do you venture to say that you are not false? *A.* How should I venture? *R.* But there is no sense without soul, no falsity without sense. Either therefore the soul operates, or co-operates with the falsity. *A.* Our preceding reasonings imply assent to this.

4. *R.* Give answer now to this, whether it appears to you possible that at some time hereafter falsity should not be. *A.* How can that seem possible to me, when the difficulty of discovering truth is so great that it is absurder to say that falsity than that Truth cannot be. *R.* Do you then think that he who does not live, can perceive and feel? *A.* It cannot be. *R.* It results then, that the soul lives ever. *A.* Thou urgest me too fast into joys: more slowly, I pray. *R.* But, if

former inferences are just, I see no ground of doubt concerning this thing. *A.* Too fast, I say. Therefore I am easier to persuade that I have made some rash concession, than to become already secure concerning the immortality of the soul. Nevertheless evolve this conclusion, and show how it has resulted. *R.* You have said that falsity cannot be without sense, and that falsity cannot but be: therefore there is always sense. But no sense without soul: therefore the soul is everlasting. Nor has it power to exercise sense, unless it lives. Therefore the soul always lives.

5. *A.* O leaden dagger! For thou mightest conclude that man is immortal if I had granted thee that this universe can never be without man, and that this universe is eternal. *R.* You keep a keen look-out. But yet it is no small thing which we have established, namely, that the frame of things cannot be without the soul, unless perchance in the frame of things at some time hereafter there shall be no falsity. *A.* This consequence indeed I allow to be involved. But now I am of opinion that we ought to consider farther, whether former inferences do not bend under pressure. For I see no small step to have been made towards the immortality of the soul. *R.* Have you sufficiently considered whether you may not have conceded something rashly? *A.* Sufficiently indeed, but I see no point at which I can accuse myself of rashness. *R.* It is therefore concluded that the frame of things cannot be without a living soul. *A.* So far as this, that in turn some souls may be born, and others die. *R.* What if from the frame of things falsity be taken away? will it not come to pass that all things are true? *A.* I admit the inference. *R.* Tell me whence this wall seems to thee to be true. *A.* Because I am not misled by its aspect. *R.* That is, because it is as it seems. *A.* Yes. *R.* If therefore anything is thereby false because it seems otherwise than it is, and thereby true because it is as it seems; take away him to whom it seems, and there is neither anything false, nor true. But if there is no falsity in the frame of things, all things are true. Nor can anything seem except to a living soul. There remains therefore soul in the frame of things, if falsity cannot be taken away; there remains, if it can. *A.* I see our former conclusions somewhat strengthened, indeed; but we have made no progress by this amplification. For none the less does that fact remain which chiefly shakes me that souls are born and pass away, and that it comes about that they are not lacking to the world, not through their immortality, but by their succession.

6. *R.* Do any corporeal, that is, sensible things, appear to you to be capable of comprehension in the intellect? *A.* They do not. *R.* What then? does God appear to use senses for the cognition of things? *A.* I dare affirm nothing unadvisedly concerning this matter; but as far as there is room for conjecture, God in no wise makes use of senses. *R.* We conclude therefore that the only possible subject of sense is the soul. *A.* Conclude provisionally as far as probability permits. *R.* Well then; do you allow that this wall, if it is not a true wall, is not a wall? *A.* I could grant nothing more willingly. *R.* And that nothing, if it be not a true body, is a body? *A.* This likewise. *R.* Therefore if nothing is true, unless it be so as it seems; and if nothing corporeal can appear, except to the senses; and if the only subject of sense is the soul; and if no body can be, unless it be a true body: it follows that there cannot be a body, unless there has first been a soul. *A.* Thou dost urge me too strongly, and means of resistance fail me.

7. *R.* Give now still greater heed. *A.* Behold me ready. *R.* Certainly this is a stone; and it is true on this condition, if it is not otherwise than it seems; and it is not a stone, if it is not true; and it cannot seem except to the senses. *A.* Yes. *R.* There are not therefore stones in the most secluded bosom of the earth, nor anywhere at all where there are not those who have the sense of them; nor would this be a stone, unless we saw it; nor will it be a stone when we shall have departed, and no one else shall be present to see it. Nor, if you lock your coffers well, however much you may have shut up in them, will they have anything. Nor indeed is wood itself wood interiorly. For that escapes all perceptions of sense which is in the depth of an absolutely opaque body, and so is in no wise compelled to be. For if it were, it would be true; nor is anything true, unless because it is so as it appears: but that does not appear; it is not therefore true: unless you have something to object to this. *A.* I see that this results from my previous concessions; but it is so absurd, that I would more readily deny any one of these, than concede that this is true. *R.* As you please. Consider then which you prefer to say: that corporeal things can appear otherwise than to the senses, or that there can be another subject of sense than the soul, or that there is a stone or something else but that it is not true, or that Truth itself is to be otherwise defined. *A.* Let us, I pray thee, consider this last position.

8. *R.* Define therefore the True. *A.* That

is true which is so as it appears to the knower, if he will and can know. *R.* That therefore will not be true which no one can know? Then, if that is false which seems otherwise than it is; how if to one this stone should seem a stone, to another wood? will the same thing be both false and true? *A.* That former position disturbs me more, how, if anything cannot be known, it results from that that it is not true. For as to this, that one thing is both true and false, I do not much care. For I see one thing, compared with diverse things, to be both greater and smaller. From which it results, that nothing is more or less of itself. For these are terms of comparison. *R.* But if you say that nothing is true of itself, do you not fear the inference, that nothing is of itself? For whereby this is wood, thereby is it also true wood. Nor can it be, that of itself, that is, without a knower, it should be wood, and should not be true wood. *A.* Therefore thus I say and so I define, nor do I fear lest my definition be disapproved on the ground of excessive brevity: for to me that seems to be true which is. *R.* Nothing then will be false, because whatever is, is true. *A.* Thou hast driven me into close straits, and I am wholly unprovided of an answer. So it comes to pass that whereas I am unwilling to be taught except by these questionings, I fear now to be questioned.

9. *R.* God, to whom we have commended ourselves, without doubt will render help, and set us free from these straits, if only we believe, and entreat Him most devoutly. *A.* Nothing, assuredly, would I do more gladly in this place; for never have I been involved in so great a darkness. God, Our Father, who exhortest us to pray, who also bringest this about, that supplication is made to Thee; since when we make supplication to Thee, we live better, and are better: hear me groping in these glooms, and stretch forth Thy right hand to me. Shed over me Thy light, revoke me from my wanderings; bring Thyself into me that I may likewise return into Thee. Amen. *R.* Be with me now, as far as thou mayest, in most diligent attention. *A.* Utter, I pray, whatever has been suggested to thee, that we perish not. *R.* Give heed. *A.* Behold, I have neither eyes nor ears but for thee.

10. *R.* First let us again and yet again ventilate this question, What is falsity? *A.* I wonder if there will turn out to be anything, except what is not so as it seems. *R.* Give heed rather, and let us first question the senses themselves. For certainly what the eyes see, is not called false, unless it have some similitude of the true. For instance, a man whom we see in sleep, is not indeed a true man, but false, by this very fact that he has the similitude of a true one. For who, seeing a dog, would have a right to say that he had dreamed of a man? Therefore too that is thereby a false dog, that it is like a true one. *A.* It is as thou sayest. *R.* And moreover, if any one waking should see a horse and think he saw a man, is he not hereby misled, that there appears to him some similitude of a man? For if nothing should appear to him except the form of a horse, he cannot think that he sees a man. *A.* I fully concede this. *R.* We call that also a false tree which we see in a picture, and a false face which is reflected from a mirror, and a false motion of buildings to men that are sailing from them, and a false break in the oar when dipped, for no other reason than the verisimilitude in all these things. *A.* True. *R.* So we make mistakes between twins, so between eggs, so between seals stamped by one ring, and other such things. *A.* I follow and agree to all. *R.* Therefore that similitude of things which pertains to the eyes, is the mother of falsity. *A.* I cannot deny it.

11. *R.* But all this forest of facts, unless I am mistaken, may be divided into two kinds. For it lies partly in equal, partly in inferior things. They are equal, when we say that this is as like to that as that to this, as is said of twins, or impressions of a ring. Inferior, when we say that the worse is like the better. For who, looking in a mirror, would dream of saying that he is like that image, and not rather that like him? And this class consists partly in what the soul undergoes, and partly in those things which are seen. And that again which the soul undergoes, it either undergoes in the sense, as the unreal motion of a building; or in itself from that which it has received from the senses, such as are the dreams of dreamers, and perhaps also of madmen. Furthermore, those things which appear in the things themselves which we see, are some of them from nature, and some expressed and framed by living creatures. Nature either by procreation or reflection effects inferior similitudes. By procreation, when to parents children like them are born; by reflection, as from mirrors of various kinds. For although it is men that make the most of the mirrors, yet it is not they that frame the images given back. On the other hand, the works of living creatures are seen in pictures, and creations of the like kind: in which may also be included (conceding their occurrence) those things which demons produce. But the shadows of bodies, because with but a slight stretch of language they may be described as like their bodies and a sort of false

bodies, nor can be disputed to be submitted to the judgment of the eyes, may reasonably be placed in that class, which are brought about by nature through reflection. For every body exposed to the light reflects, and casts a shadow in the opposite direction. Or do you see any objection to be made? *A.* None. I am only awaiting anxiously the issue of these illustrations.

12. *R.* We must, however, wait patiently, until the remaining senses also make report to us that falsity dwells in the similitude of the true. For in the sense of hearing likewise there are almost as many sorts of similitudes: as when, hearing the voice of a speaker, whom we do not see, we think it some one else, whom in voice he resembles; and in inferior similitudes Echo is a witness, or that well-known roaring of the ears themselves, or in timepieces a certain imitation of thrush or crow, or such things as dreamers or lunatics imagine themselves to hear. And it is incredible how much false tones, as they are called by musicians, bear witness to the truth, which will appear hereinafter: yet they too (which will suffice just now) are not remote from a resemblance to those which men call true. Do you follow this? *A.* And most delightedly. For here I have no trouble to understand. *R.* Then, to press on, do you think it is easy, by the smell, to distinguish lily from lily, or by the taste honey from honey, gathered alike from thyme, though brought from different hives, or by the touch to note the difference between the softness of the plumage of the goose and of the swan? *A.* It does not seem easy. *R.* And how is it when we dream that we either smell or taste, or touch such things? Are we not then deceived by a similitude of effects and images, inferior in proportion to its emptiness? *A.* Thou speakest truly. *R.* Therefore it appears that we, in all our senses, whether by equality or inferiority of likeness, are either misled by cozening similitude, or even if we are not misled, as suspending our consent, or discovering the difference, yet that we name those things false which we apprehend as like the true. *A.* I cannot doubt it.

13. *R.* Now give heed, while we run over the same things once more, that what we are endeavoring to show may come more plainly to view. *A.* Lo, here I am, speak what thou wilt. For I have once for all resolved to endure this circuitous course, nor will I be wearied out in it, hoping so ardently to arrive at length whither I perceive that we are tending. *R.* You do well. But take note whether it seems to you, when we see a resemblance in eggs, that we can justly say that any one of them is false. *A.* Far from it. For if all are eggs, they are true eggs. *R.* And when we see an image reflected from a mirror, by what signs do we apprehend it to be false? *A.* By the fact that it cannot be grasped, gives forth no sound, does not move independently, does not live, and by innumerable other properties, which it were tedious to detail. *R.* I see you are averse to delay, and regard must be borne to your haste. Then, not to recall every particular, if those men also whom we see in dreams, were able to live, speak, be grasped by waking men, and there were no difference between them and those whom when awake and sane we address and see, should we then have any reason to call them false? *A.* What possible right could we have to do so? *R.* Therefore if they were true, in exact proportion as they were likest the truth, and as no difference existed between them and the true and false so far as they were, by those or other differences, convicted of being dissimilar; must it not be confessed that similitude is the mother of truth, and dissimilitude of falsehood? *A.* I have no answer to make, and I am ashamed of my former so hasty assent.

14. *R.* It is ridiculous if you are ashamed, as if it were not for this very reason that we have chosen this mode of discourse: which, since we are talking with ourselves alone, I wish to be called and inscribed Soliloquies; a new name, it is true, and perhaps a grating one, but not ill suited for setting forth the fact. For since Truth can not be better sought than by asking and answering, and scarcely any one can be found who does not take shame to be worsted in debate, and so it almost always happens that when a matter is well brought into shape for discussion, it is exploded by some unreasonable clamor and petulance, and angry feeling, commonly dissembled, indeed, but sometimes plainly expressed; it has been, as I think, most advantageous, and most answerable to peace, that the resolution was made by thee to seek truth in the way of question by me and answer by thee: wherefore there is no reason why you should fear, if at any point you have unadvisedly tied yourself up, to return and undo the knots; for otherwise there is no escape from hence.

15. *A.* Thou speakest rightly; but what I have granted amiss I altogether fail to see: unless perchance that that is rightly called false which has some similitude of the true, since assuredly nothing else occurs to me worthy of the name of false; and yet again I am compelled to confess that those things which are called false are so called by the fact that

they differ from the true. From which it results that that very dissimilitude is the cause of the falsity. Therefore I am disquieted; for I cannot easily call to mind anything that is engendered by contrary causes. *R.* What if this is the one and only kind in the universe of things which is so? Or are you ignorant, that in running over the innumerable species of animals, the crocodile alone is found to move its upper jaw in eating; especially as scarcely anything can be discovered so like to another thing, that it is not also in some point unlike it? *A.* I see that indeed; but when I consider that that which we call false has both something like and something unlike the true, I am not able to make out on which side it chiefly merits the name of false. For if I say: on the side on which it is unlike; there will be nothing which cannot be called false: for there is nothing which is not dissimilar to some thing, which we concede to be true. And again, if I shall say, that it is to be called false on that side on which it is similar; not only will those eggs cry out against us which are true on the very ground of their excessive similarity, but even so I shall not escape from his grasp who may compel me to confess that all things are false, because I cannot deny that all things are on some side or other similar to each other. But suppose me not afraid to give this answer, that likeness and unlikeness alike give a right to call anything false; what way of escape wilt thou give me? For none the less will the fatal necessity hang over me of proclaiming all things false; since, as has been said above, all things are found to be both similar, on some side, and dissimilar, on some side, to each other. My only remaining resource would be to declare nothing else false, except what was other than it seemed, unless I shrank from again encountering all those monsters, which I flattered myself that I had long since sailed away from. For a whirlpool again seizes me at unawares, and brings me round to own that to be true which is as it seems. From which it results that without a knower nothing can be true: where I have to fear a shipwreck on deeply hidden rocks, which are true, although unknown. Or, if I shall say that that is true which is, it follows, let who will oppose, that there is nothing false anywhere. And so I see the same breakers before me again, and see that all my patience of thy delays has helped me forward nothing at all.

16. *R.* Attend rather; for never can I be persuaded, that we have implored the Divine aid in vain. For I see that, having tried all things as far as we could, we found nothing to remain, which could rightly be called false, except what either feigns itself to be what it is not, or, to include all, tends to be and is not. But that former kind of falsity is either fallacious or mendacious. For that is rightly called fallacious which has a certain appetite of deceiving; which cannot be understood as without a soul: but this results in part from reason, in part from nature; from reason, in rational creatures, as in men; from nature, in beasts, as in the fox. But what I call mendacious, proceeds from those who utter falsehood. Who in this point differ from the fallacious, that all the fallacious seek to mislead; but not every one who utters falsehood, wishes to mislead; for both mimes and comedies and many poems are full of falsehoods, rather with the purpose of delighting than of misleading, and almost all those who jest utter falsehood. But he is rightly called fallacious, whose purpose is, that somebody should be deceived. But those who do not aim to deceive, but nevertheless feign somewhat, are mendacious only, or if not even this, no one at least doubts that they are to be called pleasant falsifiers: unless you have something to object.

17. *A.* Proceed, I pray; for now perchance thou hast begun to teach concerning falsities not falsely: but now I am considering of what sort that class of falsities may be, of which thou hast said, It tends to be, and is not. *R.* Why should you not consider? They are the same things, which already we have largely passed in review. Does not thy image in the mirror appear to will to be thou thyself, but to be therefore false, because it is not? *A.* This does, in very deed, seem so. *R.* And as to pictures, and all such expressed resemblances, every such thing wrought by the artist? Do they not press to be that, after whose similitude they have been made? *A.* I must certainly own this to be true. *R.* And you will allow, I believe, that the deceits under which dreamers, or madmen suffer, are to be included in this kind. *A.* None more: for none tend more to be such things as the waking and the sane discern; and yet they are hereby false, because that which they tend to be they cannot be. *R.* Why need I now say more concerning the gliding towers, or the dipped oar, or the shadows of bodies? It is plain, as I think, that they are to be measured by this rule. *A.* Most evidently they are. *R.* I say nothing concerning the remaining senses; for no one by consideration will fail to find this, that in the various things which are subject to our sense, that is called false which tends to be anything and is not.

18. *A.* Thou speakest rightly; but I wonder why thou wouldst separate from this class those poems and jests, and other imitative trifles. *R.* Because forsooth it is one thing to will to be false, and another not to be able to be true. Therefore these works of men themselves, such as comedies or tragedies, or mimes, and other such things, we may include with the works of painters and sculptors. For a painted man cannot be so true, however much he may tend into the form of man, as those things which are written in the books of the comic poets. For neither do they will to be false, nor are they false by any appetite of their own; but by a certain necessity, so far as they have been able to follow the mind of the author. But on the stage Roscius in will was a false Hecuba, in nature a true man; but by that will also a true tragedian, in that he was fulfilling the thing proposed: but a false Priam, in that he made himself like Priam, but was not he. From which now arises a certain marvellous thing, which nevertheless no one doubts to be so. *A.* What, pray, is it? *R.* What think you, unless that all these things are in certain aspects true, by this very thing that they are in certain aspects false, and that for their quality of truth this alone avails them, that they are false in another regard? Whence to that which they either will or ought to be, they in no wise attain, if they avoid being false. For how could he whom I have mentioned have been a true tragedian, had he been unwilling to be a false Hector, a false Andromache, a false Hercules, and innumerable other things? or how would a picture, for instance, be a true picture, unless it were a false horse? or how could there be in a mirror a true image of a man, if it were not a false man? Wherefore, if it avails some things that they be somewhat false in order that they may be somewhat true; why do we so greatly dread falsity, and seek truth as the greatest good? *A.* I know not, and I greatly marvel, unless because in these examples I see nothing worthy of imitation. For not as actors, or specular reflections, or Myron's brazen cows, ought we, in order that we may be true in some character of our own, to be outlined and accommodated to the personation of another; but to seek that truth, which is not, as if laid out on a bifronted and self-repugnant plan, false on one side that it may be true on the other. *R.* High and Divine are the things which thou requirest. Yet if we shall have found them, shall we not confess that of these things is Truth itself made up, and as it were brought into being from their fusion—Truth, from which every thing derives its name which in any way is called true? *A.* I yield no unwilling assent.

19. *R.* What then think you? Is the science of debate true, or false? *A.* True, beyond controversy. But Grammar too is true. *R.* In the same sense as the former? *A.* I do not see what is truer than the true. *R.* That assuredly which has nothing of false: in view of which a little while ago thou didst take umbrage at those things which, be it in this way or that, unless they were false, could not be true. Or do you not know, that all those fabulous and openly false things appertain to Grammar? *A.* I am not ignorant of that indeed; but, as I judge, it is not through Grammar that they are false, but through it, that, whatever they may be, they are interpreted. Since a drama is a falsehood composed for utility or delight. But Grammar is a science which is the guardian and moderatrix of articulate speech: whose profession involves the necessity of collecting even all the figments of the human tongue, which have been committed to memory and letters, not making them false, but teaching and enforcing concerning these certain principles of true interpretation. *R.* Very just: I care not now, whether or not these things have been well defined and distinguished by thee; but this I ask, whether it is Grammar itself, or that science of debate which shows this to be so. *A.* I do not deny that the force and skill of definition, whereby I have now endeavored to separate these things, is to be attributed to the art of disputation.

20. *R.* How as to Grammar itself? if it is true, is it not so far true as it is a discipline? For the name of Discipline signifies something to be learnt: but no one who has learned and who retains what he learns, can be said not to know; and no one knows falsities. Therefore every discipline and science is true. *A.* I see not what rashness there can be in assenting to this brief course of reasoning. But I am disturbed lest it should bring any one to suppose those dramas to be true; for these also we learn and retain. *R.* Was then our master unwilling that we should believe what he taught, and know it? *A.* Nay, he was thoroughly in earnest that we should know it. *R.* And did he, pray, ever set out to have us believe that Dædalus flew? *A.* That, indeed, never. But assuredly unless we remembered the poem, he took such order that we were scarcely able to hold anything in our hands. *R.* Do you then deny it to be true that there is such a poem, and that such a tradition is spread abroad concerning Dædalus? *A.* I do not deny this to be true. *R.* You do not then deny that you learned the

truth, when you learned these things. For if it is true that Dædalus flew, and boys should receive and recite this as a feigning fable, they would be laying up falsities in mind by the very fact that the things were true which they recited. For from this results what we were admiring above, that there could not be a true fiction turning on the flight of Dædalus, unless it were false that Dædalus flew. *A.* I now grasp that; but what good is to come of it, I do not yet see. *R.* What, unless that course of reasoning is not false, whereby we gather that a science, unless it is true, cannot be a science? *A.* And what does this signify? *R.* Because I wish to have you tell me on what the science of Grammar rests: for the truth of the science rests on that very principle which makes it a science. *A.* I know not what to answer thee. *R.* Does it not seem to you, that if nothing in it had been defined, and nothing distributed and distinguished into classes and parts, it could not in any wise be a true science? *A.* Now I grasp thy meaning: nor does the remembrance of any science whatever occur to me, in which definitions and divisions and processes of reasoning do not, inasmuch as it is declared what each thing is, as without confusion of parts its proper attributes are ascribed to each class, nothing peculiar to it being neglected, nothing alien to it admitted, perform that whole range of functions from which it has the name of Science. *R.* That whole range of functions therefore from which it has the name of true. *A.* I see this to be implied.

21. *R.* Tell me now what science contains the principles of definitions, divisions and partitions. *A.* It has been said above that these are contained in the rules of disputation. *R.* Grammar therefore, both as a science, and as a true science, has been created by the same art which has above been defended from the charge of falsity. Which conclusion I am not required to confine to Grammar alone, but am permitted to extend to all sciences whatever. For you have said, and truly said, that no science occurs to you, in which the law of defining and distributing does not lie at the very foundation of its character as a science. But if they are true on that ground on which they are sciences, will any one deny that very thing to be truth through which all the sciences are true? *A.* Assuredly I find it hard to withhold assent: but this gives me pause, that we reckon among the sciences even that theory of disputation. Wherefore I judge that rather to be truth, whereby this theory itself is true. *R.* Your watchful accuracy is indeed most

highly to be commended: but you do not deny, I suppose, that it is true on the same ground on which it is a theory and science. *A.* Nay, that is my very ground of perplexity. For I have noted that it also is a science, and is on this account called true. *R.* What then? Do you think this could be a science on any other ground than that all things in it were defined and distributed? *A.* I have nothing else to say. *R.* But if this function appertains to it, it is in and of itself a true science. Why then should any one find it wonderful, if that truth whereby all things are true, should be through itself and in itself true? *A.* Nothing stands now in the way of my giving an unreserved assent to that opinion.

22. *R.* Attend therefore to the few things that remain. *A.* Bring forth whatever thou hast, if only it be such as I can understand, and I will willingly agree. *R.* We do not forget, that to say that anything is in anything, is capable of a double sense. It may mean that it is so in such a sense as that it can also be disjoined and be elsewhere, as this wood in this place, or the sun in the East. Or it may mean anything is so in a subject, that it cannot be separated from it, as in this wood the shape and visible appearance, as in the sun the light, as in fire heat, as in the mind discipline, and such like. Or seems it otherwise to thee? *A.* These distinctions are indeed most thoroughly familiar to us, and from early youth most studiously made an element of thought; wherefore, if asked about these, I must needs grant the position at once. *R.* But do you not concede that if the subject do not abide, that which is in the subject cannot inseparably abide? *A.* This also I see necessary: for, the subject remaining, that which is in the subject may possibly not remain, as any one with a little thought can perceive. Since the color of this body of mine may, by reason of health or age, suffer change, though the body has not yet perished. And this is not equally true of all things, but of those whose coexistence with the subject is not necessary to the existence of the subject. For it is not necessary that this wall, in order to be a wall, should be of this color, which we see in it; for even if, by some chance, it should become black or white, or should undergo some other change of color, it would nevertheless remain a wall and be so called. But if fire were without heat, it will not even be fire; nor can we talk of snow except as being white.

23. But as to thy question, who would grant, or to whom could it appear possible, that that which is in the subject should remain,

while the subject perished? For it is monstrous and most utterly foreign to the truth, that what would not be unless it were in the subject, could be even when the subject itself was no more. *R.* Then that which we were seeking is found. *A.* What dost thou mean? *R.* What you hear. *A.* And is it then now clearly made out that the mind is immortal? *R.* If these things which you have granted are true, with most indisputable clearness: unless perchance you would say that the mind, even though it die, is still the mind. *A.* I, at least, will never say that; but by this very fact that it perishes it then comes about that it is not the mind, is what I do say. Nor am I shaken in this opinion because it has been said by great philosophers that that thing which, wherever it comes, affords life, cannot admit death into itself. For although the light wheresoever it has been able to gain entrance, makes that place luminous, and, by virtue of that memorable force of contrarieties, cannot admit darkness into itself; yet it is extinguished, and that place is by its extinction made dark. So that which resisted the darkness, neither in any way admitted the darkness into it, and yet made place for it by perishing, as it could have made place for it by departing. Therefore I fear lest death should befall the body in such wise as darkness a place, the mind, like light, sometimes departing, but sometimes being extinguished on the spot; so that now not concerning every death of the body is there security, but a particular kind of death is to be chosen, by which the soul may be conducted out of the body unharmed, and guided to a place, if there is any such place, where it cannot be extinguished. Or, if not even this may be, and the mind, as it were a light, is kindled in the body itself, nor has capacity to endure elsewhere, and every death is a sort of extinction of the soul in the body, or of the light; some sort is to be chosen by which, so far as man is allowed, life, while it is lived, may be lived in security and tranquillity, although I know not how that can come to pass if the soul dies. O greatly blessed they, who, whether from themselves, or from whom you will, have gained the persuasion, that death is not to be feared, even if the soul should perish! But, wretched me, no reasonings, no books, have hitherto been able to persuade of this.

24. *R.* Groan not, the human mind is immortal. *A.* How dost thou prove it? *R.* From those things which you have granted above, with great caution. *A.* I do not indeed recall to mind any want of vigilance in my admissions when questioned by thee: but now gather all into one sum, I pray thee; let us see at what point we have arrived after so many circuits, nor would I have thee in doing so question me. For if thou art about to enumerate concisely those things which I have granted, why is my response again desired? Or is it that thou wouldst wantonly torture me by delays of joy, if we have in fact achieved any solid result? *R.* I will do that which I see that thou dost wish, but attend most diligently. *A.* Speak now, here I am; why slayest thou me? *R.* If everything which is in the subject always abides, it follows of necessity that the subject itself always abides. And every discipline is in the subject mind. It is necessary therefore that the mind should continue forever, if the science continues forever. Now Science is Truth, and always, as in the beginning of this book Reason hath convinced thee, does Truth abide. Therefore the mind lasts forever, nor dead, could it be called the mind. He therefore alone can escape absurdity in denying the mind to be immortal, who can prove that any of the foregoing concessions have been made without reason.

25. *A.* And now I am ready to plunge into the expected joys, but yet I am held hesitating by two thoughts. For, first, it makes me uneasy that we have used so long a circuit, following out I know not what chain of reasonings, when the whole matter of discourse admitted of so brief a demonstration, as has now been shown. Wherefore, it renders me anxious that the discourse has so long held so wary a step, as if with some design of setting an ambush. Next, I do not see how a science is always in the mind, when, on the one hand, so few are familiar with it, and, on the other, whoever does know it, was during so long a time of early childhood unacquainted with it. For we can neither say that the minds of the untaught are not minds, nor that that science is in their mind of which they are ignorant. And if this is utterly absurd, it results that either the science is not always in the mind, or that that science is not Truth.

26. *R.* Thou mayest note that it is not for naught that our reasoning has taken so wide a round. For we were inquiring what is Truth, which not even now, in this very forest of thoughts and things, beguiling our steps into an infinity of paths, have we, as I see, been able to track out to the end. But what are we to do? Shall we desist from our undertaking, and wait in hope that some book or other may fall into our hands, which may satisfy this question? For many, I think, have written before our age, whom we

have not read: and now, to give no guess at what we do not know, we see plainly that there is much writing upon this theme, both in verse and prose; and that by men whose writings cannot be unknown to us, and whose genius we know to be such, that we cannot despair of finding in their works what we require: especially when here before our eyes is he in whom we have recognized that eloquence for which we mourned as dead, to have revived in vigorous life. Will he suffer us, after having in his writings taught us the true manner of living, to remain ignorant of the true nature of living? *A.* I indeed do not think so, and hope much from thence, but one matter of grief I have, that we have not opportunity of opening to him our zealous affection either towards him or towards Wisdom. For assuredly he would pity our thirst, and would overflow much more quickly than now. For he is secure, because he has now won a full conviction of the immortality of the soul, and perhaps knows not that there are any, who have only too well experienced the misery of this ignorance, and whom it is cruel not to aid, especially when they entreat it. But that other knows indeed from old familiarity our ardor of longing; but he is so far removed, and we are so circumstanced, that we have scarcely the opportunity of so much as sending a letter to him. Whom I believe to have lately in Transalpine retirement composed a spell, under whose ban the fear of death is compelled to flee, and the cold stupor of the soul, indurate with lasting ice, is expelled. But in the meantime, while these helps are leisurely making their way hither, a benefit which it is not in our power to command, is it not most unworthy that our leisure should be wasting, and our very mind hang wholly dependent on the uncertain decision of another's will?

27. What shall we say to this, that we have entreated God and do entreat, that He will show us a way, not to riches, not to bodily pleasures, not to popular honors and seats of state, but to the knowledge of our own soul, and that He will likewise disclose Himself to them that seek Him? Will He, indeed, forsake us, or shall He be forsaken by us? *R.* Most utterly foreign to Him is it indeed, that He should desert them who desire such things: whence also it ought to be strange to our thoughts that we should desert so great a Guide. Wherefore, if you will, let us briefly go over the considerations from which either proposition results, either that Truth always abides, or that Truth is the theory of argumentation. For you have said that these points wavered in your mind, so as to make

us less secure of the final conclusion of the whole matter. Or shall we rather inquire this, how a science can be in an untrained mind, which yet we cannot deny to be a mind? For this seemed to give you uneasiness, so as to involve you again in doubt as to your previous concessions. *A.* Nay, let us first discuss the two former propositions, and then we will consider the nature of this latter fact. For so, as I judge, no controversy will remain. *R.* So be it, but attend with the utmost heed and caution. For I know what happens to you as you listen, namely, that while you are too intent upon the conclusion, and expecting that now, or now, it will be drawn, you grant the points implied in my questions without a sufficiently diligent scrutiny. *A.* Perchance thou speakest the truth; but I shall strive against this kind of disease as much as I can: only begin thou now to inquire of me, that we linger not over things superfluous.

28. *R.* From this truth, as I remember, that Truth cannot perish, we have concluded, that not only if the whole world should perish, but even if Truth itself should, it will still be true that both the world and Truth have perished. Now there is nothing true without truth: in no wise therefore does Truth perish. *A.* I acknowledge all this, and shall be greatly surprised if it turns out false. *R.* Let us then consider that other point. *A.* Suffer me, I pray thee, to reflect a little, lest I should soon come back in confusion. *R.* Will it therefore not be true that Truth has perished? If it will not be true, then Truth does not perish. If it were true, where, after the fall of Truth, will be the true, when now there is no truth? *A.* I have no further occasion for thought and consideration; proceed to something else. Assuredly we will take order, so far as we may, that learned and wise men may read these musings, and may correct our unadvisedness, if they shall find any: for as to myself, I do not believe that either now or hereafter I shall be able to discover what can be said against this.

29. *R.* Is Truth then so called for any other reason than as being that by which everything is true which is true? *A.* For no other reason. *R.* Is it rightly called true for any ground than that it is not false? *A.* To doubt this were madness. *R.* Is that not false which is accommodated to the similitude of anything, yet is not that the likeness of which it appears? *A.* Nothing indeed do I see which I would more willingly call false. But yet that is commonly called false, which is far removed from the similitude of the true. *R.* Who denies it? But yet because

it implies some imitation of the true. *A.* How? For when it is said, that Medea flew away with winged snakes harnessed to her car, that thing on no side imitates truth; inasmuch as the thing is naught, nor can that thing imitate aught, when itself is absolutely nothing. *R.* You say right; but you do not note that that thing which is absolutely nothing, cannot even be called false. For if it is false, it is: if it is not, it is not false. *A.* Shall we not then say that monstrous story of Medea is false? *R.* Assuredly not; for if it is false, how is it a monstrous story? *A.* Admirable! Then when I say

"The mighty winged snakes I fasten to my car,"

do I not say false? *R.* You do, assuredly: for that is which you say to be false. *A.* What, I pray? *R.* That sentence, forsooth, which is contained in the verse itself. *A.* And pray what imitation of truth has that? *R.* Because it would bear the same tenor, even if Medea had truly done that thing. Therefore in its very terms a false sentence imitates true sentences. Which, if it is not believed, in this alone does it imitate true ones, that it is expressed as they, and it is only false, it is not also misleading. But if it obtains faith, it imitates also those sentences which, being true, are believed true. *A.* Now I perceive that there is a great difference between those things which we say and those things concerning which we say aught; wherefore I now assent: for this proposition alone held me back, that whatever we call false is not rightly so called, unless it have an imitation of something true. For who, calling a stone false silver, would not be justly derided? Yet if any one should declare a stone to be silver, we say that he speaks falsely, that is, that he utters a false sentence. But it is not, I think, unreasonable that we should call tin or lead false silver, because the thing itself, as it were, imitates that: nor is our sentence declaring this therefore false, but that very thing concerning which it is pronounced.

30. *R.* You apprehend the matter well. But consider this, whether we can also with propriety call silver by the name of false lead. *A.* Not in my opinion. *R.* Why so? *A.* I know not; except that I see that it would be altogether against my will to have it so called. *R.* Is it perchance for the reason that silver is the better, and such a name would be contemptuous of it; but it confers a certain honor, as it were, on lead, if it should be called false silver? *A.* Thou hast expressed exactly what I had in mind. And therefore I believe that it is with good right that those are held infamous and incapable of bearing

witness, who flaunt themselves in female attire, whom I know not whether I should more reasonably call false women, or false men. True actors, however, and truly infamous, without doubt we can call them; or, if they lurk unseen, and if infamy implies an evil repute, we may call them not without truth, true specimens of worthlessness. *R.* We shall have another opportunity of discussing these things: for many things are done, which in the mere guise of them appear base, yet, done for some praiseworthy end, are shown to be honorable. And it is a great question whether one, for the sake of liberating his country, ought to put on a woman's garment to deceive the enemy, being, perhaps, by the very fact that he is a false woman, apt to be shown the truer man: and whether a wise man who in some way may have certainly ascertained that his life will be necessary to the interests of mankind, ought to choose rather to die of cold, than to indue himself in female vestments, if he can find no other. But concerning this, as has been said, we will consider hereafter. For unquestionably thou discernest how careful an inquisition it requires, how far such things can be carried, without falling into various inexcusable basenesses. But now—which suffices for the present question—I think it is now evident, and beyond doubt, that there is not anything false except by some imitation of the true.

31. *A.* Go on to what remains; for of this I am well convinced. *R.* Then I ask this, whether, besides the sciences in which we are instructed, and in which it is fitting that the study of wisdom itself should be included, we can find anything so true, that it is not, like that Achilles of the stage, false on one side, that it may be true on another? *A.* To me, indeed, many such things appear capable of being found. For no sciences contain this stone, nor yet, that it may be a true stone, does it imitate anything according to which it would be called false. Which one thing being mentioned, thou seest there is opportunity to dwell upon things innumerable, which of themselves occur to the thought. *R.* I see, I see. But do they not seem to thee to be included in the one name of Body? *A.* They might so seem, if either I had ascertained the inane to be nothing, or thought that the mind itself ought to be numbered among bodies, or believed that God also is a body. If all these things are, I see them not to be false and true in imitation of anything. *R.* You send us a long journey, but I will use all compendious speed. For certainly what you call the Inane is one thing, what you call Truth another. *A.* Widely diverse, indeed. For

what more inane than I, if I think Truth anything inane, or so greatly seek after aught inane? For what else than Truth do I desire to find? *R.* Therefore perchance you grant this too, that nothing is true which does not by Truth come to be true. *A.* This became manifest at an early stage. *R.* Do you doubt that nothing is inane except the Inane itself, or certainly that a body is not inane? *A.* I do not doubt it at all. *R.* I suppose therefore, you believe that Truth is some sort of body. *A.* In no wise. *R.* What is a body? *A:* I know not; no matter: for I think thou knowest that even that inane, if it is inane, is more completely so where there is no body. *R.* This assuredly is plain. *A.* Why then do we delay? *R.* Does it then seem to thee either that Truth made the inane, or that there is anything true where Truth is not? *A.* Neither seems true. *R.* The inane therefore is not true, because neither could it become inane by that which is not inane: and it is manifest that what is void of truth is not true; and, in fine, that very thing which is called inane, is so called because it is nothing. How therefore can that be true which is not? or how can that be which is absolutely nothing? *A.* Well then, let us desert the inane as being inane.

32. *R.* What sayest thou concerning the rest? *A.* What? *R.* Because you see how much stands on my side. For we have remaining the Soul and God. And if these two are true for the reason that Truth is in them, of the immortality of God no one doubts. But the mind is believed immortal, if Truth, which cannot perish, is proved to be in it. Wherefore let us consider this last point, whether the body be not truly true, that is, whether there be in it, not Truth, but a certain image of Truth. For if even in the body, which we know to be perishable, we find such an element of truth, as there is in the sciences, it does not then so certainly follow, that the art of discussion is Truth, whereby all sciences are true. For true is even the body, which does not seem to have been formed by the force of argument. But if even the body is true by a certain imitation, and is on this account, not absolutely and purely true, there will then, perchance, be nothing to hinder the theory of argument from being taught to be Truth itself. *A.* Meanwhile let us inquire concerning the body; for not even when this shall have been settled, do I see a prospect of ending this controversy. *R.* Whence knowest thou what God purposes? Therefore attend: for I at least think the body to be contained in a certain form and guise, which if it had not, it

would not be the body; if it had it in truth, it would be the mind. Or does the fact stand otherwise? *A.* I assent in part, of the rest I doubt; for, unless some figure is maintained, I grant that it is not a body. But how, if it had it in truth, it would be the mind, I do not well understand. *R.* Do you then remember nothing concerning the exordium of this book, and that Geometry of yours? *A.* Thou hast mentioned it to purpose; I do indeed remember, and am most willing to do so. *R.* Are such figures found in bodies, as that science demonstrates? *A.* Nay, it is incredible how greatly inferior they are convicted of being. *R.* Which of them, therefore, do you think true? *A.* Do not, I beg, think it necessary even to put that question to me. For who is so dull, as not to see that those figures which are taught in Geometry, dwell in Truth itself, or even Truth in these; but that those embodied figures, inasmuch as, they seem, so to speak, to tend towards these, have I know not what imitation of truth, and are therefore false? For now that whole matter which thou wert laboring to show, I understand.

33. *R.* What need is there any longer than that we should inquire concerning the science of disputation? For whether the figures of Geometry are in the Truth, or the Truth is in them, that they are contained in our soul, that, is, in our intelligence, no one calls in question, and through this fact Truth also is compelled to be in our mind. But if every science whatever is so in the mind, as in the subject inseparably, and if Truth is not able to perish; why, I ask, do we doubt concerning the perpetual life of the mind through I know not what familiarity with death? Or have that line or squareness or roundness other things which they imitate that they may be true? *A.* In no way can I believe that, unless perchance a line be something else than length without breadth, and a circle something else than a circumscribed line everywhere verging equally to the centre. *R.* Why then do we hesitate? Or is not Truth where these things are? *A.* God avert such madness. *R.* Or is not the science in the mind? *A.* Who would say that? *R.* But is it possible, the subject perishing, that that which is in the subject should perdure? *A.* When could I imagine such a thing? *R.* It remains to suppose that Truth may fail. *A.* Whence could this be brought to pass? *R.* Therefore the soul is immortal: now at last yield to thine own arguments, believe the Truth; she cries out that she dwelleth in thee, and is immortal, and that her seat cannot be withdrawn from her by any possible death of

the body. Turn away from thy shadow, return into thyself; of no meaning is the destruction thou fearest, except that thou hast forgotten that thou canst not be destroyed. *A.* I hear, I come to a better mind, I begin to recollect myself. But I beg thou wouldst expedite those things which remain; how, in an undisciplined mind, for a mortal one we cannot call it, Science and Truth are to be understood to be. *R.* That question requires another volume, if thou wouldst have it treated thoroughly: moreover also I see occasion for thee to review those things, which, after our best power, have been already examined; because if no one of those things which have been admitted is doubtful, I think that we have accomplished much, and with no small security may proceed to push our inquiries farther.

34. *A.* It is as thou sayest, and I willingly yield compliance with thine injunctions. But this at least I would entreat, before thou decreest a term to the volume, that thou wouldst summarily explain what the distinction is between the true figure, which is contained in the intelligence, and that which thought frames to itself, which in Greek is termed either Phantasia or Phantasma. *R.* Thou seekest that which no one except one of purest sight is able to see, and to the vision of which thing thou art but poorly trained; nor have we now in these wide circuits anything else in view than to exercise thee, that thou mayest be competent to see: yet how it is possible to be taught that the difference is very great, perhaps I can, with a little pains, make clear. For suppose thou hadst forgotten something, and that others were wishing that thou shouldst recall it to memory. They therefore say: Is it this, or that? bringing forward things diverse from it as if similar to it. But thou neither seest that which thou desirest to recollect, and yet seest that it is not this which is suggested. Seems this to thee, when it happens, by any means equivalent to total forgetfulness? For this very power of distinguishing, whereby the false suggestions made to thee are repelled, is a certain part of recollection. *A.* So it seems. *R.* Such therefore do not yet see the truth; yet they cannot be misled and deceived; and what they seek, they sufficiently know. But if any one should say that thou didst laugh a few days after thou wast born, thou wouldst not venture to say it was false: and if he were an authority worthy of credit, thou art ready, not, indeed, to remember, but to believe; for to thee that whole time is buried in most authentic oblivion. Or thinkest thou otherwise? *A.* I thoroughly agree with this. *R.*

This oblivion therefore differs exceedingly from that, but that stands midway. For there is another nearer and more closely neighboring to the recollection and rekindled vision of truth: the like of which is when we see something, and recognize for certain that we have seen it at some time, and affirm that we know it; but where, or when, or how, or with whom it came into our knowledge, we have enough to do to search our memory for an answer. As if this happens in regard to a man, we also inquire where we have known him: which when he has brought to mind, suddenly the whole thing flashes upon the memory like a light, and we have no more trouble to recollect. Is this sort of forgetfulness unknown to thee, or obscure? *A.* What plainer than this? or what is happening to me more frequently?

35. *R.* Such are those who are well instructed in the liberal arts; since they by learning disinter them, buried in oblivion, doubtless, within themselves, and, in a manner, dig them out afresh: nor yet are they content, nor refrain themselves until the whole aspect of Truth, of which, in those arts, a certain effulgence already gleams forth upon them, is by them most widely and most clearly beheld. But from this certain false colors and forms pour themselves as it were upon the mirror of thought, and mislead inquirers often, and deceive those who think that to be the whole which they know or which they inquire. Those imaginations themselves are to be avoided with great carefulness; which are detected as fallacious, by their varying with the varied mirror of thought, whereas that face of Truth abides one and immutable. For then thought portrays to itself, for instance, a square of this or that or the other magnitude, and, as it were, brings it before the eyes; but the inner mind which wishes to see the truth, applies itself rather to that general conception, if it can, according to which it judges all these to be squares. *A.* What if some one should say to us that the mind judges according to what it is accustomed to see with the eyes? *R.* Why then does it judge, that is, if it is well trained, that a true sphere of any conceivable size is touched by a true plane at a point? How has eye ever seen, or how can eye ever see such a thing, when anything of this kind cannot be bodied forth in the pure imagination of thought? Or do we not prove this, when we describe even the smallest imaginary circle in our mind, and from it draw lines to the centre? For when we have drawn two, between which there is scarce room for a needle's point, we are no longer able, even in imagination, to draw

others between, so that they shall arrive at the centre without any commixture; whereas reason exclaims that innumerable lines can be drawn, without being able to touch each other except in the centre, so that in every interval between them even a circle could be described. Since that Phantasy cannot accomplish this, and is more deficient than the eyes themselves, since it is through them that it is inflicted on the mind, it is manifest that it differs much from Truth, and that that, when this is seen, is not seen.

36. These points will be treated with more pains and greater subtilty, when we shall have begun to discuss the faculty of intelligence, which part of our theme is proposed by us, as something which is to be developed and discussed by us, when anything gives anxiety concerning the life of the soul. For I believe thee to stand in no slight fear lest the death of man, even if it do not slay the soul, should nevertheless induce oblivion of all things, and of Truth itself, if any shall have been discovered. *A.* It cannot be expressed how much this evil is to be feared. For of what sort will be that eternal life, or what death is not to be preferred to it, if the soul so lives, as we see it live in a child just born? to say nothing of that life which is lived in the womb; for I do not think it to be none. *R.* Be of good courage; God will be present, as we now feel, to us who seek, who promises a certain most blessed body after this, and an utter plenitude of Truth without any falsehood. *A.* May it be as we hope.

INDEXES.

ON THE GOSPEL ACCORDING TO ST. JOHN.

INDEX OF SUBJECTS

ON THE GOSPEL ACCORDING TO ST. JOHN.

INDEX OF TEXTS.

TEN HOMILIES

ON THE

EPISTLE OF JOHN TO THE PARTHIANS.

INDEX OF SUBJECTS.

TEN HOMILIES

ON THE

EPISTLE OF JOHN TO THE PARTHIANS.

INDEX OF TEXTS.

SOLILOQUIES.

INDEX OF SUBJECTS.